America Votes™ 29

America Votes™ 29

ELECTION RETURNS BY STATE

RHODES COOK

2009–2010

Los Angeles | London | New Delhi
Singapore | Washington DC

Los Angeles | London | New Delhi
Singapore | Washington DC

FOR INFORMATION:

CQ Press
An Imprint of SAGE Publications, Inc.
2455 Teller Road
Thousand Oaks, California 91320
E-mail: order@sagepub.com

SAGE Publications Ltd.
1 Oliver's Yard
55 City Road
London, EC1Y 1SP
United Kingdom

SAGE Publications India Pvt. Ltd.
B 1/I 1 Mohan Cooperative Industrial Area
Mathura Road, New Delhi 110 044
India

SAGE Publications Asia-Pacific Pte. Ltd.
33 Pekin Street #02-01
Far East Square
Singapore 048763

Associate Editor: Sarah J. Walker
Production Editor: Laura Stewart
Typesetter: C&M Digitals (P) Ltd.
Proofreader: Jennifer Gritt
Cover Designer: anne masters design, inc.
Marketing Manager: Ben Krasney

Printed in the United States of America

This book is printed on acid-free paper.

11 12 13 14 15 10 9 8 7 6 5 4 3 2 1

ISBN: 978-1-60871-738-5

ISSN: 0065-678X

Contents

List of Maps

Acknowledgments

The publishers of *America Votes* wish to recognize the creator and longtime editor of *America Votes,* Richard M. Scammon. With his wife Mary Allen Scammon, Mr. Scammon compiled and edited the first of the *America Votes* series in 1952. He brought his keen perceptions of the American electorate and his in-depth knowledge of America's voting patterns to his more than 40 years of work on the *America Votes* series.

Scammon founded and directed the nonprofit Elections Research Center and served for more than 20 years as the senior elections consultant to NBC News. His love of elections was rooted in his lifelong commitment to democracy and his firm belief that the voice of one is always bested by the voice of the many.

The publishers also wish to recognize the late *America Votes* editor, Alice V. McGillivray, who was a longtime associate at the Elections Research Center and a coauthor in the 1980s and 1990s of *America at the Polls.*

Introduction

Barely a decade ago there was talk of a "50-50" nation. The 2000 election had ended with Republican George W. Bush narrowly winning the White House in the face of a small popular vote deficit. And the Senate was split evenly between the two parties, with 50 seats for each.

Since then, though, the political advantage has swung back and forth like a pendulum. Republicans had the upper hand in the 2002 and 2004 election cycles, followed by the Democrats in 2006 and 2008. The 2010 balloting swung momentum back to the Republicans.

The GOP scored a net gain of 63 seats in the House of Representatives in 2010, six seats in the Senate and five governorships. In addition, Republicans emerged from the 2010 election controlling both houses of state legislatures in 25 states, up 11 from before.

In the process, the 2010 election made its share of history.

The Republican total of 242 House seats was the most the GOP has won since the postwar election of 1946. And conversely, the Democrats' 193 seats was the fewest that they have won since the same election.

The Republicans' net gain of 63 House seats was the largest for any party in a midterm election since 1938 and in any election (presidential or midterm) since 1948.

The total of 54 House incumbents that lost in November 2010—52 Democrats and two Republicans—was the largest number of House incumbents defeated in any general election since at least 1952.

And, according to the National Conference of State Legislatures, the Republicans emerged from the 2010 election holding more state legislative seats than at any time since the 1920s.

Still, no one these days is talking about a permanent Republican majority. Rather, the 2010 balloting can be seen as the latest sharp swing in a volatile era of American politics, in which one unusual and historic result has been followed by another.

One can place the start of this era in 1992, when Ross Perot drew nearly 20 percent of the presidential vote as an independent. It represented the largest share for an independent or third party presidential candidate since Theodore Roosevelt in 1912. Moreover, the strong Perot vote arguably helped elect Democrat Bill Clinton, who

2010: THE REPUBLICANS' TURN

Republicans dramatically redefined the nation's political landscape in 2010, easily winning control of the House of Representatives and a majority of the nation's governorships. The Senate stayed Democratic, although the GOP cut the Democrats' advantage by a half dozen seats. The chart below reflects partisan seat totals immediately before and after the 2010 general election. The preelection House totals include a Republican vacancy in Indiana that is credited to the GOP, and a Democratic vacancy in New York that is credited to the Democrats. Two Independent senators who caucus with the Democrats, Joseph I. Lieberman of Connecticut and Bernard Sanders of Vermont, are listed in the "Other" column.

	Preelection			Postelection		
	Rep.	Dem.	Other	Rep.	Dem.	Other
Governor	24	26	0	29	20	1
Senate	41	57	2	47	51	2
House	179	256	0	242	193	0

earlier in the presidential campaign had been labeled one of the party's "seven dwarfs."

Two years later, Republicans surprised the political world by abruptly winning both houses of Congress for the first time in four decades.

In the late 1990s, President Clinton was impeached by the House of Representatives, the first time that a president had been so threatened with removal from office since Andrew Johnson suffered a similar fate after the Civil War. (Both Johnson and Clinton escaped conviction in the Senate.)

Shortly thereafter was the Electoral College "misfire" of 2000, the first presidential contest in more than a century that resulted in different winners in the popular and electoral vote. Yet despite the controversial nature of the result, hardly anyone protested the nation's unique way of electing its national leader.

Counting the 2010 Vote

From one end of the ballot to the other, Republicans dominated voting in the 2009-10 election cycle. The GOP won 25 of 39 governorships at stake, 25 of 38 Senate races (including Republican incumbent Lisa Murkowski of Alaska, who won as a write-in candidate), and 242 of 435 House seats. This translated into a Republican advantage in the aggregate nationwide vote in all three categories. No blank and void ballots are included in the totals below. They are based on official returns from 39 gubernatorial contests (37 held in 2010, two in 2009) and 38 Senate races (37 decided in November 2010, one in January 2010) as well as two versions of the House vote. "All Races" feature the results from the districts in which a vote was taken in 2010, including those in which only one major party ran a candidate. "Contested Races" are those in which both the Democrats and Republicans fielded candidates. There were 406 contested races in 2010, of which Republicans won 218. Of the other 29 House races where one major party did not field a candidate, the GOP won 24.

Office		Total Vote	Republican	Democratic	Other	Rep.-Dem. Plurality	Percentage of Total Vote		
							Rep.	Dem.	Other
Governor		75,297,581	36,190,155	35,237,483	3,869,943	952,672 R	48.1%	46.8%	5.1%
Senate		73,370,076	35,933,965	33,394,962	4,041,149	2,539,003 R	49.0%	45.5%	5.5%
House	House (All Races)	86,546,310	44,839,611	38,983,649	2,723,050	5,855,962 R	51.8%	45.0%	3.1%
	(Contested)	82,101,281	41,658,389	38,291,097	2,151,795	3,367,292 R	50.7%	46.6%	2.6%

2010: Close House Races

The volume of highly competitive House races in 2010 spiked dramatically from its levels in recent years as 55 House candidates were elected with less than 52 percent of the total vote. The number of close congressional races was disproportionately higher on the Republican side, where most of those on the list were challengers or open-seat winners. In contrast, the bulk of sub-52 percent Democratic House winners in 2010 were incumbents. An asterisk (*) indicates an incumbent.

Republicans (30)	2010 Winning Percentage	Democrats (25)	2010 Winning Percentage
R. Blake Farenthold, Texas 27	47.8%	William R. Keating, Mass. 10	46.9%
Joe Heck, Nev. 3	48.1%	William L. Owens, N.Y. 23*	47.5%
Kristi Noem, S.D. AL	48.1%	Jerry McNerney, Calif. 11*	48.0%
Dennis A. Ross, Fla. 12	48.1%	Joseph S. Donnelly, Ind. 2*	48.2%
Chip Cravaack, Minn. 8	48.2%	Gabrielle Giffords, Ariz. 8*	48.8%
Charles Bass, N.H. 2	48.3%	Russ Carnahan, Mo. 3*	48.9%
Joe Walsh, Ill. 8	48.5%	Gerald E. Connolly, Va. 11*	49.2%
Francisco "Quico" Canseco, Texas 23	49.4%	Timothy J. Walz, Minn. 1*	49.3%
Renee Ellmers, N.C. 2	49.5%	Bruce Braley, Iowa 1*	49.5%
Paul Gosar, Ariz. 1	49.7%	Gary C. Peters, Mich. 9*	49.8%
Scott Tipton, Colo. 3	49.9%	Raul M. Grijalva, Ariz. 7*	50.2%
Jon Runyan, N.J. 3	50.0%	Timothy H. Bishop, N.Y. 1*	50.1%
Dan Lungren, Calif. 3*	50.1%	Ben Chandler, Ky. 6*	50.1%
Ann Marie Buerkle, N.Y. 25	50.1%	Ron Kind, Wis. 3*	50.3%
Bill Johnson, Ohio 6	50.2%	David N. Cicilline, R.I. 1	50.5%
Tim Walberg, Mich. 7	50.2%	Jim Matheson, Utah 2*	50.5%
Vicky Hartzler, Mo. 4	50.4%	Leonard L. Boswell, Iowa 3*	50.7%
David B. McKinley, W.Va. 1	50.4%	Jason Altmire, Pa. 4*	50.8%
Robert Hurt, Va. 5	50.8%	Mark Critz, Pa. 12*	50.8%
Raul R. Labrador, Idaho 1	51.0%	Dave Loebsack, Iowa 2*	51.0%
Martha Roby, Ala. 2	51.0%	Rick Larsen, Wash. 2*	51.1%
Robert Dold, Ill. 10	51.1%	Kurt Schrader, Ore. 5*	51.2%
H. Morgan Griffith, Va. 9	51.2%	Sanford D. Bishop Jr., Ga. 2*	51.4%
Michael G. Grimm, N.Y. 13	51.3%	Jim Costa, Calif. 20*	51.7%
Randall M. Hultgren, Ill. 14	51.3%	Martin Heinrich, N.M. 1*	51.9%
Steve Chabot, Ohio 1	51.5%		
Mary Bono Mack, Calif. 45*	51.5%		
Rick Crawford, Ark. 1	51.8%		
Dan Benishek, Mich. 1	51.9%		
Steven Palazzo, Miss. 4	51.9%		

A year later were the 9/11 attacks, one of the more surreal days in American history. Both World Trade Center towers in lower Manhattan were brought down by terrorist-hijacked airliners, another slammed into the Pentagon, while a fourth crashed in southwestern Pennsylvania after a passenger revolt. A month later, the United States was at war in Afghanistan. And in 2003, a larger war on

The House Since 1990: A Political Weathervane

The House of Representatives went from Democratic to Republican control in 1994 and was regained by the Democrats in 2006. But it was held by the party only until 2010, when the Republicans emerged with a larger majority than ever. Republicans hold the bulk of the House seats in the South and Midwest, while Democrats have the upper hand in the East and West. The states in each region are listed below. An "I" indicates Independent.

	South				West			Midwest			East				Total House			
	R	D	I		R	D		R	D		R	D	I		R	D	I	
1990	44	85	0	D	37	48	D	45	68	D	41	66	1	D	167	267	1	D
1992	52	85	0	D	38	55	D	44	61	D	42	57	1	D	176	258	1	D
1994	73	64	0	R	53	40	R	59	46	R	45	54	1	D	230	204	1	R
1996	82	55	0	R	51	42	R	55	50	R	39	60	1	D	227	207	1	R
1998	82	55	0	R	49	44	R	54	51	R	38	61	1	D	223	211	1	R
2000	81	55	1	R	43	50	D	57	48	R	40	59	1	D	221	212	2	R
2002	85	57	0	R	46	52	D	61	39	R	37	57	1	D	229	205	1	R
2004	91	51	0	R	45	53	D	60	40	R	36	58	1	D	232	202	1	R
2006	85	57	0	R	41	57	D	51	49	R	25	70	0	D	202	233	0	D
2008	80	62	0	R	35	63	D	45	55	D	18	77	0	D	178	257	0	D
2010	102	40	0	R	43	55	D	65	35	R	32	63	0	D	242	193	0	R
Net Change in GOP Seats, 1994-2010	+ 29				− 10			+ 6			+ 13				+ 12			

EAST - Connecticut, Delaware, Maine, Maryland, Massachusetts, New Hampshire, New Jersey, New York, Pennsylvania, Rhode Island, Vermont, West Virginia.

MIDWEST - Illinois, Indiana, Iowa, Kansas, Michigan, Minnesota, Missouri, Nebraska, North Dakota, Ohio, South Dakota, Wisconsin.

SOUTH - Alabama, Arkansas, Florida, Georgia, Kentucky, Louisiana, Mississippi, North Carolina, Oklahoma, South Carolina, Tennessee, Texas, Virginia.

WEST - Alaska, Arizona, California, Colorado, Hawaii, Idaho, Montana, Nevada, New Mexico, Oregon, Utah, Washington, Wyoming.

terror was launched in Iraq. Both Middle East conflicts have remained a prime part of the political debate.

That is, before the economy began to sour dramatically in 2008, producing what is widely regarded as the biggest downturn since the Depression. Democrats capitalized that year by padding the congressional majorities they had won two years earlier. Their success culminated with the election of the nation's first African-American president in Barack Obama.

But with Obama and the Democrats unable to quickly revive the economy, and the unemployment rate throughout much of 2010 hovering near 10 percent, it was the Republicans who scored historic gains in 2010.

In short, the nation is in an unusual era in its political history - one where independent voting is on the rise, the two major parties are held in "minimum high regard," and external events beyond the scope of any party to effectively control continually buffet the political landscape. The result of late has often been election results that boggle the mind.

As often as not over the last two decades, national elections have produced divided government. Democrats emerged from the 2010 election controlling the White House and the Senate. Republicans gained control of the House as well as a majority of governorships. But with the nation's politics as untethered as it currently is, do not get too attached to this alignment. Two years hence, it could very well change again.

The number of ballots cast in the 2010 congressional election was barely six million more than the 80 million who participated in the last midterm contest four years earlier.

Yet the partisan distribution of the vote changed dramatically between the two midterm elections. The Republican vote surged in 2010, the Democratic vote declined, as the large independent bloc of voters moved in large numbers from the Democrats in 2006 (and 2008) to the Republicans.

In 2006, the aggregate nationwide House vote decisively favored the Democrats, 42.3 million to 35.9 million for the Republicans. In 2010, the tally was close to being

2010: Defeated Incumbents

The election of 2010 was not a good one for the Democrats, particularly in the House of Representatives. Fifty-two Democratic incumbents were defeated in the November general election compared to just two Republican House members. Together, the total of 54 incumbent casualties was the most in a House general election in more than a half century. On the Senate side, the incumbent carnage was greatest in the primaries, with three sitting senators denied renomination. The number represented the most in any primary season since 1980. The chart lists the gubernatorial, Senate and House incumbents defeated in the 2010 primaries and general election, the number of full terms they had served in that office at the time of their loss in 2010, the percentage of the total vote they had received in the previous general election (2004 for senators, 2006 for governors, and 2008 for House members) and their percentage of the total vote in the 2010 general election (for those who were not eliminated in the primaries).

	Number of Terms	Previous Election Percentage	2010 Election Percentage
GOVERNOR (3)			
Primaries			
(1 — 1 Republican)			
Jim Gibbons, R-Nev.	1	47.9%	—
General Election			
(2 — 2 Democrats)			
Chet Culver, D-Iowa	1	54.0%	43.2%
Ted Strickland, D-Ohio	1	60.5%	47.0%
SENATORS (5)			
Primaries			
(3 — 2 Republicans, 1 Democrat)			
Robert F. Bennett, R-Utah*	3	68.7%	—
Lisa Murkowski, R-Alaska#	1	48.6%	39.6%
Arlen Specter, D-Pa.	5	52.6%	—
General Election			
(2 — 2 Democrats)			
Russell D. Feingold, D-Wis.	3	55.4%	47.0%
Blanche Lincoln, D-Ark.	2	55.9%	36.9%
REPRESENTATIVES (58)			
Primaries			
(4 — 2 Democrats, 2 Republicans)			
Parker Griffith, R-Ala. 5	1	51.5%	—
Bob Inglis, R-S.C. 4@	6	60.1%	—
Carolyn Cheeks Kilpatrick, D-Mich. 13	7	74.1%	—
Alan Mollohan, D-W.Va. 1	14	99.9%	—
General Election			
(54 — 52 Democrats, 2 Republicans)			
John H. Adler, D-N.J. 3	1	52.1%	47.3%
Michael A. Arcuri, D-N.Y. 24	2	52.0%	46.8%
Melissa Bean, D-Ill. 8	3	60.7%	48.3%
John A. Boccieri, D-Ohio 16	1	55.4%	41.3%
Rick Boucher, D-Va. 9	14	97.1%	46.4%
Allen Boyd, D-Fla. 2	7	61.9%	41.4%
Bobby Bright, D-Ala. 2	1	50.2%	48.8%
Anh "Joseph" Cao, R-La. 2	1	49.5%	33.5%
Christopher P. Carney, D-Pa. 10	2	56.3%	44.8%
Travis W. Childers, D-Miss. 1	1	54.5%	40.8%
Kathleen A. Dahlkemper, D-Pa. 3	1	51.2%	44.3%
Lincoln Davis, D-Tenn. 4	4	58.8%	38.6%
Charles Djou, R-Hawaii 1	@	—	46.8%
Steve Driehaus, D-Ohio 1	1	52.5%	46.0%
Chet Edwards, D-Texas 17	10	53.0%	36.6%
Bob Etheridge, D-N.C. 2	7	66.9%	48.7%
Bill Foster, D-Ill. 14	1	57.7%	45.0%
Alan Grayson, D-Fla. 8	1	52.0%	38.2%
John Hall, D-N.Y. 19	2	58.7%	47.2%
Deborah L. Halvorson, D-Ill. 11	1	58.4%	42.7%
Phil Hare, D-Ill. 17	2	99.8%	43.0%
Baron P. Hill, D-Ind. 9	5	57.8%	42.3%
Steven Kagen, D-Wis. 8	2	54.0%	45.1%
Paul E. Kanjorski, D-Pa. 11	13	51.6%	45.3%
Mary Jo Kilroy, D-Ohio 15	1	45.9%	41.3%
Ann Kirkpatrick, D-Ariz. 1	1	55.9%	43.7%
Ron Klein, D-Fla. 22	2	54.7%	45.6%
Suzanne M. Kosmas, D-Fla. 24	1	57.2%	40.3%
Frank Kravotil, Jr., D-Md. 1	1	49.1%	42.0%
Daniel B. Maffei, D-N.Y. 25	1	54.8%	49.8%
Betsy Markey, D-Colo. 4	1	56.2%	41.4%
Jim Marshall, D-Ga. 8	4	57.2%	47.3%
Michael E. McMahon, D-N.Y. 13	1	60.9%	47.9%
Walt Minnick, D-Idaho 1	1	50.6%	41.3%
Harry Mitchell, D-Ariz. 5	2	53.2%	43.2%
Patrick J. Murphy, D-Pa. 8	2	56.8%	46.5%
Scott Murphy, D-N.Y. 20	@	—	45.1%
Glenn C. Nye, D-Va. 2	1	52.4%	42.5%
James L. Oberstar, D-Minn. 8	18	67.7%	46.6%
Solomon P. Ortiz, D-Texas 27	14	58.0%	47.1%
Thomas S. P. Perriello, D-Va. 5	1	50.1%	47.0%
Earl Pomeroy, D-N.D. AL	9	62.0%	44.9%
Ciro D. Rodriguez, D-Texas 23	5	55.8%	44.4%
John Salazar, D-Colo. 3	3	61.6%	46.0%
Stephanie Herseth Sandlin, D-S.D. AL	3	67.6%	45.9%
Mark Schauer, D-Mich. 7	1	48.8%	45.4%
Carol Shea-Porter, D-N.H. 1	2	51.7%	42.4%
Ike Skelton, D-Mo. 4	17	65.9%	45.1%
Zack Space, D-Ohio 18	2	59.9%	40.5%
John M. Spratt, Jr., D-S.C. 5	14	61.6%	44.8%
Gene Taylor, D-Miss. 4	10	74.5%	46.8%
Harry Teague, D-N.M. 2	1	56.0%	44.6%
Dina Titus, D-Nev. 3	1	47.4%	47.5%
Charles A. Wilson, D-Ohio 6	2	62.3%	45.2%

Note: An asterisk (*) indicates that Sen. Robert F. Bennett (R-Utah) was defeated in a pre-primary Republican convention. A pound sign (#) denotes that Sen. Lisa Murkowski (R-Alaska) was beaten in the Republican Senate primary but won reelection in November 2010 as a write-in candidate. @ indicates House members that were elected in a post-2008 special election and had not served a full term at the time they were defeated.

the reverse of that. Republican candidates drew 44.8 million votes compared to 39.0 million for their Democratic counterparts. Put another way, the GOP vote grew by nearly 9 million from 2006, a spike of 25%, while the Democratic vote dropped by more than 3 million, or 8%.

The 2010 turnout validated the pro-Republican "enthusiasm gap" that had been evident in polling throughout the year. It was abetted by the emergence of a new political force called the "Tea Party." Spurred by the sputtering economy, the nationally decentralized group embraced an anti-tax, small-government philosophy that gained traction with a healthy dose of "attitude." Though claiming to be politically independent, most Tea Party members were much more closely akin to the Republicans than the Democrats in their political beliefs. Democratic efforts to offset the new, energized movement by motivating the young and minorities to vote in large numbers as they did in 2008 largely failed.

The result: a pro-Democratic electorate in 2006 turned into a pro-Republican one in 2010.

In some significant respects, the 2010 congressional vote mirrored that of 1994, when Republicans scored historic breakthroughs in both houses of Congress. In both elections, the nationwide tally was 52 percent Republican, 45 percent Democratic. And in both years, a decline in the number of Democratic ballots from the previous midterm election was accompanied by a significant increase in the GOP total.

But it was not as big a landslide for the Republicans in 2010 as it appeared that it might be on election eve. Some national surveys showed Republicans with a double digit lead over the Democrats among likely voters in the generic congressional ballot. Yet the actual nationwide GOP margin of 7 percentage points not only fell short of that but was not as large as that registered by congressional Democrats in the previous two elections when they won a majority of House seats. In 2008, Democrats had an edge of 11 points over the Republicans in the nationwide House vote; in 2006, it was 8 points.

Yet Republicans did score a number of impressive gains across the country in 2010, making many of the red states redder and a number of the blue states a pale aqua. Their surge started in Democratic Massachusetts, with Republican Scott P. Brown winning a special Senate election in January 2010 for the seat formerly held by Democratic icon, Edward M. Kennedy. It was the first Republican Senate victory in the Bay State since 1972.

Republican momentum continued through November, with the party sweeping both gubernatorial and Senate contests not only in Republican states such as Georgia, Kansas and Utah, but also in battleground states such as Florida, Iowa, Ohio, Pennsylvania and Wisconsin.

Yet while Republicans captured a net of 63 House seats in 2010, they still left a lot of attainable seats on the table. Democrats won 25 seats with less than 52 percent of the total vote.

It was an eclectic group of Democrats that the GOP missed defeating, from narrow 2009-10 special election winners William L. Owens of New York and Mark S. Critz of Pennsylvania to the nationally recognized Gabrielle Giffords of Arizona, the victim of an assassination attempt in January 2011.

For Republicans, it may have been a missed opportunity that will not come along again anytime soon. Certainly, the turnout in 2012 will be quite different—larger, more youthful and rainbow-hued, and quite possibly, less Republican.

The Methodology

The twenty-ninth volume of America Votes follows the general pattern used in recent editions of this series. There is an introduction with text and tables designed to help tie together various aspects of the 2010 election cycle. The front section that follows contains tables with the state-by-state voter turnout and the vote for gubernatorial, Senate and House elections in the 2010 election cycle. There is also a summary of special elections held between the general elections of 2008 and 2010 to fill vacancies in the 111th Congress, and a listing of changes in congressional membership in the 112th Congress that occurred between the 2010 general election and the middle of August 2011.

Following this introductory material is the heart of the volume, 50 chapters—one for each state. Each state chapter begins with a profile sheet listing the current governor, senators and representatives, followed by tables of the statewide vote for president, governor and senator from immediately after World War II to the present. Following this information is a map of the state showing its counties, major population centers and congressional districts for members of the House in the 111th Congress. Following the map are the county-by-county tables of gubernatorial and Senate elections. All these tables are for the 2010 general election except for the governorships in New Jersey and Virginia, where voting was conducted in 2009, as well as a special Senate election in Massachusetts held in January 2010.

The county tables for gubernatorial and Senate elections feature a three-column format (Republican, Democratic, Other). The only exceptions are for elections where another candidate received at least 10 percent of the total vote, in which case a column for their vote is also included. All the county tables include new 2010 population figures from the Census Bureau.

The county tables are followed by a listing of votes cast for candidates for the House of Representatives, arranged by congressional district. The implementation of the 2000 Census for redistricting purposes led to changes in all multi-member states before the 2002 election, with the exception of Maine, which drew new congressional district lines after 2002. There were also post-2002 district line changes in Pennsylvania and Texas, although only those in Texas had major political ramifications, as well as significant post-2004 changes in Georgia and Texas. In the latter two states, the votes listed for House members are limited to the elections since the last round of line changes. Results for elections before 2002 are not included for any state except those with a single member in the House.

The conclusion of each state chapter consists of two parts. The first is the notes section containing a breakdown of votes cast in the general election for third party, independent, and write-in candidates. For those Democratic and Republican candidates who also ran on a third party ballot line, votes are aggregated and credited to the major party in which the candidate is a member. Blank spaces in a Democratic, Republican or Other vote column indicates there were no votes cast in that particular category.

The final part of each state section provides official results for the primary elections for governor, Senate and House held in the 2010 election cycle, as well as the primary date, registration data at the time of the primary, and the rules on voter participation in the primary. In each state, blank and void ballots are excluded from the tally.

In the chapters for New England states, tables list the vote for governor and senator by larger cities and towns as well as by counties. In Rhode Island, the results are listed for all cities and towns.

The America Votes series is compiled from official results obtained from election authorities in each state. While complete accuracy is always the goal, it can sometimes prove elusive in a work such as this. On occasion, states may belatedly report changes in their vote totals that occur after publication of this volume. And human nature being what it is, there is always an example or two (or three) of self-inflicted errors. The goal is always to keep these to a minimum.

There is the desire to make these reference volumes as useful as possible to readers and researchers. Suggestions as to new materials, together with any corrections of data, are welcome.

Considerable thanks are due Sarah J. Walker, associate editor at CQ Press, who shepherded the movement of copy over the long weeks and months of this project with the patience of Job. Production Editor Laura Stewart supervised this edition of America Votes through copyediting, composition, proofreading and corrections. Their work, with that of their colleagues, was invaluable in the completion of this volume.

And as always, my thanks to my wife, Memrie McKay-Cook, whose support and forbearance has always been integral to the completion of these volumes.

Rhodes Cook
August 2011

Errata

America Votes 28

The following corrections should be made in the previous edition of *America Votes 28*, covering the 2009-2010 election cycle.

Page viii. "2008: Close House Races" chart. Column headings should read: "2008 Winning Percentage."

Page 130. Georgia map represented Congressional districts first established for elections held in 2006,

Page 131. Map of Atlanta area congressional districts was an outdated one.

Page 409. Sen. Arlen Specter announced that he was switching his party affiliation from Republican to Democratic on April 28, 2009, which became effective April 30, 2009.

Page 449. Texas map represented Congressional districts first established for elections held in 2004, with additional changes in several districts for 2006.

Page 520. In the Wisconsin 8th District, Democrat Steve Kagen was the incumbent in 2008, which should have been indicated by an asterisk (*) next to his name.

UNITED STATES

VOTER TURNOUT 2009-2010

State	2010 Voting Eligible Population	House Vote	Senate Vote	Governor Vote	High Race	Highest Vote	Turnout as Percentage of Voting Eligible Population	
							Highest Vote	House Vote
Alabama	3,431,000	1,367,747	1,485,499	1,494,273	G	1,494,273	43.6%	39.9%
Alaska	494,000	254,335	255,474	256,192	G	256,192	51.9%	51.5%
Arizona	4,349,000	1,698,145	1,708,484	1,728,081	G	1,728,081	39.7%	39.0%
Arkansas	2,101,000	774,125	779,957	781,333	G	781,333	37.2%	36.8%
California	23,059,000	9,647,813	9,999,860	10,095,185	G	10,095,185	43.8%	41.8%
Colorado	3,290,000	1,768,467	1,777,668	1,793,148	G	1,793,148	54.4%	53.8%
Connecticut	2,555,000	1,138,202	1,153,115	1,145,799	S	1,153,115	45.1%	44.5%
Delaware	649,000	305,636	307,402	—	S	307,402	47.4%	47.1%
Florida	13,515,000	5,117,420	5,411,106	5,359,735	S	5,411,106	40.0%	37.9%
Georgia	6,501,000	2,468,680	2,555,258	2,576,161	G	2,576,161	39.6%	38.0%
Hawaii	942,000	360,121	370,583	382,563	G	382,563	40.6%	38.2%
Idaho	1,067,000	447,144	449,530	452,535	G	452,535	42.4%	41.9%
Illinois	8,586,000	3,696,159	3,704,473	3,729,989	G	3,729,989	43.4%	43.0%
Indiana	4,643,000	1,747,720	1,744,481	—	H	1,747,720	37.6%	37.6%
Iowa	2,219,000	1,106,591	1,116,063	1,122,013	G	1,122,013	50.6%	49.9%
Kansas	1,989,000	835,529	837,692	838,790	G	838,790	42.2%	42.0%
Kentucky	3,194,000	1,353,790	1,356,468	—	S	1,356,468	42.5%	42.4%
Louisiana	3,383,000	1,035,947	1,264,994	—	S	1,264,994	37.4%	30.6%
Maine	1,077,000	564,368	—	572,766	G	572,766	53.2%	52.4%
Maryland	4,182,000	1,825,472	1,833,858	1,857,880	G	1,857,880	44.4%	43.7%
Massachusetts	4,674,000	2,224,255	2,252,582	2,297,039	G	2,297,039	49.1%	47.6%
Michigan	7,614,000	3,194,901	—	3,226,088	G	3,226,088	42.4%	42.0%
Minnesota	3,928,000	2,090,591	—	2,107,021	G	2,107,021	53.6%	53.2%
Mississippi	2,184,000	788,549	—	—	H	788,549	36.1%	36.1%
Missouri	4,403,000	1,920,675	1,943,899	—	S	1,943,899	44.1%	43.6%
Montana	751,000	360,341	—	—	H	360,341	48.0%	48.0%
Nebraska	1,250,000	485,546	—	487,988	G	487,988	39.0%	38.8%
Nevada	1,745,000	702,788	721,404	716,529	S	721,404	41.3%	40.3%
New Hampshire	1,053,000	450,086	455,149	456,588	G	456,588	43.4%	42.7%
New Jersey	5,984,000	2,121,584	—	2,423,792	G	2,423,792	40.5%	35.5%
New Mexico	1,383,000	597,690	—	602,827	G	602,827	43.6%	43.2%
New York	12,707,000	4,499,163	4,596,796	4,658,825	G	4,658,825	36.7%	35.4%
North Carolina	6,615,000	2,662,549	2,660,079	—	H	2,662,549	40.3%	40.3%
North Dakota	487,000	237,137	238,812	—	S	238,812	49.0%	48.7%
Ohio	8,641,000	3,825,274	3,815,098	3,852,469	G	3,852,469	44.6%	44.3%
Oklahoma	2,584,000	792,979	1,017,151	1,034,767	G	1,034,767	40.0%	30.7%
Oregon	2,676,000	1,429,356	1,442,588	1,453,548	G	1,453,548	54.3%	53.4%
Pennsylvania	9,547,000	3,959,504	3,977,661	3,989,102	G	3,989,102	41.8%	41.5%
Rhode Island	805,000	335,484	—	342,545	G	342,545	42.6%	41.7%
South Carolina	3,316,000	1,340,189	1,318,794	1,344,198	G	1,344,198	40.5%	40.4%
South Dakota	583,000	319,426	227,947	317,083	H	319,426	54.8%	54.8%
Tennessee	4,611,000	1,559,129	—	1,601,549	G	1,601,549	34.7%	33.8%
Texas	15,389,000	4,745,613	—	4,979,870	G	4,979,870	32.4%	30.8%
Utah	1,627,000	640,495	633,829	643,307	G	643,307	39.5%	39.4%
Vermont	510,000	238,521	235,178	241,605	G	241,605	47.4%	46.8%
Virginia	5,722,000	2,189,841	—	1,985,103	H	2,189,841	38.3%	38.3%
Washington	4,617,000	2,479,409	2,511,094	—	S	2,511,094	54.4%	53.7%
West Virginia	1,438,000	514,373	529,948	—	S	529,948	36.9%	35.8%
Wisconsin	4,274,000	2,140,482	2,171,331	2,160,832	S	2,171,331	50.8%	50.1%
Wyoming	397,000	186,969	—	188,463	G	188,463	47.5%	47.1%
TOTAL	212,741,000	86,546,310	68,861,305	75,297,581		89,289,999	42.0%	40.7%

"High Race" refers to the contest in each state among the following in which the highest number of votes was cast: H - House of Representatives (aggregate vote); S - Senate; G - Governor. The overall voting eligible population is limited to the 50-state total. The District of Columbia is not included since it does not elect a governor or voting members of Congress. Votes are from the November 2010 general election, with the exception of gubernatorial contests in New Jersey and Virginia, which were held in November 2009, and a special Senate election in Massachusetts held in January 2010. Two Senate races were held in New York, but only the one with the highest turnout is listed in the chart. It was for a full six-year term. The election for a short term, two years in length, drew a turnout of 4,508,771 voters.

Source: Voting eligible population figures are from the Committee for the Study of the American Electorate (CSAE), a part of the American University Center for Democracy and Election Management. Voting eligible population figures are based on the estimated citizen voting age population in each state (and nationally) eligible to vote at the time of the November 2010 general election. However, not all of these eligible voters were actually registered to vote.

GUBERNATORIAL ELECTIONS 2009 AND 2010

State	Total Vote	Republican		Democratic		Other Vote	Rep.-Dem. Plurality		Percentage Total Vote		Major Vote	
		Vote	Candidate	Vote	Candidate				Rep.	Dem.	Rep.	Dem.
Alabama	1,494,273	860,472	Bentley, Robert	625,710	Sparks, Ron	8,091	234,762	R	57.6%	41.9%	57.9%	42.1%
Alaska	256,192	151,318	Parnell, Sean R.	96,519	Berkowitz, Ethan A.	8,355	54,799	R	59.1%	37.7%	61.1%	38.9%
Arizona	1,728,081	938,934	Brewer, Jan	733,935	Goddard, Terry	55,212	204,999	R	54.3%	42.5%	56.1%	43.9%
Arkansas	781,333	262,784	Keet, Jim	503,336	Beebe, Mike D.	15,213	240,552	D	33.6%	64.4%	34.3%	65.7%
California	10,095,185	4,127,391	Whitman, Meg	5,428,149	Brown, Edmund G., Jr.	539,645	1,300,758	D	40.9%	53.8%	43.2%	56.8%
Colorado	1,793,148	199,792	Maes, Dan	915,436	Hickenlooper, John	677,920	263,060	D	11.1%	51.1%	17.9%	82.1%
Connecticut	1,145,799	560,874	Foley, Tom	567,278	Malloy, Dan	17,647	6,404	D	49.0%	49.5%	49.7%	50.3%
Florida	5,359,735	2,619,335	Scott, Rick	2,557,785	Sink, Alex	182,615	61,550	R	48.9%	47.7%	50.6%	49.4%
Georgia	2,576,161	1,365,832	Deal, Nathan	1,107,011	Barnes, Roy E.	103,318	258,821	R	53.0%	43.0%	55.2%	44.8%
Hawaii	382,563	157,311	Aiona, Duke	222,724	Abercrombie, Neil	2,528	65,413	D	41.1%	58.2%	41.4%	58.6%
Idaho	452,535	267,483	Otter, C. L. "Butch"	148,680	Allred, Keith	36,372	118,803	R	59.1%	32.9%	64.3%	35.7%
Illinois	3,729,989	1,713,385	Brady, Bill	1,745,219	Quinn, Pat	271,385	31,834	D	45.9%	46.8%	49.5%	50.5%
Iowa	1,122,013	592,494	Branstad, Terry E.	484,798	Culver, Chet	44,721	107,696	R	52.8%	43.2%	55.0%	45.0%
Kansas	838,790	530,760	Brownback, Sam	270,166	Holland, Tom	37,864	260,594	R	63.3%	32.2%	66.3%	33.7%
Maine	572,766	218,065	LePage, Paul R.	109,387	Mitchell, Elizabeth	245,314	9,795	R	38.1%	19.1%	66.6%	33.4%
Maryland	1,857,880	776,319	Ehrlich, Robert L., Jr.	1,044,961	O'Malley, Martin	36,600	268,642	D	41.8%	56.2%	42.6%	57.4%
Massachusetts	2,297,039	964,866	Baker, Charles D.	1,112,283	Patrick, Deval L.	219,890	147,417	D	42.0%	48.4%	46.5%	53.5%
Michigan	3,226,088	1,874,834	Snyder, Rick	1,287,320	Bernero, Virg	63,934	587,514	R	58.1%	39.9%	59.3%	40.7%
Minnesota	2,107,021	910,462	Emmer, Tom	919,232	Dayton, Mark	277,327	8,770	D	43.2%	43.6%	49.8%	50.2%
Nebraska	487,988	360,645	Heineman, Dave	127,343	Meister, Mike		233,302	R	73.9%	26.1%	73.9%	26.1%
Nevada	716,529	382,350	Sandoval, Brian	298,171	Reid, Rory	36,008	84,179	R	53.4%	41.6%	56.2%	43.8%
New Hampshire	456,588	205,616	Stephen, John	240,346	Lynch, John	10,626	34,730	D	45.0%	52.6%	46.1%	53.9%
New Jersey*	2,423,792	1,174,445	Christie, Chris	1,087,731	Corzine, Jon	161,616	86,714	R	48.5%	44.9%	51.9%	48.1%
New Mexico	602,827	321,219	Martinez, Susanna	280,614	Denish, Diane D.	994	40,605	R	53.3%	46.5%	53.4%	46.6%
New York	4,658,825	1,548,184	Paladino, Carl P.	2,911,721	Cuomo, Andrew M.	198,920	1,363,537	D	33.2%	62.5%	34.7%	65.3%
Ohio	3,852,469	1,889,186	Kasich, John	1,812,059	Strickland, Ted	151,224	77,127	R	49.0%	47.0%	51.0%	49.0%
Oklahoma	1,034,767	625,506	Fallin, Mary	409,261	Askins, Jari		216,245	R	60.4%	39.6%	60.4%	39.6%
Oregon	1,453,548	694,287	Dudley, Chris	716,525	Kitzhaber, John	42,736	22,238	D	47.8%	49.3%	49.2%	50.8%
Pennsylvania	3,989,102	2,172,763	Corbett, Tom	1,814,788	Onorato, Dan	1,551	357,975	R	54.5%	45.5%	54.5%	45.5%
Rhode Island#	342,545	114,911	Robitaille, John F.	78,896	Caprio, Frank T.	148,738	8,660	R	33.5%	23.0%	59.3%	40.7%
South Carolina	1,344,198	690,525	Haley, Nikki R.	630,534	Sheheen, Vincent A.	23,139	59,991	R	51.4%	46.9%	52.3%	47.7%
South Dakota	317,083	195,046	Daugaard, Dennis	122,037	Heidepriem, Scott		73,009	R	61.5%	38.5%	61.5%	38.5%
Tennessee	1,601,549	1,041,545	Haslam, Bill	529,851	McWherter, Mike	30,153	511,694	R	65.0%	33.1%	66.3%	33.7%
Texas	4,979,870	2,737,481	Perry, Rick	2,106,395	White, Bill	135,994	631,086	R	55.0%	42.3%	56.5%	43.5%
Utah (S)	643,307	412,151	Herbert, Gary R.	205,246	Corroon, Peter	25,910	206,905	R	64.1%	31.9%	66.8%	33.2%
Vermont	241,605	115,212	Dubie, Brian E.	119,543	Shumlin, Peter	6,850	4,331	D	47.7%	49.5%	49.1%	50.9%
Virginia*	1,985,103	1,163,651	McDonnell, Robert F.	818,950	Deeds, R. Creigh	2,502	344,701	R	58.6%	41.3%	58.7%	41.3%
Wisconsin	2,160,832	1,128,941	Walker, Scott	1,004,303	Barrett, Tom	27,588	124,638	R	52.2%	46.5%	52.9%	47.1%
Wyoming	188,463	123,780	Mead, Matt	43,240	Petersen, Leslie	21,443	80,540	R	65.7%	22.9%	74.1%	25.9%
TOTAL	75,297,581	36,190,155		35,237,483		3,869,943	952,672	R	48.1%	46.8%	50.7%	49.3%

All gubernatorial elections were for four-year terms, except for that in Utah which is indicated by an "S" and was for a short term to fill a vacancy. That special election was for the remaining two years of an unexpired term. In addition, the gubernatorial terms in New Hampshire and Vermont are two years each. An asterisk (*) indicates that New Jersey and Virginia held gubernatorial elections in November 2009; the remaining states voted in November 2010. In all states except Colorado, Maine and Rhode Island, the plurality is the difference between the votes cast for the major party candidates. In Colorado, the plurality measures Democrat John Hickenlooper's margin of victory over Tom Tancredo, the candidate of the American Constitution Party. In Maine, the plurality represents Republican Paul LePage's margin over Independent Eliot Cutler. In Rhode Island, which is indicated by a pound sign (#), the plurality is Independent Lincoln Chafee's margin over the Republican runner-up. Chafee was elected with 123,571 votes, which was 36.1 percent of the total vote.

SENATE ELECTIONS 2010

State	Total Vote	Republican Vote	Republican Candidate	Democratic Vote	Democratic Candidate	Other Vote	Rep.-Dem. Plurality		Total Vote Rep.	Total Vote Dem.	Major Vote Rep.	Major Vote Dem.
Alabama	1,485,499	968,181	Shelby, Richard C.	515,619	Barnes, William G.	1,699	452,562	R	65.2%	34.7%	65.3%	34.7%
Alaska	255,474	90,839	Miller, Joe	60,045	McAdams, Scott T.	104,590	10,252	M	35.6%	23.5%	60.2%	39.8%
Arizona	1,708,484	1,005,615	McCain, John	592,011	Glassman, Rodney	110,858	413,604	R	58.9%	34.7%	62.9%	37.1%
Arkansas	779,957	451,618	Boozman, John	288,156	Lincoln, Blanche	40,183	163,462	R	57.9%	36.9%	61.0%	39.0%
California	9,999,860	4,217,386	Fiorina, Carly	5,218,137	Boxer, Barbara	564,337	1,000,751	D	42.2%	52.2%	44.7%	55.3%
Colorado	1,777,668	824,789	Buck, Ken	854,685	Bennet, Michael F.	98,194	29,896	D	46.4%	48.1%	49.1%	50.9%
Connecticut	1,153,115	498,341	McMahon, Linda E.	636,040	Blumenthal, Richard	18,734	137,699	D	43.2%	55.2%	43.9%	56.1%
Delaware (S)	307,402	123,053	O'Donnell, Christine	174,012	Coons, Christopher A.	10,337	50,959	D	40.0%	56.6%	41.4%	58.6%
Florida	5,411,106	2,645,743	Rubio, Marco	1,092,936	Meek, Kendrick B.	1,672,427	1,038,194	R	48.9%	20.2%	70.8%	29.2%
Georgia	2,555,258	1,489,904	Isakson, Johnny	996,516	Thurmond, Michael	68,838	493,388	R	58.3%	39.0%	59.9%	40.1%
Hawaii	370,583	79,939	Cavasso, Cam	277,228	Inouye, Daniel K.	13,416	197,289	D	21.6%	74.8%	22.4%	77.6%
Idaho	449,530	319,953	Crapo, Michael D.	112,057	Sullivan, P. Tom	17,520	207,896	R	71.2%	24.9%	74.1%	25.9%
Illinois	3,704,473	1,778,698	Kirk, Mark	1,719,478	Giannoulias, Alexander "Alexi"	206,297	59,220	R	48.0%	46.4%	50.8%	49.2%
Indiana	1,744,481	952,116	Coats, Dan	697,775	Ellsworth, Brad	94,590	254,341	R	54.6%	40.0%	57.7%	42.3%
Iowa	1,116,063	718,215	Grassley, Charles E.	371,686	Conlin, Roxanne	26,162	346,529	R	64.4%	33.3%	65.9%	34.1%
Kansas	837,692	587,175	Moran, Jerry	220,971	Johnston, Lisa	29,546	366,204	R	70.1%	26.4%	72.7%	27.3%
Kentucky	1,356,468	755,411	Paul, Rand	599,843	Conway, Jack	1,214	155,568	R	55.7%	44.2%	55.7%	44.3%
Louisiana	1,264,994	715,415	Vitter, David	476,572	Melancon, Charlie	73,007	238,843	R	56.6%	37.7%	60.0%	40.0%
Maryland	1,833,858	655,666	Wargotz, Eric	1,140,531	Mikulski, Barbara A.	37,661	484,865	D	35.8%	62.2%	36.5%	63.5%
Massachusetts (S)*	2,252,582	1,168,178	Brown, Scott P.	1,060,861	Coakley, Martha	23,543	107,317	R	51.9%	47.1%	52.4%	47.6%
Missouri	1,943,899	1,054,160	Blunt, Roy	789,736	Carnahan, Robin	100,003	264,424	R	54.2%	40.6%	57.2%	42.8%
Nevada	721,404	321,361	Angle, Sharron	362,785	Reid, Harry	37,258	41,424	D	44.5%	50.3%	47.0%	53.0%
New Hampshire	455,149	273,218	Ayotte, Kelly	167,545	Hodes, Paul W.	14,386	105,673	R	60.0%	36.8%	62.0%	38.0%
New York	4,596,796	1,480,423	Townsend, Jay	3,047,880	Schumer, Charles E.	68,493	1,567,457	D	32.2%	66.3%	32.7%	67.3%
New York (S)	4,508,771	1,582,693	DioGuardi, Joseph J.	2,837,684	Gillibrand, Kirsten E.	88,394	1,254,991	D	35.1%	62.9%	35.8%	64.2%
North Carolina	2,660,079	1,458,046	Burr, Richard M.	1,145,074	Marshall, Elaine	56,959	312,972	R	54.8%	43.0%	56.0%	44.0%
North Dakota	238,812	181,689	Hoeven, John	52,955	Potter, Tracy	4,168	128,734	R	76.1%	22.2%	77.4%	22.6%
Ohio	3,815,098	2,168,742	Portman, Rob	1,503,297	Fisher, Lee	143,059	665,445	R	56.8%	39.4%	59.1%	40.9%
Oklahoma	1,017,151	718,482	Coburn, Tom	265,814	Rogers, Jim	32,855	452,668	R	70.6%	26.1%	73.0%	27.0%
Oregon	1,442,588	566,199	Huffman, Jim	825,507	Wyden, Ron	50,882	259,308	D	39.2%	57.2%	40.7%	59.3%
Pennsylvania	3,977,661	2,028,945	Toomey, Pat	1,948,716	Sestak, Joe		80,229	R	51.0%	49.0%	51.0%	49.0%
South Carolina	1,318,794	810,771	DeMint, Jim	364,598	Greene, Alvin M.	143,425	446,173	R	61.5%	27.6%	69.0%	31.0%
South Dakota	227,947	227,947	Thune, John		—		227,947	R	100.0%		100.0%	
Utah	633,829	390,179	Lee, Mike	207,685	Granato, Sam F.	35,965	182,494	R	61.6%	32.8%	65.3%	34.7%
Vermont	235,178	72,699	Britton, Lee	151,281	Leahy, Patrick J.	11,198	78,582	D	30.9%	64.3%	32.5%	67.5%
Washington	2,511,094	1,196,164	Rossi, Dino	1,314,930	Murray, Patty		118,766	D	47.6%	52.4%	47.6%	52.4%
West Virginia (S)	529,948	230,013	Raese, John R.	283,358	Manchin, Joe, III	16,577	53,345	D	43.4%	53.5%	44.8%	55.2%
Wisconsin	2,171,331	1,125,999	Johnson, Ron	1,020,958	Feingold, Russell D.	24,374	105,041	R	51.9%	47.0%	52.4%	47.6%
TOTAL	73,370,076	35,933,965		33,394,962		4,041,149	2,539,003	R	49.0%	45.5%	51.8%	48.2%

All Senate elections were for full six-year terms, except for those indicated by "S," which were for short terms to fill vacancies. Those short-term special elections in Massachusetts, New York and West Virginia were for two years; the election in Delaware was for four years. The Massachusetts' election was held in January 2010, and is denoted by an asterisk (*); all other Senate elections took place in November 2010. A pound sign (#) indicates that Sen. Lisa Murkowki (R-Alaska) won reelection as a write-in candidate, collecting 101,091 votes (39.6 percent of the total vote). Her vote is included in the "Other" column, and her party designation is indicated by an "M" for Murkowski, although her victory can also be considered a win for the Republican Party. In all states except Alaska and Florida, the plurality is the difference between the votes for the major party candidates. In Alaska, the plurality measures Murkowski's margin of victory over Republican nominee Joe Miller. In Florida, the plurality indicates Republican Marco Rubio's winning margin over the runner-up, Independent candidate Charlie Crist. Democrats did not run a Senate candidate in South Dakota.

HOUSE OF REPRESENTATIVES ELECTIONS 2010

State	Seats Won Republican	Seats Won Democratic	Total Vote	Republican	Democratic	Other	Rep.-Dem. Plurality		Percentage Total Vote Rep.	Total Vote Dem.	Major Vote Rep.	Major Vote Dem.
Alabama	6	1	1,367,747	914,445	418,957	34,345	495,488	R	66.9%	30.6%	68.6%	31.4%
Alaska	1	0	254,335	175,384	77,606	1,345	97,778	R	69.0%	30.5%	69.3%	30.7%
Arizona	5	3	1,698,145	900,510	711,837	85,798	188,673	R	53.0%	41.9%	55.9%	44.1%
Arkansas	3	1	774,125	435,422	317,975	20,728	117,447	R	56.2%	41.1%	57.8%	42.2%
California	19	34	9,647,813	4,195,528	5,148,511	303,774	952,983	D	43.5%	53.4%	44.9%	55.1%
Colorado	4	3	1,768,467	886,057	804,069	78,341	81,988	R	50.1%	45.5%	52.4%	47.6%
Connecticut	0	5	1,138,202	460,286	667,983	9,933	207,697	D	40.4%	58.7%	40.8%	59.2%
Delaware	0	1	305,636	125,442	173,543	6,651	48,101	D	41.0%	56.8%	42.0%	58.0%
Florida	19	6	5,117,420	3,004,225	1,853,600	259,595	1,150,625	R	58.7%	36.2%	61.8%	38.2%
Georgia	8	5	2,468,680	1,528,142	940,347	191	587,795	R	61.9%	38.1%	61.9%	38.1%
Hawaii	0	2	360,121	129,127	226,430	4,564	97,303	D	35.9%	62.9%	36.3%	63.7%
Idaho	2	0	447,144	263,699	150,884	32,561	112,815	R	59.0%	33.7%	63.6%	36.4%
Illinois	11	8	3,696,159	1,720,016	1,876,316	99,827	156,300	D	46.5%	50.8%	47.8%	52.2%
Indiana	6	3	1,747,720	972,671	679,462	95,587	293,209	R	55.7%	38.9%	58.9%	41.1%
Iowa	2	3	1,106,591	597,414	479,874	29,303	117,540	R	54.0%	43.4%	55.5%	44.5%
Kansas	4	0	835,529	528,136	274,992	32,401	253,144	R	63.2%	32.9%	65.8%	34.2%
Kentucky	4	2	1,353,790	844,010	506,170	3,610	337,840	R	62.3%	37.4%	62.5%	37.5%
Louisiana	6	1	1,035,947	675,386	311,221	49,340	364,165	R	65.2%	30.0%	68.5%	31.5%
Maine	0	2	564,368	248,170	316,156	42	67,986	D	44.0%	56.0%	44.0%	56.0%
Maryland	2	6	1,825,472	674,246	1,104,056	47,170	429,810	D	36.9%	60.5%	37.9%	62.1%
Massachusetts	0	10	2,224,255	808,305	1,335,738	80,212	527,433	D	36.3%	60.1%	37.7%	62.3%
Michigan	9	6	3,194,901	1,671,707	1,415,212	107,982	256,495	R	52.3%	44.3%	54.2%	45.8%
Minnesota	4	4	2,090,591	970,741	1,002,026	117,824	31,285	D	46.4%	47.9%	49.2%	50.8%
Mississippi	3	1	788,549	423,579	350,695	14,275	72,884	R	53.7%	44.5%	54.7%	45.3%
Missouri	6	3	1,920,675	1,103,290	708,064	109,321	395,226	R	57.4%	36.9%	60.9%	39.1%
Montana	1	0	360,341	217,696	121,954	20,691	95,742	R	60.4%	33.8%	64.1%	35.9%
Nebraska	3	0	485,546	327,986	137,524	20,036	190,462	R	67.5%	28.3%	70.5%	29.5%
Nevada	2	1	702,788	357,369	317,835	27,584	39,534	R	50.9%	45.2%	52.9%	47.1%
New Hampshire	2	0	450,086	230,265	200,563	19,258	29,702	R	51.2%	44.6%	53.4%	46.6%
New Jersey	6	7	2,121,584	1,055,299	1,024,730	41,555	30,569	R	49.7%	48.3%	50.7%	49.3%
New Mexico	1	2	597,690	289,217	308,473		19,256	D	48.4%	51.6%	48.4%	51.6%
New York	8	21	4,499,163	1,854,302	2,600,900	43,961	746,598	D	41.2%	57.8%	41.6%	58.4%
North Carolina	6	7	2,662,549	1,440,913	1,204,635	17,001	236,278	R	54.1%	45.2%	54.5%	45.5%
North Dakota	1	0	237,137	129,802	106,542	793	23,260	R	54.7%	44.9%	54.9%	45.1%
Ohio	13	5	3,825,274	2,053,075	1,611,112	161,087	441,963	R	53.7%	42.1%	56.0%	44.0%
Oklahoma	4	1	792,979	519,562	221,966	51,451	297,596	R	65.5%	28.0%	70.1%	29.9%
Oregon	1	4	1,429,356	657,007	733,369	38,980	76,362	D	46.0%	51.3%	47.3%	52.7%
Pennsylvania	12	7	3,959,504	2,034,145	1,882,202	43,157	151,943	R	51.4%	47.5%	51.9%	48.1%
Rhode Island	0	2	335,484	126,951	185,711	22,822	58,760	D	37.8%	55.4%	40.6%	59.4%
South Carolina	5	1	1,340,189	753,932	543,921	42,336	210,011	R	56.3%	40.6%	58.1%	41.9%
South Dakota	1	0	319,426	153,703	146,589	19,134	7,114	R	48.1%	45.9%	51.2%	48.8%
Tennessee	7	2	1,559,129	955,078	541,527	62,524	413,551	R	61.3%	34.7%	63.8%	36.2%
Texas	23	9	4,745,613	3,058,228	1,450,197	237,188	1,608,031	R	64.4%	30.6%	67.8%	32.2%
Utah	2	1	640,495	390,969	218,236	31,290	172,733	R	61.0%	34.1%	64.2%	35.8%
Vermont	0	1	238,521	76,403	154,006	8,112	77,603	D	32.0%	64.6%	33.2%	66.8%
Virginia	8	3	2,189,841	1,186,098	911,116	92,627	274,982	R	54.2%	41.6%	56.6%	43.4%
Washington	4	5	2,479,409	1,135,166	1,296,502	47,741	161,336	D	45.8%	52.3%	46.7%	53.3%
West Virginia	2	1	514,373	283,085	227,857	3,431	55,228	R	55.0%	44.3%	55.4%	44.6%
Wisconsin	5	3	2,140,482	1,165,761	938,690	36,031	227,071	R	54.5%	43.9%	55.4%	44.6%
Wyoming	1	0	186,969	131,661	45,768	9,540	85,893	R	70.4%	24.5%	74.2%	25.8%
TOTAL	*242*	*193*	*86,546,310*	*44,839,611*	*38,983,649*	*2,723,050*	*5,855,962*	*R*	*51.8%*	*45.0%*	*53.5%*	*46.5%*

In states such as Connecticut and New York where third parties could endorse candidates of the major parties, all such votes are credited to the major party with which the candidates identified.

UNITED STATES

SPECIAL ELECTIONS, POSTELECTION CHANGES, AND PARTY SWITCHES, 2009–2010

SPECIAL ELECTIONS TO THE 111th CONGRESS

From the beginning of 2009 through 2010, two special elections were held in the Senate and 11 in the House of Representatives to fill unexpired terms in the 111th Congress. In addition, appointments were made to fill vacancies for seven Senate seats. This table does not include special Senate elections held in conjunction with the 2010 general election that were for lengthier terms.

SENATORS

COLORADO

Ken Salazar (D) resigned January 20, 2009, to become secretary of interior. Michael Bennet (D) was appointed to fill the vacancy and was sworn in January 22, 2009.

DELAWARE

Joseph R. Biden Jr. (D) resigned January 15, 2009, following his election as vice president of the United States. Ted Kaufman (D) was appointed to fill the vacancy and was sworn in January 16, 2009.

FLORIDA

Mel Martinez (R) resigned September 9, 2009. George LeMieux (R) was appointed to fill the vacancy and was sworn in September 10, 2009.

ILLINOIS

Barack Obama (D) resigned November 16, 2008, following his election as president of the United States. Roland Burris (D) was appointed to fill the vacancy and was sworn in January 15, 2009. Mark Kirk (R) was elected November 2, 2010, to fill the remainder of the term in the 111th Congress. No primary was held. The special election was held in conjunction with the 2010 special election.

November 2, 2010 Special Election

1,677,729 Mark Steven Kirk (R); 1,641,486 Alexander "Alexi" Giannoulias (D); 129,571 LeAlan M. Jones (Green); 95,762 Mike Labno (Libertarian); 683 Robert Zadek (write-in); 415 Will Boyd (write-in); 297 Ina Pinkney (write-in); 15 Corey Dabney (write-in); 12 Susanne Atanus (write-in); 8 Shon-Tiyon "Santiago" Horton (write-in); 5 Stan Jagla (write-in); 1 Lowell M. Seida (write-in).

MASSACHUSETTS

Edward M. Kennedy (D) died August 25, 2009. Paul Kirk (D) was appointed to fill the vacancy and was sworn in September 25, 2009. Scott P. Brown (R) was elected January 19, 2010, to fill the remainder of the term in the 111th Congress and the entire 112th Congress.

December 8, 2009 Special Democratic Primary

311,548 Martha Coakley; 185,157 Michael E. Capuano; 89,294 Alan E. Khazei; 80,217 Stephen G. Pagliuca; 1,800 scattered write-in.

December 8, 2009 Special Republican Primary

146,057 Scott P. Brown; 17,344 Jack E. Robinson; 1,139 scattered write-in.

January 19, 2010 Special Election

1,168,178 Scott P. Brown (R); 1,060,861 Martha Coakley (D); 22,388 Joseph L. Kennedy (Liberty); 1,155 scattered write-in.

NEW YORK

Hillary Rodham Clinton (D) resigned January 21, 2009, to become secretary of state. Rep. Kirsten E. Gillibrand (D) was appointed to fill the vacancy and was sworn in January 27, 2009.

WEST VIRGINIA

Robert C. Byrd (D) died June 28, 2010. Carte Goodwin (D) was appointed to fill the vacancy and was sworn in July 20, 2010.

UNITED STATES

SPECIAL ELECTIONS TO THE 111th CONGRESS

REPRESENTATIVES

CALIFORNIA 10th CD

Ellen O. Tauscher (D) resigned June 26, 2009, to become undersecretary of state for arms control and international security. John Garamendi (D) was elected November 3, 2009, to fill the remainder of her term in the 111th Congress. The highest vote-getter in each party in the September 1, 2009, special primary election qualified for the November 3 special general election.

September 1, 2009 Special Primary Election

27,580 John Garamendi (D); 22,582 David Harmer (R); 18,888 Mark DeSaulnier (D); 12,896 Joan Buchanan (D); 9,388 Anthony Woods (D); 4,871 Chris Bunch (R); 4,158 Gary W. Clift (R); 3,340 John Toth (R); 1,671 David Peterson (R); 552 Jeremy Cloward (Green); 418 Mark Loos (R); 376 Adriel Hampton (D); 309 Jerome "Jerry" Denham (American Independent); 272 Mark C. McIlroy (Peace and Freedom); 2 Tiffany Rene Estrella Attwood (D).

November 3, 2009, Special General Election

72,817 John Garamendi (D); 59,017 David Harmer (R); 2,515 Jeremy Cloward (Green); 1,846 Mark C. McIlroy (Peace and Freedom); 1,591 Jerome "Jerry" Denham (American Independent).

CALIFORNIA 32nd CD

Hilda L. Solis (D) resigned February 24, 2009, to become secretary of labor. Judy Chu (D) was elected July 14, 2009, to fill the remainder of her term in the 111th Congress. The highest vote-getter in each party in the May 19, 2009, special primary election qualified for the July 14 special general election.

May 19, 2009 Special Primary Election

17,661 Judy Chu (D); 12,570 Gil Cedillo (D); 7,252 Emanuel Pleitez (D); 5,648 Betty Chu (R); 4,581 Teresa Hernandez (R); 3,303 David A. Truax (R); 1,097 Francisco Alonso (D); 659 Benita Duran (D); 654 Christopher M. Agrella (Libertarian); 246 Stefan "Contreras" Lysenko (D); 244 Nick Juan Mostert (D); 200 Rafael F. Nadal (D); 1 Larry Dean Scarborough (R write-in).

July 14, 2009 Special General Election

16,194 Judy Chu (D); 8,630 Betty Chu (R); 1,356 Christopher M. Agrella (Libertarian); 2 Eleanor Garcia (write-in).

FLORIDA 19th CD

Robert Wexler (D) resigned January 4, 2010, to become president of the Center for Middle East Peace. Ted Deutch (D) was elected April 13, 2010, to fill the remainder of his term in the 111th Congress.

February 2, 2010 Special Democratic Primary

23,959 Ted Deutch; 4,151 Ben Graber.

February 2, 2010 Special Republican Primary

3,322 Edward Lynch; 3,274 Joe Budd; 1,566 Curt Price.

April 13, 2010 Special General Election

43,269 Ted Deutch (D); 24,549 Edward Lynch (R); 1,905 Jim McCormick (No Party Affiliation).

GEORGIA 9th CD

Nathan Deal (R) resigned March 21, 2010, to focus on his campaign for governor of Georgia. Tom Graves (R) was elected June 8, 2010, to fill the remainder of his term in the 111th Congress. The highest two vote-getters, regardless of party, in the May 11, 2010, special election qualified for the June 8 special election runoff.

May 11, 2011 Special Election

18,316 Tom Graves (R); 12,012 Lee Hawkins; 7,940 Steve Tarvin (R); 6,137 Chris Cates (R); 2,891 Mike Freeman (D); 2,084 Bill Stephens (R); 1,292 Bert Loftman (R); 1,125 Eugene Moon (Independent).

UNITED STATES

SPECIAL ELECTIONS TO THE 111th CONGRESS

GEORGIA 9th CD (continued)

June 8, 2010 Special Election Runoff

22,694 Tom Graves (R); 17,509 Lee Hawkins (R).

HAWAII 1st CD

Neil Abercrombie (D) resigned February 28, 2010, to focus on his campaign for governor of Hawaii. Charles Djou (R) was elected May 22, 2010, to fill the remainder of his term in the 111th Congress. No primary or runoff was held.

May 22, 2010 Special Election

67,610 Charles Djou (R); 52,802 Colleen Hanabusa (D); 47,391 Ed Case (D); 664 Rafael "Del" Del Castillo (D); 491 Kalaeloa Strode (Nonpartisan); 273 Jim Brewer (Nonpartisan); 254 Philmund "Phil" Lee (D); 194 Charles "Googie" Collins (R); 170 C. Kaui Jochanan Amsterdam (R); 150 Vinny Browne (D); 125 Steve Tataii (Nonpartisan); 107 Douglas Crum (R); 82 John "Raghu" Giuffre; 80 Karl F. Moseley (Nonpartisan).

ILLINOIS 5th CD

Rahm Emanuel (D) resigned January 2, 2009, to become White House chief of staff. Mike Quigley (D) was elected April 7, 2009, to fill the remainder of his term in the 111th Congress. The highest vote-getter in each party in the March 3, 2009, special primary election qualified for the April 7 special general election.

March 3, 2009 Special Primary

12,118 Mike Quigley (D); 9,835 John A. Fritchey (D); 9,194 Sara Feigenholtz (D); 6,428 Victor A. Forys (D); 6,388 Patrick J. O'Connor (D); 3,681 Charles J. Wheelan (D); 3,342 Tom Geoghegan (D); 1,111 Paul J. Bryar (D); 1,006 Rosanna Pulido (R); 892 Jan H. Donatelli (D); 859 Tom Hanson (R); 755 Frank Annunzio (D); 714 Cary Capparelli (D); 712 David J. Anderson (R); 663 Gregory A. Bedell (R); 521 Carlos A. Monteagudo (D); 379 Daniel S. Kay (Karkusiewicz) (R); 368 Jon Stewart (R); 166 Matt Reichel (Green); 155 Deb Leticia Gordils (Green); 71 Mark Arnold Fredrickson (Green); 62 Alan Augustson (Green); 37 Simon Ribeiro (Green); 10 Roger A. Thompson (D write-in).

April 7, 2009 Special General Election

30,561 Mike Quigley (D); 10,662 Rosanna Pulido (R); 2,911 Matt Reichel (Green); 3 Frances Farley (Green write-in); 1 Goran Davidovac (write-in).

INDIANA 3rd CD

Mark Souder (R) resigned May 21, 2010, after admitting to an affair with a part-time staff member. Marlin A. Stutzman (R) was elected November 2, 2010, to fill the remainder of his term in the 111th Congress. No primary was held as nominations were decided by party officials. The special election was held in conjunction with the 2010 general election.

November 2, 2010 Special Election

115,415 Marlin A. Stutzman (R); 60,880 Thomas Hayhurst (D); 7,914 Scott Wise (Libertarian).

NEW YORK 20th CD

Kirsten E. Gillibrand (D) resigned January 26, 2009, to fill the Senate vacancy created by the resignation of Hillary Rodham Clinton (D). Scott Murphy (D) was elected March 31, 2009, to fill the remainder of her term in the 111th Congress. No primary was held as nominations were decided by party officials.

March 31, 2009 Special Election

80,833 Scott Murphy (D); 80,107 Jim Tedisco (R). (Murphy received votes on the ballot lines of the Democratic, Independence and Working Families parties. Tedisco received votes on the ballot lines of the Republican and Conservative parties.)

NEW YORK 23rd CD

John M. McHugh (R) resigned September 21, 2009, to become secretary of the army. William L. Owens (D) was elected November 3, 2009, to fill the remainder of his term in the 111th Congress. No primary was held as nominations were decided by party officials.

UNITED STATES

SPECIAL ELECTIONS TO THE 111th CONGRESS

NEW YORK 23rd CD (continued)

November 3, 2009 Special Election

73,137 William L. Owens (D); 69,553 Douglas L. Hoffman (Conservative); 8,582 Dede Scozzafava (R); 94 scattered write-in. (Owens received votes on the ballot lines of the Democratic and Working Families parties. Scozzafava received votes on the ballot lines of the Republican and Independence parties.)

NEW YORK 29th CD

Eric J. J. Massa (D) resigned March 8, 2010, in midst of ethics investigation into charges that he sexually harassed male staffers. Thomas W. Reed II (R) was elected November, 2, 2010, to fill the remainder of his term in the 111th Congress. No primary was held as nominations were decided by party officials. The special election was held in conjunction with the 2010 general election.

November 2, 2010 Special Election

105,907 Thomas W. Reed II (R); 80,480 Matthew C. Zeller (D); 510 scattered write-in. (Reed received votes on the ballot lines of the Republican, Conservative and Independence parties. Zeller received votes on the ballot lines of the Democratic and Working Families parties.)

PENNSYLVANIA 12th CD

John P. Murtha (D) died February 8, 2010. Mark S. Critz (D) was elected May 18, 2010, to fill the remainder of his term in the 111th Congress. No primary was held as nominations were decided by party officials.

May 18, 2010 Special Election

72,218 Mark S. Critz (D); 61,722 Tim Burns (R); 3,249 Demo Agoris (Libertarian).

UNITED STATES

SUMMARY OF SENATE, HOUSE SPECIAL ELECTIONS 2009 TO 2010

Republicans picked up ground in both the Senate and the House in special elections held to fill vacancies in the 111th Congress. Senate elections in Illinois and Massachusetts shifted seats from Democratic to Republican, as did two special House elections in Hawaii and New York. Another House seat in the Empire state shifted from Republican to Democrat. The chart below does not include special Senate elections held in conjunction with the 2010 general election that were for lengthier terms. The partisan switches are indicated below in bold. All of the results are based on the decisive round of voting in each special election when the new member was elected to Congress. The special elections are listed in the chronological order in which they were held.

SENATORS

State	Former Member	New Member	Date Elected	Winning Percentage	Voter Turnout
Massachusetts	**Paul Kirk (D)**	**Scott P. Brown (R)**	**January 19, 2010**	**51.9%**	**2,252,582**
Illinois	**Roland Burris (D)**	**Mark Steven Kirk (R)**	**November 2, 2010**	**47.3%**	**3,545,984**

REPRESENTATIVES

District	Former Member	New Member	Date Elected	Winning Percentage	Voter Turnout
New York 20th	Kirsten E. Gillibrand (D)	Scott Murphy (D)	March 31, 2009	50.2%	160,940
Illinois 5th	Rahm Emanuel (D)	Mike Quigley (D)	April 7, 2009	69.2%	44,138
California 32nd	Hilda L. Solis (D)	Judy Chu (D)	July 14, 2009	61.9%	26,182
California 10th	Ellen O. Tauscher (D)	John Garamendi (D)	November 3, 2009	52.8%	137,786
New York 23rd	**John M. McHugh (R)**	**William L. Owens (D)**	**November 3, 2009**	**48.3%**	**151,366**
Florida 19th	Robert Wexler (D)	Ted Deutch (D)	April 13, 2010	62.1%	69,723
Pennsylvania 12th	John P. Murtha (D)	Mark S. Critz (D)	May 18, 2010	52.6%	137,189
Hawaii 1st	**Neil Abercrombie (D)**	**Charles Djou (R)**	**May 22, 2010**	**39.7%**	**170,393**
Georgia 9th	Nathan Deal (R)	Tom Graves (R)	June 8, 2010	56.4%	40,203
Indiana 3rd	Mark Souder (R)	Marlin A. Stutzman (R)	November 2, 2010	62.7%	184,209
New York 29th	**Eric J.J. Massa (D)**	**Thomas W. Reed II (R)**	**November 2, 2010**	**56.7%**	**186,897**

UNITED STATES

SPECIAL ELECTIONS TO THE 111th CONGRESS

CHANGES FOLLOWING THE 2010 ELECTION

Following the 2010 general election, and through August 15, 2011, the following changes took place in the membership of the 112th Congress.

SENATORS

Nevada – John Ensign (R) resigned May 3, 2011, in the midst of a Senate Ethics Committee investigation into his affair with a female staffer and the propriety of his payment of money to the staffer's family. Dean Heller (R) was sworn in May 9, 2011, to succeed him.

REPRESENTATIVES

California 36th District – Jane Harman (D) resigned February 28, 2011, to become president of the Woodrow Wilson International Center for Politics in Washington, D.C. Janice Hahn (D) was elected July 12, 2011, to replace her.

Nevada 2nd District – Dean Heller (R) resigned May 9, 2011, to fill the remainder of John Ensign's Senate term. A special election was scheduled for September 13, 2011, to fill the seat.

New York 9th District – Anthony Weiner (D) resigned June 21, 2011, after the admission of numerous "sexting" tweets. A special election was scheduled September 13, 2011, to fill the seat.

New York 26th District – Christopher John Lee (R) resigned February 9, 2011, after a "beefcake" photo of the married congressman appeared on the Internet. Kathy Hochul (D) was elected May 24, 2011, to succeed him.

Oregon 1st District – David Wu (D) resigned August, 3, 2011, following accusations of "aggressive and unwanted sexual behavior" with a female teenager. A special primary election was scheduled for November 8, 2011, with a special general election slated for January 31, 2012.

UNITED STATES

POPULAR VOTE FOR PRESIDENT 1920 TO 2008

Year	Total Vote	Republican Vote	Republican Candidate	Democratic Vote	Democratic Candidate	Other Vote	Plurality	Total Vote Rep.	Total Vote Dem.	Major Vote Rep.	Major Vote Dem.
2008	131,313,820	59,948,323	McCain, John	69,498,516	Obama, Barack	1,866,981	9,550,193 D	45.7%	52.9%	46.3%	53.7%
2004	122,295,345	62,040,610	Bush, George W.	59,028,439	Kerry, John	1,226,296	3,012,171 R	50.7%	48.3%	51.2%	48.8%
2000	105,396,627	50,455,156	Bush, George W.	50,992,335	Gore, Al	3,949,136	537,179 D	47.9%	48.4%	49.7%	50.3%
1996	96,277,872	39,198,755	Dole, Bob	47,402,357	Clinton, Bill	9,676,760	8,203,602 D	40.7%	49.2%	45.3%	54.7%
1992	104,425,014	39,103,882	Bush, George	44,909,326	Clinton, Bill	20,411,806	5,805,444 D	37.4%	43.0%	46.5%	53.5%
1988	91,594,809	48,886,097	Bush, George	41,809,074	Dukakis, Michael S.	899,638	7,077,023 R	53.4%	45.6%	53.9%	46.1%
1984	92,652,842	54,455,075	Reagan, Ronald	37,577,185	Mondale, Walter F.	620,582	16,877,890 R	58.8%	40.6%	59.2%	40.8%
1980	86,515,221	43,904,153	Reagan, Ronald	35,483,883	Carter, Jimmy	7,127,185	8,420,270 R	50.7%	41.0%	55.3%	44.7%
1976	81,555,889	39,147,793	Ford, Gerald R.	40,830,763	Carter, Jimmy	1,577,333	1,682,970 D	48.0%	50.1%	48.9%	51.1%
1972	77,718,554	47,169,911	Nixon, Richard M.	29,170,383	McGovern, George S.	1,378,260	17,999,528 R	60.7%	37.5%	61.8%	38.2%
1968	73,211,875	31,785,480	Nixon, Richard M.	31,275,166	Humphrey, Hubert H.	10,151,229	510,314 R	43.4%	42.7%	50.4%	49.6%
1964	70,644,592	27,178,188	Goldwater, Barry M.	43,129,566	Johnson, Lyndon B.	336,838	15,951,378 D	38.5%	61.1%	38.7%	61.3%
1960	68,838,219	34,108,157	Nixon, Richard M.	34,226,731	Kennedy, John F.	503,331	118,574 D	49.5%	49.7%	49.9%	50.1%
1956	62,026,908	35,590,472	Eisenhower, Dwight D.	26,022,752	Stevenson, Adlai E.	413,684	9,567,720 R	57.4%	42.0%	57.8%	42.2%
1952	61,550,918	33,936,234	Eisenhower, Dwight D.	27,314,992	Stevenson, Adlai E.	299,692	6,621,242 R	55.1%	44.4%	55.4%	44.6%
1948	48,793,826	21,991,291	Dewey, Thomas E.	24,179,345	Truman, Harry S.	2,623,190	2,188,054 D	45.1%	49.6%	47.6%	52.4%
1944	47,976,670	22,017,617	Dewey, Thomas E.	25,612,610	Roosevelt, Franklin D.	346,443	3,594,993 D	45.9%	53.4%	46.2%	53.8%
1940	49,900,418	22,348,480	Willkie, Wendell	27,313,041	Roosevelt, Franklin D.	238,897	4,964,561 D	44.8%	54.7%	45.0%	55.0%
1936	45,654,763	16,684,231	Landon, Alfred M.	27,757,333	Roosevelt, Franklin D.	1,213,199	11,073,102 D	36.5%	60.8%	37.5%	62.5%
1932	39,758,759	15,760,684	Hoover, Herbert C.	22,829,501	Roosevelt, Franklin D.	1,168,574	7,068,817 D	39.6%	57.4%	40.8%	59.2%
1928	36,805,951	21,437,277	Hoover, Herbert C.	15,007,698	Smith, Alfred E.	360,976	6,429,579 R	58.2%	40.8%	58.8%	41.2%
1924	29,095,023	15,719,921	Coolidge, Calvin	8,386,704	Davis, John W.	4,988,398	7,333,217 R	54.0%	28.8%	65.2%	34.8%
1920	26,768,613	16,153,115	Harding, Warren G.	9,133,092	Cox, James M.	1,482,406	7,020,023 R	60.3%	34.1%	63.9%	36.1%

For detail of other vote, see note section included with each U.S. summary table that follows.

ELECTORAL COLLEGE VOTE 1920 TO 2008

Year	Total	Republican	Democratic	Other
2008	538	173	365	—
2004	538	286	251	1 EDWARDS
2000	538	271	266	1 (Blank)
1996	538	159	379	—
1992	538	168	370	—
1988	538	426	111	1 BENTSEN
1984	538	525	13	—
1980	538	489	49	—
1976	538	240	297	1 REAGAN
1972	538	520	17	1 LIBERTARIAN
1968	538	301	191	46 AIP
1964	538	52	486	—
1960	537	219	303	15 BYRD
1956	531	457	73	1 JONES
1952	531	442	89	—
1948	531	189	303	39 SR
1944	531	99	432	—
1940	531	82	449	—
1936	531	8	523	—
1932	531	59	472	—
1928	531	444	87	—
1924	531	382	136	13 PROGRESSIVE
1920	531	404	127	—

ALABAMA

Congressional districts first established for elections held in 2002
7 members

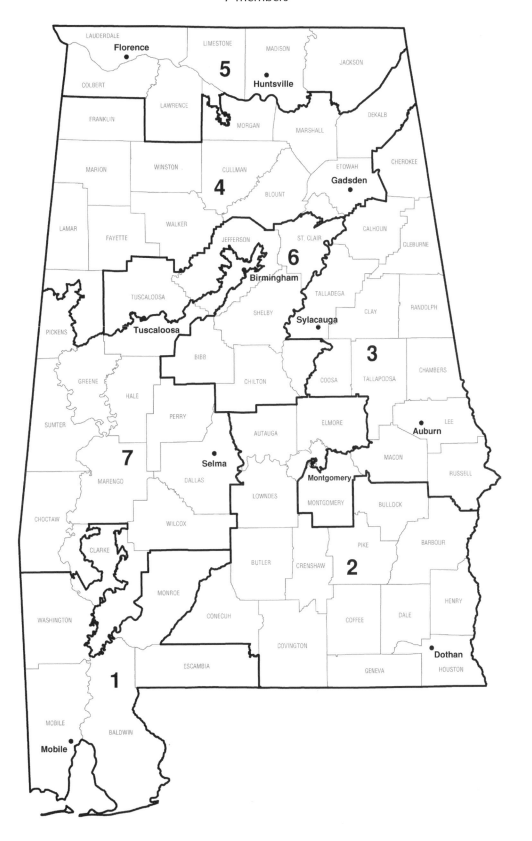

ALABAMA

GOVERNOR
Robert Bentley (R). Elected 2010 to a four-year term.

SENATORS (2 Republicans)
Jeff Sessions (R). Reelected 2008 to a six-year term. Previously elected 2002, 1996.

Richard C. Shelby (R). Reelected 2010 to a six-year term. Previously elected 2004, 1998, 1992, 1986. Changed party affiliation from Democratic to Republican in November 1994.

REPRESENTATIVES (6 Republicans, 1 Democrat)
1. Jo Bonner (R)
2. Martha Roby (R)
3. Mike D. Rogers (R)
4. Robert B. Aderholt (R)
5. Mo Brooks (R)
6. Spencer Bachus (R)
7. Terri A. Sewell (D)

POSTWAR VOTE FOR PRESIDENT

| | | Republican | | Democratic | | | | Percentage | | | |
| | | | | | | | | Total Vote | | Major Vote | |
Year	Total Vote	Vote	Candidate	Vote	Candidate	Other Vote	Rep.-Dem. Plurality	Rep.	Dem.	Rep.	Dem.
2008	2,099,819	1,266,546	McCain, John	813,479	Obama, Barack	19,794	453,067 R	60.3%	38.7%	60.9%	39.1%
2004	1,883,449	1,176,394	Bush, George W.	693,933	Kerry, John	13,122	482,461 R	62.5%	36.8%	62.9%	37.1%
2000**	1,666,272	941,173	Bush, George W.	692,611	Gore, Al	32,488	248,562 R	56.5%	41.6%	57.6%	42.4%
1996**	1,534,349	769,044	Dole, Bob	662,165	Clinton, Bill	103,140	106,879 R	50.1%	43.2%	53.7%	46.3%
1992**	1,688,060	804,283	Bush, George	690,080	Clinton, Bill	193,697	114,203 R	47.6%	40.9%	53.8%	46.2%
1988	1,378,476	815,576	Bush, George	549,506	Dukakis, Michael S.	13,394	266,070 R	59.2%	39.9%	59.7%	40.3%
1984	1,441,713	872,849	Reagan, Ronald	551,899	Mondale, Walter F.	16,965	320,950 R	60.5%	38.3%	61.3%	38.7%
1980**	1,341,929	654,192	Reagan, Ronald	636,730	Carter, Jimmy	51,007	17,462 R	48.8%	47.4%	50.7%	49.3%
1976	1,182,850	504,070	Ford, Gerald R.	659,170	Carter, Jimmy	19,610	155,100 D	42.6%	55.7%	43.3%	56.7%
1972	1,006,111	728,701	Nixon, Richard M.	256,923	McGovern, George S.	20,487	471,778 R	72.4%	25.5%	73.9%	26.1%
1968**	1,049,922	146,923	Nixon, Richard M.	196,579	Humphrey, Hubert H.	706,420	494,846 A	14.0%	18.7%	42.8%	57.2%
1964**	689,818	479,085	Goldwater, Barry M.	—	Johnson, Lyndon B.	210,733	268,353 R	69.5%		100.0%	
1960	570,225	237,981	Nixon, Richard M.	324,050	Kennedy, John F.	8,194	86,069 D	41.7%	56.8%	42.3%	57.7%
1956	496,861	195,694	Eisenhower, Dwight D.	280,844	Stevenson, Adlai E.	20,323	85,150 D	39.4%	56.5%	41.1%	58.9%
1952	426,120	149,231	Eisenhower, Dwight D.	275,075	Stevenson, Adlai E.	1,814	125,844 D	35.0%	64.6%	35.2%	64.8%
1948**	214,980	40,930	Dewey, Thomas E.	—	Truman, Harry S.	174,050	130,513 S	19.0%		100.0%	

** In past elections, the other vote included: 2000 - 18,323 Green (Ralph Nader); 1996 - 92,149 Reform (Ross Perot); 1992 - 183,109 Independent (Perot); 1980 - 16,481 Independent (John Anderson); 1968 - 691,425 American Independent (George Wallace); 1964 - 210,732 Unpledged Democratic; 1948 - 171,443 States' Rights (Strom Thurmond). In 1964 and 1948, the Democratic presidential candidates were not listed on the ballot. Wallace carried Alabama in 1968 with 65.9 percent of the total vote. Thurmond won the state in 1948 with 79.7 percent.

ALABAMA

POSTWAR VOTE FOR GOVERNOR

Year	Total Vote	Republican Vote	Republican Candidate	Democratic Vote	Democratic Candidate	Other Vote	Rep.-Dem. Plurality	Total Vote Rep.	Total Vote Dem.	Major Vote Rep.	Major Vote Dem.
2010	1,494,273	860,472	Bentley, Robert	625,710	Sparks, Ron	8,091	234,762 R	57.6%	41.9%	57.9%	42.1%
2006	1,250,401	718,327	Riley, Bob	519,827	Baxley, Lucy	12,247	198,500 R	57.4%	41.6%	58.0%	42.0%
2002	1,367,053	672,225	Riley, Bob	669,105	Siegelman, Don	25,723	3,120 R	49.2%	48.9%	50.1%	49.9%
1998	1,317,842	554,746	James, Forrest H.	760,155	Siegelman, Don	2,941	205,409 D	42.1%	57.7%	42.2%	57.8%
1994	1,201,969	604,926	James, Forrest H.	594,169	Folsom, James E.	2,874	10,757 R	50.3%	49.4%	50.4%	49.6%
1990	1,216,250	633,519	Hunt, Guy	582,106	Hubbert, Paul R.	625	51,413 R	52.1%	47.9%	52.1%	47.9%
1986	1,236,230	696,203	Hunt, Guy	537,163	Baxley, Bill	2,864	159,040 R	56.3%	43.5%	56.4%	43.6%
1982	1,128,725	440,815	Folmar, Emory	650,538	Wallace, George C.	37,372	209,723 D	39.1%	57.6%	40.4%	59.6%
1978	760,474	196,963	Hunt, Guy	551,886	James, Forrest H.	11,625	354,923 D	25.9%	72.6%	26.3%	73.7%
1974	598,305	88,381	McCary, Elvin	497,574	Wallace, George C.	12,350	409,193 D	14.8%	83.2%	15.1%	84.9%
1970**	854,952		—	637,046	Wallace, George C.	217,906	637,046 D		74.5%		100.0%
1966	848,101	262,943	Martin, James D.	537,505	Wallace, Mrs. George C.	47,653	274,562 D	31.0%	63.4%	32.8%	67.2%
1962	315,776		—	303,987	Wallace, George C.	11,789	303,987 D		96.3%		100.0%
1958	270,952	30,415	Longshore, W. L.	239,633	Patterson, John	904	209,218 D	11.2%	88.4%	11.3%	88.7%
1954	333,090	88,688	Amernethy, Tom	244,401	Folsom, James E.	1	155,713 D	26.6%	73.4%	26.6%	73.4%
1950	170,541	15,127	Crowder, John S.	155,414	Persons, Gordon		140,287 D	8.9%	91.1%	8.9%	91.1%
1946	197,324	22,362	Ward, Lyman	174,962	Folsom, James E.		152,600 D	11.3%	88.7%	11.3%	88.7%

** In past elections, the other vote included: 1970 - 125,491 National Democratic Party of Alabama (John Logan Cashin). The Republican Party did not run a candidate in the 1962 and 1970 gubernatorial elections.

POSTWAR VOTE FOR SENATOR

Year	Total Vote	Republican Vote	Republican Candidate	Democratic Vote	Democratic Candidate	Other Vote	Rep.-Dem. Plurality	Total Vote Rep.	Total Vote Dem.	Major Vote Rep.	Major Vote Dem.
2010	1,485,499	968,181	Shelby, Richard C.	515,619	Barnes, William G.	1,699	452,562 R	65.2%	34.7%	65.3%	34.7%
2008	2,060,191	1,305,383	Sessions, Jeff	752,391	Figures, Vivian Davis	2,417	552,992 R	63.4%	36.5%	63.4%	36.6%
2004	1,839,066	1,242,200	Shelby, Richard C.	595,018	Sowell, Wayne	1,848	647,182 R	67.5%	32.4%	67.6%	32.4%
2002	1,353,023	792,561	Sessions, Jeff	538,878	Parker, Susan	21,584	253,683 R	58.6%	39.8%	59.5%	40.5%
1998	1,293,405	817,973	Shelby, Richard C.	474,568	Suddith, Clayton	864	343,405 R	63.2%	36.7%	63.3%	36.7%
1996	1,499,393	786,436	Sessions, Jeff	681,651	Bedford, Roger	31,306	104,785 R	52.5%	45.5%	53.6%	46.4%
1992	1,577,799	522,015	Sellers, Richard	1,022,698	Shelby, Richard C.	33,086	500,683 D	33.1%	64.8%	33.8%	66.2%
1990	1,185,563	467,190	Cabaniss, Bill	717,814	Heflin, Howell	559	250,624 D	39.4%	60.5%	39.4%	60.6%
1986	1,211,953	602,537	Denton, Jeremiah	609,360	Shelby, Richard C.	56	6,823 D	49.7%	50.3%	49.7%	50.3%
1984	1,371,238	498,508	Smith, Albert L.	860,535	Heflin, Howell	12,195	362,027 D	36.4%	62.8%	36.7%	63.3%
1980	1,296,757	650,362	Denton, Jeremiah	610,175	Folsom, James E., Jr.	36,220	40,187 R	50.2%	47.1%	51.6%	48.4%
1978	582,025		—	547,054	Heflin, Howell	34,971	547,054 D		94.0%		100.0%
1978S	731,614	316,170	Martin, James D.	401,852	Stewart, Donald W.	13,592	85,682 D	43.2%	54.9%	44.0%	56.0%
1974	523,290		—	501,541	Allen, James B.	21,749	501,541 D		95.8%		100.0%
1972	1,051,099	347,523	Blount, Winston M.	654,491	Sparkman, John J.	49,085	306,968 D	33.1%	62.3%	34.7%	65.3%
1968	912,708	201,227	Hooper, Perry	638,774	Allen, James B.	72,707	437,547 D	22.0%	70.0%	24.0%	76.0%
1966	802,608	313,018	Grenier, John	482,138	Sparkman, John J.	7,452	169,120 D	39.0%	60.1%	39.4%	60.6%
1962	397,079	195,134	Martin, James D.	201,937	Hill, Lister	8	6,803 D	49.1%	50.9%	49.1%	50.9%
1960	554,081	164,868	Elgin, Julian	389,196	Sparkman, John J.	17	224,328 D	29.8%	70.2%	29.8%	70.2%
1956	330,191		—	330,182	Hill, Lister	9	330,182 D		100.0%		100.0%
1954	314,459	55,110	Guin, J. Foy	259,348	Sparkman, John J.	1	204,238 D	17.5%	82.5%	17.5%	82.5%
1950	164,011		—	125,534	Hill, Lister	38,477	125,534 D		76.5%		100.0%
1948	220,875	35,341	Parsons, Paul G.	185,534	Sparkman, John J.		150,193 D	16.0%	84.0%	16.0%	84.0%
1946S	163,217		—	163,217	Sparkman, John J.		163,217 D		100.0%		100.0%

The 1946 election and one of the 1978 elections were for short terms to fill vacancies. The Republican Party did not run a candidate in Senate elections in 1946, 1950, 1956, 1974 and 1978.

ALABAMA

GOVERNOR 2010

2000 Census Population	County	Total Vote	Republican	Democratic	Other	Rep.-Dem. Plurality		Percentage Total Vote Rep.	Dem.	Major Vote Rep.	Dem.
54,571	AUTAUGA	18,034	11,943	5,971	120	5,972	R	66.2%	33.1%	66.7%	33.3%
182,265	BALDWIN	57,704	44,126	12,621	957	31,505	R	76.5%	21.9%	77.8%	22.2%
27,457	BARBOUR	8,369	3,229	5,127	13	1,898	D	38.6%	61.3%	38.6%	61.4%
22,915	BIBB	6,474	4,384	2,048	42	2,336	R	67.7%	31.6%	68.2%	31.8%
57,322	BLOUNT	16,856	13,024	3,748	84	9,276	R	77.3%	22.2%	77.7%	22.3%
10,914	BULLOCK	3,892	874	3,018		2,144	D	22.5%	77.5%	22.5%	77.5%
20,947	BUTLER	7,106	3,358	3,728	20	370	D	47.3%	52.5%	47.4%	52.6%
118,572	CALHOUN	33,942	21,250	12,568	124	8,682	R	62.6%	37.0%	62.8%	37.2%
34,215	CHAMBERS	10,378	5,067	5,296	15	229	D	48.8%	51.0%	48.9%	51.1%
25,989	CHEROKEE	7,230	4,315	2,901	14	1,414	R	59.7%	40.1%	59.8%	40.2%
43,643	CHILTON	13,646	9,529	4,034	83	5,495	R	69.8%	29.6%	70.3%	29.7%
13,859	CHOCTAW	6,672	2,962	3,701	9	739	D	44.4%	55.5%	44.5%	55.5%
25,833	CLARKE	10,715	5,369	5,313	33	56	R	50.1%	49.6%	50.3%	49.7%
13,932	CLAY	5,327	3,248	2,069	10	1,179	R	61.0%	38.8%	61.1%	38.9%
14,972	CLEBURNE	5,171	3,678	1,471	22	2,207	R	71.1%	28.4%	71.4%	28.6%
49,948	COFFEE	15,218	9,535	5,647	36	3,888	R	62.7%	37.1%	62.8%	37.2%
54,428	COLBERT	16,800	9,181	7,586	33	1,595	R	54.6%	45.2%	54.8%	45.2%
13,228	CONECUH	5,303	2,311	2,982	10	671	D	43.6%	56.2%	43.7%	56.3%
11,539	COOSA	4,421	2,068	2,342	11	274	D	46.8%	53.0%	46.9%	53.1%
37,765	COVINGTON	12,196	7,832	4,328	36	3,504	R	64.2%	35.5%	64.4%	35.6%
13,906	CRENSHAW	5,529	2,880	2,632	17	248	R	52.1%	47.6%	52.2%	47.8%
80,406	CULLMAN	30,004	21,115	8,803	86	12,312	R	70.4%	29.3%	70.6%	29.4%
50,251	DALE	14,033	7,905	6,093	35	1,812	R	56.3%	43.4%	56.5%	43.5%
43,820	DALLAS	15,710	4,567	11,118	25	6,551	D	29.1%	70.8%	29.1%	70.9%
71,109	DE KALB	20,414	11,289	9,125		2,164	R	55.3%	44.7%	55.3%	44.7%
79,303	ELMORE	26,327	17,439	8,724	164	8,715	R	66.2%	33.1%	66.7%	33.3%
38,319	ESCAMBIA	10,654	6,487	4,091	76	2,396	R	60.9%	38.4%	61.3%	38.7%
104,430	ETOWAH	32,112	19,312	12,710	90	6,602	R	60.1%	39.6%	60.3%	39.7%
17,241	FAYETTE	6,102	4,200	1,885	17	2,315	R	68.8%	30.9%	69.0%	31.0%
31,704	FRANKLIN	8,714	4,751	3,947	16	804	R	54.5%	45.3%	54.6%	45.4%
26,790	GENEVA	9,708	5,605	4,079	24	1,526	R	57.7%	42.0%	57.9%	42.1%
9,045	GREENE	4,334	665	3,668	1	3,003	D	15.3%	84.6%	15.3%	84.7%
15,760	HALE	6,523	2,402	4,116	5	1,714	D	36.8%	63.1%	36.9%	63.1%
17,302	HENRY	6,824	3,286	3,522	16	236	D	48.2%	51.6%	48.3%	51.7%
101,547	HOUSTON	32,850	17,057	15,724	69	1,333	R	51.9%	47.9%	52.0%	48.0%
53,227	JACKSON	15,438	8,606	6,794	38	1,812	R	55.7%	44.0%	55.9%	44.1%
658,466	JEFFERSON	212,445	103,802	106,959	1,684	3,157	D	48.9%	50.3%	49.3%	50.7%
14,564	LAMAR	4,956	3,369	1,580	7	1,789	R	68.0%	31.9%	68.1%	31.9%
92,709	LAUDERDALE	27,994	17,074	10,849	71	6,225	R	61.0%	38.8%	61.1%	38.9%
34,339	LAWRENCE	11,607	6,036	5,547	24	489	R	52.0%	47.8%	52.1%	47.9%
140,247	LEE	33,819	19,704	13,846	269	5,858	R	58.3%	40.9%	58.7%	41.3%
82,782	LIMESTONE	25,999	17,346	8,593	60	8,753	R	66.7%	33.1%	66.9%	33.1%
11,299	LOWNDES	5,336	1,231	4,100	5	2,869	D	23.1%	76.8%	23.1%	76.9%
21,452	MACON	7,558	919	6,634	5	5,715	D	12.2%	87.8%	12.2%	87.8%
334,811	MADISON	108,376	65,963	42,090	323	23,873	R	60.9%	38.8%	61.0%	39.0%
21,027	MARENGO	8,899	3,790	5,084	25	1,294	D	42.6%	57.1%	42.7%	57.3%
30,776	MARION	8,921	5,895	2,994	32	2,901	R	66.1%	33.6%	66.3%	33.7%
93,019	MARSHALL	25,788	18,164	7,521	103	10,643	R	70.4%	29.2%	70.7%	29.3%
412,992	MOBILE	110,667	61,479	48,000	1,188	13,479	R	55.6%	43.4%	56.2%	43.8%
23,068	MONROE	7,550	4,103	3,413	34	690	R	54.3%	45.2%	54.6%	45.4%
229,363	MONTGOMERY	74,008	30,046	43,439	523	13,393	D	40.6%	58.7%	40.9%	59.1%
119,490	MORGAN	39,253	26,976	12,169	108	14,807	R	68.7%	31.0%	68.9%	31.1%
10,591	PERRY	4,458	1,143	3,303	12	2,160	D	25.6%	74.1%	25.7%	74.3%
19,746	PICKENS	7,515	4,226	3,280	9	946	R	56.2%	43.6%	56.3%	43.7%
32,899	PIKE	9,707	5,001	4,685	21	316	R	51.5%	48.3%	51.6%	48.4%
22,913	RANDOLPH	7,311	4,453	2,840	18	1,613	R	60.9%	38.8%	61.1%	38.9%
52,947	RUSSELL	11,498	4,917	6,558	23	1,641	D	42.8%	57.0%	42.8%	57.2%
83,593	ST. CLAIR	24,776	18,742	5,878	156	12,864	R	75.6%	23.7%	76.1%	23.9%
195,085	SHELBY	63,345	49,192	13,589	564	35,603	R	77.7%	21.5%	78.4%	21.6%
13,763	SUMTER	5,604	1,306	4,290	8	2,984	D	23.3%	76.6%	23.3%	76.7%

ALABAMA

GOVERNOR 2010

2000 Census Population	County	Total Vote	Republican	Democratic	Other	Rep.-Dem. Plurality		Percentage			
								Total Vote		Major Vote	
								Rep.	Dem.	Rep.	Dem.
82,291	TALLADEGA	24,059	13,200	10,773	86	2,427	R	54.9%	44.8%	55.1%	44.9%
41,616	TALLAPOOSA	15,767	9,023	6,733	11	2,290	R	57.2%	42.7%	57.3%	42.7%
194,656	TUSCALOOSA	54,575	34,206	20,146	223	14,060	R	62.7%	36.9%	62.9%	37.1%
67,023	WALKER	22,583	13,804	8,685	94	5,119	R	61.1%	38.5%	61.4%	38.6%
17,581	WASHINGTON	6,093	3,336	2,733	24	603	R	54.8%	44.9%	55.0%	45.0%
11,670	WILCOX	4,975	1,146	3,824	5	2,678	D	23.0%	76.9%	23.1%	76.9%
24,484	WINSTON	8,101	6,031	2,045	25	3,986	R	74.4%	25.2%	74.7%	25.3%
4,779,736	TOTAL	1,494,273	860,472	625,710	8,091	234,762	R	57.6%	41.9%	57.9%	42.1%

ALABAMA

SENATOR 2010

2010 Census Population	County	Total Vote	Republican	Democratic	Other	Rep.-Dem. Plurality		Percentage			
								Total Vote		Major Vote	
								Rep.	Dem.	Rep.	Dem.
54,571	AUTAUGA	17,974	13,980	3,978	16	10,002	R	77.8%	22.1%	77.8%	22.2%
182,265	BALDWIN	57,592	46,471	11,027	94	35,444	R	80.7%	19.1%	80.8%	19.2%
27,457	BARBOUR	8,274	4,242	4,030	2	212	R	51.3%	48.7%	51.3%	48.7%
22,915	BIBB	6,427	4,849	1,569	9	3,280	R	75.4%	24.4%	75.6%	24.4%
57,322	BLOUNT	16,763	14,296	2,448	19	11,848	R	85.3%	14.6%	85.4%	14.6%
10,914	BULLOCK	3,866	1,146	2,720		1,574	D	29.6%	70.4%	29.6%	70.4%
20,947	BUTLER	7,039	4,145	2,888	6	1,257	R	58.9%	41.0%	58.9%	41.1%
118,572	CALHOUN	33,724	23,643	10,046	35	13,597	R	70.1%	29.8%	70.2%	29.8%
34,215	CHAMBERS	10,305	5,594	4,705	6	889	R	54.3%	45.7%	54.3%	45.7%
25,989	CHEROKEE	7,141	5,021	2,111	9	2,910	R	70.3%	29.6%	70.4%	29.6%
43,643	CHILTON	13,557	10,801	2,735	21	8,066	R	79.7%	20.2%	79.8%	20.2%
13,859	CHOCTAW	6,620	3,510	3,108	2	402	R	53.0%	46.9%	53.0%	47.0%
25,833	CLARKE	10,557	6,063	4,483	11	1,580	R	57.4%	42.5%	57.5%	42.5%
13,932	CLAY	5,233	3,829	1,401	3	2,428	R	73.2%	26.8%	73.2%	26.8%
14,972	CLEBURNE	5,087	4,009	1,068	10	2,941	R	78.8%	21.0%	79.0%	21.0%
49,948	COFFEE	15,130	11,759	3,348	23	8,411	R	77.7%	22.1%	77.8%	22.2%
54,428	COLBERT	16,710	9,920	6,781	9	3,139	R	59.4%	40.6%	59.4%	40.6%
13,228	CONECUH	5,200	2,752	2,444	4	308	R	52.9%	47.0%	53.0%	47.0%
11,539	COOSA	4,394	2,482	1,911	1	571	R	56.5%	43.5%	56.5%	43.5%
37,765	COVINGTON	12,118	9,785	2,313	20	7,472	R	80.7%	19.1%	80.9%	19.1%
13,906	CRENSHAW	5,411	3,837	1,572	2	2,265	R	70.9%	29.1%	70.9%	29.1%
80,406	CULLMAN	29,725	23,918	5,752	55	18,166	R	80.5%	19.4%	80.6%	19.4%
50,251	DALE	13,865	10,557	3,274	34	7,283	R	76.1%	23.6%	76.3%	23.7%
43,820	DALLAS	15,627	5,372	10,248	7	4,876	D	34.4%	65.6%	34.4%	65.6%
71,109	DE KALB	19,930	14,520	5,410		9,110	R	72.9%	27.1%	72.9%	27.1%
79,303	ELMORE	26,267	20,689	5,555	23	15,134	R	78.8%	21.1%	78.8%	21.2%
38,319	ESCAMBIA	10,566	7,236	3,307	23	3,929	R	68.5%	31.3%	68.6%	31.4%
104,430	ETOWAH	31,816	22,124	9,647	45	12,477	R	69.5%	30.3%	69.6%	30.4%
17,241	FAYETTE	6,008	4,417	1,583	8	2,834	R	73.5%	26.3%	73.6%	26.4%
31,704	FRANKLIN	8,574	5,572	2,992	10	2,580	R	65.0%	34.9%	65.1%	34.9%
26,790	GENEVA	9,572	7,817	1,738	17	6,079	R	81.7%	18.2%	81.8%	18.2%
9,045	GREENE	4,305	796	3,507	2	2,711	D	18.5%	81.5%	18.5%	81.5%
15,760	HALE	6,467	2,568	3,895	4	1,327	D	39.7%	60.2%	39.7%	60.3%
17,302	HENRY	6,740	4,493	2,226	21	2,267	R	66.7%	33.0%	66.9%	33.1%
101,547	HOUSTON	32,492	24,218	8,234	40	15,984	R	74.5%	25.3%	74.6%	25.4%
53,227	JACKSON	15,119	10,507	4,589	23	5,918	R	69.5%	30.4%	69.6%	30.4%
658,466	JEFFERSON	212,150	113,144	98,773	233	14,371	R	53.3%	46.6%	53.4%	46.6%
14,564	LAMAR	4,888	3,647	1,236	5	2,411	R	74.6%	25.3%	74.7%	25.3%
92,709	LAUDERDALE	27,794	18,374	9,389	31	8,985	R	66.1%	33.8%	66.2%	33.8%
34,339	LAWRENCE	11,451	7,060	4,381	10	2,679	R	61.7%	38.3%	61.7%	38.3%

ALABAMA

SENATOR 2010

2010 Census Population	County	Total Vote	Republican	Democratic	Other	Rep.-Dem. Plurality		Percentage			
								Total Vote		Major Vote	
								Rep.	Dem.	Rep.	Dem.
140,247	LEE	33,725	21,484	12,187	54	9,297	R	63.7%	36.1%	63.8%	36.2%
82,782	LIMESTONE	25,854	19,505	6,326	23	13,179	R	75.4%	24.5%	75.5%	24.5%
11,299	LOWNDES	5,232	1,581	3,647	4	2,066	D	30.2%	69.7%	30.2%	69.8%
21,452	MACON	7,493	1,272	6,218	3	4,946	D	17.0%	83.0%	17.0%	83.0%
334,811	MADISON	108,015	73,003	34,909	103	38,094	R	67.6%	32.3%	67.7%	32.3%
21,027	MARENGO	8,830	4,359	4,462	9	103	D	49.4%	50.5%	49.4%	50.6%
30,776	MARION	8,792	6,608	2,172	12	4,436	R	75.2%	24.7%	75.3%	24.7%
93,019	MARSHALL	25,531	20,836	4,649	46	16,187	R	81.6%	18.2%	81.8%	18.2%
412,992	MOBILE	110,516	65,958	44,468	90	21,490	R	59.7%	40.2%	59.7%	40.3%
23,068	MONROE	7,531	4,474	3,052	5	1,422	R	59.4%	40.5%	59.4%	40.6%
229,363	MONTGOMERY	73,574	35,586	37,924	64	2,338	D	48.4%	51.5%	48.4%	51.6%
119,490	MORGAN	39,012	29,718	9,257	37	20,461	R	76.2%	23.7%	76.2%	23.8%
10,591	PERRY	4,443	1,265	3,177	1	1,912	D	28.5%	71.5%	28.5%	71.5%
19,746	PICKENS	7,421	4,341	3,077	3	1,264	R	58.5%	41.5%	58.5%	41.5%
32,899	PIKE	9,662	6,094	3,559	9	2,535	R	63.1%	36.8%	63.1%	36.9%
22,913	RANDOLPH	7,177	4,902	2,270	5	2,632	R	68.3%	31.6%	68.3%	31.7%
52,947	RUSSELL	11,469	5,365	6,091	13	726	D	46.8%	53.1%	46.8%	53.2%
83,593	ST. CLAIR	24,681	20,560	4,075	46	16,485	R	83.3%	16.5%	83.5%	16.5%
195,085	SHELBY	63,305	52,309	10,871	125	41,438	R	82.6%	17.2%	82.8%	17.2%
13,763	SUMTER	5,553	1,440	4,110	3	2,670	D	25.9%	74.0%	25.9%	74.1%
82,291	TALLADEGA	23,978	14,909	9,039	30	5,870	R	62.2%	37.7%	62.3%	37.7%
41,616	TALLAPOOSA	15,668	10,336	5,332		5,004	R	66.0%	34.0%	66.0%	34.0%
194,656	TUSCALOOSA	54,278	35,459	18,743	76	16,716	R	65.3%	34.5%	65.4%	34.6%
67,023	WALKER	22,412	15,916	6,470	26	9,446	R	71.0%	28.9%	71.1%	28.9%
17,581	WASHINGTON	6,052	3,864	2,181	7	1,683	R	63.8%	36.0%	63.9%	36.1%
11,670	WILCOX	4,851	1,366	3,482	3	2,116	D	28.2%	71.8%	28.2%	71.8%
24,484	WINSTON	7,966	6,508	1,449	9	5,059	R	81.7%	18.2%	81.8%	18.2%
4,779,736	TOTAL	1,485,499	968,181	515,619	1,699	452,562	R	65.2%	34.7%	65.3%	34.7%

ALABAMA

HOUSE OF REPRESENTATIVES

CD	Year	Total Vote	Republican		Democratic		Other Vote	Rep.-Dem. Plurality		Percentage			
			Vote	Candidate	Vote	Candidate				Total Vote		Major Vote	
										Rep.	Dem.	Rep.	Dem.
1	2010	156,281	129,063	BONNER, JO*	—		27,218	129,063	R	82.6%		100.0%	
1	2008	214,367	210,660	BONNER, JO*			3,707	210,660	R	98.3%		100.0%	
1	2006	165,841	112,944	BONNER, JO*	52,770	BECKERLE, VIVIAN SHEFFIELD	127	60,174	R	68.1%	31.8%	68.2%	31.8%
1	2004	255,164	161,067	BONNER, JO*	93,938	BELK, JUDY McCAIN	159	67,129	R	63.1%	36.8%	63.2%	36.8%
1	2002	178,687	108,102	BONNER, JO	67,507	BELK, JUDY McCAIN	3,078	40,595	R	60.5%	37.8%	61.6%	38.4%
2	2010	219,028	111,645	ROBY, MARTHA	106,865	BRIGHT, BOBBY*	518	4,780	R	51.0%	48.8%	51.1%	48.9%
2	2008	287,394	142,578	LOVE, JAY	144,368	BRIGHT, BOBBY	448	1,790	D	49.6%	50.2%	49.7%	50.3%
2	2006	178,919	124,302	EVERETT, TERRY*	54,450	JAMES, CHARLES "CHUCK" DEAN	167	69,852	R	69.5%	30.4%	69.5%	30.5%
2	2004	247,947	177,086	EVERETT, TERRY*	70,562	JAMES, CHARLES "CHUCK" DEAN	299	106,524	R	71.4%	28.5%	71.5%	28.5%
2	2002	187,965	129,233	EVERETT, TERRY*	55,495	WOODS, CHARLES	3,237	73,738	R	68.8%	29.5%	70.0%	30.0%
3	2010	198,139	117,736	ROGERS, MIKE D.*	80,204	SEGREST, STEVE	199	37,532	R	59.4%	40.5%	59.5%	40.5%
3	2008	264,120	142,708	ROGERS, MIKE D.*	121,080	SEGALL, JOSHUA	332	21,628	R	54.0%	45.8%	54.1%	45.9%
3	2006	165,301	98,257	ROGERS, MIKE D.*	63,559	PIERCE, GREG A.	3,485	34,698	R	59.4%	38.5%	60.7%	39.3%
3	2004	245,784	150,411	ROGERS, MIKE D.*	95,240	FULLER, BILL	133	55,171	R	61.2%	38.7%	61.2%	38.8%
3	2002	181,223	91,169	ROGERS, MIKE D.	87,351	TURNHAM, JOE	2,703	3,818	R	50.3%	48.2%	51.1%	48.9%
4	2010	169,721	167,714	ADERHOLT, ROBERT B.*		—	2,007	167,714	R	98.8%		100.0%	
4	2008	263,167	196,741	ADERHOLT, ROBERT B.*	66,077	SPARKS, NICHOLAS B.	349	130,664	R	74.8%	25.1%	74.9%	25.1%
4	2006	183,072	128,484	ADERHOLT, ROBERT B.*	54,382	BOBO, BARBARA	206	74,102	R	70.2%	29.7%	70.3%	29.7%
4	2004	255,724	191,110	ADERHOLT, ROBERT B.*	64,278	COLE, CARL	336	126,832	R	74.7%	25.1%	74.8%	25.2%
4	2002	161,101	139,705	ADERHOLT, ROBERT B.*		—	21,396	139,705	R	86.7%		100.0%	

ALABAMA

HOUSE OF REPRESENTATIVES

			Republican		Democratic		Other Vote	Rep.-Dem. Plurality	Total Vote		Major Vote	
CD	Year	Total Vote	Vote	Candidate	Vote	Candidate			Rep.	Dem.	Rep.	Dem.
5	2010	226,490	131,109	BROOKS, MO	95,192	RABY, STEVE	189	35,917 R	57.9%	42.0%	57.9%	42.1%
5	2008	307,282	147,314	PARKER, WAYNE	158,324	GRIFFITH, PARKER	1,644	11,010 D	47.9%	51.5%	48.2%	51.8%
5	2006	145,555		—	143,015	CRAMER, ROBERT E. "BUD"*	2,540	143,015 D		98.3%		100.0%
5	2004	275,459	74,145	WALLACE, GERALD "GERRY"	200,999	CRAMER, ROBERT E. "BUD"*	315	126,854 D	26.9%	73.0%	26.9%	73.1%
5	2002	195,171	48,226	ENGEL, STEPHEN P.	143,029	CRAMER, ROBERT E. "BUD"*	3,916	94,803 D	24.7%	73.3%	25.2%	74.8%
6	2010	209,364	205,288	BACHUS, SPENCER*		—	4,076	205,288 R	98.1%		100.0%	
6	2008	287,237	280,902	BACHUS, SPENCER*		—	6,335	280,902 R	97.8%		100.0%	
6	2004	166,300	163,514	BACHUS, SPENCER*		—	2,786	163,514 R	98.3%		100.0%	
6	2004	268,043	264,819	BACHUS, SPENCER*		—	3,224	264,819 R	98.8%		100.0%	
6	2002	198,346	178,171	BACHUS, SPENCER*		—	20,175	178,171 R	89.8%		100.0%	
7	2010	188,724	51,890	CHAMBERLAIN, DON	136,696	SEWELL, TERRI A.	138	84,806 D	27.5%	72.4%	27.5%	72.5%
7	2008	231,701		—	228,518	DAVIS, ARTUR*	3,183	228,518 D		98.6%		100.0%
7	2006	135,164		—	133,870	DAVIS, ARTUR*	1,294	133,870 D		99.0%		100.0%
7	2004	244,638	61,019	CAMERON, STEVE F.	183,408	DAVIS, ARTUR*	211	122,389 D	24.9%	75.0%	25.0%	75.0%
7	2002	166,309		—	153,735	DAVIS, ARTUR	12,574	153,735 D		92.4%		100.0%
TOTAL	2010	1,367,747	914,445		418,957		34,345	495,488 R	66.9%	30.6%	68.6%	31.4%
TOTAL	2008	1,855,268	1,120,903		718,367		15,998	402,536 R	60.4%	38.7%	60.9%	39.1%
TOTAL	2006	1,140,152	627,501		502,046		10,605	125,455 R	55.0%	44.0%	55.6%	44.4%
TOTAL	2004	1,792,759	1,079,657		708,425		4,677	371,232 R	60.2%	39.5%	60.4%	39.6%
TOTAL	2002	1,268,802	694,606		507,117		67,079	187,489 R	54.7%	40.0%	57.8%	42.2%

An asterisk (*) denotes incumbent. The names of unopposed candidates did not appear on the primary ballot; therefore, no votes were cast for these candidates.

ALABAMA

GENERAL AND PRIMARY ELECTIONS

2010 GENERAL ELECTIONS

Governor   Other vote was 8,091 scattered write-in.

Senator   Other vote was 1,699 scattered write-in.

House   Other vote was:

- CD 1   26,357 Constitution (David Walter); 861 scattered write-in.
- CD 2   518 scattered write-in.
- CD 3   199 scattered write-in.
- CD 4   2,007 scattered write-in.
- CD 5   189 scattered write-in.
- CD 6   4,076 scattered write-in.
- CD 7   138 scattered write-in.

2010 PRIMARY ELECTIONS

Primary   June 1, 2010   **Registration** (as of May 31, 2010 – includes 410,366 inactive registrants)   2,931,407   No Party Registration

Primary Runoff   July 13, 2010

Primary Type   Open—Any registered voter could vote in either the Democratic or Republican primary, although any voter that participated in the Republican primary could not vote in the Democratic runoff. There was no such restriction on participation in the Republican runoff.

ALABAMA

GENERAL AND PRIMARY ELECTIONS

	REPUBLICAN PRIMARIES			DEMOCRATIC PRIMARIES		
Governor	Bradley Byrne	137,451	27.9%	Ron Sparks	198,358	62.3%
	Robert Bentley	123,958	25.1%	Artur Davis	119,972	37.7%
	Tim James	123,792	25.1%			
	Roy S. Moore	95,163	19.3%			
	Bill Johnson	8,362	1.7%			
	Charles Taylor	2,622	0.5%			
	James Pott	1,549	0.3%			
	TOTAL	492,897		TOTAL	318,330	
	PRIMARY RUNOFF					
	Robert Bentley	261,233	56.1%			
	Bradley Byrne	204,503	43.9%			
	TOTAL	465,736				
Senator	Richard C. Shelby*	405,398	84.4%	William G. Barnes	160,993	60.8%
	N.C. "Clint" Moser	75,190	15.6%	Simone De Moore	103,942	39.2%
	TOTAL	480,588		TOTAL	264,935	
Congressional District 1	Jo Bonner*	56,937	75.3%	No Democratic candidate		
	Peter Gounares	18,725	24.7%			
	TOTAL	75,662				
Congressional District 2	Martha Roby	36,295	48.6%	Bobby Bright*	Unopposed	
	Rick Barber	21,313	28.5%			
	Stephanie Bell	13,797	18.5%			
	John McKinney	3,349	4.5%			
	TOTAL	74,754				
	PRIMARY RUNOFF					
	Martha Roby	39,169	60.0%			
	Rick Barber	26,091	40.0%			
	TOTAL	65,260				
Congressional District 3	Mike D. Rogers*	Unopposed		Steve Segrest	Unopposed	
Congressional District 4	Robert B. Aderholt*	Unopposed		No Democratic candidate		
Congressional District 5	Mo Brooks	35,746	50.8%	Steve Raby	27,814	61.7%
	Parker Griffith*	23,525	33.4%	Taze Shepard	10,262	22.8%
	Les Phillip	11,085	15.8%	Mitchell J. Howie	5,277	11.7%
				David J. Maker	1,751	3.9%
	TOTAL	70,356		TOTAL	45,104	
Congressional District 6	Spencer Bachus*	80,725	75.6%	No Democratic candidate		
	Stan Cooke	25,997	24.4%			
	TOTAL	106,722				
Congressional District 7	Don Chamberlain	6,166	37.6%	Terri A. Sewell	31,531	36.8%
	Chris Salter	4,826	29.4%	Shelia Smoot	24,490	28.6%
	Michele Waller	2,804	17.1%	Earl Hilliard Jr.	22,981	26.8%
	Carol F. Hendrickson	2,610	15.9%	Martha Bozeman	6,672	7.8%
	TOTAL	16,406		TOTAL	85,674	
	PRIMARY RUNOFF			PRIMARY RUNOFF		
	Don Chamberlain	11,783	55.8%	Terri A. Sewell	32,366	55.0%
	Chris Salter	9,349	44.2%	Shelia Smoot	26,481	45.0%
	TOTAL	21,132		TOTAL	58,847	

ALASKA

One member At Large

ALASKA

GOVERNOR
Sean R. Parnell (R). Elected 2010 to a four-year term. Assumed office July 26, 2009, upon the resignation of Sarah H. Palin (R).

SENATORS (1 Democrat, 1 Republican)
Mark Begich (D). Elected 2008 to a six-year term.

Lisa Murkowski (R). Reelected 2010 to a six-year term as a write-in candidate. Previously elected 2004. Had been appointed December, 20, 2002, to fill the vacancy created by the resignation of her father, Frank H. Murkowski (R), to become governor of Alaska.

REPRESENTATIVE (1 Republican)
At Large. Don Young (R)

POSTWAR VOTE FOR PRESIDENT

| | | Republican | | Democratic | | Other | Rep.-Dem. | Percentage | | | |
| | Total | | | | | | | Total Vote | | Major Vote | |
Year	Vote	Vote	Candidate	Vote	Candidate	Vote	Plurality	Rep.	Dem.	Rep.	Dem.
2008	326,197	193,841	McCain, John	123,594	Obama, Barack	8,762	70,247 R	59.4%	37.9%	61.1%	38.9%
2004	312,598	190,889	Bush, George W.	111,025	Kerry, John	10,684	79,864 R	61.1%	35.5%	63.2%	36.8%
2000**	285,560	167,398	Bush, George W.	79,004	Gore, Al	39,158	88,394 R	58.6%	27.7%	67.9%	32.1%
1996**	241,620	122,746	Dole, Bob	80,380	Clinton, Bill	38,494	42,366 R	50.8%	33.3%	60.4%	39.6%
1992**	258,506	102,000	Bush, George	78,294	Clinton, Bill	78,212	23,706 R	39.5%	30.3%	56.6%	43.4%
1988	200,116	119,251	Bush, George	72,584	Dukakis, Michael S.	8,281	46,667 R	59.6%	36.3%	62.2%	37.8%
1984	207,605	138,377	Reagan, Ronald	62,007	Mondale, Walter F.	7,221	76,370 R	66.7%	29.9%	69.1%	30.9%
1980**	158,445	86,112	Reagan, Ronald	41,842	Carter, Jimmy	30,491	44,270 R	54.3%	26.4%	67.3%	32.7%
1976	123,574	71,555	Ford, Gerald R.	44,058	Carter, Jimmy	7,961	27,497 R	57.9%	35.7%	61.9%	38.1%
1972	95,219	55,349	Nixon, Richard M.	32,967	McGovern, George S.	6,903	22,382 R	58.1%	34.6%	62.7%	37.3%
1968**	83,035	37,600	Nixon, Richard M.	35,411	Humphrey, Hubert H.	10,024	2,189 R	45.3%	42.6%	51.5%	48.5%
1964	67,259	22,930	Goldwater, Barry M.	44,329	Johnson, Lyndon B.		21,399 D	34.1%	65.9%	34.1%	65.9%
1960	60,762	30,953	Nixon, Richard M.	29,809	Kennedy, John F.		1,144 R	50.9%	49.1%	50.9%	49.1%

** In past elections, the other vote included: 2000 - 28,747 Green (Ralph Nader); 1996 - 26,333 Reform (Ross Perot); 1992 - 73,481 Independent (Perot); 1980 - 18,479 Libertarian (Ed Clark) and 11,155 Independent (John Anderson); 1968 - 10,024 American Independent (George Wallace). Alaska was formally admitted as a state in January 1959.

POSTWAR VOTE FOR GOVERNOR

| | | Republican | | Democratic | | Other | | Percentage | | | |
| | Total | | | | | | | Total Vote | | Major Vote | |
Year	Vote	Vote	Candidate	Vote	Candidate	Vote	Plurality	Rep.	Dem.	Rep.	Dem.
2010	256,192	151,318	Parnell, Sean R.	96,519	Berkowitz, Ethan A.	8,355	54,799 R	59.1%	37.7%	61.1%	38.9%
2006	237,322	114,697	Palin, Sarah H.	97,238	Knowles, Tony	25,387	17,459 R	48.3%	41.0%	54.1%	45.9%
2002	231,484	129,279	Murkowski, Frank H.	94,216	Ulmer, Fran	7,989	35,063 R	55.8%	40.7%	57.8%	42.2%
1998**	220,177	39,331	Lindauer, John	112,879	Knowles, Tony	67,967	73,548 D	17.9%	51.3%	25.8%	74.2%
1994**	213,435	87,157	Campbell, James O.	87,693	Knowles, Tony	38,585	536 D	40.8%	41.1%	49.8%	50.2%
1990**	194,750	50,991	Sturgulewski, Arliss	60,201	Knowles, Tony	83,558	15,520 AI	26.2%	30.9%	45.9%	54.1%
1986	179,555	76,515	Sturgulewski, Arliss	84,943	Cowper, Steve	18,097	8,428 D	42.6%	47.3%	47.4%	52.6%
1982**	194,885	72,291	Fink, Tom	89,918	Sheffield, Bill	32,676	17,627 D	37.1%	46.1%	44.6%	55.4%
1978**	126,910	49,580	Hammond, Jay S.	25,656	Croft, Chancy	51,674	23,924 R	39.1%	20.2%	65.9%	34.1%
1974	96,163	45,840	Hammond, Jay S.	45,553	Egan, William A.	4,770	287 R	47.7%	47.4%	50.2%	49.8%
1970	80,779	37,264	Miller, Keith	42,309	Egan, William A.	1,206	5,045 D	46.1%	52.4%	46.8%	53.2%
1966	66,294	33,145	Hickel, Walter J.	32,065	Egan, William A.	1,084	1,080 R	50.0%	48.4%	50.8%	49.2%
1962	56,681	27,054	Stepovich, Mike	29,627	Egan, William A.		2,573 D	47.7%	52.3%	47.7%	52.3%
1958	48,968	19,299	Butrovich, John	29,189	Egan, William A.	480	9,890 D	39.4%	59.6%	39.8%	60.2%

** In past elections, the other vote included: 1998 - 40,209 write-in (Robin Taylor), who finished second; 1994 - 27,838 Alaskan Independence (John B. "Jack" Coghill); 1990 - 75,721 Alaskan Independence (Walter J. Hickel); 1982 - 29,067 Libertarian (Richard L. Randolph); 1978 - 33,555 write-in (Hickel) and 15,656 Alaskans for Kelly (Tom Kelly). Hickel won the 1990 election with 38.9 percent of the total vote and finished second in 1978.

ALASKA

POSTWAR VOTE FOR SENATOR

Year	Total Vote	Republican		Democratic		Other Vote	Plurality	Percentage			
								Total Vote		Major Vote	
		Vote	Candidate	Vote	Candidate			Rep.	Dem.	Rep.	Dem.
2010**	255,474	90,839	Miller, Joe	60,045	McAdams, Scott T.	104,590	10,252 M	35.6%	23.5%	60.2%	39.8%
2008	317,723	147,814	Stevens, Ted	151,767	Begich, Mark	18,142	3,953 D	46.5%	47.8%	49.3%	50.7%
2004	308,315	149,773	Murkowski, Lisa	140,424	Knowles, Tony	18,118	9,349 R	48.6%	45.5%	51.6%	48.4%
2002	229,548	179,438	Stevens, Ted	24,133	Vondersaar, Frank	25,977	155,305 R	78.2%	10.5%	88.1%	11.9%
1998	221,807	165,227	Murkowski, Frank H.	43,743	Sonneman, Joseph	12,837	121,484 R	74.5%	19.7%	79.1%	20.9%
1996**	231,916	177,893	Stevens, Ted	23,977	Obermeyer, Theresa	30,046	148,856 R	76.7%	10.3%	88.1%	11.9%
1992	239,714	127,163	Murkowski, Frank H.	92,065	Smith, Tony	20,486	35,098 R	53.0%	38.4%	58.0%	42.0%
1990	189,957	125,806	Stevens, Ted	61,152	Beasley, Michael	2,999	64,654 R	66.2%	32.2%	67.3%	32.7%
1986	180,801	97,674	Murkowski, Frank H.	79,727	Olds, Glenn	3,400	17,947 R	54.0%	44.1%	55.1%	44.9%
1984	206,438	146,919	Stevens, Ted	58,804	Havelock, John E.	715	88,115 R	71.2%	28.5%	71.4%	28.6%
1980	156,762	84,159	Murkowski, Frank H.	72,007	Gruening, Clark S.	596	12,152 R	53.7%	45.9%	53.9%	46.1%
1978	122,741	92,783	Stevens, Ted	29,574	Hobbs, Donald W.	384	63,209 R	75.6%	24.1%	75.8%	24.2%
1974	93,275	38,914	Lewis, C. R.	54,361	Gravel, Mike		15,447 D	41.7%	58.3%	41.7%	58.3%
1972	96,007	74,216	Stevens, Ted	21,791	Guess, Gene		52,425 R	77.3%	22.7%	77.3%	22.7%
1970S	80,364	47,908	Stevens, Ted	32,456	Kay, Wendell P.		15,452 R	59.6%	40.4%	59.6%	40.4%
1968	80,931	30,286	Rasmuson, Elmer	36,527	Gravel, Mike	14,118	6,241 D	37.4%	45.1%	45.3%	54.7%
1966	65,250	15,961	McKinley, Lee L.	49,289	Bartlett, E. L.		33,328 D	24.5%	75.5%	24.5%	75.5%
1962	58,181	24,354	Stevens, Ted	33,827	Gruening, Ernest		9,473 D	41.9%	58.1%	41.9%	58.1%
1960	59,978	21,937	McKinley, Lee L.	38,041	Bartlett, E. L.		16,104 D	36.6%	63.4%	36.6%	63.4%
1958S	49,525	23,462	Stepovich, Mike	26,063	Gruening, Ernest		2,601 D	47.4%	52.6%	47.4%	52.6%
1958S	48,837	7,299	Robertson, R. E.	40,939	Bartlett, E. L.	599	33,640 D	14.9%	83.8%	15.1%	84.9%

** In past elections, the other vote included: 2010 - 101,091 write-in (Lisa Murkowski), who won reelection with 39.6 percent of the vote; 1996 - 29,037 Green (Jed Whittaker), who finished second. The 1970 election was for a short term to fill a vacancy. The two 1958 elections were held to indeterminate terms and the Senate later determined by lot that Senator Gruening would serve four years, Senator Bartlett two. Lisa Murkowski's write-in Senate victory in 2010 is indicated by an "M."

ALASKA
GOVERNOR 2010

2000 Census Population	District	Total Vote	Republican	Democratic	Other	Rep.-Dem. Plurality	Percentage			
							Total Vote		Major Vote	
							Rep.	Dem.	Rep.	Dem.
18,563	DISTRICT 1	5,324	3,464	1,650	210	1,814 R	65.1%	31.0%	67.7%	32.3%
17,131	DISTRICT 2	6,200	3,564	2,456	180	1,108 R	57.5%	39.6%	59.2%	40.8%
18,133	DISTRICT 3	7,153	3,055	3,955	143	900 D	42.7%	55.3%	43.6%	56.4%
17,837	DISTRICT 4	6,958	4,173	2,650	135	1,523 R	60.0%	38.1%	61.2%	38.8%
17,182	DISTRICT 5	5,774	2,996	2,484	294	512 R	51.9%	43.0%	54.7%	45.3%
18,398	DISTRICT 6	5,677	3,351	1,976	350	1,375 R	59.0%	34.8%	62.9%	37.1%
18,150	DISTRICT 7	9,393	5,484	3,642	267	1,842 R	58.4%	38.8%	60.1%	39.9%
18,071	DISTRICT 8	8,453	4,243	3,952	258	291 R	50.2%	46.8%	51.8%	48.2%
17,958	DISTRICT 9	5,210	3,113	1,928	169	1,185 R	59.8%	37.0%	61.8%	38.2%
17,220	DISTRICT 10	3,599	2,328	1,121	150	1,207 R	64.7%	31.1%	67.5%	32.5%
17,594	DISTRICT 11	7,456	5,727	1,451	278	4,276 R	76.8%	19.5%	79.8%	20.2%
18,026	DISTRICT 12	5,387	3,657	1,538	192	2,119 R	67.9%	28.6%	70.4%	29.6%
17,723	DISTRICT 13	9,349	6,495	2,625	229	3,870 R	69.5%	28.1%	71.2%	28.8%
17,635	DISTRICT 14	8,009	5,752	2,010	247	3,742 R	71.8%	25.1%	74.1%	25.9%
17,789	DISTRICT 15	8,694	5,832	2,515	347	3,317 R	67.1%	28.9%	69.9%	30.1%
17,799	DISTRICT 16	8,954	6,146	2,595	213	3,551 R	68.6%	29.0%	70.3%	29.7%
17,683	DISTRICT 17	7,235	5,045	2,052	138	2,993 R	69.7%	28.4%	71.1%	28.9%
17,921	DISTRICT 18	3,127	2,182	829	116	1,353 R	69.8%	26.5%	72.5%	27.5%
17,672	DISTRICT 19	5,740	3,122	2,449	169	673 R	54.4%	42.7%	56.0%	44.0%
17,678	DISTRICT 20	3,435	1,704	1,594	137	110 R	49.6%	46.4%	51.7%	48.3%
17,924	DISTRICT 21	6,881	3,863	2,853	165	1,010 R	56.1%	41.5%	57.5%	42.5%
17,768	DISTRICT 22	4,909	2,202	2,582	125	380 D	44.9%	52.6%	46.0%	54.0%
17,513	DISTRICT 23	5,489	2,202	3,156	131	954 D	40.1%	57.5%	41.1%	58.9%
17,631	DISTRICT 24	5,882	3,089	2,627	166	462 R	52.5%	44.7%	54.0%	46.0%
17,593	DISTRICT 25	4,920	2,233	2,537	150	304 D	45.4%	51.6%	46.8%	53.2%
17,991	DISTRICT 26	7,087	3,177	3,773	137	596 D	44.8%	53.2%	45.7%	54.3%
17,853	DISTRICT 27	6,974	4,193	2,623	158	1,570 R	60.1%	37.6%	61.5%	38.5%
17,995	DISTRICT 28	8,132	5,022	2,956	154	2,066 R	61.8%	36.4%	62.9%	37.1%
17,478	DISTRICT 29	5,115	2,898	2,073	144	825 R	56.7%	40.5%	58.3%	41.7%
17,822	DISTRICT 30	7,534	4,419	2,958	157	1,461 R	58.7%	39.3%	59.9%	40.1%
17,929	DISTRICT 31	8,731	5,498	3,066	167	2,432 R	63.0%	35.1%	64.2%	35.8%
17,744	DISTRICT 32	10,535	6,077	4,247	211	1,830 R	57.7%	40.3%	58.9%	41.1%
18,493	DISTRICT 33	6,906	4,835	1,840	231	2,995 R	70.0%	26.6%	72.4%	27.6%
18,159	DISTRICT 34	7,615	5,704	1,659	252	4,045 R	74.9%	21.8%	77.5%	22.5%
17,413	DISTRICT 35	7,391	3,860	3,311	220	549 R	52.2%	44.8%	53.8%	46.2%
17,219	DISTRICT 36	4,704	2,865	1,639	200	1,226 R	60.9%	34.8%	63.6%	36.4%
18,670	DISTRICT 37	3,723	1,949	1,524	250	425 R	52.4%	40.9%	56.1%	43.9%
16,969	DISTRICT 38	4,206	2,082	1,783	341	299 R	49.5%	42.4%	53.9%	46.1%
16,951	DISTRICT 39	4,562	2,086	2,064	412	22 R	45.7%	45.2%	50.3%	49.7%
16,953	DISTRICT 40	3,769	1,631	1,776	362	145 D	43.3%	47.1%	47.9%	52.1%
710,231	TOTAL	256,192	151,318	96,519	8,355	54,799 R	59.1%	37.7%	61.1%	38.9%

ALASKA
SENATOR 2010

2010 Census Population	District	Total Vote	Republican	Democratic	Murkowski (write-in)	Other	Plurality		Percentage		
									Rep.	Dem.	Murkowski
18,563	DISTRICT 1	5,372	1,776	1,043	2,475	78	699	M	33.1%	19.4%	46.1%
17,131	DISTRICT 2	6,178	1,735	2,176	2,196	71	20	M	28.1%	35.2%	35.5%
18,133	DISTRICT 3	7,153	1,201	3,268	2,612	72	656	D	16.8%	45.7%	36.5%
17,837	DISTRICT 4	6,932	2,022	2,209	2,606	95	397	M	29.2%	31.9%	37.6%
17,182	DISTRICT 5	5,709	1,524	1,646	2,431	108	785	M	26.7%	28.8%	42.6%
18,398	DISTRICT 6	5,602	2,008	947	2,523	124	515	M	35.8%	16.9%	45.0%
18,150	DISTRICT 7	9,394	3,538	2,472	3,265	119	273	R	37.7%	26.3%	34.8%
18,071	DISTRICT 8	8,428	2,602	2,803	2,923	100	120	M	30.9%	33.3%	34.7%
17,958	DISTRICT 9	5,183	1,866	1,322	1,912	83	46	M	36.0%	25.5%	36.9%
17,220	DISTRICT 10	3,591	1,514	757	1,252	68	262	R	42.2%	21.1%	34.9%
17,594	DISTRICT 11	7,434	4,268	933	2,106	127	2,162	R	57.4%	12.6%	28.3%
18,026	DISTRICT 12	5,372	2,886	942	1,431	113	1,455	R	53.7%	17.5%	26.6%
17,723	DISTRICT 13	9,340	4,604	1,486	3,129	121	1,475	R	49.3%	15.9%	33.5%
17,635	DISTRICT 14	7,997	4,342	1,163	2,394	98	1,948	R	54.3%	14.5%	29.9%
17,789	DISTRICT 15	8,702	4,477	1,511	2,599	115	1,878	R	51.4%	17.4%	·29.9%
17,799	DISTRICT 16	8,930	4,332	1,491	2,991	116	1,341	R	48.5%	16.7%	33.5%
17,683	DISTRICT 17	7,242	3,153	1,084	2,939	66	214	R	43.5%	15.0%	40.6%
17,921	DISTRICT 18	3,136	1,691	513	866	66	825	R	53.9%	16.4%	27.6%
17,672	DISTRICT 19	5,749	1,825	1,503	2,355	66	530	M	31.7%	26.1%	41.0%
17,678	DISTRICT 20	3,414	1,051	1,013	1,274	76	223	M	30.8%	29.7%	37.3%
17,924	DISTRICT 21	6,873	2,199	1,751	2,842	81	643	M	32.0%	25.5%	41.4%
17,768	DISTRICT 22	4,909	1,216	1,609	2,032	52	423	M	24.8%	32.8%	41.4%
17,513	DISTRICT 23	5,488	1,099	2,172	2,164	53	8	D	20.0%	39.6%	39.4%
17,631	DISTRICT 24	5,869	1,659	1,576	2,575	59	916	M	28.3%	26.9%	43.9%
17,593	DISTRICT 25	4,911	1,223	1,660	1,963	65	303	M	24.9%	33.8%	40.0%
17,991	DISTRICT 26	7,079	1,548	2,379	3,095	57	716	M	21.9%	33.6%	43.7%
17,853	DISTRICT 27	6,949	2,106	1,473	3,283	87	1,177	M	30.3%	21.2%	47.2%
17,995	DISTRICT 28	8,125	2,556	1,562	3,916	91	1,360	M	31.5%	19.2%	48.2%
17,478	DISTRICT 29	5,113	1,600	1,169	2,273	71	673	M	31.3%	22.9%	44.5%
17,822	DISTRICT 30	7,535	2,392	1,733	3,333	77	941	M	31.7%	23.0%	44.2%
17,929	DISTRICT 31	8,750	2,960	1,685	4,048	57	1,088	M	33.8%	19.3%	46.3%
17,744	DISTRICT 32	10,549	3,515	2,473	4,473	88	958	M	33.3%	23.4%	42.4%
18,493	DISTRICT 33	6,882	3,331	1,103	2,340	108	991	R	48.4%	16.0%	34.0%
18,159	DISTRICT 34	7,590	4,320	1,081	2,085	104	2,235	R	56.9%	14.2%	27.5%
17,413	DISTRICT 35	7,377	2,543	2,573	2,165	96	30	D	34.5%	34.9%	29.3%
17,219	DISTRICT 36	4,713	1,808	1,074	1,737	94	71	R	38.4%	22.8%	36.9%
18,670	DISTRICT 37	3,702	761	680	2,173	88	1,412	M	20.6%	18.4%	58.7%
16,969	DISTRICT 38	4,104	406	601	2,977	120	2,571	M	9.9%	14.6%	72.5%
16,951	DISTRICT 39	4,446	531	753	3,072	90	2,541	M	11.9%	16.9%	69.1%
16,953	DISTRICT 40	3,652	651	656	2,266	79	1,615	M	17.8%	18.0%	62.0%
710,231	TOTAL	255,474	90,839	60,045	101,091	3,499	10,252	M	35.6%	23.5%	39.6%

The 101,091 write-in votes for Republican Sen. Lisa Murkowski included 92,931 votes that were not challenged, and 8,160 votes that were challenged but counted. In addition, 2,035 write-in votes for Murkowski were challenged and not counted. Districts carried by Murkowski are indicated by a "M."

ALASKA

HOUSE OF REPRESENTATIVES

CD	Year	Total Vote	Republican		Democratic		Other Vote	Rep.-Dem. Plurality	Percentage			
									Total Vote		Major Vote	
			Vote	Candidate	Vote	Candidate			Rep.	Dem.	Rep.	Dem.
AL	2010	254,335	175,384	YOUNG, DON*	77,606	CRAWFORD, HARRY T.	1,345	97,778 R	69.0%	30.5%	69.3%	30.7%
AL	2008	316,978	158,939	YOUNG, DON*	142,560	BERKOWITZ, ETHAN A.	15,479	16,379 R	50.1%	45.0%	52.7%	47.3%
AL	2006	234,645	132,743	YOUNG, DON*	93,879	BENSON, DIANE E.	8,023	38,864 R	56.6%	40.0%	58.6%	41.4%
AL	2004	299,996	213,216	YOUNG, DON*	67,074	HIGGINS, THOMAS M.	19,706	146,142 R	71.1%	22.4%	76.1%	23.9%
AL	2002	227,725	169,685	YOUNG, DON*	39,357	GREENE, CLIFFORD	18,683	130,328 R	74.5%	17.3%	81.2%	18.8%
AL	2000	274,393	190,862	YOUNG, DON*	45,372	GREENE, CLIFFORD	38,159	145,490 R	69.6%	16.5%	80.8%	19.2%
AL	1998	223,300	139,676	YOUNG, DON*	77,232	DUNCAN, JIM	6,392	62,444 R	62.6%	34.6%	64.4%	35.6%
AL	1996	233,700	138,834	YOUNG, DON*	85,114	LINCOLN, GEORGIANNA	9,752	53,720 R	59.4%	36.4%	62.0%	38.0%
AL	1994	208,240	118,537	YOUNG, DON*	68,172	SMITH, TONY	21,531	50,365 R	56.9%	32.7%	63.5%	36.5%
AL	1992	239,116	111,849	YOUNG, DON*	102,378	DEVENS, JOHN S.	24,889	9,471 R	46.8%	42.8%	52.2%	47.8%
AL	1990	191,647	99,003	YOUNG, DON*	91,677	DEVENS, JOHN S.	967	7,326 R	51.7%	47.8%	51.9%	48.1%
AL	1988	192,955	120,595	YOUNG, DON*	71,881	GRUENSTEIN, PETER	479	48,714 R	62.5%	37.3%	62.7%	37.3%
AL	1986	180,277	101,799	YOUNG, DON*	74,053	BEGICH, PEGGE	4,425	27,746 R	56.5%	41.1%	57.9%	42.1%
AL	1984	206,437	113,582	YOUNG, DON*	86,052	BEGICH, PEGGE	6,803	27,530 R	55.0%	41.7%	56.9%	43.1%
AL	1982	181,084	128,274	YOUNG, DON*	52,011	CARLSON, DAVE	799	76,263 R	70.8%	28.7%	71.2%	28.8%
AL	1980	154,618	114,089	YOUNG, DON*	39,922	PARNELL, KEVIN	607	74,167 R	73.8%	25.8%	74.1%	25.9%
AL	1978	124,187	68,811	YOUNG, DON*	55,176	RODNEY, PATRICK	200	13,635 R	55.4%	44.4%	55.5%	44.5%
AL	1976	118,208	83,722	YOUNG, DON*	34,194	HOPSON, EBEN	292	49,528 R	70.8%	28.9%	71.0%	29.0%
AL	1974	95,921	51,641	YOUNG, DON*	44,280	HENSLEY, WILLIAM L.		7,361 R	53.8%	46.2%	53.8%	46.2%
AL	1972	95,401	41,750	YOUNG, DON	53,651	BEGICH, NICK*		11,901 D	43.8%	56.2%	43.8%	56.2%
AL	1970	80,084	35,947	MURKOWSKI, FRANK H.	44,137	BEGICH, NICK		8,190 D	44.9%	55.1%	44.9%	55.1%
AL	1968	80,362	43,577	POLLOCK, HOWARD W.*	36,785	BEGICH, NICK		6,792 R	54.2%	45.8%	54.2%	45.8%
AL	1966	65,907	34,040	POLLOCK, HOWARD W.	31,867	RIVERS, RALPH J.*		2,173 R	51.6%	48.4%	51.6%	48.4%
AL	1964	67,146	32,556	THOMAS, LOWELL	34,590	RIVERS, RALPH J.*		2,034 D	48.5%	51.5%	48.5%	51.5%
AL	1962	58,591	26,638	THOMAS, LOWELL	31,953	RIVERS, RALPH J.*		5,315 D	45.5%	54.5%	45.5%	54.5%
AL	1960	59,063	25,517	RETTIG, R.L.	33,546	RIVERS, RALPH J.*		8,029 D	43.2%	56.8%	43.2%	56.8%
AL	1958	48,647	20,699	BENSON, HENRY A.	27,948	RIVERS, RALPH J.		7,249 D	42.5%	57.5%	42.5%	57.5%

An asterisk (*) denotes incumbent.

ALASKA

GENERAL AND PRIMARY ELECTIONS

2010 GENERAL ELECTIONS

Governor   Other vote was 4,775 Alaskan Independence (Donald R. Wright); 2,682 Libertarian (William S. "Billy" Toien); 898 scattered write-in.

Senator   Other vote was 1,459 Libertarian (Fredrick Haase); 927 Nonaffiliated (Tim Carter); 458 Nonaffiliated (Ted Gianoutsos); 13 write-in (Sid Hill); 6 write-in (Edward D. Marin Jr); 3 write-in (Red K. Bradley); 2 write-in (Guy A. Cummins); 2 write-in (Lisa M. Lackey); 2 write-in (Richard McGahan); 2 write-in (Marvin Roger Moser); 2 write-in (Karen Perry); 2 write-in (Eileen M. Ransom); 2 write-in (Jed Whittaker); 1 write-in (Michael Ames); 1 write-in (Kevin Austin); 1 write-in (David E. Beeman); 1 write-in (Vicky L. Beeman); 1 write-in (David Boyle); 1 write-in (Michael Butler); 1 write-in (Margaret A. Crowell); 1 write-in (Chris S. Dillingham); 1 write-in (David S. George); 1 write-in (Alan D. Humphries); 1 write-in (Petter M. Johnson); 1 write-in (Eric C. Kelly); 1 write-in (Bill Klemme); 1 write-in (Marjori Landis-Beck); 1 write-in (Anthony Rice); 1 write-in (Thompson Steve); 1 write-in (Georgia Lee Tolbert); 602 scattered write-in. (Republican Senator Lisa Murkowski received 101,091 votes as a write-in candidate and was reelected with 39.6 percent of the total vote. The Murkowski vote is listed in the legislative district tables for the 2010 Senate election in Alaska.)

House   Other vote was:

At Large   1,345 scattered write-in.

ALASKA

GENERAL AND PRIMARY ELECTIONS

2010 PRIMARY ELECTIONS

Primary	August 24, 2010	**Registration** (as of August 3, 2010)	Republican	126,486	
			Democratic	74,802	
			Alaskan Independence	14,464	
			Libertarian	9,392	
			Republican Moderate	2,892	
			Green	2,373	
			Veterans	1,758	
			Nonpartisan	78,189	
			Undeclared	177,219	
			TOTAL	487,575	

Primary Type — Any registered voter could participate in the Democratic primary. The Republican primary was restricted to registered Republican, Undeclared and Nonpartisan voters. (Undeclared voters may be associated with a party, but do not wish to declare which one. Nonpartisan voters are not associated with any party.) Democratic candidates were listed on the primary ballot together with candidates of the Alaskan Independence and Libertarian parties. The high vote-getter of each party went onto the general election ballot. Republican candidates were listed on a primary ballot of their own.

	REPUBLICAN PRIMARIES			**DEMOCRATIC PRIMARIES**		
Governor	Sean R. Parnell*	54,125	50.1%	Ethan A. Berkowitz	22,607	55.6%
	Bill Walker	35,734	33.1%	Hollis S. French	18,018	44.4%
	Ralph Samuels	15,376	14.2%			
	Sam Little	1,661	1.5%			
	Merica Hlatcu	626	0.6%			
	Gerald L. Heikes	460	0.4%			
	TOTAL	107,982		TOTAL	40,625	
Senator	Joe Miller	55,878	50.9%	Scott T. McAdams	18,035	59.5%
	Lisa Murkowski*	53,872	49.1%	Jacob Seth Kern	6,913	22.8%
				Frank J. Vondersaar	5,339	17.6%
	TOTAL	109,750		TOTAL	30,287	
House At Large	Don Young*	74,310	70.4%	Harry T. Crawford	38,673	100.0%
	Sheldon Fisher	24,709	23.4%			
	John R. Cox	6,605	6.3%			
	TOTAL	105,624				

An asterisk (*) denotes incumbent.

ARIZONA

Congressional districts first established for elections held in 2002
8 members

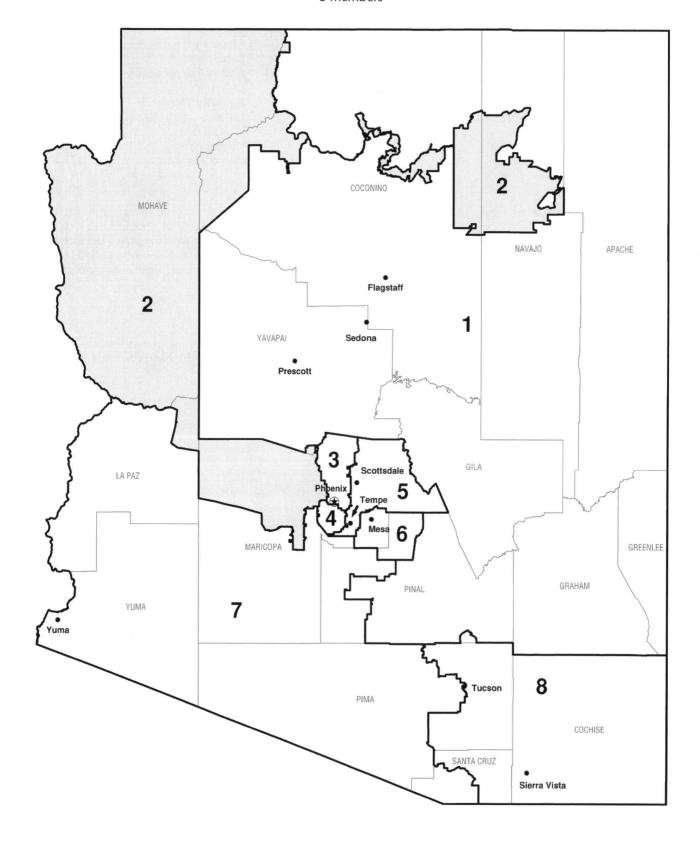

ARIZONA

GOVERNOR

Jan Brewer (R). Elected 2010 to a four-year term. Sworn in as governor January 21, 2009, to fill the vacancy created by the resignation of Janet Napolitano (D) to become U.S. Secretary of Homeland Security.

SENATORS (2 Republicans)

Jon Kyl (R). Reelected 2006 to a six-year term. Previously elected 2000, 1994.

John McCain (R). Reelected 2010 to a six-year term. Previously elected 2004, 1998, 1992, 1986.

REPRESENTATIVES (5 Republicans, 3 Democrats)

1. Paul Gosar (R)
2. Trent Franks (R)
3. Ben Quayle (R)
4. Ed Pastor (D)
5. David Schweikert (R)
6. Jeff Flake (R)
7. Raul M. Grijalva (D)
8. Gabrielle Giffords (D)

POSTWAR VOTE FOR PRESIDENT

Year	Total Vote	Republican Vote	Republican Candidate	Democratic Vote	Democratic Candidate	Other Vote	Rep.-Dem. Plurality	Total Vote Rep.	Total Vote Dem.	Major Vote Rep.	Major Vote Dem.
2008	2,293,475	1,230,111	McCain, John	1,034,707	Obama, Barack	28,657	195,404 R	53.6%	45.1%	54.3%	45.7%
2004	2,012,585	1,104,294	Bush, George W.	893,524	Kerry, John	14,767	210,770 R	54.9%	44.4%	55.3%	44.7%
2000**	1,532,016	781,652	Bush, George W.	685,341	Gore, Al	65,023	96,311 R	51.0%	44.7%	53.3%	46.7%
1996**	1,404,405	622,073	Dole, Bob	653,288	Clinton, Bill	129,044	31,215 D	44.3%	46.5%	48.8%	51.2%
1992**	1,486,975	572,086	Bush, George	543,050	Clinton, Bill	371,839	29,036 R	38.5%	36.5%	51.3%	48.7%
1988	1,171,873	702,541	Bush, George	454,029	Dukakis, Michael S.	15,303	248,512 R	60.0%	38.7%	60.7%	39.3%
1984	1,025,897	681,416	Reagan, Ronald	333,854	Mondale, Walter F.	10,627	347,562 R	66.4%	32.5%	67.1%	32.9%
1980**	873,945	529,688	Reagan, Ronald	246,843	Carter, Jimmy	97,414	282,845 R	60.6%	28.2%	68.2%	31.8%
1976	742,719	418,642	Ford, Gerald R.	295,602	Carter, Jimmy	28,475	123,040 R	56.4%	39.8%	58.6%	41.4%
1972	622,926	402,812	Nixon, Richard M.	198,540	McGovern, George S.	21,574	204,272 R	64.7%	31.9%	67.0%	33.0%
1968**	486,936	266,721	Nixon, Richard M.	170,514	Humphrey, Hubert H.	49,701	96,207 R	54.8%	35.0%	61.0%	39.0%
1964	480,770	242,535	Goldwater, Barry M.	237,753	Johnson, Lyndon B.	482	4,782 R	50.4%	49.5%	50.5%	49.5%
1960	398,491	221,241	Nixon, Richard M.	176,781	Kennedy, John F.	469	44,460 R	55.5%	44.4%	55.6%	44.4%
1956	290,173	176,990	Eisenhower, Dwight D.	112,880	Stevenson, Adlai E.	303	64,110 R	61.0%	38.9%	61.1%	38.9%
1952	260,570	152,042	Eisenhower, Dwight D.	108,528	Stevenson, Adlai E.		43,514 R	58.3%	41.7%	58.3%	41.7%
1948	177,065	77,597	Dewey, Thomas E.	95,251	Truman, Harry S.	4,217	17,654 D	43.8%	53.8%	44.9%	55.1%

** In past elections, the other vote included: 2000 - 45,645 Green (Ralph Nader); 1996 - 112,072 Reform (Ross Perot); 1992 - 353,741 Independent (Perot); 1980 - 76,952 Independent (John Anderson); 1968 - 46,573 American Independent (George Wallace).

ARIZONA

POSTWAR VOTE FOR GOVERNOR

Year	Total Vote	Republican Vote	Republican Candidate	Democratic Vote	Democratic Candidate	Other Vote	Rep.-Dem. Plurality	Total Vote Rep.	Total Vote Dem.	Major Vote Rep.	Major Vote Dem.
2010	1,728,081	938,934	Brewer, Jan	733,935	Goddard, Terry	55,212	204,999 R	54.3%	42.5%	56.1%	43.9%
2006	1,533,645	543,528	Munsil, Len	959,830	Napolitano, Janet	30,287	416,302 D	35.4%	62.6%	36.2%	63.8%
2002	1,226,111	554,465	Salmon, Matt	566,284	Napolitano, Janet	105,362	11,819 D	45.2%	46.2%	49.5%	50.5%
1998	1,017,616	620,188	Hull, Jane Dee	361,552	Johnson, Paul	35,876	258,636 R	60.9%	35.5%	63.2%	36.8%
1994	1,129,607	593,492	Symington, Fife	500,702	Basha, Eddie	35,413	92,790 R	52.5%	44.3%	54.2%	45.8%
1990**	940,737	492,569	Symington, Fife	448,168	Goddard, Terry		44,401 R	52.4%	47.6%	52.4%	47.6%
1986**	866,984	343,913	Mecham, Evan	298,986	Warner, Carolyn	224,085	44,927 R	39.7%	34.5%	53.5%	46.5%
1982	726,364	235,877	Corbet, Leo	453,795	Babbitt, Bruce	36,692	217,918 D	32.5%	62.5%	34.2%	65.8%
1978	538,556	241,093	Mecham, Evan	282,605	Babbitt, Bruce	14,858	41,512 D	44.8%	52.5%	46.0%	54.0%
1974	552,202	273,674	Williams, Russell	278,375	Castro, Raul H.	153	4,701 D	49.6%	50.4%	49.6%	50.4%
1970**	411,409	209,522	Williams, John R.	201,887	Castro, Raul H.		7,635 R	50.9%	49.1%	50.9%	49.1%
1968	483,998	279,923	Williams, John R.	204,075	Goddard, Sam		75,848 R	57.8%	42.2%	57.8%	42.2%
1966	378,342	203,438	Williams, John R.	174,904	Goddard, Sam		28,534 R	53.8%	46.2%	53.8%	46.2%
1964	473,502	221,404	Kleindienst, Richard	252,098	Goddard, Sam		30,694 D	46.8%	53.2%	46.8%	53.2%
1962	365,841	200,578	Fannin, Paul	165,263	Goddard, Sam		35,315 R	54.8%	45.2%	54.8%	45.2%
1960	397,107	235,502	Fannin, Paul	161,605	Ackerman, Lee		73,897 R	59.3%	40.7%	59.3%	40.7%
1958	290,465	160,136	Fannin, Paul	130,329	Morrison, Robert		29,807 R	55.1%	44.9%	55.1%	44.9%
1956	288,592	116,744	Griffen, Horace B.	171,848	McFarland, Ernest W.		55,104 D	40.5%	59.5%	40.5%	59.5%
1954	243,970	115,866	Pyle, Howard	128,104	McFarland, Ernest W.		12,238 D	47.5%	52.5%	47.5%	52.5%
1952	260,285	156,592	Pyle, Howard	103,693	Haldiman, Joe C.		52,899 R	60.2%	39.8%	60.2%	39.8%
1950	195,227	99,109	Pyle, Howard	96,118	Frohmiller, Ana		2,991 R	50.8%	49.2%	50.8%	49.2%
1948	175,767	70,419	Brockett, Bruce	104,008	Garvey, Dan E.	1,340	33,589 D	40.1%	59.2%	40.4%	59.6%
1946	122,462	48,867	Brockett, Bruce	73,595	Osborn, Sidney P.		24,728 D	39.9%	60.1%	39.9%	60.1%

** In 1990 neither major party candidate won an absolute majority, therefore a runoff election was held February 26, 1991; the vote above is for the February runoff. In the November 1990 election, a total of 1,055,406 votes were cast as follows: 523,984 (49.6%) Republican (Fife Symington); 519,691 (49.2%) Democratic (Terry Goddard); 11,731 (1.1%) Other. In past elections, the other vote included: 1986 - 224,085 Independent (Bill Schulz). The term of office for Arizona's Governor was increased from two to four years effective with the 1970 election.

POSTWAR VOTE FOR SENATOR

Year	Total Vote	Republican Vote	Republican Candidate	Democratic Vote	Democratic Candidate	Other Vote	Rep.-Dem. Plurality	Total Vote Rep.	Total Vote Dem.	Major Vote Rep.	Major Vote Dem.
2010	1,708,484	1,005,615	McCain, John	592,011	Glassman, Rodney	110,858	413,604 R	58.9%	34.7%	62.9%	37.1%
2006	1,526,782	814,398	Kyl, Jon	664,141	Pederson, Jim	48,243	150,257 R	53.3%	43.5%	55.1%	44.9%
2004	1,961,677	1,505,372	McCain, John	404,507	Starky, Stuart	51,798	1,100,865 R	76.7%	20.6%	78.8%	21.2%
2000	1,397,076	1,108,196	Kyl, Jon	—		288,880	1,108,196 R	79.3%		100.0%	
1998	1,013,280	696,577	McCain, John	275,224	Ranger, Ed	41,479	421,353 R	68.7%	27.2%	71.7%	28.3%
1994	1,119,060	600,999	Kyl, Jon	442,510	Coppersmith, Sam	75,551	158,489 R	53.7%	39.5%	57.6%	42.4%
1992**	1,382,051	771,395	McCain, John	436,321	Sargent, Claire	174,335	335,074 R	55.8%	31.6%	63.9%	36.1%
1988	1,164,539	478,060	DeGreen, Keith	660,403	DeConcini, Dennis	26,076	182,343 D	41.1%	56.7%	42.0%	58.0%
1986	862,921	521,850	McCain, John	340,965	Kimball, Richard	106	180,885 R	60.5%	39.5%	60.5%	39.5%
1982	723,885	291,749	Dunn, Pete	411,970	DeConcini, Dennis	20,166	120,221 D	40.3%	56.9%	41.5%	58.5%
1980	874,238	432,371	Goldwater, Barry M.	422,972	Schulz, Bill	18,895	9,399 R	49.5%	48.4%	50.5%	49.5%
1976	741,210	321,236	Steiger, Sam	400,334	DeConcini, Dennis	19,640	79,098 D	43.3%	54.0%	44.5%	55.5%
1974	549,919	320,396	Goldwater, Barry M.	229,523	Marshall, Jonathan		90,873 R	58.3%	41.7%	58.3%	41.7%
1970	407,796	228,284	Fannin, Paul	179,512	Grossman, Sam		48,772 R	56.0%	44.0%	56.0%	44.0%
1968	479,945	274,607	Goldwater, Barry M.	205,338	Elson, Roy L.		69,269 R	57.2%	42.8%	57.2%	42.8%
1964	468,801	241,089	Fannin, Paul	227,712	Elson, Roy L.		13,377 R	51.4%	48.6%	51.4%	48.6%
1962	362,605	163,388	Mecham, Evan	199,217	Hayden, Carl		35,829 D	45.1%	54.9%	45.1%	54.9%
1958	293,623	164,593	Goldwater, Barry M.	129,030	McFarland, Ernest W.		35,563 R	56.1%	43.9%	56.1%	43.9%
1956	278,263	107,447	Jones, Ross F.	170,816	Hayden, Carl		63,369 D	38.6%	61.4%	38.6%	61.4%
1952	257,401	132,063	Goldwater, Barry M.	125,338	McFarland, Ernest W.		6,725 R	51.3%	48.7%	51.3%	48.7%
1950	185,092	68,846	Brockett, Bruce	116,246	Hayden, Carl		47,400 D	37.2%	62.8%	37.2%	62.8%
1946	116,239	35,022	Powers, Ward S.	80,415	McFarland, Ernest W.	802	45,393 D	30.1%	69.2%	30.3%	69.7%

** In past elections, the other vote included: 1992 - 145,361 Independent (Evan Mecham). The Democratic Party did not run a candidate in the 2000 Senate election.

ARIZONA

GOVERNOR 2010

2010 Census Population	County	Total Vote	Republican	Democratic	Other	Rep.-Dem. Plurality		Percentage			
								Rep.	Dem.	Rep.	Dem.
71,518	APACHE	20,659	7,002	12,839	818	5,837	D	33.9%	62.1%	35.3%	64.7%
131,346	COCHISE	40,070	24,974	13,954	1,142	11,020	R	62.3%	34.8%	64.2%	35.8%
134,421	COCONINO	38,944	16,754	20,792	1,398	4,038	D	43.0%	53.4%	44.6%	55.4%
53,597	GILA	17,929	11,163	6,155	611	5,008	R	62.3%	34.3%	64.5%	35.5%
37,220	GRAHAM	9,153	5,994	2,865	294	3,129	R	65.5%	31.3%	67.7%	32.3%
8,437	GREENLEE	2,448	1,187	1,177	84	10	R	48.5%	48.1%	50.2%	49.8%
20,489	LA PAZ	4,528	3,048	1,330	150	1,718	R	67.3%	29.4%	69.6%	30.4%
3,817,117	MARICOPA	991,144	543,045	415,142	32,957	127,903	R	54.8%	41.9%	56.7%	43.3%
200,186	MOHAVE	53,715	39,026	12,777	1,912	26,249	R	72.7%	23.8%	75.3%	24.7%
107,449	NAVAJO	29,646	16,157	12,517	972	3,640	R	54.5%	42.2%	56.3%	43.7%
980,263	PIMA	315,589	148,916	158,337	8,336	9,421	D	47.2%	50.2%	48.5%	51.5%
375,770	PINAL	78,591	45,807	30,109	2,675	15,698	R	58.3%	38.3%	60.3%	39.7%
47,420	SANTA CRUZ	10,041	3,190	6,608	243	3,418	D	31.8%	65.8%	32.6%	67.4%
211,033	YAVAPAI	81,388	53,081	25,569	2,738	27,512	R	65.2%	31.4%	67.5%	32.5%
195,751	YUMA	34,236	19,590	13,764	882	5,826	R	57.2%	40.2%	58.7%	41.3%
6,392,017	TOTAL	1,728,081	938,934	733,935	55,212	204,999	R	54.3%	42.5%	56.1%	43.9%

ARIZONA

SENATOR 2010

2010 Census Population	County	Total Vote	Republican	Democratic	Other	Rep.-Dem. Plurality		Percentage			
								Total Vote		Major Vote	
								Rep.	Dem.	Rep.	Dem.
71,518	APACHE	20,556	7,371	11,785	1,400	4,414	D	35.9%	57.3%	38.5%	61.5%
131,346	COCHISE	39,615	23,445	13,119	3,051	10,326	R	59.2%	33.1%	64.1%	35.9%
134,421	COCONINO	38,624	18,995	17,164	2,465	1,831	R	49.2%	44.4%	52.5%	47.5%
53,597	GILA	17,700	11,500	4,858	1,342	6,642	R	65.0%	27.4%	70.3%	29.7%
37,220	GRAHAM	9,053	6,223	2,194	636	4,029	R	68.7%	24.2%	73.9%	26.1%
8,437	GREENLEE	2,418	1,321	947	150	374	R	54.6%	39.2%	58.2%	41.8%
20,489	LA PAZ	4,463	3,003	1,085	375	1,918	R	67.3%	24.3%	73.5%	26.5%
3,817,117	MARICOPA	979,966	599,068	319,012	61,886	280,056	R	61.1%	32.6%	65.3%	34.7%
200,186	MOHAVE	53,329	36,367	12,302	4,660	24,065	R	68.2%	23.1%	74.7%	25.3%
107,449	NAVAJO	29,223	16,157	10,737	2,329	5,420	R	55.3%	36.7%	60.1%	39.9%
980,263	PIMA	311,745	158,879	134,296	18,570	24,583	R	51.0%	43.1%	54.2%	45.8%
375,770	PINAL	77,798	47,850	24,856	5,092	22,994	R	61.5%	31.9%	65.8%	34.2%
47,420	SANTA CRUZ	9,894	3,693	5,710	491	2,017	D	37.3%	57.7%	39.3%	60.7%
211,033	YAVAPAI	80,263	52,093	21,636	6,534	30,457	R	64.9%	27.0%	70.7%	29.3%
195,751	YUMA	33,837	19,650	12,310	1,877	7,340	R	58.1%	36.4%	61.5%	38.5%
6,392,017	TOTAL	1,708,484	1,005,615	592,011	110,858	413,604	R	58.9%	34.7%	62.9%	37.1%

ARIZONA

HOUSE OF REPRESENTATIVES

| | | | Republican | | Democratic | | Other Vote | Rep.-Dem. Plurality | | Percentage | | | |
| | | | | | | | | | | Total Vote | | Major Vote | |
CD	Year	Total Vote	Vote	Candidate	Vote	Candidate				Rep.	Dem.	Rep.	Dem.
1	2010	226,918	112,816	GOSAR, PAUL	99,233	KIRKPATRICK, ANN*	14,869	13,583	R	49.7%	43.7%	53.2%	46.8%
1	2008	278,787	109,924	HAY, SYDNEY	155,791	KIRKPATRICK, ANN	13,072	45,867	D	39.4%	55.9%	41.4%	58.6%
1	2006	204,139	105,646	RENZI, RICK*	88,691	SIMON, ELLEN	9,802	16,955	R	51.8%	43.4%	54.4%	45.6%
1	2004	253,351	148,315	RENZI, RICK*	91,776	BABBITT, PAUL	13,260	56,539	R	58.5%	36.2%	61.8%	38.2%
1	2002	174,687	85,967	RENZI, RICK	79,730	CORDOVA, GEORGE	8,990	6,237	R	49.2%	45.6%	51.9%	48.1%
2	2010	266,894	173,173	FRANKS, TRENT*	82,891	THRASHER, JOHN	10,830	90,282	R	64.9%	31.1%	67.6%	32.4%
2	2008	338,023	200,914	FRANKS, TRENT*	125,611	THRASHER, JOHN	11,498	75,303	R	59.4%	37.2%	61.5%	38.5%
2	2006	230,560	135,150	FRANKS, TRENT*	89,671	THRASHER, JOHN	5,739	45,479	R	58.6%	38.9%	60.1%	39.9%
2	2004	279,303	165,260	FRANKS, TRENT*	107,406	CAMACHO, RANDY	6,637	57,854	R	59.2%	38.5%	60.6%	39.4%
2	2002	167,502	100,359	FRANKS, TRENT	61,217	CAMACHO, RANDY	5,926	39,142	R	59.9%	36.5%	62.1%	37.9%
3	2010	208,071	108,689	QUAYLE, BEN	85,610	HULBURD, JON	13,772	23,079	R	52.2%	41.1%	55.9%	44.1%
3	2008	275,161	148,800	SHADEGG, JOHN*	115,759	LORD, BOB	10,602	33,041	R	54.1%	42.1%	56.2%	43.8%
3	2006	189,849	112,519	SHADEGG, JOHN*	72,586	PAINE, HERB	4,744	39,933	R	59.3%	38.2%	60.8%	39.2%
3	2004	225,974	181,012	SHADEGG, JOHN*		-	44,962	181,012	R	80.1%		100.0%	
3	2002	155,751	104,847	SHADEGG, JOHN*	47,173	HILL, CHARLES	3,731	57,674	R	67.3%	30.3%	69.0%	31.0%
4	2010	91,907	25,300	CONTRERAS, JANET	61,524	PASTOR, ED*	5,083	36,224	D	27.5%	66.9%	29.1%	70.9%
4	2008	124,427	26,435	KARG, DON	89,721	PASTOR, ED*	8,271	63,286	D	21.2%	72.1%	22.8%	77.2%
4	2006	77,861	18,627	KARG, DON	56,464	PASTOR, ED*	2,770	37,837	D	23.9%	72.5%	24.8%	75.2%
4	2004	110,027	28,238	KARG, DON	77,150	PASTOR, ED*	4,639	48,912	D	25.7%	70.1%	26.8%	73.2%
4	2002	66,065	18,381	BARNETT, JONATHAN	44,517	PASTOR, ED*	3,167	26,136	D	27.8%	67.4%	29.2%	70.8%
5	2010	212,250	110,374	SCHWEIKERT, DAVID	91,749	MITCHELL, HARRY*	10,127	18,625	R	52.0%	43.2%	54.6%	45.4%
5	2008	280,365	122,165	SCHWEIKERT, DAVID	149,033	MITCHELL, HARRY*	9,167	26,868	D	43.6%	53.2%	45.0%	55.0%
5	2006	202,010	93,815	HAYWORTH, J.D.*	101,838	MITCHELL, HARRY	6,357	8,023	D	46.4%	50.4%	47.9%	52.1%
5	2004	268,007	159,455	HAYWORTH, J.D.*	102,363	ROGERS, ELIZABETH	6,189	57,092	R	59.5%	38.2%	60.9%	39.1%
5	2002	169,812	103,870	HAYWORTH, J.D.*	61,559	COLUMBUS, CRAIG	4,383	42,311	R	61.2%	36.3%	62.8%	37.2%
6	2010	249,383	165,649	FLAKE, JEFF*	72,615	SCHNEIDER, REBECCA	11,119	93,034	R	66.4%	29.1%	69.5%	30.5%
6	2008	334,176	208,582	FLAKE, JEFF*	115,457	SCHNEIDER, REBECCA	10,137	93,125	R	62.4%	34.5%	64.4%	35.6%
6	2006	203,486	152,201	FLAKE, JEFF*		—	51,285	152,201	R	74.8%		100.0%	
6	2004	255,577	202,882	FLAKE, JEFF*		—	52,695	202,882	R	79.4%		100.0%	
6	2002	156,337	103,094	FLAKE, JEFF*	49,355	THOMAS, DEBORAH	3,888	53,739	R	65.9%	31.6%	67.6%	32.4%
7	2010	159,144	70,385	McCLUNG, RUTH	79,935	GRIJALVA, RAUL M.*	8,824	9,550	D	44.2%	50.2%	46.8%	53.2%
7	2008	196,489	64,425	SWEENEY, JOSEPH	124,304	GRIJALVA, RAUL M.*	7,760	59,879	D	32.8%	63.3%	34.1%	65.9%
7	2006	131,525	46,498	DRAKE, RON	80,354	GRIJALVA, RAUL M.*	4,673	33,856	D	35.4%	61.1%	36.7%	63.3%
7	2004	175,437	59,066	SWEENEY, JOSEPH	108,868	GRIJALVA, RAUL M.*	7,503	49,802	D	33.7%	62.1%	35.2%	64.8%
7	2002	103,818	38,474	HIEB, ROSS	61,256	GRIJALVA, RAUL M.	4,088	22,782	D	37.1%	59.0%	38.6%	61.4%
8	2010	283,578	134,124	KELLY, JESSE	138,280	GIFFORDS, GABRIELLE*	11,174	4,156	D	47.3%	48.8%	49.2%	50.8%
8	2008	328,266	140,553	BEE, TIM	179,629	GIFFORDS, GABRIELLE*	8,084	39,076	D	42.8%	54.7%	43.9%	56.1%
8	2006	253,720	106,790	GRAF, RANDY	137,655	GIFFORDS, GABRIELLE	9,275	30,865	D	42.1%	54.3%	43.7%	56.3%
8	2004	303,769	183,363	KOLBE, JIM*	109,963	BACAL, EVA	10,443	73,400	R	60.4%	36.2%	62.5%	37.5%
8	2002	200,428	126,930	KOLBE, JIM*	67,328	RYAN, MARY JUDGE	6,170	59,602	R	63.3%	33.6%	65.3%	34.7%
TOTAL	2010	1,698,145	900,510		711,837		85,798	188,673	R	53.0%	41.9%	55.9%	44.1%
TOTAL	2008	2,155,694	1,021,798		1,055,305		78,591	33,507	D	47.4%	49.0%	49.2%	50.8%
TOTAL	2006	1,493,150	771,246		627,259		94,645	143,987	R	51.7%	42.0%	55.1%	44.9%
TOTAL	2004	1,871,445	1,127,591		597,526		146,328	530,065	R	60.3%	31.9%	65.4%	34.6%
TOTAL	2002	1,194,400	681,922		472,135		40,343	209,787	R	57.1%	39.5%	59.1%	40.9%

An asterisk (*) denotes incumbent.

ARIZONA

GENERAL AND PRIMARY ELECTIONS

2010 GENERAL ELECTIONS

Governor   Other vote was 38,722 Libertarian (Barry J. Hess); 16,128 Green (Larry Gist); 322 write-in (Janelle Wood); 28 write-in (Anton Dowls); 12 write-in (Cary Dolego).

Senator   Other vote was 80,097 Libertarian (David F. Nolan); 24,603 Green (Jerry Joslyn); 5,938 write-in (Ian Gilyeat); 160 write-in (Loyd Ellis); 39 write-in (Santps Chavez); 14 write-in (Sydney Dudikoff); 7 write-in (Ray J. Caplette).

House   Other vote was:

- CD 1   14,869 Libertarian (Nicole Patti).
- CD 2   10,820 Libertarian (Powell Gammill); 8 write-in (William Crum); 2 write-in (Mark Rankin).
- CD 3   10,478 Libertarian (Michael Schoen); 3,294 Green (Leonard Clark).
- CD 4   2,718 Libertarian (Joe Cobb); 2,365 (Rebecca DeWitt).
- CD 5   10,127 Libertarian (Nick Coons).
- CD 6   7,712 Libertarian (Darell Tapp); 3,407 Green (Richard Grayson).
- CD 7   4,506 Independent "Nonpartisan" (Harley Meyer); 4,318 Libertarian (George Keane).
- CD 8   11,174 Libertarian (Steven Stoltz).

2010 PRIMARY ELECTIONS

Primary   August 24, 2010   **Registration**
(as of August 24, 2010)

Republican	1,119,389
Democratic	856,075
Libertarian	24,143
Green	4,585
Other	953,503
TOTAL	*3,102,876*

Primary Type   Semi-open—Registered Democrats and Republicans could vote only in their party's primary. But voters not registered with any political party could participate in either the Democratic or Republican primary.

ARIZONA

GENERAL AND PRIMARY ELECTIONS

	REPUBLICAN PRIMARIES			DEMOCRATIC PRIMARIES		
Governor	Jan Brewer*	479,202	81.8%	Terry Goddard	286,565	100.0%
	Buz Mills	51,010	8.7%			
	Dean Martin	36,028	6.1%			
	Matthew Jette	19,611	3.3%			
	TOTAL	*585,851*				
Senator	John McCain*	333,744	56.3%	Rodney Glassman	100,307	34.6%
	J.D. Hayworth	190,229	32.1%	Cathy Eden	76,487	26.4%
	Jim Deakin	69,328	11.7%	John Dougherty	68,589	23.7%
				Randy Parraz	44,435	15.3%
				William Koller (write-in)	48	
	TOTAL	*593,301*		*TOTAL*	*289,866*	
Congressional District 1	Paul Gosar	21,941	30.7%	Ann Kirkpatrick*	46,902	100.0%
	Sydney Hay	16,328	22.9%			
	Bradley Beauchamp	11,356	15.9%			
	Russell "Rusty" Bowers	10,552	14.8%			
	Steve Mehta	5,846	8.2%			

ARIZONA

GENERAL AND PRIMARY ELECTIONS

	REPUBLICAN PRIMARIES			DEMOCRATIC PRIMARIES		
	Thomas J. Zaleski	2,105	2.9%			
	Jon Jensen	1,736	2.4%			
	Joe Jaraczewski	1,530	2.1%			
	TOTAL	*71,394*				
Congressional District 2	Trent Franks*	81,252	80.9%	John Thrasher	32,503	100.0%
	Charles Black	19,220	19.1%			
	TOTAL	*100,472*				
Congressional District 3	Ben Quayle	17,400	22.1%	Jon Hulburd	27,388	100.0%
	Steve Moak	14,211	18.0%			
	Jim Waring	13,850	17.6%			
	Vernon B. Parker	13,411	17.0%			
	Pamela Gorman	6,473	8.2%			
	Paulina Morris	6,138	7.8%			
	Sam Crump	3,886	4.9%			
	Ed Winkler	1,353	1.7%			
	Bob Branch	1,141	1.4%			
	LeAnn Hull	1,044	1.3%			
	TOTAL	*78,907*				
Congressional District 4	Janet Contreras	8,085	60.1%	Ed Pastor*	24,613	100.0%
	Joe Penalosa	5,368	39.9%			
	TOTAL	*13,453*				
Congressional District 5	David Schweikert	26,678	37.2%	Harry Mitchell*	29,716	100.0%
	Jim Ward	18,480	25.8%			
	Susan Bitter Smith	17,297	24.1%			
	Chris Salvino	7,156	10.0%			
	Lee Gentry	1,157	1.6%			
	Mark Spinks	884	1.2%			
	TOTAL	*71,652*				
Congressional District 6	Jeff Flake*	62,285	64.6%	Rebecca Schneider	26,220	100.0%
	Jeff Smith	34,137	35.4%			
	TOTAL	*96,422*				
Congressional District 7	Ruth McClung	15,455	51.0%	Raul M. Grijalva*	33,931	100.0%
	Terry Myers	7,044	23.2%			
	Joseph Sweeney	3,702	12.2%			
	Robert Wilson	2,737	9.0%			
	Christopher J. Flowers	1,394	4.6%			
	TOTAL	*30,332*				
Congressional District 8	Jesse Kelly	43,097	48.3%	Gabrielle Giffords*	55,530	100.0%
	Jonathan Paton	37,066	41.5%			
	Brian Miller	6,613	7.4%			
	Jay Quick	1,933	2.2%			
	Andy Goss	502	0.6%			
	TOTAL	*89,211*				

An asterisk (*) denotes incumbent.

ARKANSAS

Congressional districts first established for elections held in 2002
4 members

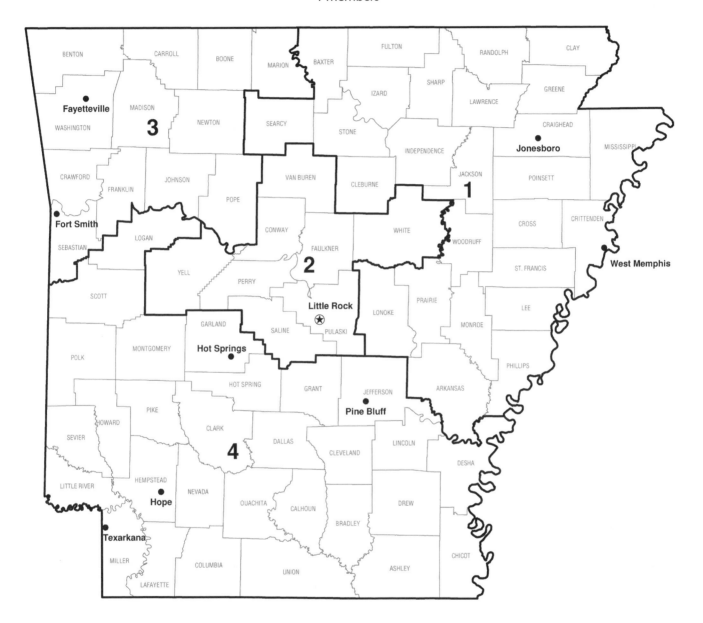

ARKANSAS

GOVERNOR
Mike D. Beebe (D). Reelected 2010 to a four-year term. Previously elected 2006.

SENATORS (1 Democrat, 1 Republican)
John Boozman (R). Elected 2010 to a six-year term.

Mark Pryor (D). Reelected 2008 to a six-year term. Previously elected 2002.

REPRESENTATIVES (3 Democrats, 1 Republican)
1. Rick Crawford (R)
2. Tim Griffin (R)
3. Steve Womack (R)
4. Mike Ross (D)

POSTWAR VOTE FOR PRESIDENT

Year	Total Vote	Republican Vote	Republican Candidate	Democratic Vote	Democratic Candidate	Other Vote	Rep.-Dem. Plurality	Total Vote Rep.	Total Vote Dem.	Major Vote Rep.	Major Vote Dem.
2008	1,086,617	638,017	McCain, John	422,310	Obama, Barack	26,290	215,707 R	58.7%	38.9%	60.2%	39.8%
2004	1,054,945	572,898	Bush, George W.	469,953	Kerry, John	12,094	102,945 R	54.3%	44.5%	54.9%	45.1%
2000**	921,781	472,940	Bush, George W.	422,768	Gore, Al	26,073	50,172 R	51.3%	45.9%	52.8%	47.2%
1996**	884,262	325,416	Dole, Bob	475,171	Clinton, Bill	83,675	149,755 D	36.8%	53.7%	40.6%	59.4%
1992**	950,653	337,324	Bush, George	505,823	Clinton, Bill	107,506	168,499 D	35.5%	53.2%	40.0%	60.0%
1988	827,738	466,578	Bush, George	349,237	Dukakis, Michael S.	11,923	117,341 R	56.4%	42.2%	57.2%	42.8%
1984	884,406	534,774	Reagan, Ronald	338,646	Mondale, Walter F.	10,986	196,128 R	60.5%	38.3%	61.2%	38.8%
1980**	837,582	403,164	Reagan, Ronald	398,041	Carter, Jimmy	36,377	5,123 R	48.1%	47.5%	50.3%	49.7%
1976	767,535	267,903	Ford, Gerald R.	498,604	Carter, Jimmy	1,028	230,701 D	34.9%	65.0%	35.0%	65.0%
1972	651,320	448,541	Nixon, Richard M.	199,892	McGovern, George S.	2,887	248,649 R	68.9%	30.7%	69.2%	30.8%
1968**	619,969	190,759	Nixon, Richard M.	188,228	Humphrey, Hubert H.	240,982	50,223 A	30.8%	30.4%	50.3%	49.7%
1964	560,426	243,264	Goldwater, Barry M.	314,197	Johnson, Lyndon B.	2,965	70,933 D	43.4%	56.1%	43.6%	56.4%
1960	428,509	184,508	Nixon, Richard M.	215,049	Kennedy, John F.	28,952	30,541 D	43.1%	50.2%	46.2%	53.8%
1956	406,572	186,287	Eisenhower, Dwight D.	213,277	Stevenson, Adlai E.	7,008	26,990 D	45.8%	52.5%	46.6%	53.4%
1952	404,800	177,155	Eisenhower, Dwight D.	226,300	Stevenson, Adlai E.	1,345	49,145 D	43.8%	55.9%	43.9%	56.1%
1948**	242,475	50,959	Dewey, Thomas E.	149,659	Truman, Harry S.	41,857	98,700 D	21.0%	61.7%	25.4%	74.6%

** In past elections, the other vote included: 2000 - 13,421 Green (Ralph Nader); 1996 - 69,884 Reform (Ross Perot); 1992 - 99,132 Independent (Perot); 1980 - 22,468 Independent (John Anderson); 1968 - 240,982 American Independent (Wallace); 1948 - 40,068 States' Rights (Strom Thurmond). Wallace carried Arkansas in 1968 with 38.9 percent of the vote.

ARKANSAS

POSTWAR VOTE FOR GOVERNOR

Year	Total Vote	Republican Vote	Republican Candidate	Democratic Vote	Democratic Candidate	Other Vote	Rep.-Dem. Plurality	Total Vote Rep.	Total Vote Dem.	Major Vote Rep.	Major Vote Dem.
2010	781,333	262,784	Keet, Jim	503,336	Beebe, Mike D.	15,213	240,552 D	33.6%	64.4%	34.3%	65.7%
2006	774,680	315,040	Hutchinson, Asa	430,765	Beebe, Mike D.	28,875	115,725 D	40.7%	55.6%	42.2%	57.8%
2002	805,696	427,082	Huckabee, Mike	378,250	Fisher, Jimmie Lou	364	48,832 R	53.0%	46.9%	53.0%	47.0%
1998	706,011	421,989	Huckabee, Mike	272,923	Bristow, Bill	11,099	149,066 R	59.8%	38.7%	60.7%	39.3%
1994	716,840	287,904	Nelson, Sheffield	428,936	Tucker, Jim Guy		141,032 D	40.2%	59.8%	40.2%	59.8%
1990	696,412	295,925	Nelson, Sheffield	400,386	Clinton, Bill	101	104,461 D	42.5%	57.5%	42.5%	57.5%
1986**	688,551	248,427	White, Frank D.	439,882	Clinton, Bill	242	191,455 D	36.1%	63.9%	36.1%	63.9%
1984	886,548	331,987	Freeman, Woody	554,561	Clinton, Bill		222,574 D	37.4%	62.6%	37.4%	62.6%
1982	789,351	357,496	White, Frank D.	431,855	Clinton, Bill		74,359 D	45.3%	54.7%	45.3%	54.7%
1980	838,925	435,684	White, Frank D.	403,241	Clinton, Bill		32,443 R	51.9%	48.1%	51.9%	48.1%
1978	528,912	193,746	Lowe, A. Lynn	335,101	Clinton, Bill	65	141,355 D	36.6%	63.4%	36.6%	63.4%
1976	726,949	121,716	Griffith, Leon	605,083	Pryor, David H.	150	483,367 D	16.7%	83.2%	16.7%	83.3%
1974	545,974	187,872	Coon, Ken	358,018	Pryor, David H.	84	170,146 D	34.4%	65.6%	34.4%	65.6%
1972	648,069	159,177	Blaylock, Len E.	488,892	Bumpers, Dale		329,715 D	24.6%	75.4%	24.6%	75.4%
1970	609,198	197,418	Rockefeller, Winthrop	375,648	Bumpers, Dale	36,132	178,230 D	32.4%	61.7%	34.4%	65.6%
1968	615,595	322,782	Rockefeller, Winthrop	292,813	Crank, Marion		29,969 R	52.4%	47.6%	52.4%	47.6%
1966	563,527	306,324	Rockefeller, Winthrop	257,203	Johnson, James D.		49,121 R	54.4%	45.6%	54.4%	45.6%
1964	592,113	254,561	Rockefeller, Winthrop	337,489	Faubus, Orval E.	63	82,928 D	43.0%	57.0%	43.0%	57.0%
1962	308,092	82,349	Ricketts, Willis	225,743	Faubus, Orval E.		143,394 D	26.7%	73.3%	26.7%	73.3%
1960	421,985	129,921	Britt, Henry M.	292,064	Faubus, Orval E.		162,143 D	30.8%	69.2%	30.8%	69.2%
1958	286,886	50,288	Johnson, George W.	236,598	Faubus, Orval E.		186,310 D	17.5%	82.5%	17.5%	82.5%
1956	399,012	77,215	Mitchell, Roy	321,797	Faubus, Orval E.		244,582 D	19.4%	80.6%	19.4%	80.6%
1954	335,176	127,004	Remmel, Pratt C.	208,121	Faubus, Orval E.	51	81,117 D	37.9%	62.1%	37.9%	62.1%
1952	391,592	49,292	Speck, Jefferson W.	342,292	Cherry, Francis	8	293,000 D	12.6%	87.4%	12.6%	87.4%
1950	317,087	50,309	Speck, Jefferson W.	266,778	McMath, Sidney S.		216,469 D	15.9%	84.1%	15.9%	84.1%
1948	249,301	26,500	Black, Charles R.	222,801	McMath, Sidney S.		196,301 D	10.6%	89.4%	10.6%	89.4%
1946	152,162	24,133	Mills, W. T.	128,029	Laney, Ben T.		103,896 D	15.9%	84.1%	15.9%	84.1%

** The term of office for Arkansas' Governor was increased from two to four years effective with the 1986 election.

POSTWAR VOTE FOR SENATOR

Year	Total Vote	Republican Vote	Republican Candidate	Democratic Vote	Democratic Candidate	Other Vote	Rep.-Dem. Plurality	Total Vote Rep.	Total Vote Dem.	Major Vote Rep.	Major Vote Dem.
2010	779,957	451,618	Boozman, John	288,156	Lincoln, Blanche	40,183	163,462 R	57.9%	36.9%	61.0%	39.0%
2008**	1,011,754		—	804,678	Pryor, Mark	207,076	804,678 D		79.5%		100.0%
2004	1,039,349	458,036	Holt, Jim	580,973	Lincoln, Blanche	340	122,937 D	44.1%	55.9%	44.1%	55.9%
2002	803,959	370,653	Hutchinson, Tim	433,306	Pryor, Mark		62,653 D	46.1%	53.9%	46.1%	53.9%
1998	700,644	295,870	Boozman, Fay	385,878	Lincoln, Blanche	18,896	90,008 D	42.2%	55.1%	43.4%	56.6%
1996	846,183	445,942	Hutchinson, Tim	400,241	Bryant, Winston		45,701 R	52.7%	47.3%	52.7%	47.3%
1992	920,008	366,373	Huckabee, Mike	553,635	Bumpers, Dale		187,262 D	39.8%	60.2%	39.8%	60.2%
1990**	494,735		—	493,910	Pryor, David H.	825	493,910 D		99.8%		100.0%
1986	695,487	262,313	Hutchinson, Asa	433,122	Bumpers, Dale	52	170,809 D	37.7%	62.3%	37.7%	62.3%
1984	875,956	373,615	Bethune, Ed	502,341	Pryor, David H.		128,726 D	42.7%	57.3%	42.7%	57.3%
1980	808,812	330,576	Clark, Bill	477,905	Bumpers, Dale	331	147,329 D	40.9%	59.1%	40.9%	59.1%
1978	522,239	84,722	Kelly, Tom	399,916	Pryor, David H.	37,601	315,194 D	16.2%	76.6%	17.5%	82.5%
1974	543,082	82,026	Jones, John H.	461,056	Bumpers, Dale		379,030 D	15.1%	84.9%	15.1%	84.9%
1972	634,636	248,238	Babbitt, Wayne H.	386,398	McClellan, John L.		138,160 D	39.1%	60.9%	39.1%	60.9%
1968	591,704	241,739	Bernard, Charles T.	349,965	Fulbright, J. W.		108,226 D	40.9%	59.1%	40.9%	59.1%
1966**			—		McClellan, John L.		D				
1962	312,880	98,013	Jones, Kenneth	214,867	Fulbright, J. W.		116,854 D	31.3%	68.7%	31.3%	68.7%
1960**			—		McClellan, John L.		D				
1956	399,695	68,016	Henley, Ben C.	331,679	Fulbright, J. W.		263,663 D	17.0%	83.0%	17.0%	83.0%
1954	291,058		—	291,058	McClellan, John L.		291,058 D		100.0%		100.0%
1950	302,582		—	302,582	Fulbright, J. W.		302,582 D		100.0%		100.0%
1948	216,401		—	216,401	McClellan, John L.		216,401 D		100.0%		100.0%

** In past elections, the other vote included: 2008 - 207,076 Green (Rebekah Kennedy), who finished second. In 1990 the vote for Senator David H. Pryor was not canvassed in seven counties because he was unopposed. Senator John L. McClellan was reelected in 1960 and in 1966, but his vote was not canvassed in many counties. The Republican Party did not run a candidate in the 1948, 1950, 1954, 1960, 1966, 1990 and 2008 Senate elections.

ARKANSAS

GOVERNOR 2010

2000 Census Population	County	Total Vote	Republican	Democratic	Other	Rep.-Dem. Plurality	Percentage			
							Total Vote		Major Vote	
							Rep.	Dem.	Rep.	Dem.
19,019	ARKANSAS	4,933	1,111	3,765	57	2,654 D	22.5%	76.3%	22.8%	77.2%
21,853	ASHLEY	5,647	1,834	3,742	71	1,908 D	32.5%	66.3%	32.9%	67.1%
41,513	BAXTER	14,907	6,468	8,128	311	1,660 D	43.4%	54.5%	44.3%	55.7%
221,339	BENTON	53,194	24,600	27,715	879	3,115 D	46.2%	52.1%	47.0%	53.0%
36,903	BOONE	14,947	5,602	8,843	502	3,241 D	37.5%	59.2%	38.8%	61.2%
11,508	BRADLEY	2,887	696	2,164	27	1,468 D	24.1%	75.0%	24.3%	75.7%
5,368	CALHOUN	1,616	448	1,143	25	695 D	27.7%	70.7%	28.2%	71.8%
27,446	CARROLL	8,309	2,876	5,166	267	2,290 D	34.6%	62.2%	35.8%	64.2%
11,800	CHICOT	3,007	573	2,404	30	1,831 D	19.1%	79.9%	19.2%	80.8%
22,995	CLARK	7,629	1,685	5,772	172	4,087 D	22.1%	75.7%	22.6%	77.4%
16,083	CLAY	4,148	1,029	3,055	64	2,026 D	24.8%	73.6%	25.2%	74.8%
25,970	CLEBURNE	9,157	3,955	5,029	173	1,074 D	43.2%	54.9%	44.0%	56.0%
8,689	CLEVELAND	2,403	807	1,539	57	732 D	33.6%	64.0%	34.4%	65.6%
24,552	COLUMBIA	7,016	2,423	4,484	109	2,061 D	34.5%	63.9%	35.1%	64.9%
21,273	CONWAY	6,153	1,595	4,439	119	2,844 D	25.9%	72.1%	26.4%	73.6%
96,443	CRAIGHEAD	21,449	6,580	14,557	312	7,977 D	30.7%	67.9%	31.1%	68.9%
61,948	CRAWFORD	14,760	6,035	8,433	292	2,398 D	40.9%	57.1%	41.7%	58.3%
50,902	CRITTENDEN	11,761	3,171	8,256	334	5,085 D	27.0%	70.2%	27.8%	72.2%
17,870	CROSS	5,159	1,435	3,651	73	2,216 D	27.8%	70.8%	28.2%	71.8%
8,116	DALLAS	2,459	628	1,807	24	1,179 D	25.5%	73.5%	25.8%	74.2%
13,008	DESHA	3,537	517	2,981	39	2,464 D	14.6%	84.3%	14.8%	85.2%
18,509	DREW	4,427	1,228	3,124	75	1,896 D	27.7%	70.6%	28.2%	71.8%
113,237	FAULKNER	27,134	10,434	16,188	512	5,754 D	38.5%	59.7%	39.2%	60.8%
18,125	FRANKLIN	5,270	1,833	3,282	155	1,449 D	34.8%	62.3%	35.8%	64.2%
12,245	FULTON	3,543	1,260	2,194	89	934 D	35.6%	61.9%	36.5%	63.5%
96,024	GARLAND	30,481	11,490	18,424	567	6,934 D	37.7%	60.4%	38.4%	61.6%
17,853	GRANT	5,228	1,816	3,319	93	1,503 D	34.7%	63.5%	35.4%	64.6%
42,090	GREENE	9,190	2,809	6,213	168	3,404 D	30.6%	67.6%	31.1%	68.9%
22,609	HEMPSTEAD	4,894	1,550	3,238	106	1,688 D	31.7%	66.2%	32.4%	67.6%
32,923	HOT SPRING	8,394	2,520	5,606	268	3,086 D	30.0%	66.8%	31.0%	69.0%
13,789	HOWARD	3,135	900	2,185	50	1,285 D	28.7%	69.7%	29.2%	70.8%
36,647	INDEPENDENCE	9,250	3,033	6,056	161	3,023 D	32.8%	65.5%	33.4%	66.6%
13,696	IZARD	4,554	1,550	2,875	129	1,325 D	34.0%	63.1%	35.0%	65.0%
17,997	JACKSON	3,949	891	2,993	65	2,102 D	22.6%	75.8%	22.9%	77.1%
77,435	JEFFERSON	18,693	3,667	14,724	302	11,057 D	19.6%	78.8%	19.9%	80.1%
25,540	JOHNSON	5,951	1,862	3,939	150	2,077 D	31.3%	66.2%	32.1%	67.9%
7,645	LAFAYETTE	2,078	706	1,342	30	636 D	34.0%	64.6%	34.5%	65.5%
17,415	LAWRENCE	4,654	1,151	3,400	103	2,249 D	24.7%	73.1%	25.3%	74.7%
10,424	LEE	3,009	461	2,509	39	2,048 D	15.3%	83.4%	15.5%	84.5%
14,134	LINCOLN	3,057	791	2,072	194	1,281 D	25.9%	67.8%	27.6%	72.4%
13,171	LITTLE RIVER	3,639	1,047	2,537	55	1,490 D	28.8%	69.7%	29.2%	70.8%
22,353	LOGAN	6,268	1,979	4,167	122	2,188 D	31.6%	66.5%	32.2%	67.8%
68,356	LONOKE	16,409	7,043	9,124	242	2,081 D	42.9%	55.6%	43.6%	56.4%
15,717	MADISON	5,048	1,831	3,097	120	1,266 D	36.3%	61.4%	37.2%	62.8%
16,653	MARION	5,725	2,222	3,267	236	1,045 D	38.8%	57.1%	40.5%	59.5%
43,462	MILLER	10,629	4,625	5,832	172	1,207 D	43.5%	54.9%	44.2%	55.8%
46,480	MISSISSIPPI	10,757	2,557	7,927	273	5,370 D	23.8%	73.7%	24.4%	75.6%
8,149	MONROE	2,695	439	2,226	30	1,787 D	16.3%	82.6%	16.5%	83.5%
9,487	MONTGOMERY	2,992	943	1,969	80	1,026 D	31.5%	65.8%	32.4%	67.6%
8,997	NEVADA	2,486	666	1,782	38	1,116 D	26.8%	71.7%	27.2%	72.8%

ARKANSAS

GOVERNOR 2010

2000 Census Population	County	Total Vote	Republican	Democratic	Other	Rep.-Dem. Plurality	Total Vote Rep.	Total Vote Dem.	Major Vote Rep.	Major Vote Dem.
8,330	NEWTON	3,369	1,329	1,916	124	587 D	39.4%	56.9%	41.0%	59.0%
26,120	OUACHITA	7,757	2,063	5,562	132	3,499 D	26.6%	71.7%	27.1%	72.9%
10,445	PERRY	3,103	1,091	1,919	93	828 D	35.2%	61.8%	36.2%	63.8%
21,757	PHILLIPS	6,361	839	5,433	89	4,594 D	13.2%	85.4%	13.4%	86.6%
11,291	PIKE	3,119	940	2,112	67	1,172 D	30.1%	67.7%	30.8%	69.2%
24,583	POINSETT	6,486	1,838	4,488	160	2,650 D	28.3%	69.2%	29.1%	70.9%
20,662	POLK	6,439	2,561	3,755	123	1,194 D	39.8%	58.3%	40.5%	59.5%
61,754	POPE	15,566	5,618	9,601	347	3,983 D	36.1%	61.7%	36.9%	63.1%
8,715	PRAIRIE	2,530	595	1,884	51	1,289 D	23.5%	74.5%	24.0%	76.0%
382,748	PULASKI	110,880	31,120	78,055	1,705	46,935 D	28.1%	70.4%	28.5%	71.5%
17,969	RANDOLPH	4,569	1,290	3,146	133	1,856 D	28.2%	68.9%	29.1%	70.9%
28,258	ST. FRANCIS	6,927	1,469	5,361	97	3,892 D	21.2%	77.4%	21.5%	78.5%
107,118	SALINE	35,147	14,078	20,488	581	6,410 D	40.1%	58.3%	40.7%	59.3%
11,233	SCOTT	3,234	1,119	2,054	61	935 D	34.6%	63.5%	35.3%	64.7%
8,195	SEARCY	3,352	1,345	1,903	104	558 D	40.1%	56.8%	41.4%	58.6%
125,744	SEBASTIAN	30,661	11,563	18,531	567	6,968 D	37.7%	60.4%	38.4%	61.6%
17,058	SEVIER	3,281	1,069	2,153	59	1,084 D	32.6%	65.6%	33.2%	66.8%
17,264	SHARP	6,054	2,279	3,607	168	1,328 D	37.6%	59.6%	38.7%	61.3%
12,394	STONE	4,992	1,684	3,177	131	1,493 D	33.7%	63.6%	34.6%	65.4%
41,639	UNION	12,135	4,540	7,412	183	2,872 D	37.4%	61.1%	38.0%	62.0%
17,295	VAN BUREN	5,472	1,824	3,493	155	1,669 D	33.3%	63.8%	34.3%	65.7%
203,065	WASHINGTON	44,652	16,585	26,987	1,080	10,402 D	37.1%	60.4%	38.1%	61.9%
77,076	WHITE	19,809	6,909	12,615	285	5,706 D	34.9%	63.7%	35.4%	64.6%
7,260	WOODRUFF	2,211	290	1,889	32	1,599 D	13.1%	85.4%	13.3%	86.7%
22,185	YELL	4,610	1,374	3,111	125	1,737 D	29.8%	67.5%	30.6%	69.4%
2,915,918	TOTAL	781,333	262,784	503,336	15,213	240,552 D	33.6%	64.4%	34.3%	65.7%

ARKANSAS

SENATOR 2010

2000 Census Population	County	Total Vote	Republican	Democratic	Other	Rep.-Dem. Plurality	Total Vote Rep.	Total Vote Dem.	Major Vote Rep.	Major Vote Dem.
19,019	ARKANSAS	4,878	2,134	2,627	117	493 D	43.7%	53.9%	44.8%	55.2%
21,853	ASHLEY	5,626	3,176	2,238	212	938 R	56.5%	39.8%	58.7%	41.3%
41,513	BAXTER	14,850	10,139	3,706	1,005	6,433 R	68.3%	25.0%	73.2%	26.8%
221,339	BENTON	53,310	39,622	11,673	2,015	27,949 R	74.3%	21.9%	77.2%	22.8%
36,903	BOONE	14,962	10,073	3,507	1,382	6,566 R	67.3%	23.4%	74.2%	25.8%
11,508	BRADLEY	2,872	1,562	1,230	80	332 R	54.4%	42.8%	55.9%	44.1%
5,368	CALHOUN	1,600	936	553	111	383 R	58.5%	34.6%	62.9%	37.1%
27,446	CARROLL	8,286	5,204	2,591	491	2,613 R	62.8%	31.3%	66.8%	33.2%
11,800	CHICOT	3,018	1,064	1,909	45	845 D	35.3%	63.3%	35.8%	64.2%
22,995	CLARK	7,604	3,382	3,782	440	400 D	44.5%	49.7%	47.2%	52.8%

ARKANSAS
SENATOR 2010

2000 Census Population	County	Total Vote	Republican	Democratic	Other	Rep.-Dem. Plurality		Percentage			
								Total Vote		Major Vote	
								Rep.	Dem.	Rep.	Dem.
16,083	CLAY	4,140	1,978	1,971	191	7	R	47.8%	47.6%	50.1%	49.9%
25,970	CLEBURNE	9,108	6,104	2,478	526	3,626	R	67.0%	27.2%	71.1%	28.9%
8,689	CLEVELAND	2,403	1,486	837	80	649	R	61.8%	34.8%	64.0%	36.0%
24,552	COLUMBIA	7,002	4,145	2,358	499	1,787	R	59.2%	33.7%	63.7%	36.3%
21,273	CONWAY	6,103	3,075	2,651	377	424	R	50.4%	43.4%	53.7%	46.3%
96,443	CRAIGHEAD	21,413	12,011	8,551	851	3,460	R	56.1%	39.9%	58.4%	41.6%
61,948	CRAWFORD	14,772	11,124	3,034	614	8,090	R	75.3%	20.5%	78.6%	21.4%
50,902	CRITTENDEN	11,527	4,820	6,219	488	1,399	D	41.8%	54.0%	43.7%	56.3%
17,870	CROSS	5,139	2,628	2,330	181	298	R	51.1%	45.3%	53.0%	47.0%
8,116	DALLAS	2,455	1,237	1,095	123	142	R	50.4%	44.6%	53.0%	47.0%
13,008	DESHA	3,531	1,240	2,177	114	937	D	35.1%	61.7%	36.3%	63.7%
18,509	DREW	4,414	2,349	1,960	105	389	R	53.2%	44.4%	54.5%	45.5%
113,237	FAULKNER	27,071	16,940	8,935	1,196	8,005	R	62.6%	33.0%	65.5%	34.5%
18,125	FRANKLIN	5,254	3,486	1,499	269	1,987	R	66.3%	28.5%	69.9%	30.1%
12,245	FULTON	3,534	1,966	1,319	249	647	R	55.6%	37.3%	59.8%	40.2%
96,024	GARLAND	30,404	18,720	9,964	1,720	8,756	R	61.6%	32.8%	65.3%	34.7%
17,853	GRANT	5,196	3,355	1,569	272	1,786	R	64.6%	30.2%	68.1%	31.9%
42,090	GREENE	9,131	5,389	3,315	427	2,074	R	59.0%	36.3%	61.9%	38.1%
22,609	HEMPSTEAD	4,861	2,760	1,829	272	931	R	56.8%	37.6%	60.1%	39.9%
32,923	HOT SPRING	8,348	4,724	3,063	561	1,661	R	56.6%	36.7%	60.7%	39.3%
13,789	HOWARD	3,132	1,769	1,188	175	581	R	56.5%	37.9%	59.8%	40.2%
36,647	INDEPENDENCE	9,217	5,390	3,248	579	2,142	R	58.5%	35.2%	62.4%	37.6%
13,696	IZARD	4,526	2,413	1,521	592	892	R	53.3%	33.6%	61.3%	38.7%
17,997	JACKSON	3,934	1,849	1,890	195	41	D	47.0%	48.0%	49.5%	50.5%
77,435	JEFFERSON	18,617	6,845	11,265	507	4,420	D	36.8%	60.5%	37.8%	62.2%
25,540	JOHNSON	5,937	3,584	1,937	416	1,647	R	60.4%	32.6%	64.9%	35.1%
7,645	LAFAYETTE	2,064	1,169	797	98	372	R	56.6%	38.6%	59.5%	40.5%
17,415	LAWRENCE	4,623	2,161	2,196	266	35	D	46.7%	47.5%	49.6%	50.4%
10,424	LEE	2,973	946	1,949	78	1,003	D	31.8%	65.6%	32.7%	67.3%
14,134	LINCOLN	3,223	1,459	1,468	296	9	D	45.3%	45.5%	49.8%	50.2%
13,171	LITTLE RIVER	3,609	2,047	1,376	186	671	R	56.7%	38.1%	59.8%	40.2%
22,353	LOGAN	6,242	4,003	1,877	362	2,126	R	64.1%	30.1%	68.1%	31.9%
68,356	LONOKE	16,362	11,204	4,551	607	6,653	R	68.5%	27.8%	71.1%	28.9%
15,717	MADISON	5,067	3,348	1,488	231	1,860	R	66.1%	29.4%	69.2%	30.8%
16,653	MARION	5,745	3,786	1,412	547	2,374	R	65.9%	24.6%	72.8%	27.2%
43,462	MILLER	10,590	7,074	3,112	404	3,962	R	66.8%	29.4%	69.4%	30.6%
46,480	MISSISSIPPI	10,697	4,404	5,661	632	1,257	D	41.2%	52.9%	43.8%	56.2%
8,149	MONROE	2,695	1,012	1,624	59	612	D	37.6%	60.3%	38.4%	61.6%
9,487	MONTGOMERY	2,976	1,785	987	204	798	R	60.0%	33.2%	64.4%	35.6%
8,997	NEVADA	2,475	1,268	1,065	142	203	R	51.2%	43.0%	54.4%	45.6%
8,330	NEWTON	3,361	2,179	882	300	1,297	R	64.8%	26.2%	71.2%	28.8%
26,120	OUACHITA	7,772	3,909	3,496	367	413	R	50.3%	45.0%	52.8%	47.2%
10,445	PERRY	3,105	1,777	1,071	257	706	R	57.2%	34.5%	62.4%	37.6%
21,757	PHILLIPS	6,332	1,832	4,203	297	2,371	D	28.9%	66.4%	30.4%	69.6%
11,291	PIKE	3,098	1,858	1,051	189	807	R	60.0%	33.9%	63.9%	36.1%
24,583	POINSETT	6,473	3,247	2,855	371	392	R	50.2%	44.1%	53.2%	46.8%
20,662	POLK	6,437	4,350	1,642	445	2,708	R	67.6%	25.5%	72.6%	27.4%
61,754	POPE	15,588	9,423	3,787	2,378	5,636	R	60.5%	24.3%	71.3%	28.7%
8,715	PRAIRIE	2,516	1,243	1,186	87	57	R	49.4%	47.1%	51.2%	48.8%
382,748	PULASKI	110,705	50,100	56,953	3,652	6,853	D	45.3%	51.4%	46.8%	53.2%

ARKANSAS

SENATOR 2010

2000 Census Population	County	Total Vote	Republican	Democratic	Other	Rep.-Dem. Plurality		Percentage			
								Total Vote		Major Vote	
								Rep.	Dem.	Rep.	Dem.
17,969	RANDOLPH	4,535	2,312	1,916	307	396	R	51.0%	42.2%	54.7%	45.3%
28,258	ST. FRANCIS	6,922	2,610	4,065	247	1,455	D	37.7%	58.7%	39.1%	60.9%
107,118	SALINE	35,102	23,484	10,035	1,583	13,449	R	66.9%	28.6%	70.1%	29.9%
11,233	SCOTT	3,221	2,234	821	166	1,413	R	69.4%	25.5%	73.1%	26.9%
8,195	SEARCY	3,355	2,115	893	347	1,222	R	63.0%	26.6%	70.3%	29.7%
125,744	SEBASTIAN	30,699	21,946	7,577	1,176	14,369	R	71.5%	24.7%	74.3%	25.7%
17,058	SEVIER	3,271	2,122	947	202	1,175	R	64.9%	29.0%	69.1%	30.9%
17,264	SHARP	6,014	3,427	2,095	492	1,332	R	57.0%	34.8%	62.1%	37.9%
12,394	STONE	4,960	2,706	1,698	556	1,008	R	54.6%	34.2%	61.4%	38.6%
41,639	UNION	12,073	7,273	4,083	717	3,190	R	60.2%	33.8%	64.0%	36.0%
17,295	VAN BUREN	5,439	2,931	1,833	675	1,098	R	53.9%	33.7%	61.5%	38.5%
203,065	WASHINGTON	44,960	27,972	15,030	1,958	12,942	R	62.2%	33.4%	65.0%	35.0%
77,076	WHITE	19,707	13,123	5,595	989	7,528	R	66.6%	28.4%	70.1%	29.9%
7,260	WOODRUFF	2,201	670	1,423	108	753	D	30.4%	64.7%	32.0%	68.0%
22,185	YELL	4,595	2,430	1,437	728	993	R	52.9%	31.3%	62.8%	37.2%
2,915,918	TOTAL	779,957	451,618	288,156	40,183	163,462	R	57.9%	36.9%	61.0%	39.0%

ARKANSAS

HOUSE OF REPRESENTATIVES

CD	Year	Total Vote	Republican		Democratic		Other Vote	Rep.-Dem. Plurality		Percentage			
			Vote	Candidate	Vote	Candidate				Total Vote		Major Vote	
										Rep.	Dem.	Rep.	Dem.
1	2010	180,016	93,224	CRAWFORD, RICK	78,267	CAUSEY, CHAD	8,525	14,957	R	51.8%	43.5%	54.4%	45.6%
1	2008			—		BERRY, MARION*			D				
1	2006	184,188	56,611	STUMBAUGH, MICKEY	127,577	BERRY, MARION*		70,966	D	30.7%	69.3%	30.7%	69.3%
1	2004	243,944	81,556	HUMPHREY, VERNON	162,388	BERRY, MARION*		80,832	D	33.4%	66.6%	33.4%	66.6%
1	2002	194,058	64,357	ROBINSON, TOMMY F.	129,701	BERRY, MARION*		65,344	D	33.2%	66.8%	33.2%	66.8%
2	2010	210,852	122,091	GRIFFIN, TIM	80,687	ELLIOTT, JOYCE	8,074	41,404	R	57.9%	38.3%	60.2%	39.8%
2	2008	277,366		—	212,303	SNYDER, VIC*	65,063	212,303	D		76.5%		100.0%
2	2006	206,303	81,432	MAYBERRY, ANDY	124,871	SNYDER, VIC*		43,439	D	39.5%	60.5%	39.5%	60.5%
2	2004	276,493	115,655	PARKS, MARVIN	160,834	SNYDER, VIC*	4	45,179	D	41.8%	58.2%	41.8%	58.2%
2	2002	153,626		—	142,752	SNYDER, VIC*	10,874	142,752	D		92.9%		100.0%
3	2010	205,123	148,581	WOMACK, STEVE	56,542	WHITAKER, DAVID		92,039	R	72.4%	27.6%	72.4%	27.6%
3	2008	274,046	215,196	BOOZMAN, JOHN*		—	58,850	215,196	R	78.5%		100.0%	
3	2006	200,924	125,039	BOOZMAN, JOHN*	75,885	ANDERSON, WOODROW		49,154	R	62.2%	37.8%	62.2%	37.8%
3	2004	270,803	160,629	BOOZMAN, JOHN*	103,158	JUDY, JAN	7,016	57,471	R	59.3%	38.1%	60.9%	39.1%
3	2002	143,055	141,478	BOOZMAN, JOHN*		—	1,577	141,478	R	98.9%		100.0%	

ARKANSAS

HOUSE OF REPRESENTATIVES

CD	Year	Total Vote	Republican		Democratic		Other Vote	Rep.-Dem. Plurality	Percentage			
									Total Vote		Major Vote	
			Vote	Candidate	Vote	Candidate			Rep.	Dem.	Rep.	Dem.
4	2010	178,134	71,526	RANKIN, BETH ANNE	102,479	ROSS, MIKE*	4,129	30,953 D	40.2%	57.5%	41.1%	58.9%
4	2008	235,781		—	203,178	ROSS, MIKE*	32,603	203,178 D		86.2%		100.0%
4	2006	171,596	43,360	ROSS, JOE	128,236	ROSS, MIKE*		84,876 D	25.3%	74.7%	25.3%	74.7%
4	2004			—		ROSS, MIKE*		D				
4	2002	197,537	77,904	DICKEY, JAY	119,633	ROSS, MIKE*		41,729 D	39.4%	60.6%	39.4%	60.6%
TOTAL	2010	774,125	435,422		317,975		20,728	117,447 R	56.2%	41.1%	57.8%	42.2%
TOTAL	2008	787,193	215,196		415,481		156,516	200,285 D	27.3%	52.8%	34.1%	65.9%
TOTAL	2006	763,011	306,442		456,569			150,127 D	40.2%	59.8%	40.2%	59.8%
TOTAL	2004	791,240	357,840		426,380		7,020	68,540 D	45.2%	53.9%	45.6%	54.4%
TOTAL	2002	688,276	283,739		392,086		12,451	108,347 D	41.2%	57.0%	42.0%	58.0%

An asterisk (*) denotes incumbent.

ARKANSAS

GENERAL AND PRIMARY ELECTIONS

2010 GENERAL ELECTIONS

Governor   Other vote was 14,513 Green (Jim Lendall); 66 write-in (Elvis D. Presley); 49 write-in (Billy Roper); 20 write-in (David E. Dinwiddie); 565 scattered write-in.

Senator   Other vote was 25,234 Independent (Trevor Drown); 14,430 Green (John Laney Gray III); 143 write-in (Stephan "Troublemaker" Hercher); 376 scattered write-in.

House   Other vote was:

CD 1   8,320 Green (Ken Adler); 196 write-in (Mickey Higgins); 9 scattered write-in.
CD 2   4,421 Independent (Lance Levi); 3,599 Green (Lewis Kennedy); 14 write-in (Danial Suits); 40 scattered write-in.
CD 3
CD 4   4,129 Green (Josh Drake).

2010 PRIMARY ELECTIONS

Primary   May 18, 2010   **Registration** (as of May 18, 2010)   1,616,143   No Party Registration

Primary Runoff   June 8, 2010

Primary Type   Open—Any registered voter could participate in either the Democratic or Republican primary. However, if they participated in one party's primary they could not vote in the runoff of the other party.

ARKANSAS

GENERAL AND PRIMARY ELECTIONS

	REPUBLICAN PRIMARIES			DEMOCRATIC PRIMARIES		
Governor	Jim Keet	Unopposed		Mike D. Beebe*	Unopposed	
Senator	John Boozman	75,010	52.7%	Blanche Lincoln*	146,579	44.5%
	Jim Holt	24,826	17.5%	Bill Halter	140,081	42.5%
	Gilbert Baker	16,540	11.6%	D.C. Morrison	42,695	13.0%
	Conrad Reynolds	7,128	5.0%			
	Curtis Coleman	6,928	4.9%			
	Kim Hendren	5,551	3.9%			
	Randy Alexander	4,389	3.1%			
	Fred Ramey	1,888	1.3%			
	TOTAL	*142,260*		*TOTAL*	*329,355*	
				PRIMARY RUNOFF		
				Blanche Lincoln*	134,756	52.0%
				Bill Halter	124,405	48.0%
				TOTAL	*259,161*	
Congressional District 1	Rick Crawford	14,461	71.8%	Tim Woolridge	36,809	38.4%
	Princella D. Smith	5,682	28.2%	Chad Causey	25,854	27.0%
				David R. Cook	14,158	14.8%
				Steve Bryles	9,650	10.1%
				Terry G. Green	5,094	5.3%
				Ben Ponder	4,270	4.5%
	TOTAL	*20,143*		*TOTAL*	*95,835*	
				PRIMARY RUNOFF		
				Chad Causey	39,402	51.5%
				Tim Woolridge	37,156	48.5%
				TOTAL	*76,558*	
Congressional District 2	Tim Griffin	24,610	61.7%	Joyce Elliott	30,420	39.7%
	Scott Wallace	15,285	38.3%	Robbie Wills	21,299	27.8%
				David Boling	14,800	19.3%
				Patrick Kennedy	5,032	6.6%
				John Adams	5,021	6.6%
	TOTAL	*39,895*		*TOTAL*	*76,572*	
				PRIMARY RUNOFF		
				Joyce Elliott	37,021	53.8%
				Robbie Wills	31,844	46.2%
				TOTAL	*68,865*	
Congressional District 3	Steve Womack	19,414	31.2%	David Whitaker	Unopposed	
	Cecile Bledsoe	8,253	13.3%			
	Gunner DeLay	8,088	13.0%			
	Bernie Skoch	7,092	11.4%			
	Doug Matayo	6,088	9.8%			
	Kurt Maddox	6,037	9.7%			
	Mike Moore	4,801	7.7%			
	Steve Lowry	2,491	4.0%			
	TOTAL	*62,264*				
	PRIMARY RUNOFF					
	Steve Womack	18,334	51.8%			
	Cecile Bledsoe	17,080	48.2%			
	TOTAL	*35,414*				
Congressional District 4	Beth Anne Rankin	9,761	55.4%	Mike Ross*	Unopposed	
	Glenn Gallas	7,867	44.6%			
	TOTAL	*17,628*				

An asterisk (*) denotes incumbent. No votes were tallied district or statewide in contests where a candidate ran unopposed.

CALIFORNIA

Congressional districts first established for elections held in 2002
53 members

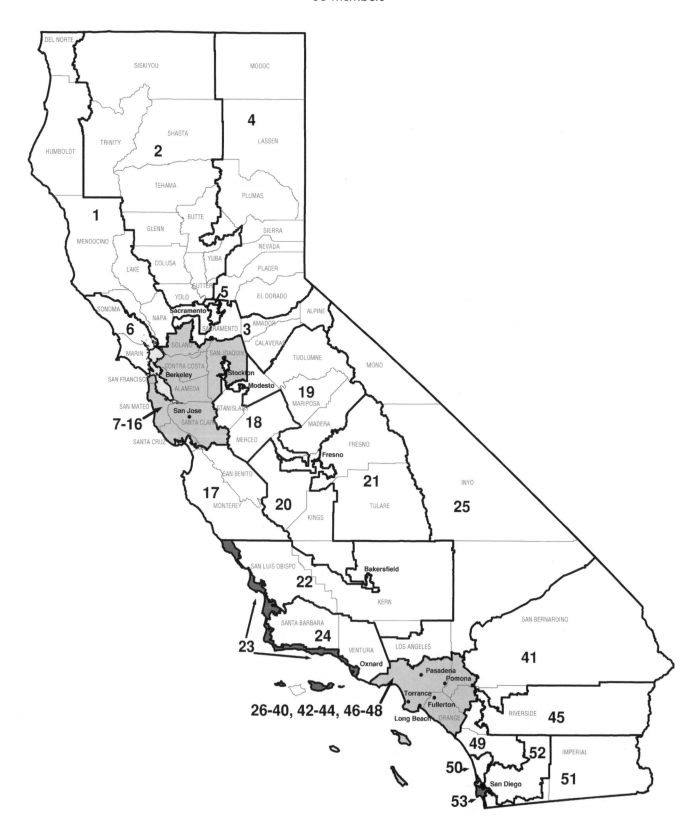

CALIFORNIA

San Francisco Bay Area

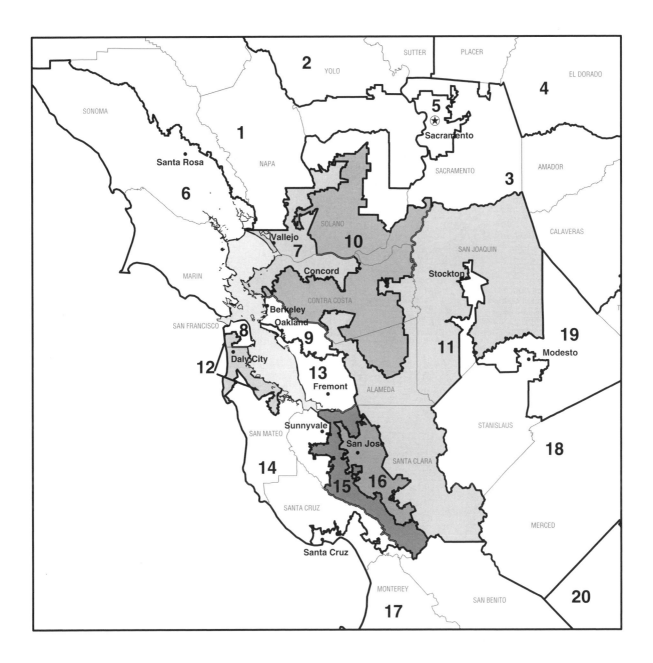

44

CALIFORNIA

Los Angeles, San Diego Areas

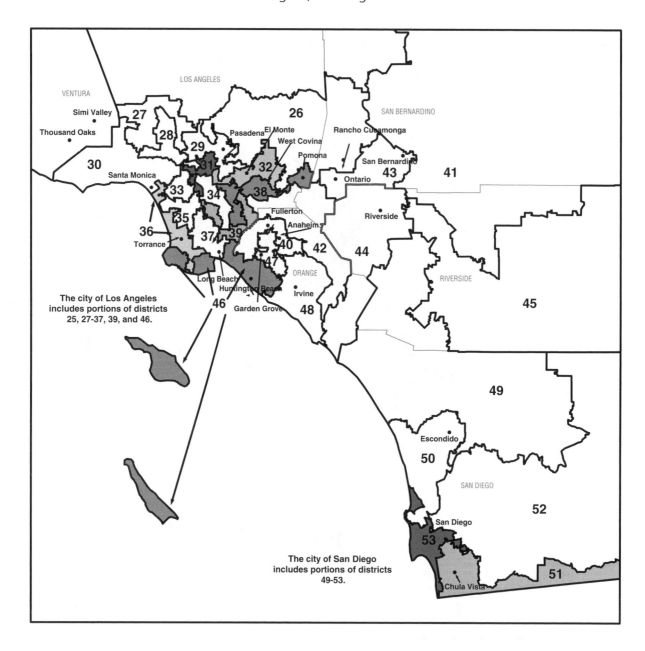

The city of Los Angeles includes portions of districts 25, 27-37, 39, and 46.

The city of San Diego includes portions of districts 49-53.

CALIFORNIA

GOVERNOR
Edmund G. "Jerry" Brown Jr. (D). Elected 2010 to a four-year term. Previously elected 1978, 1974.

SENATORS (2 Democrats)
Barbara Boxer (D). Reelected 2010 to a six-year term. Previously elected 2004, 1998, 1992.

Dianne Feinstein (D). Reelected 2006 to a six-year term. Previously elected 2000, 1994 and 1992 to fill the remaining two years of the term vacated when Senator Pete Wilson (R) was elected Governor in November 1990.

REPRESENTATIVES (34 Democrats, 19 Republicans)

1. Mike Thompson (D)
2. Wally Herger (R)
3. Dan Lungren (R)
4. Tom McClintock (R)
5. Doris Matsui (D)
6. Lynn Woolsey (D)
7. George Miller (D)
8. Nancy Pelosi (D)
9. Barbara Lee (D)
10. John Garamendi (D)
11. Jerry McNerney (D)
12. Jackie Speier (D)
13. Pete Stark (D)
14. Anna G. Eshoo (D)
15. Michael M. Honda (D)
16. Zoe Lofgren (D)
17. Sam Farr (D)
18. Dennis Cardoza (D)
19. Jeffrey Denham (R)
20. Jim Costa (D)
21. Devin Nunes (R)
22. Kevin McCarthy (R)
23. Lois Capps (D)
24. Elton Gallegly (R)
25. Howard P. "Buck" McKeon (R)
26. David Dreier (R)
27. Brad Sherman (D)
28. Howard L. Berman (D)
29. Adam B. Schiff (D)
30. Henry A. Waxman (D)
31. Xavier Becerra (D)
32. Judy Chu (D)
33. Karen Bass (D)
34. Lucille Roybal-Allard (D)
35. Maxine Waters (D)
36. Janice Hahn (D)
37. Laura Richardson (D)
38. Grace F. Napolitano (D)
39. Linda T. Sanchez (D)
40. Ed Royce (R)
41. Jerry Lewis (R)
42. Gary G. Miller (R)
43. Joe Baca (D)
44. Ken Calvert (R)
45. Mary Bono Mack (R)
46. Dana Rohrabacher (R)
47. Loretta Sanchez (D)
48. John Campbell (R)
49. Darrell Issa (R)
50. Brian P. Bilbray (R)
51. Bob Filner (D)
52. Duncan D. Hunter (R)
53. Susan A. Davis (D)

POSTWAR VOTE FOR PRESIDENT

Year	Total Vote	Republican		Democratic		Other Vote	Rep.-Dem. Plurality	Percentage			
								Total Vote		Major Vote	
		Vote	Candidate	Vote	Candidate			Rep.	Dem.	Rep.	Dem.
2008	13,561,900	5,011,781	McCain, John	8,274,473	Obama, Barack	275,646	3,262,692 D	37.0%	61.0%	37.7%	62.3%
2004	12,421,852	5,509,826	Bush, George W.	6,745,485	Kerry, John	166,541	1,235,659 D	44.4%	54.3%	45.0%	55.0%
2000**	10,965,856	4,567,429	Bush, George W.	5,861,203	Gore, Al	537,224	1,293,774 D	41.7%	53.4%	43.8%	56.2%
1996**	10,019,484	3,828,380	Dole, Bob	5,119,835	Clinton, Bill	1,071,269	1,291,455 D	38.2%	51.1%	42.8%	57.2%
1992**	11,131,721	3,630,574	Bush, George	5,121,325	Clinton, Bill	2,379,822	1,490,751 D	32.6%	46.0%	41.5%	58.5%
1988	9,887,065	5,054,917	Bush, George	4,702,233	Dukakis, Michael S.	129,915	352,684 R	51.1%	47.6%	51.8%	48.2%
1984	9,505,423	5,467,009	Reagan, Ronald	3,922,519	Mondale, Walter F.	115,895	1,544,490 R	57.5%	41.3%	58.2%	41.8%
1980**	8,587,063	4,524,858	Reagan, Ronald	3,083,661	Carter, Jimmy	978,544	1,441,197 R	52.7%	35.9%	59.5%	40.5%
1976	7,867,117	3,882,244	Ford, Gerald R.	3,742,284	Carter, Jimmy	242,589	139,960 R	49.3%	47.6%	50.9%	49.1%
1972	8,367,862	4,602,096	Nixon, Richard M.	3,475,847	McGovern, George S.	289,919	1,126,249 R	55.0%	41.5%	57.0%	43.0%
1968**	7,251,587	3,467,664	Nixon, Richard M.	3,244,318	Humphrey, Hubert H.	539,605	223,346 R	47.8%	44.7%	51.7%	48.3%
1964	7,057,586	2,879,108	Goldwater, Barry M.	4,171,877	Johnson, Lyndon B.	6,601	1,292,769 D	40.8%	59.1%	40.8%	59.2%
1960	6,506,578	3,259,722	Nixon, Richard M.	3,224,099	Kennedy, John F.	22,757	35,623 R	50.1%	49.6%	50.3%	49.7%
1956	5,466,355	3,027,668	Eisenhower, Dwight D.	2,420,135	Stevenson, Adlai E.	18,552	607,533 R	55.4%	44.3%	55.6%	44.4%
1952	5,141,849	2,897,310	Eisenhower, Dwight D.	2,197,548	Stevenson, Adlai E.	46,991	699,762 R	56.3%	42.7%	56.9%	43.1%
1948	4,021,538	1,895,269	Dewey, Thomas E.	1,913,134	Truman, Harry S.	213,135	17,865 D	47.1%	47.6%	49.8%	50.2%

**In past elections, the other vote included: 2000 - 418,707 Green (Ralph Nader); 1996 - 697,847 Reform (Ross Perot); 1992 - 2,296,006 Independent (Perot); 1980 - 739,833 Independent (John Anderson); 1968 - 487,270 American Independent (George Wallace).

CALIFORNIA

POSTWAR VOTE FOR GOVERNOR

Year	Total Vote	Republican		Democratic		Other Vote	Rep.-Dem. Plurality	Percentage			
								Total Vote		Major Vote	
		Vote	Candidate	Vote	Candidate			Rep.	Dem.	Rep.	Dem.
2010	10,095,185	4,127,391	Whitman, Meg	5,428,149	Brown, Edmund G., Jr.	539,645	1,300,758 D	40.9%	53.8%	43.2%	56.8%
2006	8,679,416	4,850,157	Schwarzenegger, Arnold	3,376,732	Angelides, Phil	452,527	1,473,425 R	55.9%	38.9%	59.0%	41.0%
2003S	8,657,915	4,206,284	Schwarzenegger, Arnold	2,724,874	Bustamante, Cruz	1,726,757	1,481,410 R	48.6%	31.5%	—	—
2002	7,476,311	3,169,801	Simon, Bill	3,533,490	Davis, Gray	773,020	363,689 D	42.4%	47.3%	47.3%	52.7%
1998	8,385,196	3,218,030	Lungren, Dan	4,860,702	Davis, Gray	306,464	1,642,672 D	38.4%	58.0%	39.8%	60.2%
1994	8,665,375	4,781,766	Wilson, Pete	3,519,799	Brown, Kathleen	363,810	1,261,967 R	55.2%	40.6%	57.6%	42.4%
1990	7,699,467	3,791,904	Wilson, Pete	3,525,197	Feinstein, Dianne	382,366	266,707 R	49.2%	45.8%	51.8%	48.2%
1986	7,443,551	4,506,601	Deukmejian, George	2,781,714	Bradley, Tom	155,236	1,724,887 R	60.5%	37.4%	61.8%	38.2%
1982	7,876,698	3,881,014	Deukmejian, George	3,787,669	Bradley, Tom	208,015	93,345 R	49.3%	48.1%	50.6%	49.4%
1978	6,922,378	2,526,534	Younger, Evelle J.	3,878,812	Brown, Edmund G., Jr.	517,032	1,352,278 D	36.5%	56.0%	39.4%	60.6%
1974	6,248,070	2,952,954	Flournoy, Houston I.	3,131,648	Brown, Edmund G., Jr.	163,468	178,694 D	47.3%	50.1%	48.5%	51.5%
1970	6,510,072	3,439,664	Reagan, Ronald	2,938,607	Unruh, Jess	131,801	501,057 R	52.8%	45.1%	53.9%	46.1%
1966	6,503,445	3,742,913	Reagan, Ronald	2,749,174	Brown, Edmund G.	11,358	993,739 R	57.6%	42.3%	57.7%	42.3%
1962	5,853,270	2,740,351	Nixon, Richard M.	3,037,109	Brown, Edmund G.	75,810	296,758 D	46.8%	51.9%	47.4%	52.6%
1958	5,255,777	2,110,911	Knowland, William F.	3,140,076	Brown, Edmund G.	4,790	1,029,165 D	40.2%	59.7%	40.2%	59.8%
1954	4,030,368	2,290,519	Knight, Goodwin J.	1,739,368	Graves, Richard P.	481	551,151 R	56.8%	43.2%	56.8%	43.2%
1950	3,796,090	2,461,754	Warren, Earl	1,333,856	Roosevelt, James	480	1,127,898 R	64.8%	35.1%	64.9%	35.1%
1946**	2,558,399	2,344,542	Warren, Earl	—		213,857	2,344,542 R	91.6%		100.0%	

**The 2003 election was for a short term to fill a vacancy created by voter approval of a measure to remove Governor Gray Davis (D) from office. The measure passed by a vote of 4,976,274 votes (55.4 percent) for recall to 4,007,783 (44.6 percent) against recall. In the same election, more than 100 candidates ran for the right to succeed Davis. No primary election was held to cull the field. All candidates, regardless of party, ran together on the same ballot. The winner, Arnold Schwarzenegger, is listed as the Republican candidate. The leading Democratic vote-getter, Cruz Bustamante, is listed as the Democratic candidate. The percentages given are for Schwarzenegger and Bustamante. The leading "Other" candidate was Republican Tom McClintock, who received 1,161,287 votes (13.4 percent of the total). In 1946 the Republican candidate won both major party nominations.

POSTWAR VOTE FOR SENATOR

Year	Total Vote	Republican		Democratic		Other Vote	Rep.-Dem. Plurality	Percentage			
								Total Vote		Major Vote	
		Vote	Candidate	Vote	Candidate			Rep.	Dem.	Rep.	Dem.
2010	9,999,860	4,217,386	Fiorina, Carly	5,218,137	Boxer, Barbara	564,337	1,000,751 D	42.2%	52.2%	44.7%	55.3%
2006	8,541,476	2,990,822	Mountjoy, Richard "Dick"	5,076,289	Feinstein, Dianne	474,365	2,085,467 D	35.0%	59.4%	37.1%	62.9%
2004	12,053,295	4,555,922	Jones, Bill	6,955,728	Boxer, Barbara	541,645	2,399,806 D	37.8%	57.7%	39.6%	60.4%
2000	10,623,614	3,886,853	Campbell, Tom	5,932,522	Feinstein, Dianne	804,239	2,045,669 D	36.6%	55.8%	39.6%	60.4%
1998	8,314,953	3,576,351	Fong, Matt	4,411,705	Boxer, Barbara	326,897	835,354 D	43.0%	53.1%	44.8%	55.2%
1994	8,514,089	3,817,025	Huffington, Michael	3,979,152	Feinstein, Dianne	717,912	162,127 D	44.8%	46.7%	49.0%	51.0%
1992	10,799,703	4,644,182	Herschensohn, Bruce	5,173,467	Boxer, Barbara	982,054	529,285 D	43.0%	47.9%	47.3%	52.7%
1992S	10,782,743	4,093,501	Seymour, John	5,853,651	Feinstein, Dianne	835,591	1,760,150 D	38.0%	54.3%	41.2%	58.8%
1988	9,743,598	5,143,409	Wilson, Pete	4,287,253	McCarthy, Leo	312,936	856,156 R	52.8%	44.0%	54.5%	45.5%
1986	7,398,549	3,541,804	Zschau, Ed	3,646,672	Cranston, Alan	210,073	104,868 D	47.9%	49.3%	49.3%	50.7%
1982	7,805,538	4,022,565	Wilson, Pete	3,494,968	Brown, Edmund G., Jr.	288,005	527,597 R	51.5%	44.8%	53.5%	46.5%
1980	8,327,481	3,093,426	Gann, Paul	4,705,399	Cranston, Alan	528,656	1,611,973 D	37.1%	56.5%	39.7%	60.3%
1976	7,472,268	3,748,973	Hayakawa, S. I.	3,502,862	Tunney, John V.	220,433	246,111 R	50.2%	46.9%	51.7%	48.3%
1974	6,102,432	2,210,267	Richardson, H. L.	3,693,160	Cranston, Alan	199,005	1,482,893 D	36.2%	60.5%	37.4%	62.6%
1970	6,492,157	2,877,617	Murphy, George	3,496,558	Tunney, John V.	117,982	618,941 D	44.3%	53.9%	45.1%	54.9%
1968	7,102,465	3,329,148	Rafferty, Max	3,680,352	Cranston, Alan	92,965	351,204 D	46.9%	51.8%	47.5%	52.5%
1964	7,041,821	3,628,555	Murphy, George	3,411,912	Salinger, Pierre	1,354	216,643 R	51.5%	48.5%	51.5%	48.5%
1962	5,647,952	3,180,483	Kuchel, Thomas H.	2,452,839	Richards, Richard	14,630	727,644 R	56.3%	43.4%	56.5%	43.5%
1958	5,135,221	2,204,337	Knight, Goodwin J.	2,927,693	Engle, Clair	3,191	723,356 D	42.9%	57.0%	43.0%	57.0%
1956	5,361,467	2,892,918	Kuchel, Thomas H.	2,445,816	Richards, Richard	22,733	447,102 R	54.0%	45.6%	54.2%	45.8%
1954S	3,929,668	2,090,836	Kuchel, Thomas H.	1,788,071	Yorty, Samuel W.	50,761	302,765 R	53.2%	45.5%	53.9%	46.1%
1952**	4,542,548	3,982,448	Knowland, William F.	—		560,100	3,982,448 R	87.7%		100.0%	
1950	3,686,315	2,183,454	Nixon, Richard M.	1,502,507	Douglas, Helen	354	680,947 R	59.2%	40.8%	59.2%	40.8%
1946	2,639,465	1,428,067	Knowland, William F.	1,167,161	Rogers, Will, Jr.	44,237	260,906 R	54.1%	44.2%	55.0%	45.0%

**In past elections, the other vote included: 1952 - 542,270 Progressive (Reuben W. Borough), who finished second. The Republican candidate that year won both major party nominations. The 1954 election was for a short term to fill a vacancy, as was one of the 1992 elections.

CALIFORNIA
GOVERNOR 2010

2010 Census Population	County	Total Vote	Republican	Democratic	Other	Rep.-Dem. Plurality		Percentage			
								Total Vote		Major Vote	
								Rep.	Dem.	Rep.	Dem.
1,510,271	ALAMEDA	461,021	103,947	340,190	16,884	236,243	D	22.5%	73.8%	23.4%	76.6%
1,175	ALPINE	564	228	319	17	91	D	40.4%	56.6%	41.7%	58.3%
38,091	AMADOR	16,253	8,511	6,750	992	1,761	R	52.4%	41.5%	55.8%	44.2%
220,000	BUTTE	76,052	37,557	32,789	5,706	4,768	R	49.4%	43.1%	53.4%	46.6%
45,578	CALAVERAS	19,807	10,655	7,737	1,415	2,918	R	53.8%	39.1%	57.9%	42.1%
21,419	COLUSA	5,227	3,063	1,878	286	1,185	R	58.6%	35.9%	62.0%	38.0%
1,049,025	CONTRA COSTA	348,151	123,606	211,125	13,420	87,519	D	35.5%	60.6%	36.9%	63.1%
28,610	DEL NORTE	8,190	3,373	4,093	724	720	D	41.2%	50.0%	45.2%	54.8%
181,058	EL DORADO	77,367	43,417	29,826	4,124	13,591	R	56.1%	38.6%	59.3%	40.7%
930,450	FRESNO	200,652	104,780	85,743	10,129	19,037	R	52.2%	42.7%	55.0%	45.0%
28,122	GLENN	7,930	4,841	2,407	682	2,434	R	61.0%	30.4%	66.8%	33.2%
134,623	HUMBOLDT	50,596	18,277	28,464	3,855	10,187	D	36.1%	56.3%	39.1%	60.9%
174,528	IMPERIAL	26,871	9,118	16,019	1,734	6,901	D	33.9%	59.6%	36.3%	63.7%
18,546	INYO	6,966	3,406	3,008	552	398	R	48.9%	43.2%	53.1%	46.9%
839,631	KERN	172,664	96,249	63,347	13,068	32,902	R	55.7%	36.7%	60.3%	39.7%
152,982	KINGS	26,324	13,868	10,607	1,849	3,261	R	52.7%	40.3%	56.7%	43.3%
64,665	LAKE	21,144	8,455	11,004	1,685	2,549	D	40.0%	52.0%	43.5%	56.5%
34,895	LASSEN	9,245	4,632	3,895	718	737	R	50.1%	42.1%	54.3%	45.7%
9,818,605	LOS ANGELES	2,321,552	749,439	1,455,184	116,929	705,745	D	32.3%	62.7%	34.0%	66.0%
150,865	MADERA	34,124	19,287	12,528	2,309	6,759	R	56.5%	36.7%	60.6%	39.4%
252,409	MARIN	113,979	30,920	80,236	2,823	49,316	D	27.1%	70.4%	27.8%	72.2%
18,251	MARIPOSA	8,231	4,513	3,077	641	1,436	R	54.8%	37.4%	59.5%	40.5%
87,841	MENDOCINO	31,897	9,524	20,186	2,187	10,662	D	29.9%	63.3%	32.1%	67.9%
255,793	MERCED	47,832	23,021	21,887	2,924	1,134	R	48.1%	45.8%	51.3%	48.7%
9,686	MODOC	3,769	2,444	1,001	324	1,443	R	64.8%	26.6%	70.9%	29.1%
14,202	MONO	4,400	2,079	2,028	293	51	R	47.3%	46.1%	50.6%	49.4%
415,057	MONTEREY	99,895	35,119	60,015	4,761	24,896	D	35.2%	60.1%	36.9%	63.1%
136,484	NAPA	46,908	17,873	26,766	2,269	8,893	D	38.1%	57.1%	40.0%	60.0%
98,764	NEVADA	45,657	22,545	20,740	2,372	1,805	R	49.4%	45.4%	52.1%	47.9%
3,010,232	ORANGE	879,937	499,878	328,663	51,396	171,215	R	56.8%	37.4%	60.3%	39.7%
348,432	PLACER	142,843	81,410	54,576	6,857	26,834	R	57.0%	38.2%	59.9%	40.1%
20,007	PLUMAS	9,203	5,168	3,444	591	1,724	R	56.2%	37.4%	60.0%	40.0%
2,189,641	RIVERSIDE	483,376	244,659	206,398	32,319	38,261	R	50.6%	42.7%	54.2%	45.8%
1,418,788	SACRAMENTO	422,308	162,369	239,599	20,340	77,230	D	38.4%	56.7%	40.4%	59.6%
55,269	SAN BENITO	16,117	6,993	8,304	820	1,311	D	43.4%	51.5%	45.7%	54.3%
2,035,210	SAN BERNARDINO	435,202	202,217	197,578	35,407	4,639	R	46.5%	45.4%	50.6%	49.4%
3,095,313	SAN DIEGO	908,222	452,205	399,845	56,172	52,360	R	49.8%	44.0%	53.1%	46.9%
805,235	SAN FRANCISCO	278,166	49,151	219,330	9,685	170,179	D	17.7%	78.8%	18.3%	81.7%
685,306	SAN JOAQUIN	158,867	71,999	77,623	9,245	5,624	D	45.3%	48.9%	48.1%	51.9%
269,637	SAN LUIS OBISPO	105,652	52,056	47,663	5,933	4,393	R	49.3%	45.1%	52.2%	47.8%
718,451	SAN MATEO	222,246	69,212	145,970	7,064	76,758	D	31.1%	65.7%	32.2%	67.8%
423,895	SANTA BARBARA	131,611	59,615	65,011	6,985	5,396	D	45.3%	49.4%	47.8%	52.2%
1,781,642	SANTA CLARA	512,358	178,695	314,022	19,641	135,327	D	34.9%	61.3%	36.3%	63.7%
262,382	SANTA CRUZ	96,251	24,390	67,107	4,754	42,717	D	25.3%	69.7%	26.7%	73.3%
177,223	SHASTA	65,276	39,702	20,797	4,777	18,905	R	60.8%	31.9%	65.6%	34.4%
3,240	SIERRA	1,827	1,042	635	150	407	R	57.0%	34.8%	62.1%	37.9%
44,900	SISKIYOU	18,378	9,839	7,274	1,265	2,565	R	53.5%	39.6%	57.5%	42.5%
413,344	SOLANO	118,390	43,323	69,597	5,470	26,274	D	36.6%	58.8%	38.4%	61.6%
483,878	SONOMA	184,050	55,472	119,079	9,499	63,607	D	30.1%	64.7%	31.8%	68.2%
514,453	STANISLAUS	120,330	60,084	52,510	7,736	7,574	R	49.9%	43.6%	53.4%	46.6%

CALIFORNIA
GOVERNOR 2010

2010 Census Population	County	Total Vote	Republican	Democratic	Other	Rep.-Dem. Plurality		Percentage Total Vote Rep.	Dem.	Major Vote Rep.	Dem.
94,737	SUTTER	25,597	14,346	9,614	1,637	4,732	R	56.0%	37.6%	59.9%	40.1%
63,463	TEHAMA	20,180	11,935	6,542	1,703	5,393	R	59.1%	32.4%	64.6%	35.4%
13,786	TRINITY	5,569	2,569	2,463	537	106	R	46.1%	44.2%	51.1%	48.9%
442,179	TULARE	81,597	46,261	30,607	4,729	15,654	R	56.7%	37.5%	60.2%	39.8%
55,365	TUOLUMNE	22,437	11,963	9,023	1,451	2,940	R	53.3%	40.2%	57.0%	43.0%
823,318	VENTURA	259,940	128,082	117,800	14,058	10,282	R	49.3%	45.3%	52.1%	47.9%
200,849	YOLO	59,894	19,456	37,894	2,544	18,438	D	32.5%	63.3%	33.9%	66.1%
72,155	YUBA	16,093	8,553	6,332	1,208	2,221	R	53.1%	39.3%	57.5%	42.5%
37,253,956	TOTAL	10,095,185	4,127,391	5,428,149	539,645	1,300,758	D	40.9%	53.8%	43.2%	56.8%

CALIFORNIA
SENATOR 2010

2010 Census Population	County	Total Vote	Republican	Democratic	Other	Rep.-Dem. Plurality		Percentage Total Vote Rep.	Dem.	Major Vote Rep.	Dem.
1,510,271	ALAMEDA	458,419	100,989	338,632	18,798	237,643	D	22.0%	73.9%	23.0%	77.0%
1,175	ALPINE	555	244	282	29	38	D	44.0%	50.8%	46.4%	53.6%
38,091	AMADOR	16,141	9,617	5,137	1,387	4,480	R	59.6%	31.8%	65.2%	34.8%
220,000	BUTTE	75,250	40,958	27,827	6,465	13,131	R	54.4%	37.0%	59.5%	40.5%
45,578	CALAVERAS	19,649	11,495	6,294	1,860	5,201	R	58.5%	32.0%	64.6%	35.4%
21,419	COLUSA	5,188	3,288	1,567	333	1,721	R	63.4%	30.2%	67.7%	32.3%
1,049,025	CONTRA COSTA	345,489	123,934	206,270	15,285	82,336	D	35.9%	59.7%	37.5%	62.5%
28,610	DEL NORTE	8,167	4,240	3,212	715	1,028	R	51.9%	39.3%	56.9%	43.1%
181,058	EL DORADO	76,760	46,771	25,085	4,904	21,686	R	60.9%	32.7%	65.1%	34.9%
930,450	FRESNO	199,498	113,583	74,705	11,210	38,878	R	56.9%	37.4%	60.3%	39.7%
28,122	GLENN	7,930	5,257	2,020	653	3,237	R	66.3%	25.5%	72.2%	27.8%
134,623	HUMBOLDT	49,671	18,659	27,081	3,931	8,422	D	37.6%	54.5%	40.8%	59.2%
174,528	IMPERIAL	26,627	9,887	14,802	1,938	4,915	D	37.1%	55.6%	40.0%	60.0%
18,546	INYO	6,962	3,909	2,353	700	1,556	R	56.1%	33.8%	62.4%	37.6%
839,631	KERN	171,712	106,448	51,364	13,900	55,084	R	62.0%	29.9%	67.5%	32.5%
152,982	KINGS	26,109	16,362	7,816	1,931	8,546	R	62.7%	29.9%	67.7%	32.3%
64,665	LAKE	20,954	8,534	10,265	2,155	1,731	D	40.7%	49.0%	45.4%	54.6%
34,895	LASSEN	9,198	6,127	2,200	871	3,927	R	66.6%	23.9%	73.6%	26.4%
9,818,605	LOS ANGELES	2,299,940	749,353	1,432,450	118,137	683,097	D	32.6%	62.3%	34.3%	65.7%
150,865	MADERA	34,046	21,413	10,308	2,325	11,105	R	62.9%	30.3%	67.5%	32.5%
252,409	MARIN	112,924	31,001	78,236	3,687	47,235	D	27.5%	69.3%	28.4%	71.6%
18,251	MARIPOSA	8,178	4,939	2,593	646	2,346	R	60.4%	31.7%	65.6%	34.4%
87,841	MENDOCINO	31,580	9,426	19,422	2,732	9,996	D	29.8%	61.5%	32.7%	67.3%
255,793	MERCED	47,426	25,280	19,058	3,088	6,222	R	53.3%	40.2%	57.0%	43.0%
9,686	MODOC	3,777	2,666	787	324	1,879	R	70.6%	20.8%	77.2%	22.8%

CALIFORNIA

SENATOR 2010

2010 Census Population	County	Total Vote	Republican	Democratic	Other	Rep.-Dem. Plurality		Percentage Total Vote Rep.	Dem.	Major Vote Rep.	Dem.
14,202	MONO	4,369	2,188	1,898	283	290	R	50.1%	43.4%	53.5%	46.5%
415,057	MONTEREY	99,203	34,721	58,574	5,908	23,853	D	35.0%	59.0%	37.2%	62.8%
136,484	NAPA	46,674	17,743	26,194	2,737	8,451	D	38.0%	56.1%	40.4%	59.6%
98,764	NEVADA	45,340	23,875	18,504	2,961	5,371	R	52.7%	40.8%	56.3%	43.7%
3,010,232	ORANGE	872,335	502,756	323,477	46,102	179,279	R	57.6%	37.1%	60.8%	39.2%
348,432	PLACER	141,268	84,905	47,331	9,032	37,574	R	60.1%	33.5%	64.2%	35.8%
20,007	PLUMAS	9,164	5,521	2,934	709	2,587	R	60.2%	32.0%	65.3%	34.7%
2,189,641	RIVERSIDE	481,044	255,738	195,418	29,888	60,320	R	53.2%	40.6%	56.7%	43.3%
1,418,788	SACRAMENTO	417,506	181,300	210,164	26,042	28,864	D	43.4%	50.3%	46.3%	53.7%
55,269	SAN BENITO	15,936	6,977	7,909	1,050	932	D	43.8%	49.6%	46.9%	53.1%
2,035,210	SAN BERNARDINO	434,370	216,441	185,164	32,765	31,277	R	49.8%	42.6%	53.9%	46.1%
3,095,313	SAN DIEGO	896,806	454,301	389,806	52,699	64,495	R	50.7%	43.5%	53.8%	46.2%
805,235	SAN FRANCISCO	266,578	43,108	213,252	10,218	170,144	D	16.2%	80.0%	16.8%	83.2%
685,306	SAN JOAQUIN	157,640	76,342	70,031	11,267	6,311	R	48.4%	44.4%	52.2%	47.8%
269,637	SAN LUIS OBISPO	104,906	53,695	44,799	6,412	8,896	R	51.2%	42.7%	54.5%	45.5%
718,451	SAN MATEO	220,522	65,803	146,537	8,182	80,734	D	29.8%	66.5%	31.0%	69.0%
423,895	SANTA BARBARA	130,266	58,817	64,771	6,678	5,954	D	45.2%	49.7%	47.6%	52.4%
1,781,642	SANTA CLARA	506,981	161,986	320,734	24,261	158,748	D	32.0%	63.3%	33.6%	66.4%
262,382	SANTA CRUZ	94,923	24,065	65,049	5,809	40,984	D	25.4%	68.5%	27.0%	73.0%
177,223	SHASTA	65,171	43,056	17,204	4,911	25,852	R	66.1%	26.4%	71.5%	28.5%
3,240	SIERRA	1,824	1,135	529	160	606	R	62.2%	29.0%	68.2%	31.8%
44,900	SISKIYOU	18,245	10,430	6,132	1,683	4,298	R	57.2%	33.6%	63.0%	37.0%
413,344	SOLANO	117,432	45,995	64,658	6,779	18,663	D	39.2%	55.1%	41.6%	58.4%
483,878	SONOMA	182,167	53,678	116,996	11,493	63,318	D	29.5%	64.2%	31.5%	68.5%
514,453	STANISLAUS	119,252	63,814	47,158	8,280	16,656	R	53.5%	39.5%	57.5%	42.5%
94,737	SUTTER	25,521	15,606	8,121	1,794	7,485	R	61.1%	31.8%	65.8%	34.2%
63,463	TEHAMA	20,166	12,950	5,352	1,864	7,598	R	64.2%	26.5%	70.8%	29.2%
13,786	TRINITY	5,478	2,813	2,029	636	784	R	51.4%	37.0%	58.1%	41.9%
442,179	TULARE	80,917	50,856	24,742	5,319	26,114	R	62.8%	30.6%	67.3%	32.7%
55,365	TUOLUMNE	22,290	13,057	7,430	1,803	5,627	R	58.6%	33.3%	63.7%	36.3%
823,318	VENTURA	257,996	128,619	115,337	14,040	13,282	R	49.9%	44.7%	52.7%	47.3%
200,849	YOLO	59,285	21,263	34,925	3,097	13,662	D	35.9%	58.9%	37.8%	62.2%
72,155	YUBA	16,135	9,452	5,212	1,471	4,240	R	58.6%	32.3%	64.5%	35.5%
37,253,956	TOTAL	9,999,860	4,217,386	5,218,137	564,337	1,000,751	D	42.2%	52.2%	44.7%	55.3%

CALIFORNIA

HOUSE OF REPRESENTATIVES

| | | | Republican | | | Democratic | | | | Percentage | | | |
| | | | | | | | | | | Total Vote | | Major Vote | |
CD	Year	Total Vote	Vote	Candidate	Vote	Candidate	Other Vote	Rep.-Dem. Plurality		Rep.	Dem.	Rep.	Dem.
1	2010	234,592	72,803	HANKS, LOREN	147,307	THOMPSON, MIKE*	14,482	74,504	D	31.0%	62.8%	33.1%	66.9%
1	2008	290,472	67,853	STARKEWOLF, ZANE	197,812	THOMPSON, MIKE*	24,807	129,959	D	23.4%	68.1%	25.5%	74.5%
1	2006	218,044	63,194	JONES, JOHN W.	144,409	THOMPSON, MIKE*	10,441	81,215	D	29.0%	66.2%	30.4%	69.6%
1	2004	282,971	79,970	WIESNER, LAWRENCE R.	189,366	THOMPSON, MIKE*	13,635	109,396	D	28.3%	66.9%	29.7%	70.3%
1	2002	185,216	60,013	WIESNER, LAWRENCE R.	118,669	THOMPSON, MIKE*	6,534	58,656	D	32.4%	64.1%	33.6%	66.4%
2	2010	228,940	130,837	HERGER, WALLY*	98,092	REED, JIM	11	32,745	R	57.1%	42.8%	57.2%	42.8%
2	2008	282,337	163,459	HERGER, WALLY*	118,878	MORRIS, JEFF		44,581	R	57.9%	42.1%	57.9%	42.1%
2	2006	210,202	134,911	HERGER, WALLY*	68,234	SEKHON, A.J.	7,057	66,677	R	64.2%	32.5%	66.4%	33.6%
2	2004	272,429	182,119	HERGER, WALLY*	90,310	JOHNSON, MIKE		91,809	R	66.9%	33.1%	66.9%	33.1%
2	2002	178,985	117,747	HERGER, WALLY*	52,455	JOHNSON, MIKE	8,783	65,292	R	65.8%	29.3%	69.2%	30.8%
3	2010	261,938	131,169	LUNGREN, DAN*	113,128	BERA, AMI	17,641	18,041	R	50.1%	43.2%	53.7%	46.3%
3	2008	314,046	155,424	LUNGREN, DAN*	137,971	DURSTON, BILL	20,651	17,453	R	49.5%	43.9%	53.0%	47.0%
3	2006	228,169	135,709	LUNGREN, DAN*	86,318	DURSTON, BILL	6,142	49,391	R	59.5%	37.8%	61.1%	38.9%
3	2004	287,073	177,738	LUNGREN, DAN	100,025	CASTILLO, GABE	9,310	77,713	R	61.9%	34.8%	64.0%	36.0%
3	2002	194,918	121,732	OSE, DOUG*	67,136	BEEMAN, HOWARD	6,050	54,596	R	62.5%	34.4%	64.5%	35.5%
4	2010	304,229	186,397	McCLINTOCK, TOM	95,653	CURTIS, CLINT	22,179	90,744	R	61.3%	31.4%	66.1%	33.9%
4	2008	369,780	185,790	McCLINTOCK, TOM	183,990	BROWN, CHARLIE		1,800	R	50.2%	49.8%	50.2%	49.8%
4	2006	276,893	135,818	DOOLITTLE, JOHN T.*	126,999	BROWN, CHARLIE	14,076	8,819	R	49.1%	45.9%	51.7%	48.3%
4	2004	339,369	221,926	DOOLITTLE, JOHN T.*	117,443	WINTERS, DAVID I.		104,483	R	65.4%	34.6%	65.4%	34.6%
4	2002	228,506	147,997	DOOLITTLE, JOHN T.*	72,860	NORBERG, MARK A.	7,649	75,137	R	64.8%	31.9%	67.0%	33.0%
5	2010	172,410	43,577	SMITH, PAUL A.	124,220	MATSUI, DORIS*	4,613	80,643	D	25.3%	72.0%	26.0%	74.0%
5	2008	221,155	46,002	SMITH, PAUL A.	164,242	MATSUI, DORIS*	10,911	118,240	D	20.8%	74.3%	21.9%	78.1%
5	2006	149,266	35,106	YAN, CLAIRE	105,676	MATSUI, DORIS*	8,484	70,570	D	23.5%	70.8%	24.9%	75.1%
5	2004	193,387	45,120	DUGAS, MIKE	138,004	MATSUI, ROBERT T.*	10,263	92,884	D	23.3%	71.4%	24.6%	75.4%
5	2002	131,578	34,749	FRANKHUIZEN, RICHARD	92,726	MATSUI, ROBERT T.*	4,103	57,977	D	26.4%	70.5%	27.3%	72.7%
6	2010	261,152	77,361	JUDD, JIM	172,216	WOOLSEY, LYNN*	11,575	94,855	D	29.6%	65.9%	31.0%	69.0%
6	2008	320,362	77,073	HALLIWELL, MIKE	229,672	WOOLSEY, LYNN*	13,617	152,599	D	24.1%	71.7%	25.1%	74.9%
6	2006	246,628	64,405	HOOPER, TODD	173,190	WOOLSEY, LYNN*	9,033	108,785	D	26.1%	70.2%	27.1%	72.9%
6	2004	311,667	85,244	ERICKSON, PAUL L.	226,423	WOOLSEY, LYNN*		141,179	D	27.4%	72.6%	27.4%	72.6%
6	2002	209,563	62,052	ERICKSON, PAUL L.	139,750	WOOLSEY, LYNN*	7,761	77,698	D	29.6%	66.7%	30.7%	69.3%
7	2010	178,916	56,798	TUBBS, RICK	122,118	MILLER, GEORGE*		65,320	D	31.7%	68.3%	31.7%	68.3%
7	2008	234,773	51,166	PETERSEN, ROGER ALLEN	170,962	MILLER, GEORGE*	12,645	119,796	D	21.8%	72.8%	23.0%	77.0%
7	2006	140,486		—	118,000	MILLER, GEORGE*	22,486	118,000	D		84.0%		100.0%
7	2004	219,277	52,446	HARGRAVE, CHARLES	166,831	MILLER, GEORGE*		114,385	D	23.9%	76.1%	23.9%	76.1%
7	2002	138,376	36,584	HARGRAVE, CHARLES	97,849	MILLER, GEORGE*	3,943	61,265	D	26.4%	70.7%	27.2%	72.8%
8	2020	209,696	31,711	DENNIS, JOHN	167,957	PELOSI, NANCY*	10,028	136,246	D	15.1%	80.1%	15.9%	84.1%
8	2008	285,247	27,614	WALSH, DANA	204,996	PELOSI, NANCY*	52,637	177,382	D	9.7%	71.9%	11.9%	88.1%
8	2006	184,639	19,800	DeNUNZIO, MIKE	148,435	PELOSI, NANCY*	16,404	128,635	D	10.7%	80.4%	11.8%	88.2%
8	2004	270,064	31,074	DEPALMA, JENNIFER	224,017	PELOSI, NANCY*	14,973	192,943	D	11.5%	82.9%	12.2%	87.8%
8	2002	160,441	20,063	GERMAN, G. MICHAEL	127,684	PELOSI, NANCY*	12,694	107,621	D	12.5%	79.6%	13.6%	86.4%
9	2010	214,085	23,054	HASHIMOTO, GERALD	180,400	LEE, BARBARA*	10,631	157,346	D	10.8%	84.3%	11.3%	88.7%
9	2008	277,600	26,917	HARGRAVE, CHARLES	238,915	LEE, BARBARA*	11,768	211,998	D	9.7%	86.1%	10.1%	89.9%
9	2006	193,686	20,786	den DULK, JOHN "J.D."	167,245	LEE, BARBARA*	5,655	146,459	D	10.7%	86.3%	11.1%	88.9%
9	2004	255,039	31,278	BERMUDEZ, CLAUDIA	215,630	LEE, BARBARA*	8,131	184,352	D	12.3%	84.5%	12.7%	87.3%
9	2002	166,917	25,333	UDINSKY, JERRY	135,893	LEE, BARBARA*	5,691	110,560	D	15.2%	81.4%	15.7%	84.3%

CALIFORNIA

HOUSE OF REPRESENTATIVES

| | | | Republican | | Democratic | | | Rep.-Dem. | | Percentage | | | |
| | | Total | | | | | | | | Total Vote | | Major Vote | |
CD	Year	Vote	Vote	Candidate	Vote	Candidate	Other Vote	Plurality		Rep.	Dem.	Rep.	Dem.
10	2010	233,806	88,512	CLIFT, GARY	137,578	GARAMENDI, JOHN*	7,716	49,066	D	37.9%	58.8%	39.1%	60.9%
10	2008	295,165	91,877	GERBER, NICHOLAS	192,226	TAUSCHER, ELLEN O.*	11,062	100,349	D	31.1%	65.1%	32.3%	67.7%
10	2006	196,978	66,069	LINN, DARCY	130,859	TAUSCHER, ELLEN O.*	50	64,790	D	33.5%	66.4%	33.5%	66.5%
10	2004	278,099	95,349	KETELSON, JEFF	182,750	TAUSCHER, ELLEN O.*		87,401	D	34.3%	65.7%	34.3%	65.7%
10	2002	167,197		—	126,390	TAUSCHER, ELLEN O.*	40,807	126,390	D		75.6%		100.0%
11	2010	240,503	112,703	HARMER, DAVID	115,361	McNERNEY, JERRY*	12,439	2,658	D	46.9%	48.0%	49.4%	50.6%
11	2008	297,616	133,104	ANDAL, DEAN	164,500	McNERNEY, JERRY*	12	31,396	D	44.7%	55.3%	44.7%	55.3%
11	2006	206,264	96,396	POMBO, RICHARD W.*	109,868	McNERNEY, JERRY		13,472	D	46.7%	53.3%	46.7%	53.3%
11	2004	267,169	163,582	POMBO, RICHARD W.*	103,587	McNERNEY, JERRY		59,995	R	61.2%	38.8%	61.2%	38.8%
11	2002	173,956	104,921	POMBO, RICHARD W.*	69,035	SHAW, ELAINE DUGGER		35,886	R	60.3%	39.7%	60.3%	39.7%
12	2010	201,162	44,475	MOLONEY, MIKE	152,044	SPEIER, JACKIE*	4,643	107,569	D	22.1%	75.6%	22.6%	77.4%
12	2008	266,853	49,258	CONLON, GREG	200,442	SPEIER, JACKIE*	17,153	151,184	D	18.5%	75.1%	19.7%	80.3%
12	2006	182,324	43,674	MOLONEY, MIKE	138,650	LANTOS, TOM*		94,976	D	24.0%	76.0%	24.0%	76.0%
12	2004	252,599	52,593	GARZA, MIKE	171,852	LANTOS, TOM*	28,154	119,259	D	20.8%	68.0%	23.4%	76.6%
12	2002	154,984	38,381	MOLONEY, MIKE	105,597	LANTOS, TOM*	11,006	67,216	D	24.8%	68.1%	26.7%	73.3%
13	2010	164,378	45,575	BAKER, FOREST	118,278	STARK, PETE*	525	72,703	D	27.7%	72.0%	27.8%	72.2%
13	2008	218,276	51,447	CHUI, RAYMOND	166,829	STARK, PETE*		115,382	D	23.6%	76.4%	23.6%	76.4%
13	2006	147,897	37,141	BRUNO, GEORGE I.	110,756	STARK, PETE*		73,615	D	25.1%	74.9%	25.1%	74.9%
13	2004	201,921	48,439	BRUNO, GEORGE I.	144,605	STARK, PETE*	8,877	96,166	D	24.0%	71.6%	25.1%	74.9%
13	2002	121,723	26,852	MAHMOOD, SYED R.	86,495	STARK, PETE*	8,376	59,643	D	22.1%	71.1%	23.7%	76.3%
14	2010	218,869	60,917	CHAPMAN, DAVE	151,217	ESHOO, ANNA G.*	6,735	90,300	D	27.8%	69.1%	28.7%	71.3%
14	2008	272,766	60,610	SANTANA, RONNY	190,301	ESHOO, ANNA G.*	21,855	129,691	D	22.2%	69.8%	24.2%	75.8%
14	2006	198,575	48,097	SMITH, ROB	141,153	ESHOO, ANNA G.*	9,325	93,056	D	24.2%	71.1%	25.4%	74.6%
14	2004	261,888	69,564	HAUGEN, CHRIS	182,712	ESHOO, ANNA G.*	9,612	113,148	D	26.6%	69.8%	27.6%	72.4%
14	2002	171,678	48,346	NIXON, JOSEPH H.	117,055	ESHOO, ANNA G.*	6,277	68,709	D	28.2%	68.2%	29.2%	70.8%
15	2010	186,615	60,468	KIRKLAND, SCOTT	126,147	HONDA, MICHAEL M.*		65,679	D	32.4%	67.6%	32.4%	67.6%
15	2008	238,589	55,489	CORDI, JOYCE STOER	170,977	HONDA, MICHAEL M.*	12,123	115,488	D	23.3%	71.7%	24.5%	75.5%
15	2006	159,718	44,186	CHUCKWU, RAYMOND L.	115,532	HONDA, MICHAEL M.*		71,346	D	27.7%	72.3%	27.7%	72.3%
15	2004	214,338	59,953	CHUCKWU, RAYMOND L.	154,385	HONDA, MICHAEL M.*		94,432	D	28.0%	72.0%	28.0%	72.0%
15	2002	133,022	41,251	HERMANN, LINDA RAE	87,482	HONDA, MICHAEL M.*	4,289	46,231	D	31.0%	65.8%	32.0%	68.0%
16	2010	156,058	37,913	SAHAGUN, DANIEL	105,841	LOFGREN, ZOE*	12,304	67,928	D	24.3%	67.8%	26.4%	73.6%
16	2008	205,327	49,399	WINSTON, CHAREL	146,481	LOFGREN, ZOE*	9,447	97,082	D	24.1%	71.3%	25.2%	74.8%
16	2006	136,059	37,130	WINSTON, CHAREL	98,929	LOFGREN, ZOE*		61,799	D	27.3%	72.7%	27.3%	72.7%
16	2004	182,281	47,992	McNEA, DOUGLAS ADAMS	129,222	LOFGREN, ZOE*	5,067	81,230	D	26.3%	70.9%	27.1%	72.9%
16	2002	107,986	32,182	McNEA, DOUGLAS ADAMS	72,370	LOFGREN, ZOE*	3,434	40,188	D	29.8%	67.0%	30.8%	69.2%
17	2010	178,139	53,176	TAYLOR, JEFF	118,734	FARR, SAM*	6,229	65,558	D	29.9%	66.7%	30.9%	69.1%
17	2008	228,626	59,037	TAYLOR, JEFF	168,907	FARR, SAM*	682	109,870	D	25.8%	73.9%	25.9%	74.1%
17	2006	159,293	35,932	DE MAIO, ANTHONY R.	120,750	FARR, SAM*	2,611	84,818	D	22.6%	75.8%	22.9%	77.1%
17	2004	223,225	65,117	RISLEY, MARK	148,958	FARR, SAM*	9,150	83,841	D	29.2%	66.7%	30.4%	69.6%
17	2002	149,296	40,334	ENGLER, CLINT C.	101,632	FARR, SAM*	7,330	61,298	D	27.0%	68.1%	28.4%	71.6%
18	2010	124,569	51,716	BERRYHILL, MICHAEL CLARE, SR.	72,853	CARDOZA, DENNIS*		21,137	D	41.5%	58.5%	41.5%	58.5%
18	2008	130,192		—	130,192	CARDOZA, DENNIS*		130,192	D		100.0%		100.0%
18	2006	108,713	37,531	KANNO, JOHN A.	71,182	CARDOZA, DENNIS*		33,651	D	34.5%	65.5%	34.5%	65.5%

CALIFORNIA

HOUSE OF REPRESENTATIVES

			Republican		Democratic			Rep.-Dem.		Percentage Total Vote		Major Vote	
CD	Year	Total Vote	Vote	Candidate	Vote	Candidate	Other Vote	Plurality		Rep.	Dem.	Rep.	Dem.
18	2004	153,705	49,973	PRINGLE, CHARLES F.	103,732	CARDOZA, DENNIS*		53,759	D	32.5%	67.5%	32.5%	67.5%
18	2002	109,593	47,528	MONTEITH, DICK	56,181	CARDOZA, DENNIS	5,884	8,653	D	43.4%	51.3%	45.8%	54.2%
19	2010	198,902	128,394	DENHAM, JEFF	69,912	GOODWIN, LORAINE	596	58,482	R	64.6%	35.1%	64.7%	35.3%
19	2008	182,101	179,245	RADANOVICH, GEORGE P.*		—	2,856	179,245	R	98.4%		100.0%	
19	2006	181,994	110,246	RADANOVICH, GEORGE P.*	71,748	COX, T.J.		38,498	R	60.6%	39.4%	60.6%	39.4%
19	2004	235,264	155,354	RADANOVICH, GEORGE P.*	64,047	BUFFORD, JAMES LEX	15,863	91,307	R	66.0%	27.2%	70.8%	29.2%
19	2002	157,802	106,209	RADANOVICH, GEORGE P.*	47,403	VEEN, JOHN	4,190	58,806	R	67.3%	30.0%	69.1%	30.9%
20	2010	89,444	43,197	VIDAK, ANDY	46,247	COSTA, JIM*		3,050	D	48.3%	51.7%	48.3%	51.7%
20	2008	125,141	32,118	LOPEZ, JIM	93,023	COSTA, JIM*		60,905	D	25.7%	74.3%	25.7%	74.3%
20	2006	61,120		—	61,120	COSTA, JIM*		61,120	D		100.0%		100.0%
20	2004	114,236	53,231	ASHBURN, ROY	61,005	COSTA, JIM		7,774	D	46.6%	53.4%	46.6%	53.4%
20	2002	74,770	25,628	MINUTH, ANDRE	47,627	DOOLEY, CAL*	1,515	21,999	D	34.3%	63.7%	35.0%	65.0%
21	2010	135,979	135,979	NUNES, DEVIN*		—		135,979	R	100.0%		100.0%	
21	2008	209,815	143,498	NUNES, DEVIN*	66,317	JOHNSON, LARRY		77,181	R	68.4%	31.6%	68.4%	31.6%
21	2006	142,661	95,214	NUNES, DEVIN*	42,718	HAZE, STEVEN	4,729	52,496	R	66.7%	29.9%	69.0%	31.0%
21	2004	192,315	140,721	NUNES, DEVIN*	51,594	DAVIS, FRED B.		89,127	R	73.2%	26.8%	73.2%	26.8%
21	2002	124,198	87,544	NUNES, DEVIN	32,584	LaPERE, DAVID G.	4,070	54,960	R	70.5%	26.2%	72.9%	27.1%
22	2010	175,663	173,490	McCARTHY, KEVIN*		—	2,173	173,490	R	98.8%		100.0%	
22	2008	224,549	224,549	McCARTHY, KEVIN*		—		224,549	R	100.0%		100.0%	
22	2006	188,504	133,278	McCARTHY, KEVIN	55,226	BEERY, SHARON M.		78,052	R	70.7%	29.3%	70.7%	29.3%
22	2004	209,384	209,384	THOMAS, BILL*		—		209,384	R	100.0%		100.0%	
22	2002	164,285	120,473	THOMAS, BILL*	38,988	CORVERA, JAIME	4,824	81,485	R	73.3%	23.7%	75.6%	24.4%
23	2010	193,463	72,744	WATSON, TOM	111,768	CAPPS, LOIS*	8,951	39,024	D	37.6%	57.8%	39.4%	60.6%
23	2008	251,788	80,385	KOKKONEN, MATT T.	171,403	CAPPS, LOIS*		91,018	D	31.9%	68.1%	31.9%	68.1%
23	2006	175,951	61,272	TOGNAZZINI, VICTOR D.	114,661	CAPPS, LOIS*	18	53,389	D	34.8%	65.2%	34.8%	65.2%
23	2004	244,297	83,926	REGAN, DON	153,980	CAPPS, LOIS*	6,391	70,054	D	34.4%	63.0%	35.3%	64.7%
23	2002	162,222	62,604	ROGERS, BETH	95,752	CAPPS, LOIS*	3,866	33,148	D	38.6%	59.0%	39.5%	60.5%
24	2010	240,334	144,055	GALLEGLY, ELTON*	96,279	ALLISON, TIMOTHY J.		47,776	R	59.9%	40.1%	59.9%	40.1%
24	2008	300,052	174,492	GALLEGLY, ELTON*	125,560	JORGENSEN, MARTA ANN		48,932	R	58.2%	41.8%	58.2%	41.8%
24	2006	209,292	129,812	GALLEGLY, ELTON*	79,461	MARTINEZ, JILL M.	19	50,351	R	62.0%	38.0%	62.0%	38.0%
24	2004	284,378	178,660	GALLEGLY, ELTON*	96,397	WAGNER, BRETT	9,321	82,263	R	62.8%	33.9%	65.0%	35.0%
24	2002	185,006	120,585	GALLEGLY, ELTON*	58,755	RUDIN, FERN	5,666	61,830	R	65.2%	31.8%	67.2%	32.8%
25	2010	191,336	118,308	McKEON, HOWARD P. "BUCK"*	73,028	CONAWAY, JACKIE		45,280	R	61.8%	38.2%	61.8%	38.2%
25	2008	250,589	144,660	McKEON, HOWARD P. "BUCK"*	105,929	CONAWAY, JACKIE		38,731	R	57.7%	42.3%	57.7%	42.3%
25	2006	156,773	93,987	McKEON, HOWARD P. "BUCK"*	55,913	RODRIGUEZ, ROBERT	6,873	38,074	R	60.0%	35.7%	62.7%	37.3%
25	2004	225,970	145,575	McKEON, HOWARD P. "BUCK"*	80,395	WILLOUGHBY, FRED "TIM"		65,180	R	64.4%	35.6%	64.4%	35.6%
25	2002	124,336	80,775	McKEON, HOWARD P. "BUCK"*	38,674	CONAWAY, BOB	4,887	42,101	R	65.0%	31.1%	67.6%	32.4%
26	2010	208,347	112,774	DREIER, DAVID*	76,093	WARNER, RUSS	19,480	36,681	R	54.1%	36.5%	59.7%	40.3%
26	2008	267,130	140,615	DREIER, DAVID*	108,039	WARNER, RUSS	18,476	32,576	R	52.6%	40.4%	56.6%	43.4%
26	2006	179,144	102,028	DREIER, DAVID*	67,878	MATTHEWS, CYNTHIA	9,238	34,150	R	57.0%	37.9%	60.0%	40.0%

CALIFORNIA

HOUSE OF REPRESENTATIVES

| | | | Republican | | Democratic | | | | | Percentage | | | |
| | | | | | | | | Rep.-Dem. | | Total Vote | | Major Vote | |
CD	Year	Total Vote	Vote	Candidate	Vote	Candidate	Other Vote	Plurality		Rep.	Dem.	Rep.	Dem.
26	2004	251,207	134,596	DREIER, DAVID*	107,522	MATTHEWS, CYNTHIA	9,089	27,074	R	53.6%	42.8%	55.6%	44.4%
26	2002	149,530	95,360	DREIER, DAVID*	50,081	MIKELS, MARJORIE MUSSER	4,089	45,279	R	63.8%	33.5%	65.6%	34.4%
27	2010	157,983	55,056	REED, MARK	102,927	SHERMAN, BRAD*		47,871	D	34.8%	65.2%	34.8%	65.2%
27	2008	212,835	52,852	SINGH, NAVRAJ	145,812	SHERMAN, BRAD*	14,171	92,960	D	24.8%	68.5%	26.6%	73.4%
27	2006	134,724	42,074	HANKWITZ, PETER	92,650	SHERMAN, BRAD*		50,576	D	31.2%	68.8%	31.2%	68.8%
27	2004	201,198	66,946	LEVY, ROBERT M.	125,296	SHERMAN, BRAD*	8,956	58,350	D	33.3%	62.3%	34.8%	65.2%
27	2002	128,811	48,996	LEVY, ROBERT M.	79,815	SHERMAN, BRAD*		30,819	D	38.0%	62.0%	38.0%	62.0%
28	2010	127,107	28,493	FROYD, MERLIN	88,385	BERMAN, HOWARD L.*	10,229	59,892	D	22.4%	69.5%	24.4%	75.6%
28	2008	137,621	—		137,471	BERMAN, HOWARD L.*	150	137,471	D		99.9%		100.0%
28	2006	108,042	20,629	KESSELMAN, STANLEY KIMMEL	79,866	BERMAN, HOWARD L.*	7,547	59,237	D	19.1%	73.9%	20.5%	79.5%
28	2004	162,510	37,868	HERNANDEZ, DAVID	115,303	BERMAN, HOWARD L.*	9,339	77,435	D	23.3%	71.0%	24.7%	75.3%
28	2002	103,326	23,926	HERNANDEZ, DAVID	73,771	BERMAN, HOWARD L.*	5,629	49,845	D	23.2%	71.4%	24.5%	75.5%
29	2010	161,126	51,534	COLBERT, JOHN P.	104,374	SCHIFF, ADAM B.*	5,218	52,840	D	32.0%	64.8%	33.1%	66.9%
29	2008	212,144	56,727	HAHN, CHARLES	146,198	SCHIFF, ADAM B.*	9,219	89,471	D	26.7%	68.9%	28.0%	72.0%
29	2006	143,404	39,321	BODELL, WILLIAM J.	91,014	SCHIFF, ADAM B.*	13,069	51,693	D	27.4%	63.5%	30.2%	69.8%
29	2004	206,832	62,871	SCOLINOS, HARRY FRANK	133,670	SCHIFF, ADAM B.*	10,291	70,799	D	30.4%	64.6%	32.0%	68.0%
29	2002	121,541	40,616	SCILEPPI, JIM	76,036	SCHIFF, ADAM B.*	4,889	35,420	D	33.4%	62.6%	34.8%	65.2%
30	2010	237,747	75,948	WILKERSON, CHARLES E.	153,663	WAXMAN, HENRY A.*	8,136	77,715	D	31.9%	64.6%	33.1%	66.9%
30	2008	242,792		—	242,792	WAXMAN, HENRY A.*		242,792	D		100.0%		100.0%
30	2006	211,734	55,904	JONES, DAVID NELSON	151,284	WAXMAN, HENRY A.*	4,546	95,380	D	26.4%	71.5%	27.0%	73.0%
30	2004	304,147	87,465	ELIZALDE, VICTOR	216,682	WAXMAN, HENRY A.*		129,217	D	28.8%	71.2%	28.8%	71.2%
30	2002	185,593	54,989	GOSS, TONY, D.	130,604	WAXMAN, HENRY A.*		75,615	D	29.6%	70.4%	29.6%	70.4%
31	2010	91,106	14,740	SMITH, STEPHEN	76,363	BECERRA, XAVIER*	3	61,623	D	16.2%	83.8%	16.2%	83.8%
31	2008	110,955		—	110,955	BECERRA, XAVIER*		110,955	D		100.0%		100.0%
31	2006	64,952		—	64,952	BECERRA, XAVIER*		64,952	D		100.0%		100.0%
31	2004	111,411	22,048	VEGA, LUIS	89,363	BECERRA, XAVIER*		67,315	D	19.8%	80.2%	19.8%	80.2%
31	2002	67,243	12,674	VEGA, LUIS	54,569	BECERRA, XAVIER*		41,895	D	18.8%	81.2%	18.8%	81.2%
32	2010	109,456	31,697	SCHMERLING, EDWARD	77,759	CHU, JUDY*		46,062	D	29.0%	71.0%	29.0%	71.0%
32	2008	130,150		—	130,142	SOLIS, HILDA L.*	8	130,142	D		100.0%		100.0%
32	2006	91,686		—	76,059	SOLIS, HILDA L.*	15,627	76,059	D		83.0%		100.0%
32	2004	140,146		—	119,144	SOLIS, HILDA L.*	21,002	119,144	D		85.0%		100.0%
32	2002	85,079	23,366	FISCHBECK, EMMA E.	58,530	SOLIS, HILDA L.*	3,183	35,164	D	27.5%	68.8%	28.5%	71.5%
33	2010	153,333	21,342	ANDION, JAMES L.	131,990	BASS, KAREN	1	110,648	D	13.9%	86.1%	13.9%	86.1%
33	2008	213,460	26,536	CROWLEY, DAVID C. II	186,924	WATSON, DIANE*		160,388	D	12.4%	87.6%	12.4%	87.6%
33	2004	113,715		—	113,715	WATSON, DIANE*		113,715	D		100.0%		100.0%
33	2004	188,314		—	166,801	WATSON, DIANE*	21,513	166,801	D		88.6%		100.0%
33	2002	118,449	16,699	KIM, ANDREW	97,779	WATSON, DIANE*	3,971	81,080	D	14.1%	82.5%	14.6%	85.4%
34	2010	89,839	20,457	MILLER, WAYNE	69,382	ROYBAL-ALLARD, LUCILLE*		48,925	D	22.8%	77.2%	22.8%	77.2%
34	2008	127,769	29,266	BALDING, CHRISTOPHER	98,503	ROYBAL-ALLARD, LUCILLE*		69,237	D	22.9%	77.1%	22.9%	77.1%
34	2006	74,819	17,359	MILLER, WAYNE	57,459	ROYBAL-ALLARD, LUCILLE*	1	40,100	D	23.2%	76.8%	23.2%	76.8%
34	2004	110,457	28,175	MILLER, WAYNE	82,282	ROYBAL-ALLARD, LUCILLE*		54,107	D	25.5%	74.5%	25.5%	74.5%
34	2002	65,824	17,090	MILLER, WAYNE	48,734	ROYBAL-ALLARD, LUCILLE*		31,644	D	26.0%	74.0%	26.0%	74.0%

CALIFORNIA

HOUSE OF REPRESENTATIVES

| | | | Republican | | Democratic | | | | | Percentage | | | |
| | | | | | | | | | | Total Vote | | Major Vote | |
CD	Year	Total Vote	Vote	Candidate	Vote	Candidate	Other Vote	Rep.-Dem. Plurality		Rep.	Dem.	Rep.	Dem.
35	2010	123,694	25,561	BROWN, K. BRUCE	98,131	WATERS, MAXINE*	2	72,570	D	20.7%	79.3%	20.7%	79.3%
35	2008	182,579	24,169	HAYES, TED	150,778	WATERS, MAXINE*	7,632	126,609	D	13.2%	82.6%	13.8%	86.2%
35	2006	98,506		—	82,498	WATERS, MAXINE*	16,008	82,498	D		83.7%		100.0%
35	2004	156,407	23,591	MOEN, ROSS	125,949	WATERS, MAXINE*	6,867	102,358	D	15.1%	80.5%	15.8%	84.2%
35	2002	93,407	18,094	MOEN, ROSS	72,401	WATERS, MAXINE*	2,912	54,307	D	19.4%	77.5%	20.0%	80.0%
36	2010	192,035	66,706	FEIN, MATTIE	114,489	HARMAN, JANE*	10,840	47,783	D	34.7%	59.6%	36.8%	63.2%
36	2008	250,491	78,543	GIBSON, BRIAN	171,948	HARMAN, JANE*		93,405	D	31.4%	68.6%	31.4%	68.6%
36	2006	166,153	53,068	GIBSON, BRIAN	105,323	HARMAN, JANE*	7,762	52,255	D	31.9%	63.4%	33.5%	66.5%
36	2004	244,044	81,666	WHITEHEAD, PAUL	151,208	HARMAN, JANE*	11,170	69,542	D	33.5%	62.0%	35.1%	64.9%
36	2002	143,751	50,328	JOHNSON, STUART	88,198	HARMAN, JANE*	5,225	37,870	D	35.0%	61.4%	36.3%	63.7%
37	2010	125,518	29,159	PARKER, STAR	85,799	RICHARDSON, LAURA*	10,560	56,640	D	23.2%	68.4%	25.4%	74.6%
37	2008	175,252		—	131,342	RICHARDSON, LAURA*	43,910	131,342	D		74.9%		100.0%
37	2006	97,962		—	80,716	MILLENDER-McDONALD, JUANITA*	17,246	80,716	D		82.4%		100.0%
37	2004	158,318	31,960	VAN, VERNON	118,823	MILLENDER-McDONALD, JUANITA*	7,535	86,863	D	20.2%	75.1%	21.2%	78.8%
37	2002	87,012	20,154	VELASCO, OSCAR A.	63,445	MILLENDER-McDONALD, JUANITA*	3,413	43,291	D	23.2%	72.9%	24.1%	75.9%
38	2010	116,342	30,883	VAUGHN, ROBERT	85,459	NAPOLITANO, GRACE F.*		54,576	D	26.5%	73.5%	26.5%	73.5%
38	2008	159,324		—	130,211	NAPOLITANO, GRACE F.*	29,113	130,211	D		81.7%		100.0%
38	2006	99,801	24,620	STREET, SIDNEY W.	75,181	NAPOLITANO, GRACE F.*		50,561	D	24.7%	75.3%	24.7%	75.3%
38	2004	116,851		—	116,851	NAPOLITANO, GRACE F.*		116,851	D		100.0%		100.0%
38	2002	88,027	23,126	BURROLA, ALEX A.	62,600	NAPOLITANO, GRACE F.*	2,301	39,474	D	26.3%	71.1%	27.0%	73.0%
39	2010	128,961	42,037	ANDRE, LARRY S.	81,590	SANCHEZ, LINDA T.*	5,334	39,553	D	32.6%	63.3%	34.0%	66.0%
39	2008	179,822	54,533	LENNING, DIANE A.	125,289	SANCHEZ, LINDA T.*		70,756	D	30.3%	69.7%	30.3%	69.7%
39	2006	109,533	37,384	ANDION, JAMES L.	72,149	SANCHEZ, LINDA T.*		34,765	D	34.1%	65.9%	34.1%	65.9%
39	2004	164,964	64,832	ESCOBAR, TIM	100,132	SANCHEZ, LINDA T.*		35,300	D	39.3%	60.7%	39.3%	60.7%
39	2002	95,346	38,925	ESCOBAR, TIM	52,256	SANCHEZ, LINDA T.	4,165	13,331	D	40.8%	54.8%	42.7%	57.3%
40	2010	178,855	119,455	ROYCE, ED*	59,400	AVALOS, CHRISTINA		60,055	R	66.8%	33.2%	66.8%	33.2%
40	2008	231,695	144,923	ROYCE, ED*	86,772	AVALOS, CHRISTINA		58,151	R	62.5%	37.5%	62.5%	37.5%
40	2006	151,289	100,995	ROYCE, ED*	46,418	HOFFMAN, FLORICE OREA	3,876	54,577	R	66.8%	30.7%	68.5%	31.5%
40	2004	217,301	147,617	ROYCE, ED*	69,684	WILLIAMS, J. TILMAN		77,933	R	67.9%	32.1%	67.9%	32.1%
40	2002	136,642	92,422	ROYCE, ED*	40,265	AVALOS, CHRISTINA	3,955	52,157	R	67.6%	29.5%	69.7%	30.3%
41	2010	202,286	127,857	LEWIS, JERRY*	74,394	MEAGHER, PAT	35	53,463	R	63.2%	36.8%	63.2%	36.8%
41	2008	258,700	159,486	LEWIS, JERRY*	99,214	PRINCE, TIM		60,272	R	61.6%	38.4%	61.6%	38.4%
41	2006	164,044	109,761	LEWIS, JERRY*	54,235	CONTRERAS, LOUIE A.	48	55,526	R	66.9%	33.1%	66.9%	33.1%
41	2004	218,937	181,605	LEWIS, JERRY*		—	37,332	181,605	R	82.9%		100.0%	
41	2002	135,533	91,326	LEWIS, JERRY*	40,155	JOHNSON, KEITH A.	4,052	51,171	R	67.4%	29.6%	69.5%	30.5%
42	2010	204,398	127,161	MILLER, GARY G.*	65,122	WILLIAMSON, MICHAEL	12,115	62,039	R	62.2%	31.9%	66.1%	33.9%
42	2008	263,313	158,404	MILLER, GARY G.*	104,909	CHAU, EDWIN "ED"		53,495	R	60.2%	39.8%	60.2%	39.8%
42	2006	129,720	129,720	MILLER, GARY G.*		—		129,720	R	100.0%		100.0%	

CALIFORNIA

HOUSE OF REPRESENTATIVES

CD	Year	Total Vote	Republican Vote	Republican Candidate	Democratic Vote	Democratic Candidate	Other Vote	Rep.-Dem. Plurality		Total Vote Rep.	Total Vote Dem.	Major Vote Rep.	Major Vote Dem.
42	2004	246,025	167,632	MILLER, GARY G.*	78,393	MYERS, LEWIS		89,239	R	68.1%	31.9%	68.1%	31.9%
42	2002	145,246	98,476	MILLER, GARY G.*	42,090	WALDRON, RICHARD	4,680	56,386	R	67.8%	29.0%	70.1%	29.9%
43	2010	106,916	36,890	FOLKENS, SCOTT	70,026	BACA, JOE*		33,136	D	34.5%	65.5%	34.5%	65.5%
43	2008	156,571	48,312	ROBERTS, JOHN	108,259	BACA, JOE*		59,947	D	30.9%	69.1%	30.9%	69.1%
43	2006	81,860	29,069	FOLKENS, SCOTT	52,791	BACA, JOE*		23,722	D	35.5%	64.5%	35.5%	64.5%
43	2004	130,834	44,004	LANING, ED	86,830	BACA, JOE*		42,826	D	33.6%	66.4%	33.6%	66.4%
43	2002	68,340	20,821	NEIGHBOR, WENDY C.	45,374	BACA, JOE*	2,145	24,553	D	30.5%	66.4%	31.5%	68.5%
44	2010	193,266	107,482	CALVERT, KEN*	85,784	HEDRICK, BILL		21,698	R	55.6%	44.4%	55.6%	44.4%
44	2008	253,827	129,937	CALVERT, KEN*	123,890	HEDRICK, BILL		6,047	R	51.2%	48.8%	51.2%	48.8%
44	2006	149,316	89,555	CALVERT, KEN*	55,275	VANDENBERG, LOUIS	4,486	34,280	R	60.0%	37.0%	61.8%	38.2%
44	2004	225,123	138,768	CALVERT, KEN*	78,796	VANDENBERG, LOUIS	7,559	59,972	R	61.6%	35.0%	63.8%	36.2%
44	2002	120,463	76,686	CALVERT, KEN*	38,021	VANDENBERG, LOUIS	5,756	38,665	R	63.7%	31.6%	66.9%	33.1%
45	2010	206,801	106,472	BONO MACK, MARY*	87,141	POUGNET, STEVE	13,188	19,331	R	51.5%	42.1%	55.0%	45.0%
45	2008	266,192	155,166	BONO MACK, MARY*	111,026	BORNSTEIN, JULIE		44,140	R	58.3%	41.7%	58.3%	41.7%
45	2006	164,251	99,638	BONO, MARY*	64,613	ROTH, DAVID		35,025	R	60.7%	39.3%	60.7%	39.3%
45	2004	230,490	153,523	BONO, MARY*	76,967	MEYER, RICHARD J.		76,556	R	66.6%	33.4%	66.6%	33.4%
45	2002	133,533	87,101	BONO, MARY*	43,692	KURPIEWSKI, ELLE K.	2,740	43,409	R	65.2%	32.7%	66.6%	33.4%
46	2010	224,782	139,822	ROHRABACHER, DANA*	84,940	ARNOLD, KEN	20	54,882	R	62.2%	37.8%	62.2%	37.8%
46	2008	285,277	149,818	ROHRABACHER, DANA*	122,891	COOK, DEBBIE	12,568	26,927	R	52.5%	43.1%	54.9%	45.1%
46	2006	195,052	116,176	ROHRABACHER, DANA*	71,573	BRANDT, JIM	7,303	44,603	R	59.6%	36.7%	61.9%	38.1%
46	2004	276,690	171,318	ROHRABACHER, DANA*	90,129	BRANDT, JIM	15,243	81,189	R	61.9%	32.6%	65.5%	34.5%
46	2002	176,265	108,807	ROHRABACHER, DANA*	60,890	SCHIPSKE, GERRIE	6,568	47,917	R	61.7%	34.5%	64.1%	35.9%
47	2010	95,954	37,679	TRAN, VAN	50,832	SANCHEZ, LORETTA*	7,443	13,153	D	39.3%	53.0%	42.6%	57.4%
47	2008	123,584	31,432	AVILA, ROSEMARIE "ROSIE"	85,878	SANCHEZ, LORETTA*	6,274	54,446	D	25.4%	69.5%	26.8%	73.2%
47	2006	75,619	28,485	NGUYEN, TAN	47,134	SANCHEZ, LORETTA*		18,649	D	37.7%	62.3%	37.7%	62.3%
47	2004	108,783	43,099	CORONADO, ALEXANDRIA A. "ALEX"	65,684	SANCHEZ, LORETTA*		22,585	D	39.6%	60.4%	39.6%	60.4%
47	2002	70,178	24,346	CHAVEZ, JEFF	42,501	SANCHEZ, LORETTA*	3,331	18,155	D	34.7%	60.6%	36.4%	63.6%
48	2010	242,719	145,481	CAMPBELL, JOHN*	88,465	KROM, BETH	8,773	57,016	R	59.9%	36.4%	62.2%	37.8%
48	2008	308,702	171,658	CAMPBELL, JOHN*	125,537	YOUNG, STEVE	11,507	46,121	R	55.6%	40.7%	57.8%	42.2%
48	2006	200,527	120,130	CAMPBELL, JOHN*	74,647	YOUNG, STEVE	5,750	45,483	R	59.9%	37.2%	61.7%	38.3%
48	2004	290,872	189,004	COX, CHRISTOPHER*	93,525	GRAHAM, JOHN	8,343	95,479	R	65.0%	32.2%	66.9%	33.1%
48	2002	179,549	122,884	COX, CHRISTOPHER*	51,058	GRAHAM, JOHN	5,607	71,826	R	68.4%	28.4%	70.6%	29.4%
49	2010	189,677	119,088	ISSA, DARRELL*	59,714	KATZ, HOWARD	10,875	59,374	R	62.8%	31.5%	66.6%	33.4%
49	2008	240,670	140,300	ISSA, DARRELL*	90,138	HAMILTON, ROBERT	10,232	50,162	R	58.3%	37.5%	60.9%	39.1%
49	2006	156,137	98,831	ISSA, DARRELL*	52,227	CRISCENZO, JEENI	5,079	46,604	R	63.3%	33.4%	65.4%	34.6%
49	2004	226,466	141,658	ISSA, DARRELL*	79,057	BYRON, MIKE	5,751	62,601	R	62.6%	34.9%	64.2%	35.8%
49	2002	122,497	94,594	ISSA, DARRELL*		—	27,903	94,594	R	77.2%		100.0%	
50	2010	251,081	142,247	BILBRAY, BRIAN P.*	97,818	BUSBY, FRANCINE	11,016	44,429	R	56.7%	39.0%	59.3%	40.7%
50	2008	313,502	157,502	BILBRAY, BRIAN P.*	141,635	LEIBHAM, NICK	14,365	15,867	R	50.2%	45.2%	52.7%	47.3%
50	2006	222,102	118,018	BILBRAY, BRIAN P.*	96,612	BUSBY, FRANCINE	7,472	21,406	R	53.1%	43.5%	55.0%	45.0%
50	2004	289,328	169,025	CUNNINGHAM, RANDY "DUKE"*	105,590	BUSBY, FRANCINE	14,713	63,435	R	58.4%	36.5%	61.5%	38.5%
50	2002	172,701	111,095	CUNNINGHAM, RANDY "DUKE"*	55,855	STEWART, DEL G.	5,751	55,240	R	64.3%	32.3%	66.5%	33.5%

CALIFORNIA

CD	Year	Total Vote	Republican Vote	Republican Candidate	Democratic Vote	Democratic Candidate	Other Vote	Rep.-Dem. Plurality		Total Vote Rep.	Total Vote Dem.	Major Vote Rep.	Major Vote Dem.
51	2010	143,916	57,488	POPADITCH, NICK	86,423	FILNER, BOB*	5	28,935	D	39.9%	60.1%	39.9%	60.1%
51	2008	203,825	49,345	JOY, DAVID LEE	148,281	FILNER, BOB*	6,199	98,936	D	24.2%	72.7%	25.0%	75.0%
51	2006	115,839	34,931	MILES, BLAKE L.	78,114	FILNER, BOB*	2,794	43,183	D	30.2%	67.4%	30.9%	69.1%
51	2004	180,879	63,526	GIORGINO, MICHAEL	111,441	FILNER, BOB*	5,912	47,915	D	35.1%	61.6%	36.3%	63.7%
51	2002	102,787	40,430	GARCIA, MARIA GUADALUPE	59,541	FILNER, BOB*	2,816	19,111	D	39.3%	57.9%	40.4%	59.6%
52	2010	221,062	139,460	HUNTER, DUNCAN D.*	70,870	LUTZ, RAY	10,732	68,590	R	63.1%	32.1%	66.3%	33.7%
52	2008	285,138	160,724	HUNTER, DUNCAN D.	111,051	LUMPKIN, MIKE	13,363	49,673	R	56.4%	38.9%	59.1%	40.9%
52	2006	191,369	123,696	HUNTER, DUNCAN*	61,208	RINALDI, JOHN	6,465	62,488	R	64.6%	32.0%	66.9%	33.1%
52	2004	271,438	187,799	HUNTER, DUNCAN*	74,857	KELIHER, BRIAN S.	8,782	112,942	R	69.2%	27.6%	71.5%	28.5%
52	2002	169,010	118,561	HUNTER, DUNCAN*	43,526	MOORE-KOCHLACS, PETER	6,923	75,035	R	70.2%	25.8%	73.1%	26.9%
53	2010	168,328	57,230	CRIMMINS, MICHAEL	104,800	DAVIS, SUSAN A.*	6,298	47,570	D	34.0%	62.3%	35.3%	64.7%
53	2008	235,542	64,658	CRIMMINS, MICHAEL	161,315	DAVIS, SUSAN A.*	9,569	96,657	D	27.5%	68.5%	28.6%	71.4%
53	2006	144,387	43,312	WOODRUM, JOHN "WOODY"	97,541	DAVIS, SUSAN A.*	3,534	54,229	D	30.0%	67.6%	30.7%	69.3%
53	2004	221,436	63,897	HUNZEKER, DARIN	146,449	DAVIS, SUSAN A.*	11,090	82,552	D	28.9%	66.1%	30.4%	69.6%
53	2002	116,180	43,891	VanDeWEGHE, BILL	72,252	DAVIS, SUSAN A.*	37	28,361	D	37.8%	62.2%	37.8%	62.2%
TOTAL	2010	9,647,813	4,195,528		5,148,511		303,774	952,983	D	43.5%	53.4%	44.9%	55.1%
TOTAL	2008	12,322,079	4,515,372		7,377,725		428,982	2,862,353	D	36.6%	59.9%	38.0%	62.0%
TOTAL	2006	8,295,816	3,314,398		4,720,164		261,254	1,405,766	D	40.0%	56.9%	41.3%	58.7%
TOTAL	2004	11,623,753	5,030,821		6,223,698		369,234	1,192,877	D	43.3%	53.5%	44.7%	55.3%
TOTAL	2002	7,258,417	3,225,666		3,731,081		301,670	505,415	D	44.4%	51.4%	46.4%	53.6%

CALIFORNIA

GENERAL AND PRIMARY ELECTIONS

2010 GENERAL ELECTIONS

Governor   Other vote was 166,312 American Independent (Chelene Nightingale); 150,895 Libertarian (Dale F. Ogden); 129,224 Green (Laura Wells); 92,851 Peace and Freedom (Carlos Alvarez); 285 write-in (Cassandra A. Lieurance); 43 write-in (Lea Sherman); 13 write-in (Rakesh Kumar Christian); 8 write-in (Nadia B. Smalley); 4 write-in (Hugh Bagley); 4 write-in (Rowan Millar); 4 write-in (Jacob Vangelisti); 2 write-in (Anselmo A. Chavez).

Senator   Other vote was 175,235 Libertarian (Gail K. Lightfoot); 135,088 Peace and Freedom (Marsha Feinland); 128,512 Green (Duane Roberts); 125,435 American Independent (Edward C. Noonan); 41 write-in (James E. Harris); 11 write-in (Connor Vlakancic); 10 write-in (Jerry Leon Carroll); 5 write-in (Hans J. Kugler).

House   Other vote was:

CD 1	8,486 Green (Carol Wolman); 5,996 Libertarian (Mike Rodrigues).
CD 2	11 write-in (Mark A. Jensen).
CD 3	6,577 American Independent (Jerry L. Leidecker); 6,275 Libertarian (Douglas Arthur Tuma); 4,789 Peace and Freedom (Mike Roskey).
CD 4	22,179 Green (Benjamin Emery).
CD 5	4,594 Peace and Freedom (Gerald Allen Frink); 19 write-in (Tony Lacy).
CD 6	5,915 Peace and Freedom (Eugene E. Ruyle); 5,660 Libertarian (Joel Smolen).
CD 7	
CD 8	5,161 Peace and Freedom (Gloria E. La Riva); 4,843 Libertarian (Philip Berg); 24 write-in (Summer Shields).
CD 9	4,848 Green (Dave Heller); 4,113 Libertarian (James Eyer); 1,670 Peace and Freedom (Larry Allen).
CD 10	7,716 Green (Jeremy Cloward).
CD 11	12,439 American Independent (David Christensen).
CD 12	4,611 Libertarian (Mark Paul Williams); 32 write-in (Joseph Michael Harding).
CD 13	525 write-in (Chris Pareja).
CD 14	6,735 Libertarian (Paul Lazaga).
CD 15	
CD 16	12,304 Libertarian (Edward Gonzalez).
CD 17	3,397 Green (Eric Petersen); 2,742 Libertarian (Mary V. Larkin); 90 write-in (Ronald P. Kabat).
CD 18	
CD 19	596 write-in (Les Marsden).
CD 20	
CD 21	
CD 22	2,173 write-in (John Uebersax).
CD 23	5,625 Independent (John V. Hager); 3,326 Libertarian (Darrell M. Stafford).
CD 24	
CD 25	
CD 26	12,784 American Independent (David L. Miller); 6,696 Libertarian (Randall Weissbuch).
CD 27	
CD 28	10,229 Libertarian (Carlos A. Rodriguez).
CD 29	5,218 Libertarian (William P. Cushing).
CD 30	5,021 Libertarian (Erich D. Miller); 3,115 Peace and Freedom (Richard R. Castaldo).
CD 31	3 write-in (Sal Genovese).
CD 32	
CD 33	1 write-in (Mervin Leon Evans).
CD 34	
CD 35	2 write-in (Suleiman Charles Edmondson).
CD 36	10,840 Libertarian (Herb Peters).
CD 37	10,560 Independent (Nicholas Dibs).
CD 38	
CD 39	5,334 American Independent (John A. Smith).
CD 40	
CD 41	35 write-in (Pamela Zander).
CD 42	12,115 Libertarian (Mark Lambert).

CALIFORNIA

GENERAL AND PRIMARY ELECTIONS

CD 43
CD 44
CD 45   13,188 American Independent (Bill Lussenheide).
CD 46   20 write-in (Jay Shah).
CD 47   7,443 Independent (Cecilia "Ceci" Iglesias).
CD 48   8,773 Libertarian (Mike Binkley).
CD 49   6,585 American Independent (Dion Clark); 4,290 Libertarian (Mike Paster).
CD 50   5,546 Libertarian (Lars Grossmith); 5,470 Peace and Freedom (Miriam E. Clark).
CD 51   5 write-in (Marcus Jay Shapiro).
CD 52   10,732 Libertarian (Michael Benoit).
CD 53   6,298 Libertarian (Paul Dekker).

2010 PRIMARY ELECTIONS

Primary   June 8, 2010   Registration   Democratic   7,553,109
                                   (as of May 24, 2010)   Republican   5,228,320
                                                          American Independent   397,136
                                                          Green   112,655
                                                          Libertarian   86,675
                                                          Peace and Freedom   56,587
                                                          Other   118,799
                                                          Decline to State   3,423,750

                                                          TOTAL   16,977,031

Primary Type   Semi-open—Registered Democrats and Republicans could vote only in their party's primary. Voters not registered with a recognized party (i.e., Decline to State) could cast a ballot in either party's primary.

CALIFORNIA

GENERAL AND PRIMARY ELECTIONS

	REPUBLICAN PRIMARIES			**DEMOCRATIC PRIMARIES**		
Governor	Meg Whitman	1,529,534	64.3%	Edmund G. Brown, Jr.	2,021,189	84.4%
	Steve Poizner	632,940	26.6%	Richard William Aguirre	95,596	4.0%
	Lawrence "Larry" Naritelli	54,202	2.3%	Charles "Chuck" Pineda, Jr.	94,669	4.0%
	Robert C. Newman II	38,462	1.6%	Vibert Greene	54,225	2.3%
	Ken Miller	36,609	1.5%	Joe Symmon	54,122	2.3%
	Bill Chambers	34,243	1.4%	Lowell Darling	39,930	1.7%
	Douglas R. Hughes	26,085	1.1%	Peter Schurman	35,450	1.5%
	David Tully-Smith	24,978	1.1%	Nadia B. Smalley (write-in)	106	
	Steven Paul Mozena (write-in)	26				
	TOTAL	*2,377,079*		*TOTAL*	*2,395,287*	
Senator	Carly Fiorina	1,315,429	56.4%	Barbara Boxer*	1,957,920	80.9%
	Tom Campbell	504,289	21.6%	Brian Quintana	338,442	14.0%
	Chuck DeVore	452,577	19.4%	Robert M. "Mickey" Kaus	123,573	5.1%
	Al Ramirez	42,149	1.8%			
	Tim Kalemkarian	19,598	0.8%			
	TOTAL	*2,334,042*		*TOTAL*	*2,419,935*	
Congressional District 1	Loren Hanks	28,155	60.5%	Mike Thompson*	74,695	100.0%
	Randy Franck	18,383	39.5%			
	TOTAL	*46,538*				

CALIFORNIA

GENERAL AND PRIMARY ELECTIONS

	REPUBLICAN PRIMARIES			DEMOCRATIC PRIMARIES		
Congressional District 2	Wally Herger*	57,272	65.3%	Jim Reed	42,334	100.0%
	Pete Stiglich	30,487	34.7%			
	TOTAL	*87,759*				
Congressional District 3	Dan Lungren*	71,918	100.0%	Ami Bera	49,022	100.0%
Congressional District 4	Tom McClintock*	89,443	78.5%	Clint Curtis	50,400	100.0%
	Michael Babich	24,528	21.5%			
	TOTAL	*113,971*				
Congressional District 5	Paul A. Smith	14,588	56.7%	Doris Matsui*	56,762	100.0%
	Erik Smitt	11,148	43.3%			
	TOTAL	*25,736*				
Congressional District 6	Jim Judd	27,770	67.9%	Lynn Woolsey*	92,204	100.0%
	Michael Halliwell	13,136	32.1%	Michael J. Halliwell (write-in)	11	
	TOTAL	*40,906*		*TOTAL*	*92,215*	
Congressional District 7	Rick Tubbs	15,245	57.1%	George Miller*	52,210	85.0%
	Roger Allen Petersen	6,242	23.4%	John Fitzgerald	9,188	15.0%
	Virginia Fuller	3,662	13.7%			
	Eugene Ray	1,564	5.9%			
	TOTAL	*26,713*		*TOTAL*	*61,398*	
Congressional District 8	John Dennis	7,013	54.9%	Nancy Pelosi*	77,175	100.0%
	Dana Walsh	5,766	45.1%			
	TOTAL	*12,779*				
Congressional District 9	Gerald Hashimoto	10,067	100.0%	Barbara Lee*	82,951	100.0%
Congressional District 10	Gary Clift	25,331	54.6%	John Garamendi*	62,138	100.0%
	Buddy Burke	21,060	45.4%			
	TOTAL	*46,391*				
Congressional District 11	David Harmer	24,626	36.4%	Jerry McNerney*	48,772	100.0%
	Brad Goehring	18,300	27.1%			
	Antonio C. "Tony" Amador	13,355	19.8%			
	Elizabeth Emken	11,306	16.7%			
	TOTAL	*67,587*				
Congressional District 12	Mike Moloney	20,460	97.3%	Jackie Speier*	64,770	100.0%
	Michael Douglas Parker (write-in)	576	2.7%			
	TOTAL	*21,036*				
Congressional District 13	Forest Baker	10,591	54.5%	Pete Stark*	48,603	84.3%
	Luis Garcia	8,831	45.5%	Justin Jelincic	9,021	15.7%
	TOTAL	*19,422*		*TOTAL*	*57,624*	
Congressional District 14	Dave Chapman	17,783	53.0%	Anna G. Eshoo*	66,978	100.0%
	Ronny Santana	15,783	47.0%			
	TOTAL	*33,566*				
Congressional District 15	Scott Kirkland	12,992	38.8%	Michael M. Honda*	57,662	100.0%
	Don Barich	12,314	36.8%			
	Raymond L. Chukwu	8,200	24.5%			
	TOTAL	*33,506*				

CALIFORNIA

GENERAL AND PRIMARY ELECTIONS

	REPUBLICAN PRIMARIES			DEMOCRATIC PRIMARIES		
Congressional District 16	Daniel Sahagun (write-in)	2,935	91.1%	Zoe Lofgren*	48,757	100.0%
	Edward Gonzalez (write-in)	285	8.9%			
	TOTAL	3,220				
Congressional District 17	Jeff Taylor	17,790	61.1%	Sam Farr*	52,689	88.8%
	Gary Richard Arnold	6,192	21.3%	Arthur V. Dunn	6,653	11.2%
	Pete Andresen	5,125	17.6%			
	Michael Robert Le Barre (write-in)	12				
	TOTAL	29,119		TOTAL	59,342	
Congressional District 18	Michael Clare Berryhill, Sr.	23,978	100.0%	Dennis Cardoza*	28,748	100.0%
Congressional District 19	Jeff Denham	26,594	36.3%	Loraine Goodwin	20,452	52.6%
	Jim Patterson	22,355	30.5%	Les Marsden	18,457	47.4%
	Richard Pombo	15,196	20.7%			
	Larry Westerlund	9,126	12.5%			
	TOTAL	73,271		TOTAL	38,909	
Congressional District 20	Andy Vidak	13,770	70.3%	Jim Costa*	19,599	79.3%
	Richard Lake	4,347	22.2%	Steve Haze	5,122	20.7%
	Serafin Quintanar	1,471	7.5%			
	TOTAL	19,588		TOTAL	24,721	
Congressional District 21	Devin Nunes*	55,299	100.0%	Ruben Macareno received 367 write-in votes but no Democratic candidate appeared on the general election ballot.		
Congressional District 22	Kevin McCarthy*	77,140	100.0%	No Democratic candidate		
Congressional District 23	Tom Watson	15,108	36.1%	Lois Capps*	52,305	100.0%
	John A. Davidson	9,429	22.5%			
	Dave Stockdale	7,044	16.8%			
	Clark Vandeventer	6,670	15.9%			
	Carole Lee Miller	3,626	8.7%			
	TOTAL	41,877				
Congressional District 24	Elton Gallegly*	71,041	100.0%	Timothy J. Allison	19,832	47.4%
				Marie T. Panec	12,526	29.9%
				Shawn Stern	9,494	22.7%
				TOTAL	41,852	
Congressional District 25	Howard P. "Buck" McKeon*	47,544	100.0%	Jackie Conaway	23,546	100.0%
Congressional District 26	David Dreier*	42,400	72.3%	Russ Warner	28,951	100.0%
	Mark Butler	16,220	27.7%			
	TOTAL	58,620				
Congressional District 27	Mark Reed	14,172	54.6%	Brad Sherman*	31,724	100.0%
	Navraj Singh	11,772	45.4%			
	TOTAL	25,944				
Congressional District 28	Merlin Froyd	10,732	100.0%	Howard L. Berman*	26,092	83.4%
				Richard A. Valdez	5,203	16.6%
				TOTAL	31,295	

CALIFORNIA

GENERAL AND PRIMARY ELECTIONS

	REPUBLICAN PRIMARIES			DEMOCRATIC PRIMARIES		
Congressional District 29	John P. Colbert	24,172	100.0%	Adam B. Schiff*	31,832	100.0%
Congressional District 30	Charles E. Wilkerson	10,270	32.6%	Henry A. Waxman*	55,952	100.0%
	David Benning	10,231	32.4%			
	Ari David	4,321	13.7%			
	Robert A. Flutie	4,264	13.5%			
	Chris Kolski	2,444	7.8%			
	TOTAL	31,530				
Congressional District 31	Stephen C. Smith	5,256	100.0%	Xavier Becerra*	20,550	88.0%
				Sal Genovese	2,795	12.0%
				TOTAL	23,345	
Congressional District 32	Edwrad Schmerling	11,567	100.0%	Judy Chu*	21,718	100.0%
Congressional District 33	James L. Andion	3,785	51.3%	Karen Bass	41,250	85.3%
	David C. Crowley, II	1,956	26.5%	Felton Newell	3,096	6.4%
	Phil Jennerjahn	1,627	22.0%	Morris F. Griffin	2,075	4.3%
	Luis Montoya (write-in)	11	0.1%	Nick Juan Mostert	1,937	4.0%
	TOTAL	7,379		TOTAL	48,358	
Congressional District 34	Wayne Miller	7,042	100.0%	Lucille Roybal-Allard*	14,309	70.7%
				David Sanchez	5,917	29.3%
				TOTAL	20,226	
Congressional District 35	Ted Hayes	5,686	100.0%	Maxine Waters*	36,685	100.0%
Congressional District 36	Mattie Fein	16,679	50.2%	Jane Harman*	27,146	59.1%
	Pete Kesterson	14,254	42.9%	Marcy Winograd	18,792	40.9%
	Andrew J. Sharp	2,278	6.9%			
	TOTAL	33,211		TOTAL	45,938	
Congressional District 37	Star Parker	9,894	100.0%	Laura Richardson*	22,574	67.3%
				Peter Mathews	6,144	18.3%
				Lee Davis	2,848	8.5%
				Terrance Ponchak	1,955	5.8%
				TOTAL	33,521	
Congressional District 38	Robert Vaughn	10,324	99.8%	Grace F. Napolitano*	22,447	100.0%
	Chris Smith (write-in)	17	0.2%			
	TOTAL	10,341				
Congressional District 39	Larry S. Andre	17,062	100.0%	Linda T. Sanchez*	23,125	100.0%
Congressional District 40	Ed Royce*	55,351	100.0%	Christina Avalos	25,518	100.0%
Congressional District 41	Jerry Lewis*	42,462	66.3%	Pat Meagher	30,159	100.0%
	Eric R. Stone	21,607	33.7%			
	TOTAL	64,069				
Congressional District 42	Gary G. Miller*	32,669	48.8%	Michael Williamson	23,366	100.0%
	Phil Liberatore	25,181	37.6%			
	Lee McGroarty	7,113	10.6%			
	David Su	2,041	3.0%			
	TOTAL	67,004				
Congressional District 43	Scott Folkens	13,232	100.0%	Joe Baca*	18,529	100.0%

CALIFORNIA

GENERAL AND PRIMARY ELECTIONS

	REPUBLICAN PRIMARIES			DEMOCRATIC PRIMARIES		
Congressional District 44	Ken Calvert*	37,327	66.3%	Bill Hedrick	27,283	100.0%
	Chris Riggs	18,994	33.7%			
	TOTAL	56,321				
Congressional District 45	Mary Bono Mack*	42,981	70.6%	Steve Pougnet	33,235	100.0%
	Clayton Thibodeau	17,940	29.4%			
	TOTAL	60,921				
Congressional District 46	Dana Rohrabacher*	67,156	100.0%	Ken Arnold	19,735	58.7%
				Jay A. Shah	13,875	41.3%
				TOTAL	33,610	
Congressional District 47	Van Tran	10,706	54.6%	Loretta Sanchez*	17,409	100.0%
	Katherine H. Smith	5,017	25.6%			
	Tan Nguyen	3,876	19.8%			
	TOTAL	19,599				
Congressional District 48	John Campbell*	72,658	100.0%	Beth Krom	30,818	100.0%
Congressional District 49	Darrell Issa*	60,447	100.0%	Howard Katz	25,948	100.0%
Congressional District 50	Brian P. Bilbray*	72,605	100.0%	Francine Busby	29,926	66.1%
				Tracy Emblem	15,370	33.9%
				TOTAL	45,296	
Congressional District 51	Nick Popaditch	27,286	100.0%	Bob Filner*	40,628	100.0%
Congressional District 52	Duncan D. Hunter	72,506	90.8%	Ray Lutz	24,639	71.3%
	Terri R. Linnell	7,355	9.2%	Connie Frankowiak	9,936	28.7%
	TOTAL	79,861		TOTAL	34,575	
Congressional District 53	Michael Crimmins	10,780	34.4%	Susan A. Davis*	42,976	100.0%
	Matt Friedman	7,251	23.2%			
	Mari Hamlin Fink	6,751	21.6%			
	C. Mason Weaver	6,527	20.8%			
	TOTAL	31,309				

An asterisk (*) denotes incumbent.

COLORADO

Congressional districts first established for elections held in 2002
7 members

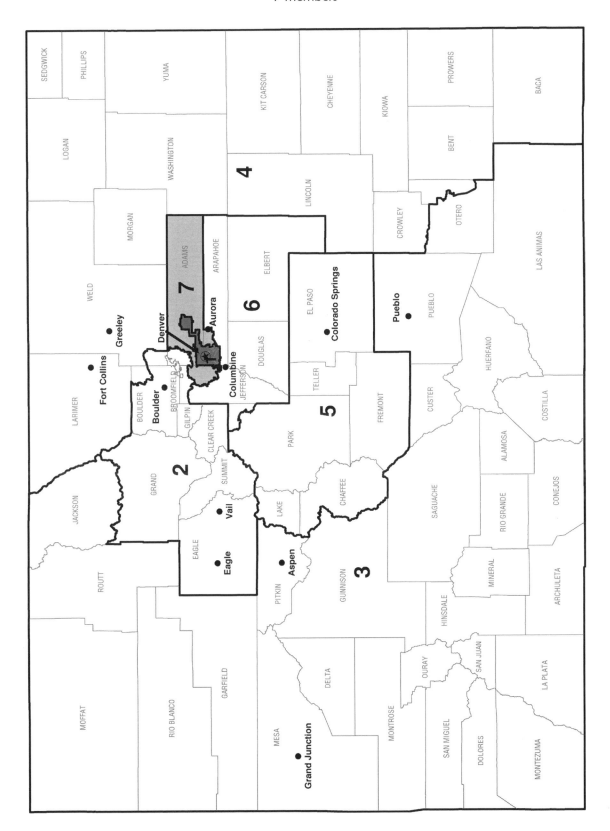

COLORADO

Denver Area

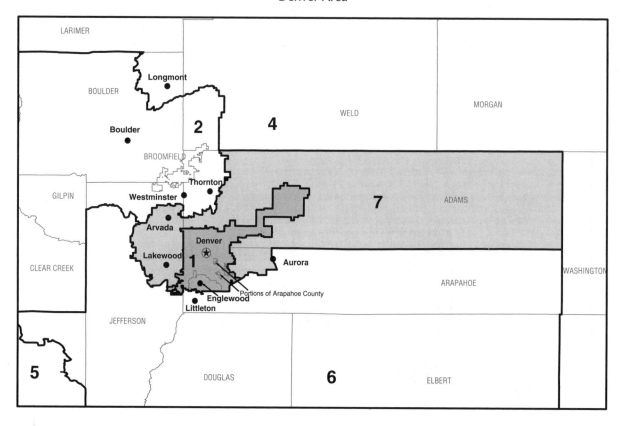

COLORADO

GOVERNOR
John Hickenlooper (D). Elected 2010 to a four-year term.

SENATORS (2 Democrats)
Michael F. Bennet (D). Elected 2010 to a six-year term. Sworn in as senator January 22, 2009, to fill the vacancy created by the resignation of Ken Salazar (D) to become U.S. Secretary of Interior.

Mark Udall (D). Elected 2008 to a six-year term.

REPRESENTATIVES (4 Republicans, 3 Democrats)
1. Diana DeGette (D)
2. Jared Polis (D)
3. Scott Tipton (R)
4. Cory Gardner (R)
5. Doug Lamborn (R)
6. Mike Coffman (R)
7. Ed Perlmutter (D)

POSTWAR VOTE FOR PRESIDENT

		Republican		Democratic		Other	Rep.-Dem.	Total Vote		Major Vote	
Year	Total Vote	Vote	Candidate	Vote	Candidate	Vote	Plurality	Rep.	Dem.	Rep.	Dem.
2008	2,401,462	1,073,629	McCain, John	1,288,633	Obama, Barack	39,200	215,004 D	44.7%	53.7%	45.4%	54.6%
2004	2,130,330	1,101,255	Bush, George W.	1,001,732	Kerry, John	27,343	99,523 R	51.7%	47.0%	52.4%	47.6%
2000**	1,741,368	883,748	Bush, George W.	738,227	Gore, Al	119,393	145,521 R	50.8%	42.4%	54.5%	45.5%
1996**	1,510,704	691,848	Dole, Bob	671,152	Clinton, Bill	147,704	20,696 R	45.8%	44.4%	50.8%	49.2%
1992**	1,569,180	562,850	Bush, George	629,681	Clinton, Bill	376,649	66,831 D	35.9%	40.1%	47.2%	52.8%
1988	1,372,394	728,177	Bush, George	621,453	Dukakis, Michael S.	22,764	106,724 R	53.1%	45.3%	54.0%	46.0%
1984	1,295,380	821,817	Reagan, Ronald	454,975	Mondale, Walter F.	18,588	366,842 R	63.4%	35.1%	64.4%	35.6%
1980**	1,184,415	652,264	Reagan, Ronald	367,973	Carter, Jimmy	164,178	284,291 R	55.1%	31.1%	63.9%	36.1%
1976	1,081,554	584,367	Ford, Gerald R.	460,353	Carter, Jimmy	36,834	124,014 R	54.0%	42.6%	55.9%	44.1%
1972	953,884	597,189	Nixon, Richard M.	329,980	McGovern, George S.	26,715	267,209 R	62.6%	34.6%	64.4%	35.6%
1968**	811,199	409,345	Nixon, Richard M.	335,174	Humphrey, Hubert H.	66,680	74,171 R	50.5%	41.3%	55.0%	45.0%
1964	776,986	296,767	Goldwater, Barry M.	476,024	Johnson, Lyndon B.	4,195	179,257 D	38.2%	61.3%	38.4%	61.6%
1960	736,236	402,242	Nixon, Richard M.	330,629	Kennedy, John F.	3,365	71,613 R	54.6%	44.9%	54.9%	45.1%
1956	657,074	394,479	Eisenhower, Dwight D.	257,997	Stevenson, Adlai E.	4,598	136,482 R	60.0%	39.3%	60.5%	39.5%
1952	630,103	379,782	Eisenhower, Dwight D.	245,504	Stevenson, Adlai E.	4,817	134,278 R	60.3%	39.0%	60.7%	39.3%
1948	515,237	239,714	Dewey, Thomas E.	267,288	Truman, Harry S.	8,235	27,574 D	46.5%	51.9%	47.3%	52.7%

**In past elections, the other vote included: 2000 - 91,434 Green (Ralph Nader); 1996 - 99,629 Reform (Ross Perot); 1992 - 366,010 Independent (Perot); 1980 - 130,633 Independent (John Anderson); 1968 - 60,813 American Independent (George Wallace).

COLORADO

POSTWAR VOTE FOR GOVERNOR

Year	Total Vote	Republican Vote	Candidate	Democratic Vote	Candidate	Other Vote	Rep.-Dem. Plurality	Total Vote Rep.	Total Vote Dem.	Major Vote Rep.	Major Vote Dem.
2010**	1,787,730	199,792	Maes, Dan	915,436	Hickenlooper, John	677,920	263,060 D	11.1%	51.0%	17.9%	82.1%
2006	1,558,387	625,886	Beauprez, Bob	888,096	Ritter, Bill Jr.	44,405	262,210 D	40.2%	57.0%	41.3%	58.7%
2002	1,412,602	884,583	Owens, Bill	475,373	Heath, Rollie	52,646	409,210 R	62.6%	33.7%	65.0%	35.0%
1998	1,321,307	648,202	Owens, Bill	639,905	Schoettler, Gail	33,200	8,297 R	49.1%	48.4%	50.3%	49.7%
1994	1,116,307	432,042	Benson, Bruce	619,205	Romer, Roy	65,060	187,163 D	38.7%	55.5%	41.1%	58.9%
1990	1,011,272	358,403	Andrews, John	626,032	Romer, Roy	26,837	267,629 D	35.4%	61.9%	36.4%	63.6%
1986	1,058,928	434,420	Strickland, Ted	616,325	Romer, Roy	8,183	181,905 D	41.0%	58.2%	41.3%	58.7%
1982	956,021	302,740	Fuhr, John D.	627,960	Lamm, Richard D.	25,321	325,220 D	31.7%	65.7%	32.5%	67.5%
1978	823,807	317,292	Strickland, Ted	483,985	Lamm, Richard D.	22,530	166,693 D	38.5%	58.7%	39.6%	60.4%
1974	828,968	378,698	Vanderhoof, John D.	441,408	Lamm, Richard D.	8,862	62,710 D	45.7%	53.2%	46.2%	53.8%
1970	668,496	350,690	Love, John A.	302,432	Hogan, Mark	15,374	48,258 R	52.5%	45.2%	53.7%	46.3%
1966	660,063	356,730	Love, John A.	287,132	Knous, Robert L.	16,201	69,598 R	54.0%	43.5%	55.4%	44.6%
1962	616,481	349,342	Love, John A.	262,890	McNichols, Stephen	4,249	86,452 R	56.7%	42.6%	57.1%	42.9%
1958**	549,808	228,643	Burch, Palmer L.	321,165	McNichols, Stephen		92,522 D	41.6%	58.4%	41.6%	58.4%
1956	645,233	313,950	Brotzman, Donald G.	331,283	McNichols, Stephen		17,333 D	48.7%	51.3%	48.7%	51.3%
1954	489,540	227,335	Brotzman, Donald G.	262,205	Johnson, Ed C.		34,870 D	46.4%	53.6%	46.4%	53.6%
1952	613,034	349,924	Thornton, Dan	260,044	Metzger, John W.	3,066	89,880 R	57.1%	42.4%	57.4%	42.6%
1950	450,994	236,472	Thornton, Dan	212,976	Johnson, Walter	1,546	23,496 R	52.4%	47.2%	52.6%	47.4%
1948	501,680	168,928	Hamil, David A.	332,752	Knous, William Lee		163,824 D	33.7%	66.3%	33.7%	66.3%
1946	335,087	160,483	Lavington, Leon E.	174,604	Knous, William Lee		14,121 D	47.9%	52.1%	47.9%	52.1%

**In past elections, the other vote included: 2010 - 651,232 American Constitution (Tom Tancredo). The term of office of Colorado's Governor was increased from two to four years effective with the 1958 election.

POSTWAR VOTE FOR SENATOR

Year	Total Vote	Republican Vote	Candidate	Democratic Vote	Candidate	Other Vote	Rep.-Dem. Plurality	Total Vote Rep.	Total Vote Dem.	Major Vote Rep.	Major Vote Dem.
2010	1,777,668	824,789	Buck, Ken	854,685	Bennet, Michael F.	98,194	28,859 D	46.4%	48.1%	49.1%	50.9%
2008	2,331,712	990,784	Schaffer, Bob	1,231,049	Udall, Mark	109,879	240,239 D	42.5%	52.8%	44.6%	55.4%
2004	2,107,554	980,668	Coors, Pete	1,081,188	Salazar, Ken	45,698	100,520 D	46.5%	51.3%	47.6%	52.4%
2002	1,416,082	717,893	Allard, Wayne	648,130	Strickland, Tom	50,059	69,763 R	50.7%	45.8%	52.6%	47.4%
1998	1,327,235	829,370	Campbell, Ben Nighthorse	464,754	Lamm, Dottie	33,111	364,616 R	62.5%	35.0%	64.1%	35.9%
1996	1,469,611	750,325	Allard, Wayne	677,600	Strickland, Tom	41,686	72,725 R	51.1%	46.1%	52.5%	47.5%
1992	1,552,289	662,893	Considine, Terry	803,725	Campbell, Ben Nighthorse	85,671	140,832 D	42.7%	51.8%	45.2%	54.8%
1990	1,022,027	569,048	Brown, Hank	425,746	Heath, Josie	27,233	143,302 R	55.7%	41.7%	57.2%	42.8%
1986	1,060,765	512,994	Kramer, Ken	529,449	Wirth, Timothy E.	18,322	16,455 D	48.4%	49.9%	49.2%	50.8%
1984	1,297,809	833,821	Armstrong, William L.	449,327	Dick, Nancy	14,661	384,494 R	64.2%	34.6%	65.0%	35.0%
1980	1,173,646	571,295	Buchanan, Mary E.	590,501	Hart, Gary W.	11,850	19,206 D	48.7%	50.3%	49.2%	50.8%
1978	819,150	480,596	Armstrong, William L.	330,247	Haskell, Floyd K.	8,307	150,349 R	58.7%	40.3%	59.3%	40.7%
1974	824,166	325,508	Dominick, Peter H.	471,691	Hart, Gary W.	26,967	146,183 D	39.5%	57.2%	40.8%	59.2%
1972	926,093	447,957	Allott, Gordon	457,545	Haskell, Floyd K.	20,591	9,588 D	48.4%	49.4%	49.5%	50.5%
1968	785,536	459,952	Dominick, Peter H.	325,584	McNichols, Stephen		134,368 R	58.6%	41.4%	58.6%	41.4%
1966	634,898	368,307	Allott, Gordon	266,259	Romer, Roy	332	102,048 R	58.0%	41.9%	58.0%	42.0%
1962	613,444	328,655	Dominick, Peter H.	279,586	Carroll, John A.	5,203	49,069 R	53.6%	45.6%	54.0%	46.0%
1960	727,633	389,428	Allott, Gordon	334,854	Knous, Robert L.	3,351	54,574 R	53.5%	46.0%	53.8%	46.2%
1956	636,974	317,102	Thornton, Dan	319,872	Carroll, John A.		2,770 D	49.8%	50.2%	49.8%	50.2%
1954	484,188	248,502	Allott, Gordon	235,686	Carroll, John A.		12,816 R	51.3%	48.7%	51.3%	48.7%
1950	450,176	239,734	Millikin, Eugene D.	210,442	Carroll, John A.		29,292 R	53.3%	46.7%	53.3%	46.7%
1948	510,121	165,069	Nicholson, W. F.	340,719	Johnson, Ed C.	4,333	175,650 D	32.4%	66.8%	32.6%	67.4%

COLORADO

GOVERNOR 2010

2010 Census Population	County	Total Vote	Republican	Democratic	Amer. Const. (Tancredo)	Other	Plurality		Percentage of Total Vote Rep.	Dem.	Amer. Const.
441,603	ADAMS	112,112	9,851	55,805	44,738	1,718	11,067	D	8.8%	49.8%	39.9%
15,445	ALAMOSA	4,977	887	2,910	1,079	101	1,831	D	17.8%	58.5%	21.7%
572,003	ARAPAHOE	195,860	15,011	104,147	76,702	0	27,445	D	7.7%	53.2%	39.2%
12,084	ARCHULETA	5,138	1,554	2,133	1,329	122	579	D	30.2%	41.5%	25.9%
3,788	BACA	1,960	512	667	738	43	71	A	26.1%	34.0%	37.7%
6,499	BENT	1,611	314	743	521	33	222	D	19.5%	46.1%	32.3%
294,567	BOULDER	125,486	6,772	87,878	29,368	1,468	58,510	D	5.4%	70.0%	23.4%
55,889	BROOMFIELD	22,898	1,987	11,996	8,666	249	3,330	D	8.7%	52.4%	37.8%
17,809	CHAFFEE	8,474	1,339	4,331	2,708	96	1,623	D	15.8%	51.1%	32.0%
1,836	CHEYENNE	961	195	237	520	9	283	A	20.3%	24.7%	54.1%
9,088	CLEAR CREEK	4,594	278	2,538	1,724	54	814	D	6.1%	55.2%	37.5%
8,256	CONEJOS	3,125	598	1,747	738	42	1,009	D	19.1%	55.9%	23.6%
3,524	COSTILLA	1,443	174	1,032	237	0	795	D	12.1%	71.5%	16.4%
5,823	CROWLEY	1,307	245	517	510	35	7	D	18.7%	39.6%	39.0%
4,255	CUSTER	2,271	478	796	952	45	156	A	21.0%	35.1%	41.9%
30,952	DELTA	13,121	3,158	4,469	5,176	318	707	A	24.1%	34.1%	39.4%
600,158	DENVER	191,853	8,068	142,645	39,009	2,131	103,636	D	4.2%	74.4%	20.3%
2,064	DOLORES	1,013	366	337	283	27	29	R	36.1%	33.3%	27.9%
285,465	DOUGLAS	116,952	12,918	46,914	56,093	1,027	9,179	A	11.0%	40.1%	48.0%
52,197	EAGLE	14,594	2,168	8,557	3,632	237	4,925	D	14.9%	58.6%	24.9%
23,086	ELBERT	11,017	1,156	2,761	6,993	107	4,232	A	10.5%	25.1%	63.5%
622,263	EL PASO	194,454	35,160	72,107	83,580	3,607	11,473	A	18.1%	37.1%	43.0%
46,824	FREMONT	16,051	3,436	5,832	6,371	412	539	A	21.4%	36.3%	39.7%
56,389	GARFIELD	17,951	3,242	8,624	5,780	305	2,844	D	18.1%	48.0%	32.2%
5,441	GILPIN	2,632	176	1,373	1,083	0	290	D	6.7%	52.2%	41.1%
14,843	GRAND	6,577	831	3,196	2,463	87	733	D	12.6%	48.6%	37.4%
15,324	GUNNISON	6,319	1,023	3,859	1,331	106	2,528	D	16.2%	61.1%	21.1%
843	HINSDALE	581	139	291	141	10	150	D	23.9%	50.1%	24.3%
6,711	HUERFANO	2,956	476	1,628	801	51	827	D	16.1%	55.1%	27.1%
1,394	JACKSON	769	175	302	279	13	23	D	22.8%	39.3%	36.3%
534,543	JEFFERSON	228,576	15,419	116,120	94,375	2,662	21,745	D	6.7%	50.8%	41.3%
1,398	KIOWA	765	167	204	374	20	170	A	21.8%	26.7%	48.9%
8,270	KIT CARSON	3,016	589	941	1,450	36	509	A	19.5%	31.2%	48.1%
7,310	LAKE	2,207	192	1,243	734	38	509	D	8.7%	56.3%	33.3%
51,334	LA PLATA	20,392	5,186	10,869	3,875	462	5,683	D	25.4%	53.3%	19.0%
299,630	LARIMER	125,601	13,813	64,538	45,397	1,853	19,141	D	11.0%	51.4%	36.1%
15,507	LAS ANIMAS	5,526	902	3,075	1,420	129	1,655	D	16.3%	55.6%	25.7%
5,467	LINCOLN	1,883	296	502	1,064	21	562	A	15.7%	26.7%	56.5%
22,709	LOGAN	7,576	1,210	2,697	3,547	122	850	A	16.0%	35.6%	46.8%
146,723	MESA	54,549	9,870	19,869	23,316	1,494	3,447	A	18.1%	36.4%	42.7%
712	MINERAL	583	138	306	127	12	168	D	23.7%	52.5%	21.8%
13,795	MOFFAT	4,612	1,393	1,021	2,092	106	699	A	30.2%	22.1%	45.4%
25,535	MONTEZUMA	9,605	3,644	3,570	2,146	245	74	R	37.9%	37.2%	22.3%
41,276	MONTROSE	15,822	4,079	5,459	5,893	391	434	A	25.8%	34.5%	37.2%
28,159	MORGAN	8,249	1,025	2,789	4,332	103	1,543	A	12.4%	33.8%	52.5%
18,831	OTERO	6,416	1,286	2,894	2,121	115	773	D	20.0%	45.1%	33.1%
4,436	OURAY	2,607	483	1,430	655	39	775	D	18.5%	54.9%	25.1%
16,206	PARK	7,584	809	3,006	3,657	112	651	A	10.7%	39.6%	48.2%
4,442	PHILLIPS	1,957	363	647	931	16	284	A	18.5%	33.1%	47.6%
17,148	PITKIN	7,257	943	5,258	954	102	4,304	D	13.0%	72.5%	13.1%
12,551	PROWERS	3,767	712	1,388	1,621	46	233	A	18.9%	36.8%	43.0%
159,063	PUEBLO	53,730	6,608	30,862	15,414	846	15,448	D	12.3%	57.4%	28.7%
6,666	RIO BLANCO	2,589	890	578	1,076	45	186	A	34.4%	22.3%	41.6%
11,982	RIO GRANDE	4,460	892	2,107	1,384	77	723	D	20.0%	47.2%	31.0%
23,509	ROUTT	4,324	683	2,685	904	52	1,781	D	15.8%	62.1%	20.9%

COLORADO

GOVERNOR 2010

2010 Census Population	County	Total Vote	Republican	Democratic	Amer. Const. (Tancredo)	Other	Plurality		Percentage of Total Vote		
									Rep.	Dem.	Amer. Const.
6,108	SAGUACHE	2,407	398	1,482	460	67	1,022	D	16.5%	61.6%	19.1%
699	SAN JUAN	458	79	267	90	22	177	D	17.2%	58.3%	19.7%
7,359	SAN MIGUEL	3,004	402	2,160	372	70	1,758	D	13.4%	71.9%	12.4%
2,379	SEDGWICK	1,119	199	466	432	22	34	D	17.8%	41.6%	38.6%
27,994	SUMMIT	10,070	919	6,455	2,571	125	3,884	D	9.1%	64.1%	25.5%
23,350	TELLER	9,827	1,995	3,168	4,503	161	1,335	A	20.3%	32.2%	45.8%
4,814	WASHINGTON	2,307	375	533	1,377	22	844	A	16.3%	23.1%	59.7%
252,825	WELD	79,818	9,652	32,056	37,149	961	5,093	A	12.1%	40.2%	46.5%
10,043	YUMA	3,910	764	1,172	1,933	41	761	A	19.5%	30.0%	49.4%
5,029,196	TOTAL	1,767,604	199,792	915,436	652,376	0	263,060	D	11.3%	51.8%	36.9%

Counties carried by Tom Tancredo of the American Constitution Party are indicated by an "A." The plurality represents the vote differential between the leading candidate and the runner-up, regardless of party.

COLORADO

SENATOR 2010

2010 Census Population	County	Total Vote	Republican	Democratic	Other	Rep.-Dem. Plurality		Percentage			
								Total Vote		Major Vote	
								Rep.	Dem.	Rep.	Dem.
441,603	ADAMS	111,081	47,446	55,601	8,034	8,155	D	42.7%	50.1%	46.0%	54.0%
15,445	ALAMOSA	4,918	1,977	2,656	285	679	D	40.2%	54.0%	42.7%	57.3%
572,003	ARAPAHOE	196,374	88,957	97,240	10,177	8,283	D	45.3%	49.5%	47.8%	52.2%
12,084	ARCHULETA	5,143	2,875	1,952	316	923	R	55.9%	38.0%	59.6%	40.4%
3,788	BACA	1,929	1,248	548	133	700	R	64.7%	28.4%	69.5%	30.5%
6,499	BENT	1,585	811	652	122	159	R	51.2%	41.1%	55.4%	44.6%
294,567	BOULDER	125,265	35,450	84,264	5,551	48,814	D	28.3%	67.3%	29.6%	70.4%
55,889	BROOMFIELD	22,643	10,382	11,034	1,227	652	D	45.9%	48.7%	48.5%	51.5%
17,809	CHAFFEE	8,376	3,892	3,936	548	44	D	46.5%	47.0%	49.7%	50.3%
1,836	CHEYENNE	943	696	187	60	509	R	73.8%	19.8%	78.8%	21.2%
9,088	CLEAR CREEK	4,561	1,876	2,385	300	509	D	41.1%	52.3%	44.0%	56.0%
8,256	CONEJOS	3,068	1,312	1,625	131	313	D	42.8%	53.0%	44.7%	55.3%
3,524	COSTILLA	1,447	348	1,004	95	656	D	24.0%	69.4%	25.7%	74.3%
5,823	CROWLEY	1,299	717	474	108	243	R	55.2%	36.5%	60.2%	39.8%
4,255	CUSTER	2,274	1,453	680	141	773	R	63.9%	29.9%	68.1%	31.9%
30,952	DELTA	12,985	8,025	3,932	1,028	4,093	R	61.8%	30.3%	67.1%	32.9%
600,158	DENVER	190,117	46,148	135,793	8,176	89,645	D	24.3%	71.4%	25.4%	74.6%
2,064	DOLORES	987	576	334	77	242	R	58.4%	33.8%	63.3%	36.7%
285,465	DOUGLAS	115,834	69,971	41,013	4,850	28,958	R	60.4%	35.4%	63.0%	37.0%
52,197	EAGLE	14,526	5,998	7,707	821	1,709	D	41.3%	53.1%	43.8%	56.2%
23,086	ELBERT	10,861	7,573	2,647	641	4,926	R	69.7%	24.4%	74.1%	25.9%
622,263	EL PASO	193,817	116,803	66,162	10,852	50,641	R	60.3%	34.1%	63.8%	36.2%
46,824	FREMONT	15,872	9,334	5,185	1,353	4,149	R	58.8%	32.7%	64.3%	35.7%
56,389	GARFIELD	17,771	8,423	8,062	1,286	361	R	47.4%	45.4%	51.1%	48.9%
5,441	GILPIN	2,659	1,100	1,358	201	258	D	41.4%	51.1%	44.8%	55.2%

COLORADO
SENATOR 2010

2010 Census Population	County	Total Vote	Republican	Democratic	Other	Rep.-Dem. Plurality		Percentage			
								Total Vote		Major Vote	
								Rep.	Dem.	Rep.	Dem.
14,843	GRAND	6,477	3,257	2,795	425	462	R	50.3%	43.2%	53.8%	46.2%
15,324	GUNNISON	6,260	2,377	3,435	448	1,058	D	38.0%	54.9%	40.9%	59.1%
843	HINSDALE	573	314	225	34	89	R	54.8%	39.3%	58.3%	41.7%
6,711	HUERFANO	2,910	1,205	1,530	175	325	D	41.4%	52.6%	44.1%	55.9%
1,394	JACKSON	728	433	218	77	215	R	59.5%	29.9%	66.5%	33.5%
534,543	JEFFERSON	225,247	103,657	108,954	12,636	5,297	D	46.0%	48.4%	48.8%	51.2%
1,398	KIOWA	756	532	181	43	351	R	70.4%	23.9%	74.6%	25.4%
8,270	KIT CARSON	2,941	2,012	740	189	1,272	R	68.4%	25.2%	73.1%	26.9%
7,310	LAKE	2,165	790	1,208	167	418	D	36.5%	55.8%	39.5%	60.5%
51,334	LA PLATA	20,493	9,301	10,327	865	1,026	D	45.4%	50.4%	47.4%	52.6%
299,630	LARIMER	123,676	56,954	59,456	7,266	2,502	D	46.1%	48.1%	48.9%	51.1%
15,507	LAS ANIMAS	5,466	2,286	2,842	338	556	D	41.8%	52.0%	44.6%	55.4%
5,467	LINCOLN	1,843	1,234	482	127	752	R	67.0%	26.2%	71.9%	28.1%
22,709	LOGAN	7,422	4,483	2,390	549	2,093	R	60.4%	32.2%	65.2%	34.8%
146,723	MESA	54,510	32,971	17,522	4,017	15,449	R	60.5%	32.1%	65.3%	34.7%
712	MINERAL	570	270	247	53	23	R	47.4%	43.3%	52.2%	47.8%
13,795	MOFFAT	4,556	3,080	1,104	372	1,976	R	67.6%	24.2%	73.6%	26.4%
25,535	MONTEZUMA	9,561	5,648	3,349	564	2,299	R	59.1%	35.0%	62.8%	37.2%
41,276	MONTROSE	15,748	9,885	4,627	1,236	5,258	R	62.8%	29.4%	68.1%	31.9%
28,159	MORGAN	8,099	4,732	2,847	520	1,885	R	58.4%	35.2%	62.4%	37.6%
18,831	OTERO	6,337	3,277	2,633	427	644	R	51.7%	41.5%	55.4%	44.6%
4,436	OURAY	2,602	1,164	1,295	143	131	D	44.7%	49.8%	47.3%	52.7%
16,206	PARK	7,499	4,089	2,848	562	1,241	R	54.5%	38.0%	58.9%	41.1%
4,442	PHILLIPS	1,932	1,274	555	103	719	R	65.9%	28.7%	69.7%	30.3%
17,148	PITKIN	7,324	1,951	5,091	282	3,140	D	26.6%	69.5%	27.7%	72.3%
12,551	PROWERS	3,696	2,271	1,182	243	1,089	R	61.4%	32.0%	65.8%	34.2%
159,063	PUEBLO	53,395	22,031	28,779	2,585	6,748	D	41.3%	53.9%	43.4%	56.6%
6,666	RIO BLANCO	2,531	1,883	480	168	1,403	R	74.4%	19.0%	79.7%	20.3%
11,982	RIO GRANDE	4,414	2,291	1,871	252	420	R	51.9%	42.4%	55.0%	45.0%
23,509	ROUTT	4,283	1,709	2,374	200	665	D	39.9%	55.4%	41.9%	58.1%
6,108	SAGUACHE	2,376	838	1,382	156	544	D	35.3%	58.2%	37.7%	62.3%
699	SAN JUAN	446	177	234	35	57	D	39.7%	52.5%	43.1%	56.9%
7,359	SAN MIGUEL	3,015	766	2,064	185	1,298	D	25.4%	68.5%	27.1%	72.9%
2,379	SEDGWICK	1,084	592	397	95	195	R	54.6%	36.6%	59.9%	40.1%
27,994	SUMMIT	10,003	3,713	5,832	458	2,119	D	37.1%	58.3%	38.9%	61.1%
23,350	TELLER	9,770	6,249	2,982	539	3,267	R	64.0%	30.5%	67.7%	32.3%
4,814	WASHINGTON	2,253	1,619	470	164	1,149	R	71.9%	20.9%	77.5%	22.5%
252,825	WELD	79,445	45,482	29,389	4,574	16,093	R	57.2%	37.0%	60.7%	39.3%
10,043	YUMA	3,829	2,614	1,010	205	1,604	R	68.3%	26.4%	72.1%	27.9%
5,029,196	TOTAL	1,777,668	824,789	854,685	98,194	29,896	D	46.4%	48.1%	49.1%	50.9%

COLORADO

HOUSE OF REPRESENTATIVES

| CD | Year | Total Vote | Republican | | Democratic | | Other Vote | Rep.-Dem. Plurality | | Percentage | | | |
| | | | | | | | | | | Total Vote | | Major Vote | |
			Vote	Candidate	Vote	Candidate				Rep.	Dem.	Rep.	Dem.
1	2010	207,751	59,747	FALLON, MIKE	140,073	DeGETTE, DIANA*	7,931	80,326	D	28.8%	67.4%	29.9%	70.1%
1	2008	283,246	67,345	LILLY, GEORGE C.	203,755	DeGETTE, DIANA*	12,146	136,410	D	23.8%	71.9%	24.8%	75.2%
1	2006	162,271		—	129,446	DeGETTE, DIANA*	32,825	129,446	D		79.8%		100.0%
1	2004	240,929	58,659	CHICAS, ROLAND	177,077	DeGETTE, DIANA*	5,193	118,418	D	24.3%	73.5%	24.9%	75.1%
1	2002	168,564	49,884	CHLOUBER, KEN	111,718	DeGETTE, DIANA*	6,962	61,834	D	29.6%	66.3%	30.9%	69.1%
2	2010	246,969	98,194	BAILEY, STEPHEN	148,768	POLIS, JARED*	7	50,574	D	39.8%	60.2%	39.8%	60.2%
2	2008	344,364	116,591	STARIN, SCOTT	215,571	POLIS, JARED	12,202	98,980	D	33.9%	62.6%	35.1%	64.9%
2	2006	231,307	65,481	MANCUSO, RICH	157,850	UDALL, MARK*	7,976	92,369	D	28.3%	68.2%	29.3%	70.7%
2	2004	309,364	94,160	HACKMAN, STEPHEN M.	207,900	UDALL, MARK*	7,304	113,740	D	30.4%	67.2%	31.2%	68.8%
2	2002	205,522	75,564	HUME, SANDY	123,504	UDALL, MARK*	6,454	47,940	D	36.8%	60.1%	38.0%	62.0%
3	2010	252,375	131,227	TIPTON, SCOTT	121,114	SALAZAR, JOHN*	34	10,113	R	52.0%	48.0%	52.0%	48.0%
3	2008	330,217	126,762	WOLF, WAYNE	203,455	SALAZAR, JOHN*		76,693	D	38.4%	61.6%	38.4%	61.6%
3	2006	237,858	86,930	TIPTON, SCOTT	146,488	SALAZAR, JOHN*	4,440	59,558	D	36.5%	61.6%	37.2%	62.8%
3	2004	303,646	141,376	WALCHER, GREG	153,500	SALAZAR, JOHN	8,770	12,124	D	46.6%	50.6%	47.9%	52.1%
3	2002	217,972	143,433	McINNIS, SCOTT*	68,160	BERCKEFELDT, DENIS	6,379	75,273	R	65.8%	31.3%	67.8%	32.2%
4	2010	264,181	138,634	GARDNER, CORY	109,249	MARKEY, BETSY*	16,298	29,385	R	52.5%	41.4%	55.9%	44.1%
4	2008	333,375	146,028	MUSGRAVE, MARILYN*	187,347	MARKEY, BETSY		41,319	D	43.8%	56.2%	43.8%	56.2%
4	2006	240,613	109,732	MUSGRAVE, MARILYN*	103,748	PACCIONE, ANGIE	27,133	5,984	R	45.6%	43.1%	51.4%	48.6%
4	2004	305,509	155,958	MUSGRAVE, MARILYN*	136,812	MATSUNAKA, STAN	12,739	19,146	R	51.0%	44.8%	53.3%	46.7%
4	2002	209,955	115,359	MUSGRAVE, MARILYN	87,499	MATSUNAKA, STAN	7,097	27,860	R	54.9%	41.7%	56.9%	43.1%
5	2010	232,434	152,829	LAMBORN, DOUG*	68,039	BRADLEY, KEVIN	11,566	84,790	R	65.8%	29.3%	69.2%	30.8%
5	2008	305,142	183,178	LAMBORN, DOUG*	113,025	BIDLACK, HAL	8,939	70,153	R	60.0%	37.0%	61.8%	38.2%
5	2004	206,756	123,264	LAMBORN, DOUG	83,431	FAWCETT, JAY	61	39,833	R	59.6%	40.4%	59.6%	40.4%
5	2004	274,058	193,333	HEFLEY, JOEL*	74,098	HARDEE, FRED	6,627	119,235	R	70.5%	27.0%	72.3%	27.7%
5	2002	184,677	128,118	HEFLEY, JOEL*	45,587	IMRIE, CURTIS	10,972	82,531	R	69.4%	24.7%	73.8%	26.2%
6	2010	321,566	217,400	COFFMAN, MIKE*	104,159	FLERLAGE, JOHN	7	113,241	R	67.6%	32.4%	67.6%	32.4%
6	2008	413,516	250,877	COFFMAN, MIKE	162,639	ENG, HANK		88,238	R	60.7%	39.3%	60.7%	39.3%
6	2006	270,931	158,806	TANCREDO, TOM*	108,007	WINTER, BILL	4,118	50,799	R	58.6%	39.9%	59.5%	40.5%
6	2004	357,741	212,778	TANCREDO, TOM*	139,870	CONTI, JOANNA L.	5,093	72,908	R	59.5%	39.1%	60.3%	39.7%
6	2002	237,501	158,851	TANCREDO, TOM*	71,327	WRIGHT, LANCE	7,323	87,524	R	66.9%	30.0%	69.0%	31.0%
7	2010	210,810	88,026	FRAZIER, RYAN	112,667	PERLMUTTER, ED*	10,117	24,641	D	41.8%	53.4%	43.9%	56.1%
7	2008	273,986	100,055	LEREW, JOHN W.	173,931	PERLMUTTER, ED*		73,876	D	36.5%	63.5%	36.5%	63.5%
7	2006	189,172	79,571	O'DONNELL, RICK	103,918	PERLMUTTER, ED	5,683	24,347	D	42.1%	54.9%	43.4%	56.6%
7	2004	247,764	135,571	BEAUPREZ, BOB*	106,026	THOMAS, DAVE	6,167	29,545	R	54.7%	42.8%	56.1%	43.9%
7	2002	172,879	81,789	BEAUPREZ, BOB	81,668	FEELEY, MIKE	9,422	121	R	47.3%	47.2%	50.0%	50.0%
TOTAL	2010	1,690,174	886,057		804,069		48	81,988	R	52.4%	47.6%	52.4%	47.6%
TOTAL	2008	2,283,846	990,836		1,259,723		33,287	268,887	D	43.4%	55.2%	44.0%	56.0%
TOTAL	2006	1,538,908	623,784		832,888		82,236	209,104	D	40.5%	54.1%	42.8%	57.2%
TOTAL	2004	2,039,011	991,835		995,283		51,893	3,448	D	48.6%	48.8%	49.9%	50.1%
TOTAL	2002	1,397,070	752,998		589,463		54,609	163,535	R	53.9%	42.2%	56.1%	43.9%

Note: An asterisk (*) denotes inclubent.

COLORADO

GENERAL AND PRIMARY ELECTIONS

2010 GENERAL ELECTIONS

Governor Other vote was 13,365 Libertarian (Jaimes Brown); 8,601 Unaffiliated (Jason R. Clark); 3,492 Unaffiliated (Paul Noel Fiorino); 43 Unaffiliated write-in (Holly Cremeens); 24 Democratic/Republican write-in (Willie Travis Chambers); 18 Unaffiliated write-in (Michael R. Moore); 1 write-in (Peter J. Carr). (The American Constitution candidate, Tom Tancredo, received 652,376 votes, 36.4 percent of the total vote. The American Constitution vote is listed in the county table for the 2010 gubernatorial election in Colorado.)

Senator Other vote was 38,884 Green (Bob Kinsey); 22,646 Libertarian (Maclyn "Mac" Stringer); 19,450 Independent Reform (Jason Napolitano); 11,351 Unaffiliated (Charley Miller); 5,780 Unaffiliated (J. Moromisato); 52 Republican write-in (Robert Rank); 20 Unaffiliated write-in (Michele M. Newman); 11 Green write-in (Bruce E. Lohmiller).

House Other vote was:

CD 1 2,923 Green (Gary Swing); 2,867 Libertarian (Clint Jones); 2,141 American Constitution (Chris Styskal).

CD 2 7,087 American Constitution (Jenna Goss); 5,056 Libertarian (Curtis Harris); 7 Democratic write-in (Henry Raibourn).

CD 3 5,745 Libertarian (Gregory Gilman); 4,982 Unaffiliated (Jake Segrest); 23 Unaffiliated write-in (John W. Hargis Sr.); 11 Unaffiliated write-in (James Fritz).

CD 4 12,312 American Constitution (Doug Aden); 3,986 Unaffiliated (Ken "Wasko" Waszkiewicz).

CD 5 5,886 American Constitution (Brian "Barron X" Scott); 5,680 Libertarian (Jerell Klaver).

CD 6 9,471 Libertarian (Rob McNealy); 5 Unaffiliated write-in (Michael Shawn Kearns).

CD 7 10,117 Libertarian (Buck Bailey).

2010 PRIMARY ELECTIONS

Primary August 10, 2010

Registration (as of August 1, 2010 includes 796,687 inactive registrants)		
Republican	1,069,238
Democratic	1,067,467
Libertarian	13,349
Green	7,124
American Constitution	2,332
Others	271
Unaffiliated	1,091,130
TOTAL	*3,250,911*

Primary Type Semi-open—Registered Democrats and Republicans could vote only in their party's primary. "Unaffiliated" voters could participate in either the Democratic or Republican primary but in the process had to declare their affiliation with that party.

COLORADO

GENERAL AND PRIMARY ELECTIONS

	REPUBLICAN PRIMARIES			DEMOCRATIC PRIMARIES		
Governor	Dan Maes	197,629	50.7%	John Hickenlooper	303,245	100.0%
	Scott McInnis	192,479	49.3%			
	TOTAL	*390,108*				
Senator	Ken Buck	211,099	51.6%	Michael F. Bennet*	184,714	54.1%
	Jane Norton	198,231	48.4%	Andrew Romanoff	156,419	45.9%
	TOTAL	*409,330*		*TOTAL*	*341,133*	
Congressional District 1	Mike Fallon	13,970	100.0%	Diana DeGette*	57,527	100.0%
Congressional District 2	Stephen Bailey	23,439	69.4%	Jared Polis*	47,347	100.0%
	Bob Brancato	10,353	30.6%			
	TOTAL	*33,792*				
Congressional District 3	Scott R. Tipton	39,346	55.8%	John Salazar*	46,148	100.0%
	Bob McConnell	31,214	44.2%			
	TOTAL	*70,560*				
Congressional District 4	Cory Gardner	57,358	100.0%	Betsy Markey*	33,982	100.0%
Congressional District 5	Doug Lamborn*	60,906	100.0%	Kevin Bradley	20,814	100.0%
Congressional District 6	Mike Coffman*	81,067	100.0%	John Flerlage	37,950	100.0%
Congressional District 7	Ryan Frazier	26,765	64.3%	Ed Perlmutter*	40,534	100.0%
	Lang Sias	14,835	35.7%			
	TOTAL	*41,600*				

An asterisk (*) denotes incumbent.

CONNECTICUT

Congressional districts first established for elections held in 2002
5 members

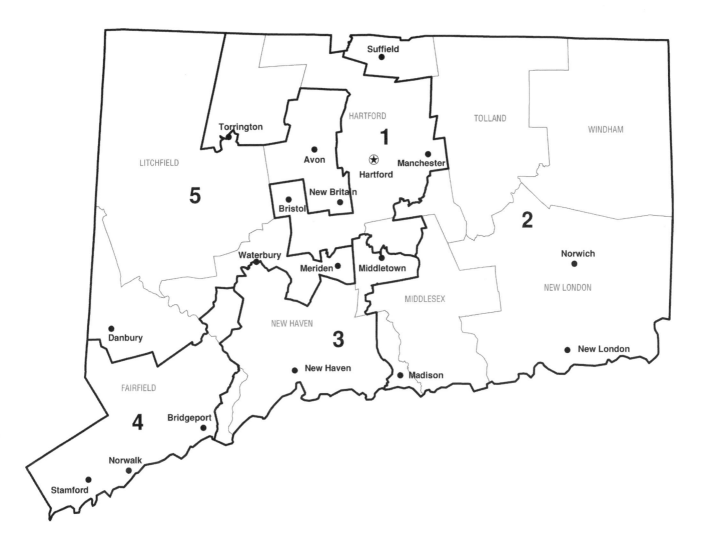

CONNECTICUT

GOVERNOR
Dan Malloy (D). Elected 2010 to a four-year term.

SENATORS (1 Democrat, 1 Independent Democrat)
Richard Blumenthal (D). Elected 2010 to a six-year term.

Joseph I. Lieberman (Ind.). Reelected 2006 to a six-year term on the Connecticut for Lieberman ballot line. Previously elected 2000, 1994, and 1988 as a Democrat.

REPRESENTATIVES (5 Democrats)
1. John B. Larson (D)
2. Joe Courtney (D)
3. Rosa L. DeLauro (D)
4. Jim Himes (D)
5. Chris Murphy (D)

POSTWAR VOTE FOR PRESIDENT

Year	Total Vote	Republican		Democratic		Other Vote	Rep.-Dem. Plurality	Total Vote Rep.	Total Vote Dem.	Major Vote Rep.	Major Vote Dem.
		Vote	Candidate	Vote	Candidate						
2008	1,646,797	629,428	McCain, John	997,772	Obama, Barack	19,597	368,344 D	38.2%	60.6%	38.7%	61.3%
2004	1,578,769	693,826	Bush, George W.	857,488	Kerry, John	27,455	163,662 D	43.9%	54.3%	44.7%	55.3%
2000**	1,459,525	561,094	Bush, George W.	816,015	Gore, Al	82,416	254,921 D	38.4%	55.9%	40.7%	59.3%
1996**	1,392,614	483,109	Dole, Bob	735,740	Clinton, Bill	173,765	252,631 D	34.7%	52.8%	39.6%	60.4%
1992**	1,616,332	578,313	Bush, George	682,318	Clinton, Bill	355,701	104,005 D	35.8%	42.2%	45.9%	54.1%
1988	1,443,394	750,241	Bush, George	676,584	Dukakis, Michael S.	16,569	73,657 R	52.0%	46.9%	52.6%	47.4%
1984	1,466,900	890,877	Reagan, Ronald	569,597	Mondale, Walter F.	6,426	321,280 R	60.7%	38.8%	61.0%	39.0%
1980**	1,406,285	677,210	Reagan, Ronald	541,732	Carter, Jimmy	187,343	135,478 R	48.2%	38.5%	55.6%	44.4%
1976	1,381,526	719,261	Ford, Gerald R.	647,895	Carter, Jimmy	14,370	71,366 R	52.1%	46.9%	52.6%	47.4%
1972	1,384,277	810,763	Nixon, Richard M.	555,498	McGovern, George S.	18,016	255,265 R	58.6%	40.1%	59.3%	40.7%
1968**	1,256,232	556,721	Nixon, Richard M.	621,561	Humphrey, Hubert H.	77,950	64,840 D	44.3%	49.5%	47.2%	52.8%
1964	1,218,578	390,996	Goldwater, Barry M.	826,269	Johnson, Lyndon B.	1,313	435,273 D	32.1%	67.8%	32.1%	67.9%
1960	1,222,883	565,813	Nixon, Richard M.	657,055	Kennedy, John F.	15	91,242 D	46.3%	53.7%	46.3%	53.7%
1956	1,117,121	711,837	Eisenhower, Dwight D.	405,079	Stevenson, Adlai E.	205	306,758 R	63.7%	36.3%	63.7%	36.3%
1952	1,096,911	611,012	Eisenhower, Dwight D.	481,649	Stevenson, Adlai E.	4,250	129,363 R	55.7%	43.9%	55.9%	44.1%
1948	883,518	437,754	Dewey, Thomas E.	423,297	Truman, Harry S.	22,467	14,457 R	49.5%	47.9%	50.8%	49.2%

**In past elections, the other vote included: 2000 - 64,452 Green (Ralph Nader); 1996 - 139,523 Reform (Ross Perot); 1992 - 348,771 Independent (Perot); 1980 - 171,807 Independent (John Anderson); 1968 - 76,650 American Independent (George Wallace).

CONNECTICUT

POSTWAR VOTE FOR GOVERNOR

Year	Total Vote	Republican Vote	Republican Candidate	Democratic Vote	Democratic Candidate	Other Vote	Rep.-Dem. Plurality	Total Vote Rep.	Total Vote Dem.	Major Vote Rep.	Major Vote Dem.
2010	1,145,799	560,874	Foley, Tom	567,278	Malloy, Dan	17,647	6,404 D	49.0%	49.5%	49.7%	50.3%
2006	1,123,466	710,048	Rell, M. Jodi	398,220	DeStefano, John	15,198	311,828 R	63.2%	35.4%	64.1%	35.9%
2002	1,022,998	573,958	Rowland, John G.	448,984	Curry, Bill	56	124,974 R	56.1%	43.9%	56.1%	43.9%
1998	999,537	628,707	Rowland, John G.	354,187	Kennelly, Barbara B.	16,643	274,520 R	62.9%	35.4%	64.0%	36.0%
1994**	1,147,084	415,201	Rowland, John G.	375,133	Curry, Bill	356,750	40,068 R	36.2%	32.7%	52.5%	47.5%
1990**	1,141,122	427,840	Rowland, John G.	236,641	Morrison, Bruce A.	476,641	32,736 C	37.5%	20.7%	64.4%	35.6%
1986	993,692	408,489	Belaga, Julie D.	575,638	O'Neill, William A.	9,565	167,149 D	41.1%	57.9%	41.5%	58.5%
1982	1,084,156	497,773	Rome, Lewis B.	578,264	O'Neill, William A.	8,119	80,491 D	45.9%	53.3%	46.3%	53.7%
1978	1,036,608	422,316	Sarasin, Ronald A.	613,109	Grasso, Ella T.	1,183	190,793 D	40.7%	59.1%	40.8%	59.2%
1974	1,102,773	440,169	Steele, Robert H.	643,490	Grasso, Ella T.	19,114	203,321 D	39.9%	58.4%	40.6%	59.4%
1970	1,082,797	582,160	Meskill, Thomas J.	500,561	Daddario, Emilio	76	81,599 R	53.8%	46.2%	53.8%	46.2%
1966	1,008,557	446,536	Gengras, E. Clayton	561,599	Dempsey, John N.	422	115,063 D	44.3%	55.7%	44.3%	55.7%
1962	1,031,902	482,852	Alsop, John	549,027	Dempsey, John N.	23	66,175 D	46.8%	53.2%	46.8%	53.2%
1958	974,509	360,644	Zeller, Fred R.	607,012	Ribicoff, Abraham A.	6,853	246,368 D	37.0%	62.3%	37.3%	62.7%
1954	936,753	460,528	Lodge, John D.	463,643	Ribicoff, Abraham A.	12,582	3,115 D	49.2%	49.5%	49.8%	50.2%
1950**	878,735	436,418	Lodge, John D.	419,404	Bowles, Chester	22,913	17,014 R	49.7%	47.7%	51.0%	49.0%
1948	875,170	429,071	Shannon, James C.	431,296	Bowles, Chester	14,803	2,225 D	49.0%	49.3%	49.9%	50.1%
1946	683,831	371,852	McConaughy, J. L.	276,335	Snow, Wilbert	35,644	95,517 R	54.4%	40.4%	57.4%	42.6%

**In past elections, the other vote included: 1994 - 216,585 A Connecticut Party (Elaine Strong Groark); 130,128 Independent (Tom Scott); 1990 - 460,576 A Connecticut Party (Lowell P. Weicker Jr.). Weicker won the 1990 election with 40.4 percent of the total vote. The term of office for Connecticut's Governor was increased from two to four years effective with the 1950 election.

POSTWAR VOTE FOR SENATOR

Year	Total Vote	Republican Vote	Republican Candidate	Democratic Vote	Democratic Candidate	Other Vote	Plurality	Total Vote Rep.	Total Vote Dem.	Major Vote Rep.	Major Vote Dem.
2010	1,153,115	498,341	McMahon, Linda E.	636,040	Blumenthal, Richard	18,734	137,699 D	43.2%	55.2%	43.9%	56.1%
2006**	1,134,780	109,198	Schlesinger, Alan	450,844	Lamont, Ned	574,738	113,251 I	9.6%	39.7%	19.5%	80.5%
2004	1,424,726	457,749	Orchulli, Jack	945,347	Dodd, Christopher J.	21,630	487,598 D	32.1%	66.4%	32.6%	67.4%
2000	1,311,261	448,077	Giordano, Philip A.	828,902	Lieberman, Joseph I.	34,282	380,825 D	34.2%	63.2%	35.1%	64.9%
1998	964,457	312,177	Franks, Gary A.	628,306	Dodd, Christopher J.	23,974	316,129 D	32.4%	65.1%	33.2%	66.8%
1994	1,079,767	334,833	Labriola, Jerry	723,842	Lieberman, Joseph I.	21,092	389,009 D	31.0%	67.0%	31.6%	68.4%
1992	1,500,709	572,036	Johnson, Brook	882,569	Dodd, Christopher J.	46,104	310,533 D	38.1%	58.8%	39.3%	60.7%
1988	1,383,526	678,454	Weicker, Lowell P.	688,499	Lieberman, Joseph I.	16,573	10,045 D	49.0%	49.8%	49.6%	50.4%
1986	976,933	340,438	Eddy, Roger W.	632,695	Dodd, Christopher J.	3,800	292,257 D	34.8%	64.8%	35.0%	65.0%
1982	1,083,613	545,987	Weicker, Lowell P.	499,146	Moffett, Anthony T.	38,480	46,841 R	50.4%	46.1%	52.2%	47.8%
1980	1,356,075	581,884	Buckley, James L.	763,969	Dodd, Christopher J.	10,222	182,085 D	42.9%	56.3%	43.2%	56.8%
1976	1,361,666	785,683	Weicker, Lowell P.	561,018	Schaffer, Gloria	14,965	224,665 R	57.7%	41.2%	58.3%	41.7%
1974	1,084,918	372,055	Brannen, James H.	690,820	Ribicoff, Abraham A.	22,043	318,765 D	34.3%	63.7%	35.0%	65.0%
1970**	1,089,353	454,721	Weicker, Lowell P.	368,111	Duffey, Joseph D.	266,521	86,610 R	41.7%	33.8%	55.3%	44.7%
1968	1,206,537	551,455	May, Edwin H.	655,043	Ribicoff, Abraham A.	39	103,588 D	45.7%	54.3%	45.7%	54.3%
1964	1,208,163	426,939	Lodge, John D.	781,008	Dodd, Thomas J.	216	354,069 D	35.3%	64.6%	35.3%	64.7%
1962	1,029,301	501,694	Seely-Brown, Horace	527,522	Ribicoff, Abraham A.	85	25,828 D	48.7%	51.3%	48.7%	51.3%
1958	965,463	410,622	Purtell, William A.	554,841	Dodd, Thomas J.		144,219 D	42.5%	57.5%	42.5%	57.5%
1956	1,113,819	610,829	Bush, Prescott	479,460	Dodd, Thomas J.	23,530	131,369 R	54.8%	43.0%	56.0%	44.0%
1952	1,093,467	573,854	Purtell, William A.	485,066	Benton, William	34,547	88,788 R	52.5%	44.4%	54.2%	45.8%
1952S	1,093,268	559,465	Bush, Prescott	530,505	Ribicoff, Abraham A.	3,298	28,960 R	51.2%	48.5%	51.3%	48.7%
1950	877,827	409,053	Talbot, Joseph E.	453,646	McMahon, Brien	15,128	44,593 D	46.6%	51.7%	47.4%	52.6%
1950S	877,135	430,311	Bush, Prescott	431,413	Benton, William	15,411	1,102 D	49.1%	49.2%	49.9%	50.1%
1946	682,921	381,328	Baldwin, Raymond	276,424	Tone, Joseph M.	25,169	104,904 R	55.8%	40.5%	58.0%	42.0%

**In past elections, the other vote included: 2006 - 564,095 Connecticut For Lieberman (Joseph I. Lieberman); 1970 - 266,497 Independent (Thomas J. Dodd). Lieberman won the 2006 election with 49.7 percent of the vote. One each of the 1950 and 1952 elections were for short terms to fill a vacancy.

CONNECTICUT

GOVERNOR 2010

2010 Census Population	County	Total Vote	Republican	Democratic	Other	Rep.-Dem. Plurality		Percentage Total Vote Rep.	Dem.	Major Vote Rep.	Dem.
916,829	FAIRFIELD	283,524	144,795	136,501	2,228	8,294	R	51.1%	48.1%	51.5%	48.5%
894,014	HARTFORD	288,598	133,159	151,191	4,248	18,032	D	46.1%	52.4%	46.8%	53.2%
189,927	LITCHFIELD	72,518	42,111	28,924	1,483	13,187	R	58.1%	39.9%	59.3%	40.7%
165,676	MIDDLESEX	65,125	32,102	31,313	1,710	789	R	49.3%	48.1%	50.6%	49.4%
862,477	NEW HAVEN	262,342	122,002	136,276	4,064	14,274	D	46.5%	51.9%	47.2%	52.8%
274,055	NEW LONDON	85,766	42,090	41,765	1,911	325	R	49.1%	48.7%	50.2%	49.8%
152,691	TOLLAND	53,720	27,501	25,096	1,123	2,405	R	51.2%	46.7%	52.3%	47.7%
118,428	WINDHAM	34,188	17,114	16,212	862	902	R	50.1%	47.4%	51.4%	48.6%
3,574,097	TOTAL	1,145,799	560,874	567,278	17,647	6,404	D	49.0%	49.5%	49.7%	50.3%

The other vote includes 18 write-in votes that were not broken down by county or town in the official returns.

2010 Census Population	City/Town	Total Vote	Republican	Democratic	Other	Rep.-Dem. Plurality		Percentage Total Vote Rep.	Dem.	Major Vote Rep.	Dem.
19,249	ANSONIA	4,973	2,260	2,616	97	356	D	45.4%	52.6%	46.3%	53.7%
20,486	BLOOMFIELD	8,743	2,024	6,657	62	4,633	D	23.1%	76.1%	23.3%	76.7%
28,026	BRANFORD	10,996	5,156	5,688	152	532	D	46.9%	51.7%	47.5%	52.5%
144,229	BRIDGEPORT	22,185	4,099	17,973	113	13,874	D	18.5%	81.0%	18.6%	81.4%
60,477	BRISTOL	17,930	9,204	8,424	302	780	R	51.3%	47.0%	52.2%	47.8%
29,261	CHESHIRE	11,881	6,696	5,007	178	1,689	R	56.4%	42.1%	57.2%	42.8%
80,893	DANBURY	18,145	9,826	8,138	181	1,688	R	54.2%	44.8%	54.7%	45.3%
20,732	DARIEN	8,187	5,650	2,496	41	3,154	R	69.0%	30.5%	69.4%	30.6%
51,252	EAST HARTFORD	11,972	4,589	7,201	182	2,612	D	38.3%	60.1%	38.9%	61.1%
29,257	EAST HAVEN	8,265	3,954	4,225	86	271	D	47.8%	51.1%	48.3%	51.7%
44,654	ENFIELD	13,289	6,929	6,122	238	807	R	52.1%	46.1%	53.1%	46.9%
59,404	FAIRFIELD	21,721	11,632	9,908	181	1,724	R	53.6%	45.6%	54.0%	46.0%
25,340	FARMINGTON	10,905	6,030	4,715	160	1,315	R	55.3%	43.2%	56.1%	43.9%
34,427	GLASTONBURY	15,074	8,127	6,750	197	1,377	R	53.9%	44.8%	54.6%	45.4%
61,171	GREENWICH	21,638	12,817	8,687	134	4,130	R	59.2%	40.1%	59.6%	40.4%
40,115	GROTON	9,946	4,820	4,910	216	90	D	48.5%	49.4%	49.5%	50.5%
22,375	GUILFORD	10,220	4,947	5,139	134	192	D	48.4%	50.3%	49.0%	51.0%
60,960	HAMDEN	19,681	6,725	12,777	179	6,052	D	34.2%	64.9%	34.5%	65.5%
124,775	HARTFORD	17,896	2,043	15,753	100	13,710	D	11.4%	88.0%	11.5%	88.5%
58,241	MANCHESTER	17,527	7,762	9,429	336	1,667	D	44.3%	53.8%	45.2%	54.8%
26,543	MANSFIELD	5,707	1,597	3,989	121	2,392	D	28.0%	69.9%	28.6%	71.4%
60,868	MERIDEN	15,380	6,520	8,609	251	2,089	D	42.4%	56.0%	43.1%	56.9%
47,648	MIDDLETOWN	14,238	5,435	8,531	272	3,096	D	38.2%	59.9%	38.9%	61.1%
52,759	MILFORD	19,293	10,086	8,873	334	1,213	R	52.3%	46.0%	53.2%	46.8%
31,862	NAUGATUCK	8,561	4,949	3,410	202	1,539	R	57.8%	39.8%	59.2%	40.8%
73,206	NEW BRITAIN	13,450	4,382	8,893	175	4,511	D	32.6%	66.1%	33.0%	67.0%
129,779	NEW HAVEN	26,181	3,679	22,285	217	18,606	D	14.1%	85.1%	14.2%	85.8%
27,620	NEW LONDON	4,975	1,502	3,365	108	1,863	D	30.2%	67.6%	30.9%	69.1%
28,142	NEW MILFORD	9,399	5,636	3,594	169	2,042	R	60.0%	38.2%	61.1%	38.9%
30,562	NEWINGTON	11,531	5,179	6,190	162	1,011	D	44.9%	53.7%	45.6%	54.4%
27,560	NEWTOWN	11,000	6,583	4,285	132	2,298	R	59.8%	39.0%	60.6%	39.4%
24,093	NORTH HAVEN	10,085	5,573	4,375	137	1,198	R	55.3%	43.4%	56.0%	44.0%
85,603	NORWALK	23,944	10,272	13,458	214	3,186	D	42.9%	56.2%	43.3%	56.7%
40,493	NORWICH	8,814	3,793	4,850	171	1,057	D	43.0%	55.0%	43.9%	56.1%
24,638	RIDGEFIELD	10,364	6,102	4,184	78	1,918	R	58.9%	40.4%	59.3%	40.7%
39,559	SHELTON	13,921	8,601	5,320		3,281	R	61.8%	38.2%	61.8%	38.2%
23,511	SIMSBURY	11,108	6,459	4,500	149	1,959	R	58.1%	40.5%	58.9%	41.1%

CONNECTICUT

GOVERNOR 2010

2010 Census Population	City/Town	Total Vote	Republican	Democratic	Other	Rep.-Dem. Plurality		Percentage			
								Total Vote		Major Vote	
								Rep.	Dem.	Rep.	Dem.
25,709	SOUTH WINDSOR	10,668	5,407	5;120	141	287	R	50.7%	48.0%	51.4%	48.6%
43,069	SOUTHINGTON	16,545	9,211	7,048	286	2,163	R	55.7%	42.6%	56.7%	43.3%
122,643	STAMFORD	33,464	13,779	19,416	269	5,637	D	41.2%	58.0%	41.5%	58.5%
51,384	STRATFORD	17,523	8,183	9,136	204	953	D	46.7%	52.1%	47.2%	52.8%
36,383	TORRINGTON	11,402	6,613	4,547	242	2,066	R	58.0%	39.9%	59.3%	40.7%
36,018	TRUMBULL	14,617	8,299	6,176	142	2,123	R	56.8%	42.3%	57.3%	42.7%
29,179	VERNON	9,558	4,846	4,504	208	342	R	50.7%	47.1%	51.8%	48.2%
45,135	WALLINGFORD	15,865	8,240	7,314	311	926	R	51.9%	46.1%	53.0%	47.0%
110,336	WATERBURY	21,526	9,607	11,335	584	1,728	D	44.6%	52.7%	45.9%	54.1%
22,514	WATERTOWN	8,590	5,488	2,860	242	2,628	R	63.9%	33.3%	65.7%	34.3%
63,268	WEST HARTFORD	25,842	10,157	15,392	293	5,235	D	39.3%	59.6%	39.8%	60.2%
55,564	WEST HAVEN	13,488	4,995	8,285	208	3,290	D	37.0%	61.4%	37.6%	62.4%
26,391	WESTPORT	11,234	5,297	5,879	58	582	D	47.2%	52.3%	47.4%	52.6%
26,668	WETHERSFIELD	10,996	5,517	5,306	173	211	R	50.2%	48.3%	51.0%	49.0%
25,268	WINDHAM	5,131	1,856	3,183	92	1,327	D	36.2%	62.0%	36.8%	63.2%
29,044	WINDSOR	11,610	4,186	7,270	154	3,084	D	36.1%	62.6%	36.5%	63.5%

CONNECTICUT

SENATOR 2010

2010 Census Population	County	Total Vote	Republican	Democratic	Other	Rep.-Dem. Plurality		Percentage			
								Total Vote		Major Vote	
								Rep.	Dem.	Rep.	Dem.
916,829	FAIRFIELD	284,723	134,242	146,926	3,555	12,684	D	47.1%	51.6%	47.7%	52.3%
894,014	HARTFORD	288,978	115,628	168,891	4,459	53,263	D	40.0%	58.4%	40.6%	59.4%
189,927	LITCHFIELD	72,979	38,888	32,824	1,267	6,064	R	53.3%	45.0%	54.2%	45.8%
165,676	MIDDLESEX	65,399	27,991	36,258	1,150	8,267	D	42.8%	55.4%	43.6%	56.4%
862,477	NEW HAVEN	264,581	107,376	153,377	3,828	46,001	D	40.6%	58.0%	41.2%	58.8%
274,055	NEW LONDON	85,928	34,810	49,286	1,832	14,476	D	40.5%	57.4%	41.4%	58.6%
152,691	TOLLAND	53,923	24,148	28,638	1,137	4,490	D	44.8%	53.1%	45.7%	54.3%
118,428	WINDHAM	35,880	15,258	19,840	782	4,582	D	42.5%	55.3%	43.5%	56.5%
3,574,097	TOTAL	1,153,115	498,341	636,040	18,734	137,699	D	43.2%	55.2%	43.9%	56.1%

The other vote includes 724 write-in votes that were not broken down by county or town in the official returns.

CONNECTICUT

SENATOR 2010

2010 Census Population	City/Town	Total Vote	Republican	Democratic	Other	Rep.-Dem. Plurality		Percentage			
								Total Vote		Major Vote	
								Rep.	Dem.	Rep.	Dem.
19,249	ANSONIA	5,067	1,956	3,043	68	1,087	D	38.6%	60.1%	39.1%	60.9%
20,486	BLOOMFIELD	8,830	1,633	7,123	74	5,490	D	18.5%	80.7%	18.7%	81.3%
28,026	BRANFORD	11,093	4,360	6,576	157	2,216	D	39.3%	59.3%	39.9%	60.1%
144,229	BRIDGEPORT	21,277	4,030	17,116	131	13,086	D	18.9%	80.4%	19.1%	80.9%
60,477	BRISTOL	18,040	7,838	9,954	248	2,116	D	43.4%	55.2%	44.1%	55.9%
29,261	CHESHIRE	11,953	5,731	6,011	211	280	D	47.9%	50.3%	48.8%	51.2%
80,893	DANBURY	17,936	8,140	9,490	306	1,350	D	45.4%	52.9%	46.2%	53.8%
20,732	DARIEN	8,213	5,416	2,705	92	2,711	R	65.9%	32.9%	66.7%	33.3%
51,252	EAST HARTFORD	11,023	3,909	6,950	164	3,041	D	35.5%	63.0%	36.0%	64.0%
29,257	EAST HAVEN	8,254	3,364	4,788	102	1,424	D	40.8%	58.0%	41.3%	58.7%
44,654	ENFIELD	13,478	5,916	7,256	306	1,340	D	43.9%	53.8%	44.9%	55.1%
59,404	FAIRFIELD	22,164	10,729	11,180	255	451	D	48.4%	50.4%	49.0%	51.0%
25,340	FARMINGTON	10,951	5,242	5,550	159	308	D	47.9%	50.7%	48.6%	51.4%
34,427	GLASTONBURY	15,104	7,127	7,735	242	608	D	47.2%	51.2%	48.0%	52.0%
61,171	GREENWICH	21,831	12,289	9,248	294	3,041	R	56.3%	42.4%	57.1%	42.9%
40,115	GROTON	9,917	3,816	5,880	221	2,064	D	38.5%	59.3%	39.4%	60.6%
22,375	GUILFORD	10,261	4,148	5,953	160	1,805	D	40.4%	58.0%	41.1%	58.9%
60,960	HAMDEN	19,925	5,760	13,942	223	8,182	D	28.9%	70.0%	29.2%	70.8%
124,775	HARTFORD	18,032	1,945	15,911	176	13,966	D	10.8%	88.2%	10.9%	89.1%
58,241	MANCHESTER	17,581	6,604	10,628	349	4,024	D	37.6%	60.5%	38.3%	61.7%
26,543	MANSFIELD	5,724	1,400	4,165	159	2,765	D	24.5%	72.8%	25.2%	74.8%
60,868	MERIDEN	15,508	5,706	9,580	222	3,874	D	36.8%	61.8%	37.3%	62.7%
47,648	MIDDLETOWN	14,291	4,833	9,205	253	4,372	D	33.8%	64.4%	34.4%	65.6%
52,759	MILFORD	19,398	8,426	10,652	320	2,226	D	43.4%	54.9%	44.2%	55.8%
31,862	NAUGATUCK	8,640	4,547	3,967	126	580	R	52.6%	45.9%	53.4%	46.6%
73,206	NEW BRITAIN	13,569	3,962	9,439	168	5,477	D	29.2%	69.6%	29.6%	70.4%
129,779	NEW HAVEN	26,423	3,266	22,865	292	19,599	D	12.4%	86.5%	12.5%	87.5%
27,620	NEW LONDON	5,106	1,215	3,778	113	2,563	D	23.8%	74.0%	24.3%	75.7%
28,142	NEW MILFORD	9,476	4,854	4,461	161	393	R	51.2%	47.1%	52.1%	47.9%
30,562	NEWINGTON	11,594	4,577	6,856	161	2,279	D	39.5%	59.1%	40.0%	60.0%
27,560	NEWTOWN	11,090	5,890	5,062	138	828	R	53.1%	45.6%	53.8%	46.2%
24,093	NORTH HAVEN	10,254	4,673	5,460	121	787	D	45.6%	53.2%	46.1%	53.9%
85,603	NORWALK	24,125	10,077	13,662	386	3,585	D	41.8%	56.6%	42.4%	57.6%
40,493	NORWICH	8,874	3,155	5,569	150	2,414	D	35.6%	62.8%	36.2%	63.8%
24,638	RIDGEFIELD	10,409	5,677	4,573	159	1,104	R	54.5%	43.9%	55.4%	44.6%
39,559	SHELTON	14,165	7,472	6,524	169	948	R	52.7%	46.1%	53.4%	46.6%
23,511	SIMSBURY	11,123	5,556	5,369	198	187	R	50.0%	48.3%	50.9%	49.1%
25,709	SOUTH WINDSOR	10,770	4,621	5,977	172	1,356	D	42.9%	55.5%	43.6%	56.4%
43,069	SOUTHINGTON	16,647	7,978	8,394	275	416	D	47.9%	50.4%	48.7%	51.3%
122,643	STAMFORD	33,931	13,861	19,718	352	5,857	D	40.9%	58.1%	41.3%	58.7%
51,384	STRATFORD	17,726	7,232	10,247	247	3,015	D	40.8%	57.8%	41.4%	58.6%
36,383	TORRINGTON	11,460	6,230	5,008	222	1,222	R	54.4%	43.7%	55.4%	44.6%
36,018	TRUMBULL	14,669	7,522	6,970	177	552	R	51.3%	47.5%	51.9%	48.1%
29,179	VERNON	9,618	4,126	5,302	190	1,176	D	42.9%	55.1%	43.8%	56.2%
45,135	WALLINGFORD	16,001	6,945	8,813	243	1,868	D	43.4%	55.1%	44.1%	55.9%
110,366	WATERBURY	21,661	9,561	11,687	413	2,126	D	44.1%	54.0%	45.0%	55.0%
22,514	WATERTOWN	8,669	5,252	3,223	194	2,029	R	60.6%	37.2%	62.0%	38.0%
63,268	WEST HARTFORD	25,809	8,590	16,773	446	8,183	D	33.3%	65.0%	33.9%	66.1%
55,564	WEST HAVEN	13,673	4,248	9,209	216	4,961	D	31.1%	67.4%	31.6%	68.4%
26,391	WESTPORT	11,400	5,048	6,229	123	1,181	D	44.3%	54.6%	44.8%	55.2%
26,668	WETHERSFIELD	10,970	4,914	5,884	172	970	D	44.8%	53.6%	45.5%	54.5%
25,268	WINDHAM	6,609	1,610	4,924	75	3,314	D	24.4%	74.5%	24.6%	75.4%
29,044	WINDSOR	11,652	3,591	7,927	134	4,336	D	30.8%	68.0%	31.2%	68.8%

CONNECTICUT

HOUSE OF REPRESENTATIVES

CD	Year	Total Vote	Republican		Democratic		Other Vote	Rep.-Dem. Plurality		Percentage			
										Total Vote		Major Vote	
			Vote	Candidate	Vote	Candidate				Rep.	Dem.	Rep.	Dem.
1	2010	226,038	84,076	BRICKLEY, ANN	138,440	LARSON, JOHN B.*	3,522	54,364	D	37.2%	61.2%	37.8%	62.2%
1	2008	295,557	76,860	VISCONTI, JOE	211,493	LARSON, JOHN B.*	7,204	134,633	D	26.0%	71.6%	26.7%	73.3%
1	2006	207,592	53,010	MacLEAN, SCOTT	154,539	LARSON, JOHN B.*	43	101,529	D	25.5%	74.4%	25.5%	74.5%
1	2004	272,403	73,601	HALSTEAD, JOHN M.	198,802	LARSON, JOHN B.*		125,201	D	27.0%	73.0%	27.0%	73.0%
1	2002	201,688	66,968	STEELE, PHIL	134,698	LARSON, JOHN B.*	22	67,730	D	33.2%	66.8%	33.2%	66.8%
2	2010	246,809	95,671	PECKINPAUGH, JANET	147,748	COURTNEY, JOE*	3,390	52,077	D	38.8%	59.9%	39.3%	60.7%
2	2008	323,041	104,574	SULLIVAN, SEAN	212,148	COURTNEY, JOE*	6,319	107,574	D	32.4%	65.7%	33.0%	67.0%
2	2006	242,413	121,165	SIMMONS, ROB*	121,248	COURTNEY, JOE		83	D	50.0%	50.0%	50.0%	50.0%
2	2004	307,078	166,412	SIMMONS, ROB*	140,536	SULLIVAN, JIM	130	25,876	R	54.2%	45.8%	54.2%	45.8%
2	2002	217,108	117,434	SIMMONS, ROB*	99,674	COURTNEY, JOE		17,760	R	54.1%	45.9%	54.1%	45.9%
3	2010	220,661	74,107	LABRIOLA, JERRY, JR.	143,565	DeLAURO, ROSA L.*	2,989	69,458	D	33.6%	65.1%	34.0%	66.0%
3	2008	297,368	58,583	ITSHAKY, BO	230,172	DeLAURO, ROSA L.*	8,613	171,589	D	19.7%	77.4%	20.3%	79.7%
3	2006	197,911	44,386	VOLLANO, JOSEPH	150,436	DeLAURO, ROSA L.*	3,089	106,050	D	22.4%	76.0%	22.8%	77.2%
3	2004	276,980	69,160	ELSER, RICHTER	200,638	DeLAURO, ROSA L.*	7,182	131,478	D	25.0%	72.4%	25.6%	74.4%
3	2002	185,364	54,757	ELSER, RICHTER	121,557	DeLAURO, ROSA L.*	9,050	66,800	D	29.5%	65.6%	31.1%	68.9%
4	2010	217,391	102,030	DEBICELLA, DAN	115,351	HIMES, JIM*	10	13,321	D	46.9%	53.1%	46.9%	53.1%
4	2008	308,776	146,854	SHAYS, CHRISTOPHER*	158,475	HIMES, JIM	3,447	11,621	D	47.6%	51.3%	48.1%	51.9%
4	2006	209,019	106,510	SHAYS, CHRISTOPHER*	99,450	FARRELL, DIANE	3,059	7,060	R	51.0%	47.6%	51.7%	48.3%
4	2004	290,830	152,493	SHAYS, CHRISTOPHER*	138,333	FARRELL, DIANE	4	14,160	R	52.4%	47.6%	52.4%	47.6%
4	2002	175,695	113,197	SHAYS, CHRISTOPHER*	62,491	SANCHEZ, STEPHANIE H.	7	50,706	R	64.4%	35.6%	64.4%	35.6%
5	2010	227,303	104,402	CALIGIURI, SAM S.F.	122,879	MURPHY, CHRIS*	22	18,477	D	45.9%	54.1%	45.9%	54.1%
5	2008	302,657	117,914	CAPPIELLO, DAVID J.	179,327	MURPHY, CHRIS*	5,416	61,413	D	39.0%	59.3%	39.7%	60.3%
5	2006	217,804	94,824	JOHNSON, NANCY L.*	122,980	MURPHY, CHRIS		28,156	D	43.5%	56.5%	43.5%	56.5%
5	2004	278,251	168,268	JOHNSON, NANCY L.*	107,438	GERRATANA, THERESA B.	2,545	60,830	R	60.5%	38.6%	61.0%	39.0%
5	2002	209,454	113,626	JOHNSON, NANCY L.*	90,616	MALONEY, JIM*	5,212	23,010	R	54.2%	43.3%	55.6%	44.4%
TOTAL	2010	1,138,202	460,286		667,983		9,933	207,697	D	40.4%	58.7%	40.8%	59.2%
TOTAL	2008	1,527,399	504,785		991,615		30,999	486,830	D	33.0%	64.9%	33.7%	66.3%
TOTAL	2006	1,074,739	419,895		648,653		6,191	228,758	D	39.1%	60.4%	39.3%	60.7%
TOTAL	2004	1,428,738	629,934		785,747		13,057	155,813	D	44.1%	55.0%	44.5%	55.5%
TOTAL	2002	989,309	465,982		509,036		14,291	43,054	D	47.1%	51.5%	47.8%	52.2%

CONNECTICUT

GENERAL AND PRIMARY ELECTIONS

2010 GENERAL ELECTIONS

Governor   Other vote was 17,629 Independent (Thomas E. Marsh); 13 write-in (Paul Copp); 5 write-in (P. Robert Thibodeau). Democrat Dan Malloy received 26,308 votes on the Working Families ballot line, which was included in his total vote.

Senator   Other vote was 11,275 Independent (Warren B. Mosler); 6,735 Connecticut for Lieberman (Dr. John Mertens); 559 write-in (Brian K. Hill); 45 write-in (Jeff Russell); 45 write-in (Todd Vachon); 31 write-in (Carl E. Vassar); 17 write-in (Jay J. Giles); 15 write-in (John Traceski); 7 write-in (Matthew Coleman); 5 write-in (Dave Olszta). Democrat Richard Blumenthal received 30,836 votes on the Working Families ballot line, which was included in his total vote.

House   Other vote was:

CD 1   2,564 Green (Kenneth J. Krayeske); 955 Socialist Action (Christopher J. Hutchinson); 3 write-in (Daniel J. Stepanek). Democrat John B. Larson received 7,902 votes on the Working Families ballot line, which was included in his total vote.

CD 2   3,344 Green (G. Scott Deshefy); 27 write-in (Daniel Reale); 19 write-in (Muriel P. Bianchi). Democrat Joe Courtney received 6,860 votes on the Working Families ballot line, which was included in his total vote.

CD 3   2,984 Green (Charles A. Pillsbury); 5 write-in (Boaz Itshaky). Democrat Rosa L. DeLauro received 9,021 votes on the Working Families ballot line, which was included in her total vote.

CD 4   10 write-in (Eugene Flanagan). Democrat Jim Himes received 4,605 votes on the Working Families ballot line, which was included in his total vote.

CD 5   20 write-in (John Pistone); 2 write-in (Elmon Smith). Democrat Chris Murphy received 4,648 votes on the Working Families ballot line, which was included in his total vote. Republican Sam S. F. Caligiuri received 2,310 votes on an Independent ballot line, which was included in his total vote.

2010 PRIMARY ELECTIONS

Primary   August 10, 2010

Registration (as of Oct. 27, 2009 - includes 123,646 inactive registrants)

Democratic	792,934
Republican	433,057
Other Parties	11,436
Unaffiliated	914,893
TOTAL	*2,152,320*

Primary Type   Closed—Only registered Democrats and Republicans could vote in their party's primary.

CONNECTICUT

GENERAL AND PRIMARY ELECTIONS

	REPUBLICAN PRIMARIES			DEMOCRATIC PRIMARIES		
Governor	Tom Foley	50,792	42.3%	Dan Malloy	103,154	57.0%
	Michael Fedele	46,989	39.1%	Ned Lamont	77,772	43.0%
	Oz Griebel	22,390	18.6%			
	TOTAL	120,171		TOTAL	180,926	
Senator	Linda E. McMahon	60,479	49.4%	Richard Blumenthal	Nominated by convention	
	Rob Simmons	34,011	27.8%			
	Peter David Schiff	27,781	22.8%			
	TOTAL	*122,321*				
Congressional District 1	Ann Brickley	11,438	59.5%	John B. Larson*	Nominated by convention	
	Mark Zydanowicz	7,791	40.5%			
	TOTAL	*19,229*				

CONNECTICUT

GENERAL AND PRIMARY ELECTIONS

	REPUBLICAN PRIMARIES			DEMOCRATIC PRIMARIES	
Congressional District 2	Janet Peckinpaugh	11,344	43.2%	Joe Courtney*	Nominated by convention
	Daria Novak	9,872	37.6%		
	Doug Dubitsky	5,044	19.2%		
	TOTAL	26,260			
Congressional District 3	Jerry Labriola Jr.	Nominated by convention		Rosa L. DeLauro*	Nominated by convention
Congressional District 4	Dan Debicella	16,494	59.9%	Jim Himes*	Nominated by convention
	Rob Merkle	6,578	23.9%		
	Rick Torres	4,465	16.2%		
	TOTAL	27,537			
Congressional District 5	Sam S.F. Caligiuri	11,287	39.2%	Chris Murphy*	Nominated by convention
	Justin Bernier	9,267	32.2%		
	Mark Greenberg	8,259	28.7%		
	TOTAL	28,813			

DELAWARE

One member At Large

Wilmington

Newark

NEW CASTLE

Dover

KENT

At Large

Rehoboth Beach

SUSSEX

Bethany Beach

DELAWARE

GOVERNOR
Jack Markell (D). Elected 2008 to a four-year term.

SENATORS (2 Democrats)
Thomas R. Carper (D). Reelected 2006 to a six-year term. Previously elected 2000.

Christopher A. Coons (D). Elected 2010 to a six-year term.

REPRESENTATIVE (1 Democrat)
At Large. John C. Carney Jr. (D)

POSTWAR VOTE FOR PRESIDENT

| | | Republican | | Democratic | | Other | Rep.-Dem. | Percentage | | | |
| | | | | | | | | Total Vote | | Major Vote | |
Year	Total Vote	Vote	Candidate	Vote	Candidate	Vote	Plurality	Rep.	Dem.	Rep.	Dem.
2008	412,412	152,374	McCain, John	255,459	Obama, Barack	4,579	103,085 D	36.9%	61.9%	37.4%	62.6%
2004	375,190	171,660	Bush, George W.	200,152	Kerry, John	3,378	28,492 D	45.8%	53.3%	46.2%	53.8%
2000**	327,622	137,288	Bush, George W.	180,068	Gore, Al	10,266	42,780 D	41.9%	55.0%	43.3%	56.7%
1996**	271,084	99,062	Dole, Bob	140,355	Clinton, Bill	31,667	41,293 D	36.5%	51.8%	41.4%	58.6%
1992**	289,735	102,313	Bush, George	126,054	Clinton, Bill	61,368	23,741 D	35.3%	43.5%	44.8%	55.2%
1988	249,891	139,639	Bush, George	108,647	Dukakis, Michael S.	1,605	30,992 R	55.9%	43.5%	56.2%	43.8%
1984	254,572	152,190	Reagan, Ronald	101,656	Mondale, Walter F.	726	50,534 R	59.8%	39.9%	60.0%	40.0%
1980**	235,900	111,252	Reagan, Ronald	105,754	Carter, Jimmy	18,894	5,498 R	47.2%	44.8%	51.3%	48.7%
1976	235,834	109,831	Ford, Gerald R.	122,596	Carter, Jimmy	3,407	12,765 D	46.6%	52.0%	47.3%	52.7%
1972	235,516	140,357	Nixon, Richard M.	92,283	McGovern, George S.	2,876	48,074 R	59.6%	39.2%	60.3%	39.7%
1968**	214,367	96,714	Nixon, Richard M.	89,194	Humphrey, Hubert H.	28,459	7,520 R	45.1%	41.6%	52.0%	48.0%
1964	201,320	78,078	Goldwater, Barry M.	122,704	Johnson, Lyndon B.	538	44,626 D	38.8%	60.9%	38.9%	61.1%
1960	196,683	96,373	Nixon, Richard M.	99,590	Kennedy, John F.	720	3,217 D	49.0%	50.6%	49.2%	50.8%
1956	177,988	98,057	Eisenhower, Dwight D.	79,421	Stevenson, Adlai E.	510	18,636 R	55.1%	44.6%	55.3%	44.7%
1952	174,025	90,059	Eisenhower, Dwight D.	83,315	Stevenson, Adlai E.	651	6,744 R	51.8%	47.9%	51.9%	48.1%
1948	139,073	69,588	Dewey, Thomas E.	67,813	Truman, Harry S.	1,672	1,775 R	50.0%	48.8%	50.6%	49.4%

**In past elections, the other vote included: 2000 - 8,307 Green (Ralph Nader); 1996 - 28,719 Reform (Ross Perot); 1992 - 59,213 Independent (Perot); 1980 - 16,288 Independent (John Anderson); 1968 - 28,459 American Independent (George Wallace).

POSTWAR VOTE FOR GOVERNOR

| | | Republican | | Democratic | | Other | Rep.-Dem. | Percentage | | | |
| | | | | | | | | Total Vote | | Major Vote | |
Year	Total Vote	Vote	Candidate	Vote	Candidate	Vote	Plurality	Rep.	Dem.	Rep.	Dem.
2008	395,204	126,662	Lee, William Swain	266,861	Markell, Jack	1,681	140,199 D	32.0%	67.5%	32.2%	67.8%
2004	365,008	167,115	Lee, William Swain	185,687	Minner, Ruth Ann	12,206	18,572 D	45.8%	50.9%	47.4%	52.6%
2000	323,688	128,603	Burris, John M.	191,695	Minner, Ruth Ann	3,390	63,092 D	39.7%	59.2%	40.2%	59.8%
1996	271,122	82,654	Rzewnicki, Janet	188,300	Carper, Thomas R.	168	105,646 D	30.5%	69.5%	30.5%	69.5%
1992	277,058	90,725	Scott, B. Gary	179,365	Carper, Thomas R.	6,968	88,640 D	32.7%	64.7%	33.6%	66.4%
1988	239,969	169,733	Castle, Michael N.	70,236	Kreshtoll, Jacob		99,497 R	70.7%	29.3%	70.7%	29.3%
1984	243,565	135,250	Castle, Michael N.	108,315	Quillen, William T.		26,935 R	55.5%	44.5%	55.5%	44.5%
1980	225,081	159,004	duPont, Pierre	64,217	Gordy, William J.	1,860	94,787 R	70.6%	28.5%	71.2%	28.8%
1976	229,563	130,531	duPont, Pierre	97,480	Tribbitt, Sherman W.	1,552	33,051 R	56.9%	42.5%	57.2%	42.8%
1972	228,722	109,583	Peterson, Russell W.	117,274	Tribbitt, Sherman W.	1,865	7,691 D	47.9%	51.3%	48.3%	51.7%
1968	206,834	104,474	Peterson, Russell W.	102,360	Terry, Charles L.		2,114 R	50.5%	49.5%	50.5%	49.5%
1964	200,171	97,374	Buckson, David P.	102,797	Terry, Charles L.		5,423 D	48.6%	51.4%	48.6%	51.4%
1960	194,835	94,043	Rollins, John W.	100,792	Carvel, Elbert N.		6,749 D	48.3%	51.7%	48.3%	51.7%
1956	177,012	91,965	Boggs, J. Caleb	85,047	McConnell, J. H. T.		6,918 R	52.0%	48.0%	52.0%	48.0%
1952	170,749	88,977	Boggs, J. Caleb	81,772	Carvel, Elbert N.		7,205 R	52.1%	47.9%	52.1%	47.9%
1948	140,335	64,996	George, Hyland P.	75,339	Carvel, Elbert N.		10,343 D	46.3%	53.7%	46.3%	53.7%

DELAWARE

POSTWAR VOTE FOR SENATOR

Year	Total Vote	Republican		Democratic		Other Vote	Rep.-Dem. Plurality	Percentage			
								Total Vote		Major Vote	
		Vote	Candidate	Vote	Candidate			Rep.	Dem.	Rep.	Dem.
2010S	307,402	123,053	O'Donnell, Christine	174,012	Coons, Christopher A.	10,337	50,959 D	40.0%	56.6%	41.4%	58.6%
2008	398,134	140,595	O'Donnell, Christine	257,539	Biden, Joseph R., Jr.		116,944 D	35.3%	64.7%	35.3%	64.7%
2006	254,099	69,734	Ting, Jan	170,567	Carper, Thomas R.	13,798	100,833 D	27.4%	67.1%	29.0%	71.0%
2002	232,314	94,793	Clatworthy, Raymond J.	135,253	Biden, Joseph R., Jr.	2,268	40,460 D	40.8%	58.2%	41.2%	58.8%
2000	327,017	142,891	Roth, William V.	181,566	Carper, Thomas R.	2,560	38,675 D	43.7%	55.5%	44.0%	56.0%
1996	275,605	105,088	Clatworthy, Raymond J.	165,465	Biden, Joseph R., Jr.	5,052	60,377 D	38.1%	60.0%	38.8%	61.2%
1994	199,029	111,088	Roth, William V.	84,554	Oberly, Charles M.	3,387	26,534 R	55.8%	42.5%	56.8%	43.2%
1990	180,152	64,554	Brady, M. Jane	112,918	Biden, Joseph R., Jr.	2,680	48,364 D	35.8%	62.7%	36.4%	63.6%
1988	243,493	151,115	Roth, William V.	92,378	Woo, S. B.		58,737 R	62.1%	37.9%	62.1%	37.9%
1984	245,932	98,101	Burris, John M.	147,831	Biden, Joseph R., Jr.		49,730 D	39.9%	60.1%	39.9%	60.1%
1982	190,960	105,357	Roth, William V.	84,413	Levinson, David N.	1,190	20,944 R	55.2%	44.2%	55.5%	44.5%
1978	162,072	66,479	Baxter, James H.	93,930	Biden, Joseph R., Jr.	1,663	27,451 D	41.0%	58.0%	41.4%	58.6%
1976	224,859	125,502	Roth, William V.	98,055	Maloney, Thomas C.	1,302	27,447 R	55.8%	43.6%	56.1%	43.9%
1972	229,828	112,844	Boggs, J. Caleb	116,006	Biden, Joseph R., Jr.	978	3,162 D	49.1%	50.5%	49.3%	50.7%
1970	161,439	94,979	Roth, William V.	64,740	Zimmerman, Jacob	1,720	30,239 R	58.8%	40.1%	59.5%	40.5%
1966	164,549	97,268	Boggs, J. Caleb	67,281	Tunnell, James M., Jr.		29,987 R	59.1%	40.9%	59.1%	40.9%
1964	200,703	103,782	Williams, John J.	96,850	Carvel, Elbert N.	71	6,932 R	51.7%	48.3%	51.7%	48.3%
1960	194,964	98,874	Boggs, J. Caleb	96,090	Frear, J. Allen		2,784 R	50.7%	49.3%	50.7%	49.3%
1958	154,432	82,280	Williams, John J.	72,152	Carvel, Elbert N.		10,128 R	53.3%	46.7%	53.3%	46.7%
1954	144,900	62,389	Warburton, H. B.	82,511	Frear, J. Allen		20,122 D	43.1%	56.9%	43.1%	56.9%
1952	170,705	93,020	Williams, John J.	77,685	Bayard, A. I. duP.		15,335 R	54.5%	45.5%	54.5%	45.5%
1948	141,362	68,246	Buck, C. Douglas	71,888	Frear, J. Allen	1,228	3,642 D	48.3%	50.9%	48.7%	51.3%
1946	113,513	62,603	Williams, John J.	50,910	Tunnell, James M.		11,693 R	55.2%	44.8%	55.2%	44.8%

The 2010 election was for a short term to fill a vacancy.

DELAWARE

SENATOR 2010

2000 Census Population	County	Total Vote	Republican	Democratic	Other	Rep.-Dem. Plurality	Percentage			
							Total Vote		Major Vote	
							Rep.	Dem.	Rep.	Dem.
162,310	KENT	49,440	25,059	22,315	2,066	2,744 R	50.7%	45.1%	52.9%	47.1%
538,479	NEW CASTLE	187,043	57,649	123,678	5,716	66,029 D	30.8%	66.1%	31.8%	68.2%
197,145	SUSSEX	70,884	40,345	28,019	2,520	12,326 R	56.9%	39.5%	59.0%	41.0%
897,934	TOTAL	307,367	123,053	174,012	10,302	50,959 D	40.0%	56.6%	41.4%	58.6%

DELAWARE

HOUSE OF REPRESENTATIVES

CD	Year	Total Vote	Republican Vote	Republican Candidate	Democratic Vote	Democratic Candidate	Other Vote	Rep.-Dem. Plurality	Percentage Total Vote Rep.	Percentage Total Vote Dem.	Percentage Major Vote Rep.	Percentage Major Vote Dem.
AL	2010	305,636	125,442	URQUHART, GLEN	173,543	CARNEY, JOHN C., JR.	6,651	48,101 D	41.0%	56.8%	42.0%	58.0%
AL	2008	385,457	235,437	CASTLE, MICHAEL N.*	146,434	HARTLEY-NAGLE, KAREN	3,586	89,003 R	61.1%	38.0%	61.7%	38.3%
AL	2006	251,694	143,897	CASTLE, MICHAEL N.*	97,565	SPIVACK, DENNIS	10,232	46,332 R	57.2%	38.8%	59.6%	40.4%
AL	2004	356,045	245,978	CASTLE, MICHAEL N.*	105,716	DONNELLY, PAUL	4,351	140,262 R	69.1%	29.7%	69.9%	30.1%
AL	2002	228,405	164,605	CASTLE, MICHAEL N.*	61,011	MILLER, MICHEAL C.	2,789	103,594 R	72.1%	26.7%	73.0%	27.0%
AL	2000	313,171	211,797	CASTLE, MICHAEL N.*	96,488	MILLER, MICHEAL C.	4,886	115,309 R	67.6%	30.8%	68.7%	31.3%
AL	1998	180,527	119,811	CASTLE, MICHAEL N.*	57,446	WILLIAMS, DENNIS E.	3,270	62,365 R	66.4%	31.8%	67.6%	32.4%
AL	1996	266,836	185,576	CASTLE, MICHAEL N.*	73,253	WILLIAMS, DENNIS E.	8,007	112,323 R	69.5%	27.5%	71.7%	28.3%
AL	1994	195,037	137,960	CASTLE, MICHAEL N.*	51,803	DESANTIS, CAROL ANN	5,274	86,157 R	70.7%	26.6%	72.7%	27.3%
AL	1992	276,157	153,037	CASTLE, MICHAEL N.	117,426	WOO, S.B.	5,694	35,611 R	55.4%	42.5%	56.6%	43.4%
AL	1990	177,432	58,037	WILLIAMS, RALPH O.	116,274	CARPER, THOMAS R.*	3,121	58,237 D	32.7%	65.5%	33.3%	66.7%
AL	1988	234,517	76,179	KRAPF, JAMES P.	158,338	CARPER, THOMAS R.*		82,159 D	32.5%	67.5%	32.5%	67.5%
AL	1986	160,757	53,767	NEUBERGER, THOMAS S.	106,351	CARPER, THOMAS R.*	639	52,584 D	33.4%	66.2%	33.6%	66.4%
AL	1984	243,014	100,650	duPONT, ELISE	142,070	CARPER, THOMAS R.*	294	41,420 D	41.4%	58.5%	41.5%	58.5%
AL	1982	188,064	87,153	EVANS, THOMAS B.*	98,533	CARPER, THOMAS R.	2,378	11,380 D	46.3%	52.4%	46.9%	53.1%
AL	1980	216,629	133,842	EVANS, THOMAS B.*	81,227	MAXWELL, ROBERT L.	1,560	52,615 R	61.8%	37.5%	62.2%	37.8%
AL	1978	157,566	91,689	EVANS, THOMAS B.*	64,863	HINDES, GARY E.	1,014	26,826 R	58.2%	41.2%	58.6%	41.4%
AL	1976	214,799	110,677	EVANS, THOMAS B.	102,431	SHIPLEY, SAMUEL L.	1,691	8,246 R	51.5%	47.7%	51.9%	48.1%
AL	1974	160,328	93,826	duPONT, PIERRE*	63,490	SOLES, JAMES	3,012	30,336 R	58.5%	39.6%	59.6%	40.4%
AL	1972	225,851	141,237	duPONT, PIERRE*	83,230	HANDLOFF, NORMA	1,384	58,007 R	62.5%	36.9%	62.9%	37.1%
AL	1970	160,313	86,125	duPONT, PIERRE	71,429	DANIELLO, JOHN D.	2,759	14,696 R	53.7%	44.6%	54.7%	45.3%
AL	1968	200,820	117,827	ROTH, WILLIAM V.*	82,993	McDOWELL, HARRIS B.		34,834 R	58.7%	41.3%	58.7%	41.3%
AL	1966	163,103	90,961	ROTH, WILLIAM V.	72,142	McDOWELL, HARRIS B.*		18,819 R	55.8%	44.2%	55.8%	44.2%
AL	1964	198,691	86,254	SNOWDEN, JAMES H.	112,361	McDOWELL, HARRIS B.*	76	26,107 D	43.4%	56.6%	43.4%	56.6%
AL	1962	153,356	71,934	WILLIAMS, WILMER F.	81,166	McDOWELL, HARRIS B.*	256	9,232 D	46.9%	52.9%	47.0%	53.0%
AL	1960	194,564	96,337	McKINSTRY, JAMES T.	98,227	McDOWELL, HARRIS B.*		1,890 D	49.5%	50.5%	49.5%	50.5%
AL	1958	152,896	76,099	HASKELL, HARRY G.*	76,797	McDOWELL, HARRIS B.		698 D	49.8%	50.2%	49.8%	50.2%
AL	1956	176,182	91,538	HASKELL, HARRY G.	84,644	McDOWELL, HARRIS B.*		6,894 R	52.0%	48.0%	52.0%	48.0%
AL	1954	144,236	65,035	MARTIN, LILLIAN	79,201	McDOWELL, HARRIS B.		14,166 D	45.1%	54.9%	45.1%	54.9%
AL	1952	170,015	88,285	WARBURTON, H.B.	81,730	SCANNELL, JOSEPH S.		6,555 R	51.9%	48.1%	51.9%	48.1%
AL	1950	129,404	73,313	BOGGS, J. CALEB*	56,091	WINCHESTER, H.M.		17,222 R	56.7%	43.3%	56.7%	43.3%
AL	1948	140,535	71,127	BOGGS, J. CALEB*	68,909	McGUIGAN, J. CARL	499	2,218 R	50.6%	49.0%	50.8%	49.2%
AL	1946	112,621	63,516	BOGGS, J. CALEB	49,105	TRAYNOR, PHILIP A.*		14,411 R	56.4%	43.6%	56.4%	43.6%

An asterisk (*) denotes incumbent.

DELAWARE

GENERAL AND PRIMARY ELECTIONS

2010 GENERAL ELECTIONS

Senator   Other vote was 8,201 Independent Party of Delaware (Glenn A. Miller); 2,101 Libertarian (James W. Rash) 25 write-in (Maurice F. Bourgeois); 10 write-in (Samtra Debard).

House   Other vote was:

At Large   3,704 Independent Party of Delaware (Earl R. Lofland); 1,986 Libertarian (Brent A. Wangen); 961 Blue Enigma (Jeffrey Brown).

DELAWARE

GENERAL AND PRIMARY ELECTIONS

2010 PRIMARY ELECTIONS

Primary	September 14, 2010	**Registration** (as of Sept. 1, 2010)	Democratic	292,738
			Republican	182,796
			Others	146,212
			TOTAL	*621,746*

Primary Type   Closed—Only registered Democrats and Republicans could vote in their party's primary.

	REPUBLICAN PRIMARIES			DEMOCRATIC PRIMARIES	
Senator	Christine O'Donnell	30,563	53.1%	Christopher A. Coons	Unopposed
	Michael N. Castle	27,021	46.9%		
	TOTAL	*57,584*			
House At Large	Glen Urquhart	27,343	48.6%	John C. Carney Jr.	Unopposed
	Michele Rollins	26,789	47.7%		
	Rose Izzo	2,082	3.7%		
	TOTAL	*56,214*			

An asterisk (*) denotes incumbent. The names of unopposed candidates did not appear on the primary ballot; therefore, no votes were cast for these candidates.

FLORIDA

Congressional districts first established for elections held in 2002
25 members

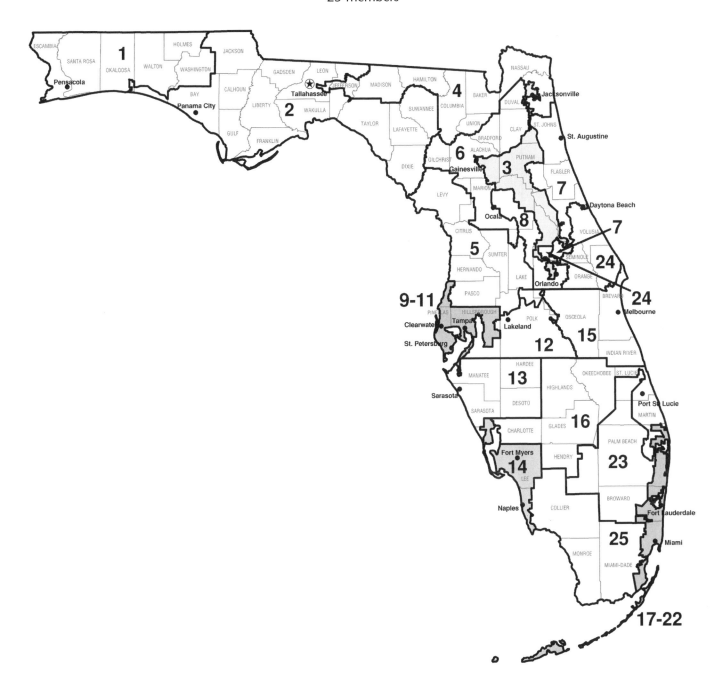

FLORIDA

St. Petersburg, Tampa, Fort Myers Areas

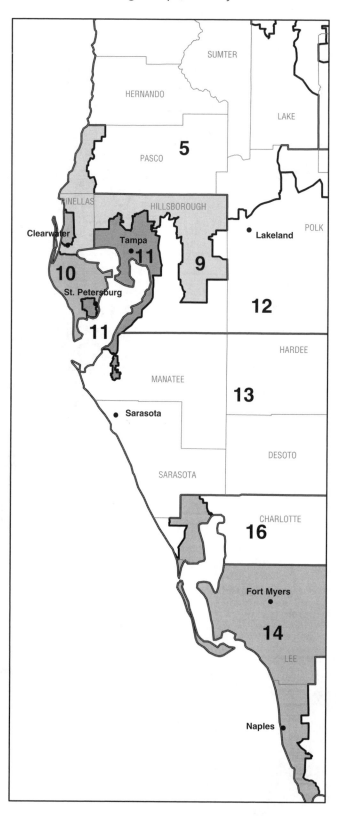

FLORIDA

Miami, Fort Lauderdale Areas

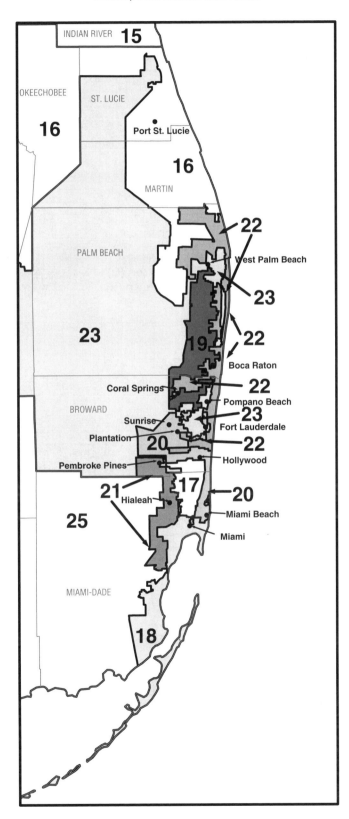

FLORIDA

GOVERNOR
Rick Scott (R). Elected 2010 to a four-year term.

SENATORS (1 Democrat,1 Republican)
Bill Nelson (D). Reelected 2006 to a six-year term. Previously elected 2000.

Marco Rubio (R). Elected 2010 to a six-year term.

REPRESENTATIVES (19 Republicans, 6 Democrats)

1. Jeff Miller (R)
2. Steve Southerland (R)
3. Corrine Brown (D)
4. Ander Crenshaw (R)
5. Richard B. Nugent (R)
6. Cliff Stearns (R)
7. John L. Mica (R)
8. Daniel Webster (R)
9. Gus Michael Bilirakis (R)
10. C. W. Bill Young (R)
11. Kathy Castor (D)
12. Dennis A. Ross (R)
13. Vern Buchanan (R)
14. Connie Mack (R)
15. Bill Posey (R)
16. Tom Rooney (R)
17. Frederica S. Wilson (D)
18. Ileana Ros-Lehtinen (R)
19. Ted Deutch (D)
20. Debbie Wasserman Schultz (D)
21. Mario Diaz-Balart (R)
22. Allen West (R)
23. Alcee L. Hastings (D)
24. Sandra "Sandy" Adams (R)
25. David Rivera (R)

POSTWAR VOTE FOR PRESIDENT

Year	Total Vote	Republican Vote	Candidate	Democratic Vote	Candidate	Other Vote	Rep.-Dem. Plurality	Total Vote Rep.	Total Vote Dem.	Major Vote Rep.	Major Vote Dem.
2008	8,390,744	4,045,624	McCain, John	4,282,074	Obama, Barack	63,046	236,450 D	48.2%	51.0%	48.6%	51.4%
2004	7,609,810	3,964,522	Bush, George W.	3,583,544	Kerry, John	61,744	380,978 R	52.1%	47.1%	52.5%	47.5%
2000**	5,963,110	2,912,790	Bush, George W.	2,912,253	Gore, Al	138,067	537 R	48.8%	48.8%	50.0%	50.0%
1996**	5,303,794	2,244,536	Dole, Bob	2,546,870	Clinton, Bill	512,388	302,334 D	42.3%	48.0%	46.8%	53.2%
1992**	5,314,392	2,173,310	Bush, George	2,072,698	Clinton, Bill	1,068,384	100,612 R	40.9%	39.0%	51.2%	48.8%
1988	4,302,313	2,618,885	Bush, George	1,656,701	Dukakis, Michael S.	26,727	962,184 R	60.9%	38.5%	61.3%	38.7%
1984	4,180,051	2,730,350	Reagan, Ronald	1,448,816	Mondale, Walter F.	885	1,281,534 R	65.3%	34.7%	65.3%	34.7%
1980**	3,686,930	2,046,951	Reagan, Ronald	1,419,475	Carter, Jimmy	220,504	627,476 R	55.5%	38.5%	59.1%	40.9%
1976	3,150,631	1,469,531	Ford, Gerald R.	1,636,000	Carter, Jimmy	45,100	166,469 D	46.6%	51.9%	47.3%	52.7%
1972	2,583,283	1,857,759	Nixon, Richard M.	718,117	McGovern, George S.	7,407	1,139,642 R	71.9%	27.8%	72.1%	27.9%
1968**	2,187,805	886,804	Nixon, Richard M.	676,794	Humphrey, Hubert H.	624,207	210,010 R	40.5%	30.9%	56.7%	43.3%
1964	1,854,481	905,941	Goldwater, Barry M.	948,540	Johnson, Lyndon B.		42,599 D	48.9%	51.1%	48.9%	51.1%
1960	1,544,176	795,476	Nixon, Richard M.	748,700	Kennedy, John F.		46,776 R	51.5%	48.5%	51.5%	48.5%
1956	1,125,762	643,849	Eisenhower, Dwight D.	480,371	Stevenson, Adlai E.	1,542	163,478 R	57.2%	42.7%	57.3%	42.7%
1952	989,337	544,036	Eisenhower, Dwight D.	444,950	Stevenson, Adlai E.	351	99,086 R	55.0%	45.0%	55.0%	45.0%
1948**	577,643	194,280	Dewey, Thomas E.	281,988	Truman, Harry S.	101,375	87,708 D	33.6%	48.8%	40.8%	59.2%

**In past elections, the other vote included: 2000 - 97,488 Green (Ralph Nader); 1996 - 483,870 Reform (Ross Perot); 1992 - 1,053,067 Independent (Perot); 1980 - 189,692 Independent (John Anderson); 1968 - 624,207 American Independent (George Wallace); 1948 - 89,755 States' Rights (Strom Thurmond).

FLORIDA

POSTWAR VOTE FOR GOVERNOR

Year	Total Vote	Republican Vote	Candidate	Democratic Vote	Candidate	Other Vote	Rep.-Dem. Plurality	Total Vote Rep.	Dem.	Major Vote Rep.	Dem.
2010	5,359,735	2,619,335	Scott, Rick	2,557,785	Sink, Alex	182,615	61,550 R	48.9%	47.7%	50.6%	49.4%
2006	4,829,270	2,519,845	Crist, Charlie	2,178,289	Davis, Jim	131,136	341,556 R	52.2%	45.1%	53.6%	46.4%
2002	5,100,581	2,856,845	Bush, Jeb	2,201,427	McBride, Bill	42,309	655,418 R	56.0%	43.2%	56.5%	43.5%
1998	3,964,441	2,191,105	Bush, Jeb	1,773,054	MacKay, Buddy	282	418,051 R	55.3%	44.7%	55.3%	44.7%
1994	4,206,659	2,071,068	Bush, Jeb	2,135,008	Chiles, Lawton	583	63,940 D	49.2%	50.8%	49.2%	50.8%
1990	3,530,871	1,535,068	Martinez, Bob	1,995,206	Chiles, Lawton	597	460,138 D	43.5%	56.5%	43.5%	56.5%
1986	3,386,171	1,847,525	Martinez, Bob	1,538,620	Pajcic, Steve	26	308,905 R	54.6%	45.4%	54.6%	45.4%
1982	2,688,566	949,013	Bafalis, L. A. "Skip"	1,739,553	Graham, Bob		790,540 D	35.3%	64.7%	35.3%	64.7%
1978	2,530,468	1,123,888	Eckerd, Jack M.	1,406,580	Graham, Bob		282,692 D	44.4%	55.6%	44.4%	55.6%
1974	1,828,392	709,438	Thomas, Jerry	1,118,954	Askew, Reubin		409,516 D	38.8%	61.2%	38.8%	61.2%
1970	1,730,813	746,243	Kirk, Claude R.	984,305	Askew, Reubin	265	238,062 D	43.1%	56.9%	43.1%	56.9%
1966	1,489,661	821,190	Kirk, Claude R.	668,233	High, Robert King	238	152,957 R	55.1%	44.9%	55.1%	44.9%
1964S	1,663,481	686,297	Holley, Charles R.	933,554	Burns, Haydon	43,630	247,257 D	41.3%	56.1%	42.4%	57.6%
1960	1,419,343	569,936	Petersen, George C.	849,407	Bryant, Farris		279,471 D	40.2%	59.8%	40.2%	59.8%
1956	1,014,733	266,980	Washburne, W. A.	747,753	Collins, LeRoy		480,773 D	26.3%	73.7%	26.3%	73.7%
1954S	357,783	69,852	Watson, J. Tom	287,769	Collins, LeRoy	162	217,917 D	19.5%	80.4%	19.5%	80.5%
1952	834,518	210,009	Swan, Harry S.	624,463	McCarty, Dan	46	414,454 D	25.2%	74.8%	25.2%	74.8%
1948	457,638	76,153	Acker, Bert Lee	381,459	Warren, Fuller	26	305,306 D	16.6%	83.4%	16.6%	83.4%

**The1964 election was for a two-year term to permit shifting the vote for governor to non-presidential years. The 1954 election was for a short term to fill a vacancy.

POSTWAR VOTE FOR SENATOR

Year	Total Vote	Republican Vote	Candidate	Democratic Vote	Candidate	Other Vote	Rep.-Dem. Plurality	Total Vote Rep.	Dem.	Major Vote Rep.	Dem.
2010**	5,411,106	2,645,743	Rubio, Marco	1,092,936	Meek, Kendrick B.	1,672,427	1,038,194 R	48.9%	20.2%	70.8%	29.2%
2006	4,793,534	1,826,127	Harris, Katherine	2,890,548	Nelson, Bill	76,859	1,064,421 D	38.1%	60.3%	38.7%	61.3%
2004	7,429,894	3,672,864	Martinez, Mel	3,590,201	Castor, Betty	166,829	82,663 R	49.4%	48.3%	50.6%	49.4%
2000	5,856,731	2,705,348	McCollum, Bill	2,989,487	Nelson, Bill	161,896	284,139 D	46.2%	51.0%	47.5%	52.5%
1998	3,900,162	1,463,755	Crist, Charlie	2,436,407	Graham, Bob		972,652 D	37.5%	62.5%	37.5%	62.5%
1994	4,106,176	2,894,726	Mack, Connie	1,210,412	Rodham, Hugh E.	1,038	1,684,314 R	70.5%	29.5%	70.5%	29.5%
1992	4,962,290	1,716,505	Grant, Bill	3,245,565	Graham, Bob	220	1,529,060 D	34.6%	65.4%	34.6%	65.4%
1988	4,068,209	2,051,071	Mack, Connie	2,016,553	MacKay, Buddy	585	34,518 R	50.4%	49.6%	50.4%	49.6%
1986	3,429,996	1,552,376	Hawkins, Paula	1,877,543	Graham, Bob	77	325,167 D	45.3%	54.7%	45.3%	54.7%
1982	2,653,419	1,015,330	Poole, Van B.	1,637,667	Chiles, Lawton	422	622,337 D	38.3%	61.7%	38.3%	61.7%
1980	3,528,028	1,822,460	Hawkins, Paula	1,705,409	Gunter, Bill	159	117,051 R	51.7%	48.3%	51.7%	48.3%
1976	2,857,534	1,057,886	Grady, John	1,799,518	Chiles, Lawton	130	741,632 D	37.0%	63.0%	37.0%	63.0%
1974**	1,800,539	736,674	Eckerd, Jack M.	781,031	Stone, Richard	282,834	44,357 D	40.9%	43.4%	48.5%	51.5%
1970	1,675,378	772,817	Cramer, William C.	902,438	Chiles, Lawton	123	129,621 D	46.1%	53.9%	46.1%	53.9%
1968	2,024,136	1,131,499	Gurney, Edward J.	892,637	Collins, LeRoy		238,862 R	55.9%	44.1%	55.9%	44.1%
1964	1,560,337	562,212	Kirk, Claude R.	997,585	Holland, Spessard L.	540	435,373 D	36.0%	63.9%	36.0%	64.0%
1962	939,207	281,381	Rupert, Emerson H.	657,633	Smathers, George A.	193	376,252 D	30.0%	70.0%	30.0%	70.0%
1958	542,069	155,956	Hyzer, Leland	386,113	Holland, Spessard L.		230,157 D	28.8%	71.2%	28.8%	71.2%
1956	655,418		—	655,418	Smathers, George A.		655,418 D		100.0%		100.0%
1952	617,800		—	616,665	Holland, Spessard L.	1,135	616,665 D		99.8%		100.0%
1950	313,487	74,228	Booth, John P.	238,987	Smathers, George A.	272	164,759 D	23.7%	76.2%	23.7%	76.3%
1946	198,640	42,408	Schad, J. Harry	156,232	Holland, Spessard L.		113,824 D	21.3%	78.7%	21.3%	78.7%

**In past elections, the other vote included: 2010 - 1,607,549 Independent (Charlie Crist), who placed second statewide; 1974 - 282,659 American (John Grady). The Republican Party did not run a candidate in the 1952 and 1956 Senate elections.

FLORIDA
GOVERNOR 2010

2010 Census Population	County	Total Vote	Republican	Democratic	Other	Rep.-Dem. Plurality		Total Vote Rep.	Total Vote Dem.	Major Vote Rep.	Major Vote Dem.
247,336	ALACHUA	73,961	28,129	43,933	1,899	15,804	D	38.0%	59.4%	39.0%	61.0%
27,115	BAKER	7,924	4,940	2,731	253	2,209	R	62.3%	34.5%	64.4%	35.6%
168,852	BAY	54,997	36,512	15,689	2,796	20,823	R	66.4%	28.5%	69.9%	30.1%
28,520	BRADFORD	8,075	4,850	2,983	242	1,867	R	60.1%	36.9%	61.9%	38.1%
543,376	BREVARD	196,391	106,838	80,865	8,688	25,973	R	54.4%	41.2%	56.9%	43.1%
1,748,066	BROWARD	420,531	140,445	271,606	8,480	131,161	D	33.4%	64.6%	34.1%	65.9%
14,625	CALHOUN	4,296	2,201	1,855	240	346	R	51.2%	43.2%	54.3%	45.7%
159,978	CHARLOTTE	59,381	32,207	23,838	3,336	8,369	R	54.2%	40.1%	57.5%	42.5%
141,236	CITRUS	54,808	29,925	21,596	3,287	8,329	R	54.6%	39.4%	58.1%	41.9%
190,865	CLAY	63,667	44,547	17,246	1,874	27,301	R	70.0%	27.1%	72.1%	27.9%
321,520	COLLIER	102,833	66,960	33,408	2,465	33,552	R	65.1%	32.5%	66.7%	33.3%
67,531	COLUMBIA	18,905	11,089	7,068	748	4,021	R	58.7%	37.4%	61.1%	38.9%
34,862	DESOTO	6,906	3,667	2,887	352	780	R	53.1%	41.8%	56.0%	44.0%
16,422	DIXIE	5,239	2,810	2,058	371	752	R	53.6%	39.3%	57.7%	42.3%
864,263	DUVAL	261,785	135,074	120,097	6,614	14,977	R	51.6%	45.9%	52.9%	47.1%
297,619	ESCAMBIA	95,916	54,607	36,873	4,436	17,734	R	56.9%	38.4%	59.7%	40.3%
95,696	FLAGLER	33,476	17,711	14,430	1,335	3,281	R	52.9%	43.1%	55.1%	44.9%
11,549	FRANKLIN	4,061	1,938	1,945	178	7	D	47.7%	47.9%	49.9%	50.1%
46,389	GADSDEN	16,698	4,324	12,067	307	7,743	D	25.9%	72.3%	26.4%	73.6%
16,939	GILCHRIST	5,382	3,321	1,797	264	1,524	R	61.7%	33.4%	64.9%	35.1%
12,884	GLADES	2,785	1,616	1,072	97	544	R	58.0%	38.5%	60.1%	39.9%
15,863	GULF	5,036	2,960	1,779	297	1,181	R	58.8%	35.3%	62.5%	37.5%
14,799	HAMILTON	3,991	1,919	1,865	207	54	R	48.1%	46.7%	50.7%	49.3%
27,731	HARDEE	5,220	3,116	1,881	223	1,235	R	59.7%	36.0%	62.4%	37.6%
39,140	HENDRY	6,517	3,551	2,743	223	808	R	54.5%	42.1%	56.4%	43.6%
172,778	HERNANDO	58,325	30,056	25,127	3,142	4,929	R	51.5%	43.1%	54.5%	45.5%
98,786	HIGHLANDS	29,847	17,171	11,143	1,533	6,028	R	57.5%	37.3%	60.6%	39.4%
1,229,226	HILLSBOROUGH	317,566	148,429	158,995	10,142	10,566	D	46.7%	50.1%	48.3%	51.7%
19,927	HOLMES	6,054	4,067	1,636	351	2,431	R	67.2%	27.0%	71.3%	28.7%
138,028	INDIAN RIVER	47,403	27,935	17,650	1,818	10,285	R	58.9%	37.2%	61.3%	38.7%
49,746	JACKSON	14,942	7,420	6,898	624	522	R	49.7%	46.2%	51.8%	48.2%
14,761	JEFFERSON	6,220	2,455	3,606	159	1,151	D	39.5%	58.0%	40.5%	59.5%
8,870	LAFAYETTE	2,502	1,405	980	117	425	R	56.2%	39.2%	58.9%	41.1%
297,052	LAKE	101,910	56,790	40,400	4,720	16,390	R	55.7%	39.6%	58.4%	41.6%
618,754	LEE	181,901	107,460	68,041	6,400	39,419	R	59.1%	37.4%	61.2%	38.8%
275,487	LEON	99,703	31,328	66,477	1,898	35,149	D	31.4%	66.7%	32.0%	68.0%
40,801	LEVY	12,731	7,405	4,711	615	2,694	R	58.2%	37.0%	61.1%	38.9%
8,365	LIBERTY	2,195	1,020	1,050	125	30	D	46.5%	47.8%	49.3%	50.7%
19,224	MADISON	6,286	2,794	3,281	211	487	D	44.4%	52.2%	46.0%	54.0%
322,833	MANATEE	105,974	57,459	44,284	4,231	13,175	R	54.2%	41.8%	56.5%	43.5%
331,298	MARION	114,361	61,978	46,449	5,934	15,529	R	54.2%	40.6%	57.2%	42.8%
146,318	MARTIN	54,246	30,416	21,946	1,884	8,470	R	56.1%	40.5%	58.1%	41.9%
2,496,435	MIAMI-DADE	487,888	204,918	274,638	8,332	69,720	D	42.0%	56.3%	42.7%	57.3%
73,090	MONROE	26,130	12,608	12,577	945	31	R	48.3%	48.1%	50.1%	49.9%
73,314	NASSAU	26,821	18,275	7,683	863	10,592	R	68.1%	28.6%	70.4%	29.6%

FLORIDA

GOVERNOR 2010

2010 Census Population	County	Total Vote	Republican	Democratic	Other	Rep.-Dem. Plurality		Percentage			
								Total Vote		Major Vote	
								Rep.	Dem.	Rep.	Dem.
180,822	OKALOOSA	60,876	42,200	14,499	4,177	27,701	R	69.3%	23.8%	74.4%	25.6%
39,996	OKEECHOBEE	8,215	4,453	3,375	387	1,078	R	54.2%	41.1%	56.9%	43.1%
1,145,956	ORANGE	271,926	117,191	147,509	7,226	30,318	D	43.1%	54.2%	44.3%	55.7%
268,685	OSCEOLA	53,395	24,053	27,469	1,873	3,416	D	45.0%	51.4%	46.7%	53.3%
1,320,134	PALM BEACH	383,853	151,406	223,194	9,253	71,788	D	39.4%	58.1%	40.4%	59.6%
464,697	PASCO	136,558	70,635	59,098	6,825	11,537	R	51.7%	43.3%	54.4%	45.6%
916,542	PINELLAS	303,380	136,657	153,865	12,858	17,208	D	45.0%	50.7%	47.0%	53.0%
602,095	POLK	160,204	85,693	68,168	6,343	17,525	R	53.5%	42.6%	55.7%	44.3%
74,364	PUTNAM	21,442	12,438	8,237	767	4,201	R	58.0%	38.4%	60.2%	39.8%
190,039	ST. JOHNS	74,754	47,573	25,054	2,127	22,519	R	63.6%	33.5%	65.5%	34.5%
277,789	ST. LUCIE	75,646	34,321	38,029	3,296	3,708	D	45.4%	50.3%	47.4%	52.6%
151,372	SANTA ROSA	49,743	34,523	12,371	2,849	22,152	R	69.4%	24.9%	73.6%	26.4%
379,448	SARASOTA	145,282	73,089	66,551	5,642	6,538	R	50.3%	45.8%	52.3%	47.7%
422,718	SEMINOLE	131,927	68,351	59,412	4,164	8,939	R	51.8%	45.0%	53.5%	46.5%
93,420	SUMTER	41,825	25,845	14,060	1,920	11,785	R	61.8%	33.6%	64.8%	35.2%
41,551	SUWANNEE	13,405	8,355	4,417	633	3,938	R	62.3%	33.0%	65.4%	34.6%
22,570	TAYLOR	6,628	3,910	2,457	261	1,453	R	59.0%	37.1%	61.4%	38.6%
15,535	UNION	3,578	1,781	1,667	130	114	R	49.8%	46.6%	51.7%	48.3%
494,593	VOLUSIA	157,444	77,039	73,765	6,640	3,274	R	48.9%	46.9%	51.1%	48.9%
30,776	WAKULLA	10,986	5,439	5,121	426	318	R	49.5%	46.6%	51.5%	48.5%
55,043	WALTON	18,876	12,744	5,072	1,060	7,672	R	67.5%	26.9%	71.5%	28.5%
24,896	WASHINGTON	8,006	4,993	2,511	502	2,482	R	62.4%	31.4%	66.5%	33.5%
18,801,310	TOTAL	5,359,735	2,619,335	2,557,785	182,615	61,550	R	48.9%	47.7%	50.6%	49.4%

FLORIDA

SENATOR 2010

2010 Census Population	County	Total Vote	Republican	Democratic	Independent (Crist)	Other	Plurality		Percentage		
									Rep.	Dem.	Ind.
247,336	ALACHUA	74,476	29,825	21,314	22,302	1,035	7,523	R	40.0%	28.6%	29.9%
27,115	BAKER	7,995	5,435	1,031	1,361	168	4,074	R	68.0%	12.9%	17.0%
168,852	BAY	55,646	40,408	6,028	8,098	1,112	32,310	R	72.6%	10.8%	14.6%
28,520	BRADFORD	8,135	5,156	1,374	1,447	158	3,709	R	63.4%	16.9%	17.8%
543,376	BREVARD	198,788	107,930	32,069	56,202	2,587	51,728	R	54.3%	16.1%	28.3%
1,748,066	BROWARD	420,243	133,264	133,026	151,125	2,828	17,861	I	31.7%	31.7%	36.0%
14,625	CALHOUN	4,313	2,772	597	787	157	1,985	R	64.3%	13.8%	18.2%
159,978	CHARLOTTE	60,199	31,258	6,932	21,269	740	9,989	R	51.9%	11.5%	35.3%
141,236	CITRUS	55,572	27,517	6,374	20,622	1,059	6,895	R	49.5%	11.5%	37.1%
190,865	CLAY	64,225	44,926	7,253	11,272	774	33,654	R	70.0%	11.3%	17.6%
321,520	COLLIER	103,275	66,349	8,876	27,188	862	39,161	R	64.2%	8.6%	26.3%
67,531	COLUMBIA	19,110	11,874	3,056	3,868	312	8,006	R	62.1%	16.0%	20.2%
34,862	DESOTO	7,002	3,608	1,104	2,151	139	1,457	R	51.5%	15.8%	30.7%
16,422	DIXIE	5,266	3,038	914	1,065	249	1,973	R	57.7%	17.4%	20.2%
864,263	DUVAL	264,036	140,447	72,184	48,323	3,082	68,263	R	53.2%	27.3%	18.3%
297,619	ESCAMBIA	97,514	55,364	18,377	22,365	1,408	32,999	R	56.8%	18.8%	22.9%
95,696	FLAGLER	33,715	17,617	6,764	8,970	364	8,647	R	52.3%	20.1%	26.6%
11,549	FRANKLIN	4,075	2,223	654	1,115	83	1,108	R	54.6%	16.0%	27.4%

FLORIDA

SENATOR 2010

2010 Census Population	County	Total Vote	Republican	Democratic	Independent (Crist)	Other	Plurality		Percentage		
									Rep.	Dem.	Ind.
46,389	GADSDEN	16,760	4,411	7,894	4,289	166	3,483	D	26.3%	47.1%	25.6%
16,939	GILCHRIST	5,425	3,531	646	1,106	142	2,425	R	65.1%	11.9%	20.4%
12,884	GLADES	2,802	1,598	341	806	57	792	R	57.0%	12.2%	28.8%
15,863	GULF	5,069	3,441	724	768	136	2,673	R	67.9%	14.3%	15.2%
14,799	HAMILTON	4,003	1,966	1,098	826	113	868	R	49.1%	27.4%	20.6%
27,731	HARDEE	5,278	2,862	771	1,543	102	1,319	R	54.2%	14.6%	29.2%
39,140	HENDRY	6,571	3,681	1,355	1,434	101	2,247	R	56.0%	20.6%	21.8%
172,778	HERNANDO	59,186	27,413	8,020	22,823	930	4,590	R	46.3%	13.6%	38.6%
98,786	HIGHLANDS	30,286	16,489	4,360	8,914	523	7,575	R	54.4%	14.4%	29.4%
1,229,226	HILLSBOROUGH	321,120	144,906	63,451	109,141	3,622	35,765	R	45.1%	19.8%	34.0%
19,927	HOLMES	6,076	4,501	570	794	211	3,707	R	74.1%	9.4%	13.1%
138,028	INDIAN RIVER	48,107	29,288	6,053	12,178	588	17,110	R	60.9%	12.6%	25.3%
49,746	JACKSON	15,067	9,115	3,434	2,188	330	5,681	R	60.5%	22.8%	14.5%
14,761	JEFFERSON	6,259	2,476	1,886	1,818	79	590	R	39.6%	30.1%	29.0%
8,870	LAFAYETTE	2,512	1,614	277	548	73	1,066	R	64.3%	11.0%	21.8%
297,052	LAKE	103,302	60,967	18,770	21,982	1,583	38,985	R	59.0%	18.2%	21.3%
618,754	LEE	180,355	103,169	18,655	56,629	1,902	46,540	R	57.2%	10.3%	31.4%
275,487	LEON	100,480	34,222	24,689	40,730	839	6,508	I	34.1%	24.6%	40.5%
40,801	LEVY	12,816	7,613	2,250	2,628	325	4,985	R	59.4%	17.6%	20.5%
8,365	LIBERTY	2,209	1,228	304	600	77	628	R	55.6%	13.8%	27.2%
19,224	MADISON	6,318	2,758	1,990	1,452	118	1,306	R	43.7%	31.5%	23.0%
322,833	MANATEE	107,297	53,127	14,363	38,667	1,140	14,460	R	49.5%	13.4%	36.0%
331,298	MARION	115,808	64,565	21,377	27,709	2,157	36,856	R	55.8%	18.5%	23.9%
146,318	MARTIN	55,061	31,935	5,922	16,606	598	15,329	R	58.0%	10.8%	30.2%
2,496,435	MIAMI-DADE	491,895	220,305	146,029	121,720	3,841	74,276	R	44.8%	29.7%	24.7%
73,090	MONROE	26,438	11,282	4,252	10,560	344	722	R	42.7%	16.1%	39.9%
73,314	NASSAU	27,098	18,458	3,153	5,150	337	13,308	R	68.1%	11.6%	19.0%
180,822	OKALOOSA	61,835	44,084	6,007	10,320	1,424	33,764	R	71.3%	9.7%	16.7%
39,996	OKEECHOBEE	8,309	4,550	1,106	2,515	138	2,035	R	54.8%	13.3%	30.3%
1,145,956	ORANGE	274,973	130,903	79,616	61,233	3,221	51,287	R	47.6%	29.0%	22.3%
268,685	OSCEOLA	53,847	26,008	15,100	11,926	813	10,908	R	48.3%	28.0%	22.1%
1,320,134	PALM BEACH	387,523	153,256	75,242	156,140	2,885	2,884	I	39.5%	19.4%	40.3%
464,697	PASCO	138,245	64,141	17,589	54,362	2,153	9,779	R	46.4%	12.7%	39.3%
916,542	PINELLAS	307,851	122,339	51,629	129,529	4,354	7,190	I	39.7%	16.8%	42.1%
602,095	POLK	162,308	79,274	30,899	49,885	2,250	29,389	R	48.8%	19.0%	30.7%
74,364	PUTNAM	21,630	12,869	4,351	3,996	414	8,518	R	59.5%	20.1%	18.5%
190,039	ST. JOHNS	75,625	49,761	8,365	16,763	736	32,998	R	65.8%	11.1%	22.2%
277,789	ST. LUCIE	76,436	36,218	16,472	22,699	1,047	13,519	R	47.4%	21.6%	29.7%
151,372	SANTA ROSA	50,413	35,461	3,837	10,227	888	25,234	R	70.3%	7.6%	20.3%
379,448	SARASOTA	147,507	68,284	18,279	59,547	1,397	8,737	R	46.3%	12.4%	40.4%
422,718	SEMINOLE	133,828	76,550	26,449	29,231	1,598	47,319	R	57.2%	19.8%	21.8%
93,420	SUMTER	42,425	26,805	5,613	9,605	402	17,200	R	63.2%	13.2%	22.6%
41,551	SUWANNEE	13,513	8,783	1,776	2,695	259	6,088	R	65.0%	13.1%	19.9%
22,570	TAYLOR	6,652	3,932	1,096	1,480	144	2,452	R	59.1%	16.5%	22.2%
15,535	UNION	3,621	2,266	585	695	75	1,571	R	62.6%	16.2%	19.2%
494,593	VOLUSIA	159,162	79,727	33,913	43,278	2,244	36,449	R	50.1%	21.3%	27.2%
30,776	WAKULLA	11,059	5,431	1,439	3,992	197	1,439	R	49.1%	13.0%	36.1%
55,043	WALTON	19,066	13,613	1,820	3,193	440	10,420	R	71.4%	9.5%	16.7%
24,896	WASHINGTON	8,095	5,556	1,192	1,099	248	4,364	R	68.6%	14.7%	13.6%
18,801,310	TOTAL	5,411,106	2,645,743	1,092,936	1,607,549	64,878	1,038,194	R	48.9%	20.2%	29.7%

Counties carried by Independent candidate Charlie Crist are indicated by an "I." The plurality represents the vote differential between the leading candidate and the runner-up, regardless of party or independent status.

FLORIDA

HOUSE OF REPRESENTATIVES

			Republican		Democratic				Percentage			
									Total Vote		Major Vote	
CD	Year	Total Vote	Vote	Candidate	Vote	Candidate	Other Vote	Rep.-Dem. Plurality	Rep.	Dem.	Rep.	Dem.
1	2010	213,526	170,821	MILLER, JEFF*	—		42,705	170,821 R	80.0%		100.0%	
1	2008	331,356	232,559	MILLER, JEFF*	98,797	BRYAN, JAMES JIM		133,762 R	70.2%	29.8%	70.2%	29.8%
1	2006	198,126	135,786	MILLER, JEFF*	62,340	ROBERTS, JOE		73,446 R	68.5%	31.5%	68.5%	31.5%
1	2004	309,110	236,604	MILLER, JEFF*	72,506	COUTO, MARK S.		164,098 R	76.5%	23.5%	76.5%	23.5%
1	2002	204,626	152,635	MILLER, JEFF*	51,972	ORAM, BERT	19	100,663 R	74.6%	25.4%	74.6%	25.4%
2	2010	254,438	136,371	SOUTHERLAND, STEVE	105,211	BOYD, ALLEN*	12,856	31,160 R	53.6%	41.4%	56.4%	43.6%
2	2008	350,367	133,404	MULLIGAN, MARK	216,804	BOYD, ALLEN*	159	83,400 D	38.1%	61.9%	38.1%	61.9%
2	2006		—			BOYD, ALLEN*		D				
2	2004	326,987	125,399	KILMER, BEV	201,577	BOYD, ALLEN*	11	76,178 D	38.3%	61.6%	38.4%	61.6%
2	2002	227,439	75,275	McGURK, TOM	152,164	BOYD, ALLEN*		76,889 D	33.1%	66.9%	33.1%	66.9%
3	2010	150,301	50,932	YOST, MICHAEL	94,744	BROWN, CORRINE*	4,625	43,812 D	33.9%	63.0%	35.0%	65.0%
3	2008		—			BROWN, CORRINE*		D				
3	2006		—			BROWN, CORRINE*		D				
3	2004	174,156		—	172,833	BROWN, CORRINE*	1,323	172,833 D		99.2%		100.0%
3	2002	149,213	60,747	CARROLL, JENIFER	88,462	BROWN, CORRINE*	4	27,715 D	40.7%	59.3%	40.7%	59.3%
4	2010	230,845	178,238	CRENSHAW, ANDER*	—		52,607	178,238 R	77.2%		100.0%	
4	2008	343,442	224,112	CRENSHAW, ANDER*	119,330	McGOVERN, JAY		104,782 R	65.3%	34.7%	65.3%	34.7%
4	2006	203,479	141,759	CRENSHAW, ANDER*	61,704	HARMS, ROBERT J.	16	80,055 R	69.7%	30.3%	69.7%	30.3%
4	2004	257,327	256,157	CRENSHAW, ANDER*	—		1,170	256,157 R	99.5%		100.0%	
4	2002	171,661	171,152	CRENSHAW, ANDER*	—		509	171,152 R	99.7%		100.0%	
5	2010	309,673	208,815	NUGENT, RICHARD B.	100,858	PICCILLO, JAMES		107,957 R	67.4%	32.6%	67.4%	32.6%
5	2008	433,632	265,186	BROWN-WAITE, GINNY*	168,446	RUSSELL, JOHN		96,740 R	61.2%	38.8%	61.2%	38.8%
5	2006	271,380	162,421	BROWN-WAITE, GINNY*	108,959	RUSSELL, JOHN		53,462 R	59.9%	40.1%	59.9%	40.1%
5	2004	364,488	240,315	BROWN-WAITE, GINNY*	124,140	WHITTEL, ROGER G.	33	116,175 R	65.9%	34.1%	65.9%	34.1%
5	2002	254,671	121,998	BROWN-WAITE, GINNY	117,758	THURMAN, KAREN L.*	14,915	4,240 R	47.9%	46.2%	50.9%	49.1%
6	2010	250,981	179,349	STEARNS, CLIFF*	—		71,632	179,349 R	71.5%		100.0%	
6	2008	374,957	228,302	STEARNS, CLIFF*	146,655	CUNHA, TIM		81,647 R	60.9%	39.1%	60.9%	39.1%
6	2006	228,129	136,601	STEARNS, CLIFF*	91,528	BRUDERLY, DAVID E.		45,073 R	59.9%	40.1%	59.9%	40.1%
6	2004	327,853	211,137	STEARNS, CLIFF*	116,680	BRUDERLY, DAVID E.	36	94,457 R	64.4%	35.6%	64.4%	35.6%
6	2002	216,616	141,570	STEARNS, CLIFF*	75,046	BRUDERLY, DAVID E.		66,524 R	65.4%	34.6%	65.4%	34.6%
7	2010	268,676	185,470	MICA, JOHN L.*	83,206	BEAVEN, HEATHER		102,264 R	69.0%	31.0%	69.0%	31.0%
7	2008	385,013	238,721	MICA, JOHN L.*	146,292	ARMITAGE, FAYE		92,429 R	62.0%	38.0%	62.0%	38.0%
7	2006	237,240	149,656	MICA, JOHN L.*	87,584	CHAGNON, JOHN F.		62,072 R	63.1%	36.9%	63.1%	36.9%
7	2004			MICA, JOHN L.*	—			R				
7	2002	238,591	142,147	MICA, JOHN L.*	96,444	HOGAN, WAYNE		45,703 R	59.6%	40.4%	59.6%	40.4%
8	2010	220,244	123,586	WEBSTER, DANIEL	84,167	GRAYSON, ALAN*	12,491	39,419 R	56.1%	38.2%	59.5%	40.5%
8	2008	332,344	159,490	KELLER, RIC*	172,854	GRAYSON, ALAN		13,364 D	48.0%	52.0%	48.0%	52.0%
8	2006	180,444	95,258	KELLER, RIC*	82,526	STUART, CHARLIE	2,660	12,732 R	52.8%	45.7%	53.6%	46.4%
8	2004	284,575	172,232	KELLER, RIC*	112,343	MURRAY, STEPHEN		59,889 R	60.5%	39.5%	60.5%	39.5%
8	2002	189,596	123,497	KELLER, RIC*	66,099	DIAZ, EDDIE		57,398 R	65.1%	34.9%	65.1%	34.9%
9	2010	231,591	165,433	BILIRAKIS, GUS MICHAEL*	66,158	DE PALMA, ANITA		99,275 R	71.4%	28.6%	71.4%	28.6%
9	2008	348,378	216,591	BILIRAKIS, GUS MICHAEL*	126,346	MITCHELL, BILL	5,441	90,245 R	62.2%	36.3%	63.2%	36.8%
9	2006	220,013	123,016	BILIRAKIS, GUS MICHAEL	96,978	BUSANSKY, PHYLLIS	19	26,038 R	55.9%	44.1%	55.9%	44.1%
9	2004	284,278	284,035	BILIRAKIS, MICHAEL*	—		243	284,035 R	99.9%		100.0%	
9	2002	237,008	169,369	BILIRAKIS, MICHAEL*	67,623	KALOGIANIS, CHUCK	16	101,746 R	71.5%	28.5%	71.5%	28.5%
10	2010	209,256	137,943	YOUNG, C.W. BILL*	71,313	JUSTICE, CHARLIE		66,630 R	65.9%	34.1%	65.9%	34.1%
10	2008	301,220	182,781	YOUNG, C.W. BILL*	118,430	HACKWORTH, BOB	9	64,351 R	60.7%	39.3%	60.7%	39.3%
10	2006	199,445	131,488	YOUNG, C.W. BILL*	67,950	SIMPSON, SAMM	7	63,538 R	65.9%	34.1%	65.9%	34.1%
10	2004	298,833	207,175	YOUNG, C.W. BILL*	91,658	DERRY, ROBERT D. "BOB"		115,517 R	69.3%	30.7%	69.3%	30.7%
10	2002			YOUNG, C.W. BILL*	—			R				

FLORIDA

HOUSE OF REPRESENTATIVES

CD	Year	Total Vote	Republican Vote	Candidate	Democratic Vote	Candidate	Other Vote	Rep.-Dem. Plurality		Total Vote Rep.	Total Vote Dem.	Major Vote Rep.	Major Vote Dem.
11	2010	153,145	61,817	PRENDERGAST, MIKE	91,328	CASTOR, KATHY*		29,511	D	40.4%	59.6%	40.4%	59.6%
11	2008	256,931	72,825	ADAMS, EDDIE JR.	184,106	CASTOR, KATHY*		111,281	D	28.3%	71.7%	28.3%	71.7%
11	2006	139,942	42,454	ADAMS, EDDIE JR.	97,470	CASTOR, KATHY	18	55,016	D	30.3%	69.7%	30.3%	69.7%
11	2004	223,481		—	191,780	DAVIS, JIM*	31,701	191,780	D		85.8%		100.0%
11	2002			—		DAVIS, JIM*			D				
12	2010	213,330	102,704	ROSS, DENNIS A.	87,769	EDWARDS, LORI	22,857	14,935	R	48.1%	41.1%	53.9%	46.1%
12	2008	323,163	185,698	PUTNAM, ADAM H.*	137,465	TUDOR, DOUG		48,233	R	57.5%	42.5%	57.5%	42.5%
12	2006	180,064	124,452	PUTNAM, ADAM H.*		—	55,612	124,452	R	69.1%		100.0%	
12	2004	276,169	179,204	PUTNAM, ADAM H.*	96,965	HAGENMAIER, BOB		82,239	R	64.9%	35.1%	64.9%	35.1%
12	2002			PUTNAM, ADAM H.*		—			R				
13	2010	266,934	183,811	BUCHANAN, VERN*	83,123	GOLDEN, JAMES T.		100,688	R	68.9%	31.1%	68.9%	31.1%
13	2008	367,996	204,382	BUCHANAN, VERN*	137,967	JENNINGS, CHRISTINE	25,647	66,415	R	55.5%	37.5%	59.7%	40.3%
13	2006	238,249	119,309	BUCHANAN, VERN	118,940	JENNINGS, CHRISTINE		369	R	50.1%	49.9%	50.1%	49.9%
13	2004	344,438	190,477	HARRIS, KATHERINE*	153,961	SCHNEIDER, JAN		36,516	R	55.3%	44.7%	55.3%	44.7%
13	2002	253,809	139,048	HARRIS, KATHERINE	114,739	SCHNEIDER, JAN	22	24,309	R	54.8%	45.2%	54.8%	45.2%
14	2010	274,691	188,341	MACK, CONNIE*	74,525	ROACH, JAMES LLOYD	11,825	113,816	R	68.6%	27.1%	71.6%	28.4%
14	2008	377,891	224,602	MACK, CONNIE*	93,590	NEELD, ROBERT M.	59,699	131,012	R	59.4%	24.8%	70.6%	29.4%
14	2006	235,539	151,615	MACK, CONNIE*	83,920	NEELD, ROBERT M.	4	67,695	R	64.4%	35.6%	64.4%	35.6%
14	2004	335,334	226,662	MACK, CONNIE	108,672	NEELD, ROBERT M.		117,990	R	67.6%	32.4%	67.6%	32.4%
14	2002			GOSS, PORTER J.*		—			R				
15	2010	242,674	157,079	POSEY, BILL*	85,595	ROBERTS, SHANNON		71,484	R	64.7%	35.3%	64.7%	35.3%
15	2008	361,871	192,151	POSEY, BILL	151,951	BLYTHE, STEPHEN	17,769	40,200	R	53.1%	42.0%	55.8%	44.2%
15	2006	223,799	125,965	WELDON, DAVE*	97,834	BOWMAN, BOB		28,131	R	56.3%	43.7%	56.3%	43.7%
15	2004	321,926	210,388	WELDON, DAVE*	111,538	PRISTOOP, SIMON		98,850	R	65.4%	34.6%	65.4%	34.6%
15	2002	231,857	146,414	WELDON, DAVE*	85,433	TSO, JIM	10	60,981	R	63.1%	36.8%	63.2%	36.8%
16	2010	242,763	162,285	ROONEY, TOM*	80,327	HORN, JIM	151	81,958	R	66.8%	33.1%	66.9%	33.1%
16	2008	349,247	209,874	ROONEY, TOM	139,373	MAHONEY, TIM*		70,501	R	60.1%	39.9%	60.1%	39.9%
16	2006	233,773	111,415	NEGRON, JOE#	115,832	MAHONEY, TIM	6,526	4,417	D	47.7%	49.5%	49.0%	51.0%
16	2004	316,810	215,563	FOLEY, MARK*	101,247	FISHER, JEFF		114,316	R	68.0%	32.0%	68.0%	32.0%
16	2002	223,340	176,171	FOLEY, MARK*		—	47,169	176,171	R	78.9%		100.0%	
17	2010	123,370		—	106,361	WILSON, FREDERICA S.	17,009	106,361	D		86.2%		100.0%
17	2008			—		MEEK, KENDRICK B.*			D				
17	2006	90,686		—	90,663	MEEK, KENDRICK B.*	23	90,663	D		100.0%		100.0%
17	2004	179,424		—	178,690	MEEK, KENDRICK B.*	734	178,690	D		99.6%		100.0%
17	2002	113,822		—	113,749	MEEK, KENDRICK B.	73	113,749	D		99.9%		100.0%
18	2010	148,595	102,360	ROS-LEHTINEN, ILEANA*	46,235	BANCIELLA, ROLANDO A.		56,125	R	68.9%	31.1%	68.9%	31.1%
18	2008	242,989	140,617	ROS-LEHTINEN, ILEANA*	102,372	TADDEO, ANNETTE		38,245	R	57.9%	42.1%	57.9%	42.1%
18	2006	128,132	79,631	ROS-LEHTINEN, ILEANA*	48,499	PATLAK, DAVID "BIG DAVE"	2	31,132	R	62.1%	37.9%	62.1%	37.9%
18	2004	221,928	143,647	ROS-LEHTINEN, ILEANA*	78,281	SHELDON, SAM		65,366	R	64.7%	35.3%	64.7%	35.3%
18	2002	149,787	103,512	ROS-LEHTINEN, ILEANA*	42,852	CHOTE, RAY	3,423	60,660	R	69.1%	28.6%	70.7%	29.3%
19	2010	211,059	78,733	BUDD, JOE	132,098	DEUTCH, TED*	228	53,365	D	37.3%	62.6%	37.3%	62.7%
19	2008	306,036	83,357	LYNCH, EDWARD J.	202,465	WEXLER, ROBERT*	20,214	119,108	D	27.2%	66.2%	29.2%	70.8%
19	2006			—		WEXLER, ROBERT*			D				
19	2004			—		WEXLER, ROBERT*			D				
19	2002	217,224	60,477	MERKL, JACK	156,747	WEXLER, ROBERT*		96,270	D	27.8%	72.2%	27.8%	72.2%
20	2010	167,570	63,845	HARRINGTON, KAREN	100,787	WASSERMAN SCHULTZ, DEBBIE*	2,938	36,942	D	38.1%	60.1%	38.8%	61.2%
20	2008	261,799		—	202,832	WASSERMAN SCHULTZ, DEBBIE*	58,967	202,832	D		77.5%		100.0%

FLORIDA

HOUSE OF REPRESENTATIVES

CD	Year	Total Vote	Republican Vote	Republican Candidate	Democratic Vote	Democratic Candidate	Other Vote	Rep.-Dem. Plurality		Total Vote Rep.	Total Vote Dem.	Major Vote Rep.	Major Vote Dem.
20	2006		—			WASSERMAN SCHULTZ, DEBBIE*			D				
20	2004	272,408	81,213	HOSTETTER, MARGARET	191,195	WASSERMAN-SCHULTZ, DEBBIE		109,982	D	29.8%	70.2%	29.8%	70.2%
20	2002		—			DEUTSCH, PETER*			D				
21	2010			DIAZ-BALART, MARIO*		—			R				
21	2008	237,002	137,226	DIAZ-BALART, LINCOLN*	99,776	MARTINEZ, RAUL L.		37,450	R	57.9%	42.1%	57.9%	42.1%
21	2006	112,306	66,784	DIAZ-BALART, LINCOLN*	45,522	GONZALEZ, FRANK J.		21,262	R	59.5%	40.5%	59.5%	40.5%
21	2004	201,243	146,507	DIAZ-BALART, LINCOLN*		—	54,736	146,507	R	72.8%		100.0%	
21	2002			DIAZ-BALART, LINCOLN*		—			R				
22	2010	218,694	118,890	WEST, ALLEN	99,804	KLEIN, RON*		19,086	R	54.4%	45.6%	54.4%	45.6%
22	2008	309,151	140,104	WEST, ALLEN	169,041	KLEIN, RON*	6	28,937	D	45.3%	54.7%	45.3%	54.7%
22	2006	213,605	100,663	SHAW, E. CLAY JR.*	108,688	KLEIN, RON	4,254	8,025	D	47.1%	50.9%	48.1%	51.9%
22	2004	306,726	192,581	SHAW, E. CLAY JR.*	108,258	RORAPAUGH, ROBIN	5,887	84,323	R	62.8%	35.3%	64.0%	36.0%
22	2002	217,115	131,930	SHAW, E. CLAY JR.*	83,265	ROBERTS, CAROL A.	1,920	48,665	R	60.8%	38.4%	61.3%	38.7%
23	2010	126,480	26,414	SANSARICQ, BERNARD	100,066	HASTINGS, ALCEE L.*		73,652	D	20.9%	79.1%	20.9%	79.1%
23	2008	210,306	37,431	THORPE, MARION D. JR.	172,835	HASTINGS, ALCEE L.*	40	135,404	D	17.8%	82.2%	17.8%	82.2%
23	2006		—			HASTINGS, ALCEE L.*			D				
23	2004		—			HASTINGS, ALCEE L.*			D				
23	2002	124,338	27,986	LAURIE, CHARLES	96,347	HASTINGS, ALCEE L.*	5	68,361	D	22.5%	77.5%	22.5%	77.5%
24	2010	245,031	146,129	ADAMS, SANDRA "SANDY"	98,787	KOSMAS, SUZANNE M.*	115	47,342	R	59.6%	40.3%	59.7%	40.3%
24	2008	369,370	151,863	FEENEY, TOM*	211,284	KOSMAS, SUZANNE M.	6,223	59,421	D	41.1%	57.2%	41.8%	58.2%
24	2006	213,658	123,795	FEENEY, TOM*	89,863	CURTIS, CLINT		33,932	R	57.9%	42.1%	57.9%	42.1%
24	2004			FEENEY, TOM*		—			R				
24	2002	219,243	135,576	FEENEY, TOM	83,667	JACOBS, HARRY		51,909	R	61.8%	38.2%	61.8%	38.2%
25	2010	143,553	74,859	RIVERA, DAVID	61,138	GARCIA, JOE	7,556	13,721	R	52.1%	42.6%	55.0%	45.0%
25	2008	246,711	130,891	DIAZ-BALART, MARIO*	115,820	GARCIA, JOE		15,071	R	53.1%	46.9%	53.1%	46.9%
25	2006	103,933	60,765	DIAZ-BALART, MARIO*	43,168	CALDERIN, MICHAEL		17,597	R	58.5%	41.5%	58.5%	41.5%
25	2004			DIAZ-BALART, MARIO*		—			R				
25	2002	126,602	81,845	DIAZ-BALART, MARIO	44,757	BETANCOURT, ANNIE		37,088	R	64.6%	35.4%	64.6%	35.4%
TOTAL	2010	5,117,420	3,004,225		1,853,600		259,595	1,150,625	R	58.7%	36.2%	61.8%	38.2%
TOTAL	2008	7,421,172	3,792,167		3,434,831		194,174	357,336	R	51.1%	46.3%	52.5%	47.5%
TOTAL	2006	3,851,942	2,182,833		1,599,968		69,141	582,865	R	56.7%	41.5%	57.7%	42.3%
TOTAL	2004	5,627,494	3,319,296		2,212,324		95,874	1,106,972	R	59.0%	39.3%	60.0%	40.0%
TOTAL	2002	3,766,558	2,161,349		1,537,124		68,085	624,225	R	57.4%	40.8%	58.4%	41.6%

In Florida districts where a candidate had no opposition, including write-ins, no vote was taken. An asterisk (*) denotes incumbent. A pound sign (#) indicates that Republican Rep. Mark Foley resigned from the House in late September2006, too late to have his name removed from the general election ballot. Votes cast for Foley were credited to Joe Negron, the candidate selected by the Republican Party to replace Foley.

98

FLORIDA

GENERAL AND PRIMARY ELECTIONS

2010 GENERAL ELECTIONS

Governor Other vote was 123,831 Independence Party of Florida (Peter Allen); 18,842 No Party Affiliation (C.C. Reed); 18,644 No Party Affiliation (Michael E. Arth);13,690 No Party Affiliation (Daniel Imperato); 7,487 No Party Affiliation (Farid Khavari); 121 write-in (Josue Larose).

Senator Other vote was 24,850 Libertarian (Alexander Andrew Snitker); 15,340 No Party Affiliation (Sue Askeland); 7,397 No Party Affiliation (Rick Tyler); 4,792 Constitution Party of Florida (Bernie DeCastro); 4,443 No Party Affiliation (Lewis Jerome Armstrong); 4,301 No Party Affiliation (Bobbie Bean); 3,647 No Party Affiliation (Bruce Ray Riggs); 47 write-in (Piotr Blass); 18 write-in (Richard Lock); 18 write-in (Belinda Gail Quarterman-Noah); 13 write-in (George Drake);6 write-in (Robert Monroe); 4 write-in (Howard Knepper); 2 write-in (Carol Ann Joyce LaRosa). (Charlie Crist, who ran with No Party Affiliation, received 1, 607,549 votes, 29.7 percent of the total vote. His vote is listed in the county table for the 2010 Senate election in Florida.)

House Other vote was:

CD1 23,250 No Party Affiliation (Joe Cantrell); 18,253 No Party Affiliation (John Krause); 1,202 write-in (Jim Bryan).
CD2 7,135 No Party Affiliation (Paul C. McKain); 5,705 No Party Affiliation (Dianne Berryhill); 16 write-in (Ray Netherwood).
CD3 4,625 No Party Affiliation (Terry Martin-Back).
CD4 52,540 No Party Affiliation (Troy D. Stanley); 40 write-in (Deborah Katz Pueschel); 27 write-in (Gary L. Koniz).
CD5
CD6 71,632 No Party Affiliation (Steve Schonberg).
CD7
CD8 8,337 Tea (Peg Dunmire); 4,143 No Party Affiliation (George L. Metcalfe); 11 write-in (Steven J. Gerritzen).
CD9
CD10
CD11
CD12 22,857 Tea (Randy Wilkinson).
CD13
CD14 11,825 No Party Affiliation (William Maverick St. Claire).
CD15
CD16 151 write-in (William Dean).
CD17 17,009 No Party Affiliation (Roderick D. Vereen).
CD18
CD19 228 write-in (Stan Smilan).
CD20 1,663 No Party Affiliation (Stanley Blumenthal); 1,272 No Party Affiliation (Robert Kunst); 3 write-in (Clayton Schock).
CD21
CD22
CD23
CD24 115 write-in (Nicholas Ruiz III).
CD25 4,312 Tea (Roly Arrojo); 3,244 Florida Whig (Craig Porter).

2010 PRIMARY ELECTIONS

Primary August 24, 2010 **Registration** (as of July 26, 2010)

Democratic	4,610,771
Republican	3,997,998
Independent Party of Florida	259,193
Independence Party of Florida	57,130
Libertarian	17,522
Independent Democrats of Florida	7,726
Green	5,785
Other Parties	9,373
No Party Affiliation	2,154,818
TOTAL	*11,120,316*

FLORIDA

GENERAL AND PRIMARY ELECTIONS

Primary Type Closed—Only registered Democrats and Republicans could vote in their party's primary, with the exception of races where there were to be no other candidates (including write-ins) on the general election ballot. Then, the contested primary would be open to all voters.

FLORIDA

GENERAL AND PRIMARY ELECTIONS

	REPUBLICAN PRIMARIES			DEMOCRATIC PRIMARIES		
Governor	Rick Scott	599,909	46.3%	Alex Sink	669,630	76.9%
	Bill McCollum	563,538	43.5%	Brian P. Moore	201,705	23.1%
	Mike McCalister	130,991	10.1%			
	TOTAL	*1,294,438*		*TOTAL*	*871,335*	
Senator	Marco Rubio	1,069,936	84.6%	Kendrick B. Meek	528,266	57.5%
	William Kogut	112,080	8.9%	Jeff Greene	284,948	31.0%
	William Escoffery III	82,426	6.5%	Glenn A. Burkett	59,840	6.5%
				Maurice A. Ferre	45,219	4.9%
	TOTAL	*1,264,442*		*TOTAL*	*918,273*	
Congressional District 1	Jeff Miller*	Unopposed		No Democratic candidate		
Congressional District 2	Steve Southerland	28,269	46.9%	Allen Boyd*	42,415	51.5%
	David Scholl	14,483	24.0%	Al Lawson	40,017	48.5%
	Ron McNeil	6,447	10.7%			
	Eddie Hendry	6,164	10.2%			
	Barbara F. Olschner	4,965	8.2%			
	TOTAL	*60,328*		*TOTAL*	*82,432*	
Congressional District 3	Michael Yost	8,919	45.7%	Corrine Brown*	35,312	80.2%
	Dean Black	6,871	35.2%	Scott Fortune	8,718	19.8%
	Chris Nwasike	3,718	19.1%			
	TOTAL	*19,508*		*TOTAL*	*44,030*	
Congressional District 4	Ander Crenshaw*	Unopposed		No Democratic candidate		
Congressional District 5	Richard B. Nugent	52,586	62.2%	James Piccillo	Unopposed	
	Jason Sager	31,969	37.8%			
	TOTAL	*84,555*				
Congressional District 6	Cliff Stearns*	50,432	71.5%	No Democratic candidate		
	Don Browning	20,111	28.5%			
	TOTAL	*70,543*				
Congressional District 7	John L. Mica*	Unopposed		Heather Beaven	Unopposed	
Congressional District 8	Daniel Webster	24,753	40.2%	Alan Grayson*	Unopposed	
	Todd Long	14,082	22.9%			
	Kurt Kelly	8,311	13.5%			
	Patricia Sullivan	6,507	10.6%			
	Bruce O'Donoghue	4,394	7.1%			
	Dan Fanelli	1,896	3.1%			
	Ross Bieling	1,645	2.7%			
	TOTAL	*61,588*				
Congressional District 9	Gus Michael Bilirakis*	Unopposed		Anita de Palma	16,646	59.4%
				Phil Hindahl	11,396	40.6%
				TOTAL	*28,042*	
Congressional District 10	C.W. Bill Young*	Unopposed		Charlie Justice	Unopposed	

FLORIDA

GENERAL AND PRIMARY ELECTIONS

	REPUBLICAN PRIMARIES			DEMOCRATIC PRIMARIES		
Congressional District 11	Mike Prendergast	11,111	47.0%	Kathy Castor*	29,556	85.3%
	Thomas C. Castellano	6,640	28.1%	Tim Curtis	5,097	14.7%
	Eddie Adams Jr.	3,093	13.1%			
	Tony Buntyn	2,777	11.8%			
	TOTAL	23,621		TOTAL	34,653	
Congressional District 12	Dennis A. Ross	33,212	69.0%	Lori Edwards	24,820	75.2%
	John W. Lindsey Jr.	14,936	31.0%	Doug Tudor	8,207	24.8%
	TOTAL	48,148		TOTAL	33,027	
Congressional District 13	Vern Buchanan*	61,517	83.5%	James T. Golden	18,325	56.7%
	Don Baldauf	12,197	16.5%	Rick Eaton	13,998	43.3%
	TOTAL	73,714		TOTAL	32,323	
Congressional District 14	Connie Mack*	Unopposed		James Lloyd Roach	Unopposed	
Congressional District 15	Bill Posey*	Unopposed		Shannon Roberts	Unopposed	
Congressional District 16	Tom Rooney*	Unopposed		Jim Horn	20,830	67.7%
				Ed Tautiva	9,917	32.3%
				TOTAL	30,747	
Congressional District 17	No Republican candidate			Frederica S. Wilson	17,047	34.5%
				Rudolph Moise	7,986	16.1%
				Shirley Gibson	5,900	11.9%
				Yolly Roberson	5,080	10.3%
				Phillip J. Brutus	4,173	8.4%
				Marleine Bastien	2,967	6.0%
				Scott Galvin	2,750	5.6%
				James Bush III	2,693	5.4%
				Andre L. Williams	856	1.7%
				TOTAL	49,452	
Congressional District 18	Ileana Ros-Lehtinen*	Unopposed		Rolando A. Banciella	Unopposed	
Congressional District 19	Joe Budd	Unopposed		Ted Deutch*	Unopposed	
Congressional District 20	Karen Harrington	7,596	39.9%	Debbie Wasserman Schultz*	Unopposed	
	Robert Lowry	7,143	37.5%			
	Donna Milo	4,284	22.5%			
	TOTAL	19,023				
Congressional District 21	Mario Diaz-Balart*	Unopposed		No Democratic candidate		
Congressional District 22	Allen West	30,024	76.7%	Ron Klein*	24,030	84.5%
	David Brady	9,137	23.3%	Paul Francis Renneisen	4,395	15.5%
	TOTAL	39,161		TOTAL	28,425	
Congressional District 23	Bernard Sansaricq	Unopposed		Alcee L. Hastings*	Unopposed	
Congressional District 24	Sandra "Sandy" Adams	19,898	30.1%	Suzanne M. Kosmas*	28,503	77.7%
	Karen Diebel	19,355	29.3%	Paul P. Partyka	8,162	22.3%
	Craig S. Miller	18,282	27.7%			
	Tom Garcia	6,446	9.8%			
	Deon Long	2,079	3.1%			
	TOTAL	66,060		TOTAL	36,665	
Congressional District 25	David Rivera	19,228	62.7%	Joe Garcia	12,459	75.9%
	Paul Crespo	8,158	26.6%	Luis Meurice	3,950	24.1%
	Mariana "Marili" Cancio	3,272	10.7%			
	TOTAL	30,658		TOTAL	16,409	

An asterisk (*) denotes incumbent. The names of unopposed candidates did not appear on the primary ballot; therefore, no votes were cast for these candidates.

GEORGIA

Congressional districts first established for elections held in 2002
13 members

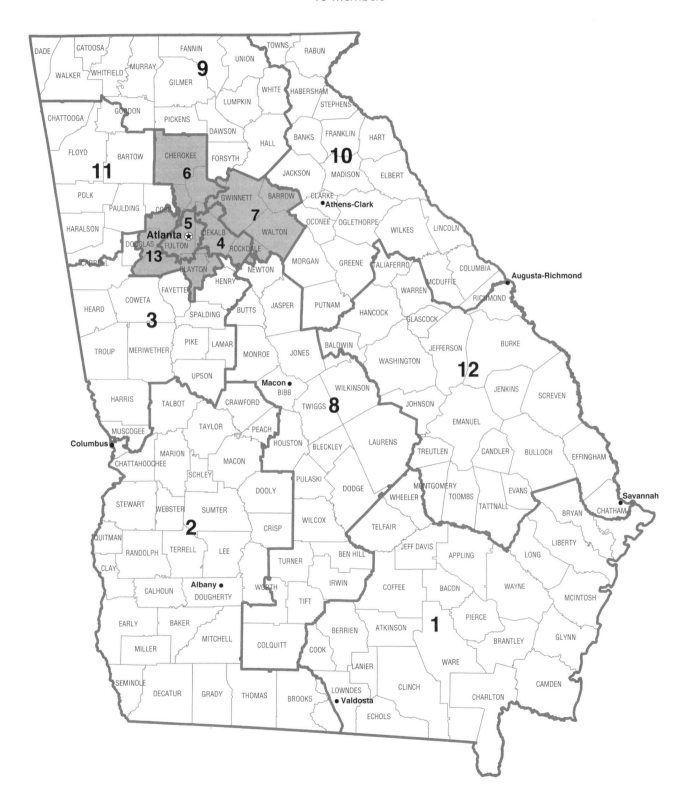

GEORGIA

Atlanta Area

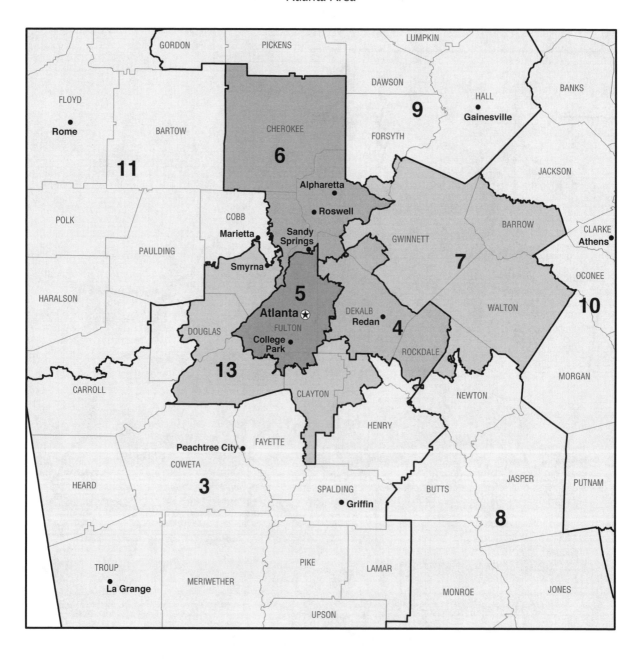

GEORGIA

GOVERNOR
Nathan Deal (R). Elected 2010 to a four-year term.

SENATORS (2 Republicans)
Saxby Chambliss (R). Reelected 2008 to a six-year term. Previously elected 2002.

Johnny Isakson (R). Reelected 2010 to a six-year term. Previously elected 2004.

REPRESENTATIVES (8 Republicans, 5 Democrats)

1. Jack Kingston (R)
2. Sanford D. Bishop Jr. (D)
3. Lynn Westmoreland (R)
4. Henry C. "Hank" Johnson Jr. (D)
5. John Lewis (D)

6. Tom Price (R)
7. Rob Woodall (R)
8. Austin Scott (R)
9. Tom Graves (R)
10. Paul C. Broun (R)

11. Phil Gingrey (R)
12. John Barrow (D)
13. David Scott (D)

POSTWAR VOTE FOR PRESIDENT

| Year | Total Vote | Republican | | Democratic | | Other Vote | Dem.-Rep. Plurality | Percentage | | | |
| | | Vote | Candidate | Vote | Candidate | | | Total Vote | | Major Vote | |
								Rep.	Dem.	Rep.	Dem.
2008	3,924,486	2,048,759	McCain, John	1,844,123	Obama, Barack	31,604	204,636 R	52.2%	47.0%	52.6%	47.4%
2004	3,301,875	1,914,254	Bush, George W.	1,366,149	Kerry, John	21,472	548,105 R	58.0%	41.4%	58.4%	41.6%
2000**	2,596,645	1,419,720	Bush, George W.	1,116,230	Gore, Al	60,695	303,490 R	54.7%	43.0%	56.0%	44.0%
1996**	2,299,071	1,080,843	Dole, Bob	1,053,849	Clinton, Bill	164,379	26,994 R	47.0%	45.8%	50.6%	49.4%
1992**	2,321,125	995,252	Bush, George	1,008,966	Clinton, Bill	316,907	13,714 D	42.9%	43.5%	49.7%	50.3%
1988	1,809,672	1,081,331	Bush, George	714,792	Dukakis, Michael S.	13,549	366,539 R	59.8%	39.5%	60.2%	39.8%
1984	1,776,120	1,068,722	Reagan, Ronald	706,628	Mondale, Walter F.	770	362,094 R	60.2%	39.8%	60.2%	39.8%
1980**	1,596,695	654,168	Reagan, Ronald	890,733	Carter, Jimmy	51,794	236,565 D	41.0%	55.8%	42.3%	57.7%
1976	1,467,458	483,743	Ford, Gerald R.	979,409	Carter, Jimmy	4,306	495,666 D	33.0%	66.7%	33.1%	66.9%
1972	1,174,772	881,496	Nixon, Richard M.	289,529	McGovern, George S.	3,747	591,967 R	75.0%	24.6%	75.3%	24.7%
1968**	1,250,266	380,111	Nixon, Richard M.	334,440	Humphrey, Hubert H.	535,715	155,439 A	30.4%	26.7%	53.2%	46.8%
1964	1,139,335	616,584	Goldwater, Barry M.	522,556	Johnson, Lyndon B.	195	94,028 R	54.1%	45.9%	54.1%	45.9%
1960	733,349	274,472	Nixon, Richard M.	458,638	Kennedy, John F.	239	184,166 D	37.4%	62.5%	37.4%	62.6%
1956	669,655	222,778	Eisenhower, Dwight D.	444,688	Stevenson, Adlai E.	2,189	221,910 D	33.3%	66.4%	33.4%	66.6%
1952	655,785	198,961	Eisenhower, Dwight D.	456,823	Stevenson, Adlai E.	1	257,862 D	30.3%	69.7%	30.3%	69.7%
1948**	418,844	76,691	Dewey, Thomas E.	254,646	Truman, Harry S.	87,507	169,511 D	18.3%	60.8%	23.1%	76.9%

**In past elections, the other vote included: 2000 - 13,273 Green (Ralph Nader); 1996 - 146,337 Reform (Ross Perot); 1992 - 309,657 Independent (Perot); 1980 - 36,055 Independent (John Anderson); 1968 - 535,550 American Independent (George Wallace); 1948 - 85,135 States' Rights (Strom Thurmond), who placed second statewide. Wallace carried Georgia in 1968 with 42.8 percent of the vote.

GEORGIA

POSTWAR VOTE FOR GOVERNOR

Year	Total Vote	Republican Vote	Republican Candidate	Democratic Vote	Democratic Candidate	Other Vote	Rep.-Dem. Plurality	Total Vote Rep.	Total Vote Dem.	Major Vote Rep.	Major Vote Dem.
2010	2,576,161	1,365,832	Deal, Nathan	1,107,011	Barnes, Roy E.	103,318	258,821 R	53.0%	43.0%	55.2%	44.8%
2006	2,122,258	1,229,724	Perdue, Sonny	811,049	Taylor, Mark	81,485	418,675 R	57.9%	38.2%	60.3%	39.7%
2002	2,027,177	1,041,700	Perdue, Sonny	937,070	Barnes, Roy E.	48,407	104,630 R	51.4%	46.2%	52.6%	47.4%
1998	1,792,808	790,201	Millner, Guy	941,076	Barnes, Roy E.	61,531	150,875 D	44.1%	52.5%	45.6%	54.4%
1994	1,545,328	756,371	Millner, Guy	788,926	Miller, Zell	31	32,555 D	48.9%	51.1%	48.9%	51.1%
1990	1,449,682	645,625	Isakson, Johnny	766,662	Miller, Zell	37,395	121,037 D	44.5%	52.9%	45.7%	54.3%
1986	1,175,114	346,512	Davis, Guy	828,465	Harris, Joe Frank	137	481,953 D	29.5%	70.5%	29.5%	70.5%
1982	1,169,041	434,496	Bell, Robert H.	734,090	Harris, Joe Frank	455	299,594 D	37.2%	62.8%	37.2%	62.8%
1978	662,862	128,139	Cook, Rodney M.	534,572	Busbee, George	151	406,433 D	19.3%	80.6%	19.3%	80.7%
1974	936,438	289,113	Thompson, Ronnie	646,777	Busbee, George	548	357,664 D	30.9%	69.1%	30.9%	69.1%
1970	1,046,663	424,983	Suit, Hal	620,419	Carter, Jimmy	1,261	195,436 D	40.6%	59.3%	40.7%	59.3%
1966**	975,019	453,665	Callaway, Howard H.	450,626	Maddox, Lester	70,728	3,039 R	46.5%	46.2%	50.2%	49.8%
1962	311,691		—	311,524	Sanders, Carl E.	167	311,524 D		99.9%		100.0%
1958	168,497		—	168,414	Vandiver, Ernest	83	168,414 D		100.0%		100.0%
1954	331,966		—	331,899	Griffin, Marvin	67	331,899 D		100.0%		100.0%
1950	234,430		—	230,771	Talmadge, Eugene	3,659	230,771 D		98.4%		100.0%
1948S	363,763		—	354,711	Talmadge, Eugene	9,052	354,711 D		97.5%		100.0%
1946	145,403		—	143,279	Talmadge, Eugene	2,124	143,279 D		98.5%		100.0%

**In 1966 in the absence of a majority for any candidate, the State Legislature elected Democrat Lester Maddox to a four-year term. The 1948 election was for a short term to fill a vacancy. The Republican Party did not run a candidate in the 1946, 1948, 1950, 1954, 1958 and 1962 gubernatorial elections.

POSTWAR VOTE FOR SENATOR

Year	Total Vote	Republican Vote	Republican Candidate	Democratic Vote	Democratic Candidate	Other Vote	Rep.-Dem. Plurality	Total Vote Rep.	Total Vote Dem.	Major Vote Rep.	Major Vote Dem.
2010	2,555,258	1,489,904	Isakson, Johnny	996,516	Thurmond, Michael	68,838	493,388 R	58.3%	39.0%	59.9%	40.1%
2008**	2,137,956	1,228,033	Chambliss, Saxby	909,923	Martin, Jim		318,110 R	57.4%	42.6%	57.4%	42.6%
2004	3,220,981	1,864,202	Isakson, Johnny	1,287,690	Majette, Denise L.	69,089	576,512 R	57.9%	40.0%	59.1%	40.9%
2002	2,030,608	1,071,464	Chambliss, Saxby	932,156	Cleland, Max	26,988	139,308 R	52.8%	45.9%	53.5%	46.5%
2000S	2,428,510	920,478	Mattingly, Mack	1,413,224	Miller, Zell	94,808	492,746 D	37.9%	58.2%	39.4%	60.6%
1998	1,753,911	918,540	Coverdell, Paul	791,904	Coles, Michael	43,467	126,636 R	52.4%	45.2%	53.7%	46.3%
1996	2,259,232	1,073,969	Millner, Guy	1,103,993	Cleland, Max	81,270	30,024 D	47.5%	48.9%	49.3%	50.7%
1992**	1,253,991	635,114	Coverdell, Paul	618,877	Fowler, Wyche		16,237 R	50.6%	49.4%	50.6%	49.4%
1990	1,033,517		—	1,033,439	Nunn, Sam	78	1,033,439 D		100.0%		100.0%
1986	1,225,008	601,241	Mattingly, Mack	623,707	Fowler, Wyche	60	22,466 D	49.1%	50.9%	49.1%	50.9%
1984	1,681,344	337,196	Hicks, Jon Michael	1,344,104	Nunn, Sam	44	1,006,908 D	20.1%	79.9%	20.1%	79.9%
1980	1,580,340	803,686	Mattingly, Mack	776,143	Talmadge, Herman	511	27,543 R	50.9%	49.1%	50.9%	49.1%
1978	645,164	108,808	Stokes, John W.	536,320	Nunn, Sam	36	427,512 D	16.9%	83.1%	16.9%	83.1%
1974	874,555	246,866	Johnson, Jerry R.	627,376	Talmadge, Herman	313	380,510 D	28.2%	71.7%	28.2%	71.8%
1972	1,178,708	542,331	Thompson, Fletcher	635,970	Nunn, Sam	407	93,639 D	46.0%	54.0%	46.0%	54.0%
1968	1,141,889	256,796	Patton, E. Earl	885,093	Talmadge, Herman		628,297 D	22.5%	77.5%	22.5%	77.5%
1966	622,371		—	622,043	Russell, Richard B.	328	622,043 D		99.9%		100.0%
1962	306,250		—	306,250	Talmadge, Herman		306,250 D		100.0%		100.0%
1960	576,495		—	576,140	Russell, Richard B.	355	576,140 D		99.9%		100.0%
1956	541,267		—	541,094	Talmadge, Herman	173	541,094 D		100.0%		100.0%
1954	333,936		—	333,917	Russell, Richard B.	19	333,917 D		100.0%		100.0%
1950	261,293		—	261,290	George, Walter F.	3	261,290 D		100.0%		100.0%
1948	362,504		—	362,104	Russell, Richard B.	400	362,104 D		99.9%		100.0%

**The 2000 election was for a short term to fill a vacancy. In 1992 and 2008, no candidate drew a majority of the general election vote required by state law, forcing runoff elections whose results are listed above for each year. In 2008 the November general election vote was 1,867,097 (49.8%) Republican (Saxby Chambliss); 1,757,393 (46.8%) Democratic (Jim Martin); and 127,995 (3.4%) Other. In 1992 the November general election vote was 1,073,282 (47.7%) Republican (Paul Coverdell); 1,108,416 (49.2%) Democratic (Wyche Fowler); and 69,889 (3.1%) Other. The 2008 runoff was held December 2; the 1992 runoff took place on November 24. The Republican Party did not run a candidate in the 1948, 1950, 1954, 1956, 1960, 1962, 1966 and 1990 Senate elections.

GEORGIA
GOVERNOR 2010

2010 Census Population	County	Total Vote	Republican	Democratic	Other	Rep.-Dem. Plurality	Percentage Total Vote Rep.	Dem.	Major Vote Rep.	Dem.
18,236	APPLING	5,105	3,514	1,430	161	2,084 R	68.8%	28.0%	71.1%	28.9%
8,375	ATKINSON	1,452	922	498	32	424 R	63.5%	34.3%	64.9%	35.1%
11,096	BACON	2,461	1,718	689	54	1,029 R	69.8%	28.0%	71.4%	28.6%
3,451	BAKER	1,230	531	668	31	137 D	43.2%	54.3%	44.3%	55.7%
45,720	BALDWIN	11,203	5,133	5,689	381	556 D	45.8%	50.8%	47.4%	52.6%
18,395	BANKS	4,475	3,744	593	138	3,151 R	83.7%	13.3%	86.3%	13.7%
69,367	BARROW	16,098	11,920	3,401	777	8,519 R	74.0%	21.1%	77.8%	22.2%
100,157	BARTOW	23,410	16,661	5,583	1,166	11,078 R	71.2%	23.8%	74.9%	25.1%
17,634	BENHILL	3,898	2,014	1,757	127	257 R	51.7%	45.1%	53.4%	46.6%
19,286	BERRIEN	4,006	2,684	1,160	162	1,524 R	67.0%	29.0%	69.8%	30.2%
155,547	BIBB	44,176	17,765	25,048	1,363	7,283 D	40.2%	56.7%	41.5%	58.5%
13,063	BLECKLEY	3,323	2,202	1,022	99	1,180 R	66.3%	30.8%	68.3%	31.7%
18,411	BRANTLEY	3,336	2,538	680	118	1,858 R	76.1%	20.4%	78.9%	21.1%
16,243	BROOKS	5,104	2,373	2,586	145	213 D	46.5%	50.7%	47.9%	52.1%
30,233	BRYAN	7,935	5,489	1,988	458	3,501 R	69.2%	25.1%	73.4%	26.6%
70,217	BULLOCH	14,338	8,852	4,978	508	3,874 R	61.7%	34.7%	64.0%	36.0%
23,316	BURKE	6,193	2,765	3,292	136	527 D	44.6%	53.2%	45.6%	54.4%
23,655	BUTTS	6,182	3,972	1,984	226	1,988 R	64.3%	32.1%	66.7%	33.3%
6,694	CALHOUN	1,645	600	1,023	22	423 D	36.5%	62.2%	37.0%	63.0%
50,513	CAMDEN	10,004	6,340	3,340	324	3,000 R	63.4%	33.4%	65.5%	34.5%
10,998	CANDLER	2,295	1,469	736	90	733 R	64.0%	32.1%	66.6%	33.4%
110,527	CARROLL	27,458	18,372	7,864	1,222	10,508 R	66.9%	28.6%	70.0%	30.0%
63,942	CATOOSA	13,611	10,192	2,926	493	7,266 R	74.9%	21.5%	77.7%	22.3%
12,171	CHARLTON	2,162	1,376	715	71	661 R	63.6%	33.1%	65.8%	34.2%
265,128	CHATHAM	67,905	30,699	34,167	3,039	3,468 D	45.2%	50.3%	47.3%	52.7%
11,267	CHATTAHOOCHEE	721	345	356	20	11 D	47.9%	49.4%	49.2%	50.8%
26,015	CHATTOOGA	4,948	3,028	1,657	263	1,371 R	61.2%	33.5%	64.6%	35.4%
214,346	CHEROKEE	65,376	49,691	12,047	3,638	37,644 R	76.0%	18.4%	80.5%	19.5%
116,714	CLARKE	26,935	9,260	16,013	1,662	6,753 D	34.4%	59.5%	36.6%	63.4%
3,183	CLAY	1,073	414	629	30	215 D	38.6%	58.6%	39.7%	60.3%
259,424	CLAYTON	61,339	10,627	48,828	1,884	38,201 D	17.3%	79.6%	17.9%	82.1%
6,798	CLINCH	1,363	554	771	38	217 D	40.6%	56.6%	41.8%	58.2%
688,078	COBB	211,459	116,506	84,638	10,315	31,868 R	55.1%	40.0%	57.9%	42.1%
42,356	COFFEE	8,163	5,209	2,722	232	2,487 R	63.8%	33.3%	65.7%	34.3%
45,498	COLQUITT	8,949	5,828	2,803	318	3,025 R	65.1%	31.3%	67.5%	32.5%
124,053	COLUMBIA	37,177	26,596	9,139	1,442	17,457 R	71.5%	24.6%	74.4%	25.6%
17,212	COOK	3,676	2,190	1,373	113	817 R	59.6%	37.4%	61.5%	38.5%
127,317	COWETA	36,739	25,984	8,946	1,809	17,038 R	70.7%	24.4%	74.4%	25.6%
12,630	CRAWFORD	3,662	2,171	1,328	163	843 R	59.3%	36.3%	62.0%	38.0%
23,439	CRISP	4,977	2,916	1,956	105	960 R	58.6%	39.3%	59.9%	40.1%
16,633	DADE	3,599	2,608	836	155	1,772 R	72.5%	23.2%	75.7%	24.3%
22,330	DAWSON	7,012	5,869	856	287	5,013 R	83.7%	12.2%	87.3%	12.7%
27,842	DECATUR	7,137	3,756	3,267	114	489 R	52.6%	45.8%	53.5%	46.5%
691,893	DEKALB	208,732	45,109	155,404	8,219	110,295 D	21.6%	74.5%	22.5%	77.5%
21,796	DODGE	5,240	3,109	1,995	136	1,114 R	59.3%	38.1%	60.9%	39.1%
14,918	DOOLY	3,143	1,350	1,724	69	374 D	43.0%	54.9%	43.9%	56.1%
94,565	DOUGHERTY	27,282	8,685	17,916	681	9,231 D	31.8%	65.7%	32.6%	67.4%
132,403	DOUGLAS	37,499	18,425	17,622	1,452	803 R	49.1%	47.0%	51.1%	48.9%
11,008	EARLY	3,782	1,754	1,962	66	208 D	46.4%	51.9%	47.2%	52.8%
4,034	ECHOLS	590	387	175	28	212 R	65.6%	29.7%	68.9%	31.1%

GEORGIA
GOVERNOR 2010

2010 Census Population	County	Total Vote	Republican	Democratic	Other	Rep.-Dem. Plurality	Percentage — Total Vote Rep.	Dem.	Major Vote Rep.	Dem.
52,250	EFFINGHAM	13,170	9,455	3,002	713	6,453 R	71.8%	22.8%	75.9%	24.1%
20,166	ELBERT	5,470	3,110	2,203	157	907 R	56.9%	40.3%	58.5%	41.5%
22,598	EMANUEL	5,062	2,932	2,012	118	920 R	57.9%	39.7%	59.3%	40.7%
11,000	EVANS	2,442	1,469	905	68	564 R	60.2%	37.1%	61.9%	38.1%
23,682	FANNIN	7,019	5,098	1,488	433	3,610 R	72.6%	21.2%	77.4%	22.6%
106,567	FAYETTE	41,887	27,070	13,032	1,785	14,038 R	64.6%	31.1%	67.5%	32.5%
96,317	FLOYD	21,722	14,209	6,525	988	7,684 R	65.4%	30.0%	68.5%	31.5%
175,511	FORSYTH	53,071	43,117	7,501	2,453	35,616 R	81.2%	14.1%	85.2%	14.8%
22,084	FRANKLIN	5,045	3,779	1,098	168	2,681 R	74.9%	21.8%	77.5%	22.5%
920,581	FULTON	256,419	90,197	156,024	10,198	65,827 D	35.2%	60.8%	36.6%	63.4%
28,292	GILMER	8,137	6,213	1,507	417	4,706 R	76.4%	18.5%	80.5%	19.5%
3,082	GLASCOCK	839	638	159	42	479 R	76.0%	19.0%	80.1%	19.9%
79,626	GLYNN	21,245	13,482	7,248	515	6,234 R	63.5%	34.1%	65.0%	35.0%
55,186	GORDON	10,841	8,023	2,267	551	5,756 R	74.0%	20.9%	78.0%	22.0%
25,011	GRADY	6,605	3,537	2,822	246	715 R	53.6%	42.7%	55.6%	44.4%
15,994	GREENE	5,892	3,641	2,075	176	1,566 R	61.8%	35.2%	63.7%	36.3%
805,321	GWINNETT	195,001	112,093	73,427	9,481	38,666 R	57.5%	37.7%	60.4%	39.6%
43,041	HABERSHAM	10,417	8,339	1,602	476	6,737 R	80.1%	15.4%	83.9%	16.1%
179,684	HALL	44,120	35,384	7,109	1,627	28,275 R	80.2%	16.1%	83.3%	16.7%
9,429	HANCOCK	3,023	610	2,358	55	1,748 D	20.2%	78.0%	20.6%	79.4%
28,780	HARALSON	7,043	5,182	1,527	334	3,655 R	73.6%	21.7%	77.2%	22.8%
32,024	HARRIS	9,870	6,721	2,803	346	3,918 R	68.1%	28.4%	70.6%	29.4%
25,213	HART	6,090	3,846	1,991	253	1,855 R	63.2%	32.7%	65.9%	34.1%
11,834	HEARD	2,839	1,950	737	152	1,213 R	68.7%	26.0%	72.6%	27.4%
203,922	HENRY	59,865	31,350	26,283	2,232	5,067 R	52.4%	43.9%	54.4%	45.6%
139,900	HOUSTON	38,531	22,156	14,833	1,542	7,323 R	57.5%	38.5%	59.9%	40.1%
9,538	IRWIN	2,621	1,485	1,073	63	412 R	56.7%	40.9%	58.1%	41.9%
60,485	JACKSON	16,317	12,917	2,628	772	10,289 R	79.2%	16.1%	83.1%	16.9%
13,900	JASPER	4,211	2,768	1,283	160	1,485 R	65.7%	30.5%	68.3%	31.7%
15,068	JEFF DAVIS	3,615	2,454	1,024	137	1,430 R	67.9%	28.3%	70.6%	29.4%
16,930	JEFFERSON	4,801	2,056	2,658	87	602 D	42.8%	55.4%	43.6%	56.4%
8,340	JENKINS	2,253	1,215	976	62	239 R	53.9%	43.3%	55.5%	44.5%
9,980	JOHNSON	2,421	1,592	760	69	832 R	65.8%	31.4%	67.7%	32.3%
28,669	JONES	8,579	4,905	3,376	298	1,529 R	57.2%	39.4%	59.2%	40.8%
18,317	LAMAR	5,045	3,162	1,706	177	1,456 R	62.7%	33.8%	65.0%	35.0%
10,078	LANIER	1,671	858	765	48	93 R	51.3%	45.8%	52.9%	47.1%
48,434	LAURENS	13,435	7,988	5,055	392	2,933 R	59.5%	37.6%	61.2%	38.8%
28,298	LEE	9,417	6,682	2,457	278	4,225 R	71.0%	26.1%	73.1%	26.9%
63,453	LIBERTY	9,875	3,528	5,975	372	2,447 D	35.7%	60.5%	37.1%	62.9%
7,996	LINCOLN	3,260	1,932	1,217	111	715 R	59.3%	37.3%	61.4%	38.6%
14,464	LONG	1,817	1,066	677	74	389 R	58.7%	37.3%	61.2%	38.8%
109,233	LOWNDES	23,438	12,715	10,116	607	2,599 R	54.2%	43.2%	55.7%	44.3%
29,966	LUMPKIN	8,121	6,087	1,530	504	4,557 R	75.0%	18.8%	79.9%	20.1%
21,875	MCDUFFIE	6,190	3,591	2,423	176	1,168 R	58.0%	39.1%	59.7%	40.3%
14,333	MCINTOSH	4,622	2,132	2,329	161	197 D	46.1%	50.4%	47.8%	52.2%
14,740	MACON	3,282	1,090	2,123	69	1,033 D	33.2%	64.7%	33.9%	66.1%
28,120	MADISON	7,620	5,491	1,772	357	3,719 R	72.1%	23.3%	75.6%	24.4%
8,742	MARION	2,065	1,115	884	66	231 R	54.0%	42.8%	55.8%	44.2%
21,992	MERIWETHER	6,353	3,368	2,785	200	583 R	53.0%	43.8%	54.7%	45.3%
6,125	MILLER	1,893	1,169	694	30	475 R	61.8%	36.7%	62.7%	37.3%

GEORGIA
GOVERNOR 2010

2010 Census Population	County	Total Vote	Republican	Democratic	Other	Rep.-Dem. Plurality	Percentage Total Vote Rep.	Dem.	Major Vote Rep.	Dem.
23,498	MITCHELL	5,752	2,667	2,970	115	303 D	46.4%	51.6%	47.3%	52.7%
26,424	MONROE	8,935	5,639	2,978	318	2,661 R	63.1%	33.3%	65.4%	34.6%
9,123	MONTGOMERY	2,516	1,707	730	79	977 R	67.8%	29.0%	70.0%	30.0%
17,868	MORGAN	6,385	4,327	1,806	252	2,521 R	67.8%	28.3%	70.6%	29.4%
39,628	MURRAY	5,877	4,296	1,284	297	3,012 R	73.1%	21.8%	77.0%	23.0%
189,885	MUSCOGEE	46,528	18,430	26,807	1,291	8,377 D	39.6%	57.6%	40.7%	59.3%
99,958	NEWTON	28,223	14,189	13,044	990	1,145 R	50.3%	46.2%	52.1%	47.9%
32,808	OCONEE	12,580	8,865	3,072	643	5,793 R	70.5%	24.4%	74.3%	25.7%
14,899	OGLETHORPE	4,261	2,742	1,317	202	1,425 R	64.4%	30.9%	67.6%	32.4%
142,324	PAULDING	32,613	22,036	9,188	1,389	12,848 R	67.6%	28.2%	70.6%	29.4%
27,695	PEACH	7,449	3,570	3,678	201	108 D	47.9%	49.4%	49.3%	50.7%
29,431	PICKENS	9,012	6,960	1,562	490	5,398 R	77.2%	17.3%	81.7%	18.3%
18,758	PIERCE	4,109	3,148	852	109	2,296 R	76.6%	20.7%	78.7%	21.3%
17,869	PIKE	5,752	4,456	1,076	220	3,380 R	77.5%	18.7%	80.5%	19.5%
41,475	POLK	8,807	5,796	2,627	384	3,169 R	65.8%	29.8%	68.8%	31.2%
12,010	PULASKI	2,579	1,604	887	88	717 R	62.2%	34.4%	64.4%	35.6%
21,218	PUTNAM	6,561	4,438	1,903	220	2,535 R	67.6%	29.0%	70.0%	30.0%
2,513	QUITMAN	797	328	445	24	117 D	41.2%	55.8%	42.4%	57.6%
16,276	RABUN	5,452	3,910	1,265	277	2,645 R	71.7%	23.2%	75.6%	24.4%
7,719	RANDOLPH	2,320	990	1,296	34	306 D	42.7%	55.9%	43.3%	56.7%
200,549	RICHMOND	49,904	17,882	30,574	1,448	12,692 D	35.8%	61.3%	36.9%	63.1%
85,215	ROCKDALE	26,762	11,794	14,018	950	2,224 D	44.1%	52.4%	45.7%	54.3%
5,010	SCHLEY	1,188	794	362	32	432 R	66.8%	30.5%	68.7%	31.3%
14,593	SCREVEN	3,824	2,056	1,676	92	380 R	53.8%	43.8%	55.1%	44.9%
8,729	SEMINOLE	2,705	1,509	1,132	64	377 R	55.8%	41.8%	57.1%	42.9%
64,073	SPALDING	16,610	10,071	5,906	633	4,165 R	60.6%	35.6%	63.0%	37.0%
26,175	STEPHENS	6,540	4,797	1,527	216	3,270 R	73.3%	23.3%	75.9%	24.1%
6,058	STEWART	1,520	518	979	23	461 D	34.1%	64.4%	34.6%	65.4%
32,819	SUMTER	8,194	3,732	4,293	169	561 D	45.5%	52.4%	46.5%	53.5%
6,865	TALBOT	2,360	825	1,473	62	648 D	35.0%	62.4%	35.9%	64.1%
1,717	TALIAFERRO	759	229	515	15	286 D	30.2%	67.9%	30.8%	69.2%
25,520	TATTNALL	4,095	2,742	1,213	140	1,529 R	67.0%	29.6%	69.3%	30.7%
8,906	TAYLOR	2,501	1,258	1,190	53	68 R	50.3%	47.6%	51.4%	48.6%
16,500	TELFAIR	2,736	1,363	1,313	60	50 R	49.8%	48.0%	50.9%	49.1%
9,315	TERRELL	3,134	1,367	1,697	70	330 D	43.6%	54.1%	44.6%	55.4%
44,720	THOMAS	13,078	7,348	5,294	436	2,054 R	56.2%	40.5%	58.1%	41.9%
40,118	TIFT	9,745	6,216	3,275	254	2,941 R	63.8%	33.6%	65.5%	34.5%
27,223	TOOMBS	6,565	4,456	1,885	224	2,571 R	67.9%	28.7%	70.3%	29.7%
10,471	TOWNS	4,228	3,025	1,013	190	2,012 R	71.5%	24.0%	74.9%	25.1%
6,885	TREUTLEN	1,793	1,088	665	40	423 R	60.7%	37.1%	62.1%	37.9%
67,044	TROUP	15,823	9,552	5,717	554	3,835 R	60.4%	36.1%	62.6%	37.4%
8,930	TURNER	2,384	1,266	1,047	71	219 R	53.1%	43.9%	54.7%	45.3%
9,023	TWIGGS	3,180	1,307	1,768	105	461 D	41.1%	55.6%	42.5%	57.5%
21,356	UNION	8,165	5,788	1,899	478	3,889 R	70.9%	23.3%	75.3%	24.7%
27,153	UPSON	7,232	4,502	2,515	215	1,987 R	62.3%	34.8%	64.2%	35.8%
68,756	WALKER	12,262	9,048	2,706	508	6,342 R	73.8%	22.1%	77.0%	23.0%
83,768	WALTON	25,489	19,639	4,798	1,052	14,841 R	77.0%	18.8%	80.4%	19.6%
36,312	WARE	6,979	4,552	2,270	157	2,282 R	65.2%	32.5%	66.7%	33.3%
5,834	WARREN	1,773	738	986	49	248 D	41.6%	55.6%	42.8%	57.2%
21,187	WASHINGTON	5,838	2,829	2,893	116	64 D	48.5%	49.6%	49.4%	50.6%

GEORGIA
GOVERNOR 2010

2010 Census Population	County	Total Vote	Republican	Democratic	Other	Rep.-Dem. Plurality	Percentage Total Vote Rep.	Dem.	Major Vote Rep.	Dem.
30,099	WAYNE	6,656	4,408	2,000	248	2,408 R	66.2%	30.0%	68.8%	31.2%
2,799	WEBSTER	938	422	504	12	82 D	45.0%	53.7%	45.6%	54.4%
7,421	WHEELER	1,341	750	556	35	194 R	55.9%	41.5%	57.4%	42.6%
27,144	WHITE	7,796	6,106	1,311	379	4,795 R	78.3%	16.8%	82.3%	17.7%
102,599	WHITFIELD	16,247	11,750	3,725	772	8,025 R	72.3%	22.9%	75.9%	24.1%
9,255	WILCOX	2,066	1,280	722	64	558 R	62.0%	34.9%	63.9%	36.1%
10,593	WILKES	3,759	2,093	1,576	90	517 R	55.7%	41.9%	57.0%	43.0%
9,563	WILKINSON	3,402	1,618	1,704	80	86 D	47.6%	50.1%	48.7%	51.3%
21,679	WORTH	5,917	3,833	1,923	161	1,910 R	64.8%	32.5%	66.6%	33.4%
9,687,653	TOTAL	2,576,161	1,365,832	1,107,011	103,318	258,821 R	53.0%	43.0%	55.2%	44.8%

GEORGIA
SENATOR 2010

2010 Census Population	County	Total Vote	Republican	Democratic	Other	Rep.-Dem. Plurality	Percentage Total Vote Rep.	Dem.	Major Vote Rep.	Dem.
18,236	APPLING	4,998	3,784	1,126	88	2,658 R	75.7%	22.5%	77.1%	22.9%
8,375	ATKINSON	1,417	982	388	47	594 R	69.3%	27.4%	71.7%	28.3%
11,096	BACON	2,401	1,890	456	55	1,434 R	78.7%	19.0%	80.6%	19.4%
3,451	BAKER	1,218	618	577	23	41 R	50.7%	47.4%	51.7%	48.3%
45,720	BALDWIN	11,055	5,689	5,085	281	604 R	51.5%	46.0%	52.8%	47.2%
18,395	BANKS	4,428	3,768	530	130	3,238 R	85.1%	12.0%	87.7%	12.3%
69,367	BARROW	16,038	12,510	2,970	558	9,540 R	78.0%	18.5%	80.8%	19.2%
100,157	BARTOW	23,292	18,039	4,453	800	13,586 R	77.4%	19.1%	80.2%	19.8%
17,634	BENHILL	3,867	2,314	1,454	99	860 R	59.8%	37.6%	61.4%	38.6%
19,286	BERRIEN	3,980	3,011	824	145	2,187 R	75.7%	20.7%	78.5%	21.5%
155,547	BIBB	44,021	20,074	23,151	796	3,077 D	45.6%	52.6%	46.4%	53.6%
13,063	BLECKLEY	3,291	2,427	786	78	1,641 R	73.7%	23.9%	75.5%	24.5%
18,411	BRANTLEY	3,267	2,636	500	131	2,136 R	80.7%	15.3%	84.1%	15.9%
16,243	BROOKS	5,000	2,686	2,190	124	496 R	53.7%	43.8%	55.1%	44.9%
30,233	BRYAN	7,922	6,023	1,619	280	4,404 R	76.0%	20.4%	78.8%	21.2%
70,217	BULLOCH	14,293	9,768	4,176	349	5,592 R	68.3%	29.2%	70.1%	29.9%
23,316	BURKE	6,051	3,098	2,855	98	243 R	51.2%	47.2%	52.0%	48.0%
23,655	BUTTS	6,118	4,279	1,679	160	2,600 R	69.9%	27.4%	71.8%	28.2%
6,694	CALHOUN	1,627	677	936	14	259 D	41.6%	57.5%	42.0%	58.0%
50,513	CAMDEN	9,972	6,582	3,001	389	3,581 R	66.0%	30.1%	68.7%	31.3%
10,998	CANDLER	2,282	1,626	610	46	1,016 R	71.3%	26.7%	72.7%	27.3%
110,527	CARROLL	27,274	19,783	6,672	819	13,111 R	72.5%	24.5%	74.8%	25.2%
63,942	CATOOSA	13,346	10,381	2,388	577	7,993 R	77.8%	17.9%	81.3%	18.7%
12,171	CHARLTON	2,147	1,424	645	78	779 R	66.3%	30.0%	68.8%	31.2%
265,128	CHATHAM	67,881	34,200	32,126	1,555	2,074 R	50.4%	47.3%	51.6%	48.4%

GEORGIA

SENATOR 2010

2010 Census Population	County	Total Vote	Republican	Democratic	Other	Rep.-Dem. Plurality	Percentage Total Vote Rep.	Dem.	Major Vote Rep.	Dem.
11,267	CHATTAHOOCHEE	725	383	315	27	68 R	52.8%	43.4%	54.9%	45.1%
26,015	CHATTOOGA	4,878	3,300	1,399	179	1,901 R	67.7%	28.7%	70.2%	29.8%
214,346	CHEROKEE	65,367	53,241	9,584	2,542	43,657 R	81.4%	14.7%	84.7%	15.3%
116,714	CLARKE	27,213	10,495	15,871	847	5,376 D	38.6%	58.3%	39.8%	60.2%
3,183	CLAY	1,054	437	593	24	156 D	41.5%	56.3%	42.4%	57.6%
259,424	CLAYTON	60,215	11,917	47,522	776	35,605 D	19.8%	78.9%	20.0%	80.0%
6,798	CLINCH	1,335	865	433	37	432 R	64.8%	32.4%	66.6%	33.4%
688,078	COBB	210,976	133,785	70,521	6,670	63,264 R	63.4%	33.4%	65.5%	34.5%
42,356	COFFEE	8,000	5,403	2,328	269	3,075 R	67.5%	29.1%	69.9%	30.1%
45,498	COLQUITT	8,887	6,444	2,148	295	4,296 R	72.5%	24.2%	75.0%	25.0%
124,053	COLUMBIA	37,168	28,109	8,129	930	19,980 R	75.6%	21.9%	77.6%	22.4%
17,212	COOK	3,638	2,364	1,161	113	1,203 R	65.0%	31.9%	67.1%	32.9%
127,317	COWETA	36,515	27,430	7,856	1,229	19,574 R	75.1%	21.5%	77.7%	22.3%
12,630	CRAWFORD	3,599	2,362	1,107	130	1,255 R	65.6%	30.8%	68.1%	31.9%
23,439	CRISP	4,931	3,231	1,607	93	1,624 R	65.5%	32.6%	66.8%	33.2%
16,633	DADE	3,472	2,558	704	210	1,854 R	73.7%	20.3%	78.4%	21.6%
22,330	DAWSON	7,012	6,081	678	253	5,403 R	86.7%	9.7%	90.0%	10.0%
27,842	DECATUR	7,047	4,165	2,713	169	1,452 R	59.1%	38.5%	60.6%	39.4%
691,893	DEKALB	206,090	53,891	147,628	4,571	93,737 D	26.1%	71.6%	26.7%	73.3%
21,796	DODGE	5,134	3,544	1,475	115	2,069 R	69.0%	28.7%	70.6%	29.4%
14,918	DOOLY	3,049	1,503	1,480	66	23 R	49.3%	48.5%	50.4%	49.6%
94,565	DOUGHERTY	26,968	9,638	16,979	351	7,341 D	35.7%	63.0%	36.2%	63.8%
132,403	DOUGLAS	37,163	20,056	16,249	858	3,807 R	54.0%	43.7%	55.2%	44.8%
11,008	EARLY	3,756	1,897	1,781	78	116 R	50.5%	47.4%	51.6%	48.4%
4,034	ECHOLS	581	439	108	34	331 R	75.6%	18.6%	80.3%	19.7%
52,250	EFFINGHAM	13,106	10,249	2,462	395	7,787 R	78.2%	18.8%	80.6%	19.4%
20,166	ELBERT	5,446	3,320	1,973	153	1,347 R	61.0%	36.2%	62.7%	37.3%
22,598	EMANUEL	4,973	3,343	1,539	91	1,804 R	67.2%	30.9%	68.5%	31.5%
11,000	EVANS	2,440	1,696	705	39	991 R	69.5%	28.9%	70.6%	29.4%
23,682	FANNIN	6,965	5,419	1,270	276	4,149 R	77.8%	18.2%	81.0%	19.0%
106,567	FAYETTE	41,820	28,798	11,806	1,216	16,992 R	68.9%	28.2%	70.9%	29.1%
96,317	FLOYD	21,652	15,787	5,294	571	10,493 R	72.9%	24.5%	74.9%	25.1%
175,511	FORSYTH	52,912	45,064	6,078	1,770	38,986 R	85.2%	11.5%	88.1%	11.9%
22,084	FRANKLIN	5,010	3,878	959	173	2,919 R	77.4%	19.1%	80.2%	19.8%
920,581	FULTON	253,475	104,472	142,999	6,004	38,527 D	41.2%	56.4%	42.2%	57.8%
28,292	GILMER	8,091	6,459	1,240	392	5,219 R	79.8%	15.3%	83.9%	16.1%
3,082	GLASCOCK	833	712	100	21	612 R	85.5%	12.0%	87.7%	12.3%
79,626	GLYNN	21,180	14,598	6,042	540	8,556 R	68.9%	28.5%	70.7%	29.3%
55,186	GORDON	10,766	8,621	1,767	378	6,854 R	80.1%	16.4%	83.0%	17.0%
25,011	GRADY	6,433	4,090	2,181	162	1,909 R	63.6%	33.9%	65.2%	34.8%
15,994	GREENE	5,876	3,895	1,867	114	2,028 R	66.3%	31.8%	67.6%	32.4%
805,321	GWINNETT	194,019	121,180	67,023	5,816	54,157 R	62.5%	34.5%	64.4%	35.6%
43,041	HABERSHAM	10,365	8,586	1,411	368	7,175 R	82.8%	13.6%	85.9%	14.1%
179,684	HALL	43,697	35,477	6,681	1,539	28,796 R	81.2%	15.3%	84.2%	15.8%
9,429	HANCOCK	2,895	695	2,148	52	1,453 D	24.0%	74.2%	24.4%	75.6%
28,780	HARALSON	7,040	5,706	1,084	250	4,622 R	81.1%	15.4%	84.0%	16.0%
32,024	HARRIS	9,844	7,233	2,326	285	4,907 R	73.5%	23.6%	75.7%	24.3%

GEORGIA
SENATOR 2010

2010 Census Population	County	Total Vote	Republican	Democratic	Other	Rep.-Dem. Plurality	Total Vote Rep.	Total Vote Dem.	Major Vote Rep.	Major Vote Dem.
25,213	HART	6,040	4,052	1,760	228	2,292 R	67.1%	29.1%	69.7%	30.3%
11,834	HEARD	2,806	2,098	601	107	1,497 R	74.8%	21.4%	77.7%	22.3%
203,922	HENRY	59,211	33,235	24,545	1,431	8,690 R	56.1%	41.5%	57.5%	42.5%
139,900	HOUSTON	38,510	24,330	13,135	1,045	11,195 R	63.2%	34.1%	64.9%	35.1%
9,538	IRWIN	2,586	1,728	797	61	931 R	66.8%	30.8%	68.4%	31.6%
60,485	JACKSON	16,264	13,434	2,287	543	11,147 R	82.6%	14.1%	85.5%	14.5%
13,900	JASPER	4,168	2,941	1,123	104	1,818 R	70.6%	26.9%	72.4%	27.6%
15,068	JEFF DAVIS	3,510	2,640	774	96	1,866 R	75.2%	22.1%	77.3%	22.7%
16,930	JEFFERSON	4,619	2,268	2,281	70	13 D	49.1%	49.4%	49.9%	50.1%
8,340	JENKINS	2,226	1,355	823	48	532 R	60.9%	37.0%	62.2%	37.8%
9,980	JOHNSON	2,361	1,659	639	63	1,020 R	70.3%	27.1%	72.2%	27.8%
28,669	JONES	8,554	5,480	2,890	184	2,590 R	64.1%	33.8%	65.5%	34.5%
18,317	LAMAR	4,959	3,351	1,473	135	1,878 R	67.6%	29.7%	69.5%	30.5%
10,078	LANIER	1,618	1,037	532	49	505 R	64.1%	32.9%	66.1%	33.9%
48,434	LAURENS	13,333	8,749	4,321	263	4,428 R	65.6%	32.4%	66.9%	33.1%
28,298	LEE	9,369	7,160	2,001	208	5,159 R	76.4%	21.4%	78.2%	21.8%
63,453	LIBERTY	9,832	4,365	5,260	207	895 D	44.4%	53.5%	45.4%	54.6%
7,996	LINCOLN	3,205	2,167	970	68	1,197 R	67.6%	30.3%	69.1%	30.9%
14,464	LONG	1,808	1,200	557	51	643 R	66.4%	30.8%	68.3%	31.7%
109,233	LOWNDES	23,082	13,782	8,669	631	5,113 R	59.7%	37.6%	61.4%	38.6%
29,966	LUMPKIN	8,103	6,401	1,339	363	5,062 R	79.0%	16.5%	82.7%	17.3%
21,875	MCDUFFIE	6,149	3,888	2,162	99	1,726 R	63.2%	35.2%	64.3%	35.7%
14,333	MCINTOSH	4,599	2,526	1,933	140	593 R	54.9%	42.0%	56.6%	43.4%
14,740	MACON	3,193	1,210	1,922	61	712 D	37.9%	60.2%	38.6%	61.4%
28,120	MADISON	7,613	5,748	1,645	220	4,103 R	75.5%	21.6%	77.7%	22.3%
8,742	MARION	2,040	1,187	798	55	389 R	58.2%	39.1%	59.8%	40.2%
21,992	MERIWETHER	6,240	3,612	2,480	148	1,132 R	57.9%	39.7%	59.3%	40.7%
6,125	MILLER	1,847	1,293	512	42	781 R	70.0%	27.7%	71.6%	28.4%
23,498	MITCHELL	5,601	2,924	2,505	172	419 R	52.2%	44.7%	53.9%	46.1%
26,424	MONROE	8,884	6,063	2,595	226	3,468 R	68.2%	29.2%	70.0%	30.0%
9,123	MONTGOMERY	2,458	1,808	593	57	1,215 R	73.6%	24.1%	75.3%	24.7%
17,868	MORGAN	6,345	4,558	1,611	176	2,947 R	71.8%	25.4%	73.9%	26.1%
39,628	MURRAY	5,757	4,331	1,143	283	3,188 R	75.2%	19.9%	79.1%	20.9%
189,885	MUSCOGEE	46,058	20,378	24,741	939	4,363 D	44.2%	53.7%	45.2%	54.8%
99,958	NEWTON	27,915	15,037	12,280	598	2,757 R	53.9%	44.0%	55.0%	45.0%
32,808	OCONEE	12,604	9,500	2,741	363	6,759 R	75.4%	21.7%	77.6%	22.4%
14,899	OGLETHORPE	4,264	2,937	1,198	129	1,739 R	68.9%	28.1%	71.0%	29.0%
142,324	PAULDING	32,459	23,676	7,779	1,004	15,897 R	72.9%	24.0%	75.3%	24.7%
27,695	PEACH	7,383	3,891	3,338	154	553 R	52.7%	45.2%	53.8%	46.2%
29,431	PICKENS	8,980	7,447	1,156	377	6,291 R	82.9%	12.9%	86.6%	13.4%
18,758	PIERCE	4,047	3,391	565	91	2,826 R	83.8%	14.0%	85.7%	14.3%
17,869	PIKE	5,697	4,695	842	160	3,853 R	82.4%	14.8%	84.8%	15.2%
41,475	POLK	8,734	6,313	2,169	252	4,144 R	72.3%	24.8%	74.4%	25.6%
12,010	PULASKI	2,529	1,710	744	75	966 R	67.6%	29.4%	69.7%	30.3%
21,218	PUTNAM	6,503	4,656	1,693	154	2,963 R	71.6%	26.0%	73.3%	26.7%
2,513	QUITMAN	771	371	378	22	7 D	48.1%	49.0%	49.5%	50.5%
16,276	RABUN	5,377	4,104	1,092	181	3,012 R	76.3%	20.3%	79.0%	21.0%
7,719	RANDOLPH	2,251	1,070	1,159	22	89 D	47.5%	51.5%	48.0%	52.0%

GEORGIA
SENATOR 2010

2010 Census Population	County	Total Vote	Republican	Democratic	Other	Rep.-Dem. Plurality	Percentage Total Vote Rep.	Dem.	Major Vote Rep.	Dem.
200,549	RICHMOND	49,448	19,552	29,102	794	9,550 D	39.5%	58.9%	40.2%	59.8%
85,215	ROCKDALE	26,690	13,034	13,133	523	99 D	48.8%	49.2%	49.8%	50.2%
5,010	SCHLEY	1,170	855	289	26	566 R	73.1%	24.7%	74.7%	25.3%
14,593	SCREVEN	3,774	2,255	1,463	56	792 R	59.8%	38.8%	60.7%	39.3%
8,729	SEMINOLE	2,668	1,635	947	86	688 R	61.3%	35.5%	63.3%	36.7%
64,073	SPALDING	16,336	10,752	5,202	382	5,550 R	65.8%	31.8%	67.4%	32.6%
26,175	STEPHENS	6,463	4,796	1,456	211	3,340 R	74.2%	22.5%	76.7%	23.3%
6,058	STEWART	1,432	590	805	37	215 D	41.2%	56.2%	42.3%	57.7%
32,819	SUMTER	8,074	4,117	3,821	136	296 R	51.0%	47.3%	51.9%	48.1%
6,865	TALBOT	2,271	891	1,324	56	433 D	39.2%	58.3%	40.2%	59.8%
1,717	TALIAFERRO	710	247	452	11	205 D	34.8%	63.7%	35.3%	64.7%
25,520	TATTNALL	4,068	3,064	905	99	2,159 R	75.3%	22.2%	77.2%	22.8%
8,906	TAYLOR	2,462	1,399	1,006	57	393 R	56.8%	40.9%	58.2%	41.8%
16,500	TELFAIR	2,680	1,540	1,088	52	452 R	57.5%	40.6%	58.6%	41.4%
9,315	TERRELL	3,081	1,482	1,545	54	63 D	48.1%	50.1%	49.0%	51.0%
44,720	THOMAS	12,926	8,070	4,545	311	3,525 R	62.4%	35.2%	64.0%	36.0%
40,118	TIFT	9,638	6,843	2,590	205	4,253 R	71.0%	26.9%	72.5%	27.5%
27,223	TOOMBS	6,482	4,806	1,506	170	3,300 R	74.1%	23.2%	76.1%	23.9%
10,471	TOWNS	4,223	3,257	836	130	2,421 R	77.1%	19.8%	79.6%	20.4%
6,885	TREUTLEN	1,743	1,162	548	33	614 R	66.7%	31.4%	68.0%	32.0%
67,044	TROUP	15,604	10,135	5,088	381	5,047 R	65.0%	32.6%	66.6%	33.4%
8,930	TURNER	2,357	1,462	838	57	624 R	62.0%	35.6%	63.6%	36.4%
9,023	TWIGGS	3,096	1,444	1,591	61	147 D	46.6%	51.4%	47.6%	52.4%
21,356	UNION	8,085	6,232	1,536	317	4,696 R	77.1%	19.0%	80.2%	19.8%
27,153	UPSON	7,125	4,860	2,130	135	2,730 R	68.2%	29.9%	69.5%	30.5%
68,756	WALKER	12,059	9,209	2,282	568	6,927 R	76.4%	18.9%	80.1%	19.9%
83,768	WALTON	25,405	20,583	4,132	690	16,451 R	81.0%	16.3%	83.3%	16.7%
36,312	WARE	6,969	4,861	1,914	194	2,947 R	69.8%	27.5%	71.7%	28.3%
5,834	WARREN	1,723	817	869	37	52 D	47.4%	50.4%	48.5%	51.5%
21,187	WASHINGTON	5,645	2,969	2,587	89	382 R	52.6%	45.8%	53.4%	46.6%
30,099	WAYNE	6,599	4,911	1,505	183	3,406 R	74.4%	22.8%	76.5%	23.5%
2,799	WEBSTER	909	457	437	15	20 R	50.3%	48.1%	51.1%	48.9%
7,421	WHEELER	1,276	798	459	19	339 R	62.5%	36.0%	63.5%	36.5%
27,144	WHITE	7,781	6,417	1,075	289	5,342 R	82.5%	13.8%	85.7%	14.3%
102,599	WHITFIELD	16,092	12,063	3,301	728	8,762 R	75.0%	20.5%	78.5%	21.5%
9,255	WILCOX	2,041	1,425	573	43	852 R	69.8%	28.1%	71.3%	28.7%
10,593	WILKES	3,668	2,245	1,374	49	871 R	61.2%	37.5%	62.0%	38.0%
9,563	WILKINSON	3,337	1,753	1,534	50	219 R	52.5%	46.0%	53.3%	46.7%
21,679	WORTH	5,889	4,075	1,656	158	2,419 R	69.2%	28.1%	71.1%	28.9%
9,687,653	TOTAL	2,555,258	1,489,904	996,516	68,838	493,388 R	58.3%	39.0%	59.9%	40.1%

GEORGIA

HOUSE OF REPRESENTATIVES

			Republican		Democratic				Percentage			
									Total Vote		Major Vote	
CD	Year	Total Vote	Vote	Candidate	Vote	Candidate	Other Vote	Rep.-Dem. Plurality	Rep.	Dem.	Rep.	Dem.
1	2010	163,719	117,270	KINGSTON, JACK*	46,449	HARRIS, OSCAR L., II		70,821 R	71.6%	28.4%	71.6%	28.4%
1	2008	249,334	165,890	KINGSTON, JACK*	83,444	GILLESPIE, BILL		82,446 R	66.5%	33.5%	66.5%	33.5%
1	2006	138,629	94,961	KINGSTON, JACK*	43,668	NELSON, JIM		51,293 R	68.5%	31.5%	68.5%	31.5%
2	2010	168,193	81,673	KEOWN, MIKE	86,520	BISHOP, SANFORD D., JR.*		4,847 D	48.6%	51.4%	48.6%	51.4%
2	2008	229,786	71,351	FERRELL, LEE	158,435	BISHOP, SANFORD D., JR.*		87,084 D	31.1%	68.9%	31.1%	68.9%
2	2006	130,629	41,967	HUGHES, BRADLEY C.	88,662	BISHOP, SANFORD D., JR.*		46,695 D	32.1%	67.9%	32.1%	67.9%
3	2010	242,239	168,304	WESTMORELAND, LYNN*	73,932	SAUNDERS, FRANK	3	94,372 R	69.5%	30.5%	69.5%	30.5%
3	2008	342,580	225,055	WESTMORELAND, LYNN*	117,522	CAMP, STEPHEN	3	107,533 R	65.7%	34.3%	65.7%	34.3%
3	2006	192,799	130,428	WESTMORELAND, LYNN*	62,371	McGRAW, MIKE		68,057 R	67.6%	32.4%	67.6%	32.4%
4	2010	176,467	44,707	CARTER, LISBETH "LIZ"	131,760	JOHNSON, HENRY C. "HANK," JR.*		87,053 D	25.3%	74.7%	25.3%	74.7%
4	2008	224,694	—		224,494	JOHNSON, HENRY C. "HANK," JR.*	200	224,494 D		99.9%		100.0%
4	2006	141,194	34,778	DAVIS, CATHERINE	106,352	JOHNSON, HENRY C. "HANK," JR.	64	71,574 D	24.6%	75.3%	24.6%	75.4%
5	2010	177,404	46,622	LITTLE, FENN	130,782	LEWIS, JOHN*		84,160 D	26.3%	73.7%	26.3%	73.7%
5	2008	231,474		—	231,368	LEWIS, JOHN*	106	231,368 D		100.0%		100.0%
5	2006	122,428		—	122,380	LEWIS, JOHN*	48	122,380 D		100.0%		100.0%
6	2010	198,288	198,100	PRICE, TOM*		—	188	198,100 R	99.9%		100.0%	
6	2008	338,071	231,520	PRICE, TOM*	106,551	JONES, BILL		124,969 R	68.5%	31.5%	68.5%	31.5%
6	2006	200,252	144,958	PRICE, TOM*	55,294	SINTON, STEVE		89,664 R	72.4%	27.6%	72.4%	27.6%
7	2010	239,894	160,898	WOODALL, ROB	78,996	HECKMAN, DOUG		81,902 R	67.1%	32.9%	67.1%	32.9%
7	2008	337,513	209,354	LINDER, JOHN*	128,159	HECKMAN, DOUG		81,195 R	62.0%	38.0%	62.0%	38.0%
7	2006	184,114	130,561	LINDER, JOHN*	53,553	BURNS, ALLAN		77,008 R	70.9%	29.1%	70.9%	29.1%
8	2010	195,020	102,770	SCOTT, AUSTIN	92,250	MARSHALL, JIM*		10,520 R	52.7%	47.3%	52.7%	47.3%
8	2008	274,687	117,446	GODDARD, RICK	157,241	MARSHALL, JIM*		39,795 D	42.8%	57.2%	42.8%	57.2%
8	2006	159,568	78,908	COLLINS, MAC	80,660	MARSHALL, JIM*		1,752 D	49.5%	50.5%	49.5%	50.5%
9	2010	173,512	173,512	GRAVES, TOM*		—		173,512 R	100.0%		100.0%	
9	2008	288,030	217,493	DEAL, NATHAN*	70,537	SCOTT, JEFF		146,956 R	75.5%	24.5%	75.5%	24.5%
9	2006	167,926	128,685	DEAL, NATHAN*	39,240	BRADBURY, JOHN D.	1	89,445 R	76.6%	23.4%	76.6%	23.4%
10	2010	204,967	138,062	BROUN, PAUL C.*	66,905	EDWARDS, RUSSELL		71,157 R	67.4%	32.6%	67.4%	32.6%
10	2008	291,903	177,265	BROUN, PAUL C.*	114,638	SAXON, BOBBY		62,627 R	60.7%	39.3%	60.7%	39.3%
10	2006	174,753	117,721	NORWOOD, CHARLIE*	57,032	HOLLEY, TERRY		60,689 R	67.4%	32.6%	67.4%	32.6%
11	2010	163,515	163,515	GINGREY, PHIL*		—		163,515 R	100.0%		100.0%	
11	2008	299,302	204,082	GINGREY, PHIL*	95,220	GAMMON, HUGH "BUD"		108,862 R	68.2%	31.8%	68.2%	31.8%
11	2006	166,788	118,524	GINGREY, PHIL*	48,261	PILLION, PATRICK SAMUEL	3	70,263 R	71.1%	28.9%	71.1%	28.9%
12	2010	163,397	70,938	McKINNEY, RAYMOND	92,459	BARROW, JOHN*		21,521 D	43.4%	56.6%	43.4%	56.6%
12	2008	249,335	84,773	STONE, JOHN	164,562	BARROW, JOHN*		79,789 D	34.0%	66.0%	34.0%	66.0%
12	2006	142,438	70,787	BURNS, MAX	71,651	BARROW, JOHN*		864 D	49.7%	50.3%	49.7%	50.3%
13	2010	202,065	61,771	CRANE, MIKE	140,294	SCOTT, DAVID*		78,523 D	30.6%	69.4%	30.6%	69.4%
13	2008	298,239	92,320	HONEYCUTT, DEBORAH	205,919	SCOTT, DAVID*		113,599 D	31.0%	69.0%	31.0%	69.0%
13	2006	148,789	45,770	HONEYCUTT, DEBORAH	103,019	SCOTT, DAVID*		57,249 D	30.8%	69.2%	30.8%	69.2%
TOTAL	2010	2,468,680	1,528,142		940,347		191	587,795 R	61.9%	38.1%	61.9%	38.1%
TOTAL	2008	3,654,948	1,796,549		1,858,090		309	61,541 D	49.2%	50.8%	49.2%	50.8%
TOTAL	2006	2,070,307	1,138,048		932,143		116	205,905 R	55.0%	45.0%	55.0%	45.0%
TOTAL	2004	2,960,763	1,819,817		1,140,869		77	678,948 R	61.5%	38.5%	61.5%	38.5%
TOTAL	2002	1,918,297	1,104,162		814,024		111	290,138 R	57.6%	42.4%	57.6%	42.4%

An asterisk (*) denotes incumbent. Georgia's congressional district lines were changed between the 2004 and 2006 elections. For general election results for 2002 and 2004, see America Votes 26, p. 139.

GEORGIA

GENERAL AND PRIMARY ELECTIONS

2010 GENERAL ELECTIONS

Governor	Other vote was 103,194 Libertarian (John H. Monds); 76 write-in (David C. Byrne); 48 write-in (Neal Horsley).
Senator	Other vote was 68,750 Libertarian (Chuck Donovan); 52 write-in (Steve Davis); 24 write-in (Raymond Beckworth); 12 write-in Brian Russell Brown).
House	Other vote was:
CD 1	
CD 2	
CD 3	3 write-in (Jagdish Agrawal).
CD 4	
CD 5	
CD 6	188 write-in (Sean Greenberg).
CD 7	
CD 8	
CD 9	
CD 10	
CD 11	
CD 12	
CD 13	

2010 PRIMARY ELECTIONS

Primary	July 20, 2010	**Registration** (includes 792,970 inactive registrants as of July 20, 2010)	5,725,884	No Party Registration

Primary Runoff August 10, 2010

Primary Type Open—Any registered voter could participate in either the Democratic or Republican primary, although if they voted in one party's primary they could not participate in a primary runoff of the other party. Voters who did not participate in the primary could vote in either party's runoff.

	REPUBLICAN PRIMARIES			DEMOCRATIC PRIMARIES		
Governor	Karen Handel	231,990	34.1%	Roy E. Barnes	259,482	65.6%
	Nathan Deal	155,946	22.9%	Thurbert Baker	85,571	21.6%
	Eric Johnson	136,792	20.1%	David Poythress	21,780	5.5%
	John W. Oxendine	115,421	17.0%	DuBose Porter	17,767	4.5%
	Jeff Chapman	20,636	3.0%	Carl Camon	4,170	1.1%
	Ray McBerry	17,171	2.5%	Bill Bolton	3,573	0.9%
	Otis Putnam	2,543	0.4%	Randal Mangham	3,124	0.8%
	TOTAL	*680,499*		*TOTAL*	*395,467*	
	PRIMARY RUNOFF					
	Nathan Deal	291,035	50.2%			
	Karen Handel	288,516	49.8%			
	TOTAL	*579,551*				
Senator	Johnny Isakson*	558,298	100%	Michael Thurmond	297,226	84.3%
				R. J. Hadley	55,159	15.7%
				TOTAL	*352,385*	
Congressional District 1	Jack Kingston*	49,787	100.0%	Oscar L. Harris II	16,828	100.0%
Congressional District 2	Mike Keown	23,945	80.8%	Sanford D. Bishop Jr.*	31,255	100.0%
	Rick Allen	3,283	11.1%			
	Lee Ferrell	2,393	8.1%			
	TOTAL	*29,621*				
Congressional District 3	Lynn Westmoreland*	63,787	100.0%	Frank Saunders	18,676	100.0%

GEORGIA

GENERAL AND PRIMARY ELECTIONS

Congressional District 4	Lisbeth "Liz" Carter	9,549	54.7%	Henry C. "Hank" Johnson Jr.*	28,095	55.2%
	Larry Gause	4,455	25.5%	Vernon Jones	13,407	26.3%
	Victor Armendariz	1,741	10.0%	Connie Stokes	9,411	18.5%
	Cory Ruth	1,697	9.7%			
	TOTAL	17,442		TOTAL	50,913	
Congressional District 5	Fenn Little	8,758	59.6%	John Lewis*	44,379	100.0%
	Kelly Nguyen	5,937	40.4%			
	TOTAL	14,695				
Congressional District 6	Tom Price*	70,049	100.0%	No Democratic candidate		
Congressional District 7	Rob Woodall	27,634	36.3%	Doug Heckman	15,130	100.0%
	Jody Hice	20,034	26.3%			
	Clay Cox	15,249	20.0%			
	Jef Fincher	4,608	6.1%			
	Tom Kirby	3,052	4.0%			
	Chuck Efstration	2,837	3.7%			
	Tom Parrott	1,648	2.2%			
	Ronnie Grist	1,083	1.4%			
	TOTAL	76,145				
	PRIMARY RUNOFF					
	Rob Woodall	39,987	56.0%			
	Jody Hice	31,426	44.0%			
	TOTAL	71,413				
Congressional District 8	Austin Scott	22,191	52.4%	Jim Marshall*	28,819	100.0%
	Ken DeLoach	13,228	31.2%			
	Diane Vann	6,959	16.4%			
	TOTAL	42,378				
Congressional District 9	Tom Graves*	38,851	49.5%	No Democratic candidate		
	Lee Hawkins	20,957	26.7%			
	Steve Tarvin	11,529	14.7%			
	Chris Cates	5,051	6.4%			
	Bobby Reese	1,362	1.7%			
	Bert Loftman	782	1.0%			
	TOTAL	78,532				
	PRIMARY RUNOFF					
	Tom Graves*	41,878	55.2%			
	Lee Hawkins	33,975	44.8%			
	TOTAL	75,853				
Congressional District 10	Paul C. Broun*	44,956	100.0%	Russell Edwards	17,075	100.0%
Congressional District 11	Phil Gingrey*	58,447	100.0%	No Democratic candidate		
Congressional District 12	Raymond McKinney	11,709	42.6%	John Barrow*	19,505	57.9%
	Carl Smith	7,677	27.9%	Regina D. Thomas	14,201	42.1%
	Jeanne Seaver	5,040	18.3%			
	Michael Horner	3,051	11.1%			
	TOTAL	27,477		TOTAL	33,706	
	PRIMARY RUNOFF					
	Raymond Mckinney	14,256	62.0%			
	Carl Smith	8,724	38.0%			
	TOTAL	22,980				
Congressional District 13	Mike Crane	7,234	29.4%	David Scott*	34,374	76.1%
	Deborah Honeycutt	6,538	26.6%	Mike Murphy	7,556	16.7%
	"Chip" Flanegan	4,137	16.8%	Michael Frisbee	3,229	7.2%
	Dave Orr	3,113	12.7%			
	Hank R. Dudek	2,322	9.4%			
	Rupert G. Parchment	1,257	5.1%			
	TOTAL	24,601		TOTAL	45,159	
	PRIMARY RUNOFF					
	Mike Crane	15,286	67.5%			
	Deborah Honeycutt	7,349	32.5%			
	TOTAL	22,635				

An asterisk (*) denotes incumbent.

HAWAII

Congressional districts first established for elections held in 2002
2 members

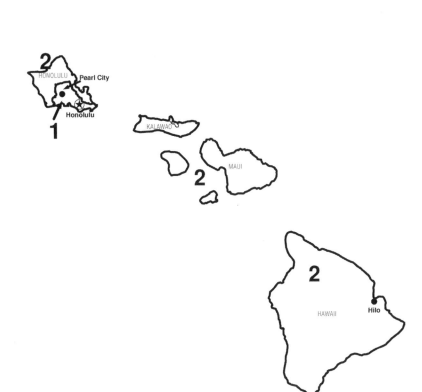

HAWAII

GOVERNOR
Neil Abercrombie (D). Elected 2010 to a four-year term.

SENATORS (2 Democrats)
Daniel K. Akaka (D). Reelected 2006 to a six-year term. Previously elected 2000,1994 and 1990 to fill out the remaining four years of the term vacated by the death of Senator Spark M. Matsunaga (D); Akaka had been previously appointed to the vacant seat and took office May 16,1990.

Daniel K. Inouye (D). Reelected 2010 to a six-year term. Previously elected 2004,1998,1992,1986,1980,1974,1968,1962.

REPRESENTATIVES (2 Democrats)
1. Colleen Hanabusa (D)   2. Mazie K. Hirono (D)

POSTWAR VOTE FOR PRESIDENT

		Republican		Democratic				Total Vote		Major Vote	
Year	Total Vote	Vote	Candidate	Vote	Candidate	Other Vote	Dem.-Rep. Plurality	Rep.	Dem.	Rep.	Dem.
2008	453,568	120,566	McCain, John	325,871	Obama, Barack	7,131	205,305 D	26.6%	71.8%	27.0%	73.0%
2004	429,013	194,191	Bush, George W.	231,708	Kerry, John	3,114	37,517 D	45.3%	54.0%	45.6%	54.4%
2000**	367,951	137,845	Bush, George W.	205,286	Gore, Al	24,820	67,441 D	37.5%	55.8%	40.2%	59.8%
1996**	360,120	113,943	Dole, Bob	205,012	Clinton, Bill	41,165	91,069 D	31.6%	56.9%	35.7%	64.3%
1992**	372,842	136,822	Bush, George	179,310	Clinton, Bill	56,710	42,488 D	36.7%	48.1%	43.3%	56.7%
1988	354,461	158,625	Bush, George	192,364	Dukakis, Michael S.	3,472	33,739 D	44.8%	54.3%	45.2%	54.8%
1984	335,846	185,050	Reagan, Ronald	147,154	Mondale, Walter F.	3,642	37,896 R	55.1%	43.8%	55.7%	44.3%
1980**	303,287	130,112	Reagan, Ronald	135,879	Carter, Jimmy	37,296	5,767 D	42.9%	44.8%	48.9%	51.1%
1976	291,301	140,003	Ford, Gerald R.	147,375	Carter, Jimmy	3,923	7,372 D	48.1%	50.6%	48.7%	51.3%
1972	270,274	168,865	Nixon, Richard M.	101,409	McGovern, George S.		67,456 R	62.5%	37.5%	62.5%	37.5%
1968**	236,218	91,425	Nixon, Richard M.	141,324	Humphrey, Hubert H.	3,469	49,899 D	38.7%	59.8%	39.3%	60.7%
1964	207,271	44,022	Goldwater, Barry M.	163,249	Johnson, Lyndon B.		119,227 D	21.2%	78.8%	21.2%	78.8%
1960	184,705	92,295	Nixon, Richard M.	92,410	Kennedy, John F.		115 D	50.0%	50.0%	50.0%	50.0%

**In past elections, the other vote included: 2000 - 21,623 Green (Ralph Nader); 1996 - 27,358 Reform (Ross Perot); 1992 - 53,003 Independent (Perot); 1980 - 32,021 Independent (John Anderson); 1968 - 3,469 American Independent (George Wallace). Hawaii was formally admitted as a state in August1959.

HAWAII

POSTWAR VOTE FOR GOVERNOR

Year	Total Vote	Republican Vote	Republican Candidate	Democratic Vote	Democratic Candidate	Other Vote	Dem.-Rep. Plurality	Percentage Total Vote Rep.	Percentage Total Vote Dem.	Percentage Major Vote Rep.	Percentage Major Vote Dem.
2010	382,563	157,311	Aiona, Duke	222,724	Abercrombie, Neil	2,528	65,413 D	41.1%	58.2%	41.4%	58.6%
2006	344,315	215,313	Lingle, Linda	121,717	Iwase, Randy	7,285	93,596 R	62.5%	35.4%	63.9%	36.1%
2002	382,110	197,009	Lingle, Linda	179,647	Hirono, Mazie K.	5,454	17,362 R	51.6%	47.0%	52.3%	47.7%
1998	407,556	198,952	Lingle, Linda	204,206	Cayetano, Benjamin J.	4,398	5,254 D	48.8%	50.1%	49.3%	50.7%
1994**	369,013	107,908	Saiki, Patricia	134,978	Cayetano, Benjamin J.	126,127	21,820 D	29.2%	36.6%	44.4%	55.6%
1990	340,132	131,310	Hemmings, Fred	203,491	Waihee, John	5,331	72,181 D	38.6%	59.8%	39.2%	60.8%
1986	334,115	160,460	Anderson, D. G.	173,655	Waihee, John		13,195 D	48.0%	52.0%	48.0%	52.0%
1982**	311,853	81,507	Anderson, D. G.	141,043	Ariyoshi, George R.	89,303	51,740 D	26.1%	45.2%	36.6%	63.4%
1978	281,587	124,610	Leopold, John	153,394	Ariyoshi, George R.	3,583	28,784 D	44.3%	54.5%	44.8%	55.2%
1974	249,650	113,388	Crossley, Randolph	136,262	Ariyoshi, George R.		22,874 D	45.4%	54.6%	45.4%	54.6%
1970	239,061	101,249	King, Samuel P.	137,812	Burns, John A.		36,563 D	42.4%	57.6%	42.4%	57.6%
1966	213,164	104,324	Crossley, Randolph	108,840	Burns, John A.		4,516 D	48.9%	51.1%	48.9%	51.1%
1962	196,015	81,707	Quinn, William F.	114,308	Burns, John A.		32,601 D	41.7%	58.3%	41.7%	58.3%
1959S	168,662	86,213	Quinn, William F.	82,074	Burns, John A.	375	4,139 R	51.1%	48.7%	51.2%	48.8%

**In past elections, the other vote included: 1994 - 113,158 Best Party (Frank F. Fasi); 1982 - 89,303 Independent Democrat (Fasi). In both 1982 and 1994, Fasi finished second. The 1959 election was for a short term pending the regular vote in 1962.

POSTWAR VOTE FOR SENATOR

Year	Total Vote	Republican Vote	Republican Candidate	Democratic Vote	Democratic Candidate	Other Vote	Rep.-Dem. Plurality	Percentage Total Vote Rep.	Percentage Total Vote Dem.	Percentage Major Vote Rep.	Percentage Major Vote Dem.
2010	370,583	79,939	Cavasso, Cam	277,228	Inouye, Daniel K.	13,416	197,289 D	21.6%	74.8%	22.4%	77.6%
2006	342,842	126,097	Thielen, Cynthia	210,330	Akaka, Daniel K.	6,415	84,233 D	36.8%	61.3%	37.5%	62.5%
2004	415,347	87,172	Cavasso, Cam	313,629	Inouye, Daniel K.	14,546	226,457 D	21.0%	75.5%	21.7%	78.3%
2000	345,623	84,701	Carroll, John S.	251,215	Akaka, Daniel K.	9,707	166,514 D	24.5%	72.7%	25.2%	74.8%
1998	398,124	70,964	Young, Crystal	315,252	Inouye, Daniel K.	11,908	244,288 D	17.8%	79.2%	18.4%	81.6%
1994	356,902	86,320	Hustace, Maria M.	256,189	Akaka, Daniel K.	14,393	169,869 D	24.2%	71.8%	25.2%	74.8%
1992**	363,662	97,928	Reed, Rick	208,266	Inouye, Daniel K.	57,468	110,338 D	26.9%	57.3%	32.0%	68.0%
1990S	349,666	155,978	Saiki, Patricia	188,901	Akaka, Daniel K.	4,787	32,923 D	44.6%	54.0%	45.2%	54.8%
1988	323,876	66,987	Hustace, Maria M.	247,941	Matsunaga, Spark M.	8,948	180,954 D	20.7%	76.6%	21.3%	78.7%
1986	328,797	86,910	Hutchinson, Frank	241,887	Inouye, Daniel K.		154,977 D	26.4%	73.6%	26.4%	73.6%
1982	306,410	52,071	Brown, Clarence J.	245,386	Matsunaga, Spark M.	8,953	193,315 D	17.0%	80.1%	17.5%	82.5%
1980	288,006	53,068	Brown, Cooper	224,485	Inouye, Daniel K.	10,453	171,417 D	18.4%	77.9%	19.1%	80.9%
1976	302,092	122,724	Quinn, William F.	162,305	Matsunaga, Spark M.	17,063	39,581 D	40.6%	53.7%	43.1%	56.9%
1974**	250,221		—	207,454	Inouye, Daniel K.	42,767	207,454 D		82.9%		100.0%
1970	240,760	124,163	Fong, Hiram L.	116,597	Heftel, Cecil		7,566 R	51.6%	48.4%	51.6%	48.4%
1968	226,927	34,008	Thiessen, Wayne C.	189,248	Inouye, Daniel K.	3,671	155,240 D	15.0%	83.4%	15.2%	84.8%
1964	208,814	110,747	Fong, Hiram L.	96,789	Gill, Thomas P.	1,278	13,958 R	53.0%	46.4%	53.4%	46.6%
1962	196,361	60,067	Dillingham, Ben F.	136,294	Inouye, Daniel K.		76,227 D	30.6%	69.4%	30.6%	69.4%
1959**	164,808	87,161	Fong, Hiram L.	77,647	Fasi, Frank F.		9,514 R	52.9%	47.1%	52.9%	47.1%
1959S	163,875	79,123	Tsukiyama, W. C.	83,700	Long, Oren E.	1,052	4,577 D	48.3%	51.1%	48.6%	51.4%

**In past elections, the other vote was: 1992 - 49,921 Green (Linda B. Martin); 1974 - 42,767 Peoples (James D. Kimmel), who finished second. The 1990 election was for a short term to fill a vacancy. The two 1959 elections were held to indeterminate terms and the Senate later determined by lot that Senator Long would serve a short term, Senator Fong a long term. The Republican Party did not run a Senate candidate in the 1974 election.

HAWAII

GOVERNOR 2010

2010 Census Population	County	Total Vote	Republican	Democratic	Other	Rep.-Dem. Plurality		Percentage			
								Total Vote		Major Vote	
								Rep.	Dem.	Rep.	Dem.
185,079	HAWAII	53,386	19,807	33,095	484	13,288	D	37.1%	62.0%	37.4%	62.6%
953,207	HONOLULU	264,573	112,527	150,554	1,492	38,027	D	42.5%	56.9%	42.8%	57.2%
67,091	KAUAI	22,668	8,953	13,559	156	4,606	D	39.5%	59.8%	39.8%	60.2%
154,834	MAUI	41,936	16,024	25,516	396	9,492	D	38.2%	60.8%	38.6%	61.4%
1,360,301	TOTAL	382,563	157,311	222,724	2,528	65,413	D	41.1%	58.2%	41.4%	58.6%

The 2010 Census included 90 people in Kalawao County; their votes are part of the Maui County returns.

HAWAII

SENATOR 2010

2010 Census Population	County	Total Vote	Republican	Democratic	Other	Rep.-Dem. Plurality		Percentage			
								Total Vote		Major Vote	
								Rep.	Dem.	Rep.	Dem.
185,079	HAWAII	52,232	10,684	39,001	2,547	28,317	D	20.5%	74.7%	21.5%	78.5%
953,207	HONOLULU	255,530	57,502	189,673	8,355	132,171	D	22.5%	74.2%	23.3%	76.7%
67,091	KAUAI	21,839	3,732	17,192	915	13,460	D	17.1%	78.7%	17.8%	82.2%
154,834	MAUI	40,905	8,006	31,301	1,598	23,295	D	19.6%	76.5%	20.4%	79.6%
	Overseas Ballots	77	15	61	1	46	D	19.5%	79.2%	19.7%	80.3%
1,360,301	TOTAL	370,583	79,939	277,228	13,416	197,289	D	21.6%	74.8%	22.4%	77.6%

The 2010 Census includes 90 people in Kalawao County; their votes are part of the Maui County returns.

HAWAII

HOUSE OF REPRESENTATIVES

CD	Year	Total Vote	Republican		Democratic		Other Vote	Rep.-Dem. Plurality		Percentage			
			Vote	Candidate	Vote	Candidate				Total Vote		Major Vote	
										Rep.	Dem.	Rep.	Dem.
1	2010	176,863	82,723	DJOU, CHARLES*	94,140	HANABUSA, COLLEEN		11,417	D	46.8%	53.2%	46.8%	53.2%
1	2008	199,917	38,115	TATAII, STEVE	154,208	ABERCROMBIE, NEIL*	7,594	116,093	D	19.1%	77.1%	19.8%	80.2%
1	2006	162,794	49,890	HOUGH, RICHARD "NOAH"	112,904	ABERCROMBIE, NEIL*		63,014	D	30.6%	69.4%	30.6%	69.4%
1	2004	204,181	69,371	TANONAKA, DALTON	128,567	ABERCROMBIE, NEIL*	6,243	59,196	D	34.0%	63.0%	35.0%	65.0%
1	2002	180,733	45,032	TERRY, MARK	131,673	ABERCROMBIE, NEIL*	4,028	86,641	D	24.9%	72.9%	25.5%	74.5%
2	2010	183, 258	46,404	WILLOUGHBY, JOHN W.	132,290	HIRONO, MAZIE K.*	4,564	85,886	D	25.3%	72.2%	26.0%	74.0%
2	2008	217,914	44,425	EVANS, ROGER B.	165,748	HIRONO, MAZIE K.*	7,741	121,323	D	20.4%	76.1%	21.1%	78.9%
2	2006	175,150	68,244	HOGUE, BOB	106,906	HIRONO, MAZIE K.		38,662	D	39.0%	61.0%	39.0%	61.0%
2	2004	212,389	79,072	GABBARD, MIKE	133,317	CASE, ED*		54,245	D	37.2%	62.8%	37.2%	62.8%
2	2002	179,251	71,661	McDERMOTT, BOB	100,671	MINK, PATSY T.*	6,919	29,010	D	40.0%	56.2%	41.6%	58.4%
TOTAL	2010	360,121	129,127		226,430		4,564	97,303	D	35.9%	62.9%	36.3%	63.7%
TOTAL	2008	417,831	82,540		319,956		15,335	237,416	D	19.8%	76.6%	20.5%	79.5%
TOTAL	2006	337,944	118,134		219,810		—	101,676	D	35.0%	65.0%	35.0%	65.0%
TOTAL	2004	416,570	148,443		261,884		6,243	113,441	D	35.6%	62.9%	36.2%	63.8%
TOTAL	2002	359,984	116,693		232,344		10,947	115,651	D	32.4%	64.5%	33.4%	66.6%

An asterisk (*) denotes incumbent.

HAWAII

GENERAL AND PRIMARY ELECTION

2010 GENERAL ELECTIONS

Governor   Other vote was 1,265 Free Energy (Daniel H. Cunningham); 1,263 Nonpartisan (Thomas Pollard).

Senator   Other vote was 7,762 Green (Jim Brewer); 2,957 Libertarian (Lloyd Jeffrey Mallan); 2,697 Nonpartisan (Jeff Jarrett).

House   Other vote was:

CD1
CD2   3,254 Libertarian (Pat Brock);1,310 Nonpartisan (Andrew Vsevolod Von Sonn).

2010 PRIMARY ELECTIONS

Primary   September 18, 2010   **Registration**   684,481   No Party Registration
(as of Sept.18, 2010)

Primary Type   Open—Any registered voter could participate in the party primary of their choice.

	REPUBLICAN PRIMARIES			DEMOCRATIC PRIMARIES		
Governor	Duke Aiona	42,520	95.3%	Neil Abercrombie	142,304	60.1%
	John S. Carroll	2,079	4.7%	Mufi Hannemann	90,590	38.3%
				Arturo "Art" P. Reyes	1,350	0.6%
				Van K. Tanabe	1,330	0.6%
				Miles Shiratori	1,033	0.4%
	TOTAL	44,599		TOTAL	236,607	
Senator	Cam Cavasso	23,033	66.9%	Daniel K. Inouye*	198,711	88.3%
	John Roco	7,483	21.7%	Andrew D. Woerner	26,411	11.7%
	Eddie Pirkowski	3,891	11.3%			
	TOTAL	34,407		TOTAL	225,122	
Congressional District1	Charles Djou*	21,622	97.4%	Colleen Hanabusa	85,732	78.9%
	C. Kaui Jochanan Amsterdam	397	1.8%	Rafael "Del" Castillo	22,874	21.1%
	John "Raghu" Giuffre	177	0.8%			
	TOTAL	22,196		TOTAL	108,606	
Congressional District2	John W. Willoughby	8,020	47.2%	Mazie K. Hirono*	88,803	100.0%
	Ramsay Puanani Wharton	7,809	46.0%			
	Antonio Gimbernat	1,163	6.8%			
	TOTAL	16,992				

An asterisk (*) denotes incumbent.

IDAHO

Congressional districts first established for elections held in 2002
2 members

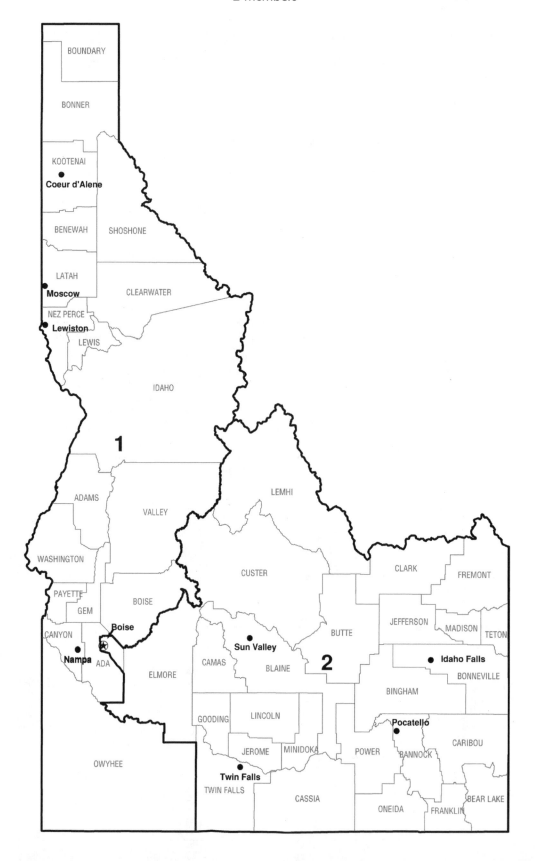

IDAHO

GOVERNOR
C. L. "Butch" Otter (R). Reelected 2010 to a four-year term. Previously elected 2006.

SENATORS (2 Republicans)
Michael D. Crapo (R). Reelected 2010 to a six-year term. Previously elected 2004, 1998.

Jim Risch (R). Elected 2008 to a six-year term.

REPRESENTATIVES (2 Republicans)
1. Raul R. Labrador (R)　　　　　2. Mike Simpson (R)

POSTWAR VOTE FOR PRESIDENT

| | | Republican | | Democratic | | | | Percentage | | | |
| | | | | | | | | Total Vote | | Major Vote | |
Year	Total Vote	Vote	Candidate	Vote	Candidate	Other Vote	Rep.-Dem. Plurality	Rep.	Dem.	Rep.	Dem.
2008	655,122	403,012	McCain, John	236,440	Obama, Barack	15,670	166,572 R	61.5%	36.1%	63.0%	37.0%
2004	598,447	409,235	Bush, George W.	181,098	Kerry, John	8,114	228,137 R	68.4%	30.3%	69.3%	30.7%
2000**	501,621	336,937	Bush, George W.	138,637	Gore, Al	26,047	198,300 R	67.2%	27.6%	70.8%	29.2%
1996**	491,719	256,595	Dole, Bob	165,443	Clinton, Bill	69,681	91,152 R	52.2%	33.6%	60.8%	39.2%
1992**	482,142	202,645	Bush, George	137,013	Clinton, Bill	142,484	65,632 R	42.0%	28.4%	59.7%	40.3%
1988	408,968	253,881	Bush, George	147,272	Dukakis, Michael S.	7,815	106,609 R	62.1%	36.0%	63.3%	36.7%
1984	411,144	297,523	Reagan, Ronald	108,510	Mondale, Walter F.	5,111	189,013 R	72.4%	26.4%	73.3%	26.7%
1980**	437,431	290,699	Reagan, Ronald	110,192	Carter, Jimmy	36,540	180,507 R	66.5%	25.2%	72.5%	27.5%
1976	344,071	204,151	Ford, Gerald R.	126,549	Carter, Jimmy	13,371	77,602 R	59.3%	36.8%	61.7%	38.3%
1972	310,379	199,384	Nixon, Richard M.	80,826	McGovern, George S.	30,169	118,558 R	64.2%	26.0%	71.2%	28.8%
1968**	291,183	165,369	Nixon, Richard M.	89,273	Humphrey, Hubert H.	36,541	76,096 R	56.8%	30.7%	64.9%	35.1%
1964	292,477	143,557	Goldwater, Barry M.	148,920	Johnson, Lyndon B.		5,363 D	49.1%	50.9%	49.1%	50.9%
1960	300,450	161,597	Nixon, Richard M.	138,853	Kennedy, John F.		22,744 R	53.8%	46.2%	53.8%	46.2%
1956	272,989	166,979	Eisenhower, Dwight D.	105,868	Stevenson, Adlai E.	142	61,111 R	61.2%	38.8%	61.2%	38.8%
1952	276,254	180,707	Eisenhower, Dwight D.	95,081	Stevenson, Adlai E.	466	85,626 R	65.4%	34.4%	65.5%	34.5%
1948	214,816	101,514	Dewey, Thomas E.	107,370	Truman, Harry S.	5,932	5,856 D	47.3%	50.0%	48.6%	51.4%

**In past elections, the other vote included: 12,292 - Green (Ralph Nader); 1996 - 62,518 Reform (Ross Perot); 1992 - 130,395 Independent (Perot); 1980 - 27,058 Independent (John Anderson); 1968 - 36,541 American Independent (George Wallace).

IDAHO

POSTWAR VOTE FOR GOVERNOR

Year	Total Vote	Republican Vote	Republican Candidate	Democratic Vote	Democratic Candidate	Other Vote	Rep.-Dem. Plurality	Total Vote Rep.	Total Vote Dem.	Major Vote Rep.	Major Vote Dem.
2010	452,535	267,483	Otter, C. L. "Butch"	148,680	Allred, Keith	36,372	118,803 R	59.1%	32.9%	64.3%	35.7%
2006	450,850	237,437	Otter, C. L. "Butch"	198,845	Brady, Jerry M.	14,568	38,592 R	52.7%	44.1%	54.4%	45.6%
2002	411,477	231,566	Kempthorne, Dirk	171,711	Brady, Jerry M.	8,200	59,855 R	56.3%	41.7%	57.4%	42.6%
1998	381,248	258,095	Kempthorne, Dirk	110,815	Huntley, Robert C.	12,338	147,280 R	67.7%	29.1%	70.0%	30.0%
1994	413,346	216,123	Batt, Phil	181,363	EchoHawk, Larry	15,860	34,760 R	52.3%	43.9%	54.4%	45.6%
1990	320,610	101,937	Fairchild, Roger	218,673	Andrus, Cecil D.		116,736 D	31.8%	68.2%	31.8%	68.2%
1986	387,426	189,794	Leroy, David H.	193,429	Andrus, Cecil D.	4,203	3,635 D	49.0%	49.9%	49.5%	50.5%
1982	326,522	161,157	Batt, Philip	165,365	Evans, John V.		4,208 D	49.4%	50.6%	49.4%	50.6%
1978	288,566	114,149	Larsen, Allan	169,540	Evans, John V.	4,877	55,391 D	39.6%	58.8%	40.2%	59.8%
1974	259,632	68,731	Murphy, Jack M.	184,142	Andrus, Cecil D.	6,759	115,411 D	26.5%	70.9%	27.2%	72.8%
1970	245,112	117,108	Samuelson, Don	128,004	Andrus, Cecil D.		10,896 D	47.8%	52.2%	47.8%	52.2%
1966**	252,593	104,586	Samuelson, Don	93,744	Andrus, Cecil D.	54,263	10,842 R	41.4%	37.1%	52.7%	47.3%
1962	255,454	139,578	Smylie, Robert E.	115,876	Smith, Vernon K.		23,702 R	54.6%	45.4%	54.6%	45.4%
1958	239,046	121,810	Smylie, Robert E.	117,236	Derr, A. M.	4,574 R		51.0%	49.0%	51.0%	49.0%
1954	228,685	124,038	Smylie, Robert E.	104,647	Hamilton, Clark		19,391 R	54.2%	45.8%	54.2%	45.8%
1950	204,792	107,642	Jordan, Len B.	97,150	Wright, Calvin E.		10,492 R	52.6%	47.4%	52.6%	47.4%
1946	181,364	102,233	Robins, C. A.	79,131	Williams, Arnold		23,102 R	56.4%	43.6%	56.4%	43.6%

**In past elections, the other vote included: 1966 - 30,913 Independent (Perry Swisher).

POSTWAR VOTE FOR SENATOR

Year	Total Vote	Republican Vote	Republican Candidate	Democratic Vote	Democratic Candidate	Other Vote	Rep.-Dem. Plurality	Total Vote Rep.	Total Vote Dem.	Major Vote Rep.	Major Vote Dem.
2010	449,530	319,953	Crapo, Michael D.	112,057	Sullivan, P. Tom	17,520	207,896 R	71.2%	24.9%	74.1%	25.9%
2008	644,780	371,744	Risch, Jim	219,903	LaRocco, Larry	53,133	151,841 R	57.7%	34.1%	62.8%	37.2%
2004**	503,932	499,796	Crapo, Michael D.	—		4,136	499,796 R	99.2%		100.0%	
2002	408,544	266,215	Craig, Larry E.	132,975	Blinken, Alan	9,354	133,240 R	65.2%	32.5%	66.7%	33.3%
1998	378,174	262,966	Crapo, Michael D.	107,375	Mauk, Bill	7,833	155,591 R	69.5%	28.4%	71.0%	29.0%
1996	497,233	283,532	Craig, Larry E.	198,422	Minnick, Walt	15,279	85,110 R	57.0%	39.9%	58.8%	41.2%
1992	478,522	270,468	Kempthorne, Dirk	208,036	Stallings, Richard	18	62,432 R	56.5%	43.5%	56.5%	43.5%
1990	315,936	193,641	Craig, Larry E.	122,295	Twilegar, Ron J.		71,346 R	61.3%	38.7%	61.3%	38.7%
1986	382,024	196,958	Symms, Steven D.	185,066	Evans, John V.		11,892 R	51.6%	48.4%	51.6%	48.4%
1984	406,168	293,193	McClure, James A.	105,591	Busch, Peter M.	7,384	187,602 R	72.2%	26.0%	73.5%	26.5%
1980	439,647	218,701	Symms, Steven D.	214,439	Church, Frank	6,507	4,262 R	49.7%	48.8%	50.5%	49.5%
1978	284,047	194,412	McClure, James A.	89,635	Jensen, Dwight		104,777 R	68.4%	31.6%	68.4%	31.6%
1974	258,847	109,072	Smith, Robert L.	145,140	Church, Frank	4,635	36,068 D	42.1%	56.1%	42.9%	57.1%
1972	309,602	161,804	McClure, James A.	140,913	Davis, William E.	6,885	20,891 R	52.3%	45.5%	53.5%	46.5%
1968	287,876	114,394	Hansen, George V.	173,482	Church, Frank		59,088 D	39.7%	60.3%	39.7%	60.3%
1966	252,456	139,819	Jordan, Len B.	112,637	Harding, Ralph R.		27,182 R	55.4%	44.6%	55.4%	44.6%
1962	258,786	117,129	Hawley, Jack	141,657	Church, Frank		24,528 D	45.3%	54.7%	45.3%	54.7%
1962S	257,677	131,279	Jordan, Len B.	126,398	Pfost, Gracie		4,881 R	50.9%	49.1%	50.9%	49.1%
1960	292,096	152,648	Dworshak, Henry C.	139,448	McLaughlin, Bob		13,200 R	52.3%	47.7%	52.3%	47.7%
1956	265,292	102,781	Welker, Herman	149,096	Church, Frank	13,415	46,315 D	38.7%	56.2%	40.8%	59.2%
1954	226,408	142,269	Dworshak, Henry C.	84,139	Taylor, Glen H.		58,130 R	62.8%	37.2%	62.8%	37.2%
1950	201,417	124,237	Welker, Herman	77,180	Clark, D. Worth		47,057 R	61.7%	38.3%	61.7%	38.3%
1950S	201,970	104,068	Dworshak, Henry C.	97,902	Burtenshaw, Claude		6,166 R	51.5%	48.5%	51.5%	48.5%
1948	214,188	103,868	Dworshak, Henry C.	107,000	Miller, Bert H.	3,320	3,132 D	48.5%	50.0%	49.3%	50.7%
1946S	180,152	105,523	Dworshak, Henry C.	74,629	Donart, George E.		30,894 R	58.6%	41.4%	58.6%	41.4%

**In 2004 there was no candidate on the Democratic line. A write-in candidate, who was a Democrat, received 4,136 votes which are listed in the Other Vote column. The 1946 election and one each of the 1950 and 1962 elections were for short terms to fill vacancies.

IDAHO

GOVERNOR 2010

2010 Census Population	County	Total Vote	Republican	Democratic	Other	Rep.-Dem. Plurality		Percentage			
								Total Vote		Major Vote	
								Rep.	Dem.	Rep.	Dem.
392,365	ADA	121,206	63,871	46,777	10,558	17,094	R	52.7%	38.6%	57.7%	42.3%
3,976	ADAMS	1,675	1,137	384	154	753	R	67.9%	22.9%	74.8%	25.2%
82,839	BANNOCK	23,555	11,308	10,613	1,634	695	R	48.0%	45.1%	51.6%	48.4%
5,986	BEAR LAKE	2,217	1,484	592	141	892	R	66.9%	26.7%	71.5%	28.5%
9,285	BENEWAH	3,015	1,969	773	273	1,196	R	65.3%	25.6%	71.8%	28.2%
45,607	BINGHAM	11,905	6,786	4,202	917	2,584	R	57.0%	35.3%	61.8%	38.2%
21,376	BLAINE	6,635	2,516	3,843	276	1,327	D	37.9%	57.9%	39.6%	60.4%
7,028	BOISE	2,763	1,756	717	290	1,039	R	63.6%	26.0%	71.0%	29.0%
40,877	BONNER	14,036	8,742	4,297	997	4,445	R	62.3%	30.6%	67.0%	33.0%
104,234	BONNEVILLE	29,448	16,204	11,438	1,806	4,766	R	55.0%	38.8%	58.6%	41.4%
10,972	BOUNDARY	3,549	2,381	892	276	1,489	R	67.1%	25.1%	72.7%	27.3%
2,891	BUTTE	1,146	724	306	116	418	R	63.2%	26.7%	70.3%	29.7%
1,117	CAMAS	452	305	103	44	202	R	67.5%	22.8%	74.8%	25.2%
188,923	CANYON	44,427	29,431	10,537	4,459	18,894	R	66.2%	23.7%	73.6%	26.4%
6,963	CARIBOU	2,281	1,434	721	126	713	R	62.9%	31.6%	66.5%	33.5%
22,952	CASSIA	5,595	4,250	929	416	3,321	R	76.0%	16.6%	82.1%	17.9%
982	CLARK	342	227	91	24	136	R	66.4%	26.6%	71.4%	28.6%
8,761	CLEARWATER	2,928	1,768	891	269	877	R	60.4%	30.4%	66.5%	33.5%
4,368	CUSTER	1,861	1,267	419	175	848	R	68.1%	22.5%	75.1%	24.9%
27,038	ELMORE	5,395	3,511	1,373	511	2,138	R	65.1%	25.4%	71.9%	28.1%
12,786	FRANKLIN	3,752	2,612	890	250	1,722	R	69.6%	23.7%	74.6%	25.4%
13,242	FREMONT	4,024	2,645	1,137	242	1,508	R	65.7%	28.3%	69.9%	30.1%
16,719	GEM	5,518	3,901	1,073	544	2,828	R	70.7%	19.4%	78.4%	21.6%
15,464	GOODING	3,969	2,544	1,024	401	1,520	R	64.1%	25.8%	71.3%	28.7%
16,267	IDAHO	6,556	4,324	1,505	727	2,819	R	66.0%	23.0%	74.2%	25.8%
26,140	JEFFERSON	7,528	5,024	1,923	581	3,101	R	66.7%	25.5%	72.3%	27.7%
22,374	JEROME	4,676	3,138	1,129	409	2,009	R	67.1%	24.1%	73.5%	26.5%
138,494	KOOTENAI	42,297	28,381	11,246	2,670	17,135	R	67.1%	26.6%	71.6%	28.4%
37,244	LATAH	12,381	5,696	5,857	828	161	D	46.0%	47.3%	49.3%	50.7%
7,936	LEMHI	3,373	2,272	729	372	1,543	R	67.4%	21.6%	75.7%	24.3%
3,821	LEWIS	1,306	827	358	121	469	R	63.3%	27.4%	69.8%	30.2%
5,208	LINCOLN	1,270	773	354	143	419	R	60.9%	27.9%	68.6%	31.4%
37,536	MADISON	7,713	4,739	2,594	380	2,145	R	61.4%	33.6%	64.6%	35.4%
20,069	MINIDOKA	4,838	3,448	1,000	390	2,448	R	71.3%	20.7%	77.5%	22.5%
39,265	NEZ PERCE	12,625	7,289	4,438	898	2,851	R	57.7%	35.2%	62.2%	37.8%
4,286	ONEIDA	1,631	1,219	308	104	911	R	74.7%	18.9%	79.8%	20.2%
11,526	OWYHEE	2,881	2,128	472	281	1,656	R	73.9%	16.4%	81.8%	18.2%
22,623	PAYETTE	6,036	4,342	1,104	590	3,238	R	71.9%	18.3%	79.7%	20.3%
7,817	POWER	2,214	1,268	811	135	457	R	57.3%	36.6%	61.0%	39.0%
12,765	SHOSHONE	3,875	2,186	1,343	346	843	R	56.4%	34.7%	61.9%	38.1%
10,170	TETON	3,385	1,470	1,706	209	236	D	43.4%	50.4%	46.3%	53.7%
77,230	TWIN FALLS	18,858	11,511	5,650	1,697	5,861	R	61.0%	30.0%	67.1%	32.9%
9,862	VALLEY	3,861	2,170	1,385	306	785	R	56.2%	35.9%	61.0%	39.0%
10,198	WASHINGTON	3,537	2,505	746	286	1,759	R	70.8%	21.1%	77.1%	22.9%
1,567,582	TOTAL	452,535	267,483	148,680	36,372	118,803	R	59.1%	32.9%	64.3%	35.7%

IDAHO

SENATOR 2010

2010 Census Population	County	Total Vote	Republican	Democratic	Other	Rep.-Dem. Plurality		Percentage			
								Total Vote		Major Vote	
								Rep.	Dem.	Rep.	Dem.
392,365	ADA	120,306	80,273	36,377	3,656	43,896	R	66.7%	30.2%	68.8%	31.2%
3,976	ADAMS	1,658	1,225	338	95	887	R	73.9%	20.4%	78.4%	21.6%
82,839	BANNOCK	23,491	14,636	7,988	867	6,648	R	62.3%	34.0%	64.7%	35.3%
5,986	BEAR LAKE	2,206	1,771	331	104	1,440	R	80.3%	15.0%	84.3%	15.7%
9,285	BENEWAH	2,998	2,140	673	185	1,467	R	71.4%	22.4%	76.1%	23.9%
45,607	BINGHAM	11,847	9,225	2,182	440	7,043	R	77.9%	18.4%	80.9%	19.1%
21,376	BLAINE	6,576	3,246	3,213	117	33	R	49.4%	48.9%	50.3%	49.7%
7,028	BOISE	2,749	2,022	580	147	1,442	R	73.6%	21.1%	77.7%	22.3%
40,877	BONNER	13,964	9,372	4,032	560	5,340	R	67.1%	28.9%	69.9%	30.1%
104,234	BONNEVILLE	29,206	22,073	5,937	1,196	16,136	R	75.6%	20.3%	78.8%	21.2%
10,972	BOUNDARY	3,507	2,495	775	237	1,720	R	71.1%	22.1%	76.3%	23.7%
2,891	BUTTE	1,139	872	209	58	663	R	76.6%	18.3%	80.7%	19.3%
1,117	CAMAS	450	343	74	33	269	R	76.2%	16.4%	82.3%	17.7%
188,923	CANYON	44,015	34,000	8,360	1,655	25,640	R	77.2%	19.0%	80.3%	19.7%
6,963	CARIBOU	2,254	1,819	323	112	1,496	R	80.7%	14.3%	84.9%	15.1%
22,952	CASSIA	5,570	4,789	537	244	4,252	R	86.0%	9.6%	89.9%	10.1%
982	CLARK	341	283	40	18	243	R	83.0%	11.7%	87.6%	12.4%
8,761	CLEARWATER	2,884	2,049	712	123	1,337	R	71.0%	24.7%	74.2%	25.8%
4,368	CUSTER	1,840	1,351	344	145	1,007	R	73.4%	18.7%	79.7%	20.3%
27,038	ELMORE	5,375	4,094	1,061	220	3,033	R	76.2%	19.7%	79.4%	20.6%
12,786	FRANKLIN	3,692	2,996	393	303	2,603	R	81.1%	10.6%	88.4%	11.6%
13,242	FREMONT	4,021	3,348	530	143	2,818	R	83.3%	13.2%	86.3%	13.7%
16,719	GEM	5,485	4,326	909	250	3,417	R	78.9%	16.6%	82.6%	17.4%
15,464	GOODING	3,956	3,015	736	205	2,279	R	76.2%	18.6%	80.4%	19.6%
16,267	IDAHO	6,526	4,933	1,162	431	3,771	R	75.6%	17.8%	80.9%	19.1%
26,140	JEFFERSON	7,511	6,230	880	401	5,350	R	82.9%	11.7%	87.6%	12.4%
22,374	JEROME	4,668	3,709	782	177	2,927	R	79.5%	16.8%	82.6%	17.4%
138,494	KOOTENAI	42,160	29,983	10,476	1,701	19,507	R	71.1%	24.8%	74.1%	25.9%
37,244	LATAH	12,270	6,736	5,162	372	1,574	R	54.9%	42.1%	56.6%	43.4%
7,936	LEMHI	3,357	2,553	642	162	1,911	R	76.1%	19.1%	79.9%	20.1%
3,821	LEWIS	1,297	963	271	63	692	R	74.2%	20.9%	78.0%	22.0%
5,208	LINCOLN	1,254	956	236	62	720	R	76.2%	18.8%	80.2%	19.8%
37,536	MADISON	7,690	6,616	734	340	5,882	R	86.0%	9.5%	90.0%	10.0%
20,069	MINIDOKA	4,765	3,846	708	211	3,138	R	80.7%	14.9%	84.5%	15.5%
39,265	NEZ PERCE	12,535	8,492	3,695	348	4,797	R	67.7%	29.5%	69.7%	30.3%
4,286	ONEIDA	1,616	1,329	213	74	1,116	R	82.2%	13.2%	86.2%	13.8%
11,526	OWYHEE	2,858	2,319	397	142	1,922	R	81.1%	13.9%	85.4%	14.6%
22,623	PAYETTE	6,007	4,684	1,001	322	3,683	R	78.0%	16.7%	82.4%	17.6%
7,817	POWER	2,205	1,599	545	61	1,054	R	72.5%	24.7%	74.6%	25.4%
12,765	SHOSHONE	3,824	2,286	1,356	182	930	R	59.8%	35.5%	62.8%	37.2%
10,170	TETON	3,382	1,766	1,564	52	202	R	52.2%	46.2%	53.0%	47.0%
77,230	TWIN FALLS	18,753	14,181	3,761	811	10,420	R	75.6%	20.1%	79.0%	21.0%
9,862	VALLEY	3,804	2,453	1,227	124	1,226	R	64.5%	32.3%	66.7%	33.3%
10,198	WASHINGTON	3,518	2,556	591	371	1,965	R	72.7%	16.8%	81.2%	18.8%
1,567,582	TOTAL	449,530	319,953	112,057	17,520	207,896	R	71.2%	24.9%	74.1%	25.9%

IDAHO

HOUSE OF REPRESENTATIVES

CD	Year	Total Vote	Republican Vote	Republican Candidate	Democratic Vote	Democratic Candidate	Other Vote	Rep.-Dem. Plurality	Total Vote Rep.	Total Vote Dem.	Major Vote Rep.	Major Vote Dem.
1	2010	247,427	126,231	LABRADOR, RAUL R.	102,135	MINNICK, WALT*	19,061	24,096 R	51.0%	41.3%	55.3%	44.7%
1	2008	347,585	171,687	SALI, BILL*	175,898	MINNICK, WALT		4,211 D	49.4%	50.6%	49.4%	50.6%
1	2006	231,974	115,843	SALI, BILL	103,935	GRANT, LARRY	12,196	11,908 R	49.9%	44.8%	52.7%	47.3%
1	2004	298,589	207,662	OTTER, C. L. "BUTCH"*	90,927	PRESTON, NAOMI		116,735 R	69.5%	30.5%	69.5%	30.5%
1	2002	206,141	120,743	OTTER, C. L. "BUTCH"*	80,269	RICHARDSON, BETTY	5,129	40,474 R	58.6%	38.9%	60.1%	39.9%
2	2010	199,717	137,468	SIMPSON, MIKE*	48,749	CRAWFORD, MIKE	13,500	88,719 R	68.8%	24.4%	73.8%	26.2%
2	2008	289,655	205,777	SIMPSON, MIKE*	83,878	HOLMES, DEBORAH		121,899 R	71.0%	29.0%	71.0%	29.0%
2	2006	213,332	132,262	SIMPSON, MIKE*	73,441	HANSEN, JIM	7,629	58,821 R	62.0%	34.4%	64.3%	35.7%
2	2004	273,837	193,704	SIMPSON, MIKE*	80,133	WITWORTH, LIN		113,571 R	70.7%	29.3%	70.7%	29.3%
2	2002	198,882	135,605	SIMPSON, MIKE*	57,769	KINGHORN, EDWARD	5,508	77,836 R	68.2%	29.0%	70.1%	29.9%
TOTAL	2010	447,144	263,699		150,884		32,561	112,815 R	59.0%	33.7%	63.6%	36.4%
TOTAL	2008	637,852	377,464		259,776		612	117,688 R	59.2%	40.7%	59.2%	40.8%
TOTAL	2006	445,306	248,105		177,376		19,825	70,729 R	55.7%	39.8%	58.3%	41.7%
TOTAL	2004	572,426	401,366		171,060			230,306 R	70.1%	29.9%	70.1%	29.9%
TOTAL	2002	405,023	256,348		138,038		10,637	118,310 R	63.3%	34.1%	65.0%	35.0%

An asterisk (*) denotes incumbent.

IDAHO

GENERAL AND PRIMARY ELECTIONS

2010 GENERAL ELECTIONS

Governor   Other vote was 26,655 Independent (Jana M. Kemp); 5,867 Libertarian (Ted Dunlap); 3,850 Independent (Pro-Life).

Senator   Other vote was 17,429 Constitution (Randy Lynn Bergquist); 91 write-in (Frederick R. Reinisch Jr.).

House   Other vote was:

CD 1   14,365 Independent (Dave Olson); 4,696 Libertarian (Mike Washburn).
CD 2   13,500 Independent (Brian Schad).

2010 PRIMARY ELECTIONS

Primary   May 25, 2010   **Registration** (as of May 25, 2010)   749,900   No Party Registration

Primary Type   Open—Any registered voter could participate in either the Democratic or Republican primary.

IDAHO

GENERAL AND PRIMARY ELECTIONS

	REPUBLICAN PRIMARIES			DEMOCRATIC PRIMARIES		
Governor	C. L. "Butch" Otter*	89,117	54.6%	Keith Allred	22,386	81.7%
	Rex Rammell	42,436	26.0%	Lee R. Chaney Sr.	5,026	18.3%
	Sharon Margaret Ullman	13,749	8.4%			
	Ron "Pete" Peterson	8,402	5.2%			
	Walt Bayes	4,825	3.0%			
	Tamara Wells	4,544	2.8%			
	Fred Nichols (write-in)	38				
	TOTAL	*163,111*		*TOTAL*	*27,412*	
Senator	Michael D. Crapo*	127,332	79.3%	P. Tom Sullivan	18,340	74.7%
	Claude M. "Skip" Davis III	33,150	20.7%	William Bryk	6,227	25.3%
	TOTAL	*160,482*		*TOTAL*	*24,567*	
Congressional District 1	Raul R. Labrador	38,711	47.6%	Walt Minnick*	11,407	100.0%
	Vaughn Ward	31,582	38.9%			
	Michael L. Chadwick	5,356	6.6%			
	Harley D. Brown	3,168	3.9%			
	Allan M. Salzberg	2,471	3.0%			
	TOTAL	*81,288*				
Congressional District 2	Mike Simpson*	45,148	58.3%	Mike Crawford	13,291	100.0%
	M. C. Chick Heileson	18,644	24.1%			
	Russell J. Mathews	7,452	9.6%			
	Katherine Burton	6,214	8.0%			
	TOTAL	*77,458*				

An asterisk (*) denotes incumbent.

ILLINOIS

Congressional districts first established for elections held in 2002
19 members

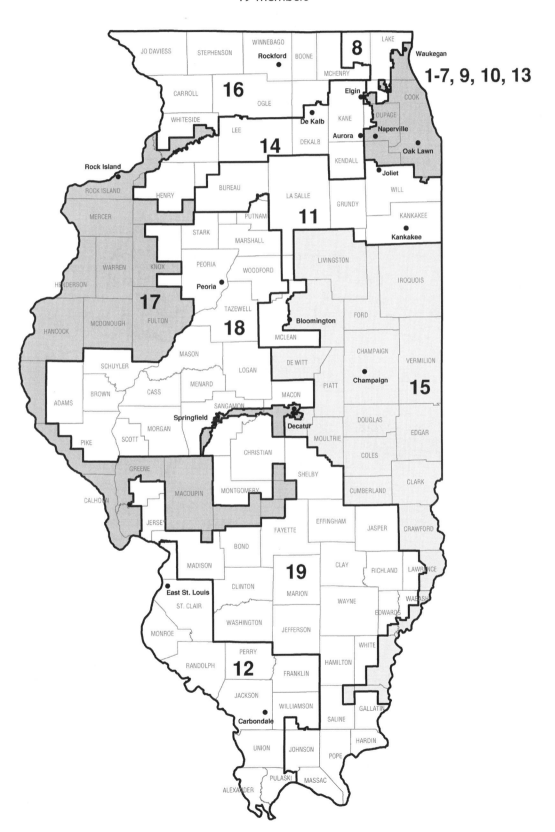

ILLINOIS

Chicago Area

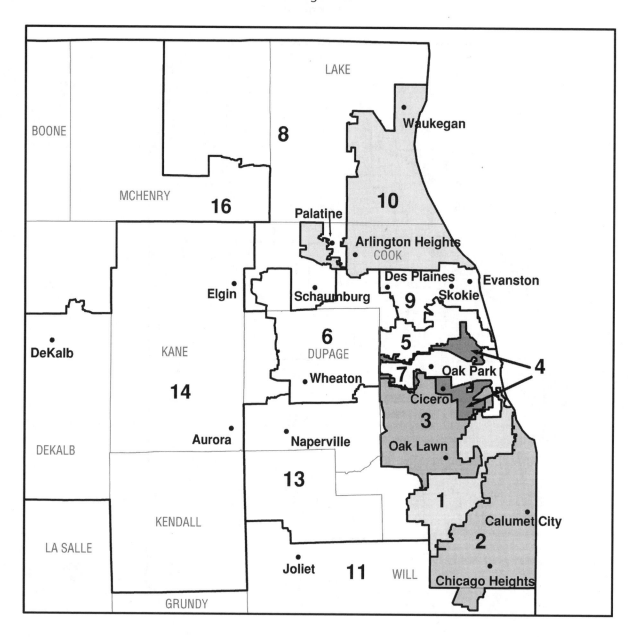

ILLINOIS

GOVERNOR

Pat Quinn (D). Elected 2010 to a four-year term. Assumed office January 29, 2009, upon the impeachment and expulsion from office of Rod R. Blagojevich (D).

SENATORS (1 Democrat, 1 Republican)

Richard J. Durbin (D). Reelected 2008 to a six-year term. Previously elected 2002, 1996.

Mark Steven Kirk (R). Elected 2010 to a six-year term. Also won special election held in conjunction with the 2010 general election to replace the appointed senator, Roland Burris (D) for the remaining weeks of the 111th Congress.

REPRESENTATIVES (11 Republicans, 8 Democrats)

1. Bobby L. Rush (D)
2. Jesse L. Jackson Jr. (D)
3. Daniel Lipinski (D)
4. Luis V. Gutierrez (D)
5. Mike Quigley (D)
6. Peter J. Roskam (R)
7. Danny K. Davis (D)
8. Joe Walsh (R)
9. Jan Schakowsky (D)
10. Robert Dold (R)
11. Adam Kinzinger (R)
12. Jerry F. Costello (D)
13. Judy Biggert (R)
14. Randall M. "Randy" Hultgren (R)
15. Timothy V. Johnson (R)
16. Donald A. Manzullo (R)
17. Bobby Schilling (R)
18. Aaron Schock (R)
19. John Shimkus (R)

POSTWAR VOTE FOR PRESIDENT

| Year | Total Vote | Republican | | Democratic | | Other Vote | Rep.-Dem. Plurality | Percentage | | | |
| | | Vote | Candidate | Vote | Candidate | | | Total Vote | | Major Vote | |
								Rep.	Dem.	Rep.	Dem.
2008	5,522,371	2,031,179	McCain, John	3,419,348	Obama, Barack	71,844	1,388,169 D	36.8%	61.9%	37.3%	62.7%
2004	5,274,322	2,345,946	Bush, George W.	2,891,550	Kerry, John	36,826	545,604 D	44.5%	54.8%	44.8%	55.2%
2000**	4,742,123	2,019,421	Bush, George W.	2,589,026	Gore, Al	133,676	569,605 D	42.6%	54.6%	43.8%	56.2%
1996**	4,311,391	1,587,021	Dole, Bob	2,341,744	Clinton, Bill	382,626	754,723 D	36.8%	54.3%	40.4%	59.6%
1992**	5,050,157	1,734,096	Bush, George	2,453,350	Clinton, Bill	862,711	719,254 D	34.3%	48.6%	41.4%	58.6%
1988	4,559,120	2,310,939	Bush, George	2,215,940	Dukakis, Michael S.	32,241	94,999 R	50.7%	48.6%	51.0%	49.0%
1984	4,819,088	2,707,103	Reagan, Ronald	2,086,499	Mondale, Walter F.	25,486	620,604 R	56.2%	43.3%	56.5%	43.5%
1980**	4,749,721	2,358,049	Reagan, Ronald	1,981,413	Carter, Jimmy	410,259	376,636 R	49.6%	41.7%	54.3%	45.7%
1976	4,718,914	2,364,269	Ford, Gerald R.	2,271,295	Carter, Jimmy	83,350	92,974 R	50.1%	48.1%	51.0%	49.0%
1972	4,723,236	2,788,179	Nixon, Richard M.	1,913,472	McGovern, George S.	21,585	874,707 R	59.0%	40.5%	59.3%	40.7%
1968**	4,619,749	2,174,774	Nixon, Richard M.	2,039,814	Humphrey, Hubert H.	405,161	134,960 R	47.1%	44.2%	51.6%	48.4%
1964	4,702,841	1,905,946	Goldwater, Barry M.	2,796,833	Johnson, Lyndon B.	62	890,887 D	40.5%	59.5%	40.5%	59.5%
1960	4,757,409	2,368,988	Nixon, Richard M.	2,377,846	Kennedy, John F.	10,575	8,858 D	49.8%	50.0%	49.9%	50.1%
1956	4,407,407	2,623,327	Eisenhower, Dwight D.	1,775,682	Stevenson, Adlai E.	8,398	847,645 R	59.5%	40.3%	59.6%	40.4%
1952	4,481,058	2,457,327	Eisenhower, Dwight D.	2,013,920	Stevenson, Adlai E.	9,811	443,407 R	54.8%	44.9%	55.0%	45.0%
1948	3,984,046	1,961,103	Dewey, Thomas E.	1,994,715	Truman, Harry S.	28,228	33,612 D	49.2%	50.1%	49.6%	50.4%

**In past elections, the other vote included: 2000 - 103,759 Green (Ralph Nader); 1996 - 346,408 Reform (Ross Perot); 1992 - 840,515 Independent (Perot); 1980 - 346,754 Independent (John Anderson); 1968 - 390,958 American Independent (George Wallace).

ILLINOIS

POSTWAR VOTE FOR GOVERNOR

Year	Total Vote	Republican Vote	Republican Candidate	Democratic Vote	Democratic Candidate	Other Vote	Plurality	Total Vote Rep.	Total Vote Dem.	Major Vote Rep.	Major Vote Dem.
2010	3,729,989	1,713,385	Brady, Bill	1,745,219	Quinn, Pat	271,385	31,834 D	45.9%	46.8%	49.5%	50.5%
2006**	3,487,989	1,369,315	Topinka, Judy Baar	1,736,731	Blagojevich, Rod R.	381,943	367,416 D	39.3%	49.8%	44.1%	55.9%
2002	3,538,891	1,594,960	Ryan, Jim	1,847,040	Blagojevich, Rod R.	96,891	252,080 D	45.1%	52.2%	46.3%	53.7%
1998	3,358,705	1,714,094	Ryan, George H.	1,594,191	Poshard, Glenn	50,420	119,903 R	51.0%	47.5%	51.8%	48.2%
1994	3,106,566	1,984,318	Edgar, Jim	1,069,850	Netsch, Dawn C.	52,398	914,468 R	63.9%	34.4%	65.0%	35.0%
1990	3,257,410	1,653,126	Edgar, Jim	1,569,217	Hartigan, Neil F.	35,067	83,909 R	50.7%	48.2%	51.3%	48.7%
1986**	3,143,978	1,655,849	Thompson, James R.	208,830	[See note below]	1,279,299	399,223 R	52.7%	6.6%	88.8%	11.2%
1982	3,673,681	1,816,101	Thompson, James R.	1,811,027	Stevenson, Adlai E., III	46,553	5,074 R	49.4%	49.3%	50.1%	49.9%
1978	3,150,095	1,859,684	Thompson, James R.	1,263,134	Bakalis, Michael	27,277	596,550 R	59.0%	40.1%	59.6%	40.4%
1976S	4,638,997	3,000,395	Thompson, James R.	1,610,258	Howlett, Michael J.	28,344	1,390,137 R	64.7%	34.7%	65.1%	34.9%
1972	4,678,804	2,293,809	Ogilvie, Richard B.	2,371,303	Walker, Daniel	13,692	77,494 D	49.0%	50.7%	49.2%	50.8%
1968	4,506,000	2,307,295	Ogilvie, Richard B.	2,179,501	Shapiro, Samuel H.	19,204	127,794 R	51.2%	48.4%	51.4%	48.6%
1964	4,657,500	2,239,095	Percy, Charles H.	2,418,394	Kerner, Otto	11	179,299 D	48.1%	51.9%	48.1%	51.9%
1960	4,674,187	2,070,479	Stratton, William G.	2,594,731	Kerner, Otto	8,977	524,252 D	44.3%	55.5%	44.4%	55.6%
1956	4,314,611	2,171,786	Stratton, William G.	2,134,909	Austin, Richard B.	7,916	36,877 R	50.3%	49.5%	50.4%	49.6%
1952	4,415,864	2,317,363	Stratton, William G.	2,089,721	Dixon, Sherwood	8,780	227,642 R	52.5%	47.3%	52.6%	47.4%
1948	3,940,257	1,678,007	Green, Dwight H.	2,250,074	Stevenson, Adlai E.	12,176	572,067 D	42.6%	57.1%	42.7%	57.3%

**In past elections, the other vote included: 2006 - 361,336 Green (Rich Whitney); 1986 - 1,256,626 Illinois Solidarity (Adlai E. Stevenson III). In 1986 there was no Democratic candidate for Governor on the ballot. Mark Fairchild, a supporter of Lyndon H. LaRouche Jr., was the "paired" Democratic candidate for Lt. Governor and the Democratic vote was cast for this ticket of "no name" and Fairchild. Running on the Illinois Solidarity line, Stevenson finished second with 40.0 percent of the vote. The 1976 vote was for a two-year term to permit shifting the election for Governor to non-presidential years.

POSTWAR VOTE FOR SENATOR

Year	Total Vote	Republican Vote	Republican Candidate	Democratic Vote	Democratic Candidate	Other Vote	Rep.-Dem. Plurality	Total Vote Rep.	Total Vote Dem.	Major Vote Rep.	Major Vote Dem.
2010	3,704,473	1,778,698	Kirk, Mark Steven	1,719,478	Giannoulias, Alexander	206,297	59,220 R	48.0%	46.4%	50.8%	49.2%
2008	5,329,884	1,520,621	Sauerberg, Steve	3,615,844	Durbin, Richard J.	193,419	2,095,223 D	28.5%	67.8%	29.6%	70.4%
2004	5,141,520	1,390,690	Keyes, Alan	3,597,456	Obama, Barack	153,374	2,206,766 D	27.0%	70.0%	27.9%	72.1%
2002	3,486,851	1,325,703	Durkin, Jim	2,103,766	Durbin, Richard J.	57,382	778,063 D	38.0%	60.3%	38.7%	61.3%
1998	3,394,521	1,709,041	Fitzgerald, Peter G.	1,610,496	Moseley-Braun, Carol	74,984	98,545 R	50.3%	47.4%	51.5%	48.5%
1996	4,250,722	1,728,824	Salvi, Al	2,384,028	Durbin, Richard J.	137,870	655,204 D	40.7%	56.1%	42.0%	58.0%
1992	4,939,558	2,126,833	Williamson, Richard S.	2,631,229	Moseley-Braun, Carol	181,496	504,396 D	43.1%	53.3%	44.7%	55.3%
1990	3,251,005	1,135,628	Martin, Lynn	2,115,377	Simon, Paul		979,749 D	34.9%	65.1%	34.9%	65.1%
1986	3,122,883	1,053,734	Koehler, Judy	2,033,783	Dixon, Alan J.	35,366	980,049 D	33.7%	65.1%	34.1%	65.9%
1984	4,787,473	2,308,039	Percy, Charles H.	2,397,303	Simon, Paul	82,131	89,264 D	48.2%	50.1%	49.1%	50.9%
1980	4,580,029	1,946,296	O'Neal, David C.	2,565,302	Dixon, Alan J.	68,431	619,006 D	42.5%	56.0%	43.1%	56.9%
1978	3,184,764	1,698,711	Percy, Charles H.	1,448,187	Seith, Alex	37,866	250,524 R	53.3%	45.5%	54.0%	46.0%
1974	2,914,666	1,084,884	Burditt, George M.	1,811,496	Stevenson, Adlai E., III	18,286	726,612 D	37.2%	62.2%	37.5%	62.5%
1972	4,608,380	2,867,078	Percy, Charles H.	1,721,031	Pucinski, Roman C.	20,271	1,146,047 R	62.2%	37.3%	62.5%	37.5%
1970S	3,599,272	1,519,718	Smith, Ralph T.	2,065,054	Stevenson, Adlai E., III	14,500	545,336 D	42.2%	57.4%	42.4%	57.6%
1968	4,449,757	2,358,947	Dirksen, Everett M.	2,073,242	Clark, William G.	17,568	285,705 R	53.0%	46.6%	53.2%	46.8%
1966	3,822,725	2,100,449	Percy, Charles H.	1,678,147	Douglas, Paul H.	44,129	422,302 R	54.9%	43.9%	55.6%	44.4%
1962	3,709,216	1,961,202	Dirksen, Everett M.	1,748,007	Yates, Sidney R.	7	213,195 R	52.9%	47.1%	52.9%	47.1%
1960	4,632,796	2,093,846	Witwer, Samuel W.	2,530,943	Douglas, Paul H.	8,007	437,097 D	45.2%	54.6%	45.3%	54.7%
1956	4,264,830	2,307,352	Dirksen, Everett M.	1,949,883	Stengel, Richard	7,595	357,469 R	54.1%	45.7%	54.2%	45.8%
1954	3,368,025	1,563,683	Meek, Joseph T.	1,804,338	Douglas, Paul H.	4	240,655 D	46.4%	53.6%	46.4%	53.6%
1950	3,622,673	1,951,984	Dirksen, Everett M.	1,657,630	Lucas, Scott W.	13,059	294,354 R	53.9%	45.8%	54.1%	45.9%
1948	3,900,285	1,740,026	Brooks, C. Wayland	2,147,754	Douglas, Paul H.	12,505	407,728 D	44.6%	55.1%	44.8%	55.2%

The 1970 election was for a short term to fill a vacancy.

ILLINOIS

GOVERNOR 2010

2010 Census Population	County	Total Vote	Republican	Democratic	Other	Rep.-Dem. Plurality		Percentage			
								Total Vote		Major Vote	
								Rep.	Dem.	Rep.	Dem.
67,103	ADAMS	23,850	17,765	4,883	1,202	12,882	R	74.5%	20.5%	78.4%	21.6%
8,238	ALEXANDER	2,754	1,248	1,371	135	123	D	45.3%	49.8%	47.7%	52.3%
17,768	BOND	5,504	3,345	1,847	312	1,498	R	60.8%	33.6%	64.4%	35.6%
54,165	BOONE	14,939	9,074	4,414	1,451	4,660	R	60.7%	29.5%	67.3%	32.7%
6,937	BROWN	2,146	1,503	499	144	1,004	R	70.0%	23.3%	75.1%	24.9%
34,978	BUREAU	12,721	7,319	4,371	1,031	2,948	R	57.5%	34.4%	62.6%	37.4%
5,089	CALHOUN	2,297	1,227	961	109	266	R	53.4%	41.8%	56.1%	43.9%
15,387	CARROLL	5,186	3,361	1,445	380	1,916	R	64.8%	27.9%	69.9%	30.1%
13,642	CASS	3,862	2,433	1,088	341	1,345	R	63.0%	28.2%	69.1%	30.9%
201,081	CHAMPAIGN	53,571	29,297	21,053	3,221	8,244	R	54.7%	39.3%	58.2%	41.8%
34,800	CHRISTIAN	12,443	7,465	3,820	1,158	3,645	R	60.0%	30.7%	66.1%	33.9%
16,335	CLARK	6,144	4,231	1,629	284	2,602	R	68.9%	26.5%	72.2%	27.8%
13,815	CLAY	4,853	3,484	1,158	211	2,326	R	71.8%	23.9%	75.1%	24.9%
37,762	CLINTON	12,914	8,547	3,653	714	4,894	R	66.2%	28.3%	70.1%	29.9%
53,873	COLES	14,838	9,713	4,100	1,025	5,613	R	65.5%	27.6%	70.3%	29.7%
5,194,675	COOK	1,399,258	400,285	900,838	98,135	500,553	D	28.6%	64.4%	30.8%	69.2%
19,817	CRAWFORD	6,905	4,864	1,691	350	3,173	R	70.4%	24.5%	74.2%	25.8%
11,048	CUMBERLAND	4,299	2,993	970	336	2,023	R	69.6%	22.6%	75.5%	24.5%
105,160	DE KALB	28,735	14,949	10,852	2,934	4,097	R	52.0%	37.8%	57.9%	42.1%
16,561	DE WITT	5,749	3,920	1,358	471	2,562	R	68.2%	23.6%	74.3%	25.7%
19,980	DOUGLAS	6,417	4,753	1,239	425	3,514	R	74.1%	19.3%	79.3%	20.7%
916,924	DU PAGE	285,383	154,986	110,117	20,280	44,869	R	54.3%	38.6%	58.5%	41.5%
18,576	EDGAR	6,895	4,890	1,607	398	3,283	R	70.9%	23.3%	75.3%	24.7%
6,721	EDWARDS	2,256	1,800	380	76	1,420	R	79.8%	16.8%	82.6%	17.4%
34,242	EFFINGHAM	13,008	9,856	2,381	771	7,475	R	75.8%	18.3%	80.5%	19.5%
22,140	FAYETTE	6,780	4,675	1,598	507	3,077	R	69.0%	23.6%	74.5%	25.5%
14,081	FORD	4,643	3,452	906	285	2,546	R	74.3%	19.5%	79.2%	20.8%
39,561	FRANKLIN	13,186	6,395	5,741	1,050	654	R	48.5%	43.5%	52.7%	47.3%
37,069	FULTON	11,637	5,786	4,748	1,103	1,038	R	49.7%	40.8%	54.9%	45.1%
5,589	GALLATIN	2,202	1,148	883	171	265	R	52.1%	40.1%	56.5%	43.5%
13,886	GREENE	4,388	2,739	1,305	344	1,434	R	62.4%	29.7%	67.7%	32.3%
50,063	GRUNDY	16,646	9,132	5,813	1,701	3,319	R	54.9%	34.9%	61.1%	38.9%
8,457	HAMILTON	3,484	2,052	1,206	226	846	R	58.9%	34.6%	63.0%	37.0%
19,104	HANCOCK	6,821	4,780	1,631	410	3,149	R	70.1%	23.9%	74.6%	25.4%
4,320	HARDIN	2,104	1,303	680	121	623	R	61.9%	32.3%	65.7%	34.3%
7,331	HENDERSON	3,426	1,888	1,297	241	591	R	55.1%	37.9%	59.3%	40.7%
50,486	HENRY	18,072	10,900	5,980	1,192	4,920	R	60.3%	33.1%	64.6%	35.4%
29,718	IROQUOIS	10,540	7,741	1,997	802	5,744	R	73.4%	18.9%	79.5%	20.5%
60,218	JACKSON	16,339	7,220	7,386	1,733	166	D	44.2%	45.2%	49.4%	50.6%
9,698	JASPER	4,044	2,837	1,008	199	1,829	R	70.2%	24.9%	73.8%	26.2%
38,827	JEFFERSON	12,406	7,500	4,030	876	3,470	R	60.5%	32.5%	65.0%	35.0%
22,985	JERSEY	7,664	4,724	2,509	431	2,215	R	61.6%	32.7%	65.3%	34.7%
22,678	JO DAVIESS	8,072	4,763	2,842	467	1,921	R	59.0%	35.2%	62.6%	37.4%
12,582	JOHNSON	4,666	3,021	1,309	336	1,712	R	64.7%	28.1%	69.8%	30.2%
515,269	KANE	127,201	68,426	48,579	10,196	19,847	R	53.8%	38.2%	58.5%	41.5%
113,449	KANKAKEE	32,512	17,207	12,046	3,259	5,161	R	52.9%	37.1%	58.8%	41.2%
114,736	KENDALL	31,167	17,130	11,158	2,879	5,972	R	55.0%	35.8%	60.6%	39.4%
52,919	KNOX	16,682	9,085	6,465	1,132	2,620	R	54.5%	38.8%	58.4%	41.6%
703,462	LAKE	204,927	102,675	86,878	15,374	15,797	R	50.1%	42.4%	54.2%	45.8%
113,924	LA SALLE	34,024	17,378	13,495	3,151	3,883	R	51.1%	39.7%	56.3%	43.7%
16,833	LAWRENCE	5,128	3,229	1,642	257	1,587	R	63.0%	32.0%	66.3%	33.7%
36,031	LEE	10,901	6,838	3,246	817	3,592	R	62.7%	29.8%	67.8%	32.2%
38,950	LIVINGSTON	12,620	8,273	3,503	844	4,770	R	65.6%	27.8%	70.3%	29.7%
30,305	LOGAN	8,878	6,304	1,953	621	4,351	R	71.0%	22.0%	76.3%	23.7%
32,612	MCDONOUGH	9,232	5,716	2,792	724	2,924	R	61.9%	30.2%	67.2%	32.8%

ILLINOIS

GOVERNOR 2010

2010 Census Population	County	Total Vote	Republican	Democratic	Other	Rep.-Dem. Plurality		Percentage			
								Total Vote		Major Vote	
								Rep.	Dem.	Rep.	Dem.
308,760	MCHENRY	94,217	53,585	31,659	8,973	21,926	R	56.9%	33.6%	62.9%	37.1%
169,572	MCLEAN	52,244	32,972	15,723	3,549	17,249	R	63.1%	30.1%	67.7%	32.3%
110,768	MACON	36,463	21,914	11,966	2,583	9,948	R	60.1%	32.8%	64.7%	35.3%
47,765	MACOUPIN	16,435	9,278	6,042	1,115	3,236	R	56.5%	36.8%	60.6%	39.4%
269,282	MADISON	82,018	44,382	33,060	4,576	11,322	R	54.1%	40.3%	57.3%	42.7%
39,437	MARION	11,996	7,016	4,168	812	2,848	R	58.5%	34.7%	62.7%	37.3%
12,640	MARSHALL	4,331	2,744	1,162	425	1,582	R	63.4%	26.8%	70.3%	29.7%
14,666	MASON	4,879	2,836	1,594	449	1,242	R	58.1%	32.7%	64.0%	36.0%
15,429	MASSAC	4,891	3,170	1,513	208	1,657	R	64.8%	30.9%	67.7%	32.3%
12,705	MENARD	4,859	3,159	1,324	376	1,835	R	65.0%	27.2%	70.5%	29.5%
16,434	MERCER	6,688	3,710	2,403	575	1,307	R	55.5%	35.9%	60.7%	39.3%
32,957	MONROE	11,934	7,639	3,849	446	3,790	R	64.0%	32.3%	66.5%	33.5%
30,104	MONTGOMERY	9,623	5,670	3,262	691	2,408	R	58.9%	33.9%	63.5%	36.5%
35,547	MORGAN	10,790	6,738	3,162	890	3,576	R	62.4%	29.3%	68.1%	31.9%
14,846	MOULTRIE	4,824	3,346	1,117	361	2,229	R	69.4%	23.2%	75.0%	25.0%
53,497	OGLE	17,201	11,318	4,542	1,341	6,776	R	65.8%	26.4%	71.4%	28.6%
186,494	PEORIA	52,517	28,955	20,039	3,523	8,916	R	55.1%	38.2%	59.1%	40.9%
22,350	PERRY	7,528	3,898	2,997	633	901	R	51.8%	39.8%	56.5%	43.5%
16,729	PIATT	6,772	4,653	1,619	500	3,034	R	68.7%	23.9%	74.2%	25.8%
16,430	PIKE	6,367	4,391	1,514	462	2,877	R	69.0%	23.8%	74.4%	25.6%
4,470	POPE	2,003	1,309	566	128	743	R	65.4%	28.3%	69.8%	30.2%
6,161	PULASKI	2,865	1,631	1,082	152	549	R	56.9%	37.8%	60.1%	39.9%
6,006	PUTNAM	2,317	1,195	913	209	282	R	51.6%	39.4%	56.7%	43.3%
33,476	RANDOLPH	11,653	6,227	4,607	819	1,620	R	53.4%	39.5%	57.5%	42.5%
16,233	RICHLAND	5,162	3,684	1,266	212	2,418	R	71.4%	24.5%	74.4%	25.6%
147,546	ROCK ISLAND	46,363	22,904	20,514	2,945	2,390	R	49.4%	44.2%	52.8%	47.2%
270,056	ST. CLAIR	80,927	37,772	39,152	4,003	1,380	D	46.7%	48.4%	49.1%	50.9%
24,913	SALINE	8,073	4,448	3,060	565	1,388	R	55.1%	37.9%	59.2%	40.8%
197,465	SANGAMON	72,905	42,278	25,038	5,589	17,240	R	58.0%	34.3%	62.8%	37.2%
7,544	SCHUYLER	2,975	1,891	845	239	1,046	R	63.6%	28.4%	69.1%	30.9%
5,355	SCOTT	1,780	1,235	422	123	813	R	69.4%	23.7%	74.5%	25.5%
22,363	SHELBY	8,180	5,638	1,819	723	3,819	R	68.9%	22.2%	75.6%	24.4%
5,994	STARK	1,947	1,242	543	162	699	R	63.8%	27.9%	69.6%	30.4%
47,711	STEPHENSON	14,692	9,293	4,209	1,190	5,084	R	63.3%	28.6%	68.8%	31.2%
135,394	TAZEWELL	45,653	29,248	13,189	3,216	16,059	R	64.1%	28.9%	68.9%	31.1%
17,808	UNION	6,652	3,676	2,411	565	1,265	R	55.3%	36.2%	60.4%	39.6%
81,625	VERMILION	22,482	14,251	6,561	1,670	7,690	R	63.4%	29.2%	68.5%	31.5%
11,947	WABASH	3,928	2,728	1,054	146	1,674	R	69.5%	26.8%	72.1%	27.9%
17,707	WARREN	6,009	3,602	1,965	442	1,637	R	59.9%	32.7%	64.7%	35.3%
14,716	WASHINGTON	5,843	3,950	1,495	398	2,455	R	67.6%	25.6%	72.5%	27.5%
16,760	WAYNE	6,783	5,404	1,123	256	4,281	R	79.7%	16.6%	82.8%	17.2%
14,665	WHITE	5,281	3,537	1,510	234	2,027	R	67.0%	28.6%	70.1%	29.9%
58,498	WHITESIDE	18,819	10,510	6,981	1,328	3,529	R	55.8%	37.1%	60.1%	39.9%
677,560	WILL	194,542	97,831	79,786	16,925	18,045	R	50.3%	41.0%	55.1%	44.9%
66,357	WILLIAMSON	22,421	12,240	8,654	1,527	3,586	R	54.6%	38.6%	58.6%	41.4%
295,266	WINNEBAGO	81,873	46,492	28,398	6,983	18,094	R	56.8%	34.7%	62.1%	37.9%
38,664	WOODFORD	13,965	10,170	2,990	805	7,180	R	72.8%	21.4%	77.3%	22.7%
12,830,632	TOTAL	3,729,989	1,713,385	1,745,219	271,385	31,834	D	45.9%	46.8%	49.5%	50.5%

ILLINOIS

SENATOR 2010

2010 Census Population	County	Total Vote	Republican	Democratic	Other	Rep.-Dem. Plurality		Percentage Total Vote Rep.	Dem.	Major Vote Rep.	Dem.
67,103	ADAMS	23,586	17,525	5,124	937	12,401	R	74.3%	21.7%	77.4%	22.6%
8,238	ALEXANDER	2,695	1,179	1,358	158	179	D	43.7%	50.4%	46.5%	53.5%
17,768	BOND	5,425	3,219	1,791	415	1,428	R	59.3%	33.0%	64.3%	35.7%
54,165	BOONE	14,764	9,029	4,408	1,327	4,621	R	61.2%	29.9%	67.2%	32.8%
6,937	BROWN	2,065	1,411	514	140	897	R	68.3%	24.9%	73.3%	26.7%
34,978	BUREAU	12,516	7,452	4,180	884	3,272	R	59.5%	33.4%	64.1%	35.9%
5,089	CALHOUN	2,220	1,140	937	143	203	R	51.4%	42.2%	54.9%	45.1%
15,387	CARROLL	5,121	3,290	1,425	406	1,865	R	64.2%	27.8%	69.8%	30.2%
13,642	CASS	3,806	2,305	1,190	311	1,115	R	60.6%	31.3%	66.0%	34.0%
201,081	CHAMPAIGN	53,077	29,321	20,205	3,551	9,116	R	55.2%	38.1%	59.2%	40.8%
34,800	CHRISTIAN	12,256	7,072	4,037	1,147	3,035	R	57.7%	32.9%	63.7%	36.3%
16,335	CLARK	6,041	4,125	1,635	281	2,490	R	68.3%	27.1%	71.6%	28.4%
13,815	CLAY	4,734	3,256	1,185	293	2,071	R	68.8%	25.0%	73.3%	26.7%
37,762	CLINTON	12,640	8,623	3,364	653	5,259	R	68.2%	26.6%	71.9%	28.1%
53,873	COLES	14,715	9,629	3,985	1,101	5,644	R	65.4%	27.1%	70.7%	29.3%
5,194,675	COOK	1,397,353	442,029	898,751	56,573	456,722	D	31.6%	64.3%	33.0%	67.0%
19,817	CRAWFORD	6,789	4,724	1,682	383	3,042	R	69.6%	24.8%	73.7%	26.3%
11,048	CUMBERLAND	4,215	2,916	944	355	1,972	R	69.2%	22.4%	75.5%	24.5%
105,160	DE KALB	28,415	15,389	10,633	2,393	4,756	R	54.2%	37.4%	59.1%	40.9%
16,561	DE WITT	5,635	3,791	1,356	488	2,435	R	67.3%	24.1%	73.7%	26.3%
19,980	DOUGLAS	6,323	4,624	1,263	436	3,361	R	73.1%	20.0%	78.5%	21.5%
916,924	DU PAGE	284,976	163,875	106,429	14,672	57,446	R	57.5%	37.3%	60.6%	39.4%
18,576	EDGAR	6,749	4,699	1,664	386	3,035	R	69.6%	24.7%	73.8%	26.2%
6,721	EDWARDS	2,194	1,685	353	156	1,332	R	76.8%	16.1%	82.7%	17.3%
34,242	EFFINGHAM	12,820	9,518	2,378	924	7,140	R	74.2%	18.5%	80.0%	20.0%
22,140	FAYETTE	6,694	4,571	1,711	412	2,860	R	68.3%	25.6%	72.8%	27.2%
14,081	FORD	4,596	3,441	823	332	2,618	R	74.9%	17.9%	80.7%	19.3%
39,561	FRANKLIN	12,979	6,636	5,222	1,121	1,414	R	51.1%	40.2%	56.0%	44.0%
37,069	FULTON	11,470	5,761	4,612	1,097	1,149	R	50.2%	40.2%	55.5%	44.5%
5,589	GALLATIN	2,092	1,013	880	199	133	R	48.4%	42.1%	53.5%	46.5%
13,886	GREENE	4,292	2,591	1,326	375	1,265	R	60.4%	30.9%	66.1%	33.9%
50,063	GRUNDY	16,554	9,418	5,814	1,322	3,604	R	56.9%	35.1%	61.8%	38.2%
8,457	HAMILTON	3,333	1,910	1,146	277	764	R	57.3%	34.4%	62.5%	37.5%
19,104	HANCOCK	6,750	4,647	1,641	462	3,006	R	68.8%	24.3%	73.9%	26.1%
4,320	HARDIN	1,981	1,133	719	129	414	R	57.2%	36.3%	61.2%	38.8%
7,331	HENDERSON	3,329	1,837	1,279	213	558	R	55.2%	38.4%	59.0%	41.0%
50,486	HENRY	17,872	11,034	5,653	1,185	5,381	R	61.7%	31.6%	66.1%	33.9%
29,718	IROQUOIS	10,403	7,763	1,871	769	5,892	R	74.6%	18.0%	80.6%	19.4%
60,218	JACKSON	16,364	7,436	7,443	1,485	7	D	45.4%	45.5%	50.0%	50.0%
9,698	JASPER	3,905	2,606	1,112	187	1,494	R	66.7%	28.5%	70.1%	29.9%
38,827	JEFFERSON	12,206	7,580	3,799	827	3,781	R	62.1%	31.1%	66.6%	33.4%
22,985	JERSEY	7,527	4,569	2,450	508	2,119	R	60.7%	32.5%	65.1%	34.9%
22,678	JO DAVIESS	7,950	4,859	2,546	545	2,313	R	61.1%	32.0%	65.6%	34.4%
12,582	JOHNSON	4,564	3,094	1,157	313	1,937	R	67.8%	25.4%	72.8%	27.2%
515,269	KANE	126,490	70,621	47,486	8,383	23,135	R	55.8%	37.5%	59.8%	40.2%
113,449	KANKAKEE	32,453	18,277	12,037	2,139	6,240	R	56.3%	37.1%	60.3%	39.7%
114,736	KENDALL	30,556	17,633	10,797	2,126	6,836	R	57.7%	35.3%	62.0%	38.0%
52,919	KNOX	16,563	9,389	6,081	1,093	3,308	R	56.7%	36.7%	60.7%	39.3%
703,462	LAKE	203,175	114,971	78,569	9,635	36,402	R	56.6%	38.7%	59.4%	40.6%
113,924	LA SALLE	33,748	18,278	12,826	2,644	5,452	R	54.2%	38.0%	58.8%	41.2%
16,833	LAWRENCE	4,994	3,198	1,535	261	1,663	R	64.0%	30.7%	67.6%	32.4%
36,031	LEE	10,838	6,869	3,072	897	3,797	R	63.4%	28.3%	69.1%	30.9%
38,950	LIVINGSTON	12,353	8,575	2,894	884	5,681	R	69.4%	23.4%	74.8%	25.2%
30,305	LOGAN	8,757	6,105	1,959	693	4,146	R	69.7%	22.4%	75.7%	24.3%
32,612	MCDONOUGH	9,102	5,656	2,859	587	2,797	R	62.1%	31.4%	66.4%	33.6%

ILLINOIS

SENATOR 2010

2010 Census Population	County	Total Vote	Republican	Democratic	Other	Rep.-Dem. Plurality		Percentage			
								Total Vote		Major Vote	
								Rep.	Dem.	Rep.	Dem.
308,760	MCHENRY	93,782	55,831	30,889	7,062	24,942	R	59.5%	32.9%	64.4%	35.6%
169,572	MCLEAN	52,082	32,958	15,448	3,676	17,510	R	63.3%	29.7%	68.1%	31.9%
110,768	MACON	36,415	21,072	12,938	2,405	8,134	R	57.9%	35.5%	62.0%	38.0%
47,765	MACOUPIN	16,108	8,823	6,182	1,103	2,641	R	54.8%	38.4%	58.8%	41.2%
269,282	MADISON	81,501	44,152	32,575	4,774	11,577	R	54.2%	40.0%	57.5%	42.5%
39,437	MARION	11,715	7,071	3,966	678	3,105	R	60.4%	33.9%	64.1%	35.9%
12,640	MARSHALL	4,254	2,679	1,106	469	1,573	R	63.0%	26.0%	70.8%	29.2%
14,666	MASON	4,809	2,753	1,571	485	1,182	R	57.2%	32.7%	63.7%	36.3%
15,429	MASSAC	4,805	3,129	1,453	223	1,676	R	65.1%	30.2%	68.3%	31.7%
12,705	MENARD	4,838	3,190	1,268	380	1,922	R	65.9%	26.2%	71.6%	28.4%
16,434	MERCER	6,635	3,806	2,321	508	1,485	R	57.4%	35.0%	62.1%	37.9%
32,957	MONROE	11,804	7,854	3,536	414	4,318	R	66.5%	30.0%	69.0%	31.0%
30,104	MONTGOMERY	9,484	5,427	3,351	706	2,076	R	57.2%	35.3%	61.8%	38.2%
35,547	MORGAN	10,733	6,818	3,101	814	3,717	R	63.5%	28.9%	68.7%	31.3%
14,846	MOULTRIE	4,776	3,189	1,241	346	1,948	R	66.8%	26.0%	72.0%	28.0%
53,497	OGLE	16,902	11,184	4,261	1,457	6,923	R	66.2%	25.2%	72.4%	27.6%
186,494	PEORIA	52,236	28,797	19,751	3,688	9,046	R	55.1%	37.8%	59.3%	40.7%
22,350	PERRY	7,345	3,960	2,754	631	1,206	R	53.9%	37.5%	59.0%	41.0%
16,729	PIATT	6,700	4,582	1,569	549	3,013	R	68.4%	23.4%	74.5%	25.5%
16,430	PIKE	6,201	4,067	1,696	438	2,371	R	65.6%	27.4%	70.6%	29.4%
4,470	POPE	1,949	1,242	602	105	640	R	63.7%	30.9%	67.4%	32.6%
6,161	PULASKI	2,700	1,429	1,155	116	274	R	52.9%	42.8%	55.3%	44.7%
6,006	PUTNAM	2,268	1,241	846	181	395	R	54.7%	37.3%	59.5%	40.5%
33,476	RANDOLPH	11,390	6,168	4,358	864	1,810	R	54.2%	38.3%	58.6%	41.4%
16,233	RICHLAND	5,047	3,501	1,270	276	2,231	R	69.4%	25.2%	73.4%	26.6%
147,546	ROCK ISLAND	46,203	23,249	20,445	2,509	2,804	R	50.3%	44.3%	53.2%	46.8%
270,056	ST. CLAIR	80,443	38,185	38,512	3,746	327	D	47.5%	47.9%	49.8%	50.2%
24,913	SALINE	7,826	4,528	2,668	630	1,860	R	57.9%	34.1%	62.9%	37.1%
197,465	SANGAMON	72,249	42,169	25,248	4,832	16,921	R	58.4%	34.9%	62.5%	37.5%
7,544	SCHUYLER	2,895	1,830	844	221	986	R	63.2%	29.2%	68.4%	31.6%
5,355	SCOTT	1,745	1,203	440	102	763	R	68.9%	25.2%	73.2%	26.8%
22,363	SHELBY	8,062	5,401	1,936	725	3,465	R	67.0%	24.0%	73.6%	26.4%
5,994	STARK	1,911	1,250	464	197	786	R	65.4%	24.3%	72.9%	27.1%
47,711	STEPHENSON	14,551	8,711	4,174	1,666	4,537	R	59.9%	28.7%	67.6%	32.4%
135,394	TAZEWELL	45,245	28,825	12,765	3,655	16,060	R	63.7%	28.2%	69.3%	30.7%
17,808	UNION	6,463	3,658	2,347	458	1,311	R	56.6%	36.3%	60.9%	39.1%
81,625	VERMILION	22,257	14,078	6,309	1,870	7,769	R	63.3%	28.3%	69.1%	30.9%
11,947	WABASH	3,832	2,645	974	213	1,671	R	69.0%	25.4%	73.1%	26.9%
17,707	WARREN	5,925	3,654	1,883	388	1,771	R	61.7%	31.8%	66.0%	34.0%
14,716	WASHINGTON	5,670	3,833	1,494	343	2,339	R	67.6%	26.3%	72.0%	28.0%
16,760	WAYNE	6,488	4,922	1,201	365	3,721	R	75.9%	18.5%	80.4%	19.6%
14,665	WHITE	5,171	3,407	1,466	298	1,941	R	65.9%	28.4%	69.9%	30.1%
58,498	WHITESIDE	18,729	10,473	7,005	1,251	3,468	R	55.9%	37.4%	59.9%	40.1%
677,560	WILL	191,073	100,616	78,787	11,670	21,829	R	52.7%	41.2%	56.1%	43.9%
66,357	WILLIAMSON	22,077	13,197	7,320	1,560	5,877	R	59.8%	33.2%	64.3%	35.7%
295,266	WINNEBAGO	80,354	44,622	29,144	6,588	15,478	R	55.5%	36.3%	60.5%	39.5%
38,664	WOODFORD	13,805	10,022	2,734	1,049	7,288	R	72.6%	19.8%	78.6%	21.4%
12,830,632	TOTAL	3,704,473	1,778,698	1,719,478	206,297	59,220	R	48.0%	46.4%	50.8%	49.2%

ILLINOIS

HOUSE OF REPRESENTATIVES

CD	Year	Total Vote	Republican Vote	Republican Candidate	Democratic Vote	Democratic Candidate	Other Vote	Rep.-Dem. Plurality		Total Vote Rep.	Total Vote Dem.	Major Vote Rep.	Major Vote Dem.
1	2010	184,386	29,253	WARDINGLEY, RAYMOND G.	148,170	RUSH, BOBBY L.*	6,963	118,917	D	15.9%	80.4%	16.5%	83.5%
1	2008	271,397	38,361	MEMBERS, ANTOINE	233,036	RUSH, BOBBY L.*		194,675	D	14.1%	85.9%	14.1%	85.9%
1	2006	174,427	27,804	TABOUR, JASON E.	146,623	RUSH, BOBBY L.*		118,819	D	15.9%	84.1%	15.9%	84.1%
1	2004	249,949	37,840	WARDINGLEY, RAYMOND G.	212,109	RUSH, BOBBY L.*		174,269	D	15.1%	84.9%	15.1%	84.9%
1	2002	183,656	29,776	WARDINGLEY, RAYMOND G.	149,068	RUSH, BOBBY L.*	4,812	119,292	D	16.2%	81.2%	16.6%	83.4%
2	2010	187,113	25,883	HAYES, ISAAC C.	150,666	JACKSON, JESSE L. JR.*	10,564	124,783	D	13.8%	80.5%	14.7%	85.3%
2	2008	280,776	29,721	WILLIAMS, ANTHONY W.	251,052	JACKSON, JESSE L. JR.*	3	221,331	D	10.6%	89.4%	10.6%	89.4%
2	2006	172,490	20,395	BELIN, ROBERT	146,347	JACKSON, JESSE L. JR.*	5,748	125,952	D	11.8%	84.8%	12.2%	87.8%
2	2004	234,525		—	207,535	JACKSON, JESSE L. JR.*	26,990	207,535	D		88.5%		100.0%
2	2002	184,010	32,567	NELSON, DOUG	151,443	JACKSON, JESSE L. JR.*		118,876	D	17.7%	82.3%	17.7%	82.3%
3	2010	166,627	40,479	BENDAS, MICHAEL A.	116,120	LIPINSKI, DANIEL*	10,028	75,641	D	24.3%	69.7%	25.8%	74.2%
3	2008	235,524	50,336	HAWKINS, MICHAEL	172,581	LIPINSKI, DANIEL*	12,607	122,245	D	21.4%	73.3%	22.6%	77.4%
3	2006	165,722	37,954	WARDINGLEY, RAYMOND G.	127,768	LIPINSKI, DANIEL*		89,814	D	22.9%	77.1%	22.9%	77.1%
3	2004	229,956	57,845	CHLADA, RYAN	167,034	LIPINSKI, DANIEL	5,077	109,189	D	25.2%	72.6%	25.7%	74.3%
3	2002	156,042		—	156,042	LIPINSKI, WILLIAM O.*		156,042	D		100.0%		100.0%
4	2010	81,792	11,711	VASQUEZ, ISRAEL	63,273	GUTIERREZ, LUIS V*	6,808	51,562	D	14.3%	77.4%	15.6%	84.4%
4	2008	139,606	16,024	CUNNINGHAM, DANIEL	112,529	GUTIERREZ, LUIS V*	11,053	96,505	D	11.5%	80.6%	12.5%	87.5%
4	2006	81,442	11,532	MELICHAR, ANN	69,910	GUTIERREZ, LUIS V*		58,378	D	14.2%	85.8%	14.2%	85.8%
4	2004	125,142	15,536	CISNEROS, TONY	104,761	GUTIERREZ, LUIS V*	4,845	89,225	D	12.4%	83.7%	12.9%	87.1%
4	2002	84,513	12,778	LOPEZ-CISNEROS, ANTHONY J. "TONY"	67,339	GUTIERREZ, LUIS V*	4,396	54,561	D	15.1%	79.7%	15.9%	84.1%
5	2010	153,435	38,935	RATOWITZ, DAVID	108,360	QUIGLEY, MIKE*	6,140	69,425	D	25.4%	70.6%	26.4%	73.6%
5	2008	230,892	50,881	HANSON, TOM	170,728	EMANUEL, RAHM*	9,283	119,847	D	22.0%	73.9%	23.0%	77.0%
5	2006	146,581	32,250	WHITE, KEVIN EDWARD	114,319	EMANUEL, RAHM*	12	82,069	D	22.0%	78.0%	22.0%	78.0%
5	2004	207,930	49,530	BEST, BRUCE	158,400	EMANUEL, RAHM*		108,870	D	23.8%	76.2%	23.8%	76.2%
5	2002	159,435	46,008	AUGUSTI, MARK A.	106,514	EMANUEL, RAHM	6,913	60,506	D	28.9%	66.8%	30.2%	69.8%
6	2010	179,835	114,456	ROSKAM, PETER J.*	65,379	LOWE, BENJAMIN S.		49,077	R	63.6%	36.4%	63.6%	36.4%
6	2008	256,913	147,906	ROSKAM, PETER J.*	109,007	MORGENTHALER, JILL		38,899	R	57.6%	42.4%	57.6%	42.4%
6	2006	177,957	91,382	ROSKAM, PETER J.	86,572	DUCKWORTH, L. TAMMY	3	4,810	R	51.4%	48.6%	51.4%	48.6%
6	2004	250,097	139,627	HYDE, HENRY J.*	110,470	CEGELIS, CHRISTINE		29,157	R	55.8%	44.2%	55.8%	44.2%
6	2002	173,872	113,174	HYDE, HENRY J.*	60,698	BERRY, TOM		52,476	R	65.1%	34.9%	65.1%	34.9%
7	2010	183,849	29,575	WEIMAN, MARK M.	149,846	DAVIS, DANNY K.*	4,428	120,271	D	16.1%	81.5%	16.5%	83.5%
7	2008	276,817	41,474	MILLER, STEVE	235,343	DAVIS, DANNY K.*		193,869	D	15.0%	85.0%	15.0%	85.0%
7	2006	165,011	21,939	HUTCHINSON, CHARLES	143,071	DAVIS, DANNY K.*	1	121,132	D	13.3%	86.7%	13.3%	86.7%
7	2004	256,736	35,603	DAVIS-FAIRMAN, ANTONIO	221,133	DAVIS, DANNY K.*		185,530	D	13.9%	86.1%	13.9%	86.1%
7	2002	165,756	25,280	TUNNEY, MARK	137,933	DAVIS, DANNY K.*	2,543	112,653	D	15.3%	83.2%	15.5%	84.5%
8	2010	202,435	98,115	WALSH, JOE	97,825	BEAN, MELISSA*	6,495	290	R	48.5%	48.3%	50.1%	49.9%
8	2008	295,525	116,081	GREENBERG, STEVE	179,444	BEAN, MELISSA*		63,363	D	39.3%	60.7%	39.3%	60.7%
8	2006	183,394	80,720	McSWEENEY, DAVID	93,355	BEAN, MELISSA*	9,319	12,635	D	44.0%	50.9%	46.4%	53.6%
8	2004	270,393	130,601	CRANE, PHILIP M.*	139,792	BEAN, MELISSA		9,191	D	48.3%	51.7%	48.3%	51.7%
8	2002	165,926	95,275	CRANE, PHILIP M.*	70,626	BEAN, MELISSA	25	24,649	R	57.4%	42.6%	57.4%	42.6%
9	2010	177,207	55,182	POLLAK, JOEL BARRY	117,553	SCHAKOWSKY, JAN*	4,472	62,371	D	31.1%	66.3%	31.9%	68.1%
9	2008	243,694	53,593	YOUNAN, MICHAEL BENJAMIN	181,948	SCHAKOWSKY, JAN*	8,153	128,355	D	22.0%	74.7%	22.8%	77.2%

ILLINOIS

HOUSE OF REPRESENTATIVES

| | | | Republican | | Democratic | | Other | Rep.-Dem. | | Percentage | | | |
| | | Total | | | | | | | | Total Vote | | Major Vote | |
CD	Year	Vote	Vote	Candidate	Vote	Candidate	Vote	Plurality		Rep.	Dem.	Rep.	Dem.
9	2006	164,713	41,858	SHANNON, MICHAEL P.	122,852	SCHAKOWSKY, JAN*	3	80,994	D	25.4%	74.6%	25.4%	74.6%
9	2004	231,417	56,135	ECKHARDT, KURT J.	175,282	SCHAKOWSKY, JAN*		119,147	D	24.3%	75.7%	24.3%	75.7%
9	2002	168,836	45,307	DURIC, NICHOLAS M.	118,642	SCHAKOWSKY, JAN*	4,887	73,335	D	26.8%	70.3%	27.6%	72.4%
10	2010	215,232	109,941	DOLD, ROBERT	105,290	SEALS, DANIEL J.	1	4,651	R	51.1%	48.9%	51.1%	48.9%
10	2008	291,258	153,082	KIRK, MARK STEVEN*	138,176	SEALS, DANIEL J.		14,906	R	52.6%	47.4%	52.6%	47.4%
10	2006	202,208	107,929	KIRK, MARK STEVEN*	94,278	SEALS, DANIEL J.	1	13,651	R	53.4%	46.6%	53.4%	46.6%
10	2004	276,711	177,493	KIRK, MARK STEVEN*	99,218	GOODMAN, LEE		78,275	R	64.1%	35.9%	64.1%	35.9%
10	2002	186,911	128,611	KIRK, MARK STEVEN*	58,300	PERRITT, HENRY H. "HANK"		70,311	R	68.8%	31.2%	68.8%	31.2%
11	2010	225,127	129,108	KINZINGER, ADAM	96,019	HALVORSON, DEBORAH L.*		33,089	R	57.3%	42.7%	57.3%	42.7%
11	2008	317,895	109,608	OZINGA, MARTY	185,652	HALVORSON, DEBORAH L.	22,635	76,044	D	34.5%	58.4%	37.1%	62.9%
11	2006	197,856	109,009	WELLER, JERRY*	88,846	PAVICH, JOHN	1	20,163	R	55.1%	44.9%	55.1%	44.9%
11	2004	294,960	173,057	WELLER, JERRY*	121,903	RENNER, TARI		51,154	R	58.7%	41.3%	58.7%	41.3%
11	2002	193,085	124,192	WELLER, JERRY*	68,893	VAN DUYNE, KEITH S.		55,299	R	64.3%	35.7%	64.3%	35.7%
12	2010	202,705	74,046	NEWMAN, TERI	121,272	COSTELLO, JERRY F.*	7,387	47,226	D	36.5%	59.8%	37.9%	62.1%
12	2008	298,181	74,382	RICHARDSON, TIMOTHY JAY, JR	212,891	COSTELLO, JERRY F.*	10,908	138,509	D	24.9%	71.4%	25.9%	74.1%
12	2006	157,809		—	157,802	COSTELLO, JERRY F.*	7	157,802	D		100.0%		100.0%
12	2004	286,435	82,677	ZWEIGART, ERIN R.	198,962	COSTELLO, JERRY F.*	4,796	116,285	D	28.9%	69.5%	29.4%	70.6%
12	2002	190,020	58,440	SADLER, DAVID	131,580	COSTELLO, JERRY F.*		73,140	D	30.8%	69.2%	30.8%	69.2%
13	2010	238,413	152,132	BIGGERT, JUDY*	86,281	HARPER, SCOTT		65,851	R	63.8%	36.2%	63.8%	36.2%
13	2008	337,771	180,888	BIGGERT, JUDY*	147,430	HARPER, SCOTT	9,453	33,458	R	53.6%	43.6%	55.1%	44.9%
13	2006	205,234	119,720	BIGGERT, JUDY*	85,507	SHANNON, JOSEPH	7	34,213	R	58.3%	41.7%	58.3%	41.7%
13	2004	308,312	200,472	BIGGERT, JUDY*	107,836	ANDERSEN, GLORIA SCHOR	4	92,636	R	65.0%	35.0%	65.0%	35.0%
13	2002	198,615	139,546	BIGGERT, JUDY*	59,069	MASON, TOM		80,477	R	70.3%	29.7%	70.3%	29.7%
14	2010	219,013	112,369	HULTGREN, RANDALL M. "RANDY"	98,645	FOSTER, BILL*	7,999	13,724	R	51.3%	45.0%	53.3%	46.7%
14	2008	321,057	135,653	OBERWEIS, JIM	185,404	FOSTER, BILL*		49,751	D	42.3%	57.7%	42.3%	57.7%
14	2006	197,144	117,870	HASTERT, J. DENNIS*	79,274	LAESCH, JONATHAN "JOHN"		38,596	R	59.8%	40.2%	59.8%	40.2%
14	2004	279,208	191,618	HASTERT, J. DENNIS*	87,590	ZAMORA, RUBEN		104,028	R	68.6%	31.4%	68.6%	31.4%
14	2002	182,363	135,198	HASTERT, J. DENNIS*	47,165	QUICK, LAURENCE J.		88,033	R	74.1%	25.9%	74.1%	25.9%
15	2010	212,863	136,915	JOHNSON, TIMOTHY V.*	75,948	GILL, DAVID		60,967	R	64.3%	35.7%	64.3%	35.7%
15	2008	291,514	187,121	JOHNSON, TIMOTHY V.*	104,393	COX, STEVE		82,728	R	64.2%	35.8%	64.2%	35.8%
15	2006	202,835	116,810	JOHNSON, TIMOTHY V.*	86,025	GILL, DAVID		30,785	R	57.6%	42.4%	57.6%	42.4%
15	2004	291,739	178,114	JOHNSON, TIMOTHY V.*	113,625	GILL, DAVID		64,489	R	61.1%	38.9%	61.1%	38.9%
15	2002	206,617	134,650	JOHNSON, TIMOTHY V.*	64,131	HARTKE, JOSHUA T.	7,836	70,519	R	65.2%	31.0%	67.7%	32.3%
16	2010	212,761	138,299	MANZULLO, DONALD A.*	66,037	GAULRAPP, GEORGE W.	8,425	72,262	R	65.0%	31.0%	67.7%	32.3%
16	2008	312,220	190,039	MANZULLO, DONALD A.*	112,648	ABBOUD, ROBERT G.	9,533	77,391	R	60.9%	36.1%	62.8%	37.2%
16	2006	198,101	125,951	MANZULLO, DONALD A.*	63,627	AUMAN, RICHARD D.	8,523	62,324	R	63.6%	32.1%	66.4%	33.6%
16	2004	295,806	204,350	MANZULLO, DONALD A.*	91,452	KUTSCH, JOHN H.	4	112,898	R	69.1%	30.9%	69.1%	30.9%
16	2002	188,827	133,339	MANZULLO, DONALD A.*	55,488	KUTSCH, JOHN H.		77,851	R	70.6%	29.4%	70.6%	29.4%
17	2010	198,898	104,583	SCHILLING, BOBBY	85,454	HARE, PHIL*	8,861	19,129	R	52.6%	43.0%	55.0%	45.0%
17	2008	221,478		—	220,961	HARE, PHIL*	517	220,961	D		99.8%		100.0%

ILLINOIS

HOUSE OF REPRESENTATIVES

CD	Year	Total Vote	Republican		Democratic		Other Vote	Rep.-Dem. Plurality		Percentage			
			Vote	Candidate	Vote	Candidate				Total Vote		Major Vote	
										Rep.	Dem.	Rep.	Dem.
17	2006	201,186	86,161	ZINGA, ANDREA	115,025	HARE, PHIL		28,864	D	42.8%	57.2%	42.8%	57.2%
17	2004	284,000	111,680	ZINGA, ANDREA	172,320	EVANS, LANE*		60,640	D	39.3%	60.7%	39.3%	60.7%
17	2002	203,612	76,519	CALDERONE, PETER	127,093	EVANS, LANE*		50,574	D	37.6%	62.4%	37.6%	62.4%
18	2010	221,170	152,868	SCHOCK, AARON*	57,046	HIRNER, DEIRDRE "DK"	11,256	95,822	R	69.1%	25.8%	72.8%	27.2%
18	2008	310,088	182,589	SCHOCK, AARON	117,642	CALLAHAN, COLLEEN	9,857	64,947	R	58.9%	37.9%	60.8%	39.2%
18	2006	223,246	150,194	LaHOOD, RAY*	73,052	WATERWORTH, STEVE		77,142	R	67.3%	32.7%	67.3%	32.7%
18	2004	307,595	216,047	LaHOOD, RAY*	91,548	WATERWORTH, STEVE		124,499	R	70.2%	29.8%	70.2%	29.8%
18	2002	192,567	192,567	LaHOOD, RAY*	—			192,567	R	100.0%		100.0%	
19	2010	233,298	166,166	SHIMKUS, JOHN*	67,132	BAGWELL, TIM		99,034	R	71.2%	28.8%	71.2%	28.8%
19	2008	315,589	203,434	SHIMKUS, JOHN*	105,338	DAVIS, DANIEL	6,817	98,096	R	64.5%	33.4%	65.9%	34.1%
19	2006	236,352	143,491	SHIMKUS, JOHN*	92,861	STOVER, DANNY L.		50,630	R	60.7%	39.3%	60.7%	39.3%
19	2004	307,754	213,451	SHIMKUS, JOHN*	94,303	BAGWELL, TIM		119,148	R	69.4%	30.6%	69.4%	30.6%
19	2002	244,473	133,956	SHIMKUS, JOHN*	110,517	PHELPS, DAVID*		23,439	R	54.8%	45.2%	54.8%	45.2%
TOTAL	2010	3,696,159	1,720,016		1,876,316		99,827	156,300	D	46.5%	50.8%	47.8%	52.2%
TOTAL	2008	5,248,195	1,961,173		3,176,203		110,819	1,215,030	D	37.4%	60.5%	38.2%	61.8%
TOTAL	2006	3,453,708	1,442,969		1,987,114		23,625	544,145	D	41.8%	57.5%	42.1%	57.9%
TOTAL	2004	4,988,665	2,271,676		2,675,273		41,716	403,597	D	45.5%	53.6%	45.9%	54.1%
TOTAL	2002	3,429,136	1,657,183		1,740,541		31,412	83,358	D	48.3%	50.8%	48.8%	51.2%

GENERAL AND PRIMARY ELECTIONS

2010 GENERAL ELECTIONS

Governor   Other vote was 135,705 Independent (Scott Lee Cohen); 100,756 Green (Rich Whitney); 34,681 Libertarian (Lex Green); 221 write-in (Michael White); 17 write-in (Steve Estill); 3 write-in (Greg Moore); 2 write-in (No candidate for governor, but Larry L. Jones listed as candidate for lieutenant governor).

Senator   Other vote was 117,914 Green (LeAlan M. Jones); 87,247 Libertarian (Mike Labno); 561 write-in (Robert L. Zadek); 468 write-in (Will Boyd); 33 write-in (Corey Dabney); 19 write-in (Susanne Atanus); 16 write-in (Shon-Tiyon "Santiago" Horton); 15 write-in (Avner Nagar); 12 write-in (Stan Jagla); 9 write-in (Darren Raichart); 3 write-in (Lowell M. Seida).

House   Other vote was:

CD 1   6,963 Green (Jeff Adams).
CD 2   10,564 Green (Anthony W. Williams).
CD 3   10,028 Green (Laurel Lambert Schmidt).
CD 4   6,808 Green (Robert J. Burns).
CD 5   6,140 Green (Matthew Reichel).
CD 6
CD 7   4,428 Independent (Clarence Desmond Clemons).
CD 8   6,495 Green (Bill Scheurer).

CD 9	4,472 Green (Simon Ribeiro).
CD 10	1 write-in (Author C. Brumfield).
CD 11	
CD 12	7,387 Green (Rodger W. Jennings).
CD 13	
CD 14	7,949 Green (Daniel J. Kairis); 50 write-in (Doug Marks).
CD 15	
CD 16	8,425 Green (Terry G. Campbell).
CD 17	8,861 Green (Roger K. Davis).
CD 18	11,256 Green (Sheldon Schafer).
CD 19	

2010 PRIMARY ELECTIONS

Primary	February 2, 2010	**Registration** (as of February 2, 2010)	7,600,962	No Party Registration
Primary Type	Open—Any registered voter could participate in the primary of either party.			

ILLINOIS

GENERAL AND PRIMARY ELECTIONS

	REPUBLICAN PRIMARIES			DEMOCRATIC PRIMARIES		
Governor	Bill Brady	155,527	20.3%	Pat Quinn*	462,049	50.5%
	Kirk W. Dillard	155,334	20.2%	Daniel W. Hynes	453,677	49.5%
	Andy McKenna	148,054	19.3%			
	Jim Ryan	130,785	17.0%			
	Adam Andrzejewski	111,030	14.5%			
	Dan Proft	59,335	7.7%			
	Robert J. Schillerstrom	7,420	1.0%			
	TOTAL	*767,485*		*TOTAL*	*915,726*	
Senator	Mark Steven Kirk	420,373	56.6%	Alexander Giannoulias	352,202	38.9%
	Patrick J. Hughes	142,928	19.3%	David Hoffman	304,757	33.7%
	Donald Lowery	66,357	8.9%	Cheryle Jackson	179,682	19.9%
	Kathleen Thomas	54,038	7.3%	Robert Marshall	51,813	5.7%
	Andy Martin	37,480	5.0%	Jacob J. Meister	16,317	1.8%
	John Arrington	21,090	2.8%	Christopher Smith (write-in)	2	
	Patricia Elaine Beard (write-in)	2				
	TOTAL	*742,268*		*TOTAL*	*904,773*	
Congressional District 1	*No Republican candidate filed for the primary. Raymond G. Wardingly received 18 write-in votes and was subsequently the party's nominee in the general election.*			Bobby L. Rush*	68,585	79.7%
				JoAnne Guillemette	8,035	9.3%
				Fred Smith	5,203	6.0%
				Harold L. Bailey	4,232	4.9%
				TOTAL	*86,055*	
Congressional District 2	Isaac C. Hayes	6,632	100.0%	Jesse L. Jackson Jr.*	79,962	100.0%
Congressional District 3	Michael A. Bendas	18,520	100.0%	Daniel Lipinksi*	57,684	77.9%
				Jorge Mujica	16,372	22.1%
				TOTAL	*74,056*	

ILLINOIS

GENERAL AND PRIMARY ELECTIONS

	REPUBLICAN PRIMARIES			DEMOCRATIC PRIMARIES		
Congressional District 4	*No Republican candidate filed for the primary. Israel Vasquez was subsequently approved by Republican district officials to fill the vacancy on the general election ballot.*			Luis V. Gutierrez*	34,000	100.0%
Congressional District 5	David Ratowitz	5,689	39.6%	Mike Quigley*	56,667	100.0%
	Rosanna Pulido	4,722	32.9%			
	Ashvin Lad	3,942	27.5%			
	TOTAL	14,353				
Congressional District 6	Peter J. Roskam*	53,081	100.0%	Benjamin S. Lowe	23,542	100.0%
Congressional District 7	Mark M. Weiman	8,365	100.0%	Danny K. Davis*	52,728	66.8%
				Sharon Denise Dixon	10,851	13.7%
				Darlena Williams-Burnett	10,173	12.9%
				Jim Ascot	5,221	6.6%
				TOTAL	78,973	
Congressional District 8	Joe Walsh	16,162	34.2%	Melissa Bean*	25,000	99.9%
	Dirk W. Beveridge	11,708	24.7%	Jonathan Farnick (write-in)	25	0.1%
	Maria Rodriguez	9,803	20.7%			
	Christopher Geissler	4,267	9.0%			
	John Dawson	3,921	8.3%			
	Gregory S. Jacobs	1,445	3.1%			
	TOTAL	47,306		TOTAL	25,025	
Congressional District 9	Joel Barry Pollak	13,566	100.0%	Jan Schakowsky*	62,763	100.0%
Congressional District 10	Robert Dold	19,691	38.0%	Daniel J. Seals	25,490	48.2%
	Elizabeth Coulson	16,149	31.2%	Julie Hamos	24,531	46.4%
	Dick Green	7,595	14.7%	Elliot Richardson	2,838	5.4%
	Arie Friedman	7,260	14.0%			
	Paul Hamann	1,078	2.1%			
	TOTAL	51,773		TOTAL	52,859	
Congressional District 11	Adam Kinzinger	32,233	63.7%	Deborah L. Halvorson*	29,015	100.0%
	Dave White	5,257	10.4%			
	David McAloon	4,880	9.6%			
	Henry W. Meers Jr.	4,555	9.0%			
	Darrel Miller	3,701	7.3%			
	TOTAL	50,626				
Congressional District 12	Teri Newman	14,995	52.6%	Jerry F. Costello*	44,913	100.0%
	Theresa Kormos	13,510	47.4%			
	TOTAL	28,505				
Congressional District 13	Judy Biggert*	58,294	100.0%	Scott Harper	33,290	100.0%
Congressional District 14	Randall M. "Randy" Hultgren	34,833	54.7%	Bill Foster*	25,446	100.0%
	Ethan A. Hastert	28,840	45.3%	Bobby G. Rose (write-in)	1	
	TOTAL	63,673		TOTAL	25,447	

ILLINOIS

GENERAL AND PRIMARY ELECTIONS

	REPUBLICAN PRIMARIES			DEMOCRATIC PRIMARIES		
Congressional District 15	Timothy V. Johnson*	68,621	100.0%	David Gill	21,617	100.0%
Congressional District 16	Donald A. Manzullo*	54,060	100.0%	George W. Gaulrapp	18,021	100.0%
Congressional District 17	Bobby Schilling	33,659	100.0%	Phil Hare*	34,427	100.0%
Congressional District 18	Aaron Schock*	60,653	100.0%	Deirdre "DK" Hirner	13,683	54.2%
				Carl Ray	11,566	45.8%
				TOTAL	*25,249*	
Congressional District 19	John Shimkus*	48,680	85.3%	Tim Bagwell	30,999	100.0%
	Michael Firsching	8,363	14.7%			
	TOTAL	*57,043*				

An asterisk (*) denotes incumbent.

INDIANA

Congressional districts first established for elections held in 2002
9 members

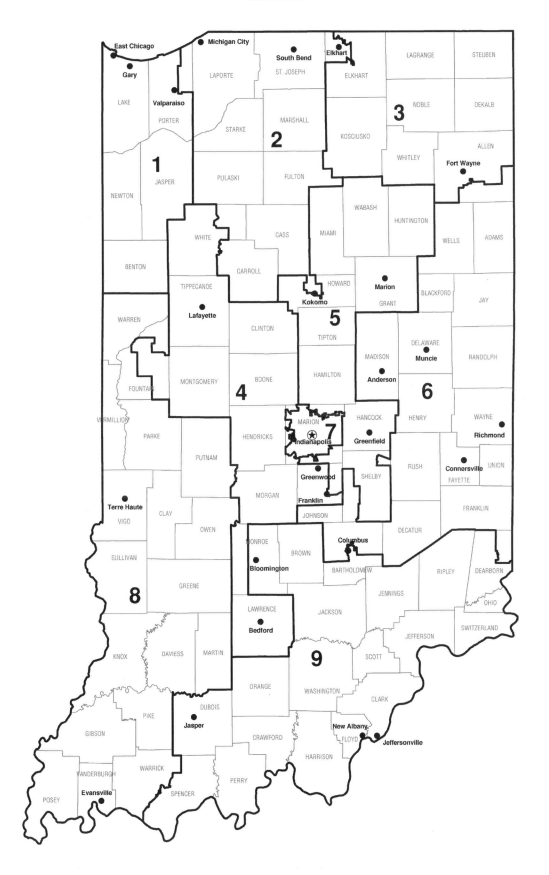

142

INDIANA

GOVERNOR
Mitch Daniels (R). Reelected 2008 to a four-year term. Previously elected 2004.

SENATORS (2 Republicans)
Dan Coats (R). Elected 2010 to a six-year term. Previously elected 1992, 1990.

Richard G. Lugar (R). Reelected 2006 to a six-year term. Previously elected 2000, 1994, 1988, 1982, 1976.

REPRESENTATIVES (6 Republicans, 3 Democrats)
1. Peter J. Visclosky (D)
2. Joseph S. Donnelly (D)
3. Marlin A. Stutzman (R)
4. Todd Rokita (R)
5. Dan Burton (R)
6. Mike Pence (R)
7. Andre D. Carson (D)
8. Larry D. Bucshon (R)
9. Todd Young (R)

POSTWAR VOTE FOR PRESIDENT

		Republican		Democratic				Total Vote		Major Vote	
Year	Total Vote	Vote	Candidate	Vote	Candidate	Other Vote	Rep.-Dem. Plurality	Rep.	Dem.	Rep.	Dem.
2008	2,751,054	1,345,648	McCain, John	1,374,039	Obama, Barack	31,367	28,391 D	48.9%	49.9%	49.5%	50.5%
2004	2,468,002	1,479,438	Bush, George W.	969,011	Kerry, John	19,553	510,427 R	59.9%	39.3%	60.4%	39.6%
2000**	2,199,302	1,245,836	Bush, George W.	901,980	Gore, Al	51,486	343,856 R	56.6%	41.0%	58.0%	42.0%
1996**	2,135,842	1,006,693	Dole, Bob	887,424	Clinton, Bill	241,725	119,269 R	47.1%	41.5%	53.1%	46.9%
1992**	2,305,871	989,375	Bush, George	848,420	Clinton, Bill	468,076	140,955 R	42.9%	36.8%	53.8%	46.2%
1988	2,168,621	1,297,763	Bush, George	860,643	Dukakis, Michael S.	10,215	437,120 R	59.8%	39.7%	60.1%	39.9%
1984	2,233,069	1,377,230	Reagan, Ronald	841,481	Mondale, Walter F.	14,358	535,749 R	61.7%	37.7%	62.1%	37.9%
1980**	2,242,033	1,255,656	Reagan, Ronald	844,197	Carter, Jimmy	142,180	411,459 R	56.0%	37.7%	59.8%	40.2%
1976	2,220,362	1,183,958	Ford, Gerald R.	1,014,714	Carter, Jimmy	21,690	169,244 R	53.3%	45.7%	53.8%	46.2%
1972	2,125,529	1,405,154	Nixon, Richard M.	708,568	McGovern, George S.	11,807	696,586 R	66.1%	33.3%	66.5%	33.5%
1968**	2,123,597	1,067,885	Nixon, Richard M.	806,659	Humphrey, Hubert H.	249,053	261,226 R	50.3%	38.0%	57.0%	43.0%
1964	2,091,606	911,118	Goldwater, Barry M.	1,170,848	Johnson, Lyndon B.	9,640	259,730 D	43.6%	56.0%	43.8%	56.2%
1960	2,135,360	1,175,120	Nixon, Richard M.	952,358	Kennedy, John F.	7,882	222,762 R	55.0%	44.6%	55.2%	44.8%
1956	1,974,607	1,182,811	Eisenhower, Dwight D.	783,908	Stevenson, Adlai E.	7,888	398,903 R	59.9%	39.7%	60.1%	39.9%
1952	1,955,049	1,136,259	Eisenhower, Dwight D.	801,530	Stevenson, Adlai E.	17,260	334,729 R	58.1%	41.0%	58.6%	41.4%
1948	1,656,212	821,079	Dewey, Thomas E.	807,831	Truman, Harry S.	27,302	13,248 R	49.6%	48.8%	50.4%	49.6%

**In past elections, the other vote included: 2000 - 18,531 Green (Ralph Nader); 1996 - 224,299 Reform (Ross Perot); 1992 - 455,934 Independent (Perot); 1980 - 111,639 Independent (John Anderson); 1968 - 243,108 American Independent (George Wallace).

INDIANA

POSTWAR VOTE FOR GOVERNOR

Year	Total Vote	Republican Vote	Republican Candidate	Democratic Vote	Democratic Candidate	Other Vote	Rep.-Dem. Plurality	Total Vote Rep.	Total Vote Dem.	Major Vote Rep.	Major Vote Dem.
2008	2,703,752	1,563,885	Daniels, Mitch	1,082,463	Thompson, Jill Long	57,404	481,422 R	57.8%	40.0%	59.1%	40.9%
2004	2,448,498	1,302,912	Daniels, Mitch	1,113,900	Kernan, Joseph E.	31,686	189,012 R	53.2%	45.5%	53.9%	46.1%
2000	2,179,413	908,285	McIntosh, David M.	1,232,525	O'Bannon, Frank L.	38,603	324,240 D	41.7%	56.6%	42.4%	57.6%
1996	2,110,047	986,982	Goldsmith, Stephen	1,087,128	O'Bannon, Frank L.	35,937	100,146 D	46.8%	51.5%	47.6%	52.4%
1992	2,229,116	822,533	Pearson, Linley E.	1,382,151	Bayh, Evan	24,432	559,618 D	36.9%	62.0%	37.3%	62.7%
1988	2,140,781	1,002,207	Mutz, John M.	1,138,574	Bayh, Evan		136,367 D	46.8%	53.2%	46.8%	53.2%
1984	2,197,988	1,146,497	Orr, Robert D.	1,036,922	Townsend, W. Wayne	14,569	109,575 R	52.2%	47.2%	52.5%	47.5%
1980	2,178,403	1,257,383	Orr, Robert D.	913,116	Hillenbrand, John A.	7,904	344,267 R	57.7%	41.9%	57.9%	42.1%
1976	2,175,324	1,236,555	Bowen, Otis R.	927,243	Conrad, Larry A.	11,526	309,312 R	56.8%	42.6%	57.1%	42.9%
1972	2,120,847	1,203,903	Bowen, Otis R.	900,489	Welsh, Matthew E.	16,455	303,414 R	56.8%	42.5%	57.2%	42.8%
1968	2,049,072	1,080,271	Whitcomb, Edgar D.	965,816	Rock, Robert L.	2,985	114,455 R	52.7%	47.1%	52.8%	47.2%
1964	2,072,915	901,342	Ristine, Richard O.	1,164,620	Branigin, Roger D.	6,953	263,278 D	43.5%	56.2%	43.6%	56.4%
1960	2,128,965	1,049,540	Parker, Crawford F.	1,072,717	Welsh, Matthew E.	6,708	23,177 D	49.3%	50.4%	49.5%	50.5%
1956	1,954,290	1,086,868	Handley, Harold W.	859,393	Tucker, Ralph	8,029	227,475 R	55.6%	44.0%	55.8%	44.2%
1952	1,931,869	1,075,685	Craig, George N.	841,984	Watkins, John A.	14,200	233,701 R	55.7%	43.6%	56.1%	43.9%
1948	1,652,321	745,892	Creighton, Hobart	884,995	Schricker, Henry F.	21,434	139,103 D	45.1%	53.6%	45.7%	54.3%

POSTWAR VOTE FOR SENATOR

Year	Total Vote	Republican Vote	Republican Candidate	Democratic Vote	Democratic Candidate	Other Vote	Rep.-Dem. Plurality	Total Vote Rep.	Total Vote Dem.	Major Vote Rep.	Major Vote Dem.
2010	1,744,481	952,116	Coats, Dan	697,775	Ellsworth, Brad	94,590	254,341 R	54.6%	40.0%	57.7%	42.3%
2006**	1,341,111	1,171,553	Lugar, Richard G.	—		169,558	1,171,553 R	87.4%		100.0%	
2004	2,428,233	903,913	Scott, Marvin	1,496,976	Bayh, Evan	27,344	593,063 D	37.2%	61.6%	37.6%	62.4%
2000	2,145,209	1,427,944	Lugar, Richard G.	683,273	Johnson, David L.	33,992	744,671 R	66.6%	31.9%	67.6%	32.4%
1998	1,588,617	552,732	Helmke, Paul	1,012,244	Bayh, Evan	23,641	459,512 D	34.8%	63.7%	35.3%	64.7%
1994	1,543,568	1,039,625	Lugar, Richard G.	470,799	Jontz, Jim	33,144	568,826 R	67.4%	30.5%	68.8%	31.2%
1992	2,211,426	1,267,972	Coats, Dan	900,148	Hogsett, Joseph H.	43,306	367,824 R	57.3%	40.7%	58.5%	41.5%
1990S	1,504,302	806,048	Coats, Dan	696,639	Hill, Baron P.	1,615	109,409 R	53.6%	46.3%	53.6%	46.4%
1988	2,099,303	1,430,525	Lugar, Richard G.	668,778	Wickes, Jack		761,747 R	68.1%	31.9%	68.1%	31.9%
1986	1,545,563	936,143	Quayle, J. Danforth	595,192	Long, Jill L.	14,228	340,951 R	60.6%	38.5%	61.1%	38.9%
1982	1,817,287	978,301	Lugar, Richard G.	828,400	Fithian, Floyd	10,586	149,901 R	53.8%	45.6%	54.1%	45.9%
1980	2,198,376	1,182,414	Quayle, J. Danforth	1,015,962	Bayh, Birch		166,452 R	53.8%	46.2%	53.8%	46.2%
1976	2,171,187	1,275,833	Lugar, Richard G.	878,522	Hartke, R. Vance	16,832	397,311 R	58.8%	40.5%	59.2%	40.8%
1974	1,752,978	814,117	Lugar, Richard G.	889,269	Bayh, Birch	49,592	75,152 D	46.4%	50.7%	47.8%	52.2%
1970	1,737,697	866,707	Roudebush, Richard	870,990	Hartke, R. Vance		4,283 D	49.9%	50.1%	49.9%	50.1%
1968	2,053,118	988,571	Ruckelshaus, William	1,060,456	Bayh, Birch	4,091	71,885 D	48.1%	51.7%	48.2%	51.8%
1964	2,076,963	941,519	Bontrager, D. Russell	1,128,505	Hartke, R. Vance	6,939	186,986 D	45.3%	54.3%	45.5%	54.5%
1962	1,800,038	894,547	Capehart, Homer E.	905,491	Bayh, Birch		10,944 D	49.7%	50.3%	49.7%	50.3%
1958	1,724,598	731,635	Handley, Harold W.	973,636	Hartke, R. Vance	19,327	242,001 D	42.4%	56.5%	42.9%	57.1%
1956	1,963,986	1,084,262	Capehart, Homer E.	871,781	Wickard, Claude	7,943	212,481 R	55.2%	44.4%	55.4%	44.6%
1952	1,946,118	1,020,605	Jenner, William E.	911,169	Schricker, Henry F.	14,344	109,436 R	52.4%	46.8%	52.8%	47.2%
1950	1,598,724	844,303	Capehart, Homer E.	741,025	Campbell, Alex M.	13,396	103,278 R	52.8%	46.4%	53.3%	46.7%
1946	1,347,434	739,809	Jenner, William E.	584,288	Townsend, M. Clifford	23,337	155,521 R	54.9%	43.4%	55.9%	44.1%

**In past elections, the other vote included: 2006 - 168,820 Libertarian (Steve Osborn), who finished second. The 1990 election was for a short term to fill a vacancy. The Democratic Party did not run a candidate in the 2006 Senate election.

INDIANA

SENATOR 2010

2010 Census Population	County	Total Vote	Republican	Democratic	Other	Rep.-Dem. Plurality		Percentage			
								Total Vote		Major Vote	
								Rep.	Dem.	Rep.	Dem.
34,387	ADAMS	9,526	6,181	2,880	465	3,301	R	64.9%	30.2%	68.2%	31.8%
355,329	ALLEN	90,957	55,454	31,347	4,156	24,107	R	61.0%	34.5%	63.9%	36.1%
76,794	BARTHOLOMEW	19,776	12,243	6,492	1,041	5,751	R	61.9%	32.8%	65.3%	34.7%
8,854	BENTON	2,261	1,432	667	162	765	R	63.3%	29.5%	68.2%	31.8%
12,766	BLACKFORD	3,849	2,068	1,551	230	517	R	53.7%	40.3%	57.1%	42.9%
56,640	BOONE	19,136	12,773	4,944	1,419	7,829	R	66.7%	25.8%	72.1%	27.9%
15,242	BROWN	6,248	3,201	2,608	439	593	R	51.2%	41.7%	55.1%	44.9%
20,155	CARROLL	5,963	3,566	1,883	514	1,683	R	59.8%	31.6%	65.4%	34.6%
38,966	CASS	10,811	6,361	3,673	777	2,688	R	58.8%	34.0%	63.4%	36.6%
110,232	CLARK	32,613	17,773	13,429	1,411	4,344	R	54.5%	41.2%	57.0%	43.0%
26,890	CLAY	8,196	4,543	3,187	466	1,356	R	55.4%	38.9%	58.8%	41.2%
33,224	CLINTON	7,412	4,618	2,222	572	2,396	R	62.3%	30.0%	67.5%	32.5%
10,713	CRAWFORD	3,750	1,803	1,755	192	48	R	48.1%	46.8%	50.7%	49.3%
31,648	DAVIESS	7,034	4,690	2,061	283	2,629	R	66.7%	29.3%	69.5%	30.5%
50,047	DEARBORN	15,032	10,589	3,776	667	6,813	R	70.4%	25.1%	73.7%	26.3%
25,740	DECATUR	7,647	4,838	2,283	526	2,555	R	63.3%	29.9%	67.9%	32.1%
42,223	DE KALB	11,501	7,351	3,479	671	3,872	R	63.9%	30.2%	67.9%	32.1%
117,671	DELAWARE	30,681	14,720	14,414	1,547	306	R	48.0%	47.0%	50.5%	49.5%
41,889	DUBOIS	13,991	7,059	6,344	588	715	R	50.5%	45.3%	52.7%	47.3%
197,559	ELKHART	46,094	30,546	13,867	1,681	16,679	R	66.3%	30.1%	68.8%	31.2%
24,277	FAYETTE	6,283	3,154	2,618	511	536	R	50.2%	41.7%	54.6%	45.4%
74,578	FLOYD	25,711	14,529	10,238	944	4,291	R	56.5%	39.8%	58.7%	41.3%
17,240	FOUNTAIN	5,379	3,178	1,837	364	1,341	R	59.1%	34.2%	63.4%	36.6%
23,087	FRANKLIN	7,223	4,858	1,976	389	2,882	R	67.3%	27.4%	71.1%	28.9%
20,836	FULTON	6,129	3,854	1,977	298	1,877	R	62.9%	32.3%	66.1%	33.9%
33,503	GIBSON	11,431	6,308	4,644	479	1,664	R	55.2%	40.6%	57.6%	42.4%
70,061	GRANT	16,011	9,684	5,433	894	4,251	R	60.5%	33.9%	64.1%	35.9%
33,165	GREENE	9,864	5,281	4,079	504	1,202	R	53.5%	41.4%	56.4%	43.6%
274,569	HAMILTON	80,724	54,675	20,658	5,391	34,017	R	67.7%	25.6%	72.6%	27.4%
70,002	HANCOCK	22,626	14,367	6,325	1,934	8,042	R	63.5%	28.0%	69.4%	30.6%
39,364	HARRISON	14,611	8,362	5,569	680	2,793	R	57.2%	38.1%	60.0%	40.0%
145,448	HENDRICKS	38,803	26,072	9,896	2,835	16,176	R	67.2%	25.5%	72.5%	27.5%
49,462	HENRY	13,243	7,192	4,944	1,107	2,248	R	54.3%	37.3%	59.3%	40.7%
82,752	HOWARD	25,739	14,212	9,734	1,793	4,478	R	55.2%	37.8%	59.4%	40.6%
37,124	HUNTINGTON	11,200	7,731	2,717	752	5,014	R	69.0%	24.3%	74.0%	26.0%
42,376	JACKSON	13,498	7,838	4,826	834	3,012	R	58.1%	35.8%	61.9%	38.1%
33,478	JASPER	8,215	5,329	2,505	381	2,824	R	64.9%	30.5%	68.0%	32.0%
21,253	JAY	5,771	3,432	1,986	353	1,446	R	59.5%	34.4%	63.3%	36.7%
32,428	JEFFERSON	10,013	5,447	3,981	585	1,466	R	54.4%	39.8%	57.8%	42.2%
28,525	JENNINGS	8,387	4,725	3,161	501	1,564	R	56.3%	37.7%	59.9%	40.1%
139,654	JOHNSON	38,268	25,462	9,813	2,993	15,649	R	66.5%	25.6%	72.2%	27.8%
38,440	KNOX	11,403	5,604	5,230	569	374	R	49.1%	45.9%	51.7%	48.3%
77,358	KOSCIUSKO	19,939	14,936	3,917	1,086	11,019	R	74.9%	19.6%	79.2%	20.8%
37,128	LAGRANGE	6,511	4,420	1,733	358	2,687	R	67.9%	26.6%	71.8%	28.2%
496,005	LAKE	112,701	44,232	65,767	2,702	21,535	D	39.2%	58.4%	40.2%	59.8%
111,467	LA PORTE	28,752	13,597	13,627	1,528	30	D	47.3%	47.4%	49.9%	50.1%
46,134	LAWRENCE	11,054	6,963	3,343	748	3,620	R	63.0%	30.2%	67.6%	32.4%
131,636	MADISON	39,099	18,848	17,694	2,557	1,154	R	48.2%	45.3%	51.6%	48.4%
903,393	MARION	214,077	88,564	113,634	11,879	25,070	D	41.4%	53.1%	43.8%	56.2%
47,051	MARSHALL	13,222	8,280	4,362	580	3,918	R	62.6%	33.0%	65.5%	34.5%
10,334	MARTIN	4,139	2,189	1,719	231	470	R	52.9%	41.5%	56.0%	44.0%
36,903	MIAMI	8,715	5,275	2,612	828	2,663	R	60.5%	30.0%	66.9%	33.1%
137,974	MONROE	35,841	14,336	19,797	1,708	5,461	D	40.0%	55.2%	42.0%	58.0%
38,124	MONTGOMERY	10,679	6,396	3,051	1,232	3,345	R	59.9%	28.6%	67.7%	32.3%
68,894	MORGAN	18,033	11,961	4,436	1,636	7,525	R	66.3%	24.6%	72.9%	27.1%

INDIANA

SENATOR 2010

2010 Census Population	County	Total Vote	Republican	Democratic	Other	Rep.-Dem. Plurality		Percentage			
								Total Vote		Major Vote	
								Rep.	Dem.	Rep.	Dem.
14,244	NEWTON	4,205	2,593	1,397	215	1,196	R	61.7%	33.2%	65.0%	35.0%
47,536	NOBLE	11,276	7,167	3,443	666	3,724	R	63.6%	30.5%	67.5%	32.5%
6,128	OHIO	2,200	1,302	789	109	513	R	59.2%	35.9%	62.3%	37.7%
19,840	ORANGE	5,843	3,405	2,142	296	1,263	R	58.3%	36.7%	61.4%	38.6%
21,575	OWEN	6,134	3,353	2,329	452	1,024	R	54.7%	38.0%	59.0%	41.0%
17,339	PARKE	5,411	2,898	2,120	393	778	R	53.6%	39.2%	57.8%	42.2%
19,338	PERRY	6,732	2,484	3,939	309	1,455	D	36.9%	58.5%	38.7%	61.3%
12,845	PIKE	4,808	2,294	2,288	226	6	R	47.7%	47.6%	50.1%	49.9%
164,343	PORTER	44,123	23,723	18,556	1,844	5,167	R	53.8%	42.1%	56.1%	43.9%
25,910	POSEY	9,880	5,144	4,418	318	726	R	52.1%	44.7%	53.8%	46.2%
13,402	PULASKI	4,523	2,762	1,512	249	1,250	R	61.1%	33.4%	64.6%	35.4%
37,963	PUTNAM	10,155	5,964	3,452	739	2,512	R	58.7%	34.0%	63.3%	36.7%
26,171	RANDOLPH	6,945	4,201	2,185	559	2,016	R	60.5%	31.5%	65.8%	34.2%
28,818	RIPLEY	8,321	5,580	2,323	418	3,257	R	67.1%	27.9%	70.6%	29.4%
17,392	RUSH	4,939	2,987	1,421	531	1,566	R	60.5%	28.8%	67.8%	32.2%
266,931	ST. JOSEPH	79,342	39,111	37,563	2,668	1,548	R	49.3%	47.3%	51.0%	49.0%
24,181	SCOTT	6,955	3,329	3,215	411	114	R	47.9%	46.2%	50.9%	49.1%
44,436	SHELBY	10,693	6,597	3,200	896	3,397	R	61.7%	29.9%	67.3%	32.7%
20,952	SPENCER	7,458	3,674	3,486	298	188	R	49.3%	46.7%	51.3%	48.7%
23,363	STARKE	6,950	3,557	3,050	343	507	R	51.2%	43.9%	53.8%	46.2%
34,185	STEUBEN	10,044	6,149	3,297	598	2,852	R	61.2%	32.8%	65.1%	34.9%
21,475	SULLIVAN	6,445	2,681	3,392	372	711	D	41.6%	52.6%	44.1%	55.9%
10,613	SWITZERLAND	2,953	1,583	1,215	155	368	R	53.6%	41.1%	56.6%	43.4%
172,780	TIPPECANOE	35,693	19,494	14,078	2,121	5,416	R	54.6%	39.4%	58.1%	41.9%
15,936	TIPTON	5,876	3,512	1,929	435	1,583	R	59.8%	32.8%	64.5%	35.5%
7,516	UNION	2,405	1,590	658	157	932	R	66.1%	27.4%	70.7%	29.3%
179,703	VANDERBURGH	50,310	26,372	22,305	1,633	4,067	R	52.4%	44.3%	54.2%	45.8%
16,212	VERMILLION	4,915	1,991	2,613	311	622	D	40.5%	53.2%	43.2%	56.8%
107,848	VIGO	28,595	12,443	14,771	1,381	2,328	D	43.5%	51.7%	45.7%	54.3%
32,888	WABASH	8,943	5,666	2,571	706	3,095	R	63.4%	28.7%	68.8%	31.2%
8,508	WARREN	2,582	1,530	896	156	634	R	59.3%	34.7%	63.1%	36.9%
59,689	WARRICK	20,639	11,771	8,207	661	3,564	R	57.0%	39.8%	58.9%	41.1%
28,262	WASHINGTON	8,318	4,844	2,975	499	1,869	R	58.2%	35.8%	62.0%	38.0%
68,917	WAYNE	16,497	9,602	5,386	1,509	4,216	R	58.2%	32.6%	64.1%	35.9%
27,636	WELLS	9,495	6,401	2,471	623	3,930	R	67.4%	26.0%	72.1%	27.9%
24,643	WHITE	7,432	4,393	2,377	662	2,016	R	59.1%	32.0%	64.9%	35.1%
33,292	WHITLEY	10,674	6,869	3,105	700	3,764	R	64.4%	29.1%	68.9%	31.1%
6,483,802	TOTAL	1,744,481	952,116	697,775	94,590	254,341	R	54.6%	40.0%	57.7%	42.3%

INDIANA

HOUSE OF REPRESENTATIVES

CD	Year	Total Vote	Republican Vote	Republican Candidate	Democratic Vote	Democratic Candidate	Other Vote	Rep.-Dem. Plurality		Total Vote Rep.	Total Vote Dem.	Major Vote Rep.	Major Vote Dem.
1	2010	169,707	65,558	LEYVA, MARK J.	99,387	VISCLOSKY, PETER J.*	4,762	33,829	D	38.6%	58.6%	39.7%	60.3%
1	2008	282,022	76,647	LEYVA, MARK J.	199,954	VISCLOSKY, PETER J.*	5,421	123,307	D	27.2%	70.9%	27.7%	72.3%
1	2006	149,607	40,146	LEYVA, MARK J.	104,195	VISCLOSKY, PETER J.*	5,266	64,049	D	26.8%	69.6%	27.8%	72.2%
1	2004	261,264	82,858	LEYVA, MARK J.	178,406	VISCLOSKY, PETER J.*		95,548	D	31.7%	68.3%	31.7%	68.3%
1	2002	135,111	41,909	LEYVA, MARK J.	90,443	VISCLOSKY, PETER J.*	2,759	48,534	D	31.0%	66.9%	31.7%	68.3%
2	2010	189,591	88,803	WALORSKI, JACKIE	91,341	DONNELLY, JOSEPH S.*	9,447	2,538	D	46.8%	48.2%	49.3%	50.7%
2	2008	279,346	84,455	PUCKETT, LUKE WAYNE	187,416	DONNELLY, JOSEPH S.*	7,475	102,961	D	30.2%	67.1%	31.1%	68.9%
2	2006	191,861	88,300	CHOCOLA, CHRIS*	103,561	DONNELLY, JOSEPH S.		15,261	D	46.0%	54.0%	46.0%	54.0%
2	2004	259,355	140,496	CHOCOLA, CHRIS*	115,513	DONNELLY, JOSEPH S.	3,346	24,983	R	54.2%	44.5%	54.9%	45.1%
2	2002	188,458	95,081	CHOCOLA, CHRIS	86,253	THOMPSON, JILL LONG	7,124	8,828	R	50.5%	45.8%	52.4%	47.6%
3	2010	185,049	116,140	STUTZMAN, MARLIN A.	61,267	HAYHURST, THOMAS	7,642	54,873	R	62.8%	33.1%	65.5%	34.5%
3	2008	282,879	155,693	SOUDER, MARK*	112,309	MONTAGANO, MICHAEL A.	14,877	43,384	R	55.0%	39.7%	58.1%	41.9%
3	2006	175,778	95,421	SOUDER, MARK*	80,357	HAYHURST, THOMAS		15,064	R	54.3%	45.7%	54.3%	45.7%
3	2004	247,621	171,389	SOUDER, MARK*	76,232	PARRA, MARIA M.		95,157	R	69.2%	30.8%	69.2%	30.8%
3	2002	146,606	92,566	SOUDER, MARK*	50,509	RIGDON, JAY	3,531	42,057	R	63.1%	34.5%	64.7%	35.3%
4	2010	202,322	138,732	ROKITA, TODD	53,167	SANDERS, DAVID	10,423	85,565	R	68.6%	26.3%	72.3%	27.7%
4	2008	321,564	192,526	BUYER, STEVE*	129,038	ACKERSON, NELS		63,488	R	59.9%	40.1%	59.9%	40.1%
4	2006	178,043	111,057	BUYER, STEVE*	66,986	SANDERS, DAVID		44,071	R	62.4%	37.6%	62.4%	37.6%
4	2004	274,136	190,445	BUYER, STEVE*	77,574	SANDERS, DAVID	6,117	112,871	R	69.5%	28.3%	71.1%	28.9%
4	2002	158,008	112,760	BUYER, STEVE*	41,314	ABBOTT, BILL	3,934	71,446	R	71.4%	26.1%	73.2%	26.8%
5	2010	236,407	146,899	BURTON, DAN*	60,024	CRAWFORD, TIM	29,484	86,875	R	62.1%	25.4%	71.0%	29.0%
5	2008	358,062	234,705	BURTON, DAN*	123,357	RULEY, MARY ETTA		111,348	R	65.5%	34.5%	65.5%	34.5%
5	2006	204,929	133,118	BURTON, DAN*	64,362	CARR, KATHERINE FOX	7,449	68,756	R	65.0%	31.4%	67.4%	32.6%
5	2004	318,363	228,718	BURTON, DAN*	82,637	CARR, KATHERINE FOX	7,008	146,081	R	71.8%	26.0%	73.5%	26.5%
5	2002	179,855	129,442	BURTON, DAN*	45,283	CARR, KATHERINE FOX	5,130	84,159	R	72.0%	25.2%	74.1%	25.9%
6	2010	189,309	126,027	PENCE, MIKE*	56,647	WELSH, BARRY A.	6,635	69,380	R	66.6%	29.9%	69.0%	31.0%
6	2008	282,412	180,608	PENCE, MIKE*	94,265	WELSH, BARRY A.	7,539	86,343	R	64.0%	33.4%	65.7%	34.3%
6	2006	192,078	115,266	PENCE, MIKE*	76,812	WELSH, BARRY A.		38,454	R	60.0%	40.0%	60.0%	40.0%
6	2004	272,049	182,529	PENCE, MIKE*	85,123	FOX, MELINA ANN	4,397	97,406	R	67.1%	31.3%	68.2%	31.8%
6	2002	185,653	118,436	PENCE, MIKE*	63,871	FOX, MELINA ANN	3,346	54,565	R	63.8%	34.4%	65.0%	35.0%
7	2010	146,039	55,213	SCOTT, MARVIN B.	86,011	CARSON, ANDRE D.*	4,815	30,798	D	37.8%	58.9%	39.1%	60.9%
7	2008	265,299	92,645	CAMPO, GABRIELLE	172,650	CARSON, ANDRE D.*	4	80,005	D	34.9%	65.1%	34.9%	65.1%
7	2006	139,054	64,304	DICKERSON, ERIC	74,750	CARSON, JULIA*		10,446	D	46.2%	53.8%	46.2%	53.8%
7	2004	223,175	97,491	HORNING, ANDREW	121,303	CARSON, JULIA*	4,381	23,812	D	43.7%	54.4%	44.6%	55.4%
7	2002	145,840	64,379	McVEY, BROSE A.	77,478	CARSON, JULIA*	3,983	13,099	D	44.1%	53.1%	45.4%	54.6%
8	2010	203,763	117,259	BUCSHON, LARRY D.	76,265	VANHAAFTEN, W. TRENT	10,240	40,994	R	57.5%	37.4%	60.6%	39.4%
8	2008	291,462	102,769	GOODE, GREGORY J.	188,693	ELLSWORTH, BRAD*		85,924	D	35.3%	64.7%	35.3%	64.7%
8	2006	214,723	83,704	HOSTETTLER, JOHN*	131,019	ELLSWORTH, BRAD		47,315	D	39.0%	61.0%	39.0%	61.0%
8	2004	272,778	145,576	HOSTETTLER, JOHN*	121,522	JENNINGS, JON P.	5,680	24,054	R	53.4%	44.5%	54.5%	45.5%
8	2002	192,865	98,952	HOSTETTLER, JOHN*	88,763	HARTKE, BRYAN L.	5,150	10,189	R	51.3%	46.0%	52.7%	47.3%
9	2010	225,532	118,040	YOUNG, TODD	95,353	HILL, BARON P.*	12,139	22,687	R	52.3%	42.3%	55.3%	44.7%
9	2008	313,804	120,529	SODREL, MIKE	181,281	HILL, BARON P.*	11,994	60,752	D	38.4%	57.8%	39.9%	60.1%
9	2006	220,849	100,469	SODREL, MIKE*	110,454	HILL, BARON P.	9,926	9,985	D	45.5%	50.0%	47.6%	52.4%
9	2004	287,510	142,197	SODREL, MIKE	140,772	HILL, BARON P.*	4,541	1,425	R	49.5%	49.0%	50.3%	49.7%
9	2002	188,957	87,169	SODREL, MIKE	96,654	HILL, BARON P.*	5,134	9,485	D	46.1%	51.2%	47.4%	52.6%
TOTAL	2010	1,747,720	972,671		679,462		95,587	293,209	R	55.7%	38.9%	58.9%	41.1%
TOTAL	2008	2,676,850	1,240,577		1,388,963		47,310	148,386	D	46.3%	51.9%	47.2%	52.8%
TOTAL	2006	1,666,922	831,785		812,496		22,641	19,289	R	49.9%	48.7%	50.6%	49.4%
TOTAL	2004	2,416,251	1,381,699		999,082		35,470	382,617	R	57.2%	41.3%	58.0%	42.0%
TOTAL	2002	1,521,353	840,694		640,568		40,091	200,126	R	55.3%	42.1%	56.8%	43.2%

An asterisk (*) denotes incumbent.

GENERAL AND PRIMARY ELECTIONS

2010 GENERAL ELECTIONS

Senator	Other vote was 94,330 Libertarian (Rebecca Sink-Burris); 161 write-in (Jim Miller); 99 Independent write-in (Jack Rooney).
House	Other vote was:

CD 1	4,762 Libertarian (Jon Morris).
CD 2	9,447 Libertarian (Mark Vogel).
CD 3	7,631 Libertarian (Scott Wise); 10 Independent write-in (Tom Metzger); 1 Independent write-in (Wes Stephens).
CD 4	10,423 Libertarian (John Duncan).
CD 5	18,266 Libertarian (Richard "Chard" Reid); 11,218 Independent (Jesse C. Trueblood).
CD 6	6,635 Libertarian (Talmage "T.J." Thompson Jr.)
CD 7	4,815 Libertarian (Dav Wilson).
CD 8	10,240 Libertarian (John Cunningham).
CD 9	12,070 Libertarian (Greg "No Bull" Knott); 69 Independent write-in (Jerry R. Lucas).

2010 PRIMARY ELECTIONS

Primary	May 4, 2010	**Registration** (as of May 4, 2010)	4,277,762		No Party Registration

Primary Type   Open—Any registered voter could participate in the primary of either party, although they could be challenged based on party affiliation. When a voter is challenged, they must execute a statement saying that they voted for a majority of the party's candidates in the previous general election. If they did not vote in the previous general election, they must indicate that they will vote for a majority of the party's candidates in the next general election.

INDIANA

GENERAL AND PRIMARY ELECTIONS

	REPUBLICAN PRIMARIES			DEMOCRATIC PRIMARIES		
Senator	Dan Coats	217,225	39.5%	*No Democratic candidate filed for the primary. Brad Ellsworth was subsequently named the nominee at a post-primary meeting of the Democratic state central committee.*		
	Marlin A. Stutzman	160,981	29.2%			
	John N. Hostettler	124,494	22.6%			
	Don Bates Jr.	24,664	4.5%			
	Richard Behney	23,005	4.2%			
	TOTAL	*550,369*				
Congressional District 1	Mark J. Levya	6,385	24.7%	Peter J. Visclosky*	41,982	100.0%
	Peter Lindemulder III	5,783	22.3%			
	Eric L. Olson	3,482	13.4%			
	Robert Pastore	3,469	13.4%			
	Adam A. Dombkowski	3,320	12.8%			

INDIANA

GENERAL AND PRIMARY ELECTIONS

		REPUBLICAN PRIMARIES		DEMOCRATIC PRIMARIES		
	Ric Holtz	1,505	5.8%			
	Jayson Reeves	1,194	4.6%			
	Michael Petyo	754	2.9%			
	TOTAL	*25,892*				
Congressional District 2	Jackie Walorski	29,118	60.8%	Joseph S. Donnelly*	26,659	100.0%
	Jack Edward Jordan	13,576	28.4%			
	Martin A. Dolan	3,762	7.9%			
	Tony Hvfvgpd Zirkle	1,415	3.0%			
	TOTAL	*47,871*				
Congressional District 3	Mark Souder*	38,441	47.8%	Thomas Hayhurst	8,759	79.8%
	Bob Thomas	27,068	33.6%	Thomas Allen Schrader	2,212	20.2%
	Phillip J. Troyer	12,851	16.0%			
	Gregory Dickman	2,127	2.6%			
	TOTAL	*80,487*		*TOTAL*	*10,971*	
Congressional District 4	Todd Rokita	36,411	42.4%	David Sanders	7,615	51.5%
	Brandt Hershman	14,712	17.1%	Tara E. Nelson	4,253	28.8%
	R. Michael Young	6,991	8.1%	Mark Powell	2,905	19.7%
	Eric L. Wathen	5,493	6.4%			
	LaRon "firefighter LaRon" Keith	3,549	4.1%			
	Charles E. Henderson	3,531	4.1%			
	Jon Acton	3,444	4.0%			
	Cheryl Denise Allen	2,972	3.5%			
	Mike Campbell	2,407	2.8%			
	James T. Hass	2,161	2.5%			
	Phillip J. "PJ" Steffen	1,737	2.0%			
	Mark Seitz	1,562	1.8%			
	Daniel L. Dunham	981	1.1%			
	TOTAL	*85,951*		*TOTAL*	*14,773*	
Congressional District 5	Dan Burton*	32,769	29.7%	Tim Crawford	9,937	60.9%
	Luke Messer	30,502	27.6%	Nasser Hanna	6,386	39.1%
	John McGoff	20,679	18.7%			
	Michael B. Murphy	9,805	8.9%			
	Brose McVey	9,372	8.5%			
	Andy Lyons	3,964	3.6%			
	Ann B. Adcook	3,352	3.0%			
	TOTAL	*110,443*		*TOTAL*	*16,323*	
Congressional District 6	Mike Pence*	61,381	100.0%	Barry A. Welsh	17,479	63.0%
				George Thomas Holland	10,287	37.0%
				TOTAL	*27,766*	
Congressional District 7	Marvin B. Scott	11,193	44.3%	Andre D. Carson*	26,364	89.1%
	Carlos May	9,325	36.9%	Bob Kern	2,150	7.3%
	Wayne E. Harmon	4,728	18.7%	Carl Kakasuleff	737	2.5%
				Pierre Quincy Pullins	354	1.2%
	TOTAL	*25,246*		*TOTAL*	*29,605*	
Congressional District 8	Larry D. Bucshon	16,262	32.7%	W. Trent VanHaaften	31,685	100.0%
	Kristi Risk	14,273	28.7%			
	John Lee Smith	4,715	9.5%			
	Dan Stockton	4,697	9.5%			
	Steve Westell	4,324	8.7%			
	John K. Snyder	2,523	5.1%			
	Bud Bernitt	1,469	3.0%			
	Billy J. Mahoney	1,410	2.8%			
	TOTAL	*49,673*				

INDIANA

GENERAL AND PRIMARY ELECTIONS

		REPUBLICAN PRIMARIES			DEMOCRATIC PRIMARIES		
Congressional	Todd Young	19,141	34.6%	Baron P. Hill*	37,493	69.6%
District 9	Travis Hankins	17,909	32.3%	John R. Bottorff	7,628	14.2%
	Mike Sodrel	16,868	30.5%	Carol Johnson-Smith	4,679	8.7%
	Rick Warren	1,453	2.6%	James R. McClure Jr.	2,399	4.5%
				Lendall B. Terry	1,685	3.1%
	TOTAL	*55,371*		*TOTAL*	*53,884*	

An asterisk (*) denotes incumbent.

IOWA

Congressional districts first established for elections held in 2002
5 members

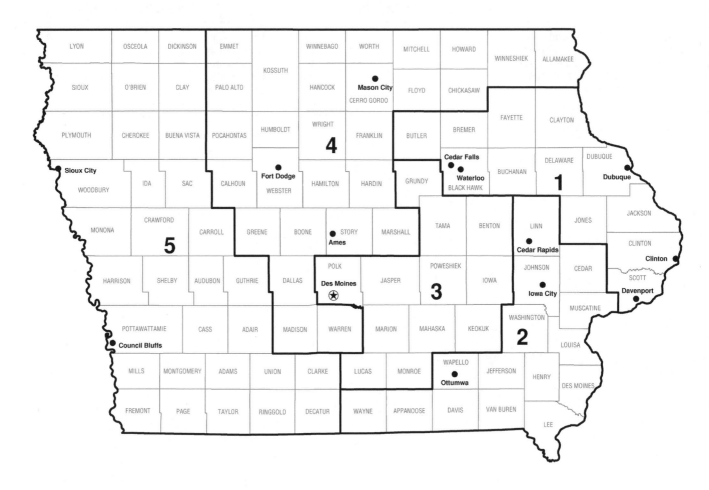

IOWA

GOVERNOR
Terry E. Branstad (R). Elected 2010 to a four-year term. Previously elected 1994, 1990, 1986, 1982.

SENATORS (1 Democrat, 1 Republican)
Charles E. Grassley (R). Reelected 2010 to a six-year term. Previously elected 2004, 1998, 1992, 1986, 1980.

Tom Harkin (D). Reelected 2008 to a six-year term. Previously elected 2002, 1996, 1990, 1984.

REPRESENTATIVES (3 Democrats, 2 Republicans)

1. Bruce Braley (D)
2. Dave Loebsack (D)
3. Leonard L. Boswell (D)
4. Tom Latham (R)
5. Steve King (R)

POSTWAR VOTE FOR PRESIDENT

Year	Total Vote	Republican Vote	Republican Candidate	Democratic Vote	Democratic Candidate	Other Vote	Rep.-Dem. Plurality	Total Vote Rep.	Total Vote Dem.	Major Vote Rep.	Major Vote Dem.
2008	1,537,123	682,379	McCain, John	828,940	Obama, Barack	25,804	146,561 D	44.4%	53.9%	45.2%	54.8%
2004	1,506,908	751,957	Bush, George W.	741,898	Kerry, John	13,053	10,059 R	49.9%	49.2%	50.3%	49.7%
2000**	1,315,563	634,373	Bush, George W.	638,517	Gore, Al	42,673	4,144 D	48.2%	48.5%	49.8%	50.2%
1996**	1,234,075	492,644	Dole, Bob	620,258	Clinton, Bill	121,173	127,614 D	39.9%	50.3%	44.3%	55.7%
1992**	1,354,607	504,891	Bush, George	586,353	Clinton, Bill	263,363	81,462 D	37.3%	43.3%	46.3%	53.7%
1988	1,225,614	545,355	Bush, George	670,557	Dukakis, Michael S.	9,702	125,202 D	44.5%	54.7%	44.9%	55.1%
1984	1,319,805	703,088	Reagan, Ronald	605,620	Mondale, Walter F.	11,097	97,468 R	53.3%	45.9%	53.7%	46.3%
1980**	1,317,661	676,026	Reagan, Ronald	508,672	Carter, Jimmy	132,963	167,354 R	51.3%	38.6%	57.1%	42.9%
1976	1,279,306	632,863	Ford, Gerald R.	619,931	Carter, Jimmy	26,512	12,932 R	49.5%	48.5%	50.5%	49.5%
1972	1,225,944	706,207	Nixon, Richard M.	496,206	McGovern, George S.	23,531	210,001 R	57.6%	40.5%	58.7%	41.3%
1968**	1,167,931	619,106	Nixon, Richard M.	476,699	Humphrey, Hubert H.	72,126	142,407 R	53.0%	40.8%	56.5%	43.5%
1964	1,184,539	449,148	Goldwater, Barry M.	733,030	Johnson, Lyndon B.	2,361	283,882 D	37.9%	61.9%	38.0%	62.0%
1960	1,273,810	722,381	Nixon, Richard M.	550,565	Kennedy, John F.	864	171,816 R	56.7%	43.2%	56.7%	43.3%
1956	1,234,564	729,187	Eisenhower, Dwight D.	501,858	Stevenson, Adlai E.	3,519	227,329 R	59.1%	40.7%	59.2%	40.8%
1952	1,268,773	808,906	Eisenhower, Dwight D.	451,513	Stevenson, Adlai E.	8,354	357,393 R	63.8%	35.6%	64.2%	35.8%
1948	1,038,264	494,018	Dewey, Thomas E.	522,380	Truman, Harry S.	21,866	28,362 D	47.6%	50.3%	48.6%	51.4%

**In past elections, the other vote included: 2000 - 29,374 Green (Ralph Nader); 1996 - 105,159 Reform (Ross Perot); 1992 - 253,468 Independent (Perot); 1980 - 115,633 Independent (John Anderson); 1968 - 66,422 American Independent (George Wallace).

IOWA

POSTWAR VOTE FOR GOVERNOR

Year	Total Vote	Republican Vote	Republican Candidate	Democratic Vote	Democratic Candidate	Other Vote	Rep.-Dem. Plurality	Total Vote Rep.	Total Vote Dem.	Major Vote Rep.	Major Vote Dem.
2010	1,122,013	592,494	Branstad, Terry E.	484,798	Culver, Chet	44,721	107,696 R	52.8%	43.2%	55.0%	45.0%
2006	1,053,255	467,425	Nussle, Jim	569,021	Culver, Chet	16,809	101,596 D	44.4%	54.0%	45.1%	54.9%
2002	1,025,802	456,612	Gross, Doug	540,449	Vilsack, Tom	28,741	83,837 D	44.5%	52.7%	45.8%	54.2%
1998	956,418	444,787	Lightfoot, Jim Ross	500,231	Vilsack, Tom	11,400	55,444 D	46.5%	52.3%	47.1%	52.9%
1994	997,248	566,395	Branstad, Terry E.	414,453	Campbell, Bonnie J.	16,400	151,942 R	56.8%	41.6%	57.7%	42.3%
1990	976,483	591,852	Branstad, Terry E.	379,372	Avenson, Donald D.	5,259	212,480 R	60.6%	38.9%	60.9%	39.1%
1986	910,623	472,712	Branstad, Terry E.	436,987	Junkins, Lowell L.	924	35,725 R	51.9%	48.0%	52.0%	48.0%
1982	1,038,229	548,313	Branstad, Terry E.	483,291	Conlin, Roxanne	6,625	65,022 R	52.8%	46.5%	53.2%	46.8%
1978	843,190	491,713	Ray, Robert	345,519	Fitzgerald, Jerome D.	5,958	146,194 R	58.3%	41.0%	58.7%	41.3%
1974**	920,458	534,518	Ray, Robert	377,553	Schaben, James, F.	8,387	156,965 R	58.1%	41.0%	58.6%	41.4%
1972	1,210,222	707,177	Ray, Robert	487,282	Franzenburg, Paul	15,763	219,895 R	58.4%	40.3%	59.2%	40.8%
1970	791,241	403,394	Ray, Robert	368,911	Fulton, Robert	18,936	34,483 R	51.0%	46.6%	52.2%	47.8%
1968	1,136,489	614,328	Ray, Robert	521,216	Franzenburg, Paul	945	93,112 R	54.1%	45.9%	54.1%	45.9%
1966	893,175	394,518	Murray, William G.	494,259	Hughes, Harold E.	4,398	99,741 D	44.2%	55.3%	44.4%	55.6%
1964	1,167,734	365,131	Hultman, Evan	794,610	Hughes, Harold E.	7,993	429,479 D	31.3%	68.0%	31.5%	68.5%
1962	819,854	388,955	Erbe, Norman A.	430,899	Hughes, Harold E.		41,944 D	47.4%	52.6%	47.4%	52.6%
1960	1,237,089	645,026	Erbe, Norman A.	592,063	McManus, E. J.		52,963 R	52.1%	47.9%	52.1%	47.9%
1958	859,095	394,071	Murray, William G.	465,024	Loveless, Herschel C.		70,953 D	45.9%	54.1%	45.9%	54.1%
1956	1,204,235	587,383	Hoegh, Leo A.	616,852	Loveless, Herschel C.		29,469 D	48.8%	51.2%	48.8%	51.2%
1954	848,592	435,944	Hoegh, Leo A.	410,255	Herring, Clyde E.	2,393	25,689 R	51.4%	48.3%	51.5%	48.5%
1952	1,230,045	638,388	Beardsley, William	587,671	Loveless, Herschel C.	3,986	50,717 R	51.9%	47.8%	52.1%	47.9%
1950	857,213	506,642	Beardsley, William	347,176	Gillette, Lester S.	3,395	159,466 R	59.1%	40.5%	59.3%	40.7%
1948	994,833	553,900	Beardsley, William	434,432	Switzer, Carroll O.	6,501	119,468 R	55.7%	43.7%	56.0%	44.0%
1946	631,681	362,592	Blue, Robert D.	266,190	Miles, Frank	2,899	96,402 R	57.4%	42.1%	57.7%	42.3%

**The term of office of Iowa's Governor was increased from two to four years effective with the 1974 election.

POSTWAR VOTE FOR SENATOR

Year	Total Vote	Republican Vote	Republican Candidate	Democratic Vote	Democratic Candidate	Other Vote	Rep.-Dem. Plurality	Total Vote Rep.	Total Vote Dem.	Major Vote Rep.	Major Vote Dem.
2010	1,116,063	718,215	Grassley, Charles E.	371,686	Conlin, Roxanne	26,162	346,529 R	64.4%	33.3%	65.9%	34.1%
2008	1,502,918	560,006	Reed, Christopher	941,665	Harkin, Tom	1,247	381,659 D	37.3%	62.7%	37.3%	62.7%
2004	1,479,228	1,038,175	Grassley, Charles E.	412,365	Small, Arthur	28,688	625,810 R	70.2%	27.9%	71.6%	28.4%
2002	1,023,075	447,892	Ganske, Greg	554,278	Harkin, Tom	20,905	106,386 D	43.8%	54.2%	44.7%	55.3%
1998	947,907	648,480	Grassley, Charles E.	289,049	Osterberg, David	10,378	359,431 R	68.4%	30.5%	69.2%	30.8%
1996	1,224,054	571,807	Lightfoot, Jim Ross	634,166	Harkin, Tom	18,081	62,359 D	46.7%	51.8%	47.4%	52.6%
1992	1,292,494	899,761	Grassley, Charles E.	351,561	Lloyd-Jones, Jean	41,172	548,200 R	69.6%	27.2%	71.9%	28.1%
1990	983,933	446,869	Tauke, Tom	535,974	Harkin, Tom	1,089	89,106 D	45.4%	54.5%	45.5%	54.5%
1986	891,762	588,880	Grassley, Charles E.	299,406	Roehrick, John P.	3,476	289,474 R	66.0%	33.6%	66.3%	33.7%
1984	1,292,700	564,381	Jepsen, Roger W.	716,883	Harkin, Tom	11,436	152,502 D	43.7%	55.5%	44.0%	56.0%
1980	1,277,034	683,014	Grassley, Charles E.	581,545	Culver, John C.	12,475	101,469 R	53.5%	45.5%	54.0%	46.0%
1978	824,654	421,598	Jepsen, Roger W.	395,066	Clark, Richard	7,990	26,532 R	51.1%	47.9%	51.6%	48.4%
1974	889,561	420,546	Stanley, David M.	462,947	Culver, John C.	6,068	42,401 D	47.3%	52.0%	47.6%	52.4%
1972	1,203,333	530,525	Miller, Jack	662,637	Clark, Richard	10,171	132,112 D	44.1%	55.1%	44.5%	55.5%
1968	1,144,086	568,469	Stanley, David M.	574,884	Hughes, Harold E.	733	6,415 D	49.7%	50.2%	49.7%	50.3%
1966	857,496	522,339	Miller, Jack	324,114	Smith, E. B.	11,043	198,225 R	60.9%	37.8%	61.7%	38.3%
1962	807,972	431,364	Hickenlooper, Bourke B.	376,602	Smith, E. B.	6	54,762 R	53.4%	46.6%	53.4%	46.6%
1960	1,237,582	642,463	Miller, Jack	595,119	Loveless, Herschel C.		47,344 R	51.9%	48.1%	51.9%	48.1%
1956	1,178,655	635,499	Hickenlooper, Bourke B.	543,156	Evans, R. M.		92,343 R	53.9%	46.1%	53.9%	46.1%
1954	847,355	442,409	Martin, Thomas E.	402,712	Gillette, Guy	2,234	39,697 R	52.2%	47.5%	52.3%	47.7%
1950	858,523	470,613	Hickenlooper, Bourke B.	383,766	Loveland, A. J.	4,144	86,847 R	54.8%	44.7%	55.1%	44.9%
1948	1,000,412	415,778	Wilson, George A.	578,226	Gillette, Guy	6,408	162,448 D	41.6%	57.8%	41.8%	58.2%

IOWA

GOVERNOR 2010

2010 Census Population	County	Total Vote	Republican	Democratic	Other	Rep.-Dem. Plurality	Percentage			
							Total Vote		Major Vote	
							Rep.	Dem.	Rep.	Dem.
7,682	ADAIR	3,090	1,799	1,147	144	652 R	58.2%	37.1%	61.1%	38.9%
4,029	ADAMS	1,756	1,077	571	108	506 R	61.3%	32.5%	65.4%	34.6%
14,330	ALLAMAKEE	5,337	2,966	2,212	159	754 R	55.6%	41.4%	57.3%	42.7%
12,887	APPANOOSE	4,622	2,809	1,553	260	1,256 R	60.8%	33.6%	64.4%	35.6%
6,119	AUDUBON	2,752	1,592	1,064	96	528 R	57.8%	38.7%	59.9%	40.1%
26,076	BENTON	10,026	5,534	4,100	392	1,434 R	55.2%	40.9%	57.4%	42.6%
131,090	BLACK HAWK	45,353	21,355	22,720	1,278	1,365 D	47.1%	50.1%	48.5%	51.5%
26,306	BOONE	10,791	5,537	4,718	536	819 R	51.3%	43.7%	54.0%	46.0%
24,276	BREMER	9,860	5,525	4,088	247	1,437 R	56.0%	41.5%	57.5%	42.5%
20,958	BUCHANAN	7,950	3,889	3,788	273	101 R	48.9%	47.6%	50.7%	49.3%
20,260	BUENA VISTA	5,613	3,633	1,741	239	1,892 R	64.7%	31.0%	67.6%	32.4%
14,867	BUTLER	5,699	3,485	1,969	245	1,516 R	61.2%	34.5%	63.9%	36.1%
9,670	CALHOUN	4,018	2,366	1,432	220	934 R	58.9%	35.6%	62.3%	37.7%
20,816	CARROLL	8,316	4,642	3,410	264	1,232 R	55.8%	41.0%	57.7%	42.3%
13,956	CASS	5,240	3,424	1,616	200	1,808 R	65.3%	30.8%	67.9%	32.1%
18,499	CEDAR	7,096	3,870	3,005	221	865 R	54.5%	42.3%	56.3%	43.7%
44,151	CERRO GORDO	17,382	8,470	8,369	543	101 R	48.7%	48.1%	50.3%	49.7%
12,072	CHEROKEE	4,746	3,003	1,575	168	1,428 R	63.3%	33.2%	65.6%	34.4%
12,439	CHICKASAW	4,961	2,555	2,230	176	325 R	51.5%	45.0%	53.4%	46.6%
9,286	CLARKE	3,723	2,195	1,318	210	877 R	59.0%	35.4%	62.5%	37.5%
16,667	CLAY	5,792	3,831	1,796	165	2,035 R	66.1%	31.0%	68.1%	31.9%
18,129	CLAYTON	7,008	3,662	3,096	250	566 R	52.3%	44.2%	54.2%	45.8%
49,116	CLINTON	17,286	8,524	8,204	558	320 R	49.3%	47.5%	51.0%	49.0%
17,096	CRAWFORD	5,140	3,309	1,669	162	1,640 R	64.4%	32.5%	66.5%	33.5%
66,135	DALLAS	25,581	15,103	9,242	1,236	5,861 R	59.0%	36.1%	62.0%	38.0%
8,753	DAVIS	3,109	1,698	1,185	226	513 R	54.6%	38.1%	58.9%	41.1%
8,457	DECATUR	2,915	1,685	1,074	156	611 R	57.8%	36.8%	61.1%	38.9%
17,764	DELAWARE	6,979	3,905	2,881	193	1,024 R	56.0%	41.3%	57.5%	42.5%
40,325	DES MOINES	14,951	7,219	7,276	456	57 D	48.3%	48.7%	49.8%	50.2%
16,667	DICKINSON	7,275	4,600	2,521	154	2,079 R	63.2%	34.7%	64.6%	35.4%
93,653	DUBUQUE	33,910	16,237	16,990	683	753 D	47.9%	50.1%	48.9%	51.1%
10,302	EMMET	3,571	2,113	1,342	116	771 R	59.2%	37.6%	61.2%	38.8%
20,880	FAYETTE	7,939	4,136	3,546	257	590 R	52.1%	44.7%	53.8%	46.2%
16,303	FLOYD	6,082	2,900	2,963	219	63 D	47.7%	48.7%	49.5%	50.5%
10,680	FRANKLIN	3,846	2,297	1,329	220	968 R	59.7%	34.6%	63.3%	36.7%
7,441	FREMONT	2,662	1,646	939	77	707 R	61.8%	35.3%	63.7%	36.3%
9,336	GREENE	3,801	2,088	1,532	181	556 R	54.9%	40.3%	57.7%	42.3%
12,453	GRUNDY	5,285	3,446	1,568	271	1,878 R	65.2%	29.7%	68.7%	31.3%
10,954	GUTHRIE	4,582	2,591	1,688	303	903 R	56.5%	36.8%	60.6%	39.4%
15,673	HAMILTON	6,234	3,450	2,480	304	970 R	55.3%	39.8%	58.2%	41.8%
11,341	HANCOCK	4,678	2,960	1,521	197	1,439 R	63.3%	32.5%	66.1%	33.9%
17,534	HARDIN	6,662	3,842	2,436	384	1,406 R	57.7%	36.6%	61.2%	38.8%
14,928	HARRISON	5,296	3,370	1,770	156	1,600 R	63.6%	33.4%	65.6%	34.4%
20,145	HENRY	6,870	4,209	2,396	265	1,813 R	61.3%	34.9%	63.7%	36.3%
9,566	HOWARD	3,438	1,693	1,636	109	57 R	49.2%	47.6%	50.9%	49.1%
9,815	HUMBOLDT	3,939	2,373	1,397	169	976 R	60.2%	35.5%	62.9%	37.1%
7,089	IDA	2,683	1,852	742	89	1,110 R	69.0%	27.7%	71.4%	28.6%
16,355	IOWA	6,561	3,693	2,516	352	1,177 R	56.3%	38.3%	59.5%	40.5%
19,848	JACKSON	7,476	3,770	3,451	255	319 R	50.4%	46.2%	52.2%	47.8%
36,842	JASPER	15,017	7,727	6,351	939	1,376 R	51.5%	42.3%	54.9%	45.1%

IOWA

GOVERNOR 2010

2010 Census Population	County	Total Vote	Republican	Democratic	Other	Rep.-Dem. Plurality	Percentage Total Vote Rep.	Dem.	Major Vote Rep.	Dem.
16,843	JEFFERSON	6,729	2,949	3,412	368	463 D	43.8%	50.7%	46.4%	53.6%
130,882	JOHNSON	51,725	17,967	31,862	1,896	13,895 D	34.7%	61.6%	36.1%	63.9%
20,638	JONES	7,735	3,971	3,471	293	500 R	51.3%	44.9%	53.4%	46.6%
10,511	KEOKUK	3,914	2,387	1,276	251	1,111 R	61.0%	32.6%	65.2%	34.8%
15,543	KOSSUTH	6,768	4,057	2,470	241	1,587 R	59.9%	36.5%	62.2%	37.8%
35,862	LEE	11,865	5,600	5,781	484	181 D	47.2%	48.7%	49.2%	50.8%
211,226	LINN	80,245	37,222	40,739	2,284	3,517 D	46.4%	50.8%	47.7%	52.3%
11,387	LOUISA	3,399	2,013	1,246	140	767 R	59.2%	36.7%	61.8%	38.2%
8,898	LUCAS	3,580	2,063	1,295	222	768 R	57.6%	36.2%	61.4%	38.6%
11,581	LYON	5,054	4,054	889	111	3,165 R	80.2%	17.6%	82.0%	18.0%
15,679	MADISON	6,811	3,894	2,444	473	1,450 R	57.2%	35.9%	61.4%	38.6%
22,381	MAHASKA	8,441	5,430	2,449	562	2,981 R	64.3%	29.0%	68.9%	31.1%
33,309	MARION	13,040	7,946	4,278	816	3,668 R	60.9%	32.8%	65.0%	35.0%
40,648	MARSHALL	14,303	7,116	6,344	843	772 R	49.8%	44.4%	52.9%	47.1%
15,059	MILLS	4,884	3,111	1,621	152	1,490 R	63.7%	33.2%	65.7%	34.3%
10,776	MITCHELL	4,512	2,622	1,783	107	839 R	58.1%	39.5%	59.5%	40.5%
9,243	MONONA	3,550	2,208	1,245	97	963 R	62.2%	35.1%	63.9%	36.1%
7,970	MONROE	2,903	1,650	1,125	128	525 R	56.8%	38.8%	59.5%	40.5%
10,740	MONTGOMERY	3,675	2,565	1,018	92	1,547 R	69.8%	27.7%	71.6%	28.4%
42,745	MUSCATINE	13,326	7,057	5,817	452	1,240 R	53.0%	43.7%	54.8%	45.2%
14,398	O'BRIEN	5,504	4,143	1,214	147	2,929 R	75.3%	22.1%	77.3%	22.7%
6,462	OSCEOLA	2,444	1,873	509	62	1,364 R	76.6%	20.8%	78.6%	21.4%
15,932	PAGE	4,836	3,526	1,191	119	2,335 R	72.9%	24.6%	74.8%	25.2%
9,421	PALO ALTO	3,909	2,270	1,455	184	815 R	58.1%	37.2%	60.9%	39.1%
24,986	PLYMOUTH	8,827	6,452	2,139	236	4,313 R	73.1%	24.2%	75.1%	24.9%
7,310	POCAHONTAS	3,037	1,874	1,008	155	866 R	61.7%	33.2%	65.0%	35.0%
430,640	POLK	160,960	76,772	76,234	7,954	538 R	47.7%	47.4%	50.2%	49.8%
93,158	POTTAWATTAMIE	26,611	15,963	9,743	905	6,220 R	60.0%	36.6%	62.1%	37.9%
18,914	POWESHIEK	7,490	3,715	3,395	380	320 R	49.6%	45.3%	52.3%	47.7%
5,131	RINGGOLD	2,151	1,271	790	90	481 R	59.1%	36.7%	61.7%	38.3%
10,350	SAC	3,937	2,471	1,292	174	1,179 R	62.8%	32.8%	65.7%	34.3%
165,224	SCOTT	56,713	29,061	26,078	1,574	2,983 R	51.2%	46.0%	52.7%	47.3%
12,167	SHELBY	4,181	2,913	1,127	141	1,786 R	69.7%	27.0%	72.1%	27.9%
33,704	SIOUX	12,823	11,238	1,385	200	9,853 R	87.6%	10.8%	89.0%	11.0%
89,542	STORY	32,337	14,729	15,795	1,813	1,066 D	45.5%	48.8%	48.3%	51.7%
17,767	TAMA	6,505	3,324	2,804	377	520 R	51.1%	43.1%	54.2%	45.8%
6,317	TAYLOR	2,539	1,607	834	98	773 R	63.3%	32.8%	65.8%	34.2%
12,534	UNION	4,804	2,790	1,800	214	990 R	58.1%	37.5%	60.8%	39.2%
7,570	VAN BUREN	2,883	1,628	1,065	190	563 R	56.5%	36.9%	60.5%	39.5%
35,625	WAPELLO	11,800	5,611	5,501	688	110 R	47.6%	46.6%	50.5%	49.5%
46,225	WARREN	20,204	10,653	8,431	1,120	2,222 R	52.7%	41.7%	55.8%	44.2%
21,704	WASHINGTON	8,754	4,935	3,391	428	1,544 R	56.4%	38.7%	59.3%	40.7%
6,403	WAYNE	2,338	1,461	756	121	705 R	62.5%	32.3%	65.9%	34.1%
38,013	WEBSTER	13,176	7,010	5,596	570	1,414 R	53.2%	42.5%	55.6%	44.4%
10,866	WINNEBAGO	4,447	2,802	1,527	118	1,275 R	63.0%	34.3%	64.7%	35.3%
21,056	WINNESHIEK	8,213	4,271	3,723	219	548 R	52.0%	45.3%	53.4%	46.6%
102,172	WOODBURY	31,133	17,990	12,079	1,064	5,911 R	57.8%	38.8%	59.8%	40.2%
7,598	WORTH	3,199	1,659	1,452	88	207 R	51.9%	45.4%	53.3%	46.7%
13,229	WRIGHT	4,900	2,945	1,756	199	1,189 R	60.1%	35.8%	62.6%	37.4%
3,046,355	TOTAL	1,122,013	592,494	484,798	44,721	107,696 R	52.8%	43.2%	55.0%	45.0%

IOWA

SENATOR 2010

2010 Census Population	County	Total Vote	Republican	Democratic	Other	Rep.-Dem. Plurality		Percentage Total Vote Rep.	Dem.	Major Vote Rep.	Dem.
7,682	ADAIR	3,061	2,220	778	63	1,442	R	72.5%	25.4%	74.0%	26.0%
4,029	ADAMS	1,727	1,234	442	51	792	R	71.5%	25.6%	73.6%	26.4%
14,330	ALLAMAKEE	5,260	3,584	1,416	260	2,168	R	68.1%	26.9%	71.7%	28.3%
12,887	APPANOOSE	4,597	3,050	1,398	149	1,652	R	66.3%	30.4%	68.6%	31.4%
6,119	AUDUBON	2,714	1,908	747	59	1,161	R	70.3%	27.5%	71.9%	28.1%
26,076	BENTON	9,981	6,936	2,796	249	4,140	R	69.5%	28.0%	71.3%	28.7%
131,090	BLACK HAWK	45,013	27,099	17,114	800	9,985	R	60.2%	38.0%	61.3%	38.7%
26,306	BOONE	10,720	7,014	3,457	249	3,557	R	65.4%	32.2%	67.0%	33.0%
24,276	BREMER	9,822	6,811	2,815	196	3,996	R	69.3%	28.7%	70.8%	29.2%
20,958	BUCHANAN	7,890	5,291	2,446	153	2,845	R	67.1%	31.0%	68.4%	31.6%
20,260	BUENA VISTA	5,590	4,237	1,239	114	2,998	R	75.8%	22.2%	77.4%	22.6%
14,867	BUTLER	5,704	4,339	1,258	107	3,081	R	76.1%	22.1%	77.5%	22.5%
9,670	CALHOUN	4,006	2,971	964	71	2,007	R	74.2%	24.1%	75.5%	24.5%
20,816	CARROLL	8,210	5,731	2,312	167	3,419	R	69.8%	28.2%	71.3%	28.7%
13,956	CASS	5,196	3,930	1,154	112	2,776	R	75.6%	22.2%	77.3%	22.7%
18,499	CEDAR	7,017	4,660	2,148	209	2,512	R	66.4%	30.6%	68.4%	31.6%
44,151	CERRO GORDO	17,227	10,421	6,440	366	3,981	R	60.5%	37.4%	61.8%	38.2%
12,072	CHEROKEE	4,724	3,632	1,001	91	2,631	R	76.9%	21.2%	78.4%	21.6%
12,439	CHICKASAW	4,939	3,331	1,508	100	1,823	R	67.4%	30.5%	68.8%	31.2%
9,286	CLARKE	3,693	2,551	1,041	101 0	1,510	R	69.1%	28.2%	71.0%	29.0%
16,667	CLAY	5,771	4,254	1,369	148	2,885	R	73.7%	23.7%	75.7%	24.3%
18,129	CLAYTON	6,951	4,632	2,106	213	2,526	R	66.6%	30.3%	68.7%	31.3%
49,116	CLINTON	17,208	10,189	6,600	419	3,589	R	59.2%	38.4%	60.7%	39.3%
17,096	CRAWFORD	5,078	3,749	1,201	128	2,548	R	73.8%	23.7%	75.7%	24.3%
66,135	DALLAS	25,473	18,126	6,736	611 0	11,390	R	71.2%	26.4%	72.9%	27.1%
8,753	DAVIS	3,079	2,042	907	130	1,135	R	66.3%	29.5%	69.2%	30.8%
8,457	DECATUR	2,875	1,937	846	92	1,091	R	67.4%	29.4%	69.6%	30.4%
17,764	DELAWARE	6,967	5,048	1,734	185	3,314	R	72.5%	24.9%	74.4%	25.6%
40,325	DES MOINES	14,858	8,083	6,365	410	1,718	R	54.4%	42.8%	55.9%	44.1%
16,667	DICKINSON	7,224	5,191	1,887	146	3,304	R	71.9%	26.1%	73.3%	26.7%
93,653	DUBUQUE	33,470	19,634	12,941	895	6,693	R	58.7%	38.7%	60.3%	39.7%
10,302	EMMET	3,538	2,419	1,050	69	1,369	R	68.4%	29.7%	69.7%	30.3%
20,880	FAYETTE	7,893	5,265	2,466	162	2,799	R	66.7%	31.2%	68.1%	31.9%
16,303	FLOYD	6,059	3,793	2,126	140	1,667	R	62.6%	35.1%	64.1%	35.9%
10,680	FRANKLIN	3,833	2,859	891	83	1,968	R	74.6%	23.2%	76.2%	23.8%
7,441	FREMONT	2,621	1,949	595	77	1,354	R	74.4%	22.7%	76.6%	23.4%
9,336	GREENE	3,773	2,610	1,073	90	1,537	R	69.2%	28.4%	70.9%	29.1%
12,453	GRUNDY	5,289	4,191	990	108	3,201	R	79.2%	18.7%	80.9%	19.1%
10,954	GUTHRIE	4,566	3,181	1,238	147	1,943	R	69.7%	27.1%	72.0%	28.0%
15,673	HAMILTON	6,205	4,226	1,856	123	2,370	R	68.1%	29.9%	69.5%	30.5%
11,341	HANCOCK	4,637	3,384	1,144	109	2,240	R	73.0%	24.7%	74.7%	25.3%
17,534	HARDIN	6,638	4,760	1,748	130	3,012	R	71.7%	26.3%	73.1%	26.9%
14,928	HARRISON	5,255	3,874	1,240	141	2,634	R	73.7%	23.6%	75.8%	24.2%
20,145	HENRY	6,811	4,723	1,916	172	2,807	R	69.3%	28.1%	71.1%	28.9%
9,566	HOWARD	3,388	2,165	1,154	69	1,011	R	63.9%	34.1%	65.2%	34.8%
9,815	HUMBOLDT	3,922	2,966	869	87	2,097	R	75.6%	22.2%	77.3%	22.7%
7,089	IDA	2,669	2,194	422	53	1,772	R	82.2%	15.8%	83.9%	16.1%
16,355	IOWA	6,530	4,673	1,673	184	3,000	R	71.6%	25.6%	73.6%	26.4%
19,848	JACKSON	7,392	4,561	2,605	226	1,956	R	61.7%	35.2%	63.6%	36.4%
36,842	JASPER	14,967	9,614	5,031	322	4,583	R	64.2%	33.6%	65.6%	34.4%
16,843	JEFFERSON	6,658	3,429	2,987	242	442	R	51.5%	44.9%	53.4%	46.6%
130,882	JOHNSON	51,656	24,347	26,047	1,262	1,700	D	47.1%	50.4%	48.3%	51.7%
20,638	JONES	7,710	5,236	2,268	206	2,968	R	67.9%	29.4%	69.8%	30.2%
10,511	KEOKUK	3,863	2,832	915	116	1,917	R	73.3%	23.7%	75.6%	24.4%
15,543	KOSSUTH	6,753	4,688	1,928	137	2,760	R	69.4%	28.6%	70.9%	29.1%

IOWA

SENATOR 2010

2010 Census Population	County	Total Vote	Republican	Democratic	Other	Rep.-Dem. Plurality		Percentage			
								Total Vote		Major Vote	
								Rep.	Dem.	Rep.	Dem.
35,862	LEE	11,758	6,050	5,276	432	774	R	51.5%	44.9%	53.4%	46.6%
211,226	LINN	80,082	48,488	29,764	1,830	18,724	R	60.5%	37.2%	62.0%	38.0%
11,387	LOUISA	3,366	2,411	859	96	1,552	R	71.6%	25.5%	73.7%	26.3%
8,898	LUCAS	3,538	2,470	967	101	1,503	R	69.8%	27.3%	71.9%	28.1%
11,581	LYON	4,995	4,269	620	106	3,649	R	85.5%	12.4%	87.3%	12.7%
15,679	MADISON	6,743	4,753	1,810	180	2,943	R	70.5%	26.8%	72.4%	27.6%
22,381	MAHASKA	8,412	6,376	1,866	170	4,510	R	75.8%	22.2%	77.4%	22.6%
33,309	MARION	13,036	9,326	3,409	301	5,917	R	71.5%	26.2%	73.2%	26.8%
40,648	MARSHALL	14,215	9,026	4,836	353	4,190	R	63.5%	34.0%	65.1%	34.9%
15,059	MILLS	4,823	3,633	1,068	122	2,565	R	75.3%	22.1%	77.3%	22.7%
10,776	MITCHELL	4,485	3,121	1,274	90	1,847	R	69.6%	28.4%	71.0%	29.0%
9,243	MONONA	3,519	2,578	881	60	1,697	R	73.3%	25.0%	74.5%	25.5%
7,970	MONROE	2,882	1,983	827	72	1,156	R	68.8%	28.7%	70.6%	29.4%
10,740	MONTGOMERY	3,644	2,824	722	98	2,102	R	77.5%	19.8%	79.6%	20.4%
42,745	MUSCATINE	13,229	7,974	4,872	383	3,102	R	60.3%	36.8%	62.1%	37.9%
14,398	O'BRIEN	5,481	4,556	831	94	3,725	R	83.1%	15.2%	84.6%	15.4%
6,462	OSCEOLA	2,404	2,013	323	68	1,690	R	83.7%	13.4%	86.2%	13.8%
15,932	PAGE	4,801	3,751	945	105	2,806	R	78.1%	19.7%	79.9%	20.1%
9,421	PALO ALTO	3,885	2,653	1,139	93	1,514	R	68.3%	29.3%	70.0%	30.0%
24,986	PLYMOUTH	8,791	7,219	1,422	150	5,797	R	82.1%	16.2%	83.5%	16.5%
7,310	POCAHONTAS	3,018	2,296	654	68	1,642	R	76.1%	21.7%	77.8%	22.2%
430,640	POLK	160,582	96,219	61,170	3,193	35,049	R	59.9%	38.1%	61.1%	38.9%
93,158	POTTAWATTAMIE	26,534	17,916	7,907	711	10,009	R	67.5%	29.8%	69.4%	30.6%
18,914	POWESHIEK	7,474	4,594	2,746	134	1,848	R	61.5%	36.7%	62.6%	37.4%
5,131	RINGGOLD	2,135	1,537	552	46 0	985	R	72.0%	25.9%	73.6%	26.4%
10,350	SAC	3,932	3,035	815	82	2,220	R	77.2%	20.7%	78.8%	21.2%
165,224	SCOTT	56,258	33,050	21,592	1,616	11,458	R	58.7%	38.4%	60.5%	39.5%
12,167	SHELBY	4,147	3,166	885	96	2,281	R	76.3%	21.3%	78.2%	21.8%
33,704	SIOUX	12,785	11,677	973	135	10,704	R	91.3%	7.6%	92.3%	7.7%
89,542	STORY	32,278	19,430	12,029	819	7,401	R	60.2%	37.3%	61.8%	38.2%
17,767	TAMA	6,496	4,323	2,023	150	2,300	R	66.5%	31.1%	68.1%	31.9%
6,317	TAYLOR	2,504	1,866	581	57	1,285	R	74.5%	23.2%	76.3%	23.7%
12,534	UNION	4,771	3,257	1,401	113	1,856	R	68.3%	29.4%	69.9%	30.1%
7,570	VAN BUREN	2,841	1,916	807	118	1,109	R	67.4%	28.4%	70.4%	29.6%
35,625	WAPELLO	11,676	6,308	5,006	362	1,302	R	54.0%	42.9%	55.8%	44.2%
46,225	WARREN	20,152	13,273	6,429	450	6,844	R	65.9%	31.9%	67.4%	32.6%
21,704	WASHINGTON	8,667	6,152	2,280	235	3,872	R	71.0%	26.3%	73.0%	27.0%
6,403	WAYNE	2,313	1,683	582	48	1,101	R	72.8%	25.2%	74.3%	25.7%
38,013	WEBSTER	13,112	8,533	4,355	224	4,178	R	65.1%	33.2%	66.2%	33.8%
10,866	WINNEBAGO	4,389	3,062	1,236	91	1,826	R	69.8%	28.2%	71.2%	28.8%
21,056	WINNESHIEK	8,154	5,179	2,766	209	2,413	R	63.5%	33.9%	65.2%	34.8%
102,172	WOODBURY	31,003	20,895	9,461	647	11,434	R	67.4%	30.5%	68.8%	31.2%
7,598	WORTH	3,193	2,046	1,067	80	979	R	64.1%	33.4%	65.7%	34.3%
13,229	WRIGHT	4,889	3,554	1,260	75	2,294	R	72.7%	25.8%	73.8%	26.2%
3,046,355	TOTAL	1,116,063	718,215	371,686	26,162	346,529	R	64.4%	33.3%	65.9%	34.1%

IOWA

HOUSE OF REPRESENTATIVES

			Republican		Democratic		Other	Rep.-Dem.	Percentage			
		Total							Total Vote		Major Vote	
CD	Year	Vote	Vote	Candidate	Vote	Candidate	Vote	Plurality	Rep.	Dem.	Rep.	Dem.
1	2010	210,902	100,219	LANGE, BENJAMIN M.	104,428	BRALEY, BRUCE*	6,255	4,209 D	47.5%	49.5%	49.0%	51.0%
1	2008	289,629	102,439	HARTSUCH, DAVID	186,991	BRALEY, BRUCE*	199	84,552 D	35.4%	64.6%	35.4%	64.6%
1	2006	207,621	89,729	WHALEN, MIKE	114,322	BRALEY, BRUCE	3,570	24,593 D	43.2%	55.1%	44.0%	56.0%
1	2004	290,054	159,993	NUSSLE, JIM*	125,490	GLUBA, BILL	4,571	34,503 R	55.2%	43.3%	56.0%	44.0%
1	2002	196,455	112,280	NUSSLE, JIM*	83,779	HUTCHINSON, ANN	396	28,501 R	57.2%	42.6%	57.3%	42.7%
2	2010	227,175	104,319	MILLER-MEEKS, MARIANNETTE	115,839	LOEBSACK, DAVE*	7,017	11,520 D	45.9%	51.0%	47.4%	52.6%
2	2008	306,358	118,778	MILLER-MEEKS, MARIANNETTE	175,218	LOEBSACK, DAVE*	12,362	56,440 D	38.8%	57.2%	40.4%	59.6%
2	2006	209,586	101,707	LEACH, JIM*	107,683	LOEBSACK, DAVE	196	5,976 D	48.5%	51.4%	48.6%	51.4%
2	2004	299,881	176,684	LEACH, JIM*	117,405	FRANKER, DAVE	5,792	59,279 R	58.9%	39.2%	60.1%	39.9%
2	2002	207,171	108,130	LEACH, JIM*	94,767	THOMAS, JULIE	4,274	13,363 R	52.2%	45.7%	53.3%	46.7%
3	2010	240,756	111,925	ZAUN, BRAD	122,147	BOSWELL, LEONARD L.*	6,684	10,222 D	46.5%	50.7%	47.8%	52.2%
3	2008	314,160	132,136	SCHMETT, KIM	176,904	BOSWELL, LEONARD L.*	5,120	44,768 D	42.1%	56.3%	42.8%	57.2%
3	2006	223,287	103,722	LAMBERTI, JEFF	115,769	BOSWELL, LEONARD L.*	3,796	12,047 D	46.5%	51.8%	47.3%	52.7%
3	2004	304,319	136,099	THOMPSON, STAN	168,007	BOSWELL, LEONARD L.*	213	31,908 D	44.7%	55.2%	44.8%	55.2%
3	2002	215,985	97,285	THOMPSON, STAN	115,367	BOSWELL, LEONARD L.*	3,333	18,082 D	45.0%	53.4%	45.7%	54.3%
4	2010	232,519	152,588	LATHAM, TOM*	74,300	MASKE, BILL	5,631	78,288 R	65.6%	32.0%	67.3%	32.7%
4	2008	306,401	185,458	LATHAM, TOM*	120,746	GREENWALD, BECKY	197	64,712 R	60.5%	39.4%	60.6%	39.4%
4	2006	212,730	121,650	LATHAM, TOM*	90,982	SPENCER, SELDEN E.	98	30,668 R	57.2%	42.8%	57.2%	42.8%
4	2004	297,566	181,294	LATHAM, TOM*	116,121	JOHNSON, PAUL W.	151	65,173 R	60.9%	39.0%	61.0%	39.0%
4	2002	210,774	115,430	LATHAM, TOM*	90,784	NORRIS, JOHN	4,560	24,646 R	54.8%	43.1%	56.0%	44.0%
5	2010	195,239	128,363	KING, STEVE*	63,160	CAMPBELL, MATTHEW	3,716	65,203 R	65.7%	32.4%	67.0%	33.0%
5	2008	266,617	159,430	KING, STEVE*	99,601	HUBLER, ROB	7,586	59,829 R	59.8%	37.4%	61.5%	38.5%
5	2006	180,464	105,580	KING, STEVE*	64,181	SCHULTE, JOYCE	10,703	41,399 R	58.5%	35.6%	62.2%	37.8%
5	2004	266,341	168,583	KING, STEVE*	97,597	SCHULTE, JOYCE	161	70,986 R	63.3%	36.6%	63.3%	36.7%
5	2002	182,237	113,257	KING, STEVE	68,853	SHOMSHOR, PAUL	127	44,404 R	62.1%	37.8%	62.2%	37.8%
TOTAL	2010	1,106,591	597,414		479,874		29,303	117,540 R	54.0%	43.4%	55.5%	44.5%
TOTAL	2008	1,483,165	698,241		759,460		25,464	61,219 D	47.1%	51.2%	47.9%	52.1%
TOTAL	2006	1,033,688	522,388		492,937		18,363	29,451 R	50.5%	47.7%	51.5%	48.5%
TOTAL	2004	1,458,161	822,653		624,620		10,888	198,033 R	56.4%	42.8%	56.8%	43.2%
TOTAL	2002	1,012,622	546,382		453,550		12,690	92,832 R	54.0%	44.8%	54.6%	45.4%

An asterisk (*) denotes incumbent.

IOWA

GENERAL AND PRIMARY ELECTIONS

2010 GENERAL ELECTIONS

Governor Other vote was 20,859 Iowa Party (Jonathan Narcisse); 14,398 Libertarian (Eric Cooper); 3,884 Nominated by Petition (Gregory James Hughes); 2,757 Socialist Workers (David Rosenfeld); 2,823 scattered write-in.

Senator Other vote was 25,290 Libertarian (John Heiderscheit); 872 scattered write-in.

House Other vote was:

IOWA

GENERAL AND PRIMARY ELECTIONS

CD 1   4,087 Libertarian (Rob J. Petsche); 2,092 Nominated by Petition (Jason A. Faulkner); 76 scattered write-in.
CD 2   4,356 Libertarian (Gary Sicard); 2,463 Constitution (Jon Tack); 198 scattered write-in.
CD 3   6,258 Socialist Workers (Rebecca Williamson); 426 scattered write-in.
CD 4   5,499 Nominated by Petition (Dan Lensing); 132 scattered write-in.
CD 5   3,622 Nominated by Petition (Martin James Monroe); 94 scattered write-in.

2010 PRIMARY ELECTIONS

Primary	June 8, 2010	Registration (as of June 1, 2010 - includes 135,280 inactive registrants)	Democratic	710,017
			Republican	607,567
			Other	1,703
			No Party	772,725
			TOTAL	2,092,012

Primary Type   Semi-open—Registered Democrats and Republicans could vote only in their party's primary, although any registered voter (including those not affiliated with either party) could participate in either party's primary by changing their registration to that party on primary day.

IOWA

GENERAL AND PRIMARY ELECTIONS

	REPUBLICAN PRIMARIES			DEMOCRATIC PRIMARIES		
Governor	Terry E. Branstad	114,450	50.3%	Chet Culver*	56,293	95.7%
	Bob Vander Plaats	93,058	40.9%	Scattered write-in	2,534	4.3%
	Rod Roberts	19,896	8.7%			
	Scattered write-in	121	0.1%			
	TOTAL	227,525		TOTAL	58,827	
Senator	Charles E. Grassley*	197,194	98.0%	Roxanne Conlin	52,715	77.5%
	Scattered write-in	3,926	2.0%	Bob Krause	8,728	12.8%
				Thomas L. Fiegen	6,357	9.4%
				Scattered write-in	177	0.3%
	TOTAL	201,120		TOTAL	67,977	
Congressional District 1	Benjamin M. Lange	14,048	52.8%	Bruce Braley*	12,316	99.4%
	Will Johnson	6,067	22.8%	Scattered write-in	70	0.6%
	James R. Budde	3,347	12.6%			
	Mike La Coste	3,076	11.6%			
	Scattered write-in	77	0.3%			
	TOTAL	26,615		TOTAL	12,386	
Congressional District 2	Mariannette Miller-Meeks	18,830	50.7%	Dave Loebsack*	13,324	99.1%
	Steven R. Rathje	8,155	22.0%	Scattered write-in	118	0.9%
	Christopher Reed	5,365	14.4%			
	Rob Gettemy	4,749	12.8%			
	Scattered write-in	47	0.1%			
	TOTAL	37,146		TOTAL	13,442	

IOWA

GENERAL AND PRIMARY ELECTIONS

	REPUBLICAN PRIMARIES			DEMOCRATIC PRIMARIES		
Congressional District 3	Brad Zaun	19,469	42.1%	Leonard L. Boswell*	13,107	97.5%
	Jim Gibbons	13,022	28.2%	Scattered write-in	338	2.5%
	Dave Funk	9,989	21.6%			
	Mark R. Rees	1,981	4.3%			
	Pat Bertroche	690	1.5%			
	Jason Lee Welch	572	1.2%			
	Scott G. Batcher	464	1.0%			
	Scattered write-in	36	0.1%			
	TOTAL	*46,223*		*TOTAL*	*13,445*	
Congressional District 4	Tom Latham*	42,605	99.4%	Bill Maske	11,374	99.5%
	Scattered write-in	267	0.6%	Scattered write-in	53	0.5%
	TOTAL	*42,872*		*TOTAL*	*11,427*	
Congressional District 5	Steve King*	47,117	99.2%	Matthew Campbell	7,119	75.7%
	Scattered write-in	370	0.8%	Mike Denklau	2,261	24.0%
				Scattered write-in	26	0.3%
	TOTAL	*47,487*		*TOTAL*	*9,406*	

KANSAS

Congressional districts first established for elections held in 2002
4 members

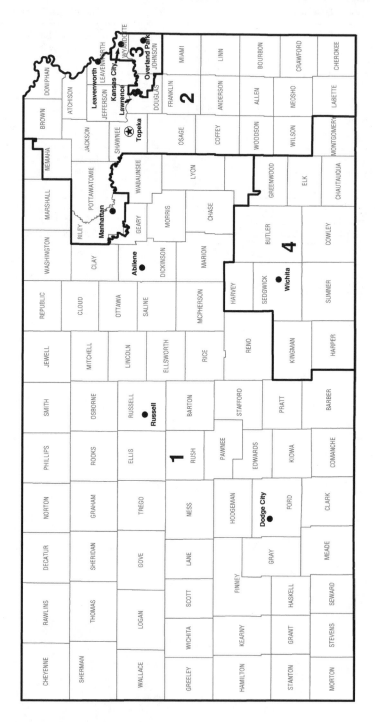

KANSAS

GOVERNOR

Sam Brownback (R). Elected 2010 to a four-year term.

SENATORS (2 Republicans)

Jerry Moran (R). Elected 2010 to a six-year term.

Pat Roberts (R). Reelected 2008 to a six-year term. Previously elected 2002, 1996.

REPRESENTATIVES (4 Republicans)

1. Tim Huelskamp (R)
2. Lynn Jenkins (R)

3. Kevin Yoder (R)

4. Mike Pompeo (R)

POSTWAR VOTE FOR PRESIDENT

| | | Republican | | Democratic | | Other | Rep.-Dem. | Percentage | | | |
| | | | | | | | | Total Vote | | Major Vote | |
Year	Total Vote	Vote	Candidate	Vote	Candidate	Vote	Plurality	Rep.	Dem.	Rep.	Dem.
2008	1,235,872	699,655	McCain, John	514,765	Obama, Barack	21,452	184,890 R	56.6%	41.7%	57.6%	42.4%
2004	1,187,756	736,456	Bush, George W.	434,993	Kerry, John	16,307	301,463 R	62.0%	36.6%	62.9%	37.1%
2000**	1,072,218	622,332	Bush, George W.	399,276	Gore, Al	50,610	223,056 R	58.0%	37.2%	60.9%	39.1%
1996**	1,074,300	583,245	Dole, Bob	387,659	Clinton, Bill	103,396	195,586 R	54.3%	36.1%	60.1%	39.9%
1992**	1,157,335	449,951	Bush, George	390,434	Clinton, Bill	316,950	59,517 R	38.9%	33.7%	53.5%	46.5%
1988	993,044	554,049	Bush, George	422,636	Dukakis, Michael S.	16,359	131,413 R	55.8%	42.6%	56.7%	43.3%
1984	1,021,991	677,296	Reagan, Ronald	333,149	Mondale, Walter F.	11,546	344,147 R	66.3%	32.6%	67.0%	33.0%
1980**	979,795	566,812	Reagan, Ronald	326,150	Carter, Jimmy	86,833	240,662 R	57.9%	33.3%	63.5%	36.5%
1976	957,845	502,752	Ford, Gerald R.	430,421	Carter, Jimmy	24,672	72,331 R	52.5%	44.9%	53.9%	46.1%
1972	916,095	619,812	Nixon, Richard M.	270,287	McGovern, George S.	25,996	349,525 R	67.7%	29.5%	69.6%	30.4%
1968**	872,783	478,674	Nixon, Richard M.	302,996	Humphrey, Hubert H.	91,113	175,678 R	54.8%	34.7%	61.2%	38.8%
1964	857,901	386,579	Goldwater, Barry M.	464,028	Johnson, Lyndon B.	7,294	77,449 D	45.1%	54.1%	45.4%	54.6%
1960	928,825	561,474	Nixon, Richard M.	363,213	Kennedy, John F.	4,138	198,261 R	60.4%	39.1%	60.7%	39.3%
1956	866,243	566,878	Eisenhower, Dwight D.	296,317	Stevenson, Adlai E.	3,048	270,561 R	65.4%	34.2%	65.7%	34.3%
1952	896,166	616,302	Eisenhower, Dwight D.	273,296	Stevenson, Adlai E.	6,568	343,006 R	68.8%	30.5%	69.3%	30.7%
1948	788,819	423,039	Dewey, Thomas E.	351,902	Truman, Harry S.	13,878	71,137 R	53.6%	44.6%	54.6%	45.4%

**In past elections, the other vote included: 2000 - 36,086 Green (Ralph Nader); 1996 - 92,639 Reform (Ross Perot);1992 - 312,358 Independent (Perot);1980 - 68,231 Independent (John Anderson); 1968 - 88,921 American Independent (George Wallace).

KANSAS

POSTWAR VOTE FOR GOVERNOR

Year	Total Vote	Republican Vote	Republican Candidate	Democratic Vote	Democratic Candidate	Other Vote	Rep.-Dem. Plurality	Total Vote Rep.	Total Vote Dem.	Major Vote Rep.	Major Vote Dem.
2010	838,790	530,760	Brownback, Sam	270,166	Holland, Tom	37,864	260,594 R	63.3%	32.2%	66.3%	33.7%
2006	849,700	343,586	Barnett, Jim	491,993	Sebelius, Kathleen	14,121	148,407 D	40.4%	57.9%	41.1%	58.9%
2002	835,692	376,830	Shallenburger, Tim	441,858	Sebelius, Kathleen	17,004	65,028 D	45.1%	52.9%	46.0%	54.0%
1998	742,665	544,882	Graves, Bill	168,243	Sawyer, Tom	29,540	376,639 R	73.4%	22.7%	76.4%	23.6%
1994	821,030	526,113	Graves, Bill	294,733	Slattery, Jim	184	231,380 R	64.1%	35.9%	64.1%	35.9%
1990	783,325	333,589	Hayden, Mike	380,609	Finney, Joan	69,127	47,020 D	42.6%	48.6%	46.7%	53.3%
1986	840,605	436,267	Hayden, Mike	404,338	Docking, Thomas R.		31,929 R	51.9%	48.1%	51.9%	48.1%
1982	763,263	339,356	Hardage, Sam	405,772	Carlin, John	18,135	66,416 D	44.5%	53.2%	45.5%	54.5%
1978	736,246	348,015	Bennett, Robert F.	363,835	Carlin, John	24,396	15,820 D	47.3%	49.4%	48.9%	51.1%
1974**	783,875	387,792	Bennett, Robert F.	384,115	Miller, Vern	11,968	3,677 R	49.5%	49.0%	50.2%	49.8%
1972	921,552	341,440	Kay, Morris	571,256	Docking, Robert	8,856	229,816 D	37.1%	62.0%	37.4%	62.6%
1970	745,196	333,227	Frizzell, Kent	404,611	Docking, Robert	7,358	71,384 D	44.7%	54.3%	45.2%	54.8%
1968	862,473	410,673	Harman, Rick	447,269	Docking, Robert	4,531	36,596 D	47.6%	51.9%	47.9%	52.1%
1966	692,955	304,325	Avery, William H.	380,030	Docking, Robert	8,600	75,705 D	43.9%	54.8%	44.5%	55.5%
1964	850,414	432,667	Avery, William H.	400,264	Wiles, Harry G.	17,483	32,403 R	50.9%	47.1%	51.9%	48.1%
1962	638,798	341,257	Anderson, John	291,285	Saffels, Dale E.	6,256	49,972 R	53.4%	45.6%	54.0%	46.0%
1960	922,522	511,534	Anderson, John	402,261	Docking, George	8,727	109,273 R	55.4%	43.6%	56.0%	44.0%
1958	735,939	313,036	Reed, Clyde M.	415,506	Docking, George	7,397	102,470 D	42.5%	56.5%	43.0%	57.0%
1956	864,935	364,340	Shaw, Warren W.	479,701	Docking, George	20,894	115,361 D	42.1%	55.5%	43.2%	56.8%
1954	622,633	329,868	Hall, Fred	286,218	Docking, George	6,547	43,650 R	53.0%	46.0%	53.5%	46.5%
1952	872,139	491,338	Arn, Edward F.	363,482	Rooney, Charles	17,319	127,856 R	56.3%	41.7%	57.5%	42.5%
1950	619,310	333,001	Arn, Edward F.	275,494	Anderson, Kenneth	10,815	57,507 R	53.8%	44.5%	54.7%	45.3%
1948	760,407	433,396	Carlson, Frank	307,485	Carpenter, Randolph	19,526	125,911 R	57.0%	40.4%	58.5%	41.5%
1946	577,694	309,064	Carlson, Frank	254,283	Woodring, Harry H.	14,347	54,781 R	53.5%	44.0%	54.9%	45.1%

**The term of office of Kansas's Governor was increased from two to four years effective with the 1974 election.

POSTWAR VOTE FOR SENATOR

Year	Total Vote	Republican Vote	Republican Candidate	Democratic Vote	Democratic Candidate	Other Vote	Rep.-Dem. Plurality	Total Vote Rep.	Total Vote Dem.	Major Vote Rep.	Major Vote Dem.
2010	837,692	587,175	Moran, Jerry	220,971	Johnston, Lisa	29,546	366,204 R	70.1%	26.4%	72.7%	27.3%
2008	1,210,690	727,121	Roberts, Pat	441,399	Slattery, Jim	42,170	285,722 R	60.1%	36.5%	62.2%	37.8%
2004	1,129,022	780,863	Brownback, Sam	310,337	Jones, Lee	37,822	470,526 R	69.2%	27.5%	71.6%	28.4%
2002	776,850	641,075	Roberts, Pat	—		135,775	641,075 R	82.5%		100.0%	
1998	727,236	474,639	Brownback, Sam	229,718	Feleciano, Paul, Jr.	22,879	244,921 R	65.3%	31.6%	67.4%	32.6%
1996	1,052,300	652,677	Roberts, Pat	362,380	Thompson, Sally	37,243	290,297 R	62.0%	34.4%	64.3%	35.7%
1996S	1,064,716	574,021	Brownback, Sam	461,344	Docking, Jill	29,351	112,677 R	53.9%	43.3%	55.4%	44.6%
1992	1,126,447	706,246	Dole, Robert	349,525	O'Dell, Gloria	70,676	356,721 R	62.7%	31.0%	66.9%	33.1%
1990	786,235	578,605	Kassebaum, Nancy Landon	207,491	Williams, Dick	139	371,114 R	73.6%	26.4%	73.6%	26.4%
1986	823,566	576,902	Dole, Robert	246,664	MacDonald, Guy		330,238 R	70.0%	30.0%	70.0%	30.0%
1984	996,729	757,402	Kassebaum, Nancy Landon	211,664	Maher, James	27,663	545,738 R	76.0%	21.2%	78.2%	21.8%
1980	938,957	598,686	Dole, Robert	340,271	Simpson, John		258,415 R	63.8%	36.2%	63.8%	36.2%
1978	748,839	403,354	Kassebaum, Nancy Landon	317,602	Roy, William R.	27,883	85,752 R	53.9%	42.4%	55.9%	44.1%
1974	794,437	403,983	Dole, Robert	390,451	Roy, William R.	3	13,532 R	50.9%	49.1%	50.9%	49.1%
1972	871,722	622,591	Pearson, James B.	200,764	Tetzlaff, Arch O.	48,367	421,827 R	71.4%	23.0%	75.6%	24.4%
1968	817,096	490,911	Dole, Robert	315,911	Robinson, William I.	10,274	175,000 R	60.1%	38.7%	60.8%	39.2%
1966	671,345	350,077	Pearson, James B.	303,223	Breeding, J. Floyd	18,045	46,854 R	52.1%	45.2%	53.6%	46.4%
1962	622,232	388,500	Carlson, Frank	223,630	Smith, K. L.	10,102	164,870 R	62.4%	35.9%	63.5%	36.5%
1962S	613,250	344,689	Pearson, James B.	260,756	Aylward, Paul L.	7,805	83,933 R	56.2%	42.5%	56.9%	43.1%
1960	888,592	485,499	Schoeppel, Andrew F.	388,895	Theis, Frank	14,198	96,604 R	54.6%	43.8%	55.5%	44.5%
1956	825,280	477,822	Carlson, Frank	333,939	Hart, George	13,519	143,883 R	57.9%	40.5%	58.9%	41.1%
1954	618,063	348,144	Schoeppel, Andrew F.	258,575	McGill, George	11,344	89,569 R	56.3%	41.8%	57.4%	42.6%
1950	619,104	335,880	Carlson, Frank	271,365	Aiken, Paul	11,859	64,515 R	54.3%	43.8%	55.3%	44.7%
1948	716,342	393,412	Schoeppel, Andrew F.	305,987	McGill, George	16,943	87,425 R	54.9%	42.7%	56.3%	43.7%

The Democratic Party did not run a candidate in the 2002 Senate election. One of the 1996 and 1962 elections was for a short term to fill a vacancy.

KANSAS

GOVERNOR 2010

2010 Census Population	County	Total Vote	Republican	Democratic	Other	Rep.-Dem. Plurality		Percentage Total Vote Rep.	Dem.	Major Vote Rep.	Dem.
13,371	ALLEN	4,536	3,080	1,242	214	1,838	R	67.9%	27.4%	71.3%	28.7%
8,102	ANDERSON	2,785	1,902	715	168	1,187	R	68.3%	25.7%	72.7%	27.3%
16,924	ATCHISON	4,666	2,865	1,593	208	1,272	R	61.4%	34.1%	64.3%	35.7%
4,861	BARBER	2,057	1,587	389	81	1,198	R	77.2%	18.9%	80.3%	19.7%
27,674	BARTON	8,156	6,304	1,504	348	4,800	R	77.3%	18.4%	80.7%	19.3%
15,173	BOURBON	4,802	3,473	1,135	194	2,338	R	72.3%	23.6%	75.4%	24.6%
9,984	BROWN	3,025	2,180	666	179	1,514	R	72.1%	22.0%	76.6%	23.4%
65,880	BUTLER	20,923	14,566	5,304	1,053	9,262	R	69.6%	25.4%	73.3%	26.7%
2,790	CHASE	1,073	747	265	61	482	R	69.6%	24.7%	73.8%	26.2%
3,669	CHAUTAUQUA	1,291	1,033	186	72	847	R	80.0%	14.4%	84.7%	15.3%
21,603	CHEROKEE	6,094	4,114	1,697	283	2,417	R	67.5%	27.8%	70.8%	29.2%
2,726	CHEYENNE	1,117	922	160	35	762	R	82.5%	14.3%	85.2%	14.8%
2,215	CLARK	920	742	142	36	600	R	80.7%	15.4%	83.9%	16.1%
8,535	CLAY	2,952	2,331	523	98	1,808	R	79.0%	17.7%	81.7%	18.3%
9,533	CLOUD	3,065	2,289	629	147	1,660	R	74.7%	20.5%	78.4%	21.6%
8,601	COFFEY	3,023	2,220	626	177	1,594	R	73.4%	20.7%	78.0%	22.0%
1,891	COMANCHE	793	655	113	25	542	R	82.6%	14.2%	85.3%	14.7%
36,311	COWLEY	10,155	6,701	2,977	477	3,724	R	66.0%	29.3%	69.2%	30.8%
39,134	CRAWFORD	11,105	6,301	4,295	509	2,006	R	56.7%	38.7%	59.5%	40.5%
2,961	DECATUR	1,165	931	193	41	738	R	79.9%	16.6%	82.8%	17.2%
19,754	DICKINSON	6,160	4,353	1,512	295	2,841	R	70.7%	24.5%	74.2%	25.8%
7,945	DONIPHAN	2,305	1,745	446	114	1,299	R	75.7%	19.3%	79.6%	20.4%
110,826	DOUGLAS	33,151	12,066	19,966	1,119	7,900	D	36.4%	60.2%	37.7%	62.3%
3,037	EDWARDS	1,052	825	184	43	641	R	78.4%	17.5%	81.8%	18.2%
2,882	ELK	1,152	863	214	75	649	R	74.9%	18.6%	80.1%	19.9%
28,452	ELLIS	8,774	6,228	2,223	323	4,005	R	71.0%	25.3%	73.7%	26.3%
6,497	ELLSWORTH	2,222	1,593	518	111	1,075	R	71.7%	23.3%	75.5%	24.5%
36,776	FINNEY	6,377	4,866	1,239	272	3,627	R	76.3%	19.4%	79.7%	20.3%
33,848	FORD	6,283	4,707	1,344	232	3,363	R	74.9%	21.4%	77.8%	22.2%
25,992	FRANKLIN	7,597	4,843	2,359	395	2,484	R	63.7%	31.1%	67.2%	32.8%
34,362	GEARY	4,931	3,157	1,580	194	1,577	R	64.0%	32.0%	66.6%	33.4%
2,695	GOVE	1,108	924	159	25	765	R	83.4%	14.4%	85.3%	14.7%
2,597	GRAHAM	1,073	839	188	46	651	R	78.2%	17.5%	81.7%	18.3%
7,829	GRANT	1,778	1,449	253	76	1,196	R	81.5%	14.2%	85.1%	14.9%
6,006	GRAY	1,575	1,293	221	61	1,072	R	82.1%	14.0%	85.4%	14.6%
1,247	GREELEY	608	511	82	15	429	R	84.0%	13.5%	86.2%	13.8%
6,689	GREENWOOD	2,315	1,620	558	137	1,062	R	70.0%	24.1%	74.4%	25.6%
2,690	HAMILTON	807	649	118	40	531	R	80.4%	14.6%	84.6%	15.4%
6,034	HARPER	2,113	1,568	405	140	1,163	R	74.2%	19.2%	79.5%	20.5%
34,684	HARVEY	11,470	7,422	3,633	415	3,789	R	64.7%	31.7%	67.1%	32.9%
4,256	HASKELL	1,154	922	112	120	810	R	79.9%	9.7%	89.2%	10.8%
1,916	HODGEMAN	903	759	115	29	644	R	84.1%	12.7%	86.8%	13.2%
13,462	JACKSON	4,277	2,618	1,340	319	1,278	R	61.2%	31.3%	66.1%	33.9%
19,126	JEFFERSON	6,233	3,583	2,284	366	1,299	R	57.5%	36.6%	61.1%	38.9%
3,077	JEWELL	1,169	912	185	72	727	R	78.0%	15.8%	83.1%	16.9%

KANSAS

GOVERNOR 2010

2010 Census Population	County	Total Vote	Republican	Democratic	Other	Rep.-Dem. Plurality		Total Vote		Major Vote	
								Rep.	Dem.	Rep.	Dem.
544,179	JOHNSON	183,459	115,994	61,212	6,253	54,782	R	63.2%	33.4%	65.5%	34.5%
3,977	KEARNY	1,054	839	170	45	669	R	79.6%	16.1%	83.2%	16.8%
7,858	KINGMAN	2,706	2,032	543	131	1,489	R	75.1%	20.1%	78.9%	21.1%
2,553	KIOWA	1,047	878	130	39	748	R	83.9%	12.4%	87.1%	12.9%
21,607	LABETTE	5,661	3,627	1,738	296	1,889	R	64.1%	30.7%	67.6%	32.4%
1,750	LANE	753	619	99	35	520	R	82.2%	13.1%	86.2%	13.8%
76,227	LEAVENWORTH	18,824	11,551	6,411	862	5,140	R	61.4%	34.1%	64.3%	35.7%
3,241	LINCOLN	1,164	835	236	93	599	R	71.7%	20.3%	78.0%	22.0%
9,656	LINN	3,318	2,384	742	192	1,642	R	71.9%	22.4%	76.3%	23.7%
2,756	LOGAN	1,090	916	136	38	780	R	84.0%	12.5%	87.1%	12.9%
33,690	LYON	8,726	5,027	3,275	424	1,752	R	57.6%	37.5%	60.6%	39.4%
29,180	MCPHERSON	9,529	6,962	2,200	367	4,762	R	73.1%	23.1%	76.0%	24.0%
12,660	MARION	4,476	3,421	899	156	2,522	R	76.4%	20.1%	79.2%	20.8%
10,117	MARSHALL	3,786	2,524	1,090	172	1,434	R	66.7%	28.8%	69.8%	30.2%
4,575	MEADE	1,497	1,267	185	45	1,082	R	84.6%	12.4%	87.3%	12.7%
32,787	MIAMI	10,029	7,028	2,553	448	4,475	R	70.1%	25.5%	73.4%	26.6%
6,373	MITCHELL	2,251	1,742	413	96	1,329	R	77.4%	18.3%	80.8%	19.2%
35,471	MONTGOMERY	9,375	6,895	2,064	416	4,831	R	73.5%	22.0%	77.0%	23.0%
5,923	MORRIS	2,072	1,397	545	130	852	R	67.4%	26.3%	71.9%	28.1%
3,233	MORTON	995	858	96	41	762	R	86.2%	9.6%	89.9%	10.1%
10,178	NEMAHA	4,200	3,019	941	240	2,078	R	71.9%	22.4%	76.2%	23.8%
16,512	NEOSHO	4,802	3,193	1,388	221	1,805	R	66.5%	28.9%	69.7%	30.3%
3,107	NESS	1,138	955	157	26	798	R	83.9%	13.8%	85.9%	14.1%
5,671	NORTON	1,744	1,364	289	91	1,075	R	78.2%	16.6%	82.5%	17.5%
16,295	OSAGE	5,603	3,423	1,725	455	1,698	R	61.1%	30.8%	66.5%	33.5%
3,858	OSBORNE	1,578	1,252	252	74	1,000	R	79.3%	16.0%	83.2%	16.8%
6,091	OTTAWA	2,191	1,693	358	140	1,335	R	77.3%	16.3%	82.5%	17.5%
6,973	PAWNEE	2,169	1,542	497	130	1,045	R	71.1%	22.9%	75.6%	24.4%
5,642	PHILLIPS	1,971	1,567	312	92	1,255	R	79.5%	15.8%	83.4%	16.6%
21,604	POTTAWATOMIE	6,912	4,986	1,506	420	3,480	R	72.1%	21.8%	76.8%	23.2%
9,656	PRATT	3,040	2,232	691	117	1,541	R	73.4%	22.7%	76.4%	23.6%
2,519	RAWLINS	1,149	984	123	42	861	R	85.6%	10.7%	88.9%	11.1%
64,511	RENO	18,372	12,605	5,070	697	7,535	R	68.6%	27.6%	71.3%	28.7%
4,980	REPUBLIC	1,911	1,499	340	72	1,159	R	78.4%	17.8%	81.5%	18.5%
10,083	RICE	2,924	2,192	640	92	1,552	R	75.0%	21.9%	77.4%	22.6%
71,115	RILEY	14,053	8,311	5,188	554	3,123	R	59.1%	36.9%	61.6%	38.4%
5,181	ROOKS	2,001	1,643	278	80	1,365	R	82.1%	13.9%	85.5%	14.5%
3,307	RUSH	1,266	946	279	41	667	R	74.7%	22.0%	77.2%	22.8%
6,970	RUSSELL	2,671	2,027	509	135	1,518	R	75.9%	19.1%	79.9%	20.1%
55,606	SALINE	17,538	11,350	5,220	968	6,130	R	64.7%	29.8%	68.5%	31.5%
4,936	SCOTT	1,795	1,516	210	69	1,306	R	84.5%	11.7%	87.8%	12.2%
498,365	SEDGWICK	134,368	83,862	43,709	6,797	40,153	R	62.4%	32.5%	65.7%	34.3%
22,952	SEWARD	3,551	2,798	606	147	2,192	R	78.8%	17.1%	82.2%	17.8%
177,934	SHAWNEE	57,572	30,106	23,613	3,853	6,493	R	52.3%	41.0%	56.0%	44.0%
2,556	SHERIDAN	1,054	889	138	27	751	R	84.3%	13.1%	86.6%	13.4%

KANSAS

GOVERNOR 2010

2010 Census Population	County	Total Vote	Republican	Democratic	Other	Rep.-Dem. Plurality		Total Vote Rep.	Dem.	Major Vote Rep.	Dem.
6,010	SHERMAN	1,921	1,539	305	77	1,234	R	80.1%	15.9%	83.5%	16.5%
3,853	SMITH	1,516	1,154	309	53	845	R	76.1%	20.4%	78.9%	21.1%
4,437	STAFFORD	1,506	1,163	286	57	877	R	77.2%	19.0%	80.3%	19.7%
2,235	STANTON	596	511	69	16	442	R	85.7%	11.6%	88.1%	11.9%
5,724	STEVENS	1,511	1,303	160	48	1,143	R	86.2%	10.6%	89.1%	10.9%
24,132	SUMNER	7,770	5,160	2,142	468	3,018	R	66.4%	27.6%	70.7%	29.3%
7,900	THOMAS	2,557	2,005	467	85	1,538	R	78.4%	18.3%	81.1%	18.9%
3,001	TREGO	1,175	906	224	45	682	R	77.1%	19.1%	80.2%	19.8%
7,053	WABAUNSEE	2,721	1,824	705	192	1,119	R	67.0%	25.9%	72.1%	27.9%
1,485	WALLACE	618	508	72	38	436	R	82.2%	11.7%	87.6%	12.4%
5,799	WASHINGTON	2,169	1,740	348	81	1,392	R	80.2%	16.0%	83.3%	16.7%
2,234	WICHITA	760	639	98	23	541	R	84.1%	12.9%	86.7%	13.3%
9,409	WILSON	2,729	2,058	544	127	1,514	R	75.4%	19.9%	79.1%	20.9%
3,309	WOODSON	1,171	804	303	64	501	R	68.7%	25.9%	72.6%	27.4%
157,505	WYANDOTTE	32,395	11,438	19,766	1,191	8,328	D	35.3%	61.0%	36.7%	63.3%
2,853,118	TOTAL	838,790	530,760	270,166	37,864	260,594	R	63.3%	32.2%	66.3%	33.7%

KANSAS

SENATOR 2010

2010 Census Population	County	Total Vote	Republican	Democratic	Other	Rep.-Dem. Plurality		Total Vote Rep.	Dem.	Major Vote Rep.	Dem.
13,371	ALLEN	4,446	3,124	1,135	187	1,989	R	70.3%	25.5%	73.4%	26.6%
8,102	ANDERSON	2,716	1,968	578	170	1,390	R	72.5%	21.3%	77.3%	22.7%
16,924	ATCHISON	4,663	3,082	1,419	162	1,663	R	66.1%	30.4%	68.5%	31.5%
4,861	BARBER	1,952	1,653	244	55	1,409	R	84.7%	12.5%	87.1%	12.9%
27,674	BARTON	8,219	7,153	856	210	6,297	R	87.0%	10.4%	89.3%	10.7%
15,173	BOURBON	4,815	3,386	1,245	184	2,141	R	70.3%	25.9%	73.1%	26.9%
9,984	BROWN	2,998	2,379	496	123	1,883	R	79.4%	16.5%	82.7%	17.3%
65,880	BUTLER	20,846	16,017	4,106	723	11,911	R	76.8%	19.7%	79.6%	20.4%
2,790	CHASE	1,075	874	163	38	711	R	81.3%	15.2%	84.3%	15.7%
3,669	CHAUTAUQUA	1,275	1,051	175	49	876	R	82.4%	13.7%	85.7%	14.3%
21,603	CHEROKEE	6,060	3,925	1,861	274	2,064	R	64.8%	30.7%	67.8%	32.2%
2,726	CHEYENNE	1,131	1,005	100	26	905	R	88.9%	8.8%	91.0%	9.0%
2,215	CLARK	924	804	98	22	706	R	87.0%	10.6%	89.1%	10.9%
8,535	CLAY	2,930	2,585	280	65	2,305	R	88.2%	9.6%	90.2%	9.8%
9,533	CLOUD	3,062	2,585	401	76	2,184	R	84.4%	13.1%	86.6%	13.4%
8,601	COFFEY	3,007	2,432	444	131	1,988	R	80.9%	14.8%	84.6%	15.4%
1,891	COMANCHE	791	716	63	12	653	R	90.5%	8.0%	91.9%	8.1%
36,311	COWLEY	10,072	7,384	2,315	373	5,069	R	73.3%	23.0%	76.1%	23.9%
39,134	CRAWFORD	10,948	6,292	4,153	503	2,139	R	57.5%	37.9%	60.2%	39.8%
2,961	DECATUR	1,170	1,057	91	22	966	R	90.3%	7.8%	92.1%	7.9%

KANSAS

SENATOR 2010

2010 Census Population	County	Total Vote	Republican	Democratic	Other	Rep.-Dem. Plurality		Percentage			
								Total Vote		Major Vote	
								Rep.	Dem.	Rep.	Dem.
19,754	DICKINSON	6,191	5,166	839	186	4,327	R	83.4%	13.6%	86.0%	14.0%
7,945	DONIPHAN	2,288	1,784	409	95	1,375	R	78.0%	17.9%	81.3%	18.7%
110,826	DOUGLAS	32,760	14,872	16,365	1,523	1,493	D	45.4%	50.0%	47.6%	52.4%
3,037	EDWARDS	1,057	927	99	31	828	R	87.7%	9.4%	90.4%	9.6%
2,882	ELK	1,133	932	164	37	768	R	82.3%	14.5%	85.0%	15.0%
28,452	ELLIS	8,851	7,863	859	129	7,004	R	88.8%	9.7%	90.2%	9.8%
6,497	ELLSWORTH	2,232	1,930	248	54	1,682	R	86.5%	11.1%	88.6%	11.4%
36,776	FINNEY	6,405	5,356	852	197	4,504	R	83.6%	13.3%	86.3%	13.7%
33,848	FORD	6,297	5,163	932	202	4,231	R	82.0%	14.8%	84.7%	15.3%
25,992	FRANKLIN	7,603	5,464	1,670	469	3,794	R	71.9%	22.0%	76.6%	23.4%
34,362	GEARY	4,941	3,408	1,365	168	2,043	R	69.0%	27.6%	71.4%	28.6%
2,695	GOVE	1,115	1,037	64	14	973	R	93.0%	5.7%	94.2%	5.8%
2,597	GRAHAM	1,077	994	72	11	922	R	92.3%	6.7%	93.2%	6.8%
7,829	GRANT	1,785	1,562	168	55	1,394	R	87.5%	9.4%	90.3%	9.7%
6,006	GRAY	1,574	1,406	114	54	1,292	R	89.3%	7.2%	92.5%	7.5%
1,247	GREELEY	639	573	44	22	529	R	89.7%	6.9%	92.9%	7.1%
6,689	GREENWOOD	2,309	1,827	371	111	1,456	R	79.1%	16.1%	83.1%	16.9%
2,690	HAMILTON	806	710	71	25	639	R	88.1%	8.8%	90.9%	9.1%
6,034	HARPER	2,109	1,758	283	68	1,475	R	83.4%	13.4%	86.1%	13.9%
34,684	HARVEY	11,457	8,319	2,828	310	5,491	R	72.6%	24.7%	74.6%	25.4%
4,256	HASKELL	1,128	1,008	85	35	923	R	89.4%	7.5%	92.2%	7.8%
1,916	HODGEMAN	912	838	60	14	778	R	91.9%	6.6%	93.3%	6.7%
13,462	JACKSON	4,281	3,061	1,008	212	2,053	R	71.5%	23.5%	75.2%	24.8%
19,126	JEFFERSON	6,191	4,205	1,651	335	2,554	R	67.9%	26.7%	71.8%	28.2%
3,077	JEWELL	1,169	1,041	90	38	951	R	89.1%	7.7%	92.0%	8.0%
544,179	JOHNSON	183,387	121,630	55,587	6,170	66,043	R	66.3%	30.3%	68.6%	31.4%
3,977	KEARNY	1,056	928	97	31	831	R	87.9%	9.2%	90.5%	9.5%
7,858	KINGMAN	2,696	2,260	335	101	1,925	R	83.8%	12.4%	87.1%	12.9%
2,553	KIOWA	1,053	967	61	25	906	R	91.8%	5.8%	94.1%	5.9%
21,607	LABETTE	5,679	3,789	1,685	205	2,104	R	66.7%	29.7%	69.2%	30.8%
1,750	LANE	759	685	54	20	631	R	90.3%	7.1%	92.7%	7.3%
76,227	LEAVENWORTH	18,753	12,433	5,492	828	6,941	R	66.3%	29.3%	69.4%	30.6%
3,241	LINCOLN	1,180	1,051	98	31	953	R	89.1%	8.3%	91.5%	8.5%
9,656	LINN	3,298	2,460	677	161	1,783	R	74.6%	20.5%	78.4%	21.6%
2,756	LOGAN	1,101	1,010	77	14	933	R	91.7%	7.0%	92.9%	7.1%
33,690	LYON	8,727	6,309	2,125	293	4,184	R	72.3%	24.3%	74.8%	25.2%
29,180	MCPHERSON	9,576	7,858	1,485	233	6,373	R	82.1%	15.5%	84.1%	15.9%
12,660	MARION	4,498	3,835	571	92	3,264	R	85.3%	12.7%	87.0%	13.0%
10,117	MARSHALL	3,781	2,941	745	95	2,196	R	77.8%	19.7%	79.8%	20.2%
4,575	MEADE	1,480	1,350	105	25	1,245	R	91.2%	7.1%	92.8%	7.2%
32,787	MIAMI	10,019	7,316	2,308	395	5,008	R	73.0%	23.0%	76.0%	24.0%
6,373	MITCHELL	2,234	1,977	205	52	1,772	R	88.5%	9.2%	90.6%	9.4%
35,471	MONTGOMERY	9,226	6,930	1,938	358	4,992	R	75.1%	21.0%	78.1%	21.9%
5,923	MORRIS	2,078	1,691	311	76	1,380	R	81.4%	15.0%	84.5%	15.5%
3,233	MORTON	999	897	70	32	827	R	89.8%	7.0%	92.8%	7.2%

KANSAS

SENATOR 2010

2010 Census Population	County	Total Vote	Republican	Democratic	Other	Rep.-Dem. Plurality		Percentage Total Vote		Major Vote	
								Rep.	Dem.	Rep.	Dem.
10,178	NEMAHA	4,187	3,420	656	111	2,764	R	81.7%	15.7%	83.9%	16.1%
16,512	NEOSHO	4,758	3,393	1,161	204	2,232	R	71.3%	24.4%	74.5%	25.5%
3,107	NESS	1,134	1,064	49	21	1,015	R	93.8%	4.3%	95.6%	4.4%
5,671	NORTON	1,753	1,548	157	48	1,391	R	88.3%	9.0%	90.8%	9.2%
16,295	OSAGE	5,601	4,021	1,241	339	2,780	R	71.8%	22.2%	76.4%	23.6%
3,858	OSBORNE	1,591	1,448	108	35	1,340	R	91.0%	6.8%	93.1%	6.9%
6,091	OTTAWA	2,174	1,907	199	68	1,708	R	87.7%	9.2%	90.6%	9.4%
6,973	PAWNEE	2,195	1,950	220	25	1,730	R	88.8%	10.0%	89.9%	10.1%
5,642	PHILLIPS	1,998	1,834	132	32	1,702	R	91.8%	6.6%	93.3%	6.7%
21,604	POTTAWATOMIE	7,047	5,401	1,100	546	4,301	R	76.6%	15.6%	83.1%	16.9%
9,656	PRATT	3,038	2,605	347	86	2,258	R	85.7%	11.4%	88.2%	11.8%
2,519	RAWLINS	1,158	1,071	56	31	1,015	R	92.5%	4.8%	95.0%	5.0%
64,511	RENO	18,258	14,524	3,166	568	11,358	R	79.5%	17.3%	82.1%	17.9%
4,980	REPUBLIC	1,913	1,691	176	46	1,515	R	88.4%	9.2%	90.6%	9.4%
10,083	RICE	2,935	2,506	352	77	2,154	R	85.4%	12.0%	87.7%	12.3%
71,115	RILEY	14,030	9,621	3,960	449	5,661	R	68.6%	28.2%	70.8%	29.2%
5,181	ROOKS	2,033	1,898	101	34	1,797	R	93.4%	5.0%	94.9%	5.1%
3,307	RUSH	1,289	1,180	83	26	1,097	R	91.5%	6.4%	93.4%	6.6%
6,970	RUSSELL	2,698	2,421	212	65	2,209	R	89.7%	7.9%	91.9%	8.1%
55,606	SALINE	17,659	14,208	2,933	518	11,275	R	80.5%	16.6%	82.9%	17.1%
4,936	SCOTT	1,803	1,657	116	30	1,541	R	91.9%	6.4%	93.5%	6.5%
498,365	SEDGWICK	134,349	93,838	36,049	4,462	57,789	R	69.8%	26.8%	72.2%	27.8%
22,952	SEWARD	3,550	3,021	425	104	2,596	R	85.1%	12.0%	87.7%	12.3%
177,934	SHAWNEE	57,443	34,995	19,981	2,467	15,014	R	60.9%	34.8%	63.7%	36.3%
2,556	SHERIDAN	1,044	964	66	14	898	R	92.3%	6.3%	93.6%	6.4%
6,010	SHERMAN	1,927	1,681	196	50	1,485	R	87.2%	10.2%	89.6%	10.4%
3,853	SMITH	1,531	1,378	134	19	1,244	R	90.0%	8.8%	91.1%	8.9%
4,437	STAFFORD	1,512	1,335	136	41	1,199	R	88.3%	9.0%	90.8%	9.2%
2,235	STANTON	591	545	40	6	505	R	92.2%	6.8%	93.2%	6.8%
5,724	STEVENS	1,515	1,389	93	33	1,296	R	91.7%	6.1%	93.7%	6.3%
24,132	SUMNER	7,754	5,891	1,544	319	4,347	R	76.0%	19.9%	79.2%	20.8%
7,900	THOMAS	2,564	2,298	225	41	2,073	R	89.6%	8.8%	91.1%	8.9%
3,001	TREGO	1,193	1,085	90	18	995	R	90.9%	7.5%	92.3%	7.7%
7,053	WABAUNSEE	2,740	2,169	449	122	1,720	R	79.2%	16.4%	82.8%	17.2%
1,485	WALLACE	615	580	22	13	558	R	94.3%	3.6%	96.3%	3.7%
5,799	WASHINGTON	2,169	1,932	188	49	1,744	R	89.1%	8.7%	91.1%	8.9%
2,234	WICHITA	767	701	55	11	646	R	91.4%	7.2%	92.7%	7.3%
9,409	WILSON	2,708	2,210	412	86	1,798	R	81.6%	15.2%	84.3%	15.7%
3,309	WOODSON	1,152	876	224	52	652	R	76.0%	19.4%	79.6%	20.4%
157,505	WYANDOTTE	32,326	11,926	19,157	1,243	7,231	D	36.9%	59.3%	38.4%	61.6%
2,853,118	TOTAL	837,692	587,175	220,971	29,546	366,204	R	70.1%	26.4%	72.7%	27.3%

KANSAS

HOUSE OF REPRESENTATIVES

					Democratic					Percentage			
										Total Vote		Major Vote	
CD	Year	Total Vote	Republican Vote	Candidate	Vote	Candidate	Other Vote	Rep.-Dem. Plurality		Rep.	Dem.	Rep.	Dem.
1	2010	192,886	142,281	HUELSKAMP, TIM	44,068	JILKA, ALAN	6,537	98,213	R	73.8%	22.8%	76.4%	23.6%
1	2008	262,027	214,549	MORAN, JERRY*	34,771	BORDONARO, JAMES	12,707	179,778	R	81.9%	13.3%	86.1%	13.9%
1	2006	199,378	156,728	MORAN, JERRY*	39,781	DOLL, JOHN	2,869	116,947	R	78.6%	20.0%	79.8%	20.2%
1	2004	264,293	239,776	MORAN, JERRY*		—	24,517	239,776	R	90.7%		100.0%	
1	2002	208,561	189,976	MORAN, JERRY*		—	18,585	189,976	R	91.1%		100.0%	
2	2010	205,975	130,034	JENKINS, LYNN*	66,588	HUDSPETH, CHERYL	9,353	63,446	R	63.1%	32.3%	66.1%	33.9%
2	2008	307,308	155,532	JENKINS, LYNN	142,013	BOYDA, NANCY*	9,763	13,519	R	50.6%	46.2%	52.3%	47.7%
2	2006	225,562	106,329	RYUN, JIM*	114,139	BOYDA, NANCY	5,094	7,810	D	47.1%	50.6%	48.2%	51.8%
2	2004	294,436	165,325	RYUN, JIM*	121,532	BOYDA, NANCY	7,579	43,793	R	56.1%	41.3%	57.6%	42.4%
2	2002	210,977	127,477	RYUN, JIM*	79,160	LYKINS, DAN	4,340	48,317	R	60.4%	37.5%	61.7%	38.3%
3	2010	233,285	136,246	YODER, KEVIN	90,193	MOORE, STEPHENE	6,846	46,053	R	58.4%	38.7%	60.2%	39.8%
3	2008	358,858	142,307	JORDAN, NICK	202,541	MOORE, DENNIS*	14,010	60,234	D	39.7%	56.4%	41.3%	58.7%
3	2006	236,980	79,824	AHNER, CHUCK	153,105	MOORE, DENNIS*	4,051	73,281	D	33.7%	64.6%	34.3%	65.7%
3	2004	335,739	145,542	KOBACH, KRIS	184,050	MOORE, DENNIS*	6,147	38,508	D	43.3%	54.8%	44.2%	55.8%
3	2002	219,389	102,882	TAFF, ADAM	110,095	MOORE, DENNIS*	6,412	7,213	D	46.9%	50.2%	48.3%	51.7%
4	2010	203,383	119,575	POMPEO, MIKE	74,143	GOYLE, RAJ	9,665	45,432	R	58.8%	36.5%	61.7%	38.3%
4	2008	280,109	177,617	TIAHRT, TODD*	90,706	BETTS, DONALD JR.	11,786	86,911	R	63.4%	32.4%	66.2%	33.8%
4	2006	183,207	116,386	TIAHRT, TODD*	62,166	McGINN, GARTH J.	4,655	54,220	R	63.5%	33.9%	65.2%	34.8%
4	2004	261,915	173,151	TIAHRT, TODD*	81,388	KINARD, MICHAEL	7,376	91,763	R	66.1%	31.1%	68.0%	32.0%
4	2002	190,963	115,691	TIAHRT, TODD*	70,656	NOLLA, CARLOS	4,616	45,035	R	60.6%	37.0%	62.1%	37.9%
TOTAL	2010	835,529	528,136		274,992		32,401	253,144	R	63.2%	32.9%	65.8%	34.2%
TOTAL	2008	1,208,302	690,005		470,031		48,266	219,974	R	57.1%	38.9%	59.5%	40.5%
TOTAL	2006	845,127	459,267		369,191		16,669	90,076	R	54.3%	43.7%	55.4%	44.6%
TOTAL	2004	1,156,383	723,794		386,970		45,619	336,824	R	62.6%	33.5%	65.2%	34.8%
TOTAL	2002	829,890	536,026		259,911		33,953	276,115	R	64.6%	31.3%	67.3%	32.7%

An asterisk (*) denotes incumbent.

KANSAS

GENERAL AND PRIMARY ELECTIONS

2010 GENERAL ELECTIONS

Governor   Other vote was 22,460 Libertarian (Andrew P. Gray); 15,397 Reform (Kenneth W. Cannon); 7 write-in (Heath Charles Norris).

Senator   Other vote was 17,922 Libertarian (Michael Wm. Dann); 11,624 Reform (Joseph K. Bellis).

House   Other vote was:

CD1   6,537 Libertarian (Jack Warner).
CD2   9,353 Libertarian (Robert Garrard).
CD3   6,846 Libertarian (Jasmin Talbert).
CD4   5,041 Reform (Susan G. Ducey); 4,624 Libertarian (Shawn Smith).

2010 PRIMARY ELECTIONS

Primary   August3,2010   **Registration**
(as of July 19,2010)

Republican	744,975
Democratic	460,318
Libertarian	9,956
Reform	1,154
Unaffiliated	490,395
TOTAL	1,706,798

Primary Type   Semi-open—Registered Democrats and Republicans could vote only in their party's primary. "Unaffiliated" voters could participate in either primary, although if they voted in the Republican primary they had to change their registration to Republican on primary day.

	REPUBLICAN PRIMARIES			DEMOCRATIC PRIMARIES		
Governor	Sam Brownback	263,920	82.2%	Tom Holland	74,754	100.0%
	Joan Heffington	57,160	17.8%			
	TOTAL	321,080				
Senator	Jerry Moran	163,483	49.7%	Lisa Johnston	25,695	31.3%
	Todd Tiahrt	146,702	44.6%	Charles Schollenberger	19,426	23.6%
	Tom Little	10,256	3.1%	David Haley	15,731	19.1%
	Robert Londerholm	8,278	2.5%	Patrick Wiesner	13,481	16.4%
				Robert A. Conroy	7,857	9.6%
	TOTAL	328,719		TOTAL	82,190	
Congressional District 1	Tim Huelskamp	34,819	34.8%	Alan Jilka	15,399	100.0%
	Jim Barnett	25,047	25.1%			
	Tracey Mann	21,161	21.2%			
	Rob Wasinger	9,296	9.3%			
	Sue "Holloway" Boldra	7,892	7.9%			
	Marck Cobb	1,768	1.8%			
	TOTAL	99,983				
Congressional District 2	Lynn Jenkins*	41,458	57.1%	Cheryl Hudspeth	10,030	44.2%
	Dennis Pyle	31,085	42.9%	Thomas Koch	8,086	35.6%
				Sean Tevis	4,579	20.2%
	TOTAL	72,543		TOTAL	22,695	

KANSAS

GENERAL AND PRIMARY ELECTIONS

	REPUBLICAN PRIMARIES			DEMOCRATIC PRIMARIES		
Congressional District 3	Kevin Yoder	32,210	44.4%	Stephene Moore	16,756	78.1%
	Patricia Lightner	26,695	36.8%	Thomas Scherer	4,709	21.9%
	Craig McPherson	2,664	3.7%			
	Dan Gilyeat	2,581	3.6%			
	Jerry M. Malone	2,099	2.9%			
	Jean Ann Uvodich	1,934	2.7%			
	Garry R. Klotz	1,873	2.6%			
	John Timothy Rysavy "Rez"	1,633	2.3%			
	Dave King	820	1.1%			
	TOTAL	*72,509*		*TOTAL*	*21,465*	
Congressional District 4	Mike Pompeo	31,180	38.7%	Raj Goyle	17,146	79.7%
	Jean Kurtis Schodorf	19,099	23.7%	Robert Tillman	4,358	20.3%
	Wink Hartman	18,365	22.8%			
	Jim Anderson	10,294	12.8%			
	Paij Rutschman	1,596	2.0%			
	TOTAL	*80,534*		*TOTAL*	*21,504*	

An asterisk (*) denotes incumbent.

KENTUCKY

Congressional districts first established for elections held in 2002
6 members

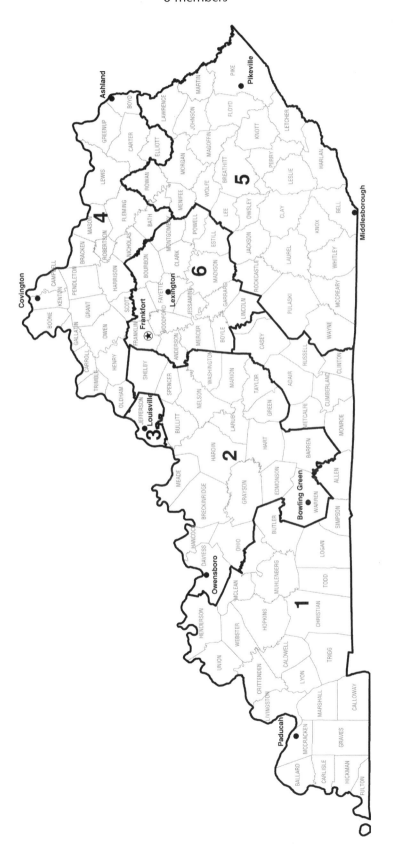

KENTUCKY

GOVERNOR
Steven L. Beshear (D). Elected 2007 to a four-year term.

SENATORS (2 Republicans)
Mitch McConnell (R). Reelected 2008 to a six-year term. Previously elected 2002, 1996, 1990, 1984.

Rand Paul (R). Elected 2010 to a six-year term.

REPRESENTATIVES (4 Republicans, 2 Democrats)
1. Edward Whitfield (R)
2. Brett Guthrie (R)
3. John Yarmuth (D)
4. Geoff Davis (R)
5. Harold Rogers (R)
6. Ben Chandler (D)

POSTWAR VOTE FOR PRESIDENT

| | | Republican | | Democratic | | | | Percentage | | | |
| | | | | | | | | Total Vote | | Major Vote | |
Year	Total Vote	Vote	Candidate	Vote	Candidate	Other Vote	Rep.-Dem. Plurality	Rep.	Dem.	Rep.	Dem.
2008	1,826,620	1,048,462	McCain, John	751,985	Obama, Barack	26,173	296,477 R	57.4%	41.2%	58.2%	41.8%
2004	1,795,882	1,069,439	Bush, George W.	712,733	Kerry, John	13,710	356,706 R	59.5%	39.7%	60.0%	40.0%
2000**	1,544,187	872,492	Bush, George W.	638,898	Gore, Al	32,797	233,594 R	56.5%	41.4%	57.7%	42.3%
1996**	1,388,708	623,283	Dole, Bob	636,614	Clinton, Bill	128,811	13,331 D	44.9%	45.8%	49.5%	50.5%
1992**	1,492,900	617,178	Bush, George	665,104	Clinton, Bill	210,618	47,926 D	41.3%	44.6%	48.1%	51.9%
1988	1,322,517	734,281	Bush, George	580,368	Dukakis, Michael S.	7,868	153,913 R	55.5%	43.9%	55.9%	44.1%
1984	1,369,345	821,702	Reagan, Ronald	539,539	Mondale, Walter F.	8,104	282,163 R	60.0%	39.4%	60.4%	39.6%
1980**	1,294,627	635,274	Reagan, Ronald	616,417	Carter, Jimmy	42,936	18,857 R	49.1%	47.6%	50.8%	49.2%
1976	1,167,142	531,852	Ford, Gerald R.	615,717	Carter, Jimmy	19,573	83,865 D	45.6%	52.8%	46.3%	53.7%
1972	1,067,499	676,446	Nixon, Richard M.	371,159	McGovern, George S.	19,894	305,287 R	63.4%	34.8%	64.6%	35.4%
1968**	1,055,893	462,411	Nixon, Richard M.	397,541	Humphrey, Hubert H.	195,941	64,870 R	43.8%	37.6%	53.8%	46.2%
1964	1,046,105	372,977	Goldwater, Barry M.	669,659	Johnson, Lyndon B.	3,469	296,682 D	35.7%	64.0%	35.8%	64.2%
1960	1,124,462	602,607	Nixon, Richard M.	521,855	Kennedy, John F.		80,752 R	53.6%	46.4%	53.6%	46.4%
1956	1,053,805	572,192	Eisenhower, Dwight D.	476,453	Stevenson, Adlai E.	5,160	95,739 R	54.3%	45.2%	54.6%	45.4%
1952	993,148	495,029	Eisenhower, Dwight D.	495,729	Stevenson, Adlai E.	2,390	700 D	49.8%	49.9%	50.0%	50.0%
1948	822,658	341,210	Dewey, Thomas E.	466,756	Truman, Harry S.	14,692	125,546 D	41.5%	56.7%	42.2%	57.8%

**In past elections, the other vote included: 2000 - 23,192 Green (Ralph Nader); 1996 - 120,396 Reform (Ross Perot); 1992 - 203,944 Independent (Perot); 1980 - 31,127 Independent (John Anderson); 1968 - 193,098 American Independent (George Wallace).

KENTUCKY

POSTWAR VOTE FOR GOVERNOR

| Year | Total Vote | Republican | | Democratic | | Other Vote | Rep.-Dem. Plurality | Percentage | | | |
| | | Vote | Candidate | Vote | Candidate | | | Total Vote | | Major Vote | |
								Rep.	Dem.	Rep.	Dem.
2007	1,055,325	435,773	Fletcher, Ernie	619,552	Beshear, Steven L.		183,779 D	41.3%	58.7%	41.3%	58.7%
2003	1,083,443	596,284	Fletcher, Ernie	487,159	Chandler, Ben		109,125 R	55.0%	45.0%	55.0%	45.0%
1999**	580,074	128,788	Martin, Peppy	352,099	Patton, Paul E.	99,187	223,311 D	22.2%	60.7%	26.8%	73.2%
1995	983,979	479,227	Forgy, Larry	500,787	Patton, Paul E.	3,965	21,560 D	48.7%	50.9%	48.9%	51.1%
1991	834,920	294,452	Hopkins, Larry J.	540,468	Jones, Brereton C.		246,016 D	35.3%	64.7%	35.3%	64.7%
1987	777,815	273,141	Harper, John	504,674	Wilkinson, Wallace G.		231,533 D	35.1%	64.9%	35.1%	64.9%
1983	1,030,671	454,650	Bunning, Jim	561,674	Collins, Martha Layne	14,347	107,024 D	44.1%	54.5%	44.7%	55.3%
1979	939,366	381,278	Nunn, Louie B.	558,088	Brown, J. Y., Jr.		176,810 D	40.6%	59.4%	40.6%	59.4%
1975	748,157	277,998	Gable, Robert E.	470,159	Carroll, Julian		192,161 D	37.2%	62.8%	37.2%	62.8%
1971	930,790	412,653	Emberton, Thomas	470,720	Ford, Wendell H.	47,417	58,067 D	44.3%	50.6%	46.7%	53.3%
1967	886,946	454,123	Nunn, Louie B.	425,674	Ward, Henry	7,149	28,449 R	51.2%	48.0%	51.6%	48.4%
1963	886,047	436,496	Nunn, Louie B.	449,551	Breathitt, Edward T.		13,055 D	49.3%	50.7%	49.3%	50.7%
1959	853,005	336,456	Robsion, John M.	516,549	Combs, Bert T.		180,093 D	39.4%	60.6%	39.4%	60.6%
1955	778,488	322,671	Denney, Edwin R.	451,647	Chandler, Albert B.	4,170	128,976 D	41.4%	58.0%	41.7%	58.3%
1951	634,359	288,014	Siler, Eugene	346,345	Wetherby, Lawrence		58,331 D	45.4%	54.6%	45.4%	54.6%
1947	672,372	287,130	Dummit, Eldon S.	385,242	Clements, Earle C.		98,112 D	42.7%	57.3%	42.7%	57.3%

**In past elections, the other vote included: 1999 - 88,930 Reform (Gatewood Galbraith).

POSTWAR VOTE FOR SENATOR

| Year | Total Vote | Republican | | Democratic | | Other Vote | Rep.-Dem. Plurality | Percentage | | | |
| | | Vote | Candidate | Vote | Candidate | | | Total Vote | | Major Vote | |
								Rep.	Dem.	Rep.	Dem.
2010	1,356,468	755,411	Paul, Rand	599,843	Conway, Jack	1,214	155,568 R	55.7%	44.2%	55.7%	44.3%
2008	1,800,821	953,816	McConnell, Mitch	847,005	Lunsford, Bruce		106,811 R	53.0%	47.0%	53.0%	47.0%
2004	1,724,362	873,507	Bunning, Jim	850,855	Mongiardo, Daniel		22,652 R	50.7%	49.3%	50.7%	49.3%
2002	1,131,475	731,679	McConnell, Mitch	399,634	Weinberg, Lois Combs	162	332,045 R	64.7%	35.3%	64.7%	35.3%
1998	1,145,414	569,817	Bunning, Jim	563,051	Baesler, Scotty	12,546	6,766 R	49.7%	49.2%	50.3%	49.7%
1996	1,307,046	724,794	McConnell, Mitch	560,012	Beshear, Steven L.	22,240	164,782 R	55.5%	42.8%	56.4%	43.6%
1992	1,330,858	476,604	Williams, David L.	836,888	Ford, Wendell H.	17,366	360,284 D	35.8%	62.9%	36.3%	63.7%
1990	916,010	478,034	McConnell, Mitch	437,976	Sloane, Harvey		40,058 R	52.2%	47.8%	52.2%	47.8%
1986	677,280	173,330	Andrews, Jackson M.	503,775	Ford, Wendell H.	175	330,445 D	25.6%	74.4%	25.6%	74.4%
1984	1,292,407	644,990	McConnell, Mitch	639,721	Huddleston, Walter	7,696	5,269 R	49.9%	49.5%	50.2%	49.8%
1980	1,106,890	386,029	Foust, Mary Louise	720,861	Ford, Wendell H.		334,832 D	34.9%	65.1%	34.9%	65.1%
1978	476,783	175,766	Guenthner, Louie	290,730	Huddleston, Walter	10,287	114,964 D	36.9%	61.0%	37.7%	62.3%
1974	745,994	328,982	Cook, Marlow W.	399,406	Ford, Wendell H.	17,606	70,424 D	44.1%	53.5%	45.2%	54.8%
1972	1,037,861	494,337	Nunn, Louie B.	528,550	Huddleston, Walter	14,974	34,213 D	47.6%	50.9%	48.3%	51.7%
1968	942,865	484,260	Cook, Marlow W.	448,960	Peden, Katherine	9,645	35,300 R	51.4%	47.6%	51.9%	48.1%
1966	749,884	483,805	Cooper, John Sherman	266,079	Brown, J. Y.		217,726 R	64.5%	35.5%	64.5%	35.5%
1962	820,088	432,648	Morton, Thruston B.	387,440	Wyatt, Wilson W.		45,208 R	52.8%	47.2%	52.8%	47.2%
1960	1,088,377	644,087	Cooper, John Sherman	444,290	Johnson, Keen		199,797 R	59.2%	40.8%	59.2%	40.8%
1956	1,006,825	506,903	Morton, Thruston B.	499,922	Clements, Earle C.		6,981 R	50.3%	49.7%	50.3%	49.7%
1956S	1,011,645	538,505	Cooper, John Sherman	473,140	Wetherby, Lawrence		65,365 R	53.2%	46.8%	53.2%	46.8%
1954	797,057	362,948	Cooper, John Sherman	434,109	Barkley, Alben W.		71,161 D	45.5%	54.5%	45.5%	54.5%
1952S	960,228	494,576	Cooper, John Sherman	465,652	Underwood, Thomas R.		28,924 R	51.5%	48.5%	51.5%	48.5%
1950	612,617	278,368	Dawson, Charles L.	334,249	Clements, Earle C.		55,881 D	45.4%	54.6%	45.4%	54.6%
1948	794,469	383,776	Cooper, John Sherman	408,256	Chapman, Virgil	2,437	24,480 D	48.3%	51.4%	48.5%	51.5%
1946S	615,119	327,652	Cooper, John Sherman	285,829	Brown, J. Y.	1,638	41,823 R	53.3%	46.5%	53.4%	46.6%

**The elections in 1946 and 1952 as well as one in 1956 were for short terms to fill vacancies.

KENTUCKY

SENATOR 2010

2010 Census Population	County	Total Vote	Republican	Democratic	Other	Rep.-Dem. Plurality		Percentage			
								Total Vote		Major Vote	
								Rep.	Dem.	Rep.	Dem.
18,656	ADAIR	6,530	4,498	2,032		2,466	R	68.9%	31.1%	68.9%	31.1%
19,956	ALLEN	6,394	4,277	2,115	2	2,162	R	66.9%	33.1%	66.9%	33.1%
21,421	ANDERSON	8,099	4,572	3,523	4	1,049	R	56.5%	43.5%	56.5%	43.5%
8,249	BALLARD	3,009	1,647	1,362		285	R	54.7%	45.3%	54.7%	45.3%
42,173	BARREN	12,843	7,458	5,385		2,073	R	58.1%	41.9%	58.1%	41.9%
11,591	BATH	3,390	1,409	1,981		572	D	41.6%	58.4%	41.6%	58.4%
28,691	BELL	8,505	5,269	3,236		2,033	R	62.0%	38.0%	62.0%	38.0%
118,811	BOONE	32,698	24,332	8,364	2	15,968	R	74.4%	25.6%	74.4%	25.6%
19,985	BOURBON	5,845	3,026	2,818	1	208	R	51.8%	48.2%	51.8%	48.2%
49,542	BOYD	14,179	7,039	7,140		101	D	49.6%	50.4%	49.6%	50.4%
28,432	BOYLE	8,841	4,960	3,880	1	1,080	R	56.1%	43.9%	56.1%	43.9%
8,488	BRACKEN	3,157	1,765	1,392		373	R	55.9%	44.1%	55.9%	44.1%
13,878	BREATHITT	4,487	2,023	2,464		441	D	45.1%	54.9%	45.1%	54.9%
20,059	BRECKINRIDGE	6,443	3,686	2,757		929	R	57.2%	42.8%	57.2%	42.8%
74,319	BULLITT	23,156	14,547	8,608	1	5,939	R	62.8%	37.2%	62.8%	37.2%
12,690	BUTLER	3,982	2,699	1,283		1,416	R	67.8%	32.2%	67.8%	32.2%
12,984	CALDWELL	4,658	2,544	2,114		430	R	54.6%	45.4%	54.6%	45.4%
37,191	CALLOWAY	10,521	6,134	4,386	1	1,748	R	58.3%	41.7%	58.3%	41.7%
90,336	CAMPBELL	28,335	18,386	9,948	1	8,438	R	64.9%	35.1%	64.9%	35.1%
5,104	CARLISLE	2,218	1,249	969		280	R	56.3%	43.7%	56.3%	43.7%
10,811	CARROLL	3,316	1,509	1,807		298	D	45.5%	54.5%	45.5%	54.5%
27,720	CARTER	8,272	3,797	4,475		678	D	45.9%	54.1%	45.9%	54.1%
15,955	CASEY	4,342	3,207	1,135		2,072	R	73.9%	26.1%	73.9%	26.1%
73,955	CHRISTIAN	14,244	8,832	5,410	2	3,422	R	62.0%	38.0%	62.0%	38.0%
35,613	CLARK	10,772	6,287	4,485		1,802	R	58.4%	41.6%	58.4%	41.6%
21,730	CLAY	4,982	3,712	1,270		2,442	R	74.5%	25.5%	74.5%	25.5%
10,272	CLINTON	3,728	2,844	884		1,960	R	76.3%	23.7%	76.3%	23.7%
9,315	CRITTENDEN	3,375	2,053	1,316	6	737	R	60.8%	39.0%	60.9%	39.1%
6,856	CUMBERLAND	2,664	1,978	686		1,292	R	74.2%	25.8%	74.2%	25.8%
96,656	DAVIESS	30,788	16,930	13,858		3,072	R	55.0%	45.0%	55.0%	45.0%
12,161	EDMONSON	4,387	2,656	1,730	1	926	R	60.5%	39.4%	60.6%	39.4%
7,852	ELLIOTT	1,484	493	991		498	D	33.2%	66.8%	33.2%	66.8%
14,672	ESTILL	4,508	2,607	1,901		706	R	57.8%	42.2%	57.8%	42.2%
295,803	FAYETTE	87,921	43,313	44,591	17	1,278	D	49.3%	50.7%	49.3%	50.7%
14,348	FLEMING	5,072	2,445	2,627		182	D	48.2%	51.8%	48.2%	51.8%
39,451	FLOYD	11,154	4,794	6,360		1,566	D	43.0%	57.0%	43.0%	57.0%
49,285	FRANKLIN	18,579	7,912	10,654	13	2,742	D	42.6%	57.3%	42.6%	57.4%
6,813	FULTON	2,054	1,045	1,009		36	R	50.9%	49.1%	50.9%	49.1%
8,589	GALLATIN	2,786	1,619	1,167		452	R	58.1%	41.9%	58.1%	41.9%
16,912	GARRARD	5,310	3,617	1,693		1,924	R	68.1%	31.9%	68.1%	31.9%
24,662	GRANT	6,029	3,882	2,147		1,735	R	64.4%	35.6%	64.4%	35.6%
37,121	GRAVES	11,991	6,818	5,169	4	1,649	R	56.9%	43.1%	56.9%	43.1%
25,746	GRAYSON	8,586	5,443	3,133	10	2,310	R	63.4%	36.5%	63.5%	36.5%
11,258	GREEN	4,548	2,926	1,622		1,304	R	64.3%	35.7%	64.3%	35.7%
36,910	GREENUP	11,616	5,862	5,750	4	112	R	50.5%	49.5%	50.5%	49.5%
8,565	HANCOCK	3,163	1,444	1,719		275	D	45.7%	54.3%	45.7%	54.3%
105,543	HARDIN	27,343	16,064	11,271	8	4,793	R	58.7%	41.2%	58.8%	41.2%
29,278	HARLAN	8,389	4,934	3,455		1,479	R	58.8%	41.2%	58.8%	41.2%
18,846	HARRISON	5,635	3,035	2,596	4	439	R	53.9%	46.1%	53.9%	46.1%
18,199	HART	5,017	2,748	2,268	1	480	R	54.8%	45.2%	54.8%	45.2%

KENTUCKY

SENATOR 2010

2010 Census Population	County	Total Vote	Republican	Democratic	Other	Rep.-Dem. Plurality		Percentage Total Vote Rep.	Dem.	Major Vote Rep.	Dem.
46,250	HENDERSON	13,541	6,650	6,885	6	235	D	49.1%	50.8%	49.1%	50.9%
15,416	HENRY	5,546	2,992	2,551	3	441	R	53.9%	46.0%	54.0%	46.0%
4,902	HICKMAN	1,680	947	733		214	R	56.4%	43.6%	56.4%	43.6%
46,920	HOPKINS	15,327	9,051	6,274	2	2,777	R	59.1%	40.9%	59.1%	40.9%
13,494	JACKSON	4,436	3,421	1,015		2,406	R	77.1%	22.9%	77.1%	22.9%
741,096	JEFFERSON	258,663	114,435	143,385	843	28,950	D	44.2%	55.4%	44.4%	55.6%
48,586	JESSAMINE	15,667	10,197	5,468	2	4,729	R	65.1%	34.9%	65.1%	34.9%
23,356	JOHNSON	7,915	5,216	2,692	7	2,524	R	65.9%	34.0%	66.0%	34.0%
159,720	KENTON	43,956	29,372	14,582	2	14,790	R	66.8%	33.2%	66.8%	33.2%
16,346	KNOTT	5,795	2,720	3,067	8	347	D	46.9%	52.9%	47.0%	53.0%
31,883	KNOX	8,934	5,664	.3,267	3	2,397	R	63.4%	36.6%	63.4%	36.6%
14,193	LARUE	4,594	2,729	1,865		864	R	59.4%	40.6%	59.4%	40.6%
58,849	LAUREL	15,401	11,472	3,927	2	7,545	R	74.5%	25.5%	74.5%	25.5%
15,860	LAWRENCE	4,892	2,685	2,207		478	R	54.9%	45.1%	54.9%	45.1%
7,887	LEE	2,679	1,639	1,040		599	R	61.2%	38.8%	61.2%	38.8%
11,310	LESLIE	4,453	3,530	916	7	2,614	R	79.3%	20.6%	79.4%	20.6%
24,519	LETCHER	7,396	3,856	3,540		316	R	52.1%	47.9%	52.1%	47.9%
13,870	LEWIS	3,516	2,436	1,080		1,356	R	69.3%	30.7%	69.3%	30.7%
24,742	LINCOLN	7,241	4,072	3,169		903	R	56.2%	43.8%	56.2%	43.8%
9,519	LIVINGSTON	3,886	2,090	1,792	4	298	R	53.8%	46.1%	53.8%	46.2%
26,835	LOGAN	8,152	5,061	3,087	4	1,974	R	62.1%	37.9%	62.1%	37.9%
8,314	LYON	3,205	1,727	1,475	3	252	R	53.9%	46.0%	53.9%	46.1%
65,565	MCCRACKEN	22,242	13,629	8,601	12	5,028	R	61.3%	38.7%	61.3%	38.7%
18,306	MCCREARY	4,792	3,417	1,375		2,042	R	71.3%	28.7%	71.3%	28.7%
9,531	MCLEAN	3,561	1,731	1,826	4	95	D	48.6%	51.3%	48.7%	51.3%
82,916	MADISON	24,255	13,737	10,401	117	3,336	R	56.6%	42.9%	56.9%	43.1%
13,333	MAGOFFIN	5,647	2,504	3,143		639	D	44.3%	55.7%	44.3%	55.7%
19,820	MARION	5,393	2,349	3,029	15	680	D	43.6%	56.2%	43.7%	56.3%
31,448	MARSHALL	11,948	6,689	5,254	5	1,435	R	56.0%	44.0%	56.0%	44.0%
12,929	MARTIN	3,682	2,453	1,226	3	1,227	R	66.6%	33.3%	66.7%	33.3%
17,490	MASON	5,007	2,724	2,282	1	442	R	54.4%	45.6%	54.4%	45.6%
28,602	MEADE	9,254	4,984	4,269	1	715	R	53.9%	46.1%	53.9%	46.1%
6,306	MENIFEE	2,389	869	1,520		651	D	36.4%	63.6%	36.4%	63.6%
21,331	MERCER	7,635	4,502	3,125	8	1,377	R	59.0%	40.9%	59.0%	41.0%
10,099	METCALFE	3,896	2,112	1,783	1	329	R	54.2%	45.8%	54.2%	45.8%
10,963	MONROE	4,586	3,488	1,098		2,390	R	76.1%	23.9%	76.1%	23.9%
26,499	MONTGOMERY	7,850	3,864	3,986		122	D	49.2%	50.8%	49.2%	50.8%
13,923	MORGAN	4,067	1,733	2,334		601	D	42.6%	57.4%	42.6%	57.4%
31,499	MUHLENBERG	8,964	4,019	4,945		926	D	44.8%	55.2%	44.8%	55.2%
43,437	NELSON	14,208	7,706	6,502		1,204	R	54.2%	45.8%	54.2%	45.8%
7,135	NICHOLAS	1,969	882	1,087		205	D	44.8%	55.2%	44.8%	55.2%
23,842	OHIO	8,520	4,498	4,021	1	477	R	52.8%	47.2%	52.8%	47.2%
60,316	OLDHAM	22,188	14,932	7,248	8	7,684	R	67.3%	32.7%	67.3%	32.7%
10,841	OWEN	3,426	1,968	1,458		510	R	57.4%	42.6%	57.4%	42.6%
4,755	OWSLEY	1,833	1,199	634		565	R	65.4%	34.6%	65.4%	34.6%
14,877	PENDLETON	3,997	2,525	1,472		1,053	R	63.2%	36.8%	63.2%	36.8%
28,712	PERRY	8,667	4,834	3,833		1,001	R	55.8%	44.2%	55.8%	44.2%
65,024	PIKE	15,134	7,663	7,470	1	193	R	50.6%	49.4%	50.6%	49.4%
12,613	POWELL	3,874	1,758	2,116		358	D	45.4%	54.6%	45.4%	54.6%
63,063	PULASKI	19,221	14,209	5,001	11	9,208	R	73.9%	26.0%	74.0%	26.0%

176

KENTUCKY

SENATOR 2010

2010 Census Population	County	Total Vote	Republican	Democratic	Other	Rep.-Dem. Plurality		Total Vote Rep.	Dem.	Major Vote Rep.	Dem.
2,282	ROBERTSON	746	373	373				50.0%	50.0%	50.0%	50.0%
17,056	ROCKCASTLE	4,483	3,182	1,301		1,881	R	71.0%	29.0%	71.0%	29.0%
23,333	ROWAN	6,635	2,883	3,752		869	D	43.5%	56.5%	43.5%	56.5%
17,565	RUSSELL	6,230	4,443	1,786	1	2,657	R	71.3%	28.7%	71.3%	28.7%
47,173	SCOTT	14,828	8,577	6,250	1	2,327	R	57.8%	42.1%	57.8%	42.2%
42,074	SHELBY	14,345	8,734	5,609	2	3,125	R	60.9%	39.1%	60.9%	39.1%
17,327	SIMPSON	4,911	2,846	2,065		781	R	58.0%	42.0%	58.0%	42.0%
17,061	SPENCER	6,857	4,295	2,562		1,733	R	62.6%	37.4%	62.6%	37.4%
24,512	TAYLOR	9,532	5,539	3,977	16	1,562	R	58.1%	41.7%	58.2%	41.8%
12,460	TODD	3,828	2,283	1,545		738	R	59.6%	40.4%	59.6%	40.4%
14,339	TRIGG	5,555	3,301	2,254		1,047	R	59.4%	40.6%	59.4%	40.6%
8,809	TRIMBLE	2,729	1,432	1,291	6	141	R	52.5%	47.3%	52.6%	47.4%
15,007	UNION	5,029	2,513	2,516		3	D	50.0%	50.0%	50.0%	50.0%
113,792	WARREN	30,338	18,651	11,686	1	6,965	R	61.5%	38.5%	61.5%	38.5%
11,717	WASHINGTON	4,385	2,480	1,904	1	576	R	56.6%	43.4%	56.6%	43.4%
20,813	WAYNE	6,703	3,868	2,835		1,033	R	57.7%	42.3%	57.7%	42.3%
13,621	WEBSTER	4,104	2,195	1,909		286	R	53.5%	46.5%	53.5%	46.5%
35,637	WHITLEY	9,063	6,469	2,594		3,875	R	71.4%	28.6%	71.4%	28.6%
7,355	WOLFE	1,859	737	1,122		385	D	39.6%	60.4%	39.6%	60.4%
24,939	WOODFORD	9,883	5,344	4,520	19	824	R	54.1%	45.7%	54.2%	45.8%
4,339,367	TOTAL	1,356,468	755,411	599,843	1,214	155,568	R	55.7%	44.2%	55.7%	44.3%

KENTUCKY

HOUSE OF REPRESENTATIVES

CD	Year	Total Vote	Republican Vote	Republican Candidate	Democratic Vote	Democratic Candidate	Other Vote	Rep.-Dem. Plurality		Total Vote Rep.	Dem.	Major Vote Rep.	Dem.
1	2010	215,479	153,519	WHITFIELD, EDWARD*	61,960	HATCHETT, CHARLES KENDALL		91,559	R	71.2%	28.8%	71.2%	28.8%
1	2008	276,786	178,107	WHITFIELD, EDWARD*	98,674	RYAN, HEATHER A.	5	79,433	R	64.3%	35.6%	64.3%	35.7%
1	2006	207,483	123,618	WHITFIELD, EDWARD*	83,865	BARLOW, TOM		39,753	R	59.6%	40.4%	59.6%	40.4%
1	2004	261,201	175,972	WHITFIELD, EDWARD*	85,229	CARTWRIGHT, BILLY R.		90,743	R	67.4%	32.6%	67.4%	32.6%
1	2002	180,217	117,600	WHITFIELD, EDWARD*	62,617	ALEXANDER, KLINT		54,983	R	65.3%	34.7%	65.3%	34.7%
2	2010	229,655	155,906	GUTHRIE, BRETT*	73,749	MARKSBERRY, ED		82,157	R	67.9%	32.1%	67.9%	32.1%
2	2008	302,315	158,936	GUTHRIE, BRETT	143,379	BOSWELL, DAVID E.		15,557	R	52.6%	47.4%	52.6%	47.4%
2	2006	213,963	118,548	LEWIS, RON*	95,415	WEAVER, MIKE		23,133	R	55.4%	44.6%	55.4%	44.6%
2	2004	272,979	185,394	LEWIS, RON*	87,585	SMITH, ADAM		97,809	R	67.9%	32.1%	67.9%	32.1%
2	2002	176,288	122,773	LEWIS, RON*	51,431	WILLIAMS, DAVID L.	2,084	71,342	R	69.6%	29.2%	70.5%	29.5%
3	2010	255,930	112,627	LALLY, TODD	139,940	YARMUTH, JOHN*	3,363	27,313	D	44.0%	54.7%	44.6%	55.4%
3	2008	343,370	139,527	NORTHUP, ANNE M.	203,843	YARMUTH, JOHN*		64,316	D	40.6%	59.4%	40.6%	59.4%
3	2006	241,965	116,568	NORTHUP, ANNE M.*	122,489	YARMUTH, JOHN	2,908	5,921	D	48.2%	50.6%	48.8%	51.2%
3	2004	328,139	197,736	NORTHUP, ANNE M.*	124,040	MILLER, TONY	6,363	73,696	R	60.3%	37.8%	61.5%	38.5%
3	2002	229,074	118,228	NORTHUP, ANNE M.*	110,846	CONWAY, JACK		7,382	R	51.6%	48.4%	51.6%	48.4%
4	2010	218,449	151,774	DAVIS, GEOFF*	66,675	WALTZ, JOHN		85,099	R	69.5%	30.5%	69.5%	30.5%
4	2008	301,759	190,210	DAVIS, GEOFF*	111,549	KELLEY, MICHAEL		78,661	R	63.0%	37.0%	63.0%	37.0%
4	2006	204,767	105,845	DAVIS, GEOFF*	88,822	LUCAS, KEN	10,100	17,023	R	51.7%	43.4%	54.4%	45.6%

KENTUCKY

HOUSE OF REPRESENTATIVES

CD	Year	Total Vote	Republican Vote	Republican Candidate	Democratic Vote	Democratic Candidate	Other Vote	Rep.-Dem. Plurality		Percentage Total Vote Rep.	Total Vote Dem.	Major Vote Rep.	Major Vote Dem.
4	2004	295,927	160,982	DAVIS, GEOFF	129,876	CLOONEY, NICK	5,069	31,106	R	54.4%	43.9%	55.3%	44.7%
4	2002	171,735	81,651	DAVIS, GEOFF	87,776	LUCAS, KEN*	2,308	6,125	D	47.5%	51.1%	48.2%	51.8%
5	2010	195,053	151,019	ROGERS, HAROLD*	44,034	HOLBERT, JAMES E.		106,985	R	77.4%	22.6%	77.4%	22.6%
5	2008	210,468	177,024	ROGERS, HAROLD*			33,444	177,024	R	84.1%		100.0%	
5	2006	199,568	147,201	ROGERS, HAROLD*	52,367	STEPP, KENNETH		94,834	R	73.8%	26.2%	73.8%	26.2%
5	2004	177,579	177,579	ROGERS, HAROLD*	—			177,579	R	100.0%		100.0%	
5	2002	176,240	137,986	ROGERS, HAROLD*	38,254	BAILEY, SIDNEY JANE		99,732	R	78.3%	21.7%	78.3%	21.7%
6	2010	239,224	119,165	BARR, GARLAND "ANDY"	119,812	CHANDLER, BEN*	247	647	D	49.8%	50.1%	49.9%	50.1%
6	2008	315,142	111,378	LARSON, JON	203,764	CHANDLER, BEN*		92,386	D	35.3%	64.7%	35.3%	64.7%
6	2006	185,780		—	158,765	CHANDLER, BEN*	27,015	158,765	D		85.5%		100.0%
6	2004	299,217	119,716	BUFORD, TOM	175,355	CHANDLER, BEN*	4,146	55,639	D	40.0%	58.6%	40.6%	59.4%
6	2002	160,688	115,622	FLETCHER, ERNIE*	—		45,066	115,622	R	72.0%		100.0%	
TOTAL	2010	1,353,790	844,010		506,170		3,610	337,840	R	62.3%	37.4%	62.5%	37.5%
TOTAL	2008	1,749,840	955,182		761,209		33,449	193,973	R	54.6%	43.5%	55.7%	44.3%
TOTAL	2006	1,253,526	611,780		601,723		40,023	10,057	R	48.8%	48.0%	50.4%	49.6%
TOTAL	2004	1,635,243	1,017,379		602,085		15,779	415,294	R	62.2%	36.8%	62.8%	37.2%
TOTAL	2002	1,094,242	693,860		350,924		49,458	342,936	R	63.4%	32.1%	66.4%	33.6%

An asterisk (*) denotes incumbent.

KENTUCKY

GENERAL AND PRIMARY ELECTIONS

2010 GENERAL ELECTIONS

Senator   Other was 1,214 scattered write-in.

House   Other vote was:

CD 1
CD 2
CD 3   2,029 Libertarian (Edward A. Martin); 1,334 Independent (Michael D. Hansen).
CD 4
CD 5
CD 6   225 write-in (C. Wes Collins); 22 write-in (Randolph S. Vance).

2010 PRIMARY ELECTIONS

Primary	May 18, 2010	**Registration** (as of May 18, 2010)	Democratic	1,618,011
			Republican	1,044,872
			Other	189,113
			TOTAL	2,851,996

Primary Type   Closed—Only registered Democrats and Republicans could vote in their party's primary.

KENTUCKY

GENERAL AND PRIMARY ELECTIONS

	REPUBLICAN PRIMARIES			DEMOCRATIC PRIMARIES		
Senator	Rand Paul	206,986	58.8%	Jack Conway	229,433	44.0%
	C.M. "Trey" Grayson	124,864	35.4%	Daniel Mongiardo	225,260	43.2%
	Bill Johnson	7,861	2.2%	Darlene F. Price	28,531	5.5%
	John Stephenson	6,885	2.0%	James Buckmaster	20,561	3.9%
	Gurley L. Martin	2,850	0.8%	Maurice M. Sweeney	17,874	3.4%
	Jon J. Scribner	2,829	0.8%			
	TOTAL	352,275		TOTAL	521,659	
Congressional District 1	Edward Whitfield*	Unopposed		Charles Kendall Hatchett	Unopposed	
Congressional District 2	Brett Guthrie*	Unopposed		Ed Marksberry	Unopposed	
Congressional District 3	Todd Lally	22,048	51.9%	John Yarmuth*	Unopposed	
	Larry Hausman	10,674	25.1%			
	Jeff Reetz	7,167	16.9%			
	Brooks Wicker	2,595	6.1%			
	TOTAL	42,484				
Congressional District 4	Geoff Davis*	Unopposed		John Waltz	Unopposed	
Congressional District 5	Harold Rogers*	Unopposed		James E. Holbert	27,552	41.0%
				Kenneth Stepp	23,323	34.7%
				David Prince	16,333	24.3%
				TOTAL	67,208	
Congressional District 6	Garland "Andy" Barr	31,255	63.9%	Ben Chandler*	Unopposed	
	Mike Templeman	4,789	9.8%			
	Matt Lockett	4,070	8.3%			
	John T. Kemper III	3,454	7.1%			
	George Pendergrass	3,438	7.0%			
	Perry Wilson Barnes	1,880	3.8%			
	TOTAL	48,886				

An asterisk (*) denotes incumbent. The names of unopposed candidates did not appear on the primary ballot; therefore, no votes were cast for these candidates.

LOUISIANA

Congressional districts first established for elections held in 2002
7 members

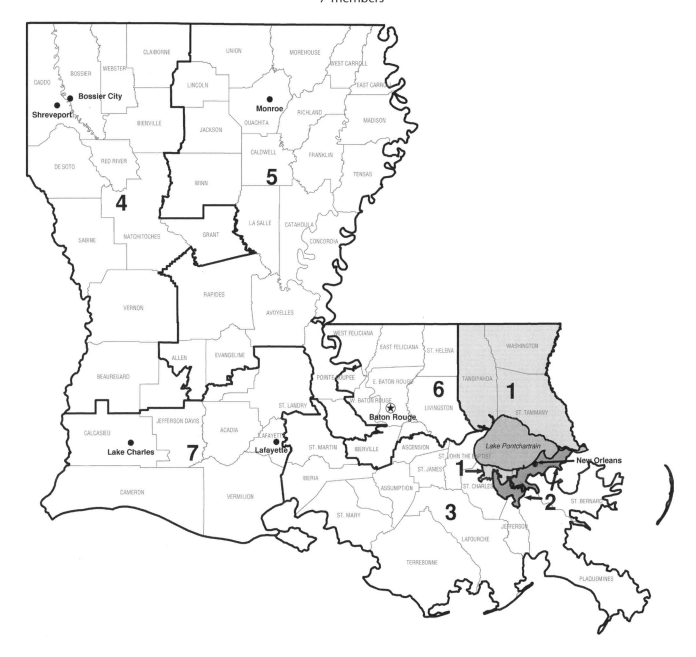

LOUISIANA

GOVERNOR
Bobby Jindal (R). Elected 2007 to a four-year term.

SENATORS (1 Democrat, 1 Republican)
Mary L. Landrieu (D). Reelected 2008 to a six-year term. Previously elected 2002, 1996.

David Vitter (R). Reelected 2010 to a six-year term. Previously elected 2004.

REPRESENTATIVES (6 Republicans, 1 Democrat)
1. Steve Scalise (R)
2. Cedric Richmond (D)
3. Jeff Landry (R)
4. John Fleming (R)
5. Rodney Alexander (R)
6. Bill Cassidy (R)
7. Charles Boustany Jr. (R)

POSTWAR VOTE FOR PRESIDENT

Year	Total Vote	Republican Vote	Republican Candidate	Democratic Vote	Democratic Candidate	Other Vote	Plurality	Total Vote Rep.	Total Vote Dem.	Major Vote Rep.	Major Vote Dem.
2008	1,960,761	1,148,275	McCain, John	782,989	Obama, Barack	29,497	365,286 R	58.6%	39.9%	59.5%	40.5%
2004	1,943,106	1,102,169	Bush, George W.	820,299	Kerry, John	20,638	281,870 R	56.7%	42.2%	57.3%	42.7%
2000**	1,765,656	927,871	Bush, George W.	792,344	Gore, Al	45,441	135,527 R	52.6%	44.9%	53.9%	46.1%
1996**	1,783,959	712,586	Dole, Bob	927,837	Clinton, Bill	143,536	215,251 D	39.9%	52.0%	43.4%	56.6%
1992**	1,790,017	733,386	Bush, George	815,971	Clinton, Bill	240,660	82,585 D	41.0%	45.6%	47.3%	52.7%
1988	1,628,202	883,702	Bush, George	717,460	Dukakis, Michael S.	27,040	166,242 R	54.3%	44.1%	55.2%	44.8%
1984	1,706,822	1,037,299	Reagan, Ronald	651,586	Mondale, Walter F.	17,937	385,713 R	60.8%	38.2%	61.4%	38.6%
1980**	1,548,591	792,853	Reagan, Ronald	708,453	Carter, Jimmy	47,285	84,400 R	51.2%	45.7%	52.8%	47.2%
1976	1,278,439	587,446	Ford, Gerald R.	661,365	Carter, Jimmy	29,628	73,919 D	46.0%	51.7%	47.0%	53.0%
1972	1,051,491	686,852	Nixon, Richard M.	298,142	McGovern, George S.	66,497	388,710 R	65.3%	28.4%	69.7%	30.3%
1968**	1,097,450	257,535	Nixon, Richard M.	309,615	Humphrey, Hubert H.	530,300	220,685 A	23.5%	28.2%	45.4%	54.6%
1964	896,293	509,225	Goldwater, Barry M.	387,068	Johnson, Lyndon B.		122,157 R	56.8%	43.2%	56.8%	43.2%
1960**	807,891	230,980	Nixon, Richard M.	407,339	Kennedy, John F.	169,572	176,359 D	28.6%	50.4%	36.2%	63.8%
1956	617,544	329,047	Eisenhower, Dwight D.	243,977	Stevenson, Adlai E.	44,520	85,070 R	53.3%	39.5%	57.4%	42.6%
1952	651,952	306,925	Eisenhower, Dwight D.	345,027	Stevenson, Adlai E.		38,102 D	47.1%	52.9%	47.1%	52.9%
1948**	416,336	72,657	Dewey, Thomas E.	136,344	Truman, Harry S.	207,335	67,946 SR	17.5%	32.7%	34.8%	65.2%

**In past elections, the other vote included: 20,473 Green (Ralph Nader); 1996 - 123,293 Reform (Ross Perot); 1992 - 211,478 Independent (Perot); 1980 - 26,345 Independent (John Anderson); 1968 - 530,300 American Independent (George Wallace); 1960 - 169,572 Unpledged Independent Electors; 1948 - 204,290 States' Rights (Strom Thurmond). Wallace carried Louisiana in 1968 with 48.3 percent of the vote. Thurmond won the state in 1948 with 49.1 percent.

LOUISIANA

POSTWAR VOTE FOR GOVERNOR

Year	Total Vote	Republican Vote	Republican Candidate	Democratic Vote	Democratic Candidate	Other Vote	Rep.-Dem. Plurality	Total Vote Rep.	Total Vote Dem.	Major Vote Rep.	Major Vote Dem.
2007**	1,297,840	699,275	Jindal, Bobby	226,476	Boasso, Walter J.	372,089	472,799 R	53.9%	17.5%		
2003*	1,407,842	676,484	Jindal, Bobby	731,358	Blanco, Kathleen Babineaux		54,874 D	48.1%	51.9%	48.1%	51.9%
1999	1,295,205	805,203	Foster, Mike	382,445	Jefferson, William J.	107,557	422,758 R	62.2%	29.5%		
1995*	1,550,360	984,499	Foster, Mike	565,861	Fields, Cleo		418,638 R	63.5%	36.5%	63.5%	36.5%
1991*	1,728,040	671,009	Duke, David E.	1,057,031	Edwards, Edwin W.		386,022 D	38.8%	61.2%	38.8%	61.2%
1987**	1,558,730	287,780	Livingston, Robert L.	516,078	Roemer, Charles	754,872	78,277 D	18.5%	33.1%		
1983	1,615,905	588,508	Treen, David C.	1,006,561	Edwards, Edwin W.	20,836	418,053 D	36.4%	62.3%		
1979*	1,371,825	690,691	Treen, David C.	681,134	Lambert, Louis		9,557 R	50.3%	49.7%	50.3%	49.7%
1975	430,095		—	430,095	Edwards, Edwin W.		430,095 D		100.0%		100.0%
1972	1,121,570	480,424	Treen, David C.	641,146	Edwards, Edwin W.		160,722 D	42.8%	57.2%	42.8%	57.2%
1968	372,762		—	372,762	McKeithen, John J.		372,762 D		100.0%		100.0%
1964	773,390	297,753	Lyons, C. H.	469,589	McKeithen, John J.	6,048	171,836 D	38.5%	60.7%	38.8%	61.2%
1960	506,562	86,135	Grevemberg, F. C.	407,907	Davis, Jimmie H.	12,520	321,772 D	17.0%	80.5%	17.4%	82.6%
1956	172,291		—	172,291	Long, Earl K.		172,291 D		100.0%		100.0%
1952	123,681	4,958	Bagwell, Harrison G.	118,723	Kennon, Robert F.		113,765 D	4.0%	96.0%	4.0%	96.0%
1948	76,566		—	76,566	Long, Earl K.		76,566 D		100.0%		100.0%

Since the 1970s, Louisiana has had a two-tier election system for governor in which all candidates, regardless of party, run together in an open election. A candidate that wins a majority of the vote is elected. If no candidate receives 50 percent, a runoff is held between the top two finishers. A single asterisk (*) indicates gubernatorial elections that were decided in a runoff, with the results of the runoff listed in this chart. In elections that did not require a runoff, the leading Democratic and Republican candidates are listed with their votes from the first-round, open election. The votes for other candidates are listed in the "Other" column, regardless of whether they were Democratic, Republican, or independent. In past elections, the other vote included: 2007 - 186,682 No Party (John Georges), 161,665 Democrat (Foster Campbell); 1987 - 437,801 Democrat (Edwin W. Edwards). In 1987, Edwards withdrew after finishing second in the initial round of voting. Democrat Charles Roemer finished first with 33.1 percent and with Edwards' withdrawal, no runoff was held. The major party vote percentages are given for those elections where there was no more than one Democratic and one Republican candidate. The Republican Party did not run a candidate in the 1948, 1956, 1968, and 1975 gubernatorial elections.

POSTWAR VOTE FOR SENATOR

Year	Total Vote	Republican Vote	Republican Candidate	Democratic Vote	Democratic Candidate	Other Vote	Rep.-Dem. Plurality	Total Vote Rep.	Total Vote Dem.	Major Vote Rep.	Major Vote Dem.
2010	1,264,994	715,415	Vitter, David	476,572	Melancon, Charlie	73,007	238,843 R	56.6%	37.7%	60.0%	40.0%
2008	1,896,574	867,177	Kennedy, John	988,298	Landrieu, Mary L.	41,099	121,121 D	45.7%	52.1%	46.7%	53.3%
2004**	1,848,056	943,014	Vitter, David	542,150	John, Chris	362,892	400,864 R	51.0%	29.3%		
2002*	1,235,296	596,642	Terrell, Suzanne Haik	638,654	Landrieu, Mary L.		42,012 D	48.3%	51.7%	48.3%	51.7%
1998	969,165	306,616	Donelon, Jim	620,502	Breaux, John B.	42,047	313,886 D	31.6%	64.0%		
1996*	1,700,102	847,157	Jenkins, Louis	852,945	Landrieu, Mary L.		5,788 D	49.8%	50.2%	49.8%	50.2%
1992	843,037	69,986	Stockstill, Lyle	616,021	Breaux, John B.	157,030	541,236 D	8.3%	73.1%		
1990	1,396,113	607,391	Duke, David E.	752,902	Johnston, J. Bennett	35,820	145,511 D	43.5%	53.9%		
1986*	1,369,897	646,311	Moore, W. Henson	723,586	Breaux, John B.		77,275 D	47.2%	52.8%	47.2%	52.8%
1984	977,473	86,546	Robert M. Ross	838,181	Johnston, J. Bennett	52,746	751,635 D	8.9%	85.7%		
1980**	841,013	13,739	Bardwell, Jerry C.	484,770	Long, Russell B.	342,504	158,848 D	1.6%	57.6%		
1978**	839,669		—	498,773	Johnston, J. Bennett	340,896	157,877 D		59.4%		
1974	434,643			434,643	Long, Russell B.		434,643 D		100.0%		100.0%
1972**	1,084,904	206,846	Toledano, Ben C.	598,987	Johnston, J. Bennett	279,071	348,826 D	19.1%	55.2%	25.7%	74.3%
1968	518,586		—	518,586	Long, Russell B.		518,586 D		100.0%		100.0%
1966	437,695		—	437,695	Ellender, Allen J.		437,695 D		100.0%		100.0%
1962	421,904	103,066	O'Hearn, Taylor W.	318,838	Long, Russell B.		215,772 D	24.4%	75.6%	24.4%	75.6%
1960	541,928	109,698	Reese, George W.	432,228	Ellender, Allen J.	2	322,530 D	20.2%	79.8%	20.2%	79.8%
1956	335,564		—	335,564	Long, Russell B.		335,564 D		100.0%		100.0%
1954	207,115		—	207,115	Ellender, Allen J.		207,115 D		100.0%		100.0%
1950	251,838	30,931	Gerth, Charles S.	220,907	Long, Russell B.		189,976 D	12.3%	87.7%	12.3%	87.7%
1948	330,124		—	330,115	Ellender, Allen J.	9	330,115 D		100.0%		100.0%
1948S	408,667	102,331	Clarke, Clem S.	306,336	Long, Russell B.		204,005 D	25.0%	75.0%	25.0%	75.0%

In 2008 Louisiana returned to the traditional system of party primaries followed by a general election to fill seats in Congress. From 1978 through 2004, Senate seats were decided in open elections in which candidates of all parties ran together on the same ballot. If no candidate won a majority of the vote in the first round, a runoff was held between the top two vote-getters, regardless of party. A single asterisk (*) indicates Senate elections that were decided in a runoff, with the results of the runoff listed in this chart. In elections that did not require a runoff, the leading Democratic and Republican candidates are listed with their votes in the first-round, open election. The votes for other candidates are listed in the "Other" column, regardless of whether they were Democratic, Republican, or independent. In past elections, the other vote included: 2004 - Democrat (John Kennedy); 1980 - 325,922 Democrat (Louis Jenkins); 1978 - 340,896 Democrat (Louis Jenkins); 1972 - 250,161 Independent (John J. McKeithen). One of the 1948 elections was for a short term to fill a vacancy. The major party vote percentages are given for those elections where there was no more than one Democratic and one Republican candidate. The Republican Party did not run a candidate in Senate elections in 1948, 1954, 1956, 1966, 1968, 1974, and 1978.

LOUISIANA

SENATOR 2010

2010 Census Population	Parish	Total Vote	Republican	Democratic	Other	Rep.-Dem. Plurality	Percentage Total Vote Rep.	Total Vote Dem.	Major Vote Rep.	Major Vote Dem.
61,773	ACADIA	17,354	11,627	4,719	1,008	6,908 R	67.0%	27.2%	71.1%	28.9%
25,764	ALLEN	4,992	3,065	1,550	377	1,515 R	61.4%	31.0%	66.4%	33.6%
107,215	ASCENSION	31,462	19,234	10,333	1,895	8,901 R	61.1%	32.8%	65.1%	34.9%
23,421	ASSUMPTION	7,125	2,981	3,848	296	867 D	41.8%	54.0%	43.7%	56.3%
42,073	AVOYELLES	8,749	4,925	3,109	715	1,816 R	56.3%	35.5%	61.3%	38.7%
35,654	BEAUREGARD	8,787	6,236	1,899	652	4,337 R	71.0%	21.6%	76.7%	23.3%
14,353	BIENVILLE	4,848	2,465	2,006	377	459 R	50.8%	41.4%	55.1%	44.9%
116,979	BOSSIER	27,887	20,144	6,620	1,123	13,524 R	72.2%	23.7%	75.3%	24.7%
254,969	CADDO	72,661	34,947	33,759	3,955	1,188 R	48.1%	46.5%	50.9%	49.1%
192,768	CALCASIEU	51,519	30,903	17,018	3,598	13,885 R	60.0%	33.0%	64.5%	35.5%
10,132	CALDWELL	2,663	1,784	680	199	1,104 R	67.0%	25.5%	72.4%	27.6%
6,839	CAMERON	2,231	1,686	400	145	1,286 R	75.6%	17.9%	80.8%	19.2%
10,407	CATAHOULA	2,873	1,926	774	173	1,152 R	67.0%	26.9%	71.3%	28.7%
17,195	CLAIBORNE	3,995	2,387	1,394	214	993 R	59.7%	34.9%	63.1%	36.9%
20,822	CONCORDIA	5,359	3,319	1,764	276	1,555 R	61.9%	32.9%	65.3%	34.7%
26,656	DE SOTO	7,363	4,213	2,774	376	1,439 R	57.2%	37.7%	60.3%	39.7%
440,171	EAST BATON ROUGE	132,723	64,298	61,561	6,864	2,737 R	48.4%	46.4%	51.1%	48.9%
7,759	EAST CARROLL	2,554	893	1,270	391	377 D	35.0%	49.7%	41.3%	58.7%
20,267	EAST FELICIANA	6,924	3,531	2,925	468	606 R	51.0%	42.2%	54.7%	45.3%
33,984	EVANGELINE	9,744	5,465	3,427	852	2,038 R	56.1%	35.2%	61.5%	38.5%
20,767	FRANKLIN	5,295	3,482	1,456	357	2,026 R	65.8%	27.5%	70.5%	29.5%
22,309	GRANT	5,087	3,699	957	431	2,742 R	72.7%	18.8%	79.4%	20.6%
73,240	IBERIA	21,347	12,964	7,350	1,033	5,614 R	60.7%	34.4%	63.8%	36.2%
33,387	IBERVILLE	10,354	3,996	5,788	570	1,792 D	38.6%	55.9%	40.8%	59.2%
16,274	JACKSON	4,775	3,059	1,416	300	1,643 R	64.1%	29.7%	68.4%	31.6%
432,552	JEFFERSON	119,268	72,054	40,887	6,327	31,167 R	60.4%	34.3%	63.8%	36.2%
31,594	JEFFERSON DAVIS	8,396	5,453	2,379	564	3,074 R	64.9%	28.3%	69.6%	30.4%
221,578	LAFAYETTE	64,326	41,666	18,768	3,892	22,898 R	64.8%	29.2%	68.9%	31.1%
96,318	LAFOURCHE	25,298	16,509	7,512	1,277	8,997 R	65.3%	29.7%	68.7%	31.3%
14,890	LA SALLE	3,950	3,092	524	334	2,568 R	78.3%	13.3%	85.5%	14.5%
46,735	LINCOLN	11,143	6,769	3,767	607	3,002 R	60.7%	33.8%	64.2%	35.8%
128,026	LIVINGSTON	34,376	26,378	5,854	2,144	20,524 R	76.7%	17.0%	81.8%	18.2%
12,093	MADISON	2,617	1,291	1,190	136	101 R	49.3%	45.5%	52.0%	48.0%
27,979	MOREHOUSE	7,431	4,002	2,962	467	1,040 R	53.9%	39.9%	57.5%	42.5%
39,566	NATCHITOCHES	9,598	5,178	3,684	736	1,494 R	53.9%	38.4%	58.4%	41.6%
343,829	ORLEANS	97,306	19,858	73,071	4,377	53,213 D	20.4%	75.1%	21.4%	78.6%
153,720	OUACHITA	39,684	23,955	13,646	2,083	10,309 R	60.4%	34.4%	63.7%	36.3%
23,042	PLAQUEMINES	6,538	3,605	1,970	963	1,635 R	55.1%	30.1%	64.7%	35.3%
22,802	POINTE COUPEE	8,514	3,867	4,018	629	151 D	45.4%	47.2%	49.0%	51.0%
131,613	RAPIDES	35,947	21,803	11,313	2,831	10,490 R	60.7%	31.5%	65.8%	34.2%
9,091	RED RIVER	2,507	1,403	958	146	445 R	56.0%	38.2%	59.4%	40.6%
20,725	RICHLAND	5,699	3,445	1,845	409	1,600 R	60.4%	32.4%	65.1%	34.9%
24,233	SABINE	5,831	4,247	1,105	479	3,142 R	72.8%	19.0%	79.4%	20.6%
35,897	ST. BERNARD	8,213	4,631	3,029	553	1,602 R	56.4%	36.9%	60.5%	39.5%
52,780	ST. CHARLES	16,387	10,061	5,582	744	4,479 R	61.4%	34.1%	64.3%	35.7%

LOUISIANA

SENATOR 2010

2010 Census Population	Parish	Total Vote	Republican	Democratic	Other	Rep.-Dem. Plurality	Percentage			
							Total Vote		Major Vote	
							Rep.	Dem.	Rep.	Dem.
11,203	ST. HELENA	4,271	1,682	2,254	335	572 D	39.4%	52.8%	42.7%	57.3%
22,102	ST. JAMES	8,342	3,145	4,895	302	1,750 D	37.7%	58.7%	39.1%	60.9%
45,924	ST. JOHN THE BAPTIST	13,122	5,134	7,435	553	2,301 D	39.1%	56.7%	40.8%	59.2%
83,384	ST. LANDRY	26,948	13,368	11,539	2,041	1,829 R	49.6%	42.8%	53.7%	46.3%
52,160	ST. MARTIN	16,507	9,332	6,331	844	3,001 R	56.5%	38.4%	59.6%	40.4%
54,650	ST. MARY	15,219	8,515	5,896	808	2,619 R	55.9%	38.7%	59.1%	40.9%
233,740	ST. TAMMANY	76,521	56,779	15,931	3,811	40,848 R	74.2%	20.8%	78.1%	21.9%
121,097	TANGIPAHOA	31,418	20,253	9,404	1,761	10,849 R	64.5%	29.9%	68.3%	31.7%
5,252	TENSAS	1,445	759	594	92	165 R	52.5%	41.1%	56.1%	43.9%
111,860	TERREBONNE	26,724	17,429	8,016	1,279	9,413 R	65.2%	30.0%	68.5%	31.5%
22,721	UNION	6,427	4,292	1,674	461	2,618 R	66.8%	26.0%	71.9%	28.1%
57,999	VERMILION	15,374	10,571	3,839	964	6,732 R	68.8%	25.0%	73.4%	26.6%
52,334	VERNON	8,724	6,269	1,645	810	4,624 R	71.9%	18.9%	79.2%	20.8%
47,168	WASHINGTON	11,519	7,294	3,533	692	3,761 R	63.3%	30.7%	67.4%	32.6%
41,207	WEBSTER	12,312	7,380	4,191	741	3,189 R	59.9%	34.0%	63.8%	36.2%
23,788	WEST BATON ROUGE	7,789	3,988	3,409	392	579 R	51.2%	43.8%	53.9%	46.1%
11,604	WEST CARROLL	2,670	1,987	485	198	1,502 R	74.4%	18.2%	80.4%	19.6%
15,625	WEST FELICIANA	3,975	2,082	1,677	216	405 R	52.4%	42.2%	55.4%	44.6%
15,313	WINN	3,987	2,660	963	364	1,697 R	66.7%	24.2%	73.4%	26.6%
4,533,372	TOTAL	1,264,994	715,415	476,572	73,007	238,843 R	56.6%	37.7%	60.0%	40.0%

LOUISIANA

HOUSE OF REPRESENTATIVES

			Republican		Democratic				Total Vote		Major Vote	
CD	Year	Total Vote	Vote	Candidate	Vote	Candidate	Other Vote	Rep.-Dem. Plurality	Rep.	Dem.	Rep.	Dem.
1	2010	200,176	157,182	SCALISE, STEVE*	38,416	KATZ, MYRON	4,578	118,766 R	78.5%	19.2%	80.4%	19.6%
1	2008	288,007	189,168	SCALISE, STEVE*	98,839	HARLAN, JIM		90,329 R	65.7%	34.3%		
1	2006	148,128	130,508	JINDAL, BOBBY*	10,919	GEREIGHTY, DAVID	6,701	119,589 R	88.1%	7.4%		
1	2004	287,897	225,708	JINDAL, BOBBY	19,266	ARMSTRONG, ROY	42,923	206,442 R	78.4%	6.7%		
1	2002	180,570	147,117	VITTER, DAVID*		—	33,453	147,117 R	81.5%			
2	2010	129,604	43,378	CAO, ANH "JOSEPH"*	83,705	RICHMOND, CEDRIC	2,521	40,327 D	33.5%	64.6%	34.1%	65.9%
2	2008@	66,882	33,132	CAO, ANH "JOSEPH"	31,318	JEFFERSON, WILLIAM J.*	2,432	1,814 R	49.5%	46.8%	51.4%	48.6%
2	2006#	62,164		—	62,164	JEFFERSON*/CARTER		8,142 D		100.0%		100.0%
2	2004	219,607	46,097	SCHWERTZ, ARTHUR L. "ART"	173,510	JEFFERSON, WILLIAM J.*		127,413 D	21.0%	79.0%	21.0%	79.0%
2	2002	142,156	15,440	SULLIVAN, "SILKY"	90,310	JEFFERSON, WILLIAM J.*	36,406	74,870 D	10.9%	63.5%		
3	2010	170,877	108,963	LANDRY, JEFF	61,914	SANGISETTY, RAVI		47,049 R	63.8%	36.2%	63.8%	36.2%
3	2008			—		MELANCON, CHARLIE*		D				
3	2006	136,331	54,950	ROMERO, CRAIG	75,023	MELANCON, CHARLIE*	6,358	20,073 D	40.3%	55.0%		
3	2004#	114,653	57,042	TAUZIN, W. J. "BILLY" III	57,611	MELANCON, CHARLIE		569 D	49.8%	50.2%	49.8%	50.2%
3	2002	150,342	130,323	TAUZIN, BILLY*		—	20,019	130,323 R	86.7%		100.0%	
4	2010	168,794	105,223	FLEMING, JOHN*	54,609	MELVILLE, DAVID	8,962	50,614 R	62.3%	32.4%	65.8%	34.2%
4	2008@	92,572	44,501	FLEMING, JOHN	44,151	CARMOUCHE, PAUL J.	3,920	350 R	48.1%	47.7%	50.2%	49.8%
4	2006	134,272	77,078	McCRERY, JIM*	22,757	CASH, ARTIS R., SR.	34,437	54,321 R	57.4%	16.9%		
4	2004			McCRERY, JIM*		—		R				
4	2002	160,093	114,649	McCRERY, JIM*	42,340	MILKOVICH, JOHN	3,104	72,309 R	71.6%	26.4%	73.0%	27.0%
5	2010	155,312	122,033	ALEXANDER, RODNEY*		—	33,279	122,033 R	78.6%		100.0%	
5	2008			ALEXANDER, RODNEY*		—		R				
5	2006	114,582	78,211	ALEXANDER, RODNEY*	33,233	HEARN, GLORIA WILLIAMS	3,138	44,978 R	68.3%	29.0%	70.2%	29.8%
5	2004	238,057	141,495	ALEXANDER, RODNEY*	58,591	BLAKES, ZELMA "TISA"	37,971	82,904 R	59.4%	24.6%		
5	2002#	172,462	85,744	FLETCHER, LEE	86,718	ALEXANDER, RODNEY		974 D	49.7%	50.3%	49.7%	50.3%
6	2010	211,184	138,607	CASSIDY, BILL*	72,577	McDONALD, MERRITT E.		66,030 R	65.6%	34.4%	65.6%	34.4%
6	2008	312,416	150,332	CASSIDY, BILL	125,886	CAZAYOUX, DON*	36,198	24,446 R	48.1%	40.3%	54.4%	45.6%
6	2006	114,306	94,658	BAKER, RICHARD H.*		—	19,648	94,658 R	82.8%		100.0%	
6	2004	261,869	189,106	BAKER, RICHARD H.*	50,732	CRAIG, RUFUS HOLT JR.	22,031	138,374 R	72.2%		100.0%	
6	2002	174,830	146,932	BAKER, RICHARD H.*		—	27,898	146,932 R	84.0%		100.0%	
7	2010			BOUSTANY, CHARLES JR.*		—		R				
7	2008	286,299	177,173	BOUSTANY, CHARLES JR.*	98,280	CRAVINS, DONALD JR.	10,846	78,893 R	61.9%	34.3%	64.3%	35.7%
7	2006	160,853	113,720	BOUSTANY, CHARLES JR.*	47,133	STAGG, MIKE		66,587 R	70.7%	29.3%	70.7%	29.3%
7	2004#	136,532	75,039	BOUSTANY, CHARLES JR.	61,493	MOUNT, WILLIELANDRY		13,546 R	55.0%	45.0%	55.0%	45.0%
7	2002	159,710		—	138,659	JOHN, CHRIS*	21,051	138,659 D		86.8%		100.0%
TOTAL	2010	1,035,947	675,386		311,221		49,340	364,165 R	65.2%	30.0%	68.5%	31.5%
TOTAL	2008	1,046,176	594,306		398,474		53,396	195,832 R	56.8%	38.1%	59.9%	40.1%
TOTAL	2006	902,498	579,702		295,762		27,034	283,940 R	64.2%	32.8%	66.2%	33.8%
TOTAL	2004	1,545,982	936,801		609,181			327,620 R	60.6%	39.4%	60.6%	39.4%
TOTAL	2002	1,152,358	707,923		361,473		82,962	346,450 R	61.4%	31.4%	66.2%	33.8%

In 2008, three of the general elections for House seats in Louisiana were held on November 4. Two others were held December 6 (following primary runoffs on November 4), and are indicated by "@." In the other two districts, no election was held as one candidate in each district ran unopposed. Previously, Louisiana had a unique two-tier electoral system for House seats, with a first round of voting that featured candidates from all parties running together on the same ballot. A candidate that won a majority of the vote in the first round was elected. Otherwise, the top two finishers met in a runoff. In 2002 and again in 2006, one runoff for the House of Representatives was required; in 2004 there were two runoffs. All four are indicated by a pound sign (#). In elections that did not require a runoff, the leading Democratic and Republican candidates are listed with their first-round votes. The votes for other candidates are listed in the "Other" column, regardless of whether they were Democratic, Republican, or unaffiliated with either party. However, the statewide vote totals represent the aggregate vote for all House candidates of each party in the November balloting, not just the top finishers. The major party vote percentages are given for those individual House elections where there was no more than one Democratic and one Republican candidate.

An asterisk (*) denotes incumbent. In 2006, the runoff in the Louisiana 2nd District featured two Democrats, with their vote as follows: William J. Jefferson 35,153 (56.5 percent); Karen Carter 27,011 (43.5%), resulting in a Jefferson plurality of 8,142 votes.

LOUISIANA

GENERAL AND PRIMARY ELECTIONS

2010 GENERAL ELECTIONS

Note: Candidates are listed as "Other" if they did not belong to a recognized political party in Louisiana. In 2010, there were five recognized parties: Democratic, Republican, Green, Libertarian and Reform.

Senator	Other vote was 13,957 Libertarian (Randall Todd Hayes); 9,973 No Party (Michael Karlton Brown); 9,190 Other (Michael Lane Spears); 8,167 Other (Ernest D. Wooton); 7,474 No Party (R.A. "Skip" Galan); 5,879 Reform (William R. McShan); 5,734 Other (William Robert Lang Jr.); 4,810 No Party (Milton Gordon); 4,043 Other (Thomas G. LaFargue); 3,780 No Party (Sam Houston Melton Jr.).
House	Other vote was:
CD 1	4,578 Other (Arden Wells).
CD 2	1,876 No Party (Anthony Marquize); 645 No Party (Jack Radosta).
CD 3	
CD 4	8,962 Other (Artis Cash).
CD 5	33,279 No Party (Tom Gibbs Jr.)
CD 6	
CD 7	

2010 PRIMARY ELECTION

Primary	August 28, 2010	**Registration** (as of August 1, 2010)	Democratic	1,488,463
			Republican	757,212
			Other	671,262
			TOTAL	*2,916,937*

Primary Runoff October 2, 2010

Primary Type Republicans held a "closed" primary limited to registered Republican voters only. Democrats held a "semi-open" primary, in which registered Democrats and registered voters not affiliated with any recognized party could participate.

LOUISIANA

GENERAL AND PRIMARY ELECTIONS

	REPUBLICAN PRIMARIES			DEMOCRATIC PRIMARIES		
Senator	David Vitter*	85,225	87.6%	Charlie Melancon	77,809	70.6%
	Chet D. Traylor	6,841	7.0%	Neeson J. Chauvin Jr.	19,521	17.7%
	Nick J. Accardo	5,232	5.4%	Cary J. Deaton	12,853	11.7%
	TOTAL	97,298		TOTAL	110,183	
Congressional District 1	Steve Scalise*	Unopposed		Myron Katz	Unopposed	
Congressional District 2	Anh "Joseph" Cao*	Unopposed		Cedric Richmond	14,678	60.5%
				Juan LaFonta	5,171	21.3%
				Eugene Green	2,500	10.3%
				Gary Johnson	1,914	7.9%
				TOTAL	24,263	
Congressional District 3	Jeff Landry	10,396	49.6%	Ravi Sangisetty	Unopposed	
	Hunt Downer	7,570	36.1%			
	Kristian Magar	2,987	14.3%			
	TOTAL	20,953				
	PRIMARY RUNOFF					
	Jeff Landry	19,657	65.1%			
	Hunt Downer	10,549	34.9%			
	TOTAL	30,206				
Congressional District 4	John Fleming*	Unopposed		David Melville	10,145	81.1%
				Steven Jude Gavi	2,365	18.9%
				TOTAL	12,510	
Congressional District 5	Rodney Alexander*	14,031	88.9%	No Democratic candidate		
	Todd Slavant	1,744	11.1%			
	TOTAL	15,775				
Congressional District 6	Bill Cassidy*	Unopposed		Merritt E. McDonald	Unopposed	
Congressional District 7	Charles Boustany Jr.*	Unopposed		No Democratic candidate		

An asterisk (*) denotes incumbent. The names of unopposed candidates did not appear on the primary ballot; therefore, no votes were cast for these candidates.

MAINE

Congressional districts first established for elections held in 2004
2 members

MAINE

GOVERNOR
Paul R. LePage (R). Elected 2010 to a four-year term.

SENATORS (2 Republicans)
Susan Collins (R). Reelected 2008 to a six-year term. Previously elected 2002,1996.

Olympia J. Snowe (R). Reelected 2006 to a six-year term. Previously elected 2000,1994.

REPRESENTATIVES (2 Democrats)
1. Chellie Pingree (D) 2. Michael H. Michaud (D)

POSTWAR VOTE FOR PRESIDENT

| Year | Total Vote | Republican | | Democratic | | Other Vote | Rep.-Dem. Plurality | Percentage | | | |
| | | Vote | Candidate | Vote | Candidate | | | Total Vote | | Major Vote | |
								Rep.	Dem.	Rep.	Dem.
2008	731,163	295,273	McCain, John	421,923	Obama, Barack	13,967	126,650 D	40.4%	57.7%	41.2%	58.8%
2004	740,752	330,201	Bush, George W.	396,842	Kerry, John	13,709	66,641 D	44.6%	53.6%	45.4%	54.6%
2000**	651,817	286,616	Bush, George W.	319,951	Gore, Al	45,250	33,335 D	44.0%	49.1%	47.3%	52.7%
1996**	605,897	186,378	Dole, Bob	312,788	Clinton, Bill	106,731	126,410 D	30.8%	51.6%	37.3%	62.7%
1992**	679,499	206,504	Bush, George	263,420	Clinton, Bill	209,575	56,600 D	30.4%	38.8%	43.9%	56.1%
1988	555,035	307,131	Bush, George	243,569	Dukakis, Michael S.	4,335	63,562 R	55.3%	43.9%	55.8%	44.2%
1984	553,144	336,500	Reagan, Ronald	214,515	Mondale, Walter F.	2,129	121,985 R	60.8%	38.8%	61.1%	38.9%
1980**	523,011	238,522	Reagan, Ronald	220,974	Carter, Jimmy	63,515	17,548 R	45.6%	42.3%	51.9%	48.1%
1976	483,216	236,320	Ford, Gerald R.	232,279	Carter, Jimmy	14,617	4,041 R	48.9%	48.1%	50.4%	49.6%
1972	417,042	256,458	Nixon, Richard M.	160,584	McGovern, George S.		95,874 R	61.5%	38.5%	61.5%	38.5%
1968**	392,936	169,254	Nixon, Richard M.	217,312	Humphrey, Hubert H.	6,370	48,058 D	43.1%	55.3%	43.8%	56.2%
1964	380,965	118,701	Goldwater, Barry M.	262,264	Johnson, Lyndon B.		143,563 D	31.2%	68.8%	31.2%	68.8%
1960	421,767	240,608	Nixon, Richard M.	181,159	Kennedy, John F.		59,449 R	57.0%	43.0%	57.0%	43.0%
1956	351,706	249,238	Eisenhower, Dwight D.	102,468	Stevenson, Adlai E.		146,770 R	70.9%	29.1%	70.9%	29.1%
1952	351,786	232,353	Eisenhower, Dwight D.	118,806	Stevenson, Adlai E.	627	113,547 R	66.0%	33.8%	66.2%	33.8%
1948	264,787	150,234	Dewey, Thomas E.	111,916	Truman, Harry S.	2,637	38,318 R	56.7%	42.3%	57.3%	42.7%

**In past elections, the other vote included: 2000 - 37,127 Green (Ralph Nader); 1996 - 85,970 Reform (Ross Perot); 1992 - 206,820 Independent (Perot), who placed second statewide; 1980 - 53,327 Independent (John Anderson); 1968 - 6,370 American Independent (George Wallace).

MAINE

POSTWAR VOTE FOR GOVERNOR

Year	Total Vote	Republican Vote	Candidate	Democratic Vote	Candidate	Other Vote	Rep.-Dem. Plurality	Total Vote Rep.	Total Vote Dem.	Major Vote Rep.	Major Vote Dem.
2010**	572,766	218,065	LePage, Paul R.	109,387	Mitchell, Elizabeth	245,314	9,795 R	38.1%	19.1%	66.6%	33.4%
2006**	550,865	166,425	Woodcock, Chandler E.	209,927	Baldacci, John	174,513	43,502 D	30.2%	38.1%	44.2%	55.8%
2002	505,190	209,496	Cianchette, Peter E.	238,179	Baldacci, John	57,515	28,683 D	41.5%	47.1%	46.8%	53.2%
1998**	421,009	79,716	Longley, James B., Jr.	50,506	Connolly, Thomas J.	290,787	167,056 I	18.9%	12.0%	61.2%	38.8%
1994**	511,308	117,990	Collins, Susan	172,951	Brennan, Joseph E.	220,367	7,878 I	23.1%	33.8%	40.6%	59.4%
1990	522,492	243,766	McKernan, John R.	230,038	Brennan, Joseph E.	48,688	13,728 R	46.7%	44.0%	51.4%	48.6%
1986**	426,861	170,312	McKernan, John R.	128,744	Tierney, James	127,805	41,568 R	39.9%	30.2%	56.9%	43.1%
1982	460,295	172,949	Cragin, Charles L.	281,066	Brennan, Joseph E.	6,280	108,117 D	37.6%	61.1%	38.1%	61.9%
1978**	370,258	126,862	Palmer, Linwood E.	176,493	Brennan, Joseph E.	66,903	49,631 D	34.3%	47.7%	41.8%	58.2%
1974**	363,945	84,176	Erwin, James S.	132,219	Mitchell, George J.	147,550	10,245 I	23.1%	36.3%	38.9%	61.1%
1970	325,386	162,248	Erwin, James S.	163,138	Curtis, Kenneth M.		890 D	49.9%	50.1%	49.9%	50.1%
1966	323,838	151,802	Reed, John H.	172,036	Curtis, Kenneth M.		20,234 D	46.9%	53.1%	46.9%	53.1%
1962	292,725	146,604	Reed, John H.	146,121	Dolloff, Maynard C.		483 R	50.1%	49.9%	50.1%	49.9%
1960S	417,315	219,768	Reed, John H.	197,547	Coffin, Frank M.		22,221 R	52.7%	47.3%	52.7%	47.3%
1958**	280,295	134,572	Hildreth, Horace A.	145,723	Clauson, Clinton A.		11,151 D	48.0%	52.0%	48.0%	52.0%
1956	304,649	124,395	Trafton, Willis A.	180,254	Muskie, Edmund S.		55,859 D	40.8%	59.2%	40.8%	59.2%
1954	248,971	113,298	Cross, Burton M.	135,673	Muskie, Edmund S.		22,375 D	45.5%	54.5%	45.5%	54.5%
1952	248,441	128,532	Cross, Burton M.	82,538	Oliver, James C.	37,371	45,994 R	51.7%	33.2%	60.9%	39.1%
1950	241,177	145,823	Payne, Frederick G.	94,304	Grant, Earl S.	1,050	51,519 R	60.5%	39.1%	60.7%	39.3%
1948	222,500	145,956	Payne, Frederick G.	76,544	Lausier, Louis B.		69,412 R	65.6%	34.4%	65.6%	34.4%
1946	179,951	110,327	Hildreth, Horace A.	69,624	Clark, F. Davis		40,703 R	61.3%	38.7%	61.3%	38.7%

**In past elections, the other vote included: 2010 - 208,270 Independent (Eliot R. Cutler), who placed second statewide; 2006 - 118,715 Independent Maine Course (Barbara Merrill); 1998 - 246,772 Independent (Angus King), who was reelected with 58.6 percent of the total vote; 1994 - 180,829 Independent (King), who was elected with 35.4 percent of the total vote; 1986 - 64,317 Independent (Sherry F. Huber), 63,474 Independent (John E. Menario); 1978 - 65,889 Independent (Herman C. Frankland); 1974 - 142,464 Independent (James B. Longley), who was elected with 39.1 percent of the total vote. The 1960 election was for a short term to fill a vacancy. The term of office of Maine's Governor was increased from two to four years effective with the 1958 election.

POSTWAR VOTE FOR SENATOR

Year	Total Vote	Republican Vote	Candidate	Democratic Vote	Candidate	Other Vote	Rep.-Dem. Plurality	Total Vote Rep.	Total Vote Dem.	Major Vote Rep.	Major Vote Dem.
2008	724,430	444,300	Collins, Susan	279,510	Allen, Tom	620	164,790 R	61.3%	38.6%	61.4%	38.6%
2006	543,981	402,598	Snowe, Olympia J.	111,984	Hay Bright, Jean	29,399	290,614 R	74.0%	20.6%	78.2%	21.8%
2002	504,899	295,041	Collins, Susan	209,858	Pingree, Chellie		85,183 R	58.4%	41.6%	58.4%	41.6%
2000	634,872	437,689	Snowe, Olympia J.	197,183	Lawrence, Mark		240,506 R	68.9%	31.1%	68.9%	31.1%
1996	606,777	298,422	Collins, Susan	266,226	Brennan, Joseph E.	42,129	32,196 R	49.2%	43.9%	52.9%	47.1%
1994	511,733	308,244	Snowe, Olympia J.	186,042	Andrews, Thomas H.	17,447	122,202 R	60.2%	36.4%	62.4%	37.6%
1990	520,320	319,167	Cohen, William S.	201,053	Rolde, Neil	100	118,114 R	61.3%	38.6%	61.4%	38.6%
1988	557,375	104,758	Wyman, Jasper S.	452,590	Mitchell, George J.	27	347,832 D	18.8%	81.2%	18.8%	81.2%
1984	551,406	404,414	Cohen, William S.	142,626	Mitchell, Elizabeth	4,366	261,788 R	73.3%	25.9%	73.9%	26.1%
1982	459,715	179,882	Emery, David F.	279,819	Mitchell, George J.	14	99,937 D	39.1%	60.9%	39.1%	60.9%
1978	375,172	212,294	Cohen, William S.	127,327	Hathaway, William D.	35,551	84,967 R	56.6%	33.9%	62.5%	37.5%
1976	486,254	193,489	Monks, Robert A. G.	292,704	Muskie, Edmund S.	61	99,215 D	39.8%	60.2%	39.8%	60.2%
1972	421,310	197,040	Smith, Margaret Chase	224,270	Hathaway, William D.		27,230 D	46.8%	53.2%	46.8%	53.2%
1970	323,860	123,906	Bishop, Neil S.	199,954	Muskie, Edmund S.		76,048 D	38.3%	61.7%	38.3%	61.7%
1966	319,535	188,291	Smith, Margaret Chase	131,136	Violette, Elmer H.	108	57,155 R	58.9%	41.0%	58.9%	41.1%
1964	380,551	127,040	McIntire, Clifford	253,511	Muskie, Edmund S.		126,471 D	33.4%	66.6%	33.4%	66.6%
1960	416,699	256,890	Smith, Margaret Chase	159,809	Cormier, Lucia M.		97,081 R	61.6%	38.4%	61.6%	38.4%
1958	284,226	111,522	Payne, Frederick G.	172,704	Muskie, Edmund S.		61,182 D	39.2%	60.8%	39.2%	60.8%
1954	246,605	144,530	Smith, Margaret Chase	102,075	Fullam, Paul A.		42,455 R	58.6%	41.4%	58.6%	41.4%
1952	237,164	139,205	Payne, Frederick G.	82,665	Dube, Roger P.	15,294	56,540 R	58.7%	34.9%	62.7%	37.3%
1948	223,256	159,182	Smith, Margaret Chase	64,074	Scolten, Adrian H.		95,108 R	71.3%	28.7%	71.3%	28.7%
1946	175,014	111,215	Brewster, Owen	63,799	MacDonald, Peter		47,416 R	63.5%	36.5%	63.5%	36.5%

MAINE

GOVERNOR 2010

2010 Census Population	County	Total Vote	Republican	Democratic	Independent (Cutler)	Other	Rep.-Dem. Plurality		Percentage		
									Rep.	Dem.	Ind. (Cutler)
107,702	ANDROSCOGGIN	41,876	18,007	6,838	13,316	3,715	4,691	R	43.0%	16.3%	31.8%
71,870	AROOSTOOK	26,752	11,353	5,307	7,478	2,614	3,875	R	42.4%	19.8%	28.0%
281,674	CUMBERLAND	128,421	38,984	27,097	53,036	9,304	14,052	I	30.4%	21.1%	41.3%
30,768	FRANKLIN	13,704	5,877	2,571	4,495	761	1,382	R	42.9%	18.8%	32.8%
54,418	HANCOCK	25,723	9,056	4,445	11,258	964	2,202	I	35.2%	17.3%	43.8%
122,151	KENNEBEC	54,221	23,567	11,406	17,146	2,102	6,421	R	43.5%	21.0%	31.6%
39,736	KNOX	18,701	6,830	3,970	7,327	574	497	I	36.5%	21.2%	39.2%
34,457	LINCOLN	17,755	7,196	3,304	6,598	657	598	R	40.5%	18.6%	37.2%
57,833	OXFORD	26,000	10,281	4,659	8,416	2,644	1,865	R	39.5%	17.9%	32.4%
153,923	PENOBSCOT	60,507	25,721	8,253	24,150	2,383	1,571	R	42.5%	13.6%	39.9%
17,535	PISCATAQUIS	7,686	3,724	837	2,809	316	915	R	48.5%	10.9%	36.5%
35,293	SAGADAHOC	17,448	6,495	3,330	6,796	827	301	I	37.2%	19.1%	39.0%
52,228	SOMERSET	20,468	9,994	2,703	6,814	957	3,180	R	48.8%	13.2%	33.3%
38,786	WALDO	17,589	7,088	3,053	6,684	764	404	R	40.3%	17.4%	38.0%
32,856	WASHINGTON	12,946	5,586	1,858	4,846	656	740	R	43.1%	14.4%	37.4%
197,131	YORK	82,370	28,103	19,456	27,031	7,780	1,072	R	34.1%	23.6%	32.8%
	Overseas Voters	599	203	300	70	26	133	D	33.9%	50.1%	11.7%
1,328,361	TOTAL	572,766	218,065	109,387	208,270	37,044	9,795	R	38.1%	19.1%	36.4%

Counties carried by Independent candidate Eliot R. Cutler are indicated by an "I." The plurality represents the vote differential between the leading candidate and the runner-up, regardless of party or independent status.

MAINE

GOVERNOR 2010

2010 Census Population	City/Town	Total Vote	Republican	Democratic	Independent (Cutler)	Other	Rep.-Dem. Plurality		Percentage		
									Rep.	Dem.	Ind. (Cutler)
23,055	AUBURN	9,043	3,452	1,583	3,067	941	385	R	38.2%	17.5%	33.9%
19,136	AUGUSTA	7,509	2,768	2,133	2,313	295	455	R	36.9%	28.4%	30.8%
33,039	BANGOR	10,984	3,857	2,179	4,578	370	721	I	35.1%	19.8%	41.7%
8,514	BATH	3,802	1,195	900	1,550	157	355	I	31.4%	23.7%	40.8%
6,668	BELFAST	3,064	930	730	1,272	132	342	I	30.4%	23.8%	41.5%
7,246	BERWICK	2,322	1,012	528	638	144	374	R	43.6%	22.7%	27.5%
21,277	BIDDEFORD	7,808	2,249	1,974	2,669	916	420	I	28.8%	25.3%	34.2%
9,482	BREWER	3,993	1,697	456	1,705	135	8	I	42.5%	11.4%	42.7%
20,278	BRUNSWICK	9,153	2,606	2,659	3,575	313	916	I	28.5%	29.1%	39.1%
8,034	BUXTON	3,602	1,281	482	998	841	283	R	35.6%	13.4%	27.7%
4,850	CAMDEN	2,680	643	745	1,240	52	495	I	24.0%	27.8%	46.3%
9,015	CAPE ELIZABETH	5,344	1,347	862	3,013	122	1,666	I	25.2%	16.1%	56.4%
8,189	CARIBOU	2,889	1,211	521	872	285	339	R	41.9%	18.0%	30.2%
7,211	CUMBERLAND TOWN	4,095	1,484	549	1,930	132	446	I	36.2%	13.4%	47.1%
6,204	ELIOT	2,869	1,022	879	878	90	143	R	35.6%	30.6%	30.6%

MAINE

GOVERNOR 2010

2010 Census Population	City/Town	Total Vote	Republican	Democratic	Independent (Cutler)	Other	Rep.-Dem. Plurality	Percentage		
								Rep.	Dem.	Ind. (Cutler)
7,741	ELLSWORTH	3,316	1,367	495	1,308	146	59 R	41.2%	14.9%	39.4%
6,735	FAIRFIELD	2,711	1,311	404	857	139	454 R	48.4%	14.9%	31.6%
11,185	FALMOUTH	6,040	2,123	967	2,740	210	617 I	35.1%	16.0%	45.4%
7,760	FARMINGTON	3,226	1,288	744	1,037	157	251 R	39.9%	23.1%	32.1%
7,879	FREEPORT	4,121	1,134	808	2,006	173	872 I	27.5%	19.6%	48.7%
5,800	GARDINER	2,506	986	529	893	98	93 R	39.3%	21.1%	35.6%
16,381	GORHAM	6,795	2,023	1,069	2,060	1,643	37 I	29.8%	15.7%	30.3%
7,761	GRAY	3,605	1,538	557	1,225	285	313 R	42.7%	15.5%	34.0%
7,257	HAMPDEN	3,483	1,422	437	1,519	105	97 I	40.8%	12.5%	43.6%
4,740	HARPSWELL	2,928	1,044	549	1,216	119	172 I	35.7%	18.8%	41.5%
6,123	HOULTON	2,022	927	311	651	133	276 R	45.8%	15.4%	32.2%
4,851	JAY	2,192	897	528	648	119	249 R	40.9%	24.1%	29.6%
10,798	KENNEBUNK	5,432	1,710	1,314	2,139	269	429 I	31.5%	24.2%	39.4%
9,490	KITTERY	3,934	1,105	1,466	1,236	127	230 D	28.1%	37.3%	31.4%
36,592	LEWISTON	11,822	4,626	2,435	3,681	1,080	945 R	39.1%	20.6%	31.1%
2,314	LIMESTONE	630	222	107	179	122	43 R	35.2%	17.0%	28.4%
5,085	LINCOLN TOWN	1,844	971	185	602	86	369 R	52.7%	10.0%	32.6%
9,009	LISBON	3,869	1,824	522	1,196	327	628 R	47.1%	13.5%	30.9%
4,506	MILLINOCKET	2,156	748	308	1,003	97	255 I	34.7%	14.3%	46.5%
6,240	OAKLAND	2,766	1,320	559	799	88	521 R	47.7%	20.2%	28.9%
8,624	OLD ORCHARD BEACH	4,038	1,195	1,044	1,443	356	248 I	29.6%	25.9%	35.7%
7,840	OLD TOWN	2,991	959	487	1,442	103	483 I	32.1%	16.3%	48.2%
10,362	ORONO	3,250	715	817	1,620	98	803 I	22.0%	25.1%	49.8%
66,194	PORTLAND	26,729	5,153	8,440	12,023	1,113	3,583 I	19.3%	31.6%	45.0%
9,692	PRESQUE ISLE	3,203	1,344	581	957	321	387 R	42.0%	18.1%	29.9%
7,297	ROCKLAND	2,741	900	698	1,031	112	131 I	32.8%	25.5%	37.6%
5,841	RUMFORD	2,401	835	623	678	265	157 R	34.8%	25.9%	28.2%
18,482	SACO	7,435	2,204	1,686	2,812	733	608 I	29.6%	22.7%	37.8%
20,798	SANFORD	7,452	2,489	1,746	2,484	733	5 R	33.4%	23.4%	33.3%
18,919	SCARBOROUGH	9,515	3,418	1,598	3,746	753	328 I	35.9%	16.8%	39.4%
8,589	SKOWHEGAN	3,163	1,377	532	1,106	148	271 R	43.5%	16.8%	35.0%
7,220	SOUTH BERWICK	2,864	1,009	910	812	133	99 R	35.2%	31.8%	28.4%
25,002	SOUTH PORTLAND	11,307	2,755	2,836	4,973	743	2,137 I	24.4%	25.1%	44.0%
9,874	STANDISH	3,996	1,555	529	1,281	631	274 R	38.9%	13.2%	32.1%
8,784	TOPSHAM	4,566	1,621	871	1,844	230	223 I	35.5%	19.1%	40.4%
15,722	WATERVILLE	5,453	2,306	1,521	1,484	142	785 R	42.3%	27.9%	27.2%
9,589	WELLS	4,437	1,575	1,020	1,529	313	46 R	35.5%	23.0%	34.5%
17,494	WESTBROOK	6,602	2,094	1,336	2,454	718	360 I	31.7%	20.2%	37.2%
17,001	WINDHAM	7,118	2,755	1,099	2,411	853	344 R	38.7%	15.4%	33.9%
7,794	WINSLOW	3,536	1,745	615	1,055	121	690 R	49.3%	17.4%	29.8%
6,092	WINTHROP	3,086	1,203	632	1,115	136	88 R	39.0%	20.5%	36.1%
8,349	YARMOUTH	4,537	1,307	648	2,418	164	1,111 I	28.8%	14.3%	53.3%
12,529	YORK TOWN	6,322	2,103	2,094	1,905	220	9 R	33.3%	33.1%	30.1%

Cities and towns carried by Independent candidate Eliot R. Cutler are indicated by an "I." The plurality represents the vote differential between the leading candidate and the runner-up, regardless of party or independent status.

MAINE

HOUSE OF REPRESENTATIVES

CD	Year	Total Vote	Republican Vote	Republican Candidate	Democratic Vote	Democratic Candidate	Other Vote	Rep.-Dem. Plurality		Total Vote Rep.	Total Vote Dem.	Major Vote Rep.	Major Vote Dem.
1	2010	297,657	128,501	SCONTRAS, DEAN PETER	169,114	PINGREE, CHELLIE*	42	40,613	D	43.2%	56.8%	43.2%	56.8%
1	2008	374,559	168,930	SUMMERS, CHARLES E.	205,629	PINGREE, CHELLIE		36,699	D	45.1%	54.9%	45.1%	54.9%
1	2006	280,987	88,009	CURLEY, DARLENE J.	170,949	ALLEN, TOM*	22,029	82,940	D	31.3%	60.8%	34.0%	66.0%
1	2004	366,740	147,663	SUMMERS, CHARLES E.	219,077	ALLEN, TOM*		71,414	D	40.3%	59.7%	40.3%	59.7%
1	2002	270,577	97,931	JOYCE, STEVEN	172,646	ALLEN, TOM*		74,715	D	36.2%	63.8%	36.2%	63.8%
2	2010	266,711	119,669	LEVESQUE, JASON J.	147,042	MICHAUD, MICHAEL H.*		27,373	D	44.9%	55.1%	44.9%	55.1%
2	2008	335,542	109,268	FRARY, JOHN N.	226,274	MICHAUD, MICHAEL H.*		117,006	D	32.6%	67.4%	32.6%	67.4%
2	2006	254,878	75,146	D'AMBOISE, LAURENCE S.	179,732	MICHAUD, MICHAEL H.*		104,586	D	29.5%	70.5%	29.5%	70.5%
2	2004	343,436	135,547	HAMEL, BRIAN N.	199,303	MICHAUD, MICHAEL H.*	8,586	63,756	D	39.5%	58.0%	40.5%	59.5%
2	2002	224,717	107,849	RAYE, KEVIN L.	116,868	MICHAUD, MICHAEL H.		9,019	D	48.0%	52.0%	48.0%	52.0%
TOTAL	2010	564,368	248,170		316,156		42	67,986	D	44.0%	56.0%	44.0%	56.0%
TOTAL	2008	710,101	278,198		431,903			153,705	D	39.2%	60.8%	39.2%	60.8%
TOTAL	2006	535,865	163,155		350,681		22,029	187,526	D	30.4%	65.4%	31.8%	68.2%
TOTAL	2004	710,176	283,210		418,380		8,586	135,170	D	39.9%	58.9%	40.4%	59.6%
TOTAL	2002	495,294	205,780		289,514			83,734	D	41.5%	58.5%	41.5%	58.5%

An asterisk (*) denotes incumbent.

MAINE

GENERAL AND PRIMARY ELECTIONS

2010 GENERAL ELECTIONS

Governor   Other vote was 28,756 Independent (Shawn H. Moody); 5,664 Independent (Kevin L. Scott); 2,624 scattered write-in. Another Independent, Eliot R. Cutler, received 208,270 votes, 36.4 percent of the total vote. The Cutler vote is listed in the county and city/town tables for the 2010 gubernatorial election in Maine.

House   Other vote was:

CD 1   42 scattered write-in.
CD 2

2010 PRIMARY ELECTIONS

Primary   June 8, 2010

Registration
(as of June 8, 2010 - includes 45,948 inactive registrants)

Democratic	337,217
Republican	283,666
Green Independent	34,484
Unenrolled	367,606
TOTAL	1,022,973

Primary Type   Semi-open—Registered voters in a political party could participate only in their party's primary. "Unenrolled" and new voters could vote in either party's primary by enrolling in that party on primary day.

MAINE

GENERAL AND PRIMARY ELECTIONS

	REPUBLICAN PRIMARIES			DEMOCRATIC PRIMARIES		
Governor	Paul R. LePage	49,126	37.4%	Elizabeth Mitchell	42,328	34.4%
	Leslie B. Otten	22,945	17.5%	G. Steven Rowe	27,932	22.7%
	S. Peter Mills	19,271	14.7%	Rosa W. Scarcelli	26,444	21.5%
	Steven W. Abbott	17,209	13.1%	Patrick K. McGowan	24,392	19.8%
	William H. Beardsley	12,061	9.2%	John G. Richardson	1,604	1.3%
	Bruce Poliquin	6,471	4.9%	Scattered write-in	236	0.2%
	Matthew C. Jacobson	4,324	3.3%			
	TOTAL	*131,407*		*TOTAL*	*122,936*	
Congressional District 1	Dean Peter Scontras	44,683	100.0%	Chellie Pingree*	57,799	100.0%
Congressional District 2	Jason J. Levesque	42,454	100.0%	Michael H. Michaud*	45,628	100.0%

An asterisk (*) denotes incumbent.

MARYLAND

Congressional districts first established for elections held in 2002
8 members

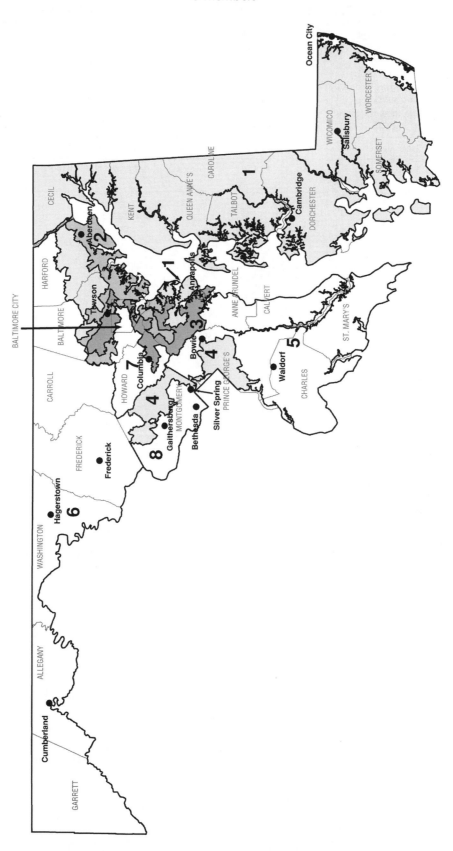

MARYLAND

Baltimore, Washington, D.C., Areas

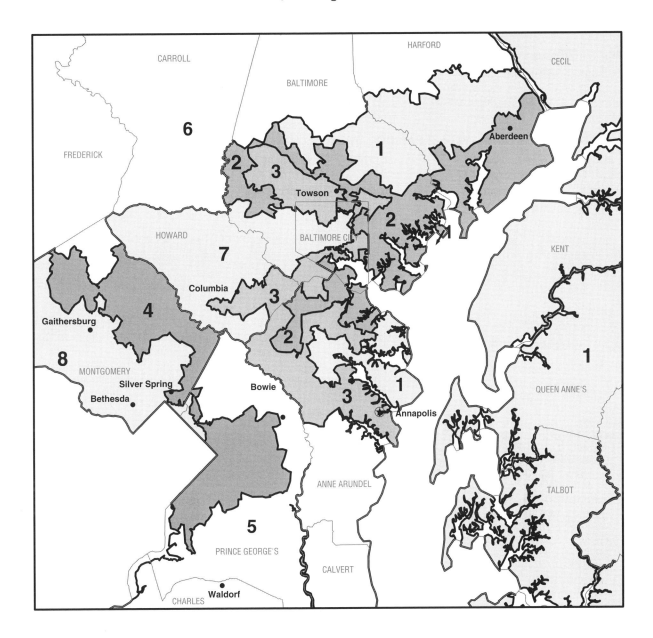

MARYLAND

GOVERNOR
Martin O'Malley (D). Reelected 2010 to a four-year term. Previously elected 2006.

SENATORS (2 Democrats)
Benjamin L. Cardin (D). Elected 2006 to a six-year term.

Barbara A. Mikulski (D). Reelected 2010 to a six-year term. Previously elected 2004, 1998, 1992, 1986.

REPRESENTATIVES (6 Democrats, 2 Republican)
1. Andy Harris (R)
2. C.A. Dutch Ruppersberger (D)
3. John P. Sarbanes (D)
4. Donna F. Edwards (D)
5. Steny H. Hoyer (D)
6. Roscoe G. Bartlett (R)
7. Elijah E. Cummings (D)
8. Chris Van Hollen (D)

POSTWAR VOTE FOR PRESIDENT

Year	Total Vote	Republican Vote	Republican Candidate	Democratic Vote	Democratic Candidate	Other Vote	Rep.-Dem. Plurality	Total Vote Rep.	Total Vote Dem.	Major Vote Rep.	Major Vote Dem.
2008	2,631,596	959,862	McCain, John	1,629,467	Obama, Barack	42,267	669,605 D	36.5%	61.9%	37.1%	62.9%
2004	2,386,678	1,024,703	Bush, George W.	1,334,493	Kerry, John	27,482	309,790 D	42.9%	55.9%	43.4%	56.6%
2000**	2,020,480	813,797	Bush, George W.	1,140,782	Gore, Al	65,901	326,985 D	40.3%	56.5%	41.6%	58.4%
1996**	1,780,870	681,530	Dole, Bob	966,207	Clinton, Bill	133,133	284,677 D	38.3%	54.3%	41.4%	58.6%
1992**	1,985,046	707,094	Bush, George	988,571	Clinton, Bill	289,381	281,477 D	35.6%	49.8%	41.7%	58.3%
1988	1,714,358	876,167	Bush, George	826,304	Dukakis, Michael S.	11,887	49,863 R	51.1%	48.2%	51.5%	48.5%
1984	1,675,873	879,918	Reagan, Ronald	787,935	Mondale, Walter F.	8,020	91,983 R	52.5%	47.0%	52.8%	47.2%
1980**	1,540,496	680,606	Reagan, Ronald	726,161	Carter, Jimmy	133,729	45,555 D	44.2%	47.1%	48.4%	51.6%
1976	1,439,897	672,661	Ford, Gerald R.	759,612	Carter, Jimmy	7,624	86,951 D	46.7%	52.8%	47.0%	53.0%
1972	1,353,812	829,305	Nixon, Richard M.	505,781	McGovern, George S.	18,726	323,524 R	61.3%	37.4%	62.1%	37.9%
1968**	1,235,039	517,995	Nixon, Richard M.	538,310	Humphrey, Hubert H.	178,734	20,315 D	41.9%	43.6%	49.0%	51.0%
1964	1,116,457	385,495	Goldwater, Barry M.	730,912	Johnson, Lyndon B.	50	345,417 D	34.5%	65.5%	34.5%	65.5%
1960	1,055,349	489,538	Nixon, Richard M.	565,808	Kennedy, John F.	3	76,270 D	46.4%	53.6%	46.4%	53.6%
1956	932,827	559,738	Eisenhower, Dwight D.	372,613	Stevenson, Adlai E.	476	187,125 R	60.0%	39.9%	60.0%	40.0%
1952	902,074	499,424	Eisenhower, Dwight D.	395,337	Stevenson, Adlai E.	7,313	104,087 R	55.4%	43.8%	55.8%	44.2%
1948	596,748	294,814	Dewey, Thomas E.	286,521	Truman, Harry S.	15,413	8,293 R	49.4%	48.0%	50.7%	49.3%

**In past elections, the other vote included: 2000 - 53,768 Green (Ralph Nader); 1996 - 115,812 Reform (Ross Perot); 1992 - 281,414 Independent (Perot); 1980 - 119,537 Independent (John Anderson); 1968 - 178,734 American Independent (George Wallace).

MARYLAND

POSTWAR VOTE FOR GOVERNOR

Year	Total Vote	Republican Vote	Republican Candidate	Democratic Vote	Democratic Candidate	Other Vote	Rep.-Dem. Plurality	Total Vote Rep.	Total Vote Dem.	Major Vote Rep.	Major Vote Dem.
2010	1,857,880	776,319	Ehrlich, Robert L. Jr.	1,044,961	O'Malley, Martin	36,600	268,642 D	41.8%	56.2%	42.6%	57.4%
2006	1,788,316	825,464	Ehrlich, Robert L. Jr.	942,279	O'Malley, Martin	20,573	116,815 D	46.2%	52.7%	46.7%	53.3%
2002	1,706,179	879,592	Ehrlich, Robert L. Jr.	813,422	Townsend, Kathleen Kennedy	13,165	66,170 R	51.6%	47.7%	52.0%	48.0%
1998	1,535,978	688,357	Sauerbrey, Ellen R.	846,972	Glendening, Parris N.	649	158,615 D	44.8%	55.1%	44.8%	55.2%
1994	1,410,300	702,101	Sauerbrey, Ellen R.	708,094	Glendening, Parris N.	105	5,993 D	49.8%	50.2%	49.8%	50.2%
1990	1,111,088	446,980	Shepard, William S.	664,015	Schaefer, William D.	93	217,035 D	40.2%	59.8%	40.2%	59.8%
1986	1,101,476	194,185	Mooney, Thomas J.	907,291	Schaefer, William D.		713,106 D	17.6%	82.4%	17.6%	82.4%
1982	1,139,149	432,826	Pascal, Robert A.	705,910	Hughes, Harry	413	273,084 D	38.0%	62.0%	38.0%	62.0%
1978	1,011,963	293,635	Beall, J. Glenn, Jr.	718,328	Hughes, Harry		424,693 D	29.0%	71.0%	29.0%	71.0%
1974	949,097	346,449	Gore, Louise	602,648	Mandel, Marvin		256,199 D	36.5%	63.5%	36.5%	63.5%
1970	973,099	314,336	Blain, C. Stanley	639,579	Mandel, Marvin	19,184	325,243 D	32.3%	65.7%	33.0%	67.0%
1966	918,761	455,318	Agnew, Spiro T.	373,543	Mahoney, George P.	89,900	81,775 R	49.6%	40.7%	54.9%	45.1%
1962	775,101	343,051	Small, Frank	432,045	Tawes, J. Millard	5	88,994 D	44.3%	55.7%	44.3%	55.7%
1958	763,234	278,173	Devereux, James	485,061	Tawes, J. Millard		206,888 D	36.4%	63.6%	36.4%	63.6%
1954	700,484	381,451	McKeldin, Theodore	319,033	Byrd, Harry C.		62,418 R	54.5%	45.5%	54.5%	45.5%
1950	645,631	369,807	McKeldin, Theodore	275,824	Lane, William P.		93,983 R	57.3%	42.7%	57.3%	42.7%
1946	489,836	221,752	McKeldin, Theodore	268,084	Lane, William P.		46,332 D	45.3%	54.7%	45.3%	54.7%

POSTWAR VOTE FOR SENATOR

Year	Total Vote	Republican Vote	Republican Candidate	Democratic Vote	Democratic Candidate	Other Vote	Rep.-Dem. Plurality	Total Vote Rep.	Total Vote Dem.	Major Vote Rep.	Major Vote Dem.
2010	1,833,858	655,666	Wargotz, Eric	1,140,531	Mikulski, Barbara A.	37,661	484,865 D	35.8%	62.2%	36.5%	63.5%
2006	1,781,139	787,182	Steele, Michael S.	965,477	Cardin, Benjamin L.	28,480	178,295 D	44.2%	54.2%	44.9%	55.1%
2004	2,323,183	783,055	Pipkin, E.J.	1,504,691	Mikulski, Barbara A.	35,437	721,636 D	33.7%	64.8%	34.2%	65.8%
2000	1,946,898	715,178	Rappaport, Paul	1,230,013	Sarbanes, Paul S.	1,707	514,835 D	36.7%	63.2%	36.8%	63.2%
1998	1,507,447	444,637	Pierpont, Ross Z.	1,062,810	Mikulski, Barbara A.		618,173 D	29.5%	70.5%	29.5%	70.5%
1994	1,369,104	559,908	Brock, William E.	809,125	Sarbanes, Paul S.	71	249,217 D	40.9%	59.1%	40.9%	59.1%
1992	1,841,735	533,688	Keyes, Alan L.	1,307,610	Mikulski, Barbara A.	437	773,922 D	29.0%	71.0%	29.0%	71.0%
1988	1,617,065	617,537	Keyes, Alan L.	999,166	Sarbanes, Paul S.	362	381,629 D	38.2%	61.8%	38.2%	61.8%
1986	1,112,637	437,411	Chavez, Linda	675,225	Mikulski, Barbara A.	1	237,814 D	39.3%	60.7%	39.3%	60.7%
1982	1,114,690	407,334	Hogan, Lawrence J.	707,356	Sarbanes, Paul S.		300,022 D	36.5%	63.5%	36.5%	63.5%
1980	1,286,088	850,970	Mathias, Charles	435,118	Conroy, Edward T.		415,852 R	66.2%	33.8%	66.2%	33.8%
1976	1,365,568	530,439	Beall, J. Glenn, Jr.	772,101	Sarbanes, Paul S.	63,028	241,662 D	38.8%	56.5%	40.7%	59.3%
1974	877,786	503,223	Mathias, Charles	374,563	Mikulski, Barbara A.		128,660 R	57.3%	42.7%	57.3%	42.7%
1970	956,370	484,960	Beall, J. Glenn, Jr.	460,422	Tydings, Joseph D.	10,988	24,538 R	50.7%	48.1%	51.3%	48.7%
1968**	1,133,727	541,893	Mathias, Charles	443,367	Brewster, Daniel B.	148,467	98,526 R	47.8%	39.1%	55.0%	45.0%
1964	1,081,049	402,393	Beall, J. Glenn	678,649	Tydings, Joseph D.	7	276,256 D	37.2%	62.8%	37.2%	62.8%
1962	714,248	270,312	Miller, Edward T.	443,935	Brewster, Daniel B.	1	173,623 D	37.8%	62.2%	37.8%	62.2%
1958	749,291	382,021	Beall, J. Glenn	367,270	D'Alesandro, Thomas		14,751 R	51.0%	49.0%	51.0%	49.0%
1956	892,167	473,059	Butler, John Marshall	419,108	Mahoney, George P.		53,951 R	53.0%	47.0%	53.0%	47.0%
1952	856,193	449,823	Beall, J. Glenn	406,370	Mahoney, George P.		43,453 R	52.5%	47.5%	52.5%	47.5%
1950	615,614	326,291	Butler, John Marshall	283,180	Tydings, Millard E.	6,143	43,111 R	53.0%	46.0%	53.5%	46.5%
1946	472,232	235,000	Markey, David John	237,232	O'Conor, Herbert R.		2,232 D	49.8%	50.2%	49.8%	50.2%

**In past elections, the other vote included: 1968 - 148,467 Independent (George P. Mahoney).

MARYLAND

GOVERNOR 2010

2010 Census Population	County	Total Vote	Republican	Democratic	Other	Rep.-Dem. Plurality		Percentage			
								Total Vote		Major Vote	
								Rep.	Dem.	Rep.	Dem.
75,087	ALLEGANY	22,124	13,394	7,933	797	5,461	R	60.5%	35.9%	62.8%	37.2%
537,656	ANNE ARUNDEL	202,960	110,002	88,161	4,797	21,841	R	54.2%	43.4%	55.5%	44.5%
620,961	BALTIMORE CITY	162,420	26,073	133,068	3,279	106,995	D	16.1%	81.9%	16.4%	83.6%
805,029	BALTIMORE COUNTY	288,254	140,476	141,802	5,976	1,326	D	48.7%	49.2%	49.8%	50.2%
88,737	CALVERT	31,990	17,444	13,864	682	3,580	R	54.5%	43.3%	55.7%	44.3%
33,066	CAROLINE	10,046	6,571	3,185	290	3,386	R	65.4%	31.7%	67.4%	32.6%
167,134	CARROLL	63,833	45,357	16,733	1,743	28,624	R	71.1%	26.2%	73.1%	26.9%
101,108	CECIL	30,160	18,273	10,833	1,054	7,440	R	60.6%	35.9%	62.8%	37.2%
146,551	CHARLES	47,009	17,531	28,818	660	11,287	D	37.3%	61.3%	37.8%	62.2%
32,618	DORCHESTER	11,793	6,780	4,756	257	2,024	R	57.5%	40.3%	58.8%	41.2%
233,385	FREDERICK	75,653	41,410	32,222	2,021	9,188	R	54.7%	42.6%	56.2%	43.8%
30,097	GARRETT	9,734	6,972	2,530	232	4,442	R	71.6%	26.0%	73.4%	26.6%
244,826	HARFORD	94,634	61,068	31,220	2,346	29,848	R	64.5%	33.0%	66.2%	33.8%
287,085	HOWARD	107,804	47,642	58,215	1,947	10,573	D	44.2%	54.0%	45.0%	55.0%
20,197	KENT	8,244	4,485	3,574	185	911	R	54.4%	43.4%	55.7%	44.3%
971,777	MONTGOMERY	292,058	89,108	198,950	4,000	109,842	D	30.5%	68.1%	30.9%	69.1%
863,420	PRINCE GEORGES	231,954	26,156	203,957	1,841	177,801	D	11.3%	87.9%	11.4%	88.6%
47,798	QUEEN ANNES	19,888	13,238	6,278	372	6,960	R	66.6%	31.6%	67.8%	32.2%
105,151	ST. MARYS	31,668	17,804	12,990	874	4,814	R	56.2%	41.0%	57.8%	42.2%
26,470	SOMERSET	7,705	4,318	3,198	189	1,120	R	56.0%	41.5%	57.5%	42.5%
37,782	TALBOT	16,357	9,707	6,331	319	3,376	R	59.3%	38.7%	60.5%	39.5%
147,430	WASHINGTON	40,384	23,651	15,155	1,578	8,496	R	58.6%	37.5%	60.9%	39.1%
98,733	WICOMICO	29,720	16,325	12,661	734	3,664	R	54.9%	42.6%	56.3%	43.7%
51,454	WORCESTER	21,488	12,534	8,527	427	4,007	R	58.3%	39.7%	59.5%	40.5%
5,773,552	TOTAL	1,857,880	776,319	1,044,961	36,600	268,642	D	41.8%	56.2%	42.6%	57.4%

MARYLAND

SENATOR 2010

2010 Census Population	County	Total Vote	Republican	Democratic	Other	Rep.-Dem. Plurality	Percentage			
							Total Vote		Major Vote	
							Rep.	Dem.	Rep.	Dem.
75,087	ALLEGANY	21,612	11,350	9,639	623	1,711 R	52.5%	44.6%	54.1%	45.9%
537,656	ANNE ARUNDEL	200,353	92,994	102,511	4,848	9,517 D	46.4%	51.2%	47.6%	52.4%
620,961	BALTIMORE CITY	159,740	18,336	138,312	3,092	119,976 D	11.5%	86.6%	11.7%	88.3%
805,029	BALTIMORE COUNTY	284,350	112,670	165,678	6,002	53,008 D	39.6%	58.3%	40.5%	59.5%
88,737	CALVERT	31,476	15,569	15,247	660	322 R	49.5%	48.4%	50.5%	49.5%
33,066	CAROLINE	9,916	5,142	4,508	266	634 R	51.9%	45.5%	53.3%	46.7%
167,134	CARROLL	62,919	39,312	21,632	1,975	17,680 R	62.5%	34.4%	64.5%	35.5%
101,108	CECIL	29,700	15,600	13,132	968	2,468 R	52.5%	44.2%	54.3%	45.7%
146,551	CHARLES	46,401	15,598	30,106	697	14,508 D	33.6%	64.9%	34.1%	65.9%
32,618	DORCHESTER	11,582	4,910	6,481	191	1,571 D	42.4%	56.0%	43.1%	56.9%
233,385	FREDERICK	74,814	38,013	34,913	1,888	3,100 R	50.8%	46.7%	52.1%	47.9%
30,097	GARRETT	9,400	5,750	3,361	289	2,389 R	61.2%	35.8%	63.1%	36.9%
244,826	HARFORD	93,584	50,513	40,712	2,359	9,801 R	54.0%	43.5%	55.4%	44.6%
287,085	HOWARD	106,749	40,853	63,738	2,158	22,885 D	38.3%	59.7%	39.1%	60.9%
20,197	KENT	8,117	3,405	4,549	163	1,144 D	41.9%	56.0%	42.8%	57.2%
971,777	MONTGOMERY	288,684	79,582	204,005	5,097	124,423 D	27.6%	70.7%	28.1%	71.9%
863,420	PRINCE GEORGES	229,436	22,607	204,441	2,388	181,834 D	9.9%	89.1%	10.0%	90.0%
47,798	QUEEN ANNES	19,650	10,561	8,575	514	1,986 R	53.7%	43.6%	55.2%	44.8%
105,151	ST. MARYS	31,303	15,911	14,669	723	1,242 R	50.8%	46.9%	52.0%	48.0%
26,470	SOMERSET	7,562	3,363	4,082	117	719 D	44.5%	54.0%	45.2%	54.8%
37,782	TALBOT	16,168	7,946	7,968	254	22 D	49.1%	49.3%	49.9%	50.1%
147,430	WASHINGTON	39,708	20,873	17,356	1,479	3,517 R	52.6%	43.7%	54.6%	45.4%
98,733	WICOMICO	29,408	14,189	14,668	551	479 D	48.2%	49.9%	49.2%	50.8%
51,454	WORCESTER	21,226	10,619	10,248	359	371 R	50.0%	48.3%	50.9%	49.1%
5,773,552	TOTAL	1,833,858	655,666	1,140,531	37,661	484,865 D	35.8%	62.2%	36.5%	63.5%

MARYLAND

HOUSE OF REPRESENTATIVES

CD	Year	Total Vote	Republican Vote	Republican Candidate	Democratic Vote	Democratic Candidate	Other Vote	Rep.-Dem. Plurality		Total Vote Rep.	Total Vote Dem.	Major Vote Rep.	Major Vote Dem.
1	2010	286,812	155,118	HARRIS, ANDY	120,400	KRATOVIL, FRANK JR.*	11,294	34,718	R	54.1%	42.0%	56.3%	43.7%
1	2008	360,480	174,213	HARRIS, ANDY	177,065	KRATOVIL, FRANK JR.	9,202	2,852	D	48.3%	49.1%	49.6%	50.4%
1	2006	269,147	185,177	GILCHREST, WAYNE T.*	83,738	CORWIN, JIM	232	101,439	R	68.8%	31.1%	68.9%	31.1%
1	2004	323,526	245,149	GILCHREST, WAYNE T.*	77,872	ALEXAKIS, KOSTAS	505	167,277	R	75.8%	24.1%	75.9%	24.1%
1	2002	250,413	192,004	GILCHREST, WAYNE T.*	57,986	TAMLYN, ANN D.	423	134,018	R	76.7%	23.2%	76.8%	23.2%
2	2010	208,904	69,523	CARDARELLI, MARCELO	134,133	RUPPERSBERGER, C. A. DUTCH*	5,248	64,610	D	33.3%	64.2%	34.1%	65.9%
2	2008	276,333	68,561	MATTHEWS, RICHARD PRYCE	198,578	RUPPERSBERGER, C. A. DUTCH*	9,194	130,017	D	24.8%	71.9%	25.7%	74.3%
2	2006	196,228	60,195	MATHIS, JIMMY	135,818	RUPPERSBERGER, C. A. DUTCH*	215	75,623	D	30.7%	69.2%	30.7%	69.3%
2	2004	247,295	75,812	BROOKS, JANE	164,751	RUPPERSBERGER, C. A. DUTCH*	6,732	88,939	D	30.7%	66.6%	31.5%	68.5%
2	2002	195,202	88,954	BENTLEY, HELEN DELICH	105,718	RUPPERSBERGER, C. A. DUTCH	530	16,764	D	45.6%	54.2%	45.7%	54.3%
3	2010	241,429	86,947	WILHELM, JIM	147,448	SARBANES, JOHN P.*	7,034	60,501	D	36.0%	61.1%	37.1%	62.9%
3	2008	292,448	87,971	HARRIS, THOMAS E. "PINKSTON"	203,711	SARBANES, JOHN P.*	766	115,740	D	30.1%	69.7%	30.2%	69.8%
3	2006	234,486	79,174	WHITE, JOHN	150,142	SARBANES, JOHN P.	5,170	70,968	D	33.8%	64.0%	34.5%	65.5%
3	2004	287,219	97,008	DUCKWORTH, ROBERT P.	182,066	CARDIN, BENJAMIN L.*	8,145	85,058	D	33.8%	63.4%	34.8%	65.2%
3	2002	221,543	75,721	CONWELL, SCOTT	145,589	CARDIN, BENJAMIN L.*	233	69,868	D	34.2%	65.7%	34.2%	65.8%
4	2010	192,020	31,467	BROADUS, ROBERT	160,228	EDWARDS, DONNA F.*	325	128,761	D	16.4%	83.4%	16.4%	83.6%
4	2008	301,431	38,739	JAMES, PETER	258,704	EDWARDS, DONNA F.*	3,988	219,965	D	12.9%	85.8%	13.0%	87.0%
4	2006	175,903	32,792	STARKMAN, MICHAEL MOSHE	141,897	WYNN, ALBERT R.*	1,214	109,105	D	18.6%	80.7%	18.8%	81.2%
4	2004	261,860	52,907	McKINNIS, JOHN	196,809	WYNN, ALBERT R.*	12,144	143,902	D	20.2%	75.2%	21.2%	78.8%
4	2002	167,555	34,890	KIMBLE, JOHN B.	131,644	WYNN, ALBERT R.*	1,021	96,754	D	20.8%	78.6%	21.0%	79.0%
5	2010	241,383	83,575	LOLLAR, CHARLES	155,110	HOYER, STENY H.*	2,698	71,535	D	34.6%	64.3%	35.0%	65.0%
5	2008	344,691	82,631	BAILEY, COLLINS	253,854	HOYER, STENY H.*	8,206	171,223	D	24.0%	73.6%	24.6%	75.4%
5	2006	203,323		—	168,114	HOYER, STENY H.*	35,209	168,114	D		82.7%		100.0%
5	2004	298,335	87,189	JEWITT, BRAD	204,867	HOYER, STENY H.*	6,279	117,678	D	29.2%	68.7%	29.9%	70.1%
5	2002	199,087	60,758	CRAWFORD, JOSEPH T.	137,903	HOYER, STENY H.*	426	77,145	D	30.5%	69.3%	30.6%	69.4%
6	2010	242,189	148,820	BARTLETT, ROSCOE G.*	80,455	DUCK, ANDREW	12,914	68,365	R	61.4%	33.2%	64.9%	35.1%
6	2008	330,535	190,926	BARTLETT, ROSCOE G.*	128,207	DOUGHERTY, JENNIFER P.	11,402	62,719	R	57.8%	38.8%	59.8%	40.2%
6	2006	239,453	141,200	BARTLETT, ROSCOE G.*	92,030	DUCK, ANDREW	6,223	49,170	R	59.0%	38.4%	60.5%	39.5%
6	2004	305,857	206,076	BARTLETT, ROSCOE G.*	90,108	BOSLEY, KENNETH T.	9,673	115,968	R	67.4%	29.5%	69.6%	30.4%
6	2002	223,611	147,825	BARTLETT, ROSCOE G.*	75,575	DeARMON, DONALD M.	211	72,250	R	66.1%	33.8%	66.2%	33.8%
7	2010	203,068	46,375	MIRABILE, FRANK JR.	152,669	CUMMINGS, ELIJAH E.*	4,024	106,294	D	22.8%	75.2%	23.3%	76.7%
7	2008	286,020	53,147	HARGADON, MICHAEL T.	227,379	CUMMINGS, ELIJAH E.*	5,494	174,232	D	18.6%	79.5%	18.9%	81.1%
7	2006	161,977		—	158,830	CUMMINGS, ELIJAH E.*	3,147	158,830	D		98.1%		100.0%
7	2004	244,183	60,102	SALAZAR, TONY	179,189	CUMMINGS, ELIJAH E.*	4,892	119,087	D	24.6%	73.4%	25.1%	74.9%
7	2002	186,394	49,172	WARD, JOSEPH E.	137,047	CUMMINGS, ELIJAH E.*	175	87,875	D	26.4%	73.5%	26.4%	73.6%
8	2010	209,667	52,421	PHILIPS, MICHAEL LEE	153,613	VAN HOLLEN, CHRIS*	3,633	101,192	D	25.0%	73.3%	25.4%	74.6%
8	2008	306,014	66,351	HUDSON, STEVE	229,740	VAN HOLLEN, CHRIS*	9,923	163,389	D	21.7%	75.1%	22.4%	77.6%
8	2006	220,685	48,324	STEIN, JEFFREY M.	168,872	VAN HOLLEN, CHRIS*	3,489	120,548	D	21.9%	76.5%	22.2%	77.8%
8	2004	287,680	71,989	FLOYD, CHUCK	215,129	VAN HOLLEN, CHRIS*	562	143,140	D	25.0%	74.8%	25.1%	74.9%
8	2002	218,113	103,587	MORELLA, CONSTANCE A.*	112,788	VAN HOLLEN, CHRIS	1,738	9,201	D	47.5%	51.7%	47.9%	52.1%
TOTAL	2010	1,825,472	674,246		1,104,056		47,170	429,810	D	36.9%	60.5%	37.9%	62.1%
TOTAL	2008	2,497,952	762,539		1,677,238		58,175	914,699	D	30.5%	67.1%	31.3%	68.7%
TOTAL	2006	1,701,202	546,862		1,099,441		54,899	552,579	D	32.1%	64.6%	33.2%	66.8%
TOTAL	2004	2,255,955	896,232		1,310,791		48,932	414,559	D	39.7%	58.1%	40.6%	59.4%
TOTAL	2002	1,661,918	752,911		904,250		4,757	151,339	D	45.3%	54.4%	45.4%	54.6%

An asterisk (*) denotes incumbent.

MARYLAND

GENERAL AND PRIMARY ELECTIONS

2010 GENERAL ELECTIONS

Governor Other vote was 14,137 Libertarian (Susan J. Gaztanaga); 11,825 Green (Maria Allwine); 8,612 Constitution (Eric Delano Knowles); 319 Democratic write-in (Ralph Jaffe); 179 Unaffiliated write-in (Corrogan R. Vaughn); 1,528 scattered write-in.

Senator Other vote was 20,717 Green (Kenniss Henry); 14,746 Constitution (Richard Shawver); 204 Republican write-in (Claud L. Asbury); 110 Unaffiliated write-in (Donald Kaplan); 84 Democratic write-in (James T. Lynch Jr.); 80 Democratic write-in (Lih Young); 56 Democratic write-in (Denise L. Whittington); 14 Unaffiliated write-in (Robert J. Evans); 6 Republican write-in (Mary Catherine Podlesak); 1,644 scattered write-in.

House Other vote was:

CD 1 10,876 Libertarian (Richard James Davis); 158 write-in (Jack N. Wilson); 18 write-in (Michael Kennedy); 242 scattered write-in.

CD 2 5,090 Libertarian (Lorenzo Gaztanaga); 158 scattered write-in.

CD 3 5,212 Libertarian (Jerry Mckinley); 1,634 Constitution (Alain Lareau); 188 scattered write-in.

CD 4 325 scattered write-in.

CD 5 2,578 Libertarian (H. Gavin Shickle); 120 scattered write-in.

CD 6 6,816 Libertarian (Dan Massey); 5,907 Constitution (Michael Reed); 191 scattered write-in.

CD 7 3,814 Libertarian (Scott Spencer); 55 write-in (Fred Donald Dickson Jr.); 20 write-in (Ray Bly); 135 scattered write-in.

CD 8 2,713 Libertarian (Mark Grannis); 696 Constitution (Fred Nordhorn); 224 scattered write-in.

2010 PRIMARY ELECTIONS

Primary September 14, 2010

Registration (active registrants as of Aug. 29, 2010)

Democratic	1,944,620
Republican	915,506
Libertarian	3,920
Green	3,503
Constitution	245
Other	23,255
Unaffiliated	276,797
TOTAL	*3,167,846*

Primary Type Closed—Only registered Democrats and Republicans could vote in their party's primary.

MARYLAND

GENERAL AND PRIMARY ELECTIONS

	REPUBLICAN PRIMARIES			DEMOCRATIC PRIMARIES		
Governor	Robert L. Ehrlich Jr.	211,428	75.8%	Martin O'Malley*	414,595	86.3%
	Brian Murphy	67,364	24.2%	J. P. Cusick	46,411	9.7%
				Ralph Jaffe	19,517	4.1%
	TOTAL	278,792		TOTAL	480,523	
Senator	Eric Wargotz	93,490	38.4%	Barbara A. Mikulski*	396,252	82.3%
	Jim Rutledge	74,404	30.6%	Christopher J. Garner	36,194	7.5%
	Joseph Alexander	14,270	5.9%	A. Billy Bob Jaworski	15,335	3.2%
	Neil H. Cohen	13,869	5.7%	Blaine Taylor	11,049	2.3%
	Stephens Dempsey	9,517	3.9%	Theresa C. Scaldaferri	8,092	1.7%
	Daniel W. McAndrew	8,611	3.5%	Sanquetta Taylor	7,684	1.6%
	John B. Kimble	8,265	3.4%	Lih Young	6,911	1.4%
	Samuel R. Graham Sr.	6,738	2.8%			
	Barry Steve Asbury	6,011	2.5%			
	Eddie Vendetti	5,161	2.1%			
	Gregory L. Kump	2,981	1.2%			
	TOTAL	243,317		TOTAL	481,517	
Congressional District 1	Andy Harris	46,227	67.4%	Frank Kratovil Jr.*	42,762	100.0%
	Rob Fisher	22,409	32.6%			
	TOTAL	68,636				
Congressional District 2	Marcelo Cardarelli	10,427	46.1%	C.A. Dutch Ruppersberger*	42,262	74.0%
	Jimmy Mathis	5,904	26.1%	Raymond Atkins	7,405	13.0%
	Francis Treadwell	2,633	11.6%	Jeff Morris	3,841	6.7%
	Troy Stouffer	2,593	11.5%	Christopher C. Boardman	3,575	6.3%
	Josh Dowlut	1,067	4.7%			
	TOTAL	22,624		TOTAL	57,083	
Congressional District 3	Jim Wilhelm	8,856	36.0%	John P. Sarbanes*	54,710	83.0%
	Thomas E. "Pinkston" Harris	6,906	28.1%	Michael Miller	5,456	8.3%
	Greg Bartosz	6,597	26.8%	John Kibler	2,989	4.5%
	Thomas Defibaugh Sr.	2,215	9.0%	Ryan Ludick	1,425	2.2%
				John Rea	1,307	2.0%
	TOTAL	24,574		TOTAL	65,887	
Congressional District 4	Robert Broadus	6,828	100.0%	Donna F. Edwards*	56,737	83.6%
				Herman Taylor	5,972	8.8%
				George McDermott	2,833	4.2%
				Kwame Gyamfi	2,355	3.5%
				TOTAL	67,897	
Congressional District 5	Charles Lollar	16,773	58.0%	Steny H. Hoyer*	58,717	85.7%
	Collins A. Bailey	9,001	31.1%	Andrew Charles Gall	6,682	9.7%
	Chris Chaffee	1,631	5.6%	Sylvanus G. Bent	3,147	4.6%
	Chris Robins	1,530	5.3%			
	TOTAL	28,935		TOTAL	68,546	
Congressional District 6	Roscoe G. Bartlett*	49,056	69.8%	Andrew Duck	21,605	65.4%
	Joseph T. Krysztoforski	11,124	15.8%	J. Casey Clark	11,449	34.6%
	Steve Taylor	4,822	6.9%			
	Seth Edward Wilson	3,860	5.5%			
	Dennis B. Janda	1,379	2.0%			
	TOTAL	70,241		TOTAL	33,054	

An asterisk (*) denotes incumbent.

MARYLAND

GENERAL AND PRIMARY ELECTIONS

	REPUBLICAN PRIMARIES			DEMOCRATIC PRIMARIES		
District 7	Frank Mirabile Jr.	7,306	56.0%	Elijah E. Cummings*	59,649	91.0%
	Michael J. Vallerie	3,982	30.5%	Charles U. Smith	5,884	9.0%
	Ray Bly	1,766	13.5%			
	TOTAL	*13,054*		*TOTAL*	*65,533*	
Congressional	Michael Lee Philips	4,717	32.1%	Chris Van Hollen*	57,847	92.9%
District 8	Bruce Stern	4,665	31.7%	Robert Long	4,392	7.1%
	Christine Thron	3,073	20.9%			
	Bill Thomas	2,242	15.3%			
	TOTAL	*14,697*		*TOTAL*	*62,239*	

MASSACHUSETTS

Congressional districts first established for elections held in 2002
10 members

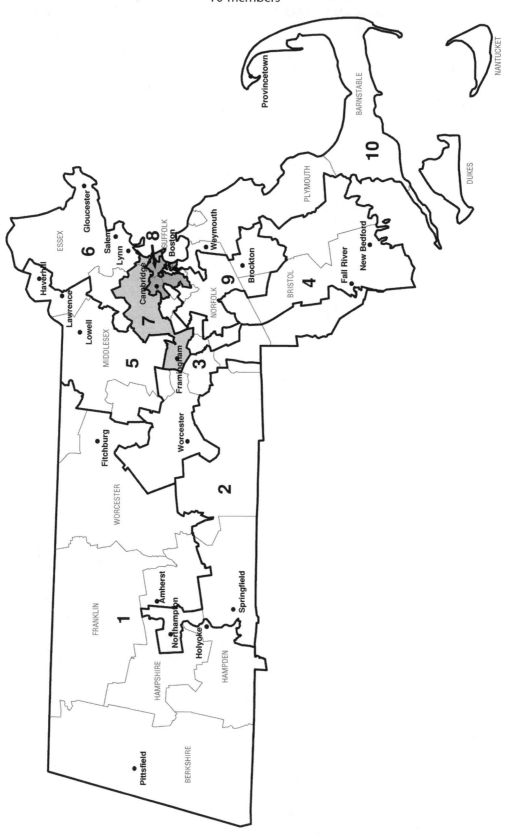

MASSACHUSETTS

Boston Area

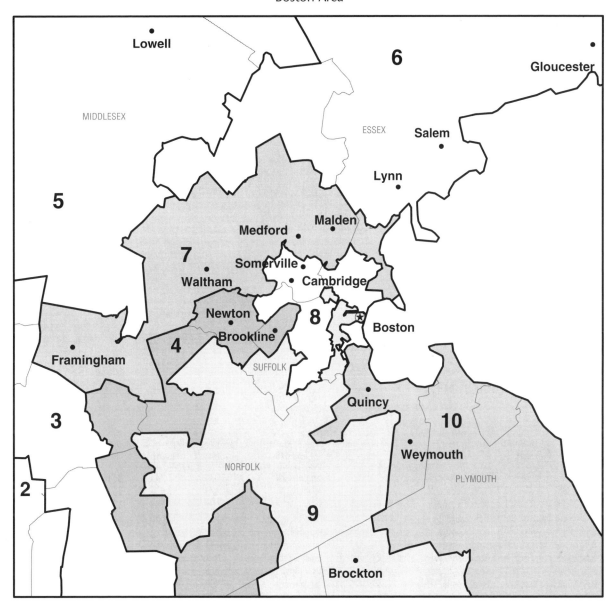

MASSACHUSETTS

GOVERNOR
Deval L. Patrick (D). Reelected 2010 to a four-year term. Previously elected 2006.

SENATORS (1 Democrat, 1 Republican)
Scott P. Brown (R). Elected January 19, 2010, to serve the remainder of the term vacated by the August 2009 death of Senator Edward M. Kennedy. Paul Kirk (D) had been appointed to serve on an interim basis until the 2010 special election was held.

John Kerry (D). Reelected 2008 to a six-year term. Previously elected 2002, 1996, 1990, 1984.

REPRESENTATIVES (10 Democrats)

1. John W. Olver (D)
2. Richard E. Neal (D)
3. Jim McGovern (D)
4. Barney Frank (D)
5. Niki Tsongas (D)
6. John F. Tierney (D)
7. Edward J. Markey (D)
8. Michael E. Capuano (D)
9. Stephen F. Lynch (D)
10. William R. Keating (D)

POSTWAR VOTE FOR PRESIDENT

		Republican		Democratic				Total Vote		Major Vote	
Year	Total Vote	Vote	Candidate	Vote	Candidate	Other Vote	Rep.-Dem. Plurality	Rep.	Dem.	Rep.	Dem.
2008	3,080,985	1,108,854	McCain, John	1,904,097	Obama, Barack	68,034	795,243 D	36.0%	61.8%	36.8%	63.2%
2004	2,912,388	1,071,109	Bush, George W.	1,803,800	Kerry, John	37,479	732,691 D	36.8%	61.9%	37.3%	62.7%
2000**	2,702,984	878,502	Bush, George W.	1,616,487	Gore, Al	207,995	737,985 D	32.5%	59.8%	35.2%	64.8%
1996**	2,556,785	718,107	Dole, Bob	1,571,763	Clinton, Bill	266,915	853,656 D	28.1%	61.5%	31.4%	68.6%
1992**	2,773,700	805,049	Bush, George	1,318,662	Clinton, Bill	649,989	513,613 D	29.0%	47.5%	37.9%	62.1%
1988	2,632,805	1,194,635	Bush, George	1,401,415	Dukakis, Michael S.	36,755	206,780 D	45.4%	53.2%	46.0%	54.0%
1984	2,559,453	1,310,936	Reagan, Ronald	1,239,606	Mondale, Walter F.	8,911	71,330 R	51.2%	48.4%	51.4%	48.6%
1980**	2,524,298	1,057,631	Reagan, Ronald	1,053,802	Carter, Jimmy	412,865	3,829 R	41.9%	41.7%	50.1%	49.9%
1976	2,547,558	1,030,276	Ford, Gerald R.	1,429,475	Carter, Jimmy	87,807	399,199 D	40.4%	56.1%	41.9%	58.1%
1972	2,458,756	1,112,078	Nixon, Richard M.	1,332,540	McGovern, George S.	14,138	220,462 D	45.2%	54.2%	45.5%	54.5%
1968**	2,331,752	766,844	Nixon, Richard M.	1,469,218	Humphrey, Hubert H.	95,690	702,374 D	32.9%	63.0%	34.3%	65.7%
1964	2,344,798	549,727	Goldwater, Barry M.	1,786,422	Johnson, Lyndon B.	8,649	1,236,695 D	23.4%	76.2%	23.5%	76.5%
1960	2,469,480	976,750	Nixon, Richard M.	1,487,174	Kennedy, John F.	5,556	510,424 D	39.6%	60.2%	39.6%	60.4%
1956	2,348,506	1,393,197	Eisenhower, Dwight D.	948,190	Stevenson, Adlai E.	7,119	445,007 R	59.3%	40.4%	59.5%	40.5%
1952	2,383,398	1,292,325	Eisenhower, Dwight D.	1,083,525	Stevenson, Adlai E.	7,548	208,800 R	54.2%	45.5%	54.4%	45.6%
1948	2,107,146	909,370	Dewey, Thomas E.	1,151,788	Truman, Harry S.	45,988	242,418 D	43.2%	54.7%	44.1%	55.9%

**In past elections, the other vote included: 2000 - 173,564 - Green (Ralph Nader); 1996 - 227,217 Reform (Ross Perot); 1992 - 630,731 Independent (Perot); 1980 - 382,539 Independent (John Anderson); 1968 - 87,088 American Independent (George Wallace).

MASSACHUSETTS

POSTWAR VOTE FOR GOVERNOR

Year	Total Vote	Republican Vote	Republican Candidate	Democratic Vote	Democratic Candidate	Other Vote	Rep.-Dem. Plurality	Total Vote Rep.	Total Vote Dem.	Major Vote Rep.	Major Vote Dem.
2010	2,297,039	964,866	Baker, Charles D.	1,112,283	Patrick, Deval L.	219,890	147,417 D	42.0%	48.4%	46.5%	53.5%
2006	2,219,779	784,342	Healey, Kerry	1,234,984	Patrick, Deval L.	200,453	450,642 D	35.3%	55.6%	38.8%	61.2%
2002	2,194,179	1,091,988	Romney, Mitt	985,981	O'Brien, Shannon P.	116,210	106,007 R	49.8%	44.9%	52.6%	47.4%
1998	1,903,336	967,160	Cellucci, Paul	901,843	Harshbarger, Scott	34,333	65,317 R	50.8%	47.4%	51.7%	48.3%
1994	2,164,318	1,533,430	Weld, William F.	611,650	Roosevelt, Mark	19,238	921,780 R	70.9%	28.3%	71.5%	28.5%
1990	2,342,927	1,175,817	Weld, William F.	1,099,878	Silber, John	67,232	75,939 R	50.2%	46.9%	51.7%	48.3%
1986	1,684,079	525,364	Kariotis, George	1,157,786	Dukakis, Michael S.	929	632,422 D	31.2%	68.7%	31.2%	68.8%
1982	2,050,254	749,679	Sears, John W.	1,219,109	Dukakis, Michael S.	81,466	469,430 D	36.6%	59.5%	38.1%	61.9%
1978	1,962,251	926,072	Hatch, Francis W.	1,030,294	King, Edward J.	5,885	104,222 D	47.2%	52.5%	47.3%	52.7%
1974	1,854,798	784,353	Sargent, Francis W.	992,284	Dukakis, Michael S.	78,161	207,931 D	42.3%	53.5%	44.1%	55.9%
1970	1,867,906	1,058,623	Sargent, Francis W.	799,269	White, Kevin H.	10,014	259,354 R	56.7%	42.8%	57.0%	43.0%
1966**	2,041,177	1,277,358	Volpe, John A.	752,720	McCormack, Edward J.	11,099	524,638 R	62.6%	36.9%	62.9%	37.1%
1964	2,340,130	1,176,462	Volpe, John A.	1,153,416	Bellotti, Francis X.	10,252	23,046 R	50.3%	49.3%	50.5%	49.5%
1962	2,109,089	1,047,891	Volpe, John A.	1,053,322	Peabody, Endicott	7,876	5,431 D	49.7%	49.9%	49.9%	50.1%
1960	2,417,133	1,269,295	Volpe, John A.	1,130,810	Ward, Joseph D.	17,028	138,485 R	52.5%	46.8%	52.9%	47.1%
1958	1,899,117	818,463	Gibbons, Charles	1,067,020	Furcolo, Foster	13,634	248,557 D	43.1%	56.2%	43.4%	56.6%
1956	2,339,884	1,096,759	Whittier, Sumner G.	1,234,618	Furcolo, Foster	8,507	137,859 D	46.9%	52.8%	47.0%	53.0%
1954	1,903,774	985,339	Herter, Christian A.	910,087	Murphy, Robert F.	8,348	75,252 R	51.8%	47.8%	52.0%	48.0%
1952	2,356,298	1,175,955	Herter, Christian A.	1,161,499	Dever, Paul A.	18,844	14,456 R	49.9%	49.3%	50.3%	49.7%
1950	1,910,180	824,069	Coolidge, Arthur W.	1,074,570	Dever, Paul A.	11,541	250,501 D	43.1%	56.3%	43.4%	56.6%
1948	2,099,250	849,895	Bradford, Robert F.	1,239,247	Dever, Paul A.	10,108	389,352 D	40.5%	59.0%	40.7%	59.3%
1946	1,683,452	911,152	Bradford, Robert F.	762,743	Tobin, Maurice	9,557	148,409 R	54.1%	45.3%	54.4%	45.6%

**The term of office of Massachusetts' Governor was increased from two to four years effective with the 1966 election.

POSTWAR VOTE FOR SENATOR

Year	Total Vote	Republican Vote	Republican Candidate	Democratic Vote	Democratic Candidate	Other Vote	Rep.-Dem. Plurality	Total Vote Rep.	Total Vote Dem.	Major Vote Rep.	Major Vote Dem.
2010S	2,252,582	1,168,178	Brown, Scott P.	1,060,861	Coakley, Martha	23,543	107,317 R	51.9%	47.1%	52.4%	47.6%
2008	2,994,247	926,044	Beatty, Jeffrey K.	1,971,974	Kerry, John	96,229	1,045,930 D	30.9%	65.9%	32.0%	68.0%
2006	2,165,490	661,532	Chase, Kenneth G.	1,500,738	Kennedy, Edward M.	3,220	839,206 D	30.5%	69.3%	30.6%	69.4%
2002**	2,006,758		—	1,605,976	Kerry, John	400,782	1,605,976 D		80.0%		100.0%
2000**	2,599,420	334,341	Robinson, Jack E.	1,889,494	Kennedy, Edward M.	375,585	1,555,153 D	12.9%	72.7%	15.0%	85.0%
1996	2,555,886	1,142,837	Weld, William F.	1,334,345	Kerry, John	78,704	191,508 D	44.7%	52.2%	46.1%	53.9%
1994	2,179,964	894,005	Romney, Mitt	1,266,011	Kennedy, Edward M.	19,948	372,006 D	41.0%	58.1%	41.4%	58.6%
1990	2,316,212	992,917	Rappaport, Jim	1,321,712	Kerry, John	1,583	328,795 D	42.9%	57.1%	42.9%	57.1%
1988	2,606,225	884,267	Malone, Joseph	1,693,344	Kennedy, Edward M.	28,614	809,077 D	33.9%	65.0%	34.3%	65.7%
1984	2,530,195	1,136,806	Shamie, Raymond	1,392,981	Kerry, John	408	256,175 D	44.9%	55.1%	44.9%	55.1%
1982	2,050,769	784,602	Shamie, Raymond	1,247,084	Kennedy, Edward M.	19,083	462,482 D	38.3%	60.8%	38.6%	61.4%
1978	1,985,700	890,584	Brooke, Edward W.	1,093,283	Tsongas, Paul E.	1,833	202,699 D	44.8%	55.1%	44.9%	55.1%
1976	2,491,255	722,641	Robertson, Michael	1,726,657	Kennedy, Edward M.	41,957	1,004,016 D	29.0%	69.3%	29.5%	70.5%
1972	2,370,676	1,505,932	Brooke, Edward W.	823,278	Droney, John J.	41,466	682,654 R	63.5%	34.7%	64.7%	35.3%
1970	1,935,607	715,978	Spaulding, Josiah A.	1,202,856	Kennedy, Edward M.	16,773	486,878 D	37.0%	62.1%	37.3%	62.7%
1966	1,999,949	1,213,473	Brooke, Edward W.	774,761	Peabody, Endicott	11,715	438,712 R	60.7%	38.7%	61.0%	39.0%
1964	2,312,028	587,663	Whitmore, Howard	1,716,907	Kennedy, Edward M.	7,458	1,129,244 D	25.4%	74.3%	25.5%	74.5%
1962S	2,097,085	877,669	Lodge, George C.	1,162,611	Kennedy, Edward M.	56,805	284,942 D	41.9%	55.4%	43.0%	57.0%
1960	2,417,813	1,358,556	Saltonstall, Leverett	1,050,725	O'Connor, Thomas J.	8,532	307,831 R	56.2%	43.5%	56.4%	43.6%
1958	1,862,041	488,318	Celeste, Vincent J.	1,362,926	Kennedy, John F.	10,797	874,608 D	26.2%	73.2%	26.4%	73.6%
1954	1,892,710	956,605	Saltonstall, Leverett	927,899	Furcolo, Foster	8,206	28,706 R	50.5%	49.0%	50.8%	49.2%
1952	2,360,425	1,141,247	Lodge, Henry Cabot	1,211,984	Kennedy, John F.	7,194	70,737 D	48.3%	51.3%	48.5%	51.5%
1948	2,055,798	1,088,475	Saltonstall, Leverett	954,398	Fitzgerald, John I.	12,925	134,077 R	52.9%	46.4%	53.3%	46.7%
1946	1,662,063	989,736	Lodge, Henry Cabot	660,200	Walsh, David I.	12,127	329,536 R	59.5%	39.7%	60.0%	40.0%

**In past elections, the other vote included: 2002 - 369,807 Libertarian (Michael E. Cloud); 2000 - 308,748 Libertarian (Carla Howell). The Republican Party did not run a candidate in the 2002 Senate election. The 1962 and 2010 elections were for short terms to fill a vacancy. The latter election was held in January 2010.

MASSACHUSETTS

GOVERNOR 2010

2010 Census Population	County	Total Vote	Republican	Democratic	Other	Rep.-Dem. Plurality		Percentage			
								Total Vote		Major Vote	
								Rep.	Dem.	Rep.	Dem.
215,888	BARNSTABLE	106,663	50,609	47,124	8,930	3,485	R	47.4%	44.2%	51.8%	48.2%
131,219	BERKSHIRE	42,541	9,266	30,269	3,006	21,003	D	21.8%	71.2%	23.4%	76.6%
548,285	BRISTOL	171,619	73,220	81,059	17,340	7,839	D	42.7%	47.2%	47.5%	52.5%
16,535	DUKES	8,409	2,757	4,908	744	2,151	D	32.8%	58.4%	36.0%	64.0%
743,159	ESSEX	267,151	127,964	116,360	22,827	11,604	R	47.9%	43.6%	52.4%	47.6%
71,372	FRANKLIN	27,774	6,838	17,068	3,868	10,230	D	24.6%	61.5%	28.6%	71.4%
463,490	HAMPDEN	136,540	54,653	62,816	19,071	8,163	D	40.0%	46.0%	46.5%	53.5%
158,080	HAMPSHIRE	56,557	15,994	33,317	7,246	17,323	D	28.3%	58.9%	32.4%	67.6%
1,503,085	MIDDLESEX	553,379	226,272	283,221	43,886	56,949	D	40.9%	51.2%	44.4%	55.6%
10,172	NANTUCKET	4,712	1,846	2,454	412	608	D	39.2%	52.1%	42.9%	57.1%
670,850	NORFOLK	271,145	119,850	119,806	31,489	44	R	44.2%	44.2%	50.0%	50.0%
494,919	PLYMOUTH	192,459	96,592	74,355	21,512	22,237	R	50.2%	38.6%	56.5%	43.5%
722,023	SUFFOLK	186,160	46,822	125,961	13,377	79,139	D	25.2%	67.7%	27.1%	72.9%
798,552	WORCESTER	271,930	132,183	113,565	26,182	18,618	R	48.6%	41.8%	53.8%	46.2%
6,547,629	TOTAL	2,297,039	964,866	1,112,283	219,890	147,417	D	42.0%	48.4%	46.5%	53.5%

2010 Census Population	City/Town	Total Vote	Republican	Democratic	Other	Rep.-Dem. Plurality		Percentage			
								Total Vote		Major Vote	
								Rep.	Dem.	Rep.	Dem.
21,924	ACTON	9,256	3,478	5,326	452	1,848	D	37.6%	57.5%	39.5%	60.5%
28,438	AGAWAM	10,702	4,975	4,019	1,708	956	R	46.5%	37.6%	55.3%	44.7%
37,819	AMHERST	7,901	879	6,284	738	5,405	D	11.1%	79.5%	12.3%	87.7%
33,201	ANDOVER	14,184	7,540	5,893	751	1,647	R	53.2%	41.5%	56.1%	43.9%
42,844	ARLINGTON	20,282	5,684	13,205	1,393	7,521	D	28.0%	65.1%	30.1%	69.9%
43,593	ATTLEBORO	13,171	6,780	4,946	1,445	1,834	R	51.5%	37.6%	57.8%	42.2%
45,193	BARNSTABLE	20,107	10,382	7,983	1,742	2,399	R	51.6%	39.7%	56.5%	43.5%
24,729	BELMONT	11,112	3,960	6,546	606	2,586	D	35.6%	58.9%	37.7%	62.3%
39,502	BEVERLY	15,652	7,132	7,100	1,420	32	R	45.6%	45.4%	50.1%	49.9%
40,243	BILLERICA	14,950	8,128	4,977	1,845	3,151	R	54.4%	33.3%	62.0%	38.0%
617,594	BOSTON	162,903	37,493	114,519	10,891	77,026	D	23.0%	70.3%	24.7%	75.3%
35,744	BRAINTREE	15,209	6,886	5,519	2,804	1,367	R	45.3%	36.3%	55.5%	44.5%
93,810	BROCKTON	22,326	7,656	12,380	2,290	4,724	D	34.3%	55.5%	38.2%	61.8%
58,732	BROOKLINE	20,446	4,765	14,909	772	10,144	D	23.3%	72.9%	24.2%	75.8%
24,498	BURLINGTON	9,415	4,815	3,777	823	1,038	R	51.1%	40.1%	56.0%	44.0%
105,162	CAMBRIDGE	33,934	4,284	26,918	2,732	22,634	D	12.6%	79.3%	13.7%	86.3%
21,561	CANTON	9,470	4,706	3,902	862	804	R	49.7%	41.2%	54.7%	45.3%
33,802	CHELMSFORD	15,095	8,040	5,717	1,338	2,323	R	53.3%	37.9%	58.4%	41.6%
55,298	CHICOPEE	16,150	6,273	6,853	3,024	580	D	38.8%	42.4%	47.8%	52.2%
17,668	CONCORD	8,722	3,110	5,280	332	2,170	D	35.7%	60.5%	37.1%	62.9%
26,493	DANVERS	10,669	5,599	4,027	1,043	1,572	R	52.5%	37.7%	58.2%	41.8%
34,032	DARTMOUTH	11,906	4,340	6,563	1,003	2,223	D	36.5%	55.1%	39.8%	60.2%
24,729	DEDHAM	10,345	4,674	4,513	1,158	161	R	45.2%	43.6%	50.9%	49.1%
29,457	DRACUT	11,058	6,306	3,428	1,324	2,878	R	57.0%	31.0%	64.8%	35.2%
23,112	EASTON	9,006	4,882	3,332	792	1,550	R	54.2%	37.0%	59.4%	40.6%

MASSACHUSETTS

GOVERNOR 2010

2010 Census Population	City/Town	Total Vote	Republican	Democratic	Other	Rep.-Dem. Plurality		Percentage			
								Total Vote		Major Vote	
								Rep.	Dem.	Rep.	Dem.
41,667	EVERETT	8,949	3,257	4,579	1,113	1,322	D	36.4%	51.2%	41.6%	58.4%
88,857	FALL RIVER	19,810	5,762	12,028	2,020	6,266	D	29.1%	60.7%	32.4%	67.6%
31,531	FALMOUTH	15,834	6,812	7,739	1,283	927	D	43.0%	48.9%	46.8%	53.2%
40,318	FITCHBURG	10,025	4,532	4,378	1,115	154	R	45.2%	43.7%	50.9%	49.1%
68,318	FRAMINGHAM	20,025	7,911	10,579	1,535	2,668	D	39.5%	52.8%	42.8%	57.2%
31,635	FRANKLIN	12,756	6,884	4,617	1,255	2,267	R	54.0%	36.2%	59.9%	40.1%
28,789	GLOUCESTER	11,333	4,749	5,588	996	839	D	41.9%	49.3%	45.9%	54.1%
60,879	HAVERHILL	19,608	9,635	7,829	2,144	1,806	R	49.1%	39.9%	55.2%	44.8%
22,157	HINGHAM	11,260	5,741	4,658	861	1,083	R	51.0%	41.4%	55.2%	44.8%
39,880	HOLYOKE	10,356	2,923	6,139	1,294	3,216	D	28.2%	59.3%	32.3%	67.7%
76,377	LAWRENCE	13,040	3,139	9,094	807	5,955	D	24.1%	69.7%	25.7%	74.3%
40,759	LEOMINSTER	13,269	6,782	5,179	1,308	1,603	R	51.1%	39.0%	56.7%	43.3%
31,394	LEXINGTON	14,430	4,529	9,330	571	4,801	D	31.4%	64.7%	32.7%	67.3%
106,519	LOWELL	22,184	8,987	10,839	2,358	1,852	D	40.5%	48.9%	45.3%	54.7%
90,329	LYNN	21,091	7,533	11,358	2,200	3,825	D	35.7%	53.9%	39.9%	60.1%
59,450	MALDEN	14,609	5,417	7,743	1,449	2,326	D	37.1%	53.0%	41.2%	58.8%
19,808	MARBLEHEAD	10,102	5,179	4,482	441	697	R	51.3%	44.4%	53.6%	46.4%
38,499	MARLBOROUGH	12,339	5,872	5,346	1,121	526	R	47.6%	43.3%	52.3%	47.7%
25,132	MARSHFIELD	11,647	6,225	4,150	1,272	2,075	R	53.4%	35.6%	60.0%	40.0%
56,173	MEDFORD	19,900	7,101	10,745	2,054	3,644	D	35.7%	54.0%	39.8%	60.2%
26,983	MELROSE	12,317	5,584	5,842	891	258	D	45.3%	47.4%	48.9%	51.1%
47,255	METHUEN	15,191	8,235	5,447	1,509	2,788	R	54.2%	35.9%	60.2%	39.8%
27,999	MILFORD	8,967	4,507	3,584	876	923	R	50.3%	40.0%	55.7%	44.3%
27,003	MILTON	12,882	4,711	7,014	1,157	2,303	D	36.6%	54.4%	40.2%	59.8%
33,006	NATICK	13,838	5,813	6,979	1,046	1,166	D	42.0%	50.4%	45.4%	54.6%
28,886	NEEDHAM	14,152	6,123	7,431	598	1,308	D	43.3%	52.5%	45.2%	54.8%
95,072	NEW BEDFORD	21,994	5,483	14,516	1,995	9,033	D	24.9%	66.0%	27.4%	72.6%
85,146	NEWTON	35,238	10,381	23,424	1,433	13,043	D	29.5%	66.5%	30.7%	69.3%
28,352	NORTH ANDOVER	11,170	6,419	3,999	752	2,420	R	57.5%	35.8%	61.6%	38.4%
28,712	NORTH ATTLEBOROUGH	9,954	5,921	3,091	942	2,830	R	59.5%	31.1%	65.7%	34.3%
28,549	NORTHAMPTON	11,886	1,843	8,751	1,292	6,908	D	15.5%	73.6%	17.4%	82.6%
28,602	NORWOOD	11,257	5,270	4,636	1,351	634	R	46.8%	41.2%	53.2%	46.8%
51,251	PEABODY	20,236	9,725	8,162	2,349	1,563	R	48.1%	40.3%	54.4%	45.6%
44,737	PITTSFIELD	12,723	2,525	9,243	955	6,718	D	19.8%	72.6%	21.5%	78.5%
56,468	PLYMOUTH	22,259	11,220	8,647	2,392	2,573	R	50.4%	38.8%	56.5%	43.5%
92,271	QUINCY	31,075	10,417	12,632	8,026	2,215	D	33.5%	40.7%	45.2%	54.8%
32,112	RANDOLPH	10,152	3,046	6,126	980	3,080	D	30.0%	60.3%	33.2%	66.8%
24,747	READING	10,984	5,657	4,548	779	1,109	R	51.5%	41.4%	55.4%	44.6%
51,755	REVERE	11,676	4,981	5,331	1,364	350	D	42.7%	45.7%	48.3%	51.7%
41,340	SALEM	13,539	5,068	7,159	1,312	2,091	D	37.4%	52.9%	41.4%	58.6%
26,628	SAUGUS	10,464	5,541	3,637	1,286	1,904	R	53.0%	34.8%	60.4%	39.6%
18,133	SCITUATE	9,102	4,600	3,704	798	896	R	50.5%	40.7%	55.4%	44.6%
35,608	SHREWSBURY	13,903	6,937	5,942	1,024	995	R	49.9%	42.7%	53.9%	46.1%
75,754	SOMERVILLE	22,742	4,397	16,486	1,859	12,089	D	19.3%	72.5%	21.1%	78.9%
153,060	SPRINGFIELD	31,967	8,035	20,297	3,635	12,262	D	25.1%	63.5%	28.4%	71.6%

MASSACHUSETTS

GOVERNOR 2010

2010 Census Population	City/Town	Total Vote	Republican	Democratic	Other	Rep.-Dem. Plurality		Percentage			
---	---	---	---	---	---	---	---	Total Vote		Major Vote	
								Rep.	Dem.	Rep.	Dem.
21,437	STONEHAM	9,307	4,859	3,619	829	1,240	R	52.2%	38.9%	57.3%	42.7%
26,962	STOUGHTON	10,281	4,598	4,518	1,165	80	R	44.7%	43.9%	50.4%	49.6%
55,874	TAUNTON	16,631	7,120	7,308	2,203	188	D	42.8%	43.9%	49.3%	50.7%
28,961	TEWKSBURY	11,572	6,475	3,701	1,396	2,774	R	56.0%	32.0%	63.6%	36.4%
24,932	WAKEFIELD	11,281	6,258	4,196	827	2,062	R	55.5%	37.2%	59.9%	40.1%
24,070	WALPOLE	10,837	6,039	3,743	1,055	2,296	R	55.7%	34.5%	61.7%	38.3%
60,632	WALTHAM	17,386	7,082	8,724	1,580	1,642	D	40.7%	50.2%	44.8%	55.2%
31,915	WATERTOWN	11,921	3,767	7,227	927	3,460	D	31.6%	60.6%	34.3%	65.7%
27,982	WELLESLEY	11,816	5,466	5,962	388	496	D	46.3%	50.5%	47.8%	52.2%
28,391	WEST SPRINGFIELD	8,677	3,899	3,479	1,299	420	R	44.9%	40.1%	52.8%	47.2%
41,094	WESTFIELD	12,528	5,847	4,725	1,956	1,122	R	46.7%	37.7%	55.3%	44.7%
53,743	WEYMOUTH	21,662	9,748	8,089	3,825	1,659	R	45.0%	37.3%	54.7%	45.3%
21,374	WINCHESTER	10,070	4,796	4,786	488	10	R	47.6%	47.5%	50.1%	49.9%
38,120	WOBURN	14,216	7,096	5,520	1,600	1,576	R	49.9%	38.8%	56.2%	43.8%
181,045	WORCESTER	42,880	14,032	25,605	3,243	11,573	D	32.7%	59.7%	35.4%	64.6%
23,793	YARMOUTH	11,024	5,332	4,679	1,013	653	R	48.4%	42.4%	53.3%	46.7%

MASSACHUSETTS

SENATOR 2010

2010 Census Population	County	Total Vote	Republican	Democratic	Other	Rep.-Dem. Plurality		Percentage			
---	---	---	---	---	---	---	---	Total Vote		Major Vote	
								Rep.	Dem.	Rep.	Dem.
215,888	BARNSTABLE	104,622	60,032	43,652	938	16,380	R	57.4%	41.7%	57.9%	42.1%
131,219	BERKSHIRE	43,614	13,298	29,869	447	16,571	D	30.5%	68.5%	30.8%	69.2%
548,285	BRISTOL	168,246	93,826	72,392	2,028	21,434	R	55.8%	43.0%	56.4%	43.6%
16,535	DUKES	7,666	2,646	4,922	98	2,276	D	34.5%	64.2%	35.0%	65.0%
743,159	ESSEX	254,835	143,969	108,430	2,436	35,539	R	56.5%	42.5%	57.0%	43.0%
71,372	FRANKLIN	27,747	9,908	17,382	457	7,474	D	35.7%	62.6%	36.3%	63.7%
463,490	HAMPDEN	131,604	71,697	57,890	2,017	13,807	R	54.5%	44.0%	55.3%	44.7%
158,080	HAMPSHIRE	56,653	21,112	34,808	733	13,696	D	37.3%	61.4%	37.8%	62.2%
1,503,085	MIDDLESEX	548,576	259,927	283,595	5,054	23,668	D	47.4%	51.7%	47.8%	52.2%
10,172	NANTUCKET	4,235	2,032	2,141	62	109	D	48.0%	50.6%	48.7%	51.3%
670,850	NORFOLK	273,499	150,890	120,198	2,411	30,692	R	55.2%	43.9%	55.7%	44.3%
494,919	PLYMOUTH	192,276	120,971	69,615	1,690	51,356	R	62.9%	36.2%	63.5%	36.5%
722,023	SUFFOLK	175,487	57,461	116,038	1,988	58,577	D	32.7%	66.1%	33.1%	66.9%
798,552	WORCESTER	263,522	160,409	99,929	3,184	60,480	R	60.9%	37.9%	61.6%	38.4%
6,547,629	TOTAL	2,252,582	1,168,178	1,060,861	23,543	107,317	R	51.9%	47.1%	52.4%	47.6%

MASSACHUSETTS

SENATOR 2010

2010 Census Population	City/Town	Total Vote	Republican	Democratic	Other	Rep.-Dem. Plurality	Percentage			
							Total Vote		Major Vote	
							Rep.	Dem.	Rep.	Dem.
21,924	ACTON	9,352	3,901	5,375	76	1,474 D	41.7%	57.5%	42.1%	57.9%
28,438	AGAWAM	10,545	6,726	3,661	158	3,065 R	63.8%	34.7%	64.8%	35.2%
37,819	AMHERST	7,802	1,180	6,554	68	5,374 D	15.1%	84.0%	15.3%	84.7%
33,201	ANDOVER	14,329	8,338	5,905	86	2,433 R	58.2%	41.2%	58.5%	41.5%
42,844	ARLINGTON	20,323	6,847	13,287	189	6,440 D	33.7%	65.4%	34.0%	66.0%
43,593	ATTLEBORO	13,563	8,607	4,831	125	3,776 R	63.5%	35.6%	64.0%	36.0%
45,193	BARNSTABLE	20,064	12,332	7,544	188	4,788 R	61.5%	37.6%	62.0%	38.0%
24,729	BELMONT	11,018	4,407	6,533	78	2,126 D	40.0%	59.3%	40.3%	59.7%
39,502	BEVERLY	15,321	8,400	6,744	177	1,656 R	54.8%	44.0%	55.5%	44.5%
40,243	BILLERICA	14,721	9,587	4,972	162	4,615 R	65.1%	33.8%	65.8%	34.2%
617,594	BOSTON	153,810	46,575	105,544	1691	58,969 D	30.3%	68.6%	30.6%	69.4%
35,744	BRAINTREE	15,103	9,320	5,612	171	3,708 R	61.7%	37.2%	62.4%	37.6%
93,810	BROCKTON	21,639	9,638	11,768	233	2,130 D	44.5%	54.4%	45.0%	55.0%
58,732	BROOKLINE	20,669	5,236	15,312	121	10,076 D	25.3%	74.1%	25.5%	74.5%
24,498	BURLINGTON	9,359	5,640	3,660	59	1,980 R	60.3%	39.1%	60.6%	39.4%
105,162	CAMBRIDGE	32,554	4,927	27,373	254	22,446 D	15.1%	84.1%	15.3%	84.7%
21,561	CANTON	9,641	5,770	3,788	83	1,982 R	59.8%	39.3%	60.4%	39.6%
33,802	CHELMSFORD	15,251	9,421	5,694	136	3,727 R	61.8%	37.3%	62.3%	37.7%
55,298	CHICOPEE	15,731	8,343	7,046	342	1,297 R	53.0%	44.8%	54.2%	45.8%
17,668	CONCORD	8,788	3,277	5,455	56	2,178 D	37.3%	62.1%	37.5%	62.5%
26,493	DANVERS	10,090	6,347	3,651	92	2,696 R	62.9%	36.2%	63.5%	36.5%
34,032	DARTMOUTH	11,030	5,815	5,115	100	700 R	52.7%	46.4%	53.2%	46.8%
24,729	DEDHAM	10,779	5,979	4,647	153	1,332 R	55.5%	43.1%	56.3%	43.7%
29,457	DRACUT	10,911	7,658	3,166	87	4,492 R	70.2%	29.0%	70.8%	29.2%
23,112	EASTON	9,299	5,940	3,297	62	2,643 R	63.9%	35.5%	64.3%	35.7%
41,667	EVERETT	8,178	3,798	4,248	132	450 D	46.4%	51.9%	47.2%	52.8%
88,857	FALL RIVER	18,281	7,520	10,388	373	2,868 D	41.1%	56.8%	42.0%	58.0%
31,531	FALMOUTH	15,323	8,045	7,139	139	906 R	52.5%	46.6%	53.0%	47.0%
40,318	FITCHBURG	9,473	5,578	3,786	109	1,792 R	58.9%	40.0%	59.6%	40.4%
68,318	FRAMINGHAM	19,682	9,169	10,341	172	1,172 D	46.6%	52.5%	47.0%	53.0%
31,635	FRANKLIN	13,416	8,828	4,470	118	4,358 R	65.8%	33.3%	66.4%	33.6%
28,789	GLOUCESTER	11,216	5,525	5,563	128	38 D	49.3%	49.6%	49.8%	50.2%
60,879	HAVERHILL	18,547	11,078	7,267	202	3,811 R	59.7%	39.2%	60.4%	39.6%
22,157	HINGHAM	11,277	6,800	4,419	58	2,381 R	60.3%	39.2%	60.6%	39.4%
39,880	HOLYOKE	8,814	3,772	4,871	171	1,099 D	42.8%	55.3%	43.6%	56.4%
76,377	LAWRENCE	9,909	3,336	6,463	110	3,127 D	33.7%	65.2%	34.0%	66.0%
40,759	LEOMINSTER	12,993	8,127	4,711	155	3,416 R	62.5%	36.3%	63.3%	36.7%
31,394	LEXINGTON	14,451	4,959	9,397	95	4,438 D	34.3%	65.0%	34.5%	65.5%
106,519	LOWELL	20,448	10,559	9,571	318	988 R	51.6%	46.8%	52.5%	47.5%
90,329	LYNN	18,614	8,597	9,802	215	1,205 D	46.2%	52.7%	46.7%	53.3%
59,450	MALDEN	13,943	5,946	7,796	201	1,850 D	42.6%	55.9%	43.3%	56.7%
19,808	MARBLEHEAD	10,015	5,290	4,659	66	631 R	52.8%	46.5%	53.2%	46.8%
38,499	MARLBOROUGH	12,001	6,817	5,042	142	1,775 R	56.8%	42.0%	57.5%	42.5%
25,132	MARSHFIELD	11,676	7,681	3,896	99	3,785 R	65.8%	33.4%	66.3%	33.7%
56,173	MEDFORD	20,051	8,387	11,428	236	3,041 D	41.8%	57.0%	42.3%	57.7%

MASSACHUSETTS

SENATOR 2010

2010 Census Population	City/Town	Total Vote	Republican	Democratic	Other	Rep.-Dem. Plurality	Percentage			
							Total Vote		Major Vote	
							Rep.	Dem.	Rep.	Dem.
26,983	MELROSE	12,075	6,098	5,871	106	227 R	50.5%	48.6%	50.9%	49.1%
47,255	METHUEN	14,131	9,175	4,838	118	4,337 R	64.9%	34.2%	65.5%	34.5%
27,999	MILFORD	9,086	5,432	3,561	93	1,871 R	59.8%	39.2%	60.4%	39.6%
27,003	MILTON	12,884	6,347	6,442	95	95 D	49.3%	50.0%	49.6%	50.4%
33,006	NATICK	14,306	6,959	7,211	136	252 D	48.6%	50.4%	49.1%	50.9%
28,886	NEEDHAM	14,620	6,899	7,658	63	759 D	47.2%	52.4%	47.4%	52.6%
95,072	NEW BEDFORD	21,042	8,068	12,614	360	4,546 D	38.3%	59.9%	39.0%	61.0%
85,146	NEWTON	35,039	11,352	23,456	231	12,104 D	32.4%	66.9%	32.6%	67.4%
28,352	NORTH ANDOVER	10,931	7,020	3,828	83	3,192 R	64.2%	35.0%	64.7%	35.3%
28,712	NORTH ATTLEBOROUGH	10,921	7,804	3,029	88	4,775 R	71.5%	27.7%	72.0%	28.0%
28,549	NORTHAMPTON	11,992	2,448	9,430	114	6,982 D	20.4%	78.6%	20.6%	79.4%
28,602	NORWOOD	11,233	6,570	4,534	129	2,036 R	58.5%	40.4%	59.2%	40.8%
51,251	PEABODY	19,267	11,441	7,620	206	3,821 R	59.4%	39.5%	60.0%	40.0%
44,737	PITTSFIELD	12,944	3,803	8,992	149	5,189 D	29.4%	69.5%	29.7%	70.3%
56,468	PLYMOUTH	22,533	14,327	8,011	195	6,316 R	63.6%	35.6%	64.1%	35.9%
92,271	QUINCY	29,298	15,609	13,337	352	2,272 R	53.3%	45.5%	53.9%	46.1%
32,112	RANDOLPH	9,809	3,701	6,001	107	2,300 D	37.7%	61.2%	38.1%	61.9%
24,747	READING	10,991	6,240	4,665	86	1,575 R	56.8%	42.4%	57.2%	42.8%
51,755	REVERE	10,959	5,786	5,023	150	763 R	52.8%	45.8%	53.5%	46.5%
41,340	SALEM	12,566	5,744	6,659	163	915 D	45.7%	53.0%	46.3%	53.7%
26,628	SAUGUS	10,002	6,317	3,588	97	2,729 R	63.2%	35.9%	63.8%	36.2%
18,133	SCITUATE	9,124	5,590	3,471	63	2,119 R	61.3%	38.0%	61.7%	38.3%
35,608	SHREWSBURY	13,235	7,876	5,249	110	2,627 R	59.5%	39.7%	60.0%	40.0%
75,754	SOMERVILLE	22,791	5,469	17,014	308	11,545 D	24.0%	74.7%	24.3%	75.7%
153,060	SPRINGFIELD	28,793	10,672	17,673	448	7,001 D	37.1%	61.4%	37.7%	62.3%
21,437	STONEHAM	9,188	5,473	3,634	81	1,839 R	59.6%	39.6%	60.1%	39.9%
26,962	STOUGHTON	10,174	5,619	4,467	88	1,152 R	55.2%	43.9%	55.7%	44.3%
55,874	TAUNTON	15,777	8,944	6,595	238	2,349 R	56.7%	41.8%	57.6%	42.4%
28,961	TEWKSBURY	10,835	7,355	3,383	97	3,972 R	67.9%	31.2%	68.5%	31.5%
24,932	WAKEFIELD	11,316	6,818	4,414	84	2,404 R	60.3%	39.0%	60.7%	39.3%
24,070	WALPOLE	11,244	7,608	3,565	71	4,043 R	67.7%	31.7%	68.1%	31.9%
60,632	WALTHAM	17,248	8,546	8,530	172	16 R	49.5%	49.5%	50.0%	50.0%
31,915	WATERTOWN	11,935	4,521	7,305	109	2,784 D	37.9%	61.2%	38.2%	61.8%
27,982	WELLESLEY	11,954	5,935	5,971	48	36 D	49.6%	49.9%	49.8%	50.2%
28,391	WEST SPRINGFIELD	8,384	5,102	3,145	137	1,957 R	60.9%	37.5%	61.9%	38.1%
41,094	WESTFIELD	12,496	7,775	4,543	178	3,232 R	62.2%	36.4%	63.1%	36.9%
53,743	WEYMOUTH	21,458	13,098	8,109	251	4,989 R	61.0%	37.8%	61.8%	38.2%
21,374	WINCHESTER	10,200	5,253	4,879	68	374 R	51.5%	47.8%	51.8%	48.2%
38,120	WOBURN	14,149	8,367	5,638	144	2,729 R	59.1%	39.8%	59.7%	40.3%
181,045	WORCESTER	38,398	17,926	19,918	554	1,992 D	46.7%	51.9%	47.4%	52.6%
23,793	YARMOUTH	10,991	6,498	4,395	98	2,103 R	59.1%	40.0%	59.7%	40.3%

MASSACHUSETTS

HOUSE OF REPRESENTATIVES

CD	Year	Total Vote	Republican Vote	Republican Candidate	Democratic Vote	Democratic Candidate	Other Vote	Rep.-Dem. Plurality		Total Vote Rep.	Total Vote Dem.	Major Vote Rep.	Major Vote Dem.
1	2010	213,364	74,418	GUNN, WILLIAM L., JR.	128,011	OLVER, JOHN W.*	10,935	53,593	D	34.9%	60.0%	36.8%	63.2%
1	2008	296,099	80,067	BECH, NATHAN A.	215,696	OLVER, JOHN W.*	336	135,629	D	27.0%	72.8%	27.1%	72.9%
1	2006	206,884		—	158,057	OLVER, JOHN W.*	48,827	158,057	D		76.4%		100.0%
1	2004	231,747		—	229,465	OLVER, JOHN W.*	2,282	229,465	D		99.0%		100.0%
1	2002	204,019	66,061	KINNAMAN, MATTHEW W.	137,841	OLVER, JOHN W.*	117	71,780	D	32.4%	67.6%	32.4%	67.6%
2	2010	214,124	91,209	WESLEY, THOMAS A.	122,751	NEAL, RICHARD E.*	164	31,542	D	42.6%	57.3%	42.6%	57.4%
2	2008	238,000		—	234,369	NEAL, RICHARD E.*	3,631	234,369	D		98.5%		100.0%
2	2006	167,193		—	164,939	NEAL, RICHARD E.*	2,254	164,939	D		98.7%		100.0%
2	2004	220,484		—	217,682	NEAL, RICHARD E.*	2,802	217,682	D		98.7%		100.0%
2	2002	154,728		—	153,387	NEAL, RICHARD E.*	1,341	153,387	D		99.1%		100.0%
3	2010	217,352	85,124	LAMB, MARTIN A.	122,708	McGOVERN, JIM*	9,520	37,584	D	39.2%	56.5%	41.0%	59.0%
3	2008	231,107		—	227,619	McGOVERN, JIM*	3,488	227,619	D		98.5%		100.0%
3	2006	168,956		—	166,973	McGOVERN, JIM*	1,983	166,973	D		98.8%		100.0%
3	2004	272,412	80,197	CREWS, RONALD A.	192,036	McGOVERN, JIM*	179	111,839	D	29.4%	70.5%	29.5%	70.5%
3	2002	157,545		—	155,697	McGOVERN, JIM*	1,848	155,697	D		98.8%		100.0%
4	2010	234,127	101,517	BIELAT, SEAN DM	126,194	FRANK, BARNEY*	6,416	24,677	D	43.4%	53.9%	44.6%	55.4%
4	2008	298,788	75,571	SHOLLEY, EARL HENRY	203,032	FRANK, BARNEY*	20,185	127,461	D	25.3%	68.0%	27.1%	72.9%
4	2006	179,243		—	176,513	FRANK, BARNEY*	2,730	176,513	D		98.5%		100.0%
4	2004	282,039		—	219,260	FRANK, BARNEY*	62,779	219,260	D		77.7%		100.0%
4	2002	167,816		—	166,125	FRANK, BARNEY*	1,691	166,125	D		99.0%		100.0%
5	2010	224,029	94,646	GOLNIK, JONATHAN A.	122,858	TSONGAS, NIKI*	6,525	28,212	D	42.2%	54.8%	43.5%	56.5%
5	2008	228,907		—	225,947	TSONGAS, NIKI*	2,960	225,947	D		98.7%		100.0%
5	2006	162,272		—	159,120	MEEHAN, MARTIN T.*	3,152	159,120	D		98.1%		100.0%
5	2004	268,189	88,232	TIERNEY, THOMAS P.	179,652	MEEHAN, MARTIN T.*	305	91,420	D	32.9%	67.0%	32.9%	67.1%
5	2002	203,777	69,337	McCARTHY, CHARLES	122,562	MEEHAN, MARTIN T.*	11,878	53,225	D	34.0%	60.1%	36.1%	63.9%
6	2010	251,081	107,930	HUDAK, BILL	142,732	TIERNEY, JOHN F.*	419	34,802	D	43.0%	56.8%	43.1%	56.9%
6	2008	321,312	94,845	BAKER, RICHARD A.	226,216	TIERNEY, JOHN F.*	251	131,371	D	29.5%	70.4%	29.5%	70.5%
6	2006	241,625	72,997	BARTON, RICHARD W.	168,056	TIERNEY, JOHN F.*	572	95,059	D	30.2%	69.6%	30.3%	69.7%
6	2004	305,522	91,597	O'MALLEY, STEPHEN P. JR.	213,458	TIERNEY, JOHN F.*	467	121,861	D	30.0%	69.9%	30.0%	70.0%
6	2002	238,615	75,462	SMITH, MARK C.	162,900	TIERNEY, JOHN F.*	253	87,438	D	31.6%	68.3%	31.7%	68.3%
7	2010	219,357	73,467	DEMBROWSKI, GERRY	145,696	MARKEY, EDWARD J.*	194	72,229	D	33.5%	66.4%	33.5%	66.5%
7	2008	280,682	67,978	CUNNINGHAM, JOHN	212,304	MARKEY, EDWARD J.*	400	144,326	D	24.2%	75.6%	24.3%	75.7%
7	2006	174,791		—	171,902	MARKEY, EDWARD J.*	2,889	171,902	D		98.3%		100.0%
7	2004	275,099	60,334	CHASE, KENNETH G.	202,399	MARKEY, EDWARD J.*	12,366	142,065	D	21.9%	73.6%	23.0%	77.0%
7	2002	174,037		—	170,968	MARKEY, EDWARD J.*	3,069	170,968	D		98.2%		100.0%
8	2010	137,660		—	134,974	CAPUANO, MICHAEL E.*	2,686	134,974	D		98.0%		100.0%
8	2008	188,252		—	185,530	CAPUANO, MICHAEL E.*	2,722	185,530	D		98.6%		100.0%
8	2006	138,455		—	125,515	CAPUANO, MICHAEL E.*	12,940	125,515	D		90.7%		100.0%
8	2004	168,081		—	165,852	CAPUANO, MICHAEL E.*	2,229	165,852	D		98.7%		100.0%
8	2002	112,356		—	111,861	CAPUANO, MICHAEL E.*	495	111,861	D		99.6%		100.0%
9	2010	229,964	59,965	HARRISON, VERNON M.	157,071	LYNCH, STEPHEN F.*	12,928	97,106	D	26.1%	68.3%	27.6%	72.4%
9	2008	245,294		—	242,166	LYNCH, STEPHEN F.*	3,128	242,166	D		98.7%		100.0%
9	2006	217,036	47,114	ROBINSON, JACK E.	169,420	LYNCH, STEPHEN F.*	502	122,306	D	21.7%	78.1%	21.8%	78.2%
9	2004	220,312		—	218,167	LYNCH, STEPHEN F.*	2,145	218,167	D		99.0%		100.0%
9	2002	168,976		—	168,055	LYNCH, STEPHEN F.*	921	168,055	D		99.5%		100.0%
10	2010	283,197	120,029	PERRY, JEFFREY DAVIS	132,743	KEATING, WILLIAM R.	30,425	12,714	D	42.4%	46.9%	47.5%	52.5%
10	2008	276,673		—	272,899	DELAHUNT, BILL*	3,774	272,899	D		98.6%		100.0%
10	2006	267,202	78,439	BEATTY, JEFFREY K.	171,812	DELAHUNT, BILL*	16,951	93,373	D	29.4%	64.3%	31.3%	68.7%
10	2004	337,070	114,879	JONES, MICHAEL J.	222,013	DELAHUNT, BILL*	178	107,134	D	34.1%	65.9%	34.1%	65.9%
10	2002	259,002	79,624	GONZAGA, LUIS	179,238	DELAHUNT, BILL*	140	99,614	D	30.7%	69.2%	30.8%	69.2%
TOTAL	2010	2,224,255	808,305		1,335,738		80,212	527,433	D	36.3%	60.1%	37.7%	62.3%
TOTAL	2008	2,605,114	318,461		2,245,778		40,875	1,927,317	D	12.2%	86.2%	12.4%	87.6%
TOTAL	2006	1,923,657	198,550		1,632,307		92,800	1,433,757	D	10.3%	84.9%	10.8%	89.2%
TOTAL	2004	2,580,955	435,239		2,059,984		85,732	1,624,745	D	16.9%	79.8%	17.4%	82.6%
TOTAL	2002	1,840,871	290,484		1,528,634		21,753	1,238,150	D	15.8%	83.0%	16.0%	84.0%

An asterisk (*) denotes incumbent.

MASSACHUSETTS

GENERAL AND PRIMARY ELECTIONS

2010 GENERAL ELECTIONS

Governor   Other vote was 184,395 Independent (Timothy P. Cahill); 32,895 Green-Rainbow (Jill Stein); 2,600 scattered write-in.

Senator   Other vote was 22,388 Liberty (Joseph L. Kennedy); 1,155 scattered write-in.

House   Other vote was:

CD 1	10,880 Independent (Michael Engel); 55 scattered write-in.
CD 2	164 scattered write-in.
CD 3	9,388 Independent (Patrick J. Barron); 132 scattered write-in.
CD 4	3,445 Independent (Susan F. Allen); 2,873 Tax Revolt Independent (Donald M. Jordan); 98 scattered write-in.
CD 5	4,387 Liberty (Dale E. Brown); 1,991 Citizen Legislator (Robert M. Clark); 147 scattered write-in.
CD 6	419 scattered write-in.
CD 7	194 scattered write-in.
CD 8	2,686 scattered write-in.
CD 9	12,572 Independent (Philip Dunkelbarger); 356 scattered write-in.
CD 10	16,705 Independent (Maryanne Lewis); 10,445 Independent (James A. Sheets); 3,084 Bring Home Troops (Joe Van Nes); 191 scattered write-in.

2010 PRIMARY ELECTIONS

Primary   December 8, 2009 (Special Senate)
September 14, 2010 (Congress)

Registration
(as of August 25, 2010)

Democratic	1,521,487
Republican	470,852
Libertarian	14,784
Other Parties	8,506
Unenrolled	2,135,446
TOTAL	*4,151,075*

Primary Type   Semi-open—Registered Democrats and Republicans could vote only in their party's primary. "Unenrolled" voters could participate in either party's primary.

	REPUBLICAN PRIMARIES			DEMOCRATIC PRIMARIES		
Governor	Charles D. Baker	215,008	98.3%	Deval L. Patrick*	345,764	96.5%
	Scott D. Lively (write-in)	1,021	0.5%	Timothy P. Cahill (write-in)	2,670	0.7%
	Timothy P. Cahill (write-in)	448	0.2%	Scattered write-in	9,712	2.7%
	Scattered write-in	2,179	1.0%			
	TOTAL	*218,656*		*TOTAL*	*358,146*	
Senator	Scott P. Brown	146,057	88.8%	Martha Coakley	311,548	46.6%
(2009 Special	Jack E. Robinson	17,344	10.5%	Michael E. Capuano	185,157	27.7%
Election Primary)	Scattered write-in	1,139	0.7%	Alan A. Khazei	89,294	13.4%
				Stephen G. Pagliuca	80,217	12.0%
				Scattered write-in	1,800	0.3%
	TOTAL	*164,540*		*TOTAL*	*668,016*	
Congressional	William L. Gunn Jr.	13,354	99.5%	John W. Olver*	43,363	99.5%
District 1	Scattered write-in	69	0.5%	Scattered write-in	199	0.5%
	TOTAL	*13,423*		*TOTAL*	*43,562*	

MASSACHUSETTS

GENERAL AND PRIMARY ELECTIONS

	REPUBLICAN PRIMARIES			DEMOCRATIC PRIMARIES		
Congressional District 2	Thomas A. Wesley	10,780	56.1%	Richard E. Neal*	31,053	98.7%
	Jay S. Fleitman	8,403	43.7%	Scattered write-in	416	1.3%
	Scattered write-in	40	0.2%			
	TOTAL	19,223		TOTAL	31,469	
Congressional District 3	Martin A. Lamb	6,963	31.1%	Jim McGovern*	32,108	99.2%
	Brian J. Herr	5,584	25.0%	Scattered write-in	275	0.8%
	Michael P. Stopa	3,701	16.5%			
	Robert J. Chipman	3,139	14.0%			
	Robert A. Delle	2,864	12.8%			
	Scattered write-in	125	0.6%			
	TOTAL	22,376		TOTAL	32,383	
Congressional District 4	Sean DM Bielat	11,797	60.0%	Barney Frank*	39,974	79.4%
	Earl H. Sholley	7,782	39.6%	Rachel E. Brown	10,289	20.4%
	Scattered write-in	79	0.4%	Scattered write-in	83	0.2%
	TOTAL	19,658		TOTAL	50,346	
Congressional District 5	Jonathan A. Golnik	11,384	38.6%	Niki Tsongas*	29,773	98.9%
	Sam S. Meas	7,601	25.7%	Scattered write-in	326	1.1%
	Thomas J.M. Weaver	6,143	20.8%			
	Robert L. Shapiro	4,351	14.7%			
	Scattered write-in	50	0.2%			
	TOTAL	29,529		TOTAL	30,099	
Congressional District 6	Bill Hudak	20,765	76.3%	John F. Tierney*	28,136	98.2%
	Robert J. McCarthy Jr.	6,345	23.3%	Scattered write-in	530	1.8%
	Scattered write-in	109	0.4%			
	TOTAL	27,219		TOTAL	28,666	
Congressional District 7	Gerry Dombrowski	9,382	56.0%	Edward J. Markey*	35,573	98.8%
	Thomas P. Tierney	7,302	43.6%	Scattered write-in	435	1.2%
	Scattered write-in	75	0.4%			
	TOTAL	16,759		TOTAL	36,008	
Congressional District 8	*No Republican candidate filed for the primary. There were 178 write-in votes for Frederick T. Golder and 650 scattered write-in votes.*			Michael E. Capuano*	32,198	98.9%
				Scattered write-in	345	1.1%
				TOTAL	32,543	
Congressional District 9	Vernon M. Harrison	10,261	62.5%	Stephen F. Lynch*	42,527	64.7%
	Keith P. Lepor	6,026	36.7%	Macdonald K. D'Alessandro	23,109	35.2%
	Scattered write-in	135	0.8%	Scattered write-in	88	0.1%
	TOTAL	16,422		TOTAL	65,724	
Congressional District 10	Jeffrey Davis Perry	31,851	60.6%	William R. Keating	29,953	50.9%
	Joseph Daniel Malone	16,060	30.5%	Robert A. O'Leary	28,656	48.7%
	Robert E. Hayden III	2,364	4.5%	Scattered write-in	208	0.4%
	Raymond Kasperowicz	2,237	4.3%			
	Scattered write-in	82	0.2%			
	TOTAL	52,594		TOTAL	58,817	

An asterisk (*) denotes incumbent.

MICHIGAN

Congressional districts first established for elections held in 2002
15 members

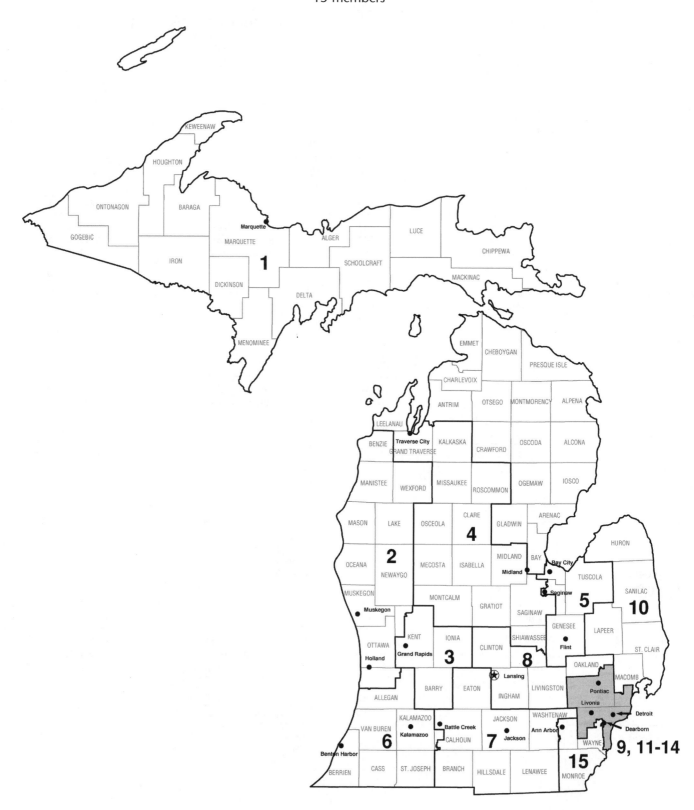

MICHIGAN

Detroit Area

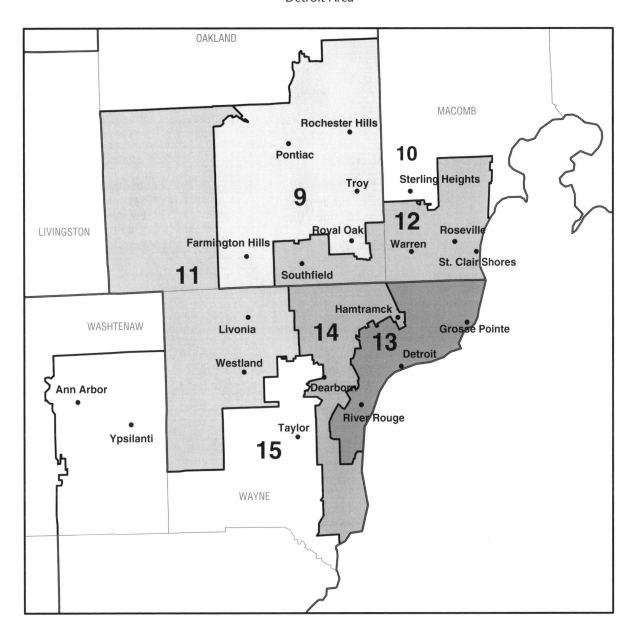

MICHIGAN

GOVERNOR
Rick Snyder (R). Elected 2010 to a four-year term.

SENATORS (2 Democrats)
Carl Levin (D). Reelected 2008 to a six-year term. Previously elected 2002, 1996, 1990, 1984, 1978.

Debbie Stabenow (D). Elected 2006 to a six-year term. Previously elected 2000.

REPRESENTATIVES (9 Republicans, 6 Democrats)

1. Dan Benishek (R)
2. Bill Huizenga (R)
3. Justin Amash (R)
4. Dave Camp (R)
5. Dale E. Kildee (D)
6. Fred Upton (R)
7. Tim Walberg (R)
8. Mike Rogers (R)
9. Gary C. Peters (D)
10. Candice S. Miller (R)
11. Thaddeus McCotter (R)
12. Sander M. Levin (D)
13. Hansen Clarke (D)
14. John Conyers Jr. (D)
15. John D. Dingell (D)

POSTWAR VOTE FOR PRESIDENT

Year	Total Vote	Republican Vote	Republican Candidate	Democratic Vote	Democratic Candidate	Other Vote	Rep.-Dem. Plurality	Total Vote Rep.	Total Vote Dem.	Major Vote Rep.	Major Vote Dem.
2008	5,001,766	2,048,639	McCain, John	2,872,579	Obama, Barack	80,548	823,940 D	41.0%	57.4%	41.6%	58.4%
2004	4,839,252	2,313,746	Bush, George W.	2,479,183	Kerry, John	46,323	165,437 D	47.8%	51.2%	48.3%	51.7%
2000**	4,232,711	1,953,139	Bush, George W.	2,170,418	Gore, Al	109,154	217,279 D	46.1%	51.3%	47.4%	52.6%
1996**	3,848,844	1,481,212	Dole, Bob	1,989,653	Clinton, Bill	377,979	508,441 D	38.5%	51.7%	42.7%	57.3%
1992**	4,274,673	1,554,940	Bush, George	1,871,182	Clinton, Bill	848,551	316,242 D	36.4%	43.8%	45.4%	54.6%
1988	3,669,163	1,965,486	Bush, George	1,675,783	Dukakis, Michael S.	27,894	289,703 R	53.6%	45.7%	54.0%	46.0%
1984	3,801,658	2,251,571	Reagan, Ronald	1,529,638	Mondale, Walter F.	20,449	721,933 R	59.2%	40.2%	59.5%	40.5%
1980**	3,909,725	1,915,225	Reagan, Ronald	1,661,532	Carter, Jimmy	332,968	253,693 R	49.0%	42.5%	53.5%	46.5%
1976	3,653,749	1,893,742	Ford, Gerald R.	1,696,714	Carter, Jimmy	63,293	197,028 R	51.8%	46.4%	52.7%	47.3%
1972	3,489,727	1,961,721	Nixon, Richard M.	1,459,435	McGovern, George S.	68,571	502,286 R	56.2%	41.8%	57.3%	42.7%
1968**	3,306,250	1,370,665	Nixon, Richard M.	1,593,082	Humphrey, Hubert H.	342,503	222,417 D	41.5%	48.2%	46.2%	53.8%
1964	3,203,102	1,060,152	Goldwater, Barry M.	2,136,615	Johnson, Lyndon B.	6,335	1,076,463 D	33.1%	66.7%	33.2%	66.8%
1960	3,318,097	1,620,428	Nixon, Richard M.	1,687,269	Kennedy, John F.	10,400	66,841 D	48.8%	50.9%	49.0%	51.0%
1956	3,080,468	1,713,647	Eisenhower, Dwight D.	1,359,898	Stevenson, Adlai E.	6,923	353,749 R	55.6%	44.1%	55.8%	44.2%
1952	2,798,592	1,551,529	Eisenhower, Dwight D.	1,230,657	Stevenson, Adlai E.	16,406	320,872 R	55.4%	44.0%	55.8%	44.2%
1948	2,109,609	1,038,595	Dewey, Thomas E.	1,003,448	Truman, Harry S.	67,566	35,147 R	49.2%	47.6%	50.9%	49.1%

**In past elections, the other vote included: 2000 - 84,165 Green (Ralph Nader); 1996 - 336,670 Reform (Ross Perot); 1992 - 824,813 Independent (Perot); 1980 - 275,223 Independent (John Anderson); 1968 - 331,968 American Independent (George Wallace).

MICHIGAN

POSTWAR VOTE FOR GOVERNOR

Year	Total Vote	Republican Vote	Republican Candidate	Democratic Vote	Democratic Candidate	Other Vote	Rep.-Dem. Plurality	Percentage Total Vote Rep.	Dem.	Major Vote Rep.	Dem.
2010	3,226,088	1,874,834	Snyder, Rick	1,287,320	Bernero, Virg	63,934	587,514 R	58.1%	39.9%	59.3%	40.7%
2006	3,801,256	1,608,086	DeVos, Dick	2,142,513	Granholm, Jennifer M.	50,657	534,427 D	42.3%	56.4%	42.9%	57.1%
2002	3,177,565	1,506,104	Posthumus, Dick	1,633,796	Granholm, Jennifer M.	37,665	127,692 D	47.4%	51.4%	48.0%	52.0%
1998	3,027,104	1,883,005	Engler, John	1,143,574	Fieger, Geoffrey	525	739,431 R	62.2%	37.8%	62.2%	37.8%
1994	3,089,077	1,899,101	Engler, John	1,188,438	Wolpe, Howard	1,538	710,663 R	61.5%	38.5%	61.5%	38.5%
1990	2,564,563	1,276,134	Engler, John	1,258,539	Blanchard, James J.	29,890	17,595 R	49.8%	49.1%	50.3%	49.7%
1986	2,396,564	753,647	Lucas, William	1,632,138	Blanchard, James J.	10,779	878,491 D	31.4%	68.1%	31.6%	68.4%
1982	3,040,008	1,369,582	Headlee, Richard H.	1,561,291	Blanchard, James J.	109,135	191,709 D	45.1%	51.4%	46.7%	53.3%
1978	2,867,212	1,628,485	Milliken, William G.	1,237,256	Fitzgerald, William	1,471	391,229 R	56.8%	43.2%	56.8%	43.2%
1974	2,657,017	1,356,865	Milliken, William G.	1,242,247	Levin, Sander	57,905	114,618 R	51.1%	46.8%	52.2%	47.8%
1970	2,656,162	1,339,047	Milliken, William G.	1,294,638	Levin, Sander	22,477	44,409 R	50.4%	48.7%	50.8%	49.2%
1966**	2,461,909	1,490,430	Romney, George W.	963,383	Ferency, Zolton A.	8,096	527,047 R	60.5%	39.1%	60.7%	39.3%
1964	3,158,102	1,764,355	Romney, George W.	1,381,442	Staebler, Neil	12,305	382,913 R	55.9%	43.7%	56.1%	43.9%
1962	2,764,839	1,420,086	Romney, George W.	1,339,513	Swainson, John B.	5,240	80,573 R	51.4%	48.4%	51.5%	48.5%
1960	3,255,991	1,602,022	Bagwell, Paul D.	1,643,634	Swainson, John B.	10,335	41,612 D	49.2%	50.5%	49.4%	50.6%
1958	2,312,184	1,078,089	Bagwell, Paul D.	1,225,533	Williams, G. Mennen	8,562	147,444 D	46.6%	53.0%	46.8%	53.2%
1956	3,049,651	1,376,376	Cobo, Albert E.	1,666,689	Williams, G. Mennen	6,586	290,313 D	45.1%	54.7%	45.2%	54.8%
1954	2,187,027	963,300	Leonard, Donald S.	1,216,308	Williams, G. Mennen	7,419	253,008 D	44.0%	55.6%	44.2%	55.8%
1952	2,865,980	1,423,275	Alger, Fred M.	1,431,893	Williams, G. Mennen	10,812	8,618 D	49.7%	50.0%	49.8%	50.2%
1950	1,879,382	933,998	Kelly, Harry F.	935,152	Williams, G. Mennen	10,232	1,154 D	49.7%	49.8%	50.0%	50.0%
1948	2,113,122	964,810	Sigler, Kim	1,128,664	Williams, G. Mennen	19,648	163,854 D	45.7%	53.4%	46.1%	53.9%
1946	1,665,475	1,003,878	Sigler, Kim	644,540	Van Wagoner, Murray	17,057	359,338 R	60.3%	38.7%	60.9%	39.1%

**The term of office of Michigan's Governor was increased from two to four years effective with the 1966 election.

POSTWAR VOTE FOR SENATOR

Year	Total Vote	Republican Vote	Republican Candidate	Democratic Vote	Democratic Candidate	Other Vote	Rep.-Dem. Plurality	Percentage Total Vote Rep.	Dem.	Major Vote Rep.	Dem.
2008	4,848,620	1,641,070	Hoogendyk, Jack	3,038,386	Levin, Carl	169,164	1,397,316 D	33.8%	62.7%	35.1%	64.9%
2006	3,780,142	1,559,597	Bouchard, Michael	2,151,278	Stabenow, Debbie	69,267	591,681 D	41.3%	56.9%	42.0%	58.0%
2002	3,129,287	1,185,545	Raczkowski, Andrew	1,896,614	Levin, Carl	47,128	711,069 D	37.9%	60.6%	38.5%	61.5%
2000	4,167,685	1,994,693	Abraham, Spencer	2,061,952	Stabenow, Debbie	111,040	67,259 D	47.9%	49.5%	49.2%	50.8%
1996	3,762,575	1,500,106	Romney, Ronna	2,195,738	Levin, Carl	66,731	695,632 D	39.9%	58.4%	40.6%	59.4%
1994	3,043,385	1,578,770	Abraham, Spencer	1,300,960	Carr, M. Robert	163,655	277,810 R	51.9%	42.7%	54.8%	45.2%
1990	2,560,494	1,055,695	Schuette, Bill	1,471,753	Levin, Carl	33,046	416,058 D	41.2%	57.5%	41.8%	58.2%
1988	3,505,985	1,348,219	Dunn, Jim	2,116,865	Riegle, Donald W.	40,901	768,646 D	38.5%	60.4%	38.9%	61.1%
1984	3,700,938	1,745,302	Lousma, Jack	1,915,831	Levin, Carl	39,805	170,529 D	47.2%	51.8%	47.7%	52.3%
1982	2,994,334	1,223,288	Ruppe, Philip E.	1,728,793	Riegle, Donald W.	42,253	505,505 D	40.9%	57.7%	41.4%	58.6%
1978	2,846,630	1,362,165	Griffin, Robert P.	1,484,193	Levin, Carl	272	122,028 D	47.9%	52.1%	47.9%	52.1%
1976	3,490,664	1,635,087	Esch, Marvin L.	1,831,031	Riegle, Donald W.	24,546	195,944 D	46.8%	52.5%	47.2%	52.8%
1972	3,406,906	1,781,065	Griffin, Robert P.	1,577,178	Kelley, Frank J.	48,663	203,887 R	52.3%	46.3%	53.0%	47.0%
1970	2,610,839	858,470	Romney, Lenore	1,744,716	Hart, Philip A.	7,653	886,246 D	32.9%	66.8%	33.0%	67.0%
1966	2,439,365	1,363,530	Griffin, Robert P.	1,069,484	Williams, G. Mennen	6,351	294,046 R	55.9%	43.8%	56.0%	44.0%
1964	3,101,667	1,096,272	Peterson, Elly M.	1,996,912	Hart, Philip A.	8,483	900,640 D	35.3%	64.4%	35.4%	64.6%
1960	3,226,647	1,548,873	Bentley, Alvin M.	1,669,179	McNamara, Patrick V.	8,595	120,306 D	48.0%	51.7%	48.1%	51.9%
1958	2,271,644	1,046,963	Potter, Charles E.	1,216,966	Hart, Philip A.	7,715	170,003 D	46.1%	53.6%	46.2%	53.8%
1954	2,144,840	1,049,420	Ferguson, Homer	1,088,550	McNamara, Patrick V.	6,870	39,130 D	48.9%	50.8%	49.1%	50.9%
1952	2,821,133	1,428,352	Potter, Charles E.	1,383,416	Moody, Blair	9,365	44,936 R	50.6%	49.0%	50.8%	49.2%
1948	2,062,097	1,045,156	Ferguson, Homer	1,000,329	Hook, Frank E.	16,612	44,827 R	50.7%	48.5%	51.1%	48.9%
1946	1,618,720	1,085,570	Vandenberg, Arthur	517,923	Lee, James H.	15,227	567,647 R	67.1%	32.0%	67.7%	32.3%

MICHIGAN
GOVERNOR 2010

2010 Census Population	County	Total Vote	Republican	Democratic	Other	Rep.-Dem. Plurality		Percentage			
								Total Vote		Major Vote	
								Rep.	Dem.	Rep.	Dem.
10,942	ALCONA	4,569	2,896	1,518	155	1,378	R	63.4%	33.2%	65.6%	34.4%
9,601	ALGER	3,777	2,075	1,559	143	516	R	54.9%	41.3%	57.1%	42.9%
111,408	ALLEGAN	37,323	26,990	9,438	895	17,552	R	72.3%	25.3%	74.1%	25.9%
29,598	ALPENA	10,068	5,753	3,982	333	1,771	R	57.1%	39.6%	59.1%	40.9%
23,580	ANTRIM	10,336	7,295	2,753	288	4,542	R	70.6%	26.6%	72.6%	27.4%
15,899	ARENAC	5,505	3,521	1,825	159	1,696	R	64.0%	33.2%	65.9%	34.1%
8,860	BARAGA	2,653	1,578	983	92	595	R	59.5%	37.1%	61.6%	38.4%
59,173	BARRY	21,013	15,300	5,243	470	10,057	R	72.8%	25.0%	74.5%	25.5%
107,771	BAY	39,637	23,622	15,147	868	8,475	R	59.6%	38.2%	60.9%	39.1%
17,525	BENZIE	7,556	4,709	2,625	222	2,084	R	62.3%	34.7%	64.2%	35.8%
156,813	BERRIEN	45,820	28,519	16,178	1,123	12,341	R	62.2%	35.3%	63.8%	36.2%
45,248	BRANCH	12,779	9,183	3,306	290	5,877	R	71.9%	25.9%	73.5%	26.5%
136,146	CALHOUN	41,348	25,967	14,572	809	11,395	R	62.8%	35.2%	64.1%	35.9%
52,293	CASS	13,951	8,879	4,661	411	4,218	R	63.6%	33.4%	65.6%	34.4%
25,949	CHARLEVOIX	10,249	7,048	2,918	283	4,130	R	68.8%	28.5%	70.7%	29.3%
26,152	CHEBOYGAN	10,076	6,775	3,016	285	3,759	R	67.2%	29.9%	69.2%	30.8%
38,520	CHIPPEWA	11,720	7,114	4,261	345	2,853	R	60.7%	36.4%	62.5%	37.5%
30,926	CLARE	9,375	6,078	3,018	279	3,060	R	64.8%	32.2%	66.8%	33.2%
75,382	CLINTON	28,130	18,425	9,239	466	9,186	R	65.5%	32.8%	66.6%	33.4%
14,074	CRAWFORD	4,881	3,233	1,477	171	1,756	R	66.2%	30.3%	68.6%	31.4%
37,069	DELTA	13,077	7,558	5,122	397	2,436	R	57.8%	39.2%	59.6%	40.4%
26,168	DICKINSON	9,310	5,910	3,134	266	2,776	R	63.5%	33.7%	65.3%	34.7%
107,759	EATON	41,747	24,927	15,899	921	9,028	R	59.7%	38.1%	61.1%	38.9%
32,694	EMMET	13,183	9,183	3,632	368	5,551	R	69.7%	27.6%	71.7%	28.3%
425,790	GENESEE	133,932	62,589	68,708	2,635	6,119	D	46.7%	51.3%	47.7%	52.3%
25,692	GLADWIN	8,989	5,756	2,986	247	2,770	R	64.0%	33.2%	65.8%	34.2%
16,427	GOGEBIC	5,314	2,511	2,627	176	116	D	47.3%	49.4%	48.9%	51.1%
86,986	GRAND TRAVERSE	33,815	23,541	9,395	879	14,146	R	69.6%	27.8%	71.5%	28.5%
42,476	GRATIOT	11,024	7,234	3,537	253	3,697	R	65.6%	32.1%	67.2%	32.8%
46,688	HILLSDALE	14,118	10,055	3,675	388	6,380	R	71.2%	26.0%	73.2%	26.8%
36,628	HOUGHTON	12,171	7,295	4,479	397	2,816	R	59.9%	36.8%	62.0%	38.0%
33,118	HURON	12,097	8,453	3,347	297	5,106	R	69.9%	27.7%	71.6%	28.4%
280,895	INGHAM	88,069	43,181	42,961	1,927	220	R	49.0%	48.8%	50.1%	49.9%
63,905	IONIA	18,381	13,269	4,754	358	8,515	R	72.2%	25.9%	73.6%	26.4%
25,887	IOSCO	9,665	5,943	3,435	287	2,508	R	61.5%	35.5%	63.4%	36.6%
11,817	IRON	4,495	2,516	1,825	154	691	R	56.0%	40.6%	58.0%	42.0%
70,311	ISABELLA	15,986	9,865	5,776	345	4,089	R	61.7%	36.1%	63.1%	36.9%
160,248	JACKSON	49,822	31,914	16,947	961	14,967	R	64.1%	34.0%	65.3%	34.7%
250,331	KALAMAZOO	78,857	46,823	30,499	1,535	16,324	R	59.4%	38.7%	60.6%	39.4%
17,153	KALKASKA	5,808	4,096	1,467	245	2,629	R	70.5%	25.3%	73.6%	26.4%
602,622	KENT	194,609	134,019	57,142	3,448	76,877	R	68.9%	29.4%	70.1%	29.9%
2,156	KEWEENAW	1,098	691	374	33	317	R	62.9%	34.1%	64.9%	35.1%
11,539	LAKE	3,672	2,220	1,354	98	866	R	60.5%	36.9%	62.1%	37.9%
88,319	LAPEER	29,595	19,771	9,072	752	10,699	R	66.8%	30.7%	68.5%	31.5%
21,708	LEELANAU	11,400	7,467	3,655	278	3,812	R	65.5%	32.1%	67.1%	32.9%

MICHIGAN

GOVERNOR 2010

2010 Census Population	County	Total Vote	Republican	Democratic	Other	Rep.-Dem. Plurality		Percentage			
								Total Vote		Major Vote	
								Rep.	Dem.	Rep.	Dem.
99,892	LENAWEE	31,664	19,611	11,284	769	8,327	R	61.9%	35.6%	63.5%	36.5%
180,967	LIVINGSTON	68,701	51,560	15,994	1,147	35,566	R	75.0%	23.3%	76.3%	23.7%
6,631	LUCE	1,950	1,285	615	50	670	R	65.9%	31.5%	67.6%	32.4%
11,113	MACKINAC	4,759	3,129	1,511	119	1,618	R	65.7%	31.8%	67.4%	32.6%
840,978	MACOMB	268,700	164,660	98,675	5,365	65,985	R	61.3%	36.7%	62.5%	37.5%
24,733	MANISTEE	9,147	5,513	3,352	282	2,161	R	60.3%	36.6%	62.2%	37.8%
67,077	MARQUETTE	21,718	10,690	10,301	727	389	R	49.2%	47.4%	50.9%	49.1%
28,705	MASON	10,262	6,871	3,152	239	3,719	R	67.0%	30.7%	68.6%	31.4%
42,798	MECOSTA	11,832	8,079	3,485	268	4,594	R	68.3%	29.5%	69.9%	30.1%
24,029	MENOMINEE	7,145	4,114	2,797	234	1,317	R	57.6%	39.1%	59.5%	40.5%
83,629	MIDLAND	28,918	20,262	8,041	615	12,221	R	70.1%	27.8%	71.6%	28.4%
14,849	MISSAUKEE	5,289	4,057	1,105	127	2,952	R	76.7%	20.9%	78.6%	21.4%
152,021	MONROE	47,967	28,911	17,917	1,139	10,994	R	60.3%	37.4%	61.7%	38.3%
63,342	MONTCALM	17,840	12,170	5,237	433	6,933	R	68.2%	29.4%	69.9%	30.1%
9,765	MONTMORENCY	3,874	2,625	1,113	136	1,512	R	67.8%	28.7%	70.2%	29.8%
172,188	MUSKEGON	51,125	27,567	22,552	1,006	5,015	R	53.9%	44.1%	55.0%	45.0%
48,460	NEWAYGO	14,968	10,503	4,101	364	6,402	R	70.2%	27.4%	71.9%	28.1%
1,202,362	OAKLAND	452,637	272,040	173,615	6,982	98,425	R	60.1%	38.4%	61.0%	39.0%
26,570	OCEANA	8,434	5,710	2,549	175	3,161	R	67.7%	30.2%	69.1%	30.9%
21,699	OGEMAW	7,556	4,866	2,442	248	2,424	R	64.4%	32.3%	66.6%	33.4%
6,780	ONTONAGON	2,885	1,585	1,176	124	409	R	54.9%	40.8%	57.4%	42.6%
23,528	OSCEOLA	7,648	5,518	1,901	229	3,617	R	72.1%	24.9%	74.4%	25.6%
8,640	OSCODA	3,110	2,079	896	135	1,183	R	66.8%	28.8%	69.9%	30.1%
24,164	OTSEGO	8,717	6,130	2,349	238	3,781	R	70.3%	26.9%	72.3%	27.7%
263,801	OTTAWA	90,818	71,847	17,534	1,437	54,313	R	79.1%	19.3%	80.4%	19.6%
13,376	PRESQUE ISLE	5,482	3,427	1,892	163	1,535	R	62.5%	34.5%	64.4%	35.6%
24,449	ROSCOMMON	9,913	6,450	3,157	306	3,293	R	65.1%	31.8%	67.1%	32.9%
200,169	SAGINAW	68,087	37,920	29,008	1,159	8,912	R	55.7%	42.6%	56.7%	43.3%
163,040	ST. CLAIR	52,268	34,503	16,425	1,340	18,078	R	66.0%	31.4%	67.7%	32.3%
61,295	ST. JOSEPH	15,294	10,794	4,126	374	6,668	R	70.6%	27.0%	72.3%	27.7%
43,114	SANILAC	13,338	9,576	3,453	309	6,123	R	71.8%	25.9%	73.5%	26.5%
8,485	SCHOOLCRAFT	3,176	1,787	1,285	104	502	R	56.3%	40.5%	58.2%	41.8%
70,648	SHIAWASSEE	23,386	14,245	8,595	546	5,650	R	60.9%	36.8%	62.4%	37.6%
55,729	TUSCOLA	18,619	12,314	5,850	455	6,464	R	66.1%	31.4%	67.8%	32.2%
76,258	VAN BUREN	21,828	13,985	7,264	579	6,721	R	64.1%	33.3%	65.8%	34.2%
344,791	WASHTENAW	120,005	58,029	59,829	2,147	1,800	D	48.4%	49.9%	49.2%	50.8%
1,820,584	WAYNE	525,750	201,424	316,514	7,812	115,090	D	38.3%	60.2%	38.9%	61.1%
32,735	WEXFORD	10,278	7,251	2,707	320	4,544	R	70.5%	26.3%	72.8%	27.2%
9,883,640	TOTAL	3,226,088	1,874,834	1,287,320	63,934	587,514	R	58.1%	39.9%	59.3%	40.7%

MICHIGAN

HOUSE OF REPRESENTATIVES

CD	Year	Total Vote	Republican Vote	Republican Candidate	Democratic Vote	Democratic Candidate	Other Vote	Rep.-Dem. Plurality		Total Vote Rep.	Total Vote Dem.	Major Vote Rep.	Major Vote Dem.
1	2010	232,037	120,523	BENISHEK, DAN	94,824	McDOWELL, GARY	16,690	25,699	R	51.9%	40.9%	56.0%	44.0%
1	2008	327,836	107,340	CASPERSON, TOM	213,216	STUPAK, BART*	7,280	105,876	D	32.7%	65.0%	33.5%	66.5%
1	2006	259,927	72,753	HOOPER, DON	180,448	STUPAK, BART*	6,726	107,695	D	28.0%	69.4%	28.7%	71.3%
1	2004	322,674	105,706	HOOPER, DON	211,571	STUPAK, BART*	5,397	105,865	D	32.8%	65.6%	33.3%	66.7%
1	2002	222,687	69,254	HOOPER, DON	150,701	STUPAK, BART*	2,732	81,447	D	31.1%	67.7%	31.5%	68.5%
2	2010	228,078	148,864	HUIZENGA, BILL	72,118	JOHNSON, FRED	7,096	76,746	R	65.3%	31.6%	67.4%	32.6%
2	2008	343,309	214,100	HOEKSTRA, PETER*	119,506	JOHNSON, FRED	9,703	94,594	R	62.4%	34.8%	64.2%	35.8%
2	2006	275,394	183,006	HOEKSTRA, PETER*	86,950	KOTOS, KIMON	5,438	96,056	R	66.5%	31.6%	67.8%	32.2%
2	2004	325,005	225,343	HOEKSTRA, PETER*	94,040	KOTOS, KIMON	5,622	131,303	R	69.3%	28.9%	70.6%	29.4%
2	2002	222,907	156,937	HOEKSTRA, PETER*	61,749	WRISLEY, JEFF	4,221	95,188	R	70.4%	27.7%	71.8%	28.2%
3	2010	224,063	133,714	AMASH, JUSTIN	83,953	MILES, PAT	6,396	49,761	R	59.7%	37.5%	61.4%	38.6%
3	2008	333,518	203,799	EHLERS, VERNON J.*	117,961	SANCHEZ, HENRY	11,758	85,838	R	61.1%	35.4%	63.3%	36.7%
3	2006	271,352	171,212	EHLERS, VERNON J.*	93,846	RINCK, JAMES	6,294	77,366	R	63.1%	34.6%	64.6%	35.4%
3	2004	322,103	214,465	EHLERS, VERNON J.*	101,395	HICKEY, PETER	6,243	113,070	R	66.6%	31.5%	67.9%	32.1%
3	2002	218,855	153,131	EHLERS, VERNON J.*	61,987	LYNNES, KATHRYN	3,737	91,144	R	70.0%	28.3%	71.2%	28.8%
4	2010	224,354	148,531	CAMP, DAVE*	68,458	CAMPBELL, JERRY	7,365	80,073	R	66.2%	30.5%	68.5%	31.5%
4	2008	329,764	204,259	CAMP, DAVE*	117,665	CONCANNON, ANDREW D.	7,840	86,594	R	61.9%	35.7%	63.4%	36.6%
4	2006	264,245	160,041	CAMP, DAVE*	100,260	HUCKLEBERRY, MIKE	3,944	59,781	R	60.6%	37.9%	61.5%	38.5%
4	2004	318,924	205,274	CAMP, DAVE*	110,885	HUCKLEBERRY, MIKE	2,765	94,389	R	64.4%	34.8%	64.9%	35.1%
4	2002	218,573	149,090	CAMP, DAVE*	65,950	HOLLENBECK, LAWRENCE	3,533	83,140	R	68.2%	30.2%	69.3%	30.7%
5	2010	202,263	89,680	KUPIEC, JOHN	107,286	KILDEE, DALE E.*	5,297	17,606	D	44.3%	53.0%	45.5%	54.5%
5	2008	315,295	85,017	SAWICKI, MATT	221,841	KILDEE, DALE E.*	8,437	136,824	D	27.0%	70.4%	27.7%	72.3%
5	2006	241,691	60,967	KLAMMER, ERIC	176,171	KILDEE, DALE E.*	4,553	115,204	D	25.2%	72.9%	25.7%	74.3%
5	2004	309,915	96,934	KIRKWOOD, MYRAH	208,163	KILDEE, DALE E.*	4,818	111,229	D	31.3%	67.2%	31.8%	68.2%
5	2002	173,339		—	158,709	KILDEE, DALE E.*	14,630	158,709	D		91.6%		100.0%
6	2010	198,696	123,142	UPTON, FRED*	66,729	COONEY, DON	8,825	56,413	R	62.0%	33.6%	64.9%	35.1%
6	2008	319,646	188,157	UPTON, FRED*	123,257	COONEY, DON	8,232	64,900	R	58.9%	38.6%	60.4%	39.6%
6	2006	234,583	142,125	UPTON, FRED*	88,978	CLARK, KIM	3,480	53,147	R	60.6%	37.9%	61.5%	38.5%
6	2004	302,158	197,425	UPTON, FRED*	97,978	ELLIOTT, SCOTT	6,755	99,447	R	65.3%	32.4%	66.8%	33.2%
6	2002	183,517	126,936	UPTON, FRED*	53,793	GIGUERE, GARY JR.	2,788	73,143	R	69.2%	29.3%	70.2%	29.8%
7	2010	225,669	113,185	WALBERG, TIM	102,402	SCHAUER, MARK H.*	10,082	10,783	R	50.2%	45.4%	52.5%	47.5%
7	2008	322,286	149,781	WALBERG, TIM*	157,213	SCHAUER, MARK H.	15,292	7,432	D	46.5%	48.8%	48.8%	51.2%
7	2006	245,026	122,348	WALBERG, TIM	112,665	RENIER, SHARON	10,013	9,683	R	49.9%	46.0%	52.1%	47.9%
7	2004	301,642	176,053	SCHWARZ, JOE	109,527	RENIER, SHARON	16,062	66,526	R	58.4%	36.3%	61.6%	38.4%
7	2002	203,069	121,142	SMITH, NICK*	78,412	SIMPSON, MIKE	3,515	42,730	R	59.7%	38.6%	60.7%	39.3%
8	2010	244,894	156,931	ROGERS, MIKE*	84,069	ENDERLE, LANCE	3,894	72,862	R	64.1%	34.3%	65.1%	34.9%
8	2008	361,607	204,408	ROGERS, MIKE*	145,491	ALEXANDER, ROBERT	11,708	58,917	R	56.5%	40.2%	58.4%	41.6%
8	2006	284,471	157,237	ROGERS, MIKE*	122,107	MARCINKOWSKI, JIM	5,127	35,130	R	55.3%	42.9%	56.3%	43.7%
8	2004	340,423	207,925	ROGERS, MIKE*	125,619	ALEXANDER, ROBERT	6,879	82,306	R	61.1%	36.9%	62.3%	37.7%
8	2002	230,597	156,525	ROGERS, MIKE*	70,920	McALPINE, FRANK	3,152	85,605	R	67.9%	30.8%	68.8%	31.2%
9	2010	252,650	119,325	RACZKOWSKI, ROCKY	125,730	PETERS, GARY C.*	7,595	6,405	D	47.2%	49.8%	48.7%	51.3%
9	2008	351,963	150,035	KNOLLENBERG, JOE*	183,311	PETERS, GARY C.	18,617	33,276	D	42.6%	52.1%	45.0%	55.0%
9	2006	276,180	142,390	KNOLLENBERG, JOE*	127,620	SKINNER, NANCY	6,170	14,770	R	51.6%	46.2%	52.7%	47.3%
9	2004	340,799	199,210	KNOLLENBERG, JOE*	134,764	REIFMAN, STEVEN	6,825	64,446	R	58.5%	39.5%	59.6%	40.4%
9	2002	242,880	141,102	KNOLLENBERG, JOE*	96,856	FINK, DAVID	4,922	44,246	R	58.1%	39.9%	59.3%	40.7%

MICHIGAN

HOUSE OF REPRESENTATIVES

CD	Year	Total Vote	Republican Vote	Republican Candidate	Democratic Vote	Democratic Candidate	Other Vote	Rep.-Dem. Plurality		Total Vote Rep.	Dem.	Major Vote Rep.	Dem.
10	2010	233,930	168,364	MILLER, CANDICE S.*	58,530	YANEZ, HENRY	7,036	109,834	R	72.0%	25.0%	74.2%	25.8%
10	2008	347,603	230,471	MILLER, CANDICE S.*	108,354	DENISON, ROBERT	8,778	122,117	R	66.3%	31.2%	68.0%	32.0%
10	2006	270,421	179,072	MILLER, CANDICE S.*	84,689	DENISON, ROBERT	6,660	94,383	R	66.2%	31.3%	67.9%	32.1%
10	2004	331,868	227,720	MILLER, CANDICE S.*	98,029	CASEY, ROB	6,119	129,691	R	68.6%	29.5%	69.9%	30.1%
10	2002	216,928	137,339	MILLER, CANDICE S.	77,053	MARLINGA, CARL	2,536	60,286	R	63.3%	35.5%	64.1%	35.9%
11	2010	238,287	141,224	McCOTTER, THADDEUS*	91,710	MOSHER, NATALIE	5,353	49,514	R	59.3%	38.5%	60.6%	39.4%
11	2008	345,182	177,461	McCOTTER, THADDEUS*	156,625	LARKIN, JOSEPH	11,096	20,836	R	51.4%	45.4%	53.1%	46.9%
11	2006	265,784	143,658	McCOTTER, THADDEUS*	114,248	TRUPIANO, TONY	7,878	29,410	R	54.1%	43.0%	55.7%	44.3%
11	2004	327,216	186,431	McCOTTER, THADDEUS*	134,301	TRURAN, PHILLIP	6,484	52,130	R	57.0%	41.0%	58.1%	41.9%
11	2002	220,405	126,050	McCOTTER, THADDEUS	87,402	KELLEY, KEVIN	6,953	38,648	R	57.2%	39.7%	59.1%	40.9%
12	2010	204,117	71,372	VOLARIC, DON	124,671	LEVIN, SANDER M.*	8,074	53,299	D	35.0%	61.1%	36.4%	63.6%
12	2008	312,344	74,565	COPPLE, BERT	225,094	LEVIN, SANDER M.*	12,685	150,529	D	23.9%	72.1%	24.9%	75.1%
12	2006	240,115	62,689	SHAFER, RANDELL	168,494	LEVIN, SANDER M.*	8,932	105,805	D	26.1%	70.2%	27.1%	72.9%
12	2004	304,134	88,256	SHAFER, RANDELL	210,827	LEVIN, SANDER M.*	5,051	122,571	D	29.0%	69.3%	29.5%	70.5%
12	2002	206,528	61,502	DEAN, HARVEY	140,970	LEVIN, SANDER M.*	4,056	79,468	D	29.8%	68.3%	30.4%	69.6%
13	2010	127,076	23,462	HAULER, JOHN	100,885	CLARKE, HANSEN	2,729	77,423	D	18.5%	79.4%	18.9%	81.1%
13	2008	225,922	43,098	GUBICS, EDWARD J.	167,481	KILPATRICK, CAROLYN CHEEKS*	15,343	124,383	D	19.1%	74.1%	20.5%	79.5%
13	2006	126,323		—	126,308	KILPATRICK, CAROLYN CHEEKS*	15	126,308	D		100.0%		100.0%
13	2004	221,654	40,935	CASSELL, CYNTHIA	173,246	KILPATRICK, CAROLYN CHEEKS*	7,473	132,311	D	18.5%	78.2%	19.1%	80.9%
13	2002	131,941		—	120,869	KILPATRICK, CAROLYN CHEEKS*	11,072	120,869	D		91.6%		100.0%
14	2010	150,478	29,902	UKRAINEC, DON	115,511	CONYERS, JOHN JR.*	5,065	85,609	D	19.9%	76.8%	20.6%	79.4%
14	2008	246,588		—	227,841	CONYERS, JOHN JR.*	18,747	227,841	D		92.4%		100.0%
14	2006	186,122	27,367	MILES, CHAD	158,755	CONYERS, JOHN JR.*		131,388	D	14.7%	85.3%	14.7%	85.3%
14	2004	254,580	35,089	PEDRAZA, VERONICA	213,681	CONYERS, JOHN JR.*	5,810	178,592	D	13.8%	83.9%	14.1%	85.9%
14	2002	174,608	26,544	STONE, DAVE	145,285	CONYERS, JOHN JR.*	2,779	118,741	D	15.2%	83.2%	15.4%	84.6%
15	2010	208,309	83,488	STEELE, ROB	118,336	DINGELL, JOHN D.*	6,485	34,848	D	40.1%	56.8%	41.4%	58.6%
15	2008	327,827	81,802	LYNCH, JOHN	231,784	DINGELL, JOHN D.*	14,241	149,982	D	25.0%	70.7%	26.1%	73.9%
15	2006	206,868		—	181,946	DINGELL, JOHN D.*	24,922	181,946	D		88.0%		100.0%
15	2004	307,963	81,828	REAMER, DAWN	218,409	DINGELL, JOHN D.*	7,726	136,581	D	26.6%	70.9%	27.3%	72.7%
15	2002	189,063	48,626	KALTENBACH, MARTIN	136,518	DINGELL, JOHN D.*	3,919	87,892	D	25.7%	72.2%	26.3%	73.7%
TOTAL	2010	3,194,901	1,671,707		1,415,212		107,982	256,495	R	52.3%	44.3%	54.2%	45.8%
TOTAL	2008	4,810,690	2,114,293		2,516,640		179,757	402,347	D	43.9%	52.3%	45.7%	54.3%
TOTAL	2006	3,648,502	1,624,865		1,923,485		100,152	298,620	D	44.5%	52.7%	45.8%	54.2%
TOTAL	2004	4,631,058	2,288,594		2,242,435		100,029	46,159	R	49.4%	48.4%	50.5%	49.5%
TOTAL	2002	3,055,897	1,474,178		1,507,174		74,545	32,996	D	48.2%	49.3%	49.4%	50.6%

An asterisk (*) denotes incumbent.

MICHIGAN

GENERAL AND PRIMARY ELECTIONS

2010 GENERAL ELECTIONS

Governor Other vote was 22,390 Libertarian (Ken Proctor); 20,818 U.S. Taxpayers (Stacey Mathia); 20,699 Green (Harley Mikkelson); 7 write-in (Linda Blauwkamp); 5 write-in (Dovelyn Waynick); 4 write-in (Thomas Neuenfeldt); 4 write-in (Mark Van Kleeck); 3 write-in (James Mote); 2 write-in (Larry Hutchinson Jr.); 1 write-in (Angelo Brown); 1 write-in (George DeLorean).

House Other vote was:

CD1   7,847 No Party Affiliation (Glenn Wilson); 4,200 U.S. Taxpayers (Patrick Lambert); 2,571 Libertarian (Keith Shelton); 2,072 Green (Ellis Boal).

CD2   2,701 Libertarian (Joseph Gillotte); 2,379 U.S. Taxpayers (Ronald E. Graeser); 2,016 Green (Lloyd Clarke).

CD3   2,677 Libertarian (James Rogers); 2,144 U.S. Taxpayers (Ted Gerrard); 1,575 Green (Charlie Shick).

CD4   3,861 U.S. Taxpayers (John Emerick); 3,504 Libertarian (Clint Foster).

CD5   2,649 Green (J. de Heus); 2,648 Libertarian (Michael Moon).

CD6   3,672 U.S. Taxpayers (Melvin Valkner); 3,369 Libertarian (Fred Strand); 1,784 Green (Pat Foster).

CD7   3,705 U.S. Taxpayers (Scott Aughney); 3,239 Libertarian (Greg Merle); 3,117 Green (Richard Wunsch); 21 write-in (Danny Davis).

CD8   3,881 Libertarian (Bhagwan Dashairya); 11 write-in (Katherine Houston); 2 write-in (Eric Harvey).

CD9   2,601 Libertarian (Adam Goodman); 2,484 Green (Douglas Campbell); 1,866 No Party Affiliation (Bob Gray); 644 No Party Affiliation (Matthew Kuofie).

CD10   3,750 Libertarian (Claude Beavers); 3,286 Green (Candace R. Caveny).

CD11   5,353 Libertarian (John J. Tatar).

CD12   3,038 Green (Julia Williams); 2,342 Libertarian (Leonard Schwartz); 2,285 U.S. Taxpayers (Les Townsend); 409 Natural Law (Alan Jacquemotte).

CD13   1,032 Green (George Corsetti); 881 No Party Affiliation (Duane Montgomery); 815 Libertarian (Heidi Peterson); 1 write-in (James Casha).

CD14   3,206 U.S. Taxpayers (Marc Sosnowski); 1,859 Libertarian (Richard Secula).

CD15   2,686 Green (Aimee Smith); 1,969 Libertarian (Kerry Morgan); 1,821 U.S. Taxpayers (Matthew Furman); 9 write-in (Louis Czako).

2010 PRIMARY ELECTIONS

Primary   August 3, 2010   **Registration**   7,244,356   No Party Registration
(as of July, 2010)

Primary Type   Open—Any registered voter could participate in the primary of either party.

MICHIGAN

GENERAL AND PRIMARY ELECTIONS

	REPUBLICAN PRIMARIES			DEMOCRATIC PRIMARIES		
Governor	Rick Snyder	381,588	36.4%	Virg Bernero	309,518	58.5%
	Peter Hoekstra	281,695	26.9%	Andy Dillon	219,304	41.5%
	Mike Cox	240,677	23.0%			
	Mike Bouchard	127,422	12.2%			
	Tom George	17,002	1.6%			
	TOTAL	*1,048,384*		*TOTAL*	*528,822*	

MICHIGAN

GENERAL AND PRIMARY ELECTIONS

	REPUBLICAN PRIMARIES			DEMOCRATIC PRIMARIES		
Congressional District 1	Dan Benishek	27,077	38.1%	Gary McDowell	27,996	100.0%
	Jason Allen	27,062	38.1%			
	Tom Stillings	5,418	7.6%			
	Linda Goldthorpe	4,980	7.0%			
	Don Hooper	3,969	5.6%			
	Patrick Donlon	2,490	3.5%			
	TOTAL	70,996				
Congressional District 2	Bill Huizenga	27,041	25.4%	Fred Johnson	12,375	59.9%
	Jay Riemersma	26,378	24.8%	Nicolette McClure	8,272	40.1%
	Wayne Kuipers	23,226	21.8%			
	Bill Cooper	20,584	19.3%			
	Fred Reichardt	4,517	4.2%			
	Ted Schendel	2,401	2.3%			
	Chris Larson	2,332	2.2%			
	TOTAL	106,479		TOTAL	20,647	
Congressional District 3	Justin Amash	38,569	40.3%	Pat Miles	14,114	68.5%
	Steve Heacock	25,157	26.3%	Paul Mayhue	6,480	31.5%
	Bill Hardiman	22,715	23.8%			
	Bob Overbeek	5,133	5.4%			
	Louise Johnson	4,020	4.2%			
	TOTAL	95,594		TOTAL	20,594	
Congressional District 4	Dave Camp*	76,619	100.0%	Jerry Campbell	20,951	100.0%
Congressional District 5	John Kupiec	22,177	55.7%	Dale E. Kildee*	34,902	78.4%
	Rick Wilson	17,643	44.3%	Scott Withers	9,596	21.6%
	TOTAL	39,820		TOTAL	44,498	
Congressional District 6	Fred Upton*	42,182	57.1%	Don Cooney	18,060	100.0%
	Jack Hoogendyk	31,660	42.9%			
	TOTAL	73,842				
Congressional District 7	Tim Walberg	41,784	57.5%	Mark H. Schauer*	23,806	100.0%
	Brian Rooney	23,505	32.3%			
	Marvin Carlson	7,413	10.2%			
	TOTAL	72,702				
Congressional District 8	Mike Rogers*	78,047	100.0%	No candidates were listed on the Democratic primary ballot. Lance Enderle won the nomination with 1,703 write-in votes.		
	Eric Harvey (write-in)	19				
	TOTAL	78,066				
Congressional District 9	Rocky Raczkowski	33,459	42.0%	Gary C. Peters*	37,843	100.0%
	Paul Welday	22,298	28.0%			
	Richard Kuhn	15,949	20.0%			
	Anna Janek	8,006	10.0%			
	TOTAL	79,712				
Congressional District 10	Candice S. Miller*	84,426	100.0%	Henry Yanez	23,310	100.0%
Congressional District 11	Thaddeus McCotter*	65,688	100.0%	Natalie Mosher	27,295	100.0%
Congressional District 12	Don Volaric	33,823	100.0%	Sander M. Levin*	42,732	76.0%
				Michael Switalski	13,480	24.0%
				TOTAL	56,212	
Congressional District 13	John Hauler	10,153	100.0%	Hansen Clarke	22,573	47.3%
				Carolyn Cheeks Kilpatrick*	19,507	40.9%

MICHIGAN

GENERAL AND PRIMARY ELECTIONS

	REPUBLICAN PRIMARIES			DEMOCRATIC PRIMARIES		
				Glenn Plummer	2,038	4.3%
				John Broad	1,872	3.9%
				Vincent Brown	893	1.9%
				Stephen Hume	820	1.7%
				TOTAL	47,703	
Congressional District 14	Don Ukrainec	7,435	55.4%	John Conyers Jr.*	44,902	100.0%
	Pauline Montie	5,978	44.6%			
	TOTAL	13,413				
Congressional District 15	Rob Steele	18,358	50.8%	John D. Dingell*	40,642	100.0%
	John Lynch	11,946	33.0%			
	Tony Ambrose	4,488	12.4%			
	Majed Moughni	1,374	3.8%			
	TOTAL	36,166				

An asterisk (*) denotes incumbent.

MINNESOTA

Congressional districts first established for elections held in 2002
8 members

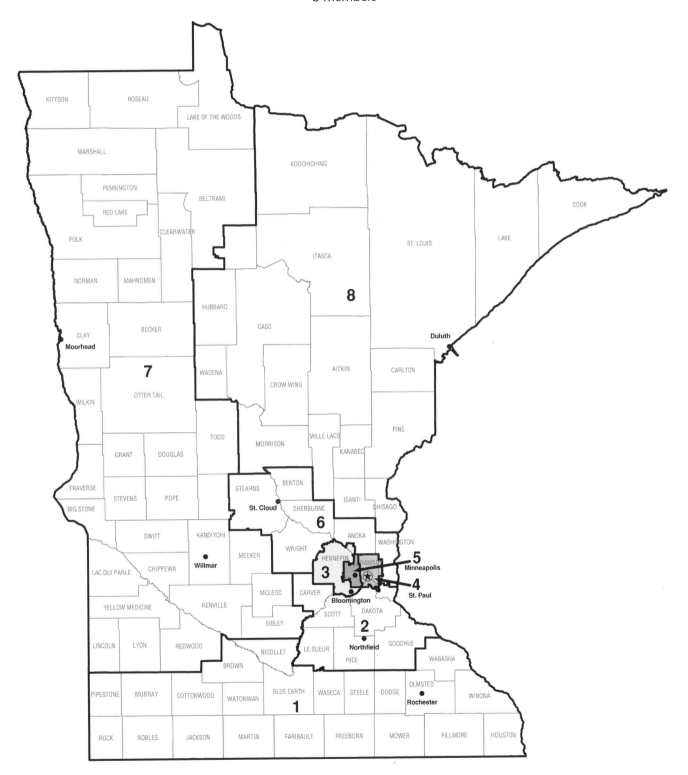

MINNESOTA

Minneapolis–St.Paul Area

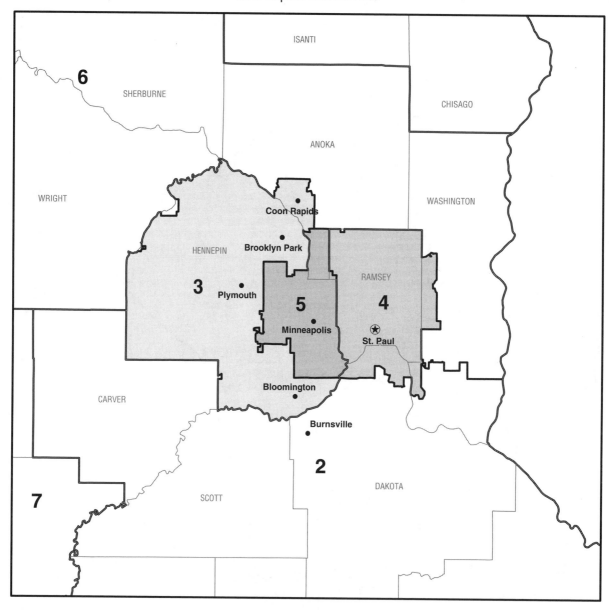

MINNESOTA

GOVERNOR
Mark Dayton (D). Elected 2010 to a four-year term.

SENATORS (2 Democrat)
Al Franken (D). Elected 2008 to a six-year term

Amy Klobuchar (D). Elected 2006 to a six-year term.

REPRESENTATIVES (4 Democrats, 4 Republicans)
1. Timothy J. Walz (D)
2. John Kline (R)
3. Erik Paulsen (R)
4. Betty McCollum (D)
5. Keith Ellison (D)
6. Michele Bachmann (R)
7. Collin C. Peterson (D)
8. Chip Cravaack (R)

POSTWAR VOTE FOR PRESIDENT

| | | Republican | | Democratic | | | | Percentage | | | |
| | Total | | | | | Other | Rep.-Dem. | Total Vote | | Major Vote | |
Year	Vote	Vote	Candidate	Vote	Candidate	Vote	Plurality	Rep.	Dem.	Rep.	Dem.
2008	2,910,369	1,275,409	McCain, John	1,573,354	Obama, Barack	61,606	297,945 D	43.8%	54.1%	44.8%	55.2%
2004	2,828,387	1,346,695	Bush, George W.	1,445,014	Kerry, John	36,678	98,319 D	47.6%	51.1%	48.2%	51.8%
2000**	2,438,685	1,109,659	Bush, George W.	1,168,266	Gore, Al	160,760	58,607 D	45.5%	47.9%	48.7%	51.3%
1996**	2,192,640	766,476	Dole, Bob	1,120,438	Clinton, Bill	305,726	353,962 D	35.0%	51.1%	40.6%	59.4%
1992**	2,347,948	747,841	Bush, George	1,020,997	Clinton, Bill	579,110	273,156 D	31.9%	43.5%	42.3%	57.7%
1988	2,096,790	962,337	Bush, George	1,109,471	Dukakis, Michael S.	24,982	147,134 D	45.9%	52.9%	46.4%	53.6%
1984	2,084,449	1,032,603	Reagan, Ronald	1,036,364	Mondale, Walter F.	15,482	3,761 D	49.5%	49.7%	49.9%	50.1%
1980**	2,051,980	873,268	Reagan, Ronald	954,174	Carter, Jimmy	224,538	80,906 D	42.6%	46.5%	47.8%	52.2%
1976	1,949,931	819,395	Ford, Gerald R.	1,070,440	Carter, Jimmy	60,096	251,045 D	42.0%	54.9%	43.4%	56.6%
1972	1,741,652	898,269	Nixon, Richard M.	802,346	McGovern, George S.	41,037	95,923 R	51.6%	46.1%	52.8%	47.2%
1968**	1,588,506	658,643	Nixon, Richard M.	857,738	Humphrey, Hubert H.	72,125	199,095 D	41.5%	54.0%	43.4%	56.6%
1964	1,554,462	559,624	Goldwater, Barry M.	991,117	Johnson, Lyndon B.	3,721	431,493 D	36.0%	63.8%	36.1%	63.9%
1960	1,541,887	757,915	Nixon, Richard M.	779,933	Kennedy, John F.	4,039	22,018 D	49.2%	50.6%	49.3%	50.7%
1956	1,340,005	719,302	Eisenhower, Dwight D.	617,525	Stevenson, Adlai E.	3,178	101,777 R	53.7%	46.1%	53.8%	46.2%
1952	1,379,483	763,211	Eisenhower, Dwight D.	608,458	Stevenson, Adlai E.	7,814	154,753 R	55.3%	44.1%	55.6%	44.4%
1948	1,212,226	483,617	Dewey, Thomas E.	692,966	Truman, Harry S.	35,643	209,349 D	39.9%	57.2%	41.1%	58.9%

**In past elections, the other vote included: 2000 - 126,696 Green (Nader); 1996 - 257,704 Reform (Ross Perot); 1992 - 562,506 Independent (Perot); 1980 - 174,990 Independent (John Anderson); 1968 - 68,931 American Independent (George Wallace).

MINNESOTA

POSTWAR VOTE FOR GOVERNOR

Year	Total Vote	Republican		Democratic		Other Vote	Plurality	Percentage			
								Total Vote		Major Vote	
		Vote	Candidate	Vote	Candidate			Rep.	Dem.	Rep.	Dem.
2010**	2,107,021	910,462	Emmer, Tom	919,232	Dayton, Mark	277,327	8,770 D	43.2%	43.6%	49.8%	50.2%
2006	2,202,937	1,028,568	Pawlenty, Tim	1,007,460	Hatch, Mike	166,909	21,108 R	46.7%	45.7%	50.5%	49.5%
2002**	2,252,473	999,473	Pawlenty, Tim	821,268	Moe, Roger D.	431,732	178,205 R	44.4%	36.5%	54.9%	45.1%
1998**	2,090,518	716,880	Coleman, Norm	587,060	Humphrey, Hubert H., III	786,578	56,523 V	34.3%	28.1%	55.0%	45.0%
1994	1,765,590	1,094,165	Carlson, Arne	589,344	Marty, John	82,081	504,821 R	62.0%	33.4%	65.0%	35.0%
1990	1,806,777	895,988	Carlson, Arne	836,218	Perpich, Rudy	74,571	59,770 R	49.6%	46.3%	51.7%	48.3%
1986	1,415,989	606,755	Ludeman, Cal R.	790,138	Perpich, Rudy	19,096	183,383 D	42.9%	55.8%	43.4%	56.6%
1982	1,789,539	715,796	Whitney, Wheelock	1,049,104	Perpich, Rudy	24,639	333,308 D	40.0%	58.6%	40.6%	59.4%
1978	1,585,702	830,019	Quie, Albert H.	718,244	Perpich, Rudy	37,439	111,775 R	52.3%	45.3%	53.6%	46.4%
1974	1,252,898	367,722	Johnson, John W.	786,787	Anderson, Wendell R.	98,389	419,065 D	29.3%	62.8%	31.9%	68.1%
1970	1,365,443	621,780	Head, Douglas M.	737,921	Anderson, Wendell R.	5,742	116,141 D	45.5%	54.0%	45.7%	54.3%
1966	1,295,058	680,593	LeVander, Harold	607,943	Rolvaag, Karl F.	6,522	72,650 R	52.6%	46.9%	52.8%	47.2%
1962**	1,246,904	619,751	Andersen, Elmer L.	619,842	Rolvaag, Karl F.	7,311	91 D	49.7%	49.7%	50.0%	50.0%
1960	1,550,265	783,813	Andersen, Elmer L.	760,934	Freeman, Orville L.	5,518	22,879 R	50.6%	49.1%	50.7%	49.3%
1958	1,159,915	490,731	MacKinnon, George	658,326	Freeman, Orville L.	10,858	167,595 D	42.3%	56.8%	42.7%	57.3%
1956	1,422,161	685,196	Nelsen, Ancher	731,180	Freeman, Orville L.	5,785	45,984 D	48.2%	51.4%	48.4%	51.6%
1954	1,151,417	538,865	Anderson, C. Elmer	607,099	Freeman, Orville L.	5,453	68,234 D	46.8%	52.7%	47.0%	53.0%
1952	1,418,869	785,125	Anderson, C. Elmer	624,480	Freeman, Orville L.	9,264	160,645 R	55.3%	44.0%	55.7%	44.3%
1950	1,046,632	635,800	Youngdahl, Luther	400,637	Peterson, Harry H.	10,195	235,163 R	60.7%	38.3%	61.3%	38.7%
1948	1,210,894	643,572	Youngdahl, Luther	545,766	Halsted, Charles L.	21,556	97,806 R	53.1%	45.1%	54.1%	45.9%
1946	880,348	519,067	Youngdahl, Luther	349,565	Barker, Harold H.	11,716	169,502 R	59.0%	39.7%	59.8%	40.2%

**In past elections, the other vote included: 2010 - 251,487 Independence (Tom Horner); 2002 - 364,534 Independence (Timothy J. Penny); 1998 - 773,403 Reform (Jesse Ventura), who was elected with 37.0 percent of the total vote. The term of office of Minnesota's Governor was increased from two to four years effective with the 1962 election.

POSTWAR VOTE FOR SENATOR

Year	Total Vote	Republican		Democratic		Other Vote	Rep.-Dem. Plurality	Percentage			
								Total Vote		Major Vote	
		Vote	Candidate	Vote	Candidate			Rep.	Dem.	Rep.	Dem.
2008**	2,887,646	1,212,317	Coleman, Norm	1,212,629	Franken, Al	462,700	312 D	42.0%	42.0%	50.0%	50.0%
2006	2,202,772	835,653	Kennedy, Mark	1,278,849	Klobuchar, Amy	88,270	443,196 D	37.9%	58.1%	39.5%	60.5%
2002**	2,254,639	1,116,697	Coleman, Norm	1,067,246	Mondale, Walter F.	70,696	49,451 R	49.5%	47.3%	51.1%	48.9%
2000	2,419,520	1,047,474	Grams, Rod	1,181,553	Dayton, Mark	190,493	134,079 D	43.3%	48.8%	47.0%	53.0%
1996	2,183,062	901,282	Boschwitz, Rudy	1,098,493	Wellstone, Paul	183,287	197,211 D	41.3%	50.3%	45.1%	54.9%
1994	1,772,929	869,653	Grams, Rod	781,860	Wynia, Ann	121,416	87,793 R	49.1%	44.1%	52.7%	47.3%
1990	1,808,045	864,375	Boschwitz, Rudy	911,999	Wellstone, Paul	31,671	47,624 D	47.8%	50.4%	48.7%	51.3%
1988	2,093,953	1,176,210	Durenberger, David	856,694	Humphrey, Hubert H. III	61,049	319,516 R	56.2%	40.9%	57.9%	42.1%
1984	2,066,143	1,199,926	Boschwitz, Rudy	852,844	Growe, Joan Anderson	13,373	347,082 R	58.1%	41.3%	58.5%	41.5%
1982	1,804,675	949,207	Durenberger, David	840,401	Dayton, Mark	15,067	108,806 R	52.6%	46.6%	53.0%	47.0%
1978	1,580,778	894,092	Boschwitz, Rudy	638,375	Anderson, Wendell R.	48,311	255,717 R	56.6%	40.4%	58.3%	41.7%
1978S	1,560,724	957,908	Durenberger, David	538,675	Short, Robert E.	64,141	419,233 R	61.4%	34.5%	64.0%	36.0%
1976	1,912,068	478,611	Brekke, Gerald W.	1,290,736	Humphrey, Hubert H.	142,721	812,125 D	25.0%	67.5%	27.1%	72.9%
1972	1,731,653	742,121	Hansen, Philip	981,340	Mondale, Walter F.	8,192	239,219 D	42.9%	56.7%	43.1%	56.9%
1970	1,364,887	568,025	MacGregor, Clark	788,256	Humphrey, Hubert H.	8,606	220,231 D	41.6%	57.8%	41.9%	58.1%
1966	1,271,426	574,568	Forsythe, Robert A.	685,840	Mondale, Walter F.	10,718	110,972 D	45.2%	53.9%	45.6%	54.4%
1964	1,543,590	605,933	Whitney, Wheelock	931,353	McCarthy, Eugene J.	6,304	325,420 D	39.3%	60.3%	39.4%	60.6%
1960	1,536,839	648,586	Peterson, P. K.	884,168	Humphrey, Hubert H.	4,085	235,582 D	42.2%	57.5%	42.3%	57.7%
1958	1,150,883	536,629	Thye, Edward J.	608,847	McCarthy, Eugene J.	5,407	72,218 D	46.6%	52.9%	46.8%	53.2%
1954	1,138,952	479,619	Bjornson, Val	642,193	Humphrey, Hubert H.	17,140	162,574 D	42.1%	56.4%	42.8%	57.2%
1952	1,387,419	785,649	Thye, Edward J.	590,011	Carlson, William E.	11,759	195,638 R	56.6%	42.5%	57.1%	42.9%
1948	1,220,250	485,801	Ball, Joseph H.	729,494	Humphrey, Hubert H.	4,955	243,693 D	39.8%	59.8%	40.0%	60.0%
1946	878,731	517,775	Thye, Edward J.	349,520	Jorgenson, Theodore	11,436	168,255 R	58.9%	39.8%	59.7%	40.3%

**In past elections, the other vote included: 2008 - 437,505 Independence (Dean Barkley). In October 2002 the Democratic incumbent, Paul Wellstone, was killed in an airplane crash. Walter F. Mondale was named to replace him on the general election ballot. One of the 1978 elections was for a short term to fill a vacancy.

MINNESOTA

GOVERNOR 2010

2010 Census Population	County	Total Vote	Republican	Democratic	Independence (Horner)	Other	Rep.-Dem. Plurality	Percentage		
								Rep.	Dem.	Independence
16,202	AITKIN	7,343	3,081	3,242	829	191	161 D	42.0%	44.2%	11.3%
330,844	ANOKA	131,166	64,826	50,669	14,166	1,505	14,157 R	49.4%	38.6%	10.8%
32,504	BECKER	11,791	5,882	4,433	1,276	200	1,449 R	49.9%	37.6%	10.8%
44,442	BELTRAMI	15,974	6,531	7,526	1,532	385	995 D	40.9%	47.1%	9.6%
38,451	BENTON	13,726	6,989	4,844	1,667	226	2,145 R	50.9%	35.3%	12.1%
5,269	BIG STONE	2,191	909	995	263	24	86 D	41.5%	45.4%	12.0%
64,013	BLUE EARTH	22,414	9,216	9,706	3,047	445	490 D	41.1%	43.3%	13.6%
25,893	BROWN	10,376	5,443	3,263	1,573	97	2,180 R	52.5%	31.4%	15.2%
35,386	CARLTON	13,643	4,274	8,010	1,156	203	3,736 D	31.3%	58.7%	8.5%
91,042	CARVER	36,999	21,589	10,249	4,866	295	11,340 R	58.4%	27.7%	13.2%
28,567	CASS	12,922	6,355	4,872	1,503	192	1,483 R	49.2%	37.7%	11.6%
12,441	CHIPPEWA	4,859	1,940	2,194	673	52	254 D	39.9%	45.2%	13.9%
53,887	CHISAGO	22,758	11,694	8,131	2,689	244	3,563 R	51.4%	35.7%	11.8%
58,999	CLAY	18,982	8,025	8,512	2,146	299	487 D	42.3%	44.8%	11.3%
8,695	CLEARWATER	3,501	1,709	1,419	308	65	290 R	48.8%	40.5%	8.8%
5,176	COOK	2,807	856	1,623	287	41	767 D	30.5%	57.8%	10.2%
11,687	COTTONWOOD	4,603	2,257	1,655	627	64	602 R	49.0%	36.0%	13.6%
62,500	CROW WING	27,382	13,442	10,559	2,934	447	2,883 R	49.1%	38.6%	10.7%
398,552	DAKOTA	161,969	76,211	63,066	21,190	1,502	13,145 R	47.1%	38.9%	13.1%
20,087	DODGE	7,877	4,117	2,579	1,015	166	1,538 R	52.3%	32.7%	12.9%
36,009	DOUGLAS	15,561	8,036	5,371	1,991	163	2,665 R	51.6%	34.5%	12.8%
14,553	FARIBAULT	6,511	3,121	2,407	858	125	714 R	47.9%	37.0%	13.2%
20,866	FILLMORE	8,332	3,648	3,535	994	155	113 R	43.8%	42.4%	11.9%
31,255	FREEBORN	13,347	5,285	6,490	1,318	254	1,205 D	39.6%	48.6%	9.9%
46,183	GOODHUE	19,381	9,178	7,247	2,730	226	1,931 R	47.4%	37.4%	14.1%
6,018	GRANT	3,021	1,297	1,279	407	38	18 R	42.9%	42.3%	13.5%
1,152,425	HENNEPIN	468,366	168,522	237,998	57,117	4,729	69,476 D	36.0%	50.8%	12.2%
19,027	HOUSTON	7,724	3,774	3,187	607	156	587 R	48.9%	41.3%	7.9%
20,428	HUBBARD	9,724	4,888	3,624	1,054	158	1,264 R	50.3%	37.3%	10.8%
37,816	ISANTI	14,791	7,905	5,247	1,482	157	2,658 R	53.4%	35.5%	10.0%
45,058	ITASCA	19,605	7,041	10,379	1,844	341	3,338 D	35.9%	52.9%	9.4%
10,266	JACKSON	4,311	2,061	1,603	561	86	458 R	47.8%	37.2%	13.0%
16,239	KANABEC	6,511	3,173	2,580	646	112	593 R	48.7%	39.6%	9.9%
42,239	KANDIYOHI	17,313	8,041	6,751	2,309	212	1,290 R	46.4%	39.0%	13.3%
4,552	KITTSON	1,961	713	1,047	180	21	334 D	36.4%	53.4%	9.2%
13,311	KOOCHICHING	5,053	1,653	2,880	415	105	1,227 D	32.7%	57.0%	8.2%
7,259	LAC QUI PARLE	3,598	1,391	1,618	525	64	227 D	38.7%	45.0%	14.6%
10,866	LAKE	5,548	1,768	3,251	449	80	1,483 D	31.9%	58.6%	8.1%
4,045	LAKE OF THE WOODS	1,844	858	750	204	32	108 R	46.5%	40.7%	11.1%
27,703	LE SUEUR	11,534	5,420	4,224	1,696	194	1,196 R	47.0%	36.6%	14.7%
5,896	LINCOLN	2,426	1,070	1,012	298	46	58 R	44.1%	41.7%	12.3%
25,857	LYON	8,907	4,153	3,261	1,338	155	892 R	46.6%	36.6%	15.0%
36,651	MCLEOD	13,396	7,365	3,967	1,891	173	3,398 R	55.0%	29.6%	14.1%
5,413	MAHNOMEN	1,897	641	1,023	165	68	382 D	33.8%	53.9%	8.7%
9,439	MARSHALL	4,205	1,708	2,028	398	71	320 D	40.6%	48.2%	9.5%
20,840	MARTIN	8,665	4,757	2,733	1,034	141	2,024 R	54.9%	31.5%	11.9%
23,300	MEEKER	9,831	4,897	3,312	1,476	146	1,585 R	49.8%	33.7%	15.0%
26,097	MILLE LACS	10,157	4,934	3,893	1,131	199	1,041 R	48.6%	38.3%	11.1%
33,198	MORRISON	12,770	6,776	4,240	1,527	227	2,536 R	53.1%	33.2%	12.0%
39,163	MOWER	14,154	5,038	7,371	1,493	252	2,333 D	35.6%	52.1%	10.5%

MINNESOTA

GOVERNOR 2010

2010 Census Population	County	Total Vote	Republican	Democratic	Independence (Horner)	Other	Rep.-Dem. Plurality	Percentage		
								Rep.	Dem.	Independence
8,725	MURRAY	3,744	1,674	1,497	519	54	177 R	44.7%	40.0%	13.9%
32,727	NICOLLET	13,289	5,433	5,759	1,901	196	326 D	40.9%	43.3%	14.3%
21,378	NOBLES	5,941	2,794	2,270	788	89	524 R	47.0%	38.2%	13.3%
6,852	NORMAN	2,627	872	1,455	253	47	583 D	33.2%	55.4%	9.6%
144,248	OLMSTED	55,027	25,228	20,813	8,175	811	4,415 R	45.8%	37.8%	14.9%
57,303	OTTER TAIL	24,822	13,295	8,702	2,450	375	4,593 R	53.6%	35.1%	9.9%
13,930	PENNINGTON	4,737	2,120	2,082	452	83	38 R	44.8%	44.0%	9.5%
29,750	PINE	10,866	4,927	4,720	1,056	163	207 R	45.3%	43.4%	9.7%
9,596	PIPESTONE	3,520	1,988	1,162	291	79	826 R	56.5%	33.0%	8.3%
31,600	POLK	10,735	4,763	4,797	1,025	150	34 D	44.4%	44.7%	9.5%
10,995	POPE	5,238	2,270	2,181	715	72	89 R	43.3%	41.6%	13.7%
508,640	RAMSEY	192,046	61,412	105,498	22,959	2,177	44,086 D	32.0%	54.9%	12.0%
4,089	RED LAKE	1,582	655	762	136	29	107 D	41.4%	48.2%	8.6%
16,059	REDWOOD	6,052	3,220	1,859	864	109	1,361 R	53.2%	30.7%	14.3%
15,730	RENVILLE	6,311	2,759	2,288	1,163	101	471 R	43.7%	36.3%	18.4%
64,142	RICE	23,303	9,740	10,382	2,895	286	642 D	41.8%	44.6%	12.4%
9,687	ROCK	3,652	2,017	1,264	317	54	753 R	55.2%	34.6%	8.7%
15,629	ROSEAU	6,500	3,218	2,577	610	95	641 R	49.5%	39.6%	9.4%
200,226	ST. LOUIS	84,635	24,187	52,312	6,999	1,137	28,125 D	28.6%	61.8%	8.3%
129,928	SCOTT	47,707	26,806	14,455	6,091	355	12,351 R	56.2%	30.3%	12.8%
88,499	SHERBURNE	32,910	18,890	10,106	3,553	361	8,784 R	57.4%	30.7%	10.8%
15,226	SIBLEY	5,935	3,128	1,760	969	78	1,368 R	52.7%	29.7%	16.3%
150,642	STEARNS	55,344	27,816	19,929	6,898	701	7,887 R	50.3%	36.0%	12.5%
36,576	STEELE	14,611	6,973	5,393	2,002	243	1,580 R	47.7%	36.9%	13.7%
9,726	STEVENS	4,388	1,942	1,932	447	67	10 R	44.3%	44.0%	10.2%
9,783	SWIFT	4,436	1,650	2,101	622	63	451 D	37.2%	47.4%	14.0%
24,895	TODD	9,292	4,734	3,411	1,012	135	1,323 R	50.9%	36.7%	10.9%
3,558	TRAVERSE	1,767	689	819	216	43	130 D	39.0%	46.3%	12.2%
21,676	WABASHA	8,913	4,341	3,272	1,182	118	1,069 R	48.7%	36.7%	13.3%
13,843	WADENA	5,414	2,906	1,922	517	69	984 R	53.7%	35.5%	9.5%
19,136	WASECA	7,826	3,577	2,853	1,280	116	724 R	45.7%	36.5%	16.4%
238,136	WASHINGTON	103,254	49,141	40,132	13,168	813	9,009 R	47.6%	38.9%	12.8%
11,211	WATONWAN	4,208	1,894	1,632	619	63	262 R	45.0%	38.8%	14.7%
6,576	WILKIN	2,407	1,249	825	305	28	424 R	51.9%	34.3%	12.7%
51,461	WINONA	18,130	7,950	8,275	1,462	443	325 D	43.8%	45.6%	8.1%
124,700	WRIGHT	47,981	27,916	14,533	5,079	453	13,383 R	58.2%	30.3%	10.6%
10,438	YELLOW MEDICINE	4,144	1,830	1,647	612	55	183 R	44.2%	39.7%	14.8%
5,303,925	TOTAL	2,107,021	910,462	919,232	251,487	25,840	8,770 D	43.2%	43.6%	11.9%

MINNESOTA

HOUSE OF REPRESENTATIVES

CD	Year	Total Vote	Republican Vote	Republican Candidate	Democratic Vote	Democratic Candidate	Other Vote	Rep.-Dem. Plurality	Total Vote Rep.	Total Vote Dem.	Major Vote Rep.	Major Vote Dem.
1	2010	248,005	109,242	DEMMER, RANDY	122,365	WALZ, TIMOTHY J.*	16,398	13,123 D	44.0%	49.3%	47.2%	52.8%
1	2008	332,400	109,453	DAVIS, BRIAN J.	207,753	WALZ, TIMOTHY J.*	15,194	98,300 D	32.9%	62.5%	34.5%	65.5%
1	2006	268,421	126,486	GUTKNECHT, GIL*	141,556	WALZ, TIMOTHY J.	379	15,070 D	47.1%	52.7%	47.2%	52.8%
1	2004	324,055	193,132	GUTKNECHT, GIL*	115,088	POMEROY, LEIGH	15,835	78,044 R	59.6%	35.5%	62.7%	37.3%
1	2002	265,982	163,570	GUTKNECHT, GIL*	92,165	ANDREASEN, STEVE	10,247	71,405 R	61.5%	34.7%	64.0%	36.0%
2	2010	286,453	181,341	KLINE, JOHN*	104,809	MADORE, SHELLEY	303	76,532 R	63.3%	36.6%	63.4%	36.6%
2	2008	385,656	220,924	KLINE, JOHN*	164,093	SARVI, STEVE	639	56,831 R	57.3%	42.5%	57.4%	42.6%
2	2006	290,540	163,269	KLINE, JOHN*	116,343	ROWLEY, COLEEN	10,928	46,926 R	56.2%	40.0%	58.4%	41.6%
2	2004	365,945	206,313	KLINE, JOHN*	147,527	DALY, TERESA	12,105	58,786 R	56.4%	40.3%	58.3%	41.7%
2	2002	286,860	152,970	KLINE, JOHN	121,121	LUTHER, BILL*	12,769	31,849 R	53.3%	42.2%	55.8%	44.2%
3	2010	274,092	161,177	PAULSEN, ERIK*	100,240	MEFFERT, JIM	12,675	60,937 R	58.8%	36.6%	61.7%	38.3%
3	2008	369,104	178,932	PAULSEN, ERIK	150,787	MADIA, ASHWIN	39,385	28,145 R	48.5%	40.9%	54.3%	45.7%
3	2006	284,244	184,333	RAMSTAD, JIM*	99,588	WILDE, WENDY	323	84,745 R	64.9%	35.0%	64.9%	35.1%
3	2004	358,892	231,871	RAMSTAD, JIM*	126,665	WATTS, DEBORAH	356	105,206 R	64.6%	35.3%	64.7%	35.3%
3	2002	296,218	213,334	RAMSTAD, JIM*	82,575	STANTON, DARRYL	309	130,759 R	72.0%	27.9%	72.1%	27.9%
4	2010	231,426	80,141	COLLETT, TERESA	136,746	McCOLLUM, BETTY*	14,539	56,605 D	34.6%	59.1%	37.0%	63.0%
4	2008	316,018	98,936	MATTHEWS, ED	216,267	McCOLLUM, BETTY*	815	117,331 D	31.3%	68.4%	31.4%	68.6%
4	2006	247,466	74,797	SIUM, OBI	172,096	McCOLLUM, BETTY*	573	97,299 D	30.2%	69.5%	30.3%	69.7%
4	2004	317,299	105,467	BATAGLIA, PATRICE	182,387	McCOLLUM, BETTY*	29,445	76,920 D	33.2%	57.5%	36.6%	63.4%
4	2002	264,540	89,705	BILLINGTON, CLYDE	164,597	McCOLLUM, BETTY*	10,238	74,892 D	33.9%	62.2%	35.3%	64.7%
5	2010	228,746	55,222	DEMOS, JOEL	154,833	ELLISON, KEITH*	18,691	99,611 D	24.1%	67.7%	26.3%	73.7%
5	2008	322,747	71,020	WHITE, BARB DAVIS	228,776	ELLISON, KEITH*	22,951	157,756 D	22.0%	70.9%	23.7%	76.3%
5	2006	244,905	52,263	FINE, ALAN	136,060	ELLISON, KEITH	56,582	83,797 D	21.3%	55.6%	27.8%	72.2%
5	2004	313,526	76,600	MATHIAS, DANIEL	218,434	SABO, MARTIN OLAV*	18,492	141,834 D	24.4%	69.7%	26.0%	74.0%
5	2002	255,982	66,271	MATHIAS, DANIEL	171,572	SABO, MARTIN OLAV*	18,139	105,301 D	25.9%	67.0%	27.9%	72.1%
6	2010	303,691	159,476	BACHMANN, MICHELE*	120,846	CLARK, TARRYL	23,369	38,630 R	52.5%	39.8%	56.9%	43.1%
6	2008	404,725	187,817	BACHMANN, MICHELE*	175,786	TINKLENBERG, EL	41,122	12,031 R	46.4%	43.4%	51.7%	48.3%
6	2006	302,188	151,248	BACHMANN, MICHELE	127,144	WETTERLING, PATTY	23,796	24,104 R	50.1%	42.1%	54.3%	45.7%
6	2004	377,224	203,669	KENNEDY, MARK*	173,309	WETTERLING, PATTY	246	30,360 R	54.0%	45.9%	54.0%	46.0%
6	2002	287,312	164,747	KENNEDY, MARK*	100,738	ROBERT, JANET	21,827	64,009 R	57.3%	35.1%	62.1%	37.9%
7	2010	241,097	90,652	BYBERG, LEE	133,096	PETERSON, COLLIN C.*	17,349	42,444 D	37.6%	55.2%	40.5%	59.5%
7	2008	314,680	87,062	MENZE, GLEN	227,187	PETERSON, COLLIN C.*	431	140,125 D	27.7%	72.2%	27.7%	72.3%
7	2006	257,194	74,557	BARRETT, MICHAEL J.	179,164	PETERSON, COLLIN C.*	3,473	104,607 D	29.0%	69.7%	29.4%	70.6%
7	2004	314,257	106,349	STURROCK, DAVID E.	207,628	PETERSON, COLLIN C.*	280	101,279 D	33.8%	66.1%	33.9%	66.1%
7	2002	260,813	90,342	STEVENS, DAN	170,234	PETERSON, COLLIN C.*	237	79,892 D	34.6%	65.3%	34.7%	65.3%
8	2010	277,081	133,490	CRAVAACK, CHIP	129,091	OBERSTAR, JAMES L.*	14,500	4,399 R	48.2%	46.6%	50.8%	49.2%
8	2008	357,284	114,871	CUMMINS, MICHAEL	241,831	OBERSTAR, JAMES L.*	582	126,960 D	32.2%	67.7%	32.2%	67.8%
8	2006	284,016	97,683	GRAMS, ROD	180,670	OBERSTAR, JAMES L.*	5,663	82,987 D	34.4%	63.6%	35.1%	64.9%
8	2004	350,483	112,693	GROETTUM, MARK	228,586	OBERSTAR, JAMES L.*	9,204	115,893 D	32.2%	65.2%	33.0%	67.0%
8	2002	283,931	88,673	LEMEN, BOB	194,909	OBERSTAR, JAMES L.*	349	106,236 D	31.2%	68.6%	31.3%	68.7%
TOTAL	2010	2,090,591	970,741		1,002,026		117,824	- 31,285 D	46.4%	47.9%	49.2%	50.8%
TOTAL	2008	2,802,614	1,069,015		1,612,480		121,119	543,465 D	38.1%	57.5%	39.9%	60.1%
TOTAL	2006	2,178,974	924,636		1,152,621		101,717	227,985 D	42.4%	52.9%	44.5%	55.5%
TOTAL	2004	2,721,681	1,236,094		1,399,624		85,963	163,530 D	45.4%	51.4%	46.9%	53.1%
TOTAL	2002	2,201,638	1,029,612		1,097,911		74,115	68,299 D	46.8%	49.9%	48.4%	51.6%

MINNESOTA

GENERAL AND PRIMARY ELECTIONS

2010 GENERAL ELECTIONS

Governor Other vote was 7,516 Grass Roots (Chris Wright); 6,188 Green (Farheen Hakeem); 6,180 Ecology Democracy (Ken Pentel); 4,092 Resource (Linda S. Eno); 30 write-in (Leslie Davis); 7 write-in (John T. Uldrich); 3 write-in (Peter Idusogie); 1 write-in (Sherif Mansour); 1 write-in (Ole Savior); 1,822 scattered write-in. (The Independence Party candidate, Tom Horner, received 251,487 votes, 11.9 percent of the total vote. The Independence Party vote is listed in the county table for the 2010 gubernatorial election in Minnesota.)

House Other vote was:

CD 1 13,242 Independence (Steven Wilson); 3,054 Party Free (Lars Johnson); 102 scattered write-in.

CD 2 303 scattered write-in.

CD 3 12,508 Independence (Jon Oleson); 167 scattered write-in.

CD 4 14,207 Independence (Steve Carlson); 39 write-in (Amber Garlan); 10 write-in (Jack Shepard); 283 scattered write-in.

CD 5 8,548 Independent (Lynne Torgerson); 7,446 Independence (Tom Schrunk); 2,468 Independent Progressive (Michael James Cavlan); 229 scattered write-in.

CD 6 17,698 Independence (Bob Anderson); 5,490 Independent (Aubrey Immelman); 3 write-in (Dennis S. Ferche); 178 scattered write-in.

CD 7 9,317 Independent (Gene Waldorf); 7,839 Independence (Glen R. Menze); 193 scattered write-in.

CD 8 11,876 Independence (Timothy Olson); 2,492 Constitution (Richard "George" Burton); 132 scattered write-in.

2010 PRIMARY ELECTIONS

Primary August 10, 2010   **Registration**   3,151,288   No Party Registration
                                 (as of August 10, 2010)

Primary Type Open—Any registered voter could participate in the party primary of their choice.

MINNESOTA

GENERAL AND PRIMARY ELECTIONS

	REPUBLICAN PRIMARIES			DEMOCRATIC PRIMARIES		
Governor	Tom Emmer	107,558	82.5%	Mark Dayton	182,738	41.3%
	Bob Carney Jr.	9,856	7.6%	Margaret Anderson Kelliher	175,767	39.8%
	Leslie Davis	8,598	6.6%	Matt Entenza	80,509	18.2%
	Ole Savior	4,396	3.4%	Peter Idusogie	3,123	0.7%
	TOTAL	*130,408*		*TOTAL*	*442,137*	
Congressional District 1	Randy Demmer	Unopposed		Timothy J. Walz*	Unopposed	
Congressional District 2	John Kline*	16,151	100.0%	Shelley Madore	19,990	54.7%
				Dan Powers	16,528	45.3%
				TOTAL	*36,518*	
Congressional District 3	Erik Paulsen*	Unopposed		Jim Meffert	Unopposed	100.0%
Congressional District 4	Teresa Collett	6,949	67.2%	Betty McCollum*	55,491	86.6%
	Jack Shepard	3,392	32.8%	Diana Longrie	8,622	13.4%
	TOTAL	*10,341*		*TOTAL*	*64,113*	

MINNESOTA

GENERAL AND PRIMARY ELECTIONS

	REPUBLICAN PRIMARIES			DEMOCRATIC PRIMARIES		
Congressional District 5	Joel Demos	4,975	100.0%	Keith Ellison*	55,424	81.6%
				Barb Davis White	7,963	11.7%
				Gregg A. Iverson	4,575	6.7%
				TOTAL	*67,962*	
Congressional District 6	Michele Bachmann*	17,237	100.0%	Tarryl Clark	28,185	69.1%
				Maureen Kennedy Reed	12,603	30.9%
				TOTAL	*40,788*	
Congressional District 7	Lee Byberg	11,417	60.9%	Collin C. Peterson*	42,104	100.0%
	Alan Roebke	7,315	39.1%			
	TOTAL	*18,732*				
Congressional District 8	Chip Cravaack	26,608		James L. Oberstar*	56,510	80.5%
				W.D. "Bill" Hamm	13,710	19.5%
				TOTAL	*70,220*	

An asterisk (*) denotes incumbent. No votes were tallied for unopposed candidates in districts where none of the parties had a contested primary.

MISSISSIPPI

Congressional districts first established for elections held in 2002
4 members

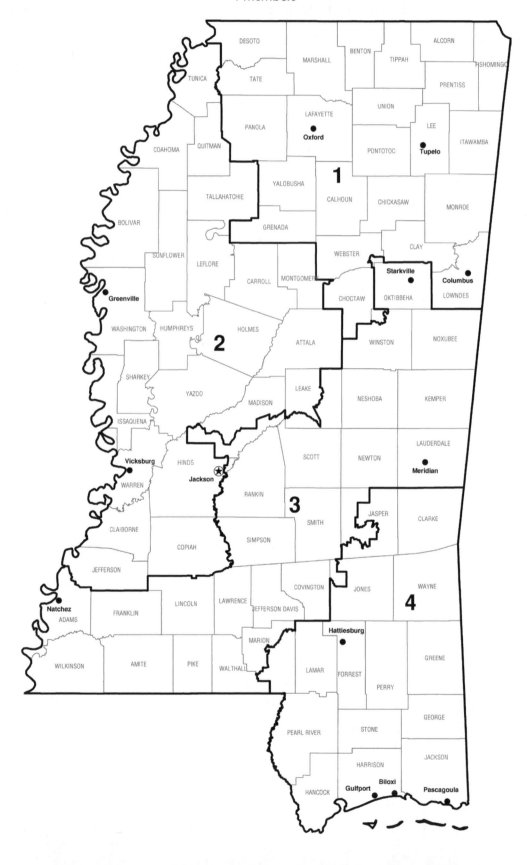

MISSISSIPPI

GOVERNOR
Haley Barbour (R). Reelected 2007 to a four-year term. Previously elected 2003.

SENATORS (2 Republicans)
Thad Cochran (R). Reelected 2008 to a six-year term. Previously elected 2002, 1996, 1990, 1984, 1978.

Roger Wicker (R). Elected 2008 to fill the final four years of the term vacated by the December 2007 resignation of Senator Trent Lott (R). Wicker had earlier been appointed to fill the vacancy and was sworn in as senator on December 31, 2007.

REPRESENTATIVES (3 Republicans, 1 Democrat)
1. Alan Nunnelee (R)
2. Bennie Thompson (D)
3. Gregg Harper (R)
4. Steven Palazzo (R)

POSTWAR VOTE FOR PRESIDENT

		Republican		Democratic				Total Vote		Major Vote	
Year	Total Vote	Vote	Candidate	Vote	Candidate	Other Vote	Rep.-Dem. Plurality	Rep.	Dem.	Rep.	Dem.
2008	1,289,865	724,597	McCain, John	554,662	Obama, Barack	10,606	169,935 R	56.2%	43.0%	56.6%	43.4%
2004	1,152,145	684,981	Bush, George W.	458,094	Kerry, John	9,070	226,887 R	59.5%	39.8%	59.9%	40.1%
2000**	994,184	572,844	Bush, George W.	404,614	Gore, Al	16,726	168,230 R	57.6%	40.7%	58.6%	41.4%
1996**	893,857	439,838	Dole, Bob	394,022	Clinton, Bill	59,997	45,816 R	49.2%	44.1%	52.7%	47.3%
1992**	981,793	487,793	Bush, George	400,258	Clinton, Bill	93,742	87,535 R	49.7%	40.8%	54.9%	45.1%
1988	931,527	557,890	Bush, George	363,921	Dukakis, Michael S.	9,716	193,969 R	59.9%	39.1%	60.5%	39.5%
1984	941,104	582,377	Reagan, Ronald	352,192	Mondale, Walter F.	6,535	230,185 R	61.9%	37.4%	62.3%	37.7%
1980**	892,620	441,089	Reagan, Ronald	429,281	Carter, Jimmy	22,250	11,808 R	49.4%	48.1%	50.7%	49.3%
1976	769,361	366,846	Ford, Gerald R.	381,309	Carter, Jimmy	21,206	14,463 D	47.7%	49.6%	49.0%	51.0%
1972	645,963	505,125	Nixon, Richard M.	126,782	McGovern, George S.	14,056	378,343 R	78.2%	19.6%	79.9%	20.1%
1968**	654,509	88,516	Nixon, Richard M.	150,644	Humphrey, Hubert H.	415,349	264,705 A	13.5%	23.0%	37.0%	63.0%
1964	409,146	356,528	Goldwater, Barry M.	52,618	Johnson, Lyndon B.		303,910 R	87.1%	12.9%	87.1%	12.9%
1960**	298,171	73,561	Nixon, Richard M.	108,362	Kennedy, John F.	116,248	7,886 U	24.7%	36.3%	40.4%	59.6%
1956	248,104	60,685	Eisenhower, Dwight D.	144,453	Stevenson, Adlai E.	42,966	83,768 D	24.5%	58.2%	29.6%	70.4%
1952	285,532	112,966	Eisenhower, Dwight D.	172,566	Stevenson, Adlai E.		59,600 D	39.6%	60.4%	39.6%	60.4%
1948**	192,190	5,043	Dewey, Thomas E.	19,384	Truman, Harry S.	167,763	148,154 SR	2.6%	10.1%	20.6%	79.4%

**In past elections, the other vote included: 2000 - 8,122 Green (Ralph Nader); 1996 - 52,222 Reform (Ross Perot); 1992 - 85,626 Independent (Perot); 1980 - 12,036 Independent (John Anderson); 1968 - 415,349 American Independent (George Wallace); 1960 - 116,248 Unpledged Independent Democratic electors; 1948 - 167,538 States' Rights (Strom Thurmond). Thurmond won Mississippi in 1948 with 87.2 percent of the vote. The slate of Unpledged Independent Democratic electors carried the state in 1960 with 39.0 percent. Wallace won Mississippi in 1968 with 63.5 percent of the vote.

MISSISSIPPI

POSTWAR VOTE FOR GOVERNOR

Year	Total Vote	Republican		Democratic		Other Vote	Rep.-Dem. Plurality	Percentage			
								Total Vote		Major Vote	
		Vote	Candidate	Vote	Candidate			Rep.	Dem.	Rep.	Dem.
2007	744,039	430,807	Barbour, Haley	313,232	Eaves, John A.		117,575 R	57.9%	42.1%	57.9%	42.1%
2003	894,487	470,404	Barbour, Haley	409,787	Musgrove, Ronnie	14,296	60,617 R	52.6%	45.8%	53.4%	46.6%
1999**	763,938	370,691	Parker, Mike	379,034	Musgrove, Ronnie	14,213	8,343 D	48.5%	49.6%	49.4%	50.6%
1995	819,471	455,261	Fordice, Kirk	364,210	Molpus, Dick		91,051 R	55.6%	44.4%	55.6%	44.4%
1991	711,188	361,500	Fordice, Kirk	338,435	Mabus, Ray	11,253	23,065 R	50.8%	47.6%	51.6%	48.4%
1987	721,695	336,006	Reed, Jack	385,689	Mabus, Ray		49,683 D	46.6%	53.4%	46.6%	53.4%
1983	742,737	288,764	Bramlett, Leon	409,209	Allain, William A.	44,764	120,445 D	38.9%	55.1%	41.4%	58.6%
1979	677,322	263,702	Carmichael, Gil	413,620	Winter, William F.		149,918 D	38.9%	61.1%	38.9%	61.1%
1975	708,033	319,632	Carmichael, Gil	369,568	Finch, Cliff	18,833	49,936 D	45.1%	52.2%	46.4%	53.6%
1971**	780,537		—	601,122	Waller, William L.	179,415	601,122 D		77.0%		100.0%
1967	448,697	133,379	Phillips, Rubel L.	315,318	Williams, John Bell		181,939 D	29.7%	70.3%	29.7%	70.3%
1963	363,971	138,515	Phillips, Rubel L.	225,456	Johnson, Paul B.		86,941 D	38.1%	61.9%	38.1%	61.9%
1959	57,671		—	57,671	Barnett, Ross R.		57,671 D		100.0%		100.0%
1955	40,707		—	40,707	Coleman, James P.		40,707 D		100.0%		100.0%
1951	43,422		—	43,422	White, Hugh		43,422 D		100.0%		100.0%
1947	166,095		—	161,993	Wright, Fielding L.	4,102	161,993 D		97.5%		100.0%

**In past elections, the other vote included: 1971 - 172,762 Independent (Charles Evers). In 1999 no candidate received a majority of the vote. Democrat Ronnie Musgrove was elected in January 2000 by the Mississippi House of Representatives. The Republican Party did not run a gubernatorial candidate in 1947, 1951, 1955, 1959 and 1971.

POSTWAR VOTE FOR SENATOR

Year	Total Vote	Republican		Democratic		Other Vote	Rep.-Dem. Plurality	Percentage			
								Total Vote		Major Vote	
		Vote	Candidate	Vote	Candidate			Rep.	Dem.	Rep.	Dem.
2008	1,247,026	766,111	Cochran, Thad	480,915	Fleming, Erik R.		285,196 R	61.4%	38.6%	61.4%	38.6%
2008S	1,243,473	683,409	Wicker, Roger	560,064	Musgrove, Ronnie		123,345 R	55.0%	45.0%	55.0%	45.0%
2006	610,921	388,399	Lott, Trent	213,000	Fleming, Erik R.	9,522	175,399 R	63.6%	34.9%	64.6%	35.4%
2002**	630,495	533,269	Cochran, Thad	—		97,226	533,269 R	84.6%		100.0%	
2000	994,144	654,941	Lott, Trent	314,090	Brown, Troy	25,113	340,851 R	65.9%	31.6%	67.6%	32.4%
1996	878,662	624,154	Cochran, Thad	240,647	Hunt, James W.	13,861	383,507 R	71.0%	27.4%	72.2%	27.8%
1994	608,085	418,333	Lott, Trent	189,752	Harper, Ken		228,581 R	68.8%	31.2%	68.8%	31.2%
1990	274,244	274,244	Cochran, Thad	—			274,244 R	100.0%		100.0%	
1988	946,719	510,380	Lott, Trent	436,339	Dowdy, Wayne		74,041 R	53.9%	46.1%	53.9%	46.1%
1984	952,240	580,314	Cochran, Thad	371,926	Winter, William F.		208,388 R	60.9%	39.1%	60.9%	39.1%
1982	645,026	230,927	Barbour, Haley	414,099	Stennis, John		183,172 D	35.8%	64.2%	35.8%	64.2%
1978**	583,936	263,089	Cochran, Thad	185,454	Dantin, Maurice	135,393	77,635 R	45.1%	31.8%	58.7%	41.3%
1976	554,433		—	554,433	Stennis, John		554,433 D		100.0%		100.0%
1972	645,746	249,779	Carmichael, Gil	375,102	Eastland, James O.	20,865	125,323 D	38.7%	58.1%	40.0%	60.0%
1970**	324,215		—	286,622	Stennis, John	37,593	286,622 D		88.4%		100.0%
1966	393,900	105,150	Walker, Prentiss	258,248	Eastland, James O.	30,502	153,098 D	26.7%	65.6%	28.9%	71.1%
1964	343,364		—	343,364	Stennis, John		343,364 D		100.0%		100.0%
1960	266,148	21,807	Moore, Joe A.	244,341	Eastland, James O.		222,534 D	8.2%	91.8%	8.2%	91.8%
1958	61,039		—	61,039	Stennis, John		61,039 D		100.0%		100.0%
1954	105,526	4,678	White, James A.	100,848	Eastland, James O.		96,170 D	4.4%	95.6%	4.4%	95.6%
1952	233,919		—	233,919	Stennis, John		233,919 D		100.0%		100.0%
1948	151,478		—	151,478	Eastland, James O.		151,478 D		100.0%		100.0%
1947S	193,709		[See note below]				D				
1946	46,747		—	46,747	Bilbo, Theodore		46,747 D		100.0%		100.0%

**In past elections, the other vote included: 2002 - 97,226 Reform (Shawn O'Hara); 1978 - 133,646 Independent (Charles Evers); 1970 - 37,593 Independent (William R. Thompson). The 1947 election and one of the 2008 elections were for a short term. Both were held without party designation or nomination. In 1947 John Stennis received 52,068 votes (26.9 percent of the total vote) and won the election with a 6,343-vote plurality. Other candidates included: 45,725 W. M. Colmer; 43,642 Forrest B. Jackson; 27,159 Paul B. Johnson; 24,492 John E. Rankin. The Republican Party did not run a candidate in Senate elections in 1946, 1948, 1952, 1958, 1964, 1970, and 1976. The Democratic Party did not run a candidate in Senate elections in 1990 and 2002.

MISSISSIPPI

HOUSE OF REPRESENTATIVES

										Percentage			
			Republican			Democratic		Other	Rep.-Dem.	Total Vote		Major Vote	
CD	Year	Total Vote	Vote	Candidate	Vote	Candidate	Vote	Plurality		Rep.	Dem.	Rep.	Dem.
1	2010	219,093	121,074	NUNNELEE, ALAN	89,388	CHILDERS, TRAVIS W.*	8,631	31,686 R		55.3%	40.8%	57.5%	42.5%
1	2008	341,389	149,818	DAVIS, GREG	185,959	CHILDERS, TRAVIS W.*	5,612	36,141 D		43.9%	54.5%	44.6%	55.4%
1	2006	144,272	95,098	WICKER, ROGER*	49,174	HURT, JAMES K. "KEN"		45,924 R		65.9%	34.1%	65.9%	34.1%
1	2004	277,584	219,328	WICKER, ROGER*		—	58,256	219,328 R		79.0%		100.0%	
1	2002	133,567	95,404	WICKER, ROGER*	32,318	WEATHERS, REX N.	5,845	63,086 R		71.4%	24.2%	74.7%	25.3%
2	2010	171,356	64,499	MARCY, BILL	105,327	THOMPSON, BENNIE*	1,530	40,828 D		37.6%	61.5%	38.0%	62.0%
2	2008	291,970	90,364	COOK, RICHARD	201,606	THOMPSON, BENNIE*		111,242 D		30.9%	69.1%	30.9%	69.1%
2	2006	155,832	55,672	BROWN, YVONNE R.	100,160	THOMPSON, BENNIE*		44,488 D		35.7%	64.3%	35.7%	64.3%
2	2004	264,869	107,647	LeSUEUR, CLINTON B.	154,626	THOMPSON, BENNIE*	2,596	46,979 D		40.6%	58.4%	41.0%	59.0%
2	2002	163,050	69,711	LeSUEUR, CLINTON B.	89,913	THOMPSON, BENNIE*	3,426	20,202 D		42.8%	55.1%	43.7%	56.3%
3	2010	194,716	132,393	HARPER, GREGG*	60,737	GILL, JOEL L.	1,586	71,656 R		68.0%	31.2%	68.6%	31.4%
3	2008	340,869	213,171	HARPER, GREGG	127,698	GILL, JOEL L.		85,473 R		62.5%	37.5%	62.5%	37.5%
3	2006	161,480	125,421	PICKERING, CHARLES W. "CHIP" JR.*		—	36,059	125,421 R		77.7%		100.0%	
3	2004	293,368	234,874	PICKERING, CHARLES W. "CHIP" JR.*		—	58,494	234,874 R		80.1%		100.0%	
3	2002	219,151	139,329	PICKERING, CHARLES W. "CHIP" JR.*	76,184	SHOWS, RONNIE*	3,638	63,145 R		63.6%	34.8%	64.6%	35.4%
4	2010	203,384	105,613	PALAZZO, STEVEN	95,243	TAYLOR, GENE*	2,528	10,370 R		51.9%	46.8%	52.6%	47.4%
4	2008	290,519	73,977	McCAY, JOHN III	216,542	TAYLOR, GENE*		142,565 D		25.5%	74.5%	25.5%	74.5%
4	2006	139,113	28,117	McDONNELL, RANDY	110,996	TAYLOR, GENE*		82,879 D		20.2%	79.8%	20.2%	79.8%
4	2004	280,382	96,740	LOTT, MICHAEL	181,614	TAYLOR, GENE*	2,028	84,874 D		34.5%	64.8%	34.8%	65.2%
4	2002	161,868	34,373	MERTZ, KARL CLEVELAND	121,742	TAYLOR, GENE*	5,753	87,369 D		21.2%	75.2%	22.0%	78.0%
TOTAL	2010	788,549	423,579		350,695		14,275	72,884 R		53.7%	44.5%	54.7%	45.3%
TOTAL	2008	1,264,747	527,330		731,805		5,612	204,475 D		41.7%	57.9%	41.9%	58.1%
TOTAL	2006	600,697	304,308		260,330		36,059	43,978 R		50.7%	43.3%	53.9%	46.1%
TOTAL	2004	1,116,203	658,589		336,240		121,374	322,349 R		59.0%	30.1%	66.2%	33.8%
TOTAL	2002	677,636	338,817		320,157		18,662	18,660 R		50.0%	47.2%	51.4%	48.6%

An asterisk (*) denotes incumbent.

MISSISSIPPI

GENERAL AND PRIMARY ELECTIONS

2010 GENERAL ELECTIONS

House   Other vote was:

CD 1   2,180 Independent (Wally Pang); 2,020 Independent (Les Green); 1,882 Independent (A.G. Baddley); 1,235 Constitution (Gail Giaramita); 478 Independent (Rick "Rico" Hoskins); 447 Libertarian (Harold M. Taylor); 389 Reform (Barbara Dale Washer).

CD 2   1,530 Reform (Ashley Norwood).

CD 3   1,586 Reform (Tracella Lou O'Hara Hill).

CD 4   1,741 Libertarian (Kenneth "Tim" Hampton); 787 Reform (Anna Jewel Revies).

2010 PRIMARY ELECTIONS

Primary	June 1, 2010	**Registration** (as of May 26, 2010 - includes 170,023 inactive registrants)	1,970,294	No Party Registration
Primary Runoff	June 22, 2010			

Primary Type   Open—Any registered voter could participate in the party primary of their choice. But any voter who cast a ballot in the primary of one party could not vote in the runoff of the other party.

	REPUBLICAN PRIMARIES			DEMOCRATIC PRIMARIES		
Congressional District 1	Alan Nunnelee	20,236	51.8%	Travis W. Childers*	Unopposed	
	Henry Ross	12,894	33.0%			
	Angela McGlowan	5,924	15.2%			
	TOTAL	39,054				
Congressional District 2	Richard Cook	2,232	34.8%	Bennie Thompson*	Unopposed	
	Bill Marcy	2,231	34.8%			
	George Bailey	1,957	30.5%			
	TOTAL	6,420				
	PRIMARY RUNOFF					
	Bill Marcy	3,126	58.4%			
	Richard Cook	2,230	41.6%			
	TOTAL	5,356				
Congressional District 3	Gregg Harper*	Unopposed		Joel L. Gill	3,805	52.3%
				James D. Jackson	2,138	29.4%
				Shawn O'Hara	1,328	18.3%
				TOTAL	7,271	
Congressional District 4	Steven Palazzo	15,556	57.2%	Gene Taylor*	Unopposed	
	Joe Tegerdine	11,663	42.8%			
	TOTAL	27,219				

An asterisk (*) denotes incumbent. If no candidate received a majority of the primary vote, a runoff was held between the top two finishers. The names of unopposed candidates did not have to appear on the primary ballot; therefore, in some races no votes were cast for these candidates.

MISSOURI

Congressional districts first established for elections held in 2002
9 members

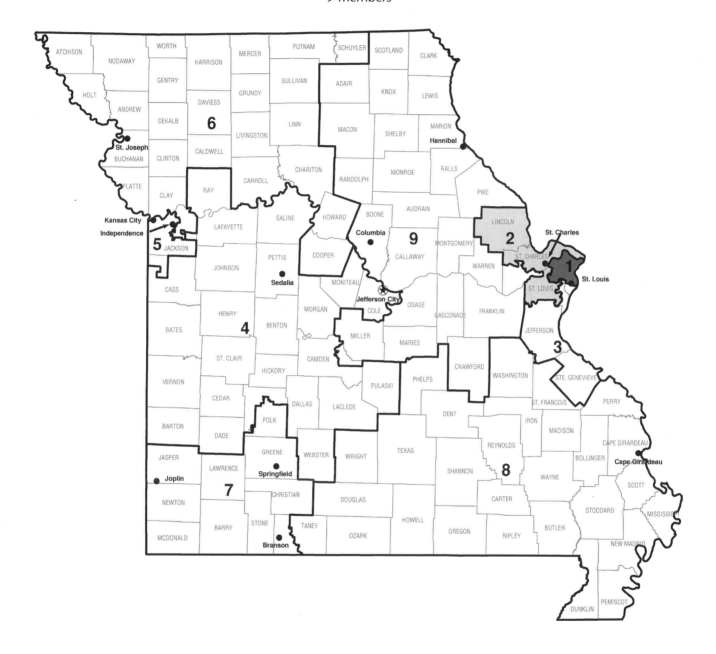

MISSOURI

GOVERNOR
Jeremiah W. "Jay" Nixon (D). Elected 2008 to a four-year term.

SENATORS (1 Democrat, 1 Republican)
Roy Blunt (R). Elected 2010 to a six-year term.

Claire McCaskill (D). Elected 2006 to a six-year term.

REPRESENTATIVES (6 Republicans, 3 Democrats)

1. William Lacy Clay (D)	4. Vicky Hartzler (R)	7. Billy Long (R)
2. Todd Akin (R)	5. Emanuel Cleaver II (D)	8. Jo Ann Emerson (R)
3. Russ Carnahan (D)	6. Sam Graves (R)	9. Blaine Luetkemeyer (R)

POSTWAR VOTE FOR PRESIDENT

		Republican		Democratic				Percentage			
								Total Vote		Major Vote	
Year	Total Vote	Vote	Candidate	Vote	Candidate	Other Vote	Rep.-Dem. Plurality	Rep.	Dem.	Rep.	Dem.
2008	2,925,205	1,445,814	McCain, John	1,441,911	Obama, Barack	37,480	3,903 R	49.4%	49.3%	50.1%	49.9%
2004	2,731,364	1,455,713	Bush, George W.	1,259,171	Kerry, John	16,480	196,542 R	53.3%	46.1%	53.6%	46.4%
2000**	2,359,892	1,189,924	Bush, George W.	1,111,138	Gore, Al	58,830	78,786 R	50.4%	47.1%	51.7%	48.3%
1996**	2,158,065	890,016	Dole, Bob	1,025,935	Clinton, Bill	242,114	135,919 D	41.2%	47.5%	46.5%	53.5%
1992**	2,391,565	811,159	Bush, George	1,053,873	Clinton, Bill	526,533	242,714 D	33.9%	44.1%	43.5%	56.5%
1988	2,093,713	1,084,953	Bush, George	1,001,619	Dukakis, Michael S.	7,141	83,334 R	51.8%	47.8%	52.0%	48.0%
1984	2,122,783	1,274,188	Reagan, Ronald	848,583	Mondale, Walter F.	12	425,605 R	60.0%	40.0%	60.0%	40.0%
1980**	2,099,824	1,074,181	Reagan, Ronald	931,182	Carter, Jimmy	94,461	142,999 R	51.2%	44.3%	53.6%	46.4%
1976	1,953,600	927,443	Ford, Gerald R.	998,387	Carter, Jimmy	27,770	70,944 D	47.5%	51.1%	48.2%	51.8%
1972	1,855,803	1,153,852	Nixon, Richard M.	697,147	McGovern, George S.	4,804	456,705 R	62.2%	37.6%	62.3%	37.7%
1968**	1,809,502	811,932	Nixon, Richard M.	791,444	Humphrey, Hubert H.	206,126	20,488 R	44.9%	43.7%	50.6%	49.4%
1964	1,817,879	653,535	Goldwater, Barry M.	1,164,344	Johnson, Lyndon B.		510,809 D	36.0%	64.0%	36.0%	64.0%
1960	1,934,422	962,221	Nixon, Richard M.	972,201	Kennedy, John F.		9,980 D	49.7%	50.3%	49.7%	50.3%
1956	1,832,562	914,289	Eisenhower, Dwight D.	918,273	Stevenson, Adlai E.		3,984 D	49.9%	50.1%	49.9%	50.1%
1952	1,892,062	959,429	Eisenhower, Dwight D.	929,830	Stevenson, Adlai E.	2,803	29,599 R	50.7%	49.1%	50.8%	49.2%
1948	1,578,628	655,039	Dewey, Thomas E.	917,315	Truman, Harry S.	6,274	262,276 D	41.5%	58.1%	41.7%	58.3%

**In past elections, the other vote included: 2000 - 38,515 Green (Ralph Nader); 1996 - 217,188 Reform (Ross Perot); 1992 - 518,741 Independent (Perot); 1980 - 77,920 Independent (John Anderson); 1968 - 206,126 American Independent (George Wallace).

MISSOURI

POSTWAR VOTE FOR GOVERNOR

| | | Republican | | Democratic | | Other Vote | Rep.-Dem. Plurality | Percentage | | | |
| | Total Vote | | | | | | | Total Vote | | Major Vote | |
Year		Vote	Candidate	Vote	Candidate			Rep.	Dem.	Rep.	Dem.
2008	2,877,778	1,136,364	Hulshof, Kenny	1,680,611	Nixon, Jeremiah W. "Jay"	60,803	544,247 D	39.5%	58.4%	40.3%	59.7%
2004	2,719,599	1,382,419	Blunt, Matt	1,301,442	McCaskill, Claire	35,738	80,977 R	50.8%	47.9%	51.5%	48.5%
2000	2,346,830	1,131,307	Talent, Jim	1,152,752	Holden, Bob	62,771	21,445 D	48.2%	49.1%	49.5%	50.5%
1996	2,142,518	866,268	Kelly, Margaret	1,224,801	Carnahan, Mel	51,449	358,533 D	40.4%	57.2%	41.4%	58.6%
1992	2,344,121	968,574	Webster, William L.	1,375,425	Carnahan, Mel	122	406,851 D	41.3%	58.7%	41.3%	58.7%
1988	2,085,928	1,339,531	Ashcroft, John	724,919	Hearnes, Betty C.	21,478	614,612 R	64.2%	34.8%	64.9%	35.1%
1984	2,108,210	1,194,506	Ashcroft, John	913,700	Rothman, Kenneth J.	4	280,806 R	56.7%	43.3%	56.7%	43.3%
1980	2,088,028	1,098,950	Bond, Christopher S.	981,884	Teasdale, Joseph P.	7,194	117,066 R	52.6%	47.0%	52.8%	47.2%
1976	1,933,575	958,110	Bond, Christopher S.	971,184	Teasdale, Joseph P.	4,281	13,074 D	49.6%	50.2%	49.7%	50.3%
1972	1,865,683	1,029,451	Bond, Christopher S.	832,751	Dowd, Edward L.	3,481	196,700 R	55.2%	44.6%	55.3%	44.7%
1968	1,764,602	691,797	Roos, Lawrence K.	1,072,805	Hearnes, Warren E.		381,008 D	39.2%	60.8%	39.2%	60.8%
1964	1,789,600	678,949	Shepley, Ethan	1,110,651	Hearnes, Warren E.		431,702 D	37.9%	62.1%	37.9%	62.1%
1960	1,887,331	792,131	Farmer, Edward G.	1,095,200	Dalton, John M.		303,069 D	42.0%	58.0%	42.0%	58.0%
1956	1,808,338	866,810	Hocker, Lon	941,528	Blair, James T.		74,718 D	47.9%	52.1%	47.9%	52.1%
1952	1,871,095	886,370	Elliott, Howard	983,166	Donnelly, Phil M.	1,559	96,796 D	47.4%	52.5%	47.4%	52.6%
1948	1,567,338	670,064	Thompson, Murray	893,092	Smith, Forrest	4,182	223,028 D	42.8%	57.0%	42.9%	57.1%

POSTWAR VOTE FOR SENATOR

| | | Republican | | Democratic | | Other Vote | Rep.-Dem. Plurality | Percentage | | | |
| | Total Vote | | | | | | | Total Vote | | Major Vote | |
Year		Vote	Candidate	Vote	Candidate			Rep.	Dem.	Rep.	Dem.
2010	1,943,899	1,054,160	Blunt, Roy	789,736	Carnahan, Robin	100,003	264,424 R	54.2%	40.6%	57.2%	42.8%
2006	2,128,459	1,006,941	Talent, Jim	1,055,255	McCaskill, Claire	66,263	48,314 D	47.3%	49.6%	48.8%	51.2%
2004	2,706,402	1,518,089	Bond, Christopher S.	1,158,261	Farmer, Nancy	30,052	359,828 R	56.1%	42.8%	56.7%	43.3%
2002S	1,877,620	935,032	Talent, Jim	913,778	Carnahan, Jean	28,810	21,254 R	49.8%	48.7%	50.6%	49.4%
2000**	2,361,586	1,142,852	Ashcroft, John	1,191,812	Carnahan, Mel	26,922	48,960 D	48.4%	50.5%	49.0%	51.0%
1998	1,576,857	830,625	Bond, Christopher S.	690,208	Nixon, Jeremiah W.	56,024	140,417 R	52.7%	43.8%	54.6%	45.4%
1994	1,775,116	1,060,149	Ashcroft, John	633,697	Wheat, Alan	81,270	426,452 R	59.7%	35.7%	62.6%	37.4%
1992	2,354,925	1,221,901	Bond, Christopher S.	1,057,967	Rothman-Serot, Geri	75,057	163,934 R	51.9%	44.9%	53.6%	46.4%
1988	2,078,875	1,407,416	Danforth, John C.	660,045	Nixon, Jeremiah W. "Jay"	11,414	747,371 R	67.7%	31.8%	68.1%	31.9%
1986	1,477,327	777,612	Bond, Christopher S.	699,624	Woods, Harriett	91	77,988 R	52.6%	47.4%	52.6%	47.4%
1982	1,543,521	784,876	Danforth, John C.	758,629	Woods, Harriett	16	26,247 R	50.8%	49.1%	50.9%	49.1%
1980	2,066,965	985,399	McNary, Gene	1,074,859	Eagleton, Thomas F.	6,707	89,460 D	47.7%	52.0%	47.8%	52.2%
1976	1,914,777	1,090,067	Danforth, John C.	813,571	Hearnes, Warren E.	11,139	276,496 R	56.9%	42.5%	57.3%	42.7%
1974	1,224,303	480,900	Curtis, Thomas B.	735,433	Eagleton, Thomas F.	7,970	254,533 D	39.3%	60.1%	39.5%	60.5%
1970	1,283,912	617,903	Danforth, John C.	655,431	Symington, Stuart	10,578	37,528 D	48.1%	51.0%	48.5%	51.5%
1968	1,737,958	850,544	Curtis, Thomas B.	887,414	Eagleton, Thomas F.		36,870 D	48.9%	51.1%	48.9%	51.1%
1964	1,783,043	596,377	Bradshaw, Jean P.	1,186,666	Symington, Stuart		590,289 D	33.4%	66.6%	33.4%	66.6%
1962	1,222,259	555,330	Kemper, Crosby	666,929	Long, Edward V.		111,599 D	45.4%	54.6%	45.4%	54.6%
1960S	1,880,232	880,576	Hocker, Lon	999,656	Long, Edward V.		119,080 D	46.8%	53.2%	46.8%	53.2%
1958	1,173,903	393,847	Palmer, Hazel	780,056	Symington, Stuart		386,209 D	33.6%	66.4%	33.6%	66.4%
1956	1,800,984	785,048	Douglas, Herbert	1,015,936	Hennings, Thomas C.		230,888 D	43.6%	56.4%	43.6%	56.4%
1952	1,868,083	858,170	Kem, James P.	1,008,523	Symington, Stuart	1,390	150,353 D	45.9%	54.0%	46.0%	54.0%
1950	1,279,414	592,922	Donnell, Forrest C.	685,732	Hennings, Thomas C.	760	92,810 D	46.3%	53.6%	46.4%	53.6%
1946	1,084,100	572,556	Kem, James P.	511,544	Briggs, Frank P.		61,012 R	52.8%	47.2%	52.8%	47.2%

**In 2000 the Democratic candidate, Mel Carnahan, was killed in an airplane crash in October but his name remained on the ballot and he won the election in November. Subsequently, his widow, Jean Carnahan, was appointed to fill the seat until an election could be held in 2002 for the remaining four years of the term. The 1960 election was for a short term to fill a vacancy.

MISSOURI

SENATOR 2010

2010 Census Population	County	Total Vote	Republican	Democratic	Other	Rep.-Dem. Plurality		Percentage			
								Total Vote		Major Vote	
								Rep.	Dem.	Rep.	Dem.
25,607	ADAIR	7,589	4,464	2,872	253	1,592	R	58.8%	37.8%	60.9%	39.1%
17,291	ANDREW	5,899	3,864	1,759	276	2,105	R	65.5%	29.8%	68.7%	31.3%
5,685	ATCHISON	2,088	1,470	527	91	943	R	70.4%	25.2%	73.6%	26.4%
25,529	AUDRAIN	7,574	4,512	2,538	524	1,974	R	59.6%	33.5%	64.0%	36.0%
35,597	BARRY	10,600	7,549	2,356	695	5,193	R	71.2%	22.2%	76.2%	23.8%
12,402	BARTON	4,571	3,651	739	181	2,912	R	79.9%	16.2%	83.2%	16.8%
17,049	BATES	5,834	3,495	1,954	385	1,541	R	59.9%	33.5%	64.1%	35.9%
19,056	BENTON	7,446	4,676	2,217	553	2,459	R	62.8%	29.8%	67.8%	32.2%
12,363	BOLLINGER	4,113	2,891	1,012	210	1,879	R	70.3%	24.6%	74.1%	25.9%
162,642	BOONE	51,454	25,253	23,117	3,084	2,136	R	49.1%	44.9%	52.2%	47.8%
89,201	BUCHANAN	24,161	13,107	9,771	1,283	3,336	R	54.2%	40.4%	57.3%	42.7%
42,794	BUTLER	11,665	8,229	2,938	498	5,291	R	70.5%	25.2%	73.7%	26.3%
9,424	CALDWELL	3,322	2,083	979	260	1,104	R	62.7%	29.5%	68.0%	32.0%
44,332	CALLAWAY	13,621	8,277	4,301	1,043	3,976	R	60.8%	31.6%	65.8%	34.2%
44,002	CAMDEN	16,727	11,035	4,558	1,134	6,477	R	66.0%	27.2%	70.8%	29.2%
75,674	CAPE GIRARDEAU	27,110	18,728	7,216	1,166	11,512	R	69.1%	26.6%	72.2%	27.8%
9,295	CARROLL	3,175	2,199	818	158	1,381	R	69.3%	25.8%	72.9%	27.1%
6,265	CARTER	2,159	1,326	727	106	599	R	61.4%	33.7%	64.6%	35.4%
99,478	CASS	35,544	21,923	11,619	2,002	10,304	R	61.7%	32.7%	65.4%	34.6%
13,982	CEDAR	4,868	3,310	1,225	333	2,085	R	68.0%	25.2%	73.0%	27.0%
7,831	CHARITON	3,050	1,807	1,021	222	786	R	59.2%	33.5%	63.9%	36.1%
77,422	CHRISTIAN	26,783	19,047	6,014	1,722	13,033	R	71.1%	22.5%	76.0%	24.0%
7,139	CLARK	2,811	1,501	1,177	133	324	R	53.4%	41.9%	56.0%	44.0%
221,939	CLAY	69,968	37,966	28,161	3,841	9,805	R	54.3%	40.2%	57.4%	42.6%
20,743	CLINTON	7,277	4,128	2,706	443	1,422	R	56.7%	37.2%	60.4%	39.6%
75,990	COLE	28,482	18,240	8,801	1,441	9,439	R	64.0%	30.9%	67.5%	32.5%
17,601	COOPER	5,451	3,480	1,555	416	1,925	R	63.8%	28.5%	69.1%	30.9%
24,696	CRAWFORD	7,202	4,346	2,280	576	2,066	R	60.3%	31.7%	65.6%	34.4%
7,883	DADE	3,225	2,329	704	192	1,625	R	72.2%	21.8%	76.8%	23.2%
16,777	DALLAS	5,874	3,823	1,511	540	2,312	R	65.1%	25.7%	71.7%	28.3%
8,433	DAVIESS	2,842	1,750	848	244	902	R	61.6%	29.8%	67.4%	32.6%
12,892	DE KALB	3,514	2,210	1,086	218	1,124	R	62.9%	30.9%	67.1%	32.9%
15,657	DENT	5,156	3,437	1,370	349	2,067	R	66.7%	26.6%	71.5%	28.5%
13,684	DOUGLAS	5,225	3,522	1,199	504	2,323	R	67.4%	22.9%	74.6%	25.4%
31,953	DUNKLIN	6,892	4,306	2,363	223	1,943	R	62.5%	34.3%	64.6%	35.4%
101,492	FRANKLIN	33,623	19,835	11,050	2,738	8,785	R	59.0%	32.9%	64.2%	35.8%
15,222	GASCONADE	5,589	3,606	1,608	375	1,998	R	64.5%	28.8%	69.2%	30.8%
6,738	GENTRY	2,320	1,371	781	168	590	R	59.1%	33.7%	63.7%	36.3%
275,174	GREENE	88,268	55,068	28,494	4,706	26,574	R	62.4%	32.3%	65.9%	34.1%
10,261	GRUNDY	3,142	2,113	744	285	1,369	R	67.3%	23.7%	74.0%	26.0%
8,957	HARRISON	2,862	1,966	678	218	1,288	R	68.7%	23.7%	74.4%	25.6%
22,272	HENRY	8,159	4,647	2,923	589	1,724	R	57.0%	35.8%	61.4%	38.6%
9,627	HICKORY	3,991	2,308	1,361	322	947	R	57.8%	34.1%	62.9%	37.1%
4,912	HOLT	1,762	1,306	372	84	934	R	74.1%	21.1%	77.8%	22.2%
10,144	HOWARD	3,676	2,199	1,263	214	936	R	59.8%	34.4%	63.5%	36.5%
40,400	HOWELL	11,761	7,752	3,176	833	4,576	R	65.9%	27.0%	70.9%	29.1%
10,630	IRON	3,016	1,388	1,346	282	42	R	46.0%	44.6%	50.8%	49.2%
674,158	JACKSON	117,078	63,870	47,634	5,574	16,236	R	54.6%	40.7%	57.3%	42.7%

MISSOURI

SENATOR 2010

2010 Census Population	County	Total Vote	Republican	Democratic	Other	Rep.-Dem. Plurality		Percentage			
								Total Vote		Major Vote	
								Rep.	Dem.	Rep.	Dem.
117,404	JASPER	31,521	23,355	6,779	1,387	16,576	R	74.1%	21.5%	77.5%	22.5%
218,733	JEFFERSON	66,089	35,585	25,689	4,815	9,896	R	53.8%	38.9%	58.1%	41.9%
52,595	JOHNSON	14,889	8,677	5,230	982	3,447	R	58.3%	35.1%	62.4%	37.6%
*See Note	KANSAS CITY	86,520	21,866	62,448	2,206	40,582	D	25.3%	72.2%	25.9%	74.1%
4,131	KNOX	1,616	1,013	546	57	467	R	62.7%	33.8%	65.0%	35.0%
35,571	LACLEDE	12,063	8,414	2,817	832	5,597	R	69.8%	23.4%	74.9%	25.1%
33,381	LAFAYETTE	11,872	7,068	4,181	623	2,887	R	59.5%	35.2%	62.8%	37.2%
38,634	LAWRENCE	12,031	8,529	2,680	822	5,849	R	70.9%	22.3%	76.1%	23.9%
10,211	LEWIS	3,415	2,095	1,182	138	913	R	61.3%	34.6%	63.9%	36.1%
52,566	LINCOLN	16,001	9,027	5,351	1,623	3,676	R	56.4%	33.4%	62.8%	37.2%
12,761	LINN	4,277	2,439	1,525	313	914	R	57.0%	35.7%	61.5%	38.5%
15,195	LIVINGSTON	4,514	2,901	1,356	257	1,545	R	64.3%	30.0%	68.1%	31.9%
23,083	MCDONALD	5,654	4,199	1,127	328	3,072	R	74.3%	19.9%	78.8%	21.2%
15,566	MACON	5,811	3,591	1,904	316	1,687	R	61.8%	32.8%	65.4%	34.6%
12,226	MADISON	3,546	2,148	1,190	208	958	R	60.6%	33.6%	64.3%	35.7%
9,176	MARIES	3,531	2,227	1,053	251	1,174	R	63.1%	29.8%	67.9%	32.1%
28,781	MARION	8,834	5,713	2,804	317	2,909	R	64.7%	31.7%	67.1%	32.9%
3,785	MERCER	1,230	863	241	126	622	R	70.2%	19.6%	78.2%	21.8%
24,748	MILLER	7,969	5,743	1,696	530	4,047	R	72.1%	21.3%	77.2%	22.8%
14,358	MISSISSIPPI	3,445	2,068	1,252	125	816	R	60.0%	36.3%	62.3%	37.7%
15,607	MONITEAU	5,402	3,585	1,427	390	2,158	R	66.4%	26.4%	71.5%	28.5%
8,840	MONROE	3,148	1,923	1,065	160	858	R	61.1%	33.8%	64.4%	35.6%
12,236	MONTGOMERY	4,334	2,565	1,372	397	1,193	R	59.2%	31.7%	65.2%	34.8%
20,565	MORGAN	7,058	4,488	2,007	563	2,481	R	63.6%	28.4%	69.1%	30.9%
18,956	NEW MADRID	4,684	2,806	1,733	145	1,073	R	59.9%	37.0%	61.8%	38.2%
58,114	NEWTON	18,031	13,625	3,739	667	9,886	R	75.6%	20.7%	78.5%	21.5%
23,370	NODAWAY	6,872	4,195	2,269	408	1,926	R	61.0%	33.0%	64.9%	35.1%
10,881	OREGON	3,490	2,029	1,214	247	815	R	58.1%	34.8%	62.6%	37.4%
13,878	OSAGE	5,693	4,018	1,323	352	2,695	R	70.6%	23.2%	75.2%	24.8%
9,723	OZARK	3,532	2,286	960	286	1,326	R	64.7%	27.2%	70.4%	29.6%
18,296	PEMISCOT	3,453	2,119	1,262	72	857	R	61.4%	36.5%	62.7%	37.3%
18,971	PERRY	6,061	4,068	1,603	390	2,465	R	67.1%	26.4%	71.7%	28.3%
42,201	PETTIS	12,623	8,027	3,763	833	4,264	R	63.6%	29.8%	68.1%	31.9%
45,156	PHELPS	13,985	8,570	4,631	784	3,939	R	61.3%	33.1%	64.9%	35.1%
18,516	PIKE	5,666	3,101	2,056	509	1,045	R	54.7%	36.3%	60.1%	39.9%
89,322	PLATTE	31,091	17,619	12,006	1,466	5,613	R	56.7%	38.6%	59.5%	40.5%
31,137	POLK	9,858	6,794	2,424	640	4,370	R	68.9%	24.6%	73.7%	26.3%
52,274	PULASKI	9,052	6,172	2,357	523	3,815	R	68.2%	26.0%	72.4%	27.6%
4,979	PUTNAM	1,967	1,426	463	78	963	R	72.5%	23.5%	75.5%	24.5%
10,167	RALLS	3,814	2,308	1,360	146	948	R	60.5%	35.7%	62.9%	37.1%
25,414	RANDOLPH	7,640	4,845	2,263	532	2,582	R	63.4%	29.6%	68.2%	31.8%
23,494	RAY	7,558	4,055	3,013	490	1,042	R	53.7%	39.9%	57.4%	42.6%
6,696	REYNOLDS	2,467	1,247	1,012	208	235	R	50.5%	41.0%	55.2%	44.8%
14,100	RIPLEY	3,977	2,526	1,169	282	1,357	R	63.5%	29.4%	68.4%	31.6%
360,485	ST. CHARLES	124,516	73,697	43,960	6,859	29,737	R	59.2%	35.3%	62.6%	37.4%
9,805	ST. CLAIR	3,918	2,408	1,242	268	1,166	R	61.5%	31.7%	66.0%	34.0%
65,359	ST. FRANCOIS	15,599	8,222	6,042	1,335	2,180	R	52.7%	38.7%	57.6%	42.4%
998,954	ST. LOUIS COUNTY	375,434	167,458	195,229	12,747	27,771	D	44.6%	52.0%	46.2%	53.8%
319,294	ST. LOUIS CITY	90,732	16,353	71,938	2,441	55,585	D	18.0%	79.3%	18.5%	81.5%
18,145	STE. GENEVIEVE	5,702	2,688	2,614	400	74	R	47.1%	45.8%	50.7%	49.3%

MISSOURI

SENATOR 2010

2010 Census Population	County	Total Vote	Republican	Democratic	Other	Rep.-Dem. Plurality		Total Vote Rep.	Total Vote Dem.	Major Vote Rep.	Major Vote Dem.
23,370	SALINE	6,887	3,763	2,667	457	1,096	R	54.6%	38.7%	58.5%	41.5%
4,431	SCHUYLER	1,634	930	624	80	306	R	56.9%	38.2%	59.8%	40.2%
4,843	SCOTLAND	1,634	991	593	50	398	R	60.6%	36.3%	62.6%	37.4%
39,191	SCOTT	11,320	7,664	3,161	495	4,503	R	67.7%	27.9%	70.8%	29.2%
8,441	SHANNON	3,007	1,533	1,235	239	298	R	51.0%	41.1%	55.4%	44.6%
6,373	SHELBY	2,801	1,727	996	78	731	R	61.7%	35.6%	63.4%	36.6%
29,968	STODDARD	9,881	6,725	2,766	390	3,959	R	68.1%	28.0%	70.9%	29.1%
32,202	STONE	12,689	8,905	2,897	887	6,008	R	70.2%	22.8%	75.5%	24.5%
6,714	SULLIVAN	2,416	1,458	818	140	640	R	60.3%	33.9%	64.1%	35.9%
51,675	TANEY	15,314	11,026	3,392	896	7,634	R	72.0%	22.1%	76.5%	23.5%
26,008	TEXAS	8,189	5,371	2,268	550	3,103	R	65.6%	27.7%	70.3%	29.7%
21,159	VERNON	6,601	4,555	1,777	269	2,778	R	69.0%	26.9%	71.9%	28.1%
32,513	WARREN	10,732	6,433	3,500	799	2,933	R	59.9%	32.6%	64.8%	35.2%
25,195	WASHINGTON	6,671	3,378	2,780	513	598	R	50.6%	41.7%	54.9%	45.1%
13,521	WAYNE	4,226	2,625	1,411	190	1,214	R	62.1%	33.4%	65.0%	35.0%
36,202	WEBSTER	12,025	7,990	3,130	905	4,860	R	66.4%	26.0%	71.9%	28.1%
2,171	WORTH	964	572	311	81	261	R	59.3%	32.3%	64.8%	35.2%
18,815	WRIGHT	6,204	4,407	1,374	423	3,033	R	71.0%	22.1%	76.2%	23.8%
5,988,927	TOTAL	1,943,899	1,054,160	789,736	100,003	264,424	R	54.2%	40.6%	57.2%	42.8%

The city of Kansas City is located in Jackson County, but its election results are listed separately by state election officials.

MISSOURI

HOUSE OF REPRESENTATIVES

CD	Year	Total Vote	Republican Vote	Republican Candidate	Democratic Vote	Democratic Candidate	Other Vote	Rep.-Dem. Plurality		Total Vote Rep.	Total Vote Dem.	Major Vote Rep.	Major Vote Dem.
1	2010	184,779	43,649	HAMLIN, ROBYN	135,907	CLAY, WILLIAM LACY*	5,223	92,258	D	23.6%	73.6%	24.3%	75.7%
1	2008	279,277	—		242,570	CLAY, WILLIAM LACY*	36,707	242,570	D		86.9%		100.0%
1	2006	194,235	47,893	BYRNE, MARK J.	141,574	CLAY, WILLIAM LACY*	4,768	93,681	D	24.7%	72.9%	25.3%	74.7%
1	2004	283,771	64,791	FARR, LESLIE L. II	213,658	CLAY, WILLIAM LACY*	5,322	148,867	D	22.8%	75.3%	23.3%	76.7%
1	2002	191,055	51,755	SCHWADRON, RICHARD	133,946	CLAY, WILLIAM LACY*	5,354	82,191	D	27.1%	70.1%	27.9%	72.1%
2	2010	265,632	180,481	AKIN, TODD*	77,467	LIEBER, ARTHUR	7,684	103,014	R	67.9%	29.2%	70.0%	30.0%
2	2008	372,972	232,276	AKIN, TODD*	132,068	HAAS, WILLIAM C. "BILL"	8,628	100,208	R	62.3%	35.4%	63.8%	36.2%
2	2006	287,617	176,452	AKIN, TODD*	105,242	WEBER, GEORGE D.	5,923	71,210	R	61.3%	36.6%	62.6%	37.4%
2	2004	349,867	228,725	AKIN, TODD*	115,366	WEBER, GEORGE D.	5,776	113,359	R	65.4%	33.0%	66.5%	33.5%
2	2002	248,828	167,057	AKIN, TODD*	77,223	HOGAN, JOHN	4,548	89,834	R	67.1%	31.0%	68.4%	31.6%
3	2010	203,085	94,757	MARTIN, ED	99,398	CARNAHAN, RUSS*	8,930	4,641	D	46.7%	48.9%	48.8%	51.2%
3	2008	305,071	92,759	SANDER, CHRIS	202,470	CARNAHAN, RUSS*	9,842	109,711	D	30.4%	66.4%	31.4%	68.6%

MISSOURI

HOUSE OF REPRESENTATIVES

			Republican		Democratic				Percentage Total Vote		Percentage Major Vote	
CD	Year	Total Vote	Vote	Candidate	Vote	Candidate	Other Vote	Rep.-Dem. Plurality		Rep.	Dem.	Rep.	Dem.
3	2006	221,448	70,189	BERTELSEN, DAVID	145,219	CARNAHAN, RUSS*	6,040	75,030	D	31.7%	65.6%	32.6%	67.4%
3	2004	277,916	125,422	FEDERER, BILL	146,894	CARNAHAN, RUSS	5,600	21,472	D	45.1%	52.9%	46.1%	53.9%
3	2002	206,878	80,551	ENZ, CATHERINE S.	122,181	GEPHARDT, RICHARD A.*	4,146	41,630	D	38.9%	59.1%	39.7%	60.3%
4	2010	225,056	113,489	HARTZLER, VICKY	101,532	SKELTON, IKE*	10,035	11,957	R	50.4%	45.1%	52.8%	47.2%
4	2008	303,455	103,446	PARNELL, JEFF	200,009	SKELTON, IKE*		96,563	D	34.1%	65.9%	34.1%	65.9%
4	2006	235,525	69,254	NOLAND, JAMES A. "JIM"	159,303	SKELTON, IKE*	6,968	90,049	D	29.4%	67.6%	30.3%	69.7%
4	2004	288,226	93,334	NOLAND, JAMES A. "JIM"	190,800	SKELTON, IKE*	4,092	97,466	D	32.4%	66.2%	32.8%	67.2%
4	2002	210,238	64,451	NOLAND, JAMES A. "JIM"	142,204	SKELTON, IKE*	3,583	77,753	D	30.7%	67.6%	31.2%	68.8%
5	2010	191,423	84,578	TURK, JACOB	102,076	CLEAVER, EMANUEL II*	4,769	17,498	D	44.2%	53.3%	45.3%	54.7%
5	2008	306,415	109,166	TURK, JACOB	197,249	CLEAVER, EMANUEL II*		88,083	D	35.6%	64.4%	35.6%	64.4%
5	2006	211,919	68,456	TURK, JACOB	136,149	CLEAVER, EMANUEL II*	7,314	67,693	D	32.3%	64.2%	33.5%	66.5%
5	2004	293,025	123,431	PATTERSON, JEANNE	161,727	CLEAVER, EMANUEL II	7,867	38,296	D	42.1%	55.2%	43.3%	56.7%
5	2002	186,167	60,245	GORDON, STEVE	122,645	McCARTHY, KAREN*	3,277	62,400	D	32.4%	65.9%	32.9%	67.1%
6	2010	221,912	154,103	GRAVES, SAM*	67,762	HYLTON, CLINT	47	86,341	R	69.4%	30.5%	69.5%	30.5%
6	2008	330,699	196,526	GRAVES, SAM*	121,894	BARNES, KAY	12,279	74,632	R	59.4%	36.9%	61.7%	38.3%
6	2006	244,795	150,882	GRAVES, SAM*	87,477	SHETTLES, SARA JO	6,436	63,405	R	61.6%	35.7%	63.3%	36.7%
6	2004	307,855	196,516	GRAVES, SAM*	106,987	BROOMFIELD, CHARLES S.	4,352	89,529	R	63.8%	34.8%	64.7%	35.3%
6	2002	208,088	131,151	GRAVES, SAM*	73,202	RINEHART, CATHY	3,735	57,949	R	63.0%	35.2%	64.2%	35.8%
7	2010	222,431	141,010	LONG, BILLY	67,545	ECKERSLEY, SCOTT	13,876	73,465	R	63.4%	30.4%	67.6%	32.4%
7	2008	323,212	219,016	BLUNT, ROY*	91,010	MONROE, RICHARD	13,186	128,006	R	67.8%	28.2%	70.6%	29.4%
7	2006	241,123	160,942	BLUNT, ROY*	72,592	TRUMAN, JACK	7,589	88,350	R	66.7%	30.1%	68.9%	31.1%
7	2004	298,205	210,080	BLUNT, ROY*	84,356	NEWBERRY, JIM	3,769	125,724	R	70.4%	28.3%	71.3%	28.7%
7	2002	199,863	149,519	BLUNT, ROY*	45,964	LAPHAM, RON	4,380	103,555	R	74.8%	23.0%	76.5%	23.5%
8	2010	195,999	128,499	EMERSON, JO ANN*	56,377	SOWERS, TOMMY	11,123	72,122	R	65.6%	28.8%	69.5%	30.5%
8	2008	278,288	198,798	EMERSON, JO ANN*	72,790	ALLEN, JOE	6,700	126,008	R	71.4%	26.2%	73.2%	26.8%
8	2006	217,989	156,164	EMERSON, JO ANN*	57,557	HAMBACKER, VERONICA J.	4,268	98,607	R	71.6%	26.4%	73.1%	26.9%
8	2004	268,711	194,039	EMERSON, JO ANN*	71,543	HENDERSON, DEAN	3,129	122,496	R	72.2%	26.6%	73.1%	26.9%
8	2002	188,321	135,144	EMERSON, JO ANN*	50,686	CURTIS, GENE	2,491	84,458	R	71.8%	26.9%	72.7%	27.3%
9	2010	210,358	162,724	LUETKEMEYER, BLAINE*	—	—	47,634	162,724	R	77.4%		100.0%	
9	2008	322,095	161,031	LUETKEMEYER, BLAINE	152,956	BAKER, JUDY	8,108	8,075	R	50.0%	47.5%	51.3%	48.7%
9	2006	242,671	149,114	HULSHOF, KENNY*	87,145	BURGHARD, DUANE N.	6,412	61,969	R	61.4%	35.9%	63.1%	36.9%
9	2004	299,447	193,429	HULSHOF, KENNY*	101,343	JACOBSEN, LINDA	4,675	92,086	R	64.6%	33.8%	65.6%	34.4%
9	2002	214,125	146,032	HULSHOF, KENNY*	61,126	DEICHMAN, DONALD M. "DON"	6,967	84,906	R	68.2%	28.5%	70.5%	29.5%
TOTAL	2010	1,920,675	1,103,290		708,064		109,321	395,226	R	57.4%	36.9%	60.9%	39.1%
TOTAL	2008	2,821,484	1,313,018		1,413,016		95,450	99,998	D	46.5%	50.1%	48.2%	51.8%
TOTAL	2006	2,097,322	1,049,346		992,258		55,718	57,088	R	50.0%	47.3%	51.4%	48.6%
TOTAL	2004	2,667,023	1,429,767		1,192,674		44,582	237,093	R	53.6%	44.7%	54.5%	45.5%
TOTAL	2002	1,853,563	985,905		829,177		38,481	156,728	R	53.2%	44.7%	54.3%	45.7%

An asterisk (*) denotes incumbent.

MISSOURI

GENERAL AND PRIMARY ELECTIONS

2010 GENERAL ELECTIONS

Senator   Other vote was 58,663 Libertarian (Jonathan Dine); 41,309 Constitution (Jerry Beck); 14 write-in (Dale M. Hoinoski); 7 write-in (Frazier Glenn Miller Jr.); 4 write-in (Jeff Wirick); 3 write-in (Charlie L. Bailey); 2 write-in (Richie L. Wolfe); 1 write-in (Mark S. Memoly).

House   Other vote was:

CD 1   5,223 Libertarian (Julie Stone).

CD 2   7,677 Libertarian (Steve Mosbacher); 7 write-in (Patrick M. Cannon).

CD 3   5,772 Libertarian (Steven R. Hedrick); 3,155 Constitution (Nicholas J. "Nick" Ivanovich); 3 write-in (Brian Wallner).

CD 4   6,123 Libertarian (Jason Michael Braun); 3,912 Constitution (Greg Cowan).

CD 5   3,077 Libertarian (Randall D. Langkraehr); 1,692 Constitution (Dave Lay).

CD 6   47 write-in (Kyle Yarber).

CD 7   13,866 Libertarian (Kevin Craig); 10 write-in (Nicholas Ivan Ladendorf).

CD 8   7,193 Independent (Larry Bill); 3,930 Libertarian (Rick Vandeven).

CD 9   46,817 Libertarian (Christopher W. Dwyer); 748 write-in (Clifford Jeffery Reed); 69 write-in (Ron Burrus).

2010 PRIMARY ELECTIONS

Primary   August 3, 2010   **Registration**   4,104,834   No Party Registration
                                 (as of August 3, 2010)

Primary Type   Open—Any registered voter could participate in the party primary of their choice.

MISSOURI

GENERAL AND PRIMARY ELECTIONS

	REPUBLICAN PRIMARIES			DEMOCRATIC PRIMARIES		
Senator	Roy Blunt	411,040	70.9%	Robin Carnahan	266,349	83.9%
	Chuck Purgason	75,663	13.1%	Richard Charles Tolbert	33,731	10.6%
	Kristi Nichols	40,744	7.0%	Francis J. Vangeli	17,511	5.5%
	Deborah Solomon	15,099	2.6%			
	Hector Maldonado	8,731	1.5%			
	Davis Conway	8,525	1.5%			
	R. L. Praprotnik	8,047	1.4%			
	Tony Laszacs	6,309	1.1%			
	Mike Vontz	5,190	0.9%			
	TOTAL	*579,348*		*TOTAL*	*317,591*	
Congressional District 1	Robyn Hamlin	10,305	63.2%	William Lacy Clay*	37,041	81.3%
	Martin D. Baker	4,532	27.8%	Candice "Britt" Britton	8,546	18.7%
	Marshall Works	1,467	9.0%			
	TOTAL	*16,304*		*TOTAL*	*45,587*	
Congressional District 2	Todd Akin*	72,269	84.6%	Arthur Lieber	24,227	100.0%
	William C. Haas	9,494	11.1%			
	Jeffrey Lowe	3,692	4.3%			
	TOTAL	*85,455*				

MISSOURI

GENERAL AND PRIMARY ELECTIONS

	REPUBLICAN PRIMARIES			DEMOCRATIC PRIMARIES		
Congressional District 3	Ed Martin	22,266	63.4%	Russ Carnahan*	36,976	80.1%
	Rusty Wallace	7,478	21.3%	David Arnold	6,467	14.0%
	John Wayne Tucker	5,379	15.3%	Edward Crim	2,697	5.8%
	TOTAL	35,123		TOTAL	46,140	
Congressional District 4	Vicky Hartzler	35,860	40.5%	Ike Skelton*	25,919	80.5%
	Bill Stouffer	26,573	30.0%	Leonard Steinman	6,268	19.5%
	Jeff Parnell	7,969	9.0%			
	James Scholz	4,259	4.8%			
	Roy Viessman	3,702	4.2%			
	Brian Riley	3,197	3.6%			
	Brian Clark	2,658	3.0%			
	Arthur John Madden	2,484	2.8%			
	Eric James McElroy	1,928	2.2%			
	TOTAL	88,630		TOTAL	32,187	
Congressional District 5	Jacob Turk	23,078	67.0%	Emanuel Cleaver II*	34,117	100.0%
	Jerry Fowler	3,963	11.5%			
	Patrick Haake	3,469	10.1%			
	Ralph Sheffield	2,748	8.0%			
	Ron Shawd	1,185	3.4%			
	TOTAL	34,443				
Congressional District 6	Sam Graves*	54,566	82.5%	Clint Hylton	30,233	100.0%
	Christopher Ryan	11,608	17.5%			
	TOTAL	66,174				
Congressional District 7	Billy Long	38,218	36.6%	Scott Eckersley	9,210	62.7%
	Jack Goodman	30,401	29.1%	Tim Davis	5,489	37.3%
	Gary Nodler	14,561	13.9%			
	Darrell L. Moore	9,312	8.9%			
	Jeff Wisdom	4,552	4.4%			
	Mike Moon	4,473	4.3%			
	Steve Hunter	2,173	2.1%			
	Michael Wardell	844	0.8%			
	TOTAL	104,534		TOTAL	14,699	
Congressional District 8	Jo Ann Emerson*	47,880	65.6%	Tommy Sowers	27,874	100.0%
	Bob Parker	25,118	34.4%			
	TOTAL	72,998				
Congressional District 9	Blaine Luetkemeyer*	59,684	83.0%	No Democratic candidate		
	James O. Baker	12,248	17.0%			
	TOTAL	71,932				

An asterisk (*) denotes incumbent.

MONTANA

One member At Large

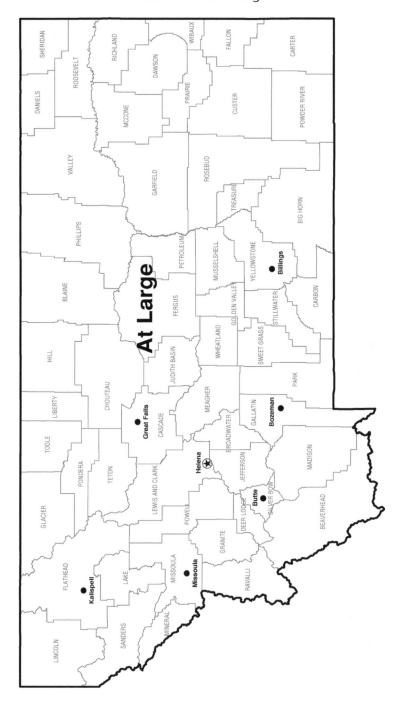

MONTANA

GOVERNOR
Brian Schweitzer (D). Reelected 2008 to a four-year term. Previously elected 2004.

SENATORS (2 Democrats)
Max Baucus (D). Reelected 2008 to a six-year term. Previously elected 2002, 1996, 1990, 1984, 1978.

Jon Tester (D). Elected 2006 to a six-year term.

REPRESENTATIVE (1 Republican)
At Large. Denny Rehberg (R)

POSTWAR VOTE FOR PRESIDENT

| | | Republican | | Democratic | | | | Percentage | | | |
| | | | | | | | | Total Vote | | Major Vote | |
Year	Total Vote	Vote	Candidate	Vote	Candidate	Other Vote	Rep.-Dem. Plurality	Rep.	Dem.	Rep.	Dem.
2008	490,302	242,763	McCain, John	231,667	Obama, Barack	15,872	11,096 R	49.5%	47.2%	51.2%	48.8%
2004	450,445	266,063	Bush, George W.	173,710	Kerry, John	10,672	92,353 R	59.1%	38.6%	60.5%	39.5%
2000**	410,997	240,178	Bush, George W.	137,126	Gore, Al	33,693	103,052 R	58.4%	33.4%	63.7%	36.3%
1996**	407,261	179,652	Dole, Bob	167,922	Clinton, Bill	59,687	11,730 R	44.1%	41.2%	51.7%	48.3%
1992**	410,611	144,207	Bush, George	154,507	Clinton, Bill	111,897	10,300 D	35.1%	37.6%	48.3%	51.7%
1988	365,674	190,412	Bush, George	168,936	Dukakis, Michael S.	6,326	21,476 R	52.1%	46.2%	53.0%	47.0%
1984	384,377	232,450	Reagan, Ronald	146,742	Mondale, Walter F.	5,185	85,708 R	60.5%	38.2%	61.3%	38.7%
1980**	363,952	206,814	Reagan, Ronald	118,032	Carter, Jimmy	39,106	88,782 R	56.8%	32.4%	63.7%	36.3%
1976	328,734	173,703	Ford, Gerald R.	149,259	Carter, Jimmy	5,772	24,444 R	52.8%	45.4%	53.8%	46.2%
1972	317,603	183,976	Nixon, Richard M.	120,197	McGovern, George S.	13,430	63,779 R	57.9%	37.8%	60.5%	39.5%
1968**	274,404	138,835	Nixon, Richard M.	114,117	Humphrey, Hubert H.	21,452	24,718 R	50.6%	41.6%	54.9%	45.1%
1964	278,628	113,032	Goldwater, Barry M.	164,246	Johnson, Lyndon B.	1,350	51,214 D	40.6%	58.9%	40.8%	59.2%
1960	277,579	141,841	Nixon, Richard M.	134,891	Kennedy, John F.	847	6,950 R	51.1%	48.6%	51.3%	48.7%
1956	271,171	154,933	Eisenhower, Dwight D.	116,238	Stevenson, Adlai E.		38,695 R	57.1%	42.9%	57.1%	42.9%
1952	265,037	157,394	Eisenhower, Dwight D.	106,213	Stevenson, Adlai E.	1,430	51,181 R	59.4%	40.1%	59.7%	40.3%
1948	224,278	96,770	Dewey, Thomas E.	119,071	Truman, Harry S.	8,437	22,301 D	43.1%	53.1%	44.8%	55.2%

**In past elections, the other vote included: 2000 - 24,437 Green (Ralph Nader); 1996 - 55,229 Reform (Ross Perot); 1992 - 107,225 Independent (Perot); 1980 - 29,281 Independent (John Anderson); 1968 - 20,015 American Independent (George Wallace).

MONTANA

POSTWAR VOTE FOR GOVERNOR

Year	Total Vote	Republican Vote	Republican Candidate	Democratic Vote	Democratic Candidate	Other Vote	Rep.-Dem. Plurality	Total Vote Rep.	Total Vote Dem.	Major Vote Rep.	Major Vote Dem.
2008	486,734	158,268	Brown, Roy	318,670	Schweitzer, Brian	9,796	160,402 D	32.5%	65.5%	33.2%	66.8%
2004	446,146	205,313	Brown, Bob	225,016	Schweitzer, Brian	15,817	19,703 D	46.0%	50.4%	47.7%	52.3%
2000	410,192	209,135	Martz, Judy	193,131	O'Keefe, Mark	7,926	16,004 R	51.0%	47.1%	52.0%	48.0%
1996**	405,175	320,768	Racicot, Marc	84,407	Jacobson, Judy		236,361 R	79.2%	20.8%	79.2%	20.8%
1992	407,842	209,401	Racicot, Marc	198,421	Bradley, Dorothy	20	10,980 R	51.3%	48.7%	51.3%	48.7%
1988	367,021	190,604	Stephens, Stan	169,313	Judge, Thomas L.	7,104	21,291 R	51.9%	46.1%	53.0%	47.0%
1984	378,970	100,070	Goodover, Pat M.	266,578	Schwinden, Ted	12,322	166,508 D	26.4%	70.3%	27.3%	72.7%
1980	360,466	160,892	Ramirez, Jack	199,574	Schwinden, Ted		38,682 D	44.6%	55.4%	44.6%	55.4%
1976	316,720	115,848	Woodahl, Robert	195,420	Judge, Thomas L.	5,452	79,572 D	36.6%	61.7%	37.2%	62.8%
1972	318,754	146,231	Smith, Ed	172,523	Judge, Thomas L.		26,292 D	45.9%	54.1%	45.9%	54.1%
1968	278,112	116,432	Babcock, Tim M.	150,481	Anderson, Forrest H.	11,199	34,049 D	41.9%	54.1%	43.6%	56.4%
1964	280,975	144,113	Babcock, Tim M.	136,862	Renne, Roland		7,251 R	51.3%	48.7%	51.3%	48.7%
1960	279,881	154,230	Nutter, Donald G.	125,651	Cannon, Paul		28,579 R	55.1%	44.9%	55.1%	44.9%
1956	270,366	138,878	Aronson, J. Hugo	131,488	Olsen, Arnold H.		7,390 R	51.4%	48.6%	51.4%	48.6%
1952	263,792	134,423	Aronson, J. Hugo	129,369	Bonner, John W.		5,054 R	51.0%	49.0%	51.0%	49.0%
1948	222,964	97,792	Ford, Sam C.	124,267	Bonner, John W.	905	26,475 D	43.9%	55.7%	44.0%	56.0%

**In 1996 the Democratic vote total included 7,936 absentee ballots cast for the party's initial gubernatorial candidate, Chet Blaylock, who died that October.

POSTWAR VOTE FOR SENATOR

Year	Total Vote	Republican Vote	Republican Candidate	Democratic Vote	Democratic Candidate	Other Vote	Rep.-Dem. Plurality	Total Vote Rep.	Total Vote Dem.	Major Vote Rep.	Major Vote Dem.
2008	477,658	129,369	Kelleher, Bob	348,289	Baucus, Max		218,920 D	27.1%	72.9%	27.1%	72.9%
2006	406,505	196,283	Burns, Conrad	199,845	Tester, Jon	10,377	3,562 D	48.3%	49.2%	49.6%	50.4%
2002	326,537	103,611	Taylor, Mike	204,853	Baucus, Max	18,073	101,242 D	31.7%	62.7%	33.6%	66.4%
2000	411,601	208,082	Burns, Conrad	194,430	Schweitzer, Brian	9,089	13,652 R	50.6%	47.2%	51.7%	48.3%
1996	407,490	182,111	Rehberg, Denny	201,935	Baucus, Max	23,444	19,824 D	44.7%	49.6%	47.4%	52.6%
1994	350,409	218,542	Burns, Conrad	131,845	Mudd, Jack	22	86,697 R	62.4%	37.6%	62.4%	37.6%
1990	319,336	93,836	Kolstad, Allen C.	217,563	Baucus, Max	7,937	123,727 D	29.4%	68.1%	30.1%	69.9%
1988	365,254	189,445	Burns, Conrad	175,809	Melcher, John		13,636 R	51.9%	48.1%	51.9%	48.1%
1984	379,155	154,308	Cozzens, Chuck	215,704	Baucus, Max	9,143	61,396 D	40.7%	56.9%	41.7%	58.3%
1982	321,062	133,789	Williams, Larry	174,861	Melcher, John	12,412	41,072 D	41.7%	54.5%	43.3%	56.7%
1978	287,942	127,589	Williams, Larry	160,353	Baucus, Max		32,764 D	44.3%	55.7%	44.3%	55.7%
1976	321,445	115,213	Burger, Stanley C.	206,232	Melcher, John		91,019 D	35.8%	64.2%	35.8%	64.2%
1972	314,925	151,316	Hibbard, Henry S.	163,609	Metcalf, Lee		12,293 D	48.0%	52.0%	48.0%	52.0%
1970	247,869	97,809	Wallace, Harold E.	150,060	Mansfield, Mike		52,251 D	39.5%	60.5%	39.5%	60.5%
1966	259,863	121,697	Babcock, Tim M.	138,166	Metcalf, Lee		16,469 D	46.8%	53.2%	46.8%	53.2%
1964	280,010	99,367	Blewett, Alex	180,643	Mansfield, Mike		81,276 D	35.5%	64.5%	35.5%	64.5%
1960	276,612	136,281	Fjare, Orvin B.	140,331	Metcalf, Lee		4,050 D	49.3%	50.7%	49.3%	50.7%
1958	229,483	54,573	Welch, Lou W.	174,910	Mansfield, Mike		120,337 D	23.8%	76.2%	23.8%	76.2%
1954	227,454	112,863	D'Ewart, Wesley A.	114,591	Murray, James E.		1,728 D	49.6%	50.4%	49.6%	50.4%
1952	262,297	127,360	Ecton, Zales N.	133,109	Mansfield, Mike	1,828	5,749 D	48.6%	50.7%	48.9%	51.1%
1948	221,003	94,458	David, Tom J.	125,193	Murray, James E.	1,352	30,735 D	42.7%	56.6%	43.0%	57.0%
1946	190,566	101,901	Ecton, Zales N.	86,476	Erickson, Leif	2,189	15,425 R	53.5%	45.4%	54.1%	45.9%

MONTANA

HOUSE OF REPRESENTATIVES

CD	Year	Total Vote	Republican Vote	Candidate	Democratic Vote	Candidate	Other Vote	Rep.-Dem. Plurality	Total Vote Rep.	Total Vote Dem.	Major Vote Rep.	Major Vote Dem.
AL	2010	360,341	217,696	REHBERG, DENNY*	121,954	McDONALD, DENNIS	20,691	95,742 R	60.4%	33.8%	64.1%	35.9%
AL	2008	480,900	308,470	REHBERG, DENNY*	155,930	DRISCOLL, JOHN	16,500	152,540 R	64.1%	32.4%	66.4%	33.6%
AL	2006	406,134	239,124	REHBERG, DENNY*	158,916	LINDEEN, MONICA	8,094	80,208 R	58.9%	39.1%	60.1%	39.9%
AL	2004	444,230	286,076	REHBERG, DENNY*	145,606	VELAZQUEZ, TRACY	12,548	140,470 R	64.4%	32.8%	66.3%	33.7%
AL	2002	331,321	214,100	REHBERG, DENNY*	108,233	KELLY, STEVE	8,988	105,867 R	64.6%	32.7%	66.4%	33.6%
AL	2000	410,523	211,418	REHBERG, DENNY	189,971	KEENAN, NANCY	9,134	21,447 R	51.5%	46.3%	52.7%	47.3%
AL	1998	331,551	175,748	HILL, RICK*	147,073	DESCHAMPS, DUSTY	8,730	28,675 R	53.0%	44.4%	54.4%	45.6%
AL	1996	404,426	211,975	HILL, RICK	174,516	YELLOWTAIL, BILL	17,935	37,459 R	52.4%	43.2%	54.8%	45.2%
AL	1994	352,133	148,715	JAMISON, CY	171,372	WILLIAMS, PAT*	32,046	22,657 D	42.2%	48.7%	46.5%	53.5%
AL	1992	403,735	189,570	MARLENEE, RON*	203,711	WILLIAMS, PAT*	10,454	14,141 D	47.0%	50.5%	48.2%	51.8%

An asterisk (*) denotes incumbent.

MONTANA

GENERAL AND PRIMARY ELECTIONS

2010 GENERAL ELECTIONS

House

At Large Other vote was: 20,691 Libertarian (Mike Fellows).

2010 PRIMARY ELECTIONS

Primary June 8, 2010 **Registration** (as of June 8, 2010) 639,309 No Party Reigstration

Primary Type Open—Any registered voter could participate in the party primary of their choice.

	REPUBLICAN PRIMARIES			DEMOCRATIC PRIMARIES		
Congressional At Large	Denny Rehberg*	96,796	74.7%	Dennis McDonald	24,014	38.4%
	Mark T. French	25,344	19.6%	Tyler Gernant	15,177	24.3%
	A.J. Otjen	7,461	5.8%	Melinda Gopher	13,170	21.1%
				Sam Rankin	10,138	16.2%
	TOTAL	129,601		TOTAL	62,499	

An asterisk (*) denotes incumbent.

NEBRASKA

Congressional districts first established for elections held in 2002
3 members

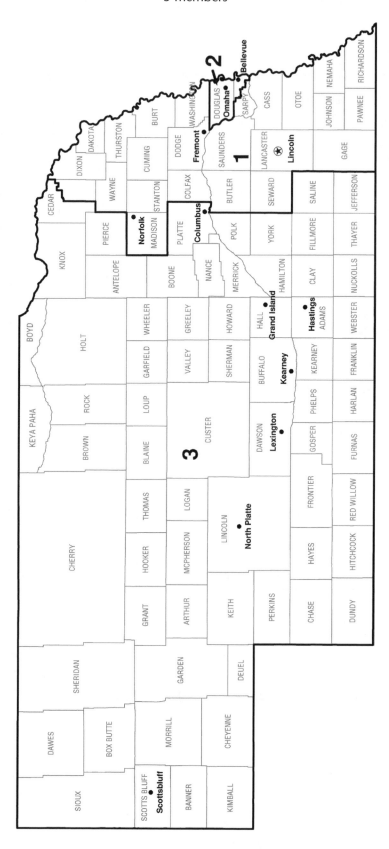

NEBRASKA

GOVERNOR
Dave Heineman (R). Reelected 2010 to a four-year term. Previously elected 2006. Became Governor January 21, 2005, upon the resignation of Mike Johanns (R) to become U.S. Secretary of Agriculture.

SENATORS (1 Democrat, 1 Republican)
Mike Johanns (R). Elected 2008 to a six-year term.

Ben Nelson (D). Reelected 2006 to a six-year term. Previously elected 2000.

REPRESENTATIVES (3 Republicans)

1. Jeff Fortenberry (R)   2. Lee Terry (R)   3. Adrian Smith (R)

POSTWAR VOTE FOR PRESIDENT

| | | Republican | | Democratic | | | | Percentage | | | |
| | | | | | | | | Total Vote | | Major Vote | |
Year	Total Vote	Vote	Candidate	Vote	Candidate	Other Vote	Rep.-Dem. Plurality	Rep.	Dem.	Rep.	Dem.
2008	801,281	452,979	McCain, John	333,319	Obama, Barack	14,983	119,660 R	56.5%	41.6%	57.6%	42.4%
2004	778,186	512,814	Bush, George W.	254,328	Kerry, John	11,044	258,486 R	65.9%	32.7%	66.8%	33.2%
2000**	697,019	433,862	Bush, George W.	231,780	Gore, Al	31,377	202,082 R	62.2%	33.3%	65.2%	34.8%
1996**	677,415	363,467	Dole, Bob	236,761	Clinton, Bill	77,187	126,706 R	53.7%	35.0%	60.6%	39.4%
1992**	737,546	343,678	Bush, George	216,864	Clinton, Bill	177,004	126,814 R	46.6%	29.4%	61.3%	38.7%
1988	661,465	397,956	Bush, George	259,235	Dukakis, Michael S.	4,274	138,721 R	60.2%	39.2%	60.6%	39.4%
1984	652,090	460,054	Reagan, Ronald	187,866	Mondale, Walter F.	4,170	272,188 R	70.6%	28.8%	71.0%	29.0%
1980**	640,854	419,937	Reagan, Ronald	166,851	Carter, Jimmy	54,066	253,086 R	65.5%	26.0%	71.6%	28.4%
1976	607,668	359,705	Ford, Gerald R.	233,692	Carter, Jimmy	14,271	126,013 R	59.2%	38.5%	60.6%	39.4%
1972	576,289	406,298	Nixon, Richard M.	169,991	McGovern, George S.		236,307 R	70.5%	29.5%	70.5%	29.5%
1968**	536,851	321,163	Nixon, Richard M.	170,784	Humphrey, Hubert H.	44,904	150,379 R	47.4%	31.8%	65.3%	34.7%
1964	584,154	276,847	Goldwater, Barry M.	307,307	Johnson, Lyndon B.		30,460 D	47.4%	52.6%	47.4%	52.6%
1960	613,095	380,553	Nixon, Richard M.	232,542	Kennedy, John F.		148,011 R	62.1%	37.9%	62.1%	37.9%
1956	577,137	378,108	Eisenhower, Dwight D.	199,029	Stevenson, Adlai E.		179,079 R	65.5%	34.5%	65.5%	34.5%
1952	609,660	421,603	Eisenhower, Dwight D.	188,057	Stevenson, Adlai E.		233,546 R	69.2%	30.8%	69.2%	30.8%
1948	488,940	264,774	Dewey, Thomas E.	224,165	Truman, Harry S.	1	40,609 R	54.2%	45.8%	54.2%	45.8%

**In past elections, the other vote included: 2000 - 24,540 Green (Ralph Nader); 1996 - 71,278 Reform (Ross Perot); 1992 - 174,104 Independent (Perot); 1980 - 44,993 Independent (John Anderson); 1968 - 44,904 American Independent (George Wallace).

NEBRASKA

POSTWAR VOTE FOR GOVERNOR

Year	Total Vote	Republican Vote	Republican Candidate	Democratic Vote	Democratic Candidate	Other Vote	Rep.-Dem. Plurality	Total Vote Rep.	Total Vote Dem.	Major Vote Rep.	Major Vote Dem.
2010	487,988	360,645	Heineman, Dave	127,343	Meister, Mike		233,302 R	73.9%	26.1%	73.9%	26.1%
2006	593,357	435,507	Heineman, Dave	145,115	Hahn, David	12,735	290,392 R	73.4%	24.5%	75.0%	25.0%
2002	480,991	330,349	Johanns, Mike	132,348	Dean, Stormy	18,294	198,001 R	68.7%	27.5%	71.4%	28.6%
1998	545,238	293,910	Johanns, Mike	250,678	Hoppner, Bill	650	43,232 R	53.9%	46.0%	54.0%	46.0%
1994	579,561	148,230	Spence, Gene	423,270	Nelson, Ben	8,061	275,040 D	25.6%	73.0%	25.9%	74.1%
1990	586,542	288,741	Orr, Kay	292,771	Nelson, Ben	5,030	4,030 D	49.2%	49.9%	49.7%	50.3%
1986	564,422	298,325	Orr, Kay	265,156	Boosalis, Helen	941	33,169 R	52.9%	47.0%	52.9%	47.1%
1982	547,902	270,203	Thone, Charles	277,436	Kerrey, Bob	263	7,233 D	49.3%	50.6%	49.3%	50.7%
1978	492,423	275,473	Thone, Charles	216,754	Whelan, Gerald T.	196	58,719 R	55.9%	44.0%	56.0%	44.0%
1974	451,306	159,780	Marvel, Richard D.	267,012	Exon, J. J.	24,514	107,232 D	35.4%	59.2%	37.4%	62.6%
1970	461,619	201,994	Tiemann, Norbert T.	248,552	Exon, J. J.	11,073	46,558 D	43.8%	53.8%	44.8%	55.2%
1966**	486,396	299,245	Tiemann, Norbert T.	186,985	Sorensen, Philip C.	166	112,260 R	61.5%	38.4%	61.5%	38.5%
1964	578,090	231,029	Burney, Dwight W.	347,026	Morrison, Frank B.	35	115,997 D	40.0%	60.0%	40.0%	60.0%
1962	464,585	221,885	Seaton, Fred A.	242,669	Morrison, Frank B.	31	20,784 D	47.8%	52.2%	47.8%	52.2%
1960	598,971	287,302	Cooper, John R.	311,344	Morrison, Frank B.	325	24,042 D	48.0%	52.0%	48.0%	52.0%
1958	421,067	209,705	Anderson, Victor E.	211,345	Brooks, Ralph G.	17	1,640 D	49.8%	50.2%	49.8%	50.2%
1956	567,933	308,293	Anderson, Victor E.	228,048	Sorrell, Frank	31,592	80,245 R	54.3%	40.2%	57.5%	42.5%
1954	414,841	250,080	Anderson, Victor E.	164,753	Ritchie, William	8	85,327 R	60.3%	39.7%	60.3%	39.7%
1952	595,714	366,009	Crosby, Robert B.	229,700	Raecke, Walter R.	5	136,309 R	61.4%	38.6%	61.4%	38.6%
1950	449,720	247,081	Peterson, Val	202,638	Raecke, Walter R.	1	44,443 R	54.9%	45.1%	54.9%	45.1%
1948	476,352	286,119	Peterson, Val	190,214	Sorrell, Frank	19	95,905 R	60.1%	39.9%	60.1%	39.9%
1946	380,835	249,468	Peterson, Val	131,367	Sorrell, Frank		118,101 R	65.5%	34.5%	65.5%	34.5%

**The term of office of Nebraska's Governor was increased from two to four years effective with the 1966 election.

POSTWAR VOTE FOR SENATOR

Year	Total Vote	Republican Vote	Republican Candidate	Democratic Vote	Democratic Candidate	Other Vote	Rep.-Dem. Plurality	Total Vote Rep.	Total Vote Dem.	Major Vote Rep.	Major Vote Dem.
2008	792,511	455,854	Johanns, Mike	317,456	Kleeb, Scott	19,201	138,398 R	57.5%	40.1%	58.9%	41.1%
2006	592,316	213,928	Ricketts, Pete	378,388	Nelson, Ben		164,460 D	36.1%	63.9%	36.1%	63.9%
2002	480,217	397,438	Hagel, Chuck	70,290	Matulka, Charlie A.	12,489	327,148 R	82.8%	14.6%	85.0%	15.0%
2000	692,344	337,967	Stenberg, Don	353,097	Nelson, Ben	1,280	15,130 D	48.8%	51.0%	48.9%	51.1%
1996	676,789	379,933	Hagel, Chuck	281,904	Nelson, Ben	14,952	98,029 R	56.1%	41.7%	57.4%	42.6%
1994	579,205	260,668	Stoney, Jan	317,297	Kerrey, Bob	1,240	56,629 D	45.0%	54.8%	45.1%	54.9%
1990	593,828	243,013	Daub, Harold J.	349,779	Exon, J. J.	1,036	106,766 D	40.9%	58.9%	41.0%	59.0%
1988	667,860	278,250	Karnes, David	378,717	Kerrey, Bob	10,893	100,467 D	41.7%	56.7%	42.4%	57.6%
1984	639,668	307,147	Hoch, Nancy	332,217	Exon, J. J.	304	25,070 D	48.0%	51.9%	48.0%	52.0%
1982	545,647	155,760	Keck, Jim	363,350	Zorinsky, Edward	26,537	207,590 D	28.5%	66.6%	30.0%	70.0%
1978	494,368	159,806	Shasteen, Donald	334,276	Exon, J. J.	286	174,470 D	32.3%	67.6%	32.3%	67.7%
1976	598,314	284,284	McCollister, John Y.	313,809	Zorinsky, Edward	221	29,525 D	47.5%	52.4%	47.5%	52.5%
1972	568,580	301,841	Curtis, Carl T.	265,922	Carpenter, Terry	817	35,919 R	53.1%	46.8%	53.2%	46.8%
1970	458,966	240,894	Hruska, Roman L.	217,681	Morrison, Frank B.	391	23,213 R	52.5%	47.4%	52.5%	47.5%
1966	485,101	296,116	Curtis, Carl T.	187,950	Morrison, Frank B.	1,035	108,166 R	61.0%	38.7%	61.2%	38.8%
1964	563,401	345,772	Hruska, Roman L.	217,605	Arndt, Raymond W.	24	128,167 R	61.4%	38.6%	61.4%	38.6%
1960	598,743	352,748	Curtis, Carl T.	245,837	Conrad, Robert	158	106,911 R	58.9%	41.1%	58.9%	41.1%
1958	417,385	232,227	Hruska, Roman L.	185,152	Morrison, Frank B.	6	47,075 R	55.6%	44.4%	55.6%	44.4%
1954	418,691	255,695	Curtis, Carl T.	162,990	Neville, Keith	6	92,705 R	61.1%	38.9%	61.1%	38.9%
1954S	411,225	250,341	Hruska, Roman L.	160,881	Green, James F.	3	89,460 R	60.9%	39.1%	60.9%	39.1%
1952	591,749	408,971	Butler, Hugh	164,660	Long, Stanley D.	18,118	244,311 R	69.1%	27.8%	71.3%	28.7%
1952S	581,750	369,841	Griswold, Dwight	211,898	Ritchie, William	11	157,943 R	63.6%	36.4%	63.6%	36.4%
1948	471,895	267,575	Wherry, Kenneth S.	204,320	Carpenter, Terry		63,255 R	56.7%	43.3%	56.7%	43.3%
1946	382,958	271,208	Butler, Hugh	111,750	Mekota, John E.		159,458 R	70.8%	29.2%	70.8%	29.2%

One each of the 1952 and 1954 elections was for a short term to fill a vacancy.

NEBRASKA
GOVERNOR 2010

2010 Census Population	County	Total Vote	Republican	Democratic	Rep.-Dem. Plurality	Percentage			
						Total Vote		Major Vote	
						Rep.	Dem.	Rep.	Dem.
31,364	ADAMS	8,144	6,321	1,823	4,498 R	77.6%	22.4%	77.6%	22.4%
6,685	ANTELOPE	2,603	2,227	376	1,851 R	85.6%	14.4%	85.6%	14.4%
460	ARTHUR	197	172	25	147 R	87.3%	12.7%	87.3%	12.7%
690	BANNER	344	288	56	232 R	83.7%	16.3%	83.7%	16.3%
478	BLAINE	285	252	33	219 R	88.4%	11.6%	88.4%	11.6%
5,505	BOONE	1,801	1,487	314	1,173 R	82.6%	17.4%	82.6%	17.4%
11,308	BOX BUTTE	3,090	2,325	765	1,560 R	75.2%	24.8%	75.2%	24.8%
2,099	BOYD	823	698	125	573 R	84.8%	15.2%	84.8%	15.2%
3,145	BROWN	1,322	1,141	181	960 R	86.3%	13.7%	86.3%	13.7%
46,102	BUFFALO	11,998	9,700	2,298	7,402 R	80.8%	19.2%	80.8%	19.2%
6,858	BURT	2,596	1,960	636	1,324 R	75.5%	24.5%	75.5%	24.5%
8,395	BUTLER	2,490	1,945	545	1,400 R	78.1%	21.9%	78.1%	21.9%
25,241	CASS	7,586	5,797	1,789	4,008 R	76.4%	23.6%	76.4%	23.6%
8,852	CEDAR	3,102	2,606	496	2,110 R	84.0%	16.0%	84.0%	16.0%
3,966	CHASE	1,586	1,400	186	1,214 R	88.3%	11.7%	88.3%	11.7%
5,713	CHERRY	2,138	1,835	303	1,532 R	85.8%	14.2%	85.8%	14.2%
9,998	CHEYENNE	3,172	2,665	507	2,158 R	84.0%	16.0%	84.0%	16.0%
6,542	CLAY	2,190	1,861	329	1,532 R	85.0%	15.0%	85.0%	15.0%
10,515	COLFAX	1,858	1,512	346	1,166 R	81.4%	18.6%	81.4%	18.6%
9,139	CUMING	2,764	2,375	389	1,986 R	85.9%	14.1%	85.9%	14.1%
10,939	CUSTER	4,190	3,532	658	2,874 R	84.3%	15.7%	84.3%	15.7%
21,006	DAKOTA	4,037	2,840	1,197	1,643 R	70.3%	29.7%	70.3%	29.7%
9,182	DAWES	2,704	2,109	595	1,514 R	78.0%	22.0%	78.0%	22.0%
24,326	DAWSON	4,892	4,138	754	3,384 R	84.6%	15.4%	84.6%	15.4%
1,941	DEUEL	774	648	126	522 R	83.7%	16.3%	83.7%	16.3%
6,000	DIXON	1,739	1,369	370	999 R	78.7%	21.3%	78.7%	21.3%
36,691	DODGE	8,832	7,247	1,585	5,662 R	82.1%	17.9%	82.1%	17.9%
517,110	DOUGLAS	124,351	82,922	41,429	41,493 R	66.7%	33.3%	66.7%	33.3%
2,008	DUNDY	811	694	117	577 R	85.6%	14.4%	85.6%	14.4%
5,890	FILLMORE	1,909	1,537	372	1,165 R	80.5%	19.5%	80.5%	19.5%
3,225	FRANKLIN	1,106	844	262	582 R	76.3%	23.7%	76.3%	23.7%
2,756	FRONTIER	992	848	144	704 R	85.5%	14.5%	85.5%	14.5%
4,959	FURNAS	1,846	1,546	300	1,246 R	83.7%	16.3%	83.7%	16.3%
22,311	GAGE	7,462	5,090	2,372	2,718 R	68.2%	31.8%	68.2%	31.8%
2,057	GARDEN	802	670	132	538 R	83.5%	16.5%	83.5%	16.5%
2,049	GARFIELD	876	749	127	622 R	85.5%	14.5%	85.5%	14.5%
2,044	GOSPER	724	599	125	474 R	82.7%	17.3%	82.7%	17.3%
614	GRANT	292	267	25	242 R	91.4%	8.6%	91.4%	8.6%
2,538	GREELEY	1,178	891	287	604 R	75.6%	24.4%	75.6%	24.4%
58,607	HALL	12,468	9,592	2,876	6,716 R	76.9%	23.1%	76.9%	23.1%
9,124	HAMILTON	2,993	2,557	436	2,121 R	85.4%	14.6%	85.4%	14.6%
3,423	HARLAN	1,567	1,248	319	929 R	79.6%	20.4%	79.6%	20.4%
967	HAYES	455	385	70	315 R	84.6%	15.4%	84.6%	15.4%
2,908	HITCHCOCK	1,237	1,009	228	781 R	81.6%	18.4%	81.6%	18.4%
10,435	HOLT	3,620	3,162	458	2,704 R	87.3%	12.7%	87.3%	12.7%
736	HOOKER	348	294	54	240 R	84.5%	15.5%	84.5%	15.5%
6,274	HOWARD	2,227	1,684	543	1,141 R	75.6%	24.4%	75.6%	24.4%
7,547	JEFFERSON	2,234	1,698	536	1,162 R	76.0%	24.0%	76.0%	24.0%
5,217	JOHNSON	1,789	1,285	504	781 R	71.8%	28.2%	71.8%	28.2%
6,489	KEARNEY	2,002	1,660	342	1,318 R	82.9%	17.1%	82.9%	17.1%
8,368	KEITH	3,430	2,865	565	2,300 R	83.5%	16.5%	83.5%	16.5%
824	KEYA PAHA	373	327	46	281 R	87.7%	12.3%	87.7%	12.3%
3,821	KIMBALL	1,316	1,028	288	740 R	78.1%	21.9%	78.1%	21.9%

NEBRASKA
GOVERNOR 2010

2010 Census Population	County	Total Vote	Republican	Democratic	Rep.-Dem. Plurality	Percentage Total Vote Rep.	Dem.	Percentage Major Vote Rep.	Dem.
8,701	KNOX	2,999	2,444	555	1,889 R	81.5%	18.5%	81.5%	18.5%
285,407	LANCASTER	69,914	43,060	26,854	16,206 R	61.6%	38.4%	61.6%	38.4%
36,288	LINCOLN	10,505	8,192	2,313	5,879 R	78.0%	22.0%	78.0%	22.0%
763	LOGAN	378	319	59	260 R	84.4%	15.6%	84.4%	15.6%
632	LOUP	252	214	38	176 R	84.9%	15.1%	84.9%	15.1%
539	MCPHERSON	233	201	32	169 R	86.3%	13.7%	86.3%	13.7%
34,876	MADISON	9,658	8,117	1,541	6,576 R	84.0%	16.0%	84.0%	16.0%
7,845	MERRICK	2,432	2,024	408	1,616 R	83.2%	16.8%	83.2%	16.8%
5,042	MORRILL	1,931	1,547	384	1,163 R	80.1%	19.9%	80.1%	19.9%
3,735	NANCE	1,302	1,026	276	750 R	78.8%	21.2%	78.8%	21.2%
7,248	NEMAHA	2,283	1,758	525	1,233 R	77.0%	23.0%	77.0%	23.0%
4,500	NUCKOLLS	1,566	1,249	317	932 R	79.8%	20.2%	79.8%	20.2%
15,740	OTOE	4,130	3,179	951	2,228 R	77.0%	23.0%	77.0%	23.0%
2,773	PAWNEE	934	704	230	474 R	75.4%	24.6%	75.4%	24.6%
2,970	PERKINS	1,106	943	163	780 R	85.3%	14.7%	85.3%	14.7%
9,188	PHELPS	2,960	2,504	456	2,048 R	84.6%	15.4%	84.6%	15.4%
7,266	PIERCE	2,222	1,955	267	1,688 R	88.0%	12.0%	88.0%	12.0%
32,237	PLATTE	8,827	7,531	1,296	6,235 R	85.3%	14.7%	85.3%	14.7%
5,406	POLK	1,574	1,319	255	1,064 R	83.8%	16.2%	83.8%	16.2%
11,055	RED WILLOW	3,782	3,165	617	2,548 R	83.7%	16.3%	83.7%	16.3%
8,363	RICHARDSON	2,849	2,308	541	1,767 R	81.0%	19.0%	81.0%	19.0%
1,526	ROCK	669	582	87	495 R	87.0%	13.0%	87.0%	13.0%
14,200	SALINE	3,396	2,254	1,142	1,112 R	66.4%	33.6%	66.4%	33.6%
158,840	SARPY	38,486	29,851	8,635	21,216 R	77.6%	22.4%	77.6%	22.4%
20,780	SAUNDERS	6,892	5,519	1,373	4,146 R	80.1%	19.9%	80.1%	19.9%
36,970	SCOTTS BLUFF	9,743	7,596	2,147	5,449 R	78.0%	22.0%	78.0%	22.0%
16,750	SEWARD	5,394	4,101	1,293	2,808 R	76.0%	24.0%	76.0%	24.0%
5,469	SHERIDAN	1,734	1,495	239	1,256 R	86.2%	13.8%	86.2%	13.8%
3,152	SHERMAN	1,263	952	311	641 R	75.4%	24.6%	75.4%	24.6%
1,311	SIOUX	587	514	73	441 R	87.6%	12.4%	87.6%	12.4%
6,129	STANTON	1,827	1,572	255	1,317 R	86.0%	14.0%	86.0%	14.0%
5,228	THAYER	1,912	1,542	370	1,172 R	80.6%	19.4%	80.6%	19.4%
647	THOMAS	316	279	37	242 R	88.3%	11.7%	88.3%	11.7%
6,940	THURSTON	1,422	910	512	398 R	64.0%	36.0%	64.0%	36.0%
4,260	VALLEY	1,528	1,263	265	998 R	82.7%	17.3%	82.7%	17.3%
20,234	WASHINGTON	7,204	5,835	1,369	4,466 R	81.0%	19.0%	81.0%	19.0%
9,595	WAYNE	2,342	1,919	423	1,496 R	81.9%	18.1%	81.9%	18.1%
3,812	WEBSTER	1,329	1,007	322	685 R	75.8%	24.2%	75.8%	24.2%
818	WHEELER	402	345	57	288 R	85.8%	14.2%	85.8%	14.2%
13,665	YORK	4,040	3,449	591	2,858 R	85.4%	14.6%	85.4%	14.6%
1,826,341	TOTAL	487,988	360,645	127,343	233,302 R	73.9%	26.1%	73.9%	26.1%

NEBRASKA

HOUSE OF REPRESENTATIVES

			Republican		Democratic		Other	Rep.-Dem.		Percentage			
										Total Vote		Major Vote	
CD	Year	Total Vote	Vote	Candidate	Vote	Candidate	Vote	Plurality		Rep.	Dem.	Rep.	Dem.
1	2010	163,977	116,871	FORTENBERRY, JEFF*	47,106	HARPER, IVY		69,765	R	71.3%	28.7%	71.3%	28.7%
1	2008	262,820	184,923	FORTENBERRY, JEFF*	77,897	YASHIRIN, MAX		107,026	R	70.4%	29.6%	70.4%	29.6%
1	2006	207,375	121,015	FORTENBERRY, JEFF*	86,360	MOUL, MAXINE B.		34,655	R	58.4%	41.6%	58.4%	41.6%
1	2004	265,072	143,756	FORTENBERRY, JEFF	113,971	CONNEALY, MATT	7,345	29,785	R	54.2%	43.0%	55.8%	44.2%
1	2002	155,844	133,013	BEREUTER, DOUG*	—		22,831	133,013	R	85.4%		100.0%	
2	2010	154,326	93,840	TERRY, LEE*	60,486	WHITE, TOM		33,354	R	60.8%	39.2%	60.8%	39.2%
2	2008	274,374	142,473	TERRY, LEE*	131,901	ESCH, JIM		10,572	R	51.9%	48.1%	51.9%	48.1%
2	2006	181,979	99,475	TERRY, LEE*	82,504	ESCH, JIM		16,971	R	54.7%	45.3%	54.7%	45.3%
2	2004	249,764	152,608	TERRY, LEE*	90,292	THOMPSON, NANCY	6,864	62,316	R	61.1%	36.2%	62.8%	37.2%
2	2002	142,014	89,917	TERRY, LEE*	46,843	SIMON, JIM	5,254	43,074	R	63.3%	33.0%	65.7%	34.3%
3	2010	167,243	117,275	SMITH, ADRIAN*	29,932	DAVIS, REBEKAH	20,036	87,343	R	70.1%	17.9%	79.7%	20.3%
3	2008	238,204	183,117	SMITH, ADRIAN*	55,087	STODDARD, JAY C.		128,030	R	76.9%	23.1%	76.9%	23.1%
3	2006	206,733	113,687	SMITH, ADRIAN	93,046	KLEEB, SCOTT		20,641	R	55.0%	45.0%	55.0%	45.0%
3	2004	250,136	218,751	OSBORNE, TOM*	26,434	ANDERSON, DONNA J.	4,951	192,317	R	87.5%	10.6%	89.2%	10.8%
3	2002	175,956	163,939	OSBORNE, TOM*	—		12,017	163,939	R	93.2%		100.0%	
TOTAL	2010	485,546	327,986		137,524		20,036	190,462	R	67.5%	28.3%	70.5%	29.5%
TOTAL	2008	775,398	510,513		264,885			245,628	R	65.8%	34.2%	65.8%	34.2%
TOTAL	2006	596,087	334,177		261,910			72,267	R	56.1%	43.9%	56.1%	43.9%
TOTAL	2004	764,972	515,115		230,697		19,160	284,418	R	67.3%	30.2%	69.1%	30.9%
TOTAL	2002	473,814	386,869		46,843		40,102	340,026	R	81.6%	9.9%	89.2%	10.8%

An asterisk (*) denotes incumbent.

NEBRASKA

GENERAL AND PRIMARY ELECTIONS

2010 GENERAL ELECTIONS

Governor

House   Other vote was:

CD 1
CD 2
CD 3   20,036 By Petition (Dan Hill).

2010 PRIMARY ELECTIONS

Primary	May 11, 2010	**Registration** (as of May 11, 2010)	Republican	546,309
			Democratic	382,239
			Nonpartisan	207,624
			TOTAL	1,136,172

Primary Type   Semi-open—Registered Democrats and Republicans could vote only in their party's primary. Voters registered as Nonpartisan could participate in either party's primary for the Senate and House (but not for governor).

NEBRASKA

GENERAL AND PRIMARY ELECTIONS

	REPUBLICAN PRIMARIES			DEMOCRATIC PRIMARIES		
Governor	Dave Heineman*	152,931	89.9%	Mark Lakers	57,463	100.0%
	Paul Anderson	8,980	5.3%			
	Christopher N. Geary	8,179		*Mark Lakers withdrew from the race after the primary and was replaced on the general election ballot by Mike Meister.*		
	TOTAL	170,090				
Congressional District 1	Jeff Fortenberry*	57,390	83.9%	Ivy Harper	12,249	37.9%
	David L. Hunt	7,000	10.2%	Jessica Lynn Turek	11,847	36.6%
	Ralph M. Bodie	4,053	5.9%	Stanley E. Krauter	4,145	12.8%
				Sherman Yates	4,100	12.7%
	TOTAL	68,443		TOTAL	32,341	
Congressional District 2	Lee Terry*	18,478	63.1%	Tom White	12,468	100.0%
	Matt Sakalosky	10,816	36.9%			
	TOTAL	29,294				
Congressional District 3	Adrian Smith*	65,664	88.0%	Rebekah Davis	16,468	100.0%
	Dennis L. Parker	8,979	12.0%			
	TOTAL	74,643				

An asterisk (*) denotes incumbent. Ballots cast by nonpartisan voters in primaries for the House were tallied separately but were combined into an overall total for each candidate, which is listed above.

NEVADA

Congressional districts first established for elections held in 2002
3 members

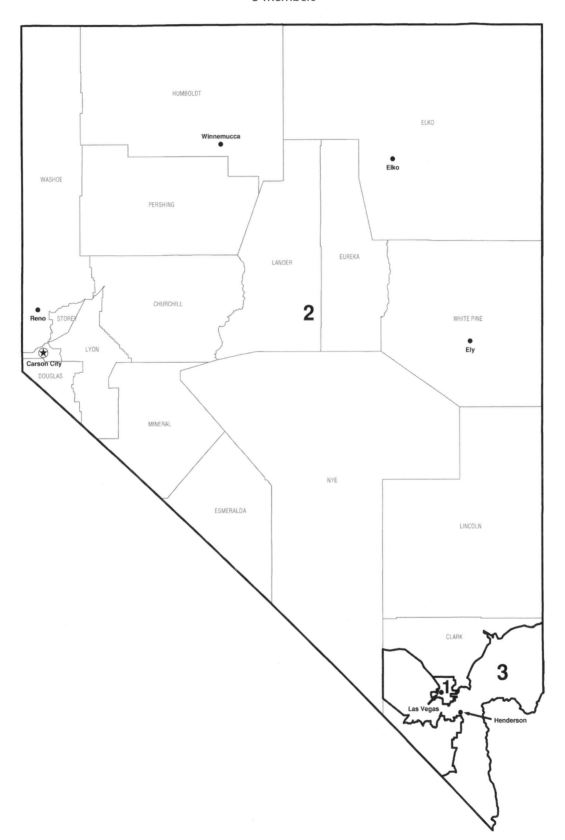

NEVADA

GOVERNOR
Brian Sandoval (R). Elected 2010 to a four-year term.

SENATORS (1 Democrat, 1 Republican)
Dean Heller (R). Sworn into office May 9, 2011, following the resignation of John Ensign (R), who was under investigation by the Senate Ethics Committee as to whether he tried to improperly cover up an extramarital affair with a former staff member.

Harry Reid (D). Reelected 2010 to a six-year term. Previously elected 2004, 1998, 1992, 1986.

REPRESENTATIVES (1 Democrat, 1 Republican, 1 Vacancy)
1. Shelley Berkley (D)   2. Vacancy   3. Joe Heck (R)

POSTWAR VOTE FOR PRESIDENT

| | | Republican | | Democratic | | Other | Rep.-Dem. | Percentage | | | |
| | | | | | | | | Total Vote | | Major Vote | |
Year	Total Vote	Vote	Candidate	Vote	Candidate	Vote	Plurality	Rep.	Dem.	Rep.	Dem.
2008	967,848	412,827	McCain, John	533,736	Obama, Barack	21,285	120,909 D	42.7%	55.1%	43.6%	56.4%
2004	829,587	418,690	Bush, George W.	397,190	Kerry, John	13,707	21,500 R	50.5%	47.9%	51.3%	48.7%
2000**	608,970	301,575	Bush, George W.	279,978	Gore, Al	27,417	21,597 R	49.5%	46.0%	51.9%	48.1%
1996**	464,279	199,244	Dole, Bob	203,974	Clinton, Bill	61,061	4,730 D	42.9%	43.9%	49.4%	50.6%
1992**	506,318	175,828	Bush, George	189,148	Clinton, Bill	141,342	13,320 D	34.7%	37.4%	48.2%	51.8%
1988	350,067	206,040	Bush, George	132,738	Dukakis, Michael S.	11,289	73,302 R	58.9%	37.9%	60.8%	39.2%
1984	286,667	188,770	Reagan, Ronald	91,655	Mondale, Walter F.	6,242	97,115 R	65.8%	32.0%	67.3%	32.7%
1980**	247,885	155,017	Reagan, Ronald	66,666	Carter, Jimmy	26,202	88,351 R	62.5%	26.9%	69.9%	30.1%
1976	201,876	101,273	Ford, Gerald R.	92,479	Carter, Jimmy	8,124	8,794 R	50.2%	45.8%	52.3%	47.7%
1972	181,766	115,750	Nixon, Richard M.	66,016	McGovern, George S.		49,734 R	63.7%	36.3%	63.7%	36.3%
1968**	154,218	73,188	Nixon, Richard M.	60,598	Humphrey, Hubert H.	20,432	12,590 R	47.5%	39.3%	54.7%	45.3%
1964	135,433	56,094	Goldwater, Barry M.	79,339	Johnson, Lyndon B.		23,245 D	41.4%	58.6%	41.4%	58.6%
1960	107,267	52,387	Nixon, Richard M.	54,880	Kennedy, John F.		2,493 D	48.8%	51.2%	48.8%	51.2%
1956	96,689	56,049	Eisenhower, Dwight D.	40,640	Stevenson, Adlai E.		15,409 R	58.0%	42.0%	58.0%	42.0%
1952	82,190	50,502	Eisenhower, Dwight D.	31,688	Stevenson, Adlai E.		18,814 R	61.4%	38.6%	61.4%	38.6%
1948	62,117	29,357	Dewey, Thomas E.	31,291	Truman, Harry S.	1,469	1,934 D	47.3%	50.4%	48.4%	51.6%

**In past elections, the other vote included: 2000 - 15,008 Green (Ralph Nader); 1996 - 43,986 Reform (Ross Perot); 1992 - 132,580 Independent (Perot); 1980 - 17,651 Independent (John Anderson); 1968 - 20,432 American Independent (George Wallace).

NEVADA

POSTWAR VOTE FOR GOVERNOR

Year	Total Vote	Republican Vote	Republican Candidate	Democratic Vote	Democratic Candidate	Other Vote	Rep.-Dem. Plurality	Total Vote Rep.	Total Vote Dem.	Major Vote Rep.	Major Vote Dem.
2010	716,529	382,350	Sandoval, Brian	298,171	Reid, Rory	36,008	84,179 R	53.4%	41.6%	56.2%	43.8%
2006	582,158	279,003	Gibbons, Jim	255,684	Titus, Dana	47,471	23,319 R	47.9%	43.9%	52.2%	47.8%
2002	504,079	344,001	Guinn, Kenny	110,935	Neal, Joe	49,143	233,066 R	68.2%	22.0%	75.6%	24.4%
1998	433,630	223,892	Guinn, Kenny	182,281	Jones, Jan Laverty	27,457	41,611 R	51.6%	42.0%	55.1%	44.9%
1994	379,676	156,875	Gibbons, Jim	200,026	Miller, Robert J.	22,775	43,151 D	41.3%	52.7%	44.0%	56.0%
1990	320,743	95,789	Gallaway, Jim	207,878	Miller, Robert J.	17,076	112,089 D	29.9%	64.8%	31.5%	68.5%
1986	260,375	65,081	Cafferata, Patty	187,268	Bryan, Richard H.	8,026	122,187 D	25.0%	71.9%	25.8%	74.2%
1982	239,751	100,104	List, Robert F.	128,132	Bryan, Richard H.	11,515	28,028 D	41.8%	53.4%	43.9%	56.1%
1978	192,445	108,097	List, Robert F.	76,361	Rose, Robert E.	7,987	31,736 R	56.2%	39.7%	58.6%	41.4%
1974**	169,358	28,959	Crumpler, Shirley	114,114	O'Callaghan, Mike	26,285	85,155 D	17.1%	67.4%	20.2%	79.8%
1970	146,991	64,400	Fike, Ed	70,697	O'Callaghan, Mike	11,894	6,297 D	43.8%	48.1%	47.7%	52.3%
1966	137,677	71,807	Laxalt, Paul	65,870	Sawyer, Grant		5,937 R	52.2%	47.8%	52.2%	47.8%
1962	96,929	32,145	Gragson, Oran K.	64,784	Sawyer, Grant		32,639 D	33.2%	66.8%	33.2%	66.8%
1958	84,889	34,025	Russell, Charles H.	50,864	Sawyer, Grant		16,839 D	40.1%	59.9%	40.1%	59.9%
1954	78,462	41,665	Russell, Charles H.	36,797	Pittman, Vail		4,868 R	53.1%	46.9%	53.1%	46.9%
1950	61,773	35,609	Russell, Charles H.	26,164	Pittman, Vail		9,445 R	57.6%	42.4%	57.6%	42.4%
1946	49,902	21,247	Jepson, Melvin E.	28,655	Pittman, Vail		7,408 D	42.6%	57.4%	42.6%	57.4%

**In past elections, the other vote included: 1974 - 26,285 Independent American (James Ray Houston).

POSTWAR VOTE FOR SENATOR

Year	Total Vote	Republican Vote	Republican Candidate	Democratic Vote	Democratic Candidate	Other Vote	Rep.-Dem. Plurality	Total Vote Rep.	Total Vote Dem.	Major Vote Rep.	Major Vote Dem.
2010	721,404	321,361	Angle, Sharron	362,785	Reid, Harry	37,258	41,424 D	44.5%	50.3%	47.0%	53.0%
2006	582,572	322,501	Ensign, John	238,796	Carter, Jack	21,275	83,705 R	55.4%	41.0%	57.5%	42.5%
2004	810,068	284,640	Ziser, Richard	494,805	Reid, Harry	30,623	210,165 D	35.1%	61.1%	36.5%	63.5%
2000	600,250	330,687	Ensign, John	238,260	Bernstein, Ed	31,303	92,427 R	55.1%	39.7%	58.1%	41.9%
1998	435,790	208,222	Ensign, John	208,650	Reid, Harry	18,918	428 D	47.8%	47.9%	49.9%	50.1%
1994	380,530	156,020	Furman, Hal	193,804	Bryan, Richard H.	30,706	37,784 D	41.0%	50.9%	44.6%	55.4%
1992	495,887	199,413	Dahl, Demar	253,150	Reid, Harry	43,324	53,737 D	40.2%	51.0%	44.1%	55.9%
1988	349,649	161,336	Hecht, Chic	175,548	Bryan, Richard H.	12,765	14,212 D	46.1%	50.2%	47.9%	52.1%
1986	261,932	116,606	Santini, James	130,955	Reid, Harry	14,371	14,349 D	44.5%	50.0%	47.1%	52.9%
1982	240,394	120,377	Hecht, Chic	114,720	Cannon, Howard W.	5,297	5,657 R	50.1%	47.7%	51.2%	48.8%
1980	246,436	144,224	Laxalt, Paul	92,129	Gojack, Mary	10,083	52,095 R	58.5%	37.4%	61.0%	39.0%
1976	201,980	63,471	Towell, David	127,295	Cannon, Howard W.	11,214	63,824 D	31.4%	63.0%	33.3%	66.7%
1974	169,473	79,605	Laxalt, Paul	78,981	Reid, Harry	10,887	624 R	47.0%	46.6%	50.2%	49.8%
1970	147,768	60,838	Raggio, William J.	85,187	Cannon, Howard W.	1,743	24,349 D	41.2%	57.6%	41.7%	58.3%
1968	152,690	69,068	Fike, Ed	83,622	Bible, Alan		14,554 D	45.2%	54.8%	45.2%	54.8%
1964	134,624	67,288	Laxalt, Paul	67,336	Cannon, Howard W.		48 D	50.0%	50.0%	50.0%	50.0%
1962	97,192	33,749	Wright, William B.	63,443	Bible, Alan		29,694 D	34.7%	65.3%	34.7%	65.3%
1958	84,492	35,760	Malone, George W.	48,732	Cannon, Howard W.		12,972 D	42.3%	57.7%	42.3%	57.7%
1956	96,389	45,712	Young, Clifton	50,677	Bible, Alan		4,965 D	47.4%	52.6%	47.4%	52.6%
1954S	77,513	32,470	Brown, Ernest S.	45,043	Bible, Alan		12,573 D	41.9%	58.1%	41.9%	58.1%
1952	81,090	41,906	Malone, George W.	39,184	Mechling, Thomas B.		2,722 R	51.7%	48.3%	51.7%	48.3%
1950	61,762	25,933	Marshall, George E.	35,829	McCarran, Pat		9,896 D	42.0%	58.0%	42.0%	58.0%
1946	50,354	27,801	Malone, George W.	22,553	Bunker, Berkeley		5,248 R	55.2%	44.8%	55.2%	44.8%

The 1954 election was for a short term to fill a vacancy.

NEVADA

GOVERNOR 2010

								Percentage			
						Rep.-Dem.		Total Vote		Major Vote	
2010 Census Population	County	Total Vote	Republican	Democratic	Other	Plurality		Rep.	Dem.	Rep.	Dem.
55,274	CARSON CITY	19,492	11,512	6,676	1,304	4,836	R	59.1%	34.2%	63.3%	36.7%
24,877	CHURCHILL	8,877	6,586	1,697	594	4,889	R	74.2%	19.1%	79.5%	20.5%
1,951,269	CLARK	462,372	224,751	217,113	20,508	7,638	R	48.6%	47.0%	50.9%	49.1%
46,997	DOUGLAS	21,708	15,001	5,345	1,362	9,656	R	69.1%	24.6%	73.7%	26.3%
48,818	ELKO	12,829	9,489	2,194	1,146	7,295	R	74.0%	17.1%	81.2%	18.8%
783	ESMERALDA	398	289	48	61	241	R	72.6%	12.1%	85.8%	14.2%
1,987	EUREKA	756	597	76	83	521	R	79.0%	10.1%	88.7%	11.3%
16,528	HUMBOLDT	4,977	3,564	994	419	2,570	R	71.6%	20.0%	78.2%	21.8%
5,775	LANDER	1,896	1,449	277	170	1,172	R	76.4%	14.6%	84.0%	16.0%
5,345	LINCOLN	1,947	1,381	380	186	1,001	R	70.9%	19.5%	78.4%	21.6%
51,980	LYON	17,437	11,937	4,331	1,169	7,606	R	68.5%	24.8%	73.4%	26.6%
4,772	MINERAL	1,897	1,136	556	205	580	R	59.9%	29.3%	67.1%	32.9%
43,946	NYE	14,359	8,829	4,224	1,306	4,605	R	61.5%	29.4%	67.6%	32.4%
6,753	PERSHING	1,731	1,140	396	195	744	R	65.9%	22.9%	74.2%	25.8%
4,010	STOREY	2,127	1,355	615	157	740	R	63.7%	28.9%	68.8%	31.2%
421,407	WASHOE	140,468	81,073	52,730	6,665	28,343	R	57.7%	37.5%	60.6%	39.4%
10,030	WHITE PINE	3,258	2,261	519	478	1,742	R	69.4%	15.9%	81.3%	18.7%
2,700,551	TOTAL	716,529	382,350	298,171	36,008	84,179	R	53.4%	41.6%	56.2%	43.8%

NEVADA

SENATOR 2010

								Percentage			
						Rep.-Dem.		Total Vote		Major Vote	
2010 Census Population	County	Total Vote	Republican	Democratic	Other	Plurality		Rep.	Dem.	Rep.	Dem.
55,274	CARSON CITY	19,519	9,362	8,714	1,443	648	R	48.0%	44.6%	51.8%	48.2%
24,877	CHURCHILL	8,895	5,639	2,473	783	3,166	R	63.4%	27.8%	69.5%	30.5%
1,951,269	CLARK	466,163	192,516	253,617	20,030	61,101	D	41.3%	54.4%	43.2%	56.8%
46,997	DOUGLAS	21,780	12,858	7,530	1,392	5,328	R	59.0%	34.6%	63.1%	36.9%
48,818	ELKO	12,859	8,173	3,246	1,440	4,927	R	63.6%	25.2%	71.6%	28.4%
783	ESMERALDA	397	268	80	49	188	R	67.5%	20.2%	77.0%	23.0%
1,987	EUREKA	759	524	137	98	387	R	69.0%	18.1%	79.3%	20.7%
16,528	HUMBOLDT	4,982	2,836	1,600	546	1,236	R	56.9%	32.1%	63.9%	36.1%
5,775	LANDER	1,902	1,201	487	214	714	R	63.1%	25.6%	71.1%	28.9%
5,345	LINCOLN	1,949	1,311	442	196	869	R	67.3%	22.7%	74.8%	25.2%
51,980	LYON	17,471	10,473	5,659	1,339	4,814	R	59.9%	32.4%	64.9%	35.1%
4,772	MINERAL	1,903	822	855	226	33	D	43.2%	44.9%	49.0%	51.0%
43,946	NYE	14,399	7,822	5,279	1,298	2,543	R	54.3%	36.7%	59.7%	40.3%
6,753	PERSHING	1,736	915	597	224	318	R	52.7%	34.4%	60.5%	39.5%
4,010	STOREY	2,134	1,124	843	167	281	R	52.7%	39.5%	57.1%	42.9%
421,407	WASHOE	141,287	63,316	70,523	7,448	7,207	D	44.8%	49.9%	47.3%	52.7%
10,030	WHITE PINE	3,269	2,201	703	365	1,498	R	67.3%	21.5%	75.8%	24.2%
2,700,551	TOTAL	721,404	321,361	362,785	37,258	41,424	D	44.5%	50.3%	47.0%	53.0%

NEVADA

HOUSE OF REPRESENTATIVES

| | | | Republican | | Democratic | | | | | Percentage | | | |
| | | | | | | | | | | Total Vote | | Major Vote | |
CD	Year	Total Vote	Vote	Candidate	Vote	Candidate	Other Vote	Rep.-Dem. Plurality		Rep.	Dem.	Rep.	Dem.
1	2010	167,206	58,995	WEGNER, KENNETH	103,246	BERKLEY, SHELLEY*	4,965	44,251	D	35.3%	61.7%	36.4%	63.6%
1	2008	228,922	64,837	WEGNER, KENNETH	154,860	BERKLEY, SHELLEY*	9,225	90,023	D	28.3%	67.6%	29.5%	70.5%
1	2006	131,124	40,917	WEGNER, KENNETH	85,025	BERKLEY, SHELLEY*	5,182	44,108	D	31.2%	64.8%	32.5%	67.5%
1	2004	202,436	63,005	MICKELSON, RUSS	133,569	BERKLEY, SHELLEY*	5,862	70,564	D	31.1%	66.0%	32.1%	67.9%
1	2002	119,714	51,148	BOGGS-McDONALD, LYNETTE MARIA	64,312	BERKLEY, SHELLEY*	4,254	13,164	D	42.7%	53.7%	44.3%	55.7%
2	2010	267,708	169,458	HELLER, DEAN*	87,421	PRICE, NANCY	10,829	82,037	R	63.3%	32.7%	66.0%	34.0%
2	2008	329,520	170,771	HELLER, DEAN*	136,548	DERBY, JILL	22,201	34,223	R	51.8%	41.4%	55.6%	44.4%
2	2006	232,724	117,168	HELLER, DEAN	104,593	DERBY, JILL	10,963	12,575	R	50.3%	44.9%	52.8%	47.2%
2	2004	291,079	195,466	GIBBONS, JIM*	79,978	COCHRAN, ANGIE G.	15,635	115,488	R	67.2%	27.5%	71.0%	29.0%
2	2002	201,200	149,574	GIBBONS, JIM*	40,189	SOUZA, TRAVIS O.	11,437	109,385	R	74.3%	20.0%	78.8%	21.2%
3	2010	267,874	128,916	HECK, JOE	127,168	TITUS, DINA*	11,790	1,748	R	48.1%	47.5%	50.3%	49.7%
3	2008	349,812	147,940	PORTER, JON*	165,912	TITUS, DINA	35,960	17,972	D	42.3%	47.4%	47.1%	52.9%
3	2006	210,979	102,232	PORTER, JON*	98,261	HAFEN, TESSA M.	10,486	3,971	R	48.5%	46.6%	51.0%	49.0%
3	2004	297,918	162,240	PORTER, JON*	120,365	GALLAGHER, TOM	15,313	41,875	R	54.5%	40.4%	57.4%	42.6%
3	2002	178,994	100,378	PORTER, JON	66,659	HERRERA, DARIO	11,957	33,719	R	56.1%	37.2%	60.1%	39.9%
TOTAL	2010	702,788	357,369		317,835		27,584	39,534	R	50.9%	45.2%	52.9%	47.1%
TOTAL	2008	908,254	383,548		457,320		67,386	73,772	D	42.2%	50.4%	45.6%	54.4%
TOTAL	2006	574,827	260,317		287,879		26,631	27,562	D	45.3%	50.1%	47.5%	52.5%
TOTAL	2004	791,433	420,711		333,912		36,810	86,799	R	53.2%	42.2%	55.8%	44.2%
TOTAL	2002	499,908	301,100		171,160		27,648	129,940	R	60.2%	34.2%	63.8%	36.2%

An asterisk (*) denotes incumbent.

NEVADA

GENERAL AND PRIMARY ELECTIONS

2010 GENERAL ELECTIONS

Governor   Other vote was 12,231 "None of these candidates"; 6,403 Independent (Eugene "Gino" Disimone); 5,049 Independent American (Floyd Fitzgibbons); 4,672 Libertarian (Arthur Forest Lampitt Jr.); 4,437 Green (David Scott Curtis); 3,216 Independent (Aaron Y. Honig).

Senator   Other vote was 16,197 "None of these candidates"; 5,811 Tea Party of Nevada (Scott Ashjian); 4,261 Independent (Michael L. Haines); 3,185 Independent American (Tim Fasano); 3,175 Independent (Jesse Holland); 2,510 Independent (Jeffrey C. Reeves); 2,119 Independent (Wil Stand).

House   Other vote was:

CD 1   2,847 Independent American (Jonathan J. Hansen); 2,118 Libertarian (Ed Klapproth).

CD 2   10,829 Independent American (Russell Best).

CD 3   6,473 Independent (Barry Michaels); 4,026 Libertarian (Joseph P. Silvestri); 1,291 Independent American (Scott David Narter).

NEVADA

GENERAL AND PRIMARY ELECTIONS

2010 PRIMARY ELECTIONS

Primary	June 8, 2010	Registration (as of May 2010—includes 274,655 inactive registrants)		

	Democratic	579,108
	Republican	471,819
	Independent American	59,115
	Libertarian	8,228
	Green	1,474
	Other	7,563
	Non-Partisan	211,904
	TOTAL	*1,339,211*

Primary Type   Closed—Only registered Democrats and Republicans could vote in their party's primary.

	REPUBLICAN PRIMARIES			DEMOCRATIC PRIMARIES		
Governor	Brian Sandoval	97,201	55.5%	Rory Reid	80,162	70.1%
	Jim Gibbons*	47,616	27.2%	"None of these candidates"	17,454	15.3%
	Michael L. Montandon	22,003	12.6%	Frederick L. Conquest	16,775	14.7%
	"None of these candidates"	4,400	2.5%			
	Tony Atwood	2,440	1.4%			
	Stanleigh Harold Lusak	1,380	0.8%			
	TOTAL	*175,040*		*TOTAL*	*114,391*	
Senator	Sharron Angle	70,424	40.1%	Harry Reid*	87,366	75.3%
	Sue Lowden	45,871	26.1%	"None of these candidates"	12,335	10.6%
	Danny Tarkanian	40,926	23.3%	Alex Miller	9,715	8.4%
	John Chachas	6,926	3.9%	Eduardo "Mr. Clean" Hamilton	4,644	4.0%
	Chad Christensen	4,803	2.7%	Carlo Poliak	1,938	1.7%
	"None of these candidates"	3,090	1.8%			
	Bill Parson	1,483	0.8%			
	Gary Bernstein	698	0.4%			
	Garn Mabey	462	0.3%			
	Cecilia Stern	355	0.2%			
	Brian Nadell	235	0.1%			
	Terry Suominen	223	0.1%			
	Gary Marinch	178	0.1%			
	TOTAL	*175,674*		*TOTAL*	*115,998*	
Congressional District 1	Kenneth Wegner	7,214	26.7%	Shelley Berkley*	Unopposed	
	Michele Fiore	5,922	22.0%			
	Craig Lake	5,277	19.6%			
	Chuck Flume	4,318	16.0%			
	David Cunningham	2,051	7.6%			
	Joseph Tatner	1,293	4.8%			
	Mike A. Monroe	456	1.7%			
	Scott Neistadt	440	1.6%			
	TOTAL	*26,971*				
Congressional District 2	Dean Heller*	72,728	83.7%	Nancy Price	18,609	45.4%
	Patrick J. Colletti	14,162	16.3%	Ken McKenna	18,259	44.5%
				Denis "Sam" Dehne	4,156	10.1%
	TOTAL	*86,890*		*TOTAL*	*41,024*	
Congressional District 3	Joe Heck	36,898	68.8%	Dina Titus*	32,119	80.4%
	Steven P. Nohrden	8,853	16.5%	John M. Beard	7,846	19.6%
	Ed Bridges	6,066	11.3%			
	Brad Leutwyler	1,812	3.4%			
	TOTAL	*53,629*		*TOTAL*	*39,965*	

NEW HAMPSHIRE

Congressional districts first established for elections held in 2002
2 members

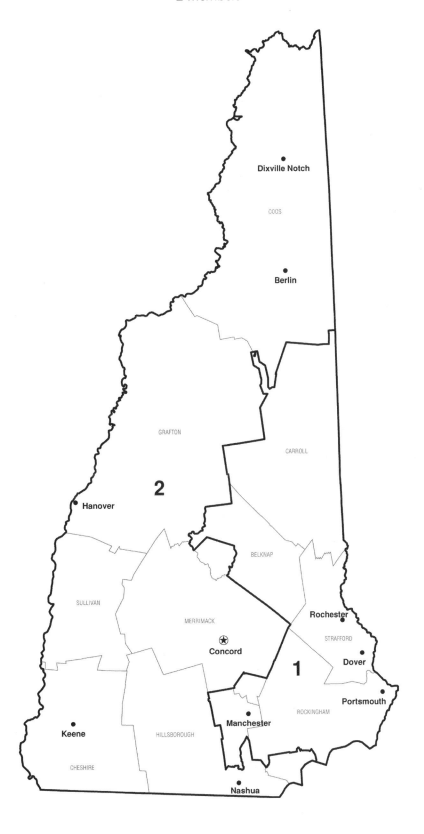

NEW HAMPSHIRE

GOVERNOR
John Lynch (D). Reelected 2010 to a two-year term. Previously elected 2008, 2006, 2004.

SENATORS (1 Democrat, 1 Republican)
Kelly Ayotte (R). Elected 2010 to a six-year term.

Jeanne Shaheen (D). Elected 2008 to a six-year term.

REPRESENTATIVES (2 Republicans)
1. Frank C. Guinta (R) 2. Charles Bass (R)

POSTWAR VOTE FOR PRESIDENT

Year	Total Vote	Republican Vote	Candidate	Democratic Vote	Candidate	Other Vote	Rep.-Dem. Plurality	Total Vote Rep.	Total Vote Dem.	Major Vote Rep.	Major Vote Dem.
2008	710,970	316,534	McCain, John	384,826	Obama, Barack	9,610	68,292 D	44.5%	54.1%	45.1%	54.9%
2004	677,738	331,237	Bush, George W.	340,511	Kerry, John	5,990	9,274 D	48.9%	50.2%	49.3%	50.7%
2000**	569,081	273,559	Bush, George W.	266,348	Gore, Al	29,174	7,211 R	48.1%	46.8%	50.7%	49.3%
1996**	499,175	196,532	Dole, Bob	246,214	Clinton, Bill	56,429	49,682 D	39.4%	49.3%	44.4%	55.6%
1992**	537,943	202,484	Bush, George	209,040	Clinton, Bill	126,419	6,556 D	37.6%	38.9%	49.2%	50.8%
1988	451,074	281,537	Bush, George	163,696	Dukakis, Michael S.	5,841	117,841 R	62.4%	36.3%	63.2%	36.8%
1984	389,066	267,051	Reagan, Ronald	120,395	Mondale, Walter F.	1,620	146,656 R	68.6%	30.9%	68.9%	31.1%
1980**	383,990	221,705	Reagan, Ronald	108,864	Carter, Jimmy	53,421	112,841 R	57.7%	28.4%	67.1%	32.9%
1976	339,618	185,935	Ford, Gerald R.	147,635	Carter, Jimmy	6,048	38,300 R	54.7%	43.5%	55.7%	44.3%
1972	334,055	213,724	Nixon, Richard M.	116,435	McGovern, George S.	3,896	97,289 R	64.0%	34.9%	64.7%	35.3%
1968**	297,298	154,903	Nixon, Richard M.	130,589	Humphrey, Hubert H.	11,806	24,314 R	52.1%	43.9%	54.3%	45.7%
1964	288,093	104,029	Goldwater, Barry M.	184,064	Johnson, Lyndon B.		80,035 D	36.1%	63.9%	36.1%	63.9%
1960	295,761	157,989	Nixon, Richard M.	137,772	Kennedy, John F.		20,217 R	53.4%	46.6%	53.4%	46.6%
1956	266,994	176,519	Eisenhower, Dwight D.	90,364	Stevenson, Adlai E.	111	86,155 R	66.1%	33.8%	66.1%	33.9%
1952	272,950	166,287	Eisenhower, Dwight D.	106,663	Stevenson, Adlai E.		59,624 R	60.9%	39.1%	60.9%	39.1%
1948	231,440	121,299	Dewey, Thomas E.	107,995	Truman, Harry S.	2,146	13,304 R	52.4%	46.7%	52.9%	47.1%

**In past elections, the other vote included: 2000 - 22,198 Green (Ralph Nader); 1996 - 48,390 Reform (Ross Perot); 1992 - 121,337 Independent (Perot); 1980 - 49,693 Independent (John Anderson); 1968 - 11,173 American Independent (George Wallace).

NEW HAMPSHIRE

POSTWAR VOTE FOR GOVERNOR

Year	Total Vote	Republican Vote	Republican Candidate	Democratic Vote	Democratic Candidate	Other Vote	Rep.-Dem. Plurality		Total Vote Rep.	Total Vote Dem.	Major Vote Rep.	Major Vote Dem.
2010	456,588	205,616	Stephen, John	240,346	Lynch, John	10,626	34,730	D	45.0%	52.6%	46.1%	53.9%
2008	682,910	188,555	Kenney, Joseph D.	479,042	Lynch, John	15,313	290,487	D	27.6%	70.1%	28.2%	71.8%
2006	403,679	104,288	Coburn, Jim	298,760	Lynch, John	631	194,472	D	25.8%	74.0%	25.9%	74.1%
2004	667,020	325,981	Benson, Craig	340,299	Lynch, John	740	14,318	D	48.9%	51.0%	48.9%	51.1%
2002	442,976	259,663	Benson, Craig	169,277	Fernald, Mark	14,036	90,386	R	58.6%	38.2%	60.5%	39.5%
2000	564,953	246,952	Humphrey, Gordon J.	275,038	Shaheen, Jeanne	42,963	28,086	D	43.7%	48.7%	47.3%	52.7%
1998	318,940	98,473	Lucas, Jay	210,769	Shaheen, Jeanne	9,698	112,296	D	30.9%	66.1%	31.8%	68.2%
1996	497,040	196,321	Lamontagne, Ovide	284,175	Shaheen, Jeanne	16,544	87,854	D	39.5%	57.2%	40.9%	59.1%
1994	311,882	218,134	Merrill, Steve	79,686	King, Wayne D.	14,062	138,448	R	69.9%	25.6%	73.2%	26.8%
1992	516,170	289,170	Merrill, Steve	206,232	Arnesen, Deborah A.	20,768	82,938	R	56.0%	40.0%	58.4%	41.6%
1990	295,018	177,773	Gregg, Judd	101,923	Grandmaison, J. Joseph	15,322	75,850	R	60.3%	34.5%	63.6%	36.4%
1988	441,923	267,064	Gregg, Judd	172,543	McEachern, Paul	2,316	94,521	R	60.4%	39.0%	60.8%	39.2%
1986	251,107	134,824	Sununu, John H.	116,142	McEachern, Paul	141	18,682	R	53.7%	46.3%	53.7%	46.3%
1984	383,910	256,574	Sununu, John H.	127,156	Spirou, Chris	180	129,418	R	66.8%	33.1%	66.9%	33.1%
1982	282,588	145,389	Sununu, John H.	132,317	Gallen, Hugh J.	4,882	13,072	R	51.4%	46.8%	52.4%	47.6%
1980	384,031	156,178	Thomson, Meldrim	226,436	Gallen, Hugh J.	1,417	70,258	D	40.7%	59.0%	40.8%	59.2%
1978	269,587	122,464	Thomson, Meldrim	133,133	Gallen, Hugh J.	13,990	10,669	D	45.4%	49.4%	47.9%	52.1%
1976	342,669	197,589	Thomson, Meldrim	145,015	Spanos, Harry V.	65	52,574	R	57.7%	42.3%	57.7%	42.3%
1974	226,665	115,933	Thomson, Meldrim	110,591	Leonard, Richard W.	141	5,342	R	51.1%	48.8%	51.2%	48.8%
1972**	323,102	133,702	Thomson, Meldrim	126,107	Crowley, Roger J.	63,293	7,595	R	41.4%	39.0%	51.5%	48.5%
1970	222,441	102,298	Peterson, Walter R.	98,098	Crowley, Roger J.	22,045	4,200	R	46.0%	44.1%	51.0%	49.0%
1968	285,342	149,902	Peterson, Walter R.	135,378	Bussiere, Emile R.	62	14,524	R	52.5%	47.4%	52.5%	47.5%
1966	233,642	107,259	Gregg, Hugh	125,882	King, John W.	501	18,623	D	45.9%	53.9%	46.0%	54.0%
1964	285,863	94,824	Pillsbury, John	190,863	King, John W.	176	96,039	D	33.2%	66.8%	33.2%	66.8%
1962	230,048	94,567	Pillsbury, John	135,481	King, John W.		40,914	D	41.1%	58.9%	41.1%	58.9%
1960	290,527	161,123	Powell, Wesley	129,404	Boutin, Bernard L.		31,719	R	55.5%	44.5%	55.5%	44.5%
1958	206,745	106,790	Powell, Wesley	99,955	Boutin, Bernard L.		6,835	R	51.7%	48.3%	51.7%	48.3%
1956	258,695	141,578	Dwinell, Lane	117,117	Shaw, John		24,461	R	54.7%	45.3%	54.7%	45.3%
1954	194,631	107,287	Dwinell, Lane	87,344	Shaw, John		19,943	R	55.1%	44.9%	55.1%	44.9%
1952	265,715	167,791	Gregg, Hugh	97,924	Craig, William H.		69,867	R	63.1%	36.9%	63.1%	36.9%
1950	191,239	108,907	Adams, Sherman	82,258	Bingham, Robert P.	74	26,649	R	56.9%	43.0%	57.0%	43.0%
1948	222,571	116,212	Adams, Sherman	105,207	Hill, Herbert W.	1,152	11,005	R	52.2%	47.3%	52.5%	47.5%
1946	163,451	103,204	Dale, Charles M.	60,247	Keefe, F. Clyde		42,957	R	63.1%	36.9%	63.1%	36.9%

**In past elections, the other vote included: 1972 - 63,199 Independent (Malcolm McLane).

NEW HAMPSHIRE

POSTWAR VOTE FOR SENATOR

Year	Total Vote	Republican Vote	Republican Candidate	Democratic Vote	Democratic Candidate	Other Vote	Rep.-Dem. Plurality	Percentage Total Vote Rep.	Percentage Total Vote Dem.	Percentage Major Vote Rep.	Percentage Major Vote Dem.
2010	455,149	273,218	Ayotte, Kelly	167,545	Hodes, Paul W.	14,386	105,673 R	60.0%	36.8%	62.0%	38.0%
2008	694,787	314,403	Sununu, John E.	358,438	Shaheen, Jeanne	21,946	44,035 D	45.3%	51.6%	46.7%	53.3%
2004	657,086	434,847	Gregg, Judd	221,549	Haddock, Doris Granny D.	690	213,298 R	66.2%	33.7%	66.2%	33.8%
2002	447,135	227,229	Sununu, John E.	207,478	Shaheen, Jeanne	12,428	19,751 R	50.8%	46.4%	52.3%	47.7%
1998	314,956	213,477	Gregg, Judd	88,883	Condodemetraky, George	12,596	124,594 R	67.8%	28.2%	70.6%	29.4%
1996	492,598	242,304	Smith, Robert C.	227,397	Swett, Dick	22,897	14,907 R	49.2%	46.2%	51.6%	48.4%
1992	518,416	249,591	Gregg, Judd	234,982	Rauh, John	33,843	14,609 R	48.1%	45.3%	51.5%	48.5%
1990	291,393	189,792	Smith, Robert C.	91,299	Durkin, John A.	10,302	98,493 R	65.1%	31.3%	67.5%	32.5%
1986	244,797	154,090	Rudman, Warren	79,225	Peabody, Endicott	11,482	74,865 R	62.9%	32.4%	66.0%	34.0%
1984	384,406	225,828	Humphrey, Gordon J.	157,447	D'Amours, Norman E.	1,131	68,381 R	58.7%	41.0%	58.9%	41.1%
1980	375,064	195,563	Rudman, Warren	179,455	Durkin, John A.	46	16,108 R	52.1%	47.8%	52.1%	47.9%
1978	263,779	133,745	Humphrey, Gordon J.	127,945	McIntyre, Thomas J.	2,089	5,800 R	50.7%	48.5%	51.1%	48.9%
1975S	262,682	113,007	Wyman, Louis C.	140,778	Durkin, John A.	8,897	27,771 D	43.0%	53.6%	44.5%	55.5%
1974**	223,363	110,926	Wyman, Louis C.	110,924	Durkin, John A.	1,513	2 R	49.7%	49.7%	50.0%	50.0%
1972	324,354	139,852	Powell, Wesley	184,495	McIntyre, Thomas J.	7	44,643 D	43.1%	56.9%	43.1%	56.9%
1968	286,989	170,163	Cotton, Norris	116,816	King, John W.	10	53,347 R	59.3%	40.7%	59.3%	40.7%
1966	229,305	105,241	Thyng, Harrison R.	123,888	McIntyre, Thomas J.	176	18,647 D	45.9%	54.0%	45.9%	54.1%
1962	224,479	134,035	Cotton, Norris	90,444	Catalfo, Alfred		43,591 R	59.7%	40.3%	59.7%	40.3%
1962S	224,811	107,199	Bass, Perkins	117,612	McIntyre, Thomas J.		10,413 D	47.7%	52.3%	47.7%	52.3%
1960	287,545	173,521	Bridges, Styles	114,024	Hill, Herbert W.		59,497 R	60.3%	39.7%	60.3%	39.7%
1956	251,943	161,424	Cotton, Norris	90,519	Pickett, Laurence M.		70,905 R	64.1%	35.9%	64.1%	35.9%
1954	194,536	117,150	Bridges, Styles	77,386	Morin, Gerard L.		39,764 R	60.2%	39.8%	60.2%	39.8%
1954S	189,558	114,068	Cotton, Norris	75,490	Bentley, Stanley J.		38,578 R	60.2%	39.8%	60.2%	39.8%
1950	190,573	106,142	Tobey, Charles W.	72,473	Kelley, Emmet J.	11,958	33,669 R	55.7%	38.0%	59.4%	40.6%
1948	222,898	129,600	Bridges, Styles	91,760	Fortin, Alfred E.	1,538	37,840 R	58.1%	41.2%	58.5%	41.5%

**Following the closely contested 1974 election, neither candidate was seated and the 1975 special election was held for the remaining years of that term. One each of the 1954 and 1962 elections were for short terms to fill vacancies.

NEW HAMPSHIRE

GOVERNOR 2010

2010 Census Population	County	Total Vote	Republican	Democratic	Other	Rep.-Dem. Plurality		Percentage Total Vote Rep.	Percentage Total Vote Dem.	Percentage Major Vote Rep.	Percentage Major Vote Dem.
60,088	BELKNAP	22,609	11,008	11,021	580	13	D	48.7%	48.7%	50.0%	50.0%
47,818	CARROLL	20,311	9,895	10,003	413	108	D	48.7%	49.2%	49.7%	50.3%
77,117	CHESHIRE	26,135	10,082	15,429	624	5,347	D	38.6%	59.0%	39.5%	60.5%
33,055	COOS	10,595	4,590	5,699	306	1,109	D	43.3%	53.8%	44.6%	55.4%
89,118	GRAFTON	31,410	11,898	18,618	894	6,720	D	37.9%	59.3%	39.0%	61.0%
400,721	HILLSBOROUGH	130,591	62,704	65,183	2,704	2,479	D	48.0%	49.9%	49.0%	51.0%
146,445	MERRIMACK	55,027	21,548	31,929	1,550	10,381	D	39.2%	58.0%	40.3%	59.7%
295,223	ROCKINGHAM	106,956	53,049	51,714	2,193	1,335	R	49.6%	48.4%	50.6%	49.4%
123,143	STRAFFORD	38,425	14,639	22,807	979	8,168	D	38.1%	59.4%	39.1%	60.9%
43,742	SULLIVAN	14,529	6,203	7,943	383	1,740	D	42.7%	54.7%	43.8%	56.2%
1,316,470	TOTAL	456,588	205,616	240,346	10,626	34,730	D	45.0%	52.6%	46.1%	53.9%

NEW HAMPSHIRE

GOVERNOR 2010

2010 Census Population	City/Town	Total Vote	Republican	Democratic	Other	Rep.-Dem. Plurality		Percentage			
								Total Vote		Major Vote	
								Rep.	Dem.	Rep.	Dem.
11,201	AMHERST	5,323	2,511	2,738	74	227	D	47.2%	51.4%	47.8%	52.2%
6,751	ATKINSON	2,953	1,736	1,171	46	565	R	58.8%	39.7%	59.7%	40.3%
8,576	BARRINGTON	3,195	1,314	1,778	103	464	D	41.1%	55.6%	42.5%	57.5%
21,203	BEDFORD	9,024	5,275	3,648	101	1,627	R	58.5%	40.4%	59.1%	40.9%
7,356	BELMONT	2,138	1,056	1,021	61	35	R	49.4%	47.8%	50.8%	49.2%
10,051	BERLIN	2,835	845	1,903	87	1,058	D	29.8%	67.1%	30.7%	69.3%
7,519	BOW	3,638	1,400	2,153	85	753	D	38.5%	59.2%	39.4%	60.6%
13,355	CLAREMONT	3,462	1,493	1,866	103	373	D	43.1%	53.9%	44.4%	55.6%
42,695	CONCORD	14,727	4,376	9,963	388	5,587	D	29.7%	67.7%	30.5%	69.5%
10,115	CONWAY	3,256	1,365	1,816	75	451	D	41.9%	55.8%	42.9%	57.1%
33,109	DERRY	9,190	5,085	3,903	202	1,182	R	55.3%	42.5%	56.6%	43.4%
29,987	DOVER	9,711	3,357	6,127	227	2,770	D	34.6%	63.1%	35.4%	64.6%
14,638	DURHAM	3,690	849	2,719	122	1,870	D	23.0%	73.7%	23.8%	76.2%
6,411	EPPING	2,021	922	1,039	60	117	D	45.6%	51.4%	47.0%	53.0%
14,306	EXETER	5,842	2,208	3,559	75	1,351	D	37.8%	60.9%	38.3%	61.7%
6,786	FARMINGTON	1,759	852	865	42	13	D	48.4%	49.2%	49.6%	50.4%
8,477	FRANKLIN	2,366	1,012	1,273	81	261	D	42.8%	53.8%	44.3%	55.7%
7,126	GILFORD	3,160	1,573	1,531	56	42	R	49.8%	48.4%	50.7%	49.3%
17,651	GOFFSTOWN	5,903	3,070	2,682	151	388	R	52.0%	45.4%	53.4%	46.6%
8,523	HAMPSTEAD	3,428	1,990	1,388	50	602	R	58.1%	40.5%	58.9%	41.1%
15,430	HAMPTON	6,378	2,869	3,414	95	545	D	45.0%	53.5%	45.7%	54.3%
11,260	HANOVER	4,423	799	3,550	74	2,751	D	18.1%	80.3%	18.4%	81.6%
7,684	HOLLIS	3,653	1,815	1,776	62	39	R	49.7%	48.6%	50.5%	49.5%
13,451	HOOKSETT	4,731	2,521	2,140	70	381	R	53.3%	45.2%	54.1%	45.9%
24,467	HUDSON	7,183	3,710	3,307	166	403	R	51.6%	46.0%	52.9%	47.1%
5,457	JAFFREY	1,891	855	1,001	35	146	D	45.2%	52.9%	46.1%	53.9%
23,409	KEENE	7,277	2,281	4,816	180	2,535	D	31.3%	66.2%	32.1%	67.9%
6,025	KINGSTON	2,130	1,137	946	47	191	R	53.4%	44.4%	54.6%	45.4%
15,951	LACONIA	5,081	2,395	2,594	92	199	D	47.1%	51.1%	48.0%	52.0%
13,151	LEBANON	4,195	1,266	2,836	93	1,570	D	30.2%	67.6%	30.9%	69.1%
8,271	LITCHFIELD	2,950	1,645	1,248	57	397	R	55.8%	42.3%	56.9%	43.1%
5,928	LITTLETON	1,866	897	945	24	48	D	48.1%	50.6%	48.7%	51.3%
24,129	LONDONDERRY	8,284	4,475	3,716	93	759	R	54.0%	44.9%	54.6%	45.4%
109,565	MANCHESTER	29,882	13,661	15,612	609	1,951	D	45.7%	52.2%	46.7%	53.3%
25,494	MERRIMACK TOWN	9,592	4,824	4,615	153	209	R	50.3%	48.1%	51.1%	48.9%
15,115	MILFORD	4,917	2,342	2,485	90	143	D	47.6%	50.5%	48.5%	51.5%
86,494	NASHUA	24,571	10,390	13,674	507	3,284	D	42.3%	55.7%	43.2%	56.8%
8,936	NEWMARKET	3,115	1,070	1,968	77	898	D	34.3%	63.2%	35.2%	64.8%
6,507	NEWPORT	1,844	883	896	65	13	D	47.9%	48.6%	49.6%	50.4%
12,897	PELHAM	3,896	2,317	1,505	74	812	R	59.5%	38.6%	60.6%	39.4%
7,115	PEMBROKE	2,614	1,074	1,466	74	392	D	41.1%	56.1%	42.3%	57.7%
6,284	PETERBOROUGH	2,757	855	1,861	41	1,006	D	31.0%	67.5%	31.5%	68.5%
7,609	PLAISTOW	2,278	1,315	915	48	400	R	57.7%	40.2%	59.0%	41.0%
6,990	PLYMOUTH	1,721	580	1,073	68	493	D	33.7%	62.3%	35.1%	64.9%
20,779	PORTSMOUTH	8,150	2,151	5,817	182	3,666	D	26.4%	71.4%	27.0%	73.0%
10,138	RAYMOND	3,087	1,681	1,299	107	382	R	54.5%	42.1%	56.4%	43.6%
29,752	ROCHESTER	8,772	3,752	4,819	201	1,067	D	42.8%	54.9%	43.8%	56.2%
28,776	SALEM	8,748	5,055	3,509	184	1,546	R	57.8%	40.1%	59.0%	41.0%
8,693	SEABROOK	2,355	1,257	1,030	68	227	R	53.4%	43.7%	55.0%	45.0%
11,766	SOMERSWORTH	3,102	1,138	1,889	75	751	D	36.7%	60.9%	37.6%	62.4%
7,230	SWANZEY	2,242	999	1,197	46	198	D	44.6%	53.4%	45.5%	54.5%
8,785	WEARE	2,958	1,521	1,335	102	186	R	51.4%	45.1%	53.3%	46.7%
13,592	WINDHAM	5,006	2,944	1,973	89	971	R	58.8%	39.4%	59.9%	40.1%

NEW HAMPSHIRE

SENATOR 2010

2010 Census Population	County	Total Vote	Republican	Democratic	Other	Rep.-Dem. Plurality		Percentage			
								Total Vote		Major Vote	
								Rep.	Dem.	Rep.	Dem.
60,088	BELKNAP	22,498	14,817	6,964	717	7,853	R	65.9%	31.0%	68.0%	32.0%
47,818	CARROLL	20,215	12,550	7,013	652	5,537	R	62.1%	34.7%	64.2%	35.8%
77,117	CHESHIRE	26,118	13,075	12,260	783	815	R	50.1%	46.9%	51.6%	48.4%
33,055	COOS	10,601	6,196	4,064	341	2,132	R	58.4%	38.3%	60.4%	39.6%
89,118	GRAFTON	31,352	15,372	15,032	948	340	R	49.0%	47.9%	50.6%	49.4%
400,721	HILLSBOROUGH	130,296	82,511	43,924	3,861	38,587	R	63.3%	33.7%	65.3%	34.7%
146,445	MERRIMACK	54,895	31,456	21,655	1,784	9,801	R	57.3%	39.4%	59.2%	40.8%
295,223	ROCKINGHAM	106,502	68,017	35,002	3,483	33,015	R	63.9%	32.9%	66.0%	34.0%
123,143	STRAFFORD	38,212	21,204	15,695	1,313	5,509	R	55.5%	41.1%	57.5%	42.5%
43,742	SULLIVAN	14,460	8,020	5,936	504	2,084	R	55.5%	41.1%	57.5%	42.5%
1,316,470	TOTAL	455,149	273,218	167,545	14,386	105,673	R	60.0%	36.8%	62.0%	38.0%

2010 Census Population	City/Town	Total Vote	Republican	Democratic	Other	Rep.-Dem. Plurality		Percentage			
								Total Vote		Major Vote	
								Rep.	Dem.	Rep.	Dem.
11,201	AMHERST	5,311	3,289	1,933	89	1,356	R	61.9%	36.4%	63.0%	37.0%
6,751	ATKINSON	2,958	2,108	759	91	1,349	R	71.3%	25.7%	73.5%	26.5%
8,576	BARRINGTON	3,173	1,901	1,133	139	768	R	59.9%	35.7%	62.7%	37.3%
21,203	BEDFORD	9,032	6,570	2,297	165	4,273	R	72.7%	25.4%	74.1%	25.9%
7,356	BELMONT	2,137	1,439	602	96	837	R	67.3%	28.2%	70.5%	29.5%
10,051	BERLIN	2,824	1,398	1,339	87	59	R	49.5%	47.4%	51.1%	48.9%
7,519	BOW	3,634	2,171	1,381	82	790	R	59.7%	38.0%	61.1%	38.9%
13,355	CLAREMONT	3,430	1,930	1,359	141	571	R	56.3%	39.6%	58.7%	41.3%
42,695	CONCORD	14,659	6,921	7,263	475	342	D	47.2%	49.5%	48.8%	51.2%
10,115	CONWAY	3,203	1,796	1,291	116	505	R	56.1%	40.3%	58.2%	41.8%
33,109	DERRY	9,132	6,145	2,695	292	3,450	R	67.3%	29.5%	69.5%	30.5%
29,987	DOVER	9,666	4,959	4,421	286	538	R	51.3%	45.7%	52.9%	47.1%
14,638	DURHAM	3,695	1,266	2,311	118	1,045	D	34.3%	62.5%	35.4%	64.6%
6,411	EPPING	2,024	1,246	679	99	567	R	61.6%	33.5%	64.7%	35.3%
14,306	EXETER	5,842	2,980	2,681	181	299	R	51.0%	45.9%	52.6%	47.4%
6,786	FARMINGTON	1,747	1,135	549	63	586	R	65.0%	31.4%	67.4%	32.6%
8,477	FRANKLIN	2,352	1,459	802	91	657	R	62.0%	34.1%	64.5%	35.5%
7,126	GILFORD	3,145	2,103	956	86	1,147	R	66.9%	30.4%	68.7%	31.3%
17,651	GOFFSTOWN	5,899	4,091	1,627	181	2,464	R	69.4%	27.6%	71.5%	28.5%
8,523	HAMPSTEAD	3,414	2,481	839	94	1,642	R	72.7%	24.6%	74.7%	25.3%
15,430	HAMPTON	6,331	3,896	2,262	173	1,634	R	61.5%	35.7%	63.3%	36.7%
11,260	HANOVER	4,449	1,068	3,303	78	2,235	D	24.0%	74.2%	24.4%	75.6%
7,684	HOLLIS	3,649	2,305	1,253	91	1,052	R	63.2%	34.3%	64.8%	35.2%
13,451	HOOKSETT	4,716	3,317	1,302	97	2,015	R	70.3%	27.6%	71.8%	28.2%
24,467	HUDSON	7,157	4,947	1,974	236	2,973	R	69.1%	27.6%	71.5%	28.5%
5,457	JAFFREY	1,894	1,101	745	48	356	R	58.1%	39.3%	59.6%	40.4%
23,409	KEENE	7,309	3,027	4,076	206	1,049	D	41.4%	55.8%	42.6%	57.4%
6,025	KINGSTON	2,117	1,430	609	78	821	R	67.5%	28.8%	70.1%	29.9%
15,951	LACONIA	5,029	3,233	1,668	128	1,565	R	64.3%	33.2%	66.0%	34.0%
13,151	LEBANON	4,188	1,694	2,399	95	705	D	40.4%	57.3%	41.4%	58.6%
8,271	LITCHFIELD	2,944	2,169	695	80	1,474	R	73.7%	23.6%	75.7%	24.3%
5,928	LITTLETON	1,868	1,160	660	48	500	R	62.1%	35.3%	63.7%	36.3%
24,129	LONDONDERRY	8,274	5,691	2,400	183	3,291	R	68.8%	29.0%	70.3%	29.7%
109,565	MANCHESTER	29,703	18,046	10,734	923	7,312	R	60.8%	36.1%	62.7%	37.3%
25,494	MERRIMACK TOWN	9,575	6,450	2,876	249	3,574	R	67.4%	30.0%	69.2%	30.8%

NEW HAMPSHIRE

SENATOR 2010

2010 Census Population	City/Town	Total Vote	Republican	Democratic	Other	Rep.-Dem. Plurality		Percentage Total Vote Rep.	Dem.	Major Vote Rep.	Dem.
15,115	MILFORD	4,895	3,090	1,650	155	1,440	R	63.1%	33.7%	65.2%	34.8%
86,494	NASHUA	24,488	14,466	9,290	732	5,176	R	59.1%	37.9%	60.9%	39.1%
8,936	NEWMARKET	3,097	1,512	1,457	128	55	R	48.8%	47.0%	50.9%	49.1%
6,507	NEWPORT	1,835	1,165	592	78	573	R	63.5%	32.3%	66.3%	33.7%
12,897	PELHAM	3,872	2,747	986	139	1,761	R	70.9%	25.5%	73.6%	26.4%
7,115	PEMBROKE	2,597	1,602	900	95	702	R	61.7%	34.7%	64.0%	36.0%
6,284	PETERBOROUGH	2,781	1,195	1,515	71	320	D	43.0%	54.5%	44.1%	55.9%
7,609	PLAISTOW	2,261	1,647	520	94	1,127	R	72.8%	23.0%	76.0%	24.0%
6,990	PLYMOUTH	1,690	774	865	51	91	D	45.8%	51.2%	47.2%	52.8%
20,779	PORTSMOUTH	8,095	3,223	4,646	226	1,423	D	39.8%	57.4%	41.0%	59.0%
10,138	RAYMOND	3,086	2,161	805	120	1,356	R	70.0%	26.1%	72.9%	27.1%
29,752	ROCHESTER	8,713	5,476	2,941	296	2,535	R	62.8%	33.8%	65.1%	34.9%
28,776	SALEM	8,682	6,055	2,279	348	3,776	R	69.7%	26.2%	72.7%	27.3%
8,693	SEABROOK	2,349	1,606	618	125	988	R	68.4%	26.3%	72.2%	27.8%
11,766	SOMERSWORTH	3,078	1,755	1,203	120	552	R	57.0%	39.1%	59.3%	40.7%
7,230	SWANZEY	2,239	1,293	882	64	411	R	57.7%	39.4%	59.4%	40.6%
8,785	WEARE	2,962	2,048	813	101	1,235	R	69.1%	27.4%	71.6%	28.4%
13,592	WINDHAM	4,960	3,558	1,247	155	2,311	R	71.7%	25.1%	74.0%	26.0%

NEW HAMPSHIRE

HOUSE OF REPRESENTATIVES

CD	Year	Total Vote	Republican Vote	Candidate	Democratic Vote	Candidate	Other Vote	Rep.-Dem. Plurality		Percentage Total Vote Rep.	Dem.	Major Vote Rep.	Dem.
1	2010	225,423	121,655	GUINTA, FRANK C.	95,503	SHEA-PORTER, CAROL*	8,265	26,152	R	54.0%	42.4%	56.0%	44.0%
1	2008	341,071	156,338	BRADLEY, JEB	176,435	SHEA-PORTER, CAROL*	8,298	20,097	D	45.8%	51.7%	47.0%	53.0%
1	2006	196,377	95,527	BRADLEY, JEB*	100,691	SHEA-PORTER, CAROL	159	5,164	D	48.6%	51.3%	48.7%	51.3%
1	2004	323,372	204,836	BRADLEY, JEB*	118,226	NADEAU, JUSTIN	310	86,610	R	63.3%	36.6%	63.4%	36.6%
1	2002	221,987	128,993	BRADLEY, JEB	85,426	CLARK, MARTHA FULLER	7,568	43,567	R	58.1%	38.5%	60.2%	39.8%
2	2010	224,663	108,610	BASS, CHARLES	105,060	KUSTER, ANN McLANE	10,993	3,550	R	48.3%	46.8%	50.8%	49.2%
2	2008	333,904	138,222	HORN, JENNIFER	188,332	HODES, PAUL W.*	7,350	50,110	D	41.4%	56.4%	42.3%	57.7%
2	2006	206,292	94,088	BASS, CHARLES*	108,743	HODES, PAUL W.	3,461	14,655	D	45.6%	52.7%	46.4%	53.6%
2	2004	328,194	191,188	BASS, CHARLES*	125,280	HODES, PAUL W.	11,726	65,908	R	58.3%	38.2%	60.4%	39.6%
2	2002	221,456	125,804	BASS, CHARLES*	90,479	SWETT, KATRINA	5,173	35,325	R	56.8%	40.9%	58.2%	41.8%
TOTAL	2010	450,086	230,265		200,563		19,258	29,702	R	51.2%	44.6%	53.4%	46.6%
TOTAL	2008	674,975	294,560		364,767		15,648	70,207	D	43.6%	54.0%	44.7%	55.3%
TOTAL	2006	402,669	189,615		209,434		3,620	19,819	D	47.1%	52.0%	47.5%	52.5%
TOTAL	2004	651,566	396,024		243,506		12,036	152,518	R	60.8%	37.4%	61.9%	38.1%
TOTAL	2002	443,443	254,797		175,905		12,741	78,892	R	57.5%	39.7%	59.2%	40.8%

An asterisk (*) denotes incumbent.

NEW HAMPSHIRE

GENERAL AND PRIMARY ELECTIONS

2010 GENERAL ELECTIONS

Governor Other vote was 10,089 Libertarian (John J. Babiarz); 537 scattered write-in.

Senator Other vote was 9,194 Independent (Chris Booth); 4,753 Libertarian (Ken Blevens); 439 scattered write-in.

House Other vote was:

CD 1 7,966 Libertarian (Philip Hodson); 299 scattered write-in.

CD 2 6,197 Independent (Tim vanBlommesteyn); 4,796 Libertarian (Howard L. Wilson). (Official returns listed 4 scattered write-in votes from the town of Andover, but the total number of scattered write-ins was not listed.)

2008 PRIMARY ELECTIONS

Primary September 14, 2010

Registration
(as of May 10, 2010)

Democratic	267,725
Republican	266,077
Undeclared	388,220
TOTAL	*922,022*

Primary Type Semi-open—Registered Democrats and Republicans could vote only in their party's primary. "Undeclared" voters could participate in either party's primary.

	REPUBLICAN PRIMARIES			DEMOCRATIC PRIMARIES		
Governor	John Stephen	78,783	61.5%	John Lynch*	50,348	87.5%
	Jack Kimball Jr.	32,121	25.1%	Timothy Robertson	3,792	6.6%
	Karen Testerman	12,787	10.0%	Frank Sullivan	3,418	5.9%
	Frank Robert Emiro Sr.	4,400	3.4%			
	TOTAL	*128,091*		*TOTAL*	*57,558*	
Senator	Kelly Ayotte	53,056	38.2%	Paul W. Hodes	49,845	100.0%
	Ovide Lamontagne	51,397	37.0%			
	Bill Binnie	19,508	14.0%			
	Jim Bender	12,611	9.1%			
	Dennis Lamare	1,388	1.0%			
	Tom Alciere	499	0.4%			
	Gerard Beloin	402	0.3%			
	TOTAL	*138,861*				
Congressional District 1	Frank C. Guinta	22,237	31.8%	Carol Shea-Porter*	19,405	96.4%
	Sean Mahoney	19,418	27.8%	Scattered write-in	717	3.6%
	Richard Ashooh	19,376	27.8%			
	Bob Bestani	5,337	7.6%			
	Peter J. Bearse	1,158	1.7%			
	Richard Charles Parent	1,051	1.5%			
	Kevin Rondeau	702	1.0%			
	Andrew P. Kohlhofer	397	0.6%			
	Scattered write-in	146	0.2%			
	TOTAL	*69,822*		*TOTAL*	*20,122*	
Congressional District 2	Charles Bass	27,457	42.5%	Ann McLane Kuster	25,431	70.9%
	Jennifer Horn	22,868	35.4%	Katrina Swett	10,100	28.2%
	Robert J. Giuda	11,145	17.2%	Scattered write-in	320	0.9%
	Joseph G. Reilly	1,757	2.7%			
	Wesley M. Sonner Jr.	1,192	1.8%			
	Scattered write-in	218	0.3%			
	TOTAL	*64,637*		*TOTAL*	*35,851*	

An asterisk (*) denotes incumbent.

NEW JERSEY

Congressional districts first established for elections held in 2002
13 members

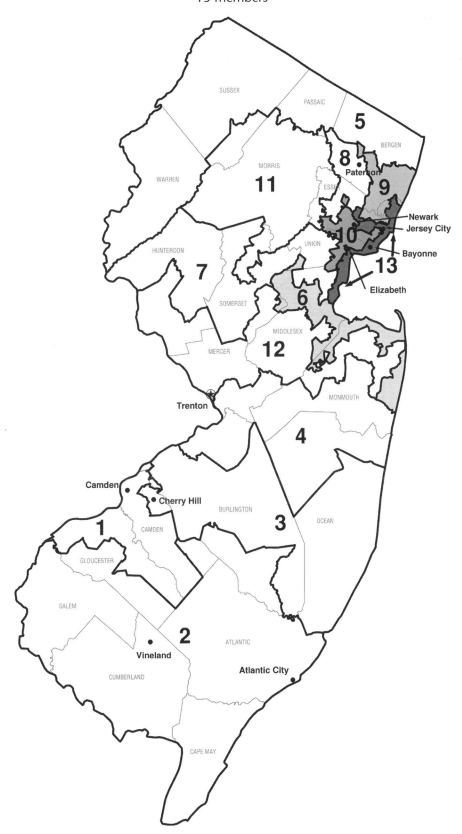

NEW JERSEY

Northern New Jersey Gateway Area

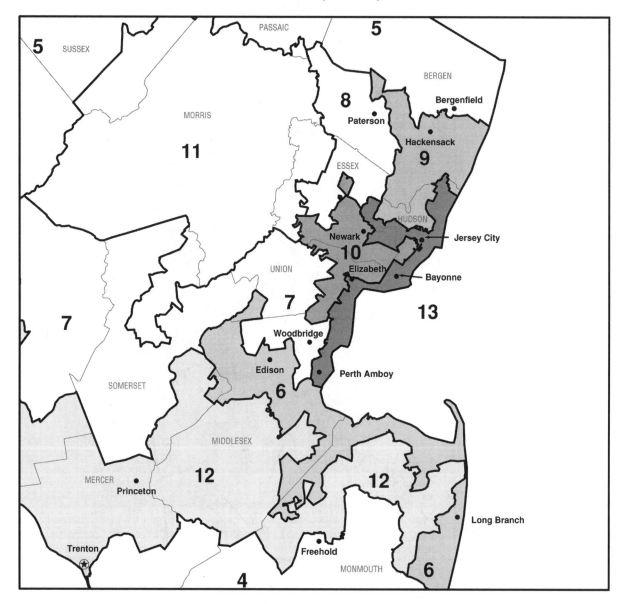

NEW JERSEY

GOVERNOR
Chris Christie (R). Elected 2009 to a four-year term.

SENATORS (2 Democrats)
Frank R. Lautenberg (D). Reelected 2008 to a six-year term. Previously elected 2002, 1994, 1988, 1982.

Robert Menendez (D). Elected 2006 to a six-year term.

REPRESENTATIVES (7 Democrats, 6 Republicans)

1. Robert E. Andrews (D)
2. Frank A. LoBiondo (R)
3. Jon Runyan (R)
4. Christopher H. Smith (R)
5. Scott Garrett (R)
6. Frank Pallone Jr. (D)
7. Leonard Lance (R)
8. Bill Pascrell Jr. (D)
9. Steven R. Rothman (D)
10. Donald M. Payne (D)
11. Rodney Frelinghuysen (R)
12. Rush D. Holt (D)
13. Albio Sires (D)

POSTWAR VOTE FOR PRESIDENT

| | | Republican | | Democratic | | | | Percentage | | | |
| | | | | | | | | Total Vote | | Major Vote | |
Year	Total Vote	Vote	Candidate	Vote	Candidate	Other Vote	Rep.-Dem. Plurality	Rep.	Dem.	Rep.	Dem.
2008	3,868,237	1,613,207	McCain, John	2,215,422	Obama, Barack	39,608	602,215 D	41.7%	57.3%	42.1%	57.9%
2004	3,611,691	1,670,003	Bush, George W.	1,911,430	Kerry, John	30,258	241,427 D	46.2%	52.9%	46.6%	53.4%
2000**	3,187,226	1,284,173	Bush, George W.	1,788,850	Gore, Al	114,203	504,677 D	40.3%	56.1%	41.8%	58.2%
1996**	3,075,807	1,103,078	Dole, Bob	1,652,329	Clinton, Bill	320,400	549,251 D	35.9%	53.7%	40.0%	60.0%
1992**	3,343,594	1,356,865	Bush, George	1,436,206	Clinton, Bill	550,523	79,341 D	40.6%	43.0%	48.6%	51.4%
1988	3,099,553	1,743,192	Bush, George	1,320,352	Dukakis, Michael S.	36,009	422,840 R	56.2%	42.6%	56.9%	43.1%
1984	3,217,862	1,933,630	Reagan, Ronald	1,261,323	Mondale, Walter F.	22,909	672,307 R	60.1%	39.2%	60.5%	39.5%
1980**	2,975,684	1,546,557	Reagan, Ronald	1,147,364	Carter, Jimmy	281,763	399,193 R	52.0%	38.6%	57.4%	42.6%
1976	3,014,472	1,509,688	Ford, Gerald R.	1,444,653	Carter, Jimmy	60,131	65,035 R	50.1%	47.9%	51.1%	48.9%
1972	2,997,229	1,845,502	Nixon, Richard M.	1,102,211	McGovern, George S.	49,516	743,291 R	61.6%	36.8%	62.6%	37.4%
1968**	2,875,395	1,325,467	Nixon, Richard M.	1,264,206	Humphrey, Hubert H.	285,722	61,261 R	46.1%	44.0%	51.2%	48.8%
1964	2,847,663	964,174	Goldwater, Barry M.	1,868,231	Johnson, Lyndon B.	15,258	904,057 D	33.9%	65.6%	34.0%	66.0%
1960	2,773,111	1,363,324	Nixon, Richard M.	1,385,415	Kennedy, John F.	24,372	22,091 D	49.2%	50.0%	49.6%	50.4%
1956	2,484,312	1,606,942	Eisenhower, Dwight D.	850,337	Stevenson, Adlai E.	27,033	756,605 R	64.7%	34.2%	65.4%	34.6%
1952	2,418,554	1,373,613	Eisenhower, Dwight D.	1,015,902	Stevenson, Adlai E.	29,039	357,711 R	56.8%	42.0%	57.5%	42.5%
1948	1,949,555	981,124	Dewey, Thomas E.	895,455	Truman, Harry S.	72,976	85,669 R	50.3%	45.9%	52.3%	47.7%

**In past elections, the other vote included: 2000 - 94,554 Green (Ralph Nader); 1996 - 262,134 Reform (Ross Perot); 1992 - 521,829 Independent (Perot); 1980 - 234,632 Independent (John Anderson); 1968 - 262,187 American Independent (George Wallace).

NEW JERSEY

POSTWAR VOTE FOR GOVERNOR

Year	Total Vote	Republican		Democratic		Other Vote	Rep.-Dem. Plurality	Percentage			
								Total Vote		Major Vote	
		Vote	Candidate	Vote	Candidate			Rep.	Dem.	Rep.	Dem.
2009	2,423,792	1,174,445	Christie, Chris	1,087,731	Corzine, Jon	161,616	86,714 R	48.5%	44.9%	51.9%	48.1%
2005	2,290,099	985,271	Forrester, Doug	1,224,551	Corzine, Jon	80,277	239,280 D	43.0%	53.5%	44.6%	55.4%
2001	2,227,165	928,174	Schundler, Bret	1,256,853	McGreevey, James E.	42,138	328,679 D	41.7%	56.4%	42.5%	57.5%
1997	2,418,344	1,133,394	Whitman, Christine T.	1,107,968	McGreevey, James E.	176,982	25,426 R	46.9%	45.8%	50.6%	49.4%
1993	2,505,964	1,236,124	Whitman, Christine T.	1,210,031	Florio, James J.	59,809	26,093 R	49.3%	48.3%	50.5%	49.5%
1989	2,253,764	838,553	Courter, James A.	1,379,937	Florio, James J.	35,274	541,384 D	37.2%	61.2%	37.8%	62.2%
1985	1,972,624	1,372,631	Kean, Thomas H.	578,402	Shapiro, Peter	21,591	794,229 R	69.6%	29.3%	70.4%	29.6%
1981	2,317,239	1,145,999	Kean, Thomas H.	1,144,202	Florio, James J.	27,038	1,797 R	49.5%	49.4%	50.0%	50.0%
1977	2,126,264	888,880	Bateman, Raymond H.	1,184,564	Byrne, Brendan T.	52,820	295,684 D	41.8%	55.7%	42.9%	57.1%
1973	2,122,009	676,235	Sandman, Charles W.	1,414,613	Byrne, Brendan T.	31,161	738,378 D	31.9%	66.7%	32.3%	67.7%
1969	2,366,606	1,411,905	Cahill, William T.	911,003	Meyner, Robert B.	43,698	500,902 R	59.7%	38.5%	60.8%	39.2%
1965	2,229,583	915,996	Dumont, Wayne	1,279,568	Hughes, Richard J.	34,019	363,572 D	41.1%	57.4%	41.7%	58.3%
1961	2,152,662	1,049,274	Mitchell, James P.	1,084,194	Hughes, Richard J.	19,194	34,920 D	48.7%	50.4%	49.2%	50.8%
1957	2,018,488	897,321	Forbes, Malcolm S.	1,101,130	Meyner, Robert B.	20,037	203,809 D	44.5%	54.6%	44.9%	55.1%
1953	1,810,812	809,068	Troast, Paul L.	962,710	Meyner, Robert B.	39,034	153,642 D	44.7%	53.2%	45.7%	54.3%
1949**	1,718,788	885,882	Driscoll, Alfred	810,022	Wene, Elmer H.	22,884	75,860 R	51.5%	47.1%	52.2%	47.8%
1946	1,414,527	807,378	Driscoll, Alfred	585,960	Hansen, Lewis G.	21,189	221,418 R	57.1%	41.4%	57.9%	42.1%

**The term of office of New Jersey's Governor was increased from three to four years effective with the 1949 election.

POSTWAR VOTE FOR SENATOR

Year	Total Vote	Republican		Democratic		Other Vote	Rep.-Dem. Plurality	Percentage			
								Total Vote		Major Vote	
		Vote	Candidate	Vote	Candidate			Rep.	Dem.	Rep.	Dem.
2008	3,482,445	1,461,025	Zimmer, Dick	1,951,218	Lautenberg, Frank R.	70,202	490,193 D	42.0%	56.0%	42.8%	57.2%
2006	2,250,070	997,775	Kean, Thomas H. Jr.	1,200,843	Menendez, Robert	51,452	203,068 D	44.3%	53.4%	45.4%	54.6%
2002	2,112,604	928,439	Forrester, Doug	1,138,193	Lautenberg, Frank R.	45,972	209,754 D	43.9%	53.9%	44.9%	55.1%
2000	3,015,662	1,420,267	Franks, Bob	1,511,237	Corzine, Jon	84,158	90,970 D	47.1%	50.1%	48.4%	51.6%
1996	2,884,106	1,227,817	Zimmer, Dick	1,519,328	Torricelli, Robert G.	136,961	291,511 D	42.6%	52.7%	44.7%	55.3%
1994	2,054,887	966,244	Haytaian, Garabed	1,033,487	Lautenberg, Frank R.	55,156	67,243 D	47.0%	50.3%	48.3%	51.7%
1990	1,938,454	918,874	Whitman, Christine T.	977,810	Bradley, Bill	41,770	58,936 D	47.4%	50.4%	48.4%	51.6%
1988	2,987,634	1,349,937	Dawkins, Peter M.	1,599,905	Lautenberg, Frank R.	37,792	249,968 D	45.2%	53.6%	45.8%	54.2%
1984	3,096,456	1,080,100	Mochary, Mary V.	1,986,644	Bradley, Bill	29,712	906,544 D	34.9%	64.2%	35.2%	64.8%
1982	2,193,945	1,047,626	Fenwick, Millicent	1,117,549	Lautenberg, Frank R.	28,770	69,923 D	47.8%	50.9%	48.4%	51.6%
1978	1,957,515	844,200	Bell, Jeffrey	1,082,960	Bradley, Bill	30,355	238,760 D	43.1%	55.3%	43.8%	56.2%
1976	2,771,390	1,054,508	Norcross, David F.	1,681,140	Williams, Harrison	35,742	626,632 D	38.0%	60.7%	38.5%	61.5%
1972	2,791,907	1,743,854	Case, Clifford P.	963,573	Krebs, Paul J.	84,480	780,281 R	62.5%	34.5%	64.4%	35.6%
1970	2,142,105	903,026	Gross, Nelson G.	1,157,074	Williams, Harrison	82,005	254,048 D	42.2%	54.0%	43.8%	56.2%
1966	2,131,188	1,279,343	Case, Clifford P.	788,021	Wilentz, Warren W.	63,824	491,322 R	60.0%	37.0%	61.9%	38.1%
1964	2,710,441	1,011,610	Shanley, Bernard M.	1,678,051	Williams, Harrison	20,780	666,441 D	37.3%	61.9%	37.6%	62.4%
1960	2,664,556	1,483,832	Case, Clifford P.	1,151,385	Lord, Thorn	29,339	332,447 R	55.7%	43.2%	56.3%	43.7%
1958	1,881,329	882,287	Kean, Robert W.	966,832	Williams, Harrison	32,210	84,545 D	46.9%	51.4%	47.7%	52.3%
1954	1,770,557	861,528	Case, Clifford P.	858,158	Howell, Charles R.	50,871	3,370 R	48.7%	48.5%	50.1%	49.9%
1952	2,318,232	1,286,782	Smith, H. Alexander	1,011,187	Alexander, Archibald	20,263	275,595 R	55.5%	43.6%	56.0%	44.0%
1948	1,869,882	934,720	Hendrickson, Robert	884,414	Alexander, Archibald	50,748	50,306 R	50.0%	47.3%	51.4%	48.6%
1946	1,367,155	799,808	Smith, H. Alexander	548,458	Brunner, George E.	18,889	251,350 R	58.5%	40.1%	59.3%	40.7%

NEW JERSEY

GOVERNOR 2009

2010 Census Population	County	Total Vote	Republican	Democratic	Other	Rep.-Dem. Plurality		Percentage			
								Total Vote		Major Vote	
								Rep.	Dem.	Rep.	Dem.
274,549	ATLANTIC	73,608	35,724	33,360	4,524	2,364	R	48.5%	45.3%	51.7%	48.3%
905,116	BERGEN	262,546	121,446	127,386	13,714	5,940	D	46.3%	48.5%	48.8%	51.2%
448,734	BURLINGTON	137,947	66,723	63,114	8,110	3,609	R	48.4%	45.8%	51.4%	48.6%
513,657	CAMDEN	133,200	52,337	73,171	7,692	20,834	D	39.3%	54.9%	41.7%	58.3%
97,265	CAPE MAY	34,948	18,992	13,379	2,577	5,613	R	54.3%	38.3%	58.7%	41.3%
156,898	CUMBERLAND	33,719	14,079	17,092	2,548	3,013	D	41.8%	50.7%	45.2%	54.8%
783,969	ESSEX	182,477	50,240	122,640	9,597	72,400	D	27.5%	67.2%	29.1%	70.9%
288,288	GLOUCESTER	84,251	39,815	37,066	7,370	2,749	R	47.3%	44.0%	51.8%	48.2%
634,266	HUDSON	118,192	30,820	82,075	5,297	51,255	D	26.1%	69.4%	27.3%	72.7%
128,349	HUNTERDON	50,738	33,360	12,893	4,485	20,467	R	65.7%	25.4%	72.1%	27.9%
366,513	MERCER	101,266	39,769	55,199	6,298	15,430	D	39.3%	54.5%	41.9%	58.1%
809,858	MIDDLESEX	199,295	94,506	89,732	15,057	4,774	R	47.4%	45.0%	51.3%	48.7%
630,380	MONMOUTH	207,321	129,039	64,672	13,610	64,367	R	62.2%	31.2%	66.6%	33.4%
492,276	MORRIS	165,023	99,085	51,586	14,352	47,499	R	60.0%	31.3%	65.8%	34.2%
576,567	OCEAN	189,022	124,238	53,761	11,023	70,477	R	65.7%	28.4%	69.8%	30.2%
501,226	PASSAIC	110,779	48,500	57,010	5,269	8,510	D	43.8%	51.5%	46.0%	54.0%
66,083	SALEM	20,344	9,599	8,323	2,422	1,276	R	47.2%	40.9%	53.6%	46.4%
323,444	SOMERSET	102,221	57,481	35,089	9,651	22,392	R	56.2%	34.3%	62.1%	37.9%
149,265	SUSSEX	49,846	31,749	12,870	5,227	18,879	R	63.7%	25.8%	71.2%	28.8%
536,499	UNION	134,693	56,769	68,867	9,057	12,098	D	42.1%	51.1%	45.2%	54.8%
108,692	WARREN	32,356	20,174	8,446	3,736	11,728	R	62.4%	26.1%	70.5%	29.5%
8,791,894	TOTAL	2,423,792	1,174,445	1,087,731	161,616	86,714	R	48.5%	44.9%	51.9%	48.1%

NEW JERSEY

HOUSE OF REPRESENTATIVES

CD	Year	Total Vote	Republican		Democratic		Other Vote	Rep.-Dem. Plurality		Percentage			
			Vote	Candidate	Vote	Candidate				Total Vote		Major Vote	
										Rep.	Dem.	Rep.	Dem.
1	2010	168,267	58,562	GLADING, DALE	106,334	ANDREWS, ROBERT E.*	3,371	47,772	D	34.8%	63.2%	35.5%	64.5%
1	2008	285,157	74,001	GLADING, DALE	206,453	ANDREWS, ROBERT E.*	4,703	132,452	D	26.0%	72.4%	26.4%	73.6%
1	2006	140,110		—	140,110	ANDREWS, ROBERT E.*		140,110	D		100.0%		100.0%
1	2004	268,203	66,109	HUTCHISON, S. DANIEL	201,163	ANDREWS, ROBERT E.*	931	135,054	D	24.6%	75.0%	24.7%	75.3%
1	2002	131,389		—	121,846	ANDREWS, ROBERT E.*	9,543	121,846	D		92.7%		100.0%
2	2010	167,120	109,460	LoBIONDO, FRANK A.*	51,690	STEIN, GARY	5,970	57,770	R	65.5%	30.9%	67.9%	32.1%
2	2008	283,965	167,701	LoBIONDO, FRANK A.*	110,990	KURKOWSKI, DAVID	5,274	56,711	R	59.1%	39.1%	60.2%	39.8%
2	2006	180,575	111,245	LoBIONDO, FRANK A.*	64,279	THOMAS-HUGHES, VIOLA	5,051	46,966	R	61.6%	35.6%	63.4%	36.6%
2	2004	265,442	172,779	LoBIONDO, FRANK A.*	86,792	ROBB, TIMOTHY J.	5,871	85,987	R	65.1%	32.7%	66.6%	33.4%
2	2002	168,799	116,834	LoBIONDO, FRANK A.*	47,735	FARKAS, STEVEN A.	4,230	69,099	R	69.2%	28.3%	71.0%	29.0%
3	2010	220,309	110,215	RUNYAN, JON	104,252	ADLER, JOHN*	5,842	5,963	R	50.0%	47.3%	51.4%	48.6%
3	2008	319,512	153,122	MYERS, CHRIS	166,390	ADLER, JOHN		13,268	D	47.9%	52.1%	47.9%	52.1%
3	2006	209,851	122,559	SAXTON, H. JAMES*	86,113	SEXTON, RICH	1,179	36,446	R	58.4%	41.0%	58.7%	41.3%
3	2004	308,862	195,938	SAXTON, H. JAMES*	107,034	CONAWAY, HERB	5,890	88,904	R	63.4%	34.7%	64.7%	35.3%
3	2002	189,739	123,375	SAXTON, H. JAMES*	64,364	STRADA, RICHARD	2,000	59,011	R	65.0%	33.9%	65.7%	34.3%
4	2010	186,938	129,752	SMITH, CHRISTOPHER H.*	52,118	KLEINHENDLER, HOWARD	5,068	77,634	R	69.4%	27.9%	71.3%	28.7%
4	2008	306,551	202,972	SMITH, CHRISTOPHER H.*	100,036	ZEITZ, JOSHUA M.	3,543	102,936	R	66.2%	32.6%	67.0%	33.0%
4	2006	189,540	124,482	SMITH, CHRISTOPHER H.*	62,905	GAY, CAROL E.	2,153	61,577	R	65.7%	33.2%	66.4%	33.6%
4	2004	287,553	192,671	SMITH, CHRISTOPHER H.*	92,826	VASQUEZ, AMY	2,056	99,845	R	67.0%	32.3%	67.5%	32.5%
4	2002	174,301	115,293	SMITH, CHRISTOPHER H.*	55,967	BRENNAN, MARY	3,041	59,326	R	66.1%	32.1%	67.3%	32.7%

NEW JERSEY

HOUSE OF REPRESENTATIVES

CD	Year	Total Vote	Republican Vote	Republican Candidate	Democratic Vote	Democratic Candidate	Other Vote	Rep.-Dem. Plurality		Total Vote Rep.	Total Vote Dem.	Major Vote Rep.	Major Vote Dem.
5	2010	190,993	124,030	GARRETT, SCOTT*	62,634	THEISE, TOD	4,329	61,396	R	64.9%	32.8%	66.4%	33.6%
5	2008	309,007	172,653	GARRETT, SCOTT*	131,033	SHULMAN, DENNIS	5,321	41,620	R	55.9%	42.4%	56.9%	43.1%
5	2006	204,242	112,142	GARRETT, SCOTT*	89,503	ARONSOHN, PAUL	2,597	22,639	R	54.9%	43.8%	55.6%	44.4%
5	2004	297,425	171,220	GARRETT, SCOTT*	122,259	WOLFE, DOROTHEA ANNE	3,946	48,961	R	57.6%	41.1%	58.3%	41.7%
5	2002	199,851	118,881	GARRETT, SCOTT	76,504	SUMERS, ANNE	4,466	42,377	R	59.5%	38.3%	60.8%	39.2%
6	2010	149,662	65,413	LITTLE, ANNA C.	81,933	PALLONE, FRANK JR.*	2,316	16,520	D	43.7%	54.7%	44.4%	55.6%
6	2008	245,077	77,469	McLEOD, ROBERT E.	164,077	PALLONE, FRANK JR.*	3,531	86,608	D	31.6%	66.9%	32.1%	67.9%
6	2006	143,773	43,539	BELLEW, LEIGH-ANN	98,615	PALLONE, FRANK JR.*	1,619	55,076	D	30.3%	68.6%	30.6%	69.4%
6	2004	230,151	70,942	FERNANDEZ, SYLVESTER	153,981	PALLONE, FRANK JR.*	5,228	83,039	D	30.8%	66.9%	31.5%	68.5%
6	2002	137,495	42,479	MEDROW, RIC	91,379	PALLONE, FRANK JR.*	3,637	48,900	D	30.9%	66.5%	31.7%	68.3%
7	2010	176,986	105,084	LANCE, LEONARD*	71,902	POTOSNAK, ED		33,182	R	59.4%	40.6%	59.4%	40.6%
7	2008	295,628	148,461	LANCE, LEONARD	124,818	STENDER, LINDA	22,349	23,643	R	50.2%	42.2%	54.3%	45.7%
7	2006	199,075	98,399	FERGUSON, MIKE*	95,454	STENDER, LINDA	5,222	2,945	R	49.4%	47.9%	50.8%	49.2%
7	2004	285,847	162,597	FERGUSON, MIKE*	119,081	BROZAK, STEVE	4,169	43,516	R	56.9%	41.7%	57.7%	42.3%
7	2002	183,002	106,055	FERGUSON, MIKE*	74,879	CARDEN, TIM	2,068	31,176	R	58.0%	40.9%	58.6%	41.4%
8	2010	141,208	51,023	STRATEN, ROLAND	88,478	PASCRELL, BILL JR.*	1,707	37,455	D	36.1%	62.7%	36.6%	63.4%
8	2008	223,986	63,107	STRATEN, ROLAND	159,279	PASCRELL, BILL JR.*	1,600	96,172	D	28.2%	71.1%	28.4%	71.6%
8	2006	137,639	39,053	SANDOVAL, JOSE M.	97,568	PASCRELL, BILL JR.*	1,018	58,515	D	28.4%	70.9%	28.6%	71.4%
8	2004	218,820	62,747	AJJAN, GEORGE	152,001	PASCRELL, BILL JR.*	4,072	89,254	D	28.7%	69.5%	29.2%	70.8%
8	2002	131,819	40,318	SILVERMAN, JARED	88,101	PASCRELL, BILL JR.*	3,400	47,783	D	30.6%	66.8%	31.4%	68.6%
9	2010	137,626	52,082	AGOSTA, MICHAEL A.	83,564	ROTHMAN, STEVEN R.*	1,980	31,482	D	37.8%	60.7%	38.4%	61.6%
9	2008	223,885	69,503	MICCO, VINCENT	151,182	ROTHMAN, STEVEN R.*	3,200	81,679	D	31.0%	67.5%	31.5%	68.5%
9	2006	148,095	40,879	MICCO, VINCENT	105,853	ROTHMAN, STEVEN R.*	1,363	64,974	D	27.6%	71.5%	27.9%	72.1%
9	2004	216,251	68,564	TRAWINSKI, EDWARD	146,038	ROTHMAN, STEVEN R.*	1,649	77,474	D	31.7%	67.5%	31.9%	68.1%
9	2002	139,196	42,088	GLASS, JOSEPH	97,108	ROTHMAN, STEVEN R.*		55,020	D	30.2%	69.8%	30.2%	69.8%
10	2010	111,877	14,357	ALONSO, MICHAEL J.	95,299	PAYNE, DONALD M.*	2,221	80,942	D	12.8%	85.2%	13.1%	86.9%
10	2008	171,793		—	169,945	PAYNE, DONALD M.*	1,848	169,945	D		98.9%		100.0%
10	2006	90,264		—	90,264	PAYNE, DONALD M.*		90,264	D		100.0%		100.0%
10	2004	160,713		—	155,697	PAYNE, DONALD M.*	5,016	155,697	D		96.9%		100.0%
10	2002	102,346	15,913	WIRTZ, ANDREW	86,433	PAYNE, DONALD M.*		70,520	D	15.5%	84.5%	15.5%	84.5%
11	2010	181,800	122,149	FRELINGHUYSEN, RODNEY*	55,472	HERBERT, DOUGLAS	4,179	66,677	R	67.2%	30.5%	68.8%	31.2%
11	2008	306,732	189,696	FRELINGHUYSEN, RODNEY*	113,510	WYKA, TOM	3,526	76,186	R	61.8%	37.0%	62.6%	37.4%
11	2006	203,071	126,085	FRELINGHUYSEN, RODNEY*	74,414	WYKA, TOM	2,572	51,671	R	62.1%	36.6%	62.9%	37.1%
11	2004	296,002	200,915	FRELINGHUYSEN, RODNEY*	91,811	BUELL, JAMES W.	3,276	109,104	R	67.9%	31.0%	68.6%	31.4%
11	2002	183,678	132,938	FRELINGHUYSEN, RODNEY*	48,477	PAWAR, VIJ	2,263	84,461	R	72.4%	26.4%	73.3%	26.7%
12	2010	204,002	93,634	SIPPRELLE, SCOTT	108,214	HOLT, RUSH D.*	2,154	14,580	D	45.9%	53.0%	46.4%	53.6%
12	2008	306,934	108,400	BATEMAN, ALAN R.	193,732	HOLT, RUSH D.*	4,802	85,332	D	35.3%	63.1%	35.9%	64.1%
12	2006	190,977	65,509	SINAGRA, JOSEPH S.	125,468	HOLT, RUSH D.*		59,959	D	34.3%	65.7%	34.3%	65.7%
12	2004	289,785	115,014	SPADEA, BILL	171,691	HOLT, RUSH D.*	3,080	56,677	D	39.7%	59.2%	40.1%	59.9%
12	2002	171,713	62,938	SOARIES, DeFOREST "BUSTER"	104,806	HOLT, RUSH D.*	3,969	41,868	D	36.7%	61.0%	37.5%	62.5%
13	2010	84,796	19,538	DWYER, HENRIETTA	62,840	SIRES, ALBIO*	2,418	43,302	D	23.0%	74.1%	23.7%	76.3%
13	2008	159,753	34,735	TURULA, JOSEPH	120,382	SIRES, ALBIO*	4,636	85,647	D	21.7%	75.4%	22.4%	77.6%
13	2006	99,630	19,284	GUARINI, JOHN J.	77,238	SIRES, ALBIO	3,108	57,954	D	19.4%	77.5%	20.0%	80.0%
13	2004	159,541	35,288	PIATKOWSKI, RICHARD W.	121,018	MENENDEZ, ROBERT*	3,235	85,730	D	22.1%	75.9%	22.6%	77.4%
13	2002	92,731	16,852	GERON, JAMES	72,605	MENENDEZ, ROBERT*	3,274	55,753	D	18.2%	78.3%	18.8%	81.2%
TOTAL	2010	2,121,584	1,055,299		1,024,730		41,555	30,569	R	49.7%	48.3%	50.7%	49.3%
TOTAL	2008	3,437,980	1,461,820		1,911,827		64,333	450,007	D	42.5%	55.6%	43.3%	56.7%
TOTAL	2006	2,136,842	903,176		1,207,784		25,882	304,608	D	42.3%	56.5%	42.8%	57.2%
TOTAL	2004	3,284,595	1,514,784		1,721,392		48,419	206,608	D	46.1%	52.4%	46.8%	53.2%
TOTAL	2002	2,006,059	933,964		1,030,204		41,891	96,240	D	46.6%	51.4%	47.6%	52.4%

An asterisk (*) denotes incumbent.

NEW JERSEY

GENERAL AND PRIMARY ELECTIONS

2009-10 GENERAL ELECTIONS

Governor (2009)	Other vote was 139,579 Independent (Christopher J. Daggett); 4,830 Independent (Kenneth R. Kaplan); 3,585 Independent (Gary T. Steele); 2,869 Independent (Jason Cullen); 2,598 Independent (David R. Meiswinkle); 2,563 Independent (Kostas Petris); 2,085 Independent (Gregory Pason); 1,625 Independent (Gary Stein); 1,021 Independent (Joshua Leinsdorf); 753 Independent (Alvin Lindsay Jr.); 108 Personal Choice (no name).
House	Other vote was:
CD 1	1,593 Green (Mark Heacock); 1,257 Time for Change (Margaret M. Chapman); 521 Defend American Constitution (Nicky I. Petrutz).
CD 2	4,120 Constitution (Peter F. Boyce); 1,123 marklovett.us (Mark Lovett); 727 American Labor (Vitov Valdes-Munoz).
CD 3	3,284 NJ Tea Party (Peter DeStefano); 1,445 Libertarian (Russ Conger); 1,113 Your Country Again (Lawrence J. Donahue).
CD 4	2,912 Libertarian (Joe Siano); 1,574 Green (Steven Welzer); 582 American Renaissance Movement (David R. Meiswinkle).
CD 5	2,347 Green (Ed Fanning); 1,646 For Americans (Mark D. Quick); 336 Be Determined (James Douglas Radigan).
CD 6	1,299 Independent (Jack Freudenheim); 1,017 Green Tea Patriots (Karen Anne Zaletel).
CD 7	
CD 8	1,707 Independent (Raymond Giangrasso).
CD 9	1,980 Green (Patricia Alessandrini).
CD 10	1,141 Action No Talk (Robert Louis Toussaint); 1,080 Agent of Change (Joanne Miller).
CD 11	4,179 Libertarian (Jim Gawron).
CD 12	2,154 Truth Vision Hope (Kenneth J. Cody).
CD 13	1,508 Independent American (Anthony Zanowic); 910 Gravity Buoyancy Solution (Maximo Gomez Nacer).

2009-10 PRIMARY ELECTIONS

Primary	June 2, 2009 (Governor) June 8, 2010 (Congress)	**Registration** (as of June 4, 2010)	Democratic	1,752,073
			Republican	1,055,896
			Libertarian	1,330
			Green	961
			Conservative	289
			Constitution	136
			Reform	67
			Natural Law	31
			Unaffiliated	2,442,329
			TOTAL	*5,253,112*

Primary Type	Semi-open—Registered Democrats and Republicans could vote only in their party's primary. "Unaffiliated" voters could participate in either party's primary if they were willing to become a member of that party.

NEW JERSEY

GENERAL AND PRIMARY ELECTIONS

	REPUBLICAN PRIMARIES			DEMOCRATIC PRIMARIES		
Governor (2009)	Chris Christie	184,085	55.1%	Jon Corzine*	154,448	77.2%
	Steven M. Lonegan	140,946	42.2%	Carl A. Bergmanson	17,125	8.6%
	Rick Merkt	9,184	2.7%	Jeff Boss	16,639	8.3%
				Roger Bacon	11,908	6.0%
	TOTAL	334,215		TOTAL	200,120	
Congressional District 1	Dale Glading	5,315	54.8%	Robert E. Andrews*	14,695	86.7%
	Loran M. Oglesby	2,718	28.0%	John Caramanna	2,262	13.3%
	Fernando Powers	1,401	14.4%			
	Lee Lucas	264	2.7%			
	TOTAL	9,698		TOTAL	16,957	
Congressional District 2	Frank A. LoBiondo*	19,337	78.1%	Gary Stein	5,441	100.0%
	Linda Biamonte	2,984	12.0%			
	Donna Ward	2,451	9.9%			
	TOTAL	24,772				
Congressional District 3	Jon Runyan	17,250	60.4%	John Adler*	11,833	75.1%
	Justin Michael Murphy	11,304	39.6%	Barry D. Bendar	3,916	24.9%
	TOTAL	28,554		TOTAL	15,749	
Congressional District 4	Christopher H. Smith*	21,723	68.8%	Howard Kleinhendler	7,976	100.0%
	Alan Bateman	9,839	31.2%			
	TOTAL	31,562				
Congressional District 5	Scott Garrett*	29,523	100.0%	Tod Theise	5,711	79.4%
				Anthony N. Iannarelli Jr.	1,478	20.6%
				TOTAL	7,189	
Congressional District 6	Anna C. Little	6,804	50.3%	Frank Pallone Jr.*	11,667	100.0%
	Diane Gooch	6,721	49.7%			
	TOTAL	13,525				
Congressional District 7	Leonard Lance*	17,200	56.1%	Ed Potosnak	8,176	100.0%
	David Larsen	9,475	30.9%			
	Alonzo "Lon" Hosford	2,534	8.3%			
	Bruce E. Baker	1,448	4.7%			
	TOTAL	30,657				
Congressional District 8	Roland Straten	5,739	81.2%	Bill Pascrell Jr.*	13,213	100.0%
	Blasé Billack	1,333	18.8%			
	TOTAL	7,072				
Congressional District 9	Michael A. Agosta	5,830	58.1%	Steven R. Rothman*	14,973	100.0%
	John Asianian	3,629	36.2%			
	Sergey Shevchuk	567	5.7%			
	TOTAL	10,026				
Congressional District 10	Michael J. Alonso	1,061	100.0%	Donald M. Payne*	22,155	100.0%
Congressional District 11	Rodney Frelinghuysen*	32,631	76.4%	Douglas Herbert	6,192	71.5%
	Richard T. Luzzi	10,060	23.6%	James D. Kelly Jr.	2,466	28.5%
	TOTAL	42,691		TOTAL	8,658	
Congressional District 12	Scott Sipprelle	8,927	54.1%	Rush D. Holt*	14,480	100.0%
	David Corsi	7,569	45.9%			
	TOTAL	16,496				
Congressional District 13	Henrietta Dwyer	2,436	100.0%	Albio Sires*	16,022	86.9%
				Jeff "Jefe" Boss	2,409	13.1%
				TOTAL	18,431	

An asterisk (*) denotes incumbent.

NEW MEXICO

Congressional districts first established for elections held in 2002
3 members

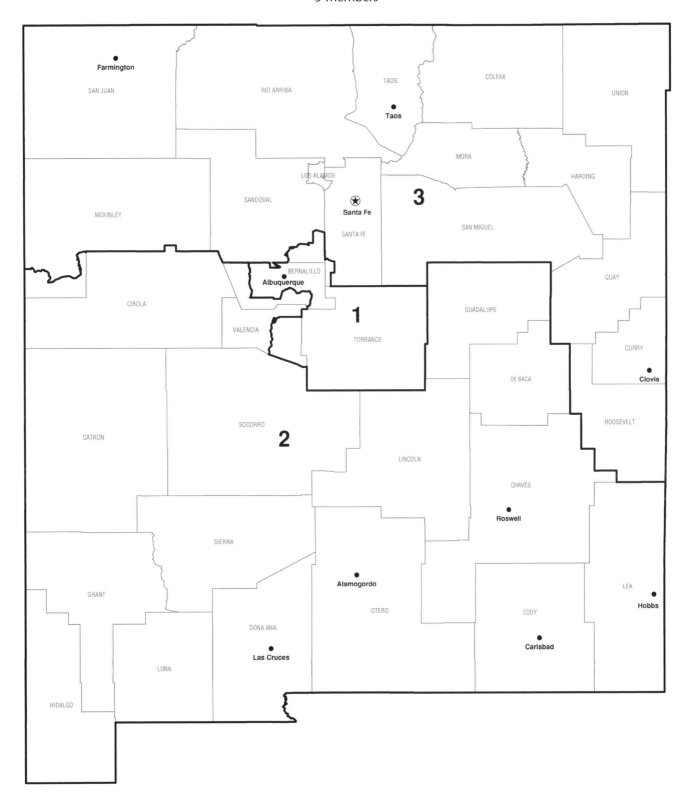

NEW MEXICO

GOVERNOR
Susana Martinez (R). Elected 2010 to a four-year term.

SENATORS (2 Democrats)
Jeff Bingaman (D). Reelected 2006 to a six-year term. Previously elected 2000, 1994, 1988, 1982.

Tom Udall (D). Elected 2008 to a six-year term.

REPRESENTATIVES (2 Democrats, 1 Republican)
1. Martin Heinrich (D)   2. Steve Pearce (R)   3. Ben Ray Lujan (D)

POSTWAR VOTE FOR PRESIDENT

| | | Republican | | Democratic | | | | Percentage | | | |
| | | | | | | | | Total Vote | | Major Vote | |
Year	Total Vote	Vote	Candidate	Vote	Candidate	Other Vote	Rep.-Dem. Plurality	Rep.	Dem.	Rep.	Dem.
2008	830,158	346,832	McCain, John	472,422	Obama, Barack	10,904	125,590 D	41.8%	56.9%	42.3%	57.7%
2004	756,304	376,930	Bush, George W.	370,942	Kerry, John	8,432	5,988 R	49.8%	49.0%	50.4%	49.6%
2000**	598,605	286,417	Bush, George W.	286,783	Gore, Al	25,405	366 D	47.8%	47.9%	50.0%	50.0%
1996**	556,074	232,751	Dole, Bob	273,495	Clinton, Bill	49,828	40,744 D	41.9%	49.2%	46.0%	54.0%
1992**	569,986	212,824	Bush, George	261,617	Clinton, Bill	95,545	48,793 D	37.3%	45.9%	44.9%	55.1%
1988	521,287	270,341	Bush, George	244,497	Dukakis, Michael S.	6,449	25,844 R	51.9%	46.9%	52.5%	47.5%
1984	514,370	307,101	Reagan, Ronald	201,769	Mondale, Walter F.	5,500	105,332 R	59.7%	39.2%	60.3%	39.7%
1980**	456,971	250,779	Reagan, Ronald	167,826	Carter, Jimmy	38,366	82,953 R	54.9%	36.7%	59.9%	40.1%
1976	418,409	211,419	Ford, Gerald R.	201,148	Carter, Jimmy	5,842	10,271 R	50.5%	48.1%	51.2%	48.8%
1972	386,241	235,606	Nixon, Richard M.	141,084	McGovern, George S.	9,551	94,522 R	61.0%	36.5%	62.5%	37.5%
1968**	327,350	169,692	Nixon, Richard M.	130,081	Humphrey, Hubert H.	27,577	39,611 R	51.8%	39.7%	56.6%	43.4%
1964	328,645	132,838	Goldwater, Barry M.	194,015	Johnson, Lyndon B.	1,792	61,177 D	40.4%	59.0%	40.6%	59.4%
1960	311,107	153,733	Nixon, Richard M.	156,027	Kennedy, John F.	1,347	2,294 D	49.4%	50.2%	49.6%	50.4%
1956	253,926	146,788	Eisenhower, Dwight D.	106,098	Stevenson, Adlai E.	1,040	40,690 R	57.8%	41.8%	58.0%	42.0%
1952	238,608	132,170	Eisenhower, Dwight D.	105,661	Stevenson, Adlai E.	777	26,509 R	55.4%	44.3%	55.6%	44.4%
1948	187,063	80,303	Dewey, Thomas E.	105,464	Truman, Harry S.	1,296	25,161 D	42.9%	56.4%	43.2%	56.8%

**In past elections, the other vote included: 2000 - 21,251 Green (Ralph Nader); 1996 - 32,257 Reform (Ross Perot); 1992 - 91,895 Independent (Perot); 1980 - 29,459 Independent (John Anderson); 1968 - 25,737 American Independent (George Wallace).

NEW MEXICO

POSTWAR VOTE FOR GOVERNOR

Year	Total Vote	Republican Vote	Republican Candidate	Democratic Vote	Democratic Candidate	Other Vote	Rep.-Dem. Plurality	Total Vote Rep.	Total Vote Dem.	Major Vote Rep.	Major Vote Dem.
2010	602,827	321,219	Martinez, Susana	280,614	Denish, Diane D.	994	40,605 R	53.3%	46.5%	53.4%	46.6%
2006	559,170	174,364	Dendahl, John	384,806	Richardson, Bill		210,442 D	31.2%	68.8%	31.2%	68.8%
2002	484,233	189,074	Sanchez, John A.	268,693	Richardson, Bill	26,466	79,619 D	39.0%	55.5%	41.3%	58.7%
1998	498,703	271,948	Johnson, Gary E.	226,755	Chavez, Martin J.		45,193 R	54.5%	45.5%	54.5%	45.5%
1994**	467,621	232,945	Johnson, Gary E.	186,686	King, Bruce	47,990	46,259 R	49.8%	39.9%	55.5%	44.5%
1990	411,236	185,692	Bond, Frank M.	224,564	King, Bruce	980	38,872 D	45.2%	54.6%	45.3%	54.7%
1986	394,833	209,455	Carruthers, Garrey E.	185,378	Powell. Ray B.		24,077 R	53.0%	47.0%	53.0%	47.0%
1982	407,466	191,626	Irick, John B.	215,840	Anaya, Toney		24,214 D	47.0%	53.0%	47.0%	53.0%
1978	345,577	170,848	Skeen, Joseph R.	174,631	King, Bruce	98	3,783 D	49.4%	50.5%	49.5%	50.5%
1974	328,742	160,430	Skeen, Joseph R.	164,172	Apodaca, Jerry	4,140	3,742 D	48.8%	49.9%	49.4%	50.6%
1970**	290,375	134,640	Domenici, Pete V.	148,835	King, Bruce	6,900	14,195 D	46.4%	51.3%	47.5%	52.5%
1968	318,975	160,140	Cargo, David F.	157,230	Chavez, Fabian	1,605	2,910 R	50.2%	49.3%	50.5%	49.5%
1966	260,232	134,625	Cargo, David F.	125,587	Lusk, Thomas E.	20	9,038 R	51.7%	48.3%	51.7%	48.3%
1964	318,042	126,540	Tucker, Merle H.	191,497	Campbell, Jack M.	5	64,957 D	39.8%	60.2%	39.8%	60.2%
1962	247,135	116,184	Mechem, Edwin L.	130,933	Campbell, Jack M.	18	14,749 D	47.0%	53.0%	47.0%	53.0%
1960	305,542	153,765	Mechem, Edwin L.	151,777	Burroughs, John		1,988 R	50.3%	49.7%	50.3%	49.7%
1958	205,048	101,567	Mechem, Edwin L.	103,481	Burroughs, John		1,914 D	49.5%	50.5%	49.5%	50.5%
1956	251,751	131,488	Mechem, Edwin L.	120,263	Simms, John F.		11,225 R	52.2%	47.8%	52.2%	47.8%
1954	193,956	83,373	Stockton, Alvin	110,583	Simms, John F.		27,210 D	43.0%	57.0%	43.0%	57.0%
1952	240,150	129,116	Mechem, Edwin L.	111,034	Grantham, Everett		18,082 R	53.8%	46.2%	53.8%	46.2%
1950	180,205	96,846	Mechem, Edwin L.	83,359	Miles, John E.		13,487 R	53.7%	46.3%	53.7%	46.3%
1948	189,992	86,023	Lujan, Manuel	103,969	Mabry, Thomas J.		17,946 D	45.3%	54.7%	45.3%	54.7%
1946	132,930	62,875	Safford, Edward L.	70,055	Mabry, Thomas J.		7,180 D	47.3%	52.7%	47.3%	52.7%

**In past elections, the other vote included: 1994 - 47,990 Green (Roberto Mondragon). The term of New Mexico's Governor was increased from two to four years effective with the 1970 election.

POSTWAR VOTE FOR SENATOR

Year	Total Vote	Republican Vote	Republican Candidate	Democratic Vote	Democratic Candidate	Other Vote	Rep.-Dem. Plurality	Total Vote Rep.	Total Vote Dem.	Major Vote Rep.	Major Vote Dem.
2008	823,650	318,522	Pearce, Steve	505,128	Udall, Tom		186,606 D	38.7%	61.3%	38.7%	61.3%
2006	558,550	163,826	McCulloch, Allen W.	394,365	Bingaman, Jeff	359	230,539 D	29.3%	70.6%	29.3%	70.7%
2002	483,340	314,301	Domenici, Pete V.	169,039	Tristani, Gloria		145,262 R	65.0%	35.0%	65.0%	35.0%
2000	589,526	225,517	Redmond, Bill	363,744	Bingaman, Jeff	265	138,227 D	38.3%	61.7%	38.3%	61.7%
1996	551,821	357,171	Domenici, Pete V.	164,356	Trujillo, Art	30,294	192,815 R	64.7%	29.8%	68.5%	31.5%
1994	463,196	213,025	McMillan, Colin R.	249,989	Bingaman, Jeff	182	36,964 D	46.0%	54.0%	46.0%	54.0%
1990	406,938	296,712	Domenici, Pete V.	110,033	Benavides, Tom R.	193	186,679 R	72.9%	27.0%	72.9%	27.1%
1988	508,598	186,579	Valentine, William	321,983	Bingaman, Jeff	36	135,404 D	36.7%	63.3%	36.7%	63.3%
1984	502,634	361,371	Domenici, Pete V.	141,253	Pratt, Judith A.	10	220,118 R	71.9%	28.1%	71.9%	28.1%
1982	404,810	187,128	Schmitt, Harrison	217,682	Bingaman, Jeff		30,554 D	46.2%	53.8%	46.2%	53.8%
1978	343,554	183,442	Domenici, Pete V.	160,045	Anaya, Toney	67	23,397 R	53.4%	46.6%	53.4%	46.6%
1976	413,141	234,681	Schmitt, Harrison	176,382	Montoya, Joseph M.	2,078	58,299 R	56.8%	42.7%	57.1%	42.9%
1972	378,330	204,253	Domenici, Pete V.	173,815	Daniels, Jack	262	30,438 R	54.0%	45.9%	54.0%	46.0%
1970	289,906	135,004	Carter, Anderson	151,486	Montoya, Joseph M.	3,416	16,482 D	46.6%	52.3%	47.1%	52.9%
1966	258,203	120,988	Carter, Anderson	137,205	Anderson, Clinton P.	10	16,217 D	46.9%	53.1%	46.9%	53.1%
1964	325,774	147,562	Mechem, Edwin L.	178,209	Montoya, Joseph M.	3	30,647 D	45.3%	54.7%	45.3%	54.7%
1960	300,551	109,897	Colwes, William F.	190,654	Anderson, Clinton P.		80,757 D	36.6%	63.4%	36.6%	63.4%
1958	203,323	75,827	Atchley, Forrest S.	127,496	Chavez, Dennis		51,669 D	37.3%	62.7%	37.3%	62.7%
1954	194,422	83,071	Mechem, Edwin L.	111,351	Anderson, Clinton P.		28,280 D	42.7%	57.3%	42.7%	57.3%
1952	239,711	117,168	Hurley, Patrick J.	122,543	Chavez, Dennis		5,375 D	48.9%	51.1%	48.9%	51.1%
1948	188,495	80,226	Hurley, Patrick J.	108,269	Anderson, Clinton P.		28,043 D	42.6%	57.4%	42.6%	57.4%
1946	133,282	64,632	Hurley, Patrick J.	68,650	Chavez, Dennis		4,018 D	48.5%	51.5%	48.5%	51.5%

NEW MEXICO
GOVERNOR 2010

2010 Census Population	County	Total Vote	Republican	Democratic	Other	Rep.-Dem. Plurality	Percentage			
							Total Vote		Major Vote	
							Rep.	Dem.	Rep.	Dem.
662,564	BERNALILLO	202,207	102,711	99,278	218	3,433 R	50.8%	49.1%	50.8%	49.2%
3,725	CATRON	1,897	1,472	420	5	1,052 R	77.6%	22.1%	77.8%	22.2%
65,645	CHAVES	16,040	11,279	4,715	46	6,564 R	70.3%	29.4%	70.5%	29.5%
27,213	CIBOLA	6,546	3,176	3,340	30	164 D	48.5%	51.0%	48.7%	51.3%
13,750	COLFAX	4,843	2,916	1,913	14	1,003 R	60.2%	39.5%	60.4%	39.6%
48,376	CURRY	9,978	7,234	2,700	44	4,534 R	72.5%	27.1%	72.8%	27.2%
2,022	DE BACA	898	619	276	3	343 R	68.9%	30.7%	69.2%	30.8%
209,233	DONA ANA	47,912	24,628	23,190	94	1,438 R	51.4%	48.4%	51.5%	48.5%
53,829	EDDY	14,654	10,144	4,498	12	5,646 R	69.2%	30.7%	69.3%	30.7%
29,514	GRANT	10,593	5,165	5,406	22	241 D	48.8%	51.0%	48.9%	51.1%
4,687	GUADALUPE	1,928	1,100	828		272 R	57.1%	42.9%	57.1%	42.9%
695	HARDING	541	337	204		133 R	62.3%	37.7%	62.3%	37.7%
4,894	HIDALGO	1,743	1,014	728	1	286 R	58.2%	41.8%	58.2%	41.8%
64,727	LEA	13,023	9,661	3,341	21	6,320 R	74.2%	25.7%	74.3%	25.7%
20,497	LINCOLN	7,543	5,544	1,990	9	3,554 R	73.5%	26.4%	73.6%	26.4%
17,950	LOS ALAMOS	8,712	4,729	3,972	11	757 R	54.3%	45.6%	54.4%	45.6%
25,095	LUNA	6,109	3,588	2,498	23	1,090 R	58.7%	40.9%	59.0%	41.0%
71,492	MCKINLEY	16,865	5,850	10,965	50	5,115 D	34.7%	65.0%	34.8%	65.2%
4,881	MORA	2,630	1,220	1,410		190 D	46.4%	53.6%	46.4%	53.6%
63,797	OTERO	15,904	11,085	4,792	27	6,293 R	69.7%	30.1%	69.8%	30.2%
9,041	QUAY	3,003	1,955	1,036	12	919 R	65.1%	34.5%	65.4%	34.6%
40,246	RIO ARRIBA	11,906	4,818	7,066	22	2,248 D	40.5%	59.3%	40.5%	59.5%
19,846	ROOSEVELT	4,417	3,162	1,244	11	1,918 R	71.6%	28.2%	71.8%	28.2%
131,561	SANDOVAL	42,647	24,097	18,478	72	5,619 R	56.5%	43.3%	56.6%	43.4%
130,044	SAN JUAN	35,720	24,857	10,777	86	14,080 R	69.6%	30.2%	69.8%	30.2%
29,393	SAN MIGUEL	9,157	3,508	5,641	8	2,133 D	38.3%	61.6%	38.3%	61.7%
144,170	SANTA FE	53,486	17,441	35,963	82	18,522 D	32.6%	67.2%	32.7%	67.3%
11,988	SIERRA	4,389	2,887	1,495	7	1,392 R	65.8%	34.1%	65.9%	34.1%
17,866	SOCORRO	6,267	3,317	2,942	8	375 R	52.9%	46.9%	53.0%	47.0%
32,937	TAOS	11,910	3,495	8,415		4,920 D	29.3%	70.7%	29.3%	70.7%
16,383	TORRANCE	5,624	3,788	1,827	9	1,961 R	67.4%	32.5%	67.5%	32.5%
4,549	UNION	1,473	1,071	400	2	671 R	72.7%	27.2%	72.8%	27.2%
76,569	VALENCIA	22,262	13,351	8,866	45	4,485 R	60.0%	39.8%	60.1%	39.9%
2,059,179	TOTAL	602,827	321,219	280,614	994	40,605 R	53.3%	46.5%	53.4%	46.6%

NEW MEXICO

HOUSE OF REPRESENTATIVES

CD	Year	Total Vote	Republican Vote	Republican Candidate	Democratic Vote	Democratic Candidate	Other Vote	Rep.-Dem. Plurality	Total Vote Rep.	Total Vote Dem.	Major Vote Rep.	Major Vote Dem.
1	2010	217,250	104,543	BARELA, JONATHAN L.	112,707	HEINRICH, MARTIN*		8,164 D	48.1%	51.9%	48.1%	51.9%
1	2008	298,756	132,485	WHITE, DARREN	166,271	HEINRICH, MARTIN		33,786 D	44.3%	55.7%	44.3%	55.7%
1	2006	211,111	105,986	WILSON, HEATHER A.*	105,125	MADRID, PATRICIA A.		861 R	50.2%	49.8%	50.2%	49.8%
1	2004	270,905	147,372	WILSON, HEATHER A.*	123,339	ROMERO, RICHARD M.	194	24,033 R	54.4%	45.5%	54.4%	45.6%
1	2002	172,945	95,711	WILSON, HEATHER A.*	77,234	ROMERO, RICHARD M.		18,477 R	55.3%	44.7%	55.3%	44.7%
2	2010	169,762	94,053	PEARCE, STEVE	75,709	TEAGUE, HARRY*		18,344 R	55.4%	44.6%	55.4%	44.6%
2	2008	231,552	101,980	TINSLEY, EDWARD R.	129,572	TEAGUE, HARRY		27,592 D	44.0%	56.0%	44.0%	56.0%
2	2006	155,874	92,620	PEARCE, STEVE*	63,119	KISSLING, ALBERT D.	135	29,501 R	59.4%	40.5%	59.5%	40.5%
2	2004	216,790	130,498	PEARCE, STEVE*	86,292	KING, GARY K.		44,206 R	60.2%	39.8%	60.2%	39.8%
2	2002	141,629	79,631	PEARCE, STEVE	61,916	SMITH, JOHN ARTHUR	82	17,715 R	56.2%	43.7%	56.3%	43.7%
3	2010	210,678	90,621	MULLINS, THOMAS E.	120,057	LUJAN, BEN RAY*		29,436 D	43.0%	57.0%	43.0%	57.0%
3	2008	284,258	86,618	EAST, DANIEL K.	161,292	LUJAN, BEN RAY	36,348	74,674 D	30.5%	56.7%	34.9%	65.1%
3	2006	194,099	49,219	DOLIN, RONALD M.	144,880	UDALL, TOM*		95,661 D	25.4%	74.6%	25.4%	74.6%
3	2004	255,204	79,935	TUCKER, GREGORY M.	175,269	UDALL, TOM*		95,334 D	31.3%	68.7%	31.3%	68.7%
3	2002	122,950		—	122,950	UDALL, TOM*		122,950 D		100.0%		100.0%
TOTAL	2010	597,690	289,217		308,473			19,256 D	48.4%	51.6%	48.4%	51.6%
TOTAL	2008	814,566	321,083		457,135		36,348	136,052 D	39.4%	56.1%	41.3%	58.7%
TOTAL	2006	561,084	247,825		313,124		135	65,299 D	44.2%	55.8%	44.2%	55.8%
TOTAL	2004	742,899	357,805		384,900		194	27,095 D	48.2%	51.8%	48.2%	51.8%
TOTAL	2002	437,524	175,342		262,100		82	86,758 D	40.1%	59.9%	40.1%	59.9%

NEW MEXICO

GENERAL AND PRIMARY ELECTIONS

2010 GENERAL ELECTIONS

Governor   Other vote was 994 Republican write-in (Kenneth A. Gomez).

House   Other vote was:

CD 1
CD 2
CD 3

2010 PRIMARY ELECTIONS

Primary   June 1, 2010

Registration
(as of May 18, 2010)

Democratic	565,718
Republican	358,074
Other Parties	32,075
Declined to State	175,158
TOTAL	1,131,025

Primary Type   Closed—Only registered Democrats and Republicans could vote in their party's primary.

NEW MEXICO

GENERAL AND PRIMARY ELECTIONS

	REPUBLICAN PRIMARIES			DEMOCRATIC PRIMARIES		
Governor	Susana Martinez	62,006	50.7%	Diane D. Denish	108,302	99.1%
	Allen Weh	33,727	27.6%	Billy J. Driggs (write-in)	1,016	0.9%
	Doug W. Turner	14,166	11.6%			
	Pete V. Domenici Jr.	8,630	7.1%			
	Janice E. Arnold-Jones	3,740	3.1%			
	TOTAL	122,269		TOTAL	109,318	
Congressional District 1	Jonathan L. Barela	32,743	100.0%	Martin Heinrich*	32,173	100.0%
Congressional District 2	Steve Pearce	33,021	84.8%	Harry Teague*	26,321	100.0%
	Cliff R. Pirtle	5,913	15.2%			
	TOTAL	38,934				
Congressional District 3	Thomas E. Mullins	23,301	71.3%	Ben Ray Lujan*	44,967	100.0%
	Adam C. Kokesh	9,372	28.7%			
	TOTAL	32,673				

An asterisk (*) denotes incumbent.

NEW YORK

Congressional districts first established for elections held in 2002
29 members

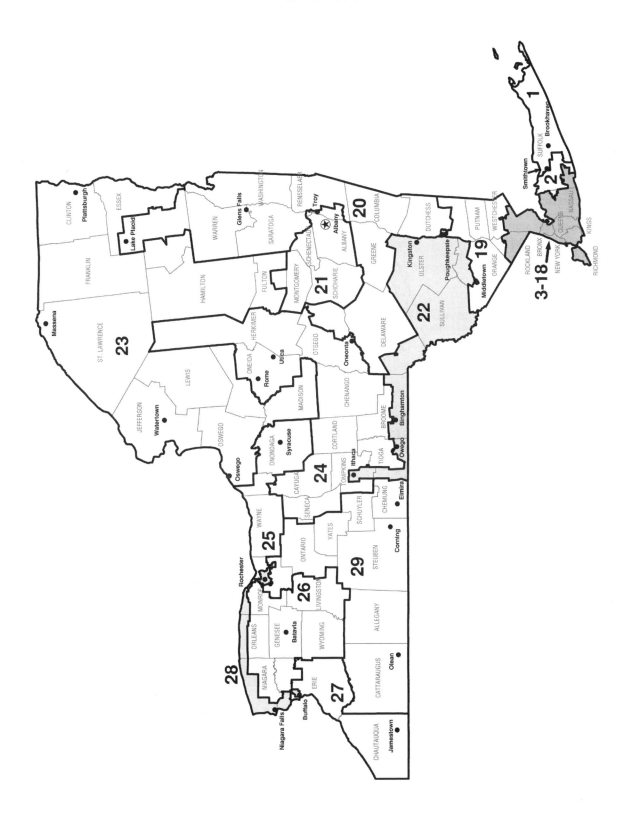

NEW YORK

New York City Area

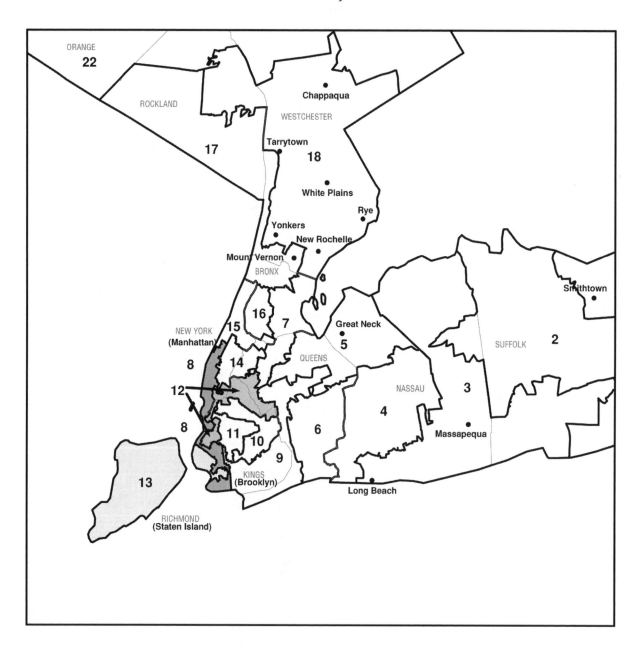

ORANGE
22

ROCKLAND

Chappaqua

WESTCHESTER

17

Tarrytown

18

White Plains

Rye

Yonkers

New Rochelle

Mount Vernon

BRONX

Smithtown

16

7

15

Great Neck

NEW YORK
(Manhattan)

5

SUFFOLK

2

QUEENS

8

14

NASSAU

3

12

4

8

11

10

6

Massapequa

9

KINGS
(Brooklyn)

13

Long Beach

RICHMOND
(Staten Island)

NEW YORK

GOVERNOR
Andrew M. Cuomo (D). Elected 2010 to a four-year term.

SENATORS (2 Democrats)
Kirsten E. Gillibrand (D). Elected 2010 to fill the remaining two years of the term vacated by Hillary Rodham Clinton (D), who resigned to become U.S. Secretary of State. Gillibrand sworn in as senator January 27, 2009, shortly after the vacancy occurred.

Charles E. Schumer (D). Reelected 2010 to a six-year term. Previously elected 2004, 1998.

REPRESENTATIVES (21 Democrats, 7 Republicans, 1 Vacancy)

1. Timothy H. Bishop (D)
2. Steve Israel (D)
3. Peter T. King (R)
4. Carolyn McCarthy (D)
5. Gary L. Ackerman (D)
6. Gregory W. Meeks (D)
7. Joseph Crowley (D)
8. Jerrold Nadler (D)
9. Vacancy
10. Edolphus Towns (D)
11. Yvette D. Clarke (D)
12. Nydia M. Velázquez
13. Michael G. Grimm (R)
14. Carolyn B. Maloney (D)
15. Charles B. Rangel (D)
16. Jose E. Serrano (D)
17. Eliot L. Engel (D)
18. Nita M. Lowey (D)
19. Nan Hayworth (R)
20. Christopher P. Gibson (R)
21. Paul Tonko (D)
22. Maurice D. Hinchey (D)
23. William L. Owens (D)
24. Richard L. Hanna (R)
25. Ann Marie Buerkle (R)
26. Kathy Hochul (D)
27. Brian Higgins (D)
28. Louise M. Slaughter (D)
29. Thomas W. Reed II (R)

POSTWAR VOTE FOR PRESIDENT

Year	Total Vote	Republican Vote	Republican Candidate	Democratic Vote	Democratic Candidate	Other Vote	Rep.-Dem. Plurality	Total Vote Rep.	Total Vote Dem.	Major Vote Rep.	Major Vote Dem.
2008	7,640,931	2,752,771	McCain, John	4,804,945	Obama, Barack	83,215	2,052,174 D	36.0%	62.9%	36.4%	63.6%
2004	7,391,036	2,962,567	Bush, George W.	4,314,280	Kerry, John	114,189	1,351,713 D	40.1%	58.4%	40.7%	59.3%
2000**	6,821,999	2,403,374	Bush, George W.	4,107,697	Gore, Al	310,928	1,704,323 D	35.2%	60.2%	36.9%	63.1%
1996**	6,316,129	1,933,492	Dole, Bob	3,756,177	Clinton, Bill	626,460	1,822,685 D	30.6%	59.5%	34.0%	66.0%
1992**	6,926,925	2,346,649	Bush, George	3,444,450	Clinton, Bill	1,135,826	1,097,801 D	33.9%	49.7%	40.5%	59.5%
1988	6,485,683	3,081,871	Bush, George	3,347,882	Dukakis, Michael S.	55,930	266,011 D	47.5%	51.6%	47.9%	52.1%
1984	6,806,810	3,664,763	Reagan, Ronald	3,119,609	Mondale, Walter F.	22,438	545,154 R	53.8%	45.8%	54.0%	46.0%
1980**	6,201,959	2,893,831	Reagan, Ronald	2,728,372	Carter, Jimmy	579,756	165,459 R	46.7%	44.0%	51.5%	48.5%
1976	6,534,170	3,100,791	Ford, Gerald R.	3,389,558	Carter, Jimmy	43,821	288,767 D	47.5%	51.9%	47.8%	52.2%
1972	7,165,919	4,192,778	Nixon, Richard M.	2,951,084	McGovern, George S.	22,057	1,241,694 R	58.5%	41.2%	58.7%	41.3%
1968**	6,791,688	3,007,932	Nixon, Richard M.	3,378,470	Humphrey, Hubert H.	405,286	370,538 D	44.3%	49.7%	47.1%	52.9%
1964	7,166,275	2,243,559	Goldwater, Barry M.	4,913,102	Johnson, Lyndon B.	9,614	2,669,543 D	31.3%	68.6%	31.3%	68.7%
1960	7,291,079	3,446,419	Nixon, Richard M.	3,830,085	Kennedy, John F.	14,575	383,666 D	47.3%	52.5%	47.4%	52.6%
1956	7,095,971	4,345,506	Eisenhower, Dwight D.	2,747,944	Stevenson, Adlai E.	2,521	1,597,562 R	61.2%	38.7%	61.3%	38.7%
1952	7,128,239	3,952,813	Eisenhower, Dwight D.	3,104,601	Stevenson, Adlai E.	70,825	848,212 R	55.5%	43.6%	56.0%	44.0%
1948**	6,177,337	2,841,163	Dewey, Thomas E.	2,780,204	Truman, Harry S.	555,970	60,959 R	46.0%	45.0%	50.5%	49.5%

**In past elections, the other vote included: 2000 - 244,030 Green (Ralph Nader); 1996 - 503,458 Reform (Ross Perot); 1992 - 1,090,721 Independent (Perot); 1980 - 467,801 Independent (John Anderson); 1968 - 358,864 American Independent (George Wallace); 1948 - 509,559 Progressive (Henry Wallace).

NEW YORK

POSTWAR VOTE FOR GOVERNOR

Year	Total Vote	Republican Vote	Republican Candidate	Democratic Vote	Democratic Candidate	Other Vote	Rep.-Dem. Plurality	Percentage Total Vote Rep.	Percentage Total Vote Dem.	Percentage Major Vote Rep.	Percentage Major Vote Dem.
2010	4,658,825	1,548,184	Paladino, Carl P.	2,911,721	Cuomo, Andrew M.	198,920	1,363,537 D	33.2%	62.5%	34.7%	65.3%
2006	4,437,220	1,274,335	Faso, John J.	3,086,709	Spitzer, Eliot	76,176	1,812,374 D	28.7%	69.6%	29.2%	70.8%
2002**	4,579,078	2,262,255	Pataki, George E.	1,534,064	McCall, H. Carl	782,759	728,191 R	49.4%	33.5%	59.6%	40.4%
1998	4,735,236	2,571,991	Pataki, George E.	1,570,317	Vallone, Peter F.	592,928	1,001,674 R	54.3%	33.2%	62.1%	37.9%
1994	5,208,762	2,538,702	Pataki, George E.	2,364,904	Cuomo, Mario M.	305,156	173,798 R	48.7%	45.4%	51.8%	48.2%
1990**	4,056,896	865,948	Rinfret, Pierre A.	2,157,087	Cuomo, Mario M.	1,033,861	1,291,139 D	21.3%	53.2%	28.6%	71.4%
1986	4,294,124	1,363,810	O'Rourke, Andrew P.	2,775,229	Cuomo, Mario M.	155,085	1,411,419 D	31.8%	64.6%	32.9%	67.1%
1982	5,254,891	2,494,827	Lehrman, Lew	2,675,213	Cuomo, Mario M.	84,851	180,386 D	47.5%	50.9%	48.3%	51.7%
1978	4,768,820	2,156,404	Duryea, Perry B.	2,429,272	Carey, Hugh L.	183,144	272,868 D	45.2%	50.9%	47.0%	53.0%
1974	5,293,176	2,219,667	Wilson, Malcolm	3,028,503	Carey, Hugh L.	45,006	808,836 D	41.9%	57.2%	42.3%	57.7%
1970	6,013,064	3,151,432	Rockefeller, Nelson A.	2,421,426	Goldberg, Arthur	440,206	730,006 R	52.4%	40.3%	56.5%	43.5%
1966**	6,031,585	2,690,626	Rockefeller, Nelson A.	2,298,363	O'Connor, Frank D.	1,042,596	392,263 R	44.6%	38.1%	53.9%	46.1%
1962	5,805,631	3,081,587	Rockefeller, Nelson A.	2,552,418	Morgenthau, Robert M.	171,626	529,169 R	53.1%	44.0%	54.7%	45.3%
1958	5,712,665	3,126,929	Rockefeller, Nelson A.	2,553,895	Harriman, Averell	31,841	573,034 R	54.7%	44.7%	55.0%	45.0%
1954	5,161,942	2,549,613	Ives, Irving M.	2,560,738	Harriman, Averell	51,591	11,125 D	49.4%	49.6%	49.9%	50.1%
1950	5,308,889	2,819,523	Dewey, Thomas E.	2,246,855	Lynch, Walter A.	242,511	572,668 R	53.1%	42.3%	55.7%	44.3%
1946	4,964,552	2,825,633	Dewey, Thomas E.	2,138,482	Mead, James M.	437	687,151 R	56.9%	43.1%	56.9%	43.1%

**In past elections, the other vote included: 2002 - 654,016 Independence (B. Thomas Golisano); 1990 - 827,614 Conservative (Herbert I. London); 1966 - 510,023 Conservative (Paul L. Adams); and 507,234 Liberal (Franklin Roosevelt Jr.).

POSTWAR VOTE FOR SENATOR

Year	Total Vote	Republican Vote	Republican Candidate	Democratic Vote	Democratic Candidate	Other Vote	Plurality	Percentage Total Vote Rep.	Percentage Total Vote Dem.	Percentage Major Vote Rep.	Percentage Major Vote Dem.
2010	4,596,796	1,480,423	Townsend, Jay	3,047,880	Schumer, Charles E.	68,493	1,567,457 D	32.2%	66.3%	32.7%	67.3%
2010S	4,508,771	1,582,693	DioGuardi, Joseph J.	2,837,684	Gillibrand, Kirsten E.	88,394	1,254,991 D	35.1%	62.9%	35.8%	64.2%
2006	4,490,053	1,392,189	Spencer, John	3,008,428	Clinton, Hillary Rodham	89,436	1,616,239 D	31.0%	67.0%	31.6%	68.4%
2004	6,702,875	1,625,069	Mills, Howard	4,769,824	Schumer, Charles E.	307,982	3,144,755 D	24.2%	71.2%	25.4%	74.6%
2000	6,779,839	2,915,730	Lazio, Rick A.	3,747,310	Clinton, Hillary Rodham	116,799	831,580 D	43.0%	55.3%	43.8%	56.2%
1998	4,670,805	2,058,988	D'Amato, Alfonse M.	2,551,065	Schumer, Charles E.	60,752	492,077 D	44.1%	54.6%	44.7%	55.3%
1994	4,794,601	1,988,308	Castro, Bernadette	2,646,541	Moynihan, Daniel P.	159,752	658,233 D	41.5%	55.2%	42.9%	57.1%
1992	6,458,826	3,166,994	D'Amato, Alfonse M.	3,086,200	Abrams, Robert	205,632	80,794 R	49.0%	47.8%	50.6%	49.4%
1988	6,040,980	1,875,784	McMillan, Robert	4,048,649	Moynihan, Daniel P.	116,547	2,172,865 D	31.1%	67.0%	31.7%	68.3%
1986	4,179,447	2,378,197	D'Amato, Alfonse M.	1,723,216	Green, Mark	78,034	654,981 R	56.9%	41.2%	58.0%	42.0%
1982	4,967,729	1,696,766	Sullivan, Florence M.	3,232,146	Moynihan, Daniel P.	38,817	1,535,380 D	34.2%	65.1%	34.4%	65.6%
1980**	6,014,914	2,699,652	D'Amato, Alfonse M.	2,618,661	Holtzman, Elizabeth	696,601	80,991 R	44.9%	43.5%	50.8%	49.2%
1976	6,319,755	2,836,633	Buckley, James L.	3,422,594	Moynihan, Daniel P.	60,528	585,961 D	44.9%	54.2%	45.3%	54.7%
1974	5,163,600	2,340,188	Javits, Jacob K.	1,973,781	Clark, Ramsey	849,631	366,407 R	45.3%	38.2%	54.2%	45.8%
1970**	5,904,782	1,434,472	Goodell, Charles	2,171,232	Ottinger, Richard L.	2,299,078	116,958 C	24.3%	36.8%	39.8%	60.2%
1968**	6,581,587	3,269,772	Javits, Jacob K.	2,150,695	O'Dwyer, Paul	1,161,120	1,119,077 R	49.7%	32.7%	60.3%	39.7%
1964	7,151,686	3,104,056	Keating, Kenneth B.	3,823,749	Kennedy, Robert F.	223,881	719,693 D	43.4%	53.5%	44.8%	55.2%
1962	5,700,186	3,269,417	Javits, Jacob K.	2,289,341	Donovan, James B.	141,428	980,076 R	57.4%	40.2%	58.8%	41.2%
1958	5,602,088	2,842,942	Keating, Kenneth B.	2,709,950	Hogan, Frank S.	49,196	132,992 R	50.7%	48.4%	51.2%	48.8%
1956	6,991,136	3,723,933	Javits, Jacob K.	3,265,159	Wagner, Robert F.	2,044	458,774 R	53.3%	46.7%	53.3%	46.7%
1952	6,980,259	3,853,934	Ives, Irving M.	2,521,736	Cashmore, John	604,589	1,332,198 R	55.2%	36.1%	60.4%	39.6%
1950	5,228,403	2,367,353	Hanley, Joe R.	2,632,313	Lehman, Herbert H.	228,737	264,960 D	45.3%	50.3%	47.4%	52.6%
1949S	4,966,878	2,384,381	Dulles, John Foster	2,582,438	Lehman, Herbert H.	59	198,057 D	48.0%	52.0%	48.0%	52.0%
1946	4,867,564	2,559,365	Ives, Irving M.	2,308,112	Lehman, Herbert H.	87	251,253 R	52.6%	47.4%	52.6%	47.4%

In past elections, the other vote included: 1980 - 664,544 Liberal (Jacob K. Javits); 1970 - 2,288,190 Conservative (James L. Buckley); 1968 - 1,139,402 Conservative (Buckley). Buckley won the 1970 election with 38.8 percent of the total vote. The 1949 election and one of the 2010 elections were for short terms to fill a vacancy.

NEW YORK

GOVERNOR 2010

2010 Census Population	County	Total Vote	Republican	Democratic	Other	Rep.-Dem. Plurality		Percentage			
								Total Vote		Major Vote	
								Rep.	Dem.	Rep.	Dem.
304,204	ALBANY	102,739	28,076	65,798	8,865	37,722	D	27.3%	64.0%	29.9%	70.1%
48,946	ALLEGANY	13,199	8,353	4,470	376	3,883	R	63.3%	33.9%	65.1%	34.9%
1,385,108	BRONX	176,200	16,032	154,500	5,668	138,468	D	9.1%	87.7%	9.4%	90.6%
200,600	BROOME	61,131	25,214	33,761	2,156	8,547	D	41.2%	55.2%	42.8%	57.2%
80,317	CATTARAUGUS	22,236	14,554	6,997	685	7,557	R	65.5%	31.5%	67.5%	32.5%
80,026	CAYUGA	22,454	9,141	12,067	1,246	2,926	D	40.7%	53.7%	43.1%	56.9%
134,905	CHAUTAUQUA	39,785	24,593	14,022	1,170	10,571	R	61.8%	35.2%	63.7%	36.3%
88,830	CHEMUNG	24,448	10,925	12,972	551	2,047	D	44.7%	53.1%	45.7%	54.3%
50,477	CHENANGO	14,005	6,126	7,231	648	1,105	D	43.7%	51.6%	45.9%	54.1%
82,128	CLINTON	22,989	7,155	15,316	518	8,161	D	31.1%	66.6%	31.8%	68.2%
63,096	COLUMBIA	23,757	8,402	13,952	1,403	5,550	D	35.4%	58.7%	37.6%	62.4%
49,336	CORTLAND	13,891	5,424	7,715	752	2,291	D	39.0%	55.5%	41.3%	58.7%
47,980	DELAWARE	13,744	6,350	6,698	696	348	D	46.2%	48.7%	48.7%	51.3%
297,488	DUTCHESS	86,342	34,874	48,165	3,303	13,291	D	40.4%	55.8%	42.0%	58.0%
919,040	ERIE	301,861	176,690	113,459	11,712	63,231	R	58.5%	37.6%	60.9%	39.1%
39,370	ESSEX	12,935	4,464	7,991	480	3,527	D	34.5%	61.8%	35.8%	64.2%
51,599	FRANKLIN	12,259	3,699	8,144	416	4,445	D	30.2%	66.4%	31.2%	68.8%
55,531	FULTON	15,027	7,307	7,009	711	298	R	48.6%	46.6%	51.0%	49.0%
60,079	GENESEE	17,876	10,619	6,668	589	3,951	R	59.4%	37.3%	61.4%	38.6%
49,221	GREENE	16,226	7,553	7,904	769	351	D	46.5%	48.7%	48.9%	51.1%
4,836	HAMILTON	2,614	1,373	1,100	141	273	R	52.5%	42.1%	55.5%	44.5%
64,519	HERKIMER	19,547	8,840	9,942	765	1,102	D	45.2%	50.9%	47.1%	52.9%
116,229	JEFFERSON	26,973	9,760	15,762	1,451	6,002	D	36.2%	58.4%	38.2%	61.8%
2,504,700	KINGS	399,644	60,198	320,222	19,224	260,024	D	15.1%	80.1%	15.8%	84.2%
27,087	LEWIS	7,361	3,210	3,842	309	632	D	43.6%	52.2%	45.5%	54.5%
65,393	LIVINGSTON	19,610	9,069	9,919	622	850	D	46.2%	50.6%	47.8%	52.2%
73,442	MADISON	21,133	8,657	10,862	1,614	2,205	D	41.0%	51.4%	44.4%	55.6%
744,344	MONROE	229,881	80,363	141,765	7,753	61,402	D	35.0%	61.7%	36.2%	63.8%
50,219	MONTGOMERY	13,969	6,487	6,805	677	318	D	46.4%	48.7%	48.8%	51.2%
1,339,532	NASSAU	385,696	139,432	233,349	12,915	93,917	D	36.2%	60.5%	37.4%	62.6%
1,585,873	NEW YORK	352,580	35,295	300,272	17,013	264,977	D	10.0%	85.2%	10.5%	89.5%
216,469	NIAGARA	65,739	42,553	21,237	1,949	21,316	R	64.7%	32.3%	66.7%	33.3%
234,878	ONEIDA	67,968	29,469	35,651	2,848	6,182	D	43.4%	52.5%	45.3%	54.7%
467,026	ONONDAGA	143,403	46,308	84,281	12,814	37,973	D	32.3%	58.8%	35.5%	64.5%
107,931	ONTARIO	34,101	14,525	18,436	1,140	3,911	D	42.6%	54.1%	44.1%	55.9%
372,813	ORANGE	96,658	38,938	53,631	4,089	14,693	D	40.3%	55.5%	42.1%	57.9%
42,883	ORLEANS	11,277	6,716	4,252	309	2,464	R	59.6%	37.7%	61.2%	38.8%
122,109	OSWEGO	31,753	12,259	17,101	2,393	4,842	D	38.6%	53.9%	41.8%	58.2%
62,259	OTSEGO	18,167	7,459	9,899	809	2,440	D	41.1%	54.5%	43.0%	57.0%
99,710	PUTNAM	31,930	14,309	16,508	1,113	2,199	D	44.8%	51.7%	46.4%	53.6%
2,230,722	QUEENS	341,287	62,003	267,266	12,018	205,263	D	18.2%	78.3%	18.8%	81.2%
159,429	RENSSELAER	54,227	19,886	30,249	4,092	10,363	D	36.7%	55.8%	39.7%	60.3%
468,730	RICHMOND	97,271	38,895	55,532	2,844	16,637	D	40.0%	57.1%	41.2%	58.8%
311,687	ROCKLAND	85,725	32,118	51,334	2,273	19,216	D	37.5%	59.9%	38.5%	61.5%
111,944	ST. LAWRENCE	29,019	9,334	18,685	1,000	9,351	D	32.2%	64.4%	33.3%	66.7%
219,607	SARATOGA	81,867	32,690	43,535	5,642	10,845	D	39.9%	53.2%	42.9%	57.1%
154,727	SCHENECTADY	48,393	17,100	27,942	3,351	10,842	D	35.3%	57.7%	38.0%	62.0%
32,749	SCHOHARIE	10,520	5,019	4,874	627	145	R	47.7%	46.3%	50.7%	49.3%
18,343	SCHUYLER	5,953	2,829	2,922	202	93	D	47.5%	49.1%	49.2%	50.8%
35,251	SENECA	10,075	4,066	5,640	369	1,574	D	40.4%	56.0%	41.9%	58.1%

294

NEW YORK

GOVERNOR 2010

2010 Census Population	County	Total Vote	Republican	Democratic	Other	Rep.-Dem. Plurality		Percentage			
								Total Vote		Major Vote	
								Rep.	Dem.	Rep.	Dem.
98,990	STEUBEN	27,520	13,787	12,928	805	859	R	50.1%	47.0%	51.6%	48.4%
1,493,350	SUFFOLK	394,149	152,813	227,374	13,962	74,561	D	38.8%	57.7%	40.2%	59.8%
77,547	SULLIVAN	21,337	8,363	11,800	1,174	3,437	D	39.2%	55.3%	41.5%	58.5%
51,125	TIOGA	16,112	8,051	7,467	594	584	R	50.0%	46.3%	51.9%	48.1%
101,564	TOMPKINS	29,205	7,237	20,314	1,654	13,077	D	24.8%	69.6%	26.3%	73.7%
182,493	ULSTER	60,247	21,027	35,750	3,470	14,723	D	34.9%	59.3%	37.0%	63.0%
65,707	WARREN	23,016	9,365	12,351	1,300	2,986	D	40.7%	53.7%	43.1%	56.9%
63,216	WASHINGTON	18,247	7,669	9,485	1,093	1,816	D	42.0%	52.0%	44.7%	55.3%
93,772	WAYNE	27,097	12,442	13,769	886	1,327	D	45.9%	50.8%	47.5%	52.5%
949,113	WESTCHESTER	264,680	80,802	175,591	8,287	94,789	D	30.5%	66.3%	31.5%	68.5%
42,155	WYOMING	12,694	8,678	3,599	417	5,079	R	68.4%	28.4%	70.7%	29.3%
25,348	YATES	7,076	3,239	3,639	198	400	D	45.8%	51.4%	47.1%	52.9%
19,378,102	TOTAL	4,658,825	1,548,184	2,911,721	198,920	1,363,537	D	33.2%	62.5%	34.7%	65.3%

NEW YORK

GOVERNOR 2010

2010 Census Population	County	Total Vote	Republican	Democratic	Other	Rep.-Dem. Plurality		Percentage			
								Total Vote		Major Vote	
								Rep.	Dem.	Rep.	Dem.
1,385,108	BRONX	176,200	16,032	154,500	5,668	138,468	D	9.1%	87.7%	9.4%	90.6%
2,504,700	KINGS	399,644	60,198	320,222	19,224	260,024	D	15.1%	80.1%	15.8%	84.2%
1,585,873	NEW YORK	352,580	35,295	300,272	17,013	264,977	D	10.0%	85.2%	10.5%	89.5%
2,230,722	QUEENS	341,287	62,003	267,266	12,018	205,263	D	18.2%	78.3%	18.8%	81.2%
468,730	RICHMOND	97,271	38,895	55,532	2,844	16,637	D	40.0%	57.1%	41.2%	58.8%
8,175,133	TOTAL	1,366,982	212,423	1,097,792	56,767	885,369	D	15.5%	80.3%	16.2%	83.8%

NEW YORK

SENATOR 2010
(Full Term)

2010 Census Population	County	Total Vote	Republican	Democratic	Other	Rep.-Dem. Plurality		Percentage Total Vote Rep.	Dem.	Major Vote Rep.	Dem.
304,204	ALBANY	100,969	31,140	67,363	2,466	36,223	D	30.8%	66.7%	31.6%	68.4%
48,946	ALLEGANY	13,005	6,354	6,432	219	78	D	48.9%	49.5%	49.7%	50.3%
1,385,108	BRONX	172,358	15,553	155,292	1,513	139,739	D	9.0%	90.1%	9.1%	90.9%
200,600	BROOME	60,437	26,569	32,768	1,100	6,199	D	44.0%	54.2%	44.8%	55.2%
80,317	CATTARAUGUS	21,796	9,561	11,874	361	2,313	D	43.9%	54.5%	44.6%	55.4%
80,026	CAYUGA	22,061	7,990	13,592	479	5,602	D	36.2%	61.6%	37.0%	63.0%
134,905	CHAUTAUQUA	39,121	16,752	21,791	578	5,039	D	42.8%	55.7%	43.5%	56.5%
88,830	CHEMUNG	24,156	9,951	13,927	278	3,976	D	41.2%	57.7%	41.7%	58.3%
50,477	CHENANGO	13,908	6,308	7,259	341	951	D	45.4%	52.2%	46.5%	53.5%
82,128	CLINTON	22,307	7,842	14,128	337	6,286	D	35.2%	63.3%	35.7%	64.3%
63,096	COLUMBIA	23,374	8,671	14,157	546	5,486	D	37.1%	60.6%	38.0%	62.0%
49,336	CORTLAND	13,670	5,369	8,046	255	2,677	D	39.3%	58.9%	40.0%	60.0%
47,980	DELAWARE	13,601	6,503	6,787	311	284	D	47.8%	49.9%	48.9%	51.1%
297,488	DUTCHESS	84,185	36,801	46,121	1,263	9,320	D	43.7%	54.8%	44.4%	55.6%
919,040	ERIE	295,534	100,302	190,417	4,815	90,115	D	33.9%	64.4%	34.5%	65.5%
39,370	ESSEX	12,255	4,949	7,057	249	2,108	D	40.4%	57.6%	41.2%	58.8%
51,599	FRANKLIN	11,886	4,266	7,428	192	3,162	D	35.9%	62.5%	36.5%	63.5%
55,531	FULTON	14,512	6,960	7,326	226	366	D	48.0%	50.5%	48.7%	51.3%
60,079	GENESEE	17,570	8,214	9,069	287	855	D	46.8%	51.6%	47.5%	52.5%
49,221	GREENE	15,895	7,547	8,076	272	529	D	47.5%	50.8%	48.3%	51.7%
4,836	HAMILTON	2,571	1,368	1,149	54	219	R	53.2%	44.7%	54.4%	45.6%
64,519	HERKIMER	19,032	8,018	10,718	296	2,700	D	42.1%	56.3%	42.8%	57.2%
116,229	JEFFERSON	26,492	9,654	16,527	311	6,873	D	36.4%	62.4%	36.9%	63.1%
2,504,700	KINGS	393,120	59,372	327,872	5,876	268,500	D	15.1%	83.4%	15.3%	84.7%
27,087	LEWIS	7,281	2,965	4,196	120	1,231	D	40.7%	57.6%	41.4%	58.6%
65,393	LIVINGSTON	19,301	8,740	10,262	299	1,522	D	45.3%	53.2%	46.0%	54.0%
73,442	MADISON	20,956	8,768	11,706	482	2,938	D	41.8%	55.9%	42.8%	57.2%
744,344	MONROE	227,310	80,992	142,858	3,460	61,866	D	35.6%	62.8%	36.2%	63.8%
50,219	MONTGOMERY	13,670	6,051	7,325	294	1,274	D	44.3%	53.6%	45.2%	54.8%
1,339,532	NASSAU	386,220	152,797	230,103	3,320	77,306	D	39.6%	59.6%	39.9%	60.1%
1,585,873	NEW YORK	351,283	45,823	298,926	6,534	253,103	D	13.0%	85.1%	13.3%	86.7%
216,469	NIAGARA	64,359	26,555	36,792	1,012	10,237	D	41.3%	57.2%	41.9%	58.1%
234,878	ONEIDA	67,417	26,472	39,924	1,021	13,452	D	39.3%	59.2%	39.9%	60.1%
467,026	ONONDAGA	142,167	47,116	91,733	3,318	44,617	D	33.1%	64.5%	33.9%	66.1%
107,931	ONTARIO	33,927	14,174	19,242	511	5,068	D	41.8%	56.7%	42.4%	57.6%
372,813	ORANGE	96,718	41,077	54,212	1,429	13,135	D	42.5%	56.1%	43.1%	56.9%
42,883	ORLEANS	10,937	5,158	5,597	182	439	D	47.2%	51.2%	48.0%	52.0%
122,109	OSWEGO	31,212	12,182	18,286	744	6,104	D	39.0%	58.6%	40.0%	60.0%
62,259	OTSEGO	17,860	7,511	9,962	387	2,451	D	42.1%	55.8%	43.0%	57.0%
99,710	PUTNAM	31,385	14,549	16,447	389	1,898	D	46.4%	52.4%	46.9%	53.1%
2,230,722	QUEENS	334,565	64,567	266,147	3,851	201,580	D	19.3%	79.6%	19.5%	80.5%
159,429	RENSSELAER	53,116	20,302	31,645	1,169	11,343	D	38.2%	59.6%	39.1%	60.9%
468,730	RICHMOND	96,276	39,443	55,897	936	16,454	D	41.0%	58.1%	41.4%	58.6%
311,687	ROCKLAND	84,276	31,847	51,652	777	19,805	D	37.8%	61.3%	38.1%	61.9%
111,944	ST. LAWRENCE	28,216	8,813	18,908	495	10,095	D	31.2%	67.0%	31.8%	68.2%
219,607	SARATOGA	80,278	34,973	43,823	1,482	8,850	D	43.6%	54.6%	44.4%	55.6%
154,727	SCHENECTADY	47,623	18,124	28,388	1,111	10,264	D	38.1%	59.6%	39.0%	61.0%
32,749	SCHOHARIE	10,350	4,948	5,182	220	234	D	47.8%	50.1%	48.8%	51.2%
18,343	SCHUYLER	5,865	2,628	3,134	103	506	D	44.8%	53.4%	45.6%	54.4%
35,251	SENECA	9,908	3,799	5,922	187	2,123	D	38.3%	59.8%	39.1%	60.9%
98,990	STEUBEN	27,094	12,525	14,180	389	1,655	D	46.2%	52.3%	46.9%	53.1%
1,493,350	SUFFOLK	389,794	160,865	224,677	4,252	63,812	D	41.3%	57.6%	41.7%	58.3%

NEW YORK

SENATOR 2010
(Full Term)

2010 Census Population	County	Total Vote	Republican	Democratic	Other	Rep.-Dem. Plurality		Percentage			
								Total Vote		Major Vote	
								Rep.	Dem.	Rep.	Dem.
77,547	SULLIVAN	20,886	8,383	12,099	404	3,716	D	40.1%	57.9%	40.9%	59.1%
51,125	TIOGA	15,956	8,563	7,096	297	1,467	R	53.7%	44.5%	54.7%	45.3%
101,564	TOMPKINS	29,113	7,599	20,728	786	13,129	D	26.1%	71.2%	26.8%	73.2%
182,493	ULSTER	59,647	21,788	36,268	1,591	14,480	D	36.5%	60.8%	37.5%	62.5%
65,707	WARREN	22,534	8,795	13,363	376	4,568	D	39.0%	59.3%	39.7%	60.3%
63,216	WASHINGTON	17,829	7,141	10,288	400	3,147	D	40.1%	57.7%	41.0%	59.0%
93,772	WAYNE	26,661	12,412	13,781	468	1,369	D	46.6%	51.7%	47.4%	52.6%
949,113	WESTCHESTER	261,552	86,785	172,103	2,664	85,318	D	33.2%	65.8%	33.5%	66.5%
42,155	WYOMING	12,405	6,092	6,018	295	74	R	49.1%	48.5%	50.3%	49.7%
25,348	YATES	7,034	3,087	3,834	113	747	D	43.9%	54.5%	44.6%	55.4%
19,378,102	TOTAL	4,596,796	1,480,423	3,047,880	68,493	1,567,457	D	32.2%	66.3%	32.7%	67.3%

2010 Census Population	County	Total Vote	Republican	Democratic	Other	Rep.-Dem. Plurality		Percentage			
								Total Vote		Major Vote	
								Rep.	Dem.	Rep.	Dem.
1,385,108	BRONX	172,358	15,553	155,292	1,513	139,739	D	9.0%	90.1%	9.1%	90.9%
2,504,700	KINGS	393,120	59,372	327,872	5,876	268,500	D	15.1%	83.4%	15.3%	84.7%
1,585,873	NEW YORK	351,283	45,823	298,926	6,534	253,103	D	13.0%	85.1%	13.3%	86.7%
2,230,722	QUEENS	334,565	64,567	266,147	3,851	201,580	D	19.3%	79.6%	19.5%	80.5%
468,730	RICHMOND	96,276	39,443	55,897	936	16,454	D	41.0%	58.1%	41.4%	58.6%
8,175,133	TOTAL	1,347,602	224,758	1,104,134	18,710	879,376	D	16.7%	81.9%	16.9%	83.1%

NEW YORK

SENATOR 2010
(Short Term)

2010 Census Population	County	Total Vote	Republican	Democratic	Other	Rep.-Dem. Plurality		Percentage			
								Total Vote		Major Vote	
								Rep.	Dem.	Rep.	Dem.
304,204	ALBANY	101,417	32,324	66,787	2,306	34,463	D	31.9%	65.9%	32.6%	67.4%
48,946	ALLEGANY	12,781	6,523	6,010	248	513	R	51.0%	47.0%	52.0%	48.0%
1,385,108	BRONX	167,267	18,401	146,356	2,510	127,955	D	11.0%	87.5%	11.2%	88.8%
200,600	BROOME	59,669	24,899	33,499	1,271	8,600	D	41.7%	56.1%	42.6%	57.4%
80,317	CATTARAUGUS	21,413	9,908	11,027	478	1,119	D	46.3%	51.5%	47.3%	52.7%
80,026	CAYUGA	21,442	9,135	11,669	638	2,534	D	42.6%	54.4%	43.9%	56.1%
134,905	CHAUTAUQUA	38,262	16,791	20,647	824	3,856	D	43.9%	54.0%	44.9%	55.1%
88,830	CHEMUNG	23,736	10,023	13,386	327	3,363	D	42.2%	56.4%	42.8%	57.2%
50,477	CHENANGO	13,682	6,156	7,103	423	947	D	45.0%	51.9%	46.4%	53.6%
82,128	CLINTON	21,805	8,034	13,326	445	5,292	D	36.8%	61.1%	37.6%	62.4%

NEW YORK

SENATOR 2010
(Short Term)

2010 Census Population	County	Total Vote	Republican	Democratic	Other	Rep.-Dem. Plurality		Percentage			
								Total Vote		Major Vote	
								Rep.	Dem.	Rep.	Dem.
63,096	COLUMBIA	23,641	8,222	14,981	438	6,759	D	34.8%	63.4%	35.4%	64.6%
49,336	CORTLAND	13,404	5,656	7,399	349	1,743	D	42.2%	55.2%	43.3%	56.7%
47,980	DELAWARE	13,495	6,086	7,114	295	1,028	D	45.1%	52.7%	46.1%	53.9%
297,488	DUTCHESS	83,563	36,457	45,740	1,366	9,283	D	43.6%	54.7%	44.4%	55.6%
919,040	ERIE	287,841	105,569	175,311	6,961	69,742	D	36.7%	60.9%	37.6%	62.4%
39,370	ESSEX	12,306	4,557	7,504	245	2,947	D	37.0%	61.0%	37.8%	62.2%
51,599	FRANKLIN	11,599	4,148	7,191	260	3,043	D	35.8%	62.0%	36.6%	63.4%
55,531	FULTON	14,604	7,106	7,203	295	97	D	48.7%	49.3%	49.7%	50.3%
60,079	GENESEE	17,175	8,675	8,056	444	619	R	50.5%	46.9%	51.8%	48.2%
49,221	GREENE	15,950	7,365	8,308	277	943	D	46.2%	52.1%	47.0%	53.0%
4,836	HAMILTON	2,555	1,314	1,175	66	139	R	51.4%	46.0%	52.8%	47.2%
64,519	HERKIMER	18,469	7,663	10,456	350	2,793	D	41.5%	56.6%	42.3%	57.7%
116,229	JEFFERSON	25,825	9,885	15,532	408	5,647	D	38.3%	60.1%	38.9%	61.1%
2,504,700	KINGS	382,512	70,454	303,779	8,279	233,325	D	18.4%	79.4%	18.8%	81.2%
27,087	LEWIS	7,000	2,987	3,841	172	854	D	42.7%	54.9%	43.7%	56.3%
65,393	LIVINGSTON	18,885	9,148	9,278	459	130	D	48.4%	49.1%	49.6%	50.4%
73,442	MADISON	20,474	8,780	11,018	676	2,238	D	42.9%	53.8%	44.3%	55.7%
744,344	MONROE	222,400	89,827	127,790	4,783	37,963	D	40.4%	57.5%	41.3%	58.7%
50,219	MONTGOMERY	13,633	6,147	7,198	288	1,051	D	45.1%	52.8%	46.1%	53.9%
1,339,532	NASSAU	379,308	171,265	202,601	5,442	31,336	D	45.2%	53.4%	45.8%	54.2%
1,585,873	NEW YORK	345,740	49,794	287,749	8,197	237,955	D	14.4%	83.2%	14.8%	85.2%
216,469	NIAGARA	63,005	27,033	34,483	1,489	7,450	D	42.9%	54.7%	43.9%	56.1%
234,878	ONEIDA	65,860	26,774	37,820	1,266	11,046	D	40.7%	57.4%	41.4%	58.6%
467,026	ONONDAGA	138,645	51,473	83,056	4,116	31,583	D	37.1%	59.9%	38.3%	61.7%
107,931	ONTARIO	33,279	15,265	17,250	764	1,985	D	45.9%	51.8%	46.9%	53.1%
372,813	ORANGE	94,676	41,468	51,411	1,797	9,943	D	43.8%	54.3%	44.6%	55.4%
42,883	ORLEANS	10,609	5,383	4,959	267	424	R	50.7%	46.7%	52.0%	48.0%
122,109	OSWEGO	30,189	12,784	16,409	996	3,625	D	42.3%	54.4%	43.8%	56.2%
62,259	OTSEGO	17,775	7,167	10,224	384	3,057	D	40.3%	57.5%	41.2%	58.8%
99,710	PUTNAM	30,975	15,560	14,951	464	609	R	50.2%	48.3%	51.0%	49.0%
2,230,722	QUEENS	327,058	73,680	247,934	5,444	174,254	D	22.5%	75.8%	22.9%	77.1%
159,429	RENSSELAER	53,631	20,726	31,836	1,069	11,110	D	38.6%	59.4%	39.4%	60.6%
468,730	RICHMOND	95,103	45,307	48,551	1,245	3,244	D	47.6%	51.1%	48.3%	51.7%
311,687	ROCKLAND	83,283	35,149	47,068	1,066	11,919	D	42.2%	56.5%	42.8%	57.2%
111,944	ST. LAWRENCE	27,285	8,890	17,789	606	8,899	D	32.6%	65.2%	33.3%	66.7%
219,607	SARATOGA	81,342	34,431	45,664	1,247	11,233	D	42.3%	56.1%	43.0%	57.0%
154,727	SCHENECTADY	47,760	18,643	28,069	1,048	9,426	D	39.0%	58.8%	39.9%	60.1%
32,749	SCHOHARIE	10,313	4,831	5,224	258	393	D	46.8%	50.7%	48.0%	52.0%
18,343	SCHUYLER	5,796	2,642	3,041	113	399	D	45.6%	52.5%	46.5%	53.5%
35,251	SENECA	9,654	4,194	5,168	292	974	D	43.4%	53.5%	44.8%	55.2%
98,990	STEUBEN	26,631	12,849	13,238	544	389	D	48.2%	49.7%	49.3%	50.7%
1,493,350	SUFFOLK	379,365	173,573	199,909	5,883	26,336	D	45.8%	52.7%	46.5%	53.5%
77,547	SULLIVAN	20,362	8,250	11,603	509	3,353	D	40.5%	57.0%	41.6%	58.4%
51,125	TIOGA	15,753	7,877	7,525	351	352	R	50.0%	47.8%	51.1%	48.9%
101,564	TOMPKINS	28,571	7,764	19,878	929	12,114	D	27.2%	69.6%	28.1%	71.9%
182,493	ULSTER	58,838	20,930	36,228	1,680	15,298	D	35.6%	61.6%	36.6%	63.4%
65,707	WARREN	22,823	8,500	14,001	322	5,501	D	37.2%	61.3%	37.8%	62.2%
63,216	WASHINGTON	18,026	6,645	11,053	328	4,408	D	36.9%	61.3%	37.5%	62.5%
93,772	WAYNE	25,905	13,019	12,221	665	798	R	50.3%	47.2%	51.6%	48.4%
949,113	WESTCHESTER	255,331	98,959	153,197	3,175	54,238	D	38.8%	60.0%	39.2%	60.8%
42,155	WYOMING	12,205	6,314	5,520	371	794	R	51.7%	45.2%	53.4%	46.6%
25,348	YATES	6,870	3,314	3,370	186	56	D	48.2%	49.1%	49.6%	50.4%
19,378,102	TOTAL	4,508,771	1,582,693	2,837,684	88,394	1,254,991	D	35.1%	62.9%	35.8%	64.2%

NEW YORK CITY

SENATOR 2010

(Short Term)

2010 Census Population	County	Total Vote	Republican	Democratic	Other	Rep.-Dem. Plurality		Percentage			
								Total Vote		Major Vote	
								Rep.	Dem.	Rep.	Dem.
1,385,108	BRONX	167,267	18,401	146,356	2,510	127,955	D	11.0%	87.5%	11.2%	88.8%
2,504,700	KINGS	382,512	70,454	303,779	8,279	233,325	D	18.4%	79.4%	18.8%	81.2%
1,585,873	NEW YORK	345,740	49,794	287,749	8,197	237,955	D	14.4%	83.2%	14.8%	85.2%
2,230,722	QUEENS	327,058	73,680	247,934	5,444	174,254	D	22.5%	75.8%	22.9%	77.1%
468,730	RICHMOND	95,103	45,307	48,551	1,245	3,244	D	47.6%	51.1%	48.3%	51.7%
8,175,133	TOTAL	1,317,680	257,636	1,034,369	25,675	776,733	D	19.6%	78.5%	19.9%	80.1%

NEW YORK

HOUSE OF REPRESENTATIVES

CD	Year	Total Vote	Republican		Democratic		Other Vote	Rep.-Dem. Plurality		Percentage			
			Vote	Candidate	Vote	Candidate				Total Vote		Major Vote	
										Rep.	Dem.	Rep.	Dem.
1	2010	196,164	97,723 # ALTSCHULER, RANDY		98,316 # BISHOP, TIMOTHY H.*		125	593	D	49.8%	50.1%	49.8%	50.2%
1	2008	277,641	115,545 # ZELDIN, LEE M.		162,083 # BISHOP, TIMOTHY H.*		13	46,538	D	41.6%	58.4%	41.6%	58.4%
1	2006	167,688	63,328 # ZANZI, ITALO A.		104,360 # BISHOP, TIMOTHY H.*			41,032	D	37.8%	62.2%	37.8%	62.2%
1	2004	278,209	121,855 # MANGER, WILLIAM M. JR.		156,354 # BISHOP, TIMOTHY H.*			34,499	D	43.8%	56.2%	43.8%	56.2%
1	2002	167,791	81,524 # GRUCCI, FELIX J. JR.*		84,276 # BISHOP, TIMOTHY H.		1,991	2,752	D	48.6%	50.2%	49.2%	50.8%
2	2010	167,909	72,029 # GOMEZ, JOHN B.		94,594 # ISRAEL, STEVE*		1,286	22,565	D	42.9%	56.3%	43.2%	56.8%
2	2008	240,932	79,641 # STALZER, FRANK J.		161,279 # ISRAEL, STEVE*		12	81,638	D	33.1%	66.9%	33.1%	66.9%
2	2006	149,488	44,212 # BUGLER, JOHN W.		105,276 # ISRAEL, STEVE*			61,064	D	29.6%	70.4%	29.6%	70.4%
2	2004	242,543	80,950 # HOFFMANN, RICHARD		161,593 # ISRAEL, STEVE*			80,643	D	33.4%	66.6%	33.4%	66.6%
2	2002	146,126	59,117 # FINLEY, JOSEPH P.		85,451 # ISRAEL, STEVE*		1,558	26,334	D	40.5%	58.5%	40.9%	59.1%
3	2010	183,087	131,674 # KING, PETER T.*		51,346 KUDLER, HOWARD		67	80,328	R	71.9%	28.0%	71.9%	28.1%
3	2008	270,303	172,774 # KING, PETER T.*		97,525 # LONG, GRAHAM E.		4	75,249	R	63.9%	36.1%	63.9%	36.1%
3	2006	181,630	101,787 # KING, PETER T.*		79,843 # MEJIAS, DAVID L.			21,944	R	56.0%	44.0%	56.0%	44.0%
3	2004	271,996	171,259 # KING, PETER T.*		100,737 MATHIES, BLAIR H. JR.			70,522	R	63.0%	37.0%	63.0%	37.0%
3	2002	169,072	121,537 # KING, PETER T.*		46,022 FINZ, STUART L.		1,513	75,515	R	71.9%	27.2%	72.5%	27.5%
4	2010	176,253	81,718 # BECKER, FRANCIS X. JR.		94,483 # McCARTHY, CAROLYN*		52	12,765	D	46.4%	53.6%	46.4%	53.6%
4	2008	256,271	92,242 # MARTINS, JACK M.		164,028 # McCARTHY, CAROLYN*		1	71,786	D	36.0%	64.0%	36.0%	64.0%
4	2006	156,911	55,050 # BLESSINGER, MARTIN W.		101,861 # McCARTHY, CAROLYN*			46,811	D	35.1%	64.9%	35.1%	64.9%
4	2004	254,110	94,141 # GARNER, JAMES A.		159,969 # McCARTHY, CAROLYN*			65,828	D	37.0%	63.0%	37.0%	63.0%
4	2002	168,540	72,882 # O'GRADY, MARILYN F.		94,806 # McCARTHY, CAROLYN*		852	21,924	D	43.2%	56.3%	43.5%	56.5%
5	2010	114,583	41,493 # MILANO, JAMES		72,239 # ACKERMAN, GARY L.*		851	30,746	D	36.2%	63.0%	36.5%	63.5%
5	2008	158,778	43,039 BERNEY, ELIZABETH		112,724 # ACKERMAN, GARY L.*		3,015	69,685	D	27.1%	71.0%	27.6%	72.4%
5	2006	77,190	—		77,190 # ACKERMAN, GARY L.*			77,190	D		100.0%		100.0%
5	2004	167,841	46,867 # GRAVES, STEPHEN		119,726 # ACKERMAN, GARY L.*		1,248	72,859	D	27.9%	71.3%	28.1%	71.9%
5	2002	74,491	—		68,773 # ACKERMAN, GARY L.*		5,718	68,773	D		92.3%		100.0%
6	2010	96,994	11,826 # TAUB, ASHER E.		85,096 MEEKS, GREGORY W.*		72	73,270	D	12.2%	87.7%	12.2%	87.8%
6	2008	141,206	—		141,180 MEEKS, GREGORY W.*		26	141,180	D		100.0%		100.0%
6	2006	69,405	—		69,405 MEEKS, GREGORY W.*			69,405	D		100.0%		100.0%
6	2004	129,688	—		129,688 # MEEKS, GREGORY W.*			129,688	D		100.0%		100.0%
6	2002	75,431	—		72,799 # MEEKS, GREGORY W.*		2,632	72,799	D		96.5%		100.0%
7	2010	88,471	16,145 # REYNOLDS, KENNETH A.		71,247 # CROWLEY, JOSEPH*		1,079	55,102	D	18.2%	80.5%	18.5%	81.5%
7	2008	139,941	21,477 # BRITT, WILLIAM E. JR.		118,459 # CROWLEY, JOSEPH*		5	96,982	D	15.3%	84.6%	15.3%	84.7%
7	2006	76,217	12,220 # BRAWLEY, KEVIN		63,997 # CROWLEY, JOSEPH*			51,777	D	16.0%	84.0%	16.0%	84.0%
7	2004	128,823	24,548 # CINQUEMAIN, JOSEPH		104,275 # CROWLEY, JOSEPH*			79,727	D	19.1%	80.9%	19.1%	80.9%
7	2002	69,539	18,572 # BRAWLEY, KEVIN		50,967 # CROWLEY, JOSEPH*			32,395	D	26.7%	73.3%	26.7%	73.3%

NEW YORK

HOUSE OF REPRESENTATIVES

CD	Year	Total Vote	Republican Vote	Republican Candidate	Democratic Vote	Democratic Candidate	Other Vote	Rep.-Dem. Plurality	Total Vote Rep.	Total Vote Dem.	Major Vote Rep.	Major Vote Dem.
8	2010	130,928	31,996	# KONE, SUSAN L.	98,839	# NADLER, JERROLD*	93	66,843 D	24.4%	75.5%	24.5%	75.5%
8	2008	199,861	39,062	# LIN, GRACE	160,775	# NADLER, JERROLD*	24	121,713 D	19.5%	80.4%	19.5%	80.5%
8	2006	127,622	17,413	FRIEDMAN, ELEANOR	108,536	# NADLER, JERROLD*	1,673	91,123 D	13.6%	85.0%	13.8%	86.2%
8	2004	201,322	39,240	# HORT, PETER	162,082	# NADLER, JERROLD*		122,842 D	19.5%	80.5%	19.5%	80.5%
8	2002	106,481	19,674	# FARRIN, JIM	81,002	# NADLER, JERROLD*	5,805	61,328 D	18.5%	76.1%	19.5%	80.5%
9	2010	110,205	43,129	# TURNER, ROBERT L.	67,011	# WEINER, ANTHONY*	65	23,882 D	39.1%	60.8%	39.2%	60.8%
9	2008	120,589		—	112,205	# WEINER, ANTHONY*	8,384	112,205 D		93.0%		100.0%
9	2006	71,762		—	71,762	# WEINER, ANTHONY*		71,762 D		100.0%		100.0%
9	2004	158,476	45,451	# CRONIN, GERARD J.	113,025	# WEINER, ANTHONY*		67,574 D	28.7%	71.3%	28.7%	71.3%
9	2002	92,435	31,698	# DONOHUE, ALFRED F.	60,737	# WEINER, ANTHONY*		29,039 D	34.3%	65.7%	34.3%	65.7%
10	2010	104,839	7,419	MUNIZ, DIANA	95,485	TOWNS, EDOLPHUS*	1,935	88,066 D	7.1%	91.1%	7.2%	92.8%
10	2008	164,669	9,565	# GRUPICO, SALVATORE	155,090	TOWNS, EDOLPHUS*	14	145,525 D	5.8%	94.2%	5.8%	94.2%
10	2006	78,307	4,666	ANDERSON, JONATHAN H.	72,171	TOWNS, EDOLPHUS*	1,470	67,505 D	6.0%	92.2%	6.1%	93.9%
10	2004	148,766	11,099	CLARKE, HARVEY R.	136,113	# TOWNS, EDOLPHUS*	1,554	125,014 D	7.5%	91.5%	7.5%	92.5%
10	2002	75,498		—	73,859	# TOWNS, EDOLPHUS*	1,639	73,859 D		97.8%		100.0%
11	2010	115,199	10,858	# CARR, HUGH C.	104,297	# CLARKE, YVETTE D.*	44	93,439 D	9.4%	90.5%	9.4%	90.6%
11	2008	181,740	11,644	CARR, HUGH C.	168,562	# CLARKE, YVETTE D.*	1,534	156,918 D	6.4%	92.7%	6.5%	93.5%
11	2006	98,102	7,447	# FINGER, STEPHEN	88,334	# CLARKE, YVETTE D.	2,321	80,887 D	7.6%	90.0%	7.8%	92.2%
11	2004	154,198		—	144,999	# OWENS, MAJOR R.*	9,199	144,999 D		94.0%		100.0%
11	2002	88,864	11,149	# CLEARY, SUSAN	76,917	# OWENS, MAJOR R.*	798	65,768 D	12.5%	86.6%	12.7%	87.3%
12	2010	73,165			68,624	# VELAZQUEZ, NYDIA M.*	4,541	68,624 D		93.8%		100.0%
12	2008	136,809	13,748	# ROMAGUERA, ALLAN	123,053	# VELAZQUEZ, NYDIA M.*	8	109,305 D	10.0%	89.9%	10.0%	90.0%
12	2006	70,029	7,182	# ROMAGUERA, ALLAN	62,847	# VELAZQUEZ, NYDIA M.*		55,665 D	10.3%	89.7%	10.3%	89.7%
12	2004	124,962	17,166	# RODRIGUEZ, PAUL A.	107,796	# VELAZQUEZ, NYDIA M.*		90,630 D	13.7%	86.3%	13.7%	86.3%
12	2002	50,527		—	48,408	# VELAZQUEZ, NYDIA M.*	2,119	48,408 D		95.8%		100.0%
13	2010	126,798	65,024	# GRIMM, MICHAEL G.	60,773	# McMAHON, MICHAEL E.*	1,001	4,251 R	51.3%	47.9%	51.7%	48.3%
13	2008	187,446	62,441	STRANIERE, ROBERT A.	114,219	# McMAHON, MICHAEL E.	10,786	51,778 D	33.3%	60.9%	35.3%	64.7%
13	2006	104,465	59,334	# FOSSELLA, VITO J.*	45,131	# HARRISON, STEPHEN A.		14,203 R	56.8%	43.2%	56.8%	43.2%
13	2004	191,434	112,934	# FOSSELLA, VITO J.*	78,500	# BARBARO, FRANK J.		34,434 R	59.0%	41.0%	59.0%	41.0%
13	2002	103,693	72,204	# FOSSELLA, VITO J.*	29,366	# MATTSSON, ARNE M.	2,123	42,838 R	69.6%	28.3%	71.1%	28.9%
14	2010	143,042	32,065	BRUMBERG, DAVID RYAN	107,327	# MALONEY, CAROLYN B.*	3,650	75,262 D	22.4%	75.0%	23.0%	77.0%
14	2008	229,308	43,385	HEIM, ROBERT G.	183,239	# MALONEY, CAROLYN B.*	2,684	139,854 D	18.9%	79.9%	19.1%	80.9%
14	2006	141,551	21,969	MAIO, DANNIEL	119,582	# MALONEY, CAROLYN B.*		97,613 D	15.5%	84.5%	15.5%	84.5%
14	2004	230,311	43,623	# SRDANOVIC, ANTON	186,688	# MALONEY, CAROLYN B.*		143,065 D	18.9%	81.1%	18.9%	81.1%
14	2002	127,479	31,548	# SRDANOVIC, ANTON	95,931	# MALONEY, CAROLYN B.*		64,383 D	24.7%	75.3%	24.7%	75.3%
15	2010	113,686	11,754	# FAULKNER, MICHEL J.	91,225	# RANGEL, CHARLES B.*	10,707	79,471 D	10.3%	80.2%	11.4%	88.6%
15	2008	198,691	15,676	DANIELS, EDWARD	177,151	# RANGEL, CHARLES B.*	5,864	161,475 D	7.9%	89.2%	8.1%	91.9%
15	2006	110,508	6,592	DANIELS, EDWARD	103,916	# RANGEL, CHARLES B.*		97,324 D	6.0%	94.0%	6.0%	94.0%
15	2004	177,051	12,355	JEFFERSON, KENNETH P. JR.	161,351	# RANGEL, CHARLES B.*	3,345	148,996 D	7.0%	91.1%	7.1%	92.9%
15	2002	95,375	11,008	# FIELDS, JESSIE A.	84,367	# RANGEL, CHARLES B.*		73,359 D	11.5%	88.5%	11.5%	88.5%
16	2010	64,438	2,758	# DELLA VALLE, FRANK	61,642	# SERRANO, JOSE E.*	38	58,884 D	4.3%	95.7%	4.3%	95.7%
16	2008	131,669	4,488	# MOHAMED, ALI	127,179	# SERRANO, JOSE E.*	2	122,691 D	3.4%	96.6%	3.4%	96.6%
16	2006	58,883	2,759	# MOHAMED, ALI	56,124	# SERRANO, JOSE E.*		53,365 D	4.7%	95.3%	4.7%	95.3%
16	2004	117,248	5,610	# MOHAMED, ALI	111,638	# SERRANO, JOSE E.*		106,028 D	4.8%	95.2%	4.8%	95.2%
16	2002	55,082	4,366	# DELLA VALLE, FRANK	50,716	# SERRANO, JOSE E.*		46,350 D	7.9%	92.1%	7.9%	92.1%
17	2010	130,881	29,792	MELE, ANTHONY	95,346	# ENGEL, ELIOT L.*	5,743	65,554 D	22.8%	72.8%	23.8%	76.2%
17	2008	202,321	40,707	# GOODMAN, ROBERT	161,594	# ENGEL, ELIOT L.*	20	120,887 D	20.1%	79.9%	20.1%	79.9%
17	2006	122,456	28,842	# FAULKNER, JIM	93,614	# ENGEL, ELIOT L.*		64,772 D	23.6%	76.4%	23.6%	76.4%
17	2004	184,536	40,524	BRENNAN, MATT I.	140,530	# ENGEL, ELIOT L.*	3,482	100,006 D	22.0%	76.2%	22.4%	77.6%
17	2002	123,843	42,634	# VANDERHOEF, C. SCOTT	77,535	# ENGEL, ELIOT L.*	3,674	34,901 D	34.4%	62.6%	35.5%	64.5%
18	2010	186,099	70,413	# RUSSELL, JIM	115,619	# LOWEY, NITA M.*	67	45,206 D	37.8%	62.1%	37.8%	62.2%
18	2008	255,311	80,498	# RUSSELL, JIM	174,791	# LOWEY, NITA M.*	22	94,293 D	31.5%	68.5%	31.5%	68.5%
18	2006	175,706	51,450	HOFFMAN, RICHARD A.	124,256	# LOWEY, NITA M.*		72,806 D	29.3%	70.7%	29.3%	70.7%

NEW YORK

HOUSE OF REPRESENTATIVES

CD	Year	Total Vote	Republican Vote	Republican Candidate	Democratic Vote	Democratic Candidate	Other Vote	Rep.-Dem. Plurality	Total Vote Rep.	Total Vote Dem.	Major Vote Rep.	Major Vote Dem.
18	2004	244,690	73,975	HOFFMAN, RICHARD A.	170,715 #	LOWEY, NITA M.*		96,740 D	30.2%	69.8%	30.2%	69.8%
18	2002	107,515	—		98,957 #	LOWEY, NITA M.*	8,558	98,957 D		92.0%		100.0%
19	2010	209,238	109,956 #	HAYWORTH, NAN	98,766 #	HALL, JOHN*	516	11,190 R	52.6%	47.2%	52.7%	47.3%
19	2008	280,994	116,120 #	LALOR, KIERAN MICHAEL	164,859 #	HALL, JOHN*	15	48,739 D	41.3%	58.7%	41.3%	58.7%
19	2006	195,478	95,359 #	KELLY, SUE W.*	100,119	HALL, JOHN		4,760 D	48.8%	51.2%	48.8%	51.2%
19	2004	262,830	175,401 #	KELLY, SUE W.*	87,429	JALIMAN, MICHAEL		87,972 R	66.7%	33.3%	66.7%	33.3%
19	2002	173,112	121,129 #	KELLY, SUE W.*	44,967	SELENDY, JANINE M.H.	7,016	76,162 R	70.0%	26.0%	72.9%	27.1%
20	2010	237,340	130,178 #	GIBSON, CHRISTOPHER P.	107,075 #	MURPHY, SCOTT*	87	23,103 R	54.8%	45.1%	54.9%	45.1%
20	2008	311,717	118,031 #	TREADWELL, SANDY	193,651 #	GILLIBRAND, KIRSTEN E.*	35	75,620 D	37.9%	62.1%	37.9%	62.1%
20	2006	235,722	110,554 #	SWEENEY, JOHN E.*	125,168 #	GILLIBRAND, KIRSTEN E.		14,614 D	46.9%	53.1%	46.9%	53.1%
20	2004	286,736	188,753 #	SWEENEY, JOHN E.*	96,630	KELLY, DORIS F.	1,353	92,123 R	65.8%	33.7%	66.1%	33.9%
20	2002	191,278	140,238 #	SWEENEY, JOHN E.*	45,878	STOPPENBACH, FRANK	5,162	94,360 R	73.3%	24.0%	75.3%	24.7%
21	2010	210,791	85,752 #	DANZ, THEODORE J. JR.	124,889 #	TONKO, PAUL*	150	39,137 D	40.7%	59.2%	40.7%	59.3%
21	2008	275,872	96,599 #	BUHRMASTER, JAMES R.	171,286 #	TONKO, PAUL	7,987	74,687 D	35.0%	62.1%	36.1%	63.9%
21	2006	214,356	46,752	REDLICH, WARREN	167,604 #	McNULTY, MICHAEL R.*		120,852 D	21.8%	78.2%	21.8%	78.2%
21	2004	274,154	80,121	REDLICH, WARREN	194,033 #	McNULTY, MICHAEL R.*		113,912 D	29.2%	70.8%	29.2%	70.8%
21	2002	214,854	53,525	ROSENSTEIN, CHARLES B.	161,329 #	McNULTY, MICHAEL R.*		107,804 D	24.9%	75.1%	24.9%	75.1%
22	2010	187,421	88,687 #	PHILLIPS, GEORGE K.	98,661 #	HINCHEY, MAURICE D.*	73	9,974 D	47.3%	52.6%	47.3%	52.7%
22	2008	253,718	85,126	PHILLIPS, GEORGE K.	168,558 #	HINCHEY, MAURICE D.*	34	83,432 D	33.6%	66.4%	33.6%	66.4%
22	2006	121,683		—	121,683 #	HINCHEY, MAURICE D.*		121,683 D		100.0%		100.0%
22	2004	249,370	81,881	BRENNER, WILLIAM A.	167,489 #	HINCHEY, MAURICE D.*		85,608 D	32.8%	67.2%	32.8%	67.2%
22	2002	176,484	58,008 #	HALL, ERIC	113,280 #	HINCHEY, MAURICE D.*	5,196	55,272 D	32.9%	64.2%	33.9%	66.1%
23	2010	173,091	80,237 #	DOHENY, MATTHEW A.	82,232 #	OWENS, WILLIAM L.*	10,622	1,995 D	46.4%	47.5%	49.4%	50.6%
23	2008	218,925	143,029 #	McHUGH, JOHN M.*	75,871 #	OOT, MICHAEL P.	25	67,158 R	65.3%	34.7%	65.3%	34.7%
23	2006	169,099	106,781 #	McHUGH, JOHN M.*	62,318	JOHNSON, ROBERT J.		44,463 R	63.1%	36.9%	63.1%	36.9%
23	2004	226,527	160,079 #	McHUGH, JOHN M.*	66,448	JOHNSON, ROBERT J.		93,631 R	70.7%	29.3%	70.7%	29.3%
23	2002	124,682	124,682 #	McHUGH, JOHN M.*		—		124,682 R	100.0%		100.0%	
24	2010	191,700	101,599 #	HANNA, RICHARD L.	89,809 #	ARCURI, MICHAEL A.*	292	11,790 R	53.0%	46.8%	53.1%	46.9%
24	2008	251,692	120,880 #	HANNA, RICHARD L.	130,799 #	ARCURI, MICHAEL A.*	13	9,919 D	48.0%	52.0%	48.0%	52.0%
24	2006	203,324	91,504 #	MEIER, RAYMOND A.	109,686 #	ARCURI, MICHAEL A.	2,134	18,182 D	45.0%	53.9%	45.5%	54.5%
24	2004	251,368	143,000 #	BOEHLERT, SHERWOOD*	85,140	MILLER, JEFFREY A.	23,228	57,860 R	56.9%	33.9%	62.7%	37.3%
24	2002	152,777	108,017	BOEHLERT, SHERWOOD*		—	44,760	108,017 R	70.7%		100.0%	
25	2010	208,734	104,602 #	BUERKLE, ANN MARIE	103,954 #	MAFFEI, DANIEL B.*	178	648 R	50.1%	49.8%	50.2%	49.8%
25	2008	287,099	120,217 #	SWEETLAND, DALE A.	157,375 #	MAFFEI, DANIEL B.	9,507	37,158 D	41.9%	54.8%	43.3%	56.7%
25	2006	217,633	110,525 #	WALSH, JAMES T.*	107,108 #	MAFFEI, DANIEL B.		3,417 R	50.8%	49.2%	50.8%	49.2%
25	2004	209,169	189,063 #	WALSH, JAMES T.*		—	20,106	189,063 R	90.4%		100.0%	
25	2002	200,031	144,610 #	WALSH, JAMES T.*	53,290	ALDERSLEY, STEPHANIE	2,131	91,320 R	72.3%	26.6%	73.1%	26.9%
26	2010	205,805	151,449 #	LEE, CHRISTOPHER JOHN*	54,307	FEDELE, PHILIP A.	49	97,142 R	73.6%	26.4%	73.6%	26.4%
26	2008	270,335	148,607 #	LEE, CHRISTOPHER JOHN	109,615	KRYZAN, ALICE	12,113	38,992 R	55.0%	40.5%	57.6%	42.4%
26	2006	210,171	109,257 #	REYNOLDS, THOMAS M.*	100,914 #	DAVIS, JACK		8,343 R	52.0%	48.0%	52.0%	48.0%
26	2004	283,079	157,466 #	REYNOLDS. THOMAS M.*	125,613 #	DAVIS, JACK		31,853 R	55.6%	44.4%	55.6%	44.4%
26	2002	183,459	135,089 #	REYNOLDS. THOMAS M.*	41,140	NARIMAN, AYESHA F.	7,230	93,949 R	73.6%	22.4%	76.7%	23.3%
27	2010	195,415	76,320 #	ROBERTO, LEONARD A.	119,085 #	HIGGINS, BRIAN*	10	42,765 D	39.1%	60.9%	39.1%	60.9%
27	2008	249,545	56,354 #	HUMISTON, DANIEL J.	185,713 #	HIGGINS, BRIAN*	7,478	129,359 D	22.6%	74.4%	23.3%	76.7%
27	2006	176,641	36,614	McHALE, MICHAEL J.	140,027 #	HIGGINS, BRIAN*		103,413 D	20.7%	79.3%	20.7%	79.3%
27	2004	282,890	139,558 #	NAPLES, NANCY A.	143,332 #	HIGGINS, BRIAN		3,774 D	49.3%	50.7%	49.3%	50.7%
27	2002	173,919	120,117 #	QUINN, JACK*	47,811 #	CROTTY, PETER	5,991	72,306 R	69.1%	27.5%	71.5%	28.5%
28	2010	157,947	55,392 #	ROWLAND, JILL A.	102,514 #	SLAUGHTER, LOUISE M.*	41	47,122 D	35.1%	64.9%	35.1%	64.9%
28	2008	221,378	48,690 #	CRIMMEN, DAVID W.	172,655 #	SLAUGHTER, LOUISE M.*	33	123,965 D	22.0%	78.0%	22.0%	78.0%
28	2006	152,230	40,844 #	DONNELLY, JOHN E.	111,386 #	SLAUGHTER, LOUISE M.*		70,542 D	26.8%	73.2%	26.8%	73.2%
28	2004	219,876	54,543 #	LABA, MICHAEL D.	159,655 #	SLAUGHTER, LOUISE M.*	5,678	105,112 D	24.8%	72.6%	25.5%	74.5%
28	2002	158,604	59,547 #	WOJTASZEK, HENRY F.	99,057 #	SLAUGHTER, LOUISE M.*		39,510 D	37.5%	62.5%	37.5%	62.5%

NEW YORK

HOUSE OF REPRESENTATIVES

CD	Year	Total Vote	Republican			Democratic			Other Vote	Rep.-Dem. Plurality	Percentage			
			Vote		Candidate	Vote		Candidate			Total Vote		Major Vote	
											Rep.	Dem.	Rep.	Dem.
29	2010	198,940	112,314	#	REED, THOMAS W. II	86,099	#	ZELLER, MATTHEW C.	527	26,215 R	56.5%	43.3%	56.6%	43.4%
29	2008	275,755	135,199	#	KUHL, JOHN R. "RANDY" JR.*	140,529	#	MASSA, ERIC J. J.	27	5,330 D	49.0%	51.0%	49.0%	51.0%
29	2006	206,121	106,077	#	KUHL, JOHN R. "RANDY" JR.*	100,044	#	MASSA, ERIC J. J.		6,033 R	51.5%	48.5%	51.5%	48.5%
29	2004	270,215	136,883		KUHL, JOHN R. "RANDY" JR.	110,241	#	BAREND, SAMARA	23,091	26,642 R	50.7%	40.8%	55.4%	44.6%
29	2002	174,631	127,657	#	HOUGHTON, AMO*	37,128		PETERS, KISUN J.	9,846	90,529 R	73.1%	21.3%	77.5%	22.5%
TOTAL	2010	4,499,163	1,854,302			2,600,900			43,961	746,598 D	41.2%	57.8%	41.6%	58.4%
TOTAL	2008	6,390,516	2,034,784			4,286,047			69,685	2,251,263 D	31.8%	67.1%	32.2%	67.8%
TOTAL	2006	4,140,378	1,338,518			2,794,262			7,598	1,455,744 D	32.3%	67.5%	32.4%	67.6%
TOTAL	2004	6,222,418	2,448,345			3,681,789			92,284	1,233,444 D	39.3%	59.2%	39.9%	60.1%
TOTAL	2002	3,821,613	1,770,532			1,924,769			126,312	154,237 D	46.3%	50.4%	47.9%	52.1%

A pound sign (#) indicates that the candidate received votes on the ballot line of one or more other parties. Each candidate's total vote is listed above. An asterisk (*) denotes incumbent.

NEW YORK

GENERAL AND PRIMARY ELECTIONS

2010 GENERAL ELECTIONS

Note: Candidates in New York can appear on the ballot line of more than one party. In the 2010 gubernatorial and Senate elections, the results broke down as follows:

	Democratic	Independence	Working Families	TOTAL VOTE
Andrew M. Cuomo (Governor)	2,610,220	146,648	154,853	2,911,721
Charles E. Schumer (Senator – Full term)	2,686,698	177,468	183,714	3,047,880
Kirsten E. Gillibrand (Senator – Short term)	2,479,393	175,636	182,655	2,837,684

	Republican	Conservative	Taxpayers	TOTAL VOTE
Carl P. Paladino (Governor)	1,290,082	232,281	25,821	1,548,184
Jay Townsend (Senator – Full term)	1,239,605	240,818	—	1,480,423
Joseph J. DioGuardi (Senator – Short term)	1,338,308	244,385 #		1,582,693

Note: A pound sign (#) indicates that Republican Senate candidate Joseph J. DioGuardi received votes on a combined ballot line of the Conservative and Taxpayers parties.

In the New York tables, votes received by each Democratic and Republican candidate on the ballot lines of other parties are combined into one overall vote, which is credited to the major party of which they are a member.

Governor Other vote was 59,929 Green (Howie Hawkins); 48,386 Libertarian (Warren Redlich); 41,131 Rent Is 2 Damn High (Jimmy McMillan); 24,572 Freedom (Charles Barron); 20,429 Anti-Prohibition (Kristin Davis); 4,473 scattered write-in.

Senator (Full term) Other vote was 42,341 Green (Colia Clark); 24,871 Libertarian/Anti-Prohibition (Randy A. Credico); 1,281 scattered write-in.

Senator (Short term) Other vote was 35,489 Green (Cecile A. Lawrence); 18,414 Libertarian (John Clifton); 17,019 Rent Is 2 Damn High (Joseph Huff); 11,787 Anti-Prohibition (Vivia Morgan); 4,516 Tax Revolt (Bruce Blakeman); 1,169 scattered write-in.

NEW YORK

GENERAL AND PRIMARY ELECTIONS

House Other vote was:

CD 1   125 scattered write-in.
CD 2   1,256 Constitution (Anthony Tolda); 30 scattered write-in.
CD 3   67 scattered write-in.
CD 4   52 scattered write-in.
CD 5   798 Tax Revolt (Elizabeth Berney); 53 scattered write-in.
CD 6   72 scattered write-in.
CD 7   1,038 Green (Anthony Gronowicz); 41 scattered write-in.
CD 8   93 scattered write-in.
CD 9   65 scattered write-in.
CD 10   1,853 Conservative (Ernest Johnson); 82 scattered write-in.
CD 11   44 scattered write-in.
CD 12   4,482 Conservative (Alice Gaffney); 59 scattered write-in.
CD 13   929 Libertarian (Tom Vendittelli); 72 scattered write-in.
CD 14   1,891 Conservative (Timothy J. Healy); 1,617 Independence (Dino L. LaVerghetta); 142 scattered write-in.
CD 15   7,803 Independence, Vote People Change (Craig Schley); 2,647 Socialist Workers (Roger Calero); 257 scattered write-in.
CD 16   38 scattered write-in.
CD 17   5,661 Conservative (York Kleinhandler); 82 scattered write-in.
CD 18   67 scattered write-in.
CD 19   516 scattered write-in.
CD 20   87 scattered write-in.
CD 21   150 scattered write-in.
CD 22   73 scattered write-in.
CD 23   10,507 Conservative (Douglas L. Hoffman); 115 scattered write-in.
CD 24   292 scattered write-in.
CD 25   178 scattered write-in.
CD 26   49 scattered write-in.
CD 27   10 scattered write-in.
CD 28   41 scattered write-in.
CD 29   527 scattered write-in.

2010 PRIMARY ELECTIONS

Primary   September 14, 2010   **Registration**
(as of April 1, 2010 -including
1,045,829 inactive registrants)

Democratic	5,789,432
Republican	2,906,393
Independence	413,855
Conservative	146,221
Working Families	40,878
Green	22,939
Libertarian	2,427
Other Parties	77
Unaffiliated	2,336,122
TOTAL	*11,658,344*

Primary Type   Closed—Only registered Democrats and Republicans could vote in their party's primary.

NEW YORK

GENERAL AND PRIMARY ELECTIONS

	REPUBLICAN PRIMARIES			DEMOCRATIC PRIMARIES		
Governor	Carl P. Paladino	295,336	61.6%	Andrew M. Cuomo	Unopposed	
	Rick A. Lazio	184,348	38.4%			
	TOTAL	*479,684*				
Senator	Jay Townsend	234,440	55.4%	Charles E. Schumer*	Unopposed	
(Full term)	Gary Berntsen	188,628	44.6%			
	TOTAL	*423,068*				
Senator	Joseph J. DioGuardi	185,483	41.8%	Kirsten E. Gillibrand*	464,512	76.1%
(Short term)	David Malpass	167,151	37.7%	Gail Goode	145,491	23.9%
	Bruce Blakeman	91,312	20.6%			
	TOTAL	*443,946*		*TOTAL*	*610,003*	
Congressional District 1	Randy Altschuler	Unopposed		Timothy H. Bishop*	Unopposed	
Congressional District 2	John B. Gomez	Unopposed		Steve Israel*	Unopposed	
Congressional District 3	Peter T. King*	21,915	90.8%	Howard A. Kudler	Unopposed	
	Robert Previdi	2,231	9.2%			
	TOTAL	*24,146*				
Congressional District 4	Francis X. Becker Jr.	Unopposed		Carolyn McCarthy*	Unopposed	
Congressional District 5	James Milano	4,489	61.1%	Gary L. Ackerman*	19,394	75.6%
	Elizabeth Berney	2,862	38.9%	Patricia M. Maher	6,258	24.4%
	TOTAL	*7,351*		*TOTAL*	*25,652*	
Congressional District 6	Asher E. Taub	Unopposed		Gregory W. Meeks*	Unopposed	
Congressional District 7	Kenneth A. Reynolds	Unopposed		Joseph Crowley*	Unopposed	
Congressional District 8	Susan L. Kone	Unopposed		Jerrold Nadler*	Unopposed	
Congressional District 9	Robert L. Turner	Unopposed		Anthony Weiner*	Unopposed	
Congressional District 10	Diana Muniz	Unopposed		Edolphus Towns*	21,846	69.1%
				Kevin Powell	9,733	30.8%
				Scattered write-in	34	0.1%
				TOTAL	*31,613*	
Congressional District 11	Hugh C. Carr	Unopposed		Yvette D. Clarke*	Unopposed	
Congressional District 12	No Republican candidate			Nydia M. Velazquez*	Unopposed	
Congressional District 13	Michael G. Grimm	Unopposed		Michael E. McMahon*	Unopposed	
Congressional District 14	David Ryan Brumberg	Unopposed		Carolyn B. Maloney*	33,499	82.8%
				Reshma M. Saujani	6,799	16.8%
				Scattered write-in	176	0.4%
				TOTAL	*40,474*	
Congressional District 15	Michel J. Faulkner	Unopposed		Charles B. Rangel*	26,101	51.1%
				Adam Clayton Powell	11,834	23.2%
				Joyce S. Johnson	6,444	12.6%
				Ruben D. Vargas	2,703	5.3%
				Jonathan Tasini	2,634	5.2%
				Vincent S. Morgan	1,210	2.4%
				Scattered write-in	142	0.3%
				TOTAL	*51,068*	
Congressional District 16	Frank Della Valle	Unopposed		Jose E. Serrano*	Unopposed	

NEW YORK

GENERAL AND PRIMARY ELECTIONS

	REPUBLICAN PRIMARIES			DEMOCRATIC PRIMARIES	
Congressional District 17	Anthony Mele	3,730	51.1%	Eliot L. Engel*	Unopposed
	York Kleinhandler	3,573	48.9%		
	TOTAL	7,303			
Congressional District 18	Jim Russell	Unopposed		Nita M. Lowey*	Unopposed
Congressional District 19	Nan Hayworth	19,483	69.3%	John Hall*	Unopposed
	Neil A. DiCarlo	8,614	30.7%		
	TOTAL	28,097			
Congressional District 20	Christopher P. Gibson	Unopposed		Scott Murphy*	Unopposed
Congressional District 21	Theodore J. Danz Jr.	Unopposed		Paul Tonko*	Unopposed
Congressional District 22	George K. Phillips	Unopposed		Maurice D. Hinchey*	Unopposed
Congressional District 23	Matthew A. Doheny	16,311	51.0%	William L. Owens*	Unopposed
	Douglas L. Hoffman	15,660	49.0%		
	TOTAL	31,971			
Congressional District 24	Richard L. Hanna	Unopposed		Michael A. Arcuri*	Unopposed
Congressional District 25	Ann Marie Buerkle	Unopposed		Daniel B. Maffei*	Unopposed
Congressional District 26	Christopher John Lee*	Unopposed		Philip A. Fedele	Unopposed
Congressional District 27	Leonard A. Roberto	Unopposed		Brian Higgins*	Unopposed
Congressional District 28	Jill A. Rowland	Unopposed		Louise M. Slaughter*	Unopposed
Congressional District 29	Thomas W. Reed II	Unopposed		Matthew C. Zeller	Unopposed

An asterisk (*) denotes incumbent. Write-in votes were broken out separately in the official tally from New York City congressional districts but not those in the rest of the state. Names of unopposed candidates did not appear on the primary ballot; therefore, no votes were cast for these candidates.

NORTH CAROLINA

Congressional districts first established for elections held in 2002
13 members

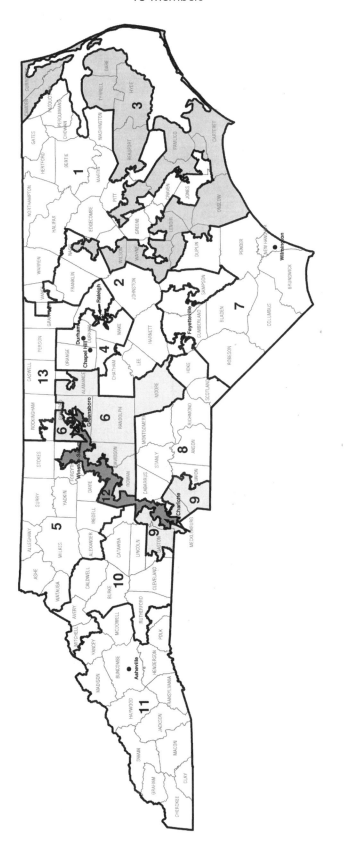

NORTH CAROLINA

Central North Carolina Area

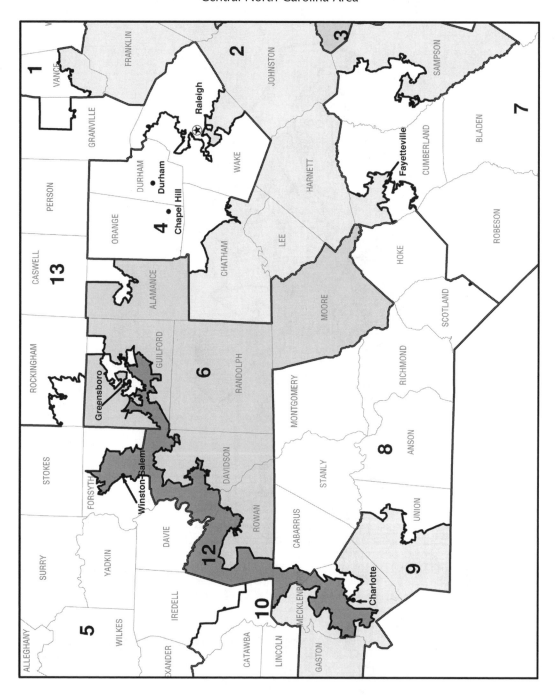

NORTH CAROLINA

GOVERNOR
Bev Perdue (D). Elected 2008 to a four-year term.

SENATORS (1 Democrat, 1 Republican)
Richard M. Burr (R). Reelected 2010 to a six-year term. Previously elected 2004.

Kay Hagan (D). Elected 2008 to a six-year term.

REPRESENTATIVES (7 Democrats, 6 Republicans)

1. G. K. Butterfield (D)
2. Renee Ellmers (R)
3. Walter B. Jones (R)
4. David E. Price (D)
5. Virginia Foxx (R)
6. Howard Coble (R)
7. Mike McIntyre (D)
8. Larry Kissell (D)
9. Sue Myrick (R)
10. Patrick T. McHenry (R)
11. Heath Shuler (D)
12. Melvin Watt (D)
13. Brad Miller (D)

POSTWAR VOTE FOR PRESIDENT

Year	Total Vote	Republican Vote	Republican Candidate	Democratic Vote	Democratic Candidate	Other Vote	Rep.-Dem. Plurality	Total Vote Rep.	Total Vote Dem.	Major Vote Rep.	Major Vote Dem.
2008	4,310,789	2,128,474	McCain, John	2,142,651	Obama, Barack	39,664	14,177 D	49.4%	49.7%	49.8%	50.2%
2004	3,501,007	1,961,166	Bush, George W.	1,525,849	Kerry, John	13,992	435,317 R	56.0%	43.6%	56.2%	43.8%
2000	2,911,262	1,631,163	Bush, George W.	1,257,692	Gore, Al	22,407	373,471 R	56.0%	43.2%	56.5%	43.5%
1996**	2,515,807	1,225,938	Dole, Bob	1,107,849	Clinton, Bill	182,020	118,089 R	48.7%	44.0%	52.5%	47.5%
1992**	2,611,850	1,134,661	Bush, George	1,114,042	Clinton, Bill	363,147	20,619 R	43.4%	42.7%	50.5%	49.5%
1988	2,134,370	1,237,258	Bush, George	890,167	Dukakis, Michael S.	6,945	347,091 R	58.0%	41.7%	58.2%	41.8%
1984	2,175,361	1,346,481	Reagan, Ronald	824,287	Mondale, Walter F.	4,593	522,194 R	61.9%	37.9%	62.0%	38.0%
1980**	1,855,833	915,018	Reagan, Ronald	875,635	Carter, Jimmy	65,180	39,383 R	49.3%	47.2%	51.1%	48.9%
1976	1,678,914	741,960	Ford, Gerald R.	927,365	Carter, Jimmy	9,589	185,405 D	44.2%	55.2%	44.4%	55.6%
1972	1,518,612	1,054,889	Nixon, Richard M.	438,705	McGovern, George S.	25,018	616,184 R	69.5%	28.9%	70.6%	29.4%
1968**	1,587,493	627,192	Nixon, Richard M.	464,113	Humphrey, Hubert H.	496,188	131,004 R	39.5%	29.2%	57.5%	42.5%
1964	1,424,983	624,844	Goldwater, Barry M.	800,139	Johnson, Lyndon B.		175,295 D	43.8%	56.2%	43.8%	56.2%
1960	1,368,556	655,420	Nixon, Richard M.	713,136	Kennedy, John F.		57,716 D	47.9%	52.1%	47.9%	52.1%
1956	1,165,592	575,062	Eisenhower, Dwight D.	590,530	Stevenson, Adlai E.		15,468 D	49.3%	50.7%	49.3%	50.7%
1952	1,210,910	558,107	Eisenhower, Dwight D.	652,803	Stevenson, Adlai E.		94,696 D	46.1%	53.9%	46.1%	53.9%
1948**	791,209	258,572	Dewey, Thomas E.	459,070	Truman, Harry S.	73,567	200,498 D	32.7%	58.0%	36.0%	64.0%

**In past elections, the other vote included: 1996 - 168,059 Reform (Ross Perot); 1992 - 357,864 Independent (Perot); 1980 - 52,800 Independent (John Anderson); 1968 - 496,188 American Independent (George Wallace), who finished second statewide; 1948 - 69,652 States' Rights (Strom Thurmond).

NORTH CAROLINA

POSTWAR VOTE FOR GOVERNOR

| Year | Total Vote | Republican | | Democratic | | Other Vote | Rep.-Dem. Plurality | Percentage | | | |
| | | | | | | | | Total Vote | | Major Vote | |
		Vote	Candidate	Vote	Candidate			Rep.	Dem.	Rep.	Dem.
2008	4,268,941	2,001,168	McCrory, Pat	2,146,189	Perdue, Bev	121,584	145,021 D	46.9%	50.3%	48.3%	51.7%
2004	3,486,688	1,495,021	Ballantine, Patrick J.	1,939,154	Easley, Michael F.	52,513	444,133 D	42.9%	55.6%	43.5%	56.5%
2000	2,942,062	1,360,960	Vinroot, Richard	1,530,324	Easley, Michael F.	50,778	169,364 D	46.3%	52.0%	47.1%	52.9%
1996	2,566,185	1,097,053	Hayes, Robin	1,436,638	Hunt, James B.	32,494	339,585 D	42.8%	56.0%	43.3%	56.7%
1992	2,595,184	1,121,955	Gardner, James C.	1,368,246	Hunt, James B.	104,983	246,291 D	43.2%	52.7%	45.1%	54.9%
1988	2,180,025	1,222,338	Martin, James G.	957,687	Jordan, Robert B.		264,651 R	56.1%	43.9%	56.1%	43.9%
1984	2,226,727	1,208,167	Martin, James G.	1,011,209	Edmisten, Rufus	7,351	196,958 R	54.3%	45.4%	54.4%	45.6%
1980	1,847,432	691,449	Lake, Beverly	1,143,145	Hunt, James B.	12,838	451,696 D	37.4%	61.9%	37.7%	62.3%
1976	1,663,824	564,102	Flaherty, David T.	1,081,293	Hunt, James B.	18,429	517,191 D	33.9%	65.0%	34.3%	65.7%
1972	1,504,785	767,470	Holshouser, James E.	729,104	Bowles, Hargrove	8,211	38,366 R	51.0%	48.5%	51.3%	48.7%
1968	1,558,308	737,075	Gardner, James C.	821,233	Scott, Robert W.		84,158 D	47.3%	52.7%	47.3%	52.7%
1964	1,396,508	606,165	Gavin, Robert L.	790,343	Moore, Dan K.		184,178 D	43.4%	56.6%	43.4%	56.6%
1960	1,350,360	613,975	Gavin, Robert L.	735,248	Sanford, Terry	1,137	121,273 D	45.5%	54.4%	45.5%	54.5%
1956	1,135,859	375,379	Hayes, Kyle	760,480	Hodges, Luther H.		385,101 D	33.0%	67.0%	33.0%	67.0%
1952	1,179,635	383,329	Seawell, H. F.	796,306	Umstead, William B.		412,977 D	32.5%	67.5%	32.5%	67.5%
1948	780,525	206,166	Pritchard, George	570,995	Scott, William Kerr	3,364	364,829 D	26.4%	73.2%	26.5%	73.5%

POSTWAR VOTE FOR SENATOR

| Year | Total Vote | Republican | | Democratic | | Other Vote | Rep.-Dem. Plurality | Percentage | | | |
| | | | | | | | | Total Vote | | Major Vote | |
		Vote	Candidate	Vote	Candidate			Rep.	Dem.	Rep.	Dem.
2010	2,660,079	1,458,046	Burr, Richard M.	1,145,074	Marshall, Elaine	56,959	312,972 R	54.8%	43.0%	56.0%	44.0%
2008	4,271,970	1,887,510	Dole, Elizabeth	2,249,311	Hagan, Kay	135,149	361,801 D	44.2%	52.7%	45.6%	54.4%
2004	3,472,082	1,791,450	Burr, Richard M.	1,632,527	Bowles, Erskine	48,105	158,923 R	51.6%	47.0%	52.3%	47.7%
2002	2,331,181	1,248,664	Dole, Elizabeth	1,047,983	Bowles, Erskine	34,534	200,681 R	53.6%	45.0%	54.4%	45.6%
1998	2,012,143	945,943	Faircloth, Lauch	1,029,237	Edwards, John	36,963	83,294 D	47.0%	51.2%	47.9%	52.1%
1996	2,556,456	1,345,833	Helms, Jesse	1,173,875	Gantt, Harvey B.	36,748	171,958 R	52.6%	45.9%	53.4%	46.6%
1992	2,577,891	1,297,892	Faircloth, Lauch	1,194,015	Sanford, Terry	85,984	103,877 R	50.3%	46.3%	52.1%	47.9%
1990	2,069,585	1,087,331	Helms, Jesse	981,573	Gantt, Harvy B.	681	105,758 R	52.5%	47.4%	52.6%	47.4%
1986	1,591,330	767,668	Broyhill, James T.	823,662	Sanford, Terry		55,994 D	48.2%	51.8%	48.2%	51.8%
1984	2,239,051	1,156,768	Helms, Jesse	1,070,488	Hunt, James B.	11,795	86,280 R	51.7%	47.8%	51.9%	48.1%
1980	1,797,665	898,064	East, John P.	887,653	Morgan, Robert	11,948	10,411 R	50.0%	49.4%	50.3%	49.7%
1978	1,135,814	619,151	Helms, Jesse	516,663	Ingram, John		102,488 R	54.5%	45.5%	54.5%	45.5%
1974	1,020,367	377,618	Stevens, William E.	633,775	Morgan, Robert	8,974	256,157 D	37.0%	62.1%	37.3%	62.7%
1972	1,472,541	795,248	Helms, Jesse	677,293	Galifianakis, Nick		117,955 R	54.0%	46.0%	54.0%	46.0%
1968	1,437,340	566,934	Somers, Robert V.	870,406	Ervin, Sam J.		303,472 D	39.4%	60.6%	39.4%	60.6%
1966	901,978	400,502	Shallcross, John S.	501,440	Jordan, B. Everett	36	100,938 D	44.4%	55.6%	44.4%	55.6%
1962	813,155	321,635	Greene, Claude L.	491,520	Ervin, Sam J.		169,885 D	39.6%	60.4%	39.6%	60.4%
1960	1,291,485	497,964	Hayes, Kyle	793,521	Jordan, B. Everett		295,557 D	38.6%	61.4%	38.6%	61.4%
1958S	616,469	184,977	Clarke, Richard C.	431,492	Jordan, B. Everett		246,515 D	30.0%	70.0%	30.0%	70.0%
1956	1,098,828	367,475	Johnson, Joel A.	731,353	Ervin, Sam J.		363,878 D	33.4%	66.6%	33.4%	66.6%
1954	619,634	211,322	West, Paul C.	408,312	Scott, William Kerr		196,990 D	34.1%	65.9%	34.1%	65.9%
1954S	410,574		—	410,574	Ervin, Sam J.		410,574 D		100.0%		100.0%
1950	548,276	171,804	Leavitt, Halsey B.	376,472	Hoey, Clyde R.		204,668 D	31.3%	68.7%	31.3%	68.7%
1950S	544,924	177,753	Gavin, E. L.	364,912	Smith, Willis	2,259	187,159 D	32.6%	67.0%	32.8%	67.2%
1948	764,559	220,307	Wilkinson, John A.	540,762	Broughton, J. M.	3,490	320,455 D	28.8%	70.7%	28.9%	71.1%

One each of the 1950 and 1954 elections as well as the 1958 election were for short terms to fill vacancies. The Republican Party did not run a Senate candidate in the 1954 election for the short term.

NORTH CAROLINA

SENATOR 2010

2010 Census Population	County	Total Vote	Republican	Democratic	Other	Rep.-Dem. Plurality		Percentage			
								Total Vote		Major Vote	
								Rep.	Dem.	Rep.	Dem.
151,131	ALAMANCE	41,512	25,012	15,446	1,054	9,566	R	60.3%	37.2%	61.8%	38.2%
37,198	ALEXANDER	12,456	8,253	3,886	317	4,367	R	66.3%	31.2%	68.0%	32.0%
11,155	ALLEGHANY	4,042	2,541	1,397	104	1,144	R	62.9%	34.6%	64.5%	35.5%
26,948	ANSON	6,732	2,628	4,024	80	1,396	D	39.0%	59.8%	39.5%	60.5%
27,281	ASHE	9,588	5,983	3,376	229	2,607	R	62.4%	35.2%	63.9%	36.1%
17,797	AVERY	5,003	3,762	1,113	128	2,649	R	75.2%	22.2%	77.2%	22.8%
47,759	BEAUFORT	16,416	10,122	5,953	341	4,169	R	61.7%	36.3%	63.0%	37.0%
21,282	BERTIE	6,463	2,563	3,836	64	1,273	D	39.7%	59.4%	40.1%	59.9%
35,190	BLADEN	12,302	5,715	6,387	200	672	D	46.5%	51.9%	47.2%	52.8%
107,431	BRUNSWICK	39,830	25,753	13,243	834	12,510	R	64.7%	33.2%	66.0%	34.0%
238,318	BUNCOMBE	77,777	36,632	39,017	2,128	2,385	D	47.1%	50.2%	48.4%	51.6%
90,912	BURKE	22,821	13,796	8,510	515	5,286	R	60.5%	37.3%	61.8%	38.2%
178,011	CABARRUS	47,736	30,758	15,922	1,056	14,836	R	64.4%	33.4%	65.9%	34.1%
83,029	CALDWELL	21,995	14,382	6,908	705	7,474	R	65.4%	31.4%	67.6%	32.4%
9,980	CAMDEN	3,095	2,005	1,014	76	991	R	64.8%	32.8%	66.4%	33.6%
66,469	CARTERET	23,269	16,677	6,064	528	10,613	R	71.7%	26.1%	73.3%	26.7%
23,719	CASWELL	7,087	3,559	3,398	130	161	R	50.2%	47.9%	51.2%	48.8%
154,358	CATAWBA	41,410	27,706	12,651	1,053	15,055	R	66.9%	30.6%	68.7%	31.3%
63,505	CHATHAM	24,580	11,711	12,310	559	599	D	47.6%	50.1%	48.8%	51.2%
27,444	CHEROKEE	9,573	6,219	2,969	385	3,250	R	65.0%	31.0%	67.7%	32.3%
14,793	CHOWAN	5,251	3,000	2,162	89	838	R	57.1%	41.2%	58.1%	41.9%
10,587	CLAY	4,793	3,029	1,557	207	1,472	R	63.2%	32.5%	66.0%	34.0%
98,078	CLEVELAND	26,520	15,752	10,259	509	5,493	R	59.4%	38.7%	60.6%	39.4%
58,098	COLUMBUS	16,412	8,598	7,513	301	1,085	R	52.4%	45.8%	53.4%	46.6%
103,505	CRAVEN	27,938	17,771	9,629	538	8,142	R	63.6%	34.5%	64.9%	35.1%
319,431	CUMBERLAND	69,053	31,205	36,692	1,156	5,487	D	45.2%	53.1%	46.0%	54.0%
23,547	CURRITUCK	7,493	5,145	2,111	237	3,034	R	68.7%	28.2%	70.9%	29.1%
33,920	DARE	11,884	7,370	4,200	314	3,170	R	62.0%	35.3%	63.7%	36.3%
162,878	DAVIDSON	41,566	29,336	11,247	983	18,089	R	70.6%	27.1%	72.3%	27.7%
41,240	DAVIE	13,987	10,340	3,363	284	6,977	R	73.9%	24.0%	75.5%	24.5%
58,505	DUPLIN	13,262	7,325	5,753	184	1,572	R	55.2%	43.4%	56.0%	44.0%
267,587	DURHAM	81,207	21,871	58,028	1,308	36,157	D	26.9%	71.5%	27.4%	72.6%
56,552	EDGECOMBE	16,102	5,621	10,318	163	4,697	D	34.9%	64.1%	35.3%	64.7%
350,670	FORSYTH	94,839	52,074	41,013	1,752	11,061	R	54.9%	43.2%	55.9%	44.1%
60,619	FRANKLIN	17,547	9,131	8,047	369	1,084	R	52.0%	45.9%	53.2%	46.8%
206,086	GASTON	49,595	32,881	15,546	1,168	17,335	R	66.3%	31.3%	67.9%	32.1%
12,197	GATES	3,281	1,686	1,559	36	127	R	51.4%	47.5%	52.0%	48.0%
8,861	GRAHAM	3,469	2,161	1,195	113	966	R	62.3%	34.4%	64.4%	35.6%
59,916	GRANVILLE	14,862	7,291	7,257	314	34	R	49.1%	48.8%	50.1%	49.9%
21,362	GREENE	5,597	2,914	2,613	70	301	R	52.1%	46.7%	52.7%	47.3%
488,406	GUILFORD	138,928	69,787	66,480	2,661	3,307	R	50.2%	47.9%	51.2%	48.8%
54,691	HALIFAX	14,516	5,416	8,934	166	3,518	D	37.3%	61.5%	37.7%	62.3%
114,678	HARNETT	26,115	15,466	10,136	513	5,330	R	59.2%	38.8%	60.4%	39.6%
59,036	HAYWOOD	20,020	11,261	8,245	514	3,016	R	56.2%	41.2%	57.7%	42.3%
106,740	HENDERSON	36,153	23,916	11,393	844	12,523	R	66.2%	31.5%	67.7%	32.3%
24,669	HERTFORD	6,515	2,053	4,401	61	2,348	D	31.5%	67.6%	31.8%	68.2%
46,952	HOKE	8,379	3,588	4,650	141	1,062	D	42.8%	55.5%	43.6%	56.4%
5,810	HYDE	1,655	847	768	40	79	R	51.2%	46.4%	52.4%	47.6%
159,437	IREDELL	42,971	28,910	12,924	1,137	15,986	R	67.3%	30.1%	69.1%	30.9%
40,271	JACKSON	11,137	5,681	5,133	323	548	R	51.0%	46.1%	52.5%	47.5%
168,878	JOHNSTON	46,954	30,901	15,115	938	15,786	R	65.8%	32.2%	67.2%	32.8%
10,153	JONES	3,780	2,051	1,657	72	394	R	54.3%	43.8%	55.3%	44.7%

NORTH CAROLINA

SENATOR 2010

2010 Census Population	County	Total Vote	Republican	Democratic	Other	Rep.-Dem. Plurality		Percentage			
								Total Vote		Major Vote	
								Rep.	Dem.	Rep.	Dem.
57,866	LEE	14,692	8,337	6,086	269	2,251	R	56.7%	41.4%	57.8%	42.2%
59,495	LENOIR	17,738	9,239	8,291	208	948	R	52.1%	46.7%	52.7%	47.3%
78,265	LINCOLN	23,186	15,653	6,958	575	8,695	R	67.5%	30.0%	69.2%	30.8%
44,996	MCDOWELL	12,234	8,104	3,794	336	4,310	R	66.2%	31.0%	68.1%	31.9%
33,922	MACON	12,316	7,672	4,188	456	3,484	R	62.3%	34.0%	64.7%	35.3%
20,764	MADISON	8,031	4,028	3,777	226	251	R	50.2%	47.0%	51.6%	48.4%
24,505	MARTIN	8,365	3,898	4,353	114	455	D	46.6%	52.0%	47.2%	52.8%
919,628	MECKLENBURG	227,203	104,168	118,876	4,159	14,708	D	45.8%	52.3%	46.7%	53.3%
15,579	MITCHELL	5,265	4,007	1,107	151	2,900	R	76.1%	21.0%	78.4%	21.6%
27,798	MONTGOMERY	7,709	4,291	3,262	156	1,029	R	55.7%	42.3%	56.8%	43.2%
88,247	MOORE	28,462	18,806	9,071	585	9,735	R	66.1%	31.9%	67.5%	32.5%
95,840	NASH	31,037	16,244	14,403	390	1,841	R	52.3%	46.4%	53.0%	47.0%
202,667	NEW HANOVER	64,009	37,472	25,089	1,448	12,383	R	58.5%	39.2%	59.9%	40.1%
22,099	NORTHAMPTON	7,550	2,780	4,669	101	1,889	D	36.8%	61.8%	37.3%	62.7%
177,772	ONSLOW	26,382	17,311	8,358	713	8,953	R	65.6%	31.7%	67.4%	32.6%
133,801	ORANGE	45,958	13,791	31,092	1,075	17,301	D	30.0%	67.7%	30.7%	69.3%
13,144	PAMLICO	4,682	2,812	1,793	77	1,019	R	60.1%	38.3%	61.1%	38.9%
40,661	PASQUOTANK	9,604	4,576	4,841	187	265	D	47.6%	50.4%	48.6%	51.4%
52,217	PENDER	16,520	10,273	5,914	333	4,359	R	62.2%	35.8%	63.5%	36.5%
13,453	PERQUIMANS	4,109	2,558	1,476	75	1,082	R	62.3%	35.9%	63.4%	36.6%
39,464	PERSON	11,592	6,308	5,032	252	1,276	R	54.4%	43.4%	55.6%	44.4%
168,148	PITT	41,627	21,291	19,828	508	1,463	R	51.1%	47.6%	51.8%	48.2%
20,510	POLK	7,676	4,418	3,051	207	1,367	R	57.6%	39.7%	59.2%	40.8%
141,752	RANDOLPH	32,757	25,067	6,667	1,023	18,400	R	76.5%	20.4%	79.0%	21.0%
46,639	RICHMOND	12,188	5,507	6,454	227	947	D	45.2%	53.0%	46.0%	54.0%
134,168	ROBESON	22,878	10,548	12,001	329	1,453	D	46.1%	52.5%	46.8%	53.2%
93,643	ROCKINGHAM	25,194	15,979	8,416	799	7,563	R	63.4%	33.4%	65.5%	34.5%
138,428	ROWAN	36,044	23,146	11,939	959	11,207	R	64.2%	33.1%	66.0%	34.0%
67,810	RUTHERFORD	18,703	12,621	5,624	458	6,997	R	67.5%	30.1%	69.2%	30.8%
63,431	SAMPSON	17,704	9,901	7,586	217	2,315	R	55.9%	42.8%	56.6%	43.4%
36,157	SCOTLAND	8,355	3,609	4,597	149	988	D	43.2%	55.0%	44.0%	56.0%
60,585	STANLY	18,643	13,014	5,271	358	7,743	R	69.8%	28.3%	71.2%	28.8%
47,401	STOKES	14,161	10,155	3,618	388	6,537	R	71.7%	25.5%	73.7%	26.3%
73,673	SURRY	18,879	12,731	5,793	355	6,938	R	67.4%	30.7%	68.7%	31.3%
13,981	SWAIN	4,172	2,142	1,878	152	264	R	51.3%	45.0%	53.3%	46.7%
33,090	TRANSYLVANIA	12,364	7,181	4,867	316	2,314	R	58.1%	39.4%	59.6%	40.4%
4,407	TYRRELL	1,328	692	609	27	83	R	52.1%	45.9%	53.2%	46.8%
201,292	UNION	49,963	34,656	14,184	1,123	20,472	R	69.4%	28.4%	71.0%	29.0%
45,422	VANCE	13,920	5,524	8,137	259	2,613	D	39.7%	58.5%	40.4%	59.6%
900,993	WAKE	276,082	136,132	133,324	6,626	2,808	R	49.3%	48.3%	50.5%	49.5%
20,972	WARREN	6,448	2,183	4,188	77	2,005	D	33.9%	65.0%	34.3%	65.7%
13,228	WASHINGTON	4,528	1,980	2,475	73	495	D	43.7%	54.7%	44.4%	55.6%
51,079	WATAUGA	16,804	9,279	7,007	518	2,272	R	55.2%	41.7%	57.0%	43.0%
122,623	WAYNE	30,931	18,336	12,206	389	6,130	R	59.3%	39.5%	60.0%	40.0%
69,340	WILKES	19,506	13,249	5,625	632	7,624	R	67.9%	28.8%	70.2%	29.8%
81,234	WILSON	26,482	12,420	13,631	431	1,211	D	46.9%	51.5%	47.7%	52.3%
38,406	YADKIN	11,584	8,924	2,374	286	6,550	R	77.0%	20.5%	79.0%	21.0%
17,818	YANCEY	9,046	4,878	3,972	196	906	R	53.9%	43.9%	55.1%	44.9%
9,535,483	TOTAL	2,660,079	1,458,046	1,145,074	56,959	312,972	R	54.8%	43.0%	56.0%	44.0%

NORTH CAROLINA

HOUSE OF REPRESENTATIVES

			Republican		Democratic				Total Vote		Major Vote	
							Other	Rep.-Dem.	Percentage			
CD	Year	Total Vote	Vote	Candidate	Vote	Candidate	Vote	Plurality	Rep.	Dem.	Rep.	Dem.
1	2010	174,161	70,867	WOOLARD, ASHLEY	103,294	BUTTERFIELD, G. K.*		32,427 D	40.7%	59.3%	40.7%	59.3%
1	2008	274,271	81,506	STEPHENS, DEAN	192,765	BUTTERFIELD, G. K.*		111,259 D	29.7%	70.3%	29.7%	70.3%
1	2006	82,510		—	82,510	BUTTERFIELD, G. K.*		82,510 D		100.0%		100.0%
1	2004	215,175	77,508	DORITY, GREG	137,667	BUTTERFIELD, G. K.*		60,159 D	36.0%	64.0%	36.0%	64.0%
1	2002	146,157	50,907	DORITY, GREG	93,157	BALANCE, FRANK W., JR.	2,093	42,250 D	34.8%	63.7%	35.3%	64.7%
2	2010	189,774	93,876	ELLMERS, RENEE	92,393	ETHERIDGE, BOB*	3,505	1,483 R	49.5%	48.7%	50.4%	49.6%
2	2008	298,430	93,323	MANSELL, DAN	199,730	ETHERIDGE, BOB*	5,377	106,407 D	31.3%	66.9%	31.8%	68.2%
2	2006	129,264	43,271	MANSELL, DAN	85,993	ETHERIDGE, BOB*		42,722 D	33.5%	66.5%	33.5%	66.5%
2	2004	232,890	87,811	CREECH, BILLY J.	145,079	ETHERIDGE, BOB*		57,268 D	37.7%	62.3%	37.7%	62.3%
2	2002	153,184	50,965	ELLEN, JOSEPH L.	100,121	ETHERIDGE, BOB*	2,098	49,156 D	33.3%	65.4%	33.7%	66.3%
3	2010	199,304	143,225	JONES, WALTER B.*	51,317	ROUSE, JOHNNY G.	4,762	91,908 R	71.9%	25.7%	73.6%	26.4%
3	2008	306,050	201,686	JONES, WALTER B.*	104,364	WEBER, CRAIG		97,322 R	65.9%	34.1%	65.9%	34.1%
3	2006	144,977	99,519	JONES, WALTER B.*	45,458	WEBER, CRAIG		54,061 R	68.6%	31.4%	68.6%	31.4%
3	2004	243,090	171,863	JONES, WALTER B.*	71,227	EATON, ROGER A.		100,636 R	70.7%	29.3%	70.7%	29.3%
3	2002	144,934	131,448	JONES, WALTER B.*		—	13,486	131,448 R	90.7%		100.0%	
4	2010	271,832	116,448	LAWSON, WILLIAM "B. J."	155,384	PRICE, DAVID E.*		38,936 D	42.8%	57.2%	42.8%	57.2%
4	2008	419,698	153,947	LAWSON, WILLIAM "B. J."	265,751	PRICE, DAVID E.*		111,804 D	36.7%	63.3%	36.7%	63.3%
4	2006	195,939	68,599	ACUFF, STEVE	127,340	PRICE, DAVID E.*		58,741 D	35.0%	65.0%	35.0%	65.0%
4	2004	339,234	121,717	BATCHELOR, TODD A.	217,441	PRICE, DAVID E.*	76	95,724 D	35.9%	64.1%	35.9%	64.1%
4	2002	216,046	78,095	NGUYEN, TUAN A.	132,185	PRICE, DAVID E.*	5,766	54,090 D	36.1%	61.2%	37.1%	62.9%
5	2010	213,287	140,525	FOXX, VIRGINIA*	72,762	KENNEDY, BILLY		67,763 R	65.9%	34.1%	65.9%	34.1%
5	2008	326,923	190,820	FOXX, VIRGINIA*	136,103	CARTER, ROY		54,717 R	58.4%	41.6%	58.4%	41.6%
5	2006	168,199	96,138	FOXX, VIRGINIA*	72,061	SHARPE, ROGER		24,077 R	57.2%	42.8%	57.2%	42.8%
5	2004	284,817	167,546	FOXX, VIRGINIA	117,271	HARRELL, JIM A., JR.		50,275 R	58.8%	41.2%	58.8%	41.2%
5	2002	196,437	137,879	BURR, RICHARD M.*	58,558	CRAWFORD, DAVID		79,321 R	70.2%	29.8%	70.2%	29.8%
6	2010	207,759	156,252	COBLE, HOWARD*	51,507	TURNER, SAM		104,745 R	75.2%	24.8%	75.2%	24.8%
6	2008	329,891	221,018	COBLE, HOWARD*	108,873	BRATTON, TERESA SUE		112,145 R	67.0%	33.0%	67.0%	33.0%
6	2006	153,094	108,433	COBLE, HOWARD*	44,661	BLAKE, RORY		63,772 R	70.8%	29.2%	70.8%	29.2%
6	2004	283,623	207,470	COBLE, HOWARD*	76,153	JORDAN, WILLIAM W.		131,317 R	73.1%	26.9%	73.1%	26.9%
6	2002	167,497	151,430	COBLE, HOWARD*		—	16,067	151,430 R	90.4%	0.0%	100.0%	0.0%
7	2010	212,285	98,328	PANTANO, ILARIO GREGORY	113,957	McINTYRE, MIKE*		15,629 D	46.3%	53.7%	46.3%	53.7%
7	2008	312,855	97,472	BREAZEALE, WILL	215,383	McINTYRE, MIKE*		117,911 D	31.2%	68.8%	31.2%	68.8%
7	2006	139,820	38,033	DAVIS, SHIRLEY	101,787	McINTYRE, MIKE*		63,754 D	27.2%	72.8%	27.2%	72.8%
7	2004	246,466	66,084	PLONK, KEN	180,382	McINTYRE, MIKE*		114,298 D	26.8%	73.2%	26.8%	73.2%
7	2002	166,654	45,537	ADAMS, JAMES R.	118,543	McINTYRE, MIKE*	2,574	73,006 D	27.3%	71.1%	27.8%	72.2%
8	2010	167,442	73,129	JOHNSON, HAROLD	88,776	KISSELL, LARRY*	5,537	15,647 D	43.7%	53.0%	45.2%	54.8%
8	2008	283,819	126,634	HAYES, ROBIN*	157,185	KISSELL, LARRY		30,551 D	44.6%	55.4%	44.6%	55.4%
8	2006	121,523	60,926	HAYES, ROBIN*	60,597	KISSELL, LARRY		329 R	50.1%	49.9%	50.1%	49.9%
8	2004	225,171	125,070	HAYES, ROBIN*	100,101	TROUTMAN, BETH		24,969 R	55.5%	44.5%	55.5%	44.5%
8	2002	149,736	80,298	HAYES, ROBIN*	66,819	KOURI, CHRIS	2,619	13,479 R	53.6%	44.6%	54.6%	45.4%
9	2010	230,240	158,790	MYRICK, SUE*	71,450	DOCTOR, JEFF		87,340 R	69.0%	31.0%	69.0%	31.0%
9	2008	386,483	241,053	MYRICK, SUE*	138,719	TAYLOR, HARRY	6,711	102,334 R	62.4%	35.9%	63.5%	36.5%
9	2006	159,643	106,206	MYRICK, SUE*	53,437	GLASS, BILL		52,769 R	66.5%	33.5%	66.5%	33.5%
9	2004	300,101	210,783	MYRICK, SUE*	89,318	FLYNN, JACK		121,465 R	70.2%	29.8%	70.2%	29.8%
9	2002	193,443	140,095	MYRICK, SUE*	49,974	McGUIRE, ED	3,374	90,121 R	72.4%	25.8%	73.7%	26.3%
10	2010	183,785	130,813	McHENRY, PATRICK T.*	52,972	GREGORY, JEFF		77,841 R	71.2%	28.8%	71.2%	28.8%
10	2008	298,473	171,774	McHENRY, PATRICK T.*	126,699	JOHNSON, DANIEL		45,075 R	57.6%	42.4%	57.6%	42.4%
10	2006	152,393	94,179	McHENRY, PATRICK T.*	58,214	CARSNER, RICHARD		35,965 R	61.8%	38.2%	61.8%	38.2%

NORTH CAROLINA

HOUSE OF REPRESENTATIVES

CD	Year	Total Vote	Republican		Democratic		Other Vote	Rep.-Dem. Plurality		Percentage			
			Vote	Candidate	Vote	Candidate				Total Vote		Major Vote	
										Rep.	Dem.	Rep.	Dem.
10	2004	246,117	157,884	McHENRY, PATRICK T.	88,233	FISCHER, ANNE N.		69,651	R	64.1%	35.9%	64.1%	35.9%
10	2002	173,292	102,768	BALLENGER, CASS*	65,587	DAUGHERTY, RON	4,937	37,181	R	59.3%	37.8%	61.0%	39.0%
11	2010	241,471	110,246	MILLER, JEFF	131,225	SHULER, HEATH*		20,979	D	45.7%	54.3%	45.7%	54.3%
11	2008	340,716	122,087	MUMPOWER, CARL	211,112	SHULER, HEATH*	7,517	89,025	D	35.8%	62.0%	36.6%	63.4%
11	2006	232,314	107,342	TAYLOR, CHARLES H.*	124,972	SHULER, HEATH		17,630	D	46.2%	53.8%	46.2%	53.8%
11	2004	290,897	159,709	TAYLOR, CHARLES H.*	131,188	KEEVER, PATSY		28,521	R	54.9%	45.1%	54.9%	45.1%
11	2002	202,260	112,335	TAYLOR, CHARLES H.*	86,664	NEILL, SAM	3,261	25,671	R	55.5%	42.8%	56.5%	43.5%
12	2010	162,007	55,315	DORITY, GREG	103,495	WATT, MELVIN*	3,197	48,180	D	34.1%	63.9%	34.8%	65.2%
12	2008	301,722	85,814	COBB, TY JR.	215,908	WATT, MELVIN*		130,094	D	28.4%	71.6%	28.4%	71.6%
12	2006	106,472	35,127	FISHER, ADA M.	71,345	WATT, MELVIN*		36,218	D	33.0%	67.0%	33.0%	67.0%
12	2004	231,806	76,898	FISHER, ADA M.	154,908	WATT, MELVIN*		78,010	D	33.2%	66.8%	33.2%	66.8%
12	2002	151,239	49,588	KISH, JEFF	98,821	WATT, MELVIN*	2,830	49,233	D	32.8%	65.3%	33.4%	66.6%
13	2010	209,202	93,099	RANDALL, WILLIAM	116,103	MILLER, BRAD*		23,004	D	44.5%	55.5%	44.5%	55.5%
13	2008	335,762	114,383	WEBSTER, HUGH	221,379	MILLER, BRAD*		106,996	D	34.1%	65.9%	34.1%	65.9%
13	2006	154,660	56,120	JOHNSON, VERNON	98,540	MILLER, BRAD*		42,420	D	36.3%	63.7%	36.3%	63.7%
13	2004	273,684	112,788	JOHNSON, VIRGINIA	160,896	MILLER, BRAD*		48,108	D	41.2%	58.8%	41.2%	58.8%
13	2002	183,270	77,688	GRANT, CAROLYN W.	100,287	MILLER, BRAD	5,295	22,599	D	42.4%	54.7%	43.7%	56.3%
TOTAL	2010	2,662,549	1,440,913		1,204,635		17,001	236,278	R	54.1%	45.2%	54.5%	45.5%
TOTAL	2008	4,215,093	1,901,517		2,293,971		19,605	392,454	D	45.1%	54.4%	45.3%	54.7%
TOTAL	2006	1,940,808	913,893		1,026,915			113,022	D	47.1%	52.9%	47.1%	52.9%
TOTAL	2004	3,413,071	1,743,131		1,669,864		76	73,267	R	51.1%	48.9%	51.1%	48.9%
TOTAL	2002	2,244,149	1,209,033		970,716		64,400	238,317	R	53.9%	43.3%	55.5%	44.5%

An asterisk (*) denotes incumbent.

NORTH CAROLINA

GENERAL AND PRIMARY ELECTIONS

2010 GENERAL ELECTIONS

Senator   Other vote was 55,687 Libertarian (Michael Beitler); 1,272 scattered write-in.

House   Other vote was:

CD 1
CD 2   3,505 Libertarian (Tom Rose).
CD 3   4,762 Libertarian (Darryl Holloman).
CD 4
CD 5
CD 6
CD 7
CD 8   5,098 Libertarian (Thomas Hill); 439 scattered write-in.
CD 9
CD 10

CD 11
CD 12   3,197 Libertarian (Lon Cecil).
CD 13

NORTH CAROLINA

GENERAL AND PRIMARY ELECTIONS

2010 PRIMARY ELECTIONS

Primary	May 4, 2010	**Registration** (as of May 4, 2010)	Democratic		2,759,502
			Republican		1,934,498
			Libertarian		7,322
			Unaffiliated		1,412,856
			TOTAL		*6,114,178*

Primary Runoff June 22, 2010

Primary Type Semi-open—Registered Democrats and Republicans could vote only in their party's primary. Unaffiliated voters could participate in the primary of either party.

	REPUBLICAN PRIMARIES			DEMOCRATIC PRIMARIES		
Senator	Richard M. Burr*	297,993	80.1%	Elaine Marshall	154,605	36.3%
	Brad Jones	37,616	10.1%	Cal Cunningham	115,851	27.2%
	Eddie Burks	22,111	5.9%	Ken Lewis	72,510	17.0%
	Larry Linney	14,248	3.8%	Marcus W. Williams	35,984	8.5%
				Susan Harris	29,738	7.0%
				Ann Worthy	16,655	3.9%
	TOTAL	*371,968*		*TOTAL*	*425,343*	
				PRIMARY RUNOFF		
				Elaine Marshall	95,390	60.0%
				Cal Cunningham	63,691	40.0%
				TOTAL	*159,081*	
Congressional District 1	Ashley Woolard	3,774	45.2%	G.K. Butterfield*	46,509	72.9%
	Jerry Grimes	2,220	26.6%	Chad Larkins	17,262	27.1%
	Jim Miller	1,252	15.0%			
	John Carter	1,097	13.1%			
	TOTAL	*8,343*		*TOTAL*	*63,771*	
Congressional District 2	Renee Ellmers	9,171	55.1%	Bob Etheridge*	Unopposed	
	Frank Deatrich	4,280	25.7%			
	Todd Gailas	3,190	19.2%			
	TOTAL	*16,641*				
Congressional District 3	Walter B. Jones*	21,551	76.9%	Johnny G. Rouse	Unopposed	
	Bob Cavanaugh	4,221	15.1%			
	Craig Weber	2,261	8.1%			
	TOTAL	*28,033*				
Congressional District 4	William "B.J." Lawson	10,449	46.0%	David E. Price*	Unopposed	
	Frank Roche	9,228	40.6%			
	David Burnett	1,967	8.7%			
	George Hutchins	1,077	4.7%			
	TOTAL	*22,721*				
Congressional District 5	Virginia Foxx*	38,174	79.8%	Billy Kennedy	Unopposed	
	Keith Gardner	9,639	20.2%			
	TOTAL	*47,813*				
Congressional District 6	Howard Coble*	31,663	63.5%	Sam Turner	Unopposed	
	Billy Yow	7,929	15.9%			
	James Taylor	7,553	15.1%			
	Cathy Brewer Hinson	1,468	2.9%			

NORTH CAROLINA

GENERAL AND PRIMARY ELECTIONS

	REPUBLICAN PRIMARIES			DEMOCRATIC PRIMARIES		
	Jeff Phillips	1,095	2.2%			
	Jon Mangin	168	0.3%			
	TOTAL	*49,876*				
Congressional District 7	Ilario Gregory Pantano	17,177	51.0%	Mike McIntyre*	Unopposed	
	Will Breazeale	11,629	34.5%			
	Randy Crow	4,862	14.4%			
	TOTAL	*33,668*				
Congressional District 8	Tim D'Annunzio	9,548	36.9%	Larry Kissell*	24,541	62.7%
	Harold Johnson	8,567	33.1%	Nancy Shakir	14,600	37.3%
	Hal Jordan	4,757	18.4%			
	Lou Huddleston	2,141	8.3%			
	Lee Cornelison	466	1.8%			
	Darrell Day	428	1.7%			
	TOTAL	*25,907*		*TOTAL*	*39,141*	
	PRIMARY RUNOFF					
	Harold Johnson	9,261	61.0%			
	Tim D'Annunzio	5,928	39.0%			
	TOTAL	*15,189*				
Congressional District 9	Sue Myrick*	Unopposed		Jeff Doctor	Unopposed	
Congressional District 10	Patrick T. McHenry*	27,657	63.1%	Jeff Gregory	9,621	50.9%
	Vance Patterson	11,392	26.0%	Anne N. Fischer	9,277	49.1%
	Scott Keadle	3,604	8.2%			
	David Michael Boldon	1,181	2.7%			
	TOTAL	*43,834*		*TOTAL*	*18,898*	
Congressional District 11	Jeff Miller	14,059	40.2%	Heath Shuler*	26,223	61.4%
	Dan Eichenbaum	11,949	34.2%	Aixa Wilson	16,507	38.6%
	Gregory A. Newman	4,103	11.7%			
	Kenny West	2,777	7.9%			
	Ed Krause	1,254	3.6%			
	James "Jake" Howard	791	2.3%			
	TOTAL	*34,933*		*TOTAL*	*42,730*	
Congressional District 12	Scott Cumbie	5,506	39.5%	Melvin Watt*	Unopposed	
	Greg Dority	4,787	34.3%			
	William Gillenwater	3,656	26.2%			
	TOTAL	*13,949*				
	PRIMARY RUNOFF					
	Greg Dority	1,449	51.7%			
	Scott Cumbie	1,352	48.3%			
	TOTAL	*2,801*				
Congressional District 13	William Randall	5,738	32.6%	Brad Miller*	Unopposed	
	Bernie Reeves	5,603	31.8%			
	Dan Huffman	4,749	27.0%			
	Frank Hurley	1,515	8.6%			
	TOTAL	*17,605*				
	PRIMARY RUNOFF					
	William Randall	3,807	58.9%			
	Bernie Reeves	2,655	41.1%			
	TOTAL	*6,462*				

An asterisk (*) denotes incumbent. The names of unopposed candidates did not appear on the primary ballot; therefore, no votes were cast for these candidates. A runoff was triggered if the leading candidate received less than a "substantial plurality" (40 percent) of the primary vote and the second-place candidate called for a runoff.

NORTH DAKOTA

One member At Large

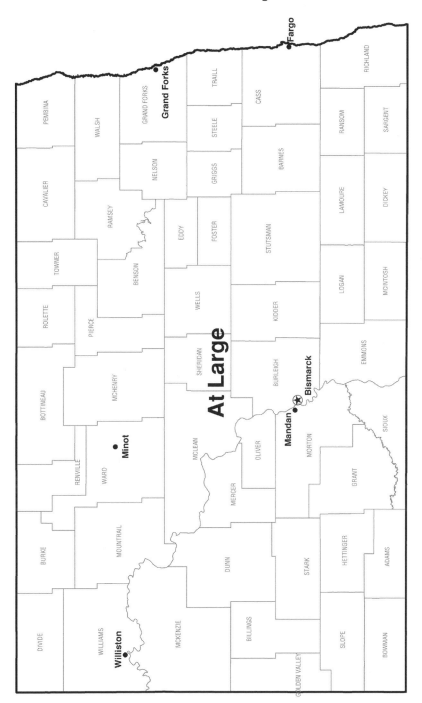

NORTH DAKOTA

GOVERNOR

Jack Dalrymple (R). Sworn in as governor December 7, 2010, to fill the vacancy created by the resignation of John Hoeven (R) following his election to the Senate.

SENATORS (1 Democrat, 1 Republican)

Kent Conrad (D). Reelected 2006 to a six-year term. Previously elected 2000, 1994 and in a special election in December 1992 to fill the remaining two years of the term vacated by the death of Senator Quentin N. Burdick (D), who died in September 1992; elected 1986 to a six-year term.

John Hoeven (R). Elected 2010 to a six-year term.

REPRESENTATIVES (1 Republican)

At Large. Rick Berg (R)

POSTWAR VOTE FOR PRESIDENT

Year	Total Vote	Republican		Democratic		Other Vote	Rep.-Dem. Plurality	Percentage			
								Total Vote		Major Vote	
		Vote	Candidate	Vote	Candidate			Rep.	Dem.	Rep.	Dem.
2008	316,621	168,601	McCain, John	141,278	Obama, Barack	6,742	27,323 R	53.3%	44.6%	54.4%	45.6%
2004	312,833	196,651	Bush, George W.	111,052	Kerry, John	5,130	85,599 R	62.9%	35.5%	63.9%	36.1%
2000**	288,256	174,852	Bush, George W.	95,284	Gore, Al	18,120	79,568 R	60.7%	33.1%	64.7%	35.3%
1996**	266,411	125,050	Dole, Bob	106,905	Clinton, Bill	34,456	18,145 R	46.9%	40.1%	53.9%	46.1%
1992**	308,133	136,244	Bush, George	99,168	Clinton, Bill	72,721	37,076 R	44.2%	32.2%	57.9%	42.1%
1988	297,261	166,559	Bush, George	127,739	Dukakis, Michael S.	2,963	38,820 R	56.0%	43.0%	56.6%	43.4%
1984	308,971	200,336	Reagan, Ronald	104,429	Mondale, Walter F.	4,206	95,907 R	64.8%	33.8%	65.7%	34.3%
1980**	301,545	193,695	Reagan, Ronald	79,189	Carter, Jimmy	28,661	114,506 R	64.2%	26.3%	71.0%	29.0%
1976	297,188	153,470	Ford, Gerald R.	136,078	Carter, Jimmy	7,640	17,392 R	51.6%	45.8%	53.0%	47.0%
1972	280,514	174,109	Nixon, Richard M.	100,384	McGovern, George S.	6,021	73,725 R	62.1%	35.8%	63.4%	36.6%
1968**	247,882	138,669	Nixon, Richard M.	94,769	Humphrey, Hubert H.	14,444	43,900 R	55.9%	38.2%	59.4%	40.6%
1964	258,389	108,207	Goldwater, Barry M.	149,784	Johnson, Lyndon B.	398	41,577 D	41.9%	58.0%	41.9%	58.1%
1960	278,431	154,310	Nixon, Richard M.	123,963	Kennedy, John F.	158	30,347 R	55.4%	44.5%	55.5%	44.5%
1956	253,991	156,766	Eisenhower, Dwight D.	96,742	Stevenson, Adlai E.	483	60,024 R	61.7%	38.1%	61.8%	38.2%
1952	270,127	191,712	Eisenhower, Dwight D.	76,694	Stevenson, Adlai E.	1,721	115,018 R	71.0%	28.4%	71.4%	28.6%
1948	220,716	115,139	Dewey, Thomas E.	95,812	Truman, Harry S.	9,765	19,327 R	52.2%	43.4%	54.6%	45.4%

**In past elections, the other vote included: 2000 - 9,486 Green (Ralph Nader); 1996 - 32,515 Reform (Ross Perot); 1992 - 71,084 Independent (Perot); 1980 - 23,640 Independent (John Anderson); 1968 - 14,244 American Independent (George Wallace).

NORTH DAKOTA

POSTWAR VOTE FOR GOVERNOR

Year	Total Vote	Republican Vote	Candidate	Democratic Vote	Candidate	Other Vote	Rep.-Dem. Plurality	Total Vote Rep.	Total Vote Dem.	Major Vote Rep.	Major Vote Dem.
2008	315,692	235,009	Hoeven, John	74,279	Mathern, Tim	6,404	160,730 R	74.4%	23.5%	76.0%	24.0%
2004	309,873	220,803	Hoeven, John	84,877	Satrom, Joseph A.	4,193	135,926 R	71.3%	27.4%	72.2%	27.8%
2000	289,412	159,255	Hoeven, John	130,144	Heitkamp, Heidi	13	29,111 R	55.0%	45.0%	55.0%	45.0%
1996	264,298	174,937	Schafer, Edward T.	89,349	Kaldor, Lee	12	85,588 R	66.2%	33.8%	66.2%	33.8%
1992	304,861	176,398	Schafer, Edward T.	123,845	Spaeth, Nicholas	4,618	52,553 R	57.9%	40.6%	58.8%	41.2%
1988	299,080	119,986	Mallberg, Leon L.	179,094	Sinner, George		59,108 D	40.1%	59.9%	40.1%	59.9%
1984	314,382	140,460	Olson, Allen I.	173,922	Sinner, George		33,462 D	44.7%	55.3%	44.7%	55.3%
1980	302,621	162,230	Olson, Allen I.	140,391	Link, Arthur A.		21,839 R	53.6%	46.4%	53.6%	46.4%
1976	297,249	138,321	Elkin, Richard	153,309	Link, Arthur A.	5,619	14,988 D	46.5%	51.6%	47.4%	52.6%
1972	281,931	138,032	Larsen, Richard	143,899	Link, Arthur A.		5,867 D	49.0%	51.0%	49.0%	51.0%
1968	248,000	108,382	McCarney, Robert P.	135,955	Guy, William L.	3,663	27,573 D	43.7%	54.8%	44.4%	55.6%
1964**	262,661	116,247	Halcrow, Donald M.	146,414	Guy, William L.		30,167 D	44.3%	55.7%	44.3%	55.7%
1962	228,509	113,251	Andrews, Mark	115,258	Guy, William L.		2,007 D	49.6%	50.4%	49.6%	50.4%
1960	275,375	122,486	Dahl, C. P.	136,148	Guy, William L.	16,741	13,662 D	44.5%	49.4%	47.4%	52.6%
1958	210,599	111,836	Davis, John E.	98,763	Lord, John F.		13,073 R	53.1%	46.9%	53.1%	46.9%
1956	252,435	147,566	Davis, John E.	104,869	Warner, Wallace E.		42,697 R	58.5%	41.5%	58.5%	41.5%
1954	193,501	124,253	Brunsdale, C. Norman	69,248	Bymers, Cornelius		55,005 R	64.2%	35.8%	64.2%	35.8%
1952	253,934	199,944	Brunsdale, C. Norman	53,990	Johnson, Ole C.		145,954 R	78.7%	21.3%	78.7%	21.3%
1950	183,772	121,822	Brunsdale, C. Norman	61,950	Byerly, Clyde G.		59,872 R	66.3%	33.7%	66.3%	33.7%
1948	214,858	131,764	Aandahl, Fred G.	80,555	Henry, Howard	2,539	51,209 R	61.3%	37.5%	62.1%	37.9%
1946	169,391	116,672	Aandahl, Fred G.	52,719	Burdick, Quentin N.		63,953 R	68.9%	31.1%	68.9%	31.1%

**The term of office of North Dakota's Governor was increased from two to four years effective with the 1964 election.

POSTWAR VOTE FOR SENATOR

Year	Total Vote	Republican Vote	Candidate	Democratic Vote	Candidate	Other Vote	Rep.-Dem. Plurality	Total Vote Rep.	Total Vote Dem.	Major Vote Rep.	Major Vote Dem.
2010	238,812	181,689	Hoeven, John	52,955	Potter, Tracy	4,168	128,734 R	76.1%	22.2%	77.4%	22.6%
2006	218,152	64,417	Grotberg, Dwight	150,146	Conrad, Kent	3,589	85,729 D	29.5%	68.8%	30.0%	70.0%
2004	310,696	98,553	Liffrig, Mike	212,143	Dorgan, Byron L.		113,590 D	31.7%	68.3%	31.7%	68.3%
2000	287,539	111,069	Sand, Duane	176,470	Conrad, Kent		65,401 D	38.6%	61.4%	38.6%	61.4%
1998	213,358	75,013	Nalewaja, Donna	134,747	Dorgan, Byron L.	3,598	59,734 D	35.2%	63.2%	35.8%	64.2%
1994	236,547	99,390	Clayburg, Ben	137,157	Conrad, Kent		37,767 D	42.0%	58.0%	42.0%	58.0%
1992	303,957	118,162	Sydness, Steve	179,347	Dorgan, Byron L.	6,448	61,185 D	38.9%	59.0%	39.7%	60.3%
1992S	163,311	55,194	Dalrymple, Jack	103,246	Conrad, Kent	4,871	48,052 D	33.8%	63.2%	34.8%	65.2%
1988	289,170	112,937	Striden, Earl	171,899	Burdick, Quentin N.	4,334	58,962 D	39.1%	59.4%	39.6%	60.4%
1986	288,998	141,797	Andrews, Mark	143,932	Conrad, Kent	3,269	2,135 D	49.1%	49.8%	49.6%	50.4%
1982	262,465	89,304	Knorr, Gene	164,873	Burdick, Quentin N.	8,288	75,569 D	34.0%	62.8%	35.1%	64.9%
1980	299,272	210,347	Andrews, Mark	86,658	Johanneson, Kent	2,267	123,689 R	70.3%	29.0%	70.8%	29.2%
1976	283,062	103,466	Stroup, Richard	175,772	Burdick, Quentin N.	3,824	72,306 D	36.6%	62.1%	37.1%	62.9%
1974	235,661	114,117	Young, Milton R.	113,931	Guy, William L.	7,613	186 R	48.4%	48.3%	50.0%	50.0%
1970	219,560	82,996	Kleppe, Tom	134,519	Burdick, Quentin N.	2,045	51,523 D	37.8%	61.3%	38.2%	61.8%
1968	239,776	154,968	Young, Milton R.	80,815	Lashkowitz, Herschel	3,993	74,153 R	64.6%	33.7%	65.7%	34.3%
1964	258,945	109,681	Kleppe, Tom	149,264	Burdick, Quentin N.		39,583 D	42.4%	57.6%	42.4%	57.6%
1962	223,737	135,705	Young, Milton R.	88,032	Lanier, William		47,673 R	60.7%	39.3%	60.7%	39.3%
1960S	210,349	103,475	Davis, John E.	104,593	Burdick, Quentin N.	2,281	1,118 D	49.2%	49.7%	49.7%	50.3%
1958	204,635	117,070	Langer, William	84,892	Vendsel, Raymond	2,673	32,178 R	57.2%	41.5%	58.0%	42.0%
1956	244,161	155,305	Young, Milton R.	87,919	Burdick, Quentin N.	937	67,386 R	63.6%	36.0%	63.9%	36.1%
1952**	237,995	157,907	Langer, William	55,347	Morrison, Harold A.	24,741	102,560 R	66.3%	23.3%	74.0%	26.0%
1950	186,716	126,209	Young, Milton R.	60,507	O'Brien, Harry		65,702 R	67.6%	32.4%	67.6%	32.4%
1946**	165,382	88,210	Langer, William	38,368	Larson, Abner B.	38,804	49,406 R	53.3%	23.2%	69.7%	30.3%
1946S**	136,852	75,998	Young, Milton R.	37,507	Lanier, William	23,347	38,491 R	55.5%	27.4%	67.0%	33.0%

**In past elections, the other vote included: 1952 - 24,741 Independent (Fred G. Aandahl); 1946 - 38,804 Independent (Arthur E. Thompson), who finished second; 1946 Special - 20,848 Independent (Gerald P. Nye). One of the 1992 elections was for a short term to fill a vacancy and the special election was held in December. The 1946 and 1960 special elections were held in June for short terms to fill vacancies.

NORTH DAKOTA

SENATOR 2010

2010 Census Population	County	Total Vote	Republican	Democratic	Other	Rep.-Dem. Plurality		Percentage			
								Total Vote		Major Vote	
								Rep.	Dem.	Rep.	Dem.
2,343	ADAMS	1,189	963	201	25	762	R	81.0%	16.9%	82.7%	17.3%
11,066	BARNES	4,765	3,538	1,140	87	2,398	R	74.2%	23.9%	75.6%	24.4%
6,660	BENSON	1,779	1,115	621	43	494	R	62.7%	34.9%	64.2%	35.8%
783	BILLINGS	501	443	48	10	395	R	88.4%	9.6%	90.2%	9.8%
6,429	BOTTINEAU	2,971	2,426	497	48	1,929	R	81.7%	16.7%	83.0%	17.0%
3,151	BOWMAN	1,457	1,234	184	39	1,050	R	84.7%	12.6%	87.0%	13.0%
1,968	BURKE	790	667	112	11	555	R	84.4%	14.2%	85.6%	14.4%
81,308	BURLEIGH	32,650	25,420	6,705	525	18,715	R	77.9%	20.5%	79.1%	20.9%
149,778	CASS	48,468	34,882	12,743	843	22,139	R	72.0%	26.3%	73.2%	26.8%
3,993	CAVALIER	1,841	1,503	322	16	1,181	R	81.6%	17.5%	82.4%	17.6%
5,289	DICKEY	2,027	1,635	364	28	1,271	R	80.7%	18.0%	81.8%	18.2%
2,071	DIVIDE	902	676	210	16	466	R	74.9%	23.3%	76.3%	23.7%
3,536	DUNN	1,554	1,236	296	22	940	R	79.5%	19.0%	80.7%	19.3%
2,385	EDDY	1,008	695	281	32	414	R	68.9%	27.9%	71.2%	28.8%
3,550	EMMONS	1,562	1,262	257	43	1,005	R	80.8%	16.5%	83.1%	16.9%
3,343	FOSTER	1,460	1,165	265	30	900	R	79.8%	18.2%	81.5%	18.5%
1,680	GOLDEN VALLEY	743	640	91	12	549	R	86.1%	12.2%	87.6%	12.4%
66,861	GRAND FORKS	20,328	14,984	5,049	295	9,935	R	73.7%	24.8%	74.8%	25.2%
2,394	GRANT	1,161	949	195	17	754	R	81.7%	16.8%	83.0%	17.0%
2,420	GRIGGS	1,138	845	274	19	571	R	74.3%	24.1%	75.5%	24.5%
2,477	HETTINGER	1,166	934	205	27	729	R	80.1%	17.6%	82.0%	18.0%
2,435	KIDDER	1,156	857	261	38	596	R	74.1%	22.6%	76.7%	23.3%
4,139	LA MOURE	2,086	1,616	426	44	1,190	R	77.5%	20.4%	79.1%	20.9%
1,990	LOGAN	967	800	146	21	654	R	82.7%	15.1%	84.6%	15.4%
5,395	MCHENRY	2,336	1,774	516	46	1,258	R	75.9%	22.1%	77.5%	22.5%
2,809	MCINTOSH	1,389	1,168	197	24	971	R	84.1%	14.2%	85.6%	14.4%
6,360	MCKENZIE	2,176	1,803	345	28	1,458	R	82.9%	15.9%	83.9%	16.1%
8,962	MCLEAN	3,957	3,030	859	68	2,171	R	76.6%	21.7%	77.9%	22.1%
8,424	MERCER	3,646	2,895	691	60	2,204	R	79.4%	19.0%	80.7%	19.3%
27,471	MORTON	9,860	7,422	2,242	196	5,180	R	75.3%	22.7%	76.8%	23.2%
7,673	MOUNTRAIL	2,167	1,450	664	53	786	R	66.9%	30.6%	68.6%	31.4%
3,126	NELSON	1,572	1,160	381	31	779	R	73.8%	24.2%	75.3%	24.7%
1,846	OLIVER	905	726	154	25	572	R	80.2%	17.0%	82.5%	17.5%
7,413	PEMBINA	2,672	2,181	447	44	1,734	R	81.6%	16.7%	83.0%	17.0%
4,357	PIERCE	1,939	1,571	339	29	1,232	R	81.0%	17.5%	82.3%	17.7%
11,451	RAMSEY	4,187	3,253	862	72	2,391	R	77.7%	20.6%	79.1%	20.9%
5,457	RANSOM	1,881	1,313	538	30	775	R	69.8%	28.6%	70.9%	29.1%
2,470	RENVILLE	1,060	832	209	19	623	R	78.5%	19.7%	79.9%	20.1%
16,321	RICHLAND	5,631	4,322	1,205	104	3,117	R	76.8%	21.4%	78.2%	21.8%
13,937	ROLETTE	3,966	2,089	1,754	123	335	R	52.7%	44.2%	54.4%	45.6%
3,829	SARGENT	1,601	1,038	546	17	492	R	64.8%	34.1%	65.5%	34.5%
1,321	SHERIDAN	781	661	111	9	550	R	84.6%	14.2%	85.6%	14.4%
4,153	SIOUX	781	426	327	28	99	R	54.5%	41.9%	56.6%	43.4%
727	SLOPE	338	279	49	10	230	R	82.5%	14.5%	85.1%	14.9%
24,199	STARK	7,748	6,421	1,179	148	5,242	R	82.9%	15.2%	84.5%	15.5%
1,975	STEELE	905	602	293	10	309	R	66.5%	32.4%	67.3%	32.7%
21,100	STUTSMAN	7,763	6,011	1,596	156	4,415	R	77.4%	20.6%	79.0%	21.0%
2,246	TOWNER	1,030	767	247	16	520	R	74.5%	24.0%	75.6%	24.4%
8,121	TRAILL	3,075	2,262	765	48	1,497	R	73.6%	24.9%	74.7%	25.3%
11,119	WALSH	4,057	3,235	767	55	2,468	R	79.7%	18.9%	80.8%	19.2%
61,675	WARD	19,193	15,465	3,453	275	12,012	R	80.6%	18.0%	81.7%	18.3%
4,207	WELLS	2,192	1,774	387	31	1,387	R	80.9%	17.7%	82.1%	17.9%
22,398	WILLIAMS	6,335	5,274	939	122	4,335	R	83.3%	14.8%	84.9%	15.1%
672,591	TOTAL	238,812	181,689	52,955	4,168	128,734	R	76.1%	22.2%	77.4%	22.6%

NORTH DAKOTA

HOUSE OF REPRESENTATIVES

| | | | Republican | | Democratic | | | | Percentage | | | |
| | | | | | | | | | Total Vote | | Major Vote | |
CD	Year	Total Vote	Vote	Candidate	Vote	Candidate	Other Vote	Rep.-Dem. Plurality	Rep.	Dem.	Rep.	Dem.
AL	2010	237,137	129,802	BERG, RICK	106,542	POMEROY, EARL*	793	23,260 R	54.7%	44.9%	54.9%	45.1%
AL	2008	313,965	119,388	SAND, DUANE	194,577	POMEROY, EARL*		75,189 D	38.0%	62.0%	38.0%	62.0%
AL	2006	217,621	74,687	MECHTEL, MATT	142,934	POMEROY, EARL*		68,247 D	34.3%	65.7%	34.3%	65.7%
AL	2004	310,814	125,684	SAND, DUANE	185,130	POMEROY, EARL*		59,446 D	40.4%	59.6%	40.4%	59.6%
AL	2002	231,030	109,957	CLAYBURGH, RICK	121,073	POMEROY, EARL*		11,116 D	47.6%	52.4%	47.6%	52.4%
AL	2000	285,658	127,251	DORSO, JOHN	151,173	POMEROY, EARL*	7,234	23,922 D	44.5%	52.9%	45.7%	54.3%
AL	1998	215,469	75,013	CRAMER, KEVIN	134,747	POMEROY, EARL*	5,709	59,734 D	34.8%	62.5%	35.8%	64.2%
AL	1996	263,010	113,684	CRAMER, KEVIN	144,833	POMEROY, EARL*	4,493	31,149 D	43.2%	55.1%	44.0%	56.0%
AL	1994	235,389	105,988	PORTER, GARY	123,134	POMEROY, EARL*	6,267	17,146 D	45.0%	52.3%	46.3%	53.7%
AL	1992	297,898	117,442	KORSMO, JOHN T.	169,273	POMEROY, EARL	11,183	51,831 D	39.4%	56.8%	41.0%	59.0%
AL	1990	233,979	81,443	SCHAFER, EDWARD	152,530	DORGAN, BYRON L.*	6	71,087 D	34.8%	65.2%	34.8%	65.2%
AL	1988	299,982	84,475	SYDNESS, STEVE	212,583	DORGAN, BYRON L.*	2,924	128,108 D	28.2%	70.9%	28.4%	71.6%
AL	1986	286,361	66,989	VINJE, SYVER	216,258	DORGAN, BYRON L.*	3,114	149,269 D	23.4%	75.5%	23.7%	76.3%
AL	1984	308,729	65,761	ALTENBURG, LOIS I.	242,968	DORGAN, BYRON L.*		177,207 D	21.3%	78.7%	21.3%	78.7%
AL	1982	260,499	72,241	JONES, KENT	186,534	DORGAN, BYRON L.*	1,724	114,293 D	27.7%	71.6%	27.9%	72.1%
AL	1980	293,076	124,707	SMYKOWSKI, JIM	166,437	DORGAN, BYRON L.	1,932	41,730 D	42.6%	56.8%	42.8%	57.2%
AL	1978	220,348	147,746	ANDREWS, MARK*	68,016	HAGEN, BRUCE	4,586	79,730 R	67.1%	30.9%	68.5%	31.5%
AL	1976	289,881	181,018	ANDREWS, MARK*	104,263	OMDAHL, LLOYD B.	4,600	76,755 R	62.4%	36.0%	63.5%	36.5%
AL	1974	233,688	130,184	ANDREWS, MARK*	103,504	DORGAN, BYRON L.		26,680 R	55.7%	44.3%	55.7%	44.3%
AL	1972	268,721	195,360	ANDREWS, MARK*	72,850	ISTA, RICHARD	511	122,510 R	72.7%	27.1%	72.8%	27.2%

An asterisk (*) denotes incumbent. North Dakota had two House seats prior to 1972.

NORTH DAKOTA

GENERAL AND PRIMARY ELECTIONS

2010 GENERAL ELECTIONS

Senator Other vote was 3,890 Libertarian (Keith J. Hanson); 278 scattered write-in.

House Other vote was

At Large 793 scattered write-in.

2010 PRIMARY ELECTIONS

Primary June 8, 2010   **Registration**   No Formal Registration

Primary Type Open—Any person of voting age (18 years old at the time of the primary election) could participate in the primary of either party. As of June 8, 2010, North Dakota's estimated voting-age population was 502,873.

	REPUBLICAN PRIMARIES			**DEMOCRATIC PRIMARIES**		
Senator	John Hoeven	65,075	99.8%	Tracy Potter	26,258	99.6%
	Scattered write-in	130	0.2%	Scattered write-in	95	0.4%
	TOTAL	*65,205*		*TOTAL*	*26,353*	
House	Rick Berg	54,662	89.3%	Earl Pomeroy*	28,329	99.7%
At Large	JD Donaghe	6,441	10.5%	Scattered write-in	75	0.3%
	Scattered write-in	87	0.1%			
	TOTAL	*61,190*		*TOTAL*	*28,404*	

An asterisk (*) denotes incumbent.

OHIO

Congressional districts first established for elections held in 2002
18 members

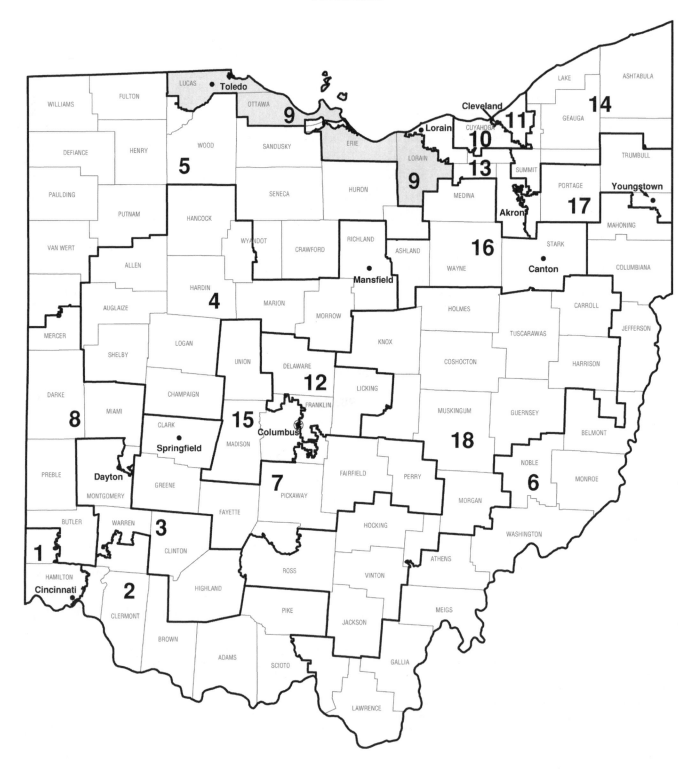

OHIO

Cleveland Area

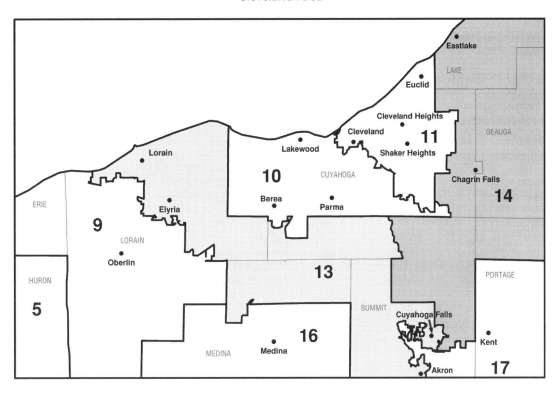

Columbus Area

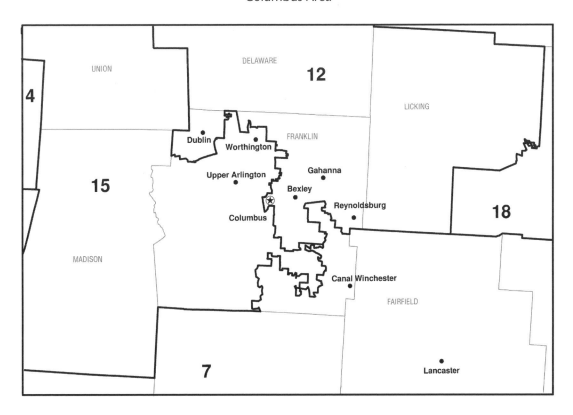

OHIO

GOVERNOR
John Kasich (R). Elected 2010 to a four-year term.

SENATORS (1 Democrat,1 Republican)
Sherrod Brown (D). Elected 2006 to a six-year term.

Rob Portman (R). Elected 2010 to a six-year term.

REPRESENTATIVES (13 Democrats, 5 Republicans)

1. Steve Chabot (R)
2. Jean Schmidt (R)
3. Michael R. Turner (R)
4. Jim Jordan (R)
5. Robert E. Latta (R)
6. Bill Johnson (R)
7. Steve Austria (R)
8. John A. Boehner (R)
9. Marcy Kaptur (D)
10. Dennis J. Kucinich (D)
11. Marcia L. Fudge (D)
12. Pat Tiberi (R)
13. Betty Sutton (D)
14. Steven C. LaTourette (R)
15. Steve Stivers (R)
16. Jim Renacci (R)
17. Tim Ryan (D)
18. Bob Gibbs (R)

POSTWAR VOTE FOR PRESIDENT

| | | Republican | | Democratic | | | | Percentage | | | |
| | | | | | | | | Total Vote | | Major Vote | |
Year	Total Vote	Vote	Candidate	Vote	Candidate	Other Vote	Rep.-Dem. Plurality	Rep.	Dem.	Rep.	Dem.
2008	5,708,350	2,677,820	McCain, John	2,940,044	Obama, Barack	90,486	262,224 D	46.9%	51.5%	47.7%	52.3%
2004	5,627,903	2,859,764	Bush, George W.	2,741,165	Kerry, John	26,974	118,599 R	50.8%	48.7%	51.1%	48.9%
2000**	4,701,998	2,350,363	Bush, George W.	2,183,628	Gore, Al	168,007	166,735 R	50.0%	46.4%	51.8%	48.2%
1996**	4,534,434	1,859,883	Dole, Bob	2,148,222	Clinton, Bill	526,329	288,339 D	41.0%	47.4%	46.4%	53.6%
1992**	4,939,967	1,894,310	Bush, George	1,984,942	Clinton, Bill	1,060,715	90,632 D	38.3%	40.2%	48.8%	51.2%
1988	4,393,699	2,416,549	Bush, George	1,939,629	Dukakis, Michael S.	37,521	476,920 R	55.0%	44.1%	55.5%	44.5%
1984	4,547,619	2,678,560	Reagan, Ronald	1,825,440	Mondale, Walter F.	43,619	853,120 R	58.9%	40.1%	59.5%	40.5%
1980**	4,283,603	2,206,545	Reagan, Ronald	1,752,414	Carter, Jimmy	324,644	454,131 R	51.5%	40.9%	55.7%	44.3%
1976	4,111,873	2,000,505	Ford, Gerald R.	2,011,621	Carter, Jimmy	99,747	11,116 D	48.7%	48.9%	49.9%	50.1%
1972	4,094,787	2,441,827	Nixon, Richard M.	1,558,889	McGovern, George S.	94,071	882,938 R	59.6%	38.1%	61.0%	39.0%
1968**	3,959,698	1,791,014	Nixon, Richard M.	1,700,586	Humphrey, Hubert H.	468,098	90,428 R	45.2%	42.9%	51.3%	48.7%
1964	3,969,196	1,470,865	Goldwater, Barry M.	2,498,331	Johnson, Lyndon B.		1,027,466 D	37.1%	62.9%	37.1%	62.9%
1960	4,161,859	2,217,611	Nixon, Richard M.	1,944,248	Kennedy, John F.		273,363 R	53.3%	46.7%	53.3%	46.7%
1956	3,702,265	2,262,610	Eisenhower, Dwight D.	1,439,655	Stevenson, Adlai E.		822,955 R	61.1%	38.9%	61.1%	38.9%
1952	3,700,758	2,100,391	Eisenhower, Dwight D.	1,600,367	Stevenson, Adlai E.		500,024 R	56.8%	43.2%	56.8%	43.2%
1948	2,936,071	1,445,684	Dewey, Thomas E.	1,452,791	Truman, Harry S.	37,596	7,107 D	49.2%	49.5%	49.9%	50.1%

**In past elections, the other vote included: 2000 - 117,799 Green (Ralph Nader);1996 - 483,207 Reform (Ross Perot); 1992 - 1,036,426 Independent (Perot); 1980 - 254,472 Independent (John Anderson); 1968 - 467,495 American Independent (George Wallace).

OHIO

POSTWAR VOTE FOR GOVERNOR

Year	Total Vote	Republican		Democratic		Other Vote	Rep.-Dem. Plurality	Percentage			
								Total Vote		Major Vote	
		Vote	Candidate	Vote	Candidate			Rep.	Dem.	Rep.	Dem.
2010	3,852,469	1,889,186	Kasich, John	1,812,059	Strickland, Ted	151,224	77,127 R	49.0%	47.0%	51.0%	49.0%
2006	4,022,754	1,474,285	Blackwell, J. Kenneth	2,435,384	Strickland, Ted	113,085	961,099 D	36.6%	60.5%	37.7%	62.3%
2002	3,228,992	1,865,007	Taft, Bob	1,236,924	Hagan, Timothy	127,061	628,083 R	57.8%	38.3%	60.1%	39.9%
1998	3,354,213	1,678,721	Taft, Bob	1,498,956	Fisher, Lee	176,536	179,765 R	50.0%	44.7%	52.8%	47.2%
1994	3,346,238	2,401,572	Voinovich, George V.	835,849	Burch, Robert L.	108,817	1,565,723 R	71.8%	25.0%	74.2%	25.8%
1990	3,477,650	1,938,103	Voinovich, George V.	1,539,416	Celebrezze, Anthony J.	131	398,687 R	55.7%	44.3%	55.7%	44.3%
1986	3,066,611	1,207,264	Rhodes, James A.	1,858,372	Celeste, Richard F.	975	651,108 D	39.4%	60.6%	39.4%	60.6%
1982	3,356,721	1,303,962	Brown, Clarence, Jr.	1,981,882	Celeste, Richard F.	70,877	677,920 D	38.8%	59.0%	39.7%	60.3%
1978	2,843,351	1,402,167	Rhodes, James A.	1,354,631	Celeste, Richard F.	86,553	47,536 R	49.3%	47.6%	50.9%	49.1%
1974	3,072,010	1,493,679	Rhodes, James A.	1,482,191	Gilligan, John J.	96,140	11,488 R	48.6%	48.2%	50.2%	49.8%
1970	3,184,133	1,382,659	Cloud, Roger	1,725,560	Gilligan, John J.	75,914	342,901 D	43.4%	54.2%	44.5%	55.5%
1966	2,887,331	1,795,277	Rhodes, James A.	1,092,054	Reams, Frazier, Jr.		703,223 R	62.2%	37.8%	62.2%	37.8%
1962	3,116,711	1,836,190	Rhodes, James A.	1,280,521	DiSalle, Michael V.		555,669 R	58.9%	41.1%	58.9%	41.1%
1958**	3,284,134	1,414,874	O'Neill, C. William	1,869,260	DiSalle, Michael V.		454,386 D	43.1%	56.9%	43.1%	56.9%
1956	3,542,091	1,984,988	O'Neill, C. William	1,557,103	DiSalle, Michael V.		427,885 R	56.0%	44.0%	56.0%	44.0%
1954	2,597,790	1,192,528	Rhodes, James A.	1,405,262	Lausche, Frank J.		212,734 D	45.9%	54.1%	45.9%	54.1%
1952	3,605,168	1,590,058	Taft, Charles P.	2,015,110	Lausche, Frank J.		425,052 D	44.1%	55.9%	44.1%	55.9%
1950	2,892,819	1,370,570	Ebright, Don H.	1,522,249	Lausche, Frank J.		151,679 D	47.4%	52.6%	47.4%	52.6%
1948	3,018,289	1,398,514	Herbert, Thomas J.	1,619,775	Lausche, Frank J.		221,261 D	46.3%	53.7%	46.3%	53.7%
1946	2,303,750	1,166,550	Herbert, Thomas J.	1,125,997	Lausche, Frank J.	11,203	40,553 R	50.6%	48.9%	50.9%	49.1%

**The term of office of Ohio's Governor was increased from two to four years effective with the 1958 election.

POSTWAR VOTE FOR SENATOR

Year	Total Vote	Republican		Democratic		Other Vote	Rep.-Dem. Plurality	Percentage			
								Total Vote		Major Vote	
		Vote	Candidate	Vote	Candidate			Rep.	Dem.	Rep.	Dem.
2010	3,815,098	2,168,742	Portman, Rob	1,503,297	Fisher, Lee	143,059	665,445 R	56.8%	39.4%	59.1%	40.9%
2006	4,019,236	1,761,037	DeWine, Mike	2,257,369	Brown, Sherrod	830	496,332 D	43.8%	56.2%	43.8%	56.2%
2004	5,425,823	3,464,356	Voinovich, George V.	1,961,171	Fingerhut, Eric D.	296	1,503,185 R	63.8%	36.1%	63.9%	36.1%
2000	4,448,801	2,665,512	DeWine, Mike	1,595,066	Celeste, Ted	188,223	1,070,446 R	59.9%	35.9%	62.6%	37.4%
1998	3,404,351	1,922,087	Voinovich, George V.	1,482,054	Boyle, Mary O.	210	440,033 R	56.5%	43.5%	56.5%	43.5%
1994	3,436,884	1,836,556	DeWine, Mike	1,348,213	Hyatt, Joel	252,115	488,343 R	53.4%	39.2%	57.7%	42.3%
1992	4,793,953	2,028,300	DeWine, Mike	2,444,419	Glenn, John H.	321,234	416,119 D	42.3%	51.0%	45.3%	54.7%
1988	4,352,905	1,872,716	Voinovich, George V.	2,480,038	Metzenbaum, Howard	151	607,322 D	43.0%	57.0%	43.0%	57.0%
1986	3,121,189	1,171,893	Kindness, Thomas N.	1,949,208	Glenn, John H.	88	777,315 D	37.5%	62.5%	37.5%	62.5%
1982	3,395,463	1,396,790	Pfeifer, Paul E.	1,923,767	Metzenbaum, Howard	74,906	526,977 D	41.1%	56.7%	42.1%	57.9%
1980	4,027,303	1,137,695	Betts, James E.	2,770,786	Glenn, John H.	118,822	1,633,091 D	28.2%	68.8%	29.1%	70.9%
1976	3,920,613	1,823,774	Taft, Robert A., Jr.	1,941,113	Metzenbaum, Howard	155,726	117,339 D	46.5%	49.5%	48.4%	51.6%
1974	2,987,951	918,133	Perk, Ralph J.	1,930,670	Glenn, John H.	139,148	1,012,537 D	30.7%	64.6%	32.2%	67.8%
1970	3,151,274	1,565,682	Taft, Robert A., Jr.	1,495,262	Metzenbaum, Howard	90,330	70,420 R	49.7%	47.4%	51.2%	48.8%
1968	3,743,121	1,928,964	Saxbe, William B.	1,814,152	Gilligan, John J.	5	114,812 R	51.5%	48.5%	51.5%	48.5%
1964	3,830,389	1,906,781	Taft, Robert A., Jr.	1,923,608	Young, Stephen M.		16,827 D	49.8%	50.2%	49.8%	50.2%
1962	2,994,986	1,151,173	Briley, John M.	1,843,813	Lausche, Frank J.		692,640 D	38.4%	61.6%	38.4%	61.6%
1958	3,149,410	1,497,199	Bricker, John W.	1,652,211	Young, Stephen M.		155,012 D	47.5%	52.5%	47.5%	52.5%
1956	3,525,499	1,660,910	Bender, George H.	1,864,589	Lausche, Frank J.		203,679 D	47.1%	52.9%	47.1%	52.9%
1954S	2,512,778	1,257,874	Bender, George H.	1,254,904	Burke, Thomas A.		2,970 R	50.1%	49.9%	50.1%	49.9%
1952	3,442,291	1,878,961	Bricker, John W.	1,563,330	DiSalle, Michael V.		315,631 R	54.6%	45.4%	54.6%	45.4%
1950	2,860,102	1,645,643	Taft, Robert A.	1,214,459	Ferguson, Joseph T.		431,184 R	57.5%	42.5%	57.5%	42.5%
1946	2,237,269	1,275,774	Bricker, John W.	947,610	Huffman, James W.	13,885	328,164 R	57.0%	42.4%	57.4%	42.6%

The 1954 election was for a short term to fill a vacancy.

OHIO

GOVERNOR 2010

2010 Census Population	County	Total Vote	Republican	Democratic	Other	Rep.-Dem. Plurality		Percentage			
								Total Vote		Major Vote	
								Rep.	Dem.	Rep.	Dem.
28,550	ADAMS	8,346	4,837	3,191	318	1,646	R	58.0%	38.2%	60.3%	39.7%
106,331	ALLEN	32,970	18,982	12,755	1,233	6,227	R	57.6%	38.7%	59.8%	40.2%
53,139	ASHLAND	17,385	10,586	5,897	902	4,689	R	60.9%	33.9%	64.2%	35.8%
101,497	ASHTABULA	29,748	12,582	15,128	2,038	2,546	D	42.3%	50.9%	45.4%	54.6%
64,757	ATHENS	17,129	4,525	12,073	531	7,548	D	26.4%	70.5%	27.3%	72.7%
45,949	AUGLAIZE	16,527	10,873	4,788	866	6,085	R	65.8%	29.0%	69.4%	30.6%
70,400	BELMONT	23,683	10,411	12,467	805	2,056	D	44.0%	52.6%	45.5%	54.5%
44,846	BROWN	13,315	7,803	4,894	618	2,909	R	58.6%	36.8%	61.5%	38.5%
368,130	BUTLER	119,539	74,942	40,153	4,444	34,789	R	62.7%	33.6%	65.1%	34.9%
28,836	CARROLL	9,966	5,002	4,272	692	730	R	50.2%	42.9%	53.9%	46.1%
40,097	CHAMPAIGN	13,514	7,688	5,137	689	2,551	R	56.9%	38.0%	59.9%	40.1%
138,333	CLARK	45,976	22,135	21,660	2,181	475	R	48.1%	47.1%	50.5%	49.5%
197,363	CLERMONT	63,070	42,763	17,490	2,817	25,273	R	67.8%	27.7%	71.0%	29.0%
42,040	CLINTON	12,123	7,621	3,836	666	3,785	R	62.9%	31.6%	66.5%	33.5%
107,841	COLUMBIANA	33,109	16,021	15,553	1,535	468	R	48.4%	47.0%	50.7%	49.3%
36,901	COSHOCTON	12,170	6,234	5,179	757	1,055	R	51.2%	42.6%	54.6%	45.4%
43,784	CRAWFORD	14,085	7,901	5,334	850	2,567	R	56.1%	37.9%	59.7%	40.3%
1,280,122	CUYAHOGA	414,785	148,611	251,251	14,923	102,640	D	35.8%	60.6%	37.2%	62.8%
52,959	DARKE	18,962	11,975	5,957	1,030	6,018	R	63.2%	31.4%	66.8%	33.2%
39,037	DEFIANCE	12,918	6,677	5,561	680	1,116	R	51.7%	43.0%	54.6%	45.4%
174,214	DELAWARE	68,792	45,285	21,988	1,519	23,297	R	65.8%	32.0%	67.3%	32.7%
77,079	ERIE	28,547	13,096	14,171	1,280	1,075	D	45.9%	49.6%	48.0%	52.0%
146,156	FAIRFIELD	50,361	29,744	18,795	1,822	10,949	R	59.1%	37.3%	61.3%	38.7%
29,030	FAYETTE	7,719	4,614	2,827	278	1,787	R	59.8%	36.6%	62.0%	38.0%
1,163,414	FRANKLIN	384,122	169,487	203,862	10,773	34,375	D	44.1%	53.1%	45.4%	54.6%
42,698	FULTON	14,599	7,798	6,131	670	1,667	R	53.4%	42.0%	56.0%	44.0%
30,934	GALLIA	9,593	4,809	4,553	231	256	R	50.1%	47.5%	51.4%	48.6%
93,389	GEAUGA	37,000	22,312	13,148	1,540	9,164	R	60.3%	35.5%	62.9%	37.1%
161,573	GREENE	58,428	34,564	21,561	2,303	13,003	R	59.2%	36.9%	61.6%	38.4%
40,087	GUERNSEY	12,150	5,900	5,594	656	306	R	48.6%	46.0%	51.3%	48.7%
802,374	HAMILTON	284,054	143,222	132,087	8,745	11,135	R	50.4%	46.5%	52.0%	48.0%
74,782	HANCOCK	24,574	15,063	8,450	1,061	6,613	R	61.3%	34.4%	64.1%	35.9%
32,058	HARDIN	8,979	4,904	3,502	573	1,402	R	54.6%	39.0%	58.3%	41.7%
15,864	HARRISON	5,672	2,548	2,840	284	292	D	44.9%	50.1%	47.3%	52.7%
28,215	HENRY	9,942	5,529	3,922	491	1,607	R	55.6%	39.4%	58.5%	41.5%
43,589	HIGHLAND	12,291	7,455	4,215	621	3,240	R	60.7%	34.3%	63.9%	36.1%
29,380	HOCKING	9,043	4,184	4,441	418	257	D	46.3%	49.1%	48.5%	51.5%
42,366	HOLMES	8,650	5,967	2,212	471	3,755	R	69.0%	25.6%	73.0%	27.0%
59,626	HURON	16,572	9,051	6,547	974	2,504	R	54.6%	39.5%	58.0%	42.0%
33,225	JACKSON	10,129	4,592	5,227	310	635	D	45.3%	51.6%	46.8%	53.2%
69,709	JEFFERSON	24,733	10,957	12,819	957	1,862	D	44.3%	51.8%	46.1%	53.9%
60,921	KNOX	20,475	12,371	7,044	1,060	5,327	R	60.4%	34.4%	63.7%	36.3%
230,041	LAKE	79,205	41,467	34,157	3,581	7,310	R	52.4%	43.1%	54.8%	45.2%
62,450	LAWRENCE	17,740	8,374	8,956	410	582	D	47.2%	50.5%	48.3%	51.7%
166,492	LICKING	59,470	35,073	21,892	2,505	13,181	R	59.0%	36.8%	61.6%	38.4%

OHIO

GOVERNOR 2010

2010 Census Population	County	Total Vote	Republican	Democratic	Other	Rep.-Dem. Plurality		Percentage			
								Total Vote		Major Vote	
								Rep.	Dem.	Rep.	Dem.
45,858	LOGAN	14,528	9,292	4,420	816	4,872	R	64.0%	30.4%	67.8%	32.2%
301,356	LORAIN	99,433	43,994	50,714	4,725	6,720	D	44.2%	51.0%	46.5%	53.5%
441,815	LUCAS	144,736	52,070	88,210	4,456	36,140	D	36.0%	60.9%	37.1%	62.9%
43,435	MADISON	12,672	7,623	4,545	504	3,078	R	60.2%	35.9%	62.6%	37.4%
238,823	MAHONING	85,506	26,566	56,228	2,712	29,662	D	31.1%	65.8%	32.1%	67.9%
66,501	MARION	20,077	10,535	8,517	1,025	2,018	R	52.5%	42.4%	55.3%	44.7%
172,332	MEDINA	63,016	36,407	23,761	2,848	12,646	R	57.8%	37.7%	60.5%	39.5%
23,770	MEIGS	6,952	3,322	3,430	200	108	D	47.8%	49.3%	49.2%	50.8%
40,814	MERCER	15,958	10,852	4,396	710	6,456	R	68.0%	27.5%	71.2%	28.8%
102,506	MIAMI	37,137	23,543	11,729	1,865	11,814	R	63.4%	31.6%	66.7%	33.3%
14,642	MONROE	5,315	2,102	3,063	150	961	D	39.5%	57.6%	40.7%	59.3%
535,153	MONTGOMERY	185,056	89,218	89,379	6,459	161	D	48.2%	48.3%	50.0%	50.0%
15,054	MORGAN	4,814	2,371	2,244	199	127	R	49.3%	46.6%	51.4%	48.6%
34,827	MORROW	11,748	7,078	3,989	681	3,089	R	60.2%	34.0%	64.0%	36.0%
86,074	MUSKINGUM	26,082	13,506	11,202	1,374	2,304	R	51.8%	42.9%	54.7%	45.3%
14,645	NOBLE	5,241	2,351	2,609	281	258	D	44.9%	49.8%	47.4%	52.6%
41,428	OTTAWA	15,890	7,350	7,945	595	595	D	46.3%	50.0%	48.1%	51.9%
19,614	PAULDING	6,877	3,695	2,795	387	900	R	53.7%	40.6%	56.9%	43.1%
36,058	PERRY	10,149	4,913	4,741	495	172	R	48.4%	46.7%	50.9%	49.1%
55,698	PICKAWAY	17,049	9,789	6,639	621	3,150	R	57.4%	38.9%	59.6%	40.4%
28,709	PIKE	8,775	3,549	4,940	286	1,391	D	40.4%	56.3%	41.8%	58.2%
161,419	PORTAGE	49,897	24,341	23,161	2,395	1,180	R	48.8%	46.4%	51.2%	48.8%
42,270	PREBLE	14,967	8,817	5,217	933	3,600	R	58.9%	34.9%	62.8%	37.2%
34,499	PUTNAM	13,226	8,210	4,446	570	3,764	R	62.1%	33.6%	64.9%	35.1%
124,475	RICHLAND	41,257	22,691	16,470	2,096	6,221	R	55.0%	39.9%	57.9%	42.1%
78,064	ROSS	22,044	10,246	10,949	849	703	D	46.5%	49.7%	48.3%	51.7%
60,944	SANDUSKY	19,678	9,326	9,261	1,091	65	R	47.4%	47.1%	50.2%	49.8%
79,499	SCIOTO	23,723	8,998	14,244	481	5,246	D	37.9%	60.0%	38.7%	61.3%
56,745	SENECA	17,661	8,716	7,790	1,155	926	R	49.4%	44.1%	52.8%	47.2%
49,423	SHELBY	17,798	11,402	5,355	1,041	6,047	R	64.1%	30.1%	68.0%	32.0%
375,586	STARK	128,267	63,779	58,492	5,996	5,287	R	49.7%	45.6%	52.2%	47.8%
541,781	SUMMIT	180,109	79,963	93,740	6,406	13,777	D	44.4%	52.0%	46.0%	54.0%
210,312	TRUMBULL	73,043	24,811	44,935	3,297	20,124	D	34.0%	61.5%	35.6%	64.4%
92,582	TUSCARAWAS	29,043	14,214	13,182	1,647	1,032	R	48.9%	45.4%	51.9%	48.1%
52,300	UNION	17,707	11,739	5,304	664	6,435	R	66.3%	30.0%	68.9%	31.1%
28,744	VAN WERT	9,897	6,396	3,014	487	3,382	R	64.6%	30.5%	68.0%	32.0%
13,435	VINTON	4,296	1,764	2,351	181	587	D	41.1%	54.7%	42.9%	57.1%
212,693	WARREN	79,762	54,536	22,271	2,955	32,265	R	68.4%	27.9%	71.0%	29.0%
61,778	WASHINGTON	21,223	10,230	10,408	585	178	D	48.2%	49.0%	49.6%	50.4%
114,520	WAYNE	36,551	21,243	13,490	1,818	7,753	R	58.1%	36.9%	61.2%	38.8%
37,642	WILLIAMS	12,188	6,610	4,931	647	1,679	R	54.2%	40.5%	57.3%	42.7%
125,488	WOOD	43,746	20,390	21,369	1,987	979	D	46.6%	48.8%	48.8%	51.2%
22,615	WYANDOT	7,215	4,103	2,666	446	1,437	R	56.9%	37.0%	60.6%	39.4%
11,536,504	TOTAL	3,852,469	1,889,186	1,812,059	151,224	77,127	R	49.0%	47.0%	51.0%	49.0%

OHIO

SENATOR 2010

2010 Census Population	County	Total Vote	Republican	Democratic	Other	Rep.-Dem. Plurality		Percentage			
								Total Vote		Major Vote	
								Rep.	Dem.	Rep.	Dem.
28,550	ADAMS	8,354	6,116	2,003	235	4,113	R	73.2%	24.0%	75.3%	24.7%
106,331	ALLEN	33,232	22,612	9,580	1,040	13,032	R	68.0%	28.8%	70.2%	29.8%
53,139	ASHLAND	17,224	12,216	4,198	810	8,018	R	70.9%	24.4%	74.4%	25.6%
101,497	ASHTABULA	29,870	15,242	12,740	1,888	2,502	R	51.0%	42.7%	54.5%	45.5%
64,757	ATHENS	16,929	5,913	10,037	979	4,124	D	34.9%	59.3%	37.1%	62.9%
45,949	AUGLAIZE	16,474	12,599	3,217	658	9,382	R	76.5%	19.5%	79.7%	20.3%
70,400	BELMONT	23,236	11,365	10,912	959	453	R	48.9%	47.0%	51.0%	49.0%
44,846	BROWN	13,531	10,013	3,143	375	6,870	R	74.0%	23.2%	76.1%	23.9%
368,130	BUTLER	118,593	83,453	31,521	3,619	51,932	R	70.4%	26.6%	72.6%	27.4%
28,836	CARROLL	9,813	5,858	3,420	535	2,438	R	59.7%	34.9%	63.1%	36.9%
40,097	CHAMPAIGN	13,484	9,289	3,631	564	5,658	R	68.9%	26.9%	71.9%	28.1%
138,333	CLARK	45,921	27,420	16,774	1,727	10,646	R	59.7%	36.5%	62.0%	38.0%
197,363	CLERMONT	64,523	50,072	12,521	1,930	37,551	R	77.6%	19.4%	80.0%	20.0%
42,040	CLINTON	12,191	9,230	2,527	434	6,703	R	75.7%	20.7%	78.5%	21.5%
107,841	COLUMBIANA	33,137	19,328	12,207	1,602	7,121	R	58.3%	36.8%	61.3%	38.7%
36,901	COSHOCTON	11,986	7,218	4,098	670	3,120	R	60.2%	34.2%	63.8%	36.2%
43,784	CRAWFORD	13,925	9,272	3,894	759	5,378	R	66.6%	28.0%	70.4%	29.6%
1,280,122	CUYAHOGA	416,500	167,763	235,795	12,942	68,032	D	40.3%	56.6%	41.6%	58.4%
52,959	DARKE	18,781	14,092	3,879	810	10,213	R	75.0%	20.7%	78.4%	21.6%
39,037	DEFIANCE	12,679	8,067	4,012	600	4,055	R	63.6%	31.6%	66.8%	33.2%
174,214	DELAWARE	67,701	47,854	17,742	2,105	30,112	R	70.7%	26.2%	73.0%	27.0%
77,079	ERIE	28,310	15,121	12,178	1,011	2,943	R	53.4%	43.0%	55.4%	44.6%
146,156	FAIRFIELD	49,445	32,989	14,189	2,267	18,800	R	66.7%	28.7%	69.9%	30.1%
29,030	FAYETTE	7,688	5,422	1,908	358	3,514	R	70.5%	24.8%	74.0%	26.0%
1,163,414	FRANKLIN	376,095	184,510	176,398	15,187	8,112	R	49.1%	46.9%	51.1%	48.9%
42,698	FULTON	14,356	9,506	4,270	580	5,236	R	66.2%	29.7%	69.0%	31.0%
30,934	GALLIA	9,241	5,753	3,149	339	2,604	R	62.3%	34.1%	64.6%	35.4%
93,389	GEAUGA	36,769	24,972	10,529	1,268	14,443	R	67.9%	28.6%	70.3%	29.7%
161,573	GREENE	58,067	39,326	16,705	2,036	22,621	R	67.7%	28.8%	70.2%	29.8%
40,087	GUERNSEY	11,942	7,162	4,174	606	2,988	R	60.0%	35.0%	63.2%	36.8%
802,374	HAMILTON	285,438	166,087	112,938	6,413	53,149	R	58.2%	39.6%	59.5%	40.5%
74,782	HANCOCK	24,300	17,833	5,545	922	12,288	R	73.4%	22.8%	76.3%	23.7%
32,058	HARDIN	8,803	5,866	2,467	470	3,399	R	66.6%	28.0%	70.4%	29.6%
15,864	HARRISON	5,588	2,880	2,426	282	454	R	51.5%	43.4%	54.3%	45.7%
28,215	HENRY	9,775	6,787	2,623	365	4,164	R	69.4%	26.8%	72.1%	27.9%
43,589	HIGHLAND	12,254	8,840	2,880	534	5,960	R	72.1%	23.5%	75.4%	24.6%
29,380	HOCKING	8,817	5,049	3,224	544	1,825	R	57.3%	36.6%	61.0%	39.0%
42,366	HOLMES	8,432	6,493	1,535	404	4,958	R	77.0%	18.2%	80.9%	19.1%
59,626	HURON	16,381	10,486	5,144	751	5,342	R	64.0%	31.4%	67.1%	32.9%
33,225	JACKSON	9,733	5,962	3,307	464	2,655	R	61.3%	34.0%	64.3%	35.7%
69,709	JEFFERSON	24,220	11,953	11,234	1,033	719	R	49.4%	46.4%	51.6%	48.4%
60,921	KNOX	20,274	13,790	5,305	1,179	8,485	R	68.0%	26.2%	72.2%	27.8%
230,041	LAKE	78,029	46,974	28,206	2,849	18,768	R	60.2%	36.1%	62.5%	37.5%
62,450	LAWRENCE	17,615	10,165	6,857	593	3,308	R	57.7%	38.9%	59.7%	40.3%
166,492	LICKING	58,236	37,997	17,156	3,083	20,841	R	65.2%	29.5%	68.9%	31.1%

OHIO

SENATOR 2010

2010 Census Population	County	Total Vote	Republican	Democratic	Other	Rep.-Dem. Plurality	Percentage			
							Total Vote		Major Vote	
							Rep.	Dem.	Rep.	Dem.
45,858	LOGAN	14,723	10,783	3,096	844	7,687 R	73.2%	21.0%	77.7%	22.3%
301,356	LORAIN	97,169	49,894	43,102	4,173	6,792 R	51.3%	44.4%	53.7%	46.3%
441,815	LUCAS	140,872	62,636	74,223	4,013	11,587 D	44.5%	52.7%	45.8%	54.2%
43,435	MADISON	12,679	8,848	3,161	670	5,687 R	69.8%	24.9%	73.7%	26.3%
238,823	MAHONING	83,928	33,152	47,708	3,068	14,556 D	39.5%	56.8%	41.0%	59.0%
66,501	MARION	19,756	12,296	6,191	1,269	6,105 R	62.2%	31.3%	66.5%	33.5%
172,332	MEDINA	61,717	40,115	19,330	2,272	20,785 R	65.0%	31.3%	67.5%	32.5%
23,770	MEIGS	6,940	4,117	2,533	290	1,584 R	59.3%	36.5%	61.9%	38.1%
40,814	MERCER	15,717	12,000	3,073	644	8,927 R	76.4%	19.6%	79.6%	20.4%
102,506	MIAMI	36,942	27,145	8,496	1,301	18,649 R	73.5%	23.0%	76.2%	23.8%
14,642	MONROE	5,270	2,315	2,738	217	423 D	43.9%	52.0%	45.8%	54.2%
535,153	MONTGOMERY	184,242	102,338	76,441	5,463	25,897 R	55.5%	41.5%	57.2%	42.8%
15,054	MORGAN	4,707	2,875	1,601	231	1,274 R	61.1%	34.0%	64.2%	35.8%
34,827	MORROW	11,542	7,915	2,909	718	5,006 R	68.6%	25.2%	73.1%	26.9%
86,074	MUSKINGUM	25,981	16,261	8,528	1,192	7,733 R	62.6%	32.8%	65.6%	34.4%
14,645	NOBLE	5,092	2,980	1,837	275	1,143 R	58.5%	36.1%	61.9%	38.1%
41,428	OTTAWA	15,997	9,299	6,193	505	3,106 R	58.1%	38.7%	60.0%	40.0%
19,614	PAULDING	6,719	4,167	2,236	316	1,931 R	62.0%	33.3%	65.1%	34.9%
36,058	PERRY	10,037	5,894	3,623	520	2,271 R	58.7%	36.1%	61.9%	38.1%
55,698	PICKAWAY	16,706	11,139	4,683	884	6,456 R	66.7%	28.0%	70.4%	29.6%
28,709	PIKE	8,612	4,602	3,689	321	913 R	53.4%	42.8%	55.5%	44.5%
161,419	PORTAGE	49,035	26,528	18,891	3,616	7,637 R	54.1%	38.5%	58.4%	41.6%
42,270	PREBLE	14,969	10,763	3,424	782	7,339 R	71.9%	22.9%	75.9%	24.1%
34,499	PUTNAM	13,201	9,950	2,833	418	7,117 R	75.4%	21.5%	77.8%	22.2%
124,475	RICHLAND	40,650	25,747	12,931	1,972	12,816 R	63.3%	31.8%	66.6%	33.4%
78,064	ROSS	21,650	12,629	7,954	1,067	4,675 R	58.3%	36.7%	61.4%	38.6%
60,944	SANDUSKY	19,628	11,939	6,754	935	5,185 R	60.8%	34.4%	63.9%	36.1%
79,499	SCIOTO	23,440	13,152	9,726	562	3,426 R	56.1%	41.5%	57.5%	42.5%
56,745	SENECA	17,716	11,069	5,732	915	5,337 R	62.5%	32.4%	65.9%	34.1%
49,423	SHELBY	17,907	13,470	3,752	685	9,718 R	75.2%	21.0%	78.2%	21.8%
375,586	STARK	126,811	72,403	49,604	4,804	22,799 R	57.1%	39.1%	59.3%	40.7%
541,781	SUMMIT	176,981	88,394	82,315	6,272	6,079 R	49.9%	46.5%	51.8%	48.2%
210,312	TRUMBULL	71,146	30,566	37,317	3,263	6,751 D	43.0%	52.5%	45.0%	55.0%
92,582	TUSCARAWAS	28,739	16,497	10,946	1,296	5,551 R	57.4%	38.1%	60.1%	39.9%
52,300	UNION	17,539	12,869	3,791	879	9,078 R	73.4%	21.6%	77.2%	22.8%
28,744	VAN WERT	9,946	7,195	2,330	421	4,865 R	72.3%	23.4%	75.5%	24.5%
13,435	VINTON	4,209	2,270	1,717	222	553 R	53.9%	40.8%	56.9%	43.1%
212,693	WARREN	79,262	60,795	16,355	2,112	44,440 R	76.7%	20.6%	78.8%	21.2%
61,778	WASHINGTON	20,923	12,512	7,572	839	4,940 R	59.8%	36.2%	62.3%	37.7%
114,520	WAYNE	36,064	24,331	10,197	1,536	14,134 R	67.5%	28.3%	70.5%	29.5%
37,642	WILLIAMS	11,990	8,082	3,410	498	4,672 R	67.4%	28.4%	70.3%	29.7%
125,488	WOOD	42,887	24,911	16,321	1,655	8,590 R	58.1%	38.1%	60.4%	39.6%
22,615	WYANDOT	7,165	4,984	1,836	345	3,148 R	69.6%	25.6%	73.1%	26.9%
11,536,504	TOTAL	3,815,098	2,168,742	1,503,297	143,059	665,445 R	56.8%	39.4%	59.1%	40.9%

OHIO

HOUSE OF REPRESENTATIVES

CD	Year	Total Vote	Republican Vote	Republican Candidate	Democratic Vote	Democratic Candidate	Other Vote	Rep.-Dem. Plurality		Total Vote Rep.	Total Vote Dem.	Major Vote Rep.	Major Vote Dem.
1	2010	201,518	103,770	CHABOT, STEVE*	92,672	DRIEHAUS, STEVE*	5,076	11,098	R	51.5%	46.0%	52.8%	47.2%
1	2008	296,290	140,683	CHABOT, STEVE*	155,455	DRIEHAUS, STEVE	152	14,772	D	47.5%	52.5%	47.5%	52.5%
1	2006	202,264	105,680	CHABOT, STEVE*	96,584	CRANLEY, JOHN		9,096	R	52.2%	47.8%	52.2%	47.8%
1	2004	289,863	173,430	CHABOT, STEVE*	116,235	HARRIS, GREG	198	57,195	R	59.8%	40.1%	59.9%	40.1%
1	2002	170,928	110,760	CHABOT, STEVE*	60,168	HARRIS, GREG		50,592	R	64.8%	35.2%	64.8%	35.2%
2	2010	237,845	139,027	SCHMIDT, JEAN*	82,431	YALAMANCHILI, SURYA	16,387	56,596	R	58.5%	34.7%	62.8%	37.2%
2	2008	331,624	148,671	SCHMIDT, JEAN*	124,213	WULSIN, VICTORIA	58,740	24,458	R	44.8%	37.5%	54.5%	45.5%
2	2006	238,081	120,112	SCHMIDT, JEAN*	117,595	WULSIN, VICTORIA	374	2,517	R	50.5%	49.4%	50.5%	49.5%
2	2004	316,760	227,102	PORTMAN, ROB*	89,598	SANDERS, CHARLES	60	137,504	R	71.7%	28.3%	71.7%	28.3%
2	2002	188,016	139,218	PORTMAN, ROB*	48,785	SANDERS, CHARLES	13	90,433	R	74.0%	25.9%	74.1%	25.9%
3	2010	224,084	152,629	TURNER, MICHAEL R.*	71,455	ROBERTS, JOE		81,174	R	68.1%	31.9%	68.1%	31.9%
3	2008	316,180	200,204	TURNER, MICHAEL R.*	115,976	MITAKIDES, JANE		84,228	R	63.3%	36.7%	63.3%	36.7%
3	2006	218,628	127,978	TURNER, MICHAEL R.*	90,650	CHEMA, RICHARD		37,328	R	58.5%	41.5%	58.5%	41.5%
3	2004	316,738	197,290	TURNER, MICHAEL R.*	119,448	MITAKIDES, JANE		77,842	R	62.3%	37.7%	62.3%	37.7%
3	2002	189,951	111,630	TURNER, MICHAEL R.	78,307	CARNE, RICK	14	33,323	R	58.8%	41.2%	58.8%	41.2%
4	2010	204,270	146,029	JORDAN, JIM*	50,533	LITT, DOUG	7,708	95,496	R	71.5%	24.7%	74.3%	25.7%
4	2008	285,653	186,154	JORDAN, JIM*	99,499	CARROLL, MIKE		86,655	R	65.2%	34.8%	65.2%	34.8%
4	2006	216,636	129,958	JORDAN, JIM	86,678	SIFERD, RICHARD E.		43,280	R	60.0%	40.0%	60.0%	40.0%
4	2004	286,345	167,807	OXLEY, MICHAEL G.*	118,538	KONOP, BEN		49,269	R	58.6%	41.4%	58.6%	41.4%
4	2002	177,727	120,001	OXLEY, MICHAEL G.*	57,726	CLARK, JIM		62,275	R	67.5%	32.5%	67.5%	32.5%
5	2010	207,453	140,703	LATTA, ROBERT E.*	54,919	FINKENBINER, CALEB	11,831	85,784	R	67.8%	26.5%	71.9%	28.1%
5	2008	294,745	188,905	LATTA, ROBERT E.*	105,840	MAYS, GEORGE F.		83,065	R	64.1%	35.9%	64.1%	35.9%
5	2006	228,357	129,813	GILLMOR, PAUL E.*	98,544	WEIRAUCH, ROBIN		31,269	R	56.8%	43.2%	56.8%	43.2%
5	2004	293,305	196,649	GILLMOR, PAUL E.*	96,656	WEIRAUCH, ROBIN		99,993	R	67.0%	33.0%	67.0%	33.0%
5	2002	188,254	126,286	GILLMOR, PAUL E.*	51,872	ANDERSON, ROGER	10,096	74,414	R	67.1%	27.6%	70.9%	29.1%
6	2010	205,575	103,170	JOHNSON, BILL	92,823	WILSON, CHARLES A.*	9,582	10,347	R	50.2%	45.2%	52.6%	47.4%
6	2008	283,110	92,968	STOBBS, RICHARD D.	176,330	WILSON, CHARLES A.*	13,812	83,362	D	32.8%	62.3%	34.5%	65.5%
6	2006	218,476	82,848	BLASDEL, CHUCK	135,628	WILSON, CHARLES A.		52,780	D	37.9%	62.1%	37.9%	62.1%
6	2004	223,989		—	223,844	STRICKLAND, TED*	145	223,844	D		99.9%		100.0%
6	2002	191,615	77,643	HALLECK, MIKE	113,972	STRICKLAND, TED*		36,329	D	40.5%	59.5%	40.5%	59.5%
7	2010	218,313	135,721	AUSTRIA, STEVE*	70,400	CONNER, BILL	12,192	65,321	R	62.2%	32.2%	65.8%	34.2%
7	2008	300,462	174,915	AUSTRIA, STEVE	125,547	NEUHARDT, SHAREN SWARTZ		49,368	R	58.2%	41.8%	58.2%	41.8%
7	2006	227,478	137,899	HOBSON, DAVID L.*	89,579	CONNER, WILLIAM R.		48,320	R	60.6%	39.4%	60.6%	39.4%
7	2004	287,151	186,534	HOBSON, DAVID L.*	100,617	ANASTASIO, KARA		85,917	R	65.0%	35.0%	65.0%	35.0%
7	2002	167,632	113,252	HOBSON, DAVID L.*	45,568	ANASTASIO, KARA	8,812	67,684	R	67.6%	27.2%	71.3%	28.7%
8	2010	217,436	142,731	BOEHNER, JOHN A.*	65,883	COUSSOULE, JUSTIN	8,822	76,848	R	65.6%	30.3%	68.4%	31.6%
8	2008	297,573	202,063	BOEHNER, JOHN A.*	95,510	VON STEIN, NICHOLAS A.		106,553	R	67.9%	32.1%	67.9%	32.1%
8	2006	214,503	136,863	BOEHNER, JOHN A.*	77,640	MEIER, MORT		59,223	R	63.8%	36.2%	63.8%	36.2%
8	2004	292,249	201,675	BOEHNER, JOHN A.*	90,574	HARDENBROOK, JEFF		111,101	R	69.0%	31.0%	69.0%	31.0%
8	2002	169,391	119,947	BOEHNER, JOHN A.*	49,444	HARDENBROOK, JEFF		70,503	R	70.8%	29.2%	70.8%	29.2%
9	2010	205,242	83,423	IOTT, RICH	121,819	KAPTUR, MARCY*		38,396	D	40.6%	59.4%	40.6%	59.4%
9	2008	298,566	76,512	LEAVITT, BRADLEY S.	222,054	KAPTUR, MARCY*		145,542	D	25.6%	74.4%	25.6%	74.4%
9	2006	208,999	55,119	LEAVITT, BRADLEY S.	153,880	KAPTUR, MARCY*		98,761	D	26.4%	73.6%	26.4%	73.6%
9	2004	301,132	95,983	KACZALA, LARRY A.	205,149	KAPTUR, MARCY*		109,166	D	31.9%	68.1%	31.9%	68.1%
9	2002	178,717	46,481	EMERY, ED	132,236	KAPTUR, MARCY*		85,755	D	26.0%	74.0%	26.0%	74.0%
10	2010	191,026	83,809	CORRIGAN, PETER	101,343	KUCINICH, DENNIS J.*	5,874	17,534	D	43.9%	53.1%	45.3%	54.7%
10	2008	275,809	107,918	TRAKAS, JIM	157,268	KUCINICH, DENNIS J.*	10,623	49,350	D	39.1%	57.0%	40.7%	59.3%
10	2006	208,389	69,996	DOVILLA, MICHAEL D.	138,393	KUCINICH, DENNIS J.*		68,397	D	33.6%	66.4%	33.6%	66.4%

OHIO

HOUSE OF REPRESENTATIVES

| CD | Year | Total Vote | Republican | | Democratic | | Other Vote | Rep.-Dem. Plurality | | Percentage | | | |
| | | | Vote | Candidate | Vote | Candidate | | | | Total Vote | | Major Vote | |
										Rep.	Dem.	Rep.	Dem.
10	2004	287,212	96,463	HERMAN, EDWARD FITZPATRICK	172,406	KUCINICH, DENNIS J.*	18,343	75,943	D	33.6%	60.0%	35.9%	64.1%
10	2002	175,536	41,778	HEBEN, JON	129,997	KUCINICH, DENNIS J.*	3,761	88,219	D	23.8%	74.1%	24.3%	75.7%
11	2010	168,447	28,754	PEKAREK, THOMAS	139,693	FUDGE, MARCIA L.*		110,939	D	17.1%	82.9%	17.1%	82.9%
11	2008	249,542	36,708	PEKAREK, THOMAS	212,667	FUDGE, MARCIA L.	167	175,959	D	14.7%	85.2%	14.7%	85.3%
11	2006	175,924	29,125	STRING, LINDSEY N.	146,799	JONES, STEPHANIE TUBBS*		117,674	D	16.6%	83.4%	16.6%	83.4%
11	2004	222,371		—	222,371	JONES, STEPHANIE TUBBS*		222,371	D		100.0%		100.0%
11	2002	152,736	36,146	PAPPANO, PATRICK	116,590	JONES, STEPHANIE TUBBS*		80,444	D	23.7%	76.3%	23.7%	76.3%
12	2010	269,180	150,163	TIBERI, PAT*	110,307	BROOKS, PAULA	8,710	39,856	R	55.8%	41.0%	57.7%	42.3%
12	2008	360,388	197,447	TIBERI, PAT*	152,234	ROBINSON, DAVID	10,707	45,213	R	54.8%	42.2%	56.5%	43.5%
12	2006	254,689	145,943	TIBERI, PAT*	108,746	SHAMANSKY, BOB		37,197	R	57.3%	42.7%	57.3%	42.7%
12	2004	321,046	198,912	TIBERI, PAT*	122,109	BROWN, EDWARD	25	76,803	R	62.0%	38.0%	62.0%	38.0%
12	2002	181,689	116,982	TIBERI, PAT*	64,707	BROWN, EDWARD		52,275	R	64.4%	35.6%	64.4%	35.6%
13	2010	213,173	94,367	GANLEY, TOM	118,806	SUTTON, BETTY*		24,439	D	44.3%	55.7%	44.3%	55.7%
13	2008	297,680	105,050	POTTER, DAVID S.	192,593	SUTTON, BETTY*	37	87,543	D	35.3%	64.7%	35.3%	64.7%
13	2006	221,561	85,922	FOLTIN, CRAIG	135,639	SUTTON, BETTY		49,717	D	38.8%	61.2%	38.8%	61.2%
13	2004	298,094	97,090	LUCAS, ROBERT	201,004	BROWN, SHERROD*		103,914	D	32.6%	67.4%	32.6%	67.4%
13	2002	178,382	55,357	OLIVEROS, ED	123,025	BROWN, SHERROD*		67,668	D	31.0%	69.0%	31.0%	69.0%
14	2010	230,865	149,878	LaTOURETTE, STEVEN C.*	72,604	O'NEILL, BILL	8,383	77,274	R	64.9%	31.4%	67.4%	32.6%
14	2008	323,213	188,488	LaTOURETTE, STEVEN C.*	125,214	O'NEILL, BILL	9,511	63,274	R	58.3%	38.7%	60.1%	39.9%
14	2006	250,322	144,069	LaTOURETTE, STEVEN C.*	97,753	KATZ, LEWIS R.	8,500	46,316	R	57.6%	39.1%	59.6%	40.4%
14	2004	321,366	201,652	LaTOURETTE, STEVEN C.*	119,714	CAFARO, CAPRI S.		81,938	R	62.7%	37.3%	62.7%	37.3%
14	2002	186,372	134,413	LaTOURETTE, STEVEN C.*	51,846	BLANCHARD, DALE	113	82,567	R	72.1%	27.8%	72.2%	27.8%
15	2010	220,596	119,471	STIVERS, STEVE	91,077	KILROY, MARY JO*	10,048	28,394	R	54.2%	41.3%	56.7%	43.3%
15	2008	303,838	137,272	STIVERS, STEVE	139,584	KILROY, MARY JO	26,982	2,312	D	45.2%	45.9%	49.6%	50.4%
15	2006	220,567	110,714	PRYCE, DEBORAH*	109,659	KILROY, MARY JO	194	1,055	R	50.2%	49.7%	50.2%	49.8%
15	2004	277,435	166,520	PRYCE, DEBORAH*	110,915	BROWN, MARK		55,605	R	60.0%	40.0%	60.0%	40.0%
15	2002	162,479	108,193	PRYCE, DEBORAH*	54,286	BROWN, MARK		53,907	R	66.6%	33.4%	66.6%	33.4%
16	2010	220,137	114,652	RENACCI, JIM	90,833	BOCCIERI, JOHN A.*	14,652	23,819	R	52.1%	41.3%	55.8%	44.2%
16	2008	305,337	136,293	SCHURING, KIRK	169,044	BOCCIERI, JOHN A.		32,751	D	44.6%	55.4%	44.6%	55.4%
16	2006	235,122	137,167	REGULA, RALPH*	97,955	SHAW, THOMAS		39,212	R	58.3%	41.7%	58.3%	41.7%
16	2004	304,361	202,544	REGULA, RALPH*	101,817	SEEMANN, JEFF		100,727	R	66.5%	33.5%	66.5%	33.5%
16	2002	188,378	129,734	REGULA, RALPH*	58,644	RICE, JIM		71,090	R	68.9%	31.1%	68.9%	31.1%
17	2010	190,666	57,352	GRAHAM, JIM	102,758	RYAN, TIM*	30,556	45,406	D	30.1%	53.9%	35.8%	64.2%
17	2008	280,112	61,216	GRASSELL, DUANE V.	218,896	RYAN, TIM*		157,680	D	21.9%	78.1%	21.9%	78.1%
17	2006	212,294	41,925	MANNING, DON, III	170,369	RYAN, TIM*		128,444	D	19.7%	80.3%	19.7%	80.3%
17	2004	275,671	62,871	CUSIMANO, FRANK V.	212,800	RYAN, TIM*		149,929	D	22.8%	77.2%	22.8%	77.2%
17	2002	184,674	62,188	BENJAMIN, ANN WOMER	94,441	RYAN, TIM	28,045	32,253	D	33.7%	51.1%	39.7%	60.3%
18	2010	199,448	107,426	GIBBS, BOB	80,756	SPACE, ZACK*	11,266	26,670	R	53.9%	40.5%	57.1%	42.9%
18	2008	274,218	110,031	DAILEY, FRED	164,187	SPACE, ZACK*		54,156	D	40.1%	59.9%	40.1%	59.9%
18	2006	208,905	79,259	PADGETT, JOY	129,646	SPACE, ZACK		50,387	D	37.9%	62.1%	37.9%	62.1%
18	2004	268,420	177,600	NEY, BOB*	90,820	THOMAS, BRIAN R.		86,780	R	66.2%	33.8%	66.2%	33.8%
18	2002	125,546	125,546	NEY, BOB*		—		125,546	R	100.0%		100.0%	
TOTAL	2010	3,825,274	2,053,075		1,611,112		161,087	441,963	R	53.7%	42.1%	56.0%	44.0%
TOTAL	2008	5,374,340	2,491,498		2,752,111		130,731	260,613	D	46.4%	51.2%	47.5%	52.5%
TOTAL	2006	3,961,195	1,870,390		2,081,737		9,068	211,347	D	47.2%	52.6%	47.3%	52.7%
TOTAL	2004	5,183,508	2,650,122		2,514,615		18,771	135,507	R	51.1%	48.5%	51.3%	48.7%
TOTAL	2002	3,158,023	1,775,555		1,331,614		50,854	443,941	R	56.2%	42.2%	57.1%	42.9%

An asterisk (*) denotes incumbent.

OHIO

GENERAL AND PRIMARY ELECTION

2010 GENERAL ELECTION:

Governor Other vote was 92,116 Libertarian (Ken Matesz); 58,475 Green (Dennis Spisak); 633 write-in (David Sargent).

Senator Other vote was 65,856 Constitution (Eric Deaton); 50,101 Independent (Michael Pryce); 26,454 Socialist (Daniel LaBotz); 648 write-in (Arthur Sullivan).

House Other vote was:

CD 1 3,076 Libertarian (Jim Berns);2,000 Green (Rich Stevenson).
CD 2 16,259 Libertarian (Marc Johnston);128 write-in (Randy Conover).
CD 3
CD 4 7,708 Libertarian (Donald Kissick).
CD 5 11,831 Libertarian (Brian Smith).
CD 6 5,077 Constitution (Richard Cadle); 4,505 Libertarian (Martin Elsass).
CD 7 9,381 Libertarian (John Anderson); 2,811 Constitution (David Easton).
CD 8 5,121 Libertarian (David Harlow); 3,701 Constitution (James Condit).
CD 9
CD 10 5,874 Libertarian (Jeff Goggins).
CD 11
CD 12 8,710 Libertarian (Travis Irvine).
CD 13
CD 14 8,383 Libertarian (John Jelenic).
CD 15 6,116 Libertarian (William Kammerer); 3,887 Constitution (David Ryon); 45 write-in (Bill Buckel).
CD 16 14,585 Libertarian (Jeffrey Blevins); 67 write-in (Robert Ross).
CD 17 30,556 Independent (James Traficant).
CD 18 11,246 Constitution (Lindsey Sutton); 20 write-in (Mark Pitrone).

2010 PRIMARY ELECTIONS

Primary	May 4, 2010	**Registration** (as of May 4, 2010)	8,013,558	No Formal System of Party Registration

Primary Type Open—Any registered voter could participate in the primary of either party. However, records are kept of voter participation in recent primaries, and voters who recently cast a ballot in one party's primary could be challenged if they attempted to participate in the other party's primary. They could be asked to sign an affidavit affirming the fact that they were voting in the opposing party's primary and would become identified with that party because of their primary ballot cast.

OHIO

GENERAL AND PRIMARY ELECTIONS

	REPUBLICAN PRIMARIES			DEMOCRATIC PRIMARIES		
Governor	John Kasich	746,719	100.0%	Ted Strickland*	630,785	100.0%
Senator	Rob Portman	667,369	100.0%	Lee Fisher	380,189	55.6%
				Jennifer Brunner	304,026	44.4%
				TOTAL	*684,215*	
Congressional District 1	Steve Chabot	33,544	100.0%	Steve Driehaus*	20,628	82.9%
				Eric Wilson	4,241	17.1%
				TOTAL	*24,869*	
Congressional District 2	Jean Schmidt*	36,214	61.7%	Surya Yalamanchili	10,342	41.1%
	C. Michael Kilburn	13,007	22.2%	David Krikorian	9,388	37.4%
	Debbi Alsfelder	5,235	8.9%	Jim Parker	5,404	21.5%
	Tim Martz	4,225	7.2%			
	TOTAL	*58,681*		*TOTAL*	*25,134*	
Congressional District 3	Michael R. Turner*	50,317	85.9%	Mark MacNealy	25,365	100.0%
	Rene Oberer	8,267	14.1%			
	TOTAL	*58,584*		*Mark MacNealy withdrew from the race after the primary and a special primary election was held to select a new Democratic nominee.*		
				SPECIAL PRIMARY		
				Joe Roberts	2,561	44.5%
				Guy Fogle	2,123	36.9%
				David Esrati	1,077	18.7%
				TOTAL	*5,761*	
Congressional District 4	Jim Jordan*	56,093	100.0%	Doug Litt	18,250	100.0%
Congressional District 5	Robert E. Latta*	42,827	83.0%	Caleb Finkenbiner	18,442	100.0%
	Robert Wallis	8,754	17.0%			
	TOTAL	*51,581*				
Congressional District 6	Bill Johnson	14,103	42.5%	Charles A. Wilson*	34,772	68.9%
	Donald Allen	12,406	37.4%	Jim Renner	15,674	31.1%
	Richard Stobbs	6,637	20.0%			
	TOTAL	*33,146*		*TOTAL*	*50,446*	
Congressional District 7	Steve Austria*	46,072	82.9%	Bill Conner	12,780	46.4%
	John Mitchel	9,535	17.1%	Olivia Freeman	10,760	39.1%
				James Barton	4,010	14.6%
	TOTAL	*55,607*		*TOTAL*	*27,550*	
Congressional District 8	John A. Boehner*	50,555	84.7%	Justin Coussoule	18,118	100.0%
	Thomas McMasters	6,266	10.5%			
	Manfred Schreyer	2,890	4.8%			
	TOTAL	*59,711*				
Congressional District 9	Rich Iott	20,675	71.2%	Marcy Kaptur*	33,637	86.5%
	Jack Smith	8,348	28.8%	Dale Terry	5,256	13.5%
	TOTAL	*29,023*		*TOTAL*	*38,893*	
Congressional District 10	Peter Corrigan	16,678	76.0%	Dennis J. Kucinich*	47,976	100.0%
	W. Benjamin Franklin	5,275	24.0%			
	TOTAL	*21,953*				
Congressional District 11	Thomas Pekarek	237	100.0%	Marcia L. Fudge*	47,773	85.4%
				Daniel Reilly	5,385	9.6%
				Isaac Powell	2,783	5.0%
				TOTAL	*55,941*	

332

OHIO

GENERAL AND PRIMARY ELECTIONS

	REPUBLICAN PRIMARIES			DEMOCRATIC PRIMARIES		
Congressional District 12	Pat Tiberi*	53,632	86.4%	Paula Brooks	37,802	
	Andrew Zukowski	8,442	13.6%			
	TOTAL	62,074				
Congressional District 13	Tom Ganley	24,757	74.3%	Betty Sutton*	37,460	79.4%
	Bill Haney	2,278	6.8%	Justin Wooden	9,706	20.6%
	Todd Sharkey	2,221	6.7%			
	Jason Meade	1,761	5.3%			
	Jim Hrubik	1,704	5.1%			
	James Brihan	607	1.8%			
	TOTAL	33,328		TOTAL	47,166	
Congressional District 14	Steven C. LaTourette*	39,190	100.0%	Bill O'Neill	19,013	62.4%
				John Greene	5,737	18.8%
				Dale Blanchard	5,704	18.7%
				TOTAL	30,454	
Congressional District 15	Steve Stivers	39,963	82.3%	Mary Jo Kilroy*	36,435	100.0%
	John Adams	5,894	12.1%			
	Ralph Applegate	2,708	5.6%			
	TOTAL	48,565				
Congressional District 16	Jim Renacci	30,358	49.2%	John A. Boccieri*	31,507	100.0%
	Matt Miller	24,322	39.5%			
	Paul Schiffer	5,048	8.2%			
	H. Doyle Smith	1,919	3.1%			
	TOTAL	61,647				
Congressional District 17	Jim Graham	12,922	71.7%	Tim Ryan*	48,750	78.7%
	M. Henderson	5,097	28.3%	Dan Moadus	7,520	12.1%
				Robert Crow	5,638	9.1%
	TOTAL	18,019		TOTAL	61,908	
Congressional District 18	Bob Gibbs	11,037	20.9%	Zack Space*	28,743	100.0%
	Fred Dailey	10,881	20.6%			
	Jeanette Moll	10,013	19.0%			
	Ron Hood	8,204	15.6%			
	Dave Daubenmire	6,288	11.9%			
	Hombre Liggett	4,065	7.7%			
	Michael Royer	1,318	2.5%			
	Beau Bromberg	894	1.7%			
	TOTAL	52,700				

An asterisk (*) denotes incumbent. A special Democratic primary was held in the 3rd Congressional District July 13, 2010, to fill a vacancy on the general election ballot.

OKLAHOMA

Congressional districts first established for elections held in 2002
5 members

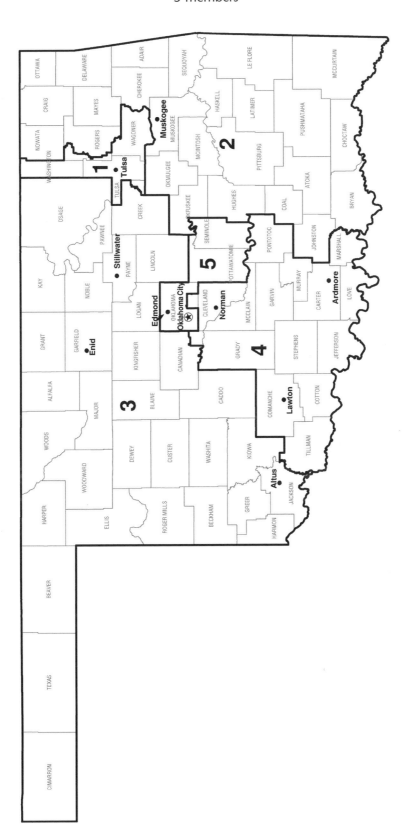

OKLAHOMA

GOVERNOR
Mary Fallin (R). Elected 2010 to a four-year term.

SENATORS (2 Republicans)
Tom Coburn (R). Reelected 2010 to a six-year term. Previously elected 2004.

James M. Inhofe (R). Reelected 2008 to a six-year term. Previously elected 2002,1996 and 1994 to fill out the remaining two years of the term vacated when David L. Boren (D) resigned to become president of the University of Oklahoma.

REPRESENTATIVES (4 Republicans,1 Democrat)

1. John Sullivan (R)
2. Dan Boren (D)

3. Frank D. Lucas (R)
4. Tom Cole (R)

5. James Lankford (R)

POSTWAR VOTE FOR PRESIDENT

		Republican		Democratic		Other	Rep.-Dem.	Total Vote		Major Vote	
Year	Total Vote	Vote	Candidate	Vote	Candidate	Vote	Plurality	Rep.	Dem.	Rep.	Dem.
2008	1,462,661	960,165	McCain, John	502,496	Obama, Barack		457,669 R	65.6%	34.4%	65.6%	34.4%
2004	1,463,758	959,792	Bush, George W.	503,966	Kerry, John		455,826 R	65.6%	34.4%	65.6%	34.4%
2000	1,234,229	744,337	Bush, George W.	474,276	Gore, Al	15,616	270,061 R	60.3%	38.4%	61.1%	38.9%
1996**	1,206,713	582,315	Dole, Bob	488,105	Clinton, Bill	136,293	94,210 R	48.3%	40.4%	54.4%	45.6%
1992**	1,390,359	592,929	Bush, George	473,066	Clinton, Bill	324,364	119,863 R	42.6%	34.0%	55.6%	44.4%
1988	1,171,036	678,367	Bush, George	483,423	Dukakis, Michael S.	9,246	194,944 R	57.9%	41.3%	58.4%	41.6%
1984	1,255,676	861,530	Reagan, Ronald	385,080	Mondale, Walter F.	9,066	476,450 R	68.6%	30.7%	69.1%	30.9%
1980**	1,149,708	695,570	Reagan, Ronald	402,026	Carter, Jimmy	52,112	293,544 R	60.5%	35.0%	63.4%	36.6%
1976	1,092,251	545,708	Ford, Gerald R.	532,442	Carter, Jimmy	14,101	13,266 R	50.0%	48.7%	50.6%	49.4%
1972	1,029,900	759,025	Nixon, Richard M.	247,147	McGovern, George S.	23,728	511,878 R	73.7%	24.0%	75.4%	24.6%
1968**	943,086	449,697	Nixon, Richard M.	301,658	Humphrey, Hubert H.	191,731	148,039 R	47.7%	32.0%	59.9%	40.1%
1964	932,499	412,665	Goldwater, Barry M.	519,834	Johnson, Lyndon B.		107,169 D	44.3%	55.7%	44.3%	55.7%
1960	903,150	533,039	Nixon, Richard M.	370,111	Kennedy, John F.		162,928 R	59.0%	41.0%	59.0%	41.0%
1956	859,350	473,769	Eisenhower, Dwight D.	385,581	Stevenson, Adlai E.		88,188 R	55.1%	44.9%	55.1%	44.9%
1952	948,984	518,045	Eisenhower, Dwight D.	430,939	Stevenson, Adlai E.		87,106 R	54.6%	45.4%	54.6%	45.4%
1948	721,599	268,817	Dewey, Thomas E.	452,782	Truman, Harry S.		183,965 D	37.3%	62.7%	37.3%	62.7%

**In past elections, the other vote included: 1996 -130,788 Reform (Ross Perot); 1992 - 319,878 Independent (Perot); 1980 - 38,284 Independent (John Anderson); 1968 - 191,731 American Independent (George Wallace).

OKLAHOMA

POSTWAR VOTE FOR GOVERNOR

		Republican		Democratic		Other	Rep.-Dem.	Percentage			
	Total							Total Vote		Major Vote	
Year	Vote	Vote	Candidate	Vote	Candidate	Vote	Plurality	Rep.	Dem.	Rep.	Dem.
2010	1,034,767	625,506	Fallin, Mary	409,261	Askins, Jari		216,245 R	60.4%	39.6%	60.4%	39.6%
2006	926,462	310,327	Istook, Ernest	616,135	Henry, Brad		305,808 D	33.5%	66.5%	33.5%	66.5%
2002**	1,035,620	441,277	Largent, Steve	448,143	Henry, Brad	146,200	6,866 D	42.6%	43.3%	49.6%	50.4%
1998	873,585	505,498	Keating, Frank	357,552	Boyd, Laura	10,535	147,946 R	57.9%	40.9%	58.6%	41.4%
1994**	995,012	466,740	Keating, Frank	294,936	Mildren, Jack	233,336	171,804 R	46.9%	29.6%	61.3%	38.7%
1990	911,314	297,584	Price, Bill	523,196	Walters, David	90,534	225,612 D	32.7%	57.4%	36.3%	63.7%
1986	909,925	431,762	Bellmon, Henry	405,295	Walters, David	72,868	26,467 R	47.5%	44.5%	51.6%	48.4%
1982	883,130	332,207	Daxon, Tom	548,159	Nigh, George	2,764	215,952 D	37.6%	62.1%	37.7%	62.3%
1978	777,414	367,055	Shotts, Ron	402,240	Nigh, George	8,119	35,185 D	47.2%	51.7%	47.7%	52.3%
1974	804,848	290,459	Inhofe, James M.	514,389	Boren, David L.		223,930 D	36.1%	63.9%	36.1%	63.9%
1970	698,790	336,157	Bartlett, Dewey F.	338,338	Hall, David	24,295	2,181 D	48.1%	48.4%	49.8%	50.2%
1966	677,258	377,078	Bartlett, Dewey F.	296,328	Moore, Preston J.	3,852	80,750 R	55.7%	43.8%	56.0%	44.0%
1962	709,763	392,316	Bellmon, Henry	315,357	Atkinson, W. P.	2,090	76,959 R	55.3%	44.4%	55.4%	44.6%
1958	538,839	107,495	Ferguson, Phil	399,504	Edmondson, J. Howard	31,840	292,009 D	19.9%	74.1%	21.2%	78.8%
1954	609,194	251,808	Sparks, Reuben K.	357,386	Gary, Raymond		105,578 D	41.3%	58.7%	41.3%	58.7%
1950	644,276	313,205	Ferguson, Jo O.	329,308	Murray, Johnston	1,763	16,103 D	48.6%	51.1%	48.7%	51.3%
1946	494,599	227,426	Flynn, Olney F.	259,491	Turner, Roy J.	7,682	32,065 D	46.0%	52.5%	46.7%	53.3%

**In past elections, the other vote included: 2002 - 146,200 Independent (Gary L. Richardson); 1994 - 233,336 Independent (Wes Watkins).

POSTWAR VOTE FOR SENATOR

		Republican		Democratic		Other	Rep.-Dem.	Percentage			
	Total							Total Vote		Major Vote	
Year	Vote	Vote	Candidate	Vote	Candidate	Vote	Plurality	Rep.	Dem.	Rep.	Dem.
2010	1,017,151	718,482	Coburn, Tom	265,814	Rogers, Jim	32,855	452,668 R	70.6%	26.1%	73.0%	27.0%
2008	1,346,819	763,375	Inhofe, James M.	527,736	Rice, Andrew	55,708	235,639 R	56.7%	39.2%	59.1%	40.9%
2004	1,446,846	763,433	Coburn, Tom	596,750	Carson, Brad	86,663	166,683 R	52.8%	41.2%	43.9%	56.1%
2002	1,018,424	583,579	Inhofe, James M.	369,789	Walters, David	65,056	213,790 R	57.3%	36.3%	61.2%	38.8%
1998	859,713	570,682	Nickles, Don	268,898	Carroll, Don E.	20,133	301,784 R	66.4%	31.3%	68.0%	32.0%
1996	1,183,150	670,610	Inhofe, James M.	474,162	Boren, Jim	38,378	196,448 R	56.7%	40.1%	58.6%	41.4%
1994S	982,430	542,390	Inhofe, James M.	392,488	McCurdy, Dave	47,552	149,902 R	55.2%	40.0%	58.0%	42.0%
1992	1,294,423	757,876	Nickles, Don	494,350	Lewis, Steve	42,197	263,526 R	58.5%	38.2%	60.5%	39.5%
1990	884,498	148,814	Jones, Stephen	735,684	Boren, David L.		586,870 D	16.8%	83.2%	16.8%	83.2%
1986	893,666	493,436	Nickles, Don	400,230	Jones, James R.		93,206 R	55.2%	44.8%	55.2%	44.8%
1984	1,197,937	280,638	Crozier, Will E.	906,131	Boren, David L.	11,168	625,493 D	23.4%	75.6%	23.6%	76.4%
1980	1,098,294	587,252	Nickles, Don	478,283	Coats, Andrew	32,759	108,969 R	53.5%	43.5%	55.1%	44.9%
1978	754,264	247,857	Kamm, Robert B.	493,953	Boren, David L.	12,454	246,096 D	32.9%	65.5%	33.4%	66.6%
1974	791,809	390,997	Bellmon, Henry	387,162	Edmondson, Ed	13,650	3,835 R	49.4%	48.9%	50.2%	49.8%
1972	1,005,148	516,934	Bartlett, Dewey F.	478,212	Edmondson, Ed	10,002	38,722 R	51.4%	47.6%	51.9%	48.1%
1968	909,119	470,120	Bellmon, Henry	419,658	Monroney, A. S. Mike	19,341	50,462 R	51.7%	46.2%	52.8%	47.2%
1966	638,742	295,585	Patterson, Pat J.	343,157	Harris, Fred R.		47,572 D	46.3%	53.7%	46.3%	53.7%
1964S	912,174	445,392	Wilkinson, Bud	466,782	Harris, Fred R.		21,390 D	48.8%	51.2%	48.8%	51.2%
1962	664,712	307,966	Crawford, B. Hayden	353,890	Monroney, A. S. Mike	2,856	45,924 D	46.3%	53.2%	46.5%	53.5%
1960	864,475	385,646	Crawford, B. Hayden	474,116	Kerr, Robert S.	4,713	88,470 D	44.6%	54.8%	44.9%	55.1%
1956	831,142	371,146	McKeever, Douglas	459,996	Monroney, A. S. Mike		88,850 D	44.7%	55.3%	44.7%	55.3%
1954	600,120	262,013	Mock, Fred M.	335,127	Kerr, Robert S.	2,980	73,114 D	43.7%	55.8%	43.9%	56.1%
1950	631,177	285,224	Alexander, W. H.	345,953	Monroney, A. S. Mike		60,729 D	45.2%	54.8%	45.2%	54.8%
1948	708,931	265,169	Rizley, Ross	441,654	Kerr, Robert S.	2,108	176,485 D	37.4%	62.3%	37.5%	62.5%

**The 1964 and 1994 elections were for short terms to fill vacancies.

OKLAHOMA
GOVERNOR 2010

2000 Census Population	County	Total Vote	Republican	Democratic	Other	Rep.-Dem. Plurality	Percentage Total Vote Rep.	Dem.	Major Vote Rep.	Dem.
22,683	ADAIR	5,524	3,023	2,501		522 R	54.7%	45.3%	54.7%	45.3%
5,642	ALFALFA	2,038	1,301	737		564 R	63.8%	36.2%	63.8%	36.2%
14,182	ATOKA	3,731	2,231	1,500		731 R	59.8%	40.2%	59.8%	40.2%
5,636	BEAVER	1,885	1,564	321		1,243 R	83.0%	17.0%	83.0%	17.0%
22,119	BECKHAM	5,465	3,471	1,994		1,477 R	63.5%	36.5%	63.5%	36.5%
11,943	BLAINE	3,161	2,061	1,100		961 R	65.2%	34.8%	65.2%	34.8%
42,416	BRYAN	10,461	6,115	4,346		1,769 R	58.5%	41.5%	58.5%	41.5%
29,600	CADDO	7,325	3,723	3,602		121 R	50.8%	49.2%	50.8%	49.2%
115,541	CANADIAN	34,928	24,964	9,964		15,000 R	71.5%	28.5%	71.5%	28.5%
47,557	CARTER	12,939	8,478	4,461		4,017 R	65.5%	34.5%	65.5%	34.5%
46,987	CHEROKEE	11,459	5,850	5,609		241 R	51.1%	48.9%	51.1%	48.9%
15,205	CHOCTAW	4,070	2,227	1,843		384 R	54.7%	45.3%	54.7%	45.3%
2,475	CIMARRON	997	734	263		471 R	73.6%	26.4%	73.6%	26.4%
255,755	CLEVELAND	73,264	42,797	30,467		12,330 R	58.4%	41.6%	58.4%	41.6%
5,925	COAL	2,010	1,052	958		94 R	52.3%	47.7%	52.3%	47.7%
124,098	COMANCHE	21,777	10,827	10,950		123 D	49.7%	50.3%	49.7%	50.3%
6,193	COTTON	1,825	818	1,007		189 D	44.8%	55.2%	44.8%	55.2%
15,029	CRAIG	4,304	2,470	1,834		636 R	57.4%	42.6%	57.4%	42.6%
69,967	CREEK	20,411	13,377	7,034		6,343 R	65.5%	34.5%	65.5%	34.5%
27,469	CUSTER	7,715	5,061	2,654		2,407 R	65.6%	34.4%	65.6%	34.4%
41,487	DELAWARE	11,431	7,304	4,127		3,177 R	63.9%	36.1%	63.9%	36.1%
4,810	DEWEY	1,864	1,307	557		750 R	70.1%	29.9%	70.1%	29.9%
4,151	ELLIS	1,520	1,105	415		690 R	72.7%	27.3%	72.7%	27.3%
60,580	GARFIELD	16,833	11,515	5,318		6,197 R	68.4%	31.6%	68.4%	31.6%
27,576	GARVIN	8,895	5,254	3,641		1,613 R	59.1%	40.9%	59.1%	40.9%
52,431	GRADY	15,772	10,031	5,741		4,290 R	63.6%	36.4%	63.6%	36.4%
4,527	GRANT	1,812	1,199	613		586 R	66.2%	33.8%	66.2%	33.8%
6,239	GREER	1,575	892	683		209 R	56.6%	43.4%	56.6%	43.4%
2,922	HARMON	754	420	334		86 R	55.7%	44.3%	55.7%	44.3%
3,685	HARPER	1,230	899	331		568 R	73.1%	26.9%	73.1%	26.9%
12,769	HASKELL	3,426	1,901	1,525		376 R	55.5%	44.5%	55.5%	44.5%
14,003	HUGHES	3,523	1,881	1,642		239 R	53.4%	46.6%	53.4%	46.6%
26,446	JACKSON	6,000	3,950	2,050		1,900 R	65.8%	34.2%	65.8%	34.2%
6,472	JEFFERSON	1,824	881	943		62 D	48.3%	51.7%	48.3%	51.7%
10,957	JOHNSTON	2,944	1,713	1,231		482 R	58.2%	41.8%	58.2%	41.8%
46,562	KAY	13,626	8,656	4,970		3,686 R	63.5%	36.5%	63.5%	36.5%
15,034	KINGFISHER	4,799	3,504	1,295		2,209 R	73.0%	27.0%	73.0%	27.0%
9,446	KIOWA	2,674	1,424	1,250		174 R	53.3%	46.7%	53.3%	46.7%
11,154	LATIMER	3,077	1,610	1,467		143 R	52.3%	47.7%	52.3%	47.7%
50,384	LE FLORE	12,990	7,040	5,950		1,090 R	54.2%	45.8%	54.2%	45.8%
34,273	LINCOLN	10,814	6,976	3,838		3,138 R	64.5%	35.5%	64.5%	35.5%
41,848	LOGAN	12,946	8,848	4,098		4,750 R	68.3%	31.7%	68.3%	31.7%
9,423	LOVE	2,661	1,554	1,107		447 R	58.4%	41.6%	58.4%	41.6%
34,506	MCCLAIN	11,065	7,248	3,817		3,431 R	65.5%	34.5%	65.5%	34.5%
33,151	MCCURTAIN	8,347	4,312	4,035		277 R	51.7%	48.3%	51.7%	48.3%
20,252	MCINTOSH	6,165	3,244	2,921		323 R	52.6%	47.4%	52.6%	47.4%
7,527	MAJOR	3,012	2,221	791		1,430 R	73.7%	26.3%	73.7%	26.3%
15,840	MARSHALL	4,013	2,528	1,485		1,043 R	63.0%	37.0%	63.0%	37.0%
41,259	MAYES	11,760	6,992	4,768		2,224 R	59.5%	40.5%	59.5%	40.5%
13,488	MURRAY	3,979	2,177	1,802		375 R	54.7%	45.3%	54.7%	45.3%

OKLAHOMA
GOVERNOR 2010

2000 Census Population	County	Total Vote	Republican	Democratic	Other	Rep.-Dem. Plurality		Percentage			
								Total Vote		Major Vote	
								Rep.	Dem.	Rep.	Dem.
70,990	MUSKOGEE	17,753	9,405	8,348		1,057	R	53.0%	47.0%	53.0%	47.0%
11,561	NOBLE	3,982	2,782	1,200		1,582	R	69.9%	30.1%	69.9%	30.1%
10,536	NOWATA	3,281	1,981	1,300		681	R	60.4%	39.6%	60.4%	39.6%
12,191	OKFUSKEE	3,024	1,619	1,405		214	R	53.5%	46.5%	53.5%	46.5%
718,633	OKLAHOMA	193,930	111,614	82,316		29,298	R	57.6%	42.4%	57.6%	42.4%
40,069	OKMULGEE	10,299	5,393	4,906		487	R	52.4%	47.6%	52.4%	47.6%
47,472	OSAGE	14,411	7,938	6,473		1,465	R	55.1%	44.9%	55.1%	44.9%
31,848	OTTAWA	7,123	3,985	3,138		847	R	55.9%	44.1%	55.9%	44.1%
16,577	PAWNEE	4,843	3,030	1,813		1,217	R	62.6%	37.4%	62.6%	37.4%
77,350	PAYNE	19,891	11,633	8,258		3,375	R	58.5%	41.5%	58.5%	41.5%
45,837	PITTSBURG	12,479	6,808	5,671		1,137	R	54.6%	45.4%	54.6%	45.4%
37,492	PONTOTOC	9,777	5,365	4,412		953	R	54.9%	45.1%	54.9%	45.1%
69,442	POTTAWATOMIE	18,368	11,832	6,536		5,296	R	64.4%	35.6%	64.4%	35.6%
11,572	PUSHMATAHA	3,426	1,901	1,525		376	R	55.5%	44.5%	55.5%	44.5%
3,647	ROGER MILLS	1,336	923	413		510	R	69.1%	30.9%	69.1%	30.9%
86,905	ROGERS	28,045	18,874	9,171		9,703	R	67.3%	32.7%	67.3%	32.7%
25,482	SEMINOLE	6,326	3,637	2,689		948	R	57.5%	42.5%	57.5%	42.5%
42,391	SEQUOYAH	10,156	5,659	4,497		1,162	R	55.7%	44.3%	55.7%	44.3%
45,048	STEPHENS	14,675	6,458	8,217		1,759	D	44.0%	56.0%	44.0%	56.0%
20,640	TEXAS	4,434	3,545	889		2,656	R	80.0%	20.0%	80.0%	20.0%
7,992	TILLMAN	2,103	1,083	1,020		63	R	51.5%	48.5%	51.5%	48.5%
603,403	TULSA	168,618	105,060	63,558		41,502	R	62.3%	37.7%	62.3%	37.7%
73,085	WAGONER	20,992	14,314	6,678		7,636	R	68.2%	31.8%	68.2%	31.8%
50,976	WASHINGTON	16,587	11,548	5,039		6,509	R	69.6%	30.4%	69.6%	30.4%
11,629	WASHITA	3,598	2,265	1,333		932	R	63.0%	37.0%	63.0%	37.0%
8,878	WOODS	3,085	2,042	1,043		999	R	66.2%	33.8%	66.2%	33.8%
20,081	WOODWARD	5,605	4,082	1,523		2,559	R	72.8%	27.2%	72.8%	27.2%
3,751,351	TOTAL	1,034,767	625,506	409,261		216,245	R	60.4%	39.6%	60.4%	39.6%

OKLAHOMA
SENATOR 2010

2010 Census Population	County	Total Vote	Republican	Democratic	Other	Rep.-Dem. Plurality		Percentage			
								Total Vote		Major Vote	
								Rep.	Dem.	Rep.	Dem.
22,683	ADAIR	5,468	3,601	1,706	161	1,895	R	65.9%	31.2%	67.9%	32.1%
5,642	ALFALFA	2,013	1,654	284	75	1,370	R	82.2%	14.1%	85.3%	14.7%
14,182	ATOKA	3,671	2,449	1,087	135	1,362	R	66.7%	29.6%	69.3%	30.7%
5,636	BEAVER	1,848	1,620	162	66	1,458	R	87.7%	8.8%	90.9%	9.1%
22,119	BECKHAM	5,387	4,205	1,054	128	3,151	R	78.1%	19.6%	80.0%	20.0%
11,943	BLAINE	3,093	2,404	600	89	1,804	R	77.7%	19.4%	80.0%	20.0%
42,416	BRYAN	10,264	6,884	3,053	327	3,831	R	67.1%	29.7%	69.3%	30.7%
29,600	CADDO	7,215	4,810	2,185	220	2,625	R	66.7%	30.3%	68.8%	31.2%
115,541	CANADIAN	34,241	27,655	5,603	983	22,052	R	80.8%	16.4%	83.2%	16.8%
47,557	CARTER	12,709	9,027	3,284	398	5,743	R	71.0%	25.8%	73.3%	26.7%
46,987	CHEROKEE	11,345	7,020	3,971	354	3,049	R	61.9%	35.0%	63.9%	36.1%
15,205	CHOCTAW	3,974	2,514	1,304	156	1,210	R	63.3%	32.8%	65.8%	34.2%
2,475	CIMARRON	978	839	108	31	731	R	85.8%	11.0%	88.6%	11.4%
255,755	CLEVELAND	71,970	48,970	20,185	2815	28,785	R	68.0%	28.0%	70.8%	29.2%
5,925	COAL	1,968	1,232	687	49	545	R	62.6%	34.9%	64.2%	35.8%
124,098	COMANCHE	21,336	14,459	6,114	763	8,345	R	67.8%	28.7%	70.3%	29.7%
6,193	COTTON	1,779	1,238	468	73	770	R	69.6%	26.3%	72.6%	27.4%
15,029	CRAIG	4,225	2,924	1,169	132	1,755	R	69.2%	27.7%	71.4%	28.6%
69,967	CREEK	20,178	15,154	4,400	624	10,754	R	75.1%	21.8%	77.5%	22.5%
27,469	CUSTER	7,637	6,072	1,387	178	4,685	R	79.5%	18.2%	81.4%	18.6%
41,487	DELAWARE	11,219	8,243	2,593	383	5,650	R	73.5%	23.1%	76.1%	23.9%
4,810	DEWEY	1,839	1,514	279	46	1,235	R	82.3%	15.2%	84.4%	15.6%
4,151	ELLIS	1,493	1,258	202	33	1,056	R	84.3%	13.5%	86.2%	13.8%
60,580	GARFIELD	16,324	13,096	2,720	508	10,376	R	80.2%	16.7%	82.8%	17.2%
27,576	GARVIN	8,710	6,118	2,257	335	3,861	R	70.2%	25.9%	73.1%	26.9%
52,431	GRADY	15,526	11,746	3,237	543	8,509	R	75.7%	20.8%	78.4%	21.6%
4,527	GRANT	1,763	1,389	308	66	1,081	R	78.8%	17.5%	81.9%	18.1%
6,239	GREER	1,528	1,064	410	54	654	R	69.6%	26.8%	72.2%	27.8%
2,922	HARMON	716	505	190	21	315	R	70.5%	26.5%	72.7%	27.3%
3,685	HARPER	1,209	1,039	136	34	903	R	85.9%	11.2%	88.4%	11.6%
12,769	HASKELL	3,387	2,269	1,030	88	1,239	R	67.0%	30.4%	68.8%	31.2%
14,003	HUGHES	3,437	2,265	1,057	115	1,208	R	65.9%	30.8%	68.2%	31.8%
26,446	JACKSON	5,898	4,598	1,136	164	3,462	R	78.0%	19.3%	80.2%	19.8%
6,472	JEFFERSON	1,747	1,136	548	63	588	R	65.0%	31.4%	67.5%	32.5%
10,957	JOHNSTON	2,895	1,868	913	114	955	R	64.5%	31.5%	67.2%	32.8%
46,562	KAY	13,460	9,782	3,177	501	6,605	R	72.7%	23.6%	75.5%	24.5%
15,034	KINGFISHER	4,656	4,019	541	96	3,478	R	86.3%	11.6%	88.1%	11.9%
9,446	KIOWA	2,581	1,833	688	60	1,145	R	71.0%	26.7%	72.7%	27.3%
11,154	LATIMER	3,016	1,942	959	115	983	R	64.4%	31.8%	66.9%	33.1%
50,384	LE FLORE	12,787	7,888	4,424	475	3,464	R	61.7%	34.6%	64.1%	35.9%
34,273	LINCOLN	10,655	8,025	2,262	368	5,763	R	75.3%	21.2%	78.0%	22.0%
41,848	LOGAN	12,784	9,842	2,569	373	7,273	R	77.0%	20.1%	79.3%	20.7%
9,423	LOVE	2,592	1,719	775	98	944	R	66.3%	29.9%	68.9%	31.1%
34,506	MCCLAIN	10,889	8,482	2,100	307	6,382	R	77.9%	19.3%	80.2%	19.8%
33,151	MCCURTAIN	8,149	5,573	2,260	316	3,313	R	68.4%	27.7%	71.1%	28.9%

OKLAHOMA

SENATOR 2010

2010 Census Population	County	Total Vote	Republican	Democratic	Other	Rep.-Dem. Plurality		Percentage Total Vote Rep.	Percentage Total Vote Dem.	Percentage Major Vote Rep.	Percentage Major Vote Dem.
20,252	MCINTOSH	6,094	3,912	2,012	170	1,900	R	64.2%	33.0%	66.0%	34.0%
7,527	MAJOR	2,979	2,556	353	70	2,203	R	85.8%	11.8%	87.9%	12.1%
15,840	MARSHALL	3,933	2,763	1,038	132	1,725	R	70.3%	26.4%	72.7%	27.3%
41,259	MAYES	11,544	7,924	3,257	363	4,667	R	68.6%	28.2%	70.9%	29.1%
13,488	MURRAY	3,905	2,679	1,086	140	1,593	R	68.6%	27.8%	71.2%	28.8%
70,990	MUSKOGEE	17,498	11,572	5,481	445	6,091	R	66.1%	31.3%	67.9%	32.1%
11,561	NOBLE	3,949	3,125	686	138	2,439	R	79.1%	17.4%	82.0%	18.0%
10,536	NOWATA	3,248	2,307	831	110	1,476	R	71.0%	25.6%	73.5%	26.5%
12,191	OKFUSKEE	2,967	1,973	909	85	1,064	R	66.5%	30.6%	68.5%	31.5%
718,633	OKLAHOMA	190,141	126,541	57,415	6185	69,126	R	66.6%	30.2%	68.8%	31.2%
40,069	OKMULGEE	10,191	6,442	3,469	280	2,973	R	63.2%	34.0%	65.0%	35.0%
47,472	OSAGE	14,229	9,140	4,638	451	4,502	R	64.2%	32.6%	66.3%	33.7%
31,848	OTTAWA	6,895	4,518	2,107	270	2,411	R	65.5%	30.6%	68.2%	31.8%
16,577	PAWNEE	4,783	3,395	1,207	181	2,188	R	71.0%	25.2%	73.8%	26.2%
77,350	PAYNE	19,600	13,623	5,266	711	8,357	R	69.5%	26.9%	72.1%	27.9%
45,837	PITTSBURG	12,303	8,060	3,840	403	4,220	R	65.5%	31.2%	67.7%	32.3%
37,492	PONTOTOC	9,510	6,706	2,510	294	4,196	R	70.5%	26.4%	72.8%	27.2%
69,442	POTTAWATOMIE	18,018	13,068	4,340	610	8,728	R	72.5%	24.1%	75.1%	24.9%
11,572	PUSHMATAHA	3,319	2,101	1,047	171	1,054	R	63.3%	31.5%	66.7%	33.3%
3,647	ROGER MILLS	1,304	1,083	188	33	895	R	83.1%	14.4%	85.2%	14.8%
86,905	ROGERS	27,701	21,238	5,661	802	15,577	R	76.7%	20.4%	79.0%	21.0%
25,482	SEMINOLE	6,239	4,215	1,821	203	2,394	R	67.6%	29.2%	69.8%	30.2%
42,391	SEQUOYAH	10,000	6,549	3,114	337	3,435	R	65.5%	31.1%	67.8%	32.2%
45,048	STEPHENS	14,398	10,576	3,377	445	7,199	R	73.5%	23.5%	75.8%	24.2%
20,640	TEXAS	4,342	3,666	491	185	3,175	R	84.4%	11.3%	88.2%	11.8%
7,992	TILLMAN	2,032	1,391	578	63	813	R	68.5%	28.4%	70.6%	29.4%
603,403	TULSA	166,227	116,824	44,253	5150	72,571	R	70.3%	26.6%	72.5%	27.5%
73,085	WAGONER	20,787	15,973	4,254	560	11,719	R	76.8%	20.5%	79.0%	21.0%
50,976	WASHINGTON	16,367	12,806	3,065	496	9,741	R	78.2%	18.7%	80.7%	19.3%
11,629	WASHITA	3,549	2,758	684	107	2,074	R	77.7%	19.3%	80.1%	19.9%
8,878	WOODS	3,045	2,440	522	83	1,918	R	80.1%	17.1%	82.4%	17.6%
20,081	WOODWARD	5,495	4,614	732	149	3,882	R	84.0%	13.3%	86.3%	13.7%
3,751,351	TOTAL	1,017,151	718,482	265,814	32,855	452,668	R	70.6%	26.1%	73.0%	27.0%

OKLAHOMA

HOUSE OF REPRESENTATIVES

CD	Year	Total Vote	Republican Vote	Republican Candidate	Democratic Vote	Democratic Candidate	Other Vote	Rep.-Dem. Plurality	Percentage Total Vote Rep.	Dem.	Major Vote Rep.	Dem.
1	2010	196,829	151,173	SULLIVAN, JOHN*		—	45,656	151,173 R	76.8%		100.0%	
1	2008	292,294	193,404	SULLIVAN, JOHN*	98,890	OLIVER, GEORGIANNA W.		94,514 R	66.2%	33.8%	66.2%	33.8%
1	2006	183,729	116,920	SULLIVAN, JOHN*	56,724	GENTGES, ALAN	10,085	60,196 R	63.6%	30.9%	67.3%	32.7%
1	2004	310,934	187,145	SULLIVAN, JOHN*	116,731	DODD, DOUG	7,058	70,414 R	60.2%	37.5%	61.6%	38.4%
1	2002	214,955	119,566	SULLIVAN, JOHN*	90,649	DODD, DOUG	4,740	28,917 R	55.6%	42.2%	56.9%	43.1%
2	2010	191,429	83,226	THOMPSON, CHARLES	108,203	BOREN, DAN*		24,977 D	43.5%	56.5%	43.5%	56.5%
2	2008	246,572	72,815	WICKSON, RAYMOND J.	173,757	BOREN, DAN*		100,942 D	29.5%	70.5%	29.5%	70.5%
2	2006	168,208	45,861	MILLER, PATRICK	122,347	BOREN, DAN*		76,486 D	27.3%	72.7%	27.3%	72.7%
2	2004	272,542	92,963	SMALLEY, WAYLAND	179,579	BOREN, DAN		86,616 D	34.1%	65.9%	34.1%	65.9%
2	2002	197,982	51,234	PHAROAH, KENT	146,748	CARSON, BRAD*		95,514 D	25.9%	74.1%	25.9%	74.1%
3	2010	207,616	161,927	LUCAS, FRANK D.*	45,689	ROBBINS, FRANKIE		116,238 R	78.0%	22.0%	78.0%	22.0%
3	2008	264,359	184,306	LUCAS, FRANK D.*	62,297	ROBBINS, FRANKIE	17,756	122,009 R	69.7%	23.6%	74.7%	25.3%
3	2006	189,791	128,042	LUCAS, FRANK D.*	61,749	BARTON, SUE		66,293 R	67.5%	32.5%	67.5%	32.5%
3	2004	262,131	215,510	LUCAS, FRANK D.*		—	46,621	215,510 R	82.2%		100.0%	
3	2002	196,090	148,206	LUCAS, FRANK D.*		—	47,884	148,206 R	75.6%		100.0%	
4	2010			COLE, TOM*		—		R				
4	2008	272,781	180,080	COLE, TOM*	79,674	CUMMINGS, BLAKE	13,027	100,406 R	66.0%	29.2%	69.3%	30.7%
4	2006	183,041	118,266	COLE, TOM*	64,775	SPAKE, HAL		53,491 R	64.6%	35.4%	64.6%	35.4%
4	2004	255,854	198,985	COLE, TOM*		—	56,869	198,985 R	77.8%		100.0%	
4	2002	197,774	106,452	COLE, TOM	91,322	ROBERTS, DARRYL		15,130 R	53.8%	46.2%	53.8%	46.2%
5	2010	197,105	123,236	LANKFORD, JAMES	68,074	COYLE, BILLY	5,795	55,162 R	62.5%	34.5%	64.4%	35.6%
5	2008	260,921	171,925	FALLIN, MARY*	88,996	PERRY, STEVEN L.		82,929 R	65.9%	34.1%	65.9%	34.1%
5	2006	180,425	108,936	FALLIN, MARY	67,293	HUNTER, DAVID	4,196	41,643 R	60.4%	37.3%	61.8%	38.2%
5	2004	273,149	180,430	ISTOOK, ERNEST*	92,719	SMITH, BERT		87,711 R	66.1%	33.9%	66.1%	33.9%
5	2002	195,051	121,374	ISTOOK, ERNEST*	63,208	BARLOW, LOU	10,469	58,166 R	62.2%	32.4%	65.8%	34.2%
TOTAL	2010	792,979	519,562		221,966		51,451	297,596 R	65.5%	28.0%	70.1%	29.9%
TOTAL	2008	1,336,927	802,530		503,614		30,783	298,916 R	60.0%	37.7%	61.4%	38.6%
TOTAL	2006	905,194	518,025		372,888		14,281	145,137 R	57.2%	41.2%	58.1%	41.9%
TOTAL	2004	1,374,610	875,033		389,029		110,548	486,004 R	63.7%	28.3%	69.2%	30.8%
TOTAL	2002	1,001,852	546,832		391,927		63,093	154,905 R	54.6%	39.1%	58.3%	41.7%

An asterisk (*) denotes incumbent.

OKLAHOMA

GENERAL AND PRIMARY ELECTIONS

2010 GENERAL ELECTIONS

Governor

Senator   Other vote was 25,048 Independent (Stephen P. Wallace); 7,807 Independent (Ronald F. Dwyer).

House   Other vote was:

CD 1   45,656 Independent (Angelia O'Dell).
CD 2
CD 3
CD 4
CD 5   3,067 Independent (Clark Duffe); 2,728 Independent (Dave White).

2010 PRIMARY ELECTIONS

Primary	July 27, 2010	**Registration**	Democratic	999,855
		(as of January 15, 2010)	Republican	813,158
Primary Runoff	August 24, 2010		Independent	225,607
			TOTAL	*2,038,620*
Primary Type	Closed—Only registered Democrats and Republicans could vote in their party's primary.			

OKLAHOMA

GENERAL AND PRIMARY ELECTIONS

	REPUBLICAN PRIMARIES			DEMOCRATIC PRIMARIES		
Governor	Mary Fallin	136,477	54.8%	Jari Askins	132,591	50.3%
	Randy Brogdon	98,170	39.4%	Drew Edmondson	131,097	49.7%
	Robert Hubbard	8,132	3.3%			
	Roger L. Jackson	6,290	2.5%			
	TOTAL	249,069		TOTAL	263,688	
Senator	Tom Coburn*	223,997	90.4%	Jim Rogers	157,955	65.4%
	Evelyn L. Rogers	15,093	6.1%	Mark Myles	83,715	34.6%
	Lewis Kelly Spring	8,812	3.6%			
	TOTAL	247,902		TOTAL	241,670	
Congressional District 1	John Sullivan*	38,673	62.1%	No Democratic candidate		
	Kenneth Rice	10,394	16.7%			
	Nathan Dahm	8,871	14.2%			
	Patrick K. Haworth	1,737	2.8%			
	Craig Allen	1,421	2.3%			
	Fran Moghaddam	1,213	1.9%			
	TOTAL	62,309				
Congressional District 2	Charles Thompson	8,161	33.6%	Dan Boren*	66,439	75.6%
	Daniel Edmonds	6,886	28.3%	Jim Wilson	21,496	24.4%
	Daniel Arnett	3,863	15.9%			
	Howard Houchen	2,785	11.5%			
	Chester Clem Falling	1,527	6.3%			
	Raymond Wickson	1,095	4.5%			
	TOTAL	24,317		TOTAL	87,935	
	PRIMARY RUNOFF					
	Charles Thompson	7,492	67.3%			
	Daniel Edmonds	3,645	32.7%			
	TOTAL	11,137				
Congressional District 3	Frank D. Lucas*	Unopposed		Frankie Robbins	Unopposed	
Congressional District 4	Tom Cole*	32,589	77.3%	No Democratic candidate		
	R. J. Harris	9,593	22.7%			
	TOTAL	42,182				
Congressional District 5	James Lankford	18,760	33.6%	Billy Coyle	21,143	56.8%
	Kevin Calvey	18,147	32.5%	Tom Guild	16,063	43.2%
	Mike Thompson	10,008	17.9%			
	Shane Jett	5,956	10.7%			
	Johnny B. Roy	1,548	2.8%			
	Rick Flanigan	762	1.4%			
	Harry Johnson	686	1.2%			
	TOTAL	55,867		TOTAL	37,206	
	PRIMARY RUNOFF					
	James Lankford	29,817	65.2%			
	Kevin Calvey	15,902	34.8%			
	TOTAL	45,719				

An asterisk (*) denotes incumbent. The names of unopposed candidates did not appear on the primary ballot; therefore, no votes were cast for these candidates. A runoff was triggered if the leading candidate received less than 50 percent of the primary vote.

OREGON

Congressional districts first established for elections held in 2002
5 members

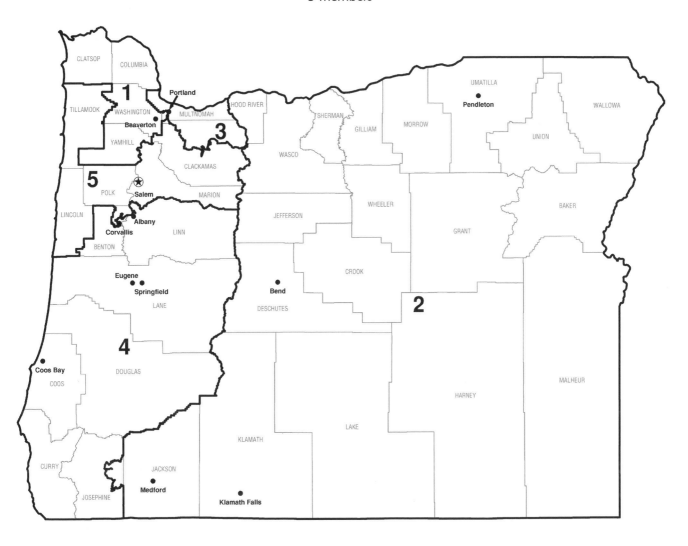

OREGON

GOVERNOR
John Kitzhaber (D). Elected 2010 to a four-year term. Previously elected 1998, 1994.

SENATORS (2 Democrats)
Jeff Merkley (D). Elected 2008 to a six-year term.

Ron Wyden (D). Reelected 2010 to a six-year term. Previously elected 2004, 1998 and in a special election January 30, 1996, to serve the remaining three years of the term vacated when Senator Robert W. Packwood (R) resigned.

REPRESENTATIVES (4 Democrats, 1 Republican)

1. David Wu (D)
2. Greg Walden (R)
3. Earl Blumenauer (D)
4. Peter A. DeFazio (D)
5. Kurt Schrader (D)

POSTWAR VOTE FOR PRESIDENT

Year	Total Vote	Republican Vote	Republican Candidate	Democratic Vote	Democratic Candidate	Other Vote	Rep.-Dem. Plurality	Total Vote Rep.	Total Vote Dem.	Major Vote Rep.	Major Vote Dem.
2008	1,827,864	738,475	McCain, John	1,037,291	Obama, Barack	52,098	298,816 D	40.4%	56.7%	41.6%	58.4%
2004	1,836,782	866,831	Bush, George W.	943,163	Kerry, John	26,788	76,332 D	47.2%	51.3%	47.9%	52.1%
2000**	1,533,968	713,577	Bush, George W.	720,342	Gore, Al	100,049	6,765 D	46.5%	47.0%	49.8%	50.2%
1996**	1,377,760	538,152	Dole, Bob	649,641	Clinton, Bill	189,967	111,489 D	39.1%	47.2%	45.3%	54.7%
1992**	1,462,643	475,757	Bush, George	621,314	Clinton, Bill	365,572	145,557 D	32.5%	42.5%	43.4%	56.6%
1988	1,201,694	560,126	Bush, George	616,206	Dukakis, Michael S.	25,362	56,080 D	46.6%	51.3%	47.6%	52.4%
1984	1,226,527	685,700	Reagan, Ronald	536,479	Mondale, Walter F.	4,348	149,221 R	55.9%	43.7%	56.1%	43.9%
1980**	1,181,516	571,044	Reagan, Ronald	456,890	Carter, Jimmy	153,582	114,154 R	48.3%	38.7%	55.6%	44.4%
1976	1,029,876	492,120	Ford, Gerald R.	490,407	Carter, Jimmy	47,349	1,713 R	47.8%	47.6%	50.1%	49.9%
1972	927,946	486,686	Nixon, Richard M.	392,760	McGovern, George S.	48,500	93,926 R	52.4%	42.3%	55.3%	44.7%
1968**	819,622	408,433	Nixon, Richard M.	358,866	Humphrey, Hubert H.	52,323	49,567 R	49.8%	43.8%	53.2%	46.8%
1964	786,305	282,779	Goldwater, Barry M.	501,017	Johnson, Lyndon B.	2,509	218,238 D	36.0%	63.7%	36.1%	63.9%
1960	776,421	408,060	Nixon, Richard M.	367,402	Kennedy, John F.	959	40,658 R	52.6%	47.3%	52.6%	47.4%
1956	736,132	406,393	Eisenhower, Dwight D.	329,204	Stevenson, Adlai E.	535	77,189 R	55.2%	44.7%	55.2%	44.8%
1952	695,059	420,815	Eisenhower, Dwight D.	270,579	Stevenson, Adlai E.	3,665	150,236 R	60.5%	38.9%	60.9%	39.1%
1948	524,080	260,904	Dewey, Thomas E.	243,147	Truman, Harry S.	20,029	17,757 R	49.8%	46.4%	51.8%	48.2%

**In past elections, the other vote included: 77,357 Green (Ralph Nader); 1996 - 121,221 Reform (Ross Perot); 1992 - 354,091 Independent (Perot); 1980 - 112,389 Independent (John Anderson); 1968 - 49,683 American Independent (George Wallace).

OREGON

POSTWAR VOTE FOR GOVERNOR

Year	Total Vote	Republican Vote	Republican Candidate	Democratic Vote	Democratic Candidate	Other Vote	Rep.-Dem. Plurality	Percentage Total Vote Rep.	Percentage Total Vote Dem.	Percentage Major Vote Rep.	Percentage Major Vote Dem.
2010	1,453,548	694,287	Dudley, Chris	716,525	Kitzhaber, John	42,736	22,238 D	47.8%	49.3%	49.2%	50.8%
2006	1,379,475	589,748	Saxton, Ron	699,786	Kulongoski, Theodore R.	89,941	110,038 D	42.8%	50.7%	45.7%	54.3%
2002	1,260,497	581,785	Mannix, Kevin L.	618,004	Kulongoski, Theodore R.	60,708	36,219 D	46.2%	49.0%	48.5%	51.5%
1998	1,113,098	334,001	Sizemore, Bill	717,061	Kitzhaber, John	62,036	383,060 D	30.0%	64.4%	31.8%	68.2%
1994	1,221,010	517,874	Smith, Denny	622,083	Kitzhaber, John	81,053	104,209 D	42.4%	50.9%	45.4%	54.6%
1990**	1,112,847	444,646	Frohnmayer, Dave	508,749	Roberts, Barbara	159,452	64,103 D	40.0%	45.7%	46.6%	53.4%
1986	1,059,630	506,986	Paulus, Norma	549,456	Goldschmidt, Neil	3,188	42,470 D	47.8%	51.9%	48.0%	52.0%
1982	1,042,009	639,841	Atiyeh, Victor	374,316	Kulongoski, Theodore R.	27,852	265,525 R	61.4%	35.9%	63.1%	36.9%
1978	911,143	498,452	Atiyeh, Victor	409,411	Straub, Robert W.	3,280	89,041 R	54.7%	44.9%	54.9%	45.1%
1974	770,574	324,751	Atiyeh, Victor	444,812	Straub, Robert W.	1,011	120,061 D	42.1%	57.7%	42.2%	57.8%
1970	666,394	369,964	McCall, Tom	293,892	Straub, Robert W.	2,538	76,072 R	55.5%	44.1%	55.7%	44.3%
1966	682,862	377,346	McCall, Tom	305,008	Straub, Robert W.	508	72,338 R	55.3%	44.7%	55.3%	44.7%
1962	637,407	345,497	Hatfield, Mark	265,359	Thornton, Robert Y.	26,551	80,138 R	54.2%	41.6%	56.6%	43.4%
1958	599,994	331,900	Hatfield, Mark	267,934	Holmes, Robert D.	160	63,966 R	55.3%	44.7%	55.3%	44.7%
1956S	731,279	361,840	Smith, Elmo E.	369,439	Holmes, Robert D.		7,599 D	49.5%	50.5%	49.5%	50.5%
1954	566,701	322,522	Patterson, Paul	244,179	Carson, Joseph K.		78,343 R	56.9%	43.1%	56.9%	43.1%
1950	505,910	334,160	McKay, Douglas	171,750	Flegel, Austin F.		162,410 R	66.1%	33.9%	66.1%	33.9%
1948S	509,633	271,295	McKay, Douglas	226,958	Wallace, Lew	11,380	44,337 R	53.2%	44.5%	54.4%	45.6%
1946	344,155	237,681	Snell, Earl	106,474	Donaugh, Carl C.		131,207 R	69.1%	30.9%	69.1%	30.9%

**In past elections, the other vote included: 1990 - 144,062 Independent (Al Mobley). The 1948 and 1956 elections were for short terms to fill a vacany.

POSTWAR VOTE FOR SENATOR

Year	Total Vote	Republican Vote	Republican Candidate	Democratic Vote	Democratic Candidate	Other Vote	Rep.-Dem. Plurality	Percentage Total Vote Rep.	Percentage Total Vote Dem.	Percentage Major Vote Rep.	Percentage Major Vote Dem.
2010	1,442,588	566,199	Huffman, Jim	825,507	Wyden, Ron	50,882	259,308 D	39.2%	57.2%	40.7%	59.3%
2008	1,767,504	805,159	Smith, Gordon H.	864,392	Merkley, Jeff	97,953	59,233 D	45.6%	48.9%	48.2%	51.8%
2004	1,780,550	565,254	King, Al	1,128,728	Wyden, Ron	86,568	563,474 D	31.7%	63.4%	33.4%	66.6%
2002	1,267,221	712,287	Smith, Gordon H.	501,898	Bradbury, Bill	53,036	210,389 R	56.2%	39.6%	58.7%	41.3%
1998	1,117,747	377,739	Lim, John	682,425	Wyden, Ron	57,583	304,686 D	33.8%	61.1%	35.6%	64.4%
1996	1,360,230	677,336	Smith, Gordon H.	624,370	Bruggere, Tom	58,524	52,966 R	49.8%	45.9%	52.0%	48.0%
1996S	1,196,608	553,519	Smith, Gordon H.	571,739	Wyden, Ron	71,350	18,220 D	46.3%	47.8%	49.2%	50.8%
1992	1,376,033	717,455	Packwood, Robert W.	639,851	AuCoin, Les	18,727	77,604 R	52.1%	46.5%	52.9%	47.1%
1990	1,099,255	590,095	Hatfield, Mark	507,743	Lonsdale, Harry	1,417	82,352 R	53.7%	46.2%	53.8%	46.2%
1986	1,042,555	656,317	Packwood, Robert W.	375,735	Bauman, Rick	10,503	280,582 R	63.0%	36.0%	63.6%	36.4%
1984	1,214,735	808,152	Hatfield, Mark	406,122	Hendriksen, Margie	461	402,030 R	66.5%	33.4%	66.6%	33.4%
1980	1,140,494	594,290	Packwood, Robert W.	501,963	Kulongoski, Theodore R.	44,241	92,327 R	52.1%	44.0%	54.2%	45.8%
1978	892,518	550,165	Hatfield, Mark	341,616	Cook, Vernon	737	208,549 R	61.6%	38.3%	61.7%	38.3%
1974	766,414	420,984	Packwood, Robert W.	338,591	Roberts, Betty	6,839	82,393 R	54.9%	44.2%	55.4%	44.6%
1972	920,833	494,671	Hatfield, Mark	425,036	Morse, Wayne L.	1,126	69,635 R	53.7%	46.2%	53.8%	46.2%
1968	814,176	408,646	Packwood, Robert W.	405,353	Morse, Wayne L.	177	3,293 R	50.2%	49.8%	50.2%	49.8%
1966	685,067	354,391	Hatfield, Mark	330,374	Duncan, Robert B.	302	24,017 R	51.7%	48.2%	51.8%	48.2%
1962	636,558	291,587	Unander, Sig	344,716	Morse, Wayne L.	255	53,129 D	45.8%	54.2%	45.8%	54.2%
1960	755,875	343,009	Smith, Elmo E.	412,757	Neuberger, Maurine	109	69,748 D	45.4%	54.6%	45.4%	54.6%
1956	732,254	335,405	McKay, Douglas	396,849	Morse, Wayne L.		61,444 D	45.8%	54.2%	45.8%	54.2%
1954	569,088	283,313	Cordon, Guy	285,775	Neuberger, Richard L.		2,462 D	49.8%	50.2%	49.8%	50.2%
1950	503,455	376,510	Morse, Wayne L.	116,780	Latourette, Howard	10,165	259,730 R	74.8%	23.2%	76.3%	23.7%
1948	498,570	299,295	Cordon, Guy	199,275	Wilson, Manley J.		100,020 R	60.0%	40.0%	60.0%	40.0%

The January 1996 election was for a short term to fill a vacancy.

OREGON

GOVERNOR 2010

2010 Census Population	County	Total Vote	Republican	Democratic	Other	Rep.-Dem. Plurality		Percentage Total Vote Rep.	Dem.	Major Vote Rep.	Dem.
16,134	BAKER	7,276	4,953	1,949	374	3,004	R	68.1%	26.8%	71.8%	28.2%
85,579	BENTON	36,189	13,767	21,498	924	7,731	D	38.0%	59.4%	39.0%	61.0%
375,992	CLACKAMAS	156,287	83,516	69,250	3,521	14,266	R	53.4%	44.3%	54.7%	45.3%
37,039	CLATSOP	14,913	6,792	7,654	467	862	D	45.5%	51.3%	47.0%	53.0%
49,351	COLUMBIA	20,190	10,302	8,973	915	1,329	R	51.0%	44.4%	53.4%	46.6%
63,043	COOS	25,343	13,652	10,456	1,235	3,196	R	53.9%	41.3%	56.6%	43.4%
20,978	CROOK	8,862	6,231	2,314	317	3,917	R	70.3%	26.1%	72.9%	27.1%
22,364	CURRY	10,281	5,761	3,986	534	1,775	R	56.0%	38.8%	59.1%	40.9%
157,733	DESCHUTES	63,783	37,706	24,289	1,788	13,417	R	59.1%	38.1%	60.8%	39.2%
107,667	DOUGLAS	43,335	27,438	14,072	1,825	13,366	R	63.3%	32.5%	66.1%	33.9%
1,871	GILLIAM	962	620	308	34	312	R	64.4%	32.0%	66.8%	33.2%
7,445	GRANT	3,469	2,576	749	144	1,827	R	74.3%	21.6%	77.5%	22.5%
7,422	HARNEY	3,368	2,436	800	132	1,636	R	72.3%	23.8%	75.3%	24.7%
22,346	HOOD RIVER	8,427	3,434	4,778	215	1,344	D	40.7%	56.7%	41.8%	58.2%
203,206	JACKSON	77,690	42,715	32,360	2,615	10,355	R	55.0%	41.7%	56.9%	43.1%
21,720	JEFFERSON	6,602	4,240	2,132	230	2,108	R	64.2%	32.3%	66.5%	33.5%
82,713	JOSEPHINE	33,290	20,025	11,558	1,707	8,467	R	60.2%	34.7%	63.4%	36.6%
66,380	KLAMATH	23,158	16,295	5,820	1,043	10,475	R	70.4%	25.1%	73.7%	26.3%
7,895	LAKE	3,131	2,323	658	150	1,665	R	74.2%	21.0%	77.9%	22.1%
351,715	LANE	143,513	57,394	81,731	4,388	24,337	D	40.0%	57.0%	41.3%	58.7%
46,034	LINCOLN	19,791	8,540	10,484	767	1,944	D	43.2%	53.0%	44.9%	55.1%
116,672	LINN	41,552	25,370	14,466	1,716	10,904	R	61.1%	34.8%	63.7%	36.3%
31,313	MALHEUR	7,732	5,440	1,884	408	3,556	R	70.4%	24.4%	74.3%	25.7%
315,335	MARION	100,936	53,177	44,795	2,964	8,382	R	52.7%	44.4%	54.3%	45.7%
11,173	MORROW	3,175	2,184	850	141	1,334	R	68.8%	26.8%	72.0%	28.0%
735,334	MULTNOMAH	280,850	76,915	198,157	5,778	121,242	D	27.4%	70.6%	28.0%	72.0%
75,403	POLK	29,724	15,966	12,899	859	3,067	R	53.7%	43.4%	55.3%	44.7%
1,765	SHERMAN	905	634	238	33	396	R	70.1%	26.3%	72.7%	27.3%
25,250	TILLAMOOK	11,031	5,604	5,072	355	532	R	50.8%	46.0%	52.5%	47.5%
75,889	UMATILLA	19,703	12,574	6,321	808	6,253	R	63.8%	32.1%	66.5%	33.5%
25,748	UNION	10,652	6,869	3,366	417	3,503	R	64.5%	31.6%	67.1%	32.9%
7,008	WALLOWA	3,800	2,581	1,088	131	1,493	R	67.9%	28.6%	70.3%	29.7%
25,213	WASCO	9,306	4,938	4,024	344	914	R	53.1%	43.2%	55.1%	44.9%
529,710	WASHINGTON	187,033	89,926	92,811	4,296	2,885	D	48.1%	49.6%	49.2%	50.8%
1,441	WHEELER	754	500	216	38	284	R	66.3%	28.6%	69.8%	30.2%
99,193	YAMHILL	36,535	20,893	14,519	1,123	6,374	R	57.2%	39.7%	59.0%	41.0%
3,831,074	TOTAL	1,453,548	694,287	716,525	42,736	22,238	D	47.8%	49.3%	49.2%	50.8%

OREGON

SENATOR 2010

2010 Census Population	County	Total Vote	Republican	Democratic	Other	Rep.-Dem. Plurality		Percentage			
								Total Vote		Major Vote	
								Rep.	Dem.	Rep.	Dem.
16,134	BAKER	7,266	4,012	2,929	325	1,083	R	55.2%	40.3%	57.8%	42.2%
85,579	BENTON	35,953	11,696	22,822	1,435	11,126	D	32.5%	63.5%	33.9%	66.1%
375,992	CLACKAMAS	155,123	67,197	83,696	4,230	16,499	D	43.3%	54.0%	44.5%	55.5%
37,039	CLATSOP	14,738	5,324	8,861	553	3,537	D	36.1%	60.1%	37.5%	62.5%
49,351	COLUMBIA	20,035	8,307	10,904	824	2,597	D	41.5%	54.4%	43.2%	56.8%
63,043	COOS	25,084	11,447	12,323	1,314	876	D	45.6%	49.1%	48.2%	51.8%
20,978	CROOK	8,845	4,884	3,663	298	1,221	R	55.2%	41.4%	57.1%	42.9%
22,364	CURRY	10,272	5,257	4,475	540	782	R	51.2%	43.6%	54.0%	46.0%
157,733	DESCHUTES	63,490	30,831	30,809	1,850	22	R	48.6%	48.5%	50.0%	50.0%
107,667	DOUGLAS	43,035	24,081	17,095	1,859	6,986	R	56.0%	39.7%	58.5%	41.5%
1,871	GILLIAM	957	425	504	28	79	D	44.4%	52.7%	45.7%	54.3%
7,445	GRANT	3,430	2,289	1,041	100	1,248	R	66.7%	30.3%	68.7%	31.3%
7,422	HARNEY	3,347	1,958	1,264	125	694	R	58.5%	37.8%	60.8%	39.2%
22,346	HOOD RIVER	8,364	2,544	5,575	245	3,031	D	30.4%	66.7%	31.3%	68.7%
203,206	JACKSON	77,488	34,912	39,839	2,737	4,927	D	45.1%	51.4%	46.7%	53.3%
21,720	JEFFERSON	6,603	3,374	3,036	193	338	R	51.1%	46.0%	52.6%	47.4%
82,713	JOSEPHINE	33,150	17,563	14,179	1,408	3,384	R	53.0%	42.8%	55.3%	44.7%
66,380	KLAMATH	23,120	13,383	8,798	939	4,585	R	57.9%	38.1%	60.3%	39.7%
7,895	LAKE	3,115	1,864	1,138	113	726	R	59.8%	36.5%	62.1%	37.9%
351,715	LANE	142,242	49,316	87,717	5,209	38,401	D	34.7%	61.7%	36.0%	64.0%
46,034	LINCOLN	19,651	6,766	12,027	858	5,261	D	34.4%	61.2%	36.0%	64.0%
116,672	LINN	41,238	21,131	18,296	1,811	2,835	R	51.2%	44.4%	53.6%	46.4%
31,313	MALHEUR	7,687	5,078	2,215	394	2,863	R	66.1%	28.8%	69.6%	30.4%
315,335	MARION	99,993	44,869	51,879	3,245	7,010	D	44.9%	51.9%	46.4%	53.6%
11,173	MORROW	3,168	1,650	1,372	146	278	R	52.1%	43.3%	54.6%	45.4%
735,334	MULTNOMAH	279,041	56,513	212,371	10,157	155,858	D	20.3%	76.1%	21.0%	79.0%
75,403	POLK	29,467	13,640	14,834	993	1,194	D	46.3%	50.3%	47.9%	52.1%
1,765	SHERMAN	906	495	387	24	108	R	54.6%	42.7%	56.1%	43.9%
25,250	TILLAMOOK	10,926	4,342	6,233	351	1,891	D	39.7%	57.0%	41.1%	58.9%
75,889	UMATILLA	19,618	10,541	8,218	859	2,323	R	53.7%	41.9%	56.2%	43.8%
25,748	UNION	10,560	5,270	4,892	398	378	R	49.9%	46.3%	51.9%	48.1%
7,008	WALLOWA	3,769	2,150	1,492	127	658	R	57.0%	39.6%	59.0%	41.0%
25,213	WASCO	9,315	3,710	5,323	282	1,613	D	39.8%	57.1%	41.1%	58.9%
529,710	WASHINGTON	184,757	71,926	107,225	5,606	35,299	D	38.9%	58.0%	40.1%	59.9%
1,441	WHEELER	748	388	324	36	64	R	51.9%	43.3%	54.5%	45.5%
99,193	YAMHILL	36,087	17,066	17,751	1,270	685	D	47.3%	49.2%	49.0%	51.0%
3,831,074	TOTAL	1,442,588	566,199	825,507	50,882	259,308	D	39.2%	57.2%	40.7%	59.3%

OREGON

HOUSE OF REPRESENTATIVES

CD	Year	Total Vote	Republican Vote	Republican Candidate	Democratic Vote	Democratic Candidate	Other Vote	Rep.-Dem. Plurality		Percentage Total Vote Rep.	Percentage Total Vote Dem.	Percentage Major Vote Rep.	Percentage Major Vote Dem.
1	2010	292,909	122,858	CORNILLES, ROB	160,357	WU, DAVID*	9,694	37,499	D	41.9%	54.7%	43.4%	56.6%
1	2008	332,248		—	237,567	WU, DAVID*	94,681	237,567	D	—	71.5%	0%	100.0%
1	2006	269,627	90,904	KITTS, DERRICK	169,409	WU, DAVID*	9,314	78,505	D	33.7%	62.8%	34.9%	65.1%
1	2004	354,338	135,164	GOLI, AMERI	203,771	WU, DAVID*	15,403	68,607	D	38.1%	57.5%	39.9%	60.1%
1	2002	238,036	80,917	GREENFIELD, JIM	149,215	WU, DAVID*	7,904	68,298	D	34.0%	62.7%	35.2%	64.8%
2	2010	279,037	206,245	WALDEN, GREG*	72,173	SEGERS, JOYCE B.	619	134,072	R	73.9%	25.9%	74.1%	25.9%
2	2008	340,379	236,560	WALDEN, GREG*	87,649	LEMAS, NOAH	16,170	148,911	R	69.5%	25.8%	73.0%	27.0%
2	2006	271,719	181,529	WALDEN, GREG*	82,484	VOISON, CAROL	7,706	99,045	R	66.8%	30.4%	68.8%	31.2%
2	2004	346,865	248,461	WALDEN, GREG*	88,914	McCOLGAN, JOHN C.	9,490	159,547	R	71.6%	25.6%	73.6%	26.4%
2	2002	252,284	181,295	WALDEN, GREG*	64,991	BUCKLEY, PETER	5,998	116,304	R	71.9%	25.8%	73.6%	26.4%
3	2010	275,802	67,714	LOPEZ, DELIA	193,104	BLUMENAUER, EARL*	14,984	125,390	D	24.6%	70.0%	26.0%	74.0%
3	2008	341,062	71,063	LOPEZ, DELIA	254,235	BLUMENAUER, EARL*	15,764	183,172	D	20.8%	74.5%	21.8%	78.2%
3	2006	253,610	59,529	BROUSSARD, BRUCE	186,380	BLUMENAUER, EARL*	7,701	126,851	D	23.5%	73.5%	24.2%	75.8%
3	2004	346,560	82,045	MARS, TAMI	245,559	BLUMENAUER, EARL*	18,956	163,514	D	23.7%	70.9%	25.0%	75.0%
3	2002	234,977	62,821	SEALE, SARAH	156,851	BLUMENAUER, EARL*	15,305	94,030	D	26.7%	66.8%	28.6%	71.4%
4	2010	298,052	129,877	ROBINSON, ART	162,416	DeFAZIO, PETER A.*	5,759	32,539	D	43.6%	54.5%	44.4%	55.6%
4	2008	334,146		—	275,143	DeFAZIO, PETER A.*	59,003	275,143	D		82.3%		100.0%
4	2006	290,244	109,105	FELDKAMP, JIM	180,607	DeFAZIO, PETER A.*	532	71,502	D	37.6%	62.2%	37.7%	62.3%
4	2004	374,909	140,882	FELDKAMP, JIM	228,611	DeFAZIO, PETER A.*	5,416	87,729	D	37.6%	61.0%	38.1%	61.9%
4	2002	263,481	90,523	VanLEEUWEN, LIZ	168,150	DeFAZIO, PETER A.*	4,808	77,627	D	34.4%	63.8%	35.0%	65.0%
5	2010	283,556	130,313	BRUUN, SCOTT	145,319	SCHRADER, KURT*	7,924	15,006	D	46.0%	51.2%	47.3%	52.7%
5	2008	334,674	128,297	ERICKSON, MIKE	181,577	SCHRADER, KURT	24,800	53,280	D	38.3%	54.3%	41.4%	58.6%
5	2006	272,234	116,424	ERICKSON, MIKE	146,973	HOOLEY, DARLENE*	8,837	30,549	D	42.8%	54.0%	44.2%	55.8%
5	2004	349,634	154,993	ZUPANCIC, JIM	184,833	HOOLEY, DARLENE*	9,808	29,840	D	44.3%	52.9%	45.6%	54.4%
5	2002	251,537	113,441	BOQUIST, BRIAN J.	137,713	HOOLEY, DARLENE*	383	24,272	D	45.1%	54.7%	45.2%	54.8%
TOTAL	2010	1,429,356	657,007		733,369		38,980	76,362	D	46.0%	51.3%	47.3%	52.7%
TOTAL	2008	1,682,509	435,920		1,036,171		210,418	600,251	D	25.9%	61.6%	29.6%	70.4%
TOTAL	2006	1,357,434	557,491		765,853		34,090	208,362	D	41.1%	56.4%	42.1%	57.9%
TOTAL	2004	1,772,306	761,545		951,688		59,073	190,143	D	43.0%	53.7%	44.5%	55.5%
TOTAL	2002	1,240,315	528,997		676,920		34,398	147,923	D	42.7%	54.6%	43.9%	56.1%

An asterisk (*) denotes incumbent.

OREGON

GENERAL AND PRIMARY ELECTIONS

2010 GENERAL ELECTIONS

Governor Other vote was 20,475 Constitution (Greg Kord); 19,048 Libertarian (Wes Wagner); 3,213 scattered write-in.

Senator Other vote was 18,940 Working Families (Bruce Cronk); 16,028 Libertarian (Marc Delphine); 14,466 Progressive (Rick Staggenborg); 1,448 scattered write-in.

House Other vote was:

CD 1 3,855 Constitution (Don LaMunyon); 2,955 Pacific Green (Chris Henry); 2,492 Libertarian (H. Joe Tabor); 392 scattered write-in.

CD 2 619 scattered write-in.

CD 3 8,380 Libertarian, Independent (Jeff Lawrence); 6,197 Pacific Green, Progressive (Michael Meo); 407 scattered write-in.

CD 4 5,215 Pacific Green (Mike Beilstein); 544 scattered write-in.

CD 5 7,557 Pacific Green, Progressive (Chris Lugo); 367 scattered write-in.

2010 PRIMARY ELECTIONS

Primary May 18, 2010 **Registration** (as of May 18, 2010)

Democratic	863,800
Republican	656,794
Others	104,791
Non-Affiliated	408,566
TOTAL	*2,033,951*

Primary Type Closed—Only registered Democrats and Republicans could vote in their party's primary.

OREGON

GENERAL AND PRIMARY ELECTIONS

	REPUBLICAN PRIMARIES			DEMOCRATIC PRIMARIES		
Governor	Chris Dudley	122,855	39.1%	John Kitzhaber	242,545	64.8%
	Allen Alley	99,753	31.8%	Bill Bradbury	110,298	29.5%
	John Lim	47,339	15.1%	Roger Obrist	16,057	4.3%
	Bill Sizemore	23,522	7.5%	Scattered write-in	5,504	1.5%
	William Ames Curtright	12,497	4.0%			
	Rex O. Watkins	3,060	1.0%			
	Clark Colvin	1,206	0.4%			
	Darren Karr	1,127	0.4%			
	Bob Forthan	727	0.2%			
	Scattered write-in	2,001	0.6%			
	TOTAL	*314,087*		*TOTAL*	*374,404*	
Senator	Jim Huffman	110,450	41.7%	Ron Wyden*	333,652	89.6%
	Loren Later	39,753	15.0%	Loren Hooker	25,152	6.8%
	G. Shane Dinkel	36,760	13.9%	Pavel Goberman	9,985	2.7%
	Tom Stutzman	31,859	12.0%	Scattered write-in	3,782	1.0%
	Keith Waldron	24,602	9.3%			
	Robin S. Parker	14,637	5.5%			
	Walter H. Woodland	4,417	1.7%			
	Scattered write-in	2,363	0.9%			
	TOTAL	*264,841*		*TOTAL*	*372,571*	

OREGON

GENERAL AND PRIMARY ELECTIONS

	REPUBLICAN PRIMARIES			DEMOCRATIC PRIMARIES		
Congressional District 1	Rob Cornilles	21,441	41.1%	David Wu*	61,439	80.9%
	Douglas Fitzgerald Keller	14,785	28.3%	David Robinson	14,102	18.6%
	John Kuzmanich	14,464	27.7%	Scattered write-in	383	0.5%
	Stephan Andrew Brodhead	1,213	2.3%			
	Scattered write-in	299	0.6%			
	TOTAL	52,202		TOTAL	75,924	
Congressional District 2	Greg Walden*	74,970	98.9%	Joyce B. Segers	37,609	97.5%
	Scattered write-in	818	1.1%	Scattered write-in	971	2.5%
	TOTAL	75,788		TOTAL	38,580	
Congressional District 3	Delia Lopez	20,007	97.6%	Earl Blumenauer*	73,962	91.2%
	Scattered write-in	482	2.4%	John Sweeney	6,774	8.4%
				Scattered write-in	337	0.4%
	TOTAL	20,489		TOTAL	81,073	
Congressional District 4	Art Robinson	49,401	79.2%	Peter A. DeFazio*	74,568	97.8%
	Jaynee Germond	12,495	20.0%	Scattered write-in	1,677	2.2%
	Scattered write-in	512	0.8%			
	TOTAL	62,408		TOTAL	76,245	
Congressional District 5	Scott Bruun	37,778	62.3%	Kurt Schrader*	57,282	98.4%
	Fred Thompson	22,616	37.3%	Scattered write-in	945	1.6%
	Scattered write-in	235	0.4%			
	TOTAL	60,629		TOTAL	58,227	

An asterisk (*) denotes incumbent. The primary and general elections were conducted entirely by mail.

PENNSYLVANIA

Congressional districts first established for elections held in 2004
19 members

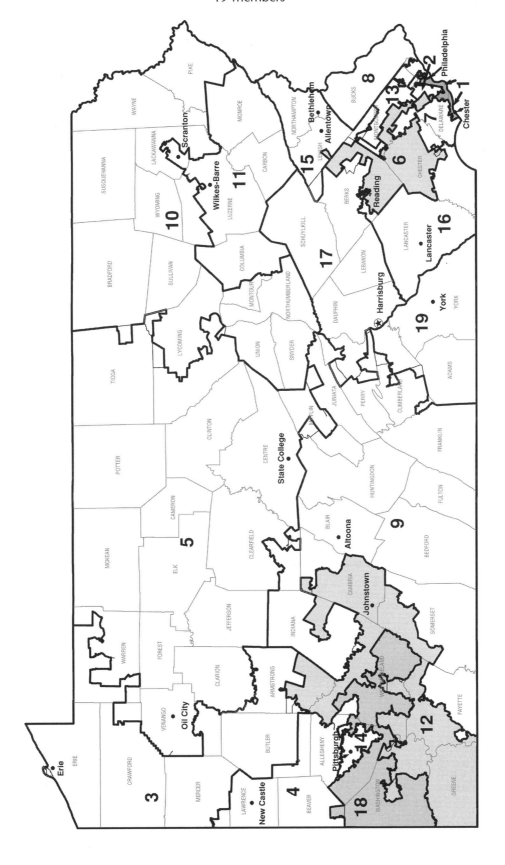

PENNSYLVANIA

Philadelphia Area

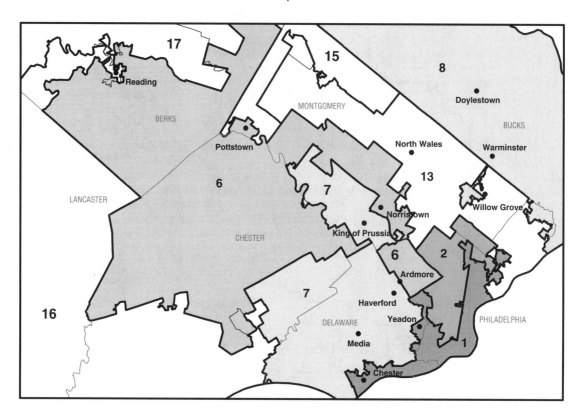

Pittsburgh Area

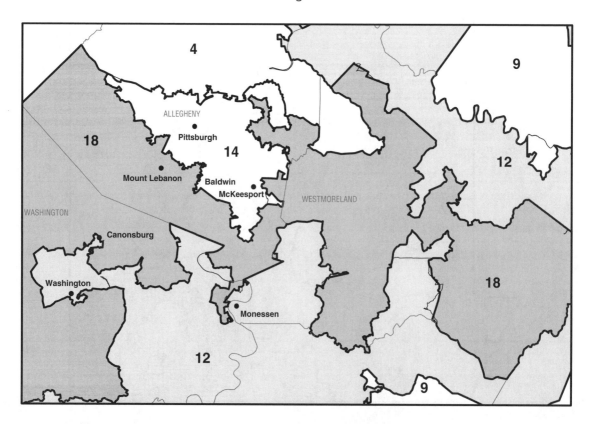

PENNSYLVANIA

GOVERNOR
Tom Corbett (R). Elected 2010 to a four-year term.

SENATORS (1 Democrat, 1 Republican)
Bob Casey Jr. (D). Elected 2006 to a six-year term.

Pat Toomey (R). Elected 2010 to a six-year term.

REPRESENTATIVES (12 Republicans, 7 Democrats)

1. Robert A. Brady (D)
2. Chaka Fattah (D)
3. Mike Kelly (R)
4. Jason Altmire (D)
5. Glenn Thompson (R)
6. Jim Gerlach (R)
7. Patrick Meehan (R)

8. Michael G. Fitzpatrick (R)
9. Bill Shuster (R)
10. Thomas A. Marino (R)
11. Lou Barletta (R)
12. Mark S. Critz (D)
13. Allyson Y. Schwartz (D)
14. Mike Doyle (D)

15. Charlie Dent (R)
16. Joe Pitts (R)
17. Tim Holden (D)
18. Tim Murphy (R)
19. Todd R. Platts (R)

POSTWAR VOTE FOR PRESIDENT

Year	Total Vote	Republican		Democratic		Other Vote	Rep.-Dem. Plurality	Total Vote		Major Vote	
		Vote	Candidate	Vote	Candidate			Rep.	Dem.	Rep.	Dem.
2008	6,013,272	2,655,885	McCain, John	3,276,363	Obama, Barack	81,024	620,478 D	44.2%	54.5%	44.8%	55.2%
2004	5,769,590	2,793,847	Bush, George W.	2,938,095	Kerry, John	37,648	144,248 D	48.4%	50.9%	48.7%	51.3%
2000**	4,913,119	2,281,127	Bush, George W.	2,485,967	Gore, Al	146,025	204,840 D	46.4%	50.6%	47.9%	52.1%
1996**	4,506,118	1,801,169	Dole, Bob	2,215,819	Clinton, Bill	489,130	414,650 D	40.0%	49.2%	44.8%	55.2%
1992**	4,959,810	1,791,841	Bush, George	2,239,164	Clinton, Bill	928,805	447,323 D	36.1%	45.1%	44.5%	55.5%
1988	4,536,251	2,300,087	Bush, George	2,194,944	Dukakis, Michael S.	41,220	105,143 R	50.7%	48.4%	51.2%	48.8%
1984	4,844,903	2,584,323	Reagan, Ronald	2,228,131	Mondale, Walter F.	32,449	356,192 R	53.3%	46.0%	53.7%	46.3%
1980**	4,561,501	2,261,872	Reagan, Ronald	1,937,540	Carter, Jimmy	362,089	324,332 R	49.6%	42.5%	53.9%	46.1%
1976	4,620,787	2,205,604	Ford, Gerald R.	2,328,677	Carter, Jimmy	86,506	123,073 D	47.7%	50.4%	48.6%	51.4%
1972	4,592,106	2,714,521	Nixon, Richard M.	1,796,951	McGovern, George S.	80,634	917,570 R	59.1%	39.1%	60.2%	39.8%
1968**	4,747,928	2,090,017	Nixon, Richard M.	2,259,405	Humphrey, Hubert H.	398,506	169,388 D	44.0%	47.6%	48.1%	51.9%
1964	4,822,690	1,673,657	Goldwater, Barry M.	3,130,954	Johnson, Lyndon B.	18,079	1,457,297 D	34.7%	64.9%	34.8%	65.2%
1960	5,006,541	2,439,956	Nixon, Richard M.	2,556,282	Kennedy, John F.	10,303	116,326 D	48.7%	51.1%	48.8%	51.2%
1956	4,576,503	2,585,252	Eisenhower, Dwight D.	1,981,769	Stevenson, Adlai E.	9,482	603,483 R	56.5%	43.3%	56.6%	43.4%
1952	4,580,969	2,415,789	Eisenhower, Dwight D.	2,146,269	Stevenson, Adlai E.	18,911	269,520 R	52.7%	46.9%	53.0%	47.0%
1948	3,735,348	1,902,197	Dewey, Thomas E.	1,752,426	Truman, Harry S.	80,725	149,771 R	50.9%	46.9%	52.0%	48.0%

**In past elections, the other vote included: 2000 - 103,392 Green (Ralph Nader); 1996 - 430,984 Reform (Ross Perot); 1992 - 902,667 Independent (Perot); 1980 - 292,921 Independent (John Anderson); 1968 - 378,582 American Independent (George Wallace).

PENNSYLVANIA

POSTWAR VOTE FOR GOVERNOR

Year	Total Vote	Republican		Democratic		Other Vote	Rep.-Dem. Plurality	Percentage			
								Total Vote		Major Vote	
		Vote	Candidate	Vote	Candidate			Rep.	Dem.	Rep.	Dem.
2010	3,989,102	2,172,763	Corbett, Tom	1,814,788	Onorato, Dan	1,551	357,975 R	54.5%	45.5%	54.5%	45.5%
2006	4,096,077	1,622,135	Swann, Lynn	2,470,517	Rendell, Edward G.	3,425	848,382 D	39.6%	60.3%	39.6%	60.4%
2002	3,583,179	1,589,408	Fisher, Mike	1,913,235	Rendell, Edward G.	80,536	323,827 D	44.4%	53.4%	45.4%	54.6%
1998**	3,025,152	1,736,844	Ridge, Thomas J.	938,745	Itkin, Ivan	349,563	798,099 R	57.4%	31.0%	64.9%	35.1%
1994**	3,585,526	1,627,976	Ridge, Thomas J.	1,430,099	Singel, Mark S.	527,451	197,877 R	45.4%	39.9%	53.2%	46.8%
1990	3,052,760	987,516	Hafer, Barbara	2,065,244	Casey, Robert		1,077,728 D	32.3%	67.7%	32.3%	67.7%
1986	3,388,275	1,638,268	Scranton, William W., III	1,717,484	Casey, Robert	32,523	79,216 D	48.4%	50.7%	48.8%	51.2%
1982	3,683,985	1,872,784	Thornburgh, Richard L.	1,772,353	Ertel, Allen E.	38,848	100,431 R	50.8%	48.1%	51.4%	48.6%
1978	3,741,969	1,966,042	Thornburgh, Richard L.	1,737,888	Flaherty, Peter	38,039	228,154 R	52.5%	46.4%	53.1%	46.9%
1974	3,491,234	1,578,917	Lewis, Andrew L.	1,878,252	Shapp, Milton	34,065	299,335 D	45.2%	53.8%	45.7%	54.3%
1970	3,700,060	1,542,854	Broderick, Raymond	2,043,029	Shapp, Milton	114,177	500,175 D	41.7%	55.2%	43.0%	57.0%
1966	4,050,668	2,110,349	Shafer, Raymond P.	1,868,719	Shapp, Milton	71,600	241,630 R	52.1%	46.1%	53.0%	47.0%
1962	4,378,042	2,424,918	Scranton, William W.	1,938,627	Dilworth, Richardson	14,497	486,291 R	55.4%	44.3%	55.6%	44.4%
1958	3,986,918	1,948,769	McGonigle, A. T.	2,024,852	Lawrence, David	13,297	76,083 D	48.9%	50.8%	49.0%	51.0%
1954	3,720,457	1,717,070	Wood, Lloyd H.	1,996,266	Leader, George M.	7,121	279,196 D	46.2%	53.7%	46.2%	53.8%
1950	3,540,059	1,796,119	Fine, John S.	1,710,355	Dilworth, Richardson	33,585	85,764 R	50.7%	48.3%	51.2%	48.8%
1946	3,123,994	1,828,462	Duff, James H.	1,270,947	Rice, John S.	24,585	557,515 R	58.5%	40.7%	59.0%	41.0%

**In past elections, the other vote included: 1998 - 315,761 Constitutional (Peg Luksik); 1994 - 460,269 Constitutional (Luksik).

POSTWAR VOTE FOR SENATOR

Year	Total Vote	Republican		Democratic		Other Vote	Rep.-Dem. Plurality	Percentage			
								Total Vote		Major Vote	
		Vote	Candidate	Vote	Candidate			Rep.	Dem.	Rep.	Dem.
2010	3,977,661	2,028,945	Toomey, Pat	1,948,716	Sestak, Joe		80,229 R	51.0%	49.0%	51.0%	49.0%
2006	4,081,043	1,684,778	Santorum, Rick	2,392,984	Casey, Bob, Jr.	3,281	708,206 D	41.3%	58.6%	41.3%	58.7%
2004	5,559,105	2,925,080	Specter, Arlen	2,334,126	Hoeffel, Joseph M.	299,899	590,954 R	52.6%	42.0%	55.6%	44.4%
2000	4,735,504	2,481,962	Santorum, Rick	2,154,908	Klink, Ron	98,634	327,054 R	52.4%	45.5%	53.5%	46.5%
1998	2,957,772	1,814,180	Specter, Arlen	1,028,839	Lloyd, Bill	114,753	785,341 R	61.3%	34.8%	63.8%	36.2%
1994	3,513,361	1,735,691	Santorum, Rick	1,648,481	Wofford, Harris	129,189	87,210 R	49.4%	46.9%	51.3%	48.7%
1992	4,802,410	2,358,125	Specter, Arlen	2,224,966	Yeakel, Lynn	219,319	133,159 R	49.1%	46.3%	51.5%	48.5%
1991S	3,382,746	1,521,986	Thornburgh, Richard	1,860,760	Wofford, Harris		338,774 D	45.0%	55.0%	45.0%	55.0%
1988	4,366,598	2,901,715	Heinz, H. John	1,416,764	Vignola, Joseph C.	48,119	1,484,951 R	66.5%	32.4%	67.2%	32.8%
1986	3,378,226	1,906,537	Specter, Arlen	1,448,219	Edgar, Robert W.	23,470	458,318 R	56.4%	42.9%	56.8%	43.2%
1982	3,604,108	2,136,418	Heinz, H. John	1,412,965	Wecht, Cyril H.	54,725	723,453 R	59.3%	39.2%	60.2%	39.8%
1980	4,418,042	2,230,404	Specter, Arlen	2,122,391	Flaherty, Peter	65,247	108,013 R	50.5%	48.0%	51.2%	48.8%
1976	4,546,353	2,381,891	Heinz, H. John	2,126,977	Green, William J., III	37,485	254,914 R	52.4%	46.8%	52.8%	47.2%
1974	3,477,812	1,843,317	Schweiker, Richard S.	1,596,121	Flaherty, Peter	38,374	247,196 R	53.0%	45.9%	53.6%	46.4%
1970	3,644,305	1,874,106	Scott, Hugh	1,653,774	Sesler, William G.	116,425	220,332 R	51.4%	45.4%	53.1%	46.9%
1968	4,624,218	2,399,762	Schweiker, Richard S.	2,117,662	Clark, Joseph S.	106,794	282,100 R	51.9%	45.8%	53.1%	46.9%
1964	4,803,835	2,429,858	Scott, Hugh	2,359,223	Blatt, Genevieve	14,754	70,635 R	50.6%	49.1%	50.7%	49.3%
1962	4,383,475	2,134,649	Van Zandt, James E.	2,238,383	Clark, Joseph S.	10,443	103,734 D	48.7%	51.1%	48.8%	51.2%
1958	3,988,622	2,042,586	Scott, Hugh	1,929,821	Leader, George M.	16,215	112,765 R	51.2%	48.4%	51.4%	48.6%
1956	4,529,874	2,250,671	Duff, James H.	2,268,641	Clark, Joseph S.	10,562	17,970 D	49.7%	50.1%	49.8%	50.2%
1952	4,519,761	2,331,034	Martin, Edward	2,168,546	Bard, Guy Kurtz	20,181	162,488 R	51.6%	48.0%	51.8%	48.2%
1950	3,548,703	1,820,400	Duff, James H.	1,694,076	Myers, Francis J.	34,227	126,324 R	51.3%	47.7%	51.8%	48.2%
1946	3,127,860	1,853,458	Martin, Edward	1,245,338	Guffey, Joseph F.	29,064	608,120 R	59.3%	39.8%	59.8%	40.2%

**The 1991 election was for a short term to fill a vacancy.

PENNSYLVANIA

GOVERNOR 2010

2010 Census Population	County	Total Vote	Republican	Democratic	Other	Rep.-Dem. Plurality	Percentage Total Vote Rep.	Dem.	Percentage Major Vote Rep.	Dem.
101,407	ADAMS	31,170	22,696	8,474		14,222 R	72.8%	27.2%	72.8%	27.2%
1,223,348	ALLEGHENY	427,318	213,889	213,429		460 R	50.1%	49.9%	50.1%	49.9%
68,941	ARMSTRONG	22,691	16,096	6,595		9,501 R	70.9%	29.1%	70.9%	29.1%
170,539	BEAVER	57,833	32,670	25,163		7,507 R	56.5%	43.5%	56.5%	43.5%
49,762	BEDFORD	16,512	12,873	3,639		9,234 R	78.0%	22.0%	78.0%	22.0%
411,442	BERKS	112,504	66,758	45,746		21,012 R	59.3%	40.7%	59.3%	40.7%
127,089	BLAIR	35,949	26,199	9,750		16,449 R	72.9%	27.1%	72.9%	27.1%
62,622	BRADFORD	17,215	12,474	4,741		7,733 R	72.5%	27.5%	72.5%	27.5%
625,249	BUCKS	228,334	126,190	102,144		24,046 R	55.3%	44.7%	55.3%	44.7%
183,862	BUTLER	65,555	47,151	18,404		28,747 R	71.9%	28.1%	71.9%	28.1%
143,679	CAMBRIA	47,546	27,444	20,102		7,342 R	57.7%	42.3%	57.7%	42.3%
5,085	CAMERON	1,561	1,100	461		639 R	70.5%	29.5%	70.5%	29.5%
65,249	CARBON	19,131	11,297	7,834		3,463 R	59.1%	40.9%	59.1%	40.9%
153,990	CENTRE	44,865	24,458	20,407		4,051 R	54.5%	45.5%	54.5%	45.5%
498,886	CHESTER	173,552	97,112	76,440		20,672 R	56.0%	44.0%	56.0%	44.0%
39,988	CLARION	12,393	8,827	3,566		5,261 R	71.2%	28.8%	71.2%	28.8%
81,642	CLEARFIELD	24,692	15,685	9,007		6,678 R	63.5%	36.5%	63.5%	36.5%
39,238	CLINTON	9,301	5,676	3,625		2,051 R	61.0%	39.0%	61.0%	39.0%
67,295	COLUMBIA	18,287	12,151	6,136		6,015 R	66.4%	33.6%	66.4%	33.6%
88,765	CRAWFORD	26,774	17,883	8,891		8,992 R	66.8%	33.2%	66.8%	33.2%
235,406	CUMBERLAND	80,815	56,284	24,531		31,753 R	69.6%	30.4%	69.6%	30.4%
268,100	DAUPHIN	88,074	53,261	34,813		18,448 R	60.5%	39.5%	60.5%	39.5%
558,979	DELAWARE	202,152	95,448	106,704		11,256 D	47.2%	52.8%	47.2%	52.8%
31,946	ELK	10,309	6,374	3,935		2,439 R	61.8%	38.2%	61.8%	38.2%
280,566	ERIE	85,333	42,752	42,581		171 R	50.1%	49.9%	50.1%	49.9%
136,606	FAYETTE	34,100	18,994	15,106		3,888 R	55.7%	44.3%	55.7%	44.3%
7,716	FOREST	1,890	1,257	633		624 R	66.5%	33.5%	66.5%	33.5%
149,618	FRANKLIN	43,854	33,559	10,295		23,264 R	76.5%	23.5%	76.5%	23.5%
14,845	FULTON	4,466	3,521	945		2,576 R	78.8%	21.2%	78.8%	21.2%
38,686	GREENE	11,153	6,000	5,153		847 R	53.8%	46.2%	53.8%	46.2%
45,913	HUNTINGDON	13,393	9,764	3,629		6,135 R	72.9%	27.1%	72.9%	27.1%
88,880	INDIANA	25,362	16,520	8,842		7,678 R	65.1%	34.9%	65.1%	34.9%
45,200	JEFFERSON	13,437	10,017	3,420		6,597 R	74.5%	25.5%	74.5%	25.5%
24,636	JUNIATA	7,368	5,834	1,534		4,300 R	79.2%	20.8%	79.2%	20.8%
214,437	LACKAWANNA	69,642	31,342	38,300		6,958 D	45.0%	55.0%	45.0%	55.0%
519,445	LANCASTER	149,698	106,430	43,268		63,162 R	71.1%	28.9%	71.1%	28.9%
91,108	LAWRENCE	27,988	16,489	11,499		4,990 R	58.9%	41.1%	58.9%	41.1%
133,568	LEBANON	39,874	29,534	10,340		19,194 R	74.1%	25.9%	74.1%	25.9%
349,497	LEHIGH	96,030	52,769	43,261		9,508 R	55.0%	45.0%	55.0%	45.0%
320,918	LUZERNE	93,126	49,734	43,392		6,342 R	53.4%	46.6%	53.4%	46.6%
116,111	LYCOMING	34,432	25,154	9,278		15,876 R	73.1%	26.9%	73.1%	26.9%
43,450	MCKEAN	9,880	7,117	2,763		4,354 R	72.0%	28.0%	72.0%	28.0%
116,638	MERCER	36,193	21,146	15,047		6,099 R	58.4%	41.6%	58.4%	41.6%
46,682	MIFFLIN	12,229	9,642	2,587		7,055 R	78.8%	21.2%	78.8%	21.2%
169,842	MONROE	39,244	21,162	18,082		3,080 R	53.9%	46.1%	53.9%	46.1%
799,874	MONTGOMERY	288,324	139,244	149,080		9,836 D	48.3%	51.7%	48.3%	51.7%
18,267	MONTOUR	5,711	3,896	1,815		2,081 R	68.2%	31.8%	68.2%	31.8%
297,735	NORTHAMPTON	84,857	45,986	38,871		7,115 R	54.2%	45.8%	54.2%	45.8%
94,528	NORTHUMBERLAND	26,174	17,781	8,393		9,388 R	67.9%	32.1%	67.9%	32.1%
45,969	PERRY	14,587	11,568	3,019		8,549 R	79.3%	20.7%	79.3%	20.7%
1,526,006	PHILADELPHIA	422,783	72,352	350,431		278,079 D	17.1%	82.9%	17.1%	82.9%
57,369	PIKE	15,366	9,894	5,472		4,422 R	64.4%	35.6%	64.4%	35.6%
17,457	POTTER	5,310	4,053	1,257		2,796 R	76.3%	23.7%	76.3%	23.7%
148,289	SCHUYLKILL	45,194	28,659	16,535		12,124 R	63.4%	36.6%	63.4%	36.6%
39,702	SNYDER	11,303	8,591	2,712		5,879 R	76.0%	24.0%	76.0%	24.0%

PENNSYLVANIA

GOVERNOR 2010

2010 Census Population	County	Total Vote	Republican	Democratic	Other	Rep.-Dem. Plurality	Total Vote Rep.	Total Vote Dem.	Major Vote Rep.	Major Vote Dem.
77,742	SOMERSET	25,836	18,542	7,294		11,248 R	71.8%	28.2%	71.8%	28.2%
6,428	SULLIVAN	2,336	1,654	682		972 R	70.8%	29.2%	70.8%	29.2%
43,356	SUSQUEHANNA	14,006	9,612	4,394		5,218 R	68.6%	31.4%	68.6%	31.4%
41,981	TIOGA	12,002	9,069	2,933		6,136 R	75.6%	24.4%	75.6%	24.4%
44,947	UNION	11,789	8,121	3,668		4,453 R	68.9%	31.1%	68.9%	31.1%
54,984	VENANGO	15,892	10,937	4,955		5,982 R	68.8%	31.2%	68.8%	31.2%
41,815	WARREN	12,190	8,194	3,996		4,198 R	67.2%	32.8%	67.2%	32.8%
207,820	WASHINGTON	70,195	41,984	28,211		13,773 R	59.8%	40.2%	59.8%	40.2%
52,822	WAYNE	15,834	10,747	5,087		5,660 R	67.9%	32.1%	67.9%	32.1%
365,169	WESTMORELAND	125,202	84,762	40,440		44,322 R	67.7%	32.3%	67.7%	32.3%
28,276	WYOMING	8,918	5,901	3,017		2,884 R	66.2%	33.8%	66.2%	33.8%
434,972	YORK	130,517	92,483	38,034		54,449 R	70.9%	29.1%	70.9%	29.1%
12,702,379	TOTAL	3,989,102	2,172,763	1,814,788	1,551	357,975 R	54.5%	45.5%	54.5%	45.5%

The statewide totals for "Total Vote" and "Other" include 1,551 scattered write-in votes that were not a part of the county-by-county returns.

PENNSYLVANIA

SENATOR 2010

2010 Census Population	County	Total Vote	Republican	Democratic	Other	Rep.-Dem. Plurality	Total Vote Rep.	Total Vote Dem.	Major Vote Rep.	Major Vote Dem.
101,407	ADAMS	31,101	21,567	9,534		12,033 R	69.3%	30.7%	69.3%	30.7%
1,223,348	ALLEGHENY	425,253	192,257	232,996		40,739 D	45.2%	54.8%	45.2%	54.8%
68,941	ARMSTRONG	22,493	14,693	7,800		6,893 R	65.3%	34.7%	65.3%	34.7%
170,539	BEAVER	57,475	30,136	27,339		2,797 R	52.4%	47.6%	52.4%	47.6%
49,762	BEDFORD	16,443	12,315	4,128		8,187 R	74.9%	25.1%	74.9%	25.1%
411,442	BERKS	112,505	62,534	49,971		12,563 R	55.6%	44.4%	55.6%	44.4%
127,089	BLAIR	35,669	24,411	11,258		13,153 R	68.4%	31.6%	68.4%	31.6%
62,622	BRADFORD	17,156	12,076	5,080		6,996 R	70.4%	29.6%	70.4%	29.6%
625,249	BUCKS	228,539	121,331	107,208		14,123 R	53.1%	46.9%	53.1%	46.9%
183,862	BUTLER	64,900	44,429	20,471		23,958 R	68.5%	31.5%	68.5%	31.5%
143,679	CAMBRIA	47,282	24,254	23,028		1,226 R	51.3%	48.7%	51.3%	48.7%
5,085	CAMERON	1,561	1,005	556		449 R	64.4%	35.6%	64.4%	35.6%
65,249	CARBON	18,885	10,326	8,559		1,767 R	54.7%	45.3%	54.7%	45.3%
153,990	CENTRE	44,713	23,111	21,602		1,509 R	51.7%	48.3%	51.7%	48.3%
498,886	CHESTER	173,405	92,667	80,738		11,929 R	53.4%	46.6%	53.4%	46.6%
39,988	CLARION	12,265	8,266	3,999		4,267 R	67.4%	32.6%	67.4%	32.6%
81,642	CLEARFIELD	24,480	14,798	9,682		5,116 R	60.4%	39.6%	60.4%	39.6%
39,238	CLINTON	9,216	5,409	3,807		1,602 R	58.7%	41.3%	58.7%	41.3%
67,295	COLUMBIA	18,155	11,287	6,868		4,419 R	62.2%	37.8%	62.2%	37.8%
88,765	CRAWFORD	26,710	16,725	9,985		6,740 R	62.6%	37.4%	62.6%	37.4%
235,406	CUMBERLAND	80,719	52,890	27,829		25,061 R	65.5%	34.5%	65.5%	34.5%
268,100	DAUPHIN	87,934	49,021	38,913		10,108 R	55.7%	44.3%	55.7%	44.3%
558,979	DELAWARE	202,799	88,955	113,844		24,889 D	43.9%	56.1%	43.9%	56.1%
31,946	ELK	10,229	5,638	4,591		1,047 R	55.1%	44.9%	55.1%	44.9%
280,566	ERIE	84,997	38,146	46,851		8,705 D	44.9%	55.1%	44.9%	55.1%

PENNSYLVANIA

SENATOR 2010

2010 Census Population	County	Total Vote	Republican	Democratic	Other	Rep.-Dem. Plurality	Percentage Total Vote Rep.	Dem.	Major Vote Rep.	Dem.
136,606	FAYETTE	33,789	16,960	16,829		131 R	50.2%	49.8%	50.2%	49.8%
7,716	FOREST	1,871	1,121	750		371 R	59.9%	40.1%	59.9%	40.1%
149,618	FRANKLIN	43,851	32,364	11,487		20,877 R	73.8%	26.2%	73.8%	26.2%
14,845	FULTON	4,471	3,434	1,037		2,397 R	76.8%	23.2%	76.8%	23.2%
38,686	GREENE	10,985	5,502	5,483		19 R	50.1%	49.9%	50.1%	49.9%
45,913	HUNTINGDON	13,357	9,134	4,223		4,911 R	68.4%	31.6%	68.4%	31.6%
88,880	INDIANA	25,218	15,133	10,085		5,048 R	60.0%	40.0%	60.0%	40.0%
45,200	JEFFERSON	13,208	9,326	3,882		5,444 R	70.6%	29.4%	70.6%	29.4%
24,636	JUNIATA	7,333	5,504	1,829		3,675 R	75.1%	24.9%	75.1%	24.9%
214,437	LACKAWANNA	69,069	27,742	41,327		13,585 D	40.2%	59.8%	40.2%	59.8%
519,445	LANCASTER	149,762	102,113	47,649		54,464 R	68.2%	31.8%	68.2%	31.8%
91,108	LAWRENCE	27,810	15,493	12,317		3,176 R	55.7%	44.3%	55.7%	44.3%
133,568	LEBANON	39,719	27,881	11,838		16,043 R	70.2%	29.8%	70.2%	29.8%
349,497	LEHIGH	95,796	50,341	45,455		4,886 R	52.6%	47.4%	52.6%	47.4%
320,918	LUZERNE	91,879	45,313	46,566		1,253 D	49.3%	50.7%	49.3%	50.7%
116,111	LYCOMING	34,195	23,944	10,251		13,693 R	70.0%	30.0%	70.0%	30.0%
43,450	MCKEAN	9,908	6,801	3,107		3,694 R	68.6%	31.4%	68.6%	31.4%
116,638	MERCER	36,095	20,095	16,000		4,095 R	55.7%	44.3%	55.7%	44.3%
46,682	MIFFLIN	12,157	9,182	2,975		6,207 R	75.5%	24.5%	75.5%	24.5%
169,842	MONROE	39,216	20,295	18,921		1,374 R	51.8%	48.2%	51.8%	48.2%
799,874	MONTGOMERY	287,368	131,955	155,413		23,458 D	45.9%	54.1%	45.9%	54.1%
18,267	MONTOUR	5,695	3,627	2,068		1,559 R	63.7%	36.3%	63.7%	36.3%
297,735	NORTHAMPTON	84,530	44,209	40,321		3,888 R	52.3%	47.7%	52.3%	47.7%
94,528	NORTHUMBERLAND	25,849	16,032	9,817		6,215 R	62.0%	38.0%	62.0%	38.0%
45,969	PERRY	14,538	10,972	3,566		7,406 R	75.5%	24.5%	75.5%	24.5%
1,526,006	PHILADELPHIA	425,977	67,996	357,981		289,985 D	16.0%	84.0%	16.0%	84.0%
57,369	PIKE	15,305	9,678	5,627		4,051 R	63.2%	36.8%	63.2%	36.8%
17,457	POTTER	5,290	3,919	1,371		2,548 R	74.1%	25.9%	74.1%	25.9%
148,289	SCHUYLKILL	44,726	26,348	18,378		7,970 R	58.9%	41.1%	58.9%	41.1%
39,702	SNYDER	11,220	8,072	3,148		4,924 R	71.9%	28.1%	71.9%	28.1%
77,742	SOMERSET	25,697	17,209	8,488		8,721 R	67.0%	33.0%	67.0%	33.0%
6,428	SULLIVAN	2,315	1,561	754		807 R	67.4%	32.6%	67.4%	32.6%
43,356	SUSQUEHANNA	14,001	9,141	4,860		4,281 R	65.3%	34.7%	65.3%	34.7%
41,981	TIOGA	12,003	8,651	3,352		5,299 R	72.1%	27.9%	72.1%	27.9%
44,947	UNION	11,677	7,618	4,059		3,559 R	65.2%	34.8%	65.2%	34.8%
54,984	VENANGO	15,744	10,147	5,597		4,550 R	64.4%	35.6%	64.4%	35.6%
41,815	WARREN	12,108	7,615	4,493		3,122 R	62.9%	37.1%	62.9%	37.1%
207,820	WASHINGTON	69,646	37,957	31,689		6,268 R	54.5%	45.5%	54.5%	45.5%
52,822	WAYNE	15,774	10,348	5,426		4,922 R	65.6%	34.4%	65.6%	34.4%
365,169	WESTMORELAND	124,340	76,002	48,338		27,664 R	61.1%	38.9%	61.1%	38.9%
28,276	WYOMING	8,852	5,569	3,283		2,286 R	62.9%	37.1%	62.9%	37.1%
434,972	YORK	130,433	88,394	42,039		46,355 R	67.8%	32.2%	67.8%	32.2%
12,702,379	TOTAL	3,977,661	2,028,945	1,948,716		80,229 R	51.0%	49.0%	51.0%	49.0%

PENNSYLVANIA

HOUSE OF REPRESENTATIVES

CD	Year	Total Vote	Republican		Democratic		Other Vote	Rep.-Dem. Plurality		Percentage Total Vote		Percentage Major Vote	
			Vote	Candidate	Vote	Candidate				Rep.	Dem.	Rep.	Dem.
1	2010	149,949		—	149,944	BRADY, ROBERT A.*	5	149,944	D		100.0%		100.0%
1	2008	267,513	24,714	MUHAMMAD, MIKE	242,799	BRADY, ROBERT A.*		218,085	D	9.2%	90.8%	9.2%	90.8%
1	2006	137,999		—	137,987	BRADY, ROBERT A.*	12	137,987	D		100.0%		100.0%
1	2004	248,587	33,266	WILLIAMS, DEBORAH L.	214,462	BRADY, ROBERT A.*	859	181,196	D	13.4%	86.3%	13.4%	86.6%
1	2002	140,090	17,444	DELANEY, MARIE G.	121,076	BRADY, ROBERT A.*	1,570	103,632	D	12.5%	86.4%	12.6%	87.4%
2	2010	204,707	21,907	HELLBERG, RICK	182,800	FATTAH, CHAKA*		160,893	D	10.7%	89.3%	10.7%	89.3%
2	2008	311,336	34,466	LANG, ADAM A.	276,870	FATTAH, CHAKA*		242,404	D	11.1%	88.9%	11.1%	88.9%
2	2006	187,283	17,291	GESSNER, MICHAEL	165,867	FATTAH, CHAKA*	4,125	148,576	D	9.2%	88.6%	9.4%	90.6%
2	2004	287,637	34,411	BOLNO, STEWART	253,226	FATTAH, CHAKA*		218,815	D	12.0%	88.0%	12.0%	88.0%
2	2002	171,611	20,988	DOUGHERTY, THOMAS G.	150,623	FATTAH, CHAKA*		129,635	D	12.2%	87.8%	12.2%	87.8%
3	2010	200,958	111,909	KELLY, MIKE	88,924	DAHLKEMPER, KATHLEEN A.*	125	22,985	R	55.7%	44.3%	55.7%	44.3%
3	2008	286,603	139,757	ENGLISH, PHIL*	146,846	DAHLKEMPER, KATHLEEN A.		7,089	D	48.8%	51.2%	48.8%	51.2%
3	2006	202,518	108,525	ENGLISH, PHIL*	85,110	PORTER, STEVEN	8,883	23,415	R	53.6%	42.0%	56.0%	44.0%
3	2004	277,323	166,580	ENGLISH, PHIL*	110,684	PORTER, STEVEN	59	55,896	R	60.1%	39.9%	60.1%	39.9%
3	2002	150,329	116,763	ENGLISH, PHIL*		—	33,566	116,763	R	77.7%	0.0%	100.0%	0.0%
4	2010	238,049	116,958	ROTHFUS, KEITH	120,827	ALTMIRE, JASON*	264	3,869	D	49.1%	50.8%	49.2%	50.8%
4	2008	333,947	147,411	HART, MELISSA A.*	186,536	ALTMIRE, JASON*		39,125	D	44.1%	55.9%	44.1%	55.9%
4	2006	254,084	122,049	HART, MELISSA A.*	131,847	ALTMIRE, JASON	188	9,798	D	48.0%	51.9%	48.1%	51.9%
4	2004	323,945	204,329	HART, MELISSA A.*	116,303	DROBAC, STEVAN, JR.	3,313	88,026	R	63.1%	35.9%	63.7%	36.3%
4	2002	202,218	130,534	HART, MELISSA A.*	71,674	DROBAC, STEVAN, JR.	10	58,860	R	64.6%	35.4%	64.6%	35.4%
5	2010	185,648	127,427	THOMPSON, GLENN*	52,375	PIPE, MICHAEL	5,846	75,052	R	68.6%	28.2%	70.9%	29.1%
5	2008	274,177	155,513	THOMPSON, GLENN	112,509	McCRACKEN, MARK B.	6,155	43,004	R	56.7%	41.0%	58.0%	42.0%
5	2006	191,727	115,126	PETERSON, JOHN E.*	76,456	HILLIARD, DONALD L.	145	38,670	R	60.0%	39.9%	60.1%	39.9%
5	2004	219,198	192,852	PETERSON, JOHN E.*		—	26,346	192,852	R	88.0%		100.0%	
5	2002	143,211	124,942	PETERSON, JOHN E.*		—	18,269	124,942	R	87.2%		100.0%	
6	2010	234,455	133,770	GERLACH, JIM*	100,493	TRIVEDI, MANAN	192	33,277	R	57.1%	42.9%	57.1%	42.9%
6	2008	344,375	179,423	GERLACH, JIM*	164,952	ROGGIO, BOB		14,471	R	52.1%	47.9%	52.1%	47.9%
6	2006	238,939	121,047	GERLACH, JIM*	117,892	MURPHY, LOIS		3,155	R	50.7%	49.3%	50.7%	49.3%
6	2004	314,386	160,348	GERLACH, JIM*	153,977	MURPHY, LOIS	61	6,371	R	51.0%	49.0%	51.0%	49.0%
6	2002	201,791	103,648	GERLACH, JIM	98,128	WOFFORD, DAN	15	5,520	R	51.4%	48.6%	51.4%	48.6%
7	2010	250,926	137,825	MEEHAN, PATRICK	110,314	LENTZ, BRYAN	2,787	27,511	R	54.9%	44.0%	55.5%	44.5%
7	2008	352,317	142,362	WILLIAMS, W. CRAIG	209,955	SESTAK, JOE*		67,593	D	40.4%	59.6%	40.4%	59.6%
7	2006	262,434	114,426	WELDON, CURT*	147,898	SESTAK, JOE	110	33,472	D	43.6%	56.4%	43.6%	56.4%
7	2004	334,547	196,556	WELDON, CURT*	134,932	SCOLES, PAUL	3,059	61,624	R	58.8%	40.3%	59.3%	40.7%
7	2002	221,351	146,296	WELDON, CURT*	75,055	LENNON, PETER A.		71,241	R	66.1%	33.9%	66.1%	33.9%
8	2010	244,306	130,759	FITZPATRICK, MICHAEL G.	113,547	MURPHY, PATRICK J.*		17,212	R	53.5%	46.5%	53.5%	46.5%
8	2008	348,515	145,103	MANION, TOM	197,869	MURPHY, PATRICK J.*	5,543	52,766	D	41.6%	56.8%	42.3%	57.7%
8	2006	249,817	124,138	FITZPATRICK, MICHAEL G.*	125,656	MURPHY, PATRICK J.	23	1,518	D	49.7%	50.3%	49.7%	50.3%
8	2004	331,276	183,229	FITZPATRICK, MICHAEL G.	143,427	SCHRADER, VIRGINIA WATERS	4,620	39,802	R	55.3%	43.3%	56.1%	43.9%
8	2002	203,687	127,475	GREENWOOD, JAMES C.*	76,178	REECE, TIMOTHY T.	34	51,297	R	62.6%	37.4%	62.6%	37.4%
9	2010	194,379	141,904	SHUSTER, BILL*	52,322	CONNERS, TOM	153	89,582	R	73.0%	26.9%	73.1%	26.9%
9	2008	273,686	174,951	SHUSTER, BILL*	98,735	BARR, TONY		76,216	R	63.9%	36.1%	63.9%	36.1%
9	2006	200,820	121,069	SHUSTER, BILL*	79,610	BARR, TONY	141	41,459	R	60.3%	39.6%	60.3%	39.7%
9	2004	265,272	184,320	SHUSTER, BILL*	80,787	POLITIS, PAUL I.	165	103,533	R	69.5%	30.5%	69.5%	30.5%
9	2002	174,849	124,184	SHUSTER, BILL*	50,558	HENRY, JOHN R.	107	73,626	R	71.0%	28.9%	71.1%	28.9%
10	2010	200,655	110,599	MARINO, THOMAS A.	89,846	CARNEY, CHRISTOPHER P.*	210	20,753	R	55.1%	44.8%	55.2%	44.8%
10	2008	285,518	124,681	HACKETT, CHRIS	160,837	CARNEY, CHRISTOPHER P.*		36,156	D	43.7%	56.3%	43.7%	56.3%
10	2006	208,173	97,862	SHERWOOD, DON*	110,115	CARNEY, CHRISTOPHER P.	196	12,253	D	47.0%	52.9%	47.1%	52.9%
10	2004	206,839	191,967	SHERWOOD, DON*		—	14,872	191,967	R	92.8%		100.0%	
10	2002	164,159	152,017	SHERWOOD, DON*		—	12,142	152,017	R	92.6%		100.0%	

PENNSYLVANIA

HOUSE OF REPRESENTATIVES

CD	Year	Total Vote	Republican Vote	Candidate	Democratic Vote	Candidate	Other Vote	Rep.-Dem. Plurality		Percentage Total Vote Rep.	Dem.	Major Vote Rep.	Dem.
11	2010	186,961	102,179	BARLETTA, LOU	84,618	KANJORSKI, PAUL E.*	164	17,561	R	54.7%	45.3%	54.7%	45.3%
11	2008	283,530	137,151	BARLETTA, LOU	146,379	KANJORSKI, PAUL E.*		9,228	D	48.4%	51.6%	48.4%	51.6%
11	2006	185,413	51,033	LEONARDI, JOSEPH F.	134,340	KANJORSKI, PAUL E.*	40	83,307	D	27.5%	72.5%	27.5%	72.5%
11	2004	181,285		—	171,147	KANJORSKI, PAUL E.*	10,138	171,147	D		94.4%		100.0%
11	2002	168,615	71,543	BARLETTA, LOU	93,758	KANJORSKI, PAUL E.*	3,314	22,215	D	42.4%	55.6%	43.3%	56.7%
12	2010	185,306	91,170	BURNS, TIM	94,056	CRITZ, MARK S.*	80	2,886	D	49.2%	50.8%	49.2%	50.8%
12	2008	268,388	113,120	RUSSELL, WILLIAM	155,268	MURTHA, JOHN P.*		42,148	D	42.1%	57.9%	42.1%	57.9%
12	2006	203,163	79,612	IREY, DIANA	123,472	MURTHA, JOHN P.*	79	43,860	D	39.2%	60.8%	39.2%	60.8%
12	2004	204,710		—	204,504	MURTHA, JOHN P.*	206	204,504	D		99.9%		100.0%
12	2002	169,028	44,818	CHOBY, BILL	124,201	MURTHA, JOHN P.*	9	79,383	D	26.5%	73.5%	26.5%	73.5%
13	2010	210,697	91,987	ADCOCK, CARSON DEE	118,710	SCHWARTZ, ALLYSON Y.*		26,723	D	43.7%	56.3%	43.7%	56.3%
13	2008	313,513	108,271	KATS, MARINA	196,868	SCHWARTZ, ALLYSON Y.*	8,374	88,597	D	34.5%	62.8%	35.5%	64.5%
13	2006	222,860	75,492	BHAKTA, RAJ PETER	147,368	SCHWARTZ, ALLYSON Y.*		71,876	D	33.9%	66.1%	33.9%	66.1%
13	2004	308,124	127,205	BROWN, MELISSA	171,763	SCHWARTZ, ALLYSON Y.	9,156	44,558	D	41.3%	55.7%	42.5%	57.5%
13	2002	211,867	100,295	BROWN, MELISSA	107,945	HOEFFEL, JOSEPH M.*	3,627	7,650	D	47.3%	50.9%	48.2%	51.8%
14	2010	178,509	49,997	HALUSZCZAK, MELISSA	122,073	DOYLE, MIKE*	6,439	72,076	D	28.0%	68.4%	29.1%	70.9%
14	2008	265,540		—	242,326	DOYLE, MIKE*	23,214	242,326	D		91.3%		100.0%
14	2006	179,401		—	161,075	DOYLE, MIKE*	18,326	161,075	D		89.8%		100.0%
14	2004	220,299		—	220,139	DOYLE, MIKE*	160	220,139	D		99.9%		100.0%
14	2002	123,412		—	123,323	DOYLE, MIKE*	89	123,323	D		99.9%		100.0%
15	2010	204,549	109,534	DENT, CHARLIE*	79,766	CALLAHAN, JOHN B.	15,249	29,768	R	53.5%	39.0%	57.9%	42.1%
15	2008	309,766	181,433	DENT, CHARLIE*	128,333	BENNETT, SAM		53,100	R	58.6%	41.4%	58.6%	41.4%
15	2006	198,173	106,153	DENT, CHARLIE*	86,186	DERTINGER, CHARLES	5,834	19,967	R	53.6%	43.5%	55.2%	44.8%
15	2004	291,147	170,634	DENT, CHARLIE	114,646	DRISCOLL, JOE	5,867	55,988	R	58.6%	39.4%	59.8%	40.2%
15	2002	171,713	98,493	TOOMEY, PATRICK J.*	73,212	O'BRIEN, EDWARD J.	8	25,281	R	57.4%	42.6%	57.4%	42.6%
16	2010	205,304	134,113	PITTS, JOE*	70,994	HERR, LOIS	197	63,119	R	65.3%	34.6%	65.4%	34.6%
16	2008	305,167	170,329	PITTS, JOE*	120,193	SLATER, BRUCE A.	14,645	50,136	R	55.8%	39.4%	58.6%	41.4%
16	2006	204,669	115,741	PITTS, JOE*	80,915	HERR, LOIS	8,013	34,826	R	56.6%	39.5%	58.9%	41.1%
16	2004	285,313	183,620	PITTS, JOE*	98,410	HERR, LOIS	3,283	85,210	R	64.4%	34.5%	65.1%	34.9%
16	2002	134,597	119,046	PITTS, JOE*		—	15,551	119,046	R	88.4%		100.0%	
17	2010	213,528	95,000	ARGALL, DAVE	118,486	HOLDEN, TIM*	42	23,486	D	44.5%	55.5%	44.5%	55.5%
17	2008	302,608	109,909	GILHOOLEY, TONI	192,699	HOLDEN, TIM*		82,790	D	36.3%	63.7%	36.3%	63.7%
17	2006	212,777	75,455	WERTZ, MATTHEW A.	137,253	HOLDEN, TIM*	69	61,798	D	35.5%	64.5%	35.5%	64.5%
17	2004	291,793	113,592	PATERNO, SCOTT	172,412	HOLDEN, TIM*	5,789	58,820	D	38.9%	59.1%	39.7%	60.3%
17	2002	201,291	97,802	GEKAS, GEORGE W.*	103,483	HOLDEN, TIM*	6	5,681	D	48.6%	51.4%	48.6%	51.4%
18	2010	240,708	161,888	MURPHY, TIM*	78,558	CONNOLLY, DAN	262	83,330	R	67.3%	32.6%	67.3%	32.7%
18	2008	333,010	213,349	MURPHY, TIM*	119,661	O'DONNELL, STEVE		93,688	R	64.1%	35.9%	64.1%	35.9%
18	2006	250,240	144,632	MURPHY, TIM*	105,419	KLUKO, CHAD	189	39,213	R	57.8%	42.1%	57.8%	42.2%
18	2004	315,342	197,894	MURPHY, TIM*	117420	BOLES, MARK G.	28	80,474	R	62.8%	37.2%	62.8%	37.2%
18	2002	199,349	119,885	MURPHY, TIM	79,451	MACHEK, JACK	13	40,434	R	60.1%	39.9%	60.1%	39.9%
19	2010	229,910	165,219	PLATTS, TODD R.*	53,549	SANDERS, RYAN S.	11,142	111,670	R	71.9%	23.3%	75.5%	24.5%
19	2008	328,395	218,862	PLATTS, TODD R.*	109,533	AVILLO, PHILIP J., JR.		109,329	R	66.6%	33.4%	66.6%	33.4%
19	2006	222,898	142,512	PLATTS, TODD R.*	74,625	AVILLO, PHILIP J., JR.	5,761	67,887	R	63.9%	33.5%	65.6%	34.4%
19	2004	245,251	224,274	PLATTS, TODD R.*		—	20,977	224,274	R	91.4%		100.0%	
19	2002	157,145	143,097	PLATTS, TODD R.*		—	14,048	143,097	R	91.1%		100.0%	
TOTAL	2010	3,959,504	2,034,145		1,882,202		43,157	151,943	R	51.4%	47.5%	51.9%	48.1%
TOTAL	2008	5,791,284	2,520,805		3,209,168		61,311	688,363	D	43.5%	55.4%	44.0%	56.0%
TOTAL	2006	4,013,388	1,732,163		2,229,091		52,134	496,928	D	43.2%	55.5%	43.7%	56.3%
TOTAL	2004	5,152,274	2,565,077		2,478,239		108,958	86,838	R	49.8%	48.1%	50.9%	49.1%
TOTAL	2002	3,310,313	1,859,270		1,348,665		102,378	510,605	R	56.2%	40.7%	58.0%	42.0%

The aggregate totals in 2008 for "Total Vote" and "Other Vote" include 3,380 write-in votes that were not a part of the district-by-district returns. Some of the congressional district lines underwent revision before the 2004 election, but the changes were minor in nature.

An asterisk (*) denotes incumbent.

PENNSYLVANIA

GENERAL AND PRIMARY ELECTIONS

2010 GENERAL ELECTIONS

Governor Other vote was 1,551 scattered write-in.

Senator

House Other vote was:

CD 1	5 scattered write-in.
CD 2	
CD 3	125 scattered write-in.
CD 4	264 scattered write-in.
CD 5	5,710 Libertarian (Vernon L. Etzel); 136 scattered write-in.
CD 6	192 scattered write-in.
CD 7	2,708 American Congress (James D. Schneller); 79 scattered write-in.
CD 8	
CD 9	153 scattered write-in.
CD 10	210 scattered write-in.
CD 11	164 scattered write-in.
CD 12	80 scattered write-in.
CD 13	
CD 14	5,400 Green (Ed Bortz); 1,039 scattered write-in.
CD 15	15,248 Towne for Congress (Jake Towne); 1 scattered write-in.
CD 16	197 scattered write-in.
CD 17	42 scattered write-in.
CD 18	262 scattered write-in.
CD 19	10,988 Independent Patriot (Joshua A. Monighan); 154 scattered write-in.

2010 PRIMARY ELECTIONS

Primary May 18, 2010

Registration (as of May 18, 2010)		
Democratic	4,311,604
Republican	3,119,468
Libertarian	36,712
Other and No Affiliation	977,211
TOTAL	*8,444,995*

Primary Type Closed—Only registered Democrats and Republicans could vote in their party's primary.

	REPUBLICAN PRIMARIES			DEMOCRATIC PRIMARIES		
Governor	Tom Corbett	589,249	68.6%	Dan Onorato	463,575	44.9%
	Samuel E. Rohrer	267,893	31.2%	Jack Wagner	248,338	24.0%
	Scattered write-in	1,601	0.2%	Anthony Hardy Williams	185,784	18.0%
				Joseph M. Hoeffel	130,799	12.7%
				Scattered write-in	4,438	0.4%
	TOTAL	*858,743*		*TOTAL*	*1,032,934*	
Senator	Pat Toomey	671,591	81.1%	Joe Sestak	568,563	53.7%
	Peg Luksik	153,154	18.5%	Arlen Specter*	487,217	46.0%
	Scattered write-in	3,472	0.4%	Scattered write-in	3,071	0.3%
	TOTAL	*828,217*		*TOTAL*	*1,058,851*	

PENNSYLVANIA

GENERAL AND PRIMARY ELECTIONS

	REPUBLICAN PRIMARIES			DEMOCRATIC PRIMARIES		
Congressional District 1	No Republican candidate			Robert A. Brady*	48,505	100.0%
				Scattered write-in	3	
				TOTAL	*48,508*	
Congressional District 2	Rick Hellberg	3,781	100.0%	Chaka Fattah*	72,417	100.0%
Congressional District 3	Mike Kelly	15,428	28.0%	Kathleen A. Dahlkemper*	34,932	72.8%
	Paul L. Huber	14,474	26.3%	Mel M. Marin	12,764	26.6%
	Clayton W. Grabb	7,486	13.6%	Scattered write-in	269	0.6%
	Steven M. Fisher	6,499	11.8%			
	Ed Franz	5,838	10.6%			
	Martha Moore	5,151	9.4%			
	Scattered write-in	134	0.2%			
	TOTAL	*55,010*		*TOTAL*	*47,965*	
Congressional District 4	Keith Rothfus	34,996	66.2%	Jason Altmire*	53,019	96.1%
	Mary Beth Buchanan	17,701	33.5%	Scattered write-in	2,172	3.9%
	Scattered write-in	185	0.3%			
	TOTAL	*52,882*		*TOTAL*	*55,191*	
Congressional District 5	Glenn Thompson*	52,856	99.6%	Michael Pipe	31,120	98.9%
	Scattered write-in	211	0.4%	Scattered write-in	348	1.1%
	TOTAL	*53,067*		*TOTAL*	*31,468*	
Congressional District 6	Jim Gerlach*	35,575	79.8%	Manan Trivedi	21,585	50.8%
	Patrick Henry Sellers	8,998	20.2%	Doug Pike	20,871	49.1%
	Scattered write-in	4		Scattered write-in	12	
	TOTAL	*44,577*		*TOTAL*	*42,468*	
Congressional District 7	Patrick Meehan	48,604	100.0%	Bryan Lentz	39,206	99.8%
	Scattered write-in	20		Scattered write-in	81	0.2%
	TOTAL	*48,624*		*TOTAL*	*39,287*	
Congressional District 8	Michael G. Fitzpatrick	33,671	76.7%	Patrick J. Murphy*	40,783	99.9%
	Gloria Carlineo	6,529	14.9%	Scattered write-in	28	0.1%
	Ira Hoffman	2,424	5.5%			
	James Jones	1,249	2.8%			
	Scattered write-in	15				
	TOTAL	*43,888*		*TOTAL*	*40,811*	
Congressional District 9	Bill Shuster*	56,828	99.6%	No candidate filed for the Democratic primary. Tom Conners received 2,023 write-in votes and was the party's candidate on the general election ballot. Bill Shuster (R) drew 1,287 write-ins in the Democratic primary, and there were 1,658 scattered write-in votes.		
	Tom Conners (write-in)	72	0.1%			
	Scattered write-in	163	0.3%			
	TOTAL	*57,063*				
Congressional District 10	Thomas A. Marino	24,435	40.9%	Christopher P. Carney*	38,928	98.4%
	David Madeira	18,524	31.0%	Scattered write-in	622	1.6%
	Malcolm L. Derk	16,690	27.9%			
	Scattered write-in	163	0.3%			
	TOTAL	*59,812*		*TOTAL*	*39,550*	
Congressional District 11	Lou Barletta	28,397	99.5%	Paul E. Kanjorski*	33,900	49.2%
	Scattered write-in	132	0.5%	Corey D. O'Brien	23,267	33.8%
				Brian Kelly	11,519	16.7%
				Scattered write-in	240	0.3%
	TOTAL	*28,529*		*TOTAL*	*68,926*	

PENNSYLVANIA

GENERAL AND PRIMARY ELECTIONS

	REPUBLICAN PRIMARIES			DEMOCRATIC PRIMARIES		
Congressional District 12	Tim Burns	26,577	56.8%	Mark S. Critz	58,817	70.9%
	William Russell	20,078	42.9%	Ryan Bucchianeri	16,965	20.4%
	Scattered write-in	137	0.3%	Ronald Mackell Jr.	6,525	7.9%
				Scattered write-in	680	0.8%
	TOTAL	46,792		TOTAL	82,987	
Congressional District 13	Carson Dee Adcock	14,416	48.0%	Allyson Y. Schwartz*	44,402	100.0%
	Joshua C. Quinter	8,334	27.7%			
	Brian P. Haughton	7,293	24.3%			
	TOTAL	30,043				
Congressional District 14	Melissa Haluszczak	11,585	98.5%	Mike Doyle*	71,511	99.1%
	Scattered write-in	177	1.5%	Scattered write-in	641	0.9%
	TOTAL	11,762		TOTAL	72,152	
Congressional District 15	Charlie Dent*	31,618	82.9%	John B. Callahan	32,825	99.8%
	Mat Benol	6,514	17.1%	Scattered write-in	56	0.2%
	TOTAL	38,132		TOTAL	32,881	
Congressional District 16	Joe Pitts*	50,629	99.4%	Lois Herr	24,541	99.5%
	Scattered write-in	330	0.6%	Scattered write-in	132	0.5%
	TOTAL	50,959		TOTAL	24,673	
Congressional District 17	Dave Argall	20,712	32.2%	Tim Holden*	30,630	65.2%
	Frank Ryan	19,890	30.9%	Sheila Dow-Ford	16,296	34.7%
	Josh First	14,955	23.2%	Scattered write-in	61	0.1%
	Allen Griffith	8,503	13.2%			
	Scattered write-in	314	0.5%			
	TOTAL	64,374		TOTAL	46,987	
Congressional District 18	Tim Murphy*	47,785	99.4%	Dan Connolly	58,081	99.3%
	Scattered write-in	308	0.6%	Scattered write-in	431	0.7%
	TOTAL	48,093		TOTAL	58,512	
Congressional District 19	Todd R. Platts*	51,792	70.0%	Ryan S. Sanders	33,283	98.7%
	Michael Smeltzer	22,210	30.0%	Scattered write-in	446	1.3%
	Scattered write-in	6				
	TOTAL	74,008		TOTAL	33,729	

An asterisk (*) denotes incumbent.

RHODE ISLAND

Congressional districts first established for elections held in 2002
2 members

RHODE ISLAND

GOVERNOR
Lincoln Chafee (Independent). Elected 2010 to a four-year term.

SENATORS (2 Democrats)
Jack Reed (D). Reelected 2008 to a six-year term. Previously elected 2002, 1996.

Sheldon Whitehouse (D). Elected 2006 to a six-year term.

REPRESENTATIVES (2 Democrats)
1. David N. Cicilline (D)　　　　2. Jim Langevin (D)

POSTWAR VOTE FOR PRESIDENT

| | | Republican | | Democratic | | | | Percentage | | | |
| | | | | | | | | Total Vote | | Major Vote | |
Year	Total Vote	Vote	Candidate	Vote	Candidate	Other Vote	Rep.-Dem. Plurality	Rep.	Dem.	Rep.	Dem.
2008	471,766	165,391	McCain, John	296,571	Obama, Barack	9,804	131,180 D	35.1%	62.9%	35.8%	64.2%
2004	437,134	169,046	Bush, George W.	259,760	Kerry, John	8,328	90,714 D	38.7%	59.4%	39.4%	60.6%
2000**	409,047	130,555	Bush, George W.	249,508	Gore, Al	28,984	118,953 D	31.9%	61.0%	34.4%	65.6%
1996**	390,284	104,683	Dole, Bob	233,050	Clinton, Bill	52,551	128,367 D	26.8%	59.7%	31.0%	69.0%
1992**	453,477	131,601	Bush, George	213,299	Clinton, Bill	108,577	81,698 D	29.0%	47.0%	38.2%	61.8%
1988	404,620	177,761	Bush, George	225,123	Dukakis, Michael S.	1,736	47,362 D	43.9%	55.6%	44.1%	55.9%
1984	410,492	212,080	Reagan, Ronald	197,106	Mondale, Walter F.	1,306	14,974 R	51.7%	48.0%	51.8%	48.2%
1980**	416,072	154,793	Reagan, Ronald	198,342	Carter, Jimmy	62,937	43,549 D	37.2%	47.7%	43.8%	56.2%
1976	411,170	181,249	Ford, Gerald R.	227,636	Carter, Jimmy	2,285	46,387 D	44.1%	55.4%	44.3%	55.7%
1972	415,808	220,383	Nixon, Richard M.	194,645	McGovern, George S.	780	25,738 R	53.0%	46.8%	53.1%	46.9%
1968**	385,000	122,359	Nixon, Richard M.	246,518	Humphrey, Hubert H.	16,123	124,159 D	31.8%	64.0%	33.2%	66.8%
1964	390,091	74,615	Goldwater, Barry M.	315,463	Johnson, Lyndon B.	13	240,848 D	19.1%	80.9%	19.1%	80.9%
1960	405,535	147,502	Nixon, Richard M.	258,032	Kennedy, John F.	1	110,530 D	36.4%	63.6%	36.4%	63.6%
1956	387,609	225,819	Eisenhower, Dwight D.	161,790	Stevenson, Adlai E.		64,029 R	58.3%	41.7%	58.3%	41.7%
1952	414,498	210,935	Eisenhower, Dwight D.	203,293	Stevenson, Adlai E.	270	7,642 R	50.9%	49.0%	50.9%	49.1%
1948	327,702	135,787	Dewey, Thomas E.	188,736	Truman, Harry S.	3,179	52,949 D	41.4%	57.6%	41.8%	58.2%

**In past elections, the other vote included: 2000 - 25,052 Green (Ralph Nader); 1996 - 43,723 Reform (Ross Perot); 1992 - 105,045 Independent (Perot); 1980 - 59,819 Independent (John Anderson); 1968 - 15,678 American Independent (George Wallace).

RHODE ISLAND

POSTWAR VOTE FOR GOVERNOR

Year	Total Vote	Republican Vote	Republican Candidate	Democratic Vote	Democratic Candidate	Other Vote	Rep.-Dem. Plurality		Total Vote Rep.	Total Vote Dem.	Major Vote Rep.	Major Vote Dem.
2010**	342,545	114,911	Robitaille, John F.	78,896	Caprio, Frank T.	148,738	8,660	I	33.5%	23.0%	59.3%	40.7%
2006	387,010	197,366	Carcieri, Donald L.	189,562	Fogarty, Charles J.	82	7,804	R	51.0%	49.0%	51.0%	49.0%
2002	332,655	181,827	Carcieri, Donald L.	150,229	York, Myrth	599	31,598	R	54.7%	45.2%	54.8%	45.2%
1998	306,445	156,180	Almond, Lincoln C.	129,105	York, Myrth	21,160	27,075	R	51.0%	42.1%	54.7%	45.3%
1994**	361,377	171,194	Almond, Lincoln C.	157,361	York, Myrth	32,822	13,833	R	47.4%	43.5%	52.1%	47.9%
1992	425,026	145,590	Leonard, Elizabeth Ann	261,484	Sundlun, Bruce G.	17,952	115,894	D	34.3%	61.5%	35.8%	64.2%
1990	356,672	92,177	DiPrete, Edward	264,411	Sundlun, Bruce G.	84	172,234	D	25.8%	74.1%	25.8%	74.2%
1988	400,516	203,550	DiPrete, Edward	196,936	Sundlun, Bruce G.	30	6,614	R	50.8%	49.2%	50.8%	49.2%
1986	322,724	208,822	DiPrete, Edward	104,508	Sundlun, Bruce G.	9,394	104,314	R	64.7%	32.4%	66.6%	33.4%
1984	408,375	245,059	DiPrete, Edward	163,311	Solomon, Anthony J.	5	81,748	R	60.0%	40.0%	60.0%	40.0%
1982	337,259	79,602	Marzullo, Vincent	247,208	Garrahy, J. Joseph	10,449	167,606	D	23.6%	73.3%	24.4%	75.6%
1980	405,916	106,729	Cianci, Vincent A.	299,174	Garrahy, J. Joseph	13	192,445	D	26.3%	73.7%	26.3%	73.7%
1978	314,363	96,596	Almond, Lincoln C.	197,386	Garrahy, J. Joseph	20,381	100,790	D	30.7%	62.8%	32.9%	67.1%
1976	398,683	178,254	Taft, James L.	218,561	Garrahy, J. Joseph	1,868	40,307	D	44.7%	54.8%	44.9%	55.1%
1974	321,660	69,224	Nugent, James W.	252,436	Noel, Philip W.		183,212	D	21.5%	78.5%	21.5%	78.5%
1972	412,866	194,315	DeSimone, Herbert F.	216,953	Noel, Philip W.	1,598	22,638	D	47.1%	52.5%	47.2%	52.8%
1970	346,342	171,549	DeSimone, Herbert F.	173,420	Licht, Frank	1,373	1,871	D	49.5%	50.1%	49.7%	50.3%
1968	383,725	187,958	Chafee, John H.	195,766	Licht, Frank	1	7,808	D	49.0%	51.0%	49.0%	51.0%
1966	332,064	210,202	Chafee, John H.	121,862	Hobbs, Horace E.		88,340	R	63.3%	36.7%	63.3%	36.7%
1964	391,668	239,501	Chafee, John H.	152,165	Gallogly, Edward P.	2	87,336	R	61.1%	38.9%	61.1%	38.9%
1962	327,506	163,952	Chafee, John H.	163,554	Notte, John A.		398	R	50.1%	49.9%	50.1%	49.9%
1960	401,362	174,044	Del Sesto, Christopher	227,318	Notte, John A.		53,274	D	43.4%	56.6%	43.4%	56.6%
1958	346,780	176,505	Del Sesto, Christopher	170,275	Roberts, Dennis J.		6,230	R	50.9%	49.1%	50.9%	49.1%
1956	383,919	191,604	Del Sesto, Christopher	192,315	Roberts, Dennis J.		711	D	49.9%	50.1%	49.9%	50.1%
1954	328,670	137,131	Lewis, Dean J.	189,595	Roberts, Dennis J.	1,944	52,464	D	41.7%	57.7%	42.0%	58.0%
1952	409,689	194,102	Archambault, Raoul	215,587	Roberts, Dennis J.		21,485	D	47.4%	52.6%	47.4%	52.6%
1950	296,809	120,684	Lachapelle, E. T.	176,125	Roberts, Dennis J.		55,441	D	40.7%	59.3%	40.7%	59.3%
1948	323,863	124,441	Ruerat, Albert P.	198,056	Pastore, John O.	1,366	73,615	D	38.4%	61.2%	38.6%	61.4%
1946	275,341	126,456	Murphy, John G.	148,885	Pastore, John O.		22,429	D	45.9%	54.1%	45.9%	54.1%

**In past elections, the other vote included: 2010 - 123,571 Independent (Lincoln Chafee), who was elected with 36.1 percent of the total vote. The term of office of Rhode Island's Governor was increased from two to four years effective with the 1994 election.

POSTWAR VOTE FOR SENATOR

Year	Total Vote	Republican Vote	Republican Candidate	Democratic Vote	Democratic Candidate	Other Vote	Rep.-Dem. Plurality		Total Vote Rep.	Total Vote Dem.	Major Vote Rep.	Major Vote Dem.
2008	438,812	116,174	Tingle, Robert G.	320,644	Reed, Jack	1,994	204,470	D	26.5%	73.1%	26.6%	73.4%
2006	385,451	179,001	Chafee, Lincoln	206,110	Whitehouse, Sheldon	340	27,109	D	46.4%	53.5%	46.5%	53.5%
2002	323,912	69,881	Tingle, Robert G.	253,922	Reed, Jack	109	184,041	D	21.6%	78.4%	21.6%	78.4%
2000	391,537	222,588	Chafee, Lincoln	161,023	Weygand, Bob	7,926	61,565	R	56.8%	41.1%	58.0%	42.0%
1996	363,378	127,368	Mayer, Nancy	230,676	Reed, Jack	5,334	103,308	D	35.1%	63.5%	35.6%	64.4%
1994	345,388	222,856	Chafee, John H.	122,532	Kushner, Linda J.		100,324	R	64.5%	35.5%	64.5%	35.5%
1990	364,062	138,947	Schneider, Claudine	225,105	Pell, Claiborne	10	86,158	D	38.2%	61.8%	38.2%	61.8%
1988	397,996	217,273	Chafee, John H.	180,717	Licht, Richard A.	6	36,556	R	54.6%	45.4%	54.6%	45.4%
1984	395,285	108,492	Leonard, Barbara	286,780	Pell, Claiborne	13	178,288	D	27.4%	72.6%	27.4%	72.6%
1982	342,779	175,495	Chafee, John H.	167,283	Michaelson, Julius C.	1	8,212	R	51.2%	48.8%	51.2%	48.8%
1978	305,618	76,061	Reynolds, James G.	229,557	Pell, Claiborne		153,496	D	24.9%	75.1%	24.9%	75.1%
1976	398,906	230,329	Chafee, John H.	167,665	Lorber, Richard P.	912	62,664	R	57.7%	42.0%	57.9%	42.1%
1972	413,432	188,990	Chafee, John H.	221,942	Pell, Claiborne	2,500	32,952	D	45.7%	53.7%	46.0%	54.0%
1970	341,222	107,351	McLaughlin, John	230,469	Pastore, John O.	3,402	123,118	D	31.5%	67.5%	31.8%	68.2%
1966	324,173	104,838	Briggs, Ruth M.	219,331	Pell, Claiborne	4	114,493	D	32.3%	67.7%	32.3%	67.7%
1964	386,322	66,715	Lagueux, Ronald R.	319,607	Pastore, John O.		252,892	D	17.3%	82.7%	17.3%	82.7%
1960	399,983	124,408	Archambault, Raoul	275,575	Pell, Claiborne		151,167	D	31.1%	68.9%	31.1%	68.9%
1958	344,519	122,353	Ewing, Bayard	222,166	Pastore, John O.		99,813	D	35.5%	64.5%	35.5%	64.5%
1954	326,624	132,970	Sundlun, Walter I.	193,654	Green, Theodore F.		60,684	D	40.7%	59.3%	40.7%	59.3%
1952	410,978	185,850	Ewing, Bayard	225,128	Pastore, John O.		39,278	D	45.2%	54.8%	45.2%	54.8%
1950S	297,909	114,184	Levy, Austin T.	183,725	Pastore, John O.		69,541	D	38.3%	61.7%	38.3%	61.7%
1948	320,420	130,262	Hazard, Thomas P.	190,158	Green, Theodore F.		59,896	D	40.7%	59.3%	40.7%	59.3%
1946	273,528	122,780	Dyer, W. Gurnee	150,748	McGrath, J. Howard		27,968	D	44.9%	55.1%	44.9%	55.1%

The 1950 election was for a short term to fill a vacancy.

RHODE ISLAND

GOVERNOR 2010

2010 Census Population	County	Total Vote	Republican	Democratic	Independent (Chafee)	Other	Plurality		Percentage		
									Rep.	Dem.	Independent
49,875	BRISTOL	19,771	6,796	3,950	7,323	1,702	527	I	34.4%	20.0%	37.0%
166,158	KENT	63,344	23,303	12,199	22,564	5,278	739	R	36.8%	19.3%	35.6%
82,888	NEWPORT	30,124	11,885	5,165	11,313	1,761	572	R	39.5%	17.1%	37.6%
626,667	PROVIDENCE	179,385	55,258	49,266	62,608	12,253	7,350	I	30.8%	27.5%	34.9%
126,979	WASHINGTON	49,577	17,637	8,292	19,733	3,915	2,096	I	35.6%	16.7%	39.8%
	State Ballots	89	32	24	30	3	2	R	36.0%	27.0%	33.7%
1,052,567	TOTAL	342,545	114,911	78,896	123,571	25,167	8,660	I	33.5%	23.0%	36.1%

The statewide totals for "Total Vote" and "Other" include 255 write-in votes that were not part of the county or city/town returns.

2010 Census Population	City/Town	Total Vote	Republican	Democratic	Independent (Chafee)	Other	Plurality		Percentage		
									Rep.	Dem.	Independent
16,310	BARRINGTON	7,834	2,738	1,042	3,248	806	510	I	35.0%	13.3%	41.5%
22,954	BRISTOL TOWN	8,046	2,762	1,947	2,750	587	12	R	34.3%	24.2%	34.2%
15,955	BURRILLVILLE	5,458	2,286	1,170	1,503	499	783	R	41.9%	21.4%	27.5%
19,376	CENTRAL FALLS	2,143	491	798	756	98	42	D	22.9%	37.2%	35.3%
7,827	CHARLESTOWN	3,264	1,131	511	1,337	285	206	I	34.7%	15.7%	41.0%
35,014	COVENTRY	13,005	5,424	2,433	3,934	1,214	1,490	R	41.7%	18.7%	30.2%
80,387	CRANSTON	27,513	8,851	7,118	9,499	2,045	648	I	32.2%	25.9%	34.5%
33,506	CUMBERLAND	13,047	5,583	2,834	3,685	945	1,898	R	42.8%	21.7%	28.2%
13,146	EAST GREENWICH	5,973	2,655	744	2,120	454	535	R	44.5%	12.5%	35.5%
47,037	EAST PROVIDENCE	15,806	4,443	4,413	5,777	1,173	1,334	I	28.1%	27.9%	36.5%
6,425	EXETER	2,581	1,056	337	959	229	97	R	40.9%	13.1%	37.2%
4,606	FOSTER	2,076	864	292	740	180	124	R	41.6%	14.1%	35.6%
9,746	GLOCESTER	4,163	1,862	675	1,262	364	600	R	44.7%	16.2%	30.3%
8,188	HOPKINTON	2,867	1,096	435	1,057	279	39	R	38.2%	15.2%	36.9%
5,405	JAMESTOWN	2,983	960	391	1,428	204	468	I	32.2%	13.1%	47.9%
28,769	JOHNSTON	11,312	3,603	4,290	2,634	785	687	D	31.9%	37.9%	23.3%
21,105	LINCOLN	8,678	3,679	1,780	2,639	580	1,040	R	42.4%	20.5%	30.4%
3,492	LITTLE COMPTON	1,806	728	206	795	77	67	I	40.3%	11.4%	44.0%
16,150	MIDDLETOWN	5,210	2,161	891	1,832	326	329	R	41.5%	17.1%	35.2%
15,868	NARRAGANSETT	6,543	2,198	1,394	2,513	438	315	I	33.6%	21.3%	38.4%
24,672	NEWPORT CITY	6,974	2,212	1,311	3,061	390	849	I	31.7%	18.8%	43.9%
1,051	NEW SHOREHAM	810	207	114	423	66	216	I	25.6%	14.1%	52.2%
26,486	NORTH KINGSTOWN	11,682	4,661	1,638	4,458	925	203	R	39.9%	14.0%	38.2%
32,078	NORTH PROVIDENCE	12,340	3,689	4,332	3,490	829	643	D	29.9%	35.1%	28.3%
11,967	NORTH SMITHFIELD	4,796	2,215	913	1,346	322	869	R	46.2%	19.0%	28.1%
71,148	PAWTUCKET	16,024	4,299	4,927	5,674	1,124	747	I	26.8%	30.7%	35.4%
17,389	PORTSMOUTH	7,459	3,568	1,102	2,392	397	1,176	R	47.8%	14.8%	32.1%
178,042	PROVIDENCE CITY	34,455	4,648	10,500	17,581	1,726	7,081	I	13.5%	30.5%	51.0%
7,708	RICHMOND	2,963	1,151	403	1,089	320	62	R	38.8%	13.6%	36.8%
10,329	SCITUATE	4,742	2,160	807	1,378	397	782	R	45.6%	17.0%	29.1%
21,430	SMITHFIELD	8,282	3,372	1,843	2,428	639	944	R	40.7%	22.3%	29.3%
30,639	SOUTH KINGSTOWN	11,060	3,426	1,510	5,270	854	1,844	I	31.0%	13.7%	47.6%

RHODE ISLAND

GOVERNOR 2010

2010 Census Population	City/Town	Total Vote	Republican	Democratic	Independent (Chafee)	Other	Plurality		Percentage Rep.	Dem.	Independent
15,780	TIVERTON	5,692	2,256	1,264	1,805	367	451	R	39.6%	22.2%	31.7%
10,611	WARREN	3,891	1,296	961	1,325	309	29	I	33.3%	24.7%	34.1%
82,672	WARWICK	32,986	10,894	6,490	12,954	2,648	2,060	I	33.0%	19.7%	39.3%
22,787	WESTERLY	7,807	2,711	1,950	2,627	519	84	R	34.7%	25.0%	33.6%
6,135	WEST GREENWICH	2,547	1,165	312	852	218	313	R	45.7%	12.2%	33.5%
29,191	WEST WARWICK	8,833	3,165	2,220	2,704	744	461	R	35.8%	25.1%	30.6%
41,186	WOONSOCKET	8,550	3,213	2,574	2,216	547	997	R	37.6%	30.1%	25.9%
	State Ballots	89	32	24	30	3	2	R	36.0%	27.0%	33.7%
1,052,567	TOTAL	342,545	114,911	78,896	123,571	25,167	8,660	I	33.5%	23.0%	36.1%

The plurality is based on the difference in the vote between the first and second-place finishers, which in all counties and most cities and towns was the Republican candidate and Independent Lincoln Chafee. State ballots are those cast by voters who were qualified to vote in state and congressional elections, but not local ones, often due to a change in residence shortly before Election Day.

RHODE ISLAND

HOUSE OF REPRESENTATIVES

CD	Year	Total Vote	Republican Vote	Candidate	Democratic Vote	Candidate	Other Vote	Rep.-Dem. Plurality	Total Vote Rep.	Dem.	Major Vote Rep.	Dem.
1	2010	160,814	71,542	LOUGHLIN, JOHN J., II	81,269	CICILLINE, DAVID N.	8,003	9,727 D	44.5%	50.5%	46.8%	53.2%
1	2008	211,998	51,340	SCOTT, JONATHAN P.	145,254	KENNEDY, PATRICK J.*	15,404	93,914 D	24.2%	68.5%	26.1%	73.9%
1	2006	180,185	41,856	SCOTT, JONATHAN P.	124,676	KENNEDY, PATRICK J.*	13,653	82,820 D	23.2%	69.2%	25.1%	74.9%
1	2004	195,010	69,819	ROGERS, DAVID W.	124,923	KENNEDY, PATRICK J.*	268	55,104 D	35.8%	64.1%	35.9%	64.1%
1	2002	159,066	59,370	ROGERS, DAVID W.	95,286	KENNEDY, PATRICK J.*	4,410	35,916 D	37.3%	59.9%	38.4%	61.6%
2	2010	174,670	55,409	ZACCARIA, MARK S.	104,442	LANGEVIN, JIM*	14,819	49,033 D	31.7%	59.8%	34.7%	65.3%
2	2008	226,234	67,433	ZACCARIA, MARK S.	158,416	LANGEVIN, JIM*	385	90,983 D	29.8%	70.0%	29.9%	70.1%
2	2006	193,197		—	140,352	LANGEVIN, JIM*	52,845	140,352 D		72.6%		100.0%
2	2004	207,165	43,139	BARTON, ARTHUR CHUCK, III	154,392	LANGEVIN, JIM*	9,634	111,253 D	20.8%	74.5%	21.8%	78.2%
2	2002	169,580	37,767	MATSON, JOHN O.	129,390	LANGEVIN, JIM*	2,423	91,623 D	22.3%	76.3%	22.6%	77.4%
TOTAL	2010	335,484	126,951		185,711		22,822	58,760 D	37.8%	55.4%	40.6%	59.4%
TOTAL	2008	438,232	118,773		303,670		15,789	184,897 D	27.1%	69.3%	28.1%	71.9%
TOTAL	2006	373,382	41,856		265,028		66,498	223,172 D	11.2%	71.0%	13.6%	86.4%
TOTAL	2004	402,175	112,958		279,315		9,902	166,357 D	28.1%	69.5%	28.8%	71.2%
TOTAL	2002	328,646	97,137		224,676		6,833	127,539 D	29.6%	68.4%	30.2%	69.8%

RHODE ISLAND

GENERAL AND PRIMARY ELECTIONS

2010 GENERAL ELECTIONS

Governor Other vote was 22,146 Moderate (Kenneth J. Block); 1,091 Independent (Joseph M. Lusi); 882 Independent (Todd Giroux); 793 Independent (Ronald Algieri); 8 write-in (None of the Above); 6 write-in (Patrick Lynch); 6 write-in (Victor Moffitt); 6 write-in (Mickey Mouse); 5 write-in (Robert Healy); 224 scattered write-in. Independent candidate Lincoln Chafee received 123,571 votes and was elected with 36.1 percent of the total vote. Chafee's vote is listed in the county and city/town tables for the 2010 gubernatorial election in Rhode Island.

House Other vote was:

CD 1 6,424 Independent (Kenneth A. Capalbo); 1,334 Vigilant Fox (Gregory Raposa); 13 write-in (David Segal); 9 write-in (Anthony Gemma); 6 write-in (Patrick Kennedy); 6 write-in (Mickey Mouse); 211 scattered write-in.

CD 2 14,584 Independent (John O. Matson); 24 write-in (Elizabeth Dennigan); 5 write-in (David Cicilline); 206 scattered write-in.

2010 PRIMARY ELECTIONS

Primary September 14, 2010

Registration (as of August 10, 2010 - includes 58,634 inactive registrants)		
Democratic		286,612
Republican		72,603
Moderate		330
Unaffiliated		340,081
TOTAL		*699,626*

Primary Type Semi-open—Registered Democrats and Republicans could vote only in their party's primary. Unaffiliated voters could participate in either party's primary if they were willing to remain a member of that party for a period of at least 90 days.

	REPUBLICAN PRIMARIES			**DEMOCRATIC PRIMARIES**		
Governor	John F. Robitaille	13,204	70.2%	Frank T. Caprio	73,142	100.0%
	Victor G. Moffitt	5,613	29.8%			
	TOTAL	*18,817*				
Congressional **District 1**	John J. Loughlin II	6,497	83.3%	David N. Cicilline	21,142	37.2%
	Kara D. Russo	1,301	16.7%	Anthony P. Gemma	13,112	23.1%
				David A. Segal	11,397	20.1%
				William J. Lynch	11,161	19.6%
	TOTAL	*7,798*		*TOTAL*	*56,812*	
Congressional **District 2**	Mark S. Zaccaria	5,674	54.9%	Jim Langevin*	25,603	57.4%
	William J. Clegg III	2,233	21.6%	Elizabeth M. Dennigan	15,146	34.0%
	Michael J. Gardiner	1,468	14.2%	Ernest A. Greco	3,833	8.6%
	Donald F. Robbio	965	9.3%			
	TOTAL	*10,340*		*TOTAL*	*44,582*	

An asterisk (*) denotes incumbent.

SOUTH CAROLINA

Congressional districts first established for elections held in 2002
6 members

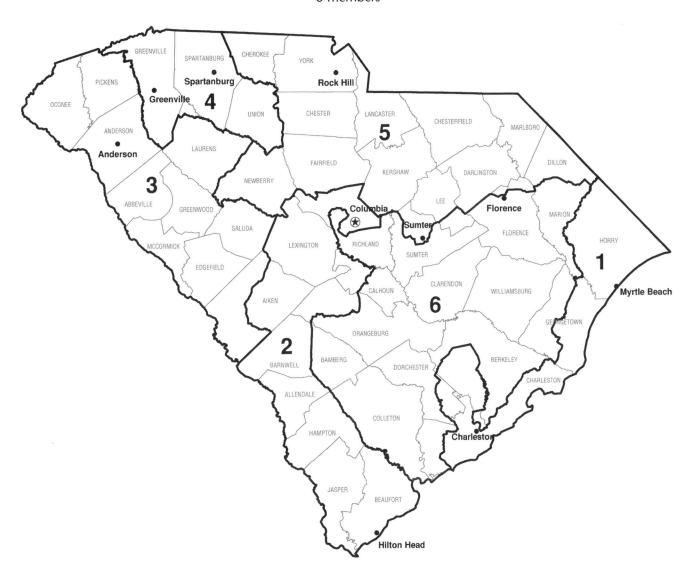

SOUTH CAROLINA

GOVERNOR
Nikki R. Haley (R). Elected 2010 to a four-year term.

SENATORS (2 Republicans)
Jim DeMint (R). Reelected 2010 to a six-year term. Previously elected 2004.

Lindsey Graham (R). Reelected 2008 to a six-year term. Previously elected 2002.

REPRESENTATIVES (5 Republicans, 1 Democrat)
1. Tim Scott (R)
2. Joe Wilson (R)
3. Jeff Duncan (R)
4. Trey Gowdy (R)
5. Mike Mulvaney (R)
6. James E. Clyburn (D)

POSTWAR VOTE FOR PRESIDENT

Year	Total Vote	Republican Vote	Republican Candidate	Democratic Vote	Democratic Candidate	Other Vote	Plurality	Total Vote Rep.	Total Vote Dem.	Major Vote Rep.	Major Vote Dem.
2008	1,920,969	1,034,896	McCain, John	862,449	Obama, Barack	23,624	172,447 R	53.9%	44.9%	54.5%	45.5%
2004	1,617,730	937,974	Bush, George W.	661,699	Kerry, John	18,057	276,275 R	58.0%	40.9%	58.6%	41.4%
2000**	1,382,717	785,937	Bush, George W.	565,561	Gore, Al	31,219	220,376 R	56.8%	40.9%	58.2%	41.8%
1996**	1,151,689	573,458	Dole, Bob	506,283	Clinton, Bill	71,948	67,175 R	49.8%	44.0%	53.1%	46.9%
1992**	1,202,527	577,507	Bush, George	479,514	Clinton, Bill	145,506	97,993 R	48.0%	39.9%	54.6%	45.4%
1988	986,009	606,443	Bush, George	370,554	Dukakis, Michael S.	9,012	235,889 R	61.5%	37.6%	62.1%	37.9%
1984	968,529	615,539	Reagan, Ronald	344,459	Mondale, Walter F.	8,531	271,080 R	63.6%	35.6%	64.1%	35.9%
1980**	894,071	441,841	Reagan, Ronald	430,385	Carter, Jimmy	21,845	11,456 R	49.4%	48.1%	50.7%	49.3%
1976	802,583	346,149	Ford, Gerald R.	450,807	Carter, Jimmy	5,627	104,658 D	43.1%	56.2%	43.4%	56.6%
1972	673,960	477,044	Nixon, Richard M.	186,824	McGovern, George S.	10,092	290,220 R	70.8%	27.7%	71.9%	28.1%
1968**	666,978	254,062	Nixon, Richard M.	197,486	Humphrey, Hubert H.	215,430	38,632 R	38.1%	29.6%	56.3%	43.7%
1964	524,779	309,048	Goldwater, Barry M.	215,723	Johnson, Lyndon B.	8	93,325 R	58.9%	41.1%	58.9%	41.1%
1960	386,688	188,558	Nixon, Richard M.	198,129	Kennedy, John F.	1	9,571 D	48.8%	51.2%	48.8%	51.2%
1956**	300,583	75,700	Eisenhower, Dwight D.	136,372	Stevenson, Adlai E.	88,511	47,863 D	25.2%	45.4%	35.7%	64.3%
1952	341,087	168,082	Eisenhower, Dwight D.	173,004	Stevenson, Adlai E.	1	4,922 D	49.3%	50.7%	49.3%	50.7%
1948**	142,571	5,386	Dewey, Thomas E.	34,423	Truman, Harry S.	102,762	68,184 SR	3.8%	24.1%	13.5%	86.5%

**In past elections, the other vote included: 2000 - 20,200 Green (Ralph Nader); 1996 - 64,386 Reform (Ross Perot); 1992 - 138,872 Independent (Perot); 1980 - 14,153 Independent (John Anderson); 1968 - 215,430 American Independent (George Wallace), who finished second in South Carolina; 1956 - 88,509 Uncommitted States' Rights electors, which placed second; 1948 - 102,607 States' Rights (Strom Thurmond), who won South Carolina with 72.0 percent of the total vote.

SOUTH CAROLINA

POSTWAR VOTE FOR GOVERNOR

Year	Total Vote	Republican Vote	Republican Candidate	Democratic Vote	Democratic Candidate	Other Vote	Rep.-Dem. Plurality	Total Vote Rep.	Total Vote Dem.	Major Vote Rep.	Major Vote Dem.
2010	1,344,198	690,525	Haley, Nikki R.	630,534	Sheheen, Vincent A.	23,139	59,991 R	51.4%	46.9%	52.3%	47.7%
2006	1,091,952	601,868	Sanford, Mark	489,076	Moore, Tommy	1,008	112,792 R	55.1%	44.8%	55.2%	44.8%
2002	1,107,725	585,422	Sanford, Mark	521,140	Hodges, Jim	1,163	64,282 R	52.8%	47.0%	52.9%	47.1%
1998	1,070,869	484,088	Beasley, David	570,070	Hodges, Jim	16,711	85,982 D	45.2%	53.2%	45.9%	54.1%
1994	933,850	470,756	Beasley, David	447,002	Theodore, Nick A.	16,092	23,754 R	50.4%	47.9%	51.3%	48.7%
1990	760,965	528,831	Campbell, Carroll	212,034	Mitchell, Theo	20,100	316,797 R	69.5%	27.9%	71.4%	28.6%
1986	753,751	384,565	Campbell, Carroll	361,325	Daniel, Mike	7,861	23,240 R	51.0%	47.9%	51.6%	48.4%
1982	671,625	202,806	Workman, W. D.	468,819	Riley, Richard W.		266,013 D	30.2%	69.8%	30.2%	69.8%
1978	627,182	236,946	Young, Edward L.	384,898	Riley, Richard W.	5,338	147,952 D	37.8%	61.4%	38.1%	61.9%
1974	523,199	266,109	Edwards, James B.	248,938	Dorn, W. J. Bryan	8,152	17,171 R	50.9%	47.6%	51.7%	48.3%
1970	484,857	221,233	Watson, Albert W.	250,551	West, John C.	13,073	29,318 D	45.6%	51.7%	46.9%	53.1%
1966	439,942	184,088	Rogers, Joseph O.	255,854	McNair, Robert E.		71,766 D	41.8%	58.2%	41.8%	58.2%
1962	253,721		—	253,704	Russell, Donald S.	17	253,704 D		100.0%		100.0%
1958	77,740		—	77,714	Hollings, Ernest F.	26	77,714 D		100.0%		100.0%
1954	214,212		—	214,204	Timmerman, George B.	8	214,204 D		100.0%		100.0%
1950	50,642		—	50,633	Byrnes, James F.	9	50,633 D		100.0%		100.0%
1946	26,520		—	26,520	Thurmond, Strom		26,520 D		100.0%		100.0%

The Republican Party did not run a candidate in the gubernatorial elections of 1946, 1950, 1954, 1958 and 1962.

POSTWAR VOTE FOR SENATOR

Year	Total Vote	Republican Vote	Republican Candidate	Democratic Vote	Democratic Candidate	Other Vote	Rep.-Dem. Plurality	Total Vote Rep.	Total Vote Dem.	Major Vote Rep.	Major Vote Dem.
2010	1,318,794	810,771	DeMint, Jim	364,598	Greene, Alvin M.	143,425	446,173 R	61.5%	27.6%	69.0%	31.0%
2008	1,871,431	1,076,534	Graham, Lindsey	790,621	Conley, Bob	4,276	285,913 R	57.5%	42.2%	57.7%	42.3%
2004	1,597,221	857,167	DeMint, Jim	704,384	Tenenbaum, Inez	35,670	152,783 R	53.7%	44.1%	54.9%	45.1%
2002	1,102,948	600,010	Graham, Lindsey	487,359	Sanders, Alex	15,579	112,651 R	54.4%	44.2%	55.2%	44.8%
1998	1,068,367	488,132	Inglis, Bob	562,791	Hollings, Ernest F.	17,444	74,659 D	45.7%	52.7%	46.4%	53.6%
1996	1,161,372	619,859	Thurmond, Strom	510,951	Close, Elliott Springs	30,562	108,908 R	53.4%	44.0%	54.8%	45.2%
1992	1,180,438	554,175	Hartnett, Thomas F.	591,030	Hollings, Ernest F.	35,233	36,855 D	46.9%	50.1%	48.4%	51.6%
1990	750,716	482,032	Thurmond, Strom	244,112	Cunningham, Bob	24,572	237,920 R	64.2%	32.5%	66.4%	33.6%
1986	737,962	262,886	McMaster, Henry D.	465,500	Hollings, Ernest F.	9,576	202,614 D	35.6%	63.1%	36.1%	63.9%
1984	965,130	644,815	Thurmond, Strom	306,982	Purvis, Melvin	13,333	337,833 R	66.8%	31.8%	67.7%	32.3%
1980	870,594	257,946	Mays, Marshall T.	612,554	Hollings, Ernest F.	94	354,608 D	29.6%	70.4%	29.6%	70.4%
1978	632,852	351,733	Thurmond, Strom	281,119	Ravenel, Charles D.		70,614 R	55.6%	44.4%	55.6%	44.4%
1974	512,397	146,645	Bush, Gwenyfred	356,126	Hollings, Ernest F.	9,626	209,481 D	28.6%	69.5%	29.2%	70.8%
1972	672,246	426,601	Thurmond, Strom	245,457	Zeigler, Eugene N.	188	181,144 R	63.5%	36.5%	63.5%	36.5%
1968	652,855	248,780	Parker, Marshall	404,060	Hollings, Ernest F.	15	155,280 D	38.1%	61.9%	38.1%	61.9%
1966	436,252	271,297	Thurmond, Strom	164,955	Morrah, Bradley		106,342 R	62.2%	37.8%	62.2%	37.8%
1966S	435,822	212,032	Parker, Marshall	223,790	Hollings, Ernest F.		11,758 D	48.7%	51.3%	48.7%	51.3%
1962	312,647	133,930	Workman, W.D.	178,712	Johnston, Olin D.	5	44,782 D	42.8%	57.2%	42.8%	57.2%
1960	330,266		—	330,164	Thurmond, Strom	102	330,164 D		100.0%		100.0%
1956	279,845	49,695	Crawford, Leon P.	230,150	Johnston, Olin D.		180,455 D	17.8%	82.2%	17.8%	82.2%
1956S	251,907		—	251,907	Thurmond, Strom		251,907 D		100.0%		100.0%
1954**	227,232		—	83,525	Brown, Edgar A.	143,707	59,919 ID		36.8%		100.0%
1950	50,277		—	50,240	Johnston, Olin D.	37	50,240 D		99.9%		100.0%
1948	141,006	5,008	Gerald, J. Bates	135,998	Maybank, Burnet R.		130,990 D	3.6%	96.4%	3.6%	96.4%

**In past elections, the other vote included: 1954 - 143,444 Independent Democratic (Strom Thurmond). Thurmond ran as a write-in candidate and won with 63.1 percent of the total vote. One each of the 1956 and 1966 elections was for a short term to fill a vacancy. The Republican Party did not run a Senate candidate in 1950, 1954, 1956 (for the short term) and 1960.

SOUTH CAROLINA

GOVERNOR 2010

2010 Census Population	County	Total Vote	Republican	Democratic	Other	Rep.-Dem. Plurality		Percentage			
								Total Vote		Major Vote	
								Rep.	Dem.	Rep.	Dem.
25,417	ABBEVILLE	7,321	3,359	3,807	155	448	D	45.9%	52.0%	46.9%	53.1%
160,099	AIKEN	48,988	30,268	17,874	846	12,394	R	61.8%	36.5%	62.9%	37.1%
10,419	ALLENDALE	2,551	564	1,926	61	1,362	D	22.1%	75.5%	22.7%	77.3%
187,126	ANDERSON	49,799	28,682	19,954	1,163	8,728	R	57.6%	40.1%	59.0%	41.0%
15,987	BAMBERG	4,826	1,661	3,086	79	1,425	D	34.4%	63.9%	35.0%	65.0%
22,621	BARNWELL	6,939	3,327	3,469	143	142	D	47.9%	50.0%	49.0%	51.0%
162,233	BEAUFORT	51,081	29,958	20,229	894	9,729	R	58.6%	39.6%	59.7%	40.3%
177,843	BERKELEY	43,070	24,164	17,979	927	6,185	R	56.1%	41.7%	57.3%	42.7%
15,175	CALHOUN	5,853	2,642	3,126	85	484	D	45.1%	53.4%	45.8%	54.2%
350,209	CHARLESTON	102,672	48,905	51,917	1,850	3,012	D	47.6%	50.6%	48.5%	51.5%
55,342	CHEROKEE	14,302	8,066	5,931	305	2,135	R	56.4%	41.5%	57.6%	42.4%
33,140	CHESTER	9,423	4,007	5,231	185	1,224	D	42.5%	55.5%	43.4%	56.6%
46,734	CHESTERFIELD	11,146	4,797	6,232	117	1,435	D	43.0%	55.9%	43.5%	56.5%
34,971	CLARENDON	11,306	4,733	6,383	190	1,650	D	41.9%	56.5%	42.6%	57.4%
38,892	COLLETON	13,045	6,227	6,535	283	308	D	47.7%	50.1%	48.8%	51.2%
68,681	DARLINGTON	21,355	9,844	11,284	227	1,440	D	46.1%	52.8%	46.6%	53.4%
32,062	DILLON	7,843	3,127	4,621	95	1,494	D	39.9%	58.9%	40.4%	59.6%
136,555	DORCHESTER	35,906	20,811	14,395	700	6,416	R	58.0%	40.1%	59.1%	40.9%
26,985	EDGEFIELD	8,180	4,447	3,623	110	824	R	54.4%	44.3%	55.1%	44.9%
23,956	FAIRFIELD	8,840	2,754	5,931	155	3,177	D	31.2%	67.1%	31.7%	68.3%
136,885	FLORENCE	40,378	19,253	20,594	531	1,341	D	47.7%	51.0%	48.3%	51.7%
60,158	GEORGETOWN	21,236	11,285	9,661	290	1,624	R	53.1%	45.5%	53.9%	46.1%
451,225	GREENVILLE	133,039	78,235	52,376	2,428	25,859	R	58.8%	39.4%	59.9%	40.1%
69,661	GREENWOOD	20,128	10,221	9,521	386	700	R	50.8%	47.3%	51.8%	48.2%
21,090	HAMPTON	6,345	2,195	4,030	120	1,835	D	34.6%	63.5%	35.3%	64.7%
269,291	HORRY	70,108	45,001	23,778	1,329	21,223	R	64.2%	33.9%	65.4%	34.6%
24,777	JASPER	6,241	2,469	3,643	129	1,174	D	39.6%	58.4%	40.4%	59.6%
61,697	KERSHAW	22,251	9,393	12,662	196	3,269	D	42.2%	56.9%	42.6%	57.4%
76,652	LANCASTER	22,340	11,650	10,358	332	1,292	R	52.1%	46.4%	52.9%	47.1%
66,537	LAURENS	17,469	9,260	7,872	337	1,388	R	53.0%	45.1%	54.1%	45.9%
19,220	LEE	6,607	1,985	4,532	90	2,547	D	30.0%	68.6%	30.5%	69.5%
262,391	LEXINGTON	83,373	50,167	31,787	1,419	18,380	R	60.2%	38.1%	61.2%	38.8%
10,233	MCCORMICK	3,990	1,995	1,933	62	62	R	50.0%	48.4%	50.8%	49.2%
33,062	MARION	10,342	3,391	6,822	129	3,431	D	32.8%	66.0%	33.2%	66.8%
28,933	MARLBORO	7,203	2,269	4,833	101	2,564	D	31.5%	67.1%	31.9%	68.1%
37,508	NEWBERRY	12,106	6,237	5,705	164	532	R	51.5%	47.1%	52.2%	47.8%
74,273	OCONEE	21,153	12,361	8,072	720	4,289	R	58.4%	38.2%	60.5%	39.5%
92,501	ORANGEBURG	28,564	8,352	19,861	351	11,509	D	29.2%	69.5%	29.6%	70.4%
119,224	PICKENS	30,227	19,435	10,033	759	9,402	R	64.3%	33.2%	66.0%	34.0%
384,504	RICHLAND	117,710	36,899	79,378	1,433	42,479	D	31.3%	67.4%	31.7%	68.3%
19,875	SALUDA	6,281	3,268	2,909	104	359	R	52.0%	46.3%	52.9%	47.1%
284,307	SPARTANBURG	73,960	41,593	31,074	1,293	10,519	R	56.2%	42.0%	57.2%	42.8%
107,456	SUMTER	29,558	12,396	16,769	393	4,373	D	41.9%	56.7%	42.5%	57.5%
28,961	UNION	9,176	4,014	4,966	196	952	D	43.7%	54.1%	44.7%	55.3%
34,423	WILLIAMSBURG	11,579	3,393	7,977	209	4,584	D	29.3%	68.9%	29.8%	70.2%
226,073	YORK	68,388	41,465	25,855	1,068	15,610	R	60.6%	37.8%	61.6%	38.4%
4,625,364	TOTAL	1,344,198	690,525	630,534	23,139	59,991	R	51.4%	46.9%	52.3%	47.7%

SOUTH CAROLINA

SENATOR 2010

2010 Census Population	County	Total Vote	Republican	Democratic	Other	Rep.-Dem. Plurality		Percentage			
								Total Vote		Major Vote	
								Rep.	Dem.	Rep.	Dem.
25,417	ABBEVILLE	7,236	4,342	2,425	469	1,917	R	60.0%	33.5%	64.2%	35.8%
160,099	AIKEN	48,448	32,651	12,024	3,773	20,627	R	67.4%	24.8%	73.1%	26.9%
10,419	ALLENDALE	2,489	695	1,707	87	1,012	D	27.9%	68.6%	28.9%	71.1%
187,126	ANDERSON	49,388	35,578	9,304	4,506	26,274	R	72.0%	18.8%	79.3%	20.7%
15,987	BAMBERG	4,748	1,850	2,693	205	843	D	39.0%	56.7%	40.7%	59.3%
22,621	BARNWELL	6,865	3,658	2,911	296	747	R	53.3%	42.4%	55.7%	44.3%
162,233	BEAUFORT	49,967	32,333	11,194	6,440	21,139	R	64.7%	22.4%	74.3%	25.7%
177,843	BERKELEY	42,207	26,970	11,016	4,221	15,954	R	63.9%	26.1%	71.0%	29.0%
15,175	CALHOUN	5,720	3,069	2,170	481	899	R	53.7%	37.9%	58.6%	41.4%
350,209	CHARLESTON	99,809	55,147	27,092	17,570	28,055	R	55.3%	27.1%	67.1%	32.9%
55,342	CHEROKEE	14,239	9,732	3,712	795	6,020	R	68.3%	26.1%	72.4%	27.6%
33,140	CHESTER	9,345	4,828	4,032	485	796	R	51.7%	43.1%	54.5%	45.5%
46,734	CHESTERFIELD	10,992	6,097	4,329	566	1,768	R	55.5%	39.4%	58.5%	41.5%
34,971	CLARENDON	11,086	5,344	4,845	897	499	R	48.2%	43.7%	52.4%	47.6%
38,892	COLLETON	12,733	7,498	4,418	817	3,080	R	58.9%	34.7%	62.9%	37.1%
68,681	DARLINGTON	21,074	10,919	9,011	1,144	1,908	R	51.8%	42.8%	54.8%	45.2%
32,062	DILLON	7,752	3,785	3,658	309	127	R	48.8%	47.2%	50.9%	49.1%
136,555	DORCHESTER	35,269	22,998	8,359	3,912	14,639	R	65.2%	23.7%	73.3%	26.7%
26,985	EDGEFIELD	8,146	4,850	2,966	330	1,884	R	59.5%	36.4%	62.1%	37.9%
23,956	FAIRFIELD	8,539	3,555	4,034	950	479	D	41.6%	47.2%	46.8%	53.2%
136,885	FLORENCE	40,052	22,432	14,784	2,836	7,648	R	56.0%	36.9%	60.3%	39.7%
60,158	GEORGETOWN	20,777	12,214	6,664	1,899	5,550	R	58.8%	32.1%	64.7%	35.3%
451,225	GREENVILLE	131,252	91,786	25,558	13,908	66,228	R	69.9%	19.5%	78.2%	21.8%
69,661	GREENWOOD	19,792	12,875	5,384	1,533	7,491	R	65.1%	27.2%	70.5%	29.5%
21,090	HAMPTON	6,240	2,524	3,428	288	904	D	40.4%	54.9%	42.4%	57.6%
269,291	HORRY	68,955	48,386	14,096	6,473	34,290	R	70.2%	20.4%	77.4%	22.6%
24,777	JASPER	6,182	2,618	3,277	287	659	D	42.3%	53.0%	44.4%	55.6%
61,697	KERSHAW	21,512	14,038	5,051	2,423	8,987	R	65.3%	23.5%	73.5%	26.5%
76,652	LANCASTER	21,887	14,305	6,164	1,418	8,141	R	65.4%	28.2%	69.9%	30.1%
66,537	LAURENS	17,292	11,075	5,039	1,178	6,036	R	64.0%	29.1%	68.7%	31.3%
19,220	LEE	6,467	2,392	3,661	414	1,269	D	37.0%	56.6%	39.5%	60.5%
262,391	LEXINGTON	81,909	61,157	10,381	10,371	50,776	R	74.7%	12.7%	85.5%	14.5%
10,233	MCCORMICK	3,927	2,121	1,546	260	575	R	54.0%	39.4%	57.8%	42.2%
33,062	MARION	10,284	4,079	5,760	445	1,681	D	39.7%	56.0%	41.5%	58.5%
28,933	MARLBORO	7,082	2,801	3,934	347	1,133	D	39.6%	55.5%	41.6%	58.4%
37,508	NEWBERRY	11,925	7,700	3,137	1,088	4,563	R	64.6%	26.3%	71.1%	28.9%
74,273	OCONEE	20,898	15,642	3,004	2,252	12,638	R	74.8%	14.4%	83.9%	16.1%
92,501	ORANGEBURG	27,862	9,710	16,334	1,818	6,624	D	34.9%	58.6%	37.3%	62.7%
119,224	PICKENS	29,866	23,108	3,620	3,138	19,488	R	77.4%	12.1%	86.5%	13.5%
384,504	RICHLAND	111,985	49,730	38,164	24,091	11,566	R	44.4%	34.1%	56.6%	43.4%
19,875	SALUDA	6,224	3,980	1,820	424	2,160	R	63.9%	29.2%	68.6%	31.4%
284,307	SPARTANBURG	72,995	50,091	15,976	6,928	34,115	R	68.6%	21.9%	75.8%	24.2%
107,456	SUMTER	29,418	14,456	11,429	3,533	3,027	R	49.1%	38.9%	55.8%	44.2%
28,961	UNION	9,111	5,265	3,290	556	1,975	R	57.8%	36.1%	61.5%	38.5%
34,423	WILLIAMSBURG	11,310	3,819	7,002	489	3,183	D	33.8%	61.9%	35.3%	64.7%
226,073	YORK	67,538	46,568	14,195	6,775	32,373	R	69.0%	21.0%	76.6%	23.4%
4,625,364	TOTAL	1,318,794	810,771	364,598	143,425	446,173	R	61.5%	27.6%	69.0%	31.0%

SOUTH CAROLINA

HOUSE OF REPRESENTATIVES

			Republican		Democratic				Percentage			
									Total Vote		Major Vote	
CD	Year	Total Vote	Vote	Candidate	Vote	Candidate	Other Vote	Rep.-Dem. Plurality	Rep.	Dem.	Rep.	Dem.
1	2010	233,695	152,755	SCOTT, TIM	67,008	FRASIER, BEN	13,932	85,747 R	65.4%	28.7%	69.5%	30.5%
1	2008	341,879	177,540	BROWN, HENRY E., JR.*	163,724	KETNER, LINDA	615	13,816 R	51.9%	47.9%	52.0%	48.0%
1	2006	193,375	115,766	BROWN, HENRY E., JR.*	73,218 #	MAATTA, RANDY	4,391	42,548 R	59.9%	37.9%	61.3%	38.7%
1	2004	212,308	186,448	BROWN, HENRY E., JR.*		—	25,860	186,448 R	87.8%		100.0%	
1	2002	142,425	127,562	BROWN, HENRY E., JR.*		—	14,863	127,562 R	89.6%		100.0%	
2	2010	259,672	138,861	WILSON, JOE*	113,625	MILLER, ROB	7,186	25,236 R	53.5%	43.8%	55.0%	45.0%
2	2008	343,486	184,583	WILSON, JOE*	158,627	MILLER, ROB	276	25,956 R	53.7%	46.2%	53.8%	46.2%
2	2006	204,052	127,811	WILSON, JOE*	76,090	ELLISOR, MICHAEL R.	151	51,721 R	62.6%	37.3%	62.7%	37.3%
2	2004	279,870	181,862	WILSON, JOE*	93,249	ELLISOR, MICHAEL R.	4,759	88,613 R	65.0%	33.3%	66.1%	33.9%
2	2002	171,359	144,149	WILSON, JOE*		—	27,210	144,149 R	84.1%		100.0%	
3	2010	202,108	126,235	DUNCAN, JEFF	73,095 #	DYER, JANE BALLARD	2,778	53,140 R	62.5%	36.2%	63.3%	36.7%
3	2008	288,741	186,799	BARRETT, J. GRESHAM*	101,724	DYER, JANE BALLARD	218	85,075 R	64.7%	35.2%	64.7%	35.3%
3	2006	177,988	111,882	BARRETT, J. GRESHAM*	66,039 #	BALLENGER, LEE	67	45,843 R	62.9%	37.1%	62.9%	37.1%
3	2004	191,999	191,052	BARRETT, J. GRESHAM*		—	947	191,052 R	99.5%		100.0%	
3	2002	178,195	119,644	BARRETT, J. GRESHAM	55,743	BRIGHTHARP, GEORGE L.	2,808	63,901 R	67.1%	31.3%	68.2%	31.8%
4	2010	216,838	137,586	GOWDY, TREY	62,438	CORDEN, PAUL	16,814	75,148 R	63.5%	28.8%	68.8%	31.2%
4	2008	306,928	184,440	INGLIS, BOB*	113,291	CORDEN, PAUL	9,197	71,149 R	60.1%	36.9%	61.9%	38.1%
4	2006	179,931	115,553	INGLIS, BOB*	57,490	GRIFFITH, WILLIAM GRIFF	6,888	58,063 R	64.2%	32.0%	66.8%	33.2%
4	2004	270,594	188,795	INGLIS, BOB	78,376	BROWN, BRANDON P.	3,423	110,419 R	69.8%	29.0%	70.7%	29.3%
4	2002	177,417	122,422	DeMINT, JIM*	52,635 #	ASHY, PETER J.	2,360	69,787 R	69.0%	29.7%	69.9%	30.1%
5	2010	228,286	125,834	MULVANEY, MIKE	102,296	SPRATT, JOHN M., JR.*	156	23,538 R	55.1%	44.8%	55.2%	44.8%
5	2008	306,285	113,282	SPENCER, ALBERT F.	188,785	SPRATT, JOHN M., JR.*	4,218	75,503 D	37.0%	61.6%	37.5%	62.5%
5	2006	175,154	75,422	NORMAN, RALPH	99,669	SPRATT, JOHN M., JR.*	63	24,247 D	43.1%	56.9%	43.1%	56.9%
5	2004	242,518	89,568	SPENCER, ALBERT F.	152,867	SPRATT, JOHN M., JR.*	83	63,299 D	36.9%	63.0%	36.9%	63.1%
5	2002	141,972		—	121,912	SPRATT, JOHN M., JR.*	20,060	121,912 D		85.9%		100.0%
6	2010	199,590	72,661	PRATT, JIM	125,459	CLYBURN, JAMES E.*	1,470	52,798 D	36.4%	62.9%	36.7%	63.3%
6	2008	286,571	93,059	HARRELSON, NANCY	193,378	CLYBURN, JAMES E.*	134	100,319 D	32.5%	67.5%	32.5%	67.5%
6	2006	155,706	53,181	McLEOD, GARY	100,213	CLYBURN, JAMES E.*	2,312	47,032 D	34.2%	64.4%	34.7%	65.3%
6	2004	241,829	79,600 #	McLEOD, GARY	161,987	CLYBURN, JAMES E.*	242	82,387 D	32.9%	67.0%	32.9%	67.1%
6	2002	174,066	55,760	McLEOD, GARY	116,586	CLYBURN, JAMES E.*	1,720	60,826 D	32.0%	67.0%	32.4%	67.6%
TOTAL	2010	1,340,189	753,932		543,921		42,336	210,011 R	56.3%	40.6%	58.1%	41.9%
TOTAL	2008	1,873,890	939,703		919,529		14,658	20,174 R	50.1%	49.1%	50.5%	49.5%
TOTAL	2006	1,086,206	599,615		472,719		13,872	126,896 R	55.2%	43.5%	55.9%	44.1%
TOTAL	2004	1,439,118	917,325		486,479		35,314	430,846 R	63.7%	33.8%	65.3%	34.7%
TOTAL	2002	985,434	569,537		346,876		69,021	222,661 R	57.8%	35.2%	62.1%	37.9%

A pound sign (#) indicates that the candidate received votes on the ballot line of another party. An asterisk (*) denotes incumbent.

SOUTH CAROLINA

GENERAL AND PRIMARY ELECTIONS

2010 GENERAL ELECTIONS

Governor   Other vote was 12,483 Green (Morgan Bruce Reeves); 7,631 United Citizens (Reeves), for a combined total of 20,114 votes for Reeves; 3,025 scattered write-in.

Senator   Other vote was 121,472 Green (Tom Clements); 21,953 scattered write-in.

House   Other vote was:

CD 1   4,148 Working Families (Rob Groce); 3,369 Green (Robert Dobbs); 2,750 Libertarian (Keith Blandford); 2,489 Independence (Jimmy Wood); 1,013 United Citizens (M. E. Mac McCullough); 163 scattered write-in.

CD 2   4,228 Libertarian (Eddie McCain); 2,856 Constitution (Marc Beaman); 102 scattered write-in.

CD 3   2,682 Constitution (John Dalen); 96 scattered write-in. Democrat Jane Ballard Dyer received 6,598 votes on the Working Families ballot line, which were included in her total vote.

CD 4   11,059 Constitution (Dave Edwards); 3,010 Libertarian (Rick Mahler); 2,564 Green (C. Faye Walters); 181 scattered write-in.

CD 5   156 scattered write-in.

CD 6   1,389 Green (Nammu Y. Muhammad); 81 scattered write-in.

2010 PRIMARY ELECTIONS

Primary	June 8, 2010	**Registration** (as of June 8, 2010)	2,585,911	No Party Registration

Primary Runoff   June 22, 2010

Primary Type   Open—Any registered voter could participate in either the Democratic or Republican primary, although any voter who participated in one party's primary could not vote in a primary runoff of the other party.

	REPUBLICAN PRIMARIES			**DEMOCRATIC PRIMARIES**		
Governor	Nikki R. Haley	206,326	48.9%	Vincent A. Sheheen	111,637	59.0%
	J. Gresham Barrett	91,824	21.7%	Jim Rex	43,590	23.0%
	Henry McMaster	71,494	16.9%	Robert Ford	34,121	18.0%
	Andre Bauer	52,607	12.5%			
	TOTAL	422,251		TOTAL	189,348	
	PRIMARY RUNOFF					
	Nikki R. Haley	233,733	65.0%			
	J. Gresham Barrett	125,601	35.0%			
	TOTAL	359,334				
Senator	Jim DeMint*	342,464	83.0%	Alvin M. Greene	100,362	59.0%
	Susan McDonald Gaddy	70,194	17.0%	Vic Rawl	69,853	41.0%
	TOTAL	412,658		TOTAL	170,215	
Congressional District 1	Tim Scott	25,457	31.5%	Ben Frasier	10,566	55.7%
	Paul Thurmond	13,149	16.3%	Robert D. Burton	8,402	44.3%
	Carroll Campbell	11,665	14.4%			
	Larry Kobrovsky	8,521	10.5%			
	Stovall Witte	7,192	8.9%			
	Clark B. Parker	6,769	8.4%			
	Katherine Jenerette	3,849	4.8%			
	Mark Lutz	3,237	4.0%			
	Ken Glasson	1,006	1.2%			
	TOTAL	80,845		TOTAL	18,968	

SOUTH CAROLINA

GENERAL AND PRIMARY ELECTIONS

	REPUBLICAN PRIMARIES			DEMOCRATIC PRIMARIES		
	PRIMARY RUNOFF					
	Tim Scott	46,989	68.3%			
	Paul Thurmond	21,799	31.7%			
	TOTAL	*68,788*				
Congressional District 2	Joe Wilson*	64,973	83.4%	Rob Miller	Unopposed	
	Phil Black	12,923	16.6%			
	TOTAL	*77,896*				
Congressional District 3	Richard Cash	20,923	25.3%	Jane Ballard Dyer	10,551	65.2%
	Jeff Duncan	19,051	23.1%	Brian Ryan B. Doyle	5,639	34.8%
	Rex Rice	16,071	19.5%			
	Joe Grimaud	15,503	18.8%			
	Neal Collins	6,787	8.2%			
	Frank Michael Vasovski	4,216	5.1%			
	TOTAL	*82,551*		*TOTAL*	*16,190*	
	PRIMARY RUNOFF					
	Jeff Duncan	37,352	51.5%			
	Richard Cash	35,185	48.5%			
	TOTAL	*72,537*				
Congressional District 4	Trey Gowdy	34,103	39.2%	Paul Corden	Unopposed	
	Bob Inglis*	23,877	27.5%			
	Jim Lee	11,854	13.6%			
	David Thomas	11,073	12.7%			
	Christina Jeffrey	6,041	6.9%			
	TOTAL	*86,948*				
	PRIMARY RUNOFF					
	Trey Gowdy	54,412	70.7%			
	Bob Inglis*	22,590	29.3%			
	TOTAL	*77,002*				
Congressional District 5	Mike Mulvaney	Unopposed		John M. Spratt Jr.*	Unopposed	
Congressional District 6	Jim Pratt	15,709	48.9%	James E. Clyburn*	50,138	90.1%
	Nancy Harrelson	13,487	42.0%	Gregory Brown	5,527	9.9%
	Colleen Payne	2,911	9.1%			
	TOTAL	*32,107*		*TOTAL*	*55,665*	
	PRIMARY RUNOFF					
	Jim Pratt	13,689	50.2%			
	Nancy Harrelson	13,578	49.8%			
	TOTAL	*27,267*				

An asterisk (*) denotes incumbent. The names of unopposed candidates did not appear on the primary ballot; therefore, no votes were cast for these candidates. A runoff was triggered if the leading candidate received less than a majority of the primary vote.

SOUTH DAKOTA

One member At Large

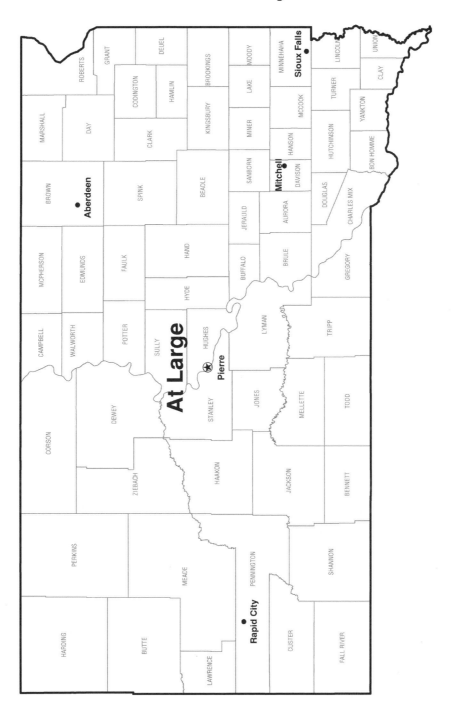

SOUTH DAKOTA

GOVERNOR
Dennis Daugaard (R). Elected 2010 to a four-year term.

SENATORS (1 Democrat, 1 Republican)
Tim Johnson (D). Reelected 2008 to a six-year term. Previously elected 2002, 1996.

John Thune (R). Reelected 2010 to a six-year term. Previously elected 2004.

REPRESENTATIVE (1 Republican)
At Large. Kristi Noem (R)

POSTWAR VOTE FOR PRESIDENT

| | | Republican | | Democratic | | | | Percentage | | | |
| | | | | | | | | Total Vote | | Major Vote | |
Year	Total Vote	Vote	Candidate	Vote	Candidate	Other Vote	Rep.-Dem. Plurality	Rep.	Dem.	Rep.	Dem.
2008	381,975	203,054	McCain, John	170,924	Obama, Barack	7,997	32,130 R	53.2%	44.7%	54.3%	45.7%
2004	388,215	232,584	Bush, George W.	149,244	Kerry, John	6,387	83,340 R	59.9%	38.4%	60.9%	39.1%
2000	316,269	190,700	Bush, George W.	118,804	Gore, Al	6,765	71,896 R	60.3%	37.6%	61.6%	38.4%
1996**	323,826	150,543	Dole, Bob	139,333	Clinton, Bill	33,950	11,210 R	46.5%	43.0%	51.9%	48.1%
1992**	336,254	136,718	Bush, George	124,888	Clinton, Bill	74,648	11,830 R	40.7%	37.1%	52.3%	47.7%
1988	312,991	165,415	Bush, George	145,560	Dukakis, Michael S.	2,016	19,855 R	52.8%	46.5%	53.2%	46.8%
1984	317,867	200,267	Reagan, Ronald	116,113	Mondale, Walter F.	1,487	84,154 R	63.0%	36.5%	63.3%	36.7%
1980**	327,703	198,343	Reagan, Ronald	103,855	Carter, Jimmy	25,505	94,488 R	60.5%	31.7%	65.6%	34.4%
1976	300,678	151,505	Ford, Gerald R.	147,068	Carter, Jimmy	2,105	4,437 R	50.4%	48.9%	50.7%	49.3%
1972	307,415	166,476	Nixon, Richard M.	139,945	McGovern, George S.	994	26,531 R	54.2%	45.5%	54.3%	45.7%
1968**	281,264	149,841	Nixon, Richard M.	118,023	Humphrey, Hubert H.	13,400	31,818 R	53.3%	42.0%	55.9%	44.1%
1964	293,118	130,108	Goldwater, Barry M.	163,010	Johnson, Lyndon B.		32,902 D	44.4%	55.6%	44.4%	55.6%
1960	306,487	178,417	Nixon, Richard M.	128,070	Kennedy, John F.		50,347 R	58.2%	41.8%	58.2%	41.8%
1956	293,857	171,569	Eisenhower, Dwight D.	122,288	Stevenson, Adlai E.		49,281 R	58.4%	41.6%	58.4%	41.6%
1952	294,283	203,857	Eisenhower, Dwight D.	90,426	Stevenson, Adlai E.		113,431 R	69.3%	30.7%	69.3%	30.7%
1948	250,105	129,651	Dewey, Thomas E.	117,653	Truman, Harry S.	2,801	11,998 R	51.8%	47.0%	52.4%	47.6%

**In past elections, the other vote included: 1996 - 31,250 Reform (Ross Perot); 1992 - 73,295 Independent (Perot); 1980 - 21,431 Independent (John Anderson); 1968 - 13,400 American Independent (George Wallace).

SOUTH DAKOTA

POSTWAR VOTE FOR GOVERNOR

Year	Total Vote	Republican		Democratic		Other Vote	Rep.-Dem. Plurality	Percentage			
								Total Vote		Major Vote	
		Vote	Candidate	Vote	Candidate			Rep.	Dem.	Rep.	Dem.
2010	317,083	195,046	Daugaard, Dennis	122,037	Heidepriem, Scott		73,009 R	61.5%	38.5%	61.5%	38.5%
2006	335,508	206,990	Rounds, Michael	121,226	Billion, Jack	7,292	85,764 R	61.7%	36.1%	63.1%	36.9%
2002	334,559	189,920	Rounds, Michael	140,263	Abbott, Jim	4,376	49,657 R	56.8%	41.9%	57.5%	42.5%
1998	260,187	166,621	Janklow, Bill	85,473	Hunhoff, Bernie	8,093	81,148 R	64.0%	32.9%	66.1%	33.9%
1994	311,613	172,515	Janklow, Bill	126,273	Beddow, Jim	12,825	46,242 R	55.4%	40.5%	57.7%	42.3%
1990	256,723	151,198	Mickelson, George S.	105,525	Samuelson, Bob L.		45,673 R	58.9%	41.1%	58.9%	41.1%
1986	294,441	152,543	Mickelson, George S.	141,898	Herseth, R. Lars		10,645 R	51.8%	48.2%	51.8%	48.2%
1982	278,562	197,426	Janklow, Bill	81,136	O'Connor, Michael J.		116,290 R	70.9%	29.1%	70.9%	29.1%
1978	259,795	147,116	Janklow, Bill	112,679	McKellips, Roger		34,437 R	56.6%	43.4%	56.6%	43.4%
1974**	278,228	129,077	Olson, John E.	149,151	Kneip, Richard F.		20,074 D	46.4%	53.6%	46.4%	53.6%
1972	308,177	123,165	Thompson, Carveth	185,012	Kneip, Richard F.		61,847 D	40.0%	60.0%	40.0%	60.0%
1970	239,963	108,347	Farrar, Frank	131,616	Kneip, Richard F.		23,269 D	45.2%	54.8%	45.2%	54.8%
1968	276,906	159,646	Farrar, Frank	117,260	Chamberlin, Robert		42,386 R	57.7%	42.3%	57.7%	42.3%
1966	228,214	131,710	Boe, Nils A.	96,504	Chamberlin, Robert		35,206 R	57.7%	42.3%	57.7%	42.3%
1964	290,570	150,151	Boe, Nils A.	140,419	Lindley, John F.		9,732 R	51.7%	48.3%	51.7%	48.3%
1962	256,120	143,682	Gubbrud, Archie M.	112,438	Herseth, Ralph		31,244 R	56.1%	43.9%	56.1%	43.9%
1960	304,625	154,530	Gubbrud, Archie M.	150,095	Herseth, Ralph		4,435 R	50.7%	49.3%	50.7%	49.3%
1958	258,281	125,520	Saunders, Phil	132,761	Herseth, Ralph		7,241 D	48.6%	51.4%	48.6%	51.4%
1956	292,017	158,819	Foss, Joe J.	133,198	Herseth, Ralph		25,621 R	54.4%	45.6%	54.4%	45.6%
1954	236,255	133,878	Foss, Joe J.	102,377	Martin, Ed C.		31,501 R	56.7%	43.3%	56.7%	43.3%
1952	289,515	203,102	Anderson, Sigurd	86,413	Iverson, Sherman A.		116,689 R	70.2%	29.8%	70.2%	29.8%
1950	253,316	154,254	Anderson, Sigurd	99,062	Robbie, Joseph		55,192 R	60.9%	39.1%	60.9%	39.1%
1948	245,372	149,883	Mickelson, George	95,489	Volz, Harold J.		54,394 R	61.1%	38.9%	61.1%	38.9%
1946	162,292	108,998	Mickelson, George	53,294	Haeder, Richard		55,704 R	67.2%	32.8%	67.2%	32.8%

**The term of office of South Dakota's governor was increased from two to four years effective with the 1974 election.

POSTWAR VOTE FOR SENATOR

Year	Total Vote	Republican		Democratic		Other Vote	Rep.-Dem. Plurality	Percentage			
								Total Vote		Major Vote	
		Vote	Candidate	Vote	Candidate			Rep.	Dem.	Rep.	Dem.
2010	227,947	227,947	Thune, John	—			227,947 R	100.0%		100.0%	
2008	380,673	142,784	Dykstra, Joel	237,889	Johnson, Tim		95,105 D	37.5%	62.5%	37.5%	62.5%
2004	391,188	197,848	Thune, John	193,340	Daschle, Tom		4,508 R	50.6%	49.4%	50.6%	49.4%
2002	337,508	166,957	Thune, John	167,481	Johnson, Tim	3,070	524 D	49.5%	49.6%	49.9%	50.1%
1998	262,111	95,431	Schmidt, Ron	162,884	Daschle, Tom	3,796	67,453 D	36.4%	62.1%	36.9%	63.1%
1996	324,487	157,954	Pressler, Larry	166,533	Johnson, Tim		8,579 D	48.7%	51.3%	48.7%	51.3%
1992	334,495	108,733	Haar, Charlene	217,095	Daschle, Tom	8,667	108,362 D	32.5%	64.9%	33.4%	66.6%
1990	258,976	135,682	Pressler, Larry	116,727	Muenster, Ted	6,567	18,955 R	52.4%	45.1%	53.8%	46.2%
1986	295,830	143,173	Abdnor, James	152,657	Daschle, Tom		9,484 D	48.4%	51.6%	48.4%	51.6%
1984	315,713	235,176	Pressler, Larry	80,537	Cunningham, George V.		154,639 R	74.5%	25.5%	74.5%	25.5%
1980	327,478	190,594	Abdnor, James	129,018	McGovern, George S.	7,866	61,576 R	58.2%	39.4%	59.6%	40.4%
1978	255,599	170,832	Pressler, Larry	84,767	Barnett, Don		86,065 R	66.8%	33.2%	66.8%	33.2%
1974	278,884	130,955	Thorsness, Leo K.	147,929	McGovern, George S.		16,974 D	47.0%	53.0%	47.0%	53.0%
1972	306,386	131,613	Hirsch, Robert W.	174,773	Abourezk, James		43,160 D	43.0%	57.0%	43.0%	57.0%
1968	279,912	120,951	Gubbrud, Archie M.	158,961	McGovern, George S.		38,010 D	43.2%	56.8%	43.2%	56.8%
1966	227,080	150,517	Mundt, Karl E.	76,563	Wright, Donn H.		73,954 R	66.3%	33.7%	66.3%	33.7%
1962	254,319	126,861	Bottum, Joe H.	127,458	McGovern, George S.		597 D	49.9%	50.1%	49.9%	50.1%
1960	305,442	160,181	Mundt, Karl E.	145,261	McGovern, George S.		14,920 R	52.4%	47.6%	52.4%	47.6%
1956	290,622	147,621	Case, Francis	143,001	Holum, Kenneth		4,620 R	50.8%	49.2%	50.8%	49.2%
1954	235,745	135,071	Mundt, Karl E.	100,674	Holum, Kenneth		34,397 R	57.3%	42.7%	57.3%	42.7%
1950	251,362	160,670	Case, Francis	90,692	Engel, John A.		69,978 R	63.9%	36.1%	63.9%	36.1%
1948	242,833	144,084	Mundt, Karl E.	98,749	Engel, John A.		45,335 R	59.3%	40.7%	59.3%	40.7%

The Democratic Party did not run a Senate candidate in the 2010 election.

SOUTH DAKOTA

GOVERNOR 2010

2010 Census Population	County	Total Vote	Republican	Democratic	Other	Rep.-Dem. Plurality	Total Vote		Major Vote	
							Rep.	Dem.	Rep.	Dem.
2,710	AURORA	1,380	788	592		196 R	57.1%	42.9%	57.1%	42.9%
17,398	BEADLE	6,883	3,931	2,952		979 R	57.1%	42.9%	57.1%	42.9%
3,431	BENNETT	1,034	619	415		204 R	59.9%	40.1%	59.9%	40.1%
7,070	BON HOMME	2,810	1,553	1,257		296 R	55.3%	44.7%	55.3%	44.7%
31,965	BROOKINGS	11,026	6,555	4,471		2,084 R	59.5%	40.5%	59.5%	40.5%
36,531	BROWN	14,357	8,541	5,816		2,725 R	59.5%	40.5%	59.5%	40.5%
5,255	BRULE	2,128	1,301	827		474 R	61.1%	38.9%	61.1%	38.9%
1,912	BUFFALO	447	124	323		199 D	27.7%	72.3%	27.7%	72.3%
10,110	BUTTE	3,670	2,575	1,095		1,480 R	70.2%	29.8%	70.2%	29.8%
1,466	CAMPBELL	782	616	166		450 R	78.8%	21.2%	78.8%	21.2%
9,129	CHARLES MIX	3,498	2,107	1,391		716 R	60.2%	39.8%	60.2%	39.8%
3,691	CLARK	1,681	979	702		277 R	58.2%	41.8%	58.2%	41.8%
13,864	CLAY	4,641	2,302	2,339		37 D	49.6%	50.4%	49.6%	50.4%
27,227	CODINGTON	10,260	6,352	3,908		2,444 R	61.9%	38.1%	61.9%	38.1%
4,050	CORSON	851	425	426		1 D	49.9%	50.1%	49.9%	50.1%
8,216	CUSTER	3,940	2,598	1,342		1,256 R	65.9%	34.1%	65.9%	34.1%
19,504	DAVISON	7,243	4,575	2,668		1,907 R	63.2%	36.8%	63.2%	36.8%
5,710	DAY	2,734	1,321	1,413		92 D	48.3%	51.7%	48.3%	51.7%
4,364	DEUEL	2,037	1,184	853		331 R	58.1%	41.9%	58.1%	41.9%
5,301	DEWEY	1,537	655	882		227 D	42.6%	57.4%	42.6%	57.4%
3,002	DOUGLAS	1,651	1,255	396		859 R	76.0%	24.0%	76.0%	24.0%
4,071	EDMUNDS	1,781	1,131	650		481 R	63.5%	36.5%	63.5%	36.5%
7,094	FALL RIVER	3,067	2,025	1,042		983 R	66.0%	34.0%	66.0%	34.0%
2,364	FAULK	1,087	693	394		299 R	63.8%	36.2%	63.8%	36.2%
7,356	GRANT	3,457	2,087	1,370		717 R	60.4%	39.6%	60.4%	39.6%
4,271	GREGORY	2,044	1,307	737		570 R	63.9%	36.1%	63.9%	36.1%
1,937	HAAKON	1,029	783	246		537 R	76.1%	23.9%	76.1%	23.9%
5,903	HAMLIN	2,634	1,692	942		750 R	64.2%	35.8%	64.2%	35.8%
3,431	HAND	1,839	967	872		95 R	52.6%	47.4%	52.6%	47.4%
3,331	HANSON	1,726	1,170	556		614 R	67.8%	32.2%	67.8%	32.2%
1,255	HARDING	671	465	206		259 R	69.3%	30.7%	69.3%	30.7%
17,022	HUGHES	7,713	5,626	2,087		3,539 R	72.9%	27.1%	72.9%	27.1%
7,343	HUTCHINSON	3,171	2,091	1,080		1,011 R	65.9%	34.1%	65.9%	34.1%
1,420	HYDE	717	483	234		249 R	67.4%	32.6%	67.4%	32.6%
3,031	JACKSON	949	614	335		279 R	64.7%	35.3%	64.7%	35.3%
2,071	JERAULD	1,127	611	516		95 R	54.2%	45.8%	54.2%	45.8%
1,006	JONES	579	427	152		275 R	73.7%	26.3%	73.7%	26.3%
5,148	KINGSBURY	2,462	1,426	1,036		390 R	57.9%	42.1%	57.9%	42.1%
11,200	LAKE	5,150	3,225	1,925		1,300 R	62.6%	37.4%	62.6%	37.4%
24,097	LAWRENCE	10,123	6,397	3,726		2,671 R	63.2%	36.8%	63.2%	36.8%
44,828	LINCOLN	17,918	11,831	6,087		5,744 R	66.0%	34.0%	66.0%	34.0%
3,755	LYMAN	1,382	840	542		298 R	60.8%	39.2%	60.8%	39.2%
5,618	MCCOOK	2,504	1,517	987		530 R	60.6%	39.4%	60.6%	39.4%
2,459	MCPHERSON	1,195	901	294		607 R	75.4%	24.6%	75.4%	24.6%
4,656	MARSHALL	1,839	965	874		91 R	52.5%	47.5%	52.5%	47.5%
25,434	MEADE	9,290	6,447	2,843		3,604 R	69.4%	30.6%	69.4%	30.6%
2,048	MELLETTE	744	402	342		60 R	54.0%	46.0%	54.0%	46.0%
2,389	MINER	1,117	595	522		73 R	53.3%	46.7%	53.3%	46.7%
169,468	MINNEHAHA	64,842	38,314	26,528		11,786 R	59.1%	40.9%	59.1%	40.9%
6,486	MOODY	2,730	1,534	1,196		338 R	56.2%	43.8%	56.2%	43.8%

SOUTH DAKOTA

GOVERNOR 2010

2010 Census Population	County	Total Vote	Republican	Democratic	Other	Rep.-Dem. Plurality	Percentage			
							Total Vote		Major Vote	
							Rep.	Dem.	Rep.	Dem.
100,948	PENNINGTON	36,762	24,443	12,319		12,124 R	66.5%	33.5%	66.5%	33.5%
2,982	PERKINS	1,352	843	509		334 R	62.4%	37.6%	62.4%	37.6%
2,329	POTTER	1,310	936	374		562 R	71.5%	28.5%	71.5%	28.5%
10,149	ROBERTS	3,808	1,852	1,956		104 D	48.6%	51.4%	48.6%	51.4%
2,355	SANBORN	1,157	673	484		189 R	58.2%	41.8%	58.2%	41.8%
13,586	SHANNON	2,382	423	1,959		1,536 D	17.8%	82.2%	17.8%	82.2%
6,415	SPINK	2,921	1,644	1,277		367 R	56.3%	43.7%	56.3%	43.7%
2,966	STANLEY	1,421	950	471		479 R	66.9%	33.1%	66.9%	33.1%
1,373	SULLY	740	529	211		318 R	71.5%	28.5%	71.5%	28.5%
9,612	TODD	1,954	630	1,324		694 D	32.2%	67.8%	32.2%	67.8%
5,644	TRIPP	2,510	1,745	765		980 R	69.5%	30.5%	69.5%	30.5%
8,347	TURNER	3,795	2,290	1,505		785 R	60.3%	39.7%	60.3%	39.7%
14,399	UNION	5,976	3,874	2,102		1,772 R	64.8%	35.2%	64.8%	35.2%
5,438	WALWORTH	2,225	1,595	630		965 R	71.7%	28.3%	71.7%	28.3%
22,438	YANKTON	8,626	5,406	3,220		2,186 R	62.7%	37.3%	62.7%	37.3%
2,801	ZIEBACH	667	291	376		85 D	43.6%	56.4%	43.6%	56.4%
814,180	TOTAL	317,083	195,046	122,037		73,009 R	61.5%	38.5%	61.5%	38.5%

SOUTH DAKOTA

SENATOR 2010

2010 Census Population	County	Total Vote	Republican	Democratic	Other	Rep.-Dem. Plurality	Percentage			
							Total Vote		Major Vote	
							Rep.	Dem.	Rep.	Dem.
2,710	AURORA	926	926			926 R	100.0%		100.0%	
17,398	BEADLE	4,897	4,897			4,897 R	100.0%		100.0%	
3,431	BENNETT	728	728			728 R	100.0%		100.0%	
7,070	BON HOMME	1,965	1,965			1,965 R	100.0%		100.0%	
31,965	BROOKINGS	7,721	7,721			7,721 R	100.0%		100.0%	
36,531	BROWN	9,862	9,862			9,862 R	100.0%		100.0%	
5,255	BRULE	1,525	1,525			1,525 R	100.0%		100.0%	
1,912	BUFFALO	208	208			208 R	100.0%		100.0%	
10,110	BUTTE	2,975	2,975			2,975 R	100.0%		100.0%	
1,466	CAMPBELL	642	642			642 R	100.0%		100.0%	
9,129	CHARLES MIX	2,518	2,518			2,518 R	100.0%		100.0%	
3,691	CLARK	1,190	1,190			1,190 R	100.0%		100.0%	
13,864	CLAY	2,756	2,756			2,756 R	100.0%		100.0%	
27,227	CODINGTON	7,504	7,504			7,504 R	100.0%		100.0%	
4,050	CORSON	577	577			577 R	100.0%		100.0%	
8,216	CUSTER	3,018	3,018			3,018 R	100.0%		100.0%	
19,504	DAVISON	5,480	5,480			5,480 R	100.0%		100.0%	
5,710	DAY	1,673	1,673			1,673 R	100.0%		100.0%	
4,364	DEUEL	1,427	1,427			1,427 R	100.0%		100.0%	
5,301	DEWEY	943	943			943 R	100.0%		100.0%	

SOUTH DAKOTA
SENATOR 2010

2010 Census Population	County	Total Vote	Republican	Democratic	Other	Rep.-Dem. Plurality	Percentage Total Vote Rep.	Dem.	Major Vote Rep.	Dem.
3,002	DOUGLAS	1,360	1,360			1,360 R	100.0%		100.0%	
4,071	EDMUNDS	1,275	1,275			1,275 R	100.0%		100.0%	
7,094	FALL RIVER	2,336	2,336			2,336 R	100.0%		100.0%	
2,364	FAULK	798	798			798 R	100.0%		100.0%	
7,356	GRANT	2,538	2,538			2,538 R	100.0%		100.0%	
4,271	GREGORY	1,549	1,549			1,549 R	100.0%		100.0%	
1,937	HAAKON	890	890			890 R	100.0%		100.0%	
5,903	HAMLIN	1,969	1,969			1,969 R	100.0%		100.0%	
3,431	HAND	1,393	1,393			1,393 R	100.0%		100.0%	
3,331	HANSON	1,323	1,323			1,323 R	100.0%		100.0%	
1,255	HARDING	583	583			583 R	100.0%		100.0%	
17,022	HUGHES	5,893	5,893			5,893 R	100.0%		100.0%	
7,343	HUTCHINSON	2,486	2,486			2,486 R	100.0%		100.0%	
1,420	HYDE	558	558			558 R	100.0%		100.0%	
3,031	JACKSON	734	734			734 R	100.0%		100.0%	
2,071	JERAULD	759	759			759 R	100.0%		100.0%	
1,006	JONES	507	507			507 R	100.0%		100.0%	
5,148	KINGSBURY	1,707	1,707			1,707 R	100.0%		100.0%	
11,200	LAKE	3,700	3,700			3,700 R	100.0%		100.0%	
24,097	LAWRENCE	7,491	7,491			7,491 R	100.0%		100.0%	
44,828	LINCOLN	13,642	13,642			13,642 R	100.0%		100.0%	
3,755	LYMAN	1,012	1,012			1,012 R	100.0%		100.0%	
5,618	MCCOOK	1,759	1,759			1,759 R	100.0%		100.0%	
2,459	MCPHERSON	990	990			990 R	100.0%		100.0%	
4,656	MARSHALL	1,186	1,186			1,186 R	100.0%		100.0%	
25,434	MEADE	7,360	7,360			7,360 R	100.0%		100.0%	
2,048	MELLETTE	543	543			543 R	100.0%		100.0%	
2,389	MINER	725	725			725 R	100.0%		100.0%	
169,468	MINNEHAHA	44,085	44,085			44,085 R	100.0%		100.0%	
6,486	MOODY	1,822	1,822			1,822 R	100.0%		100.0%	
100,948	PENNINGTON	27,928	27,928			27,928 R	100.0%		100.0%	
2,982	PERKINS	1,088	1,088			1,088 R	100.0%		100.0%	
2,329	POTTER	1,035	1,035			1,035 R	100.0%		100.0%	
10,149	ROBERTS	2,498	2,498			2,498 R	100.0%		100.0%	
2,355	SANBORN	854	854			854 R	100.0%		100.0%	
13,586	SHANNON	854	854			854 R	100.0%		100.0%	
6,415	SPINK	2,055	2,055			2,055 R	100.0%		100.0%	
2,966	STANLEY	1,062	1,062			1,062 R	100.0%		100.0%	
1,373	SULLY	600	600			600 R	100.0%		100.0%	
9,612	TODD	1,009	1,009			1,009 R	100.0%		100.0%	
5,644	TRIPP	1,925	1,925			1,925 R	100.0%		100.0%	
8,347	TURNER	2,778	2,778			2,778 R	100.0%		100.0%	
14,399	UNION	4,522	4,522			4,522 R	100.0%		100.0%	
5,438	WALWORTH	1,745	1,745			1,745 R	100.0%		100.0%	
22,438	YANKTON	6,063	6,063			6,063 R	100.0%		100.0%	
2,801	ZIEBACH	423	423			423 R	100.0%		100.0%	
814,180	TOTAL	227,947	227,947			227,947 R	100.0%		100.0%	

SOUTH DAKOTA

HOUSE OF REPRESENTATIVES

			Republican		Democratic		Other	Rep.-Dem.	Total Vote		Major Vote	
									Percentage			
CD	Year	Total Vote	Vote	Candidate	Vote	Candidate	Vote	Plurality	Rep.	Dem.	Rep.	Dem.
AL	2010	319,426	153,703	NOEM, KRISTI	146,589	HERSETH SANDLIN, STEPHANIE*	19,134	7,114 R	48.1%	45.9%	51.2%	48.8%
AL	2008	379,007	122,966	LIEN, CHRIS	256,041	HERSETH SANDLIN, STEPHANIE*		133,075 D	32.4%	67.6%	32.4%	67.6%
AL	2006	333,562	97,864	WHALEN, BRUCE W.	230,468	HERSETH, STEPHANIE*	5,230	132,604 D	29.3%	69.1%	29.8%	70.2%
AL	2004	389,468	178,823	DIEDRICH, LARRY	207,837	HERSETH, STEPHANIE*	2,808	29,014 D	45.9%	53.4%	46.2%	53.8%
AL	2002	336,807	180,023	JANKLOW, BILL	153,656	HERSETH, STEPHANIE	3,128	26,367 R	53.4%	45.6%	54.0%	46.0%
AL	2000	314,761	231,083	THUNE, JOHN*	78,321	HOHN, CURT	5,357	152,762 R	73.4%	24.9%	74.7%	25.3%
AL	1998	258,590	194,157	THUNE, JOHN*	64,433	MOSER, JEFF		129,724 R	75.1%	24.9%	75.1%	24.9%
AL	1996	323,203	186,393	THUNE, JOHN	119,547	WEILAND, RICK	17,263	66,846 R	57.7%	37.0%	60.9%	39.1%
AL	1994	305,922	112,054	BERKHOUT, JAN	183,036	JOHNSON, TIM*	10,832	70,982 D	36.6%	59.8%	38.0%	62.0%
AL	1992	332,902	89,375	TIMMER, JOHN	230,070	JOHNSON, TIM*	13,457	140,695 D	26.8%	69.1%	28.0%	72.0%
AL	1990	257,298	83,484	FRANKENFELD, DON	173,814	JOHNSON, TIM*		90,330 D	32.4%	67.6%	32.4%	67.6%
AL	1988	311,916	88,157	VOLK, DAVID	223,759	JOHNSON, TIM*		135,602 D	28.3%	71.7%	28.3%	71.7%
AL	1986	289,723	118,261	BELL, DALE	171,462	JOHNSON, TIM		53,201 D	40.8%	59.2%	40.8%	59.2%
AL	1984	316,222	134,821	BELL, DALE	181,401	DASCHLE, TOM*		46,580 D	42.6%	57.4%	42.6%	57.4%
AL	1982	275,652	133,530	ROBERTS, CLINT	142,122	DASCHLE, TOM*		8,592 D	48.4%	51.6%	48.4%	51.6%

An asterisk (*) denotes incumbent. South Dakota had two House seats before 1982.

SOUTH DAKOTA

GENERAL AND PRIMARY ELECTIONS

2010 GENERAL ELECTIONS

Governor

House Other vote was:

At Large 19,134 Independent (B. Thomas Marking).

2010 PRIMARY ELECTIONS

Primary	June 8, 2010	**Registration** (as of May 24, 2010 - does not include 53,425 inactive Registrants)	Republican	234,785
			Democratic	194,023
			Libertarian	1,055
			Constitution	328
			Other	609
			Independent	82,403
			TOTAL	*513,203*

Primary Type Republicans held a "closed" primary, with only registered Republicans allowed to vote in it. Democrats held a "semi-open" primary, with both registered Democrats and independents eligible to cast a Democratic primary ballot.

SOUTH DAKOTA

GENERAL AND PRIMARY ELECTIONS

	REPUBLICAN PRIMARIES			DEMOCRATIC PRIMARIES	
Governor	Dennis Daugaard	42,261	50.4%	Scott Heidepriem	Unopposed
	Scott Munsterman	14,726	17.6%		
	Dave Knudson	13,218	15.8%		
	Gordon Howie	10,426	12.4%		
	Ken Knuppe	3,186	3.8%		
	TOTAL	*83,817*			
House At Large	Kristi Noem	34,527	42.1%	Stephanie Herseth Sandlin*	Unopposed
	Chris Nelson	28,380	34.6%		
	Blake Curd	19,134	23.3%		
	TOTAL	*82,041*			

An asterisk (*) denotes incumbent. The names of unopposed candidates did not appear on the primary ballot; therefore, no votes were cast for these candidates.

TENNESSEE

Congressional districts first established for elections held in 2002
9 members

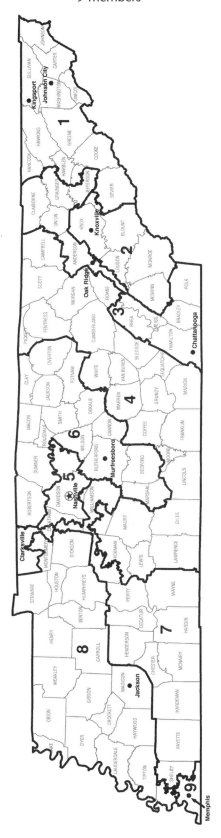

TENNESSEE

GOVERNOR

Bill Haslam (R). Elected 2010 to a four-year term.

SENATORS (2 Republicans)

Lamar Alexander (R). Reelected 2008 to a six-year term. Previously elected 2002.

Bob Corker (R). Elected 2006 to a six-year term.

REPRESENTATIVES (7 Republicans, 2 Democrats)

1. Phil Roe (R)
2. John J. "Jimmy" Duncan Jr. (R)
3. Chuck Fleischmann (R)
4. Scott DesJarlais (R)
5. Jim Cooper (D)
6. Diane Black (R)
7. Marsha Blackburn (R)
8. Stephen Lee Fincher (R)
9. Steve Cohen (D)

POSTWAR VOTE FOR PRESIDENT

Year	Total Vote	Republican Vote	Republican Candidate	Democratic Vote	Democratic Candidate	Other Vote	Rep.-Dem. Plurality	Total Vote Rep.	Total Vote Dem.	Major Vote Rep.	Major Vote Dem.
2008	2,599,749	1,479,178	McCain, John	1,087,437	Obama, Barack	33,134	391,741 R	56.9%	41.8%	57.6%	42.4%
2004	2,437,319	1,384,375	Bush, George W.	1,036,477	Kerry, John	16,467	347,898 R	56.8%	42.5%	57.2%	42.8%
2000**	2,076,181	1,061,949	Bush, George W.	981,720	Gore, Al	32,512	80,229 R	51.1%	47.3%	52.0%	48.0%
1996**	1,894,105	863,530	Dole, Bob	909,146	Clinton, Bill	121,429	45,616 D	45.6%	48.0%	48.7%	51.3%
1992**	1,982,638	841,300	Bush, George	933,521	Clinton, Bill	207,817	92,221 D	42.4%	47.1%	47.4%	52.6%
1988	1,636,250	947,233	Bush, George	679,794	Dukakis, Michael S.	9,223	267,439 R	57.9%	41.5%	58.2%	41.8%
1984	1,711,994	990,212	Reagan, Ronald	711,714	Mondale, Walter F.	10,068	278,498 R	57.8%	41.6%	58.2%	41.8%
1980**	1,617,616	787,761	Reagan, Ronald	783,051	Carter, Jimmy	46,804	4,710 R	48.7%	48.4%	50.1%	49.9%
1976	1,476,345	633,969	Ford, Gerald R.	825,879	Carter, Jimmy	16,497	191,910 D	42.9%	55.9%	43.4%	56.6%
1972	1,201,182	813,147	Nixon, Richard M.	357,293	McGovern, George S.	30,742	455,854 R	67.7%	29.7%	69.5%	30.5%
1968**	1,248,617	472,592	Nixon, Richard M.	351,233	Humphrey, Hubert H.	424,792	47,800 R	37.8%	28.1%	57.4%	42.6%
1964	1,143,946	508,965	Goldwater, Barry M.	634,947	Johnson, Lyndon B.	34	125,982 D	44.5%	55.5%	44.5%	55.5%
1960	1,051,792	556,577	Nixon, Richard M.	481,453	Kennedy, John F.	13,762	75,124 R	52.9%	45.8%	53.6%	46.4%
1956	939,404	462,288	Eisenhower, Dwight D.	456,507	Stevenson, Adlai E.	20,609	5,781 R	49.2%	48.6%	50.3%	49.7%
1952	892,553	446,147	Eisenhower, Dwight D.	443,710	Stevenson, Adlai E.	2,696	2,437 R	50.0%	49.7%	50.1%	49.9%
1948**	550,283	202,914	Dewey, Thomas E.	270,402	Truman, Harry S.	76,967	67,488 D	36.9%	49.1%	42.9%	57.1%

**In past elections, the other vote included: 2000 - 19,781 Green (Ralph Nader); 1996 - 105,918 Reform (Ross Perot); 1992 - 199,968 Independent (Perot); 1980 - 35,991 Independent (John Anderson); 1968 - 424,792 American Independent (George Wallace), who finished second; 1948 - 73,815 States' Rights (Strom Thurmond).

TENNESSEE

POSTWAR VOTE FOR GOVERNOR

Year	Total Vote	Republican Vote	Republican Candidate	Democratic Vote	Democratic Candidate	Other Vote	Rep.-Dem. Plurality	Total Vote Rep.	Total Vote Dem.	Major Vote Rep.	Major Vote Dem.
2010	1,601,549	1,041,545	Haslam, Bill	529,851	McWherter, Mike	30,153	511,694 R	65.0%	33.1%	66.3%	33.7%
2006	1,818,549	540,853	Bryson, Jim	1,247,491	Bredesen, Phil	30,205	706,638 D	29.7%	68.6%	30.2%	69.8%
2002	1,653,167	786,803	Hilleary, Van	837,284	Bredesen, Phil	29,080	50,481 D	47.6%	50.6%	48.4%	51.6%
1998	976,236	669,973	Sundquist, Don	287,750	Hooker, John J.	18,513	382,223 R	68.6%	29.5%	70.0%	30.0%
1994	1,487,130	807,104	Sundquist, Don	664,252	Bredesen, Phil	15,774	142,852 R	54.3%	44.7%	54.9%	45.1%
1990	790,441	289,348	Henry, Dwight	480,885	McWherter, Ned	20,208	191,537 D	36.6%	60.8%	37.6%	62.4%
1986	1,210,339	553,449	Dunn, Winfield	656,602	McWherter, Ned	288	103,153 D	45.7%	54.2%	45.7%	54.3%
1982	1,238,927	737,963	Alexander, Lamar	500,937	Tyree, Randy	27	237,026 R	59.6%	40.4%	59.6%	40.4%
1978	1,189,695	661,959	Alexander, Lamar	523,495	Butcher, Jake	4,241	138,464 R	55.6%	44.0%	55.8%	44.2%
1974	1,040,714	455,467	Alexander, Lamar	576,833	Blanton, Ray	8,414	121,366 D	43.8%	55.4%	44.1%	55.9%
1970	1,108,247	575,777	Dunn, Winfield	509,521	Hooker, John J.	22,949	66,256 R	52.0%	46.0%	53.1%	46.9%
1966	656,566			532,998	Ellington, Buford	123,568	532,998 D		81.2%		100.0%
1962**	621,064	100,190	Patty, Hubert D.	315,648	Clement, Frank G.	205,226	215,458 D	16.1%	50.8%	24.1%	75.9%
1958**	432,545	35,938	Wall, Thomas P.	248,874	Ellington, Buford	147,733	212,936 D	8.3%	57.5%	12.6%	87.4%
1954**	322,586		—	281,291	Clement, Frank G.	41,295	281,291 D		87.2%		100.0%
1952	806,771	166,377	Witt, R. Beecher	640,290	Clement, Frank G.	104	473,913 D	20.6%	79.4%	20.6%	79.4%
1950**	236,194		—	184,437	Browning, Gordon	51,757	184,437 D		78.1%		100.0%
1948	543,881	179,957	Acuff, Roy	363,903	Browning, Gordon	21	183,946 D	33.1%	66.9%	33.1%	66.9%
1946	229,456	73,222	Lowe, W. O.	149,937	McCord, Jim Nance	6,297	76,715 D	31.9%	65.3%	32.8%	67.2%

**In past elections, the other vote included: 1962 - 203,765 Independent (William R. Anderson), who finished second; 1958 - 136,399 Independent (Jim Nance McCord), who finished second; 1954 - 39,574 Independent (John R. Neal); 1950 - 51,757 Independent (Neal). The Republican Party did not run a gubernatorial candidate in 1950, 1954 and 1966. The term of office of Tennessee's Governor was increased from two to four years effective with the 1954 election.

POSTWAR VOTE FOR SENATOR

Year	Total Vote	Republican Vote	Republican Candidate	Democratic Vote	Democratic Candidate	Other Vote	Rep.-Dem. Plurality	Total Vote Rep.	Total Vote Dem.	Major Vote Rep.	Major Vote Dem.
2008	2,424,585	1,579,477	Alexander, Lamar	767,236	Tuke, Robert D.	77,872	812,241 R	65.1%	31.6%	67.3%	32.7%
2006	1,833,695	929,911	Corker, Bob	879,976	Ford, Harold E., Jr.	23,808	49,935 R	50.7%	48.0%	51.4%	48.6%
2002	1,642,421	891,420	Alexander, Lamar	728,295	Clement, Bob	22,706	163,125 R	54.3%	44.3%	55.0%	45.0%
2000	1,928,613	1,255,444	Frist, Bill	621,152	Clark, Jeff	52,017	634,292 R	65.1%	32.2%	66.9%	33.1%
1996	1,778,664	1,091,554	Thompson, Fred	654,937	Gordon, Houston	32,173	436,617 R	61.4%	36.8%	62.5%	37.5%
1994	1,480,391	834,226	Frist, Bill	623,164	Sasser, James R.	23,001	211,062 R	56.4%	42.1%	57.2%	42.8%
1994S	1,465,862	885,998	Thompson, Fred	565,930	Cooper, Jim	13,934	320,068 R	60.4%	38.6%	61.0%	39.0%
1990	783,922	233,703	Hawkins, William R.	530,898	Gore, Al	19,321	297,195 D	29.8%	67.7%	30.6%	69.4%
1988	1,567,181	541,033	Anderson, Bill	1,020,061	Sasser, James R.	6,087	479,028 D	34.5%	65.1%	34.7%	65.3%
1984	1,648,064	557,016	Ashe, Victor	1,000,607	Gore, Al	90,441	443,591 D	33.8%	60.7%	35.8%	64.2%
1982	1,259,785	479,642	Beard, Robin L.	780,113	Sasser, James R.	30	300,471 D	38.1%	61.9%	38.1%	61.9%
1978	1,157,094	642,644	Baker, Howard H., Jr.	466,228	Eskind, Jane	48,222	176,416 R	55.5%	40.3%	58.0%	42.0%
1976	1,432,046	673,231	Brock, William E.	751,180	Sasser, James R.	7,635	77,949 D	47.0%	52.5%	47.3%	52.7%
1972	1,164,195	716,539	Baker, Howard H., Jr.	440,599	Blanton, Ray	7,057	275,940 R	61.5%	37.8%	61.9%	38.1%
1970	1,097,041	562,645	Brock, William E.	519,858	Gore, Albert	14,538	42,787 R	51.3%	47.4%	52.0%	48.0%
1966	866,961	483,063	Baker, Howard H., Jr.	383,843	Clement, Frank G.	55	99,220 R	55.7%	44.3%	55.7%	44.3%
1964	1,064,018	493,475	Kuykendall, Daniel H.	570,542	Gore, Albert	1	77,067 D	46.4%	53.6%	46.4%	53.6%
1964S	1,091,093	517,330	Baker, Howard H., Jr.	568,905	Bass, Ross	4,858	51,575 D	47.4%	52.1%	47.6%	52.4%
1960	828,519	234,053	Frazier, A. Bradley	594,460	Kefauver, Estes	6	360,407 D	28.2%	71.7%	28.2%	71.8%
1958	401,666	76,371	Atkins, Hobart F.	317,324	Gore, Albert	7,971	240,953 D	19.0%	79.0%	19.4%	80.6%
1954	356,094	106,971	Wall, Thomas P.	249,121	Kefauver, Estes	2	142,150 D	30.0%	70.0%	30.0%	70.0%
1952	735,219	153,479	Atkins, Hobart F.	545,432	Gore, Albert	36,308	391,953 D	20.9%	74.2%	22.0%	78.0%
1948	499,218	166,947	Reece, B. Carroll	326,142	Kefauver, Estes	6,129	159,195 D	33.4%	65.3%	33.9%	66.1%
1946	218,714	57,238	Ladd, William B.	145,654	McKellar, Kenneth	15,822	88,416 D	26.2%	66.6%	28.2%	71.8%

One each of the 1964 and 1994 elections was for a short term to fill a vacancy.

TENNESSEE

GOVERNOR 2010

2010 Census Population	County	Total Vote	Republican	Democratic	Other	Rep.-Dem. Plurality		Percentage			
								Total Vote		Major Vote	
								Rep.	Dem.	Rep.	Dem.
75,129	ANDERSON	19,225	13,938	4,785	502	9,153	R	72.5%	24.9%	74.4%	25.6%
45,058	BEDFORD	9,796	6,808	2,773	215	4,035	R	69.5%	28.3%	71.1%	28.9%
16,489	BENTON	5,043	2,590	2,382	71	208	R	51.4%	47.2%	52.1%	47.9%
12,876	BLEDSOE	3,814	2,527	1,214	73	1,313	R	66.3%	31.8%	67.5%	32.5%
123,010	BLOUNT	29,963	23,786	5,449	728	18,337	R	79.4%	18.2%	81.4%	18.6%
98,963	BRADLEY	21,343	17,522	3,477	344	14,045	R	82.1%	16.3%	83.4%	16.6%
40,716	CAMPBELL	8,672	6,309	2,149	214	4,160	R	72.8%	24.8%	74.6%	25.4%
13,801	CANNON	3,921	2,412	1,415	94	997	R	61.5%	36.1%	63.0%	37.0%
28,522	CARROLL	8,328	4,724	3,484	120	1,240	R	56.7%	41.8%	57.6%	42.4%
57,424	CARTER	14,007	10,783	3,001	223	7,782	R	77.0%	21.4%	78.2%	21.8%
39,105	CHEATHAM	10,181	7,017	2,969	195	4,048	R	68.9%	29.2%	70.3%	29.7%
17,131	CHESTER	3,982	2,763	1,147	72	1,616	R	69.4%	28.8%	70.7%	29.3%
32,213	CLAIBORNE	6,404	4,768	1,463	173	3,305	R	74.5%	22.8%	76.5%	23.5%
7,861	CLAY	1,996	1,179	778	39	401	R	59.1%	39.0%	60.2%	39.8%
35,662	COCKE	8,436	6,385	1,863	188	4,522	R	75.7%	22.1%	77.4%	22.6%
52,796	COFFEE	13,591	9,436	3,872	283	5,564	R	69.4%	28.5%	70.9%	29.1%
14,586	CROCKETT	4,370	2,818	1,504	48	1,314	R	64.5%	34.4%	65.2%	34.8%
56,053	CUMBERLAND	20,010	15,550	4,061	399	11,489	R	77.7%	20.3%	79.3%	20.7%
626,681	DAVIDSON	155,618	75,381	76,427	3,810	1,046	D	48.4%	49.1%	49.7%	50.3%
11,757	DECATUR	3,232	1,820	1,351	61	469	R	56.3%	41.8%	57.4%	42.6%
18,723	DE KALB	4,914	2,870	1,947	97	923	R	58.4%	39.6%	59.6%	40.4%
49,666	DICKSON	12,190	7,812	4,150	228	3,662	R	64.1%	34.0%	65.3%	34.7%
38,335	DYER	9,891	6,576	2,848	467	3,728	R	66.5%	28.8%	69.8%	30.2%
38,413	FAYETTE	12,344	8,490	3,667	187	4,823	R	68.8%	29.7%	69.8%	30.2%
17,959	FENTRESS	5,081	3,630	1,374	77	2,256	R	71.4%	27.0%	72.5%	27.5%
41,052	FRANKLIN	12,300	7,792	4,272	236	3,520	R	63.3%	34.7%	64.6%	35.4%
49,683	GIBSON	15,049	8,664	6,152	233	2,512	R	57.6%	40.9%	58.5%	41.5%
29,485	GILES	8,193	4,936	3,074	183	1,862	R	60.2%	37.5%	61.6%	38.4%
22,657	GRAINGER	4,545	3,399	1,034	112	2,365	R	74.8%	22.8%	76.7%	23.3%
68,831	GREENE	15,705	12,066	3,315	324	8,751	R	76.8%	21.1%	78.4%	21.6%
13,703	GRUNDY	3,074	1,693	1,292	89	401	R	55.1%	42.0%	56.7%	43.3%
62,544	HAMBLEN	13,587	10,798	2,608	181	8,190	R	79.5%	19.2%	80.5%	19.5%
336,463	HAMILTON	87,039	57,090	28,556	1,393	28,534	R	65.6%	32.8%	66.7%	33.3%
6,819	HANCOCK	1,260	923	305	32	618	R	73.3%	24.2%	75.2%	24.8%
27,253	HARDEMAN	6,442	3,250	3,044	148	206	R	50.5%	47.3%	51.6%	48.4%
26,026	HARDIN	6,245	4,315	1,810	120	2,505	R	69.1%	29.0%	70.4%	29.6%
56,833	HAWKINS	12,378	9,320	2,817	241	6,503	R	75.3%	22.8%	76.8%	23.2%
18,787	HAYWOOD	5,387	2,462	2,853	72	391	D	45.7%	53.0%	46.3%	53.7%
27,769	HENDERSON	6,234	4,328	1,791	115	2,537	R	69.4%	28.7%	70.7%	29.3%
32,330	HENRY	9,530	5,261	4,129	140	1,132	R	55.2%	43.3%	56.0%	44.0%
24,690	HICKMAN	5,278	3,156	2,000	122	1,156	R	59.8%	37.9%	61.2%	38.8%
8,426	HOUSTON	2,121	1,016	1,055	50	39	D	47.9%	49.7%	49.1%	50.9%
18,538	HUMPHREYS	5,015	2,689	2,232	94	457	R	53.6%	44.5%	54.6%	45.4%
11,638	JACKSON	2,993	1,587	1,333	73	254	R	53.0%	44.5%	54.3%	45.7%
51,407	JEFFERSON	11,183	8,895	2,040	248	6,855	R	79.5%	18.2%	81.3%	18.7%
18,244	JOHNSON	4,567	3,452	1,033	82	2,419	R	75.6%	22.6%	77.0%	23.0%
432,226	KNOX	104,742	84,915	17,869	1,958	67,046	R	81.1%	17.1%	82.6%	17.4%
7,832	LAKE	1,395	661	688	46	27	D	47.4%	49.3%	49.0%	51.0%
27,815	LAUDERDALE	6,155	3,369	2,686	100	683	R	54.7%	43.6%	55.6%	44.4%
41,869	LAWRENCE	11,605	7,722	3,714	169	4,008	R	66.5%	32.0%	67.5%	32.5%

TENNESSEE

GOVERNOR 2010

2010 Census Population	County	Total Vote	Republican	Democratic	Other	Rep.-Dem. Plurality		Percentage Total Vote Rep.	Dem.	Major Vote Rep.	Dem.
12,161	LEWIS	3,524	2,235	1,197	92	1,038	R	63.4%	34.0%	65.1%	34.9%
33,361	LINCOLN	8,570	6,196	2,070	304	4,126	R	72.3%	24.2%	75.0%	25.0%
48,556	LOUDON	15,295	12,552	2,413	330	10,139	R	82.1%	15.8%	83.9%	16.1%
52,266	MCMINN	11,367	8,711	2,462	194	6,249	R	76.6%	21.7%	78.0%	22.0%
26,075	MCNAIRY	6,803	4,357	2,343	103	2,014	R	64.0%	34.4%	65.0%	35.0%
22,248	MACON	4,910	3,349	1,465	96	1,884	R	68.2%	29.8%	69.6%	30.4%
98,294	MADISON	28,276	15,762	12,214	300	3,548	R	55.7%	43.2%	56.3%	43.7%
28,237	MARION	7,330	4,579	2,616	135	1,963	R	62.5%	35.7%	63.6%	36.4%
30,617	MARSHALL	7,575	4,810	2,620	145	2,190	R	63.5%	34.6%	64.7%	35.3%
80,956	MAURY	23,191	15,190	7,612	389	7,578	R	65.5%	32.8%	66.6%	33.4%
11,753	MEIGS	2,642	1,804	780	58	1,024	R	68.3%	29.5%	69.8%	30.2%
44,519	MONROE	10,390	7,795	2,399	196	5,396	R	75.0%	23.1%	76.5%	23.5%
172,331	MONTGOMERY	31,112	19,227	11,159	726	8,068	R	61.8%	35.9%	63.3%	36.7%
6,362	MOORE	2,092	1,435	579	78	856	R	68.6%	27.7%	71.3%	28.7%
21,987	MORGAN	4,343	3,032	1,187	124	1,845	R	69.8%	27.3%	71.9%	28.1%
31,807	OBION	9,378	5,063	4,052	263	1,011	R	54.0%	43.2%	55.5%	44.5%
22,083	OVERTON	5,262	3,088	2,065	109	1,023	R	58.7%	39.2%	59.9%	40.1%
7,915	PERRY	1,910	1,057	799	54	258	R	55.3%	41.8%	57.0%	43.0%
5,077	PICKETT	2,157	1,428	683	46	745	R	66.2%	31.7%	67.6%	32.4%
16,825	POLK	3,961	2,569	1,295	97	1,274	R	64.9%	32.7%	66.5%	33.5%
72,321	PUTNAM	18,660	13,031	5,306	323	7,725	R	69.8%	28.4%	71.1%	28.9%
31,809	RHEA	7,168	5,452	1,547	169	3,905	R	76.1%	21.6%	77.9%	22.1%
54,181	ROANE	15,615	11,523	3,707	385	7,816	R	73.8%	23.7%	75.7%	24.3%
66,283	ROBERTSON	17,885	12,151	5,416	318	6,735	R	67.9%	30.3%	69.2%	30.8%
262,604	RUTHERFORD	61,071	41,999	17,912	1,160	24,087	R	68.8%	29.3%	70.1%	29.9%
22,228	SCOTT	4,729	3,522	1,107	100	2,415	R	74.5%	23.4%	76.1%	23.9%
14,112	SEQUATCHIE	3,530	2,497	966	67	1,531	R	70.7%	27.4%	72.1%	27.9%
89,889	SEVIER	19,751	16,592	2,692	467	13,900	R	84.0%	13.6%	86.0%	14.0%
927,644	SHELBY	229,404	107,227	118,977	3,200	11,750	D	46.7%	51.9%	47.4%	52.6%
19,166	SMITH	5,773	3,369	2,290	114	1,079	R	58.4%	39.7%	59.5%	40.5%
13,324	STEWART	3,861	2,120	1,662	79	458	R	54.9%	43.0%	56.1%	43.9%
156,823	SULLIVAN	39,423	30,529	8,359	535	22,170	R	77.4%	21.2%	78.5%	21.5%
160,645	SUMNER	44,473	32,543	11,251	679	21,292	R	73.2%	25.3%	74.3%	25.7%
61,081	TIPTON	15,853	10,880	4,706	267	6,174	R	68.6%	29.7%	69.8%	30.2%
7,870	TROUSDALE	2,087	1,170	875	42	295	R	56.1%	41.9%	57.2%	42.8%
18,313	UNICOI	4,417	3,334	1,001	82	2,333	R	75.5%	22.7%	76.9%	23.1%
19,109	UNION	3,807	2,861	869	77	1,992	R	75.2%	22.8%	76.7%	23.3%
5,548	VAN BUREN	1,625	931	654	40	277	R	57.3%	40.2%	58.7%	41.3%
39,839	WARREN	9,638	5,745	3,640	253	2,105	R	59.6%	37.8%	61.2%	38.8%
122,979	WASHINGTON	29,114	22,403	6,296	415	16,107	R	76.9%	21.6%	78.1%	21.9%
17,021	WAYNE	3,557	2,606	894	57	1,712	R	73.3%	25.1%	74.5%	25.5%
35,021	WEAKLEY	9,449	4,891	4,393	165	498	R	51.8%	46.5%	52.7%	47.3%
25,841	WHITE	6,994	4,542	2,260	192	2,282	R	64.9%	32.3%	66.8%	33.2%
183,182	WILLIAMSON	60,603	48,518	11,085	1,000	37,433	R	80.1%	18.3%	81.4%	18.6%
113,993	WILSON	34,600	25,217	8,724	659	16,493	R	72.9%	25.2%	74.3%	25.7%
6,346,105	TOTAL	1,601,549	1,041,545	529,851	30,153	511,694	R	65.0%	33.1%	66.3%	33.7%

TENNESSEE

HOUSE OF REPRESENTATIVES

			Republican		Democratic		Other	Rep.-Dem.	Percentage			
									Total Vote		Major Vote	
CD	Year	Total Vote	Vote	Candidate	Vote	Candidate	Vote	Plurality	Rep.	Dem.	Rep.	Dem.
1	2010	152,161	123,006	ROE, PHIL*	26,045	CLARK, MICHAEL EDWARD	3,110	96,961 R	80.8%	17.1%	82.5%	17.5%
1	2008	234,381	168,343	ROE, PHIL	57,525	RUSSELL, ROB	8,513	110,818 R	71.8%	24.5%	74.5%	25.5%
1	2006	177,278	108,336	DAVIS, DAVID	65,538	TRENT, RICK	3,404	42,798 R	61.1%	37.0%	62.3%	37.7%
1	2004	233,560	172,543	JENKINS, BILL*	56,361	LEONARD, GRAHAM	4,656	116,182 R	73.9%	24.1%	75.4%	24.6%
1	2002	128,886	127,300	JENKINS, BILL*		—	1,586	127,300 R	98.8%		100.0%	
2	2010	173,380	141,796	DUNCAN, JOHN J. "JIMMY," JR.*	25,400	HANCOCK, DAVE	6,184	116,396 R	81.8%	14.6%	84.8%	15.2%
2	2008	290,759	227,120	DUNCAN, JOHN J. "JIMMY," JR.*	63,639	SCOTT, BOB		163,481 R	78.1%	21.9%	78.1%	21.9%
2	2006	202,120	157,095	DUNCAN, JOHN J. "JIMMY," JR.*	45,025	GREENE, JOHN		112,070 R	77.7%	22.3%	77.7%	22.3%
2	2004	272,928	215,795	DUNCAN, JOHN J. "JIMMY," JR.*	52,155	GREENE, JOHN	4,978	163,640 R	79.1%	19.1%	80.5%	19.5%
2	2002	185,981	146,887	DUNCAN, JOHN J. "JIMMY," JR.*	37,035	GREENE, JOHN	2,059	109,852 R	79.0%	19.9%	79.9%	20.1%
3	2010	162,056	92,032	FLEISCHMANN, CHUCK	45,387	WOLFE, JOHN	24,637	46,645 R	56.8%	28.0%	67.0%	33.0%
3	2008	266,628	184,964	WAMP, ZACH*	73,059	VANDAGRIFF, DOUG	8,605	111,905 R	69.4%	27.4%	71.7%	28.3%
3	2006	199,115	130,791	WAMP, ZACH*	68,324	BENEDICT, BRENT		62,467 R	65.7%	34.3%	65.7%	34.3%
3	2004	256,636	166,154	WAMP, ZACH*	84,295	WOLFE, JOHN	6,187	81,859 R	64.7%	32.8%	66.3%	33.7%
3	2002	173,921	112,254	WAMP, ZACH*	58,824	WOLFE, JOHN	2,843	53,430 R	64.5%	33.8%	65.6%	34.4%
4	2010	182,191	103,969	DESJARLAIS, SCOTT	70,254	DAVIS, LINCOLN*	7,968	33,715 R	57.1%	38.6%	59.7%	40.3%
4	2008	249,805	94,447	LANKFORD, MONTY J.	146,776	DAVIS, LINCOLN*	8,582	52,329 D	37.8%	58.8%	39.2%	60.8%
4	2006	186,115	62,449	MARTIN, KENNETH	123,666	DAVIS, LINCOLN*		61,217 D	33.6%	66.4%	33.6%	66.4%
4	2004	252,646	109,993	BOWLING, JANICE	138,459	DAVIS, LINCOLN*	4,194	28,466 D	43.5%	54.8%	44.3%	55.7%
4	2002	184,300	85,680	BOWLING, JANICE	95,989	DAVIS, LINCOLN	2,631	10,309 D	46.5%	52.1%	47.2%	52.8%
5	2010	176,362	74,204	HALL, DAVID	99,162	COOPER, JIM*	2,996	24,958 D	42.1%	56.2%	42.8%	57.2%
5	2008	275,602	85,471	DONOVAN, GERARD	181,467	COOPER, JIM*	8,664	95,996 D	31.0%	65.8%	32.0%	68.0%
5	2006	178,142	49,702	KOVACH, THOMAS F.	122,919	COOPER, JIM*	5,521	73,217 D	27.9%	69.0%	28.8%	71.2%
5	2004	243,963	74,978	KNAPP, SCOTT	168,970	COOPER, JIM*	15	93,992 D	30.7%	69.3%	30.7%	69.3%
5	2002	170,886	56,825	DUVALL, ROBERT	108,903	COOPER, JIM	5,158	52,078 D	33.3%	63.7%	34.3%	65.7%
6	2010	191,084	128,517	BLACK, DIANE	56,145	CARTER, BRETT	6,422	72,372 R	67.3%	29.4%	69.6%	30.4%
6	2008	261,028		—	194,264	GORDON, BART*	66,764	194,264 D		74.4%		100.0%
6	2006	192,380	60,392	DAVIS, DAVID R.	129,069	GORDON, BART*	2,919	68,677 D	31.4%	67.1%	31.9%	68.1%
6	2004	260,642	87,523	DEMAS, NICK	167,448	GORDON, BART*	5,671	79,925 D	33.6%	64.2%	34.3%	65.7%
6	2002	177,547	57,401	GARRISON, ROBERT L.	117,034	GORDON, BART*	3,112	59,633 D	32.3%	65.9%	32.9%	67.1%
7	2010	219,583	158,916	BLACKBURN, MARSHA*	54,347	RABIDOUX, GREG	6,320	104,569 R	72.4%	24.8%	74.5%	25.5%
7	2008	316,881	217,332	BLACKBURN, MARSHA*	99,549	MORRIS, RANDY G.		117,783 R	68.6%	31.4%	68.6%	31.4%
7	2006	230,582	152,288	BLACKBURN, MARSHA*	73,369	MORRISON, BILL	4,925	78,919 R	66.0%	31.8%	67.5%	32.5%
7	2004	232,404	232,404	BLACKBURN, MARSHA*		—		232,404 R	100.0%		100.0%	
7	2002	195,558	138,314	BLACKBURN, MARSHA	51,790	BARRON, TIM	5,454	86,524 R	70.7%	26.5%	72.8%	27.2%
8	2010	167,405	98,759	FINCHER, STEPHEN LEE	64,960	HERRON, ROY	3,686	33,799 R	59.0%	38.8%	60.3%	39.7%
8	2008	180,519		—	180,465	TANNER, JOHN*	54	180,465 D		100.0%		100.0%
8	2006	177,108	47,492	FARMER, JOHN	129,610	TANNER, JOHN*	6	82,118 D	26.8%	73.2%	26.8%	73.2%
8	2004	233,567	59,853	HART, JAMES L.	173,623	TANNER, JOHN*	91	113,770 D	25.6%	74.3%	25.6%	74.4%
8	2002	167,970	45,853	McCLAIN, MAT	117,811	TANNER, JOHN*	4,306	71,958 D	27.3%	70.1%	28.0%	72.0%
9	2010	134,907	33,879	BERGMANN, CHARLOTTE	99,827	COHEN, STEVE*	1,201	65,948 D	25.1%	74.0%	25.3%	74.7%
9	2008	226,282		—	198,798	COHEN, STEVE*	27,484	198,798 D		87.9%		100.0%
9	2006	172,586	31,002	WHITE, MARK	103,341	COHEN, STEVE	38,243	72,339 D	18.0%	59.9%	23.1%	76.9%
9	2004	232,392	41,578	FORT, RUBEN M.	190,648	FORD, HAROLD E., JR.*	166	149,070 D	17.9%	82.0%	17.9%	82.1%
9	2002	144,260		—	120,904	FORD, HAROLD E., JR.*	23,356	120,904 D		83.8%		100.0%
TOTAL	2010	1,559,129	955,078		541,527		62,524	413,551 R	61.3%	34.7%	63.8%	36.2%
TOTAL	2008	2,301,885	977,677		1,195,542		128,666	217,865 D	42.5%	51.9%	45.0%	55.0%
TOTAL	2006	1,715,426	799,547		860,861		55,018	61,314 D	46.6%	50.2%	48.2%	51.8%
TOTAL	2004	2,218,738	1,160,821		1,031,959		25,958	128,862 R	52.3%	46.5%	52.9%	47.1%
TOTAL	2002	1,529,309	770,514		708,290		50,505	62,224 R	50.4%	46.3%	52.1%	47.9%

An asterisk (*) denotes incumbent.

TENNESSEE

GENERAL AND PRIMARY ELECTIONS

2010 GENERAL ELECTIONS

Governor   Other vote was 6,536 Independent (Carl Twofeathers Whitaker); 4,728 Independent (Brandon Dodds); 4,663 Independent (Bayron Binkley); 2,587 Independent (June Griffin); 2,057 Independent (Linda Kay Perry); 1,887 Independent (Howard K. Switzer); 1,755 Independent (Samuel David Duck); 1,207 Independent (Thomas Smith II); 993 Independent (Toni K. Hall); 859 Independent (David Gatchell); 828 Independent (Boyce T. McCall); 809 Independent (James Reesor); 600 Independent (Mike Knois); 583 Independent (Donald Ray McFolin); 58 write-in (Basil Marceaux); 3 write-in (James Lee).

House

CD 1	3,110 Independent (Kermit E. Steck).
CD 2	2,497 Independent (Joseph R. Leinweber Jr.); 1,993 Independent (D. H. "Andy" Andrew); 1,185 Independent (Greg Samples); 509 Independent (H. James Headings).
CD 3	17,077 Independent (Savas T. Kyriakidis); 5,773 Independent (Mark DeVol); 811 Independent (Don Barkman); 380 Independent (Gregory C. Goodwin); 380 Independent (Robert Humphries); 216 Independent (Mo Kiah).
CD 4	3,178 Independent (Paul H. Curtis); 2,159 Independent (Gerald York); 1,714 Independent (James Gray); 917 Independent (Richard S. Johnson).
CD 5	584 Independent (Stephen W. Collings); 533 Independent (John "Big John" Smith); 444 Independent (Jackie Miller); 396 Independent (John P. Miglietta); 391 Independent (Bill Crook); 333 Independent (James G. Whitfield II); 159 Independent (Joe D. Moore Jr.); 156 Independent (Clark Taylor).
CD 6	2,157 Independent (Jim Boyd); 1,296 Independent (David Purcell); 1,270 Independent (Tommy N. Hay); 1,103 Independent (Brandon E. Gore); 596 Independent (Stephen R. Sprague).
CD 7	6,320 Independent (J. W. "Bill" Stone).
CD 8	2,440 Independent (Donn Janes); 1,237 Independent (Mark J. Rawles); 9 write-in (James Hart).
CD 9	673 Independent (Sandra Sullivan); 528 Independent (Perry Steele).

In Tennessee all third-party candidates were listed as Independents regardless of party affiliation. Candidates could run simultaneously for more than one office.

2010 PRIMARY ELECTIONS

Primary	August 5, 2010	**Registration** (as of June 1, 2010 - includes 345,002 inactive registrants)	3,892,747	No Party Registration

Primary Type   Open—Any registered voter could participate in either the Democratic or Republican primary, although state party rules can spell out the grounds for a challenge to primary voters who were not party "members."

	REPUBLICAN PRIMARIES			DEMOCRATIC PRIMARIES		
Governor	Bill Haslam	343,817	47.4%	Mike McWherter	284,894	100.0%
	Zach Wamp	211,735	29.2%			
	Ron Ramsey	159,555	22.0%			
	Joe Kirkpatrick	6,787	0.9%			
	Basil Marceaux	3,514	0.5%			
	TOTAL	*725,408*				

TENNESSEE

GENERAL AND PRIMARY ELECTIONS

	REPUBLICAN PRIMARIES			DEMOCRATIC PRIMARIES		
Congressional District 1	Phil Roe*	78,862	95.7%	Michael Edward Clark	9,012	100.0%
	Mahmood "Michael" Sabri	3,546	4.3%			
	TOTAL	82,408				
Congressional District 2	John J. "Jimmy" Duncan Jr.*	92,414	100.0%	Dave Hancock	9,778	100.0%
Congressional District 3	Chuck Fleischmann	26,869	29.7%	John Wolfe	7,006	38.9%
	Robin Smith	25,454	28.1%	Brenda Freeman Short	4,530	25.2%
	Tim Gobble	14,274	15.8%	Brent Davis Staton	3,814	21.2%
	Van Irion	10,492	11.6%	Alicia Mitchell	2,647	14.7%
	Tommy Crangle	5,149	5.7%	Larry J. Abeare (write-in)	3	
	Art Rhodes	4,552	5.0%			
	Jean Howard-Hill	1,259	1.4%			
	Rick Kernea	739	0.8%			
	Harvey Howard	670	0.7%			
	Basil Marceaux	655	0.7%			
	Grover Travillian	440	0.5%			
	TOTAL	90,553		TOTAL	18,000	
Congressional District 4	Scott DesJarlais	27,812	37.1%	Lincoln Davis*	41,573	100.0%
	Jack Bailey	20,420	27.3%			
	Kent Greenough	11,413	15.2%			
	Ronald L. Harwell	9,237	12.3%			
	Donald Strong	5,992	8.0%			
	TOTAL	74,874				
Congressional District 5	David Hall	11,933	27.5%	Jim Cooper*	28,660	89.3%
	Jeffery Alan Hartline	10,009	23.1%	Eric Pearson	2,214	6.9%
	CeCe Heil	9,767	22.5%	Eric Schechter	1,213	3.8%
	Vijay Kumar	3,158	7.3%			
	Bob Schwartz	2,375	5.5%			
	Lonnie Spivak	1,530	3.5%			
	Jarod D. Scott	1,385	3.2%			
	Patrick Miranda	1,212	2.8%			
	Tracy C. Tarum	1,129	2.6%			
	Bob Ries	562	1.3%			
	Alvin M. Strauss	319	0.7%			
	TOTAL	43,379		TOTAL	32,087	
Congressional District 6	Diane Black	24,374	30.5%	Brett Carter	9,430	30.3%
	Lou Ann Zelenik	24,091	30.2%	Ben Leming	9,208	29.6%
	Jim Tracy	23,808	29.8%	Henry Clay Barry	8,917	28.6%
	Dave Evans	3,974	5.0%	Devora E. Butler	2,777	8.9%
	Kerry E. Roberts	2,482	3.1%	George T. Erdel	817	2.6%
	Bruce McLellan	695	0.9%			
	Gary Dewitt Mann	465	0.6%			
	TOTAL	79,889		TOTAL	31,149	
Congressional District 7	Marsha Blackburn*	97,088	100.0%	Greg Rabidoux	23,235	100.0%

TENNESSEE

GENERAL AND PRIMARY ELECTIONS

	REPUBLICAN PRIMARIES			DEMOCRATIC PRIMARIES		
Congressional	Stephen Lee Fincher	35,024	48.5%	Roy Herron	27,139	67.7%
District 8	Ron Kirkland	17,637	24.4%	Kimberlee E. Smith	12,971	32.3%
	George Flinn	17,308	24.0%			
	Randy Smith	1,546	2.1%			
	Ben Watts	720	1.0%			
	James Hart (write-in)	4				
	TOTAL	*72,239*		*TOTAL*	*40,110*	
Congressional	Charlotte Bergmann	13,295	61.4%	Steve Cohen*	63,402	78.7%
District 9	Jim Harrell	7,165	33.1%	Willie W. Herenton	17,153	21.3%
	Kevin Millen	1,199	5.5%			
	TOTAL	*21,659*		*TOTAL*	*80,555*	

An asterisk (*) denotes incumbent.

394

TEXAS

Congressional districts first established for elections held in 2004
32 members

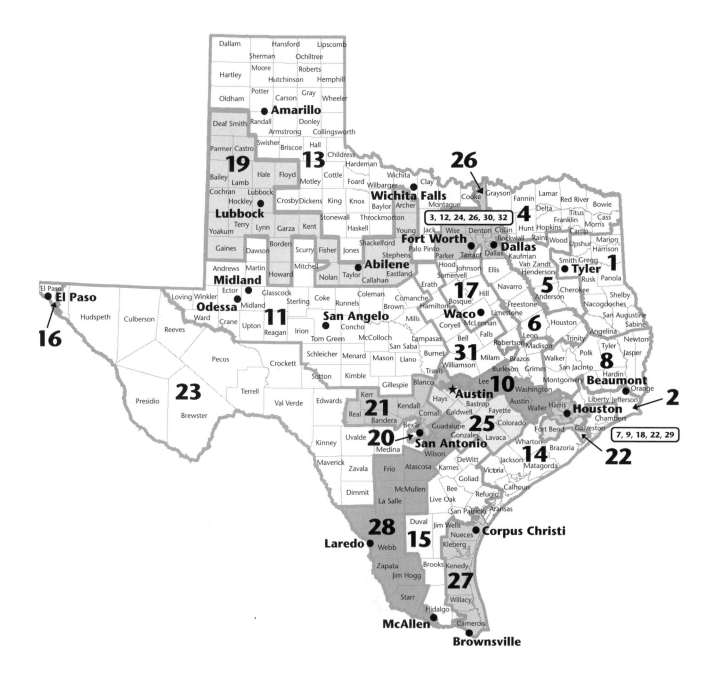

TEXAS

Houston Area

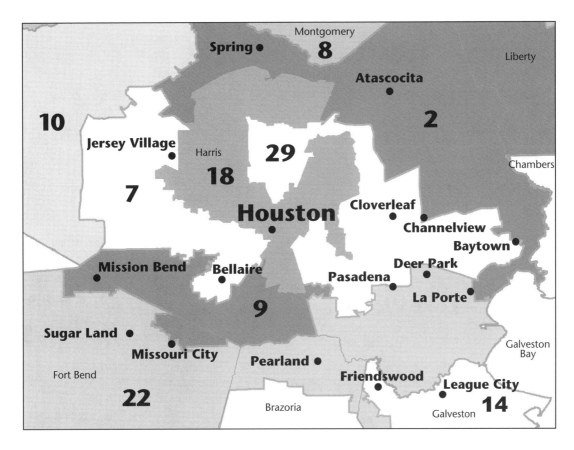

TEXAS

Dallas-Fort Worth Area

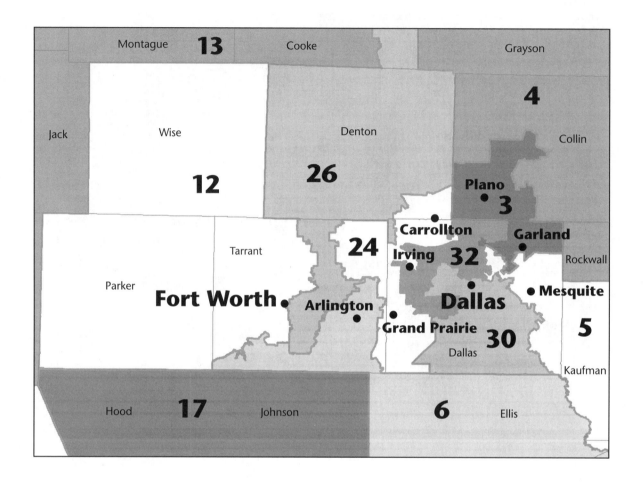

TEXAS

GOVERNOR

Rick Perry (R). Reelected 2010 to a four-year term. Previously elected 2006, 2002. Assumed office December 21, 2000, following the resignation of president-elect George W. Bush.

SENATORS (2 Republicans)

John Cornyn (R). Reelected 2008 to a six-year term. Previously elected 2002.

Kay Bailey Hutchison (R). Reelected 2006 to a six-year term. Previously elected 2000, 1994 and in a special election June 5, 1993, to fill out the remaining year and a half of the term vacated when Senator Lloyd Bentsen (D) resigned to become Secretary of the Treasury.

REPRESENTATIVES (23 Republicans, 9 Democrats)

1. Louie Gohmert (R)
2. Ted Poe (R)
3. Sam Johnson (R)
4. Ralph M. Hall (R)
5. Jeb Hensarling (R)
6. Joe L. Barton (R)
7. John Culberson (R)
8. Kevin Brady (R)
9. Al Green (D)
10. Michael McCaul (R)
11. K. Michael Conaway (R)
12. Kay Granger (R)
13. William M. "Mac" Thornberry (R)
14. Ron Paul (R)
15. Ruben Hinojosa (D)
16. Silvestre Reyes (D)
17. Bill Flores (R)
18. Sheila Jackson Lee (D)
19. Randy Neugebauer (R)
20. Charlie Gonzalez (D)
21. Lamar Smith (R)
22. Pete Olson (R)
23. Francisco "Quico" Canseco (R)
24. Kenny Marchant (R)
25. Lloyd Doggett (D)
26. Michael C. Burgess (R)
27. R. Blake Farenthold (R)
28. Henry Cuellar (D)
29. Gene Green (D)
30. Eddie Bernice Johnson (D)
31. John Carter (R)
32. Pete Sessions (R)

POSTWAR VOTE FOR PRESIDENT

Year	Total Vote	Republican		Democratic		Other Vote	Rep.-Dem. Plurality	Percentage			
								Total Vote		Major Vote	
		Vote	Candidate	Vote	Candidate			Rep.	Dem.	Rep.	Dem.
2008	8,077,795	4,479,328	McCain, John	3,528,633	Obama, Barack	69,834	950,695 R	55.5%	43.7%	55.9%	44.1%
2004	7,410,765	4,526,917	Bush, George W.	2,832,704	Kerry, John	51,144	1,694,213 R	61.1%	38.2%	61.5%	38.5%
2000**	6,407,637	3,799,639	Bush, George W.	2,433,746	Gore, Al	174,252	1,365,893 R	59.3%	38.0%	61.0%	39.0%
1996**	5,611,644	2,736,167	Dole, Bob	2,459,683	Clinton, Bill	415,794	276,484 R	48.8%	43.8%	52.7%	47.3%
1992**	6,154,018	2,496,071	Bush, George	2,281,815	Clinton, Bill	1,376,132	214,256 R	40.6%	37.1%	52.2%	47.8%
1988	5,427,410	3,036,829	Bush, George	2,352,748	Dukakis, Michael S.	37,833	684,081 R	56.0%	43.3%	56.3%	43.7%
1984	5,397,571	3,433,428	Reagan, Ronald	1,949,276	Mondale, Walter F.	14,867	1,484,152 R	63.6%	36.1%	63.8%	36.2%
1980**	4,541,636	2,510,705	Reagan, Ronald	1,881,147	Carter, Jimmy	149,784	629,558 R	55.3%	41.4%	57.2%	42.8%
1976	4,071,884	1,953,300	Ford, Gerald R.	2,082,319	Carter, Jimmy	36,265	129,019 D	48.0%	51.1%	48.4%	51.6%
1972	3,471,281	2,298,896	Nixon, Richard M.	1,154,289	McGovern, George S.	18,096	1,144,607 R	66.2%	33.3%	66.6%	33.4%
1968**	3,079,216	1,227,844	Nixon, Richard M.	1,266,804	Humphrey, Hubert H.	584,568	38,960 D	39.9%	41.1%	49.2%	50.8%
1964	2,626,811	958,566	Goldwater, Barry M.	1,663,185	Johnson, Lyndon B.	5,060	704,619 D	36.5%	63.3%	36.6%	63.4%
1960	2,311,084	1,121,310	Nixon, Richard M.	1,167,567	Kennedy, John F.	22,207	46,257 D	48.5%	50.5%	49.0%	51.0%
1956	1,955,168	1,080,619	Eisenhower, Dwight D.	859,958	Stevenson, Adlai E.	14,591	220,661 R	55.3%	44.0%	55.7%	44.3%
1952	2,075,946	1,102,878	Eisenhower, Dwight D.	969,228	Stevenson, Adlai E.	3,840	133,650 R	53.1%	46.7%	53.2%	46.8%
1948**	1,249,577	303,467	Dewey, Thomas E.	824,235	Truman, Harry S.	121,875	520,768 D	24.3%	66.0%	26.9%	73.1%

** In past elections, the other vote included: 2000 - 137,994 Green (Ralph Nader); 1996 - 378,537 Reform (Ross Perot); 1992 - 1,354,781 Independent (Perot); 1980 - 111,613 Independent (John Anderson); 1968 - 584,269 American Independent (George Wallace); 1948 - 113,920 States' Rights (Strom Thurmond).

TEXAS

POSTWAR VOTE FOR GOVERNOR

Year	Total Vote	Republican Vote	Republican Candidate	Democratic Vote	Democratic Candidate	Other Vote	Rep.-Dem. Plurality	Total Vote Rep.	Total Vote Dem.	Major Vote Rep.	Major Vote Dem.
2010	4,979,870	2,737,481	Perry, Rick	2,106,395	White, Bill	135,994	631,086 R	55.0%	42.3%	56.5%	43.5%
2006**	4,399,116	1,716,792	Perry, Rick	1,310,337	Bell, Chris	1,371,987	406,455 R	39.0%	29.8%	56.7%	43.3%
2002	4,553,987	2,632,591	Perry, Rick	1,819,798	Sanchez, Tony	101,598	812,793 R	57.8%	40.0%	59.1%	40.9%
1998	3,738,483	2,551,454	Bush, George W.	1,165,444	Mauro, Garry	21,585	1,386,010 R	68.2%	31.2%	68.6%	31.4%
1994	4,396,242	2,350,994	Bush, George W.	2,016,928	Richards, Ann	28,320	334,066 R	53.5%	45.9%	53.8%	46.2%
1990	3,892,746	1,826,431	Williams, Clayton	1,925,670	Richards, Ann	140,645	99,239 D	46.9%	49.5%	48.7%	51.3%
1986	3,441,460	1,813,779	Clements, William P.	1,584,515	White, Mark	43,166	229,264 R	52.7%	46.0%	53.4%	46.6%
1982	3,191,091	1,465,937	Clements, William P.	1,697,870	White, Mark	27,284	231,933 D	45.9%	53.2%	46.3%	53.7%
1978	2,369,764	1,183,839	Clements, William P.	1,166,979	Hill, John	18,946	16,860 R	50.0%	49.2%	50.4%	49.6%
1974**	1,654,984	514,725	Granberry, Jim	1,016,334	Briscoe, Dolph	123,925	501,609 D	31.1%	61.4%	33.6%	66.4%
1972	3,410,128	1,534,060	Grover, Henry C.	1,633,970	Briscoe, Dolph	242,098	99,910 D	45.0%	47.9%	48.4%	51.6%
1970	2,235,847	1,037,723	Eggers, Paul W.	1,197,726	Smith, Preston	398	160,003 D	46.4%	53.6%	46.4%	53.6%
1968	2,916,509	1,254,333	Eggers, Paul W.	1,662,019	Smith, Preston	157	407,686 D	43.0%	57.0%	43.0%	57.0%
1966	1,425,861	368,025	Kennerly, T. E.	1,037,517	Connally, John B.	20,319	669,492 D	25.8%	72.8%	26.2%	73.8%
1964	2,544,753	661,675	Crichton, Jack	1,877,793	Connally, John B.	5,285	1,216,118 D	26.0%	73.8%	26.1%	73.9%
1962	1,569,181	715,025	Cox, Jack	847,036	Connally, John B.	7,120	132,011 D	45.6%	54.0%	45.8%	54.2%
1960	2,250,718	612,963	Steger, William M.	1,637,755	Daniel, Price		1,024,792 D	27.2%	72.8%	27.2%	72.8%
1958	789,133	94,098	Mayer, Edwin S.	695,035	Daniel, Price		600,937 D	11.9%	88.1%	11.9%	88.1%
1956	1,828,161	271,088	Bryant, William R.	1,433,051	Daniel, Price	124,022	1,161,963 D	14.8%	78.4%	15.9%	84.1%
1954	636,892	66,154	Adams, Tod R.	569,533	Shivers, Allan	1,205	503,379 D	10.4%	89.4%	10.4%	89.6%
1952	1,881,202		—	1,844,530	Shivers, Allan	36,672	1,844,530 D		98.1%		100.0%
1950	394,747	39,737	Currie, Ralph W.	355,010	Shivers, Allan		315,273 D	10.1%	89.9%	10.1%	89.9%
1948	1,208,860	177,399	Lane, Alvin H.	1,024,160	Jester, Beauford	7,301	846,761 D	14.7%	84.7%	14.8%	85.2%
1946	378,744	33,231	Nolte, Eugene	345,513	Jester, Beauford		312,282 D	8.8%	91.2%	8.8%	91.2%

** In past elections, the other vote included: 2006 - 796,851 Independent (Carole Keeton Strayhorn); 547,674 Independent (Richard "Kinky" Friedman). The term of office of Texas' Governor was increased from two to four years effective with the 1974 election. The Republican Party did not run a candidate in the 1952 gubernatorial election.

TEXAS

POSTWAR VOTE FOR SENATOR

Year	Total Vote	Republican		Democratic		Other Vote	Rep.-Dem. Plurality	Percentage			
								Total Vote		Major Vote	
		Vote	Candidate	Vote	Candidate			Rep.	Dem.	Rep.	Dem.
2008	7,912,075	4,337,469	Cornyn, John	3,389,365	Noriega, Richard J. "Rick"	185,241	948,104 R	54.8%	42.8%	56.1%	43.9%
2006	4,314,663	2,661,789	Hutchison, Kay Bailey	1,555,202	Radnofsky, Barbara Ann	97,672	1,106,587 R	61.7%	36.0%	63.1%	36.9%
2002	4,514,012	2,496,243	Cornyn, John	1,955,758	Kirk, Ron	62,011	540,485 R	55.3%	43.3%	56.1%	43.9%
2000	6,276,652	4,082,091	Hutchison, Kay Bailey	2,030,315	Kelly, Gene	164,246	2,051,776 R	65.0%	32.3%	66.8%	33.2%
1996	5,527,441	3,027,680	Gramm, Phil	2,428,776	Morales, Victor M.	70,985	598,904 R	54.8%	43.9%	55.5%	44.5%
1994	4,279,940	2,604,218	Hutchison, Kay Bailey	1,639,615	Fisher, Richard	36,107	964,603 R	60.8%	38.3%	61.4%	38.6%
1993S	1,765,254	1,188,716	Hutchison, Kay Bailey	576,538	Krueger, Robert		612,178 R	67.3%	32.7%	67.3%	32.7%
1990	3,822,157	2,302,357	Gramm, Phil	1,429,986	Parmer, Hugh	89,814	872,371 R	60.2%	37.4%	61.7%	38.3%
1988	5,323,606	2,129,228	Boulter, Beau	3,149,806	Bentsen, Lloyd	44,572	1,020,578 D	40.0%	59.2%	40.3%	59.7%
1984	5,319,178	3,116,348	Gramm, Phil	2,202,557	Doggett, Lloyd	273	913,791 R	58.6%	41.4%	58.6%	41.4%
1982	3,103,167	1,256,759	Collins, James M.	1,818,223	Bentsen, Lloyd	28,185	561,464 D	40.5%	58.6%	40.9%	59.1%
1978	2,312,540	1,151,376	Tower, John G.	1,139,149	Krueger, Robert	22,015	12,227 R	49.8%	49.3%	50.3%	49.7%
1976	3,874,516	1,636,370	Steelman, Alan	2,199,956	Bentsen, Lloyd	38,190	563,586 D	42.2%	56.8%	42.7%	57.3%
1972	3,413,903	1,822,877	Tower, John G.	1,511,985	Sanders, Barefoot	79,041	310,892 R	53.4%	44.3%	54.7%	45.3%
1970	2,231,671	1,035,794	Bush, George	1,194,069	Bentsen, Lloyd	1,808	158,275 D	46.4%	53.5%	46.5%	53.5%
1966	1,493,182	842,501	Tower, John G.	643,855	Carr, Waggoner	6,826	198,646 R	56.4%	43.1%	56.7%	43.3%
1964	2,603,856	1,134,337	Bush, George	1,463,958	Yarborough, Ralph	5,561	329,621 D	43.6%	56.2%	43.7%	56.3%
1961S	886,091	448,217	Tower, John G.	437,874	Blakley, William A.		10,343 R	50.6%	49.4%	50.6%	49.4%
1960	2,253,784	926,653	Tower, John G.	1,306,625	Johnson, Lyndon B.	20,506	379,972 D	41.1%	58.0%	41.5%	58.5%
1958	787,128	185,926	Whittenburg, Roy	587,030	Yarborough, Ralph	14,172	401,104 D	23.6%	74.6%	24.1%	75.9%
1957S	957,298		[See note below]				D				
1954	636,475	94,131	Watson, Carlos G.	539,319	Johnson, Lyndon B.	3,025	445,188 D	14.8%	84.7%	14.9%	85.1%
1952	1,895,192		—	1,895,192	Daniel, Price		1,895,192 D		100.0%		100.0%
1948	1,061,563	349,665	Porter, Jack	702,985	Johnson, Lyndon B.	8,913	353,320 D	32.9%	66.2%	33.2%	66.8%
1946	380,681	43,750	Sells, Murray C.	336,931	Connally, Tom		293,181 D	11.5%	88.5%	11.5%	88.5%

The June 1993 election was for a short term to fill a vacancy; the vote above was for the special election runoff. The April 1957 and May 1961 elections were also for short terms to fill vacancies. Although neither vote was held with official party designations, the 1961 vote above reflected the result of a runoff between unofficial party candidates. In 1957 there was a single ballot without a runoff and Democrat Ralph Yarborough polled 364,605 votes (38.1 percent of the total vote) and won the election with a 73,802-vote plurality over Democrat Martin Dies. The Republican Party did not run a candidate in the 1952 Senate election.

TEXAS

GOVERNOR 2010

2010 Census Population	County	Total Vote	Republican	Democratic	Other	Rep.-Dem. Plurality	Percentage Total Vote Rep.	Dem.	Major Vote Rep.	Dem.
58,458	ANDERSON	10,968	6,973	3,643	352	3,330 R	63.6%	33.2%	65.7%	34.3%
14,786	ANDREWS	4,053	2,906	987	160	1,919 R	71.7%	24.4%	74.6%	25.4%
86,771	ANGELINA	19,305	11,942	6,892	471	5,050 R	61.9%	35.7%	63.4%	36.6%
23,158	ARANSAS	6,895	4,829	1,892	174	2,937 R	70.0%	27.4%	71.8%	28.2%
9,054	ARCHER	2,865	2,107	672	86	1,435 R	73.5%	23.5%	75.8%	24.2%
1,901	ARMSTRONG	661	499	135	27	364 R	75.5%	20.4%	78.7%	21.3%
44,911	ATASCOSA	8,430	4,450	3,714	266	736 R	52.8%	44.1%	54.5%	45.5%
28,417	AUSTIN	8,675	5,901	2,525	249	3,376 R	68.0%	29.1%	70.0%	30.0%
7,165	BAILEY	1,107	810	241	56	569 R	73.2%	21.8%	77.1%	22.9%
20,485	BANDERA	6,729	4,745	1,646	338	3,099 R	70.5%	24.5%	74.2%	25.8%
74,171	BASTROP	18,973	9,426	8,587	960	839 R	49.7%	45.3%	52.3%	47.7%
3,726	BAYLOR	1,120	739	339	42	400 R	66.0%	30.3%	68.6%	31.4%
31,861	BEE	5,750	2,994	2,612	144	382 R	52.1%	45.4%	53.4%	46.6%
310,235	BELL	46,478	26,318	17,159	3,001	9,159 R	56.6%	36.9%	60.5%	39.5%
1,714,773	BEXAR	304,062	146,760	148,452	8,850	1,692 D	48.3%	48.8%	49.7%	50.3%
10,497	BLANCO	3,966	2,589	1,200	177	1,389 R	65.3%	30.3%	68.3%	31.7%
641	BORDEN	334	241	74	19	167 R	72.2%	22.2%	76.5%	23.5%
18,212	BOSQUE	5,898	3,691	1,956	251	1,735 R	62.6%	33.2%	65.4%	34.6%
92,565	BOWIE	22,648	13,886	8,274	488	5,612 R	61.3%	36.5%	62.7%	37.3%
313,166	BRAZORIA	70,616	43,360	25,450	1,806	17,910 R	61.4%	36.0%	63.0%	37.0%
194,851	BRAZOS	37,695	23,809	12,733	1,153	11,076 R	63.2%	33.8%	65.2%	34.8%
9,232	BREWSTER	2,739	1,316	1,315	108	1 R	48.0%	48.0%	50.0%	50.0%
1,637	BRISCOE	485	314	143	28	171 R	64.7%	29.5%	68.7%	31.3%
7,223	BROOKS	1,204	260	936	8	676 D	21.6%	77.7%	21.7%	78.3%
38,106	BROWN	9,425	7,115	1,951	359	5,164 R	75.5%	20.7%	78.5%	21.5%
17,187	BURLESON	4,521	3,050	1,368	103	1,682 R	67.5%	30.3%	69.0%	31.0%
42,750	BURNET	12,071	8,302	3,292	477	5,010 R	68.8%	27.3%	71.6%	28.4%
38,066	CALDWELL	8,294	4,035	3,913	346	122 R	48.6%	47.2%	50.8%	49.2%
21,381	CALHOUN	4,553	2,573	1,870	110	703 R	56.5%	41.1%	57.9%	42.1%
13,544	CALLAHAN	3,556	2,701	747	108	1,954 R	76.0%	21.0%	78.3%	21.7%
406,220	CAMERON	40,964	16,722	23,474	768	6,752 D	40.8%	57.3%	41.6%	58.4%
12,401	CAMP	3,090	1,666	1,337	87	329 R	53.9%	43.3%	55.5%	44.5%
6,182	CARSON	1,907	1,369	446	92	923 R	71.8%	23.4%	75.4%	24.6%
30,464	CASS	7,254	4,404	2,667	183	1,737 R	60.7%	36.8%	62.3%	37.7%
8,062	CASTRO	1,393	834	515	44	319 R	59.9%	37.0%	61.8%	38.2%
35,096	CHAMBERS	9,913	7,106	2,537	270	4,569 R	71.7%	25.6%	73.7%	26.3%
50,845	CHEROKEE	11,519	7,373	3,768	378	3,605 R	64.0%	32.7%	66.2%	33.8%
7,041	CHILDRESS	1,103	774	293	36	481 R	70.2%	26.6%	72.5%	27.5%
10,752	CLAY	3,454	2,407	943	104	1,464 R	69.7%	27.3%	71.9%	28.1%
3,127	COCHRAN	570	387	160	23	227 R	67.9%	28.1%	70.7%	29.3%
3,320	COKE	1,088	793	260	35	533 R	72.9%	23.9%	75.3%	24.7%
8,895	COLEMAN	2,641	1,935	617	89	1,318 R	73.3%	23.4%	75.8%	24.2%
782,341	COLLIN	156,668	100,359	51,890	4,419	48,469 R	64.1%	33.1%	65.9%	34.1%
3,057	COLLINGSWORTH	837	547	259	31	288 R	65.4%	30.9%	67.9%	32.1%
20,874	COLORADO	6,248	3,845	2,256	147	1,589 R	61.5%	36.1%	63.0%	37.0%
108,472	COMAL	34,581	24,916	8,271	1,394	16,645 R	72.1%	23.9%	75.1%	24.9%
13,974	COMANCHE	3,644	2,250	1,250	144	1,000 R	61.7%	34.3%	64.3%	35.7%
4,087	CONCHO	871	566	269	36	297 R	65.0%	30.9%	67.8%	32.2%
38,437	COOKE	9,226	6,261	2,573	392	3,688 R	67.9%	27.9%	70.9%	29.1%
75,388	CORYELL	9,610	5,984	3,146	480	2,838 R	62.3%	32.7%	65.5%	34.5%
1,505	COTTLE	434	291	113	30	178 R	67.1%	26.0%	72.0%	28.0%
4,375	CRANE	811	599	184	28	415 R	73.9%	22.7%	76.5%	23.5%

TEXAS
GOVERNOR 2010

2010 Census Population	County	Total Vote	Republican	Democratic	Other	Rep.-Dem. Plurality		Percentage			
								Total Vote		Major Vote	
								Rep.	Dem.	Rep.	Dem.
3,719	CROCKETT	949	616	302	31	314	R	64.9%	31.8%	67.1%	32.9%
6,059	CROSBY	1,176	709	428	39	281	R	60.3%	36.4%	62.4%	37.6%
2,398	CULBERSON	733	323	388	22	65	D	44.1%	52.9%	45.4%	54.6%
6,703	DALLAM	930	683	195	52	488	R	73.4%	21.0%	77.8%	22.2%
2,368,139	DALLAS	424,511	180,665	234,478	9,368	53,813	D	42.6%	55.2%	43.5%	56.5%
13,833	DAWSON	2,955	1,824	988	143	836	R	61.7%	33.4%	64.9%	35.1%
19,372	DEAF SMITH	2,497	1,792	633	72	1,159	R	71.8%	25.4%	73.9%	26.1%
5,231	DELTA	1,555	864	640	51	224	R	55.6%	41.2%	57.4%	42.6%
662,614	DENTON	131,143	83,726	43,073	4,344	40,653	R	63.8%	32.8%	66.0%	34.0%
20,097	DE WITT	4,554	3,162	1,230	162	1,932	R	69.4%	27.0%	72.0%	28.0%
2,444	DICKENS	877	590	241	46	349	R	67.3%	27.5%	71.0%	29.0%
9,996	DIMMIT	1,982	604	1,350	28	746	D	30.5%	68.1%	30.9%	69.1%
3,677	DONLEY	1,158	781	333	44	448	R	67.4%	28.8%	70.1%	29.9%
11,782	DUVAL	3,010	738	2,213	59	1,475	D	24.5%	73.5%	25.0%	75.0%
18,583	EASTLAND	4,392	3,224	999	169	2,225	R	73.4%	22.7%	76.3%	23.7%
137,130	ECTOR	19,585	14,466	4,481	638	9,985	R	73.9%	22.9%	76.3%	23.7%
2,002	EDWARDS	941	556	366	19	190	R	59.1%	38.9%	60.3%	39.7%
149,610	ELLIS	31,011	20,411	9,236	1,364	11,175	R	65.8%	29.8%	68.8%	31.2%
800,647	EL PASO	88,505	32,536	54,247	1,722	21,711	D	36.8%	61.3%	37.5%	62.5%
37,890	ERATH	8,695	5,990	2,385	320	3,605	R	68.9%	27.4%	71.5%	28.5%
17,866	FALLS	3,972	1,854	1,940	178	86	D	46.7%	48.8%	48.9%	51.1%
33,915	FANNIN	7,322	4,453	2,599	270	1,854	R	60.8%	35.5%	63.1%	36.9%
24,554	FAYETTE	8,038	5,256	2,534	248	2,722	R	65.4%	31.5%	67.5%	32.5%
3,974	FISHER	1,333	686	607	40	79	R	51.5%	45.5%	53.1%	46.9%
6,446	FLOYD	1,530	1,023	471	36	552	R	66.9%	30.8%	68.5%	31.5%
1,336	FOARD	315	148	153	14	5	D	47.0%	48.6%	49.2%	50.8%
585,375	FORT BEND	139,071	71,658	65,432	1,981	6,226	R	51.5%	47.0%	52.3%	47.7%
10,605	FRANKLIN	3,417	2,203	1,095	119	1,108	R	64.5%	32.0%	66.8%	33.2%
19,816	FREESTONE	5,014	3,326	1,563	125	1,763	R	66.3%	31.2%	68.0%	32.0%
17,217	FRIO	2,095	940	1,110	45	170	D	44.9%	53.0%	45.9%	54.1%
17,526	GAINES	2,432	1,847	507	78	1,340	R	75.9%	20.8%	78.5%	21.5%
291,309	GALVESTON	75,891	43,051	31,186	1,654	11,865	R	56.7%	41.1%	58.0%	42.0%
6,461	GARZA	1,251	879	311	61	568	R	70.3%	24.9%	73.9%	26.1%
24,837	GILLESPIE	9,448	7,008	2,034	406	4,974	R	74.2%	21.5%	77.5%	22.5%
1,226	GLASSCOCK	392	320	45	27	275	R	81.6%	11.5%	87.7%	12.3%
7,210	GOLIAD	2,599	1,438	1,031	130	407	R	55.3%	39.7%	58.2%	41.8%
19,807	GONZALES	5,274	3,062	2,056	156	1,006	R	58.1%	39.0%	59.8%	40.2%
22,535	GRAY	4,699	3,777	766	156	3,011	R	80.4%	16.3%	83.1%	16.9%
120,877	GRAYSON	26,903	18,308	7,771	824	10,537	R	68.1%	28.9%	70.2%	29.8%
121,730	GREGG	25,409	17,259	7,607	543	9,652	R	67.9%	29.9%	69.4%	30.6%
26,604	GRIMES	6,145	3,663	2,276	206	1,387	R	59.6%	37.0%	61.7%	38.3%
131,533	GUADALUPE	30,386	19,837	9,488	1,061	10,349	R	65.3%	31.2%	67.6%	32.4%
36,273	HALE	6,072	3,974	1,875	223	2,099	R	65.4%	30.9%	67.9%	32.1%
3,353	HALL	762	522	217	23	305	R	68.5%	28.5%	70.6%	29.4%
8,517	HAMILTON	2,656	1,671	871	114	800	R	62.9%	32.8%	65.7%	34.3%
5,613	HANSFORD	1,324	1,126	163	35	963	R	85.0%	12.3%	87.4%	12.6%
4,139	HARDEMAN	922	612	290	20	322	R	66.4%	31.5%	67.8%	32.2%
54,635	HARDIN	14,506	10,652	3,553	301	7,099	R	73.4%	24.5%	75.0%	25.0%
4,092,459	HARRIS	788,234	379,516	395,952	12,766	16,436	D	48.1%	50.2%	48.9%	51.1%
65,631	HARRISON	17,364	10,508	6,464	392	4,044	R	60.5%	37.2%	61.9%	38.1%

TEXAS
GOVERNOR 2010

2010 Census Population	County	Total Vote	Republican	Democratic	Other	Rep.-Dem. Plurality		Percentage Total Vote Rep.	Dem.	Major Vote Rep.	Dem.
6,062	HARTLEY	1,333	1,041	251	41	790	R	78.1%	18.8%	80.6%	19.4%
5,899	HASKELL	391	262	117	12	145	R	67.0%	29.9%	69.1%	30.9%
157,107	HAYS	39,608	20,499	17,333	1,776	3,166	R	51.8%	43.8%	54.2%	45.8%
3,807	HEMPHILL	1,101	764	286	51	478	R	69.4%	26.0%	72.8%	27.2%
78,532	HENDERSON	18,872	12,342	5,957	573	6,385	R	65.4%	31.6%	67.4%	32.6%
774,769	HIDALGO	73,166	23,232	48,895	1,039	25,663	D	31.8%	66.8%	32.2%	67.8%
35,089	HILL	8,970	5,447	3,187	336	2,260	R	60.7%	35.5%	63.1%	36.9%
22,935	HOCKLEY	4,233	3,085	963	185	2,122	R	72.9%	22.7%	76.2%	23.8%
51,182	HOOD	16,041	11,490	3,954	597	7,536	R	71.6%	24.6%	74.4%	25.6%
35,161	HOPKINS	8,797	5,457	3,111	229	2,346	R	62.0%	35.4%	63.7%	36.3%
23,732	HOUSTON	6,100	3,822	2,096	182	1,726	R	62.7%	34.4%	64.6%	35.4%
35,012	HOWARD	5,988	4,054	1,695	239	2,359	R	67.7%	28.3%	70.5%	29.5%
3,476	HUDSPETH	671	376	276	19	100	R	56.0%	41.1%	57.7%	42.3%
86,129	HUNT	17,806	11,593	5,465	748	6,128	R	65.1%	30.7%	68.0%	32.0%
22,150	HUTCHINSON	5,311	4,166	947	198	3,219	R	78.4%	17.8%	81.5%	18.5%
1,599	IRION	647	476	153	18	323	R	73.6%	23.6%	75.7%	24.3%
9,044	JACK	2,154	1,604	475	75	1,129	R	74.5%	22.1%	77.2%	22.8%
14,075	JACKSON	3,665	2,218	1,352	95	866	R	60.5%	36.9%	62.1%	37.9%
35,710	JASPER	8,408	5,689	2,557	162	3,132	R	67.7%	30.4%	69.0%	31.0%
2,342	JEFF DAVIS	981	539	384	58	155	R	54.9%	39.1%	58.4%	41.6%
252,273	JEFFERSON	54,901	27,710	26,437	754	1,273	R	50.5%	48.2%	51.2%	48.8%
5,300	JIM HOGG	1,069	288	777	4	489	D	26.9%	72.7%	27.0%	73.0%
40,838	JIM WELLS	6,421	2,657	3,674	90	1,017	D	41.4%	57.2%	42.0%	58.0%
150,934	JOHNSON	30,891	20,827	8,716	1,348	12,111	R	67.4%	28.2%	70.5%	29.5%
20,202	JONES	3,855	2,444	1,267	144	1,177	R	63.4%	32.9%	65.9%	34.1%
14,824	KARNES	3,020	1,730	1,211	79	519	R	57.3%	40.1%	58.8%	41.2%
103,350	KAUFMAN	19,936	12,990	6,363	583	6,627	R	65.2%	31.9%	67.1%	32.9%
33,410	KENDALL	12,871	9,744	2,702	425	7,042	R	75.7%	21.0%	78.3%	21.7%
416	KENEDY	199	109	88	2	21	R	54.8%	44.2%	55.3%	44.7%
808	KENT	300	189	101	10	88	R	63.0%	33.7%	65.2%	34.8%
49,625	KERR	16,486	12,025	3,913	548	8,112	R	72.9%	23.7%	75.4%	24.6%
4,607	KIMBLE	1,328	1,042	231	55	811	R	78.5%	17.4%	81.9%	18.1%
286	KING	118	93	23	2	70	R	78.8%	19.5%	80.2%	19.8%
3,598	KINNEY	1,354	769	533	52	236	R	56.8%	39.4%	59.1%	40.9%
32,061	KLEBERG	5,647	2,660	2,859	128	199	D	47.1%	50.6%	48.2%	51.8%
3,719	KNOX	885	547	312	26	235	R	61.8%	35.3%	63.7%	36.3%
49,793	LAMAR	11,933	7,329	4,290	314	3,039	R	61.4%	36.0%	63.1%	36.9%
13,977	LAMB	2,705	1,873	740	92	1,133	R	69.2%	27.4%	71.7%	28.3%
19,677	LAMPASAS	4,971	3,487	1,239	245	2,248	R	70.1%	24.9%	73.8%	26.2%
6,886	LA SALLE	1,301	534	744	23	210	D	41.0%	57.2%	41.8%	58.2%
19,263	LAVACA	6,446	4,383	1,904	159	2,479	R	68.0%	29.5%	69.7%	30.3%
16,612	LEE	4,282	2,600	1,491	191	1,109	R	60.7%	34.8%	63.6%	36.4%
16,801	LEON	5,032	3,820	1,092	120	2,728	R	75.9%	21.7%	77.8%	22.2%
75,643	LIBERTY	16,134	10,309	5,467	358	4,842	R	63.9%	33.9%	65.3%	34.7%
23,384	LIMESTONE	5,572	3,197	2,198	177	999	R	57.4%	39.4%	59.3%	40.7%
3,302	LIPSCOMB	869	644	195	30	449	R	74.1%	22.4%	76.8%	23.2%
11,531	LIVE OAK	2,788	2,034	656	98	1,378	R	73.0%	23.5%	75.6%	24.4%
19,301	LLANO	7,428	5,330	1,835	263	3,495	R	71.8%	24.7%	74.4%	25.6%
82	LOVING	68	51	12	5	39	R	75.0%	17.6%	81.0%	19.0%
278,831	LUBBOCK	53,675	35,578	15,887	2,210	19,691	R	66.3%	29.6%	69.1%	30.9%
5,915	LYNN	1,296	857	375	64	482	R	66.1%	28.9%	69.6%	30.4%

TEXAS

GOVERNOR 2010

2010 Census Population	County	Total Vote	Republican	Democratic	Other	Rep.-Dem. Plurality	Percentage Total Vote Rep.	Dem.	Major Vote Rep.	Dem.
8,283	MCCULLOCH	2,084	1,479	544	61	935 R	71.0%	26.1%	73.1%	26.9%
234,906	MCLENNAN	54,756	30,694	22,515	1,547	8,179 R	56.1%	41.1%	57.7%	42.3%
707	MCMULLEN	308	216	78	14	138 R	70.1%	25.3%	73.5%	26.5%
13,664	MADISON	3,166	2,042	1,027	97	1,015 R	64.5%	32.4%	66.5%	33.5%
10,546	MARION	2,705	1,474	1,121	110	353 R	54.5%	41.4%	56.8%	43.2%
4,799	MARTIN	1,183	858	275	50	583 R	72.5%	23.2%	75.7%	24.3%
4,012	MASON	1,413	994	355	64	639 R	70.3%	25.1%	73.7%	26.3%
36,702	MATAGORDA	8,600	4,923	3,448	229	1,475 R	57.2%	40.1%	58.8%	41.2%
54,258	MAVERICK	7,155	1,877	5,142	136	3,265 D	26.2%	71.9%	26.7%	73.3%
46,006	MEDINA	11,043	7,077	3,578	388	3,499 R	64.1%	32.4%	66.4%	33.6%
2,242	MENARD	585	410	154	21	256 R	70.1%	26.3%	72.7%	27.3%
136,872	MIDLAND	27,863	21,864	5,085	914	16,779 R	78.5%	18.3%	81.1%	18.9%
24,757	MILAM	5,989	3,225	2,539	225	686 R	53.8%	42.4%	56.0%	44.0%
4,936	MILLS	1,650	1,110	460	80	650 R	67.3%	27.9%	70.7%	29.3%
9,403	MITCHELL	1,584	966	582	36	384 R	61.0%	36.7%	62.4%	37.6%
19,719	MONTAGUE	5,448	3,806	1,413	229	2,393 R	69.9%	25.9%	72.9%	27.1%
455,746	MONTGOMERY	114,560	86,178	25,919	2,463	60,259 R	75.2%	22.6%	76.9%	23.1%
21,904	MOORE	3,490	2,643	693	154	1,950 R	75.7%	19.9%	79.2%	20.8%
12,934	MORRIS	3,434	1,715	1,633	86	82 R	49.9%	47.6%	51.2%	48.8%
1,210	MOTLEY	534	385	113	36	272 R	72.1%	21.2%	77.3%	22.7%
64,524	NACOGDOCHES	13,115	8,216	4,553	346	3,663 R	62.6%	34.7%	64.3%	35.7%
47,735	NAVARRO	9,780	6,033	3,450	297	2,583 R	61.7%	35.3%	63.6%	36.4%
14,445	NEWTON	3,347	2,033	1,247	67	786 R	60.7%	37.3%	62.0%	38.0%
15,216	NOLAN	3,486	2,104	1,235	147	869 R	60.4%	35.4%	63.0%	37.0%
340,223	NUECES	61,872	32,593	27,921	1,358	4,672 R	52.7%	45.1%	53.9%	46.1%
10,223	OCHILTREE	1,895	1,679	188	28	1,491 R	88.6%	9.9%	89.9%	10.1%
2,052	OLDHAM	694	525	140	29	385 R	75.6%	20.2%	78.9%	21.1%
81,837	ORANGE	19,107	12,750	5,928	429	6,822 R	66.7%	31.0%	68.3%	31.7%
28,111	PALO PINTO	6,420	4,139	2,041	240	2,098 R	64.5%	31.8%	67.0%	33.0%
23,796	PANOLA	6,470	4,348	2,004	118	2,344 R	67.2%	31.0%	68.5%	31.5%
116,927	PARKER	30,425	22,167	7,000	1,258	15,167 R	72.9%	23.0%	76.0%	24.0%
10,269	PARMER	1,668	1,293	324	51	969 R	77.5%	19.4%	80.0%	20.0%
15,507	PECOS	3,296	1,794	1,405	97	389 R	54.4%	42.6%	56.1%	43.9%
45,413	POLK	12,555	7,989	4,203	363	3,786 R	63.6%	33.5%	65.5%	34.5%
121,073	POTTER	16,014	10,631	4,716	667	5,915 R	66.4%	29.4%	69.3%	30.7%
7,818	PRESIDIO	1,192	325	842	25	517 D	27.3%	70.6%	27.8%	72.2%
10,914	RAINS	2,715	1,835	827	53	1,008 R	67.6%	30.5%	68.9%	31.1%
120,725	RANDALL	30,785	23,381	6,233	1,171	17,148 R	75.9%	20.2%	79.0%	21.0%
3,367	REAGAN	532	405	112	15	293 R	76.1%	21.1%	78.3%	21.7%
3,309	REAL	1,245	901	290	54	611 R	72.4%	23.3%	75.7%	24.3%
12,860	RED RIVER	3,120	1,764	1,293	63	471 R	56.5%	41.4%	57.7%	42.3%
13,783	REEVES	1,913	740	1,131	42	391 D	38.7%	59.1%	39.6%	60.4%
7,383	REFUGIO	1,762	1,091	630	41	461 R	61.9%	35.8%	63.4%	36.6%
929	ROBERTS	353	282	54	17	228 R	79.9%	15.3%	83.9%	16.1%
16,622	ROBERTSON	4,970	2,663	2,175	132	488 R	53.6%	43.8%	55.0%	45.0%
78,337	ROCKWALL	18,810	13,550	4,705	555	8,845 R	72.0%	25.0%	74.2%	25.8%
10,501	RUNNELS	2,653	2,017	569	67	1,448 R	76.0%	21.4%	78.0%	22.0%
53,330	RUSK	12,054	8,087	3,643	324	4,444 R	67.1%	30.2%	68.9%	31.1%
10,834	SABINE	3,434	2,387	971	76	1,416 R	69.5%	28.3%	71.1%	28.9%
8,865	SAN AUGUSTINE	2,555	1,508	995	52	513 R	59.0%	38.9%	60.2%	39.8%
26,384	SAN JACINTO	7,205	4,284	2,704	217	1,580 R	59.5%	37.5%	61.3%	38.7%
64,804	SAN PATRICIO	12,836	7,648	4,904	284	2,744 R	59.6%	38.2%	60.9%	39.1%

TEXAS

GOVERNOR 2010

2010 Census Population	County	Total Vote	Republican	Democratic	Other	Rep.-Dem. Plurality		Percentage			
								Total Vote		Major Vote	
								Rep.	Dem.	Rep.	Dem.
6,131	SAN SABA	1,787	1,305	406	76	899	R	73.0%	22.7%	76.3%	23.7%
3,461	SCHLEICHER	772	567	184	21	383	R	73.4%	23.8%	75.5%	24.5%
16,921	SCURRY	3,462	2,424	881	157	1,543	R	70.0%	25.4%	73.3%	26.7%
3,378	SHACKELFORD	1,051	824	192	35	632	R	78.4%	18.3%	81.1%	18.9%
25,448	SHELBY	5,769	3,669	1,991	109	1,678	R	63.6%	34.5%	64.8%	35.2%
3,034	SHERMAN	662	504	143	15	361	R	76.1%	21.6%	77.9%	22.1%
209,714	SMITH	51,663	35,565	14,641	1,457	20,924	R	68.8%	28.3%	70.8%	29.2%
8,490	SOMERVELL	2,742	1,757	900	85	857	R	64.1%	32.8%	66.1%	33.9%
60,968	STARR	3,728	737	2,970	21	2,233	D	19.8%	79.7%	19.9%	80.1%
9,630	STEPHENS	2,468	1,823	553	92	1,270	R	73.9%	22.4%	76.7%	23.3%
1,143	STERLING	384	298	69	17	229	R	77.6%	18.0%	81.2%	18.8%
1,490	STONEWALL	600	329	241	30	88	R	54.8%	40.2%	57.7%	42.3%
4,128	SUTTON	1,160	808	329	23	479	R	69.7%	28.4%	71.1%	28.9%
7,854	SWISHER	1,546	818	657	71	161	R	52.9%	42.5%	55.5%	44.5%
1,809,034	TARRANT	347,489	194,583	142,392	10,514	52,191	R	56.0%	41.0%	57.7%	42.3%
131,506	TAYLOR	26,788	19,216	6,652	920	12,564	R	71.7%	24.8%	74.3%	25.7%
984	TERRELL	577	293	257	27	36	R	50.8%	44.5%	53.3%	46.7%
12,651	TERRY	2,570	1,663	802	105	861	R	64.7%	31.2%	67.5%	32.5%
1,641	THROCKMORTON	697	513	164	20	349	R	73.6%	23.5%	75.8%	24.2%
32,334	TITUS	6,310	3,594	2,538	178	1,056	R	57.0%	40.2%	58.6%	41.4%
110,224	TOM GREEN	22,708	16,005	6,003	700	10,002	R	70.5%	26.4%	72.7%	27.3%
1,024,266	TRAVIS	238,148	87,509	142,345	8,294	54,836	D	36.7%	59.8%	38.1%	61.9%
14,585	TRINITY	4,672	2,189	2,338	145	149	D	46.9%	50.0%	48.4%	51.6%
21,766	TYLER	5,562	3,434	1,964	164	1,470	R	61.7%	35.3%	63.6%	36.4%
39,309	UPSHUR	9,879	6,529	2,906	444	3,623	R	66.1%	29.4%	69.2%	30.8%
3,355	UPTON	831	566	224	41	342	R	68.1%	27.0%	71.6%	28.4%
26,405	UVALDE	6,122	3,144	2,848	130	296	R	51.4%	46.5%	52.5%	47.5%
48,879	VAL VERDE	7,148	3,365	3,636	147	271	D	47.1%	50.9%	48.1%	51.9%
52,579	VAN ZANDT	12,956	8,797	3,686	473	5,111	R	67.9%	28.5%	70.5%	29.5%
86,793	VICTORIA	19,463	12,560	6,266	637	6,294	R	64.5%	32.2%	66.7%	33.3%
67,861	WALKER	13,389	7,232	5,695	462	1,537	R	54.0%	42.5%	55.9%	44.1%
43,205	WALLER	10,430	5,862	4,306	262	1,556	R	56.2%	41.3%	57.7%	42.3%
10,658	WARD	2,673	1,593	955	125	638	R	59.6%	35.7%	62.5%	37.5%
33,718	WASHINGTON	10,577	6,939	3,387	251	3,552	R	65.6%	32.0%	67.2%	32.8%
250,304	WEBB	29,507	6,774	22,322	411	15,548	D	23.0%	75.6%	23.3%	76.7%
41,280	WHARTON	9,943	5,243	4,486	214	757	R	52.7%	45.1%	53.9%	46.1%
5,410	WHEELER	1,541	1,172	321	48	851	R	76.1%	20.8%	78.5%	21.5%
131,500	WICHITA	25,490	17,483	7,210	797	10,273	R	68.6%	28.3%	70.8%	29.2%
13,535	WILBARGER	2,764	1,813	865	86	948	R	65.6%	31.3%	67.7%	32.3%
22,134	WILLACY	2,527	929	1,560	38	631	D	36.8%	61.7%	37.3%	62.7%
422,679	WILLIAMSON	101,141	59,271	37,319	4,551	21,952	R	58.6%	36.9%	61.4%	38.6%
42,918	WILSON	11,301	6,925	3,881	495	3,044	R	61.3%	34.3%	64.1%	35.9%
7,110	WINKLER	1,132	827	260	45	567	R	73.1%	23.0%	76.1%	23.9%
59,127	WISE	12,732	8,972	3,103	657	5,869	R	70.5%	24.4%	74.3%	25.7%
41,964	WOOD	12,522	8,994	3,106	422	5,888	R	71.8%	24.8%	74.3%	25.7%
7,879	YOAKUM	1,679	1,218	376	85	842	R	72.5%	22.4%	76.4%	23.6%
18,550	YOUNG	5,373	4,025	1,212	136	2,813	R	74.9%	22.6%	76.9%	23.1%
14,018	ZAPATA	1,233	319	902	12	583	D	25.9%	73.2%	26.1%	73.9%
11,677	ZAVALA	2,513	532	1,939	42	1,407	D	21.2%	77.2%	21.5%	78.5%
25,145,561	TOTAL	4,979,870	2,737,481	2,106,395	135,994	631,086	R	55.0%	42.3%	56.5%	43.5%

TEXAS

HOUSE OF REPRESENTATIVES

			Republican		Democratic				Total Vote		Major Vote	
									Percentage			
CD	Year	Total Vote	Vote	Candidate	Vote	Candidate	Other Vote	Rep.-Dem. Plurality	Rep.	Dem.	Rep.	Dem.
1	2010	144,209	129,398	GOHMERT, LOUIE*		—	14,811	129,398 R	89.7%		100.0%	
1	2008	215,826	189,012	GOHMERT, LOUIE*		—	26,814	189,012 R	87.6%		100.0%	
1	2006	153,070	104,099	GOHMERT, LOUIE*	46,303	OWEN, ROGER L.	2,668	57,796 R	68.0%	30.2%	69.2%	30.8%
1	2004	255,507	157,068	GOHMERT, LOUIE	96,281	SANDLIN, MAX*	2,158	60,787 R	61.5%	37.7%	62.0%	38.0%
2	2010	146,731	130,020	POE, TED*		—	16,711	130,020 R	88.6%		100.0%	
2	2008	196,914	175,101	POE, TED*		—	21,813	175,101 R	88.9%		100.0%	
2	2006	137,865	90,490	POE, TED*	45,080	BINDERIM, GARY E.	2,295	45,410 R	65.6%	32.7%	66.7%	33.3%
2	2004	252,038	139,951	POE, TED	108,156	LAMPSON, NICK*	3,931	31,795 R	55.5%	42.9%	56.4%	43.6%
3	2010	152,652	101,180	JOHNSON, SAM*	47,848	LINGENFELDER, JOHN	3,624	53,332 R	66.3%	31.3%	67.9%	32.1%
3	2008	285,783	170,742	JOHNSON, SAM*	108,693	DALEY, TOM	6,348	62,049 R	59.7%	38.0%	61.1%	38.9%
3	2006	141,881	88,690	JOHNSON, SAM*	49,529	DODD, DAN	3,662	39,161 R	62.5%	34.9%	64.2%	35.8%
3	2004	210,352	180,099	JOHNSON, SAM*		—	30,253	180,099 R	85.6%		100.0%	
4	2010	186,286	136,338	HALL, RALPH M.*	40,975	HATHCOX, VALINDA	8,973	95,363 R	73.2%	22.0%	76.9%	23.1%
4	2008	300,744	206,906	HALL, RALPH M.*	88,067	MELANCON, GLENN	5,771	118,839 R	68.8%	29.3%	70.1%	29.9%
4	2006	165,269	106,495	HALL, RALPH M.*	55,278	MELANCON, GLENN	3,496	51,217 R	64.4%	33.4%	65.8%	34.2%
4	2004	267,942	182,866	HALL, RALPH M.*	81,585	NICKERSON, JIM	3,491	101,281 R	68.2%	30.4%	69.1%	30.9%
5	2010	151,349	106,742	HENSARLING, JEB*	41,649	BERRY, TOM	2,958	65,093 R	70.5%	27.5%	71.9%	28.1%
5	2008	194,861	162,894	HENSARLING, JEB*		—	31,967	162,894 R	83.6%		100.0%	
5	2006	143,252	88,478	HENSARLING, JEB*	50,983	THOMPSON, CHARLIE	3,791	37,495 R	61.8%	35.6%	63.4%	36.6%
5	2004	230,845	148,816	HENSARLING, JEB*	75,911	BERNSTEIN, BILL	6,118	72,905 R	64.5%	32.9%	66.2%	33.8%
6	2010	162,557	107,140	BARTON, JOE L.*	50,717	COZAD, DAVID E.	4,700	56,423 R	65.9%	31.2%	67.9%	32.1%
6	2008	280,582	174,008	BARTON, JOE L.*	99,919	OTTO, LUDWIG	6,655	74,089 R	62.0%	35.6%	63.5%	36.5%
6	2006	152,036	91,927	BARTON, JOE L.*	56,369	HARRIS, DAVID T.	3,740	35,558 R	60.5%	37.1%	62.0%	38.0%
6	2004	255,627	168,767	BARTON, JOE L.*	83,609	MEYER, MORRIS	3,251	85,158 R	66.0%	32.7%	66.9%	33.1%
7	2010	176,378	143,655	CULBERSON, JOHN*		—	32,723	143,655 R	81.4%		100.0%	
7	2008	290,934	162,635	CULBERSON, JOHN*	123,242	SKELLY, MICHAEL	5,057	39,393 R	55.9%	42.4%	56.9%	43.1%
7	2006	167,785	99,318	CULBERSON, JOHN*	64,514	HENLEY, JIM	3,953	34,804 R	59.2%	38.5%	60.6%	39.4%
7	2004	273,651	175,440	CULBERSON, JOHN*	91,126	MARTINEZ, JOHN	7,085	84,314 R	64.1%	33.3%	65.8%	34.2%
8	2010	201,099	161,417	BRADY, KEVIN*	34,694	HARGETT, KENT	4,988	126,723 R	80.3%	17.3%	82.3%	17.7%
8	2008	285,451	207,128	BRADY, KEVIN*	70,758	HARGETT, KENT	7,565	136,370 R	72.6%	24.8%	74.5%	25.5%
8	2006	157,058	105,665	BRADY, KEVIN*	51,393	WRIGHT, JAMES "JIM"		54,272 R	67.3%	32.7%	67.3%	32.7%
8	2004	260,628	179,599	BRADY, KEVIN*	77,324	WRIGHT, JAMES "JIM"	3,705	102,275 R	68.9%	29.7%	69.9%	30.1%
9	2010	105,767	24,201	MUELLER, STEVE	80,107	GREEN, AL*	1,459	55,906 D	22.9%	75.7%	23.2%	76.8%
9	2008	153,628		—	143,868	GREEN, AL*	9,760	143,868 D		93.6%		100.0%
9	2006	60,253		—	60,253	GREEN, AL*		60,253 D		100.0%		100.0%
9	2004	158,566	42,132	MOLINA, ARLETTE	114,462	GREEN, AL	1,972	72,330 D	26.6%	72.2%	26.9%	73.1%
10	2010	224,171	144,980	McCAUL, MICHAEL*	74,086	ANKRUM, TED	5,105	70,894 R	64.7%	33.0%	66.2%	33.8%
10	2008	333,083	179,493	McCAUL, MICHAEL*	143,719	DOHERTY, LARRY JOE	9,871	35,774 R	53.9%	43.1%	55.5%	44.5%
10	2006	176,755	97,726	McCAUL, MICHAEL*	71,415	ANKRUM, TED	7,614	26,311 R	55.3%	40.4%	57.8%	42.2%
10	2004	231,643	182,113	McCAUL, MICHAEL		—	49,530	182,113 R	78.6%		100.0%	
11	2010	155,340	125,581	CONAWAY, K. MICHAEL*	23,989	QUILLIAN, JAMES	5,770	101,592 R	80.8%	15.4%	84.0%	16.0%
11	2008	214,676	189,625	CONAWAY, K. MICHAEL*		—	25,051	189,625 R	88.3%		100.0%	
11	2006	107,268	107,268	CONAWAY, K. MICHAEL*		—		107,268 R	100.0%		100.0%	
11	2004	230,977	177,291	CONAWAY, K. MICHAEL	50,339	RAASCH, WAYNE	3,347	126,952 R	76.8%	21.8%	77.9%	22.1%
12	2010	152,917	109,882	GRANGER, KAY*	38,434	SMITH, TRACEY	4,601	71,448 R	71.9%	25.1%	74.1%	25.9%
12	2008	268,754	181,662	GRANGER, KAY*	82,250	SMITH, TRACEY	4,842	99,412 R	67.6%	30.6%	68.8%	31.2%
12	2006	146,935	98,371	GRANGER, KAY*	45,676	MORRIS, JOHN R.	2,888	52,695 R	66.9%	31.1%	68.3%	31.7%
12	2004	239,538	173,222	GRANGER, KAY*	66,316	ALVARADO, FELIX		106,906 R	72.3%	27.7%	72.3%	27.7%

TEXAS

HOUSE OF REPRESENTATIVES

CD	Year	Total Vote	Republican Vote	Republican Candidate	Democratic Vote	Democratic Candidate	Other Vote	Rep.-Dem. Plurality	Total Vote Rep.	Total Vote Dem.	Major Vote Rep.	Major Vote Dem.
13	2010	130,043	113,201	THORNBERRY, WILLIAM M. "MAC"*	—		16,842	113,201 R	87.0%		100.0%	
13	2008	231,919	180,078	THORNBERRY, WILLIAM M. "MAC"*	51,841	WAUN, ROGER JAMES		128,237 R	77.6%	22.4%	77.6%	22.4%
13	2006	145,396	108,107	THORNBERRY, WILLIAM M. "MAC"*	33,460	WAUN, ROGER JAMES	3,829	74,647 R	74.4%	23.0%	76.4%	23.6%
13	2004	205,241	189,448	THORNBERRY, WILLIAM M. "MAC"*	—		15,793	189,448 R	92.3%		100.0%	
14	2010	185,054	140,623	PAUL, RON*	44,431	PRUETT, ROBERT		96,192 R	76.0%	24.0%	76.0%	24.0%
14	2008	191,293	191,293	PAUL, RON*	—			191,293 R	100.0%		100.0%	
14	2006	156,809	94,380	PAUL, RON*	62,429	SKLAR, SHANE		31,951 R	60.2%	39.8%	60.2%	39.8%
14	2004	173,668	173,668	PAUL, RON*	—			173,668 R	100.0%		100.0%	
15	2010	96,080	39,964	ZAMORA, EDDIE	53,546	HINOJOSA, RUBEN*	2,570	13,582 D	41.6%	55.7%	42.7%	57.3%
15	2008	163,708	52,303	ZAMORA, EDDIE	107,578	HINOJOSA, RUBEN*	3,827	55,275 D	31.9%	65.7%	32.7%	67.3%
15	2006	69,987	26,751	HARING/ZAMORA	43,236	HINOJOSA, RUBEN*		26,635 D	38.2%	61.8%	38.2%	61.8%
16	2010	84,892	31,051	BESCO, TIM	49,301	REYES, SILVESTRE*	4,540	18,250 D	36.6%	58.1%	38.6%	61.4%
16	2008	158,723		—	130,375	REYES, SILVESTRE*	28,348	130,375 D		82.1%		100.0%
16	2006	77,688		—	61,116	REYES, SILVESTRE*	16,572	61,116 D		78.7%		100.0%
16	2004	160,773	49,972	BRIGHAM, DAVID	108,577	REYES, SILVESTRE*	2,224	58,605 D	31.1%	67.5%	31.5%	68.5%
17	2010	172,642	106,696	FLORES, BILL	63,138	EDWARDS, CHET*	2,808	43,558 R	61.8%	36.6%	62.8%	37.2%
17	2008	254,022	115,581	CURNOCK, ROB	134,592	EDWARDS, CHET*	3,849	19,011 D	45.5%	53.0%	46.2%	53.8%
17	2006	159,124	64,142	TAYLOR, VAN	92,478	EDWARDS, CHET*	2,504	28,336 D	40.3%	58.1%	41.0%	59.0%
17	2004	244,748	116,049	WOHLGEMUTH, ARLENE	125,309	EDWARDS, CHET*	3,390	9,260 D	47.4%	51.2%	48.1%	51.9%
18	2010	121,321	33,067	FAULK, JOHN	85,108	JACKSON LEE, SHEILA*	3,146	52,041 D	27.3%	70.2%	28.0%	72.0%
18	2008	192,198	39,095	FAULK, JOHN	148,617	JACKSON-LEE, SHEILA*	4,486	109,522 D	20.3%	77.3%	20.8%	79.2%
18	2006	86,051	16,448	HASSAN, AHMAD	65,936	JACKSON-LEE, SHEILA*	3,667	49,488 D	19.1%	76.6%	20.0%	80.0%
18	2004	152,988		—	136,018	JACKSON-LEE, SHEILA*	16,970	136,018 D		88.9%		100.0%
19	2010	136,358	106,059	NEUGEBAUER, RANDY*	25,984	WILSON, ANDY	4,315	80,075 R	77.8%	19.1%	80.3%	19.7%
19	2008	232,611	168,501	NEUGEBAUER, RANDY*	58,030	FULLINGIM, DWIGHT	6,080	110,471 R	72.4%	24.9%	74.4%	25.6%
19	2006	140,007	94,785	NEUGEBAUER, RANDY*	41,676	RICKETTS, ROBERT	3,546	53,109 R	67.7%	29.8%	69.5%	30.5%
19	2004	233,514	136,459	NEUGEBAUER, RANDY*	93,531	STENHOLM, CHARLES W.*	3,524	42,928 R	58.4%	40.1%	59.3%	40.7%
20	2010	92,185	31,757	TROTTER, CLAYTON	58,645	GONZALEZ, CHARLIE*	1,783	26,888 D	34.4%	63.6%	35.1%	64.9%
20	2008	177,055	44,585	LITOFF, ROBERT	127,298	GONZALEZ, CHARLIE*	5,172	82,713 D	25.2%	71.9%	25.9%	74.1%
20	2006	78,245		—	68,348	GONZALEZ, CHARLIE*	9,897	68,348 D		87.4%		100.0%
20	2004	171,804	54,976	SCOTT, ROGER	112,480	GONZALEZ, CHARLIE*	4,348	57,504 D	32.0%	65.5%	32.8%	67.2%
21	2010	236,545	162,924	SMITH, LAMAR*	65,927	MELNICK, LAINEY	7,694	96,997 R	68.9%	27.9%	71.2%	28.8%
21	2008	304,350	243,471	SMITH, LAMAR*	—		60,879	243,471 R	80.0%		100.0%	
21	2006	203,782	122,486	SMITH, LAMAR*	68,312	COURAGE/KELLY	12,984	72,529 R	60.1%	33.5%	64.2%	35.8%
22	2010	208,223	140,537	OLSON, PETE*	62,082	ROGERS, KESHA	5,604	78,455 R	67.5%	29.8%	69.4%	30.6%
22	2008	308,995	161,996	OLSON, PETE	140,160	LAMPSON, NICK*	6,839	21,836 R	52.4%	45.4%	53.6%	46.4%
22	2006	148,239	61,938	GIBBS, SHELLEY SEKULA	76,775	LAMPSON, NICK	9,526	14,837 D	41.8%	51.8%	44.7%	55.3%
22	2004	272,620	150,386	DeLAY, TOM*	112,034	MORRISON, RICHARD R.	10,200	38,352 R	55.2%	41.1%	57.3%	42.7%
23	2010	151,534	74,853	CANSECO, FRANCISCO "QUICO"	67,348	RODRIGUEZ, CIRO D.*	9,333	7,505 R	49.4%	44.4%	52.6%	47.4%
23	2008	240,470	100,799	LARSON, LYLE	134,090	RODRIGUEZ, CIRO D.*	5,581	33,291 D	41.9%	55.8%	42.9%	57.1%
23	2006	70,473	32,217	BONILLA, HENRY*	38,256	RODRIGUEZ, CIRO D.	3,341	6,039 D	45.7%	54.3%	45.7%	54.3%
24	2010	122,687	100,078	MARCHANT, KENNY*	—		22,609	100,078 R	81.6%		100.0%	
24	2008	270,495	151,434	MARCHANT, KENNY*	111,089	LOVE, TOM	7,972	40,345 R	56.0%	41.1%	57.7%	42.3%

TEXAS

HOUSE OF REPRESENTATIVES

			Republican			Democratic		Other	Rep.-Dem.	Percentage			
										Total Vote		Major Vote	
CD	Year	Total Vote	Vote	Candidate	Vote	Candidate	Vote	Plurality	Rep.	Dem.	Rep.	Dem.	
24	2006	140,138	83,835	MARCHANT, KENNY*	52,075	PAGE, GARY R.	4,228	31,760 R	59.8%	37.2%	61.7%	38.3%
24	2004	241,374	154,435	MARCHANT, KENNY	82,599	PAGE, GARY R.	4,340	71,836 R	64.0%	34.2%	65.2%	34.8%
25	2010	189,247	84,849	CAMPBELL, DONNA	99,967	DOGGETT, LLOYD*	4,431	15,118 D	44.8%	52.8%	45.9%	54.1%
25	2008	291,296	88,693	MOROVICH, GEORGE L.	191,755	DOGGETT, LLOYD*	10,848	103,062 D	30.4%	65.8%	31.6%	68.4%
25	2006	163,424	42,975	ROSTIG, GRANT	109,911	DOGGETT, LLOYD*	10,538	66,936 D	26.3%	67.3%	28.1%	71.9%
26	2010	180,431	120,984	BURGESS, MICHAEL C.*	55,385	DURRANCE, NEIL L.	4,062	65,599 R	67.1%	30.7%	68.6%	31.4%
26	2008	324,376	195,181	BURGESS, MICHAEL C.*	118,167	LEACH, KEN	11,028	77,014 R	60.2%	36.4%	62.3%	37.7%
26	2006	156,483	94,219	BURGESS, MICHAEL C.*	58,271	BARNWELL, TIM	3,993	35,948 R	60.2%	37.2%	61.8%	38.2%
26	2004	274,539	180,519	BURGESS, MICHAEL C.*	89,809	REYES, LICO	4,211	90,710 R	65.8%	32.7%	66.8%	33.2%
27	2010	106,599	51,001	FARENTHOLD, R. BLAKE	50,226	ORTIZ, SOLOMON P.*	5,372	775 R	47.8%	47.1%	50.4%	49.6%
27	2008	180,951	69,458	VADEN, WILLIAM "WILLIE"	104,864	ORTIZ, SOLOMON P.*	6,629	35,406 D	38.4%	58.0%	39.8%	60.2%
27	2006	109,314	42,538	VADEN, WILLIAM "WILLIE"	62,058	ORTIZ, SOLOMON P.*	4,718	19,520 D	38.9%	56.8%	40.7%	59.3%
27	2004	177,536	61,955	VADEN, WILLIAM "WILLIE"	112,081	ORTIZ, SOLOMON P.*	3,500	50,126 D	34.9%	63.1%	35.6%	64.4%
28	2010	111,402	46,740	UNDERWOOD, BRYAN	62,773	CUELLAR, HENRY*	1,889	16,033 D	42.0%	56.3%	42.7%	57.3%
28	2008	179,740	52,524	FISH, JIM	123,494	CUELLAR, HENRY*	3,722	70,970 D	29.2%	68.7%	29.8%	70.2%
28	2006	77,755		—	68,372	CUELLAR, HENRY*	9,383	68,372 D		87.9%		100.0%
29	2010	66,948	22,825	MORALES, ROY	43,257	GREEN, GENE*	866	20,432 D	34.1%	64.6%	34.5%	65.5%
29	2008	106,794	25,512	STORY, ERIC	79,718	GREEN, GENE*	1,564	54,206 D	23.9%	74.6%	24.2%	75.8%
29	2006	50,550	12,347	STORY, ERIC	37,174	GREEN, GENE*	1,029	24,827 D	24.4%	73.5%	24.9%	75.1%
29	2004	83,124		—	78,256	GREEN, GENE*	4,868	78,256 D		94.1%		100.0%
30	2010	113,978	24,668	BRODEN, STEPHEN E.	86,322	JOHNSON, EDDIE BERNICE*	2,988	61,654 D	21.6%	75.7%	22.2%	77.8%
30	2008	203,976	32,361	WOOD, FRED	168,249	JOHNSON, EDDIE BERNICE*	3,366	135,888 D	15.9%	82.5%	16.1%	83.9%
30	2006	101,448	17,850	AURBACH, WILSON	81,348	JOHNSON, EDDIE BERNICE*	2,250	63,498 D	17.6%	80.2%	18.0%	82.0%
30	2004	155,334		—	144,513	JOHNSON, EDDIE BERNICE*	10,821	144,513 D		93.0%		100.0%
31	2010	153,119	126,384	CARTER, JOHN*		—	26,735	126,384 R	82.5%		100.0%	
31	2008	291,304	175,563	CARTER, JOHN*	106,559	RUIZ, BRIAN P.	9,182	69,004 R	60.3%	36.6%	62.2%	37.8%
31	2006	155,383	90,869	CARTER, JOHN*	60,293	HARRELL, MARY BETH	4,221	30,576 R	58.5%	38.8%	60.1%	39.9%
31	2004	247,427	160,247	CARTER, JOHN*	80,292	PORTER, JON	6,888	79,955 R	64.8%	32.5%	66.6%	33.4%
32	2010	126,869	79,433	SESSIONS, PETE*	44,258	RAGGIO, GRIER	3,178	35,175 R	62.6%	34.9%	64.2%	35.8%
32	2008	203,110	116,283	SESSIONS, PETE*	82,406	ROBERSON, ERIC	4,421	33,877 R	57.3%	40.6%	58.5%	41.5%
32	2006	126,652	71,461	SESSIONS, PETE*	52,269	PRYOR, WILL	2,922	19,192 R	56.4%	41.3%	57.8%	42.2%
32	2004	202,236	109,859	SESSIONS, PETE*	89,030	FROST, MARTIN*	3,347	20,829 R	54.3%	44.0%	55.2%	44.8%
TOTAL	2010	4,745,613	3,058,228		1,450,197		237,188	1,608,031 R	64.4%	30.6%	67.8%	32.2%
TOTAL	2008	7,528,622	4,203,917		2,979,398		345,307	1,224,519 R	55.8%	39.6%	58.5%	41.5%
TOTAL	2006	4,179,701	2,183,833		1,852,613		143,255	331,220 R	52.2%	44.3%	54.1%	45.9%
TOTAL	2004	6,958,603	4,012,534		2,713,968		232,101	1,298,566 R	57.7%	39.0%	59.7%	40.3%
TOTAL	2002	4,295,210	2,290,723		1,885,178		119,309	405,545 R	53.3%	43.9%	54.9%	45.1%

An asterisk (*) denotes incumbent.

Congressional district lines in Texas were redrawn between the elections of 2002 and 2004, and for Districts 15, 21, 23, 25 and 28 between the 2006 primary and general elections. In each of these five districts, candidates of all parties ran together in a special election on the November ballot, with the plurality measured as the difference between the vote for the winner and the vote for the runner-up, regardless of party. The designated Republican candidate in the 22nd District in 2006 was a write-in candidate, Shelley Sekula Gibbs. The results listed for the 23rd District are from a December runoff, required when no candidate won a majority of the vote in November voting. The statewide vote totals represent the aggregate vote for all House candidates of each party in the November balloting. The results from 2002, and a map of the Texas congressional district lines that year, can be found in America Votes 25. The results from 2004, and a map of the Texas congressional district lines that year, can be found in *America Votes 26*.

TEXAS

GENERAL AND PRIMARY ELECTIONS

2010 GENERAL ELECTIONS

Governor   Other vote was 109,211 Libertarian (Kathie Glass); 19,516 Green (Deb Shafto); 7,267 write-in (Andy Barron).

House   Other vote was:

CD 1   14,811 Libertarian (Charles F. Parkes III).
CD 2   16,711 Libertarian (David W. Smith).
CD 3   3,602 Libertarian (Christopher J. Claytor); 22 write-in (Harry Pierce).
CD 4   4,729 Libertarian (Jim D. Prindle); 4,244 Independent (Shane Shepard).
CD 5   2,958 Libertarian (Ken Ashby).
CD 6   4,700 Libertarian (Byron Severns).
CD 7   31,704 Libertarian (Bob Townsend); 1,019 write-in (Lissa Squiers).
CD 8   4,988 Libertarian (Bruce West).
CD 9   1,459 Libertarian (Michael W. Hope).
CD 10   5,105 Libertarian (Jeremiah "JP" Perkins).
CD 11   4,321 Libertarian (James A. Powell); 1,449 Green (Jim Howe).
CD 12   4,601 Libertarian (Matthew Solodow).
CD 13   11,192 Independent (Keith Dyer); 5,650 Libertarian (John T. Burwell Jr.)
CD 14
CD 15   2,570 Libertarian (Aaron I. Cohn).
CD 16   4,319 Libertarian (Bill Collins); 221 write-in (Tim Collins).
CD 17   2,808 Libertarian (Richard B. Kelly).
CD 18   3,118 Libertarian (Mike Taylor); 28 write-in (Charles B. "Chuck M" Meyer).
CD 19   4,315 Libertarian (Richard "Chip" Peterson).
CD 20   1,783 Libertarian (Michael "Commander" Idrogo).
CD 21   7,694 Libertarian (James Arthur Strohm).
CD 22   5,538 Libertarian (Steven Susman); 66 write-in (Johnny Williams).
CD 23   5,432 Independent (Craig T. Stephens); 2,482 Libertarian (Martin Nitschke); 1,419 Green (Ed Scharf).
CD 24   22,609 Libertarian (David Sparks).
CD 25   4,431 Libertarian (Jim Stutsman).
CD 26   4,062 Libertarian (Mark Boler).
CD 27   5,372 Libertarian (Ed Mishou).
CD 28   1,889 Libertarian (Stephen Kaat).
CD 29   866 Libertarian (Brad Walters).
CD 30   2,988 Libertarian (J. B. Oswalt).
CD 31   26,735 Libertarian (Bill Oliver).
CD 32   3,178 Libertarian (John Jay Myers).

2010 PRIMARY ELECTIONS

Primary   March 2, 2010   Registration   13,023,358   No Party Registration
Primary Runoff   April 13, 2010   (as of March 2, 2010)

Primary Type   Open—Any registered voter could participate in the Democratic or Republican primary, although if they voted in the primary of one party they could not vote in the runoff of the other party.

TEXAS

GENERAL AND PRIMARY ELECTIONS

	REPUBLICAN PRIMARIES			DEMOCRATIC PRIMARIES		
Governor	Rick Perry*	759,296	51.1%	Bill White	517,487	76.0%
	Kay Bailey Hutchison	450,087	30.3%	Farouk Shami	87,411	12.8%
	Debra Medina	275,159	18.5%	Felix "Rodriguez" Alvarado	33,714	5.0%
				Alma Ludivina Aguado	19,273	2.8%
				Clement E. Green	9,836	1.4%
				Bill Dear	6,551	1.0%
				Star Locke	6,276	0.9%
	TOTAL	1,484,542		TOTAL	680,548	
Congressional District 1	Louie Gohmert*	54,478	100.0%	No Democratic candidate		
Congressional District 2	Ted Poe*	39,685	100.0%	No Democratic candidate		
Congressional District 3	Sam Johnson*	40,661	100.0%	John Lingenfelder	5,306	100.0%
Congressional District 4	Ralph M. Hall*	39,579	57.4%	VaLinda Hathcox	13,783	100.0%
	Steve Clark	20,496	29.7%			
	John Cooper	3,748	5.4%			
	Jerry Ray "Tea" Hall	3,190	4.6%			
	Lou Gigliotti	1,044	1.5%			
	Joshua Kowert	947	1.4%			
	TOTAL	69,004				
Congressional District 5	Jeb Hensarling*	49,295	100.0%	Tom Berry	17,262	100.0%
Congressional District 6	Joe L. Barton*	46,095	100.0%	David E. Cozad	8,743	100.0%
Congressional District 7	John Culberson*	43,567	100.0%	No Democratic candidate		
Congressional District 8	Kevin Brady*	52,595	79.3%	Kent Hargett	15,030	100.0%
	Scott Baker	8,614	13.0%			
	Tyler Russell	3,542	5.3%			
	Melecio Franco	1,565	2.4%			
	TOTAL	66,316				
Congressional District 9	Steve Mueller	4,629	66.6%	Al Green*	21,465	100.0%
	Dave Bannen	2,317	33.4%			
	TOTAL	6,946				
Congressional District 10	Michael McCaul*	46,881	82.9%	Ted Ankrum	15,373	100.0%
	Rick Martin	5,038	8.9%			
	Joe Petronis	4,656	8.2%			
	TOTAL	56,575				
Congressional District 11	K. Michael Conaway*	55,610	77.4%	James Quillian	8,378	100.0%
	Chris Younts	9,586	13.3%			
	Al Cowan	6,680	9.3%			
	TOTAL	71,876				

TEXAS

GENERAL AND PRIMARY ELECTIONS

	REPUBLICAN PRIMARIES			DEMOCRATIC PRIMARIES		
Congressional District 12	Kay Granger*	40,325	70.0%	Tracey Smith	6,849	100.0%
	Mike Brasovan	10,943	19.0%			
	Matthew E. Kelly	6,361	11.0%			
	TOTAL	57,629				
Congressional District 13	William M. "Mac" Thornberry*	59,070	100.0%	No Democratic candidate		
Congressional District 14	Ron Paul*	45,990	80.8%	Robert Pruett	6,842	41.6%
	Tim Graney	5,499	9.7%	Winston Cochran	5,112	31.1%
	John Gay	3,004	5.3%	Jeff Cherry	4,498	27.3%
	Gerald D. Wall	2,448	4.3%			
	TOTAL	56,941		TOTAL	16,452	
				PRIMARY RUNOFF		
				Robert Pruett	1,575	54.6%
				Winston Cochran	1,309	45.4%
				TOTAL	2,884	
Congressional District 15	Paul B. Haring	5,401	41.8%	Ruben Hinojosa*	37,430	83.7%
	Eddie Zamora	4,201	32.5%	Doug "La Perla" Purl	7,282	16.3%
	Daniel Garza	3,310	25.6%			
	TOTAL	12,912		TOTAL	44,712	
	PRIMARY RUNOFF					
	Eddie Zamora	1,558	56.8%			
	Paul B. Haring	1,187	43.2%			
	TOTAL	2,745				
Congressional District 16	Tim Besco	9,817		Silvestre Reyes*	26,066	100.0%
Congressional District 17	Bill Flores	21,479	33.0%	Chet Edwards*	11,244	100.0%
	Rob Curnock	18,679	28.7%			
	Dave McIntyre	11,870	18.3%			
	Chuck Wilson	9,853	15.2%			
	Timothy Delasandro	3,119	4.8%			
	TOTAL	65,000				
	PRIMARY RUNOFF					
	Bill Flores	21,913	65.1%			
	Rob Curnock	11,730	34.9%			
	TOTAL	33,643				
Congressional District 18	John Faulk	5,188	56.8%	Sheila Jackson Lee*	21,570	67.0%
	Brenda Page	2,743	30.0%	Jarvis Johnson	9,133	28.4%
	Tex Christopher	1,199	13.1%	Sean Roberts	1,508	4.7%
	TOTAL	9,130		TOTAL	32,211	
Congressional District 19	Randy Neugebauer*	63,780	100.0%	Andy Wilson	8,256	100.0%
Congressional District 20	Clayton Trotter	3,838	32.5%	Charlie Gonzalez*	16,935	100.0%
	Joseph "Jamie" Martinez	3,510	29.7%			
	Charles A. Shipp Jr.	2,479	21.0%			
	Alan Strack	1,997	16.9%			
	TOTAL	11,824				

TEXAS

GENERAL AND PRIMARY ELECTIONS

	REPUBLICAN PRIMARIES			DEMOCRATIC PRIMARIES		
	PRIMARY RUNOFF					
	Clayton Trotter	2,430	71.7%			
	Joseph "Jamie" Martinez	957	28.3%			
	TOTAL	3,387				
Congressional District 21	Lamar Smith*	61,923	81.4%	Lainey Melnick	14,773	100.0%
	Stephen Schoppe	14,166	18.6%			
	TOTAL	76,089				
Congressional District 22	Pete Olson*	43,418	100.0%	Kesha Rogers	7,467	52.3%
				Doug Blatt	3,956	27.7%
				Freddie John Wieder Jr.	2,858	20.0%
				TOTAL	14,281	
Congressional District 23	Will Hurd	9,695	33.7%	Ciro D. Rodriguez*	34,104	83.4%
	Francisco "Quico" Canseco	9,250	32.2%	Miguel Ortiz	6,799	16.6%
	Robert "Doc" Lowry	6,369	22.1%			
	Mike Kueber	1,990	6.9%			
	Joseph Mack "Doc" Gould	1,459	5.1%			
	TOTAL	28,763		TOTAL	40,903	
	PRIMARY RUNOFF					
	Francisco "Quico" Canseco	7,210	52.6%			
	Will Hurd	6,488	47.4%			
	TOTAL	13,698				
Congressional District 24	Kenny Marchant*	33,283	84.1%	No Democratic candidate		
	Frank Roszell	6,298	15.9%			
	TOTAL	39,581				
Congressional District 25	Donna Campbell	23,955	69.4%	Lloyd Doggett*	29,949	100.0%
	George Morovich	10,541	30.6%			
	TOTAL	34,496				
Congressional District 26	Michael C. Burgess*	44,047	85.8%	Neil L. Durrance	7,450	100.0%
	James Herford	7,284	14.2%			
	TOTAL	51,331				
Congressional District 27	James Duerr	6,368	32.4%	Solomon P. Ortiz*	21,948	100.0%
	R. Blake Farenthold	5,921	30.1%			
	William Willie Vaden	4,268	21.7%			
	Jessica Puente-Bradshaw	3,097	15.8%			
	TOTAL	19,654				
	PRIMARY RUNOFF					
	R. Blake Farenthold	4,742	51.3%			
	James Duerr	4,496	48.7%			
	TOTAL	9,238				
Congressional District 28	Bryan Underwood	13,629	74.0%	Henry Cuellar*	48,634	100.0%
	Daniel Chavez	4,792	26.0%			
	TOTAL	18,421				
Congressional District 29	Roy Morales	4,137	58.4%	Gene Green*	9,567	100.0%
	Eric Story	1,514	21.4%			
	Tom Stevens	657	9.3%			
	George A. Young	474	6.7%			
	Frank "Mazz" Mazzapica	307	4.3%			
	TOTAL	7,089				

TEXAS

GENERAL AND PRIMARY ELECTIONS

	REPUBLICAN PRIMARIES			DEMOCRATIC PRIMARIES		
Congressional District 30	Stephen E. Broden	3,681	49.5%	Eddie Bernice Johnson*	23,725	100.0%
	Sheldon Goldstein	2,809	37.8%			
	Charles Lingerfelt	944	12.7%			
	TOTAL	7,434				
	PRIMARY RUNOFF					
	Stephen E. Broden	2,126	67.5%			
	Sheldon Goldstein	1,023	32.5%			
	TOTAL	3,149				
Congressional District 31	John Carter*	52,321	89.9%	No Democratic candidate		
	Raymond Yamka	5,910	10.1%			
	TOTAL	58,231				
Congressional District 32	Pete Sessions*	30,509	83.7%	Grier Raggio	7,461	100.0%
	David Smith	5,937	16.3%			
	TOTAL	36,446				

Note: An asterisk (*) denotes incumbent. A runoff was triggered if the leading vote-getter in the primary received less than a majority of the primary vote.

UTAH

Congressional districts first established for elections held in 2002
3 members

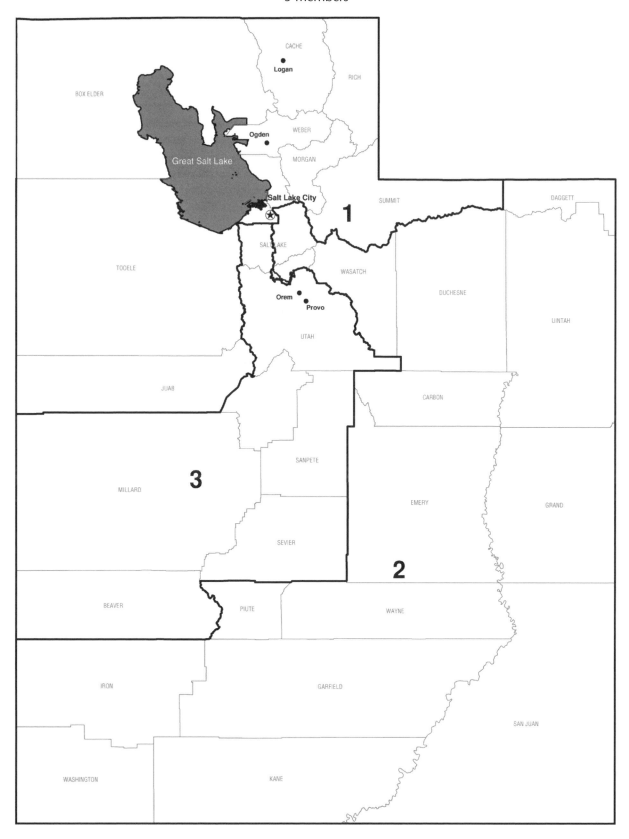

UTAH

GOVERNOR

Gary R. Herbert (R). Elected 2010 to remaining two years of term vacated by resignation of Jon Huntsman Jr. (R) to become ambassador to China. Herbert sworn in as governor August 11, 2009.

SENATORS (2 Republicans)

Orrin G. Hatch (R). Reelected 2006 to a six-year term. Previously elected 2000, 1994, 1988, 1982, 1976.

Mike Lee (R). Elected 2010 to a six-year term.

REPRESENTATIVES (2 Republicans, 1 Democrat)

1. Rob Bishop (R)   2. Jim Matheson (D)   3. Jason Chaffetz (R)

POSTWAR VOTE FOR PRESIDENT

| | | Republican | | Democratic | | | | Percentage | | | |
| | | | | | | | | Total Vote | | Major Vote | |
Year	Total Vote	Vote	Candidate	Vote	Candidate	Other Vote	Rep.-Dem. Plurality	Rep.	Dem.	Rep.	Dem.
2008	952,370	596,030	McCain, John	327,670	Obama, Barack	28,670	268,360 R	62.6%	34.4%	64.5%	35.5%
2004	927,844	663,742	Bush, George W.	241,199	Kerry, John	22,903	422,543 R	71.5%	26.0%	73.3%	26.7%
2000**	770,754	515,096	Bush, George W.	203,053	Gore, Al	52,605	312,043 R	66.8%	26.3%	71.7%	28.3%
1996**	665,629	361,911	Dole, Bob	221,633	Clinton, Bill	82,085	140,278 R	54.4%	33.3%	62.0%	38.0%
1992**	743,999	322,632	Bush, George	183,429	Clinton, Bill	237,938	119,232 R	43.4%	24.7%	63.8%	36.2%
1988	647,008	428,442	Bush, George	207,343	Dukakis, Michael S.	11,223	221,099 R	66.2%	32.0%	67.4%	32.6%
1984	629,656	469,105	Reagan, Ronald	155,369	Mondale, Walter F.	5,182	313,736 R	74.5%	24.7%	75.1%	24.9%
1980**	604,222	439,687	Reagan, Ronald	124,266	Carter, Jimmy	40,269	315,421 R	72.8%	20.6%	78.0%	22.0%
1976	541,198	337,908	Ford, Gerald R.	182,110	Carter, Jimmy	21,180	155,798 R	62.4%	33.6%	65.0%	35.0%
1972	478,476	323,643	Nixon, Richard M.	126,284	McGovern, George S.	28,549	197,359 R	67.6%	26.4%	71.9%	28.1%
1968**	422,568	238,728	Nixon, Richard M.	156,665	Humphrey, Hubert H.	27,175	82,063 R	56.5%	37.1%	60.4%	39.6%
1964	401,413	181,785	Goldwater, Barry M.	219,628	Johnson, Lyndon B.		37,843 D	45.3%	54.7%	45.3%	54.7%
1960	374,709	205,361	Nixon, Richard M.	169,248	Kennedy, John F.	100	36,113 R	54.8%	45.2%	54.8%	45.2%
1956	333,995	215,631	Eisenhower, Dwight D.	118,364	Stevenson, Adlai E.		97,267 R	64.6%	35.4%	64.6%	35.4%
1952	329,554	194,190	Eisenhower, Dwight D.	135,364	Stevenson, Adlai E.		58,826 R	58.9%	41.1%	58.9%	41.1%
1948	276,306	124,402	Dewey, Thomas E.	149,151	Truman, Harry S.	2,753	24,749 D	45.0%	54.0%	45.5%	54.5%

** In past elections, the other vote included: 2000 - 35,850 Green (Ralph Nader); 1996 - 66,461 Reform (Ross Perot); 1992 - 203,400 Independent (Perot), who finished second; 1980 - 30,284 Independent (John Anderson); 1968 - 26,906 American Independent (George Wallace).

UTAH

POSTWAR VOTE FOR GOVERNOR

Year	Total Vote	Republican		Democratic		Other Vote	Rep.-Dem. Plurality	Percentage			
		Vote	Candidate	Vote	Candidate			Total Vote		Major Vote	
								Rep.	Dem.	Rep.	Dem.
2010s	643,307	412,151	Herbert, Gary R.	205,246	Corroon, Peter	25,910	206,905 R	64.1%	31.9%	66.8%	33.2%
2008	945,525	734,049	Huntsman, Jon, Jr.	186,503	Springmeyer, Bob	24,973	548,546 R	77.6%	19.7%	79.7%	20.3%
2004	919,960	531,190	Huntsman, Jon, Jr.	380,359	Matheson, Scott M., Jr.	8,411	150,831 R	57.7%	41.3%	58.3%	41.7%
2000	761,806	424,837	Leavitt, Michael O.	321,979	Orton, Bill	14,990	102,858 R	55.8%	42.3%	56.9%	43.1%
1996	671,879	503,693	Leavitt, Michael O.	156,616	Bradley, Jim	11,570	347,077 R	75.0%	23.3%	76.3%	23.7%
1992**	762,549	321,713	Leavitt, Michael O.	177,181	Hanson, Stewart	263,655	65,960 R	42.2%	23.2%	64.5%	35.5%
1988**	649,114	260,462	Bangerter, Norman H.	249,321	Wilson, Ted	139,331	11,141 R	40.1%	38.4%	51.1%	48.9%
1984	629,619	351,792	Bangerter, Norman H.	275,669	Owens, Wayne	2,158	76,123 R	55.9%	43.8%	56.1%	43.9%
1980	600,019	266,578	Wright, Bob	330,974	Matheson, Scott M.	2,467	64,396 D	44.4%	55.2%	44.6%	55.4%
1976	539,649	248,027	Romney, Vernon B.	280,706	Matheson, Scott M.	10,916	32,679 D	46.0%	52.0%	46.9%	53.1%
1972	476,447	144,449	Strike, Nicholas L.	331,998	Rampton, Calvin L.		187,549 D	30.3%	69.7%	30.3%	69.7%
1968	421,012	131,729	Buehner, Carl W.	289,283	Rampton, Calvin L.		157,554 D	31.3%	68.7%	31.3%	68.7%
1964	398,256	171,300	Melich, Mitchell	226,956	Rampton, Calvin L.		55,656 D	43.0%	57.0%	43.0%	57.0%
1960	371,489	195,634	Clyde, George D.	175,855	Barlocker, W. A.		19,779 R	52.7%	47.3%	52.7%	47.3%
1956**	332,889	127,164	Clyde, George D.	111,297	Romney, L. C.	94,428	15,867 R	38.2%	33.4%	53.3%	46.7%
1952	327,704	180,516	Lee, J. Bracken	147,188	Glade, Earl J.		33,328 R	55.1%	44.9%	55.1%	44.9%
1948	275,067	151,253	Lee, J. Bracken	123,814	Maw, Herbert B.		27,439 R	55.0%	45.0%	55.0%	45.0%

** In past elections, the other vote included: 1992 - 255,753 Independent (Merrill Cook), who finished second; 1988 - 136,651 Independent (Cook); 1956 - 94,428 Independent (J. Bracken Lee). The 2010 election was for a short term to fill a vacancy.

POSTWAR VOTE FOR SENATOR

Year	Total Vote	Republican		Democratic		Other Vote	Rep.-Dem. Plurality	Percentage			
		Vote	Candidate	Vote	Candidate			Total Vote		Major Vote	
								Rep.	Dem.	Rep.	Dem.
2010	633,829	390,179	Lee, Mike	207,685	Granato, Sam F.	35,965	182,494 R	61.6%	32.8%	65.3%	34.7%
2006	571,252	356,238	Hatch, Orrin G.	177,459	Ashdown, Pete	37,555	178,779 R	62.4%	31.1%	66.7%	33.3%
2004	911,726	626,640	Bennett, Robert F.	258,955	Van Dam, R. Paul	26,131	367,685 R	68.7%	28.4%	70.8%	29.2%
2000	769,704	504,803	Hatch, Orrin G.	242,569	Howell, Scott N.	22,332	262,234 R	65.6%	31.5%	67.5%	32.5%
1998	494,909	316,652	Bennett, Robert F.	163,172	Leckman, Scott	15,085	153,480 R	64.0%	33.0%	66.0%	34.0%
1994	519,323	357,297	Hatch, Orrin G.	146,938	Shea, Patrick A.	15,088	210,359 R	68.8%	28.3%	70.9%	29.1%
1992	758,479	420,069	Bennett, Robert F.	301,228	Owens, Wayne	37,182	118,841 R	55.4%	39.7%	58.2%	41.8%
1988	640,702	430,089	Hatch, Orrin G.	203,364	Moss, Brian H.	7,249	226,725 R	67.1%	31.7%	67.9%	32.1%
1986	435,111	314,608	Garn, E. J.	115,523	Oliver, Craig	4,980	199,085 R	72.3%	26.6%	73.1%	26.9%
1982	530,802	309,332	Hatch, Orrin G.	219,482	Wilson, Ted	1,988	89,850 R	58.3%	41.3%	58.5%	41.5%
1980	594,298	437,675	Garn, E. J.	151,454	Berman, Dan	5,169	286,221 R	73.6%	25.5%	74.3%	25.7%
1976	540,108	290,221	Hatch, Orrin G.	241,948	Moss, Frank E.	7,939	48,273 R	53.7%	44.8%	54.5%	45.5%
1974	420,642	210,299	Garn, E. J.	185,377	Owens, Wayne	24,966	24,922 R	50.0%	44.1%	53.1%	46.9%
1970	374,303	159,004	Burton, Laurence J.	210,207	Moss, Frank E.	5,092	51,203 D	42.5%	56.2%	43.1%	56.9%
1968	419,262	225,075	Bennett, Wallace F.	192,168	Weilenmann, Milton	2,019	32,907 R	53.7%	45.8%	53.9%	46.1%
1964	397,384	169,562	Wilkinson, Ernest L.	227,822	Moss, Frank E.		58,260 D	42.7%	57.3%	42.7%	57.3%
1962	318,411	166,755	Bennett, Wallace F.	151,656	King, David S.		15,099 R	52.4%	47.6%	52.4%	47.6%
1958**	291,311	101,471	Watkins, Arthur V.	112,827	Moss, Frank E.	77,013	11,356 D	34.8%	38.7%	47.4%	52.6%
1956	330,381	178,261	Bennett, Wallace F.	152,120	Hopkin, Alonzo F.		26,141 R	54.0%	46.0%	54.0%	46.0%
1952	327,033	177,435	Watkins, Arthur V.	149,598	Granger, Walter K.		27,837 R	54.3%	45.7%	54.3%	45.7%
1950	264,440	142,427	Bennett, Wallace F.	121,198	Thomas, Elbert D.	815	21,229 R	53.9%	45.8%	54.0%	46.0%
1946	197,399	101,142	Watkins, Arthur V.	96,257	Murdock, Abe		4,885 R	51.2%	48.8%	51.2%	48.8%

** In past elections, the other vote included: 1958 - 77,013 Independent (J. Bracken Lee).

UTAH

GOVERNOR 2010

2010 Census Population	County	Total Vote	Republican	Democratic	Other	Rep.-Dem. Plurality		Percentage			
								Total Vote		Major Vote	
								Rep.	Dem.	Rep.	Dem.
6,629	BEAVER	2,217	1,640	482	95	1,158	R	74.0%	21.7%	77.3%	22.7%
49,975	BOX ELDER	12,760	9,940	2,240	580	7,700	R	77.9%	17.6%	81.6%	18.4%
112,656	CACHE	24,540	17,081	5,906	1,553	11,175	R	69.6%	24.1%	74.3%	25.7%
21,403	CARBON	5,315	2,929	2,149	237	780	R	55.1%	40.4%	57.7%	42.3%
1,059	DAGGETT	491	339	129	23	210	R	69.0%	26.3%	72.4%	27.6%
306,479	DAVIS	69,917	49,800	17,529	2,588	32,271	R	71.2%	25.1%	74.0%	26.0%
18,607	DUCHESNE	4,642	3,780	675	187	3,105	R	81.4%	14.5%	84.8%	15.2%
10,976	EMERY	3,789	2,862	777	150	2,085	R	75.5%	20.5%	78.6%	21.4%
5,172	GARFIELD	1,656	1,292	309	55	983	R	78.0%	18.7%	80.7%	19.3%
9,225	GRAND	3,341	1,638	1,532	171	106	R	49.0%	45.9%	51.7%	48.3%
46,163	IRON	10,888	8,148	1,949	791	6,199	R	74.8%	17.9%	80.7%	19.3%
10,246	JUAB	2,837	2,091	593	153	1,498	R	73.7%	20.9%	77.9%	22.1%
7,125	KANE	2,433	1,772	534	127	1,238	R	72.8%	21.9%	76.8%	23.2%
12,503	MILLARD	4,167	3,121	724	322	2,397	R	74.9%	17.4%	81.2%	18.8%
9,469	MORGAN	3,163	2,432	591	140	1,841	R	76.9%	18.7%	80.4%	19.6%
1,556	PIUTE	571	460	84	27	376	R	80.6%	14.7%	84.6%	15.4%
2,264	RICH	779	609	152	18	457	R	78.2%	19.5%	80.0%	20.0%
1,029,655	SALT LAKE	252,884	129,024	115,319	8,541	13,705	R	51.0%	45.6%	52.8%	47.2%
14,746	SAN JUAN	4,098	2,349	1,576	173	773	R	57.3%	38.5%	59.8%	40.2%
27,822	SANPETE	6,041	4,555	1,100	386	3,455	R	75.4%	18.2%	80.5%	19.5%
20,802	SEVIER	5,996	4,779	966	251	3,813	R	79.7%	16.1%	83.2%	16.8%
36,324	SUMMIT	11,452	5,050	6,051	351	1,001	D	44.1%	52.8%	45.5%	54.5%
58,218	TOOELE	11,960	7,965	3,469	526	4,496	R	66.6%	29.0%	69.7%	30.3%
32,588	UINTAH	7,399	6,068	980	351	5,088	R	82.0%	13.2%	86.1%	13.9%
516,564	UTAH	101,740	82,205	15,372	4,163	66,833	R	80.8%	15.1%	84.2%	15.8%
23,530	WASATCH	6,195	4,165	1,808	222	2,357	R	67.2%	29.2%	69.7%	30.3%
138,115	WASHINGTON	35,397	26,668	6,961	1,768	19,707	R	75.3%	19.7%	79.3%	20.7%
2,778	WAYNE	1,138	848	256	34	592	R	74.5%	22.5%	76.8%	23.2%
231,236	WEBER	45,501	28,541	15,033	1,927	13,508	R	62.7%	33.0%	65.5%	34.5%
2,763,885	TOTAL	643,307	412,151	205,246	25,910	206,905	R	64.1%	31.9%	66.8%	33.2%

UTAH

SENATOR 2010

2010 Census Population	County	Total Vote	Republican	Democratic	Other	Rep.-Dem. Plurality		Percentage			
								Total Vote		Major Vote	
								Rep.	Dem.	Rep.	Dem.
6,629	BEAVER	2,127	1,540	421	166	1,119	R	72.4%	19.8%	78.5%	21.5%
49,975	BOX ELDER	12,621	9,122	2,435	1,064	6,687	R	72.3%	19.3%	78.9%	21.1%
112,656	CACHE	24,435	14,774	5,273	4,388	9,501	R	60.5%	21.6%	73.7%	26.3%
21,403	CARBON	5,210	2,628	2,254	328	374	R	50.4%	43.3%	53.8%	46.2%
1,059	DAGGETT	473	312	130	31	182	R	66.0%	27.5%	70.6%	29.4%
306,479	DAVIS	69,257	46,513	19,079	3,665	27,434	R	67.2%	27.5%	70.9%	29.1%
18,607	DUCHESNE	4,585	3,622	572	391	3,050	R	79.0%	12.5%	86.4%	13.6%
10,976	EMERY	3,666	2,599	827	240	1,772	R	70.9%	22.6%	75.9%	24.1%
5,172	GARFIELD	1,633	1,314	262	57	1,052	R	80.5%	16.0%	83.4%	16.6%
9,225	GRAND	3,284	1,645	1,476	163	169	R	50.1%	44.9%	52.7%	47.3%

UTAH

SENATOR 2010

2010 Census Population	County	Total Vote	Republican	Democratic	Other	Rep.-Dem. Plurality		Percentage			
								Total Vote		Major Vote	
								Rep.	Dem.	Rep.	Dem.
46,163	IRON	10,681	8,178	1,651	852	6,527	R	76.6%	15.5%	83.2%	16.8%
10,246	JUAB	2,767	1,952	558	257	1,394	R	70.5%	20.2%	77.8%	22.2%
7,125	KANE	2,404	1,772	487	145	1,285	R	73.7%	20.3%	78.4%	21.6%
12,503	MILLARD	4,035	2,806	685	544	2,121	R	69.5%	17.0%	80.4%	19.6%
9,469	MORGAN	3,127	2,198	623	306	1,575	R	70.3%	19.9%	77.9%	22.1%
1,556	PIUTE	549	441	84	24	357	R	80.3%	15.3%	84.0%	16.0%
2,264	RICH	756	585	144	27	441	R	77.4%	19.0%	80.2%	19.8%
1,029,655	SALT LAKE	247,585	121,419	116,534	9,632	4,885	R	49.0%	47.1%	51.0%	49.0%
14,746	SAN JUAN	4,057	2,375	1,519	163	856	R	58.5%	37.4%	61.0%	39.0%
27,822	SANPETE	5,928	4,270	1,051	607	3,219	R	72.0%	17.7%	80.2%	19.8%
20,802	SEVIER	5,929	4,671	871	387	3,800	R	78.8%	14.7%	84.3%	15.7%
36,324	SUMMIT	11,281	4,955	6,000	326	1,045	D	43.9%	53.2%	45.2%	54.8%
58,218	TOOELE	11,830	7,219	3,696	915	3,523	R	61.0%	31.2%	66.1%	33.9%
32,588	UINTAH	7,314	5,908	833	573	5,075	R	80.8%	11.4%	87.6%	12.4%
516,564	UTAH	100,691	78,770	16,098	5,823	62,672	R	78.2%	16.0%	83.0%	17.0%
23,530	WASATCH	6,052	3,895	1,853	304	2,042	R	64.4%	30.6%	67.8%	32.2%
138,115	WASHINGTON	35,175	27,480	6,043	1,652	21,437	R	78.1%	17.2%	82.0%	18.0%
2,778	WAYNE	1,092	786	263	43	523	R	72.0%	24.1%	74.9%	25.1%
231,236	WEBER	45,285	26,430	15,963	2,892	10,467	R	58.4%	35.3%	62.3%	37.7%
2,763,885	TOTAL	633,829	390,179	207,685	35,965	182,494	R	61.6%	32.8%	65.3%	34.7%

UTAH

HOUSE OF REPRESENTATIVES

CD	Year	Total Vote	Republican		Democratic		Other Vote	Rep.-Dem. Plurality		Percentage			
			Vote	Candidate	Vote	Candidate				Total Vote		Major Vote	
										Rep.	Dem.	Rep.	Dem.
1	2010	195,462	135,247	BISHOP, ROB*	46,765	BOWEN, MORGAN	13,450	88,482	R	69.2%	23.9%	74.3%	25.7%
1	2008	303,445	196,799	BISHOP, ROB*	92,469	BOWEN, MORGAN	14,177	104,330	R	64.9%	30.5%	68.0%	32.0%
1	2006	178,474	112,546	BISHOP, ROB*	57,922	OLSEN, STEVEN	8,006	54,624	R	63.1%	32.5%	66.0%	34.0%
1	2004	293,961	199,615	BISHOP, ROB*	85,630	THOMPSON, STEVEN	8,716	113,985	R	67.9%	29.1%	70.0%	30.0%
1	2002	179,412	109,265	BISHOP, ROB	66,104	THOMAS, DAVE	4,043	43,161	R	60.9%	36.8%	62.3%	37.7%
2	2010	251,847	116,001	PHILPOT, MORGAN	127,151	MATHESON, JIM*	8,695	11,150	D	46.1%	50.5%	47.7%	52.3%
2	2008	348,325	120,083	DEW, BILL	220,666	MATHESON, JIM*	7,576	100,583	D	34.5%	63.4%	35.2%	64.8%
2	2006	225,818	84,234	CHRISTENSEN, LAVAR	133,231	MATHESON, JIM*	8,353	48,997	D	37.3%	59.0%	38.7%	61.3%
2	2004	341,968	147,778	SWALLOW, JOHN	187,250	MATHESON, JIM*	6,940	39,472	D	43.2%	54.8%	44.1%	55.9%
2	2002	224,098	109,123	SWALLOW, JOHN	110,764	MATHESON, JIM*	4,211	1,641	D	48.7%	49.4%	49.6%	50.4%
3	2010	193,186	139,721	CHAFFETZ, JASON*	44,320	HYER, KAREN	9,145	95,401	R	72.3%	22.9%	75.9%	24.1%
3	2008	285,069	187,035	CHAFFETZ, JASON	80,626	SPENCER, BENNION L.	17,408	106,409	R	65.6%	28.3%	69.9%	30.1%
3	2006	165,398	95,455	CANNON, CHRIS*	53,330	BURRIDGE, CHRISTIAN	16,613	42,125	R	57.7%	32.2%	64.2%	35.8%
3	2004	272,928	173,010	CANNON, CHRIS*	88,748	BABKA, BEAU	11,170	84,262	R	63.4%	32.5%	66.1%	33.9%
3	2002	153,643	103,598	CANNON, CHRIS*	44,533	WOODSIDE, NANCY JANE	5,512	59,065	R	67.4%	29.0%	69.9%	30.1%
TOTAL	2010	640,495	390,969		218,236		31,290	172,733	R	61.0%	34.1%	64.2%	35.8%
TOTAL	2008	936,839	503,917		393,761		39,161	110,156	R	53.8%	42.0%	56.1%	43.9%
TOTAL	2006	569,690	292,235		244,483		32,972	47,752	R	51.3%	42.9%	54.4%	45.6%
TOTAL	2004	908,857	520,403		361,628		26,826	158,775	R	57.3%	39.8%	59.0%	41.0%
TOTAL	2002	557,153	321,986		221,401		13,766	100,585	R	57.8%	39.7%	59.3%	40.7%

An asterisk (*) denotes incumbent.

UTAH

GENERAL AND PRIMARY ELECTIONS

2010 GENERAL ELECTIONS

Governor	Other vote was 13,038 Unaffiliated (Farley Anderson); 12,871 Libertarian (Andrew McCullough); 1 write-in (Michael William Heath).
Senator	Other vote was 35,937 Constitution (Scott N. Bradley); 20 write-in (Brian E. Kamerath); 6 write-in (Loy Brunson); 2 write-in (Cody Judy).
House	Other vote was:
CD 1	9,143 Constitution (Kirk D. Pearson); 4,307 Libertarian (Jared Paul Stratton).
CD 2	4,578 Constitution (Randall Hinton); 2,391 Unaffiliated (Dave Glissmeyer); 1,726 Unaffiliated (Wayne L. Hill).
CD 3	4,596 Constitution (Douglas Sligting); 2,945 Libertarian (Jake Shannon); 1,604 Unaffiliated (Joseph L. Puente).

2010 PRIMARY ELECTIONS

Primary	June 22, 2010	**Registration** (as of June 22, 2010)	Republican	664,189
			Democratic	155,609
			Libertarian	4,294
			Constitution	2,687
			Other	30,570
			Unaffiliated	985,989
			TOTAL	*1,843,338*

Primary Type　Registered Democrats and unaffiliated voters could participate in the Democratic primary. Registered Republicans and unaffiliated voters who chose to change their registration to Republican on primary day could vote in the Republican primary.

	REPUBLICAN PRIMARIES			DEMOCRATIC PRIMARIES		
Governor	Gary R. Herbert*	Nominated by convention		Peter Corroon	Nominated by convention	
Senator	Mike Lee	98,512	51.2%	Sam F. Granato	Nominated by convention	
	Tim Bridgewater	93,905	48.8%			
	TOTAL	*192,417*				
Congressional District 1	Rob Bishop*	Nominated by convention		Morgan Bowen	Nominated by convention	
Congressional District 2	Morgan Philpot	Nominated by convention		Jim Matheson*	23,067	67.3%
				Claudia Wright	11,227	32.7%
				TOTAL	*34,294*	
Congressional District 3	Jason Chaffetz*	Nominated by convention		Karen Hyer	Nominated by convention	

An asterisk (*) denotes incumbent. Candidates in Utah are usually nominated by convention. It is up to each party to determine the percentage of the convention vote that is needed to force a primary.

VERMONT

One member At Large

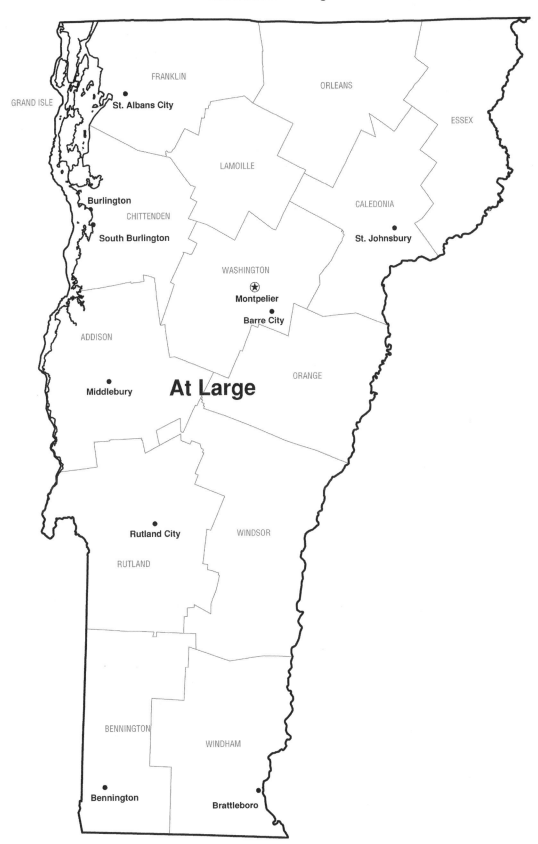

GRAND ISLE

FRANKLIN

● St. Albans City

ORLEANS

ESSEX

LAMOILLE

CALEDONIA

Burlington

CHITTENDEN

● St. Johnsbury

South Burlington

WASHINGTON

⊛
Montpelier

● Barre City

ADDISON

ORANGE

● Middlebury

At Large

● Rutland City

WINDSOR

RUTLAND

BENNINGTON

WINDHAM

● Bennington

● Brattleboro

VERMONT

GOVERNOR
Peter Shumlin (D). Elected January 2011 by the State Legislature to a two-year term. Shumlin had finished first in the 2010 general election but failed to win a majority of the vote as required by Vermont law.

SENATORS (1 Democrat, 1 Independent)
Patrick J. Leahy (D). Reelected 2010 to a six-year term. Previously elected 2004, 1998, 1992, 1986, 1980, 1974.

Bernard Sanders (I). Elected 2006 to a six-year term.

REPRESENTATIVE (1 Democrat)
At Large. Peter Welch (D)

POSTWAR VOTE FOR PRESIDENT

| | | Republican | | Democratic | | | | Percentage | | | |
| | | | | | | | | Total Vote | | Major Vote | |
Year	Total Vote	Vote	Candidate	Vote	Candidate	Other Vote	Rep.-Dem. Plurality	Rep.	Dem.	Rep.	Dem.
2008	325,046	98,974	McCain, John	219,262	Obama, Barack	6,810	120,288 D	30.4%	67.5%	31.1%	68.9%
2004	312,309	121,180	Bush, George W.	184,067	Kerry, John	7,062	62,887 D	38.8%	58.9%	39.7%	60.3%
2000**	294,308	119,775	Bush, George W.	149,022	Gore, Al	25,511	29,247 D	40.7%	50.6%	44.6%	55.4%
1996**	258,449	80,352	Dole, Bob	137,894	Clinton, Bill	40,203	57,542 D	31.1%	53.4%	36.8%	63.2%
1992**	289,701	88,122	Bush, George	133,592	Clinton, Bill	67,987	45,470 D	30.4%	46.1%	39.7%	60.3%
1988	243,328	124,331	Bush, George	115,775	Dukakis, Michael S.	3,222	8,556 R	51.1%	47.6%	51.8%	48.2%
1984	234,561	135,865	Reagan, Ronald	95,730	Mondale, Walter F.	2,966	40,135 R	57.9%	40.8%	58.7%	41.3%
1980**	213,299	94,628	Reagan, Ronald	81,952	Carter, Jimmy	36,719	12,676 R	44.4%	38.4%	53.6%	46.4%
1976	187,765	102,085	Ford, Gerald R.	80,954	Carter, Jimmy	4,726	21,131 R	54.4%	43.1%	55.8%	44.2%
1972	186,947	117,149	Nixon, Richard M.	68,174	McGovern, George S.	1,624	48,975 R	62.7%	36.5%	63.2%	36.8%
1968**	161,404	85,142	Nixon, Richard M.	70,255	Humphrey, Hubert H.	6,007	14,887 R	52.8%	43.5%	54.8%	45.2%
1964	163,089	54,942	Goldwater, Barry M.	108,127	Johnson, Lyndon B.	20	53,185 D	33.7%	66.3%	33.7%	66.3%
1960	167,324	98,131	Nixon, Richard M.	69,186	Kennedy, John F.	7	28,945 R	58.6%	41.3%	58.6%	41.4%
1956	152,978	110,390	Eisenhower, Dwight D.	42,549	Stevenson, Adlai E.	39	67,841 R	72.2%	27.8%	72.2%	27.8%
1952	153,557	109,717	Eisenhower, Dwight D.	43,355	Stevenson, Adlai E.	485	66,362 R	71.5%	28.2%	71.7%	28.3%
1948	123,382	75,926	Dewey, Thomas E.	45,557	Truman, Harry S.	1,899	30,369 R	61.5%	36.9%	62.5%	37.5%

** In past elections, the other vote included: 2000 - 20,374 Green (Ralph Nader); 1996 - 31,024 Reform (Ross Perot); 1992 - 65,991 Independent (Perot); 1980 - 31,761 Independent (John Anderson); 1968 - 5,104 American Independent (George Wallace).

VERMONT

POSTWAR VOTE FOR GOVERNOR

Year	Total Vote	Republican Vote	Republican Candidate	Democratic Vote	Democratic Candidate	Other Vote	Rep.-Dem. Plurality	Percentage Total Vote Rep.	Percentage Total Vote Dem.	Percentage Major Vote Rep.	Percentage Major Vote Dem.
2010**	241,605	115,212	Dubie, Brian E.	119,543	Shumlin, Peter	6,850	4,331 D	47.7%	49.5%	49.1%	50.9%
2008**	319,085	170,492	Douglas, Jim	69,534	Symington, Gaye	79,059	100,701 R	53.4%	21.8%	71.0%	29.0%
2006	262,524	148,014	Douglas, Jim	108,090	Parker, Scudder	6,420	39,924 R	56.4%	41.2%	57.8%	42.2%
2004	309,285	181,540	Douglas, Jim	117,327	Clavelle, Peter	10,418	64,213 R	58.7%	37.9%	60.7%	39.3%
2002**	230,161	103,436	Douglas, Jim	97,565	Racine, Doug	29,160	5,871 R	44.9%	42.4%	51.5%	48.5%
2000	293,473	111,359	Dwyer, Ruth	148,059	Dean, Howard B.	34,055	36,700 D	37.9%	50.5%	42.9%	57.1%
1998	218,120	89,726	Dwyer, Ruth	121,425	Dean, Howard B.	6,969	31,699 D	41.1%	55.7%	42.5%	57.5%
1996	254,648	57,161	Gropper, John L.	179,544	Dean, Howard B.	17,943	122,383 D	22.4%	70.5%	24.1%	75.9%
1994	212,046	40,292	Kelley, David F.	145,661	Dean, Howard B.	26,093	105,369 D	19.0%	68.7%	21.7%	78.3%
1992	285,728	65,837	McClaughry, John	213,523	Dean, Howard B.	6,368	147,686 D	23.0%	74.7%	23.6%	76.4%
1990	211,422	109,540	Snelling, Richard A.	97,321	Welch, Peter	4,561	12,219 R	51.8%	46.0%	53.0%	47.0%
1988	243,130	105,319	Bernhardt, Michael	134,594	Kunin, Madeleine M.	3,253	29,275 D	43.3%	55.4%	43.9%	56.1%
1986**	196,716	75,162	Smith, Peter	92,379	Kunin, Madeleine M.	29,175	17,217 D	38.2%	47.0%	44.9%	55.1%
1984	233,753	113,264	Easton, John J.	116,938	Kunin, Madeleine M.	3,551	3,674 D	48.5%	50.0%	49.2%	50.8%
1982	169,251	93,111	Snelling, Richard A.	74,394	Kunin, Madeleine M.	1,746	18,717 R	55.0%	44.0%	55.6%	44.4%
1980	210,381	123,229	Snelling, Richard A.	77,363	Diamond, J. Jerome	9,789	45,866 R	58.6%	36.8%	61.4%	38.6%
1978	124,482	78,181	Snelling, Richard A.	42,482	Granai, Edwin C.	3,819	35,699 R	62.8%	34.1%	64.8%	35.2%
1976	185,929	99,268	Snelling, Richard A.	75,262	Hackel, Stella B.	11,399	24,006 R	53.4%	40.5%	56.9%	43.1%
1974	141,156	53,672	Kennedy, Walter L.	79,842	Salmon, Thomas P.	7,642	26,170 D	38.0%	56.6%	40.2%	59.8%
1972	189,237	82,491	Hackett, Luther F.	104,533	Salmon, Thomas P.	2,213	22,042 D	43.6%	55.2%	44.1%	55.9%
1970	153,528	87,458	Davis, Deane C.	66,028	O'Brien, Leo	42	21,430 R	57.0%	43.0%	57.0%	43.0%
1968	161,089	89,387	Davis, Deane C.	71,656	Daley, John J.	46	17,731 R	55.5%	44.5%	55.5%	44.5%
1966	136,262	57,577	Snelling, Richard A.	78,669	Hoff, Philip H.	16	21,092 D	42.3%	57.7%	42.3%	57.7%
1964	164,199	57,576	Foote, Ralph A.	106,611	Hoff, Philip H.	12	49,035 D	35.1%	64.9%	35.1%	64.9%
1962	121,422	60,035	Keyser, F. Ray	61,383	Hoff, Philip H.	4	1,348 D	49.4%	50.6%	49.4%	50.6%
1960	164,632	92,861	Keyser, F. Ray	71,755	Niquette, Russell F.	16	21,106 R	56.4%	43.6%	56.4%	43.6%
1958	123,728	62,222	Stafford, Robert T.	61,503	Leddy, Bernard J.	3	719 R	50.3%	49.7%	50.3%	49.7%
1956	153,809	88,379	Johnson, Joseph B.	65,420	Branon, E. Frank	10	22,959 R	57.5%	42.5%	57.5%	42.5%
1954	114,360	59,778	Johnson, Joseph B.	54,554	Branon, E. Frank	28	5,224 R	52.3%	47.7%	52.3%	47.7%
1952	150,862	78,338	Emerson, Lee E.	60,051	Larrow, Robert W.	12,473	18,287 R	51.9%	39.8%	56.6%	43.4%
1950	87,155	64,915	Emerson, Lee E.	22,227	Moran, J. Edward	13	42,688 R	74.5%	25.5%	74.5%	25.5%
1948	120,183	86,394	Gibson, Ernest W., Jr.	33,588	Ryan, Charles F.	201	52,806 R	71.9%	27.9%	72.0%	28.0%
1946	72,044	57,849	Gibson, Ernest W., Jr.	14,096	Coburn, Berthold	99	43,753 R	80.3%	19.6%	80.4%	19.6%

** In past elections, the other vote included: 2008 - 69,791 Independent (Anthony Pollina), who finished second; 1986 - 28,430 Independent (Bernard Sanders). In 1986, 2002, and 2010, in the absence of a majority of the total vote for any candidate, the State Legislature elected the governor—Democrat Madeleine M. Kunin in January 1987, Republican Jim Douglas in January 2003, and Democrat Peter Shumlin in January 2011.

VERMONT

POSTWAR VOTE FOR SENATOR

Year	Total Vote	Republican		Democratic		Other Vote	Plurality	Percentage			
								Total Vote		Major Vote	
		Vote	Candidate	Vote	Candidate			Rep.	Dem.	Rep.	Dem.
2010	235,178	72,699	Britton, Len	151,281	Leahy, Patrick J.	11,198	78,582 D	30.9%	64.3%	32.5%	67.5%
2006**	262,419	84,924	Tarrant, Rich	—		177,495	86,714 I	32.4%		100.0%	
2004	307,208	75,398	McMullen, Jack	216,972	Leahy, Patrick J.	14,838	141,574 D	24.5%	70.6%	25.8%	74.2%
2000	288,500	189,133	Jeffords, James M.	73,352	Flanagan, Ed	26,015	115,781 R	65.6%	25.4%	72.1%	27.9%
1998	214,036	48,051	Tuttle, Fred H.	154,567	Leahy, Patrick J.	11,418	106,516 D	22.4%	72.2%	23.7%	76.3%
1994	211,672	106,505	Jeffords, James M.	85,868	Backus, Jan	19,299	20,637 R	50.3%	40.6%	55.4%	44.6%
1992	285,739	123,854	Douglas, Jim	154,762	Leahy, Patrick J.	7,123	30,908 D	43.3%	54.2%	44.5%	55.5%
1988	240,111	163,203	Jeffords, James M.	71,469	Gray, William	5,439	91,736 R	68.0%	29.8%	69.5%	30.5%
1986	196,532	67,798	Snelling, Richard A.	124,123	Leahy, Patrick J.	4,611	56,325 D	34.5%	63.2%	35.3%	64.7%
1982	168,003	84,450	Stafford, Robert T.	79,340	Guest, James A.	4,213	5,110 R	50.3%	47.2%	51.6%	48.4%
1980	209,124	101,421	Ledbetter, Stewart M.	104,176	Leahy, Patrick J.	3,527	2,755 D	48.5%	49.8%	49.3%	50.7%
1976	189,060	94,481	Stafford, Robert T.	85,682	Salmon, Thomas P.	8,897	8,799 R	50.0%	45.3%	52.4%	47.6%
1974	142,772	66,223	Mallary, Richard W.	70,629	Leahy, Patrick J.	5,920	4,406 D	46.4%	49.5%	48.4%	51.6%
1972S	71,348	45,888	Stafford, Robert T.	23,842	Major, Randolph T.	1,618	22,046 R	64.3%	33.4%	65.8%	34.2%
1970	154,899	91,198	Prouty, Winston L.	62,271	Hoff, Philip H.	1,430	28,927 R	58.9%	40.2%	59.4%	40.6%
1968**	157,375	157,154	Aiken, George D.		—	221	157,154 R	99.9%		100.0%	
1964	164,350	87,879	Prouty, Winston L.	76,457	Fayette, Frederick J.	14	11,422 R	53.5%	46.5%	53.5%	46.5%
1962	121,571	81,241	Aiken, George D.	40,134	Johnson, W. Robert	196	41,107 R	66.8%	33.0%	66.9%	33.1%
1958	124,442	64,900	Prouty, Winston L.	59,536	Fayette, Frederick J.	6	5,364 R	52.2%	47.8%	52.2%	47.8%
1956	155,289	103,101	Aiken, George D.	52,184	O'Shea, Bernard G.	4	50,917 R	66.4%	33.6%	66.4%	33.6%
1952	154,052	111,406	Flanders, Ralph E.	42,630	Johnston, Allan R.	16	68,776 R	72.3%	27.7%	72.3%	27.7%
1950	89,171	69,543	Aiken, George D.	19,608	Bigelow, James E.	20	49,935 R	78.0%	22.0%	78.0%	22.0%
1946	73,340	54,729	Flanders, Ralph E.	18,594	McDevitt, Charles P.	17	36,135 R	74.6%	25.4%	74.6%	25.4%

** In past elections, the other vote included: 2006 - 171,638 Independent (Bernard Sanders), who received 65.4 percent of the total vote and was elected. Sanders also won the Democratic primary in 2006, but declined the nomination in order to run as an independent. The January 1972 election was for a short term to fill a vacancy. In 1968 the Republican candidate won both major party nominations.

VERMONT

GOVERNOR 2010

2010 Census Population	County	Total Vote	Republican	Democratic	Other	Rep.-Dem. Plurality	Percentage Total Vote Rep.	Dem.	Major Vote Rep.	Dem.
36,821	ADDISON	15,238	7,129	7,739	370	610 D	46.8%	50.8%	47.9%	52.1%
37,125	BENNINGTON	13,846	5,700	7,662	484	1,962 D	41.2%	55.3%	42.7%	57.3%
31,227	CALEDONIA	11,154	6,392	4,353	409	2,039 R	57.3%	39.0%	59.5%	40.5%
156,545	CHITTENDEN	61,546	28,050	32,280	1,216	4,230 D	45.6%	52.4%	46.5%	53.5%
6,306	ESSEX	2,317	1,413	797	107	616 R	61.0%	34.4%	63.9%	36.1%
47,746	FRANKLIN	16,290	9,840	5,999	451	3,841 R	60.4%	36.8%	62.1%	37.9%
6,970	GRAND ISLE	3,493	1,906	1,495	92	411 R	54.6%	42.8%	56.0%	44.0%
24,475	LAMOILLE	9,593	4,755	4,564	274	191 R	49.6%	47.6%	51.0%	49.0%
28,936	ORANGE	11,468	5,412	5,678	378	266 D	47.2%	49.5%	48.8%	51.2%
27,231	ORLEANS	9,434	5,235	3,874	325	1,361 R	55.5%	41.1%	57.5%	42.5%
61,642	RUTLAND	22,804	12,583	9,483	738	3,100 R	55.2%	41.6%	57.0%	43.0%
59,534	WASHINGTON	25,006	10,973	13,275	758	2,302 D	43.9%	53.1%	45.3%	54.7%
44,513	WINDHAM	17,235	6,278	10,442	515	4,164 D	36.4%	60.6%	37.5%	62.5%
56,670	WINDSOR	22,181	9,546	11,902	733	2,356 D	43.0%	53.7%	44.5%	55.5%
625,741	TOTAL	241,605	115,212	119,543	6,850	4,331 D	47.7%	49.5%	49.1%	50.9%

2010 Census Population	City/Town	Total Vote	Republican	Democratic	Other	Rep.-Dem. Plurality	Percentage Total Vote Rep.	Dem.	Major Vote Rep.	Dem.
9,052	BARRE CITY	2,693	1,431	1,168	94	263 R	53.1%	43.4%	55.1%	44.9%
7,924	BARRE TOWN	3,349	2,145	1,090	114	1,055 R	64.0%	32.5%	66.3%	33.7%
15,764	BENNINGTON	5,175	1,870	3,092	213	1,222 D	36.1%	59.7%	37.7%	62.3%
12,046	BRATTLEBORO	4,356	1,172	3,073	111	1,901 D	26.9%	70.5%	27.6%	72.4%
42,417	BURLINGTON	12,993	3,539	9,129	325	5,590 D	27.2%	70.3%	27.9%	72.1%
17,067	COLCHESTER	5,869	3,278	2,491	100	787 R	55.9%	42.4%	56.8%	43.2%
4,621	DERBY	1,761	1,041	660	60	381 R	59.1%	37.5%	61.2%	38.8%
19,587	ESSEX	8,511	4,928	3,421	162	1,507 R	57.9%	40.2%	59.0%	41.0%
9,952	HARTFORD	3,314	1,427	1,797	90	370 D	43.1%	54.2%	44.3%	55.7%
5,009	JERICHO	2,587	1,230	1,312	45	82 D	47.5%	50.7%	48.4%	51.6%
5,981	LYNDON	1,667	1,076	526	65	550 R	64.5%	31.6%	67.2%	32.8%
4,391	MANCHESTER	1,697	868	792	37	76 R	51.1%	46.7%	52.3%	47.7%
8,496	MIDDLEBURY	2,703	895	1,757	51	862 D	33.1%	65.0%	33.7%	66.3%
10,352	MILTON	3,719	2,377	1,263	79	1,114 R	63.9%	34.0%	65.3%	34.7%
7,855	MONTPELIER	3,893	994	2,812	87	1,818 D	25.5%	72.2%	26.1%	73.9%
5,227	MORRISTOWN	2,070	1,023	975	72	48 R	49.4%	47.1%	51.2%	48.8%
6,207	NORTHFIELD	1,697	907	729	61	178 R	53.4%	43.0%	55.4%	44.6%
4,778	RANDOLPH	1,818	855	895	68	40 D	47.0%	49.2%	48.9%	51.1%
4,081	RICHMOND	2,012	846	1,120	46	274 D	42.0%	55.7%	43.0%	57.0%
5,282	ROCKINGHAM	1,677	574	1,024	79	450 D	34.2%	61.1%	35.9%	64.1%
16,495	RUTLAND CITY	5,519	2,890	2,462	167	428 R	52.4%	44.6%	54.0%	46.0%
4,054	RUTLAND TOWN	1,937	1,215	674	48	541 R	62.7%	34.8%	64.3%	35.7%
7,144	SHELBURNE	3,781	1,703	2,028	50	325 D	45.0%	53.6%	45.6%	54.4%
17,904	SOUTH BURLINGTON	7,583	3,463	3,967	153	504 D	45.7%	52.3%	46.6%	53.4%
9,373	SPRINGFIELD	2,857	1,394	1,343	120	51 R	48.8%	47.0%	50.9%	49.1%
6,918	ST. ALBANS CITY	1,959	1,058	843	58	215 R	54.0%	43.0%	55.7%	44.3%
5,999	ST. ALBANS TOWN	2,271	1,482	736	53	746 R	65.3%	32.4%	66.8%	33.2%
7,603	ST. JOHNSBURY	2,362	1,404	871	87	533 R	59.4%	36.9%	61.7%	38.3%
4,314	STOWE	2,024	1,077	900	47	177 R	53.2%	44.5%	54.5%	45.5%
6,427	SWANTON	1,998	1,280	672	46	608 R	64.1%	33.6%	65.6%	34.4%
5,064	WATERBURY	2,230	978	1,197	55	219 D	43.9%	53.7%	45.0%	55.0%
8,698	WILLISTON	4,202	2,214	1,916	72	298 R	52.7%	45.6%	53.6%	46.4%
7,267	WINOOSKI	1,881	758	1,078	45	320 D	40.3%	57.3%	41.3%	58.7%
3,048	WOODSTOCK	1,522	603	884	35	281 D	39.6%	58.1%	40.6%	59.4%

VERMONT

SENATOR 2010

2010 Census Population	County	Total Vote	Republican	Democratic	Other	Rep.-Dem. Plurality	Percentage			
							Total Vote		Major Vote	
							Rep.	Dem.	Rep.	Dem.
36,821	ADDISON	14,883	4,397	9,904	582	5,507 D	29.5%	66.5%	30.7%	69.3%
37,125	BENNINGTON	13,486	3,873	8,517	1,096	4,644 D	28.7%	63.2%	31.3%	68.7%
31,227	CALEDONIA	10,811	4,247	6,058	506	1,811 D	39.3%	56.0%	41.2%	58.8%
156,545	CHITTENDEN	59,867	16,716	40,837	2,314	24,121 D	27.9%	68.2%	29.0%	71.0%
6,306	ESSEX	2,253	939	1,173	141	234 D	41.7%	52.1%	44.5%	55.5%
47,746	FRANKLIN	15,904	5,582	9,629	693	4,047 D	35.1%	60.5%	36.7%	63.3%
6,970	GRAND ISLE	3,442	1,159	2,083	200	924 D	33.7%	60.5%	35.7%	64.3%
24,475	LAMOILLE	9,397	2,844	6,205	348	3,361 D	30.3%	66.0%	31.4%	68.6%
28,936	ORANGE	11,142	3,777	6,894	471	3,117 D	33.9%	61.9%	35.4%	64.6%
27,231	ORLEANS	9,148	3,176	5,517	455	2,341 D	34.7%	60.3%	36.5%	63.5%
61,642	RUTLAND	22,156	8,808	12,265	1,083	3,457 D	39.8%	55.4%	41.8%	58.2%
59,534	WASHINGTON	24,312	6,541	16,682	1,089	10,141 D	26.9%	68.6%	28.2%	71.8%
44,513	WINDHAM	16,715	3,931	11,587	1,197	7,656 D	23.5%	69.3%	25.3%	74.7%
56,670	WINDSOR	21,662	6,709	13,930	1,023	7,221 D	31.0%	64.3%	32.5%	67.5%
625,741	TOTAL	235,178	72,699	151,281	11,198	78,582 D	30.9%	64.3%	32.5%	67.5%

2010 Census Population	City/Town	Total Vote	Republican	Democratic	Other	Rep.-Dem. Plurality	Percentage			
							Total Vote		Major Vote	
							Rep.	Dem.	Rep.	Dem.
9,052	BARRE CITY	2,642	860	1,636	146	776 D	32.6%	61.9%	34.5%	65.5%
7,924	BARRE TOWN	3,250	1,348	1,794	108	446 D	41.5%	55.2%	42.9%	57.1%
15,764	BENNINGTON	5,021	1,092	3,446	483	2,354 D	21.7%	68.6%	24.1%	75.9%
12,046	BRATTLEBORO	4,215	669	3,270	276	2,601 D	15.9%	77.6%	17.0%	83.0%
42,417	BURLINGTON	12,560	1,960	9,891	709	7,931 D	15.6%	78.8%	16.5%	83.5%
17,067	COLCHESTER	5,771	1,867	3,713	191	1,846 D	32.4%	64.3%	33.5%	66.5%
4,621	DERBY	1,719	626	1,016	77	390 D	36.4%	59.1%	38.1%	61.9%
19,587	ESSEX	8,271	2,969	5,092	210	2,123 D	35.9%	61.6%	36.8%	63.2%
9,952	HARTFORD	3,232	999	2,105	128	1,106 D	30.9%	65.1%	32.2%	67.8%
5,009	JERICHO	2,540	835	1,620	85	785 D	32.9%	63.8%	34.0%	66.0%
5,981	LYNDON	1,619	706	832	81	126 D	43.6%	51.4%	45.9%	54.1%
4,391	MANCHESTER	1,658	666	904	88	238 D	40.2%	54.5%	42.4%	57.6%
8,496	MIDDLEBURY	2,666	560	2,002	104	1,442 D	21.0%	75.1%	21.9%	78.1%
10,352	MILTON	3,635	1,467	2,022	146	555 D	40.4%	55.6%	42.0%	58.0%
7,855	MONTPELIER	3,767	566	3,024	177	2,458 D	15.0%	80.3%	15.8%	84.2%
5,227	MORRISTOWN	2,032	599	1,344	89	745 D	29.5%	66.1%	30.8%	69.2%
6,207	NORTHFIELD	1,660	512	1,072	76	560 D	30.8%	64.6%	32.3%	67.7%
4,778	RANDOLPH	1,778	550	1,158	70	608 D	30.9%	65.1%	32.2%	67.8%
4,081	RICHMOND	1,952	512	1,381	59	869 D	26.2%	70.7%	27.0%	73.0%
5,282	ROCKINGHAM	1,626	344	1,157	125	813 D	21.2%	71.2%	22.9%	77.1%
16,495	RUTLAND CITY	5,342	1,928	3,149	265	1,221 D	36.1%	58.9%	38.0%	62.0%
4,054	RUTLAND TOWN	1,863	874	930	59	56 D	46.9%	49.9%	48.4%	51.6%
7,144	SHELBURNE	3,683	1,048	2,506	129	1,458 D	28.5%	68.0%	29.5%	70.5%
17,904	SOUTH BURLINGTON	7,391	2,102	5,009	280	2,907 D	28.4%	67.8%	29.6%	70.4%
9,373	SPRINGFIELD	2,792	950	1,662	180	712 D	34.0%	59.5%	36.4%	63.6%
6,918	ST. ALBANS CITY	1,904	540	1,272	92	732 D	28.4%	66.8%	29.8%	70.2%
5,999	ST. ALBANS TOWN	2,232	803	1,340	89	537 D	36.0%	60.0%	37.5%	62.5%
7,603	ST. JOHNSBURY	2,334	935	1,302	97	367 D	40.1%	55.8%	41.8%	58.2%
4,314	STOWE	1,983	650	1,263	70	613 D	32.8%	63.7%	34.0%	66.0%
6,427	SWANTON	1,953	748	1,139	66	391 D	38.3%	58.3%	39.6%	60.4%
5,064	WATERBURY	2,192	511	1,615	66	1,104 D	23.3%	73.7%	24.0%	76.0%
8,698	WILLISTON	4,087	1,324	2,646	117	1,322 D	32.4%	64.7%	33.4%	66.6%
7,267	WINOOSKI	1,838	399	1,338	101	939 D	21.7%	72.8%	23.0%	77.0%
3,048	WOODSTOCK	1,499	447	992	60	545 D	29.8%	66.2%	31.1%	68.9%

VERMONT

HOUSE OF REPRESENTATIVES

| | | | Republican | | Democratic | | | | Percentage | | | |
| | | | | | | | | | Total Vote | | Major Vote | |
CD	Year	Total Vote	Vote	Candidate	Vote	Candidate	Other Vote	Plurality**	Rep.	Dem.	Rep.	Dem.
AL	2010	238,521	76,403	BEAUDRY, PAUL D.	154,006	WELCH, PETER*	8,112	77,603 D	32.0%	64.6%	33.2%	66.8%
AL	2008	298,151	—		248,203	WELCH, PETER*	49,948	248,203 D		83.2%		100.0%
AL	2006	262,726	117,023	RAINVILLE, MARTHA	139,815	WELCH, PETER	5,888	22,792 D	44.5%	53.2%	45.6%	54.4%
AL	2004	305,008	74,271	PARKE, GREG	21,684	DROWN, LARRY	209,053	131,503 I	24.4%	67.5% (I)		
AL	2002	225,476	72,813	MEUB, WILLIAM "BILL"	—		152,663	72,067 I	32.3%	64.3% (I)		
AL	2000	283,366	51,977	KERIN, KAREN ANN	14,918	DIAMONDSTONE, PETE	216,471	144,141 I	18.3%	69.2% (I)		
AL	1998	215,133	70,740	CANDON, MARK	—		144,393	65,663 I	32.9%	63.4% (I)		
AL	1996	254,706	83,021	SWEETSER, SUSAN W.	23,830	LONG, JACK	147,855	57,657 I	32.6%	55.2% (I)		
AL	1994	211,449	98,523	CARROLL, JOHN	—		112,926	6,979 I	46.6%	49.9% (I)		
AL	1992	281,626	86,901	PHILBIN, TIMOTHY	22,279	YOUNG, LEWIS E.	172,446	75,823 I	30.9%	57.8% (I)		
AL	1990	209,856	82,938	SMITH, PETER*	6,315	SANDOVAL, DOLORES	120,603	34,584 I	39.5%	56.0% (I)		
AL	1988	240,131	98,937	SMITH, PETER	45,330	POIRIER, PAUL N.	95,864	8,911 R	41.2%	37.5% (I)	68.6%	31.4%
AL	1986	188,954	168,403	JEFFORDS, JAMES M.*	—		20,551	168,403 R	89.1%		100.0%	
AL	1984	226,297	148,025	JEFFORDS, JAMES M.*	60,360	POLLINA, ANTHONY	17,912	87,665 R	65.4%	26.7%	71.0%	29.0%
AL	1982	164,951	114,191	JEFFORDS, JAMES M.*	38,296	KAPLAN, MARK A.	12,464	75,895 R	69.2%	23.2%	74.9%	25.1%
AL	1980	194,697	154,274	JEFFORDS, JAMES M.*	—		40,423	154,274 R	79.2%		100.0%	
AL	1978	120,502	90,688	JEFFORDS, JAMES M.*	23,228	DIETZ, S. MARIE	6,586	67,460 R	75.3%	19.3%	79.6%	20.4%
AL	1976	184,783	124,458	JEFFORDS, JAMES M.*	60,202	BURGESS, JOHN A.	123	64,256 R	67.4%	32.6%	67.4%	32.6%
AL	1974	140,899	74,561	JEFFORDS, JAMES M.	56,342	CAIN, FRANCIS J.	9,996	18,219 R	52.9%	40.0%	57.0%	43.0%
AL	1972	186,028	120,924	MALLARY, RICHARD W.	65,062	MEYER, WILLIAM H.	42	55,862 R	65.0%	35.0%	65.0%	35.0%
AL	1970	152,557	103,806	STAFFORD, ROBERT T.*	44,415	O'SHEA, BERNARD G.	4,336	59,391 R	68.0%	29.1%	70.0%	30.0%
AL	1968	157,133	156,956	STAFFORD, ROBERT T.*	—		177	156,956 R	99.9%		100.0%	
AL	1966	135,748	89,097	STAFFORD, ROBERT T.*	46,643	RYAN, WILLIAM J.	8	42,454 R	65.6%	34.4%	65.6%	34.4%
AL	1964	163,452	92,252	STAFFORD, ROBERT T.*	71,193	O'SHEA, BERNARD G.	7	21,059 R	56.4%	43.6%	56.4%	43.6%
AL	1962	121,381	68,822	STAFFORD, ROBERT T.*	52,535	RAYNOLDS, HAROLD	24	16,287 R	56.7%	43.3%	56.7%	43.3%
AL	1960	166,035	94,905	STAFFORD, ROBERT T.	71,111	MEYER, WILLIAM H.	19	23,794 R	57.2%	42.8%	57.2%	42.8%
AL	1958	122,702	59,536	ARTHUR, HAROLD J.	63,131	MEYER, WILLIAM H.	35	3,595 D	48.5%	51.5%	48.5%	51.5%
AL	1956	154,536	103,736	PROUTY, WINSTON L.*	50,797	ST. AMOUR, CAMILLE	3	52,939 R	67.1%	32.9%	67.1%	32.9%
AL	1954	114,289	70,143	PROUTY, WINSTON L.*	44,141	BAYLAN, JOHN J.	5	26,002 R	61.4%	38.6%	61.4%	38.6%
AL	1952	153,060	109,871	PROUTY, WINSTON L.*	43,187	COMINGS, HERBERT B.	2	66,684 R	71.8%	28.2%	71.8%	28.2%
AL	1950	88,851	65,248	PROUTY, WINSTON L.	22,709	COMINGS, HERBERT B.	894	42,539 R	73.4%	25.6%	74.2%	25.8%
AL	1948	121,968	74,076	PLUMLEY, CHARLES A.*	47,767	READY, ROBERT W.	125	26,309 R	60.7%	39.2%	60.8%	39.2%
AL	1946	73,066	46,985	PLUMLEY, CHARLES A.*	26,056	CALDBECK, MATTHEW J.	25	20,929 R	64.3%	35.7%	64.3%	35.7%

An asterisk (*) denotes incumbent. Seat was won in 1990, 1992, 1994, 1996, 1998, 2000, 2002 and 2004 by Bernard Sanders, an independent. Sanders also finished second in 1988. "Other Vote" for those years includes the total for Sanders and other independent and third party candidates. A double asterisk (**) indicates the plurality and percentage of Total Vote figures from 1988 through 2004 compare the vote for the Republican candidate and Sanders, whose percentage is indicated with an (I). For other years, the plurality reflects the difference between the vote for the Republican and Democratic candidates. A pound sign (#) indicates that a candidate received the nomination of another party. Democratic candidates from 1988 through 2004 received the following shares of the total vote: 2004 - Larry Drown, 7.1 percent; 2000 - Pete Diamondstone, 5.3 percent; 1996 - Jack Long, 9.4 percent; 1992 - Lewis E. Young, 7.9 percent; 1990 - Dolores Sandoval, 3.0 percent; 1988 - Paul N. Poirier, 18.9 percent.

VERMONT

GENERAL AND PRIMARY ELECTIONS

2010 GENERAL ELECTIONS

Governor   Other vote was 1,917 Independent (Dennis Steele); 1,819 United States Marijuana (Cris Ericson); 1,341 Independent (Dan Feliciano); 684 Independent (Em Peyton); 429 Liberty Union (Ben Mitchell); 660 scattered write-in. (Democrat Peter Shumlin was also backed by the Working Families Party.)

Senator   Other vote was 3,544 Independent (Daniel Freilich); 2,731 United States Marijuana (Cris Ericson); 2,356 Independent (Stephen J. Cain); 1,433 Socialist (Pete Diamondstone); 1,021 Independent (Johenry Nunes); 113 scattered write-in.

House   Other vote was:

   At Large   4,704 Independent (Gus Jaccaci); 3,222 Socialist (Jane Newton); 186 scattered write-in.

2010 PRIMARY ELECTIONS

Primary	August 24, 2010	**Registration** (as of August 24, 2010)	442,783	No Party Registration

Primary Type   Open—Any registered voter could participate in the primary of any recognized party.

	REPUBLICAN PRIMARIES			**DEMOCRATIC PRIMARIES**		
Governor	Brian E. Dubie	28,452	98.6%	Peter Shumlin	18,276	24.8%
	Scattered write-in	416	1.4%	Doug Racine	18,079	24.6%
				Deb Markowitz	17,579	23.9%
				Matt Dunne	15,323	20.8%
				Susan Bartlett	3,759	5.1%
				Scattered write-in	560	0.8%
	TOTAL	*28,868*		*TOTAL*	*73,576*	
Senator	Len Britton	22,750	95.1%	Patrick J. Leahy*	64,515	88.9%
	Scattered write-in	1,176	4.9%	Daniel Freilich	7,892	10.9%
				Scattered write-in	175	0.2%
	TOTAL	*23,926*		*TOTAL*	*72,582*	
House **At Large**	Paul D. Beaudry	10,797	43.8%	Peter Welch*	65,920	98.6%
	John M. Mitchell	9,631	39.1%	Scattered write-in	913	1.4%
	Keith Stern	3,545	14.4%			
	Scattered write-in	659	2.7%			
	TOTAL	*24,632*		*TOTAL*	*66,833*	

An asterisk (*) denotes incumbent.

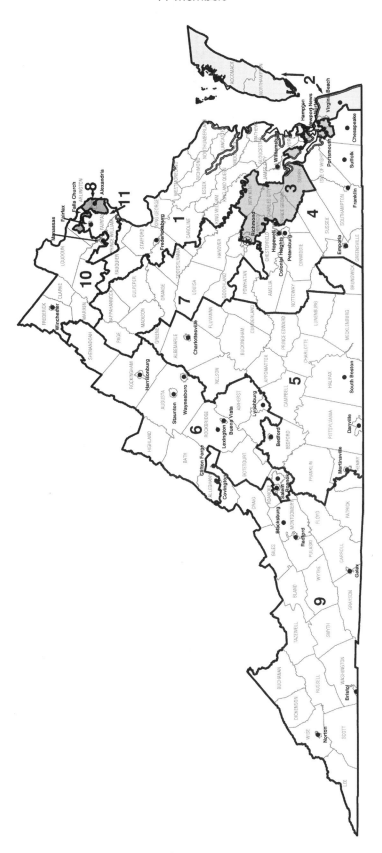

VIRGINIA

Congressional districts first established for elections held in 2002
11 members

VIRGINIA

Northern Virginia Area

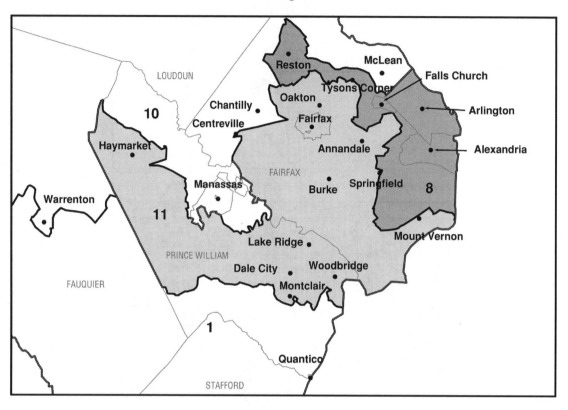

Hampton Roads, Virginia Beach Area

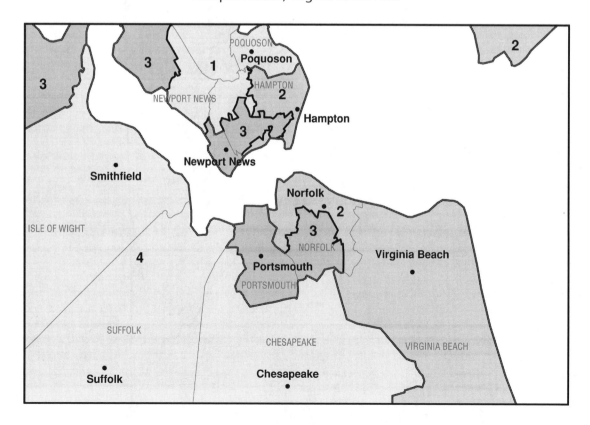

VIRGINIA

GOVERNOR
Robert F. McDonnell (R). Elected 2009 to a four-year term.

SENATORS (2 Democrats)
Mark R. Warner (D). Elected 2008 to a six-year term.

James Webb (D). Elected 2006 to a six-year term.

REPRESENTATIVES (8 Republicans, 3 Democrats)

1. Robert J. Wittman (R)
2. E. Scott Rigell (R)
3. Robert C. Scott (D)
4. J. Randy Forbes (R)
5. Robert Hurt (R)
6. Robert W. Goodlatte (R)
7. Eric Cantor (R)
8. James P. Moran (D)
9. H. Morgan Griffith (R)
10. Frank R. Wolf (R)
11. Gerald E. Connolly (D)

POSTWAR VOTE FOR PRESIDENT

Year	Total Vote	Republican Vote	Republican Candidate	Democratic Vote	Democratic Candidate	Other Vote	Rep.-Dem. Plurality	Total Vote Rep.	Total Vote Dem.	Major Vote Rep.	Major Vote Dem.
2008	3,723,260	1,725,005	McCain, John	1,959,532	Obama, Barack	38,723	234,527 D	46.3%	52.6%	46.8%	53.2%
2004	3,198,367	1,716,959	Bush, George W.	1,454,742	Kerry, John	26,666	262,217 R	53.7%	45.5%	54.1%	45.9%
2000**	2,739,447	1,437,490	Bush, George W.	1,217,290	Gore, Al	84,667	220,200 R	52.5%	44.4%	54.1%	45.9%
1996**	2,416,642	1,138,350	Dole, Bob	1,091,060	Clinton, Bill	187,232	47,290 R	47.1%	45.1%	51.1%	48.9%
1992**	2,558,665	1,150,517	Bush, George	1,038,650	Clinton, Bill	369,498	111,867 R	45.0%	40.6%	52.6%	47.4%
1988	2,191,609	1,309,162	Bush, George	859,799	Dukakis, Michael S.	22,648	449,363 R	59.7%	39.2%	60.4%	39.6%
1984	2,146,635	1,337,078	Reagan, Ronald	796,250	Mondale, Walter F.	13,307	540,828 R	62.3%	37.1%	62.7%	37.3%
1980**	1,866,032	989,609	Reagan, Ronald	752,174	Carter, Jimmy	124,249	237,435 R	53.0%	40.3%	56.8%	43.2%
1976	1,697,094	836,554	Ford, Gerald R.	813,896	Carter, Jimmy	46,644	22,658 R	49.3%	48.0%	50.7%	49.3%
1972	1,457,019	988,493	Nixon, Richard M.	438,887	McGovern, George S.	29,639	549,606 R	67.8%	30.1%	69.3%	30.7%
1968**	1,361,491	590,319	Nixon, Richard M.	442,387	Humphrey, Hubert H.	328,785	147,932 R	43.4%	32.5%	57.2%	42.8%
1964	1,042,267	481,334	Goldwater, Barry M.	558,038	Johnson, Lyndon B.	2,895	76,704 D	46.2%	53.5%	46.3%	53.7%
1960	771,449	404,521	Nixon, Richard M.	362,327	Kennedy, John F.	4,601	42,194 R	52.4%	47.0%	52.8%	47.2%
1956	697,978	386,459	Eisenhower, Dwight D.	267,760	Stevenson, Adlai E.	43,759	118,699 R	55.4%	38.4%	59.1%	40.9%
1952	619,689	349,037	Eisenhower, Dwight D.	268,677	Stevenson, Adlai E.	1,975	80,360 R	56.3%	43.4%	56.5%	43.5%
1948**	419,256	172,070	Dewey, Thomas E.	200,786	Truman, Harry S.	46,400	28,716 D	41.0%	47.9%	46.1%	53.9%

**In past elections, the other vote included: 2000 - 59,398 Green (Ralph Nader); 1996 - 159,861 Reform (Ross Perot); 1992 - 348,639 Independent (Perot); 1980 - 95,418 Independent (John Anderson); 1968 - 321,833 American Independent (George Wallace); 1948 - 43,393 States' Rights (Strom Thurmond).

VIRGINIA

POSTWAR VOTE FOR GOVERNOR

Year	Total Vote	Republican		Democratic		Other Vote	Rep.-Dem. Plurality	Percentage			
		Vote	Candidate	Vote	Candidate			Total Vote		Major Vote	
								Rep.	Dem.	Rep.	Dem.
2009	1,985,103	1,163,651	McDonnell, Robert F.	818,950	Deeds, R. Creigh	2,502	344,701 R	58.6%	41.3%	58.7%	41.3%
2005	1,983,778	912,327	Kilgore, Jerry W.	1,025,942	Kaine, Timothy M.	45,509	113,615 D	46.0%	51.7%	47.1%	52.9%
2001	1,886,721	887,234	Earley, Mark L.	984,177	Warner, Mark R.	15,310	96,943 D	47.0%	52.2%	47.4%	52.6%
1997	1,736,314	969,062	Gilmore, James S. "Jim," III	738,971	Beyer, Donald S., Jr.	28,281	230,091 R	55.8%	42.6%	56.7%	43.3%
1993	1,793,916	1,045,319	Allen, George	733,527	Terry, Mary Sue	15,070	311,792 R	58.3%	40.9%	58.8%	41.2%
1989	1,789,078	890,195	Coleman, J. Marshall	896,936	Wilder, L. Douglas	1,947	6,741 D	49.8%	50.1%	49.8%	50.2%
1985	1,343,243	601,652	Durrette, Wyatt B.	741,438	Baliles, Gerald L.	153	139,786 D	44.8%	55.2%	44.8%	55.2%
1981	1,420,611	659,398	Coleman, J. Marshall	760,357	Robb, Charles S.	856	100,959 D	46.4%	53.5%	46.4%	53.6%
1977	1,250,940	699,302	Dalton, John	541,319	Howell, Henry	10,319	157,983 R	55.9%	43.3%	56.4%	43.6%
1973**	1,035,495	525,075	Godwin, Mills E.	—		510,420	14,972 R	50.7%		100.0%	
1969	915,764	480,869	Holton, Linwood	415,695	Battle, William C.	19,200	65,174 R	52.5%	45.4%	53.6%	46.4%
1965**	562,789	212,207	Holton, Linwood	269,526	Godwin, Mills E.	81,056	57,319 D	37.7%	47.9%	44.1%	55.9%
1961	394,490	142,567	Pearson, H. Clyde	251,861	Harrison, Albertis	62	109,294 D	36.1%	63.8%	36.1%	63.9%
1957	517,655	188,628	Dalton, Ted	326,921	Almond, J. Lindsay	2,106	138,293 D	36.4%	63.2%	36.6%	63.4%
1953	414,025	183,328	Dalton, Ted	226,998	Stanley, Thomas B.	3,699	43,670 D	44.3%	54.8%	44.7%	55.3%
1949	262,350	71,991	Johnson, Walter	184,772	Battle, John S.	5,587	112,781 D	27.4%	70.4%	28.0%	72.0%
1945	168,783	52,386	Landreth, S. Floyd	112,355	Tuck, William M.	4,042	59,969 D	31.0%	66.6%	31.8%	68.2%

**In past elections, the other vote included: 1973 - 510,103 Independent (Henry Howell); 1965 - 75,307 Conservative (William J. Story Jr.). In 1973 the plurality reflects the difference in the vote for the Republican candidate and Howell. In other elections, the plurality is the difference between the Republican and Democratic vote. The Democratic Party did not run a candidate in the 1973 gubernatorial election.

POSTWAR VOTE FOR SENATOR

Year	Total Vote	Republican		Democratic		Other Vote	Plurality	Percentage			
		Vote	Candidate	Vote	Candidate			Total Vote		Major Vote	
								Rep.	Dem.	Rep.	Dem.
2008	3,643,294	1,228,830	Gilmore, James S. "Jim," III	2,369,327	Warner, Mark R.	45,137	1,140,497 D	33.7%	65.0%	34.2%	65.8%
2006	2,370,445	1,166,277	Allen, George	1,175,606	Webb, James	28,562	9,329 D	49.2%	49.6%	49.8%	50.2%
2002	1,489,422	1,229,894	Warner, John W.	—		259,528	1,229,894 R	82.6%		100.0%	
2000	2,718,301	1,420,460	Allen, George	1,296,093	Robb, Charles S.	1,748	124,367 R	52.3%	47.7%	52.3%	47.7%
1996	2,354,715	1,235,744	Warner, John W.	1,115,982	Warner, Mark R.	2,989	119,762 R	52.5%	47.4%	52.5%	47.5%
1994**	2,057,463	882,213	North, Oliver L.	938,376	Robb, Charles S.	236,874	56,163 D	42.9%	45.6%	48.5%	51.5%
1990**	1,083,690	876,782	Warner, John W.	—		206,908	876,782 R	80.9%		100.0%	
1988	2,068,897	593,652	Dawkins, Maurice A.	1,474,086	Robb, Charles S.	1,159	880,434 D	28.7%	71.2%	28.7%	71.3%
1984	2,007,478	1,406,194	Warner, John W.	601,142	Harrison, Edythe C.	151	805,052 R	70.0%	29.9%	70.1%	29.9%
1982	1,415,622	724,571	Trible, Paul	690,839	Davis, Richard	212	33,732 R	51.2%	48.8%	51.2%	48.8%
1978	1,222,256	613,232	Warner, John W.	608,511	Miller, Andrew P.	513	4,721 R	50.2%	49.8%	50.2%	49.8%
1976**	1,557,500		—	596,009	Zumwalt, Elmo R.	961,491	294,769 I		38.3%		100.0%
1972	1,396,268	718,337	Scott, William L.	643,963	Spong, William B.	33,968	74,374 R	51.4%	46.1%	52.7%	47.3%
1970**	946,751	145,031	Garland, Ray	295,057	Rawlings, George C.	506,663	211,576 I	15.3%	31.2%	33.0%	67.0%
1966	733,879	245,681	Ould, James P.	429,855	Spong, William B.	58,343	184,174 D	33.5%	58.6%	36.4%	63.6%
1966S	729,839	272,804	Traylor, Lawrence M.	389,028	Byrd, Harry Flood, Jr.	68,007	116,224 D	37.4%	53.3%	41.2%	58.8%
1964**	928,363	176,624	May, Richard A.	592,260	Byrd, Harry Flood	159,479	415,636 D	19.0%	63.8%	23.0%	77.0%
1960**	622,820		—	506,169	Robertson, A. Willis	116,651	506,169 D		81.3%		100.0%
1958**	457,640		—	317,221	Byrd, Harry Flood	140,419	317,221 D		69.3%		100.0%
1954**	306,510		—	244,844	Robertson, A. Willis	61,666	244,844 D		79.9%		100.0%
1952**	543,516		—	398,677	Byrd, Harry Flood	144,839	398,677 D		73.4%		100.0%
1948	386,178	118,546	Woods, Robert	253,865	Robertson, A. Willis	13,767	135,319 D	30.7%	65.7%	31.8%	68.2%
1946	252,863	77,005	Parsons, Lester S.	163,960	Byrd, Harry Flood	11,898	86,955 D	30.5%	64.8%	32.0%	68.0%
1946S	248,962	72,253	Woods, Robert	169,680	Robertson, A. Willis	7,029	97,427 D	29.0%	68.2%	29.9%	70.1%

** In past elections, the other vote included: 1994 - 235,324 Independent (J. Marshall Coleman); 1990 - 196,755 Independent (Nancy Spannaus); 1976 - 890,778 Independent (Harry Flood Byrd Jr.), who won the election with 57.2 percent of the total vote; 1970 - 506,633 Independent (Harry Flood Byrd Jr.), who won the election with 53.5 percent of the total vote; 1964 - 95,526 Independent (James W. Respess); 1960 - 88,718 Independent Democrat (Stuart D. Baker); 1958 - 120,224 Independent (Louis Wensel); 1954 - 32,681 Independent Democrat (Charles William Lewis Jr.); 1952 - 69,133 Independent Democrat (H. M. Vise Sr.); 67,281 Social Democrat (Clarke T. Robb). In the 1970 and 1976 elections Byrd's plurality is compared with the Democratic candidate, who in each case finished second. In other elections the plurality is the difference between the Republican and Democratic vote. One each of the 1946 and 1966 elections was for a short term to fill a vacancy. The Democratic Party did not run a candidate in the Senate elections of 1990 and 2002. The Republican Party did not run a candidate in the Senate elections of 1952, 1954, 1958, 1960 and 1976.

VIRGINIA
GOVERNOR 2010

2010 Census Population	County	Total Vote	Republican	Democratic	Other	Rep.-Dem. Plurality	Total Vote Rep.	Dem.	Major Vote Rep.	Dem.
33,164	ACCOMACK	8,651	5,400	3,249	2	2,151 R	62.4%	37.6%	62.4%	37.6%
98,970	ALBEMARLE	31,235	15,767	15,433	35	334 R	50.5%	49.4%	50.5%	49.5%
16,250	ALLEGHANY	5,210	2,017	3,190	3	1,173 D	38.7%	61.2%	38.7%	61.3%
12,690	AMELIA	4,048	2,878	1,168	2	1,710 R	71.1%	28.9%	71.1%	28.9%
32,353	AMHERST	8,807	5,976	2,827	4	3,149 R	67.9%	32.1%	67.9%	32.1%
14,973	APPOMATTOX	4,570	3,397	1,172	1	2,225 R	74.3%	25.6%	74.3%	25.7%
207,627	ARLINGTON	56,415	19,325	36,949	141	17,624 D	34.3%	65.5%	34.3%	65.7%
73,750	AUGUSTA	20,235	15,661	4,558	16	11,103 R	77.4%	22.5%	77.5%	22.5%
4,731	BATH	1,826	666	1,159	1	493 D	36.5%	63.5%	36.5%	63.5%
68,676	BEDFORD COUNTY	21,904	16,881	5,009	14	11,872 R	77.1%	22.9%	77.1%	22.9%
6,824	BLAND	1,837	1,394	442	1	952 R	75.9%	24.1%	75.9%	24.1%
33,148	BOTETOURT	10,842	7,726	3,097	19	4,629 R	71.3%	28.6%	71.4%	28.6%
17,434	BRUNSWICK	4,173	2,107	2,062	4	45 R	50.5%	49.4%	50.5%	49.5%
24,098	BUCHANAN	5,158	3,261	1,895	2	1,366 R	63.2%	36.7%	63.2%	36.8%
17,146	BUCKINGHAM	3,648	2,313	1,335		978 R	63.4%	36.6%	63.4%	36.6%
54,842	CAMPBELL	15,094	11,611	3,457	26	8,154 R	76.9%	22.9%	77.1%	22.9%
28,545	CAROLINE	6,568	3,709	2,855	4	854 R	56.5%	43.5%	56.5%	43.5%
30,042	CARROLL	7,166	5,229	1,932	5	3,297 R	73.0%	27.0%	73.0%	27.0%
7,256	CHARLES CITY	2,151	890	1,259	2	369 D	41.4%	58.5%	41.4%	58.6%
12,586	CHARLOTTE	3,523	2,347	1,171	5	1,176 R	66.6%	33.2%	66.7%	33.3%
316,236	CHESTERFIELD	89,875	59,558	30,161	156	29,397 R	66.3%	33.6%	66.4%	33.6%
14,034	CLARKE	4,334	2,744	1,586	4	1,158 R	63.3%	36.6%	63.4%	36.6%
5,190	CRAIG	1,610	1,091	518	1	573 R	67.8%	32.2%	67.8%	32.2%
46,689	CULPEPER	10,324	7,253	3,057	14	4,196 R	70.3%	29.6%	70.3%	29.7%
10,052	CUMBERLAND	2,696	1,728	967	1	761 R	64.1%	35.9%	64.1%	35.9%
15,903	DICKENSON	3,599	2,176	1,420	3	756 R	60.5%	39.5%	60.5%	39.5%
28,001	DINWIDDIE	7,126	4,461	2,661	4	1,800 R	62.6%	37.3%	62.6%	37.4%
11,151	ESSEX	2,682	1,631	1,051		580 R	60.8%	39.2%	60.8%	39.2%
1,081,726	FAIRFAX COUNTY	273,282	138,655	134,189	438	4,466 R	50.7%	49.1%	50.8%	49.2%
65,203	FAUQUIER	17,898	12,309	5,566	23	6,743 R	68.8%	31.1%	68.9%	31.1%
15,279	FLOYD	4,487	2,951	1,529	7	1,422 R	65.8%	34.1%	65.9%	34.1%
25,691	FLUVANNA	7,651	4,850	2,791	10	2,059 R	63.4%	36.5%	63.5%	36.5%
56,159	FRANKLIN COUNTY	14,951	10,283	4,656	12	5,627 R	68.8%	31.1%	68.8%	31.2%
78,305	FREDERICK	17,755	13,274	4,456	25	8,818 R	74.8%	25.1%	74.9%	25.1%
17,286	GILES	4,603	2,916	1,683	4	1,233 R	63.3%	36.6%	63.4%	36.6%
36,858	GLOUCESTER	11,272	8,126	3,130	16	4,996 R	72.1%	27.8%	72.2%	27.8%
21,717	GOOCHLAND	8,248	5,837	2,401	10	3,436 R	70.8%	29.1%	70.9%	29.1%
15,533	GRAYSON	4,305	3,026	1,279		1,747 R	70.3%	29.7%	70.3%	29.7%
18,403	GREENE	4,845	3,514	1,326	5	2,188 R	72.5%	27.4%	72.6%	27.4%
12,243	GREENSVILLE	2,709	1,283	1,426		143 D	47.4%	52.6%	47.4%	52.6%
36,241	HALIFAX	8,862	5,453	3,390	19	2,063 R	61.5%	38.3%	61.7%	38.3%
99,863	HANOVER	34,627	26,401	8,180	46	18,221 R	76.2%	23.6%	76.3%	23.7%
306,935	HENRICO	87,996	49,462	38,420	114	11,042 R	56.2%	43.7%	56.3%	43.7%
54,151	HENRY	12,952	8,160	4,791	1	3,369 R	63.0%	37.0%	63.0%	37.0%
2,321	HIGHLAND	1,124	619	505		114 R	55.1%	44.9%	55.1%	44.9%
35,270	ISLE OF WIGHT	11,673	7,684	3,981	8	3,703 R	65.8%	34.1%	65.9%	34.1%
67,009	JAMES CITY	23,163	15,193	7,945	25	7,248 R	65.6%	34.3%	65.7%	34.3%
6,945	KING AND QUEEN	1,996	1,175	819	2	356 R	58.9%	41.0%	58.9%	41.1%
23,584	KING GEORGE	5,470	3,839	1,624	7	2,215 R	70.2%	29.7%	70.3%	29.7%
15,935	KING WILLIAM	4,768	3,411	1,354	3	2,057 R	71.5%	28.4%	71.6%	28.4%

VIRGINIA

GOVERNOR 2010

2010 Census Population	County	Total Vote	Republican	Democratic	Other	Rep.-Dem. Plurality	Percentage Total Vote Rep.	Dem.	Major Vote Rep.	Dem.
11,391	LANCASTER	4,724	3,051	1,661	12	1,390 R	64.6%	35.2%	64.7%	35.3%
25,587	LEE	5,056	3,755	1,300	1	2,455 R	74.3%	25.7%	74.3%	25.7%
312,311	LOUDOUN	65,521	39,996	25,430	95	14,566 R	61.0%	38.8%	61.1%	38.9%
33,153	LOUISA	8,743	5,713	3,023	7	2,690 R	65.3%	34.6%	65.4%	34.6%
12,914	LUNENBURG	3,263	2,040	1,222	1	818 R	62.5%	37.5%	62.5%	37.5%
13,308	MADISON	4,163	2,892	1,268	3	1,624 R	69.5%	30.5%	69.5%	30.5%
8,978	MATHEWS	3,561	2,490	1,067	4	1,423 R	69.9%	30.0%	70.0%	30.0%
32,727	MECKLENBURG	7,200	4,872	2,327	1	2,545 R	67.7%	32.3%	67.7%	32.3%
10,959	MIDDLESEX	3,815	2,652	1,161	2	1,491 R	69.5%	30.4%	69.6%	30.4%
94,392	MONTGOMERY	20,868	11,378	9,455	35	1,923 R	54.5%	45.3%	54.6%	45.4%
15,020	NELSON	4,999	2,683	2,311	5	372 R	53.7%	46.2%	53.7%	46.3%
18,429	NEW KENT	6,081	4,526	1,549	6	2,977 R	74.4%	25.5%	74.5%	25.5%
12,389	NORTHAMPTON	3,872	1,976	1,892	4	84 R	51.0%	48.9%	51.1%	48.9%
12,330	NORTHUMBERLAND	4,842	3,167	1,665	10	1,502 R	65.4%	34.4%	65.5%	34.5%
15,853	NOTTOWAY	4,144	2,415	1,723	6	692 R	58.3%	41.6%	58.4%	41.6%
33,481	ORANGE	9,287	6,248	3,033	6	3,215 R	67.3%	32.7%	67.3%	32.7%
24,042	PAGE	7,477	5,245	2,223	9	3,022 R	70.1%	29.7%	70.2%	29.8%
18,490	PATRICK	4,830	3,383	1,442	5	1,941 R	70.0%	29.9%	70.1%	29.9%
63,506	PITTSYLVANIA	16,428	11,739	4,689		7,050 R	71.5%	28.5%	71.5%	28.5%
28,046	POWHATAN	9,126	7,287	1,828	11	5,459 R	79.8%	20.0%	79.9%	20.1%
23,368	PRINCE EDWARD	5,006	2,752	2,250	4	502 R	55.0%	44.9%	55.0%	45.0%
35,725	PRINCE GEORGE	8,487	5,846	2,634	7	3,212 R	68.9%	31.0%	68.9%	31.1%
402,002	PRINCE WILLIAM	74,940	43,993	30,847	100	13,146 R	58.7%	41.2%	58.8%	41.2%
34,872	PULASKI	8,736	5,689	3,044	3	2,645 R	65.1%	34.8%	65.1%	34.9%
7,373	RAPPAHANNOCK	2,884	1,664	1,217	3	447 R	57.7%	42.2%	57.8%	42.2%
9,254	RICHMOND COUNTY	2,234	1,525	708	1	817 R	68.3%	31.7%	68.3%	31.7%
92,376	ROANOKE COUNTY	30,305	20,617	9,643	45	10,974 R	68.0%	31.8%	68.1%	31.9%
22,307	ROCKBRIDGE	6,826	3,964	2,859	3	1,105 R	58.1%	41.9%	58.1%	41.9%
76,314	ROCKINGHAM	21,140	16,519	4,599	22	11,920 R	78.1%	21.8%	78.2%	21.8%
28,897	RUSSELL	7,709	4,812	2,895	2	1,917 R	62.4%	37.6%	62.4%	37.6%
23,177	SCOTT	5,545	4,370	1,172	3	3,198 R	78.8%	21.1%	78.9%	21.1%
41,993	SHENANDOAH	12,196	9,129	3,049	18	6,080 R	74.9%	25.0%	75.0%	25.0%
32,208	SMYTH	7,377	5,424	1,946	7	3,478 R	73.5%	26.4%	73.6%	26.4%
18,570	SOUTHAMPTON	5,005	2,992	2,011	2	981 R	59.8%	40.2%	59.8%	40.2%
122,397	SPOTSYLVANIA	26,087	17,831	8,220	36	9,611 R	68.4%	31.5%	68.4%	31.6%
128,961	STAFFORD	28,436	19,164	9,226	46	9,938 R	67.4%	32.4%	67.5%	32.5%
7,058	SURRY	2,393	1,105	1,283	5	178 D	46.2%	53.6%	46.3%	53.7%
12,087	SUSSEX	2,914	1,528	1,386		142 R	52.4%	47.6%	52.4%	47.6%
45,078	TAZEWELL	10,344	7,588	2,749	7	4,839 R	73.4%	26.6%	73.4%	26.6%
37,575	WARREN	8,171	5,604	2,559	8	3,045 R	68.6%	31.3%	68.7%	31.3%
54,876	WASHINGTON	13,822	10,348	3,469	5	6,879 R	74.9%	25.1%	74.9%	25.1%
17,454	WESTMORELAND	4,135	2,422	1,711	2	711 R	58.6%	41.4%	58.6%	41.4%
41,452	WISE	7,874	5,538	2,327	9	3,211 R	70.3%	29.6%	70.4%	29.6%
29,235	WYTHE	7,779	5,650	2,119	10	3,531 R	72.6%	27.2%	72.7%	27.3%
65,464	YORK	19,282	13,420	5,839	23	7,581 R	69.6%	30.3%	69.7%	30.3%
	City/Town									
139,966	ALEXANDRIA	35,229	13,050	22,108	71	9,058 D	37.0%	62.8%	37.1%	62.9%
6,222	BEDFORD CITY	1,569	1,016	553		463 R	64.8%	35.2%	64.8%	35.2%
17,835	BRISTOL	3,810	2,760	1,047	3	1,713 R	72.4%	27.5%	72.5%	27.5%
6,650	BUENA VISTA	1,352	824	528		296 R	60.9%	39.1%	60.9%	39.1%
43,475	CHARLOTTESVILLE	10,056	2,636	7,406	14	4,770 D	26.2%	73.6%	26.2%	73.8%

VIRGINIA

GOVERNOR 2010

2010 Census Population	County	Total Vote	Republican	Democratic	Other	Rep.-Dem. Plurality	Percentage Total Vote Rep.	Dem.	Major Vote Rep.	Dem.
222,209	CHESAPEAKE	53,937	32,518	21,376	43	11,142 R	60.3%	39.6%	60.3%	39.7%
17,411	COLONIAL HEIGHTS	5,212	4,333	877	2	3,456 R	83.1%	16.8%	83.2%	16.8%
5,961	COVINGTON	1,488	507	979	2	472 D	34.1%	65.8%	34.1%	65.9%
43,055	DANVILLE	10,918	6,001	4,906	11	1,095 R	55.0%	44.9%	55.0%	45.0%
5,927	EMPORIA	1,318	690	627	1	63 R	52.4%	47.6%	52.4%	47.6%
22,565	FAIRFAX CITY	6,201	3,285	2,909	7	376 R	53.0%	46.9%	53.0%	47.0%
12,332	FALLS CHURCH	4,187	1,463	2,718	6	1,255 D	34.9%	64.9%	35.0%	65.0%
8,582	FRANKLIN CITY	2,230	1,013	1,216	1	203 D	45.4%	54.5%	45.4%	54.6%
24,286	FREDERICKSBURG	4,559	2,231	2,318	10	87 D	48.9%	50.8%	49.0%	51.0%
7,042	GALAX	1,311	818	490	3	328 R	62.4%	37.4%	62.5%	37.5%
137,436	HAMPTON	32,302	13,559	18,696	47	5,137 D	42.0%	57.9%	42.0%	58.0%
48,914	HARRISONBURG	6,617	3,816	2,790	11	1,026 R	57.7%	42.2%	57.8%	42.2%
22,591	HOPEWELL	4,690	2,926	1,753	11	1,173 R	62.4%	37.4%	62.5%	37.5%
7,042	LEXINGTON	1,505	592	911	2	319 D	39.3%	60.5%	39.4%	60.6%
75,568	LYNCHBURG	20,242	12,503	7,713	26	4,790 R	61.8%	38.1%	61.8%	38.2%
37,821	MANASSAS	6,889	4,266	2,618	5	1,648 R	61.9%	38.0%	62.0%	38.0%
14,273	MANASSAS PARK	1,672	1,006	666		340 R	60.2%	39.8%	60.2%	39.8%
13,821	MARTINSVILLE	3,248	1,565	1,678	5	113 D	48.2%	51.7%	48.3%	51.7%
180,719	NEWPORT NEWS	36,857	18,401	18,415	41	14 D	49.9%	50.0%	50.0%	50.0%
242,803	NORFOLK	39,988	15,913	24,025	50	8,112 D	39.8%	60.1%	39.8%	60.2%
3,958	NORTON	938	568	369	1	199 R	60.6%	39.3%	60.6%	39.4%
32,420	PETERSBURG	6,438	1,221	5,214	3	3,993 D	19.0%	81.0%	19.0%	81.0%
12,150	POQUOSON	4,662	3,737	922	3	2,815 R	80.2%	19.8%	80.2%	19.8%
95,535	PORTSMOUTH	21,963	8,824	13,124	15	4,300 D	40.2%	59.8%	40.2%	59.8%
16,408	RADFORD	2,848	1,554	1,291	3	263 R	54.6%	45.3%	54.6%	45.4%
204,214	RICHMOND CITY	45,127	13,785	31,241	101	17,456 D	30.5%	69.2%	30.6%	69.4%
97,032	ROANOKE CITY	20,681	9,929	10,731	21	802 D	48.0%	51.9%	48.1%	51.9%
24,802	SALEM	7,082	4,706	2,365	11	2,341 R	66.5%	33.4%	66.6%	33.4%
23,746	STAUNTON	6,346	3,715	2,627	4	1,088 R	58.5%	41.4%	58.6%	41.4%
84,585	SUFFOLK	19,907	11,095	8,798	14	2,297 R	55.7%	44.2%	55.8%	44.2%
437,994	VIRGINIA BEACH	100,363	63,964	36,303	96	27,661 R	63.7%	36.2%	63.8%	36.2%
21,006	WAYNESBORO	5,002	3,447	1,549	6	1,898 R	68.9%	31.0%	69.0%	31.0%
14,068	WILLIAMSBURG	3,489	1,579	1,905	5	326 D	45.3%	54.6%	45.3%	54.7%
26,203	WINCHESTER	5,299	3,215	2,076	8	1,139 R	60.7%	39.2%	60.8%	39.2%
8,001,024	TOTAL	1,985,103	1,163,651	818,950	2,502	344,701 R	58.6%	41.3%	58.7%	41.3%

VIRGINIA

HOUSE OF REPRESENTATIVES

CD	Year	Total Vote	Republican Vote	Republican Candidate	Democratic Vote	Democratic Candidate	Other Vote	Rep.-Dem. Plurality	Percentage Total Vote Rep.	Total Vote Dem.	Major Vote Rep.	Major Vote Dem.
1	2010	212,236	135,564	WITTMAN, ROBERT J.*	73,824	BALL, KRYSTAL M.	2,848	61,740 R	63.9%	34.8%	64.7%	35.3%
1	2008	360,292	203,839	WITTMAN, ROBERT J.*	150,432	DAY, BILL S., JR.	6,021	53,407 R	56.6%	41.8%	57.5%	42.5%
1	2006	228,534	143,889	DAVIS, JO ANN*	81,083	O'DONNELL, SHAWN M.	3,562	62,806 R	63.0%	35.5%	64.0%	36.0%
1	2004	286,534	225,071	DAVIS, JO ANN*		—	61,463	225,071 R	78.5%		100.0%	
1	2002	117,997	113,168	DAVIS, JO ANN*		—	4,829	113,168 R	95.9%		100.0%	
2	2010	166,289	88,340	RIGELL, E. SCOTT	70,591	NYE, GLENN C.*	7,358	17,749 R	53.1%	42.5%	55.6%	44.4%
2	2008	270,711	128,486	DRAKE, THELMA*	141,857	NYE, GLENN C.	368	13,371 D	47.5%	52.4%	47.5%	52.5%
2	2006	173,159	88,777	DRAKE, THELMA*	83,901	KELLAM, PHILIP J.	481	4,876 R	51.3%	48.5%	51.4%	48.6%
2	2004	241,380	132,946	DRAKE, THELMA	108,180	ASHE, DAVID B.	254	24,766 R	55.1%	44.8%	55.1%	44.9%
2	2002	124,846	103,807	SCHROCK, ED*			21,039	103,807 R	83.1%		100.0%	
3	2010	163,900	44,553	SMITH, C. L. "CHUCK"	114,754	SCOTT, ROBERT C.*	4,593	70,201 D	27.2%	70.0%	28.0%	72.0%
3	2008	247,288		—	239,911	SCOTT, ROBERT C.*	7,377	239,911 D		97.0%		100.0%
3	2006	138,994			133,546	SCOTT, ROBERT C.*	5,448	133,546 D		96.1%		100.0%
3	2004	229,892	70,194	SEARS, WINSOME E.	159,373	SCOTT, ROBERT C.*	325	89,179 D	30.5%	69.3%	30.6%	69.4%
3	2002	91,073		—	87,521	SCOTT, ROBERT C.*	3,552	87,521 D		96.1%		100.0%
4	2010	198,389	123,659	FORBES, J. RANDY*	74,298	LeGROW, WYNNE V. E.	432	49,361 R	62.3%	37.5%	62.5%	37.5%
4	2008	334,521	199,075	FORBES, J. RANDY*	135,041	MILLER, ANDREA R.	405	64,034 R	59.5%	40.4%	59.6%	40.4%
4	2006	198,340	150,967	FORBES, J. RANDY*		—	47,373	150,967 R	76.1%		100.0%	
4	2004	283,027	182,444	FORBES, J. RANDY*	100,413	MENEFEE, JONATHAN R.	170	82,031 R	64.5%	35.5%	64.5%	35.5%
4	2002	111,041	108,733	FORBES, J. RANDY*		—	2,308	108,733 R	97.9%		100.0%	
5	2010	235,299	119,560	HURT, ROBERT	110,562	PERRIELLO, TOM S. P.*	5,177	8,998 R	50.8%	47.0%	52.0%	48.0%
5	2008	317,076	158,083	GOODE, VIRGIL H., JR.*	158,810	PERRIELLO, TOM S. P.	183	727 D	49.9%	50.1%	49.9%	50.1%
5	2006	212,079	125,370	GOODE, VIRGIL H., JR.*	84,682	WEED, AL C., II	2,027	40,688 R	59.1%	39.9%	59.7%	40.3%
5	2004	270,758	172,431	GOODE, VIRGIL H., JR.*	98,237	WEED, AL C., II	90	74,194 R	63.7%	36.3%	63.7%	36.3%
5	2002	150,233	95,360	GOODE, VIRGIL H., JR.*	54,805	RICHARDS, MEREDITH M.	68	40,555 R	63.5%	36.5%	63.5%	36.5%
6	2010	167,154	127,487	GOODLATTE, ROBERT W.*		—	39,667	127,487 R	76.3%		100.0%	
6	2008	312,392	192,350	GOODLATTE, ROBERT W.*	114,367	RASOUL, S. "SAM"	5,675	77,983 R	61.6%	36.6%	62.7%	37.3%
6	2006	203,995	153,187	GOODLATTE, ROBERT W.*		—	50,808	153,187 R	75.1%		100.0%	
6	2004	213,648	206,560	GOODLATTE, ROBERT W.*		—	7,088	206,560 R	96.7%		100.0%	
6	2002	108,732	105,530	GOODLATTE, ROBERT W.*		—	3,202	105,530 R	97.1%		100.0%	
7	2010	233,402	138,209	CANTOR, ERIC*	79,616	WAUGH, RICK E. JR.	15,577	58,593 R	59.2%	34.1%	63.4%	36.6%
7	2008	372,337	233,531	CANTOR, ERIC*	138,123	HARTKE, ANITA	683	95,408 R	62.7%	37.1%	62.8%	37.2%
7	2006	256,397	163,706	CANTOR, ERIC*	88,206	NACHMAN, JAMES M.	4,485	75,500 R	63.8%	34.4%	65.0%	35.0%
7	2004	305,658	230,765	CANTOR, ERIC*		—	74,893	230,765 R	75.5%		100.0%	
7	2002	163,665	113,658	CANTOR, ERIC*	49,854	JONES, BEN L. "COOTER"	153	63,804 R	69.4%	30.5%	69.5%	30.5%
8	2010	190,748	71,145	MURRAY, J. PATRICK	116,404	MORAN, JAMES P.*	3,199	45,259 D	37.3%	61.0%	37.9%	62.1%
8	2008	328,197	97,425	ELLMORE, MARK W.	222,986	MORAN, JAMES P.*	7,786	125,561 D	29.7%	67.9%	30.4%	69.6%
8	2006	217,909	66,639	O'DONOGHUE, TOM M.	144,700	MORAN, JAMES P.*	6,570	78,061 D	30.6%	66.4%	31.5%	68.5%
8	2004	287,919	106,231	CHENEY, LISA MARIE	171,986	MORAN, JAMES P.*	9,702	65,755 D	36.9%	59.7%	38.2%	61.8%
8	2002	171,799	64,121	TATE, SCOTT C.	102,759	MORAN, JAMES P.*	4,919	38,638 D	37.3%	59.8%	38.4%	61.6%
9	2010	186,917	95,726	GRIFFITH, H. MORGAN	86,743	BOUCHER, RICK*	4,448	8,983 R	51.2%	46.4%	52.5%	47.5%
9	2008	213,570			207,306	BOUCHER, RICK*	6,264	207,306 D		97.1%		100.0%
9	2006	191,415	61,574	CARRICO, C. W. "BILL"	129,705	BOUCHER, RICK*	136	68,131 D	32.2%	67.8%	32.2%	67.8%
9	2004	252,947	98,499	TRIPLETT, KEVIN R.	150,039	BOUCHER, RICK*	4,409	51,540 D	38.9%	59.3%	39.6%	60.4%
9	2002	152,183	52,076	KATZEN, JAY K.	100,075	BOUCHER, RICK*	32	47,999 D	34.2%	65.8%	34.2%	65.8%
10	2010	208,556	131,116	WOLF, FRANK R.*	72,604	BARNETT, JEFFERY R.	4,836	58,512 R	62.9%	34.8%	64.4%	35.6%
10	2008	379,480	223,140	WOLF, FRANK R.*	147,357	FEDER, JUDY M.	8,983	75,783 R	58.8%	38.8%	60.2%	39.8%
10	2006	241,134	138,213	WOLF, FRANK R.*	98,769	FEDER, JUDY M.	4,152	39,444 R	57.3%	41.0%	58.3%	41.7%
10	2004	323,011	205,982	WOLF, FRANK R.*	116,654	SOCAS, JAMES R.	375	89,328 R	63.8%	36.1%	63.8%	36.2%
10	2002	161,615	115,917	WOLF, FRANK R.*	45,464	STEVENS, JOHN B., JR.	234	70,453 R	71.7%	28.1%	71.8%	28.2%

VIRGINIA

HOUSE OF REPRESENTATIVES

CD	Year	Total Vote	Republican Vote	Republican Candidate	Democratic Vote	Democratic Candidate	Other Vote	Rep.-Dem. Plurality	Total Vote Rep.	Total Vote Dem.	Major Vote Rep.	Major Vote Dem.
11	2010	226,951	110,739	FIMIAN, KEITH S.	111,720	CONNOLLY, GERALD E.*	4,492	981 D	48.8%	49.2%	49.8%	50.2%
11	2008	359,491	154,758	FIMIAN, KEITH S.	196,598	CONNOLLY, GERALD E.	8,135	41,840 D	43.0%	54.7%	44.0%	56.0%
11	2006	235,280	130,468	DAVIS, THOMAS M., III*	102,511	HURST, ANDREW L.	2,301	27,957 R	55.5%	43.6%	56.0%	44.0%
11	2004	309,233	186,299	DAVIS, THOMAS M., III*	118,305	LONGMYER, KEN	4,629	67,994 R	60.2%	38.3%	61.2%	38.8%
11	2002	163,298	135,379	DAVIS, THOMAS M., III*	—		27,919	135,379 R	82.9%		100.0%	
TOTAL	2010	2,189,841	1,186,098		911,116		92,627	274,982 R	54.2%	41.6%	56.6%	43.4%
TOTAL	2008	3,495,355	1,590,687		1,852,788		51,880	262,101 D	45.5%	53.0%	46.2%	53.8%
TOTAL	2006	2,297,236	1,222,790		947,103		127,343	275,687 R	53.2%	41.2%	56.4%	43.6%
TOTAL	2004	3,004,007	1,817,422		1,023,187		163,398	794,235 R	60.5%	34.1%	64.0%	36.0%
TOTAL	2002	1,516,482	1,007,749		440,478		68,255	567,271 R	66.5%	29.0%	69.6%	30.4%

An asterisk (*) denotes incumbent.

VIRGINIA

GENERAL AND PRIMARY ELECTIONS

2009-10 GENERAL ELECTIONS

Governor (2009) Other vote was 2,502 scattered write-in.

House   Other vote was:

CD 1   2,544 Independent Green (G. Gail "for Rail" Parker); 304 scattered write-in.
CD 2   7,194 Independent (Kenny E. Golden); 164 scattered write-in.
CD 3   2,383 Libertarian (James J. Quigley); 2,039 Independent (John D. Kelly); 171 scattered write-in.
CD 4   432 scattered write-in.
CD 5   4,992 Independent (Jeffrey A. Clark); 185 scattered write-in.
CD 6   21,649 Independent (Jeffrey W. Vanke); 15,309 Libertarian (Stuart M. Bain); 2,709 scattered write-in.
CD 7   15,164 Independent Green (Floyd C. Bayne); 413 scattered write-in.
CD 8   2,707 Independent Green (J. Ron Fisher); 492 scattered write-in.
CD 9   4,282 Independent (Jeremiah D. Heaton); 166 scattered write-in.
CD 10   4,607 Libertarian (William B. Redpath); 229 scattered write-in.
CD 11   1,846 Independent (Christopher F. DeCarlo); 1,382 Libertarian (David L. Dotson); 959 Independent Green (David William Gillis Jr.); 305 scattered write-in.

2009-10 PRIMARY ELECTIONS

Primary   June 9, 2009 (Governor)   **Registration**   4,999,423   No Party Registration
              June 8, 2010 (Congress)   (as of May 31, 2010)

Primary Type   Open—Any registered voter could participate in the primary of either party.

VIRGINIA

GENERAL AND PRIMARY ELECTIONS

	REPUBLICAN PRIMARIES			DEMOCRATIC PRIMARIES		
Governor (2009)	Robert F. McDonnell	Nominated by convention		R. Creigh Deeds	158,845	49.8%
				Terry R. McAuliffe	84,387	26.4%
				Brian J. Moran	75,936	23.8%
				TOTAL	*319,168*	
Congressional District 1	Robert J. Wittman*	28,956	88.0%	Krystal M. Ball	Nominated by convention	
	Catherine T. Crabill	3,963	12.0%			
	TOTAL	*32,919*				
Congressional District 2	E. Scott Rigell	14,396	39.5%	Glenn C. Nye*	Unopposed	
	Ben Loyola Jr.	9,762	26.8%			
	Bert K. Mizusawa	6,342	17.4%			
	Scott W. Taylor	2,950	8.1%			
	Jessica D. Sandlin	1,620	4.4%			
	Ed C. Maulbeck	1,372	3.8%			
	TOTAL	*36,442*				
Congressional District 3	C. L. "Chuck" Smith	Nominated by convention		Robert C. Scott*	Unopposed	
Congressional District 4	J. Randy Forbes*	Unopposed		Wynne V. E. LeGrow	Unopposed	
Congressional District 5	Robert Hurt	17,120	48.4%	Tom S. P. Perriello*	Nominated by convention	
	James K. McKelvey	9,153	25.9%			
	Mike G. McPadden	3,460	9.8%			
	Kenneth C. Boyd	2,608	7.4%			
	Feda Kidd Morton	1,626	4.6%			
	Laurence Paul Verga	802	2.3%			
	Ron L. Ferrin	583	1.6%			
	TOTAL	*35,352*				
Congressional District 6	Robert W. Goodlatte*	Unopposed		No Democratic candidate		
Congressional District 7	Eric Cantor*	Unopposed		Rick E. Waugh Jr.	Nominated by convention	
Congressional District 8	J. Patrick Murray	7,136	51.7%	James P. Moran*	Unopposed	
	Matthew B. Berry	6,654	48.3%			
	TOTAL	*13,790*				
Congressional District 9	H. Morgan Griffith	Nominated by convention		Rick Boucher*	Nominated by convention	
Congressional District 10	Frank R. Wolf*	Unopposed		Jeffery R. Barnett	Unopposed	
Congressional District 11	Keith S. Fimian	20,075	55.9%	Gerald E. Connolly*	Unopposed	
	Patrick S. Herrity	15,815	44.1%			
	TOTAL	*35,890*				

An asterisk (*) denotes incumbent. The state parties and local party committees traditionally have the option of holding a primary or nominating candidates by convention or committee. If a primary was called and only one candidate filed to run in it, then no primary was held.

WASHINGTON

Congressional districts first established for elections held in 2002
9 members

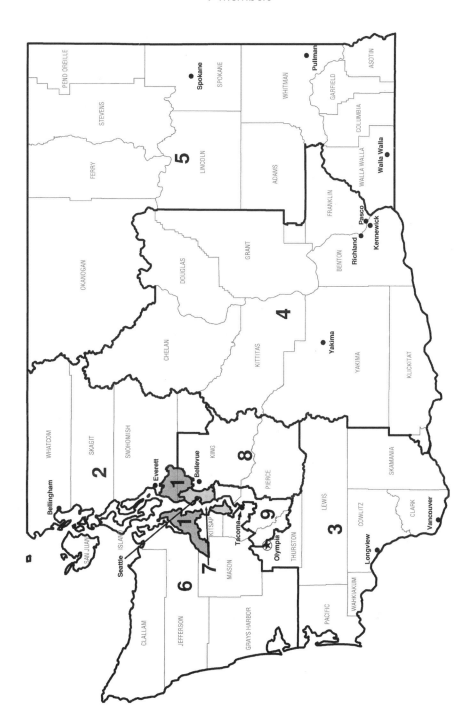

WASHINGTON

Seattle, Puget Sound Area

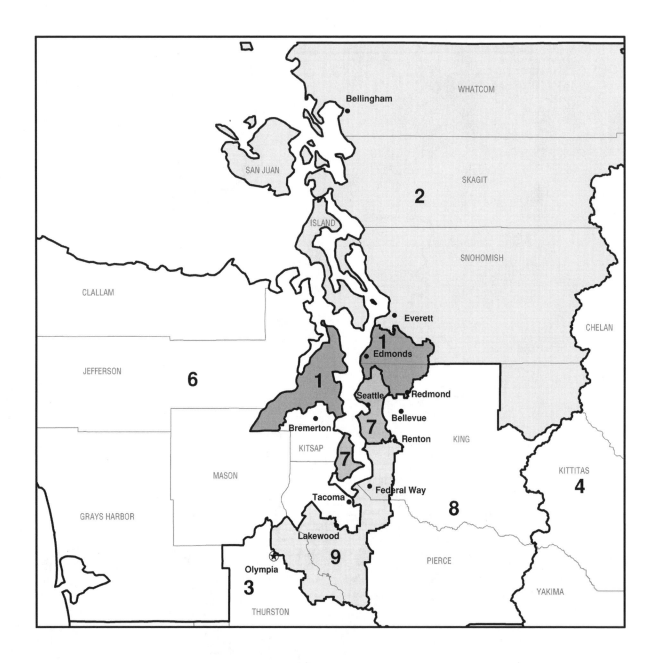

WASHINGTON

GOVERNOR

Christine Gregoire (D). Reelected 2008 to a four-year term. Previously elected 2004.

SENATORS (2 Democrats)

Maria Cantwell (D). Reelected 2006 to a six-year term. Previously elected 2000.

Patty Murray (D). Reelected 2010 to a six-year term. Previously elected 2004, 1998, 1992.

REPRESENTATIVES (5 Democrats, 4 Republicans)

1. Jay Inslee (D)
2. Rick Larsen (D)
3. Jaime Herrera (R)
4. Doc Hastings (R)
5. Cathy McMorris Rodgers (R)
6. Norm Dicks (D)
7. Jim McDermott (D)
8. Dave Reichert (R)
9. Adam Smith (D)

POSTWAR VOTE FOR PRESIDENT

		Republican		Democratic				Total Vote		Major Vote	
Year	Total Vote	Vote	Candidate	Vote	Candidate	Other Vote	Rep.-Dem. Plurality	Rep.	Dem.	Rep.	Dem.
2008	3,036,878	1,229,216	McCain, John	1,750,848	Obama, Barack	56,814	521,632 D	40.5%	57.7%	41.2%	58.8%
2004	2,859,084	1,304,894	Bush, George W.	1,510,201	Kerry, John	43,989	205,307 D	45.6%	52.8%	46.4%	53.6%
2000**	2,487,433	1,108,864	Bush, George W.	1,247,652	Gore, Al	130,917	138,788 D	44.6%	50.2%	47.1%	52.9%
1996**	2,253,837	840,712	Dole, Bob	1,123,323	Clinton, Bill	289,802	282,611 D	37.3%	49.8%	42.8%	57.2%
1992**	2,288,230	731,234	Bush, George	993,037	Clinton, Bill	563,959	261,803 D	32.0%	43.4%	42.4%	57.6%
1988	1,865,253	903,835	Bush, George	933,516	Dukakis, Michael S.	27,902	29,681 D	48.5%	50.0%	49.2%	50.8%
1984	1,883,910	1,051,670	Reagan, Ronald	807,352	Mondale, Walter F.	24,888	244,318 R	55.8%	42.9%	56.6%	43.4%
1980**	1,742,394	865,244	Reagan, Ronald	650,193	Carter, Jimmy	226,957	215,051 R	49.7%	37.3%	57.1%	42.9%
1976	1,555,534	777,732	Ford, Gerald R.	717,323	Carter, Jimmy	60,479	60,409 R	50.0%	46.1%	52.0%	48.0%
1972	1,470,847	837,135	Nixon, Richard M.	568,334	McGovern, George S.	65,378	268,801 R	56.9%	38.6%	59.6%	40.4%
1968**	1,304,281	588,510	Nixon, Richard M.	616,037	Humphrey, Hubert H.	99,734	27,527 D	45.1%	47.2%	48.9%	51.1%
1964	1,258,556	470,366	Goldwater, Barry M.	779,881	Johnson, Lyndon B.	8,309	309,515 D	37.4%	62.0%	37.6%	62.4%
1960	1,241,572	629,273	Nixon, Richard M.	599,298	Kennedy, John F.	13,001	29,975 R	50.7%	48.3%	51.2%	48.8%
1956	1,150,889	620,430	Eisenhower, Dwight D.	523,002	Stevenson, Adlai E.	7,457	97,428 R	53.9%	45.4%	54.3%	45.7%
1952	1,102,708	599,107	Eisenhower, Dwight D.	492,845	Stevenson, Adlai E.	10,756	106,262 R	54.3%	44.7%	54.9%	45.1%
1948	905,058	386,314	Dewey, Thomas E.	476,165	Truman, Harry S.	42,579	89,851 D	42.7%	52.6%	44.8%	55.2%

** In past elections, the other vote included: 2000 - 103,002 Green (Ralph Nader); 1996 - 201,003 Reform (Ross Perot); 1992 - 541,780 Independent (Perot); 1980 - 185,073 Independent (John Anderson); 1968 - 96,990 American Independent (George Wallace).

WASHINGTON

POSTWAR VOTE FOR GOVERNOR

Year	Total Vote	Republican Vote	Republican Candidate	Democratic Vote	Democratic Candidate	Other Vote	Rep.-Dem. Plurality		Total Vote Rep.	Total Vote Dem.	Major Vote Rep.	Major Vote Dem.
2008	3,002,862	1,404,124	Rossi, Dino	1,598,738	Gregoire, Christine		194,614	D	46.8%	53.2%	46.8%	53.2%
2004**	2,810,058	1,373,232	Rossi, Dino	1,373,361	Gregoire, Christine	63,465	129	D	48.9%	48.9%	50.0%	50.0%
2000	2,469,852	980,060	Carlson, John	1,441,973	Locke, Gary	47,819	461,913	D	39.7%	58.4%	40.5%	59.5%
1996	2,237,030	940,538	Craswell, Ellen	1,296,492	Locke, Gary		355,954	D	42.0%	58.0%	42.0%	58.0%
1992	2,270,826	1,086,216	Eikenberry, Ken	1,184,315	Lowry, Mike	295	98,099	D	47.8%	52.2%	47.8%	52.2%
1988	1,874,929	708,481	Williams, Bob	1,166,448	Gardner, Booth		457,967	D	37.8%	62.2%	37.8%	62.2%
1984	1,888,987	881,994	Spellman, John D.	1,006,993	Gardner, Booth		124,999	D	46.7%	53.3%	46.7%	53.3%
1980	1,730,896	981,083	Spellman, John D.	749,813	McDermott, James A.		231,270	R	56.7%	43.3%	56.7%	43.3%
1976	1,546,382	687,039	Spellman, John D.	821,797	Ray, Dixy Lee	37,546	134,758	D	44.4%	53.1%	45.5%	54.5%
1972	1,472,542	747,825	Evans, Daniel J.	630,613	Rosellini, Albert D.	94,104	117,212	R	50.8%	42.8%	54.3%	45.7%
1968	1,265,355	692,378	Evans, Daniel J.	560,262	O'Connell, John J.	12,715	132,116	R	54.7%	44.3%	55.3%	44.7%
1964	1,250,274	697,256	Evans, Daniel J.	548,692	Rosellini, Albert D.	4,326	148,564	R	55.8%	43.9%	56.0%	44.0%
1960	1,215,748	594,122	Andrews, Lloyd J.	611,987	Rosellini, Albert D.	9,639	17,865	D	48.9%	50.3%	49.3%	50.7%
1956	1,128,977	508,041	Anderson, Emmett T.	616,773	Rosellini, Albert D.	4,163	108,732	D	45.0%	54.6%	45.2%	54.8%
1952	1,078,497	567,822	Langlie, Arthur B.	510,675	Mitchell, Hugh B.		57,147	R	52.6%	47.4%	52.6%	47.4%
1948	883,141	445,958	Langlie, Arthur B.	417,035	Wallgren, Mon C.	20,148	28,923	R	50.5%	47.2%	51.7%	48.3%

** In 2004, the initial official vote count put Republican Dino Rossi ahead by 261 votes. A machine recount reduced Rossi's margin to 42 votes. A subsequent manual recount gave Democrat Christine Gregoire the election by a margin of 129 votes (see above), and she was inaugurated governor.

POSTWAR VOTE FOR SENATOR

Year	Total Vote	Republican Vote	Republican Candidate	Democratic Vote	Democratic Candidate	Other Vote	Rep.-Dem. Plurality		Total Vote Rep.	Total Vote Dem.	Major Vote Rep.	Major Vote Dem.
2010	2,511,094	1,196,164	Rossi, Dino	1,314,930	Murray, Patty		118,766	D	47.6%	52.4%	47.6%	52.4%
2006	2,083,734	832,106	McGavick, Mike	1,184,659	Cantwell, Maria	66,969	352,553	D	39.9%	56.9%	41.3%	58.7%
2004	2,818,651	1,204,584	Nethercutt, George	1,549,708	Murray, Patty	64,359	345,124	D	42.7%	55.0%	43.7%	56.3%
2000	2,461,379	1,197,208	Gorton, Slade	1,199,437	Cantwell, Maria	64,734	2,229	D	48.6%	48.7%	50.0%	50.0%
1998	1,888,561	785,377	Smith, Linda	1,103,184	Murray, Patty		317,807	D	41.6%	58.4%	41.6%	58.4%
1994	1,700,173	947,821	Gorton, Slade	752,352	Sims, Ron		195,469	R	55.7%	44.3%	55.7%	44.3%
1992	2,219,162	1,020,829	Chandler, Rod	1,197,973	Murray, Patty	360	177,144	D	46.0%	54.0%	46.0%	54.0%
1988	1,848,542	944,359	Gorton, Slade	904,183	Lowry, Mike		40,176	R	51.1%	48.9%	51.1%	48.9%
1986	1,337,367	650,931	Gorton, Slade	677,471	Adams, Brock	8,965	26,540	D	48.7%	50.7%	49.0%	51.0%
1983S	1,213,307	672,326	Evans, Daniel J.	540,981	Lowry, Mike		131,345	R	55.4%	44.6%	55.4%	44.6%
1982	1,368,476	332,273	Jewett, Doug	943,655	Jackson, Henry M.	92,548	611,382	D	24.3%	69.0%	26.0%	74.0%
1980	1,728,369	936,317	Gorton, Slade	792,052	Magnuson, Warren G.		144,265	R	54.2%	45.8%	54.2%	45.8%
1976	1,491,111	361,546	Brown, George M.	1,071,219	Jackson, Henry M.	58,346	709,673	D	24.2%	71.8%	25.2%	74.8%
1974	1,007,847	363,626	Metcalf, Jack	611,811	Magnuson, Warren G.	32,410	248,185	D	36.1%	60.7%	37.3%	62.7%
1970	1,066,807	170,790	Elicker, Charles W.	879,385	Jackson, Henry M.	16,632	708,595	D	16.0%	82.4%	16.3%	83.7%
1968	1,236,063	435,894	Metcalf, Jack	796,183	Magnuson, Warren G.	3,986	360,289	D	35.3%	64.4%	35.4%	64.6%
1964	1,213,088	337,138	Andrews, Lloyd J.	875,950	Jackson, Henry M.		538,812	D	27.8%	72.2%	27.8%	72.2%
1962	943,229	446,204	Christensen, Richard G.	491,365	Magnuson, Warren G.	5,660	45,161	D	47.3%	52.1%	47.6%	52.4%
1958	886,822	278,271	Bantz, William B.	597,040	Jackson, Henry M.	11,511	318,769	D	31.4%	67.3%	31.8%	68.2%
1956	1,122,217	436,652	Langlie, Arthur B.	685,565	Magnuson, Warren G.		248,913	D	38.9%	61.1%	38.9%	61.1%
1952	1,058,735	460,884	Cain, Harry P.	595,288	Jackson, Henry M.	2,563	134,404	D	43.5%	56.2%	43.6%	56.4%
1950	744,783	342,464	Williams, Walter	397,719	Magnuson, Warren G.	4,600	55,255	D	46.0%	53.4%	46.3%	53.7%
1946	660,342	358,847	Cain, Harry P.	298,683	Mitchell, Hugh B.	2,812	60,164	R	54.3%	45.2%	54.6%	45.4%

The 1983 election was for a short term to fill a vacancy.

WASHINGTON

SENATOR 2010

2010 Census Population	County	Total Vote	Republican	Democratic	Rep.-Dem. Plurality	Percentage			
						Total Vote		Major Vote	
						Rep.	Dem.	Rep.	Dem.
18,728	ADAMS	3,771	2,743	1,028	1,715 R	72.7%	27.3%	72.7%	27.3%
21,623	ASOTIN	8,397	5,105	3,292	1,813 R	60.8%	39.2%	60.8%	39.2%
175,177	BENTON	62,535	40,230	22,305	17,925 R	64.3%	35.7%	64.3%	35.7%
72,453	CHELAN	27,431	17,349	10,082	7,267 R	63.2%	36.8%	63.2%	36.8%
71,404	CLALLAM	33,241	17,602	15,639	1,963 R	53.0%	47.0%	53.0%	47.0%
425,363	CLARK	146,551	79,499	67,052	12,447 R	54.2%	45.8%	54.2%	45.8%
4,078	COLUMBIA	2,131	1,466	665	801 R	68.8%	31.2%	68.8%	31.2%
102,410	COWLITZ	36,774	19,443	17,331	2,112 R	52.9%	47.1%	52.9%	47.1%
38,431	DOUGLAS	13,125	8,838	4,287	4,551 R	67.3%	32.7%	67.3%	32.7%
7,551	FERRY	3,177	2,033	1,144	889 R	64.0%	36.0%	64.0%	36.0%
78,163	FRANKLIN	17,121	11,209	5,912	5,297 R	65.5%	34.5%	65.5%	34.5%
2,266	GARFIELD	1,162	822	340	482 R	70.7%	29.3%	70.7%	29.3%
89,120	GRANT	23,764	16,880	6,884	9,996 R	71.0%	29.0%	71.0%	29.0%
72,797	GRAYS HARBOR	25,295	12,209	13,086	877 D	48.3%	51.7%	48.3%	51.7%
78,506	ISLAND	35,774	17,980	17,794	186 R	50.3%	49.7%	50.3%	49.7%
29,872	JEFFERSON	17,330	6,413	10,917	4,504 D	37.0%	63.0%	37.0%	63.0%
1,931,249	KING	753,558	264,368	489,190	224,822 D	35.1%	64.9%	35.1%	64.9%
251,133	KITSAP	103,366	50,414	52,952	2,538 D	48.8%	51.2%	48.8%	51.2%
40,915	KITTITAS	15,114	9,276	5,838	3,438 R	61.4%	38.6%	61.4%	38.6%
20,318	KLICKITAT	8,667	4,950	3,717	1,233 R	57.1%	42.9%	57.1%	42.9%
75,455	LEWIS	30,706	20,354	10,352	10,002 R	66.3%	33.7%	66.3%	33.7%
10,570	LINCOLN	5,334	3,668	1,666	2,002 R	68.8%	31.2%	68.8%	31.2%
60,699	MASON	24,629	12,568	12,061	507 R	51.0%	49.0%	51.0%	49.0%
41,120	OKANOGAN	14,647	8,881	5,766	3,115 R	60.6%	39.4%	60.6%	39.4%
20,920	PACIFIC	9,708	4,552	5,156	604 D	46.9%	53.1%	46.9%	53.1%
13,001	PEND OREILLE	5,764	3,599	2,165	1,434 R	62.4%	37.6%	62.4%	37.6%
795,225	PIERCE	266,949	134,025	132,924	1,101 R	50.2%	49.8%	50.2%	49.8%
15,769	SAN JUAN	9,188	3,194	5,994	2,800 D	34.8%	65.2%	34.8%	65.2%
116,901	SKAGIT	47,832	24,609	23,223	1,386 R	51.4%	48.6%	51.4%	48.6%
11,066	SKAMANIA	4,533	2,415	2,118	297 R	53.3%	46.7%	53.3%	46.7%
713,335	SNOHOMISH	264,896	127,531	137,365	9,834 D	48.1%	51.9%	48.1%	51.9%
471,221	SPOKANE	180,612	101,628	78,984	22,644 R	56.3%	43.7%	56.3%	43.7%
43,531	STEVENS	19,455	13,076	6,379	6,697 R	67.2%	32.8%	67.2%	32.8%
252,264	THURSTON	104,964	46,014	58,950	12,936 D	43.8%	56.2%	43.8%	56.2%
3,978	WAHKIAKUM	2,027	1,112	915	197 R	54.9%	45.1%	54.9%	45.1%
58,781	WALLA WALLA	21,062	12,882	8,180	4,702 R	61.2%	38.8%	61.2%	38.8%
201,140	WHATCOM	85,322	40,539	44,783	4,244 D	47.5%	52.5%	47.5%	52.5%
44,776	WHITMAN	13,420	7,644	5,776	1,868 R	57.0%	43.0%	57.0%	43.0%
243,231	YAKIMA	61,762	39,044	22,718	16,326 R	63.2%	36.8%	63.2%	36.8%
6,724,540	TOTAL	2,511,094	1,196,164	1,314,930	118,766 D	47.6%	52.4%	47.6%	52.4%

WASHINGTON

HOUSE OF REPRESENTATIVES

| | | | Republican | | Democratic | | | | Percentage | | | |
| | | Total | | | | | Other | Rep.-Dem. | Total Vote | | Major Vote | |
CD	Year	Vote	Vote	Candidate	Vote	Candidate	Vote	Plurality	Rep.	Dem.	Rep.	Dem.
1	2010	299,379	126,737	WATKINS, JAMES	172,642	INSLEE, JAY*		45,905 D	42.3%	57.7%	42.3%	57.7%
1	2008	345,020	111,240	ISHMAEL, LARRY W.	233,780	INSLEE, JAY*		122,540 D	32.2%	67.8%	32.2%	67.8%
1	2006	241,937	78,105	ISHMAEL, LARRY W.	163,832	INSLEE, JAY*		85,727 D	32.3%	67.7%	32.3%	67.7%
1	2004	327,769	117,850	EASTWOOD, RANDY	204,121	INSLEE, JAY*	5,798	86,271 D	36.0%	62.3%	36.6%	63.4%
1	2002	205,034	84,696	MARINE, JOE	114,087	INSLEE, JAY*	6,251	29,391 D	41.3%	55.6%	42.6%	57.4%
2	2010	303,963	148,722	KOSTER, JOHN	155,241	LARSEN, RICK*		6,519 D	48.9%	51.1%	48.9%	51.1%
2	2008	348,467	131,051	BART, RICK	217,416	LARSEN, RICK*		86,365 D	37.6%	62.4%	37.6%	62.4%
2	2006	244,794	87,730	ROULSTONE, DOUG	157,064	LARSEN, RICK*		69,334 D	35.8%	64.2%	35.8%	64.2%
2	2004	316,682	106,333	SINCLAIR, SUZANNE	202,383	LARSEN, RICK*	7,966	96,050 D	33.6%	63.9%	34.4%	65.6%
2	2002	202,150	92,528	SMITH, NORMA	101,219	LARSEN, RICK*	8,403	8,691 D	45.8%	50.1%	47.8%	52.2%
3	2010	288,453	152,799	HERRERA, JAIME	135,654	HECK, DENNY		17,145 R	53.0%	47.0%	53.0%	47.0%
3	2008	338,529	121,828	DELAVAR, MICHAEL	216,701	BAIRD, BRIAN*		94,873 D	36.0%	64.0%	36.0%	64.0%
3	2006	232,980	85,915	MESSMORE, MICHAEL	147,065	BAIRD, BRIAN*		61,150 D	36.9%	63.1%	36.9%	63.1%
3	2004	312,653	119,027	CROWSON, THOMAS A.	193,626	BAIRD, BRIAN*		74,599 D	38.1%	61.9%	38.1%	61.9%
3	2002	193,329	74,065	ZARELLI, JOSEPH	119,264	BAIRD, BRIAN*		45,199 D	38.3%	61.7%	38.3%	61.7%
4	2010	231,699	156,726	HASTINGS, DOC*	74,973	CLOUGH, JAY		81,753 R	67.6%	32.4%	67.6%	32.4%
4	2008	269,370	169,940	HASTINGS, DOC*	99,430	FEARING, GEORGE		70,510 R	63.1%	36.9%	63.1%	36.9%
4	2006	192,300	115,246	HASTINGS, DOC*	77,054	WRIGHT, RICHARD		38,192 R	59.9%	40.1%	59.9%	40.1%
4	2004	247,113	154,627	HASTINGS, DOC*	92,486	MATHESON, SANDY		62,141 R	62.6%	37.4%	62.6%	37.4%
4	2002	161,829	108,257	HASTINGS, DOC*	53,572	MASON, CRAIG		54,685 R	66.9%	33.1%	66.9%	33.1%
5	2010	278,381	177,235	McMORRIS RODGERS, CATHY*	101,146	ROMEYN, DARYL		76,089 R	63.7%	36.3%	63.7%	36.3%
5	2008	323,687	211,305	McMORRIS RODGERS, CATHY*	112,382	MAYS, MARK		98,923 R	65.3%	34.7%	65.3%	34.7%
5	2006	239,324	134,967	McMORRIS, CATHY*	104,357	GOLDMARK, PETER J.		30,610 R	56.4%	43.6%	56.4%	43.6%
5	2004	300,933	179,600	McMORRIS, CATHY	121,333	BARBIERI, DON		58,267 R	59.7%	40.3%	59.7%	40.3%
5	2002	202,282	126,757	NETHERCUTT, GEORGE*	65,146	HAGGIN, BART	10,379	61,611 R	62.7%	32.2%	66.1%	33.9%
6	2010	261,673	109,800	CLOUD, DOUG	151,873	DICKS, NORM*		42,073 D	42.0%	58.0%	42.0%	58.0%
6	2008	308,072	102,081	CLOUD, DOUG	205,991	DICKS, NORM*		103,910 D	33.1%	66.9%	33.1%	66.9%
6	2006	224,085	65,883	CLOUD, DOUG	158,202	DICKS, NORM*		92,319 D	29.4%	70.6%	29.4%	70.6%
6	2004	294,147	91,228	CLOUD, DOUG	202,919	DICKS, NORM*		111,691 D	31.0%	69.0%	31.0%	69.0%
6	2002	196,444	61,584	LAWRENCE, BOB	126,116	DICKS, NORM*	8,744	64,532 D	31.3%	64.2%	32.8%	67.2%
7	2010	280,390		—	232,649	McDERMOTT, JIM*	47,741	232,649 D		83.0%		100.0%
7	2008	349,017	57,054	BEREN, STEVE	291,963	McDERMOTT, JIM*		234,909 D	16.3%	83.7%	16.3%	83.7%
7	2006	246,133	38,715	BEREN, STEVE	195,462	McDERMOTT, JIM*	11,956	156,747 D	15.7%	79.4%	16.5%	83.5%
7	2004	337,528	65,226	CASSADY, CAROL	272,302	McDERMOTT, JIM*		207,076 D	19.3%	80.7%	19.3%	80.7%
7	2002	211,003	46,256	CASSADY, CAROL	156,300	McDERMOTT, JIM*	8,447	110,044 D	21.9%	74.1%	22.8%	77.2%
8	2010	309,877	161,296	REICHERT, DAVE*	148,581	DELBENE, SUZAN		12,715 R	52.1%	47.9%	52.1%	47.9%
8	2008	362,926	191,568	REICHERT, DAVE*	171,358	BURNER, DARCY		20,210 R	52.8%	47.2%	52.8%	47.2%
8	2006	251,383	129,362	REICHERT, DAVE*	122,021	BURNER, DARCY		7,341 R	51.5%	48.5%	51.5%	48.5%
8	2004	336,499	173,298	REICHERT, DAVE	157,148	ROSS, DAVE	6,053	16,150 R	51.5%	46.7%	52.4%	47.6%
8	2002	203,335	121,633	DUNN, JENNIFER*	75,931	BEHRENS-BENEDICT, HEIDI	5,771	45,702 R	59.8%	37.3%	61.6%	38.4%
9	2010	225,594	101,851	MURI, RICHARD	123,743	SMITH, ADAM*		21,892 D	45.1%	54.9%	45.1%	54.9%
9	2008	269,375	93,080	POSTMA, JAMES	176,295	SMITH, ADAM*		83,215 D	34.6%	65.4%	34.6%	65.4%
9	2006	181,120	62,082	COFCHIN, STEVEN C.	119,038	SMITH, ADAM*		56,956 D	34.3%	65.7%	34.3%	65.7%
9	2004	256,671	88,304	LORD, PAUL J.	162,433	SMITH, ADAM*	5,934	74,129 D	34.4%	63.3%	35.2%	64.8%
9	2002	163,710	63,146	CASADA, SARAH	95,805	SMITH, ADAM*	4,759	32,659 D	38.6%	58.5%	39.7%	60.3%
TOTAL	2010	2,479,409	1,135,166		1,296,502		47,741	161,336 D	45.8%	52.3%	46.7%	53.3%
TOTAL	2008	2,914,463	1,189,147		1,725,316			536,169 D	40.8%	59.2%	40.8%	59.2%
TOTAL	2006	2,054,056	798,005		1,244,095		11,956	446,090 D	38.9%	60.6%	39.1%	60.9%
TOTAL	2004	2,729,995	1,095,493		1,608,751		25,751	513,258 D	40.1%	58.9%	40.5%	59.5%
TOTAL	2002	1,739,116	778,922		907,440		52,754	128,518 D	44.8%	52.2%	46.2%	53.8%

An asterisk (*) denotes incumbent.

WASHINGTON

GENERAL AND PRIMARY ELECTIONS

2010 GENERAL ELECTIONS

Senator

House   Other vote was:

CD 1
CD 2
CD 3
CD 4
CD 5
CD 6
CD 7   47,741 Independent (Bob Jeffers-Schroder).
CD 8
CD 9

2010 PRIMARY ELECTIONS

Primary   August 17, 2010   **Registration**   3,592,079   No Party Registration
(as of August 17, 2010)

Primary Type   Open—Any registered voter could participate in the primary.

ALL-PARTY PRIMARIES			
Senator	Patty Murray (D)*#	670,284	46.2%
	Dino Rossi (R)#	483,305	33.3%
	Clint Didier (R)	185,034	12.8%
	Paul Akers (R)	37,231	2.6%
	James "Skip" Mercer (No Party)	12,122	0.8%
	Charles Allen (D)	11,525	0.8%
	Bob Burr (D)	11,344	0.8%
	Norma D. Gruber (R)	9,162	0.6%
	Mike Latimer (R)	6,545	0.5%
	Mike The Mover (D)	6,019	0.4%
	Goodspaceguy (D)	4,718	0.3%
	Will Baker (Reform)	4,593	0.3%
	Mohammad H. Said (Centrist)	3,387	0.2%
	Schalk Leonard (No Party)	2,818	0.2%
	William Edward Chovil (R)	2,039	0.1%
	TOTAL	1,450,126	
Congressional District 1	Jay Inslee (D)*#	90,208	55.8%
	James Watkins (R)#	44,269	27.4%
	Matthew Burke (R)	20,185	12.5%
	David D. Schirle (Independent Party)	6,864	4.2%
	TOTAL	161,526	
Congressional District 2	John Koster (R)#	74,032	42.2%
	Rick Larsen (D)*#	73,734	42.0%
	Diana McGinness (D)	10,548	6.0%
	John Carmack (R)	9,566	5.5%
	Larry Kalb (D)	7,627	4.3%
	TOTAL	175,507	

WASHINGTON

GENERAL AND PRIMARY ELECTIONS

ALL-PARTY PRIMARIES

Congressional District 3	Denny Heck (D)#	51,895	31.4%
	Jaime Herrera (R)#	46,001	27.8%
	David W. Hedrick (R)	22,621	13.7%
	David B. Castillo (R)	19,995	12.1%
	Cheryl Crist (D)	18,453	11.2%
	Norma Jean Stevens (Independent Party)	6,309	3.8%
	TOTAL	165,274	
Congressional District 4	Doc Hastings (R)*#	82,909	58.7%
	Jay Clough (D)#	31,782	22.5%
	Rex A. Brocki (Tea Party)	9,826	7.0%
	Shane Fast (R)	9,214	6.5%
	Mary Ruth Edwards (Constitution)	4,270	3.0%
	Leland Yialelis (Independent)	3,136	2.2%
	TOTAL	141,137	
Congressional District 5	Cathy McMorris Rodgers (R)*#	106,191	62.5%
	Daryl Romeyn (D)#	21,091	12.4%
	Barbara Lampert (D)	15,538	9.2%
	Clyde Cordero (D)	10,787	6.4%
	Randall Yearout (Constitution)	10,635	6.3%
	David R. Fox (D)	5,569	3.3%
	TOTAL	169,811	
Congressional District 6	Norm Dicks (D)*#	90,596	56.6%
	Doug Cloud (R)#	45,959	28.7%
	Jesse Young (R)	23,410	14.6%
	TOTAL	159,965	
Congressional District 7	Jim McDermott (D)*#	110,914	79.8%
	Bob Jeffers-Schroder (Independent)#	8,860	6.4%
	Bill Hoffman (D)	6,135	4.4%
	S. Sutherland (No Party)	4,999	3.6%
	Don Rivers (D)	4,781	3.4%
	Scott Sizemore	3,220	2.3%
	TOTAL	138,909	
Congressional District 8	Dave Reichert (R)*#	76,118	47.2%
	Suzan DelBene (D)#	43,272	26.8%
	Tom Cramer (D)	15,313	9.5%
	Ernest Huber (R)	9,376	5.8%
	Tim Dillon (R)	8,291	5.1%
	Keith Arnold (D)	3,405	2.1%
	Robin Adair (Independent Party)	2,648	1.6%
	Boleslaw "John" Orlinski (D)	1,761	1.1%
	Caleb Love Mardini (No Party)	987	0.6%
	TOTAL	161,171	
Congressional District 9	Adam Smith (D)*#	63,866	51.2%
	Richard Muri (R)#	32,116	25.8%
	Jim Postma (R)	24,509	19.7%
	Roy Olson (Green)	4,159	3.3%
	TOTAL	124,650	

An asterisk (*) denotes incumbent. Washington held an all-party primary, in which candidates of all parties ran together on a single ballot. The top two vote-getters, regardless of party, advanced to the November general election. They are indicated in the chart below by a pound sign (#). Candidates identified themselves on the ballot as "preferring" a particular party (or independent, non-party status), whether or not they were a member of that party or were supported by that party. Virtually all counties in Washington in 2010 voted by mail.

WEST VIRGINIA

Congressional districts first established for elections held in 2002
3 members

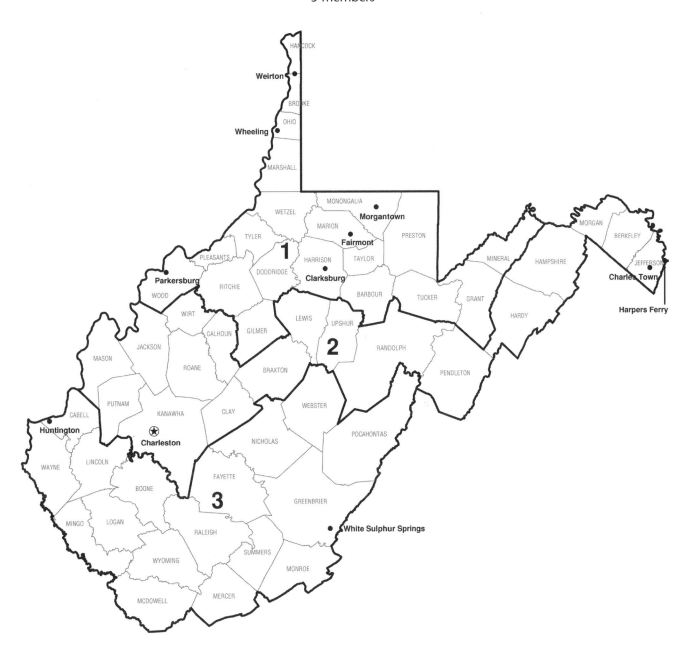

WEST VIRGINIA

GOVERNOR

Earl Ray Tomblin (D). Sworn in as acting governor November 15, 2010, to fill the vacancy created by the resignation of Joe Manchin III (D) following his election to the U.S. Senate.

SENATORS (2 Democrats)

Joe Manchin III (D). Elected 2010 to fill the remaining two years of the term vacated by the death of Robert C. Byrd (D) in June 2010. Carte Goodwin (D) was appointed to fill the vacancy until the special election could be held in November 2010.

John D. Rockefeller IV (D). Reelected 2008 to a six-year term. Previously elected 2002, 1996, 1990, 1984.

REPRESENTATIVES (2 Republicans, 1 Democrat)

1. David B. McKinley (R)   2. Shelley Moore Capito (R)   3. Nick J. Rahall II (D)

POSTWAR VOTE FOR PRESIDENT

Year	Total Vote	Republican		Democratic		Other Vote	Rep.-Dem Plurality	Percentage			
								Total Vote		Major Vote	
		Vote	Candidate	Vote	Candidate			Rep.	Dem.	Rep.	Dem.
2008	713,451	397,466	McCain, John	303,857	Obama, Barack	12,128	93,609 R	55.7%	42.6%	56.7%	43.3%
2004	755,887	423,778	Bush, George W.	326,541	Kerry, John	5,568	97,237 R	56.1%	43.2%	56.5%	43.5%
2000**	648,124	336,475	Bush, George W.	295,497	Gore, Al	16,152	40,978 R	51.9%	45.6%	53.2%	46.8%
1996**	636,459	233,946	Dole, Bob	327,812	Clinton, Bill	74,701	93,866 D	36.8%	51.5%	41.6%	58.4%
1992**	683,762	241,974	Bush, George	331,001	Clinton, Bill	110,787	89,027 D	35.4%	48.4%	42.2%	57.8%
1988	653,311	310,065	Bush, George	341,016	Dukakis, Michael S.	2,230	30,951 D	47.5%	52.2%	47.6%	52.4%
1984	735,742	405,483	Reagan, Ronald	328,125	Mondale, Walter F.	2,134	77,358 R	55.1%	44.6%	55.3%	44.7%
1980**	737,715	334,206	Reagan, Ronald	367,462	Carter, Jimmy	36,047	33,256 D	45.3%	49.8%	47.6%	52.4%
1976	750,964	314,760	Ford, Gerald R.	435,914	Carter, Jimmy	290	121,154 D	41.9%	58.0%	41.9%	58.1%
1972	762,399	484,964	Nixon, Richard M.	277,435	McGovern, George S.		207,529 R	63.6%	36.4%	63.6%	36.4%
1968**	754,206	307,555	Nixon, Richard M.	374,091	Humphrey, Hubert H.	72,560	66,536 D	40.8%	49.6%	45.1%	54.9%
1964	792,040	253,953	Goldwater, Barry M.	538,087	Johnson, Lyndon B.		284,134 D	32.1%	67.9%	32.1%	67.9%
1960	837,781	395,995	Nixon, Richard M.	441,786	Kennedy, John F.		45,791 D	47.3%	52.7%	47.3%	52.7%
1956	830,831	449,297	Eisenhower, Dwight D.	381,534	Stevenson, Adlai E.		67,763 R	54.1%	45.9%	54.1%	45.9%
1952	873,548	419,970	Eisenhower, Dwight D.	453,578	Stevenson, Adlai E.		33,608 D	48.1%	51.9%	48.1%	51.9%
1948	748,750	316,251	Dewey, Thomas E.	429,188	Truman, Harry S.	3,311	112,937 D	42.2%	57.3%	42.4%	57.6%

** In past elections, the other vote included: 2000 - 10,680 Green (Ralph Nader); 1996 - 71,639 Reform (Ross Perot); 1992 - 108,829 Independent (Perot); 1980 - 31,691 Independent (John Anderson); 1968 - 72,560 American Independent (George Wallace).

WEST VIRGINIA

POSTWAR VOTE FOR GOVERNOR

Year	Total Vote	Republican Vote	Republican Candidate	Democratic Vote	Democratic Candidate	Other Vote	Rep.-Dem Plurality	Percentage Total Vote Rep.	Percentage Total Vote Dem.	Percentage Major Vote Rep.	Percentage Major Vote Dem.
2008	706,046	181,612	Weeks, Russ	492,697	Manchin, Joe, III	31,737	311,085 D	25.7%	69.8%	26.9%	73.1%
2004	744,433	253,131	Warner, Monty	472,758	Manchin, Joe, III	18,544	219,627 D	34.0%	63.5%	34.9%	65.1%
2000	648,047	305,926	Underwood, Cecil H.	324,822	Wise, Bob	17,299	18,896 D	47.2%	50.1%	48.5%	51.5%
1996	628,559	324,518	Underwood, Cecil H.	287,870	Pritt, Charlotte	16,171	36,648 R	51.6%	45.8%	53.0%	47.0%
1992	657,193	240,390	Benedict, Cleveland K.	368,302	Caperton, Gaston	48,501	127,912 D	36.6%	56.0%	39.5%	60.5%
1988	649,593	267,172	Moore, Arch A.	382,421	Caperton, Gaston		115,249 D	41.1%	58.9%	41.1%	58.9%
1984	741,502	394,937	Moore, Arch A.	346,565	See, Clyde M.		48,372 R	53.3%	46.7%	53.3%	46.7%
1980	742,150	337,240	Moore, Arch A.	401,863	Rockefeller, John D., IV	3,047	64,623 D	45.4%	54.1%	45.6%	54.4%
1976	749,270	253,420	Underwood, Cecil H.	495,661	Rockefeller, John D., IV	189	242,241 D	33.8%	66.2%	33.8%	66.2%
1972	774,279	423,817	Moore, Arch A.	350,462	Rockefeller, John D., IV		73,355 R	54.7%	45.3%	54.7%	45.3%
1968	743,845	378,315	Moore, Arch A.	365,530	Sprouse, James M.		12,785 R	50.9%	49.1%	50.9%	49.1%
1964	788,582	355,559	Underwood, Cecil H.	433,023	Smith, Hulett C.		77,464 D	45.1%	54.9%	45.1%	54.9%
1960	827,420	380,665	Neely, Harold E.	446,755	Barron, W. W.		66,090 D	46.0%	54.0%	46.0%	54.0%
1956	817,623	440,502	Underwood, Cecil H.	377,121	Mollohan, Robert H.		63,381 R	53.9%	46.1%	53.9%	46.1%
1952	882,527	427,629	Holt, Rush D.	454,898	Marland, William C.		27,269 D	48.5%	51.5%	48.5%	51.5%
1948	768,061	329,309	Boreman, Herbert	438,752	Patteson, Okey L.		109,443 D	42.9%	57.1%	42.9%	57.1%

POSTWAR VOTE FOR SENATOR

Year	Total Vote	Republican Vote	Republican Candidate	Democratic Vote	Democratic Candidate	Other Vote	Rep.-Dem Plurality	Percentage Total Vote Rep.	Percentage Total Vote Dem.	Percentage Major Vote Rep.	Percentage Major Vote Dem.
2010S	529,948	230,013	Raese, John R.	283,358	Manchin, Joe, III	16,577	53,345 D	43.4%	53.5%	44.8%	55.2%
2008	702,308	254,629	Wolfe, Jay	447,560	Rockefeller, John D., IV	119	192,931 D	36.3%	63.7%	36.3%	63.7%
2006	459,884	155,043	Raese, John R.	296,276	Byrd, Robert C.	8,565	141,233 D	33.7%	64.4%	34.4%	65.6%
2002	436,183	160,902	Wolfe, Jay	275,281	Rockefeller, John D., IV		114,379 D	36.9%	63.1%	36.9%	63.1%
2000	603,477	121,635	Gallaher, David T.	469,215	Byrd, Robert C.	12,627	347,580 D	20.2%	77.8%	20.6%	79.4%
1996	595,614	139,088	Burks, Betty A.	456,526	Rockefeller, John D., IV		317,438 D	23.4%	76.6%	23.4%	76.6%
1994	420,936	130,441	Klos, Stan	290,495	Byrd, Robert C.		160,054 D	31.0%	69.0%	31.0%	69.0%
1990	404,305	128,071	Yoder, John	276,234	Rockefeller, John D., IV		148,163 D	31.7%	68.3%	31.7%	68.3%
1988	634,547	223,564	Wolfe, Jay	410,983	Byrd, Robert C.		187,419 D	35.2%	64.8%	35.2%	64.8%
1984	722,212	344,680	Raese, John R.	374,233	Rockefeller, John D., IV	3,299	29,553 D	47.7%	51.8%	47.9%	52.1%
1982	565,314	173,910	Benedict, Cleveland K.	387,170	Byrd, Robert C.	4,234	213,260 D	30.8%	68.5%	31.0%	69.0%
1978	493,351	244,317	Moore, Arch A.	249,034	Randolph, Jennings		4,717 D	49.5%	50.5%	49.5%	50.5%
1976	566,790		—	566,423	Byrd, Robert C.	367	566,423 D		99.9%		100.0%
1972	731,841	245,531	Leonard, Louise	486,310	Randolph, Jennings		240,779 D	33.5%	66.5%	33.5%	66.5%
1970	445,623	99,658	Dodson, Elmer H.	345,965	Byrd, Robert C.		246,307 D	22.4%	77.6%	22.4%	77.6%
1966	491,216	198,891	Love, Francis J.	292,325	Randolph, Jennings		93,434 D	40.5%	59.5%	40.5%	59.5%
1964	761,087	246,072	Benedict, Cooper P.	515,015	Byrd, Robert C.		268,943 D	32.3%	67.7%	32.3%	67.7%
1960	828,292	369,935	Underwood, Cecil H.	458,355	Randolph, Jennings	2	88,420 D	44.7%	55.3%	44.7%	55.3%
1958	644,917	263,172	Revercomb, Chapman	381,745	Byrd, Robert C.		118,573 D	40.8%	59.2%	40.8%	59.2%
1958S	630,677	256,510	Hoblitzell, John D.	374,167	Randolph, Jennings		117,657 D	40.7%	59.3%	40.7%	59.3%
1956S	805,174	432,123	Revercomb, Chapman	373,051	Marland, William C.		59,072 R	53.7%	46.3%	53.7%	46.3%
1954	593,329	268,066	Sweeney, Tom	325,263	Neely, Matthew M.		57,197 D	45.2%	54.8%	45.2%	54.8%
1952	876,573	406,554	Revercomb, Chapman	470,019	Kilgore, Harley M.		63,465 D	46.4%	53.6%	46.4%	53.6%
1948	763,888	328,534	Revercomb, Chapman	435,354	Neely, Matthew M.		106,820 D	43.0%	57.0%	43.0%	57.0%
1946	542,768	269,617	Sweeney, Tom	273,151	Kilgore, Harley M.		3,534 D	49.7%	50.3%	49.7%	50.3%

The 1956 election, one of the 1958 elections, and the 2010 election were for short terms to fill a vacancy. The Republican Party did not run a candidate in the 1976 Senate election.

WEST VIRGINIA

SENATOR 2010

2000 Census Population	County	Total Vote	Republican	Democratic	Other	Rep.-Dem. Plurality		Percentage Total Vote Rep.	Dem.	Major Vote Rep.	Dem.
16,589	BARBOUR	4,896	2,097	2,652	147	555	D	42.8%	54.2%	44.2%	55.8%
104,169	BERKELEY	24,775	13,145	10,697	933	2,448	R	53.1%	43.2%	55.1%	44.9%
24,629	BOONE	6,477	1,902	4,361	214	2,459	D	29.4%	67.3%	30.4%	69.6%
14,523	BRAXTON	4,045	1,367	2,578	100	1,211	D	33.8%	63.7%	34.7%	65.3%
24,069	BROOKE	7,169	2,650	4,310	209	1,660	D	37.0%	60.1%	38.1%	61.9%
96,319	CABELL	25,304	10,099	14,639	566	4,540	D	39.9%	57.9%	40.8%	59.2%
7,627	CALHOUN	1,793	785	937	71	152	D	43.8%	52.3%	45.6%	54.4%
9,386	CLAY	2,446	927	1,421	98	494	D	37.9%	58.1%	39.5%	60.5%
8,202	DODDRIDGE	2,335	1,448	807	80	641	R	62.0%	34.6%	64.2%	35.8%
46,039	FAYETTE	11,219	4,065	6,723	431	2,658	D	36.2%	59.9%	37.7%	62.3%
8,693	GILMER	2,351	954	1,277	120	323	D	40.6%	54.3%	42.8%	57.2%
11,937	GRANT	3,524	2,522	925	77	1,597	R	71.6%	26.2%	73.2%	26.8%
35,480	GREENBRIER	9,793	4,086	5,294	413	1,208	D	41.7%	54.1%	43.6%	56.4%
23,964	HAMPSHIRE	6,179	3,429	2,577	173	852	R	55.5%	41.7%	57.1%	42.9%
30,676	HANCOCK	10,297	4,250	5,704	343	1,454	D	41.3%	55.4%	42.7%	57.3%
14,025	HARDY	3,889	2,099	1,661	129	438	R	54.0%	42.7%	55.8%	44.2%
69,099	HARRISON	22,530	9,329	12,482	719	3,153	D	41.4%	55.4%	42.8%	57.2%
29,211	JACKSON	9,734	4,563	4,833	338	270	D	46.9%	49.7%	48.6%	51.4%
53,498	JEFFERSON	15,624	7,082	7,861	681	779	D	45.3%	50.3%	47.4%	52.6%
193,063	KANAWHA	60,148	25,120	33,064	1,964	7,944	D	41.8%	55.0%	43.2%	56.8%
16,372	LEWIS	5,267	2,447	2,621	199	174	D	46.5%	49.8%	48.3%	51.7%
21,720	LINCOLN	5,141	1,974	3,053	114	1,079	D	38.4%	59.4%	39.3%	60.7%
36,743	LOGAN	9,154	2,618	6,373	163	3,755	D	28.6%	69.6%	29.1%	70.9%
22,113	MCDOWELL	4,610	1,216	3,282	112	2,066	D	26.4%	71.2%	27.0%	73.0%
56,418	MARION	18,768	5,876	12,349	543	6,473	D	31.3%	65.8%	32.2%	67.8%
33,107	MARSHALL	10,466	4,320	5,833	313	1,513	D	41.3%	55.7%	42.5%	57.5%
27,324	MASON	7,585	2,736	4,603	246	1,867	D	36.1%	60.7%	37.3%	62.7%
62,264	MERCER	15,582	7,326	7,769	487	443	D	47.0%	49.9%	48.5%	51.5%
28,212	MINERAL	8,365	4,596	3,567	202	1,029	R	54.9%	42.6%	56.3%	43.7%
26,839	MINGO	7,025	2,146	4,774	105	2,628	D	30.5%	68.0%	31.0%	69.0%
96,189	MONONGALIA	24,452	10,765	12,817	870	2,052	D	44.0%	52.4%	45.6%	54.4%
13,502	MONROE	4,126	1,829	2,134	163	305	D	44.3%	51.7%	46.2%	53.8%
17,541	MORGAN	5,587	3,125	2,215	247	910	R	55.9%	39.6%	58.5%	41.5%
26,233	NICHOLAS	7,306	2,839	4,270	197	1,431	D	38.9%	58.4%	39.9%	60.1%
44,443	OHIO	14,430	6,597	7,486	347	889	D	45.7%	51.9%	46.8%	53.2%
7,695	PENDLETON	2,724	1,521	1,134	69	387	R	55.8%	41.6%	57.3%	42.7%
7,605	PLEASANTS	2,535	1,042	1,405	88	363	D	41.1%	55.4%	42.6%	57.4%
8,719	POCAHONTAS	2,773	1,199	1,436	138	237	D	43.2%	51.8%	45.5%	54.5%
33,520	PRESTON	9,979	5,466	4,071	442	1,395	R	54.8%	40.8%	57.3%	42.7%
55,486	PUTNAM	18,943	9,578	8,908	457	670	R	50.6%	47.0%	51.8%	48.2%
78,859	RALEIGH	21,473	9,924	10,922	627	998	D	46.2%	50.9%	47.6%	52.4%
29,405	RANDOLPH	8,536	3,261	5,000	275	1,739	D	38.2%	58.6%	39.5%	60.5%
10,449	RITCHIE	3,037	1,738	1,213	86	525	R	57.2%	39.9%	58.9%	41.1%
14,926	ROANE	4,245	1,794	2,277	174	483	D	42.3%	53.6%	44.1%	55.9%
13,927	SUMMERS	3,835	1,474	2,198	163	724	D	38.4%	57.3%	40.1%	59.9%
16,895	TAYLOR	5,112	2,153	2,790	169	637	D	42.1%	54.6%	43.6%	56.4%
7,141	TUCKER	2,727	1,127	1,501	99	374	D	41.3%	55.0%	42.9%	57.1%
9,208	TYLER	2,772	1,470	1,216	86	254	R	53.0%	43.9%	54.7%	45.3%
24,254	UPSHUR	6,764	3,270	3,259	235	11	R	48.3%	48.2%	50.1%	49.9%
42,481	WAYNE	11,640	4,609	6,776	255	2,167	D	39.6%	58.2%	40.5%	59.5%
9,154	WEBSTER	2,332	753	1,487	92	734	D	32.3%	63.8%	33.6%	66.4%
16,583	WETZEL	4,854	1,889	2,820	145	931	D	38.9%	58.1%	40.1%	59.9%
5,717	WIRT	1,734	748	917	69	169	D	43.1%	52.9%	44.9%	55.1%
86,956	WOOD	26,094	12,403	13,043	648	640	D	47.5%	50.0%	48.7%	51.3%
23,796	WYOMING	5,447	2,265	3,036	146	771	D	41.6%	55.7%	42.7%	57.3%
1,852,994	TOTAL	529,948	230,013	283,358	16,577	53,345	D	43.4%	53.5%	44.8%	55.2%

WEST VIRGINIA

HOUSE OF REPRESENTATIVES

| | | | Republican | | Democratic | | Other | Rep.-Dem. | Percentage | | | |
| | | Total | | | | | | | Total Vote | | Major Vote | |
CD	Year	Vote	Vote	Candidate	Vote	Candidate	Vote	Plurality	Rep.	Dem.	Rep.	Dem.
1	2010	179,880	90,660	McKINLEY, DAVID B.	89,220	OLIVERIO, MIKE		1,440 R	50.4%	49.6%	50.4%	49.6%
1	2008	187,864		—	187,734	MOLLOHAN, ALAN B.*	130	187,734 D		99.9%		100.0%
1	2006	157,000	55,963	WAKIM, CHRIS	100,939	MOLLOHAN, ALAN B.*	98	44,976 D	35.6%	64.3%	35.7%	64.3%
1	2004	245,779	79,196	PARKS, ALAN LEE	166,583	MOLLOHAN, ALAN B.*		87,387 D	32.2%	67.8%	32.2%	67.8%
1	2002	111,261		—	110,941	MOLLOHAN, ALAN B.*	320	110,941 D		99.7%		100.0%
2	2010	185,246	126,814	CAPITO, SHELLEY MOORE*	55,001	GRAF, VIRGINIA LYNCH	3,431	71,813 R	68.5%	29.7%	69.7%	30.3%
2	2008	258,169	147,334	CAPITO, SHELLEY MOORE*	110,819	BARTH, ANNE	16	36,515 R	57.1%	42.9%	57.1%	42.9%
2	2006	164,580	94,110	CAPITO, SHELLEY MOORE*	70,470	CALLAGHAN, MIKE		23,640 R	57.2%	42.8%	57.2%	42.8%
2	2004	257,025	147,676	CAPITO, SHELLEY MOORE*	106,131	WELLS, ERIK	3,218	41,545 R	57.5%	41.3%	58.2%	41.8%
2	2002	163,676	98,276	CAPITO, SHELLEY MOORE*	65,400	HUMPHREYS, JIM		32,876 R	60.0%	40.0%	60.0%	40.0%
3	2010	149,247	65,611	MAYNARD, ELIOTT E.	83,636	RAHALL, NICK J., II*		18,025 D	44.0%	56.0%	44.0%	56.0%
3	2008	199,527	66,005	GEARHEART, MARTY	133,522	RAHALL, NICK J., II*		67,517 D	33.1%	66.9%	33.1%	66.9%
3	2006	133,233	40,820	WOLFE, KIM	92,413	RAHALL, NICK J., II*		51,593 D	30.6%	69.4%	30.6%	69.4%
3	2004	218,852	76,170	SNUFFER, RICK	142,682	RAHALL, NICK J., II*		66,512 D	34.8%	65.2%	34.8%	65.2%
3	2002	125,012	37,229	CHAPMAN, PAUL E.	87,783	RAHALL, NICK J., II*		50,554 D	29.8%	70.2%	29.8%	70.2%
TOTAL	2010	514,373	283,085		227,857		3,431	55,228 R	55.0%	44.3%	55.4%	44.6%
TOTAL	2008	645,560	213,339		432,075		146	218,736 D	33.0%	66.9%	33.1%	66.9%
TOTAL	2006	454,813	190,893		263,822		98	72,929 D	42.0%	58.0%	42.0%	58.0%
TOTAL	2004	721,656	303,042		415,396		3,218	112,354 D	42.0%	57.6%	42.2%	57.8%
TOTAL	2002	399,949	135,505		264,124		320	128,619 D	33.9%	66.0%	33.9%	66.1%

An asterisk (*) denotes incumbent.

WEST VIRGINIA

GENERAL AND PRIMARY ELECTIONS

2010 GENERAL ELECTIONS

Senator Other vote was 10,152 Mountain (Jesse Clarence Johnson Jr.); 6,425 Constitution (Jeffrey Conrad Becker).

House Other vote was:

CD 1
CD 2 3,431 Constitution (Phil Hudok).
CD 3

2010 PRIMARY ELECTIONS

Primary May 11, 2010 (Congress) **Registration** Democratic 658,132
August 28, 2010 (Senate) (as of April 2010) Republican 347,231
Mountain 1,063
Other 17,237
No Party Affiliation 181,282

TOTAL 1,204,945

Primary Type Semi-open—Registered Democrats and registered Republicans could vote only in their party's primary. Those voters registered with no party could participate in either the Democratic or Republican primary.

WEST VIRGINIA

GENERAL AND PRIMARY ELECTIONS

	REPUBLICAN PRIMARIES			DEMOCRATIC PRIMARIES		
Senator	John R. Raese	38,568	71.3%	Joe Manchin III	68,827	73.1%
	Andrew M. Warner	8,015	14.8%	Ken Hechler	16,267	17.3%
	Scott Harold Williams	1,546	2.9%	Sheirl Lee Fletcher	9,108	9.7%
	Kenneth Allen Culp	1,389	2.6%			
	Harry C. Bruner Jr.	1,312	2.4%			
	Thomas Elwood Ressler II	1,207	2.2%			
	Lynette Kennedy McQuain	937	1.7%			
	Frank Kubic	475	0.9%			
	Daniel Scott Rebich	459	0.8%			
	Albert Benjamine Howard	176	0.3%			
	TOTAL	*54,084*		*TOTAL*	*94,202*	
Congressional District 1	David B. McKinley	14,783	34.9%	Mike Oliverio	36,135	55.9%
	Andrew M. Warner	11,353	26.8%	Alan B. Mollohan*	28,500	44.1%
	Sarah M. Minear	8,994	21.2%			
	Thomas Fredrick Stark	3,636	8.6%			
	Patricia Carol Levenson	2,110	5.0%			
	Cynthia Hall	1,533	3.6%			
	TOTAL	*42,409*		*TOTAL*	*64,635*	
Congressional District 2	Shelley Moore Capito*	27,958	100.0%	Virginia Lynch Graf	29,579	100.0%
Congressional District 3	Eliott E. Maynard	5,056	30.1%	Nick J. Rahall II*	44,929	67.5%
	Gary Martin Gearheart	4,623	27.5%	Bruce Barilla	21,620	32.5%
	Conrad Gale Lucas II	4,238	25.2%			
	Lee Allen Bias	2,906	17.3%			
	TOTAL	*16,823*		*TOTAL*	*66,549*	

An asterisk (*) denotes incumbent.

WISCONSIN

Congressional districts first established for elections held in 2002
8 members

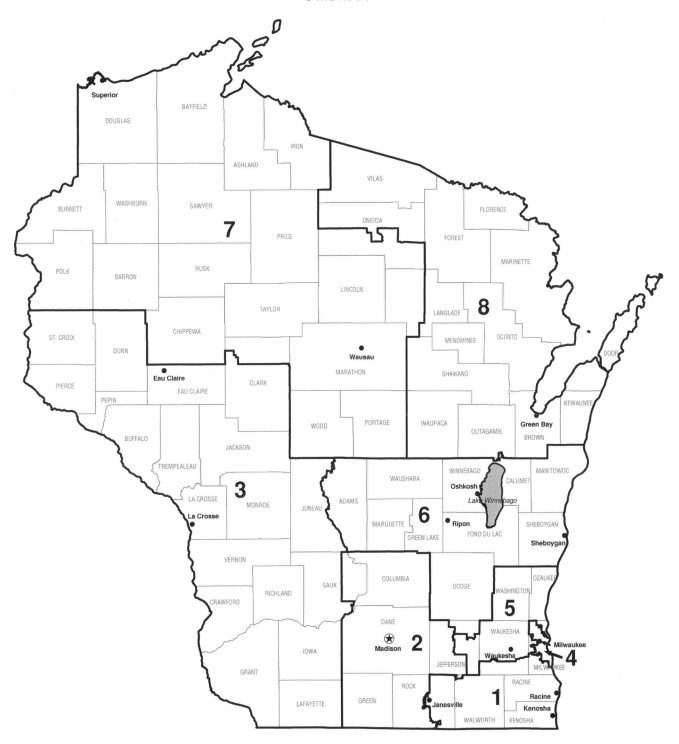

WISCONSIN

GOVERNOR
Scott Walker (R). Elected 2010 to a four-year term.

SENATORS (1 Democrat, 1 Republican)
Ron Johnson (R). Elected 2010 to a six-year term.

Herb Kohl (D). Reelected 2006 to a six-year term. Previously elected 2000, 1994, 1988.

REPRESENTATIVES (5 Republicans, 3 Democrats)

1. Paul D. Ryan (R)
2. Tammy Baldwin (D)
3. Ron Kind (D)

4. Gwen Moore (D)
5. F. James Sensenbrenner Jr. (R)
6. Tom Petri (R)

7. Sean Duffy (R)
8. Reid J. Ribble (R)

POSTWAR VOTE FOR PRESIDENT

| | | Republican | | Democratic | | | | Percentage | | | |
| | | | | | | | | Total Vote | | Major Vote | |
Year	Total Vote	Vote	Candidate	Vote	Candidate	Other Vote	Rep.-Dem. Plurality	Rep.	Dem.	Rep.	Dem.
2008	2,983,417	1,262,393	McCain, John	1,677,211	Obama, Barack	43,813	414,818 D	42.3%	56.2%	42.9%	57.1%
2004	2,997,007	1,478,120	Bush, George W.	1,489,504	Kerry, John	29,383	11,384 D	49.3%	49.7%	49.8%	50.2%
2000**	2,598,607	1,237,279	Bush, George W.	1,242,987	Gore, Al	118,341	5,708 D	47.6%	47.8%	49.9%	50.1%
1996**	2,196,169	845,029	Dole, Bob	1,071,971	Clinton, Bill	279,169	226,942 D	38.5%	48.8%	44.1%	55.9%
1992**	2,531,114	930,855	Bush, George	1,041,066	Clinton, Bill	559,193	110,211 D	36.8%	41.1%	47.2%	52.8%
1988	2,191,608	1,047,499	Bush, George	1,126,794	Dukakis, Michael S.	17,315	79,295 D	47.8%	51.4%	48.2%	51.8%
1984	2,211,689	1,198,584	Reagan, Ronald	995,740	Mondale, Walter F.	17,365	202,844 R	54.2%	45.0%	54.6%	45.4%
1980**	2,273,221	1,088,845	Reagan, Ronald	981,584	Carter, Jimmy	202,792	107,261 R	47.9%	43.2%	52.6%	47.4%
1976	2,104,175	1,004,987	Ford, Gerald R.	1,040,232	Carter, Jimmy	58,956	35,245 D	47.8%	49.4%	49.1%	50.9%
1972	1,852,890	989,430	Nixon, Richard M.	810,174	McGovern, George S.	53,286	179,256 R	53.4%	43.7%	55.0%	45.0%
1968**	1,691,538	809,997	Nixon, Richard M.	748,804	Humphrey, Hubert H.	132,737	61,193 R	47.9%	44.3%	52.0%	48.0%
1964	1,691,815	638,495	Goldwater, Barry M.	1,050,424	Johnson, Lyndon B.	2,896	411,929 D	37.7%	62.1%	37.8%	62.2%
1960	1,729,082	895,175	Nixon, Richard M.	830,805	Kennedy, John F.	3,102	64,370 R	51.8%	48.0%	51.9%	48.1%
1956	1,550,558	954,844	Eisenhower, Dwight D.	586,768	Stevenson, Adlai E.	8,946	368,076 R	61.6%	37.8%	61.9%	38.1%
1952	1,607,370	979,744	Eisenhower, Dwight D.	622,175	Stevenson, Adlai E.	5,451	357,569 R	61.0%	38.7%	61.2%	38.8%
1948	1,276,800	590,959	Dewey, Thomas E.	647,310	Truman, Harry S.	38,531	56,351 D	46.3%	50.7%	47.7%	52.3%

** In past elections, the other vote included: 2000 - 94,070 Green (Ralph Nader); 1996 - 227,339 Reform (Ross Perot); 1992 - 544,479 Independent (Perot); 1980 - 160,657 Independent (John Anderson); 1968 - 127,835 American Independent (George Wallace).

WISCONSIN

POSTWAR VOTE FOR GOVERNOR

| | | Republican | | Democratic | | | | Percentage | | | |
| | | | | | | | | Total Vote | | Major Vote | |
Year	Total Vote	Vote	Candidate	Vote	Candidate	Other Vote	Rep.-Dem. Plurality	Rep.	Dem.	Rep.	Dem.
2010	2,160,832	1,128,941	Walker, Scott	1,004,303	Barrett, Tom	27,588	124,638 R	52.2%	46.5%	52.9%	47.1%
2006	2,161,700	979,427	Green, Mark	1,139,115	Doyle, James E.	43,158	159,688 D	45.3%	52.7%	46.2%	53.8%
2002**	1,775,349	734,779	McCallum, Scott	800,515	Doyle, James E.	240,055	65,736 D	41.4%	45.1%	47.9%	52.1%
1998	1,756,014	1,047,716	Thompson, Tommy G.	679,553	Garvey, Edward R.	28,745	368,163 R	59.7%	38.7%	60.7%	39.3%
1994	1,563,835	1,051,326	Thompson, Tommy G.	482,850	Chvala, Chuck	29,659	568,476 R	67.2%	30.9%	68.5%	31.5%
1990	1,379,727	802,321	Thompson, Tommy G.	576,280	Loftus, Thomas	1,126	226,041 R	58.2%	41.8%	58.2%	41.8%
1986	1,526,960	805,090	Thompson, Tommy G.	705,578	Earl, Anthony S.	16,292	99,512 R	52.7%	46.2%	53.3%	46.7%
1982	1,580,344	662,838	Kohler, Terry J.	896,812	Earl, Anthony S.	20,694	233,974 D	41.9%	56.7%	42.5%	57.5%
1978	1,500,996	816,056	Dreyfus, Lee S.	673,813	Schreiber, Martin J.	11,127	142,243 R	54.4%	44.9%	54.8%	45.2%
1974	1,181,976	497,195	Dyke, William D.	628,639	Lucey, Patrick J.	56,142	131,444 D	42.1%	53.2%	44.2%	55.8%
1970**	1,343,160	602,617	Olson, Jack B.	728,403	Lucey, Patrick J.	12,140	125,786 D	44.9%	54.2%	45.3%	54.7%
1968	1,689,738	893,463	Knowles, Warren P.	791,100	LaFollette, Bronson C.	5,175	102,363 R	52.9%	46.8%	53.0%	47.0%
1966	1,170,173	626,041	Knowles, Warren P.	539,258	Lucey, Patrick J.	4,874	86,783 R	53.5%	46.1%	53.7%	46.3%
1964	1,694,887	856,779	Knowles, Warren P.	837,901	Reynolds, John W.	207	18,878 R	50.6%	49.4%	50.6%	49.4%
1962	1,265,900	625,536	Kuehn, Philip G.	637,491	Reynolds, John W.	2,873	11,955 D	49.4%	50.4%	49.5%	50.5%
1960	1,728,009	837,123	Kuehn, Philip G.	890,868	Nelson, Gaylord A.	18	53,745 D	48.4%	51.6%	48.4%	51.6%
1958	1,202,219	556,391	Thomson, Vernon W.	644,296	Nelson, Gaylord A.	1,532	87,905 D	46.3%	53.6%	46.3%	53.7%
1956	1,557,788	808,273	Thomson, Vernon W.	749,421	Proxmire, William	94	58,852 R	51.9%	48.1%	51.9%	48.1%
1954	1,158,666	596,158	Kohler, Walter J.	560,747	Proxmire, William	1,761	35,411 R	51.5%	48.4%	51.5%	48.5%
1952	1,615,214	1,009,171	Kohler, Walter J.	601,844	Proxmire, William	4,199	407,327 R	62.5%	37.3%	62.6%	37.4%
1950	1,138,148	605,649	Kohler, Walter J.	525,319	Thompson, Carl W.	7,180	80,330 R	53.2%	46.2%	53.6%	46.4%
1948	1,266,139	684,839	Rennebohm, Oscar	558,497	Thompson, Carl W.	22,803	126,342 R	54.1%	44.1%	55.1%	44.9%
1946	1,040,444	621,970	Goodland, Walter	406,499	Hoan, Daniel W.	11,975	215,471 R	59.8%	39.1%	60.5%	39.5%

** In past elections, the other vote included: 2002 - 185,455 Libertarian (Ed Thompson). The term of office of Wisconsin's Governor was increased from two to four years effective with the 1970 election.

POSTWAR VOTE FOR SENATOR

| | | Republican | | Democratic | | | | Percentage | | | |
| | | | | | | | | Total Vote | | Major Vote | |
Year	Total Vote	Vote	Candidate	Vote	Candidate	Other Vote	Rep.-Dem. Plurality	Rep.	Dem.	Rep.	Dem.
2010	2,171,331	1,125,999	Johnson, Ron	1,020,958	Feingold, Russell D.	24,374	105,041 R	51.9%	47.0%	52.4%	47.6%
2006	2,138,297	630,299	Lorge, Robert Gerald	1,439,214	Kohl, Herb	68,784	808,915 D	29.5%	67.3%	30.5%	69.5%
2004	2,949,743	1,301,183	Michels, Tim	1,632,697	Feingold, Russell D.	15,863	331,514 D	44.1%	55.4%	44.4%	55.6%
2000	2,540,083	940,744	Gillespie, John	1,563,238	Kohl, Herb	36,101	622,494 D	37.0%	61.5%	37.6%	62.4%
1998	1,760,836	852,272	Neumann, Mark W.	890,059	Feingold, Russell D.	18,505	37,787 D	48.4%	50.5%	48.9%	51.1%
1994	1,565,628	636,989	Welch, Robert T.	912,662	Kohl, Herb	15,977	175,673 D	40.7%	58.3%	41.1%	58.9%
1992	2,455,124	1,129,599	Kasten, Robert W.	1,290,662	Feingold, Russell D.	34,863	161,063 D	46.0%	52.6%	46.7%	53.3%
1988	2,168,190	1,030,440	Engeleiter, Susan	1,128,625	Kohl, Herb	9,125	98,185 D	47.5%	52.1%	47.7%	52.3%
1986	1,483,174	754,573	Kasten, Robert W.	702,963	Garvey, Edward R.	25,638	51,610 R	50.9%	47.4%	51.8%	48.2%
1982	1,544,981	527,355	McCallum, Scott	983,311	Proxmire, William	34,315	455,956 D	34.1%	63.6%	34.9%	65.1%
1980	2,204,202	1,106,311	Kasten, Robert W.	1,065,487	Nelson, Gaylord A.	32,404	40,824 R	50.2%	48.3%	50.9%	49.1%
1976	1,935,183	521,902	York, Stanley	1,396,970	Proxmire, William	16,311	875,068 D	27.0%	72.2%	27.2%	72.8%
1974	1,199,495	429,327	Petri, Tom	740,700	Nelson, Gaylord A.	29,468	311,373 D	35.8%	61.8%	36.7%	63.3%
1970	1,338,967	381,297	Erickson, John E.	948,445	Proxmire, William	9,225	567,148 D	28.5%	70.8%	28.7%	71.3%
1968	1,654,861	633,910	Leonard, Jerris	1,020,931	Nelson, Gaylord A.	20	387,021 D	38.3%	61.7%	38.3%	61.7%
1964	1,673,776	780,116	Renk, Wilbur N.	892,013	Proxmire, William	1,647	111,897 D	46.6%	53.3%	46.7%	53.3%
1962	1,260,168	594,846	Wiley, Alexander	662,342	Nelson, Gaylord A.	2,980	67,496 D	47.2%	52.6%	47.3%	52.7%
1958	1,194,678	510,398	Steinle, Roland J.	682,440	Proxmire, William	1,840	172,042 D	42.7%	57.1%	42.8%	57.2%
1957S	772,620	312,931	Kohler, Walter J.	435,985	Proxmire, William	23,704	123,054 D	40.5%	56.4%	41.8%	58.2%
1956	1,523,356	892,473	Wiley, Alexander	627,903	Maier, Henry W.	2,980	264,570 R	58.6%	41.2%	58.7%	41.3%
1952	1,605,228	870,444	McCarthy, Joseph R.	731,402	Fairchild, Thomas E.	3,382	139,042 R	54.2%	45.6%	54.3%	45.7%
1950	1,116,135	595,283	Wiley, Alexander	515,539	Fairchild, Thomas E.	5,313	79,744 R	53.3%	46.2%	53.6%	46.4%
1946	1,014,594	620,430	McCarthy, Joseph R.	378,772	McMurray, Howard J.	15,392	241,658 R	61.2%	37.3%	62.1%	37.9%

The August 1957 election was for a short term to fill a vacancy.

WISCONSIN

GOVERNOR 2010

2010 Census Population	County	Total Vote	Republican	Democratic	Other	Rep.-Dem. Plurality		Percentage			
								Total Vote		Major Vote	
								Rep.	Dem.	Rep.	Dem.
20,875	ADAMS	7,170	3,748	3,298	124	450	R	52.3%	46.0%	53.2%	46.8%
16,157	ASHLAND	5,949	2,205	3,664	80	1,459	D	37.1%	61.6%	37.6%	62.4%
45,870	BARRON	15,520	8,486	6,746	288	1,740	R	54.7%	43.5%	55.7%	44.3%
15,014	BAYFIELD	7,242	2,961	4,185	96	1,224	D	40.9%	57.8%	41.4%	58.6%
248,007	BROWN	88,390	49,567	37,549	1,274	12,018	R	56.1%	42.5%	56.9%	43.1%
13,587	BUFFALO	4,879	2,610	2,174	95	436	R	53.5%	44.6%	54.6%	45.4%
15,457	BURNETT	6,119	3,479	2,555	85	924	R	56.9%	41.8%	57.7%	42.3%
48,971	CALUMET	18,505	11,152	7,065	288	4,087	R	60.3%	38.2%	61.2%	38.8%
62,415	CHIPPEWA	21,158	11,901	8,753	504	3,148	R	56.2%	41.4%	57.6%	42.4%
34,690	CLARK	10,505	6,368	3,844	293	2,524	R	60.6%	36.6%	62.4%	37.6%
56,833	COLUMBIA	21,385	11,059	10,014	312	1,045	R	51.7%	46.8%	52.5%	47.5%
16,644	CRAWFORD	5,961	2,792	3,062	107	270	D	46.8%	51.4%	47.7%	52.3%
488,073	DANE	220,273	68,238	149,699	2,336	81,461	D	31.0%	68.0%	31.3%	68.7%
88,759	DODGE	31,133	20,568	10,138	427	10,430	R	66.1%	32.6%	67.0%	33.0%
27,785	DOOR	13,870	6,932	6,719	219	213	R	50.0%	48.4%	50.8%	49.2%
44,159	DOUGLAS	15,193	6,255	8,703	235	2,448	D	41.2%	57.3%	41.8%	58.2%
43,857	DUNN	13,558	7,282	5,972	304	1,310	R	53.7%	44.0%	54.9%	45.1%
98,736	EAU CLAIRE	37,133	18,018	18,454	661	436	D	48.5%	49.7%	49.4%	50.6%
4,423	FLORENCE	1,833	1,197	612	24	585	R	65.3%	33.4%	66.2%	33.8%
101,633	FOND DU LAC	37,957	24,407	13,145	405	11,262	R	64.3%	34.6%	65.0%	35.0%
9,304	FOREST	3,400	1,790	1,565	45	225	R	52.6%	46.0%	53.4%	46.6%
51,208	GRANT	16,494	8,611	7,573	310	1,038	R	52.2%	45.9%	53.2%	46.8%
36,842	GREEN	13,187	6,391	6,567	229	176	D	48.5%	49.8%	49.3%	50.7%
19,051	GREEN LAKE	6,982	4,488	2,262	232	2,226	R	64.3%	32.4%	66.5%	33.5%
23,687	IOWA	8,746	3,867	4,750	129	883	D	44.2%	54.3%	44.9%	55.1%
5,916	IRON	2,503	1,336	1,139	28	197	R	53.4%	45.5%	54.0%	46.0%
20,449	JACKSON	6,776	3,428	3,219	129	209	R	50.6%	47.5%	51.6%	48.4%
83,686	JEFFERSON	31,530	19,155	11,909	466	7,246	R	60.8%	37.8%	61.7%	38.3%
26,664	JUNEAU	7,988	4,502	3,358	128	1,144	R	56.4%	42.0%	57.3%	42.7%
166,426	KENOSHA	49,010	25,136	23,312	562	1,824	R	51.3%	47.6%	51.9%	48.1%
20,574	KEWAUNEE	8,074	4,577	3,345	152	1,232	R	56.7%	41.4%	57.8%	42.2%
114,638	LA CROSSE	42,077	20,754	20,639	684	115	R	49.3%	49.1%	50.1%	49.9%
16,836	LAFAYETTE	5,594	2,926	2,566	102	360	R	52.3%	45.9%	53.3%	46.7%
19,977	LANGLADE	7,325	4,481	2,754	90	1,727	R	61.2%	37.6%	61.9%	38.1%
28,743	LINCOLN	11,331	6,201	4,872	258	1,329	R	54.7%	43.0%	56.0%	44.0%
81,442	MANITOWOC	30,375	18,234	11,784	357	6,450	R	60.0%	38.8%	60.7%	39.3%
134,063	MARATHON	49,514	28,516	20,028	970	8,488	R	57.6%	40.4%	58.7%	41.3%
41,749	MARINETTE	14,556	8,222	6,127	207	2,095	R	56.5%	42.1%	57.3%	42.7%
15,404	MARQUETTE	6,000	3,483	2,384	133	1,099	R	58.1%	39.7%	59.4%	40.6%
4,232	MENOMINEE	752	166	586	0	420	D	22.1%	77.9%	22.1%	77.9%
947,735	MILWAUKEE	341,017	128,612	209,932	2,473	81,320	D	37.7%	61.6%	38.0%	62.0%
44,673	MONROE	13,089	7,570	5,199	320	2,371	R	57.8%	39.7%	59.3%	40.7%
37,660	OCONTO	13,700	8,131	5,380	189	2,751	R	59.4%	39.3%	60.2%	39.8%
35,998	ONEIDA	15,866	8,773	6,762	331	2,011	R	55.3%	42.6%	56.5%	43.5%
176,695	OUTAGAMIE	65,259	35,143	29,223	893	5,920	R	53.9%	44.8%	54.6%	45.4%
86,395	OZAUKEE	43,381	29,879	13,233	269	16,646	R	68.9%	30.5%	69.3%	30.7%
7,469	PEPIN	2,407	1,279	1,093	35	186	R	53.1%	45.4%	53.9%	46.1%
41,019	PIERCE	13,308	7,067	5,925	316	1,142	R	53.1%	44.5%	54.4%	45.6%
44,205	POLK	14,892	8,842	5,752	298	3,090	R	59.4%	38.6%	60.6%	39.4%
70,019	PORTAGE	27,677	12,794	14,463	420	1,669	D	46.2%	52.3%	46.9%	53.1%
14,159	PRICE	6,290	3,284	2,858	148	426	R	52.2%	45.4%	53.5%	46.5%
195,408	RACINE	72,791	40,813	31,333	645	9,480	R	56.1%	43.0%	56.6%	43.4%
18,021	RICHLAND	6,246	3,293	2,866	87	427	R	52.7%	45.9%	53.5%	46.5%

WISCONSIN

GOVERNOR 2010

2010 Census Population	County	Total Vote	Republican	Democratic	Other	Rep.-Dem. Plurality		Percentage			
								Total Vote		Major Vote	
								Rep.	Dem.	Rep.	Dem.
160,331	ROCK	52,213	23,813	27,424	976	3,611	D	45.6%	52.5%	46.5%	53.5%
14,755	RUSK	5,402	3,045	2,170	187	875	R	56.4%	40.2%	58.4%	41.6%
84,345	ST. CROIX	28,137	17,298	10,329	510	6,969	R	61.5%	36.7%	62.6%	37.4%
61,976	SAUK	22,166	11,044	10,741	381	303	R	49.8%	48.5%	50.7%	49.3%
16,557	SAWYER	6,497	3,766	2,650	81	1,116	R	58.0%	40.8%	58.7%	41.3%
41,949	SHAWANO	14,373	8,663	5,487	223	3,176	R	60.3%	38.2%	61.2%	38.8%
115,507	SHEBOYGAN	46,874	29,657	16,720	497	12,937	R	63.3%	35.7%	63.9%	36.1%
20,689	TAYLOR	6,775	4,212	2,370	193	1,842	R	62.2%	35.0%	64.0%	36.0%
28,816	TREMPEALEAU	10,021	4,898	4,928	195	30	D	48.9%	49.2%	49.8%	50.2%
29,773	VERNON	10,930	5,441	5,278	211	163	R	49.8%	48.3%	50.8%	49.2%
21,430	VILAS	10,539	6,595	3,773	171	2,822	R	62.6%	35.8%	63.6%	36.4%
102,228	WALWORTH	35,119	22,733	11,870	516	10,863	R	64.7%	33.8%	65.7%	34.3%
15,911	WASHBURN	6,612	3,533	2,974	105	559	R	53.4%	45.0%	54.3%	45.7%
131,887	WASHINGTON	58,973	44,222	14,276	475	29,946	R	75.0%	24.2%	75.6%	24.4%
389,891	WAUKESHA	188,278	134,608	52,684	986	81,924	R	71.5%	28.0%	71.9%	28.1%
52,410	WAUPACA	17,924	10,596	7,072	256	3,524	R	59.1%	39.5%	60.0%	40.0%
24,496	WAUSHARA	8,614	5,178	3,284	152	1,894	R	60.1%	38.1%	61.2%	38.8%
166,994	WINNEBAGO	61,241	33,044	27,141	1,056	5,903	R	54.0%	44.3%	54.9%	45.1%
74,749	WOOD	28,274	15,626	12,023	625	3,603	R	55.3%	42.5%	56.5%	43.5%
5,686,986	TOTAL	2,160,832	1,128,941	1,004,303	27,588	124,638	R	52.2%	46.5%	52.9%	47.1%

WISCONSIN

SENATOR 2010

2010 Census Population	County	Total Vote	Republican	Democratic	Other	Rep.-Dem. Plurality		Percentage			
								Total Vote		Major Vote	
								Rep.	Dem.	Rep.	Dem.
20,875	ADAMS	7,212	3,761	3,349	102	412	R	52.1%	46.4%	52.9%	47.1%
16,157	ASHLAND	5,979	2,156	3,734	89	1,578	D	36.1%	62.5%	36.6%	63.4%
45,870	BARRON	15,764	8,446	6,855	463	1,591	R	53.6%	43.5%	55.2%	44.8%
15,014	BAYFIELD	7,281	2,882	4,270	129	1,388	D	39.6%	58.6%	40.3%	59.7%
248,007	BROWN	89,059	50,748	37,374	937	13,374	R	57.0%	42.0%	57.6%	42.4%
13,587	BUFFALO	4,919	2,631	2,196	92	435	R	53.5%	44.6%	54.5%	45.5%
15,457	BURNETT	6,131	3,452	2,550	129	902	R	56.3%	41.6%	57.5%	42.5%
48,971	CALUMET	18,616	11,224	7,156	236	4,068	R	60.3%	38.4%	61.1%	38.9%
62,415	CHIPPEWA	21,338	11,801	9,173	364	2,628	R	55.3%	43.0%	56.3%	43.7%
34,690	CLARK	10,641	6,163	4,183	295	1,980	R	57.9%	39.3%	59.6%	40.4%
56,833	COLUMBIA	21,507	10,748	10,525	234	223	R	50.0%	48.9%	50.5%	49.5%
16,644	CRAWFORD	6,030	2,792	3,145	93	353	D	46.3%	52.2%	47.0%	53.0%
488,073	DANE	221,445	65,894	153,912	1,639	88,018	D	29.8%	69.5%	30.0%	70.0%
88,759	DODGE	31,250	20,503	10,421	326	10,082	R	65.6%	33.3%	66.3%	33.7%
27,785	DOOR	14,008	7,081	6,809	118	272	R	50.5%	48.6%	51.0%	49.0%
44,159	DOUGLAS	15,252	6,289	8,653	310	2,364	D	41.2%	56.7%	42.1%	57.9%
43,857	DUNN	13,622	7,224	6,087	311	1,137	R	53.0%	44.7%	54.3%	45.7%
98,736	EAU CLAIRE	37,404	17,946	18,916	542	970	D	48.0%	50.6%	48.7%	51.3%
4,423	FLORENCE	1,851	1,187	645	19	542	R	64.1%	34.8%	64.8%	35.2%
101,633	FOND DU LAC	38,098	24,867	12,834	397	12,033	R	65.3%	33.7%	66.0%	34.0%
9,304	FOREST	3,439	1,722	1,687	30	35	R	50.1%	49.1%	50.5%	49.5%
51,208	GRANT	16,726	8,472	7,948	306	524	R	50.7%	47.5%	51.6%	48.4%

WISCONSIN

SENATOR 2010

2010 Census Population	County	Total Vote	Republican	Democratic	Other	Rep.-Dem. Plurality		Percentage			
								Total Vote		Major Vote	
								Rep.	Dem.	Rep.	Dem.
36,842	GREEN	13,299	6,102	7,045	152	943	D	45.9%	53.0%	46.4%	53.6%
19,051	GREEN LAKE	7,034	4,693	2,249	92	2,444	R	66.7%	32.0%	67.6%	32.4%
23,687	IOWA	8,787	3,730	4,974	83	1,244	D	42.4%	56.6%	42.9%	57.1%
5,916	IRON	2,514	1,321	1,175	18	146	R	52.5%	46.7%	52.9%	47.1%
20,449	JACKSON	6,835	3,438	3,301	96	137	R	50.3%	48.3%	51.0%	49.0%
83,686	JEFFERSON	31,604	18,801	12,344	459	6,457	R	59.5%	39.1%	60.4%	39.6%
26,664	JUNEAU	8,015	4,594	3,311	110	1,283	R	57.3%	41.3%	58.1%	41.9%
166,426	KENOSHA	49,100	25,479	22,996	625	2,483	R	51.9%	46.8%	52.6%	47.4%
20,574	KEWAUNEE	8,242	4,612	3,470	160	1,142	R	56.0%	42.1%	57.1%	42.9%
114,638	LA CROSSE	42,370	20,481	21,316	573	835	D	48.3%	50.3%	49.0%	51.0%
16,836	LAFAYETTE	5,656	2,891	2,693	72	198	R	51.1%	47.6%	51.8%	48.2%
19,977	LANGLADE	7,399	4,432	2,883	84	1,549	R	59.9%	39.0%	60.6%	39.4%
28,743	LINCOLN	11,384	6,202	4,946	236	1,256	R	54.5%	43.4%	55.6%	44.4%
81,442	MANITOWOC	30,585	17,713	12,458	414	5,255	R	57.9%	40.7%	58.7%	41.3%
134,063	MARATHON	49,710	27,716	21,160	834	6,556	R	55.8%	42.6%	56.7%	43.3%
41,749	MARINETTE	14,675	8,317	6,214	144	2,103	R	56.7%	42.3%	57.2%	42.8%
15,404	MARQUETTE	6,034	3,525	2,430	79	1,095	R	58.4%	40.3%	59.2%	40.8%
4,232	MENOMINEE	761	159	595	7	436	D	20.9%	78.2%	21.1%	78.9%
947,735	MILWAUKEE	341,563	129,839	209,394	2,330	79,555	D	38.0%	61.3%	38.3%	61.7%
44,673	MONROE	13,253	7,518	5,433	302	2,085	R	56.7%	41.0%	58.0%	42.0%
37,660	OCONTO	13,773	8,191	5,387	195	2,804	R	59.5%	39.1%	60.3%	39.7%
35,998	ONEIDA	15,958	8,610	7,008	340	1,602	R	54.0%	43.9%	55.1%	44.9%
176,695	OUTAGAMIE	65,741	36,190	28,758	793	7,432	R	55.0%	43.7%	55.7%	44.3%
86,395	OZAUKEE	43,451	29,753	13,496	202	16,257	R	68.5%	31.1%	68.8%	31.2%
7,469	PEPIN	2,431	1,280	1,118	33	162	R	52.7%	46.0%	53.4%	46.6%
41,019	PIERCE	13,395	7,093	5,973	329	1,120	R	53.0%	44.6%	54.3%	45.7%
44,205	POLK	14,967	8,719	5,884	364	2,835	R	58.3%	39.3%	59.7%	40.3%
70,019	PORTAGE	27,805	12,647	14,820	338	2,173	D	45.5%	53.3%	46.0%	54.0%
14,159	PRICE	6,446	3,222	3,089	135	133	R	50.0%	47.9%	51.1%	48.9%
195,408	RACINE	73,162	40,761	31,779	622	8,982	R	55.7%	43.4%	56.2%	43.8%
18,021	RICHLAND	6,326	3,294	2,980	52	314	R	52.1%	47.1%	52.5%	47.5%
160,331	ROCK	52,415	23,181	28,361	873	5,180	D	44.2%	54.1%	45.0%	55.0%
14,755	RUSK	5,471	2,988	2,363	120	625	R	54.6%	43.2%	55.8%	44.2%
84,345	ST. CROIX	28,223	17,162	10,585	476	6,577	R	60.8%	37.5%	61.9%	38.1%
61,976	SAUK	22,392	10,856	11,188	348	332	D	48.5%	50.0%	49.2%	50.8%
16,557	SAWYER	6,514	3,701	2,743	70	958	R	56.8%	42.1%	57.4%	42.6%
41,949	SHAWANO	14,491	8,772	5,504	215	3,268	R	60.5%	38.0%	61.4%	38.6%
115,507	SHEBOYGAN	47,020	29,359	17,175	486	12,184	R	62.4%	36.5%	63.1%	36.9%
20,689	TAYLOR	6,846	4,085	2,596	165	1,489	R	59.7%	37.9%	61.1%	38.9%
28,816	TREMPEALEAU	10,153	5,027	4,979	147	48	R	49.5%	49.0%	50.2%	49.8%
29,773	VERNON	11,046	5,323	5,547	176	224	D	48.2%	50.2%	49.0%	51.0%
21,430	VILAS	10,612	6,552	3,949	111	2,603	R	61.7%	37.2%	62.4%	37.6%
102,228	WALWORTH	35,201	22,432	12,380	389	10,052	R	63.7%	35.2%	64.4%	35.6%
15,911	WASHBURN	6,541	3,485	2,957	99	528	R	53.3%	45.2%	54.1%	45.9%
131,887	WASHINGTON	59,078	44,107	14,645	326	29,462	R	74.7%	24.8%	75.1%	24.9%
389,891	WAUKESHA	188,874	134,051	53,492	1,331	80,559	R	71.0%	28.3%	71.5%	28.5%
52,410	WAUPACA	17,997	10,731	7,062	204	3,669	R	59.6%	39.2%	60.3%	39.7%
24,496	WAUSHARA	8,655	5,248	3,290	117	1,958	R	60.6%	38.0%	61.5%	38.5%
166,994	WINNEBAGO	61,502	33,967	26,869	666	7,098	R	55.2%	43.7%	55.8%	44.2%
74,749	WOOD	28,453	15,660	12,172	621	3,488	R	55.0%	42.8%	56.3%	43.7%
5,686,986	TOTAL	2,171,331	1,125,999	1,020,958	24,374	105,041	R	51.9%	47.0%	52.4%	47.6%

WISCONSIN

HOUSE OF REPRESENTATIVES

CD	Year	Total Vote	Republican		Democratic		Other Vote	Rep.-Dem. Plurality	Percentage			
									Total Vote		Major Vote	
			Vote	Candidate	Vote	Candidate			Rep.	Dem.	Rep.	Dem.
1	2010	263,627	179,819	RYAN, PAUL D.*	79,363	HECKENLIVELY, JOHN	4,445	100,456 R	68.2%	30.1%	69.4%	30.6%
1	2008	361,107	231,009	RYAN, PAUL D.*	125,268	KRUPP, MARGE	4,830	105,741 R	64.0%	34.7%	64.8%	35.2%
1	2006	257,596	161,320	RYAN, PAUL D.*	95,761	THOMAS, JEFFREY C.	515	65,559 R	62.6%	37.2%	62.8%	37.2%
1	2004	356,976	233,372	RYAN, PAUL D.*	116,250	THOMAS, JEFFREY C.	7,354	117,122 R	65.4%	32.6%	66.7%	33.3%
1	2002	208,613	140,176	RYAN, PAUL D.*	63,895	THOMAS, JEFFREY C.	4,542	76,281 R	67.2%	30.6%	68.7%	31.3%
2	2010	309,460	118,099	LEE, CHAD	191,164	BALDWIN, TAMMY*	197	73,065 D	38.2%	61.8%	38.2%	61.8%
2	2008	400,841	122,513	THERON, PETER	277,914	BALDWIN, TAMMY*	414	155,401 D	30.6%	69.3%	30.6%	69.4%
2	2006	304,688	113,015	MAGNUM, DAVE	191,414	BALDWIN, TAMMY*	259	78,399 D	37.1%	62.8%	37.1%	62.9%
2	2004	397,724	145,810	MAGNUM, DAVE	251,637	BALDWIN, TAMMY*	277	105,827 D	36.7%	63.3%	36.7%	63.3%
2	2002	247,410	83,694	GREER, RON	163,313	BALDWIN, TAMMY*	403	79,619 D	33.8%	66.0%	33.9%	66.1%
3	2010	251,340	116,838	KAPANKE, DAN	126,380	KIND, RON*	8,122	9,542 D	46.5%	50.3%	48.0%	52.0%
3	2008	356,400	122,760	STARK, PAUL	225,208	KIND, RON*	8,432	102,448 D	34.4%	63.2%	35.3%	64.7%
3	2006	252,087	88,523	NELSON, PAUL R.	163,322	KIND, RON*	242	74,799 D	35.1%	64.8%	35.1%	64.9%
3	2004	363,008	157,866	SCHULTZ, DALE W.	204,856	KIND, RON*	286	46,990 D	43.5%	56.4%	43.5%	56.5%
3	2002	208,581	69,955	ARNDT, BILL	131,038	KIND, RON*	7,588	61,083 D	33.5%	62.8%	34.8%	65.2%
4	2010	208,103	61,543	SEBRING, DAN	143,559	MOORE, GWEN*	3,001	82,016 D	29.6%	69.0%	30.0%	70.0%
4	2008	254,179		—	222,728	MOORE, GWEN*	31,451	222,728 D		87.6%		100.0%
4	2006	191,742	54,486	RIVERA, PERFECTO	136,735	MOORE, GWEN*	521	82,249 D	28.4%	71.3%	28.5%	71.5%
4	2004	305,142	85,928	BOYLE, GERALD H.	212,382	MOORE, GWEN	6,832	126,454 D	28.2%	69.6%	28.8%	71.2%
4	2002	141,367		—	122,031	KLECZKA, GERALD D.*	19,336	122,031 D		86.3%		100.0%
5	2010	331,258	229,642	SENSENBRENNER, F. JAMES, JR.*	90,634	KOLOSSO, TODD P.	10,982	139,008 R	69.3%	27.4%	71.7%	28.3%
5	2008	345,899	275,271	SENSENBRENNER, F. JAMES, JR.*		—	70,628	275,271 R	79.6%		100.0%	
5	2006	315,180	194,669	SENSENBRENNER, F. JAMES, JR.*	112,451	KENNEDY, BRYAN	8,060	82,218 R	61.8%	35.7%	63.4%	36.6%
5	2004	407,291	271,153	SENSENBRENNER, F. JAMES, JR.*	129,384	KENNEDY, BRYAN	6,754	141,769 R	66.6%	31.8%	67.7%	32.3%
5	2002	222,012	191,224	SENSENBRENNER, F. JAMES, JR.*		—	30,788	191,224 R	86.1%		100.0%	
6	2010	259,367	183,271	PETRI, TOM*	75,926	KALLAS, JOSEPH C.	170	107,345 R	70.7%	29.3%	70.7%	29.3%
6	2008	348,264	221,875	PETRI, TOM*	126,090	KITTELSON, ROGER A.	299	95,785 R	63.7%	36.2%	63.8%	36.2%
6	2006	203,557	201,367	PETRI, TOM*		—	2,190	201,367 R	98.9%		100.0%	
6	2004	355,995	238,620	PETRI, TOM*	107,209	HALL, JEF	10,166	131,411 R	67.0%	30.1%	69.0%	31.0%
6	2002	171,161	169,834	PETRI, TOM*		—	1,327	169,834 R	99.2%		100.0%	
7	2010	254,389	132,551	DUFFY, SEAN	113,018	LASSA, JULIE M.	8,820	19,533 R	52.1%	44.4%	54.0%	46.0%
7	2008	349,837	136,938	MIELKE, DAN	212,666	OBEY, DAVID R.*	233	75,728 D	39.1%	60.8%	39.2%	60.8%
7	2006	260,428	91,069	REID, NICK	161,903	OBEY, DAVID R.*	7,456	70,834 D	35.0%	62.2%	36.0%	64.0%
7	2004	281,752		—	241,306	OBEY, DAVID R.*	40,446	241,306 D		85.6%		100.0%
7	2002	227,955	81,518	ROTHBAUER, JOE	146,364	OBEY, DAVID R.*	73	64,846 D	35.8%	64.2%	35.8%	64.2%
8	2010	262,938	143,998	RIBBLE, REID J.	118,646	KAGEN, STEVE*	294	25,352 R	54.8%	45.1%	54.8%	45.2%
8	2008	358,647	164,621	GARD, JOHN	193,662	KAGEN, STEVE*	364	29,041 D	45.9%	54.0%	45.9%	54.1%
8	2006	278,135	135,622	GARD, JOHN	141,570	KAGEN, STEVE	943	5,948 D	48.8%	50.9%	48.9%	51.1%
8	2004	353,725	248,070	GREEN, MARK*	105,513	LE CLAIR, DOTTIE	142	142,557 R	70.1%	29.8%	70.2%	29.8%
8	2002	210,447	152,745	GREEN, MARK*	50,284	BECKER, ANDREW M.	7,418	102,461 R	72.6%	23.9%	75.2%	24.8%
TOTAL	2010	2,140,482	1,165,761		938,690		36,031	227,071 R	54.5%	43.9%	55.4%	44.6%
TOTAL	2008	2,775,174	1,274,987		1,383,536		116,651	108,549 D	45.9%	49.9%	48.0%	52.0%
TOTAL	2006	2,063,413	1,040,071		1,003,156		20,186	36,915 R	50.4%	48.6%	50.9%	49.1%
TOTAL	2004	2,821,613	1,380,819		1,368,537		72,257	12,282 R	48.9%	48.5%	50.2%	49.8%
TOTAL	2002	1,637,546	889,146		676,925		71,475	212,221 R	54.3%	41.3%	56.8%	43.2%

An asterisk (*) denotes incumbent.

WISCONSIN

GENERAL AND PRIMARY ELECTIONS

2010 GENERAL ELECTIONS

Governor   Other vote was 10,608 Independent (Jim Langer); 8,273 Common Sense (James James); 6,790 Libertarian (no candidate for governor, Terry Virgil for lieutenant governor); 22 write-in (Patricia Messicci); 19 write-in (Leslie Ervin Smetak); 18 write-in (Hari Trivedi); 1,858 scattered write-in.

Senator   Other vote was 23,473 Constitution (Rob Taylor); 134 Republican write-in (Ernest J. Pagels Jr.); 129 write-in (Michael D. LaForest); 638 scattered write-in.

House   Other vote was:

CD 1   4,311 Libertarian (Joseph Kexel); 134 scattered write-in.
CD 2   197 scattered write-in.
CD 3   8,001 Independent Citizen for Constitutional Government (Michael Krsiean); 121 scattered write-in.
CD 4   2,802 Coalition on Government Reform (Eddie Ahmad Ayyash); 199 scattered write-in.
CD 5   10,813 Independent (Robert R. Raymond); 169 scattered write-in.
CD 6   170 scattered write-in.
CD 7   8,397 Independent No War No Bailout (Gary Kauther); 423 scattered write-in.
CD 8   294 scattered write-in.

2010 PRIMARY ELECTIONS

Primary   September 14, 2010   **Registration**   3,419,127   No Party Registration
                                        (as of August 2, 2010)

Primary Type   Open—Any registered voter could participate in the party primary of their choice.

	REPUBLICAN PRIMARIES			DEMOCRATIC PRIMARIES		
Governor	Scott Walker	362,913	58.6%	Tom Barrett	213,145	90.4%
	Mark W. Neumann	239,022	38.6%	Tim John	22,296	9.5%
	Scott S. Paterick	16,646	2.7%	Scattered write-in	321	0.1%
	Scattered write-in	247				
	TOTAL	*618,828*		*TOTAL*	*235,762*	
Senator	Ron Johnson	504,644	84.7%	Russell D. Feingold*	223,688	99.7%
	Dave Westlake	61,633	10.3%	Scattered write-in	746	0.3%
	Stephen M. Finn	28,929	4.9%			
	Ernest J. Pagels Jr. (write-in)	23				
	Scattered write-in	601	0.1%			
	TOTAL	*595,830*		*TOTAL*	*224,434*	
Congressional District 1	Paul D. Ryan*	76,542	99.7%	John Heckenlively	18,657	99.7%
	Scattered write-in	241	0.3%	Scattered write-in	59	0.3%
	TOTAL	*76,783*		*TOTAL*	*18,716*	
Congressional District 2	Chad Lee	24,885	52.1%	Tammy Baldwin*	38,041	99.8%
	Peter Theron	22,783	47.7%	Scattered write-in	76	0.2%
	Scattered write-in	73	0.2%			
	TOTAL	*47,741*		*TOTAL*	*38,117*	
Congressional District 3	Dan Kapanke	41,216	76.9%	Ron Kind*	24,514	99.8%
	Bruce F. Evers	12,312	23.0%	Scattered write-in	51	0.2%
	Scattered write-in	42	0.1%			
	TOTAL	*53,570*		*TOTAL*	*24,565*	

WISCONSIN

GENERAL AND PRIMARY ELECTIONS

REPUBLICAN PRIMARIES				DEMOCRATIC PRIMARIES		
Congressional District 4	Dan Sebring	14,077	55.5%	Gwen Moore*	33,107	83.6%
	Kenneth Lipinski	11,164	44.0%	Paul Morel	6,430	16.2%
	Scattered write-in	111	0.4%	Scattered write-in	52	0.1%
	TOTAL	25,352		TOTAL	39,589	
Congressional District 5	F. James Sensenbrenner Jr.*	119,713	99.6%	Todd P. Kolosso	18,242	99.7%
	Scattered write-in	534	0.4%	Scattered write-in	51	0.3%
	TOTAL	120,247		TOTAL	18,293	
Congressional District 6	Tom Petri*	77,992	99.6%	Joseph C. Kallas	17,405	99.8%
	Scattered write-in	280	0.4%	Scattered write-in	31	0.2%
	TOTAL	78,272		TOTAL	17,436	
Congressional District 7	Sean Duffy	41,032	66.0%	Julie M. Lassa	28,585	85.3%
	Dan Mielke	21,075	33.9%	Don Raihala	4,920	14.7%
	Scattered write-in	25		Scattered write-in	16	0.0%
	TOTAL	62,132		TOTAL	33,521	
Congressional District 8	Reid J. Ribble	38,521	47.9%	Steve Kagen*	23,307	99.8%
	Roger Roth	25,704	32.0%	Scattered write-in	44	0.2%
	Terri McCormick	14,107	17.6%			
	Marc Savard	1,968	2.4%			
	Scattered write-in	36				
	TOTAL	80,336		TOTAL	23,351	

An asterisk (*) denotes incumbent.

WYOMING

One member At Large

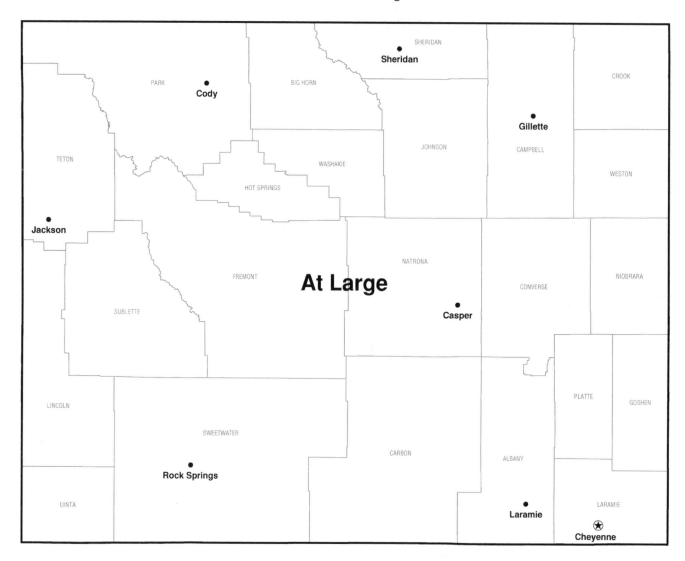

WYOMING

GOVERNOR

Matt Mead (R). Elected 2010 to a four-year term.

SENATORS (2 Republicans)

John Barrasso (R). Elected 2008 to fill out the remaining four years of the term vacated by the June 2007 death of Senator Craig Thomas (R); sworn in as Thomas' successor June 25, 2007.

Michael B. Enzi (R). Reelected 2008 to a six-year term. Previously elected 2002, 1996.

REPRESENTATIVE (1 Republican)

At Large. Cynthia M. Lummis (R)

POSTWAR VOTE FOR PRESIDENT

Year	Total Vote	Republican		Democratic		Other Vote	Rep.-Dem. Plurality	Percentage			
								Total Vote		Major Vote	
		Vote	Candidate	Vote	Candidate			Rep.	Dem.	Rep.	Dem.
2008	254,658	164,958	McCain, John	82,868	Obama, Barack	6,832	82,090 R	64.8%	32.5%	66.6%	33.4%
2004	243,428	167,629	Bush, George W.	70,776	Kerry, John	5,023	96,853 R	68.9%	29.1%	70.3%	29.7%
2000**	218,351	147,947	Bush, George W.	60,481	Gore, Al	9,923	87,466 R	67.8%	27.7%	71.0%	29.0%
1996**	211,571	105,388	Dole, Bob	77,934	Clinton, Bill	28,249	27,454 R	49.8%	36.8%	57.5%	42.5%
1992**	200,598	79,347	Bush, George	68,160	Clinton, Bill	53,091	11,187 R	39.6%	34.0%	53.8%	46.2%
1988	176,551	106,867	Bush, George	67,113	Dukakis, Michael S.	2,571	39,754 R	60.5%	38.0%	61.4%	38.6%
1984	188,968	133,241	Reagan, Ronald	53,370	Mondale, Walter F.	2,357	79,871 R	70.5%	28.2%	71.4%	28.6%
1980**	176,713	110,700	Reagan, Ronald	49,427	Carter, Jimmy	16,586	61,273 R	62.6%	28.0%	69.1%	30.9%
1976	156,343	92,717	Ford, Gerald R.	62,239	Carter, Jimmy	1,387	30,478 R	59.3%	39.8%	59.8%	40.2%
1972	145,570	100,464	Nixon, Richard M.	44,358	McGovern, George S.	748	56,106 R	69.0%	30.5%	69.4%	30.6%
1968**	127,205	70,927	Nixon, Richard M.	45,173	Humphrey, Hubert H.	11,105	25,754 R	55.8%	35.5%	61.1%	38.9%
1964	142,716	61,998	Goldwater, Barry M.	80,718	Johnson, Lyndon B.		18,720 D	43.4%	56.6%	43.4%	56.6%
1960	140,782	77,451	Nixon, Richard M.	63,331	Kennedy, John F.		14,120 R	55.0%	45.0%	55.0%	45.0%
1956	124,127	74,573	Eisenhower, Dwight D.	49,554	Stevenson, Adlai E.		25,019 R	60.1%	39.9%	60.1%	39.9%
1952	129,253	81,049	Eisenhower, Dwight D.	47,934	Stevenson, Adlai E.	270	33,115 R	62.7%	37.1%	62.8%	37.2%
1948	101,425	47,947	Dewey, Thomas E.	52,354	Truman, Harry S.	1,124	4,407 D	47.3%	51.6%	47.8%	52.2%

** In past elections, the other vote included: 2000 - 4,625 Green (Ralph Nader); 1996 - 25,928 Reform (Ross Perot); 1992 - 51,263 Independent (Perot); 1980 - 12,072 Independent (John Anderson); 1968 - 11,105 American Independent (George Wallace).

WYOMING

POSTWAR VOTE FOR GOVERNOR

Year	Total Vote	Republican Vote	Republican Candidate	Democratic Vote	Democratic Candidate	Other Vote	Rep.-Dem. Plurality	Total Vote Rep.	Total Vote Dem.	Major Vote Rep.	Major Vote Dem.
2010	188,463	123,780	Mead, Matt	43,240	Petersen, Leslie	21,443	80,540 R	65.7%	22.9%	74.1%	25.9%
2006	193,892	58,100	Hunkins, Ray	135,516	Freudenthal, Dave	276	77,416 D	30.0%	69.9%	30.0%	70.0%
2002	185,459	88,873	Bebout, Eli	92,662	Freudenthal, Dave	3,924	3,789 D	47.9%	50.0%	49.0%	51.0%
1998	174,888	97,235	Geringer, Jim	70,754	Vinich, John P.	6,899	26,481 R	55.6%	40.5%	57.9%	42.1%
1994	200,990	118,016	Geringer, Jim	80,747	Karpan, Kathy	2,227	37,269 R	58.7%	40.2%	59.4%	40.6%
1990	160,109	55,471	Mead, Mary	104,638	Sullivan, Mike		49,167 D	34.6%	65.4%	34.6%	65.4%
1986	164,720	75,841	Simpson, Peter	88,879	Sullivan, Mike		13,038 D	46.0%	54.0%	46.0%	54.0%
1982	168,555	62,128	Morton, Warren A.	106,427	Herschler, Ed		44,299 D	36.9%	63.1%	36.9%	63.1%
1978	137,567	67,595	Ostlund, John C.	69,972	Herschler, Ed		2,377 D	49.1%	50.9%	49.1%	50.9%
1974	128,386	56,645	Jones, Dick	71,741	Herschler, Ed		15,096 D	44.1%	55.9%	44.1%	55.9%
1970	118,257	74,249	Hathaway, Stan	44,008	Rooney, John J.		30,241 R	62.8%	37.2%	62.8%	37.2%
1966	120,873	65,624	Hathaway, Stan	55,249	Wilkerson, Ernest		10,375 R	54.3%	45.7%	54.3%	45.7%
1962	119,268	64,970	Hansen, Clifford P.	54,298	Gage, Jack R.		10,672 R	54.5%	45.5%	54.5%	45.5%
1958	112,537	52,488	Simpson, Milward L.	55,070	Hickey, J. J.	4,979	2,582 D	46.6%	48.9%	48.8%	51.2%
1954	111,438	56,275	Simpson, Milward L.	55,163	Jack, William		1,112 R	50.5%	49.5%	50.5%	49.5%
1950	96,959	54,441	Barrett, Frank A.	42,518	McIntyre, John J.		11,923 R	56.1%	43.9%	56.1%	43.9%
1946	81,353	38,333	Wright, Earl	43,020	Hunt, Lester C.		4,687 D	47.1%	52.9%	47.1%	52.9%

POSTWAR VOTE FOR SENATOR

Year	Total Vote	Republican Vote	Republican Candidate	Democratic Vote	Democratic Candidate	Other Vote	Rep.-Dem. Plurality	Total Vote Rep.	Total Vote Dem.	Major Vote Rep.	Major Vote Dem.
2008	249,946	189,046	Enzi, Michael B.	60,631	Rothfuss, Chris	269	128,415 R	75.6%	24.3%	75.7%	24.3%
2008S	249,558	183,063	Barrasso, John	66,202	Carter, Nick	293	116,861 R	73.4%	26.5%	73.4%	26.6%
2006	193,136	135,174	Thomas, Craig	57,671	Groutage, Dale	291	77,503 R	70.0%	29.9%	70.1%	29.9%
2002	183,280	133,710	Enzi, Michael B.	49,570	Corcoran, Joyce Jansa		84,140 R	73.0%	27.0%	73.0%	27.0%
2000	213,659	157,622	Thomas, Craig	47,087	Logan, Mel	8,950	110,535 R	73.8%	22.0%	77.0%	23.0%
1996	211,077	114,116	Enzi, Michael B.	89,103	Karpan, Kathy	7,858	25,013 R	54.1%	42.2%	56.2%	43.8%
1994	201,710	118,754	Thomas, Craig	79,287	Sullivan, Mike	3,669	39,467 R	58.9%	39.3%	60.0%	40.0%
1990	157,632	100,784	Simpson, Alan K.	56,848	Helling, Kathy		43,936 R	63.9%	36.1%	63.9%	36.1%
1988	180,964	91,143	Wallop, Malcolm	89,821	Vinich, John P.		1,322 R	50.4%	49.6%	50.4%	49.6%
1984	186,898	146,373	Simpson, Alan K.	40,525	Ryan, Victor A.		105,848 R	78.3%	21.7%	78.3%	21.7%
1982	167,191	94,725	Wallop, Malcolm	72,466	McDaniel, Rodger		22,259 R	56.7%	43.3%	56.7%	43.3%
1978	133,364	82,908	Simpson, Alan K.	50,456	Whitaker, Raymond B.		32,452 R	62.2%	37.8%	62.2%	37.8%
1976	155,368	84,810	Wallop, Malcolm	70,558	McGee, Gale		14,252 R	54.6%	45.4%	54.6%	45.4%
1972	142,067	101,314	Hansen, Clifford P.	40,753	Vinich, Mike		60,561 R	71.3%	28.7%	71.3%	28.7%
1970	120,486	53,279	Wold, John S.	67,207	McGee, Gale		13,928 D	44.2%	55.8%	44.2%	55.8%
1966	122,689	63,548	Hansen, Clifford P.	59,141	Roncalio, Teno		4,407 R	51.8%	48.2%	51.8%	48.2%
1964	141,670	65,185	Wold, John S.	76,485	McGee, Gale		11,300 D	46.0%	54.0%	46.0%	54.0%
1962S	119,372	69,043	Simpson, Milward L.	50,329	Hickey, J. J.		18,714 R	57.8%	42.2%	57.8%	42.2%
1960	138,550	78,103	Thomson, E. Keith	60,447	Whitaker, Ray		17,656 R	56.4%	43.6%	56.4%	43.6%
1958	114,157	56,122	Barrett, Frank A.	58,035	McGee, Gale		1,913 D	49.2%	50.8%	49.2%	50.8%
1954	112,252	54,407	Harrison, William H.	57,845	O'Mahoney, Joseph C.		3,438 D	48.5%	51.5%	48.5%	51.5%
1952	130,097	67,176	Barrett, Frank A.	62,921	O'Mahoney, Joseph C.		4,255 R	51.6%	48.4%	51.6%	48.4%
1948	101,480	43,527	Robertson, Edward V.	57,953	Hunt, Lester C.		14,426 D	42.9%	57.1%	42.9%	57.1%
1946	81,557	35,714	Henderson, Harry B.	45,843	O'Mahoney, Joseph C.		10,129 D	43.8%	56.2%	43.8%	56.2%

The 1962 election and one of the 2008 elections were for short terms to fill a vacancy.

WYOMING

GOVERNOR 2010

| 2010 Census Population | County | Total Vote | Republican | Democratic | Other | Rep.-Dem. Plurality | | Percentage | | | |
| | | | | | | | | Total Vote | | Major Vote | |
								Rep.	Dem.	Rep.	Dem.
36,299	ALBANY	11,455	6,374	4,352	729	2,022	R	55.6%	38.0%	59.4%	40.6%
11,668	BIG HORN	4,348	3,217	613	518	2,604	R	74.0%	14.1%	84.0%	16.0%
46,133	CAMPBELL	11,274	6,934	1,179	3,161	5,755	R	61.5%	10.5%	85.5%	14.5%
15,885	CARBON	5,196	3,585	1,308	303	2,277	R	69.0%	25.2%	73.3%	26.7%
13,833	CONVERSE	4,942	3,202	761	979	2,441	R	64.8%	15.4%	80.8%	19.2%
7,083	CROOK	3,137	2,048	388	701	1,660	R	65.3%	12.4%	84.1%	15.9%
40,123	FREMONT	13,638	8,439	3,323	1,876	5,116	R	61.9%	24.4%	71.7%	28.3%
13,249	GOSHEN	4,871	3,493	893	485	2,600	R	71.7%	18.3%	79.6%	20.4%
4,812	HOT SPRINGS	2,220	1,596	401	223	1,195	R	71.9%	18.1%	79.9%	20.1%
8,569	JOHNSON	3,797	2,804	578	415	2,226	R	73.8%	15.2%	82.9%	17.1%
91,738	LARAMIE	29,884	19,323	7,507	3,054	11,816	R	64.7%	25.1%	72.0%	28.0%
18,106	LINCOLN	6,582	4,710	1,023	849	3,687	R	71.6%	15.5%	82.2%	17.8%
75,450	NATRONA	23,137	15,077	5,761	2,299	9,316	R	65.2%	24.9%	72.4%	27.6%
2,484	NIOBRARA	1,152	753	124	275	629	R	65.4%	10.8%	85.9%	14.1%
28,205	PARK	11,478	8,312	1,813	1,353	6,499	R	72.4%	15.8%	82.1%	17.9%
8,667	PLATTE	3,827	2,303	905	619	1,398	R	60.2%	23.6%	71.8%	28.2%
29,116	SHERIDAN	10,684	7,632	2,336	716	5,296	R	71.4%	21.9%	76.6%	23.4%
10,247	SUBLETTE	3,451	2,465	554	432	1,911	R	71.4%	16.1%	81.6%	18.4%
43,806	SWEETWATER	12,550	8,218	3,532	800	4,686	R	65.5%	28.1%	69.9%	30.1%
21,294	TETON	8,548	4,407	3,856	285	551	R	51.6%	45.1%	53.3%	46.7%
21,118	UINTA	6,053	4,462	1,075	516	3,387	R	73.7%	17.8%	80.6%	19.4%
8,533	WASHAKIE	3,415	2,574	597	244	1,977	R	75.4%	17.5%	81.2%	18.8%
7,208	WESTON	2,824	1,852	361	611	1,491	R	65.6%	12.8%	83.7%	16.3%
563,626	TOTAL	188,463	123,780	43,240	21,443	80,540	R	65.7%	22.9%	74.1%	25.9%

WYOMING

HOUSE OF REPRESENTATIVES

| CD | Year | Total Vote | Republican | | Democratic | | Other Vote | Rep.-Dem. Plurality | | Percentage | | | |
| | | | | | | | | | | Total Vote | | Major Vote | |
			Vote	Candidate	Vote	Candidate				Rep.	Dem.	Rep.	Dem.
AL	2010	186,969	131,661	LUMMIS, CYNTHIA M.*	45,768	WENDT, DAVID	9,540	85,893	R	70.4%	24.5%	74.2%	25.8%
AL	2008	249,395	131,244	LUMMIS, CYNTHIA M.	106,758	TRAUNER, GARY	11,393	24,486	R	52.6%	42.8%	55.1%	44.9%
AL	2006	193,369	93,336	CUBIN, BARBARA*	92,324	TRAUNER, GARY	7,709	1,012	R	48.3%	47.7%	50.3%	49.7%
AL	2004	239,034	132,107	CUBIN, BARBARA*	99,989	LADD, TED	6,938	32,118	R	55.3%	41.8%	56.9%	43.1%
AL	2002	182,152	110,229	CUBIN, BARBARA*	65,961	AKIN, RON	5,962	44,268	R	60.5%	36.2%	62.6%	37.4%
AL	2000	212,312	141,848	CUBIN, BARBARA*	60,638	GREEN, MICHAEL ALLEN	9,826	81,210	R	66.8%	28.6%	70.1%	29.9%
AL	1998	174,219	100,687	CUBIN, BARBARA*	67,399	FARRIS, SCOTT	6,133	33,288	R	57.8%	38.7%	59.9%	40.1%
AL	1996	209,983	116,004	CUBIN, BARBARA*	85,724	MAXFIELD, PETE	8,255	30,280	R	55.2%	40.8%	57.5%	42.5%
AL	1994	196,197	104,426	CUBIN, BARBARA	81,022	SCHUSTER, BOB	10,749	23,404	R	53.2%	41.3%	56.3%	43.7%
AL	1992	196,977	113,882	THOMAS, CRAIG*	77,418	HERSCHLER, JON	5,677	36,464	R	57.8%	39.3%	59.5%	40.5%
AL	1990	158,055	87,078	THOMAS, CRAIG*	70,977	MAXFIELD, PETE		16,101	R	55.1%	44.9%	55.1%	44.9%
AL	1988	177,651	118,350	CHENEY, RICHARD*	56,527	SHARRATT, BRYAN	2,774	61,823	R	66.6%	31.8%	67.7%	32.3%
AL	1986	159,787	111,007	CHENEY, RICHARD*	48,780	GILMORE, RICK		62,227	R	69.5%	30.5%	69.5%	30.5%
AL	1984	187,904	138,234	CHENEY, RICHARD*	45,857	MCFADDEN, HUGH B.	3,813	92,377	R	73.6%	24.4%	75.1%	24.9%
AL	1982	159,277	113,236	CHENEY, RICHARD*	46,041	HOMMEL, THEODORE H.		67,195	R	71.1%	28.9%	71.1%	28.9%

WYOMING

HOUSE OF REPRESENTATIVES

| | | | Republican | | Democratic | | | | Percentage | | | |
| | | Total | | | | | Other | Rep.-Dem. | Total Vote | | Major Vote | |
CD	Year	Vote	Vote	Candidate	Vote	Candidate	Vote	Plurality	Rep.	Dem.	Rep.	Dem.
AL	1980	169,699	116,361	CHENEY, RICHARD*	53,338	ROGERS, JIM		63,023 R	68.6%	31.4%	68.6%	31.4%
AL	1978	129,377	75,855	CHENEY, RICHARD	53,522	BAGLEY, BILL		22,333 R	58.6%	41.4%	58.6%	41.4%
AL	1976	151,868	66,147	HART, LARRY	85,721	RONCALIO, TENO*		19,574 D	43.6%	56.4%	43.6%	56.4%
AL	1974	126,933	57,499	STROOK, TOM	69,434	RONCALIO, TENO*		11,935 D	45.3%	54.7%	45.3%	54.7%
AL	1972	146,299	70,667	KIDD, WILLIAM	75,632	RONCALIO, TENO*		4,965 D	48.3%	51.7%	48.3%	51.7%
AL	1970	116,304	57,848	ROBERTS, HARRY	58,456	RONCALIO, TENO		608 D	49.7%	50.3%	49.7%	50.3%
AL	1968	123,313	77,363	WOLD, JOHN S.	45,950	LINFORD, VELMA		31,413 R	62.7%	37.3%	62.7%	37.3%
AL	1966	119,426	62,984	HARRISON, WILLIAM H.	56,442	CHRISTIAN, AL		6,542 R	52.7%	47.3%	52.7%	47.3%
AL	1964	139,175	68,482	HARRISON, WILLIAM H.*	70,693	RONCALIO, TENO		2,211 D	49.2%	50.8%	49.2%	50.8%
AL	1962	116,474	71,489	HARRISON, WILLIAM H.*	44,985	MANKUS, LOUIS A.		26,504 R	61.4%	38.6%	61.4%	38.6%
AL	1960	134,331	70,241	HARRISON, WILLIAM H.	64,090	ARMSTONG, H.T.		6,151 R	52.3%	47.7%	52.3%	47.7%
AL	1958	111,780	59,894	THOMSON, E. KEITH*	51,886	WHITAKER, RAY		8,008 R	53.6%	46.4%	53.6%	46.4%
AL	1956	120,128	69,903	THOMSON, E. KEITH*	50,225	O'CALLAGHAN, JERRY		19,678 R	58.2%	41.8%	58.2%	41.8%
AL	1954	108,771	61,111	THOMSON, E. KEITH	47,660	TULLY, SAM		13,451 R	56.2%	43.8%	56.2%	43.8%
AL	1952	126,720	76,161	HARRISON, WILLIAM H.*	50,559	ROSE, ROBERT R.		25,602 R	60.1%	39.9%	60.1%	39.9%
AL	1950	93,348	50,865	HARRISON, WILLIAM H.	42,483	CLARK, JOHN B.		8,382 R	54.5%	45.5%	54.5%	45.5%
AL	1948	97,464	50,218	BARRETT, FRANK A.*	47,246	FLANNERY, L. G.		2,972 R	51.5%	48.5%	51.5%	48.5%
AL	1946	79,438	44,482	BARRETT, FRANK A.*	34,956	MCINTYRE, JOHN J.		9,526 R	56.0%	44.0%	56.0%	44.0%

An asterisk (*) denotes incumbent.

WYOMING

GENERAL AND PRIMARY ELECTIONS

2010 GENERAL ELECTIONS

Governor Other vote was 5,362 Libertarian (Mike Wheeler); 16,081 scattered write-in.

House Other vote was:

At Large 9,253 Libertarian (John V. Love); 287 scattered write-in.

2010 PRIMARY ELECTIONS

Primary	August 17, 2010	**Registration** (as of August 2, 2010)	Republican	157,750
			Democratic	65,404
			Libertarian	1,334
			Other	26
			Unaffiliated	36,895
			TOTAL	*261,409*

Primary Type Only registered Democrats and Republicans could vote in their party's primary, although on primary day any new voter could register with the party of their choice and any previously registered voter could participate in another party's primary by changing their registration to that party.

WYOMING

GENERAL AND PRIMARY ELECTIONS

		REPUBLICAN PRIMARIES			DEMOCRATIC PRIMARIES		
Governor	Matt Mead	30,308	28.7%	Leslie Petersen	10,785	47.2%
	Rita Meyer	29,605	28.0%	Peter Gosar	8,409	36.8%
	Ron Micheli	27,630	26.1%	Chris L. Zachary	1,139	5.0%
	Colin Simpson	16,722	15.8%	Al Hamburg	1,092	4.8%
	Alan Kousoulos	566	0.5%	Rex Wilde	1,042	4.6%
	Tom A. Ubben	432	0.4%	Scattered write-in	384	1.7%
	John H. Self	295	0.3%			
	Scattered write-in	202	0.2%			
	TOTAL	*105,760*		*TOTAL*	*22,851*	
House	Cynthia M. Lummis*	84,063	82.8%	David Wendt	20,410	99.0%
At Large	Evan Liam Slafter	17,148	16.9%	Scattered write-in	198	1.0%
	Scattered write-in	289	0.3%			
	TOTAL	*101,500*		*TOTAL*	*20,608*	

An asterisk (*) denotes incumbent.